LONGINES®

Longines DolceVita

The elegance of watchmaking attains new heights in the Eternal City

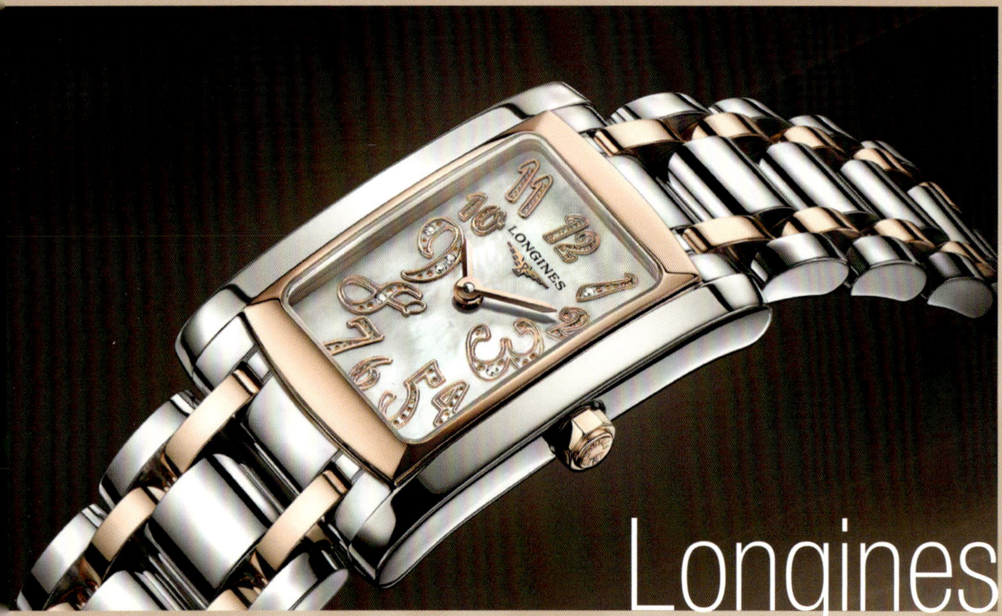

Longines DolceVita

L5.158.5.88.7
This quartz watch (calibre L963) in steel and rose gold is characterised by a rectangular case with pleasing proportions. The white mother-of-pearl dial features 13 diamonds indices and the blued hands show the hours and minutes. This elegant, contemporary model is mounted on a steel and rose gold bracelet. Water-resistant to 3 bar (30 m / ~ 100 ft).

L5.155.5.19.7
This quartz watch (calibre L178) in steel and rose gold is set with 32 diamonds (0.269 carat, Top Wesselton VVS) whose sparkle emphasises the rectangular form and harmonious proportions of the case. The white dial features ten indices, an Arabic numeral 12 and rose hands that indicate the hours and minutes, with a small seconds at 6 o'clock. This elegant, contemporary model is mounted on a steel and rose gold bracelet. Water-resistant to 3 bar (30 m / ~ 100 ft).

L5.155.5.99.7
This quartz watch (calibre L178) in steel and rose gold is set with 32 diamonds (0.269 carat, Top Wesselton VVS) whose sparkle emphasises the rectangular form and harmonious proportions of the case. The white mother-of-pearl dial features 12 rose Arabic numerals set with six diamonds, and rose hands that indicate the hours and minutes. The case is beautifully combined with a steel and rose gold bracelet to match the case. Water-resistant to 3 bar (30 m / ~ 100 ft).

L5.502.5.78.7
This quartz watch (calibre L176) in steel and yellow gold is set with 32 diamonds (0.384 carat, Top Wesselton VVS) whose sparkle emphasises the rectangular form and harmonious proportions of the case. The silvered "flinqué" dial features blue Roman numerals and hands that indicate the hours and minutes, as well as a small seconds at 6 o'clock. The watch is beautifully combined with a steel and yellow gold bracelet to match the case. Water-resistant to 3 bar (30 m / ~ 100 ft).

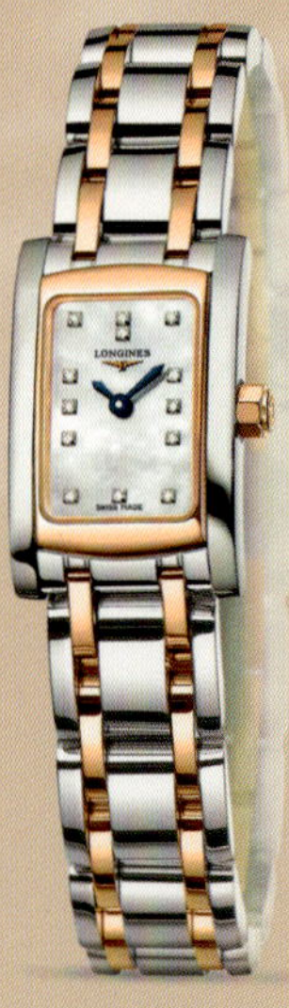

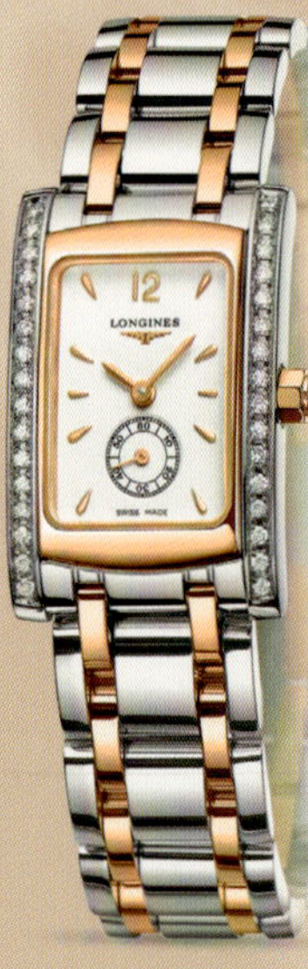

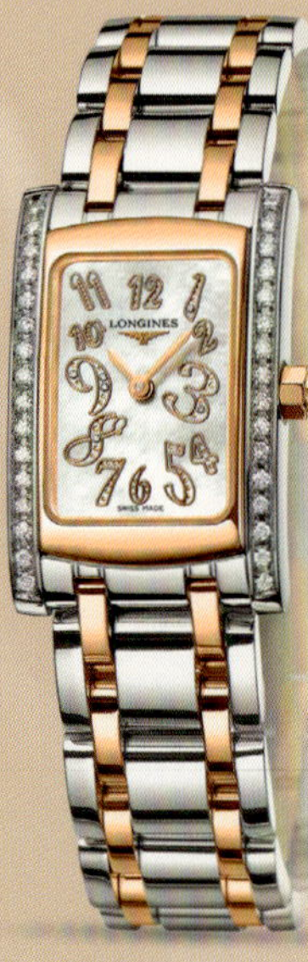

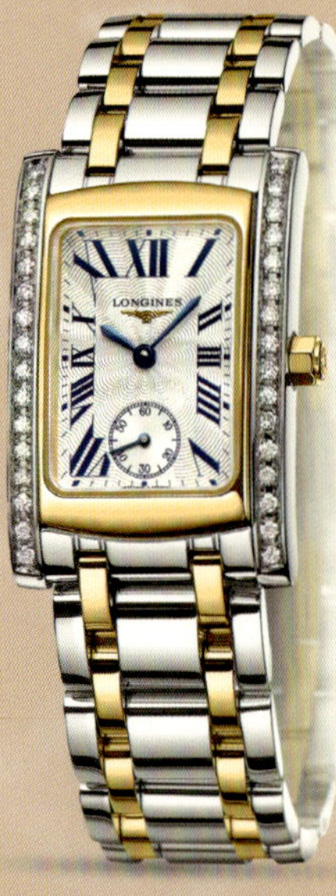

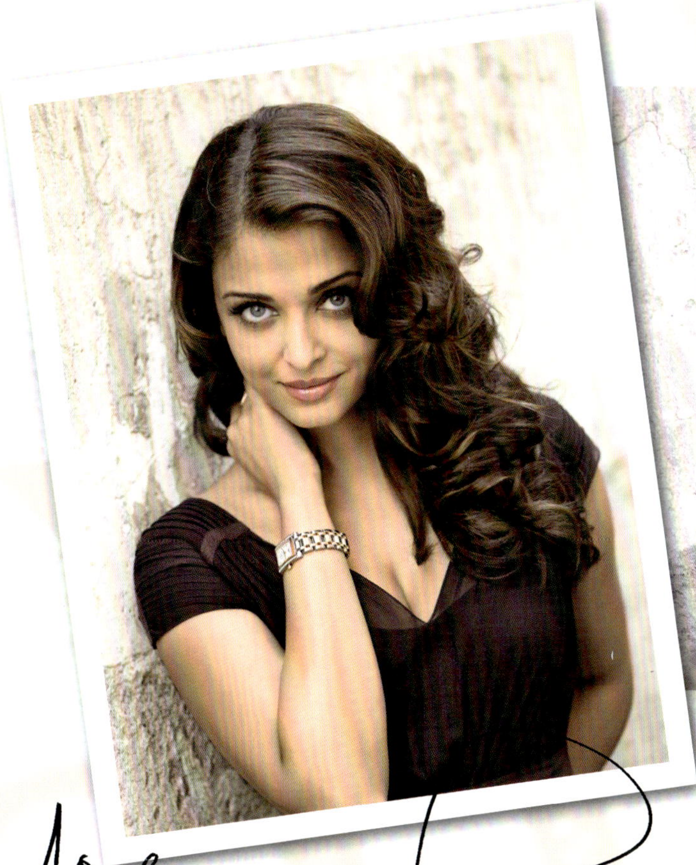

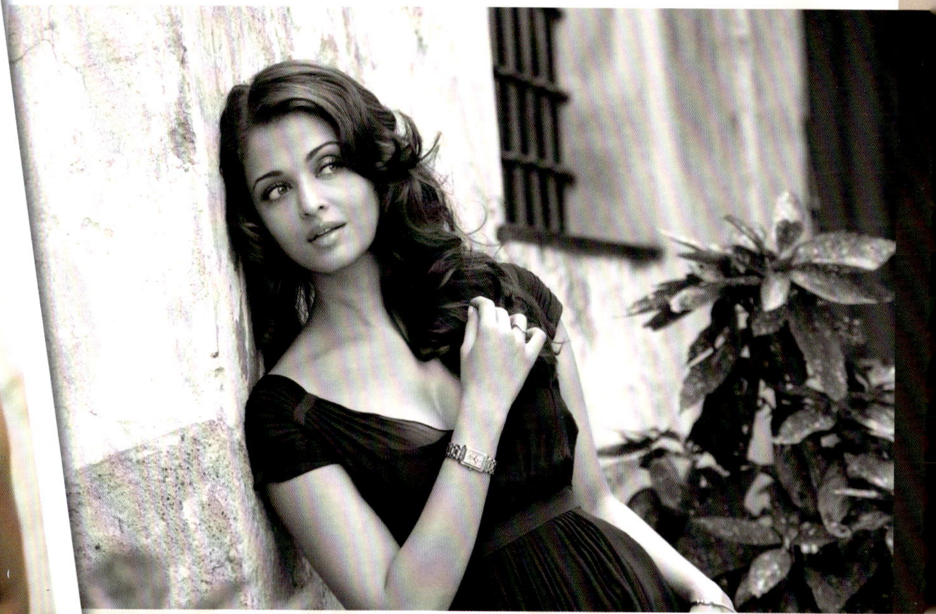

Aishwarya Rai Bachchan

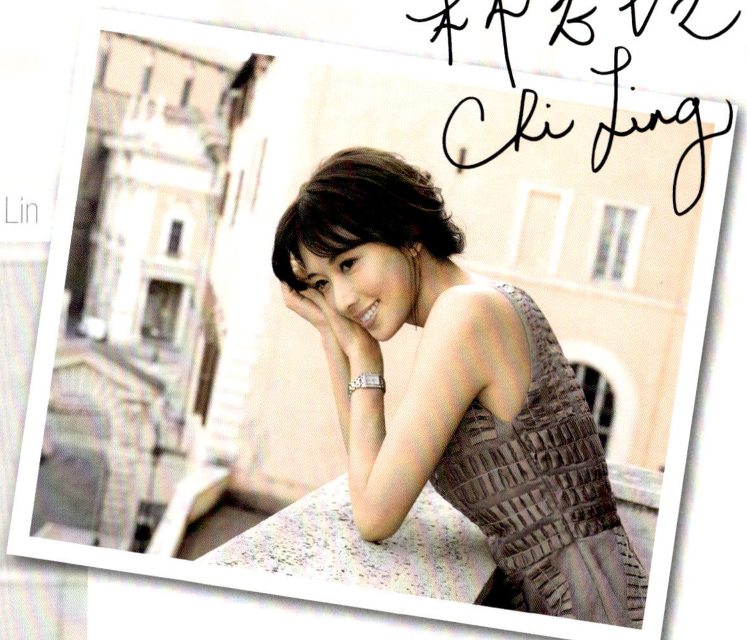

Chi Ling Lin

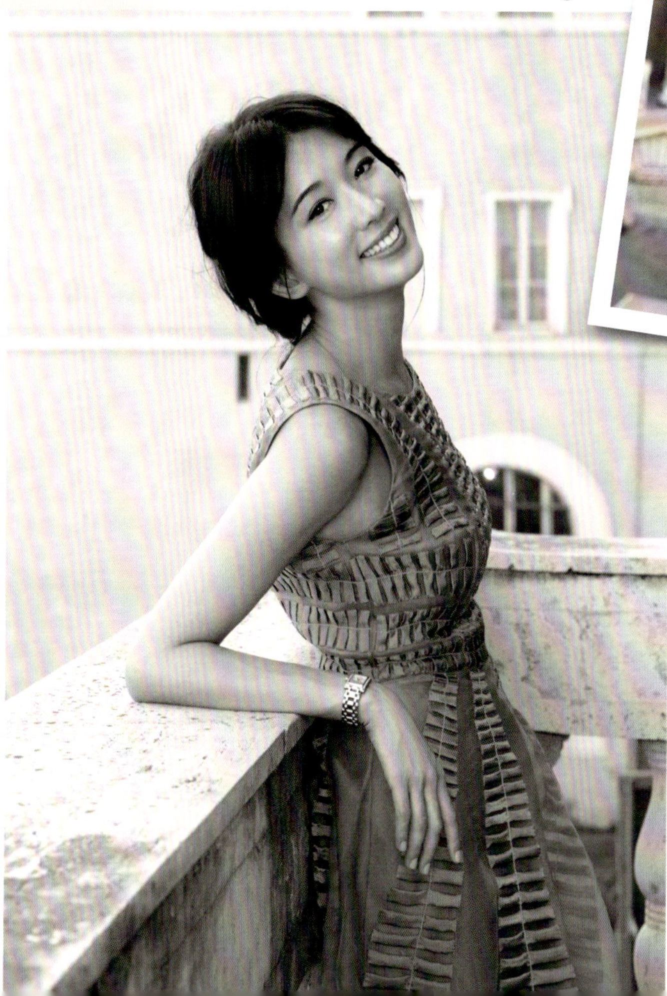

The Longines DolceVita collection embodies the brand's vision of contemporary elegance. Created in 1997, this collection has been immensely successful all around the world and today adorns the wrists of many women who appreciate refinement. The models in the collection typically have a rectangular case which offers great potential for variation. Now Longines has decided to create a new version of this example of contemporary elegance by using different colours of gold to enhance the brilliance of the steel.

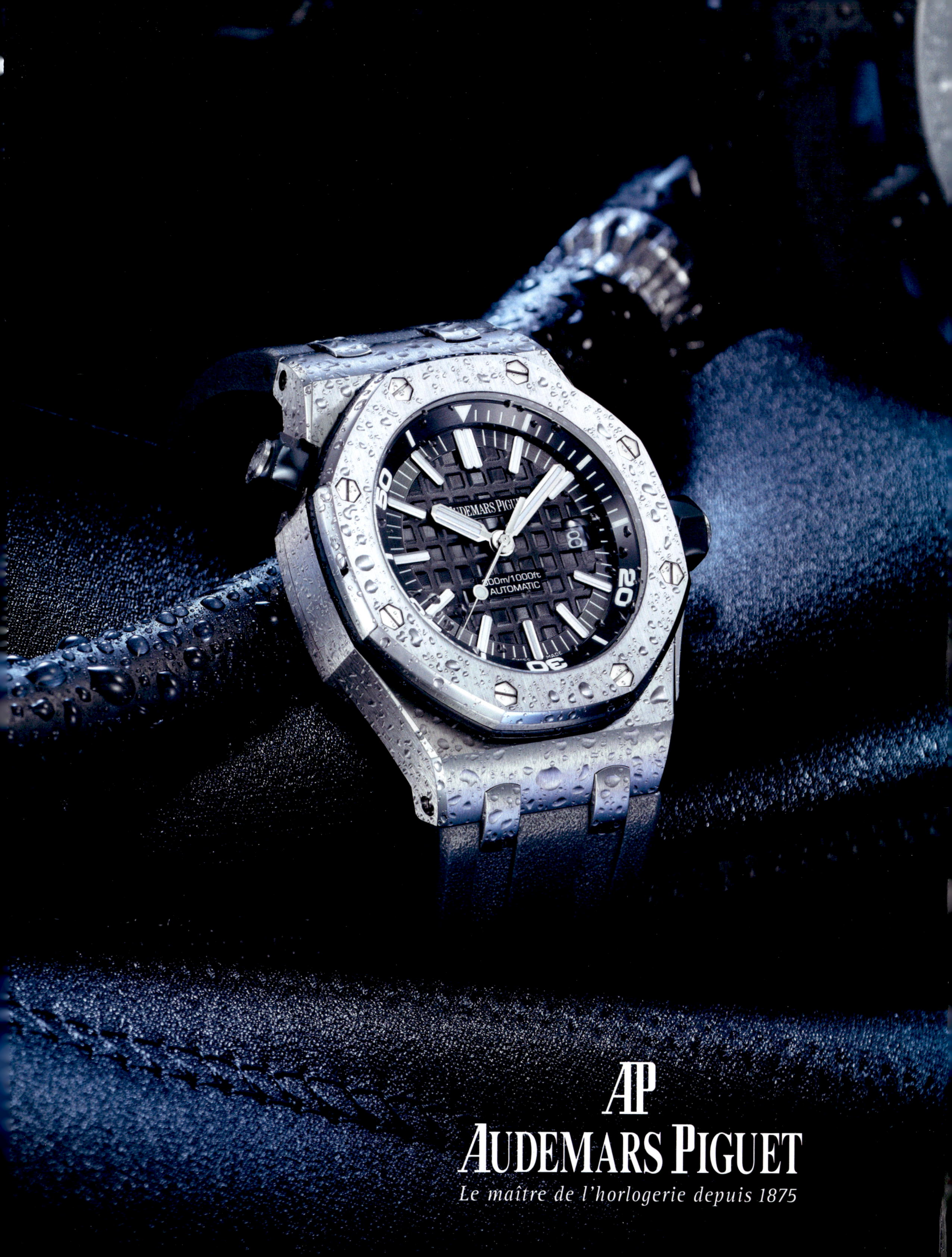
AUDEMARS PIGUET
Le maître de l'horlogerie depuis 1875

WATCHES XII INTERNATIONAL®

THE ORIGINAL ANNUAL OF THE WORLD'S FINEST WRISTWATCHES

First published in the United States in 2011 by

TOURBILLON INTERNATIONAL
A MODERN LUXURY MEDIA COMPANY

7 West 51st Street, 8th Floor
New York, NY 10019
Tel: +1 (212) 627-7732 Fax +1 (312) 274-8418
www.modernluxury.com/watches

In association with RIZZOLI INTERNATIONAL PUBLICATIONS, INC.

300 Park Avenue South, New York, NY 10010

ISBN: 978-0-8478-3602-4

PRINTED IN ITALY

COVER: PORTUGUESE PERPETUAL CALENDAR REF. IW502121 (IWC)

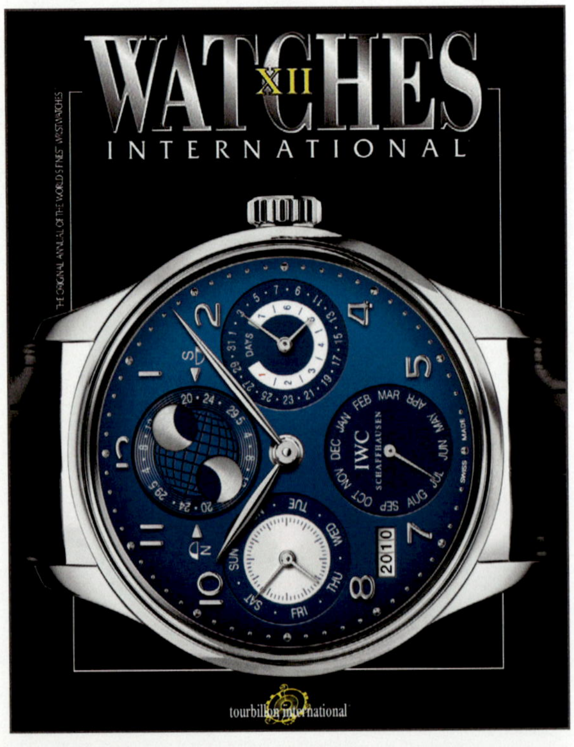

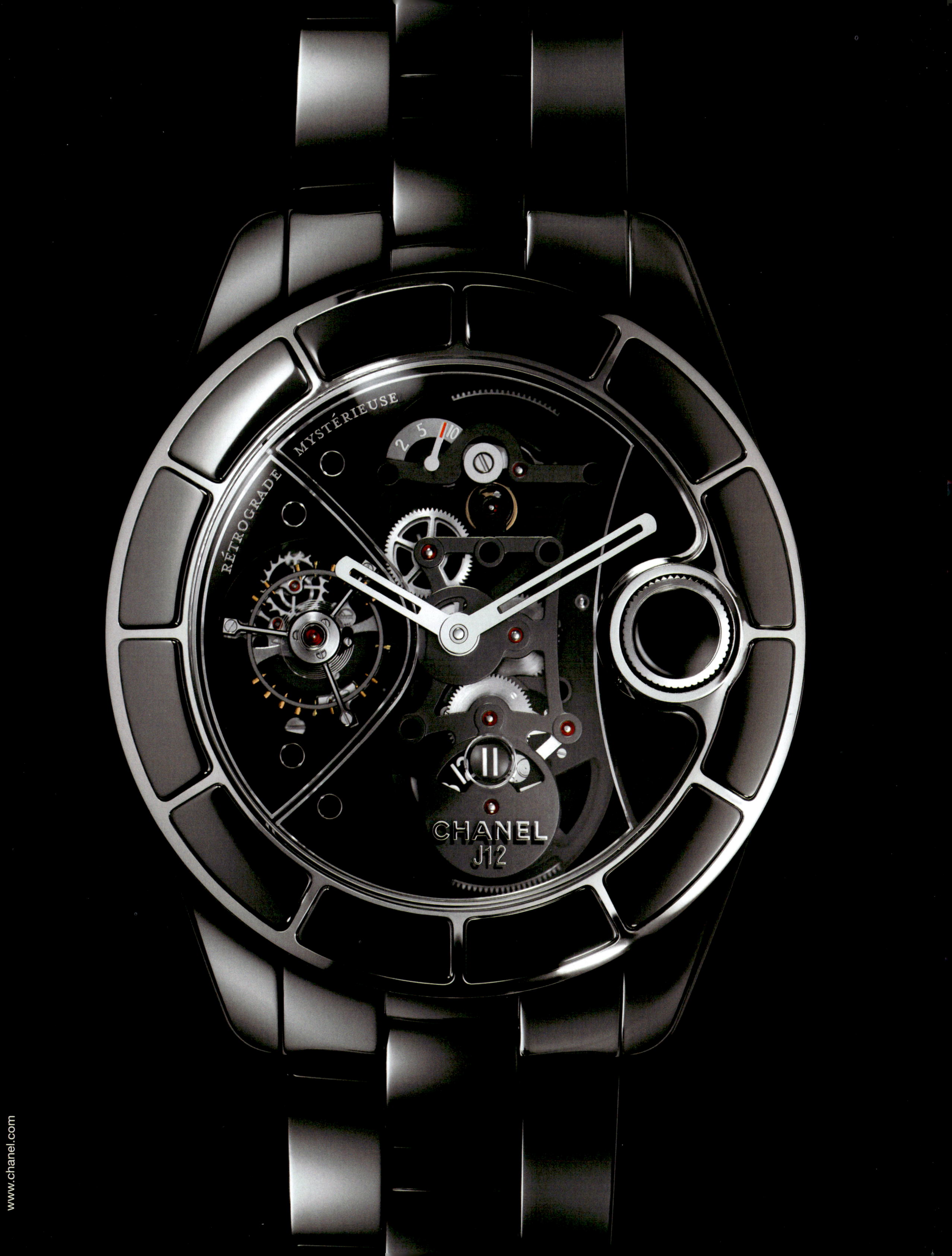
MYSTÉRIEUSE
RÉTROGRADE
CHANEL
J12
www.chanel.com

Letter from the President

About Time

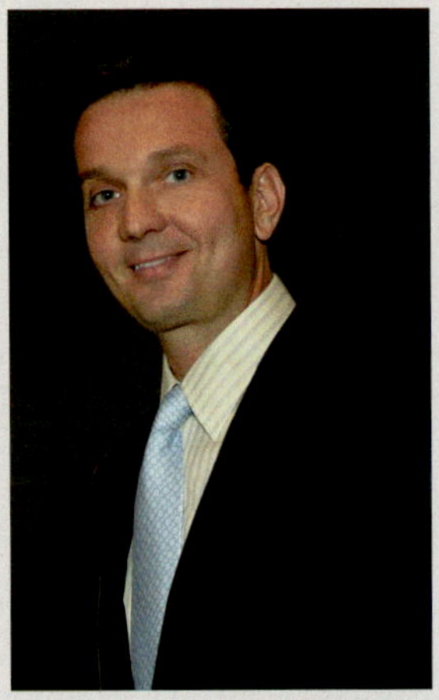

Timing really is everything. As luxury watches begin to regain the thrilling heights of popularity attained in the mid-aughts, it is my absolute pleasure to join you between these pages. I am delighted to be afforded the opportunity to join an editorial conversation that stimulates, provokes, and engages a readership—one that Modern Luxury Media and its portfolio of upmarket city magazines covering the nation's top luxury markets so brilliantly facilitates. And it is a downright thrill to announce Dickey Publishing's acquisition of the country's largest city magazine publisher.

Dickey Publishing looks forward to working closely with the dedicated and talented team at Modern Luxury Media to build upon the success this great company has worked tirelessly and creatively to achieve in its first decade. While no one can predict what the future will bequeath, I can tell you without hesitation that Dickey Publishing shares Modern Luxury's commitment to producing best-in-class publications and to partnering closely with our valued clients to maximize their return on investment and brand activation.

One of the perks of partnership is that I am able to introduce the latest edition of Watches International, which features the latest luxury timekeepers and the ongoing developments in the craft of fine watchmaking. Watches International will be available for the first time this year online as a digital edition, and we will also be producing a version especially for the iPad. This multimedia approach tracks the resurgence of the mechanical timepiece. Investment watches continue to enjoy immense popularity with both consumers and collectors, and we are pleased to bring you the market elite; products brilliantly conceived, aesthetically striking, technologically astute, and precisely engineered.

What is it about a luxury watch that in an age of instantaneous timekeeping still excites? Is it the class, the craftsmanship, the weight of expertise on the wrist? For me it is these attributes and the simple fact that excellence and legacy can be worn. A finely crafted timepiece is eminence measured in ounces, the quintessential definition of quality.

In the spirit of distinction, enjoy the issue.

Michael Dickey

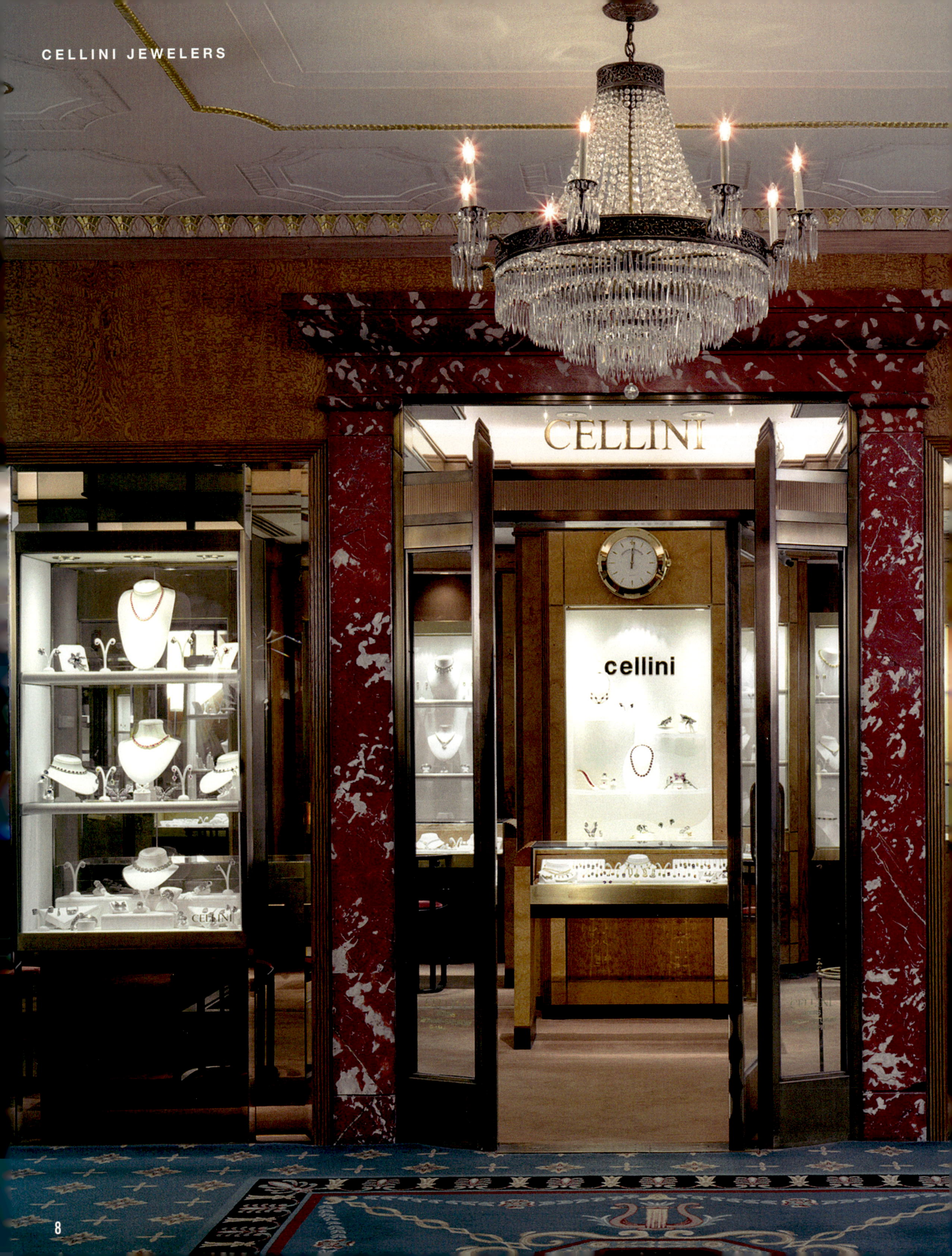
CELLINI
cellini

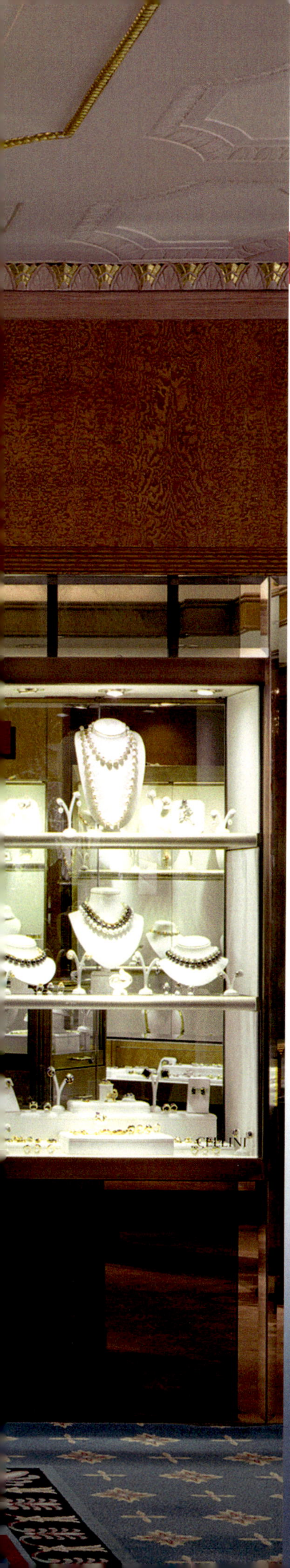

cellini

NEW YORK, NEW YORK

A New York City institution for more than a generation, Cellini Jewelers exceeds even the highest expectations with an impeccable collection of timepieces and jewelry that reflects a deep appreciation for the rareness of both handmade authenticity and natural beauty.

"Our considerable range is what sets us apart," says Cellini Jewelers President Leon Adams. "We carry an in-depth selection of the world's finest watches and a truly extensive array of jewelry. We believe it's important to have many choices, and an opportunity to select from a broad spectrum of pieces."

DEEP FOCUS

An extraordinary gathering of historic and emerging watchmakers finds a home at Cellini where it serves as the foundation for one of the world's largest and most prestigious collections of mechanical timepieces.

Dedicated watch enthusiasts have long cherished the unparalleled selection of timepieces Cellini offers. "If we believe enough in a brand to carry it, we do our best to carry the entire collection; not just every model, but more importantly, every metal that model is made in. Very few can say that," Adams says.

To help collectors navigate the eccentricities of high horology, Cellini's watch experts are as well versed in emerging trends as they are in past traditions and welcome the opportunity to answer your questions.

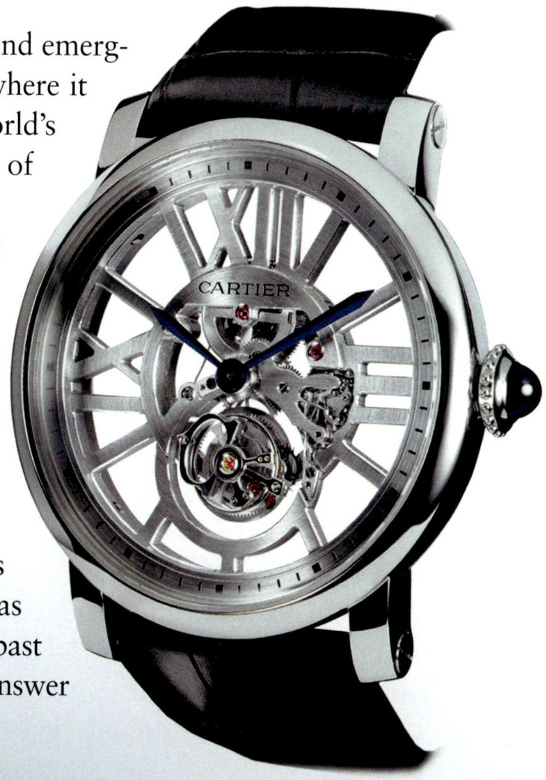

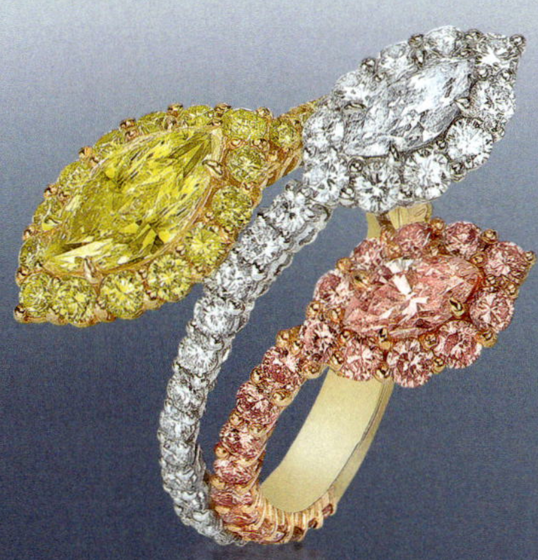

FACING PAGE

Cellini's flagship store was established in 1977 at the Hotel Waldorf-Astoria.

ABOVE

The Rotonde Skeleton Tourbillon is part of Cartier's new Fine Watchmaking collection, which is available on the East Coast exclusively at Cellini and Cartier.

LEFT

Cellini offers rings with natural fancy pink, yellow and white diamonds in platinum and 18-karat gold.

"We carry an in-depth selection of the world's finest watches and a truly extensive array of jewelry," Adams says. "We believe it's important to have many choices, and an opportunity to select from a broad spectrum of pieces."

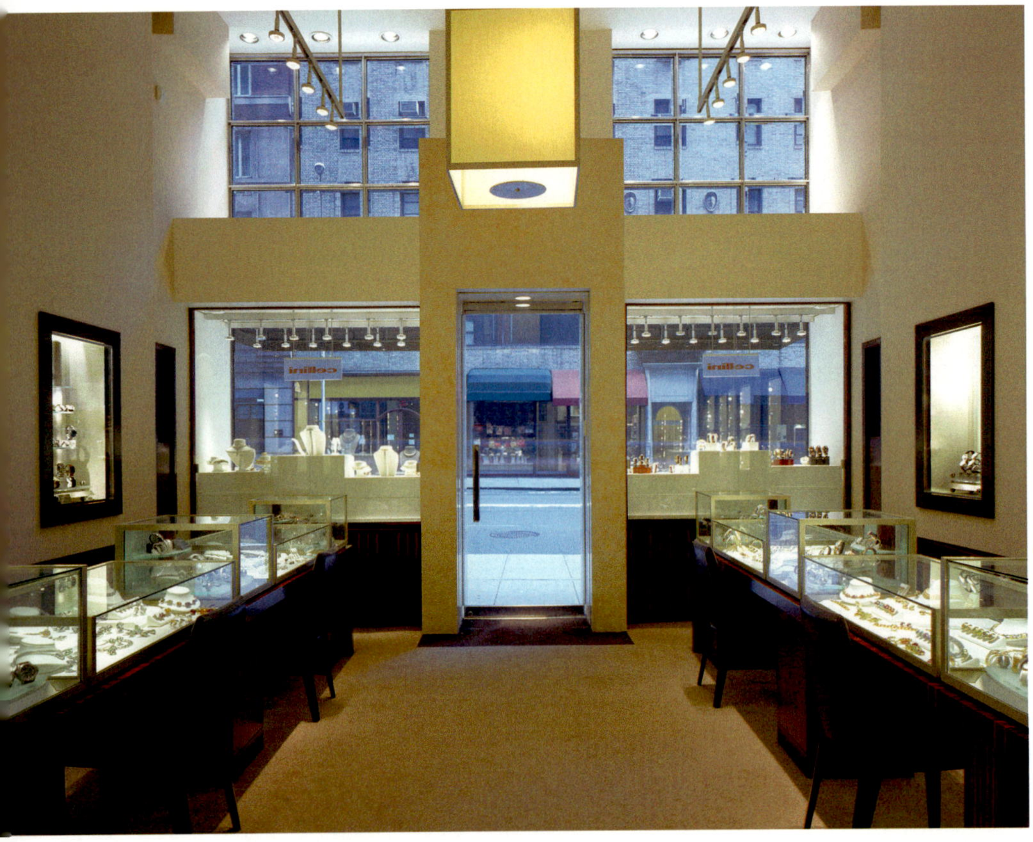

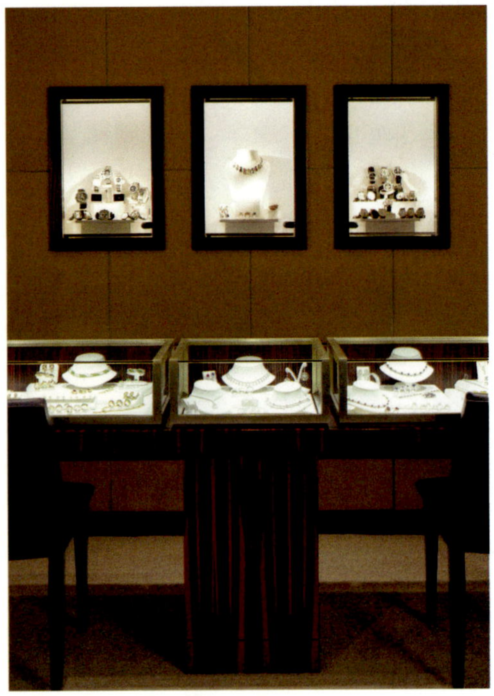

ABOVE AND LEFT

Cellini's second boutique was established in 1987 at the epicenter of the world's most elite shopping district.

FANTASTIC DISCOVERY

Along with the range of its watch collection, Cellini's dedication to rarity appeals to savvy connoisseurs who value exclusivity.

"You can walk into Cellini and see watches you won't see anywhere else," Adams says. "Beyond the best-known watchmakers, we also showcase some of the more exotic brands like Maîtres du Temps, Jean Dunand, Parmigiani, H. Moser, and just this year, Ludovic Ballouard's Upside Down watch."

In a nod to its reputation as an influential tastemaker, Cellini is also the only location on the East Coast where you can see Cartier's new Fine Watchmaking Collection other than Cartier's New York boutique.

GUIDED BY PASSION

More than just a bastion of high horology, Cellini has also cultivated a diverse collection of jewelry that ranks among the finest in New York City. Cellini is among an elite coterie of jewelers that specialize in exotic jewels, exhibiting an ambitious assortment that ranges from natural fancy color diamonds and alexandrite to Burmese rubies and Kashmir sapphires. "The same competitive spirit that drives our clients to demand the best from themselves is what inspires us to maintain such a high standard," Adams says.

For exceptional glamour, nothing outshines the supreme splendor of a bespoke setting. Cellini's gemologists and designers combine expertise with imagination to create jewelry tailored exclusively to your unique style, whether you are looking for a unique engagement ring or a one-of-a-kind necklace. "Because we have the experience and selection, the possibilities are endless," Adams says.

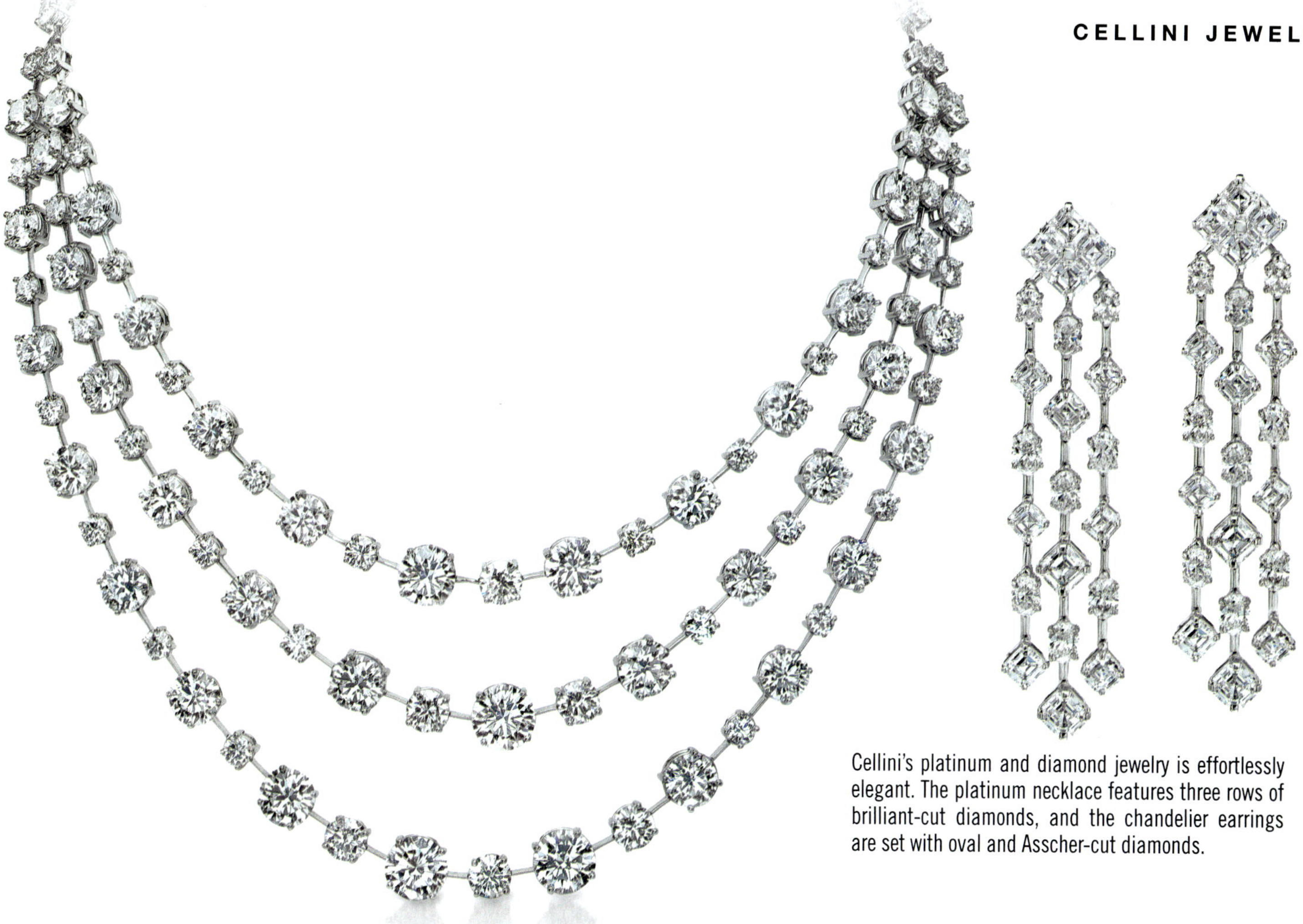

Cellini's platinum and diamond jewelry is effortlessly elegant. The platinum necklace features three rows of brilliant-cut diamonds, and the chandelier earrings are set with oval and Asscher-cut diamonds.

HANDLE WITH CARE

To maintain the beauty of your jewelry and extend the longevity of your watches, regular care is essential. Cellini invites you to visit our Waldorf-Astoria and Madison Avenue boutiques where our specialists stand ready to assist you.

Jewelry devotees will be able to relax as our experts scrutinize each stone's setting and evaluate the reliability of each clasp before returning the piece to you immaculately cleaned. Watch enthusiasts can rest assured that when the time comes every four years to service your mechanical timepiece that a master watchmaker will care for your watch as if it were their own.

Whether *haute couture* or *haute horlogerie* fuels your passion, come to Cellini and discover the best of both worlds.

BRANDS CARRIED

A. Lange & Söhne
Audemars Piguet
Bell & Ross
Cartier
Chopard
De Bethune
DeWitt
Franck Muller
Girard-Perregaux
Guy Ellia
H. Moser & Cie.
Hublot
IWC Schaffhausen
Jaeger-LeCoultre
Jean Dunand
Maîtres du Temps
Panerai
Parmigiani
Piaget
Richard Mille
Roger Dubuis
Ulysse Nardin
Vacheron Constantin

CELLINI

Hotel Waldorf-Astoria • 301 Park Avenue at 50th Street
New York, NY 10022 • 212-751-9824

509 Madison Avenue at 53rd Street
New York, NY 10022 • 212-888-0505

800-CELLINI • www.CelliniJewelers.com

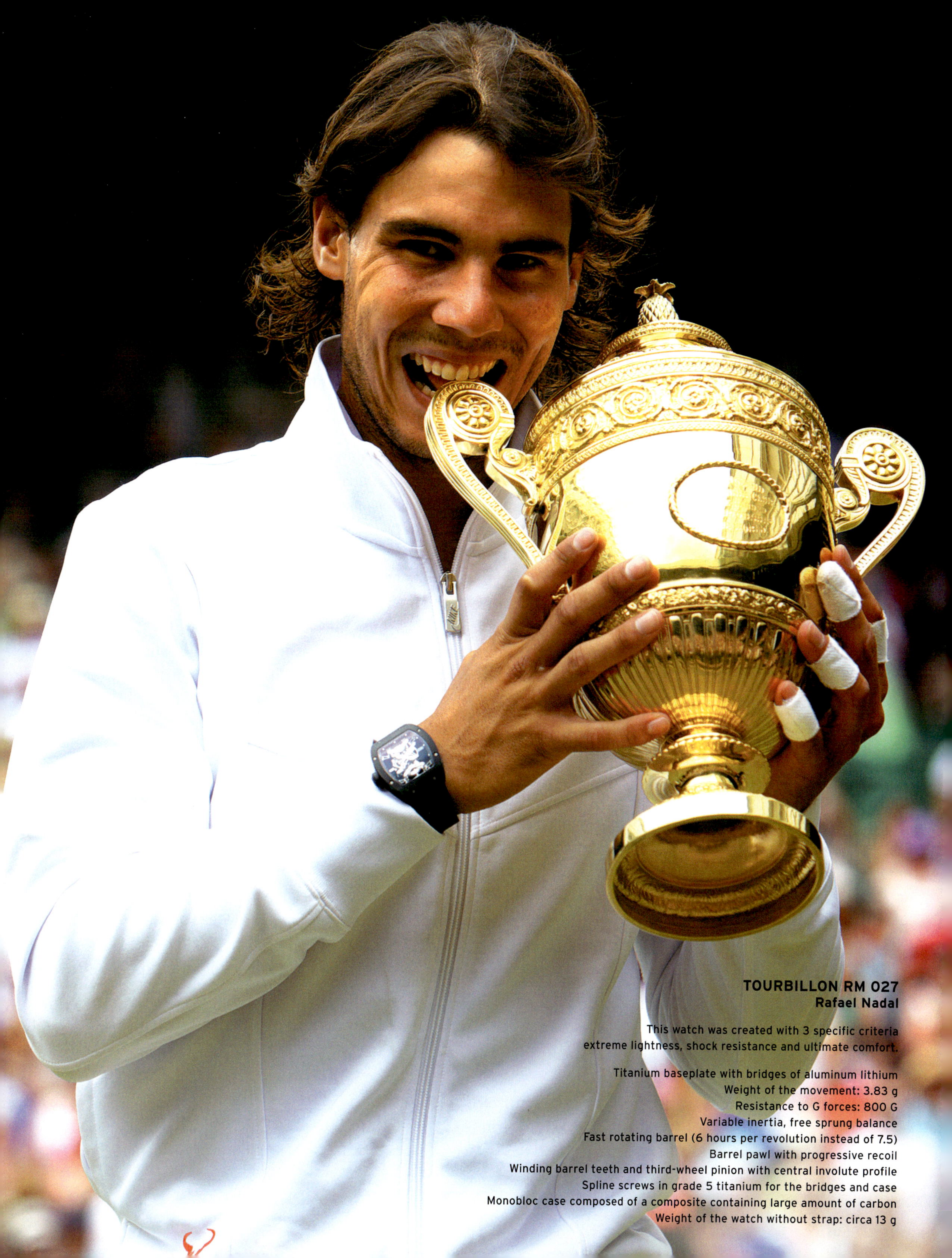

TOURBILLON RM 027
Rafael Nadal

This watch was created with 3 specific criteria
extreme lightness, shock resistance and ultimate comfort.

Titanium baseplate with bridges of aluminum lithium
Weight of the movement: 3.83 g
Resistance to G forces: 800 G
Variable inertia, free sprung balance
Fast rotating barrel (6 hours per revolution instead of 7.5)
Barrel pawl with progressive recoil
Winding barrel teeth and third-wheel pinion with central involute profile
Spline screws in grade 5 titanium for the bridges and case
Monobloc case composed of a composite containing large amount of carbon
Weight of the watch without strap: circa 13 g

Letter from the Publisher

The Conquering Cavalcade

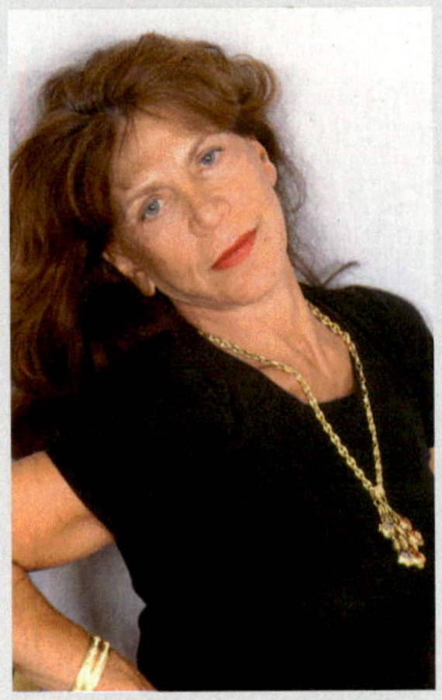

The storm clouds are breaking rank and the gloom that had surrounded the watch industry for many long months has fought its last battle. Two years of striving to see daylight once more, and at last newly claimed victories in which the cavalry has played a predominant role! The combat has left scars, and some have even had to resort to a scorched earth policy. It is almost as if the only ones left standing would necessarily be of noble lineage, along with mercenaries representing survivors from another age. Outstanding figureheads were needed, and their virtue had lain in their ability to embody Swiss Made toughness. Undeniably suffering from a lack of heroes, the industry was in dire need of reassurance.

Since 2008, it had been beaten into submission by a two-year cataclysm that wreaked havoc on the economy and on the luxury world in general, causing widespread collateral damage. Eager for release from the bondage of the crisis, the Swiss watch industry took up arms in an attempt to launch a mainly economic counter-offensive targeting Asia. It was nonetheless a very close call. The cavalry arrived just in time, led not by John Wayne, but by Hu Jintao. China will forever remain the greatest ally in this struggle. While this thought may provoke a certain amount of irritation, as if the legend had succumbed to the horn of plenty, any such hint of heresy is soon forgotten in light of the double-digit growth figures promised by the coalition.

Both in Switzerland and abroad, legions of disciples are currently marching on Shanghai. It is the new path trodden by soldiers who have become pilgrims pursuing specific industrial and financial goals, yet nonetheless driven by a Napoleonic desire for conquest! History is reversed, as troops move steadily eastward, and the watchmaking cause has found itself an amazingly efficient armed wing.

In the 1970s, war was waged against Japan in order to push back the quartz invasion. In 2011, it is all about fighting for market share in a neighboring eastern land. While the offensive is peaceable in itself, it is nonetheless guided by extremely skilled and strategic military-type maneuvers. Fortunately, many in the watch industry have learned important lessons from the past: if you want peace, prepare for war.

Caroline Childers

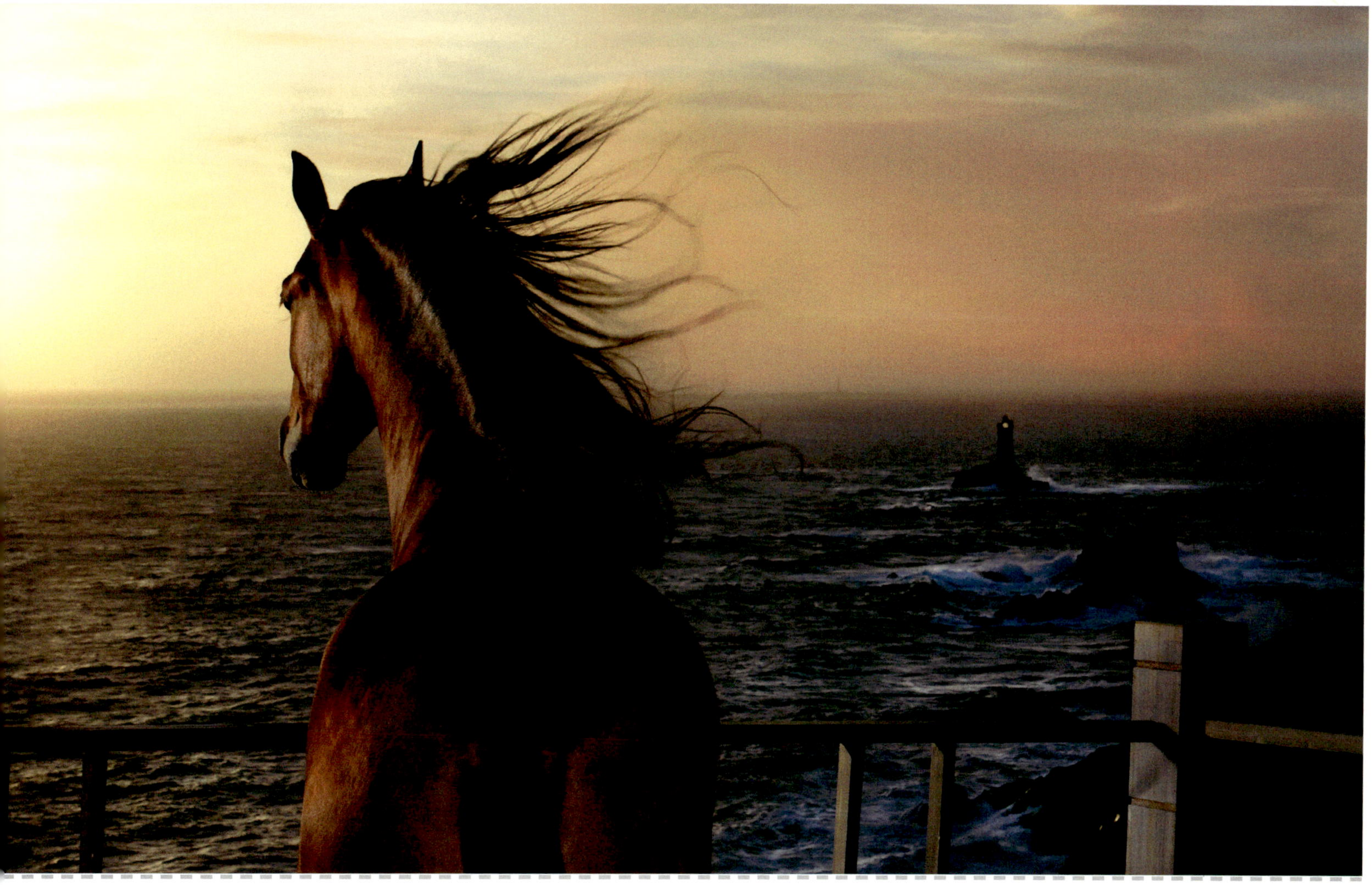

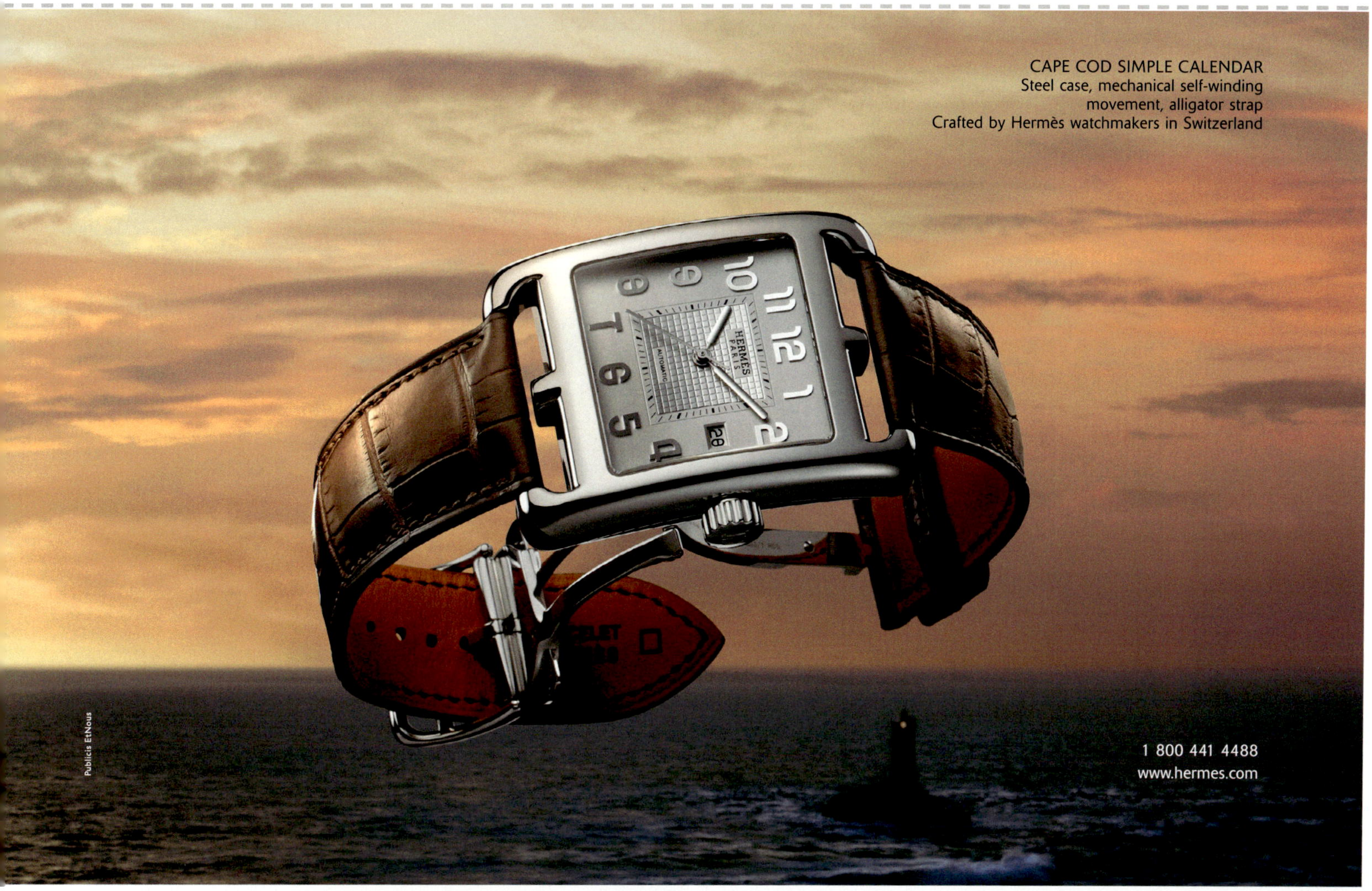
CAPE COD SIMPLE CALENDAR
Steel case, mechanical self-winding
movement, alligator strap
Crafted by Hermès watchmakers in Switzerland
1 800 441 4488
www.hermes.com
Publicis EtNous

arije

PARIS • LONDON • CANNES

Arije provides everyone who walks through its doors with the utmost in personalized service and acts as a congenial liaison between luxury watchmakers and their exclusive clientele.

For 30 years, Arije has been a fixture in the City of Lights, reinventing the aesthetic codes of jewelry and watchmaking. The first shop was established on rue Pierre Charron in the Golden Triangle of Paris, the section bordered by the avenue des Champs-Elysées, avenue Marceau and avenue Montaigne. Due to its extraordinary success and near-legendary status among Parisian watch aficionados, a sister store opened on avenue George V, a stone's throw away. The same year, 2009, Arije leapt even more emphatically into its expansion, opening two boutiques in Cannes and one in London as well.

The shops in Cannes, both on the Promenade de la Croisette—close to the esteemed Film Festival—enchant and soothe with marble-inflected interiors similar to the store in London. Taupe and chestnut accents on the walls and floor induce a state of relaxation and echo the sand just steps away on the beach. In a Paris location, the aura of luxury is tangible, and the walls themselves seem to exude golden light. A third approach, seen on the ground floor, combines the clean, simple lines of the taupe interior and the extravagance of Paris's "Golden Triangle" in a sleek modern design. Recessed displays devoted to the likes of Rolex and Audemars Piguet beckon to the passer-by, and immaculate white couches around delicate flames reinterpret the conversation pit for an upscale clientele.

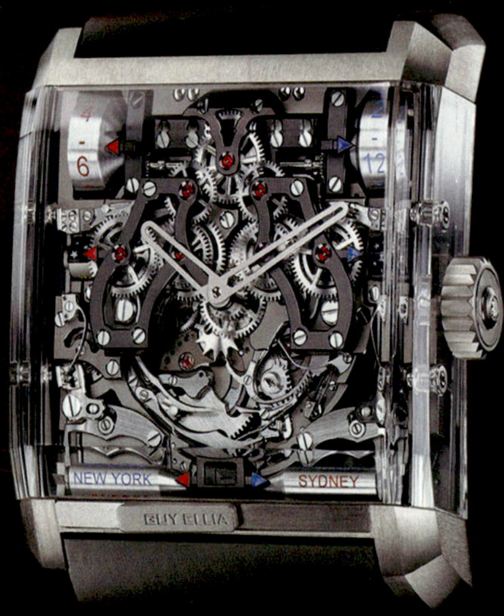

Répétition Minute Zephyr (Guy Ellia)

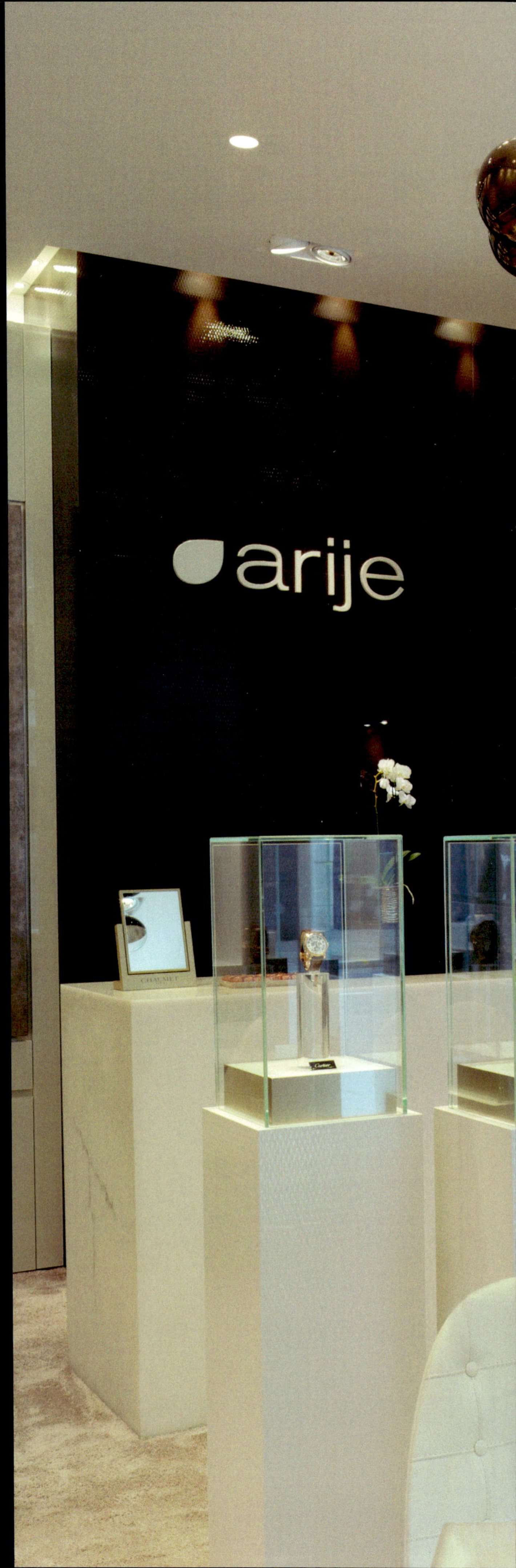

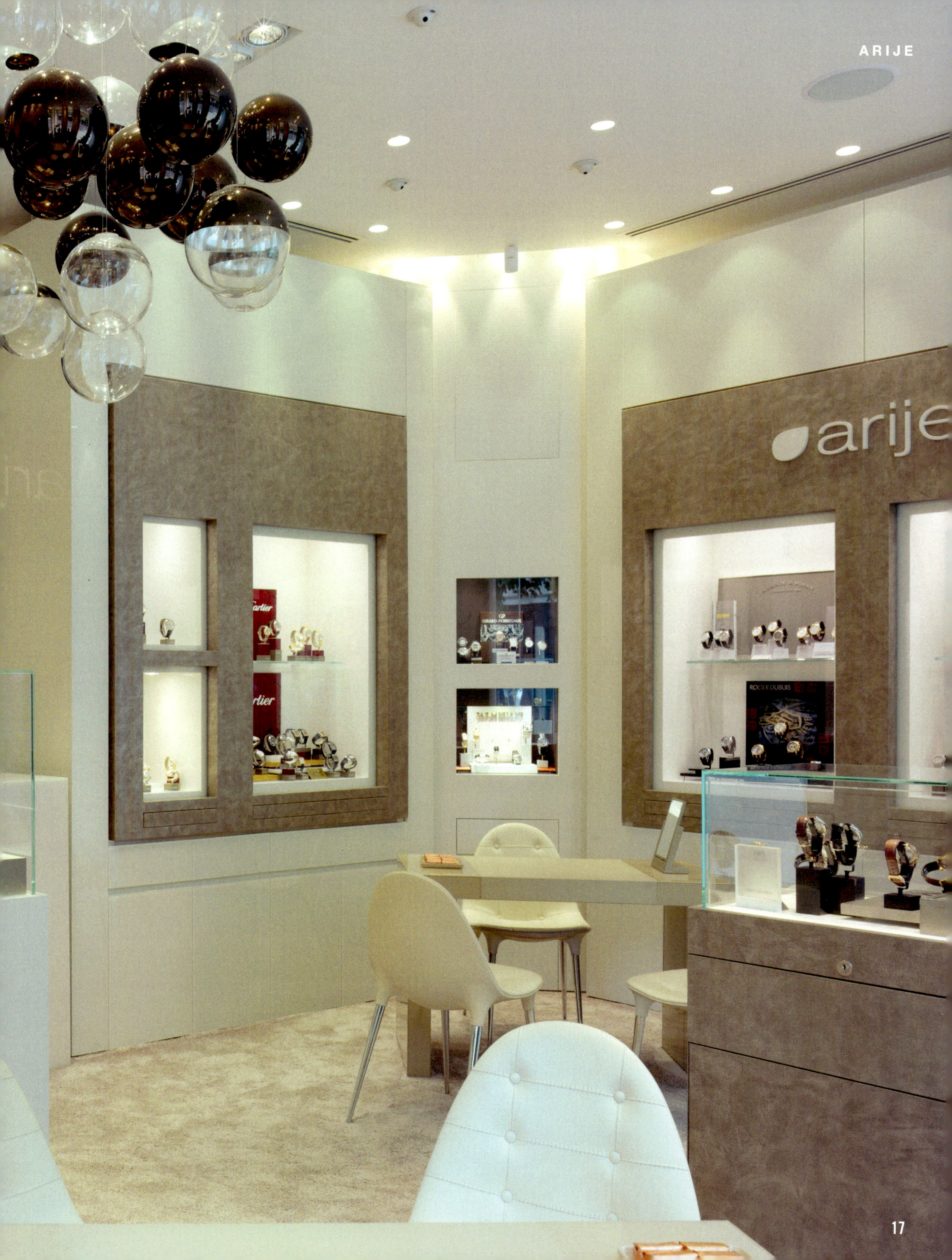
arije
ROGER DUBUIS

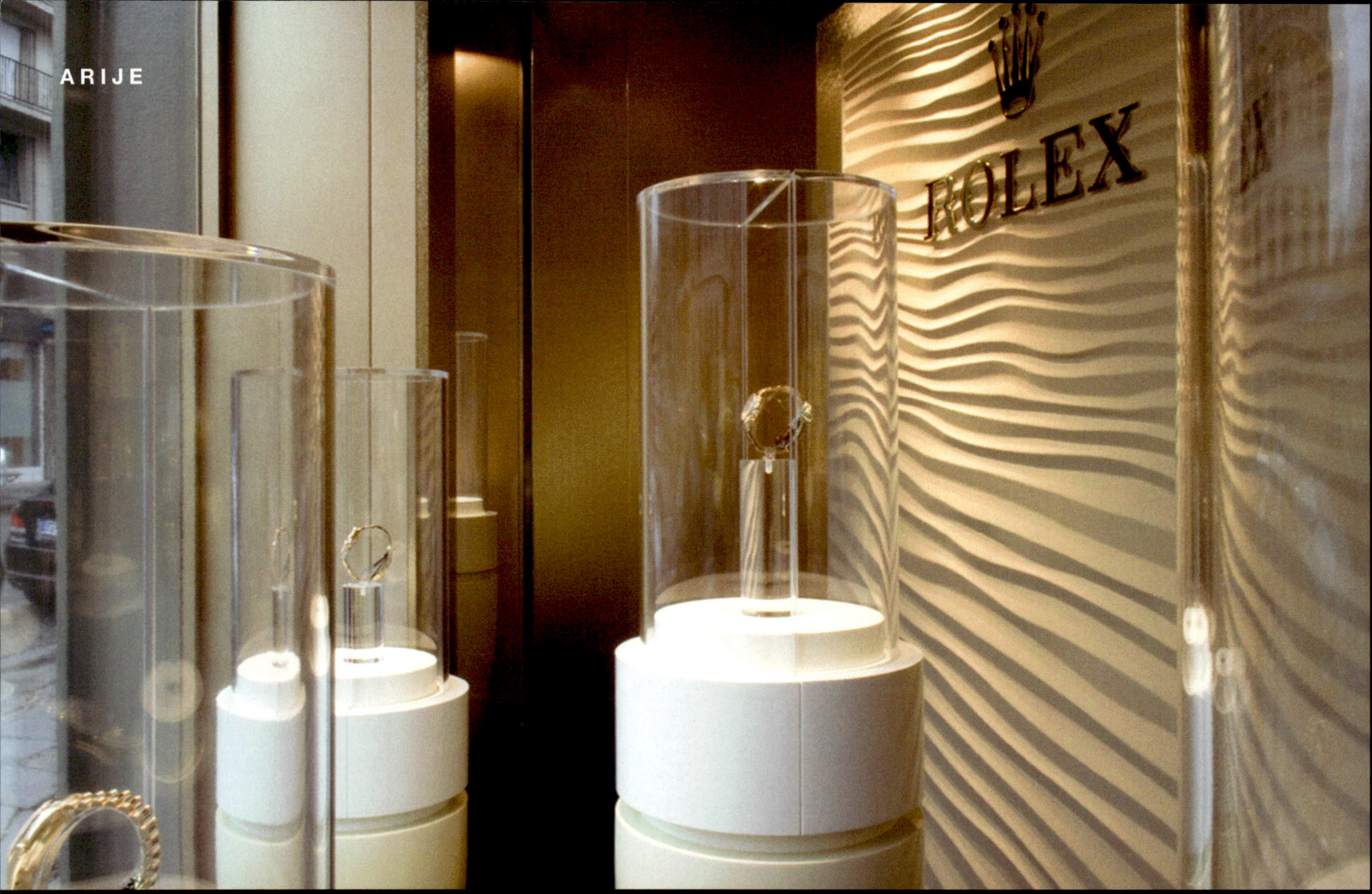

To wander inside an Arije boutique is like stumbling into a magical world made of gold and light. Five boutiques in three different cities—Paris, London and Cannes—all follow a distinct blueprint of luxury while developing their own identities.

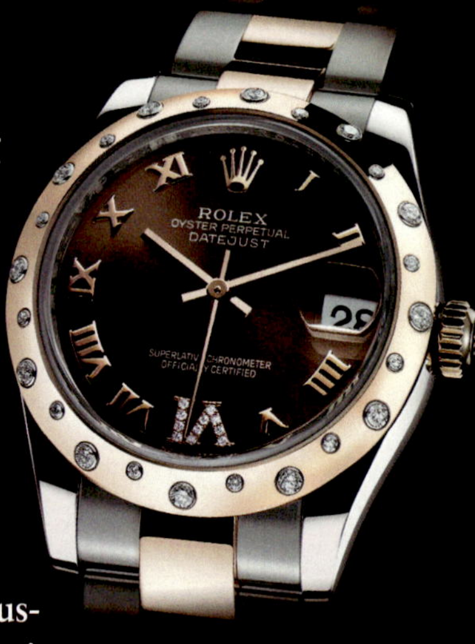

DateJust Lady
(Rolex)

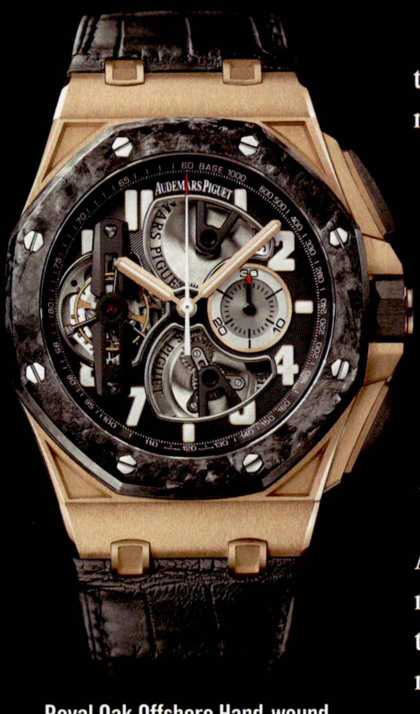

Royal Oak Offshore Hand-wound Tourbillon with chronograph (Audemars Piguet)

The décor of Arije's boutiques, however, is only the beginning of a brand-new experience. One of the reasons for Arije's standing is its uncanny ability to predict trends in the watchmaking world. Of course, high quality is hardly a trend, and Arije carries the most prestigious names in the industry, names like Audemars Piguet, Breguet, Cartier, Chopard, IWC, Rolex, Vacheron Constantin, etc. The selection of watches, as well as a bent for daring, unpredictable haute jewelry, has built a reputation for Arije predicated on combining tradition and modernity. Major watch companies partner with Arije to showcase the latest word in exclusive series and limited editions.

This dedication is evident in the welcome the customer receives from Arije's staff. Acting as a congenial liaison between the highest-end watchmakers and their exclusive clientele, Arije provides everyone who walks through its doors with the utmost in personalized service. Of course, the relationship between the customer and the boutique is far from over once the watch lover happily holds his or her new Rolex or Audemars Piguet in hand.

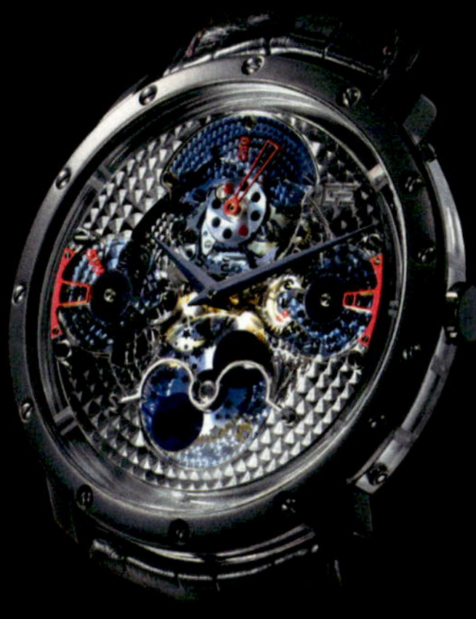

Time Space Quantième Perpétuel (Guy Ellia)

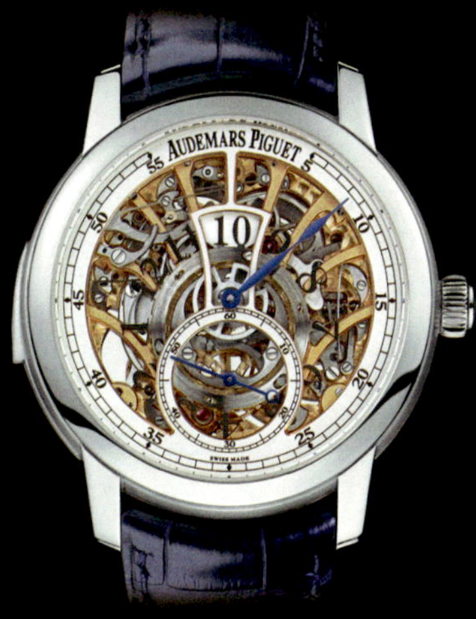

Skeleton Manual Winding Repeater with Jumping Hour (Audemars Piguet)

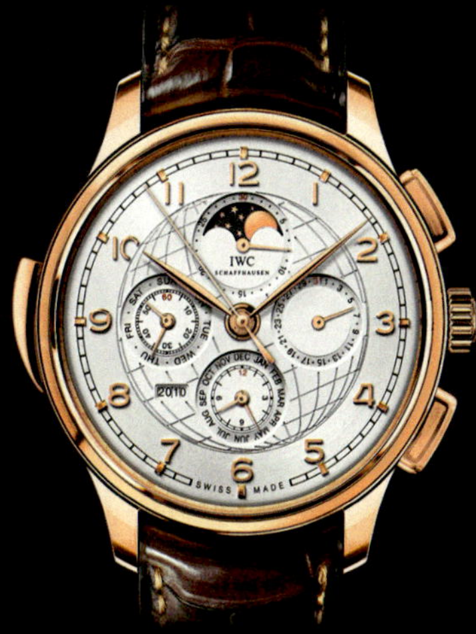

Portuguese Grand Complication (IWC)

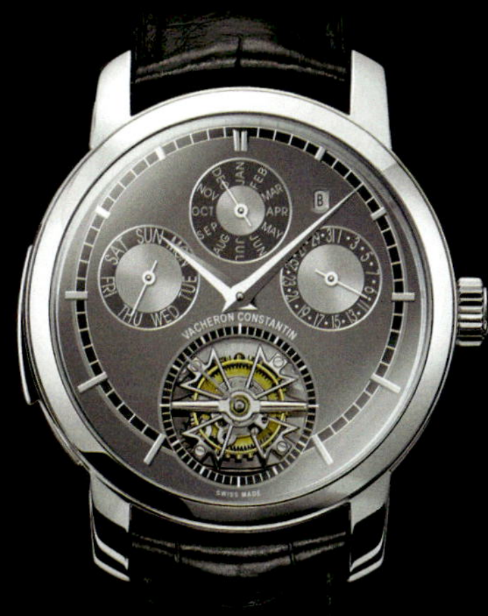

Patrimony Traditionnelle Calibre 2755 (Vacheron Constantin)

Each shop dedicates a portion of its qualified staff to customer service. Handpicked watchmakers and reparation experts are approved by most major horological brands, where they undergo regular training. For the most delicate operations on the most complicated pieces, timepieces go to the ultra-modern servicing center at the boutique on Avenue George V. Just as a sapphire caseback reveals the workings of a watch, a glass window separates the servicing center from the rest of the boutique, allowing customers to observe the high-tech, high-precision work of consummate watchmaking professionals.

Of course, Arije would not be Arije without the spirit and efforts of Carla Chalouhi, its CEO. Daughter of Arije's founder, a cosmopolitan business-woman with her finger on the pulse of the watch industry, Carla is at the heart of it all, the woman behind the watches.

BRANDS CARRIED

A. Lange & Söhne**
Audemars Piguet***
Baume & Mercier**
Bell & Ross*
Blancpain*
Breguet*
Cartier***
Chanel*
Chaumet*
Chopard*
Cvstos*
de Grisogono*
Dior*
Ebel*
Franck Muller**
Girard-Perregaux***
Glashütte*
Guy Ellia***
Harry Winston**
Hautlence**
Hublot*
IWC***
Jaeger-LeCoultre*
Jaquet Droz*
Montblanc*
Omega*
Panerai*
Parmigiani**
Piaget**
Pierre Kunz*
Roger Dubuis***
Rolex*
TAG Heuer*
Tudor*
Ulysse Nardin**
Vacheron Constantin*
Van Cleef & Arpels**
Zenith*

* Paris
* London
* Cannes

ARIJE

PARIS

50 rue Pierre Charron - Tel +33 (0)1 47 20 72 40
30 avenue George V - Tel +33 (0)1 49 52 98 88

LONDON

165 Sloane Street - Tel +44 (0)20 7752 0246

CANNES

50 boulevard de la Croisette - Tel +33 (0)4 93 68 47 73

SAINT-JEAN-CAP-FERRAT

Grand-Hôtel du Cap-Ferrat • 71 boulevard du Général de Gaulle - Tel +33 (0)4 93 76 50 24

www.arije.com
contact: shop@arije.com

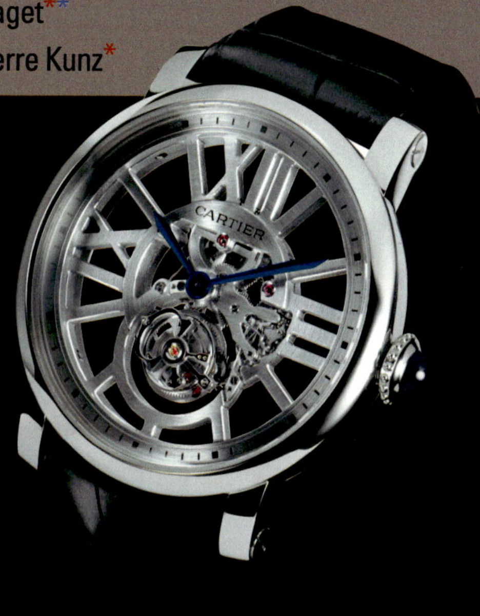

Rotonde Tourbillon Squelette (Cartier)

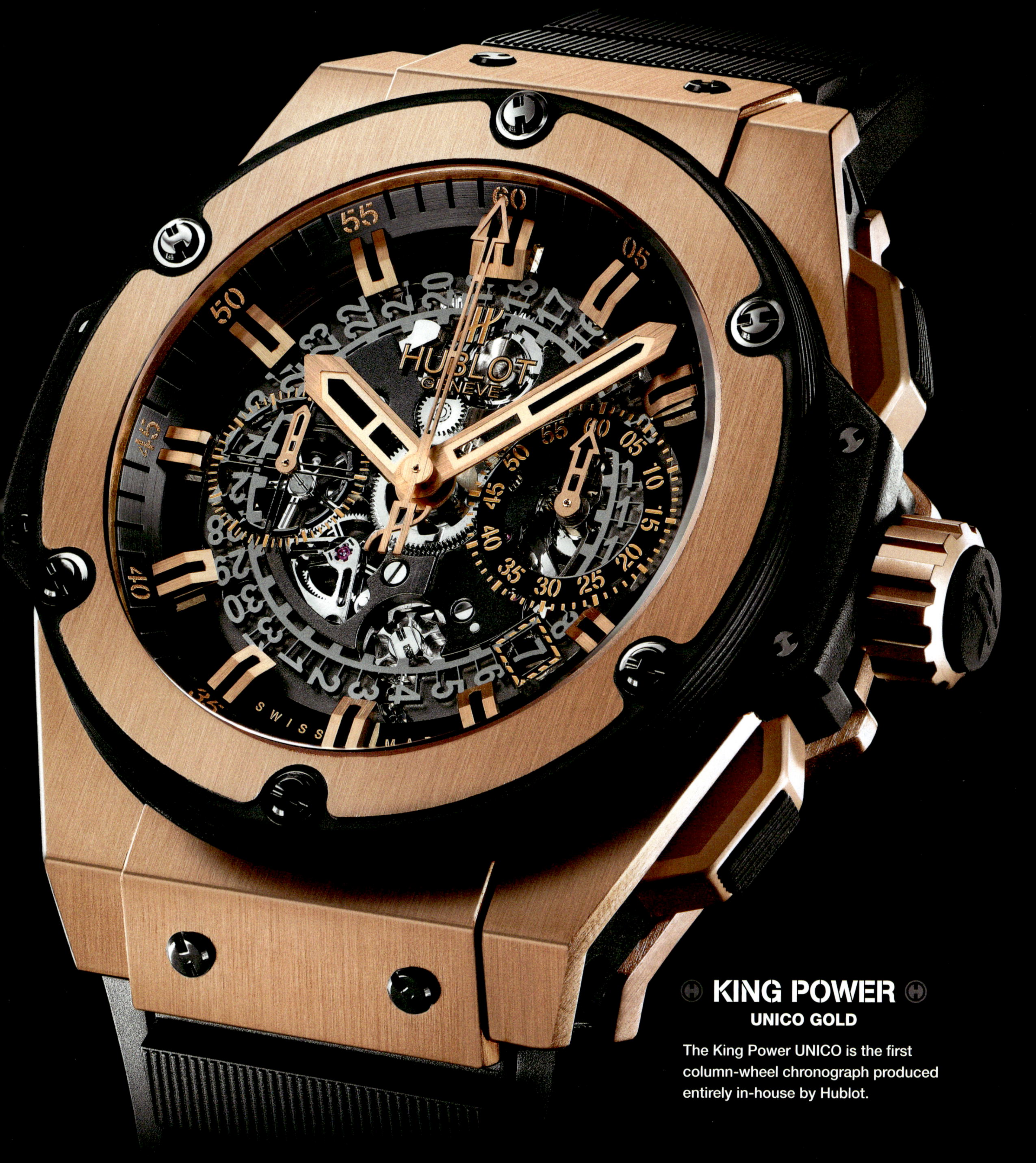

KING POWER
UNICO GOLD

The King Power UNICO is the first column-wheel chronograph produced entirely in-house by Hublot.

Letter from the Editor in Chief

The Age of Transparency

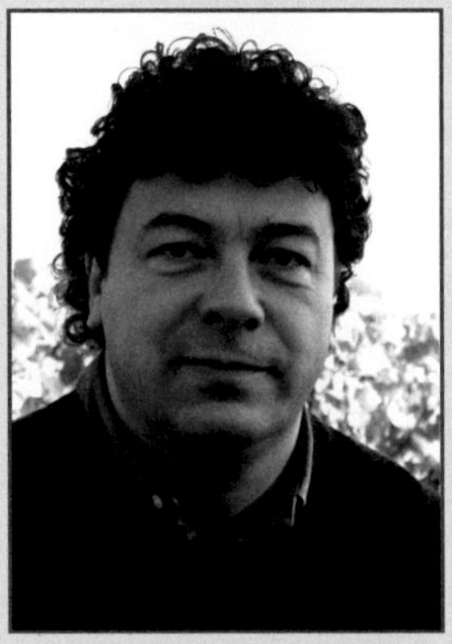

Every era brings its own challenge: after having concentrated its seductive efforts on gold and diamonds during the 1990s, and on mechanical movements and complications during the following decade, horology is preparing for an entirely different battle in the years to come: the field of competition, in the near future, will certainly be that of ethics and honesty.

The signs are clear. It started in April 2009, when Patek Philippe slammed the door on the Geneva Seal to create its own label of quality: the Patek Philippe Seal. Between the lines of the civilized, carefully worded official press release, observers quickly understood that the problem lay in the sloppiness that had crept into the Geneva Seal process in recent years and led it to grant this noble pedigree to certain undeserving brands.

Another significant development is the increasingly keen connoisseurship that watch lovers bring to the table, which inspires brands to produce ever more high-performance, exclusive timepieces. A growing number of watchmakers are developing new in-house movements that distinguish their pieces from any standard production. This adds to the need for transparency, to the resounding benefit of horolophiles everywhere.

October 2010 brought new revelations, when Swiss public television aired a shocking documentary on the nauseating practices of certain tanners in Asia. Viewers saw how lizards and snakes were skinned alive and their skins used by the luxury industry, and in particular for straps of high-end watches. The program provoked a powerful reaction of shock from the public, followed by expressions of disgust from the Swatch Group and the Federation of the Swiss Watch Industry.

The latest alert also came in October 2010 and was issued by a Swiss laboratory concerning the new European legislation known as REACH (Registration, Evaluation, Authorization and Restriction of Chemicals). This law, which took effect at the beginning of 2011, requires the Swiss watch industry—among other businesses—to do some serious introspection in order to eliminate all harmful substances from its products. To ensure the good faith of the watch brands, the consumers themselves stand ready to verify the information for themselves.

More and more informed, and less and less gullible, today's watch lover is no longer inclined to buy any watch at any price! Whether it concerns quality control for industry standards, the origins of the movements, the conditions of production of the leathers, metals and gemstones that compose the models, today's active consumer wants an "ethical" watch—and the industry is preparing to rise to the challenge.

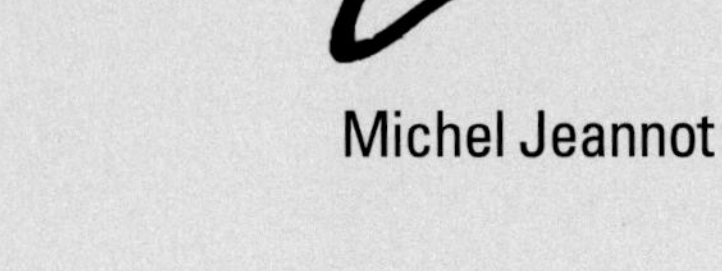

Michel Jeannot

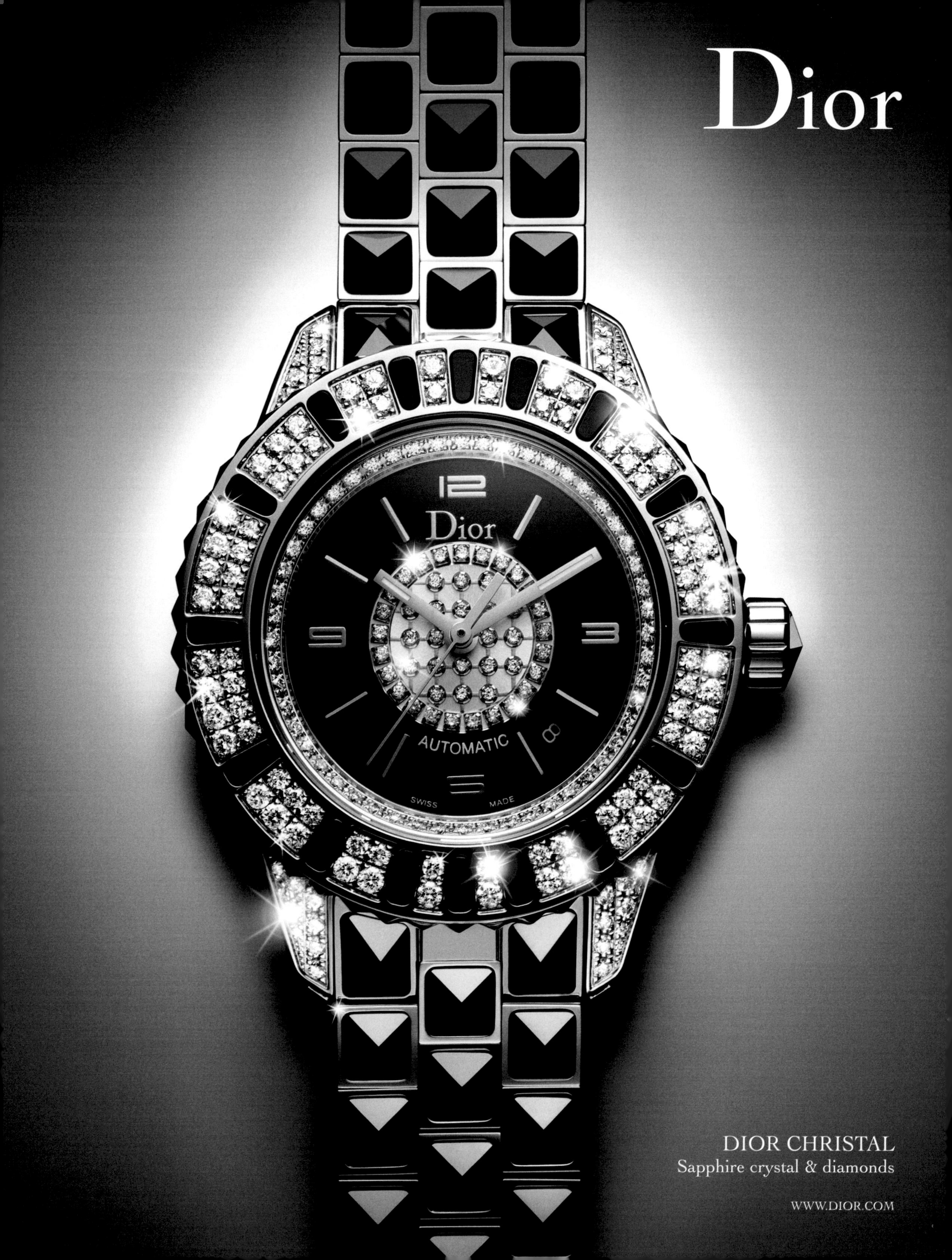
Dior
Dior
AUTOMATIC
SWISS MADE
DIOR CHRISTAL
Sapphire crystal & diamonds
WWW.DIOR.COM

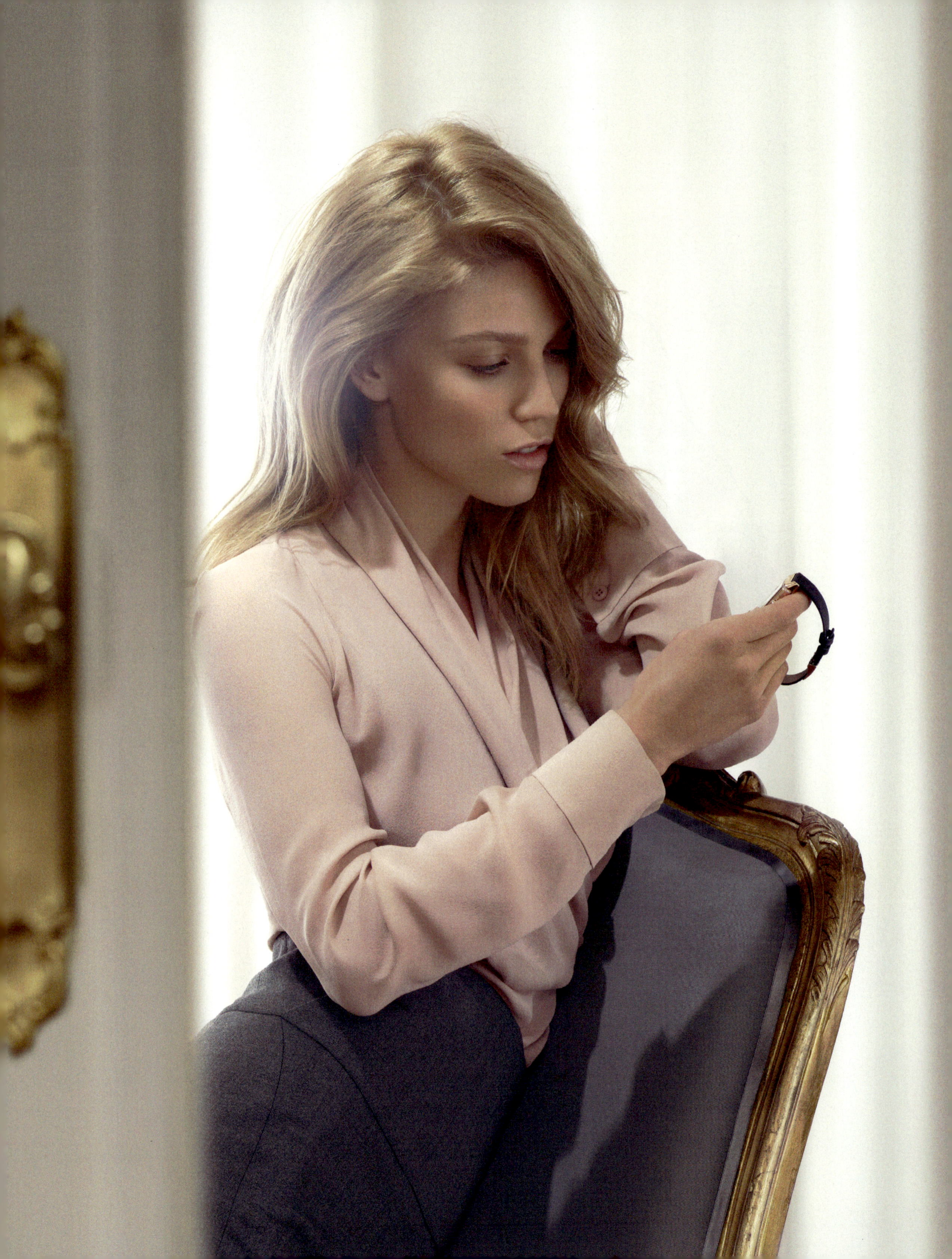

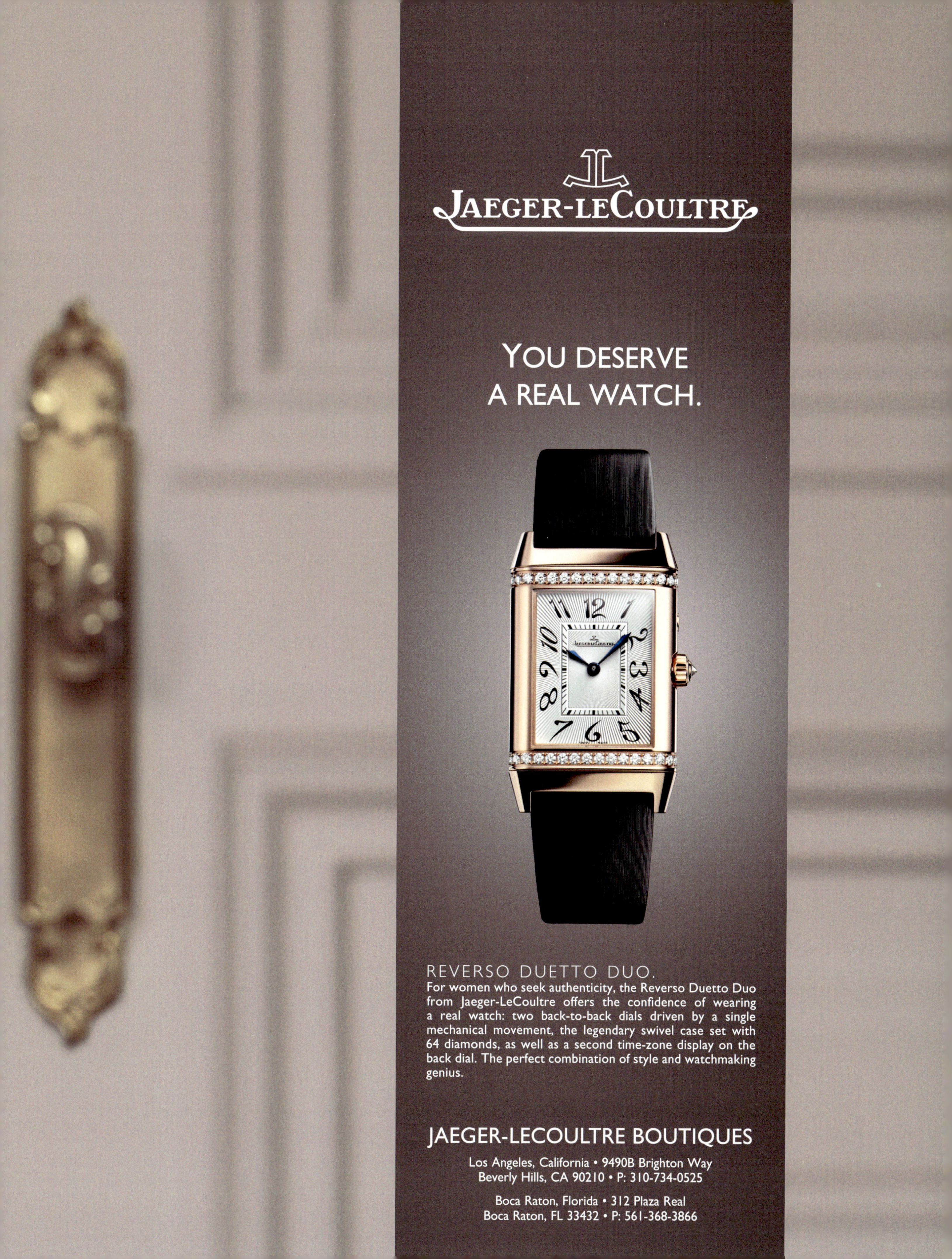

JAEGER-LECOULTRE
YOU DESERVE
A REAL WATCH.
REVERSO DUETTO DUO.
For women who seek authenticity, the Reverso Duetto Duo from Jaeger-LeCoultre offers the confidence of wearing a real watch: two back-to-back dials driven by a single mechanical movement, the legendary swivel case set with 64 diamonds, as well as a second time-zone display on the back dial. The perfect combination of style and watchmaking genius.
JAEGER-LECOULTRE BOUTIQUES
Los Angeles, California • 9490B Brighton Way
Beverly Hills, CA 90210 • P: 310-734-0525
Boca Raton, Florida • 312 Plaza Real
Boca Raton, FL 33432 • P: 561-368-3866

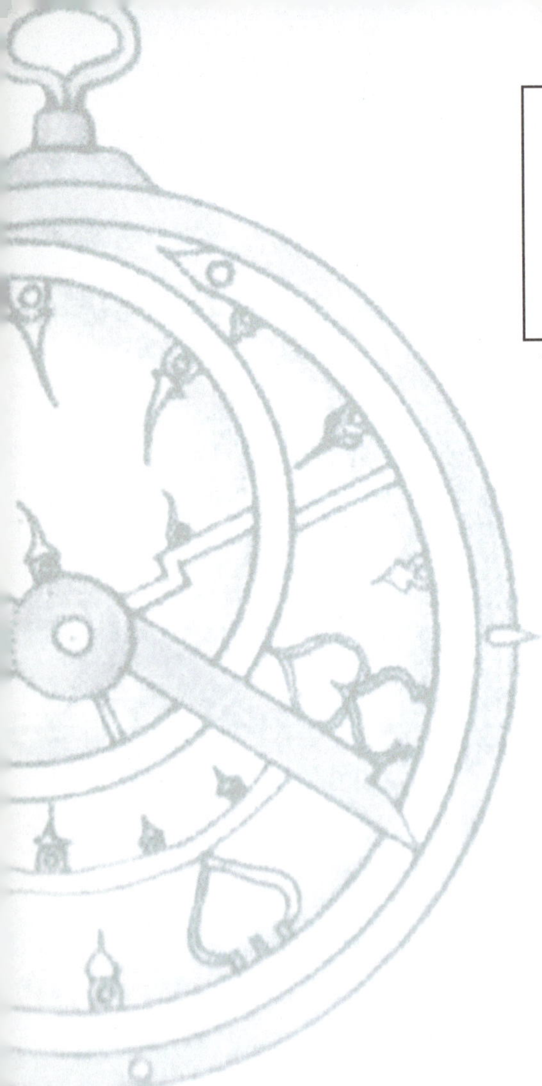

WATCHES XII INTERNATIONAL®

THE ORIGINAL ANNUAL OF THE WORLD'S FINEST WRISTWATCHES

TOURBILLON INTERNATIONAL
A MODERN LUXURY MEDIA COMPANY
ADMINISTRATION, ADVERTISING SALES, EDITORIAL, BOOK SALES

7 West 51st Street, 8th Floor • New York, NY 10019
Tel: +1 (212) 627-7732 Fax: +1 (312) 274-8418

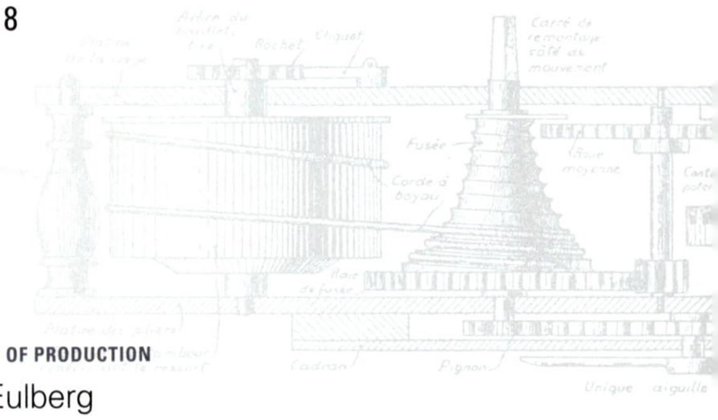

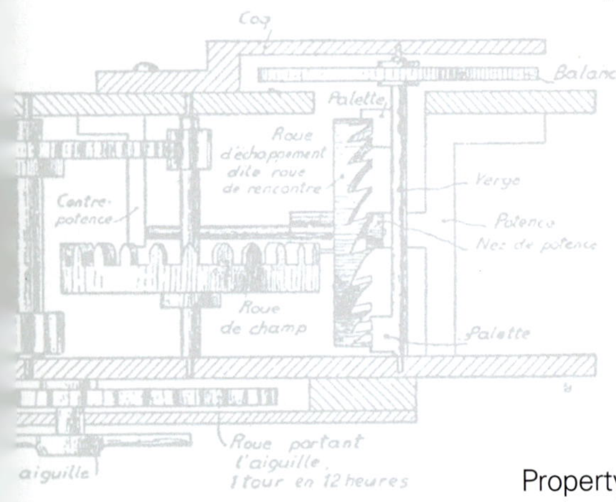

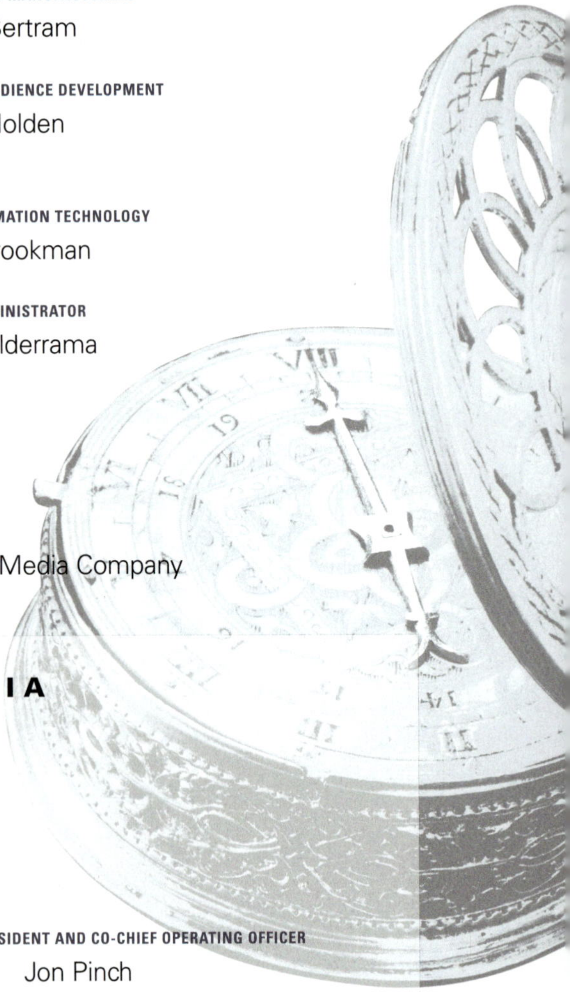

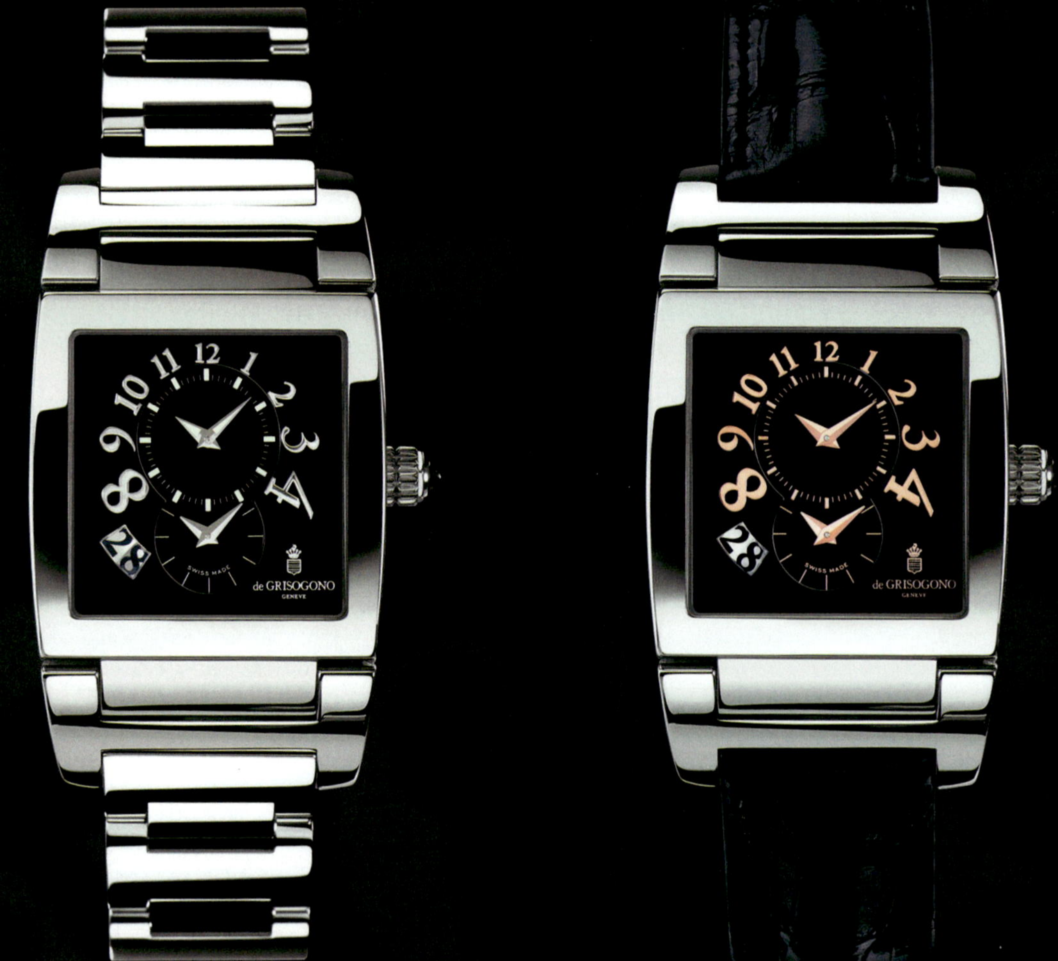
de GRISOGONO
GENEVE
de GRISOGONO
GENEVE

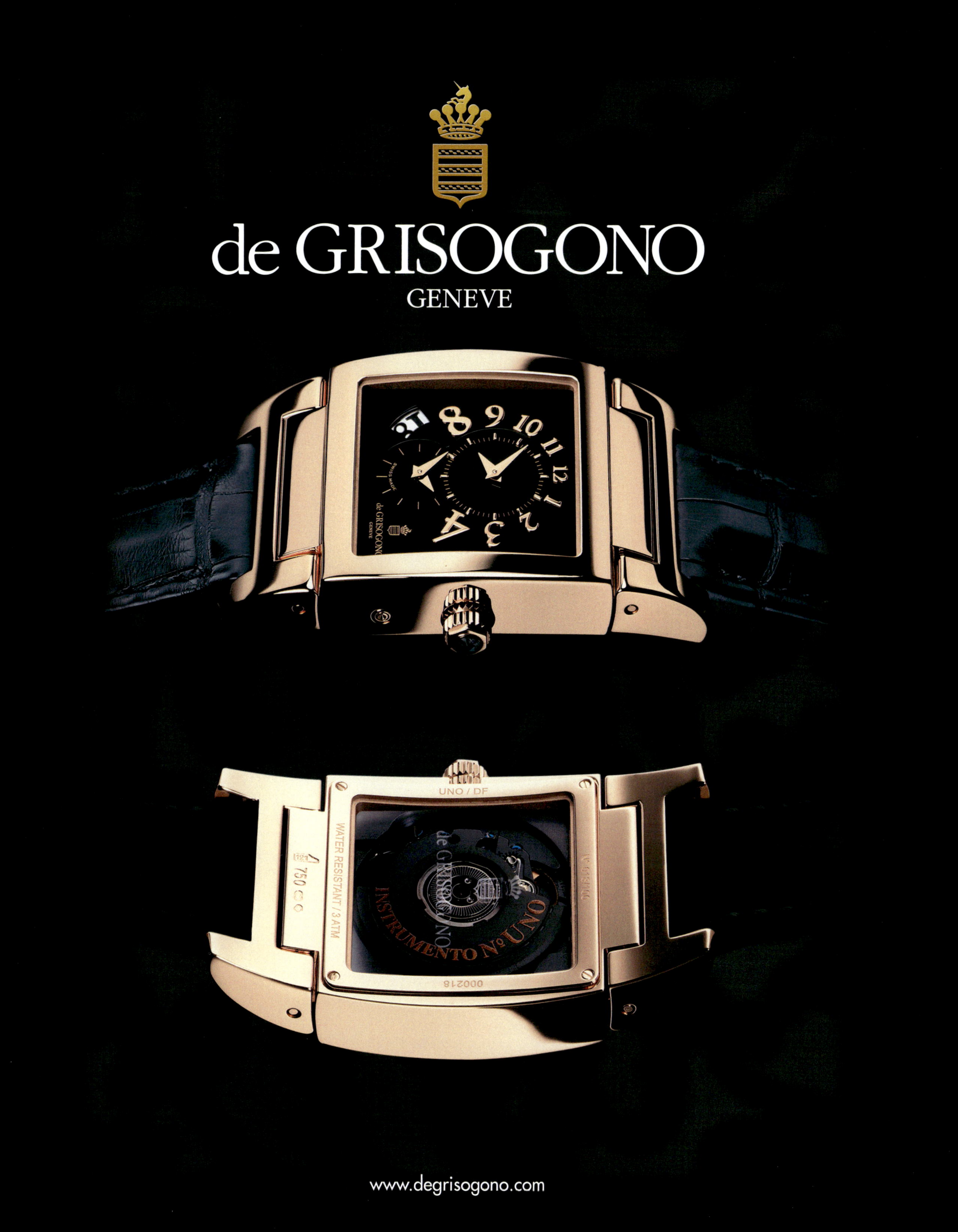
de GRISOGONO
GENEVE
UNO / DF
WATER RESISTANT / 3 ATM
INSTRUMENTO Nº UNO
000218
www.degrisogono.com

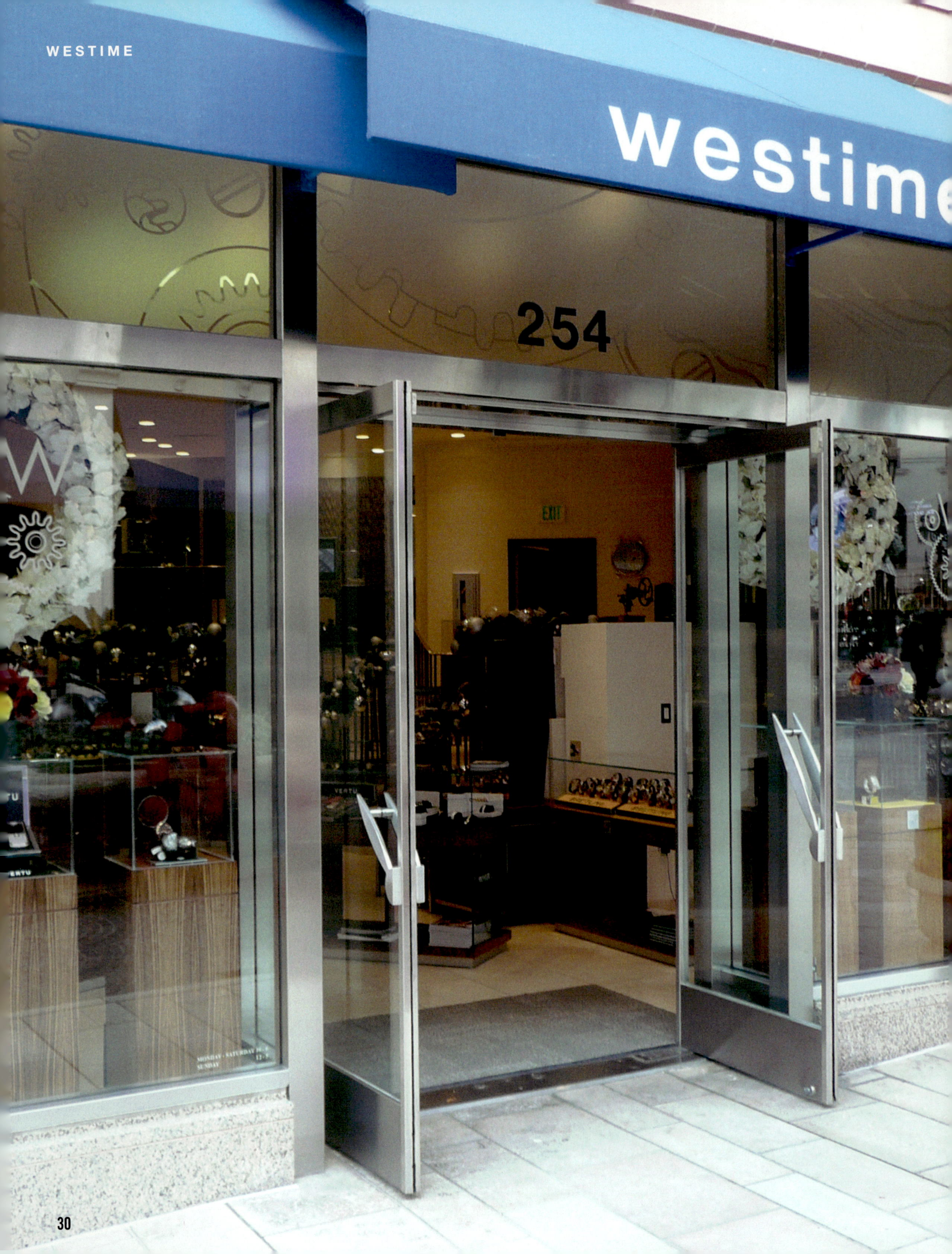
westime
254
EXIT

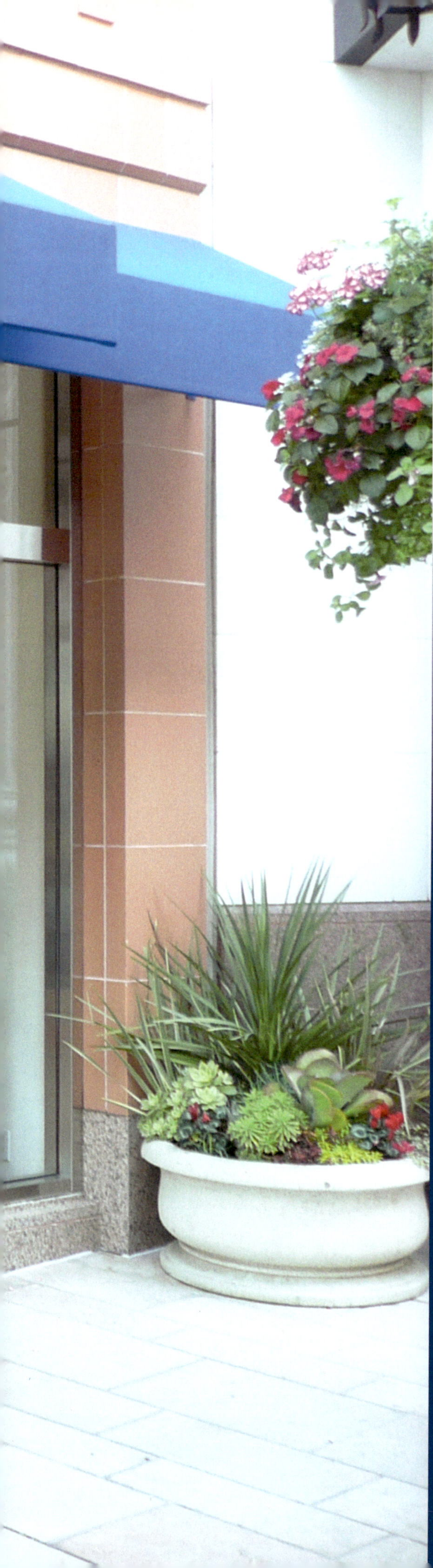

Westime

LOS ANGELES & BEVERLY HILLS, CA

For more than two decades, family-owned and operated Westime has distinguished itself as the ultimate retail destination for finding extraordinary watches. Year after year, Westime earns the return business of discriminating clients from around the world who value Westime's superior service and watch selection.

Westime's two elegant boutiques make watch shopping a true VIP experience. At the Westime Los Angeles location, which is a 6,000-square-foot showroom adjacent to the Westside Pavilion, clients will find a wide range of watches representing every price point. Here, expansive showcases, comfortable seating arrangements and two specialty boutiques make browsing easy and personal. Two master watchmakers are on site at all times, and they have state-of-the-art equipment at their disposal to provide fast service and repairs. In Beverly Hills, Westime's intimate multi-level boutique resides at the heart of the city's most glamorous shopping district. Here, watch collectors and those following the latest fashion trends will find the most sought-after timepieces in the world.

Westime prides itself on offering highly regarded and rare watches from the most acclaimed watch brands. Limited editions, unique pieces, and even custom models created exclusively for Westime take pride of place in the boutiques' showcases. Westime is frequently selected by brands to carry their most complicated timepieces on an exclusive basis.

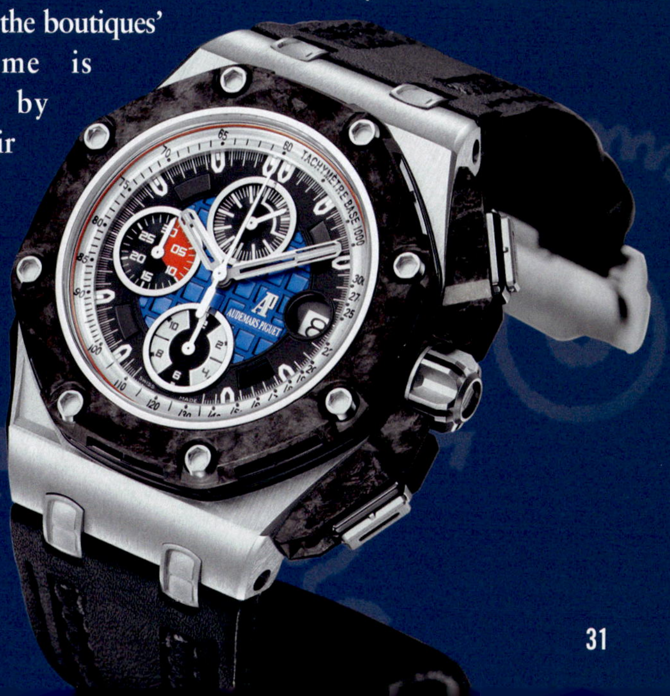

Royal Oak Offshore Grand Prix (Audemars Piguet)

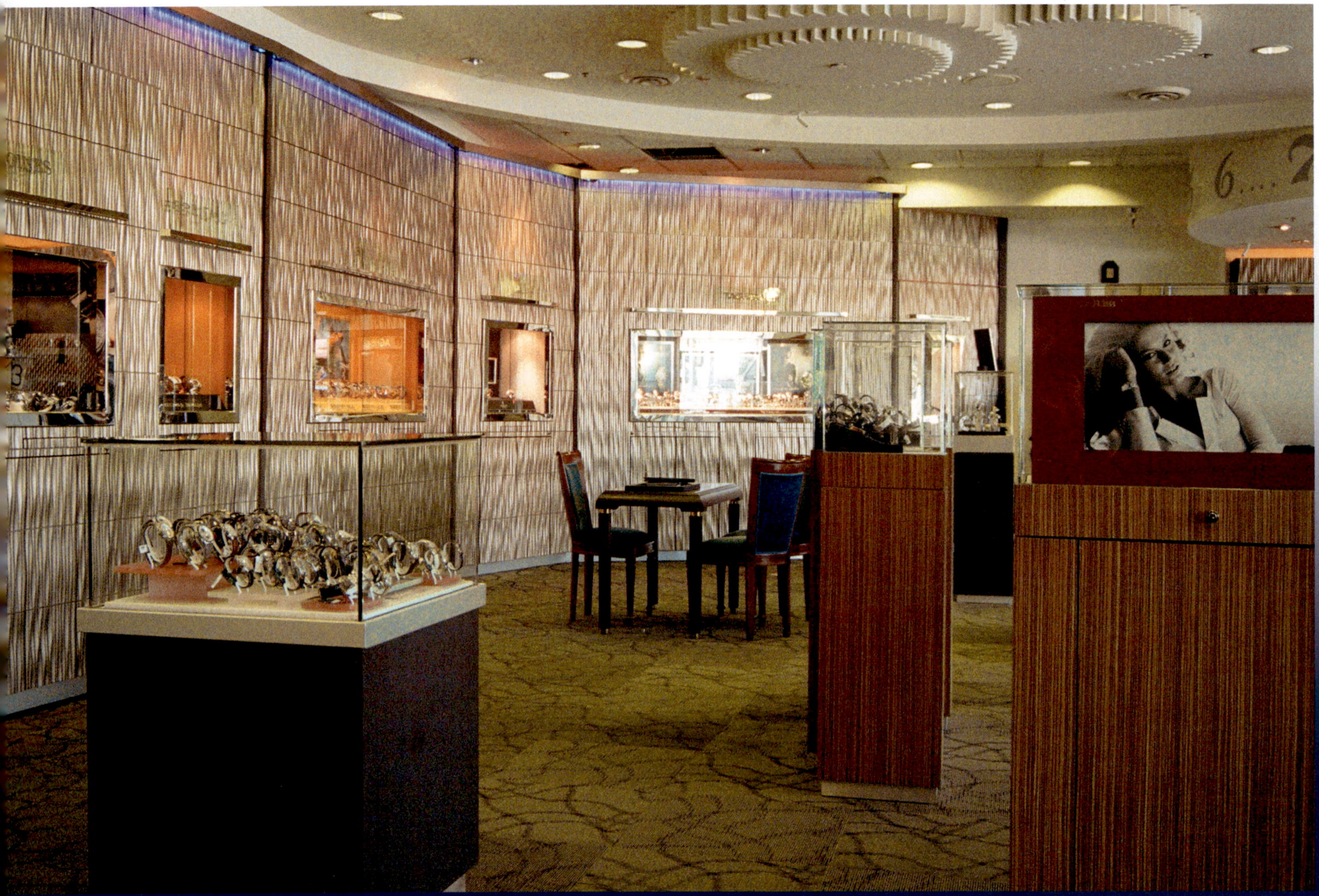

From day one, Westime has also dedicated itself to seeking the new guard in haute horology by presenting the finest creations of contemporary watchmakers. Three brands stand powerfully for the new watchmaking vanguard. Richard Mille is regarded as the master of materials that are redefining the vocabulary of luxury; Greubel Forsey hails as the tourbillon revolutionary; and URWERK has emerged as the king of kinetic sculpture.

Throughout the year, Westime hosts unique customer events to introduce preferred clients to the newest watches, as well as the visionaries behind these complicated creations. The company is also a proud supporter of charities and their local fund-raising events. And the boutiques' multi-lingual staff members are dedicated to providing the ideal service to their clients—from explaining the specifics of complications, to hand-delivering a watch across the country.

Westime is owned by a third-generation watch connoisseur with a passion for mechanical timepieces and a true love of the business. With Greg Simonian, a member of the family's fourth generation, leading the business, Westime's horizons are expanding. During 2011, Westime will open a new flagship location on Sunset Boulevard, and continue to offer an even greater selection of watches and luxurious accessories.

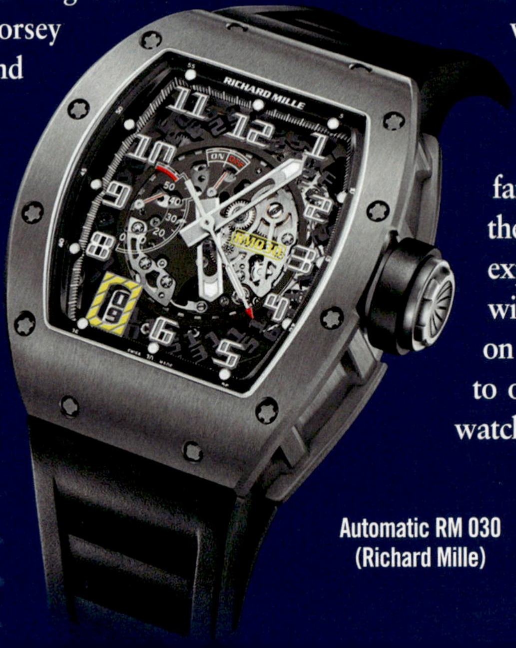

Automatic RM 030
(Richard Mille)

Westime offers highly regarded and rare watches from the most acclaimed watch brands, displaying limited editions, unique pieces, and even custom models created exclusively for Westime in its showcases.

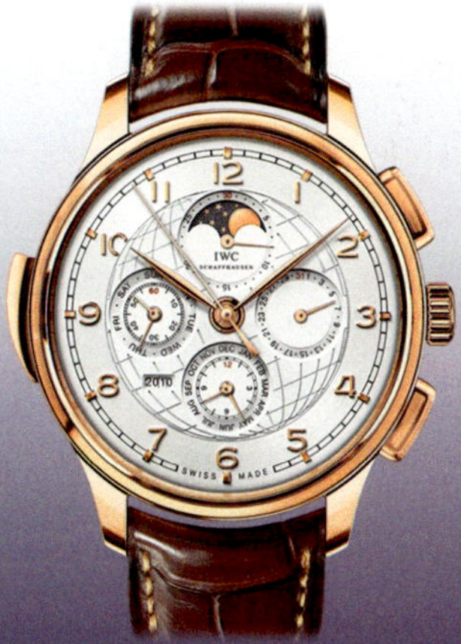

Portuguese Grande Complication (IWC)

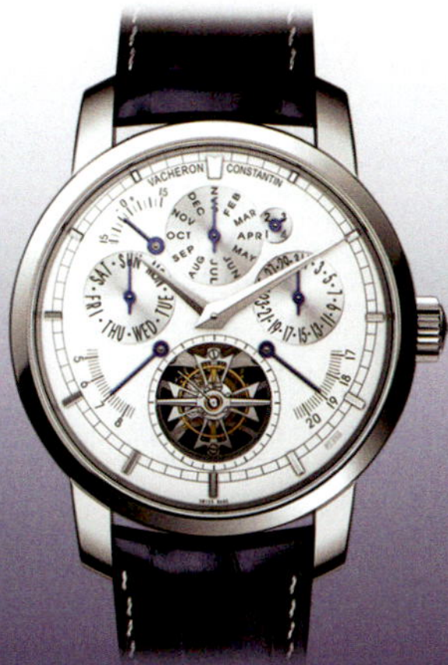

Patrimony Traditionnelle Calibre 2253 (Vacheron Constantin)

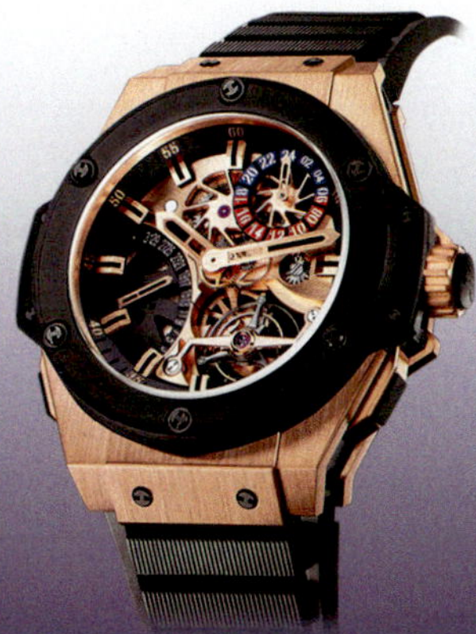

King Power Gold Tourbillon GMT (Hublot)

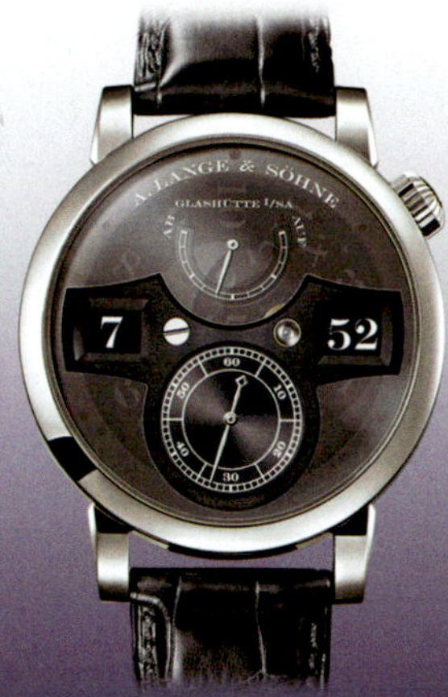

Lange Zeitwerk "Luminous" (A. Lange & Söhne)

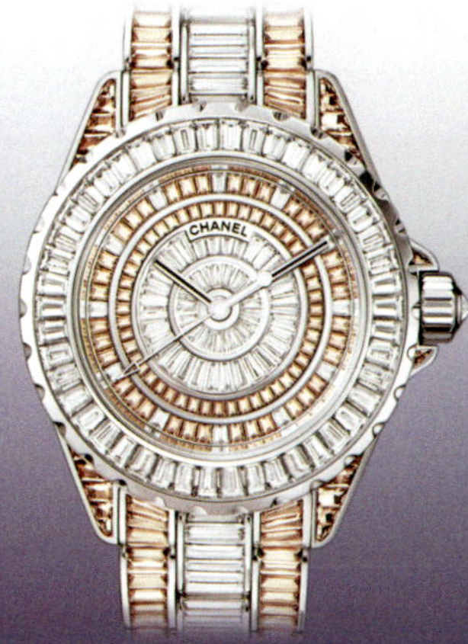

J12 Haute Joaillerie (Chanel)

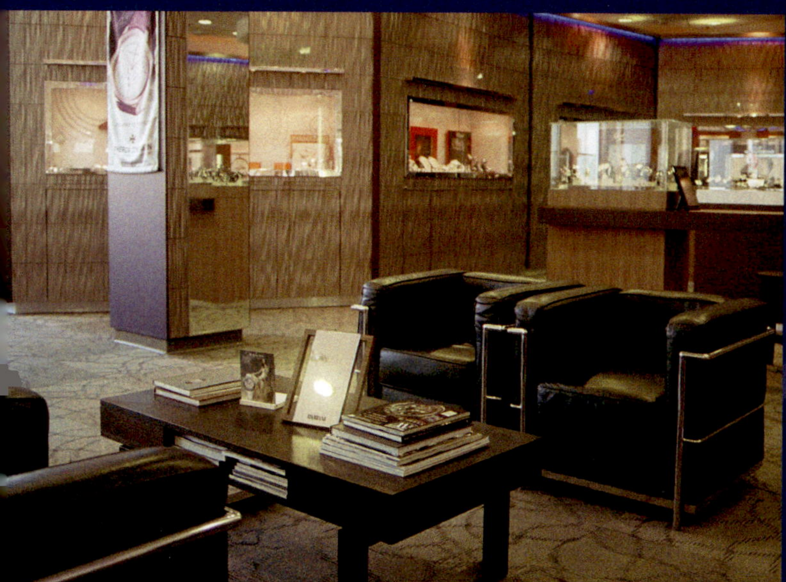

WESTIME

10800 West Pico Blvd., #197 • Los Angeles, CA 90064
tel: 310-470-1388 • fax: 310-475-0628

254 North Rodeo Drive • Beverly Hills, CA 90210
tel: 310-271-0000 • fax: 310-271-3091

www.westime.com

BRANDS CARRIED

- A. Lange & Söhne
- Alain Silberstein
- Audemars Piguet
- Bell & Ross
- Blancpain
- Breguet
- Breitling
- Buben & Zörweg
- Chanel
- Chopard
- Concord
- DeWitt
- Ebel
- FP Journe
- Franck Muller
- Frédérique Constant
- Girard-Perregaux
- Glashütte Original
- Graham-London
- Greubel Forsey
- Guy Ellia
- Hamilton
- Harry Winston
- HD3
- Hermès
- Hublot
- Ikepod
- IWC Schaffhausen
- Longines
- Ludovic Ballouard
- MB&F
- MCT
- Milus
- Nixon
- Omega
- Richard Mille
- Roland Iten
- Romain Jerome
- TAG Heuer
- Tiffany & Co.
- Tissot
- URWERK
- Vacheron Constantin
- Vertu
- Zenith

Q&A:

WESTIME PRESIDENT

GREG SIMONIAN

You represent your family's fourth generation in the watch business. How have your parents, and earlier generations, prepared you for your position as the president of Westime?

You don't really prepare yourself for a position as president of a family company. I just grew up in the business. A job in a family business—especially one that has grown as rapidly as Westime has—is not like having any other job. You don't do it without being anything less than totally involved, and all members of the family have been. When I was a kid, and we only had our flagship location on Los Angeles's Westside, that neighborhood became my second home, and it was a given that I would spend my whole weekend at the Westside Pavilion, where our store was. During the week, my mom would pick me up from school, and we would both return to the store and close it for the night. And at home, all of our conversations revolved around the business. And it really was exciting. So it's not like I ever went into the Swatch store with the intention of become a sales person. I was a middle school student, in the store on Saturdays, simply doing inventory for a time.

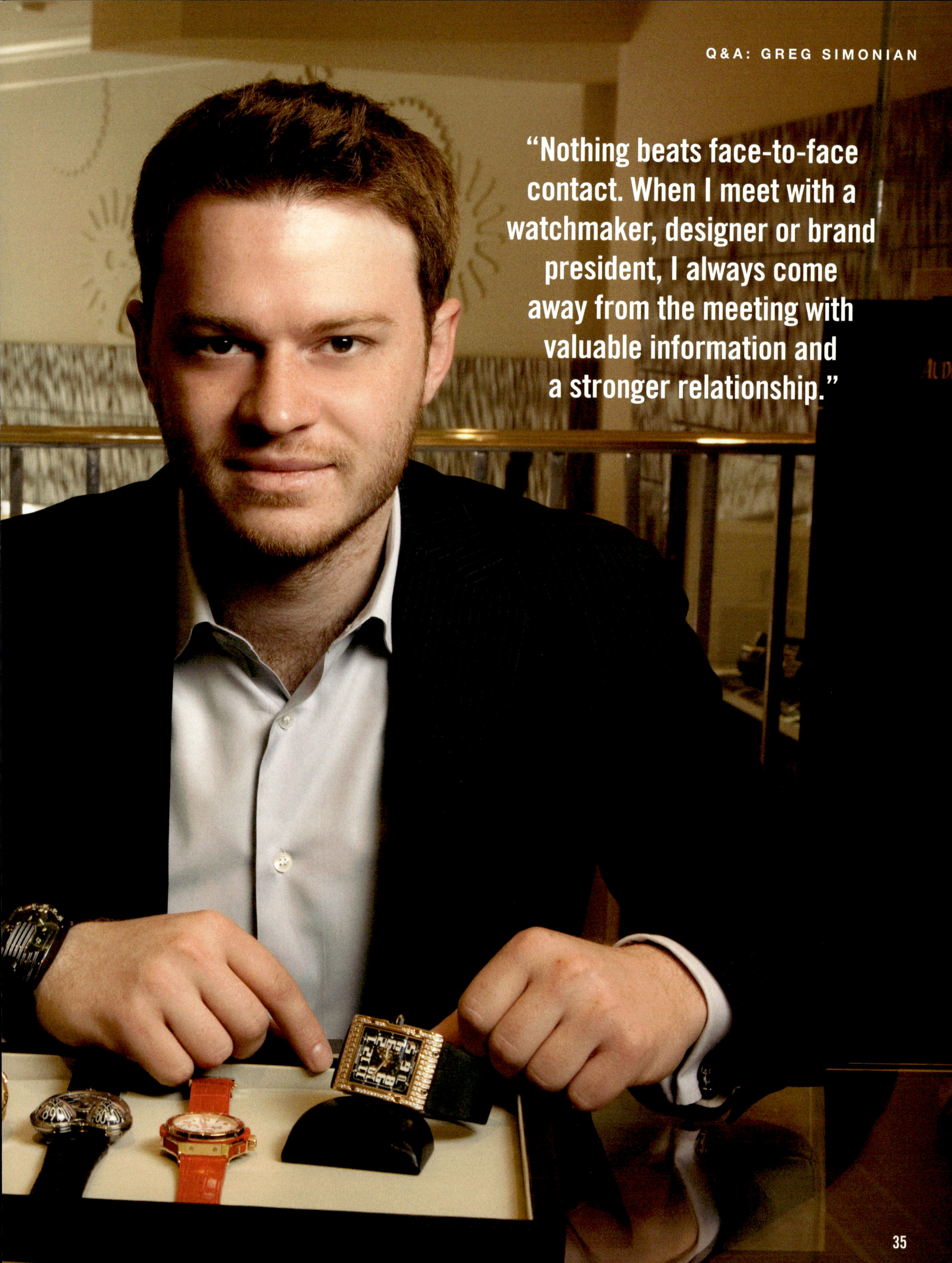

“Nothing beats face-to-face contact. When I meet with a watchmaker, designer or brand president, I always come away from the meeting with valuable information and a stronger relationship.”

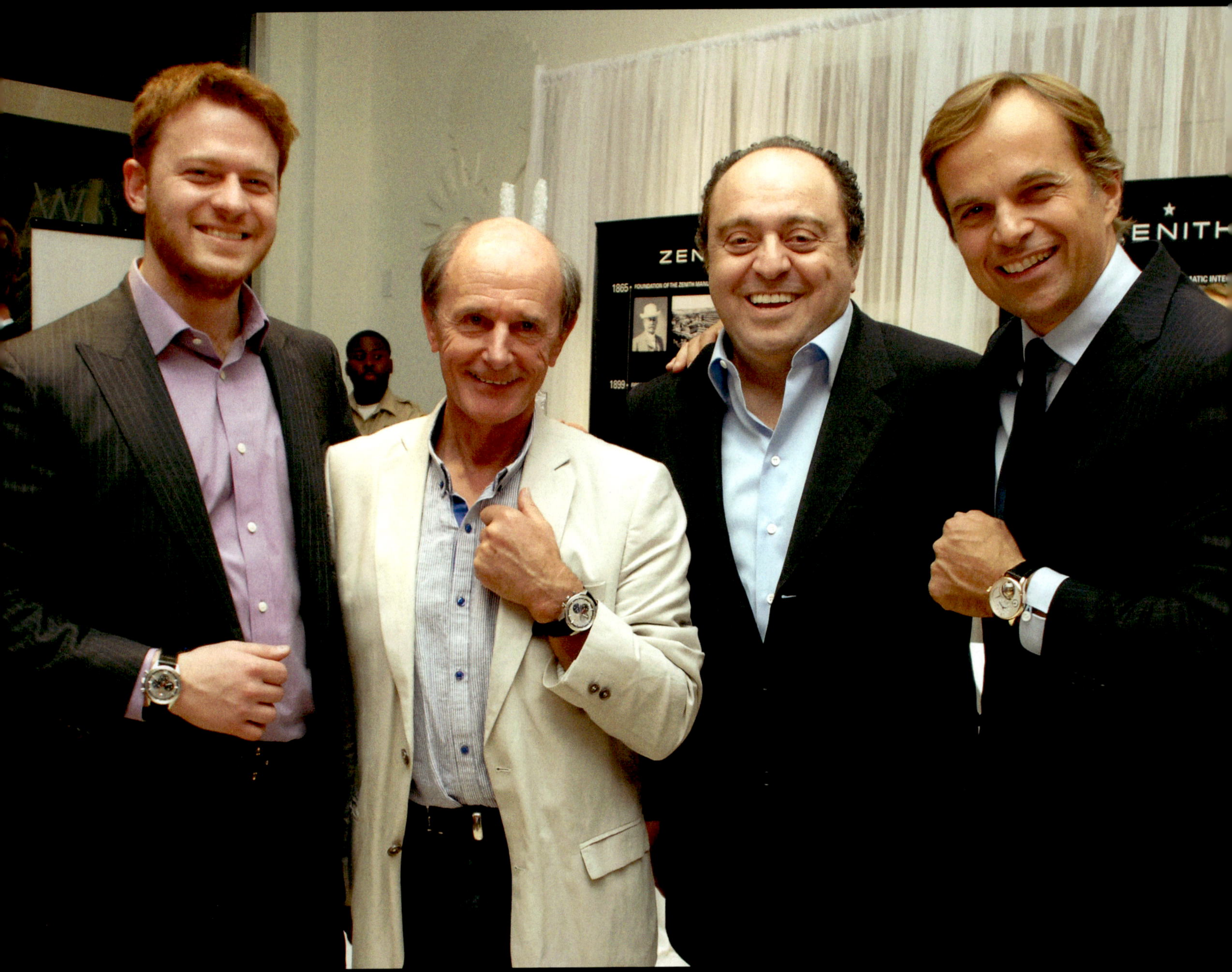

Has the role of the watch retailer changed? How is leading Westime today different from what it would have been like for your father two decades ago?

The customer has become more sophisticated and knowledgeable about watches, and they are also a lot more demanding now. I've witnessed Westime become a different store over the last two decades as well.

How is Westime distinguishing itself from other retailers, and even online points of sale today?

We serve our customers very professionally, but we're fun about it. It's not a stuffy environment at Westime. Also, we focus almost exclusively on watches in the stores, and have supported the independent watchmakers in a very strong way for years, which is something I am very proud of.

You have a very experienced staff with extensive knowledge of the watches they sell. Is it still important for you to be on the sales floor too?

Of course. It is especially important when a customer is buying a very high-end watch. For them to not just see a sales person, but the actual owner of the store standing behind the watch—the family that will always be there—that gives them confidence in the purchase they are making and the ongoing service that they will receive.

What are you hoping to see from watch brands at the 2011 fairs in Switzerland?

Other than novelties? I would like to see more of the watch companies show a better understanding of the American market.

You worked in Switzerland for two watch brands, and you continue to visit the manufactures regularly. Why is it important for you to see the watchmaking process in person?

Nothing beats face-to-face contact in our electronic age. We are all making the most of email, mobile phones, text messages, Facebook, apps, and web sites. But there is still nothing that replaces the face-to-face meeting. When I am able to meet with a watchmaker, designer, diamond setter, engraver, brand president or technician, I always come away from the meeting with valuable information and a stronger relationship.

Are there certain styles of watches, or particular complications, that Westime's clients are seeking today?

When it comes to the style of the watch, big is still in, though the most popular watches are not as thick as they once were. Sports watches are very popular with Westime's clientele. As for complications, sales of the most expensive complications declined during the economic crisis. Strong demand remains for tourbillons though, and we see a growing popularity of minute repeaters and both annual and perpetual calendars.

Recently, many watch brands have opened their own boutiques in Los Angeles. How does it affect business for a multi-brand boutique like Westime?

The more stores, the more opportunity there is for the consumer to be exposed to watches. And that is what is necessary for a consumer to decide to purchase a watch. The addition of watch stores nearby has actually enhanced Westime's business. And, we are partnering with certain watch brands to open mono-brand boutiques in Los Angeles, which will be under Westime management.

What will Westime's new flagship location on Sunset Boulevard be like?

Soon enough there will be photos, news, and lots of details. At this point all I can say is, it will be different!

What do you enjoy most about the watch business?

The relationships.

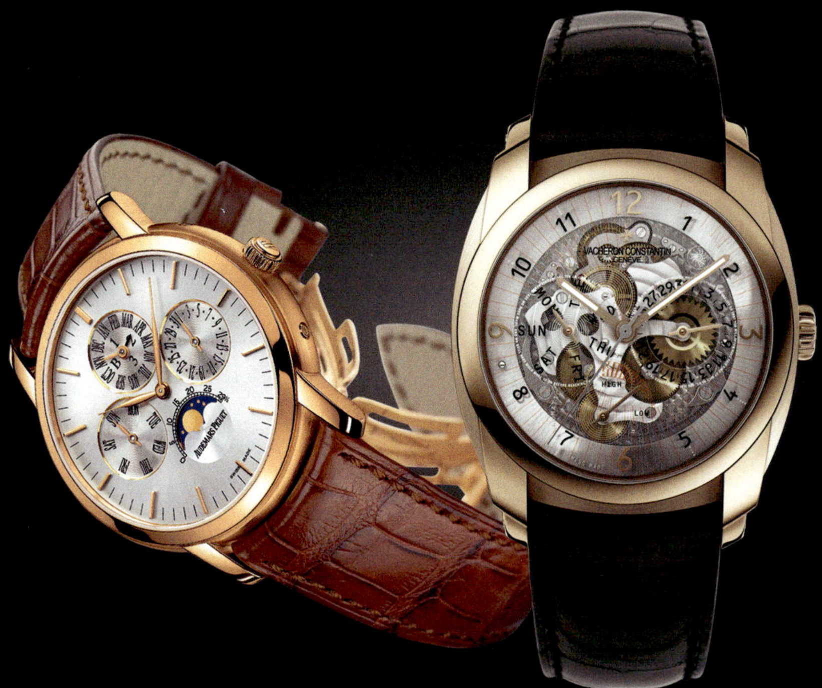

FACING PAGE

From left to right: Greg Simonian, Jean-Louis Etienne (a French explorer who inspired a Zenith watch), John Simonian, and Zenith CEO Jean-Frédéric Dufour, all attending an event in the Westime Beverly Hills boutique this fall.

FAR LEFT

Jules Audemars Perpetual Calendar (Audemars Piguet)

LEFT

Quai de L'Ile Day-Date and Power Reserve (Vacheron Constantin)

Summary

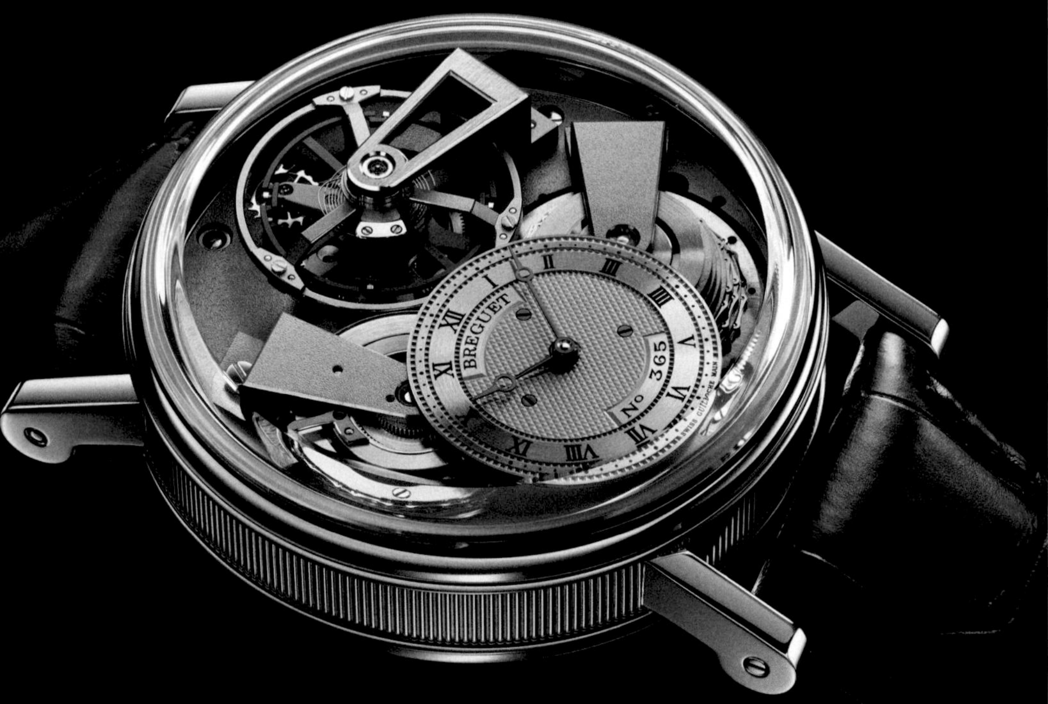

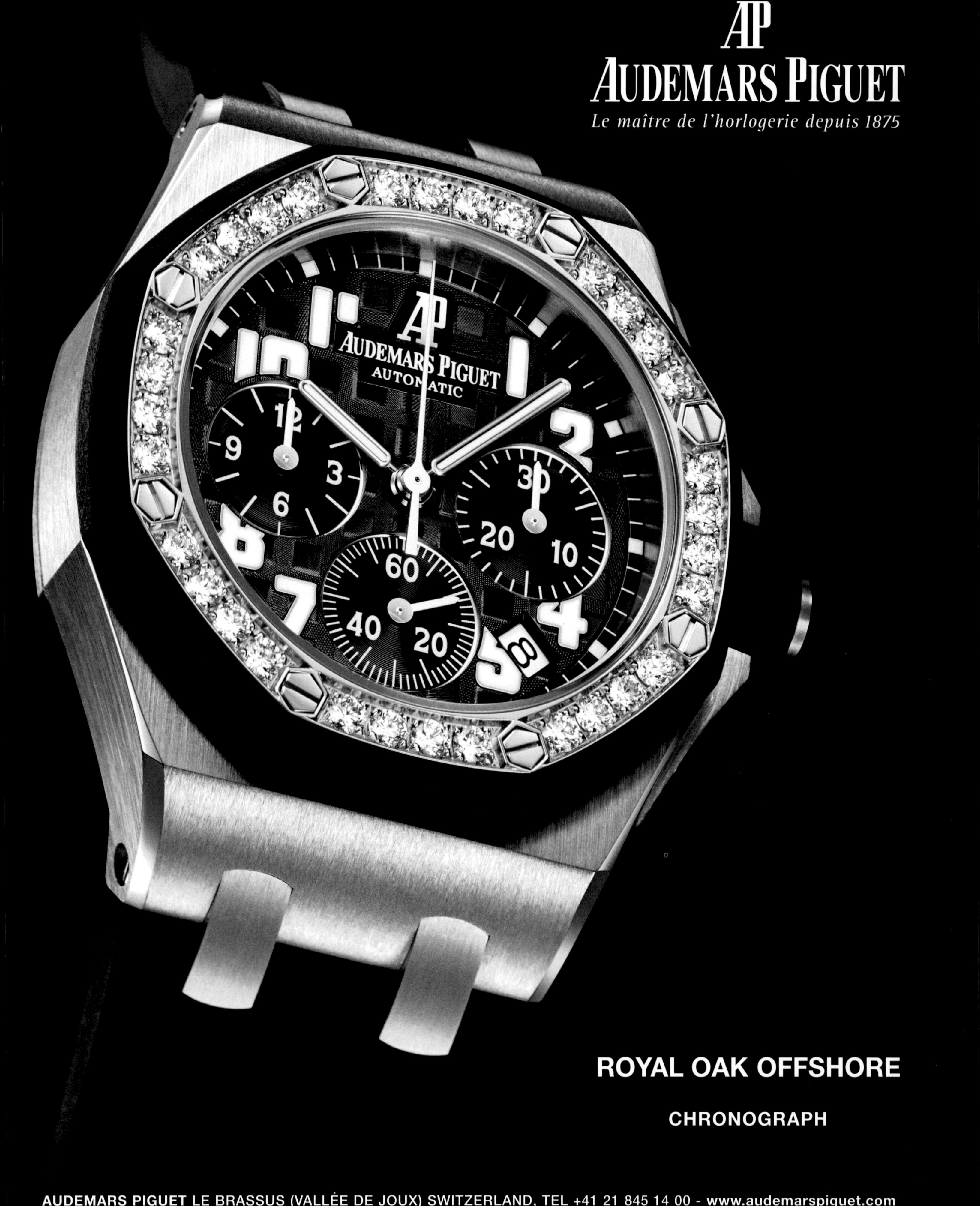
AP
AUDEMARS PIGUET
Le maître de l'horlogerie depuis 1875
ROYAL OAK OFFSHORE
CHRONOGRAPH
AUDEMARS PIGUET LE BRASSUS (VALLÉE DE JOUX) SWITZERLAND, TEL +41 21 845 14 00 - www.audemarspiguet.com

TWO WORLD RECORDS

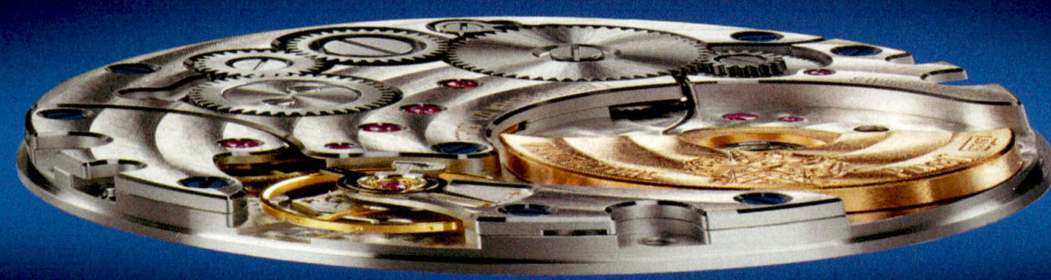

To celebrate the 50th anniversary of its legendary Calibre 12P launched in 1960, the Manufacture de Haute Horlogerie Piaget sets two new records in the ultra-thin quest.

Featuring an off-centred oscillating weight, the new generation 1208P is the world's thinnest automatic movement on the market at just 2.35 mm thick - a first record.

Thanks to this new Calibre 1208P, the Piaget Altiplano watch measures just 5.25 mm thick, making it the world's thinnest automatic watch - a second record.

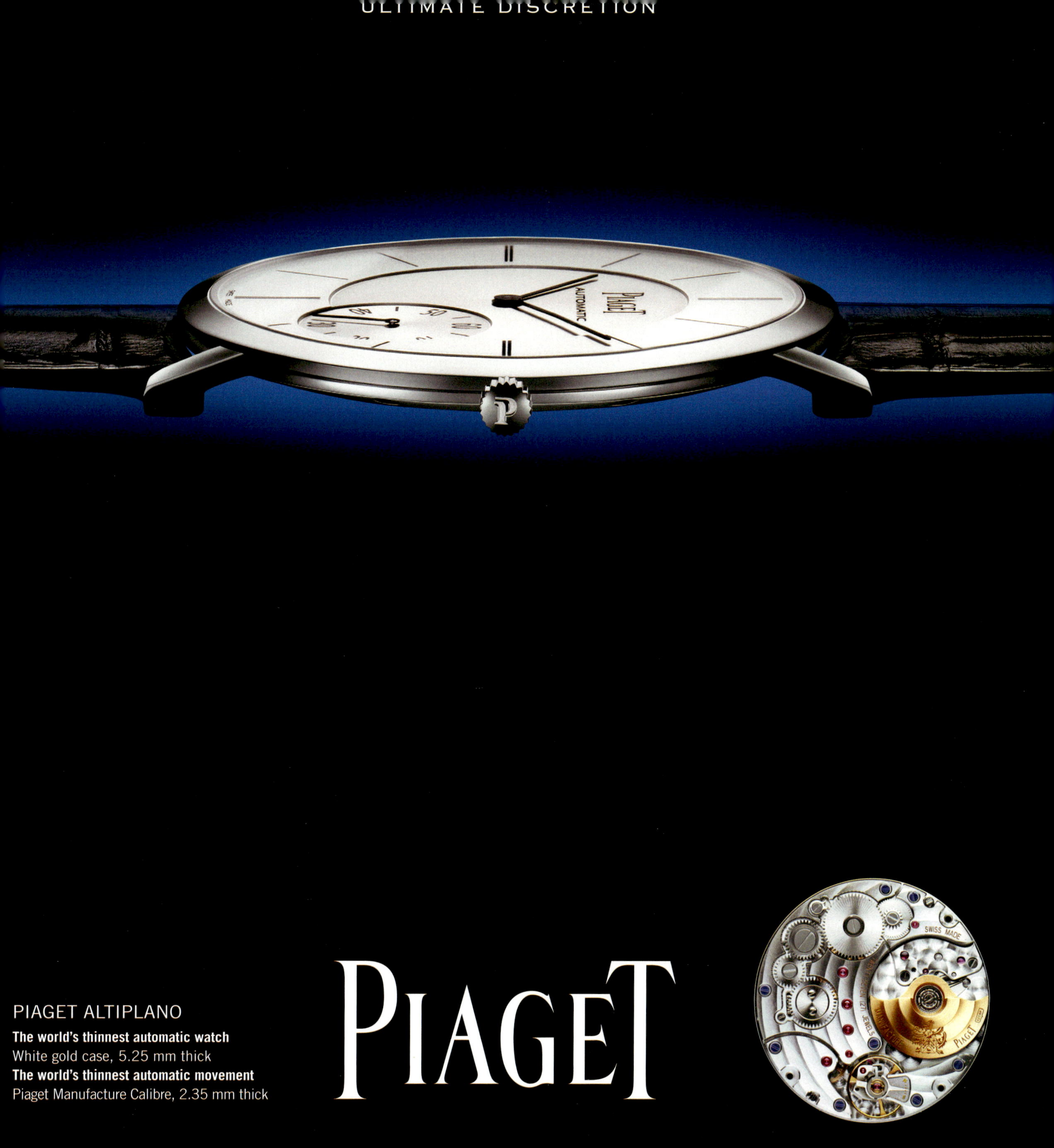
ULTIMATE DISCRETION
PIAGET
PIAGET ALTIPLANO
The world's thinnest automatic watch
White gold case, 5.25 mm thick
The world's thinnest automatic movement
Piaget Manufacture Calibre, 2.35 mm thick

Web Site Directory

A. LANGE & SÖHNE	www.alange-soehne.com
ALPINA	www.alpina-watches.com
AUDEMARS PIGUET	www.audemarspiguet.com
BEDAT & CO.	www.bedat.com
BELL & ROSS	www.bellross.com
BLANCPAIN	www.blancpain.com
BOUCHERON	www.boucheron.com
BREGUET	www.breguet.com
BUBEN & ZÖRWEG	www.buben-zorweg.com
BVLGARI	www.bulgari.com
CARL F. BUCHERER	www.carl-f-bucherer.com
CARTIER SA	www.cartier.com
CHANEL	www.chanel.com
CHOPARD	www.chopard.com
CHRISTOPHE CLARET	www.claret.ch
CLERC	www.clercwatches.com
CONCORD	www.concord.ch
DE GRISOGONO	www.degrisogono.com
DEWITT	www.dewitt.ch
DIOR HORLOGERIE	www.diorhorlogerie.com
ETERNA	www.eterna.ch
FRANCK MULLER	www.franckmullerusa.com
FRÉDÉRIQUE CONSTANT SA	www.frederique-constant.com
GIANTTO	www.giantto.com
GIRARD-PERREGAUX	www.girard-perregaux.ch
GRAHAM-LONDON	www.graham-london.com
GREUBEL FORSEY	www.greubelforsey.com
GUY ELLIA	www.guyellia.com
H. MOSER & CIE.	www.h-moser.com
HAMILTON WATCHES	www.hamiltonwatch.com
HARRY WINSTON SA	www.harrywinston.com
HERMÈS	www.hermes.com
HUBLOT	www.hublot.com
IWC SCHAFFHAUSEN	www.iwc.com
JACOB & CO	www.jacobandco.com
JAEGER-LECOULTRE	www.jaeger-lecoultre.com
LONGINES	www.longines.com
LOUIS VUITTON	www.louisvuitton.com
MONTBLANC MONTRE	www.montblanc.com
PANERAI	www.panerai.com
PARMIGIANI	www.parmigiani.ch
PATEK PHILIPPE	www.patek.com
PIAGET	www.piaget.com
PORSCHE DESIGN	www.porsche-design.com
RALPH LAUREN	www.ralphlauren.com
RAYMOND WEIL SA	www.raymond-weil.com
REBELLION TIMEPIECES	www.rebellion-timepieces.com
RICHARD MILLE	www.richardmille.com
ROGER DUBUIS	www.rogerdubuis.com
ROLAND ITEN	www.rolanditen.com
ROLEX	www.rolex.com
TAG HEUER	www.tagheuer.com
ULYSSE NARDIN	www.ulysse-nardin.com
URWERK	www.urwerk.com
VACHERON CONSTANTIN	www.vacheron-constantin.com
VAN CLEEF & ARPELS	www.vancleef-arpels.com
ZANNETTI	www.zannettiwatches.it
ZENITH	www.zenith-watches.com
RELATED SITES	
BASELWORLD	www.baselworld.com
SIHH	www.sihh.ch
AUCTION HOUSES	
CHRISTIE'S	www.christies.com
SOTHEBY'S	www.sothebys.com

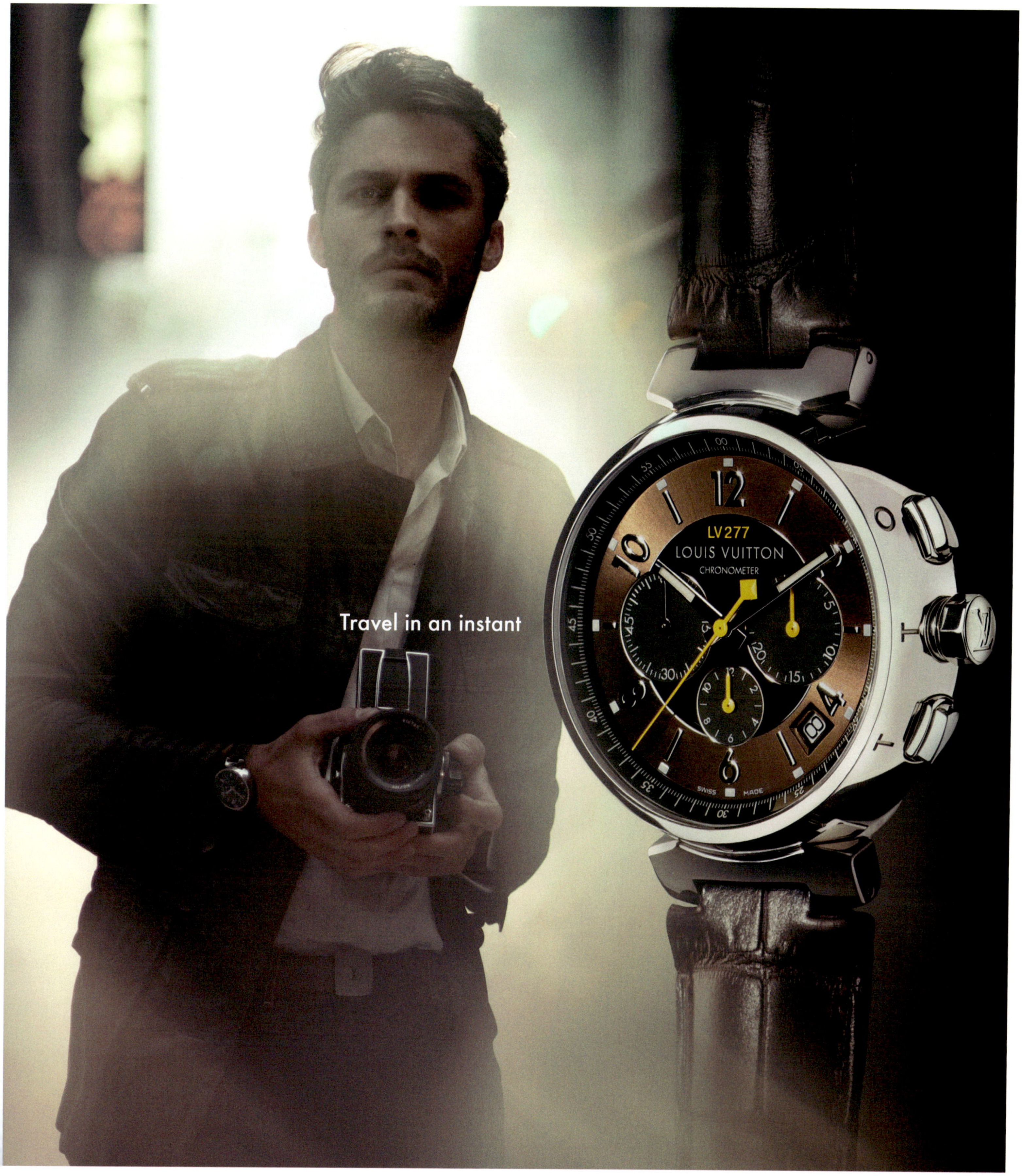
Travel in an instant
LV277
LOUIS VUITTON
CHRONOMETER

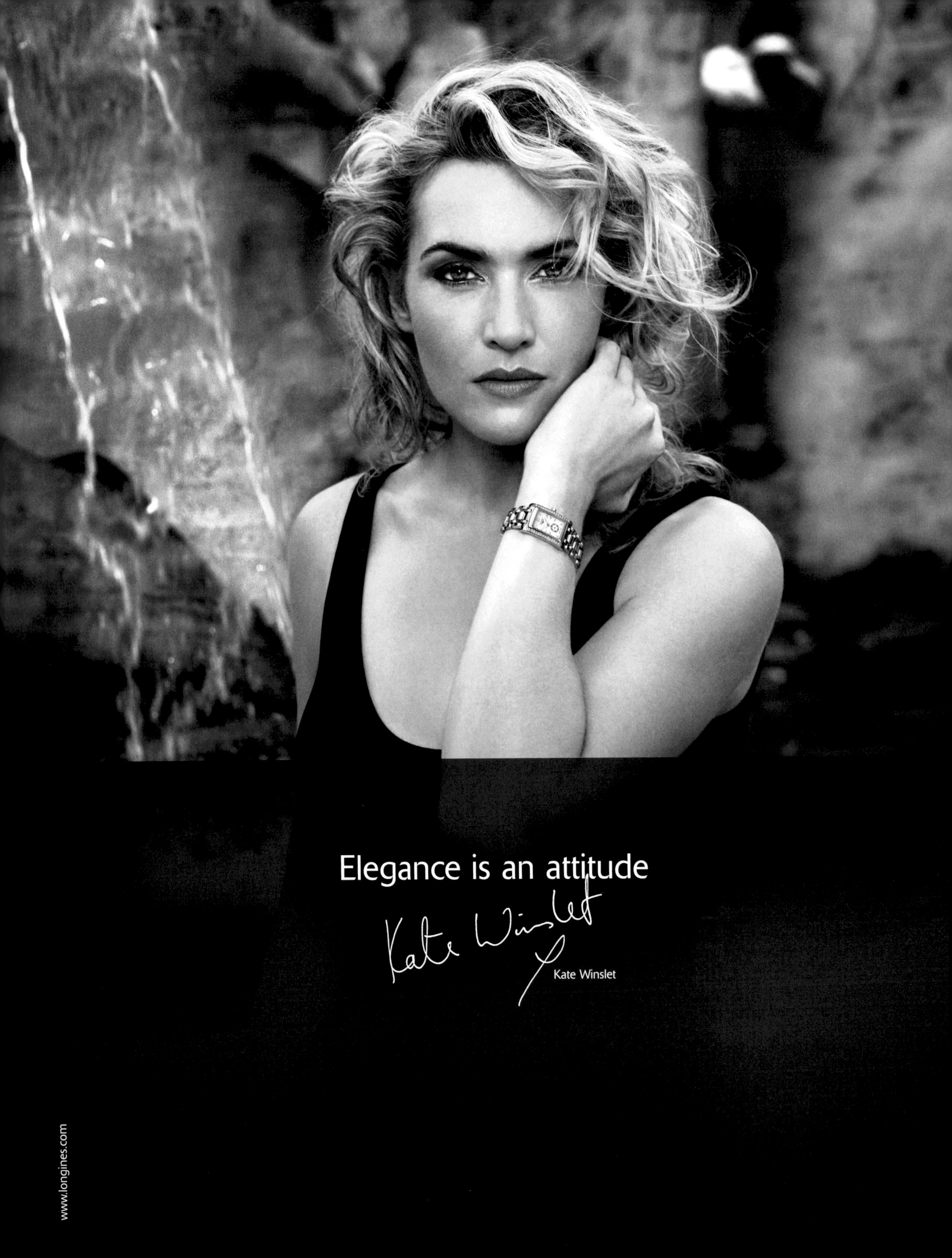
Elegance is an attitude
Kate Winslet
www.longines.com

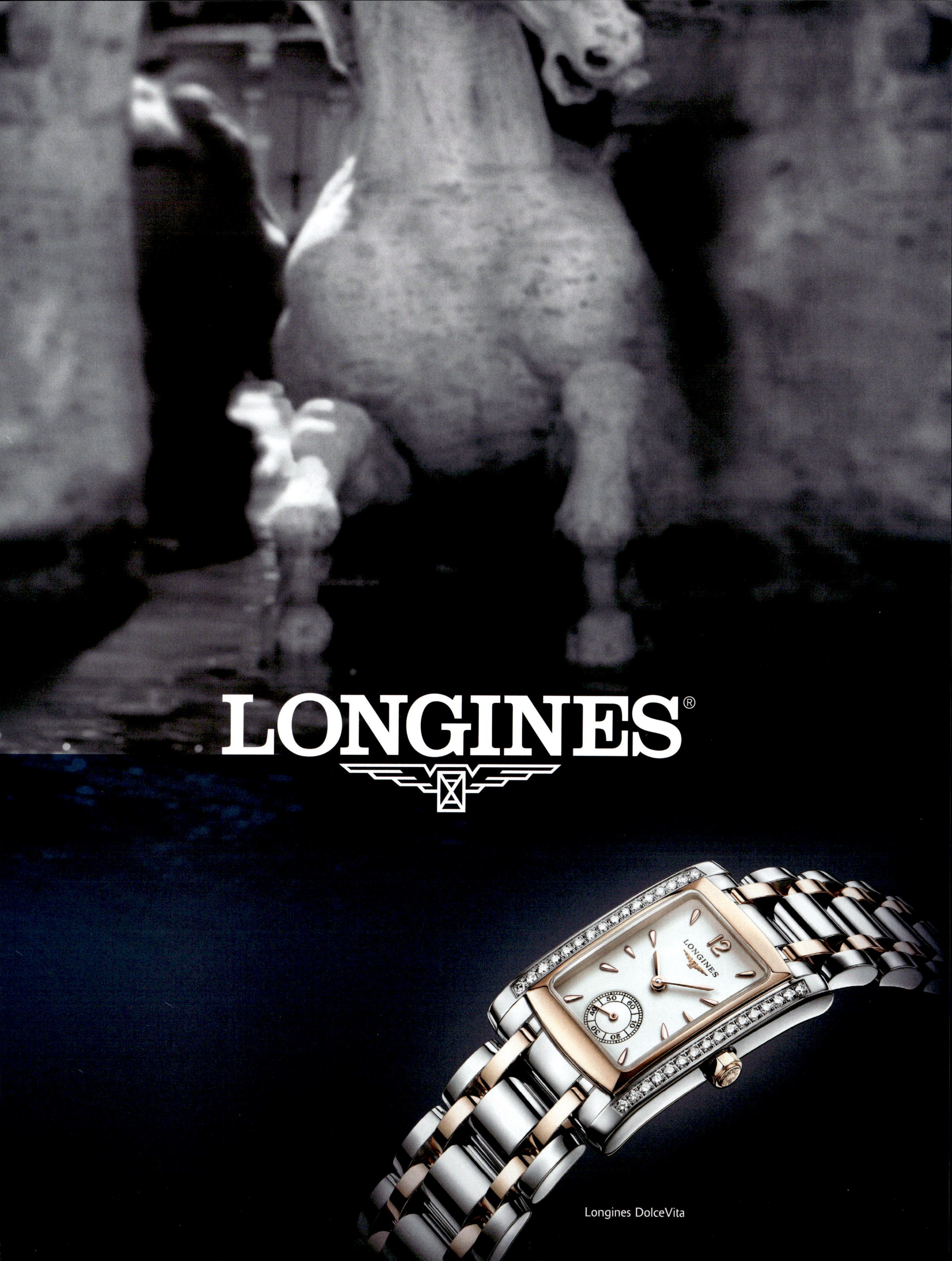
LONGINES®
Longines DolceVita

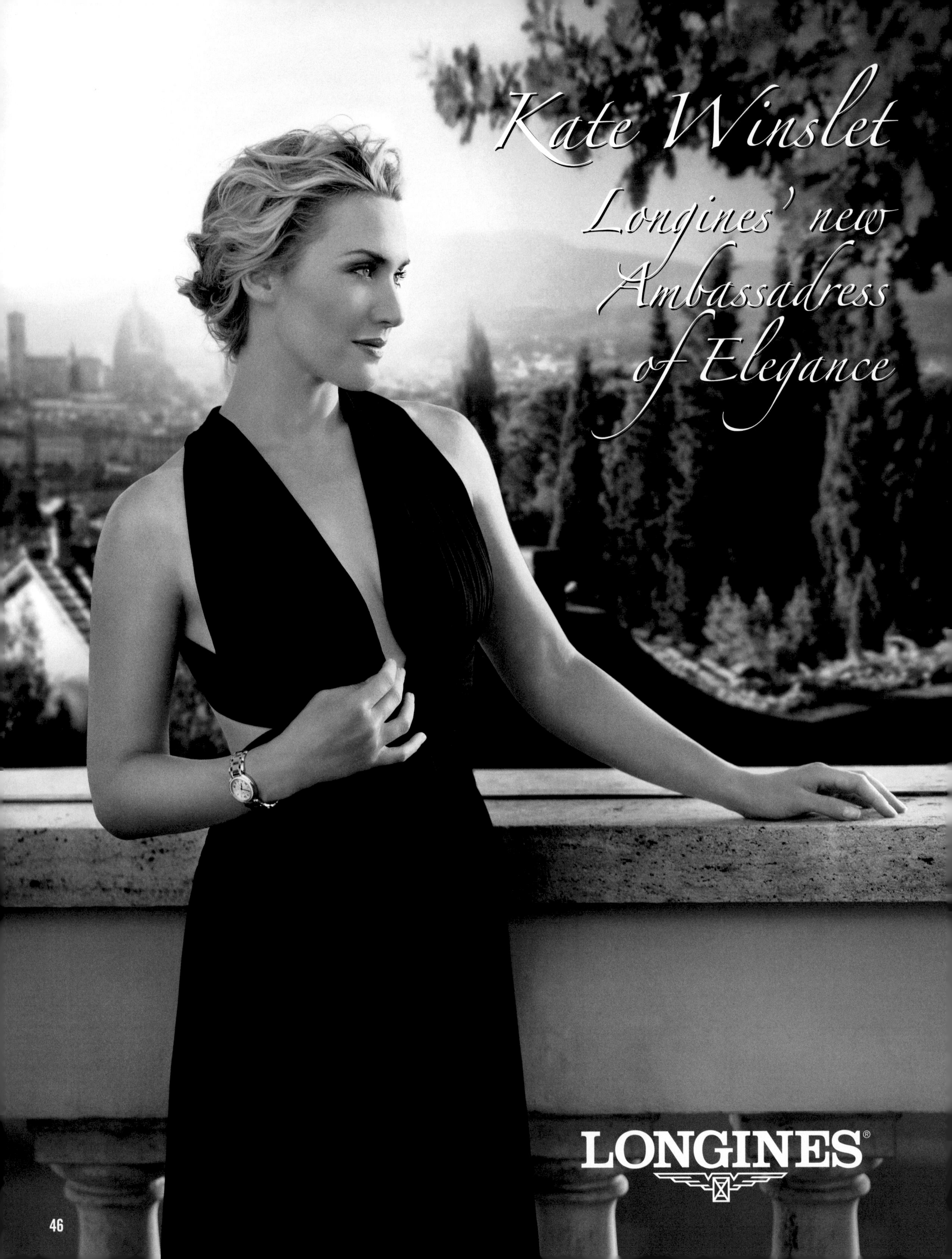
Kate Winslet
Longines' new
Ambassadress
of Elegance
LONGINES®

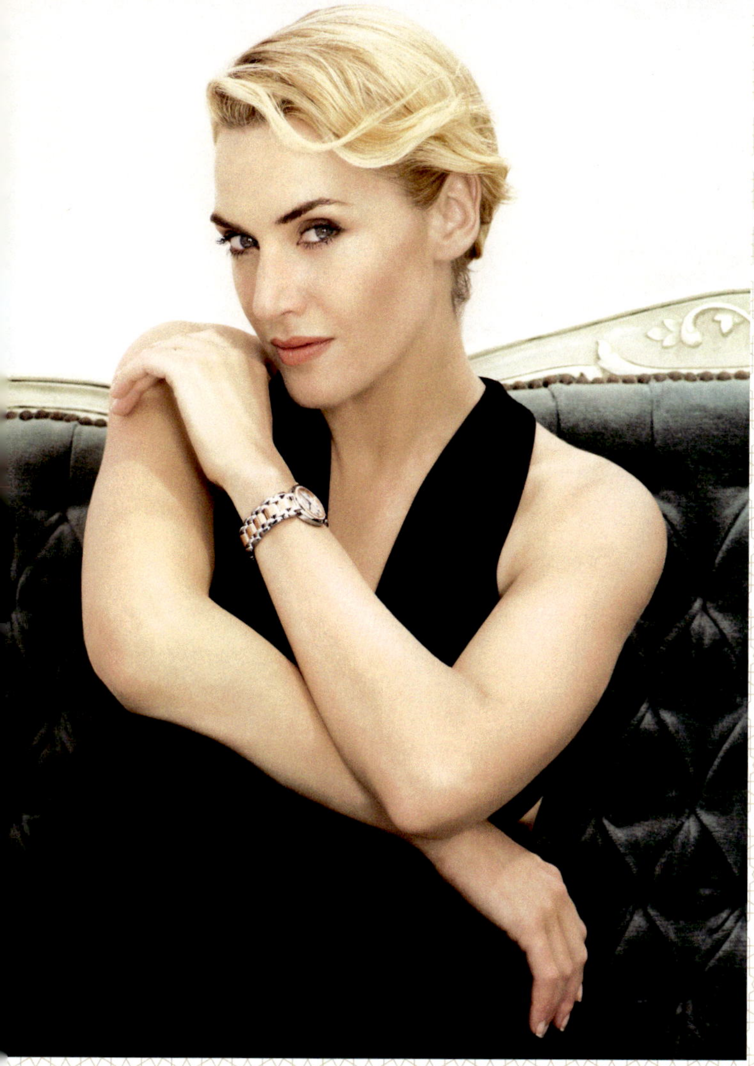

What does *la dolce vita* evoke to you?

Sun, style and elegance.

What are you working on lately? What are your future plans?

I've just finished filming a five-hour TV series for HBO called *Mildred Pierce* which will come out next year. I'm filming a new thriller with Steven Soderbergh later this year called *Contagion,* in which I'm part of a really great ensemble cast.

How do you feel about your new partnership with Longines?

I love working with Longines and am very excited about what's ahead. I have been a fan of their watches for a long time so it made great sense to accept their invitation to become an Ambassadress.

Did you enjoy the filming in Rome with Aishwarya Rai Bachchan and Chi Ling Lin?

It was such fun—I loved working with them and it was so interesting to have such a mix of different cultures.

Growing up in a family of actors, have you always wanted to become an actress yourself or did you have other dreams as a child?

I have always wanted to be an actress for as long as I can remember and I'm incredibly blessed that my career has turned out in the very fortunate way that it has.

You have played so many different roles in both film and television but who has been your favorite character?

My favorite character is always the one I am playing at the time but if I were to name one, it would be Hannah Schmidt in *The Reader.*

What or who has been your guiding force so far in your career?

I've always been able to rely on the wealth of resource that my own life experience has given me, but my good friend Emma Thompson has always been someone I can turn to.

What has been the highlight of your career to date? What further aspirations do you have to achieve in your career?

The highlight of my career to date was being cast in my very first film (*Heavenly Creatures*) at the age of 17, and the only aspiration I have is to remain as passionate about my job as I always have been.

What do you consider your greatest strength as a person?

You should probably ask my friends and family but I would say that loyalty is up there on my list of moral priorities.

Longines has named you its ambassador of elegance—what does elegance mean to you?

Relaxed, stylish and not trying to be noticed.

What are your red carpet style secrets?

Finding the right dress is key and never wearing patterns. It doesn't work for me at all.

Which is your favourite Longines watch in the collections you have seen?

So far, besides the Longines DolceVita, I would say it is the Flagship Heritage Chronograph, because it reminds me of a family heirloom.

What does time mean to you?

In my twenties it meant doing as much as I could very quickly and in my thirties I'm discovering that this needs to change.

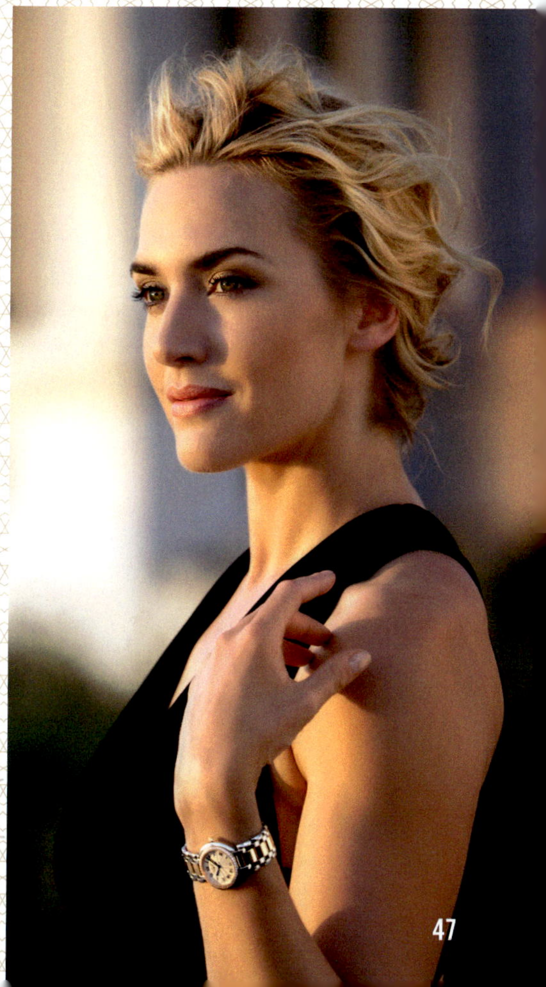

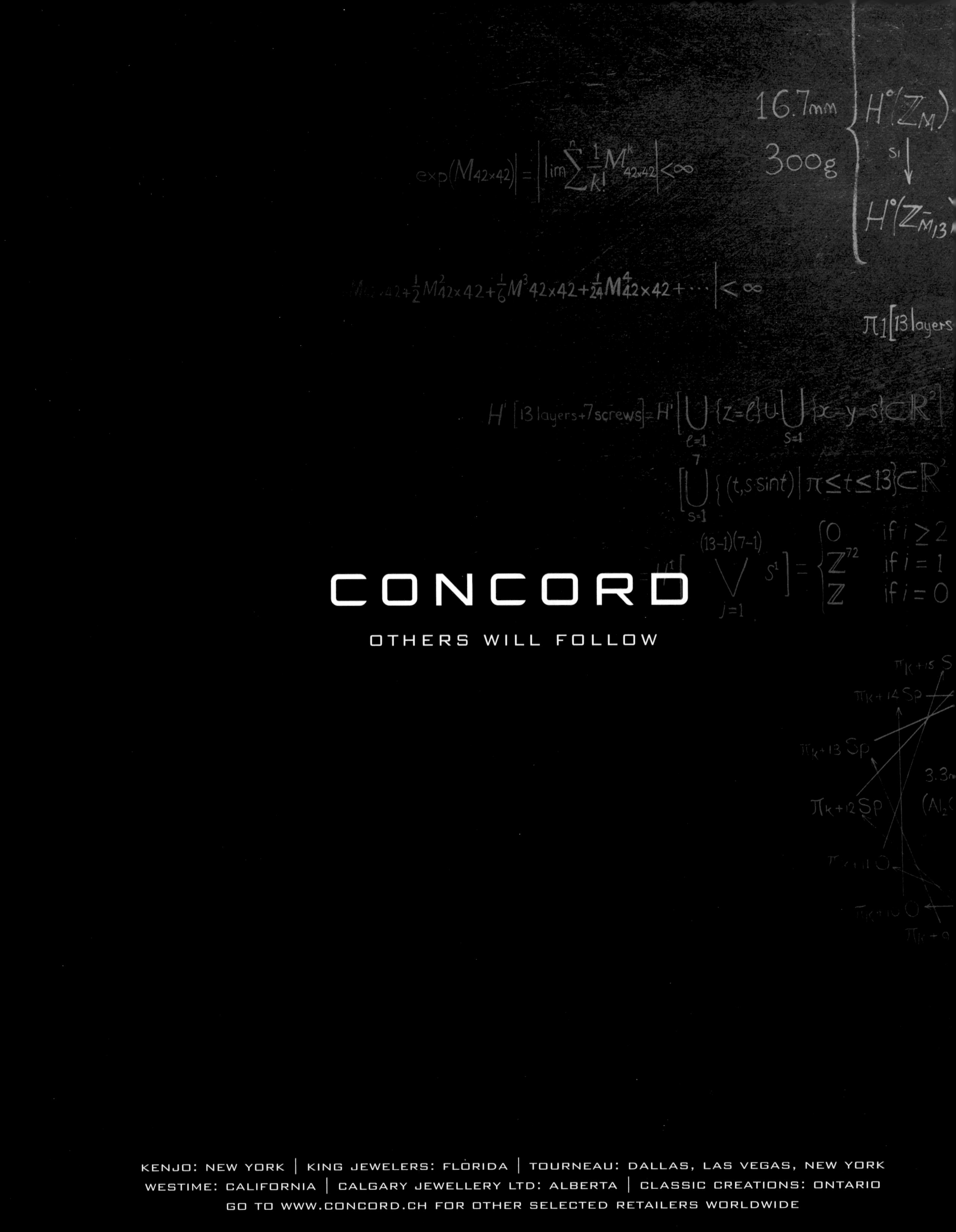
CONCORD
OTHERS WILL FOLLOW
KENJO: NEW YORK | KING JEWELERS: FLORIDA | TOURNEAU: DALLAS, LAS VEGAS, NEW YORK
WESTIME: CALIFORNIA | CALGARY JEWELLERY LTD: ALBERTA | CLASSIC CREATIONS: ONTARIO
GO TO WWW.CONCORD.CH FOR OTHER SELECTED RETAILERS WORLDWIDE

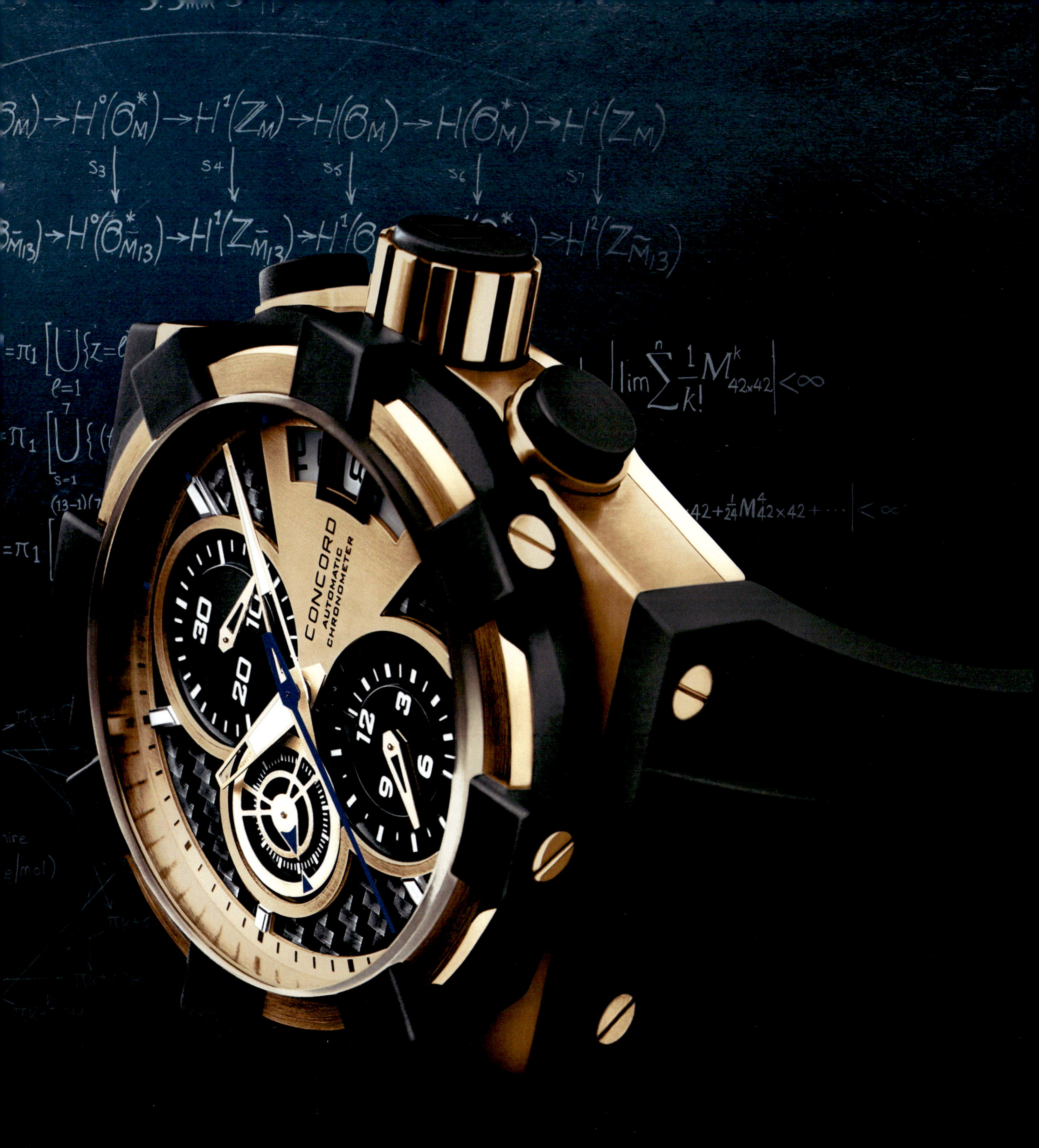
CONCORD
AUTOMATIC
CHRONOMETER

A BRIEF HISTORY OF TIME MEASUREMENT

Mechanical horology, a defining stage in human development

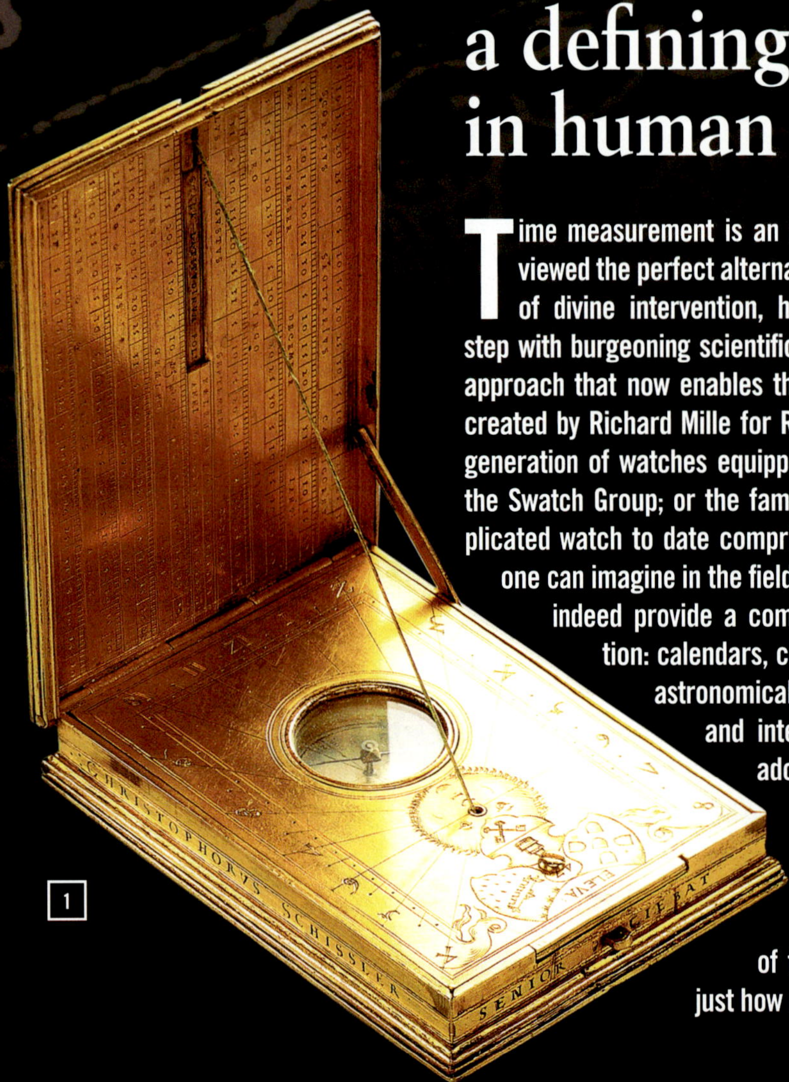

1

Time measurement is an art almost as old as humankind itself. After having long viewed the perfect alternation of seasons, lunar cycles, days and nights as the result of divine intervention, human beings progressively abandoned these beliefs in step with burgeoning scientific thought. In doing so, they were adopting the very same approach that now enables the creation of timepieces such as the RM 027 Tourbillon created by Richard Mille for Rafael Nadal and weighing less than 20 grams; the future generation of watches equipped with Bluetooth technology currently in the pipeline of the Swatch Group; or the famous Caliber 89 by Patek Philippe, the world's most complicated watch to date comprising 1,728 parts and incorporating just about everything one can imagine in the field of mechanical horological complications. Caliber 89 does indeed provide a comprehensive expression of the three main types of function: calendars, chronographs and striking mechanisms, along with a set of astronomical complications. In addition to its sidereal time indication and integrated Gregorian calendar function, Caliber 89 is also adorned with a sky chart depicting the Milky Way and enabling observers to distinguish 2,800 stars visible from the Northern Hemisphere, as well as their magnitude. Among the rarest complications it houses is its capability to provide an annual display, on midnight of December 31st, of the day on which Easter will fall in the coming year. But just how did we attain such heights of sophistication?

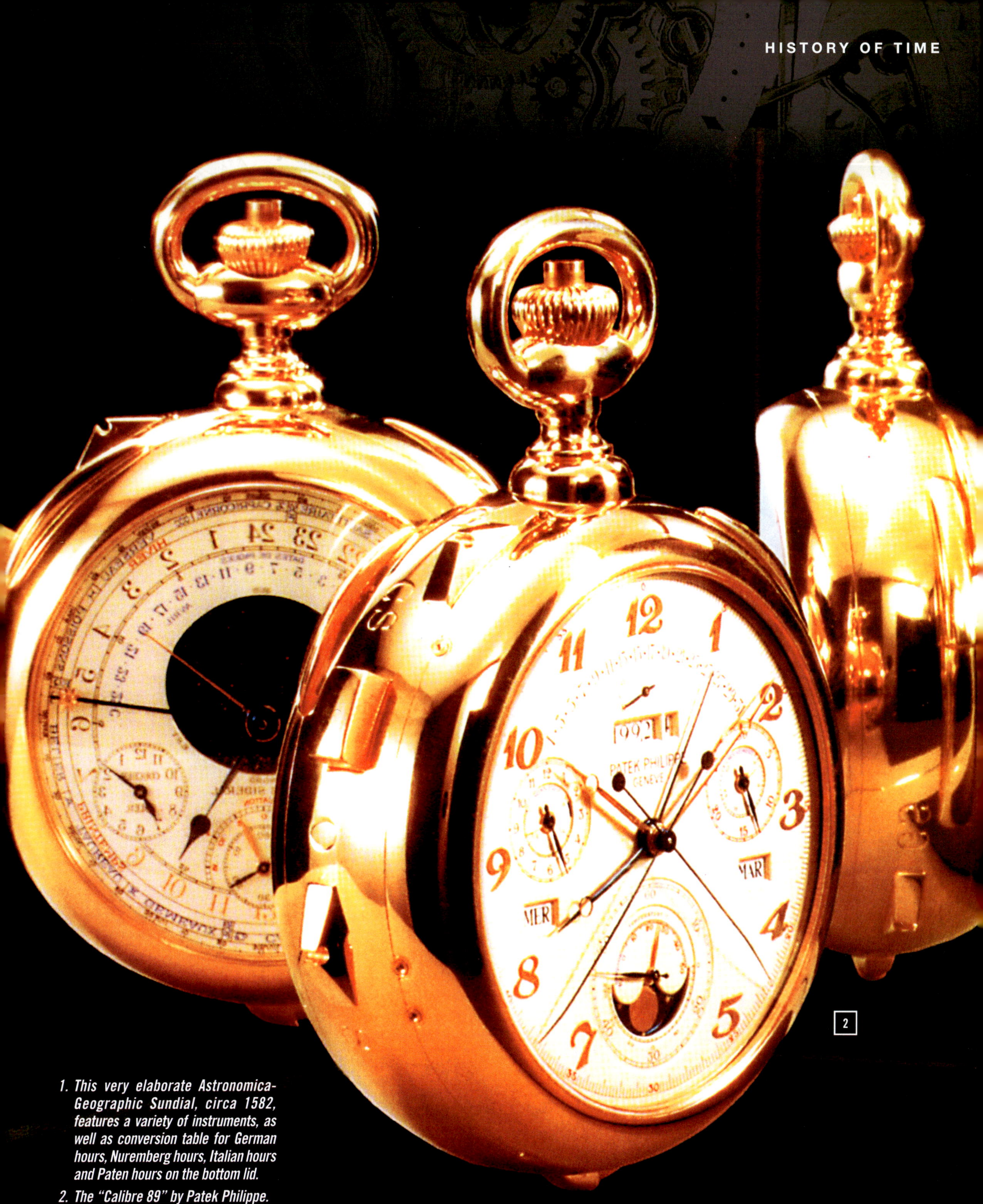

2

1. This very elaborate Astronomica-Geographic Sundial, circa 1582, features a variety of instruments, as well as conversion table for German hours, Nuremberg hours, Italian hours and Paten hours on the bottom lid.
2. The "Calibre 89" by Patek Philippe.

BABYLON DIVIDES TIME INTO 24 HOURS

The very fact that astronomical functions now hold such an important place among horological complications is largely due to the fact that the study of the stars resulted in the first attempts to divide time into fragments. The Aztec, Maya and Egyptian civilizations introduced the first calendars, stemming from research conducted by priests who occupied a dominant position in society. These dignitaries soon grasped the fact that farming activities coincided with the position of certain specific heavenly bodies. In Egypt, for example, the large annual flooding of the Nile was associated with the heliacal rise of Sirius, an event that occurs every 364 days. They derived from such observations a calendar that defined the year as "the time required for a harvest," featuring a division into 12 months of 30 days corresponding to lunar cycles, plus five additional or "epagomenal" days.

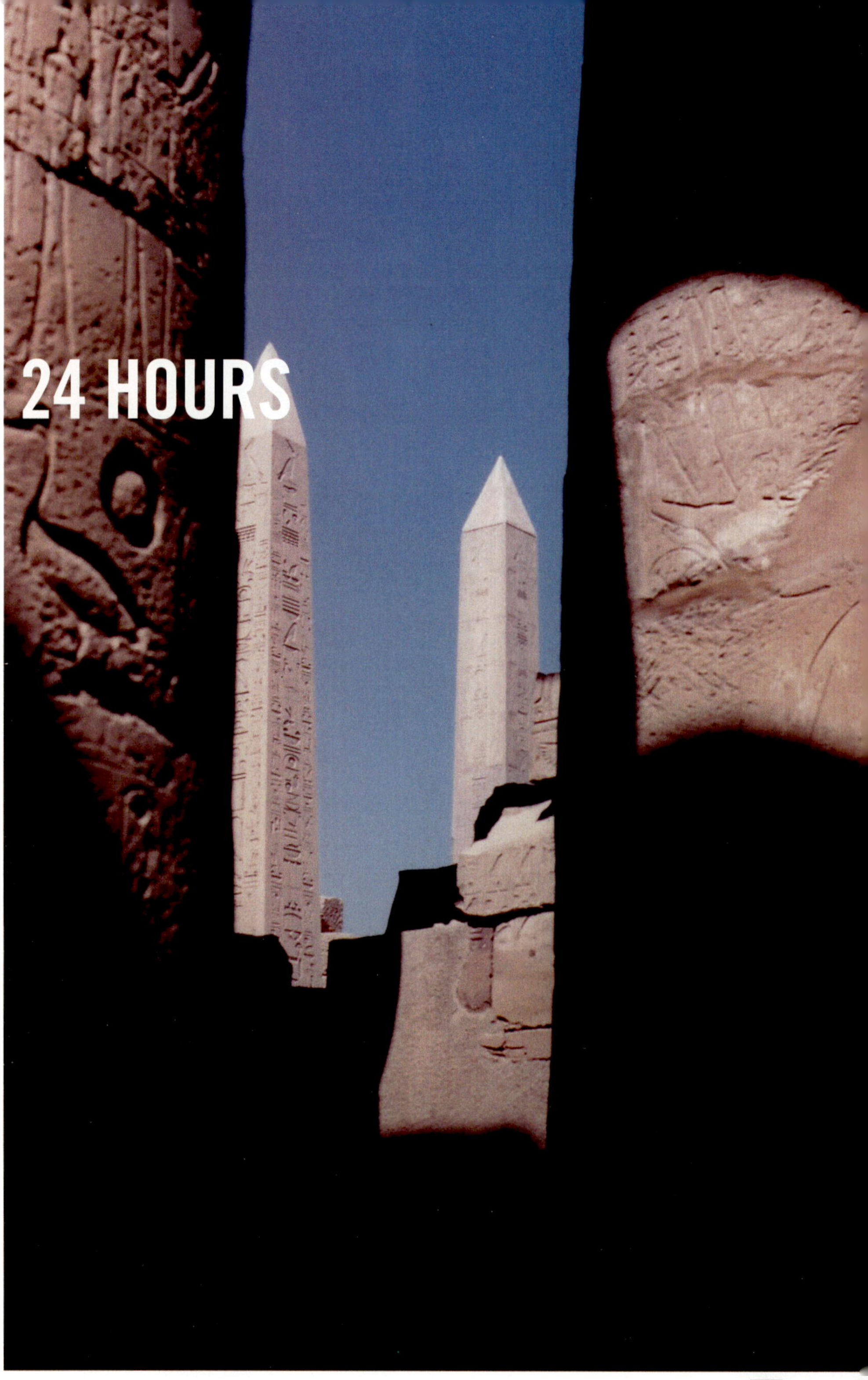

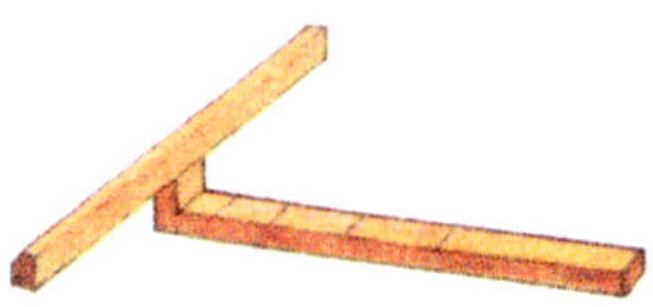

1

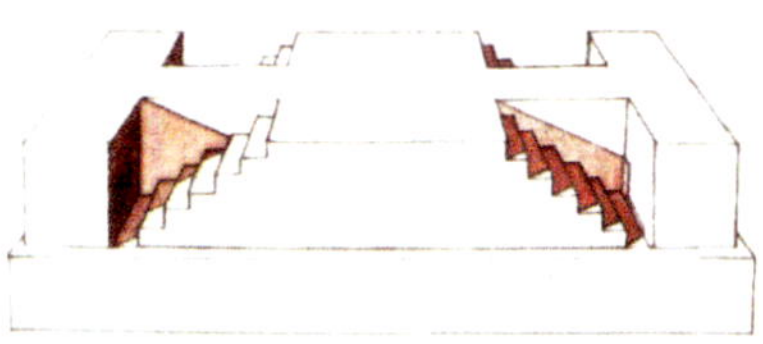

2

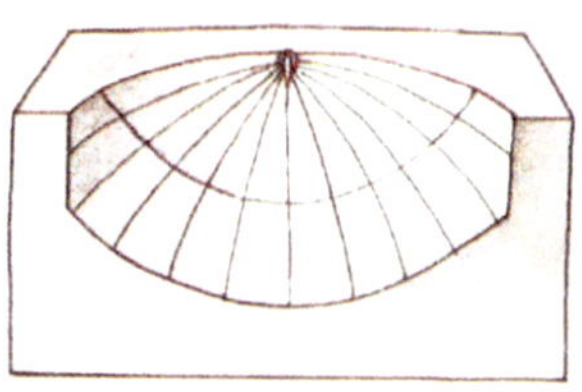

3

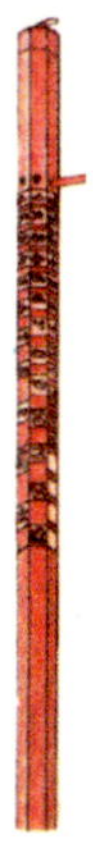

4

5

1. *This perpendicular bar casting a shadow on the dial was one of the earliest known Egyptian sundials from the 15th century B.C.*
2. *An example of an Egyptian step sundial.*
3. *The Egyptian suspension sundial dated from about A.D. 100.*
4. *This Indian pilgrim's sundial was known as the "fakir's stick." A shadow was cast by a peg shifted to one of its engraved eight scales according to the season.*
5. *It is believed that the earliest obelisks date back to 2,000 B.C. Egyptians measured time based on the shadows of the obelisk.*

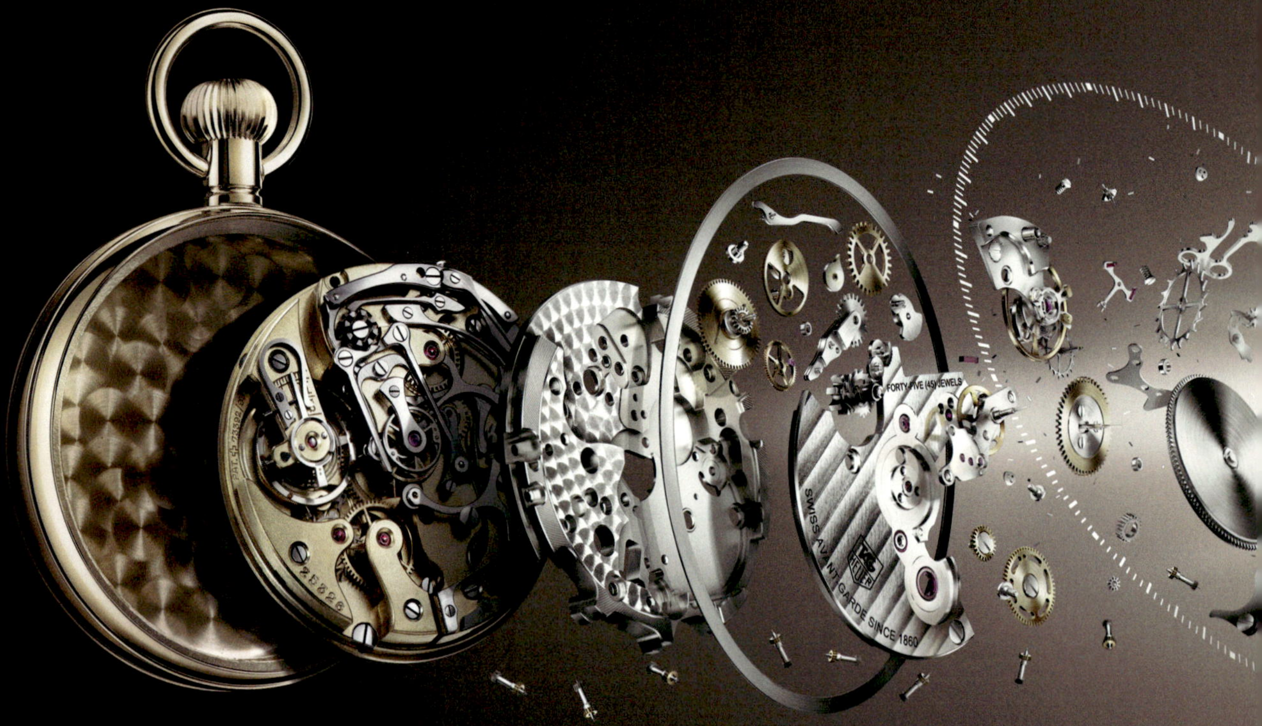

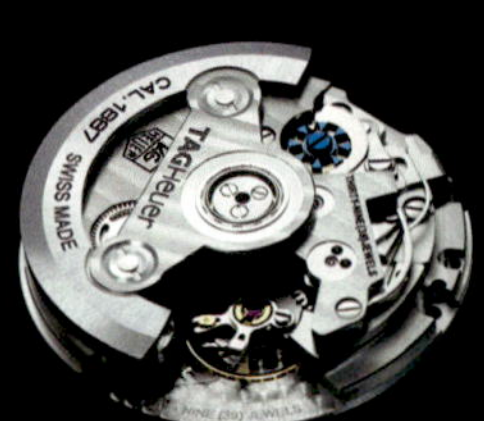

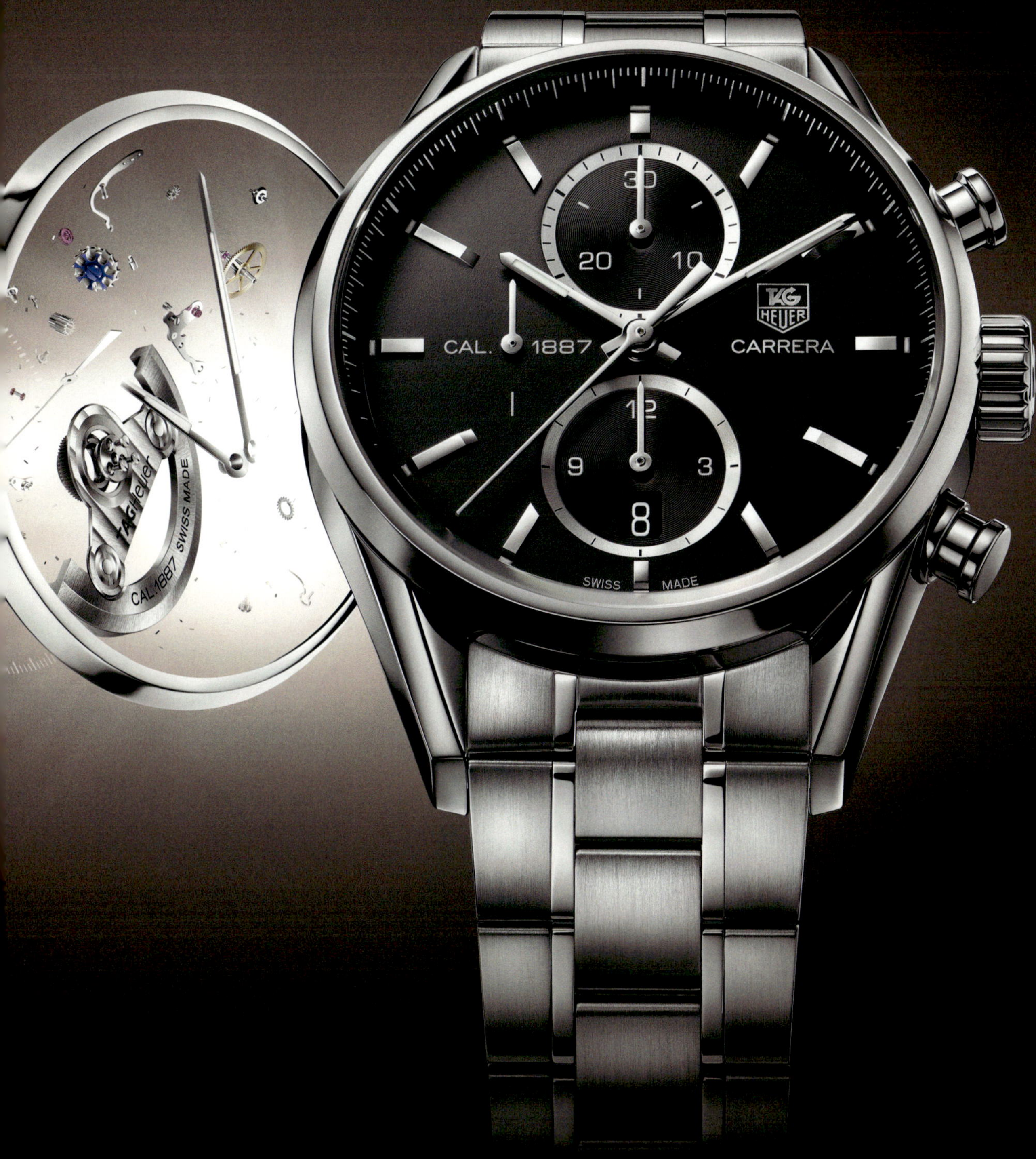
CAL. 1887
CARRERA
SWISS MADE
CAL.1887 SWISS MADE

It was also during ancient times that the idea of the hour first emerged. The decision to divide the day into 24 hours is attributed to the Babylonians, who used a sexagesimal system based on the symbolism of the circle. The Egyptians and subsequently the Greeks perpetuated this practice, involving 12 daytime hours and 12 nighttime hours, which naturally varied with the seasons. The Romans followed suit by measuring time in watches, meaning four by night and two by day: ante meridiem and post meridiem (am and pm). Given that these were basically agrarian societies, the cadence of the days echoed that of sunrises and sunsets. As the societies gradually became organized in new and different ways, including the emergence of major urban centers and of political life implying rigorous demands, the necessity of more accurate time measurement began to be keenly felt. This in turn led to the development of instruments capable of meeting these demands.

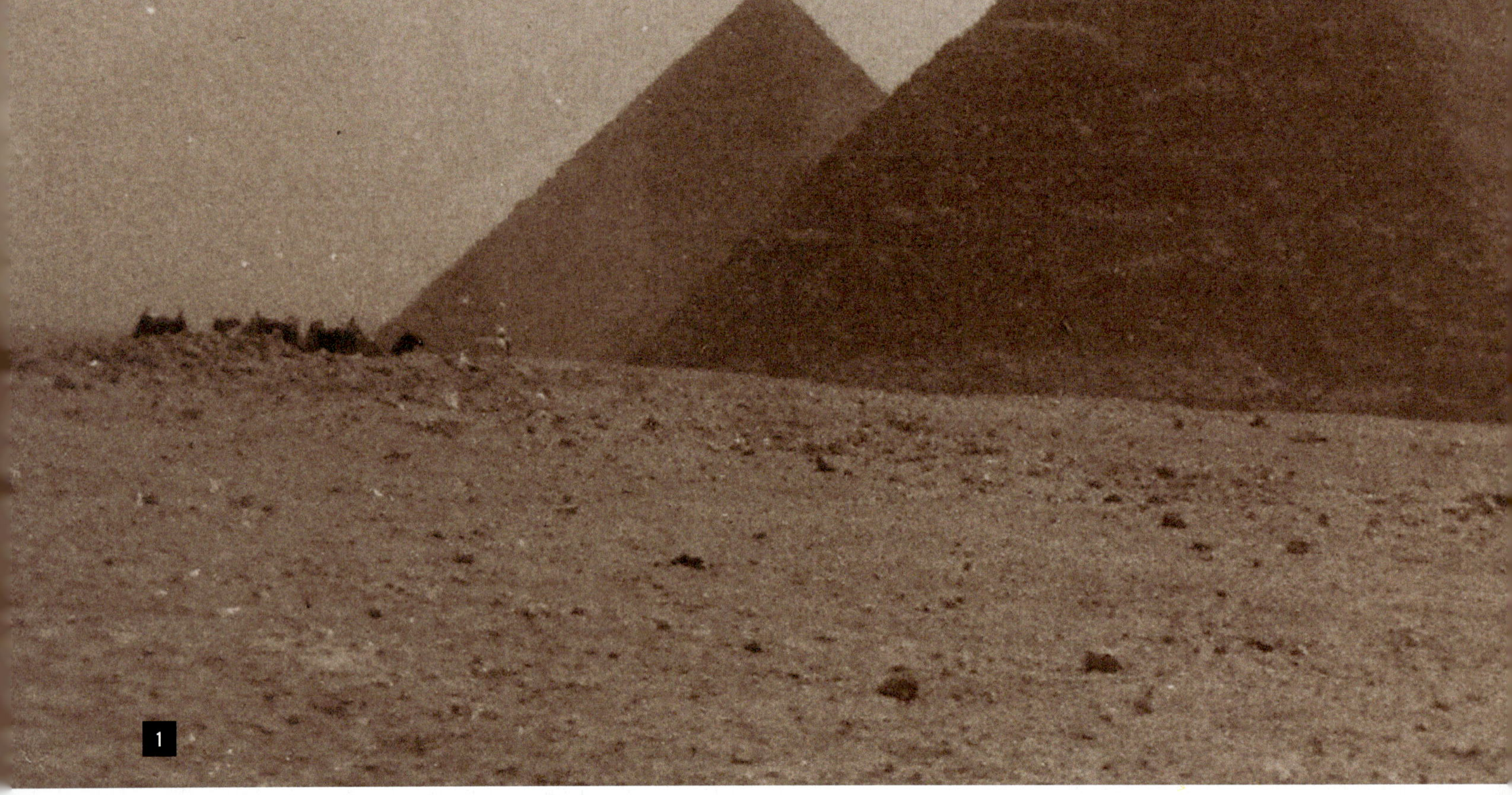

1

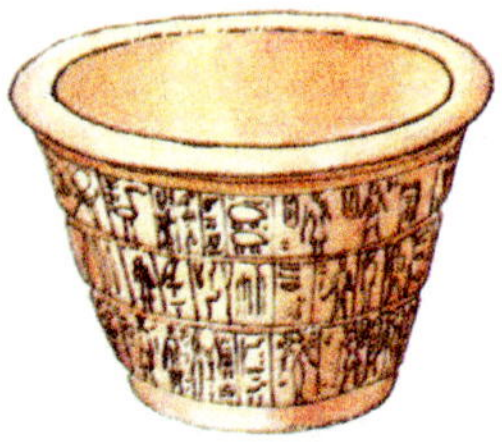

2

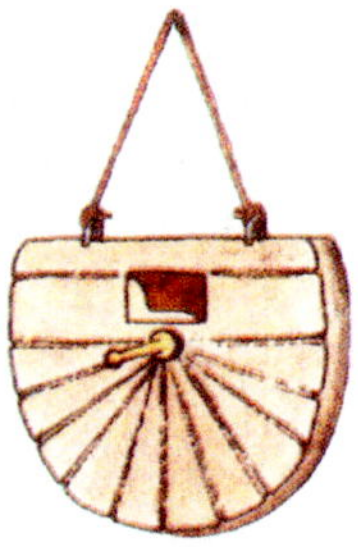

3

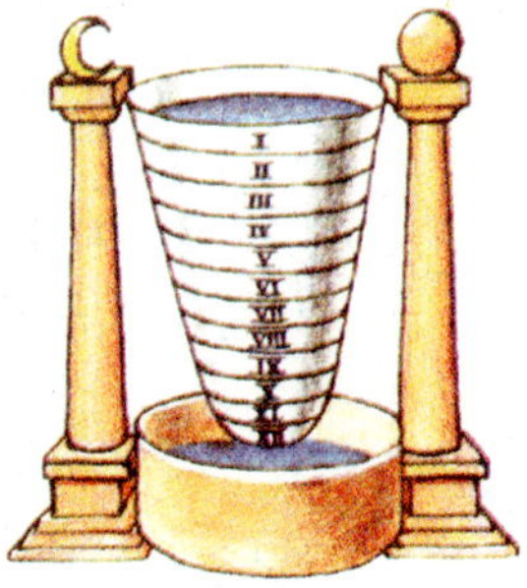

4

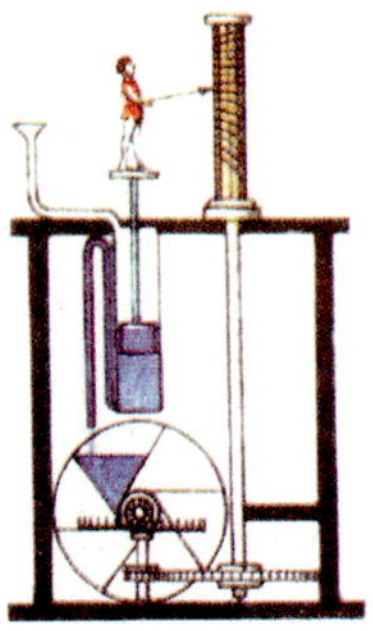

5

1. *Sometimes, the Egyptians built steps on the pyramids and determined the time based on where the shadows fell across the steps.*
2. *One of the earliest and most refined designs of the Egyptian water-clock, dating from the 14th century B.C.*
3. *The solarium was the perfected Roman version of the sundial.*
4. *The klepsydra, ancient water-clock, was also a very sought-after decorative item.*
5. *A drawing of the spectacular Ktesibios water-clock dating from the 2nd century B.C. A little statue was shifted by a float mechanism where a water-wheel turned the column with the time scale. A special device bounced a stone into a little dish and thus sounded the hours.*

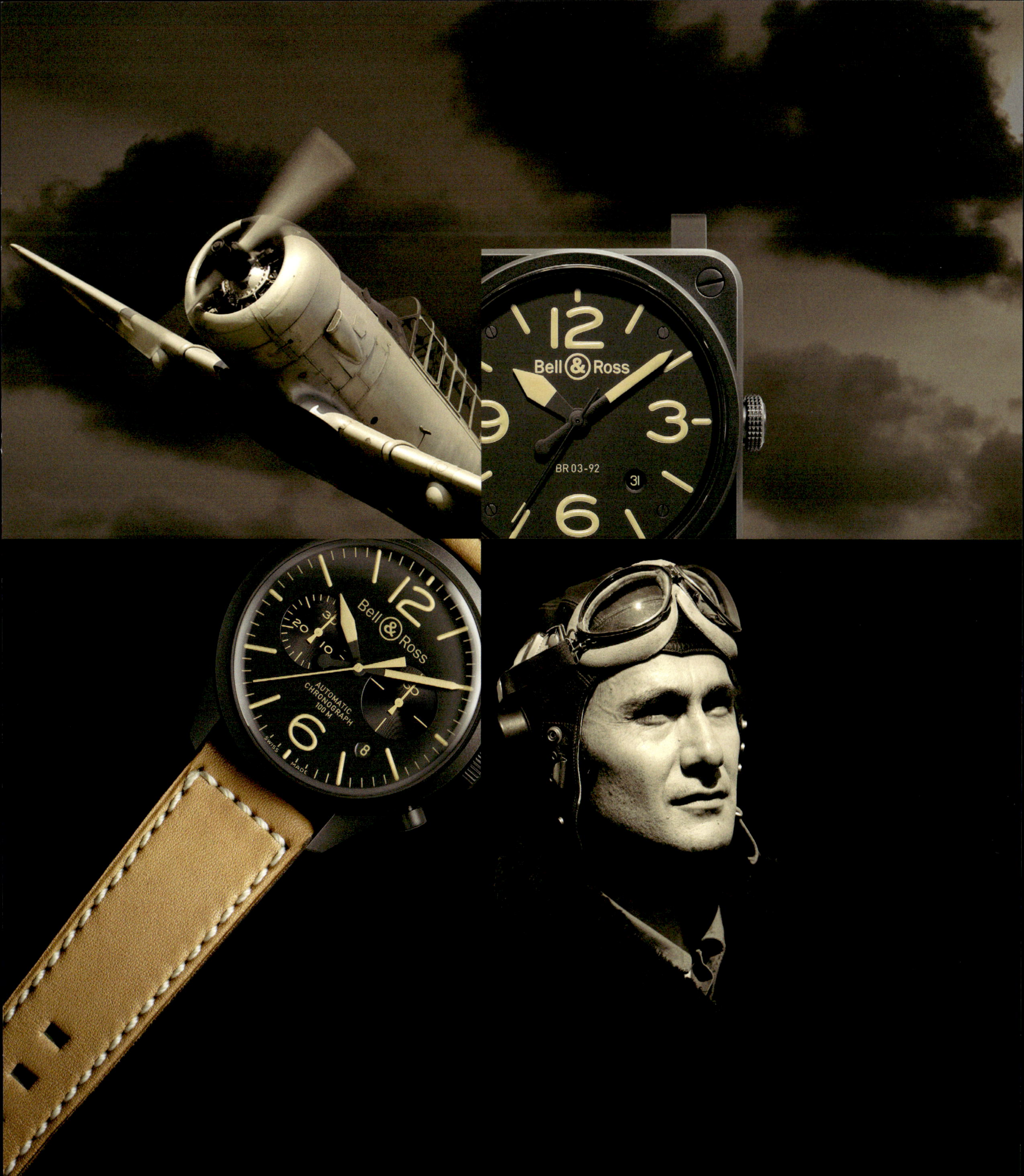
Bell & Ross
BR 03-92
Bell & Ross
AUTOMATIC
CHRONOGRAPH
100 M
SWISS MADE

THE FIRST ARTIFACTS

The gnomon is the first artifact specifically designed to evaluate the daily passing of time. It consists of planting a stick in the ground in order to measure its shadow according to the position of the sun, and appears in records of early civilizations on every continent. Its direct descendant, the sundial, was probably developed by the Egyptians. If the stylus of a sundial is positioned parallel to the Earth's rotation axis, and if the surface on which it casts a shadow is graduated with regular divisions, this instrument is perfectly capable of displaying a sufficiently accurate indication of time measurement. It is therefore hardly surprising that it has found its way unscathed through the centuries, was often used in medieval times as the only means of time measurement, and is still considered by some as a basic survival instrument.

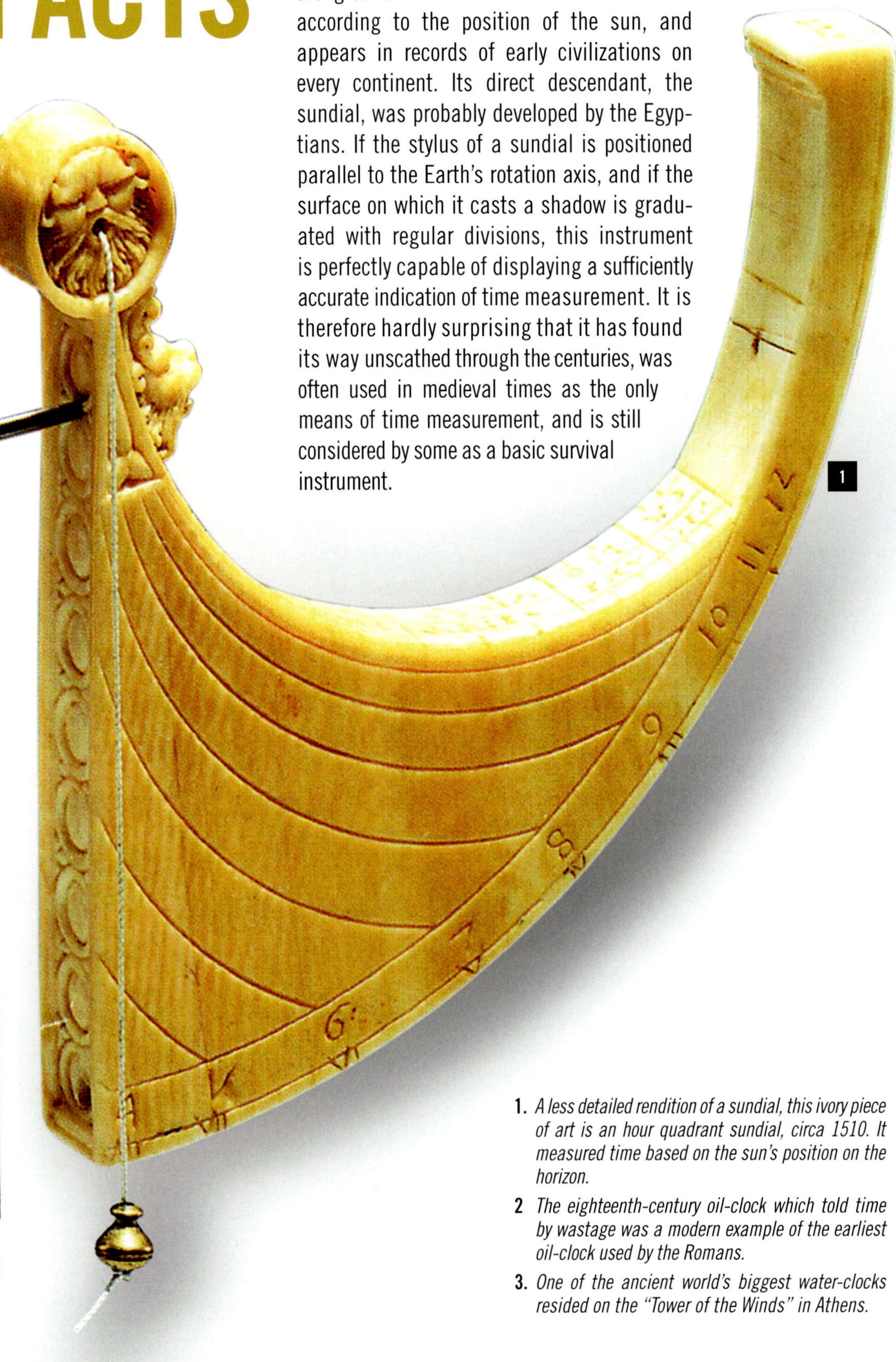

1

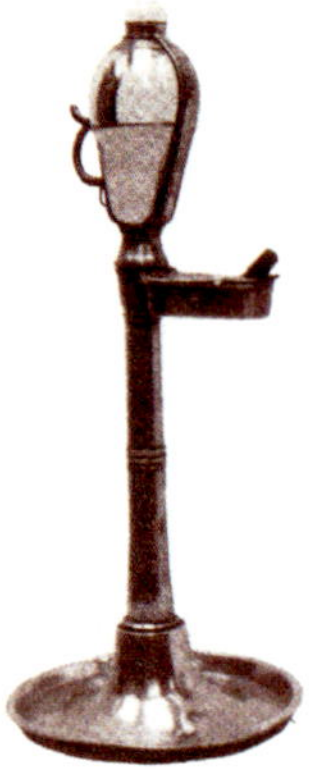

2

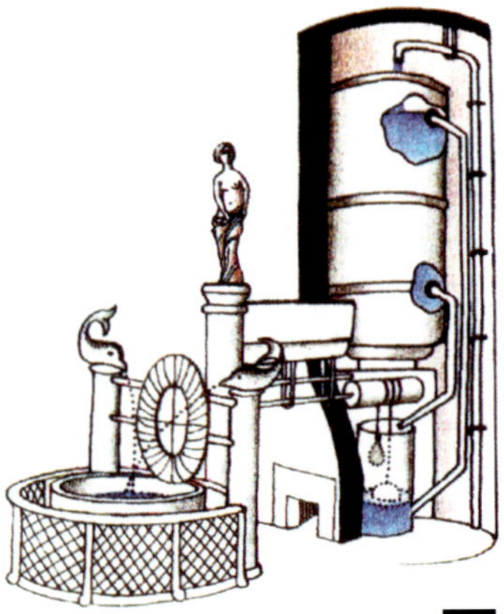

3

1. *A less detailed rendition of a sundial, this ivory piece of art is an hour quadrant sundial, circa 1510. It measured time based on the sun's position on the horizon.*
2. *The eighteenth-century oil-clock which told time by wastage was a modern example of the earliest oil-clock used by the Romans.*
3. *One of the ancient world's biggest water-clocks resided on the "Tower of the Winds" in Athens.*

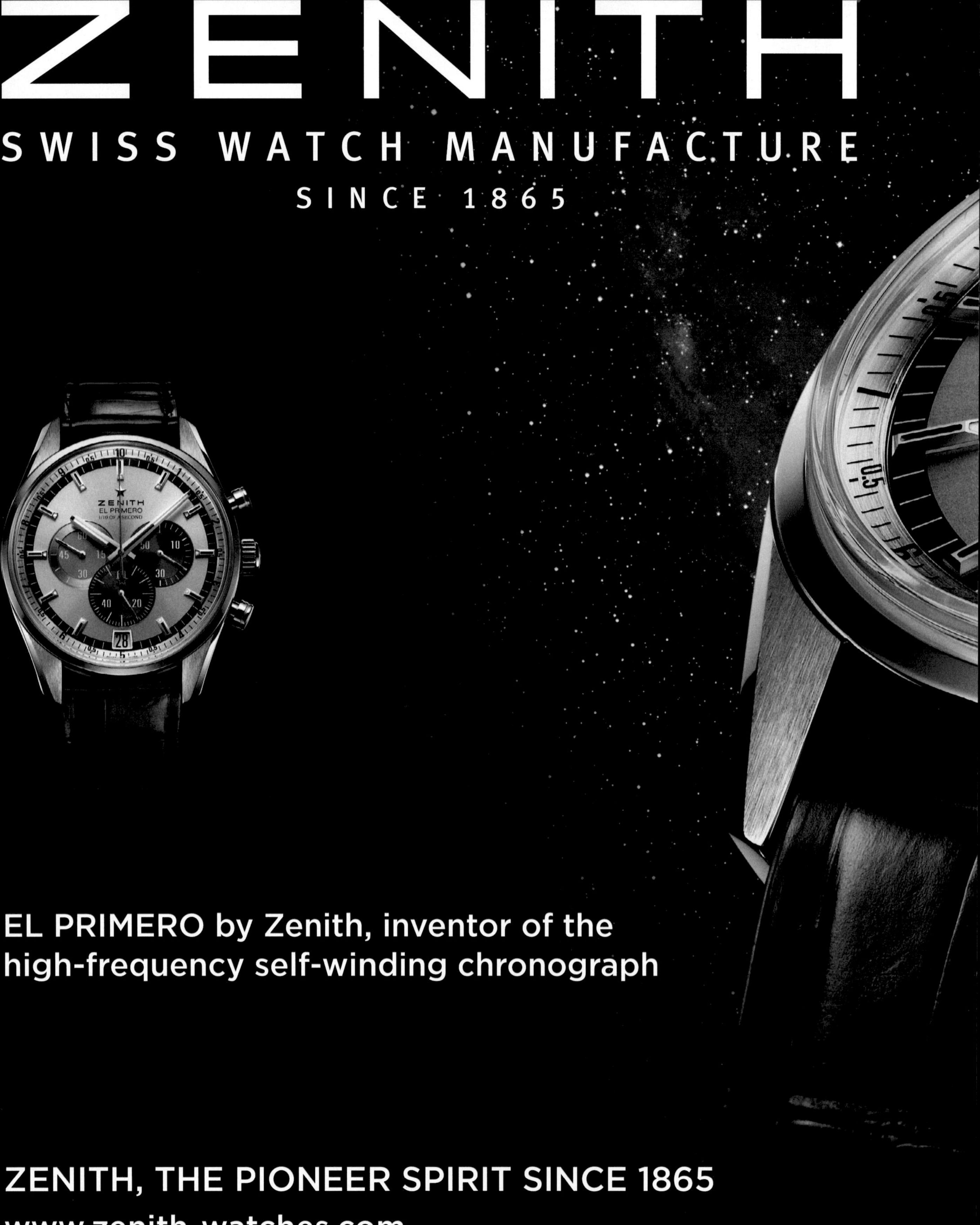
ZENITH
SWISS WATCH MANUFACTURE
SINCE 1865
EL PRIMERO by Zenith, inventor of the
high-frequency self-winding chronograph
ZENITH, THE PIONEER SPIRIT SINCE 1865

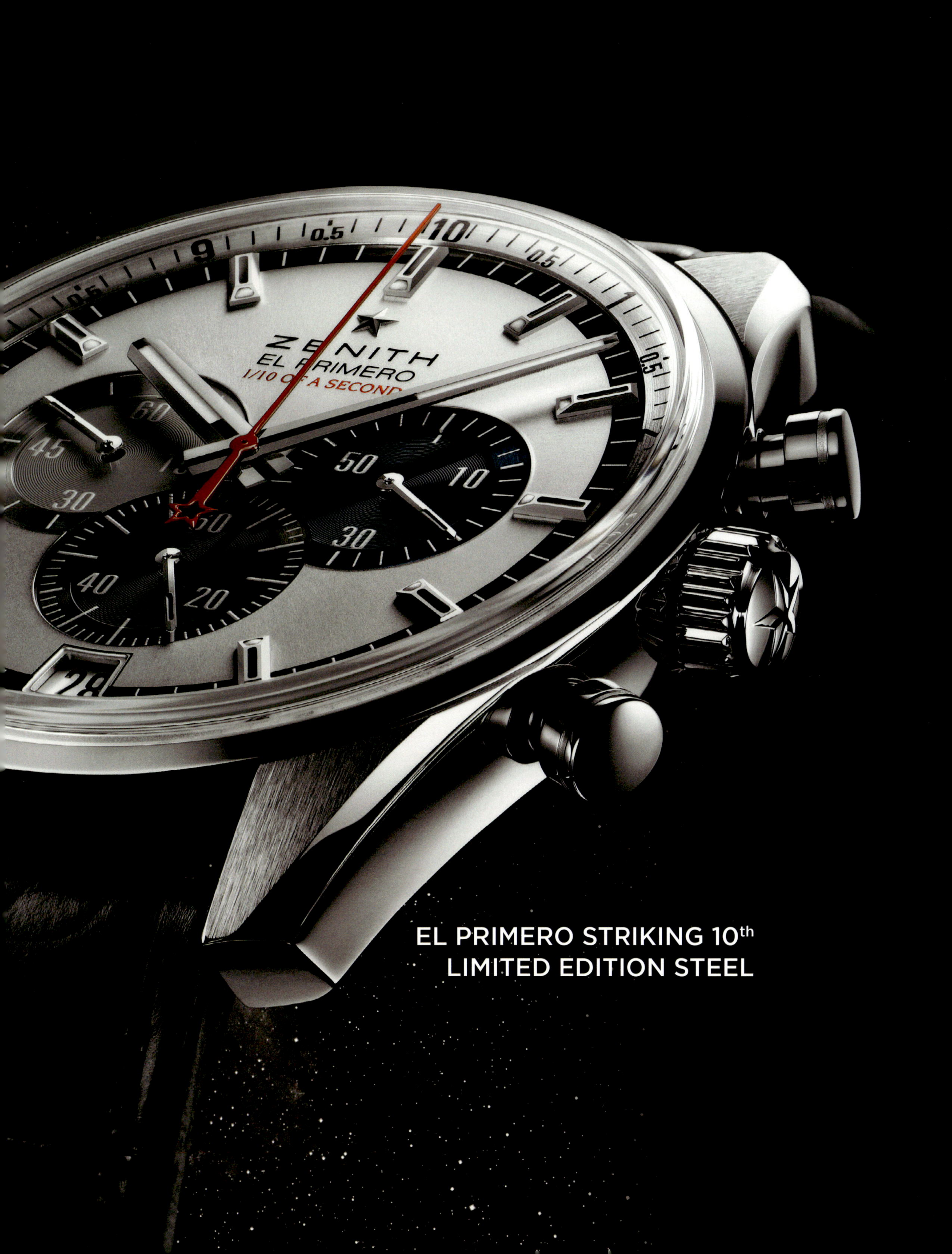
ZENITH
EL PRIMERO STRIKING 10th
LIMITED EDITION STEEL

The sundial nonetheless had a major drawback, because it was of no use whatsoever at night. Other instruments thus emerged, including the clepsydra or water clock. Originally designed to measure relatively short durations, it became widely used because of its practical nature and the possibility of applying the same concept to all 24 hours of the day. In the 18th century, water clocks operating on the same principle as paddle wheels and indicating the time along the rotation axis were still being made. These devices were not, however, very accurate, due to the variation in the water flow rates depending on the temperature, not to mention the fact that they could not be used in areas where water was scarce. The hourglass successfully made up for these shortcomings. Simpler and less expensive to make, as well as totally impervious to changes in temperature, the hourglass became widely used, particularly in the navy as an indispensable instrument in calculating speeds.

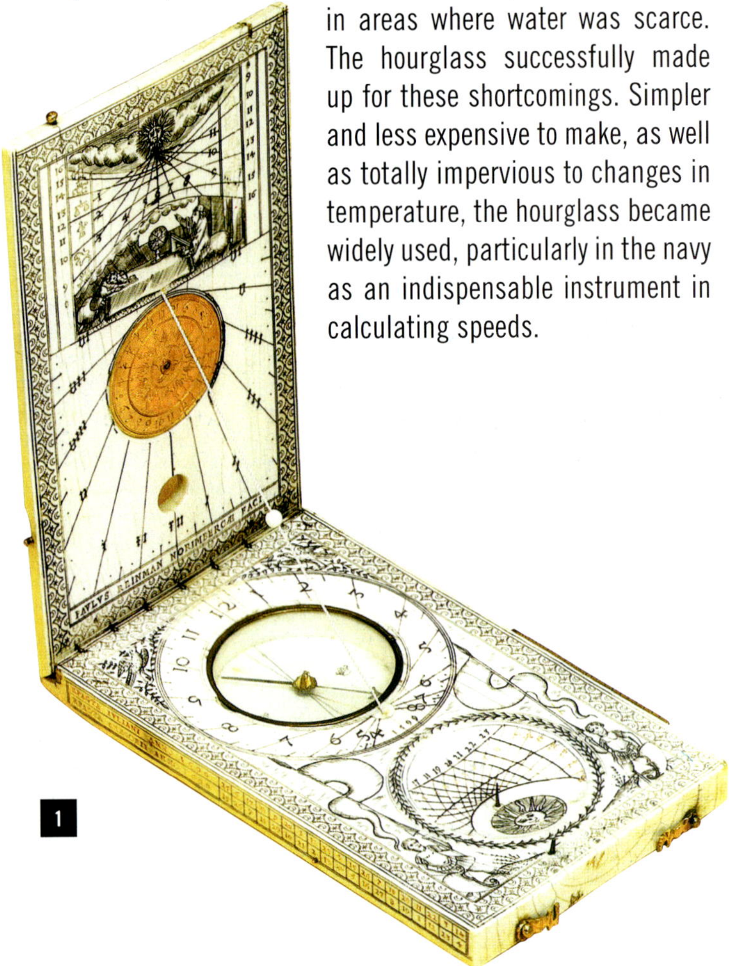

1

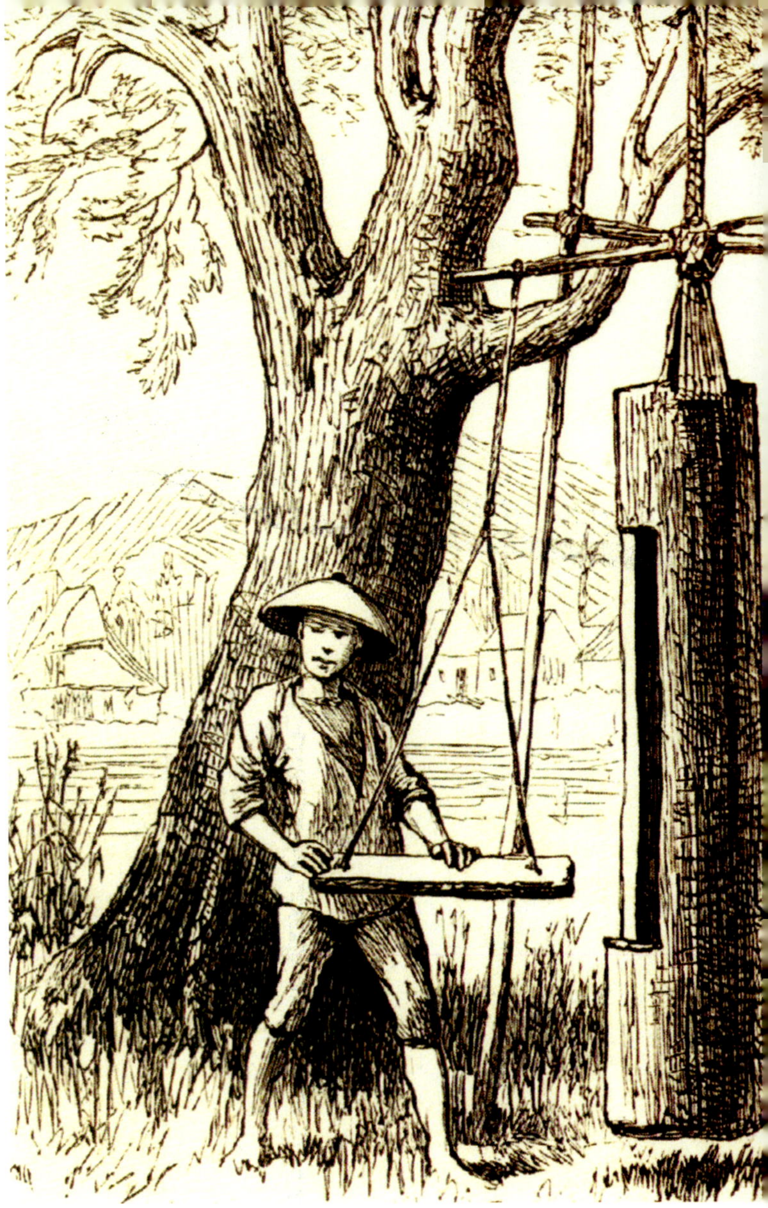

2

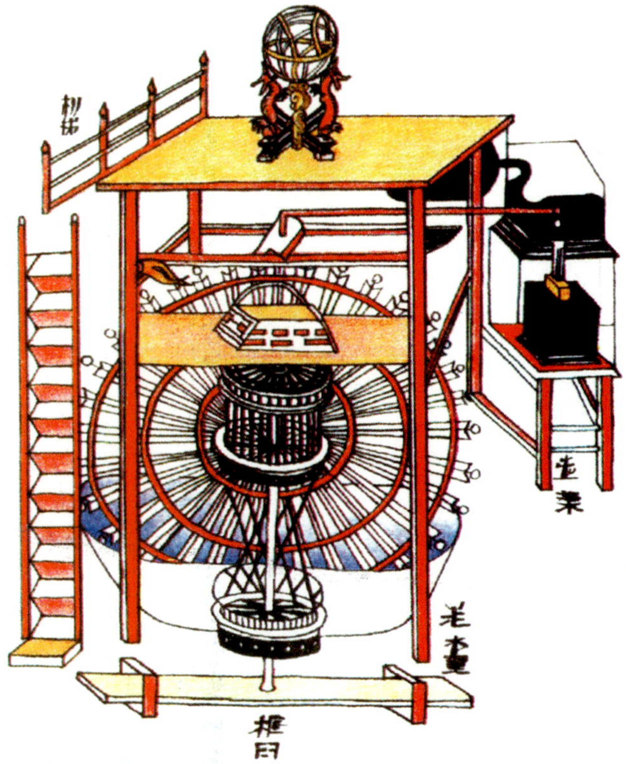

3

1. *Sundials represented the most widely used method of telling time both before and after the inception of the water clock. This sundial, circa 1599, is crafted in ivory.*
2. *Earliest time telling in China consisted of a dedicated priest who regulated village life through indicating the proper times to work, eat and pray.*
3. *This highly complicated Chinese water-clock dating from the 11th century A.D. was the ancestor of Sung's first escapement clock.*

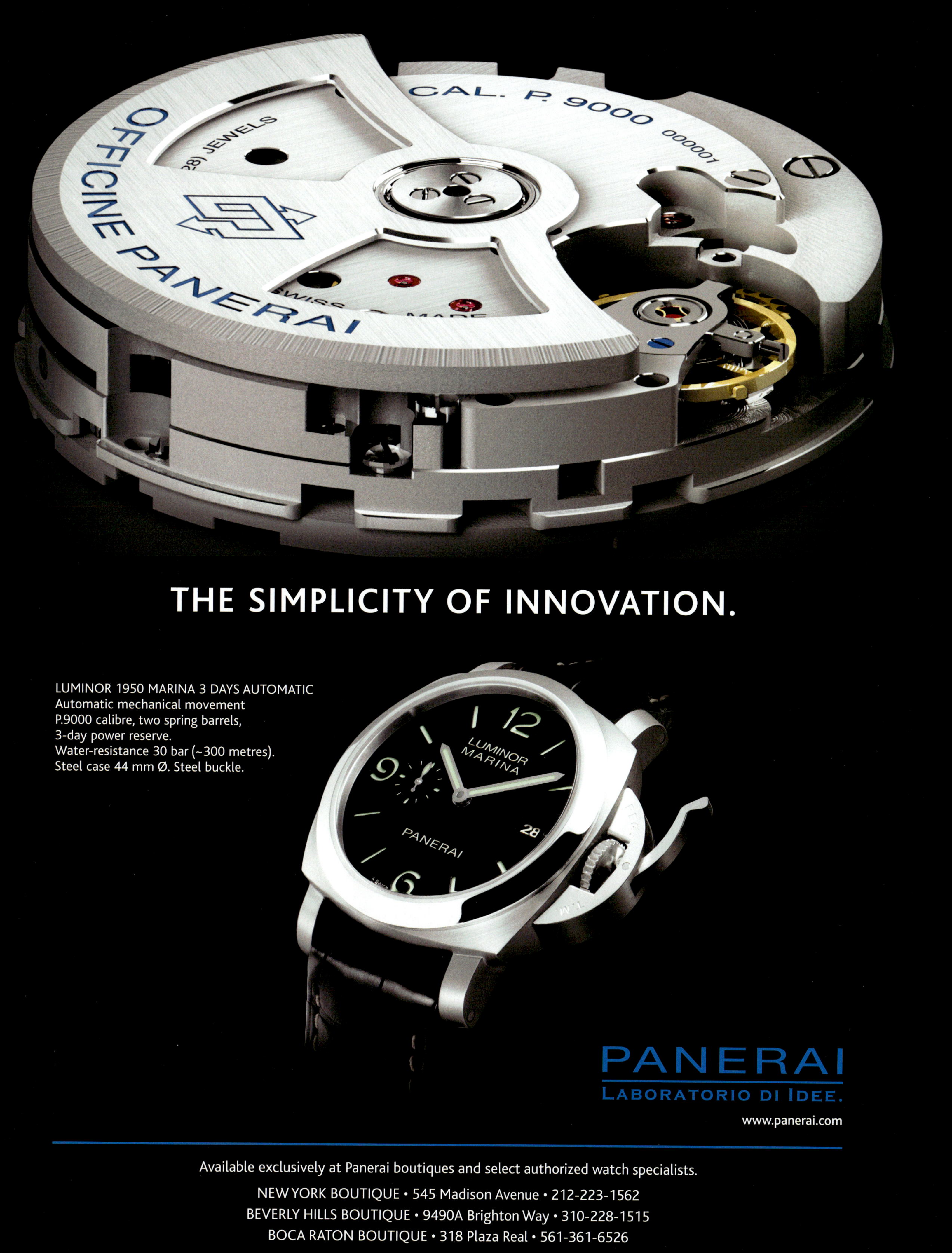
OFFICINE PANERAI
CAL. P. 9000
000001
LUMINOR MARINA
PANERAI
THE SIMPLICITY OF INNOVATION.
LUMINOR 1950 MARINA 3 DAYS AUTOMATIC
Automatic mechanical movement
P.9000 calibre, two spring barrels,
3-day power reserve.
Water-resistance 30 bar (~300 metres).
Steel case 44 mm Ø. Steel buckle.
PANERAI
LABORATORIO DI IDEE.
www.panerai.com
Available exclusively at Panerai boutiques and select authorized watch specialists.
NEW YORK BOUTIQUE • 545 Madison Avenue • 212-223-1562
BEVERLY HILLS BOUTIQUE • 9490A Brighton Way • 310-228-1515
BOCA RATON BOUTIQUE • 318 Plaza Real • 561-361-6526

Mobilizing its energy reserves.

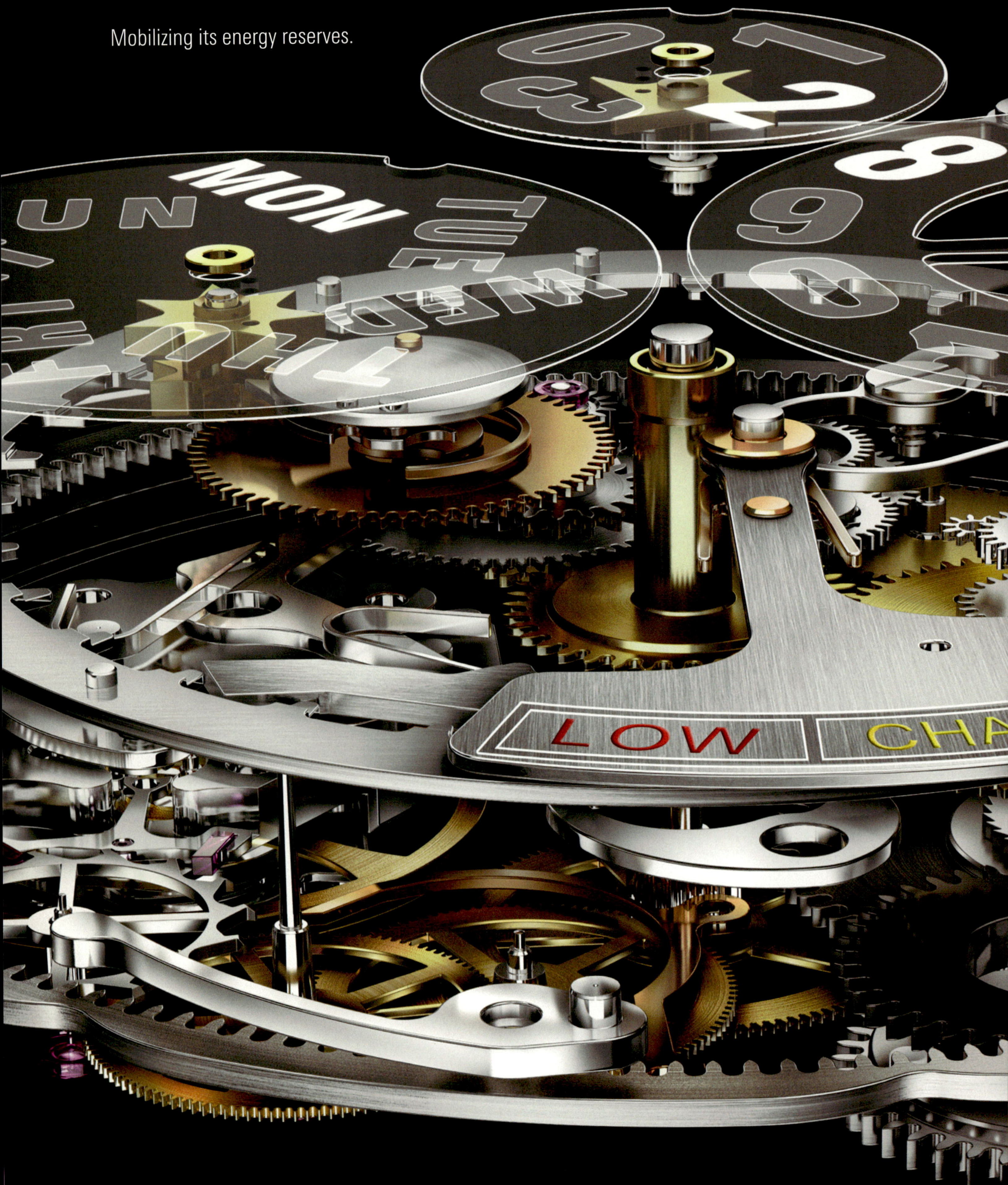

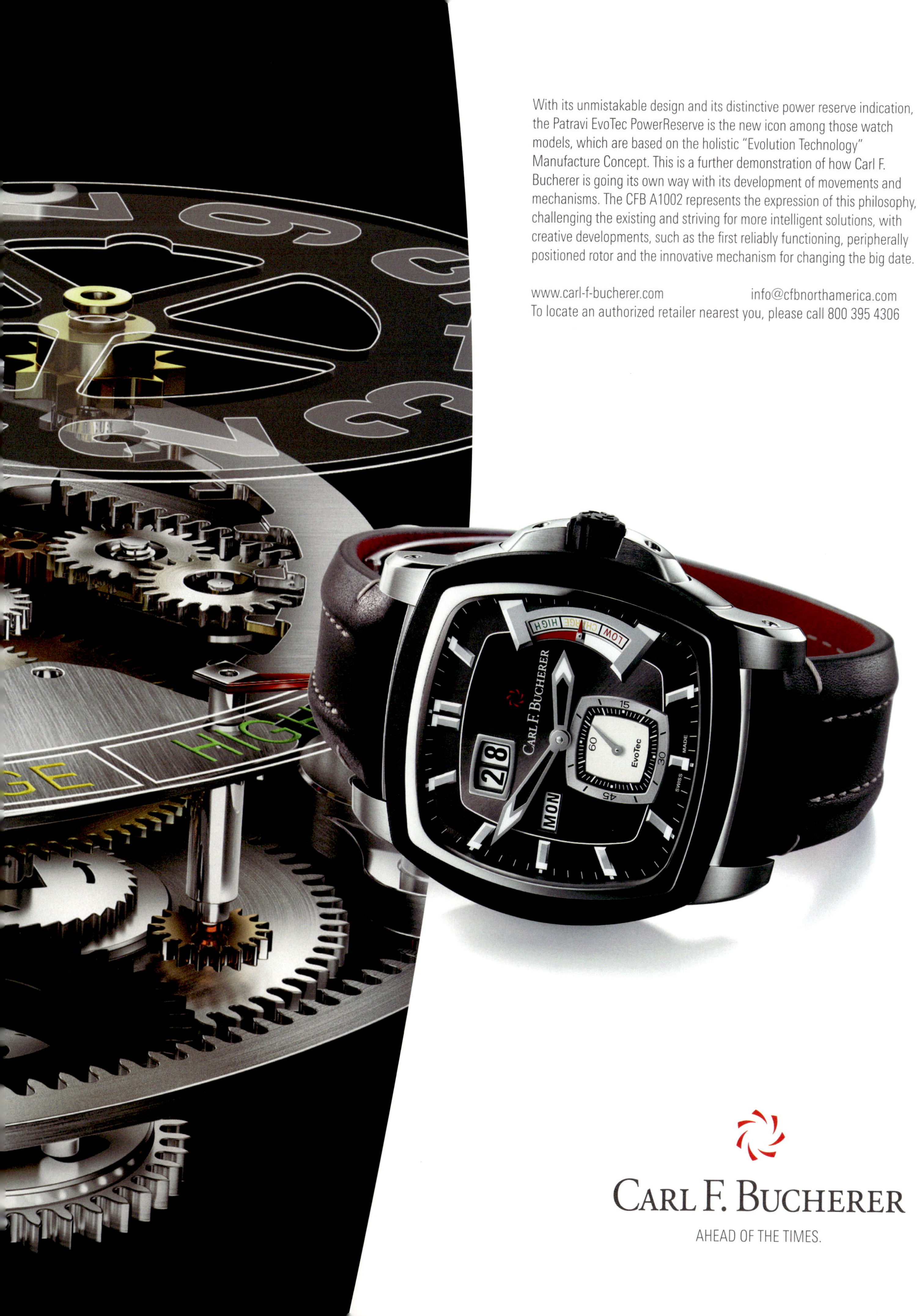
HIGH
CARL F. BUCHERER
LOW CHARGE HIGH
28
MON
EvoTec
SWISS MADE

A REVOLUTION IN THE PERCEPTION OF TIME

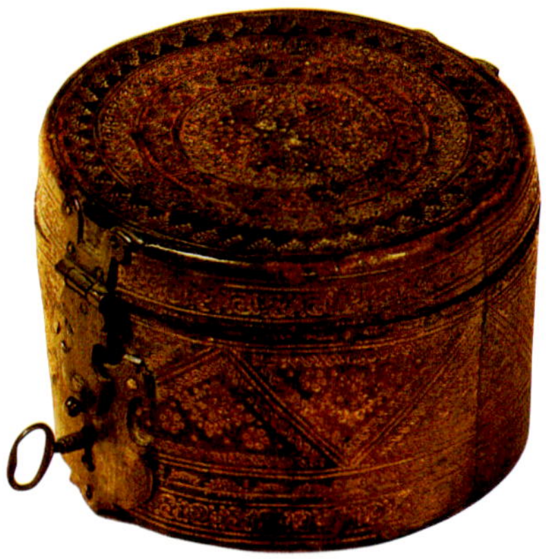

It was not until the 16th century that the hour was defined as one twenty-fourth of the time between two successive passages of the sun through the zenith. This historical period witnessed a major breakthrough in time measurement due to the invention of mechanical horology, in which the weight of water was replaced by that of a solid body. But the conception of such "machines" called for several major innovations including the invention and regulation of the escapement. In its initial form, the escapement consisted in a mechanism that locked and released a toothed wheel of which the rotation was driven by a falling weight. Regulating it via an oscillator was done by a foliot, or a heavy vertical bar on which the horizontal part, or verge, was fitted with two pallets alternately engaging and disengaging with a toothed wheel in order to hold it back, while receiving the necessary impulse to maintain the steady oscillating motion of the foliot.

1

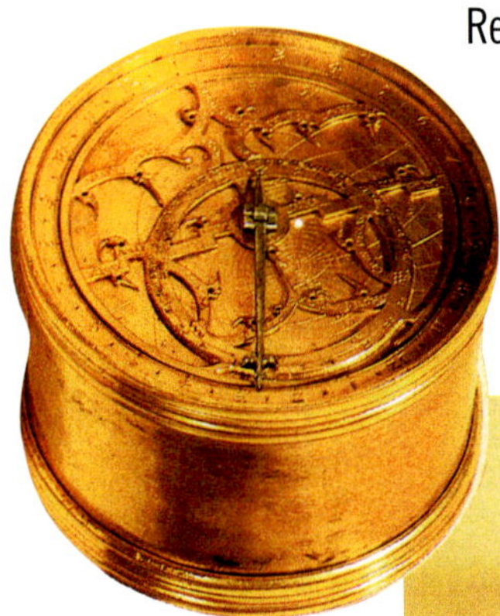

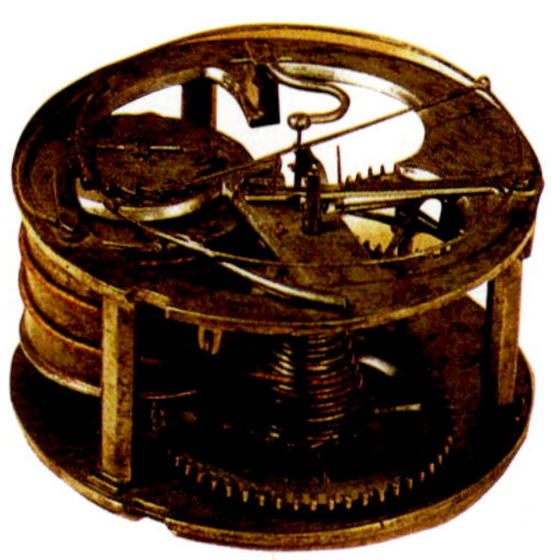

2

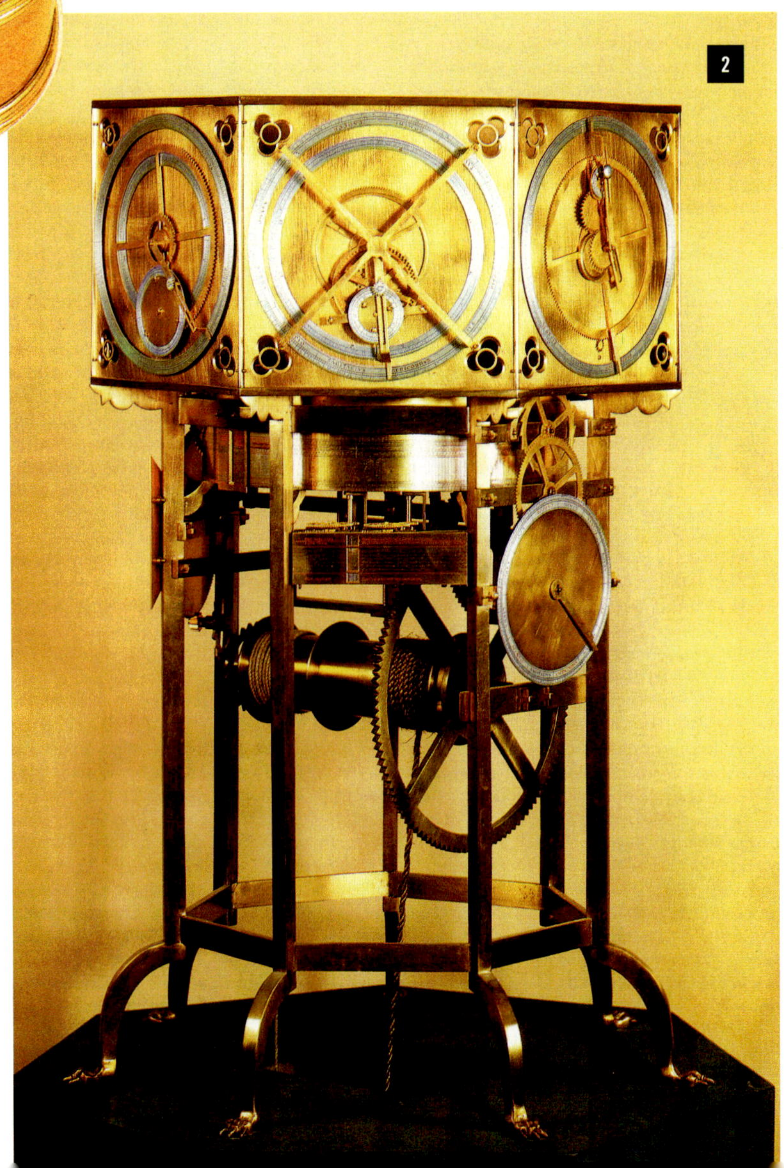

1. *In the 16th century, as people traveled more frequently, it became necessary to create portable clocks. This one, circa 1525 and shown in three views, is a circular clock with Astrolabe and traveling case. It is crafted of iron, but the case is tooled leather.*
2. *Modern reconstruction of de Dondi's astronomical clock. It took de Dondi from 1348 to 1364 to design and construct the clock.*

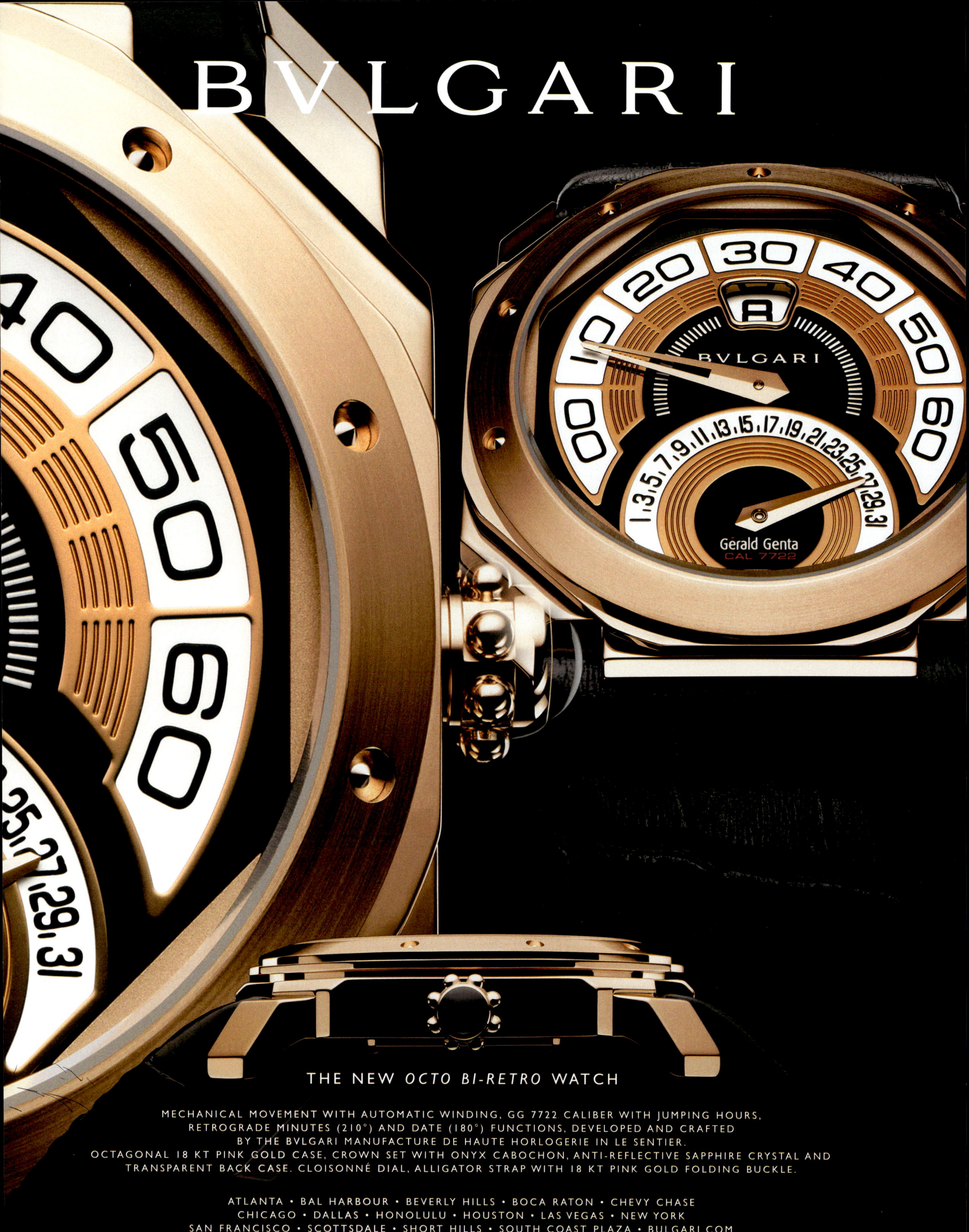
BVLGARI
BVLGARI
Gerald Genta
CAL 7722
THE NEW *OCTO BI-RETRO* WATCH
MECHANICAL MOVEMENT WITH AUTOMATIC WINDING, GG 7722 CALIBER WITH JUMPING HOURS, RETROGRADE MINUTES (210°) AND DATE (180°) FUNCTIONS, DEVELOPED AND CRAFTED BY THE BVLGARI MANUFACTURE DE HAUTE HORLOGERIE IN LE SENTIER.
OCTAGONAL 18 KT PINK GOLD CASE, CROWN SET WITH ONYX CABOCHON, ANTI-REFLECTIVE SAPPHIRE CRYSTAL AND TRANSPARENT BACK CASE. CLOISONNÉ DIAL, ALLIGATOR STRAP WITH 18 KT PINK GOLD FOLDING BUCKLE.
ATLANTA • BAL HARBOUR • BEVERLY HILLS • BOCA RATON • CHEVY CHASE
CHICAGO • DALLAS • HONOLULU • HOUSTON • LAS VEGAS • NEW YORK
SAN FRANCISCO • SCOTTSDALE • SHORT HILLS • SOUTH COAST PLAZA • BULGARI.COM

This new approach to time measurement, albeit initially very imprecise with a variation in rate of up to several hours a day, nonetheless represented a genuine revolution. The cyclical time of our ancestors, marked off by the recurrence of days and seasons, was now viewed from a new perspective, as a linear flow composed of successive moments. These fleeting moments were now measurable thanks to clocks capable of operating according to mechanical principles determined by human reasoning. In this respect, while Gutenberg's 15th-century invention of printing is rightly considered a watershed event in the development of knowledge, the advent of mechanical horology also represents a pivotal stage in human progress.

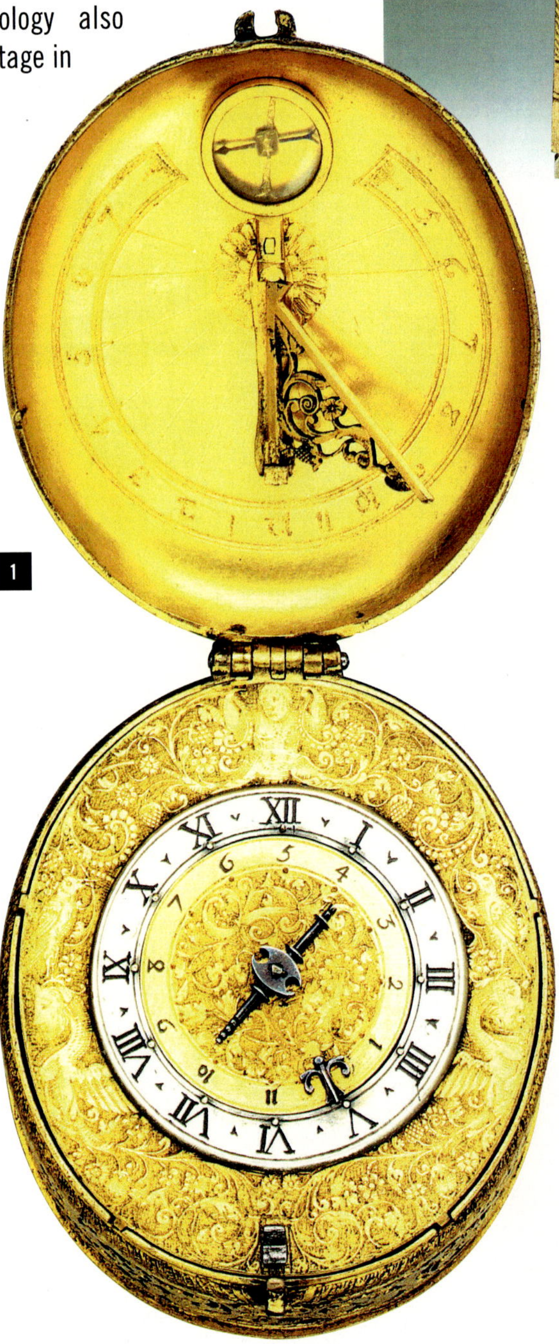

1

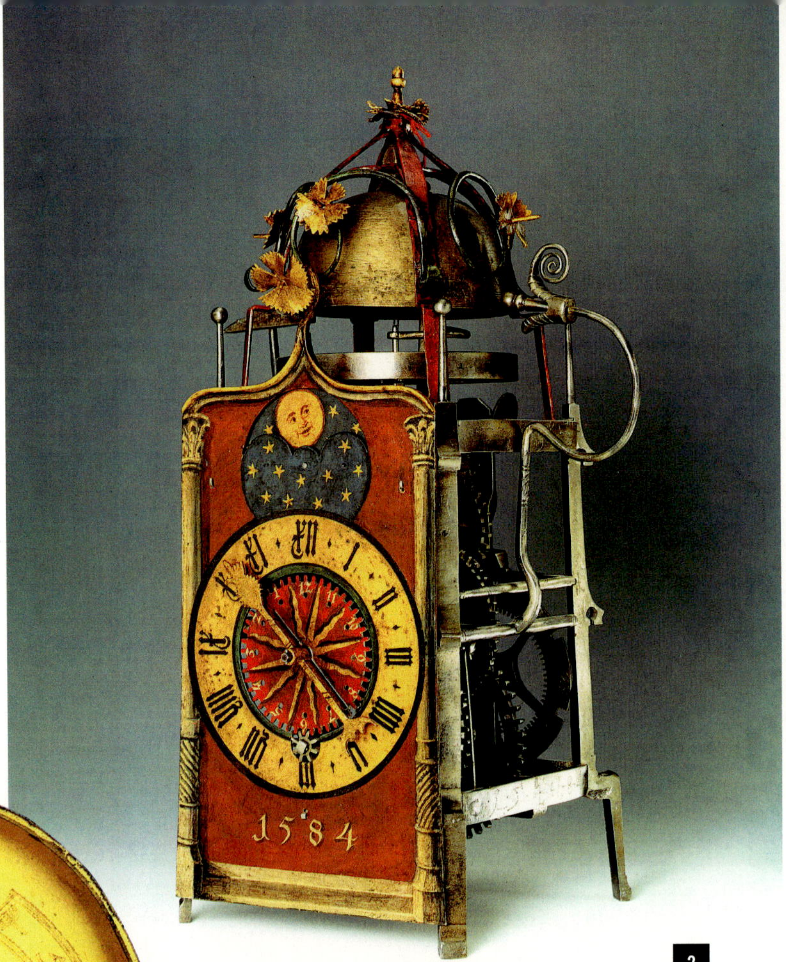

2

1. *This Renaissance neck watch in oval format, circa 1590, features an alarm. The watch has a small horizontal sundial and is created in gold.*

2. *Early clocks were forged by blacksmiths, and typically made of iron. This iron wall clock, circa 1584, features a gothic dial and movable moon plate to show phases of the moon.*

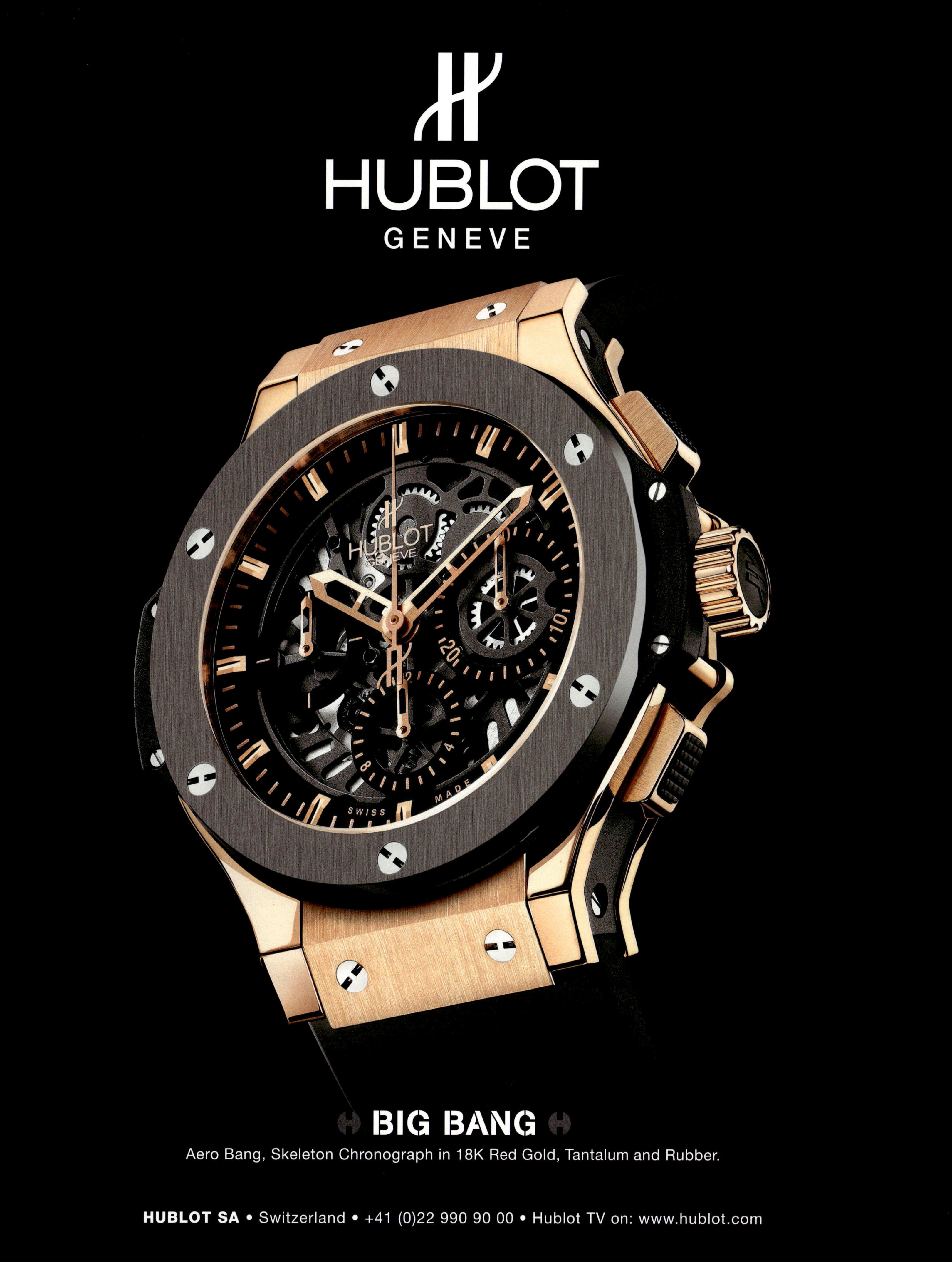
HUBLOT
GENEVE
BIG BANG
Aero Bang, Skeleton Chronograph in 18K Red Gold, Tantalum and Rubber.
HUBLOT SA • Switzerland • +41 (0)22 990 90 00 • Hublot TV on: www.hublot.com

A GENIUS NAMED GALILEO

This new way of considering the flow of time was also confirmed by the progress achieved in the field of astronomy, which contradicted the geocentric theories that were commonly upheld until that point. Thanks to the work of Copernicus (1473-1543), especially as expounded in his *De revolutionibus orbium caelestium*, a new vision of the world began to assert itself, based on the key principles of the solar system. Galileo (1564-1642) was the first to derive practical lessons from these theoretical elements. He can also be credited with considerable advances in the field of mechanics, which was to earn the status of a science in its own right.

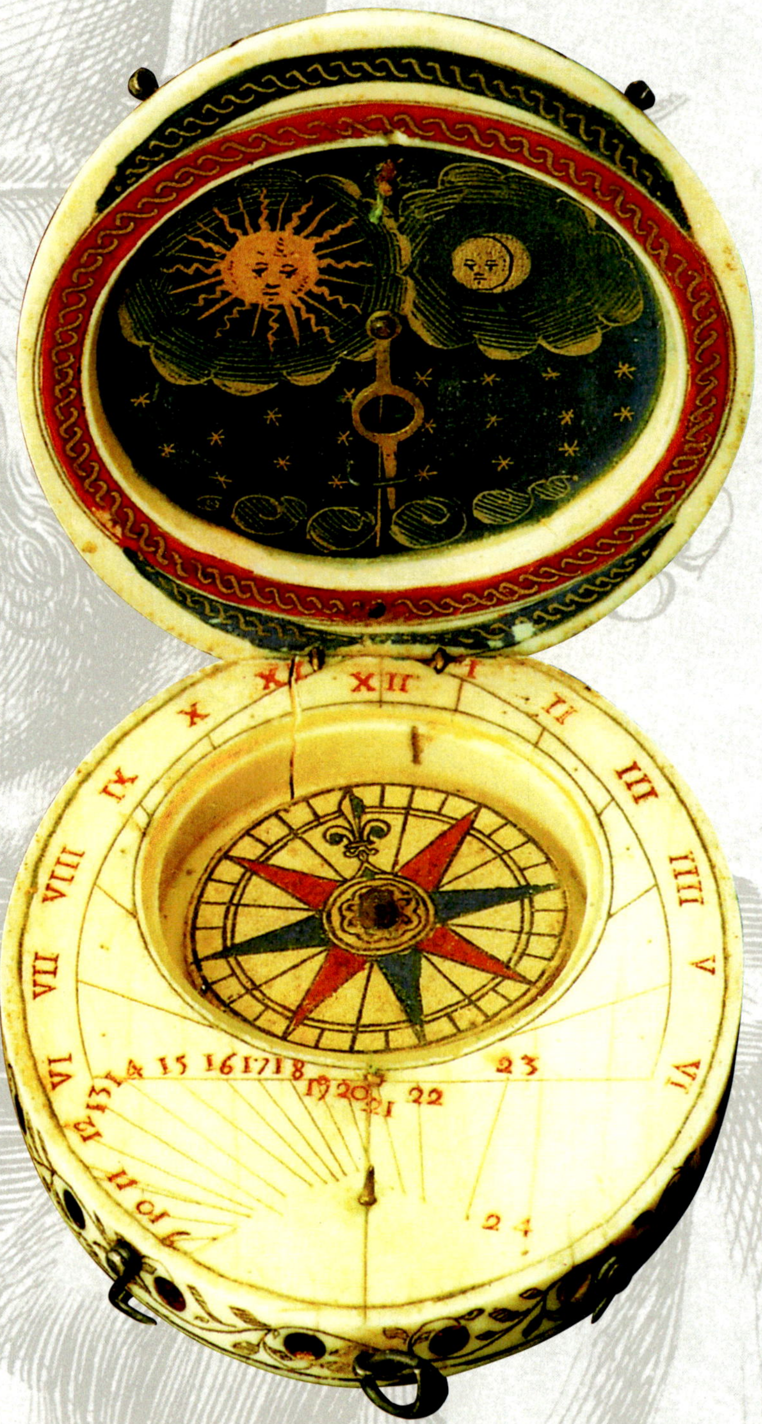

Created around the year 1600, this ivory portable sundial is decorated with garnets and emeralds.

In around 1588, he discovered the isochronism principle governing the oscillating pendulum, meaning that the duration of the oscillations of the pendulum is independent of the amplitude imparted to it. Thanks to the discovery of constant and regular pendulum oscillations, Galileo provided horology with dependable and easily reproducible norms, thereby providing a foundation that would enable a major leap forward. Galileo himself set about making a pendulum clock equipped with an escapement that freed it from the traditional foliot crown wheel. His work was not completed at the time of his death, and his son, who was charged with finishing this construction, also died before finalizing the concept.

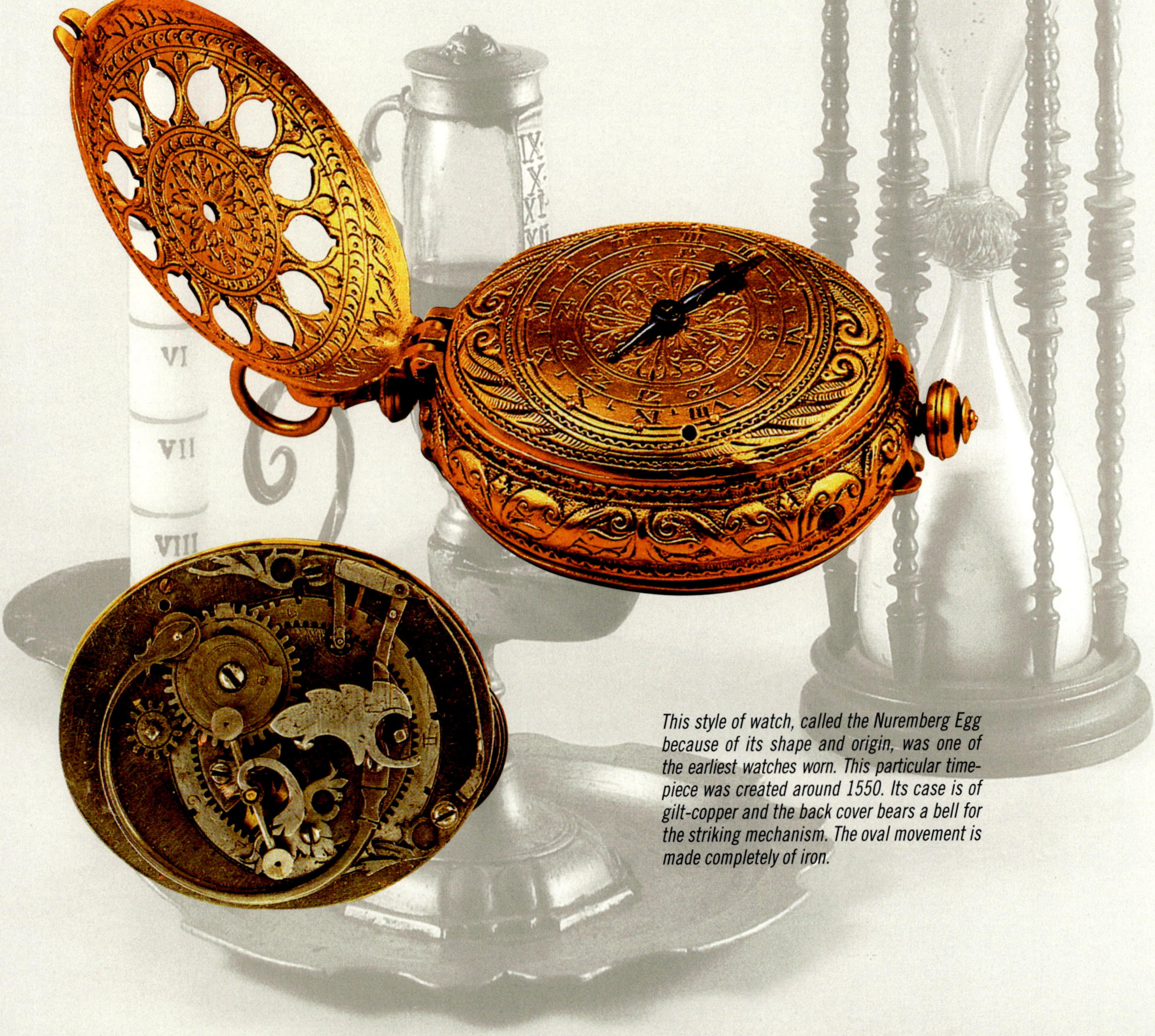

This style of watch, called the Nuremberg Egg because of its shape and origin, was one of the earliest watches worn. This particular timepiece was created around 1550. Its case is of gilt-copper and the back cover bears a bell for the striking mechanism. The oval movement is made completely of iron.

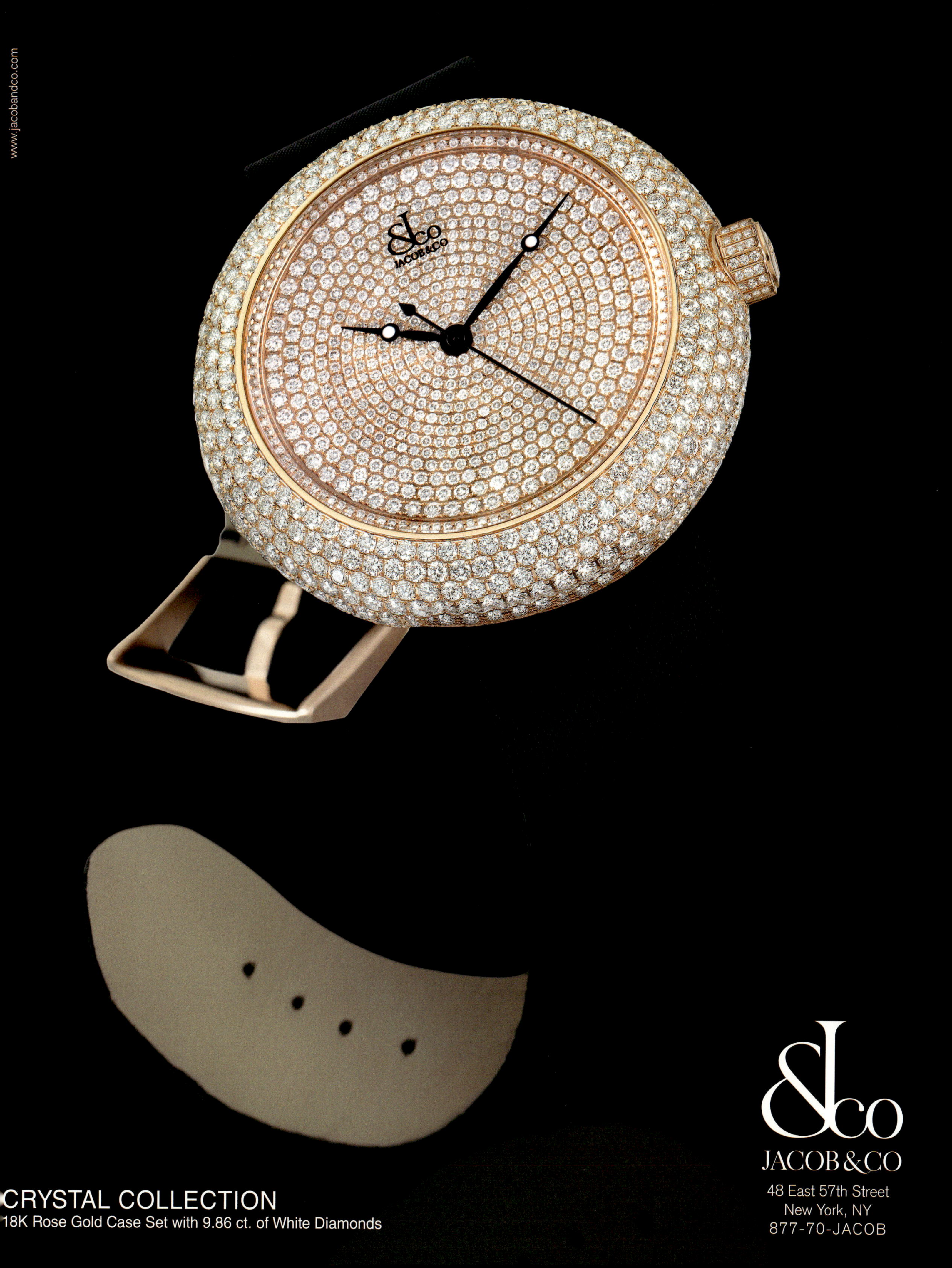
www.jacobandco.com
JACOB&CO
CRYSTAL COLLECTION
18K Rose Gold Case Set with 9.86 ct. of White Diamonds
JACOB&CO
48 East 57th Street
New York, NY
877-70-JACOB

HUYGENS MARCHES IN GALILEO'S FOOTSTEPS

While Galileo based his work on the mathematical precision of pendulum oscillations in order to design a mechanical movement, it was the Dutch physicist and astronomer Christiaan Huygens (1629-1695) who drew all the practical lessons from this invention. In 1657, based on the plans drawn up by Huygens, the horologer Salomon Coster made a mechanical clock with a cycloidal pendular balance controlling an oscillating escapement. It is also to Huygens that we owe the first watch with a balance-spring, made by Isaac Thuret in 1675. The regulating organ was composed of a balance-wheel, a tiny mechanical flywheel, coupled with a thin steel spring coiled like a spring and exercising the same effect on the balance-wheel as gravity had on the pendulum. The lack of accuracy of these first attempts subsequently led to the idea of giving new shapes to the end curves of the balance-springs in order to ensure their isochronism.

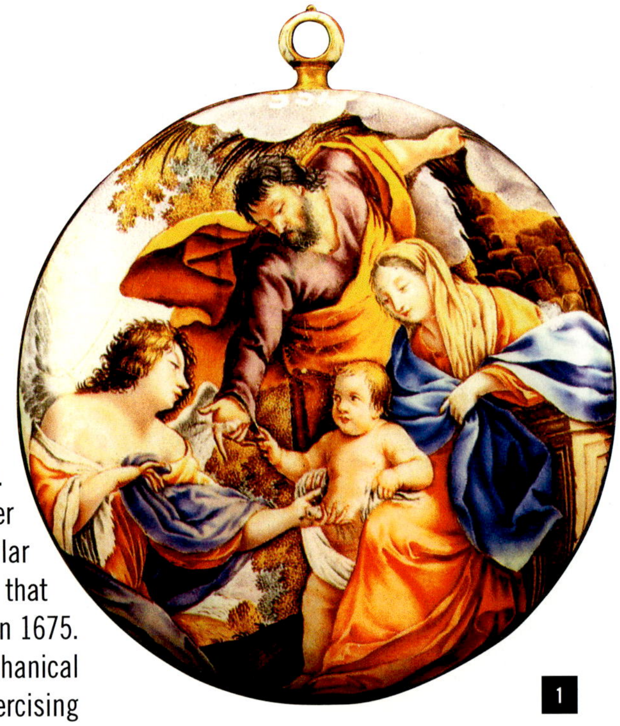

1

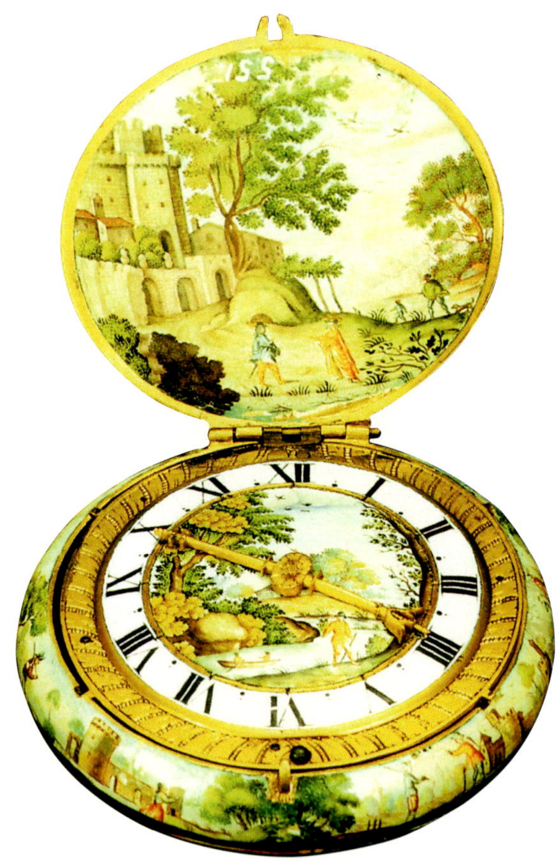

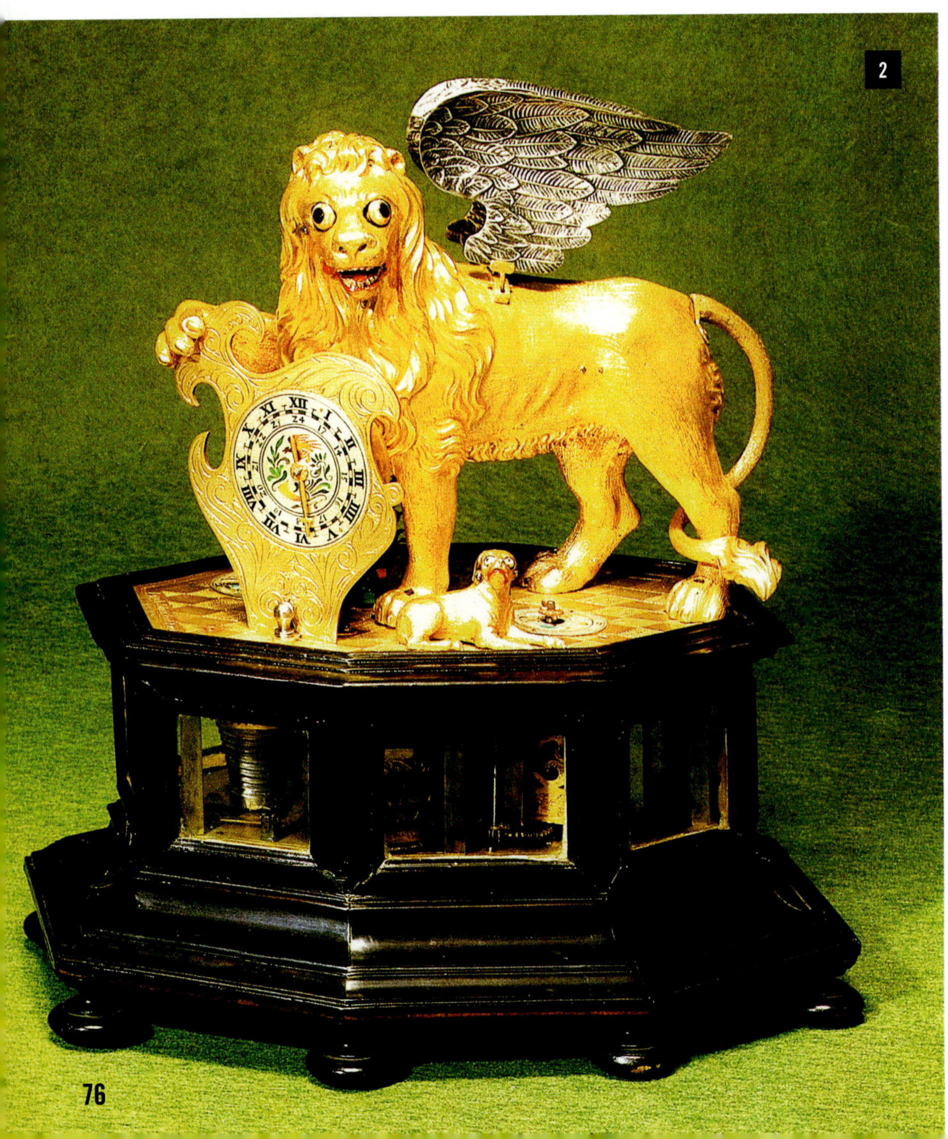

2

1. *Interior and exterior of enamel timepiece from the 17th century. Enamel work became an important decorative function of watches and clocks.*
2. *This Renaissance table clock, circa 1640, is crafted of a bronze lion and small dog. As the clock works, both the lion and the dog move their eyes in time with the clock. As the hour strikes, the lion opens its mouth and moves its wings.*

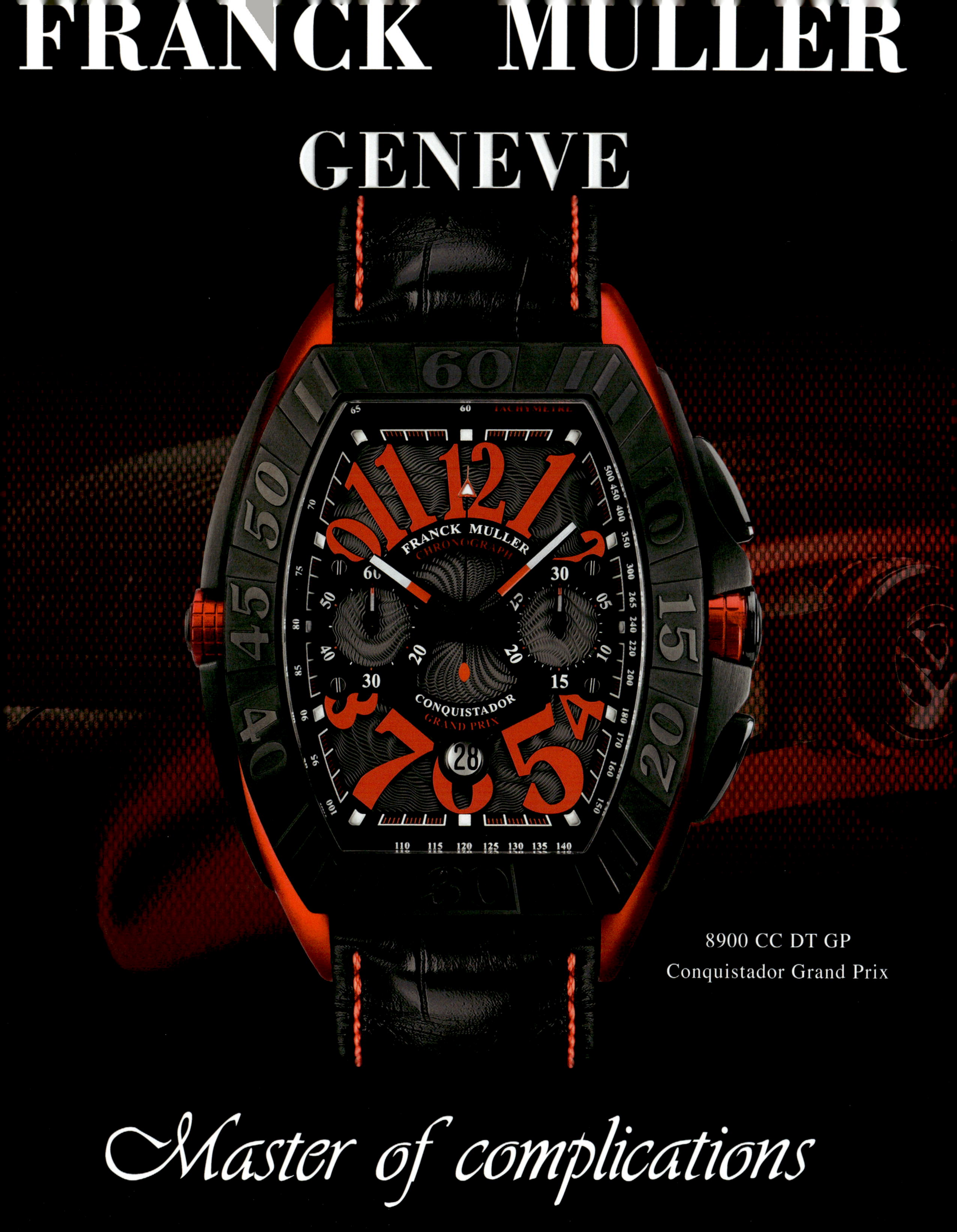
FRANCK MULLER
GENEVE
8900 CC DT GP
Conquistador Grand Prix
Master of complications

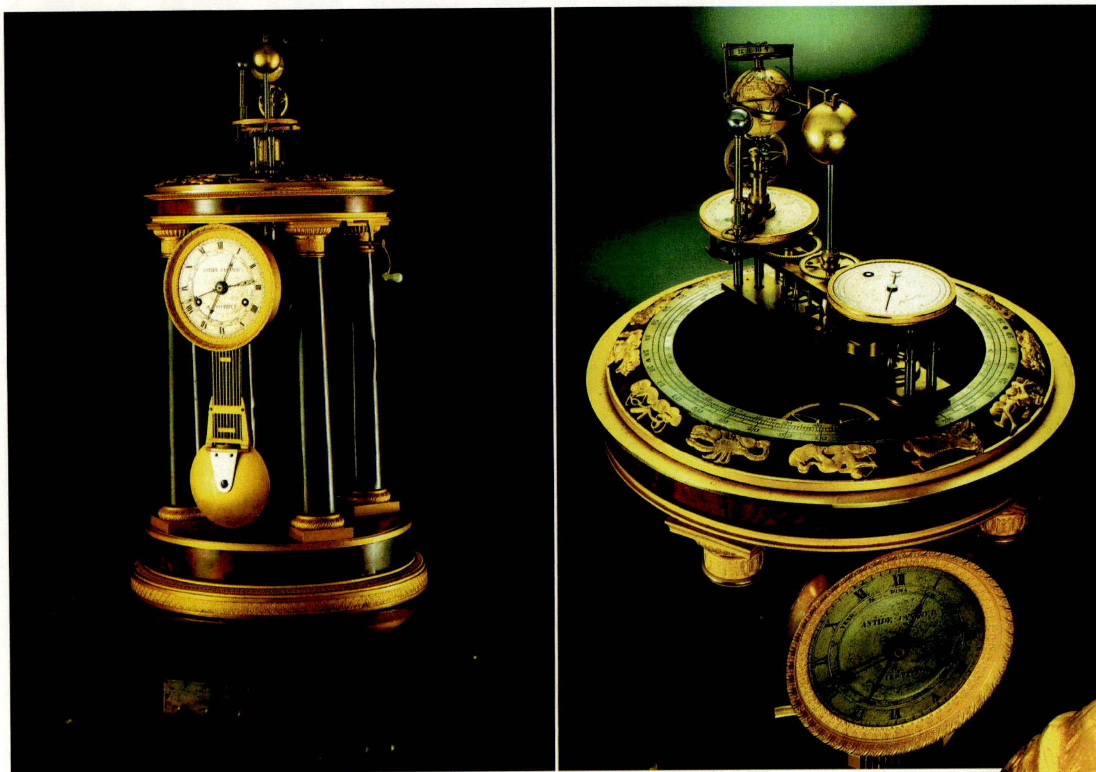

1

Despite the substantial improvements to the field of horology, civil time was not officially adopted as an alternative to astronomical time until the late 18th century. Subsequently, with the industrial revolution of the 19th century and the development of railway networks, local time also became completely obsolete—hence the necessity of establishing a reference time. At an international conference held in Washington in 1884, the 0 meridian would follow the axis of the earth passing through Greenwich, considered by most navigators as the benchmark observatory. This meant that the hours would be counted off from 0 to 23 as of midnight, meaning 12 hours after the sun had passed through the zenith. The international convention that met in Paris in 1911 officially ratified the choice of the Greenwich Meridian and of the system which divided the earth into 24 time zones, each covering a longitude of 15° and numbered 0 to 23 running from West to East.

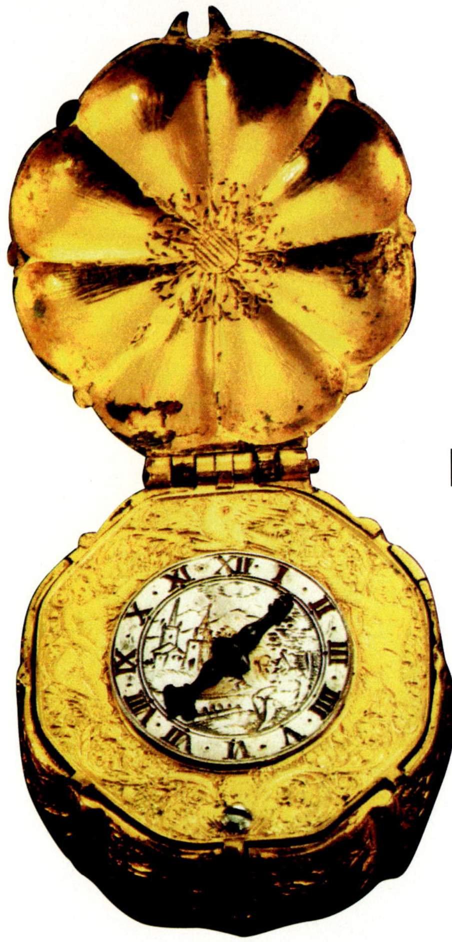

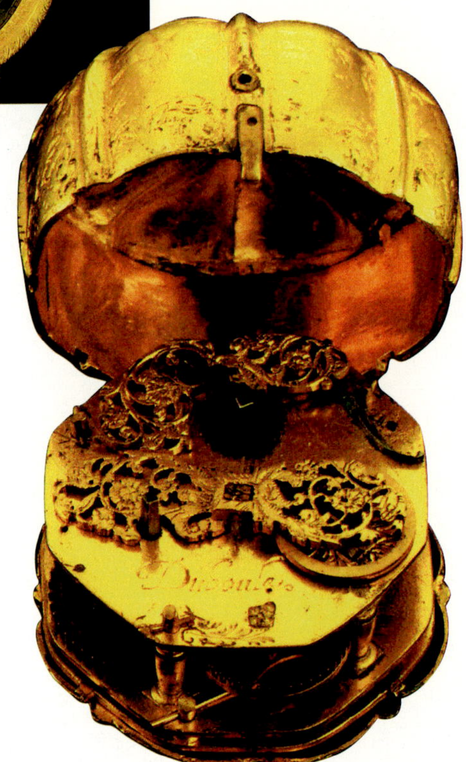

2

1. *This planetary clock with musical mechanism dates to the first quarter of the 19th century. The clock bears two signatures: Watchmaker Antide Janvier and Raingo. The clock is made up of four columns with chapters that support the round top and hold the signs of the Zodiac.*
2. *Two views of a Swiss watch, dating from the beginning of the 17th century. The movement is signed Martin Duboule who was a Geneva horologist important during his time. The dial is engraved with the view of Saint Peter's Cathedral in Geneva. The fine engraving around the center dial features flowering foliage, two children, a bird and a mask, all indicative of the Louis XIII period.*

THE CENTRAL ROLE OF THE NAVY

The navy played a central role in the pursuit of horological precision. In order to calculate a ship's longitude, an extremely difficult task for sailors of the time, navigators needed to have accurate measuring instruments, which were sadly lacking. Since antiquity, latitude had been fairly easily determined thanks to calculations based on the sun's position at noon and the polestar's position at night. Nothing equivalent was possible for longitude, because doing so necessarily involved determining the distance a ship sails between two points. Such a calculation was virtually impossible without a reliable means of time measurement. So the fact that the navy took such a keen interest in horology stemmed from the high stakes involved. The mastery of time brought with it conquest of the high seas, thus controlling international trade, which was rapidly expanding in the 16th century.

The best means of determining longitude at sea was to take a clock on board. Ships had previously taken along a sundial mounted on a compass. In 1658 Huygens believed he could adapt a pendulum clock to maritime needs thanks to his discoveries regarding devices fitted with a balance-wheel and spring, the forerunners of marine chronometers. This was a brilliant idea, but results proved disappointing, because variations in temperature had a detrimental influence on the elasticity of the balance-spring.

Astronomical Table Clock

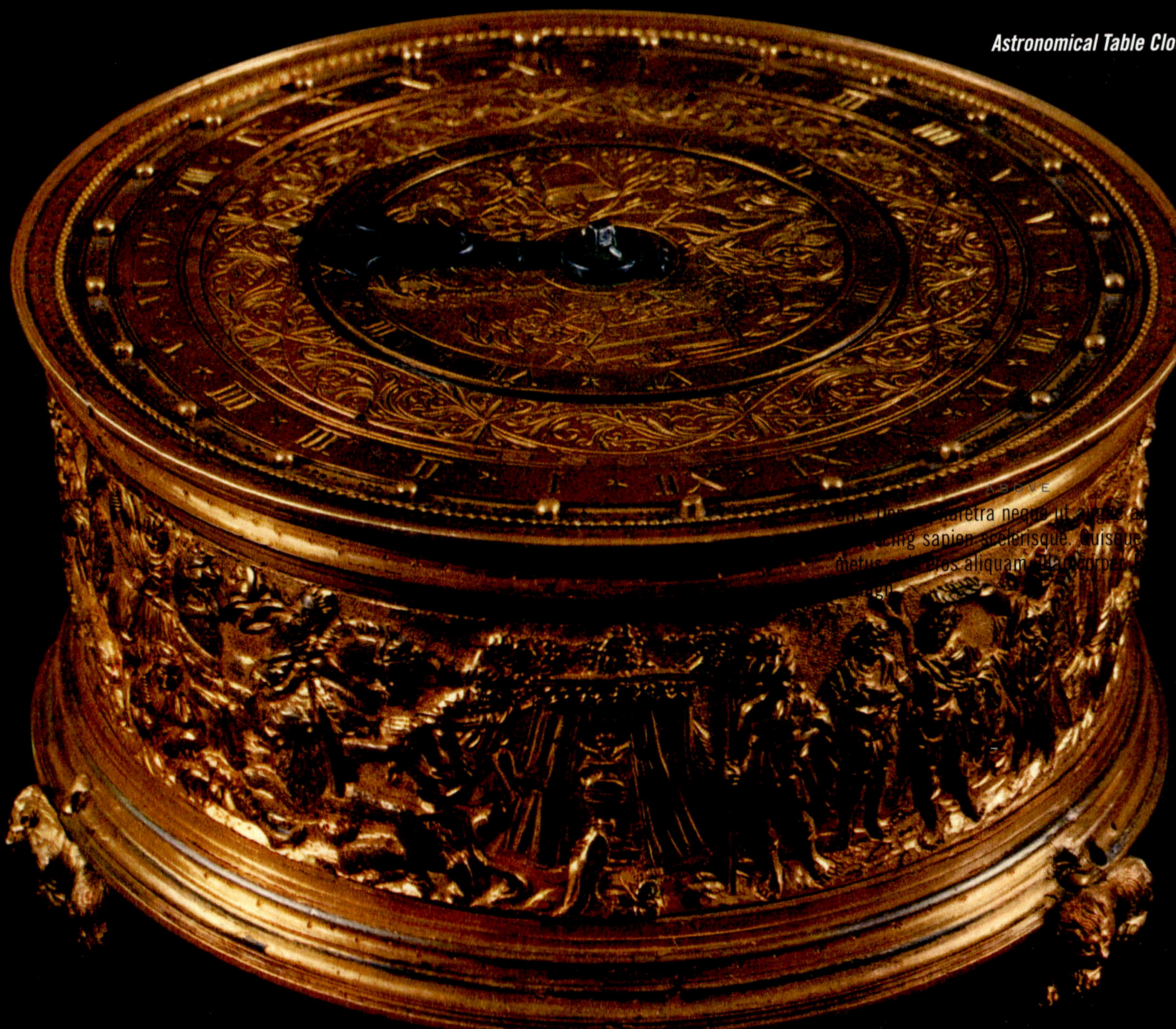

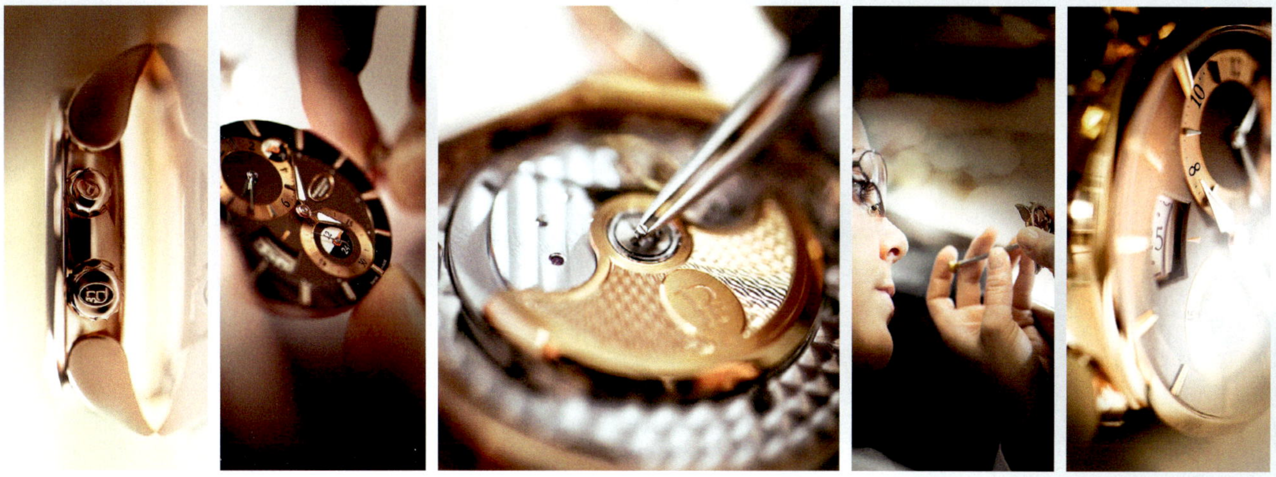

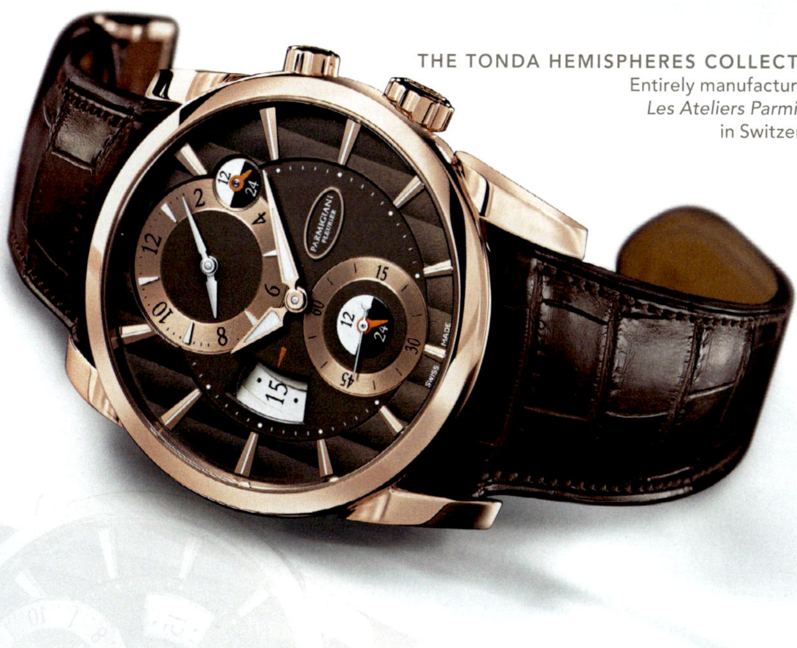

THE LONGITUDE ACT

In attempt to solve the problem, the Paris Observatory was founded in 1667 and mainly dedicated to the study of longitudes, followed by the Greenwich Observatory in 1675. This did not, however, prevent four British warships being needlessly wrecked on the Cornish coast due to a calculation error that caused the loss of 2,000 sailors. This humiliating event incited the British Parliament to issue the Longitude Act, which offered a 20,000 pound reward—a huge sum for the time—to anyone able to develop a method of determining longitude to within one degree for a voyage from Great Britain to the West Indies and back. The Academy of Paris did likewise in 1718, and the British and French were the star players in this fiercely fought contest.

A large number of master horologers were thus to contribute to developing and perfecting marine chronometers. All were aiming towards the threefold goal of creating an efficient escapement, inventing a balance impervious to variations in temperature, and stabilizing chronometers to cope with the rocking and swaying of ships. In the end, it was an English carpenter and watchmaker, John Harrison, who solved the problem in 1734 by building a huge marine chronometer weighing a massive 32 kilograms. He subsequently perfected his invention to the point where, in 1764, over a two-month journey, his chronometer recorded an angular error of just 5.2 seconds, corresponding to a distance of 1,850 meters.

Also in working towards this challenge, the Frenchman Pierre Le Roy designed a "detent escapement" suitable for maritime timekeeping, and in 1766 made the final prototype incorporating his system of compensating for variations in temperature. These chronometers were produced according to highly demanding technical specifications by workshops such as those of A. Lange & Söhne, Henri Perregaux, Constant Girard-Perregaux, and Vacheron & Constantin. Meanwhile, back in England, John Arnold had patented his discoveries, including the cylinder-shaped balance-spring featuring concentric development—a device that would enable Girard-Perregaux to create his high-precision tourbillon under three gold bridges in 1880.

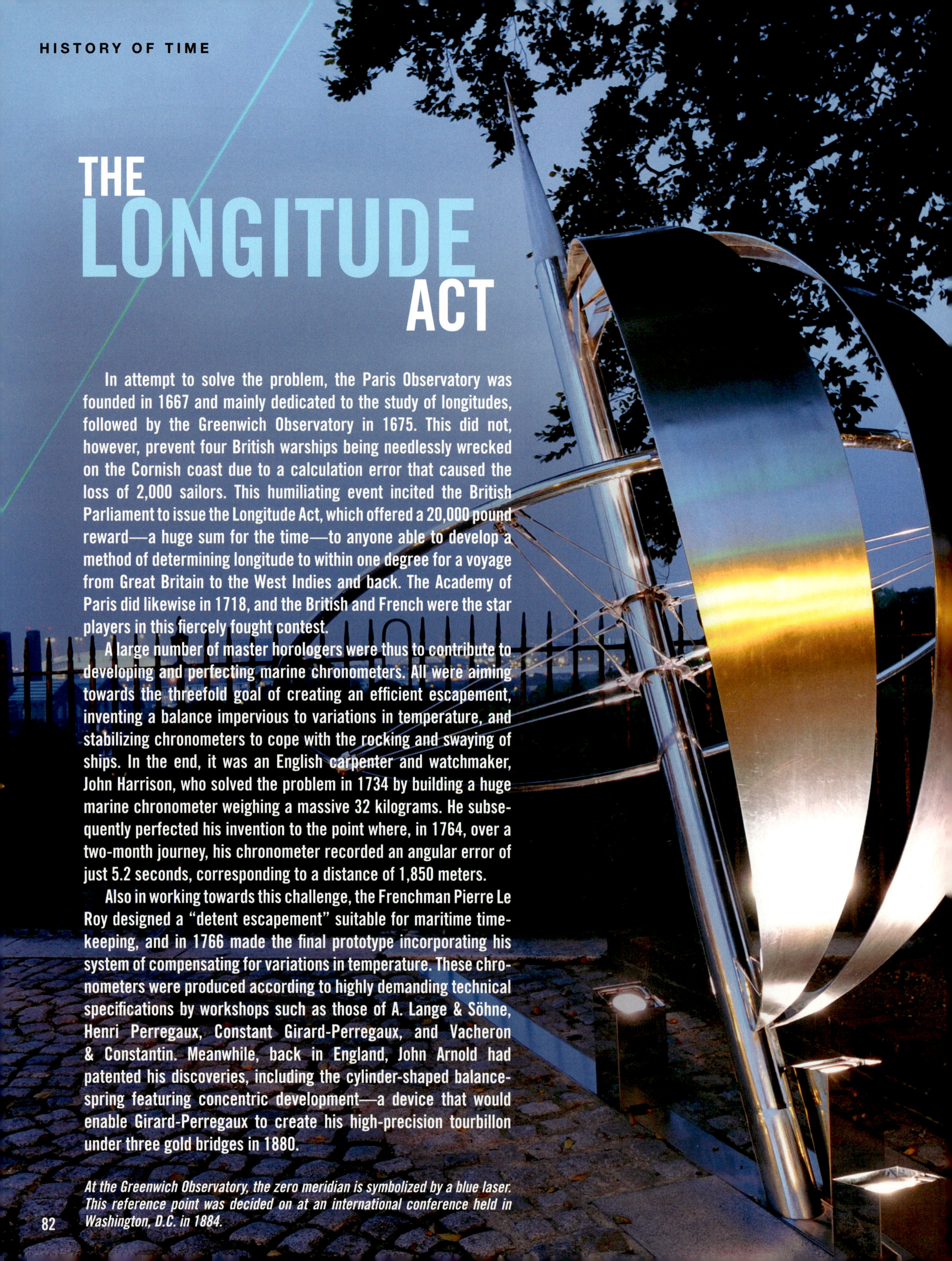

At the Greenwich Observatory, the zero meridian is symbolized by a blue laser. This reference point was decided on at an international conference held in Washington, D.C. in 1884.

THE ENGINEERS OF TIME

a depth of 1000 metres, time is especially precious. e treat it with the utmost care.

esign and engineering right down to the last detail has been the philosophy Porsche Design since 1972. This is now perfectly combined with the Swiss watch-aking tradition to create timepieces that do more than just set a global standard. ey prove themselves at a depth of 1000 metres. On the P´6780 Diver, the move-ent, rotating bezel and crown are protected in a hinged container that prevents the ne or diving time from being altered unintentionally. The functional design and minescent dial ensure optimum readability. In every situation – for every dive.

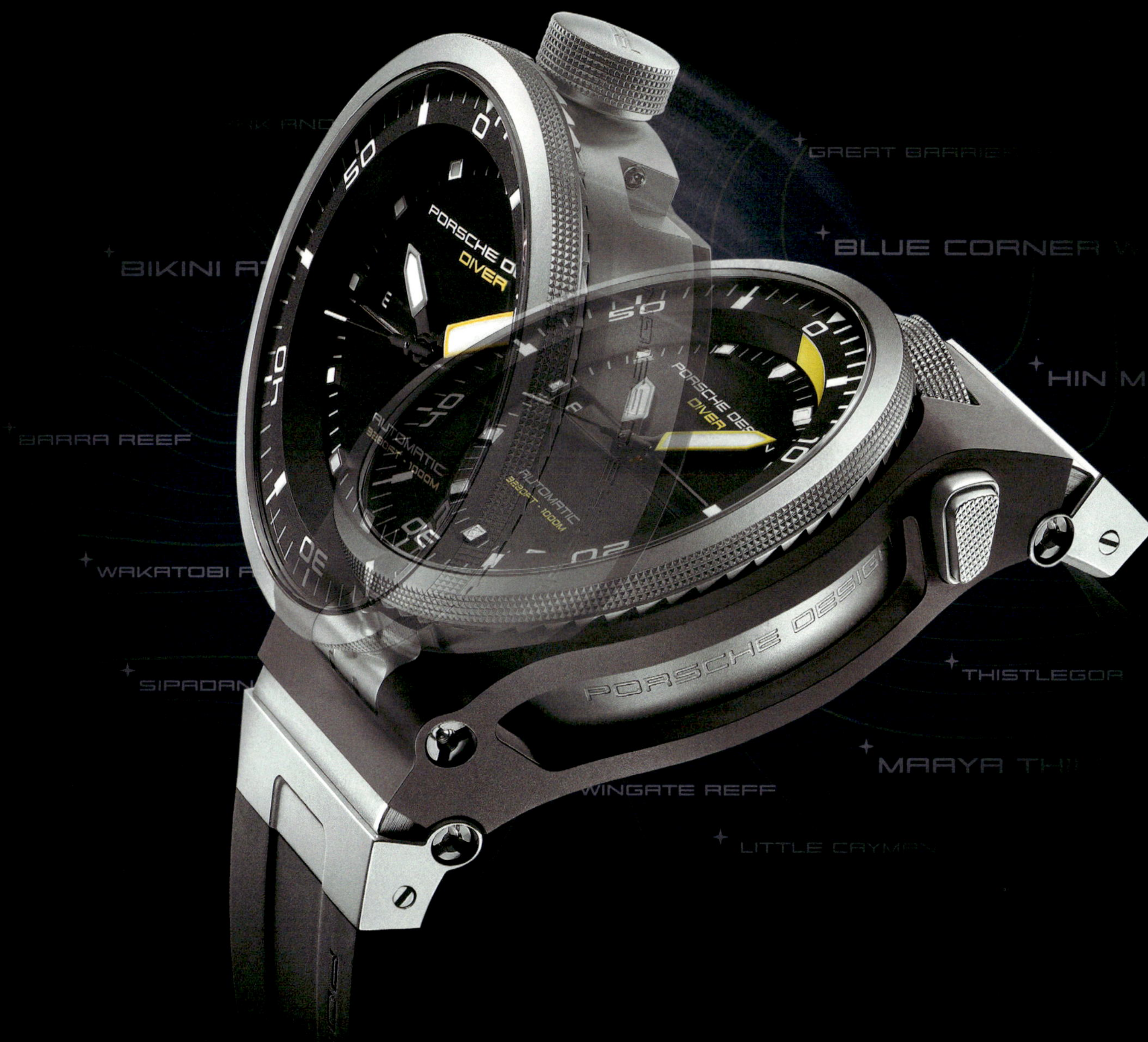

PORSCHE DESIGN
DIVER
P'6780

ww.porsche-design.com/diver

THE FIRST PORTABLE WATCHES

The first portable watches appeared in the early 16th century. The invention of the spring enabled such achievements on the basis of constructions developed for table clocks. According to certain watch history theoreticians, the first pocket watches were made to meet the needs of the great merchants of the Renaissance period, who needed a time-measuring instrument that could follow them in their constant travels. Thanks to the reduction in the size of the mechanisms inside, timepieces could be first made as pendants and later as pocket watches. It is worth noting that these early watches only rarely carried the watchmaker's signature. With the profession being strictly divided between the many different craftsmen who made the various components, such an approach was simply not justified. It was not until the 19th century that this practice of anonymity began to disappear, heralding the birth of the watch brands.

These Renaissance models nonetheless represent the culmination of a mechanical conception of time measurement that opened up whole new areas of scientific research such as astronomy, physics and mathematics, as well as promoting artistic crafts. In a nutshell, horology set off to conquer technological and artistic excellence. Between 1500 and 1700, the clock- and watch-making craft became a full-fledged profession that duly established itself in various European centers such as Blois, Lyon, Rouen, Strasbourg, as well as London, Geneva and the Netherlands. This new organization of the profession into corporations was due to the fact that the products had found a market, particularly among the prominent families of the era. In the early 16th century, the mechanical approach to measuring time reached a peak with the invention of the watch, and the following two centuries would be devoted to the quest for precision that was made feasible by Huygens's work on the balance-spring for watches.

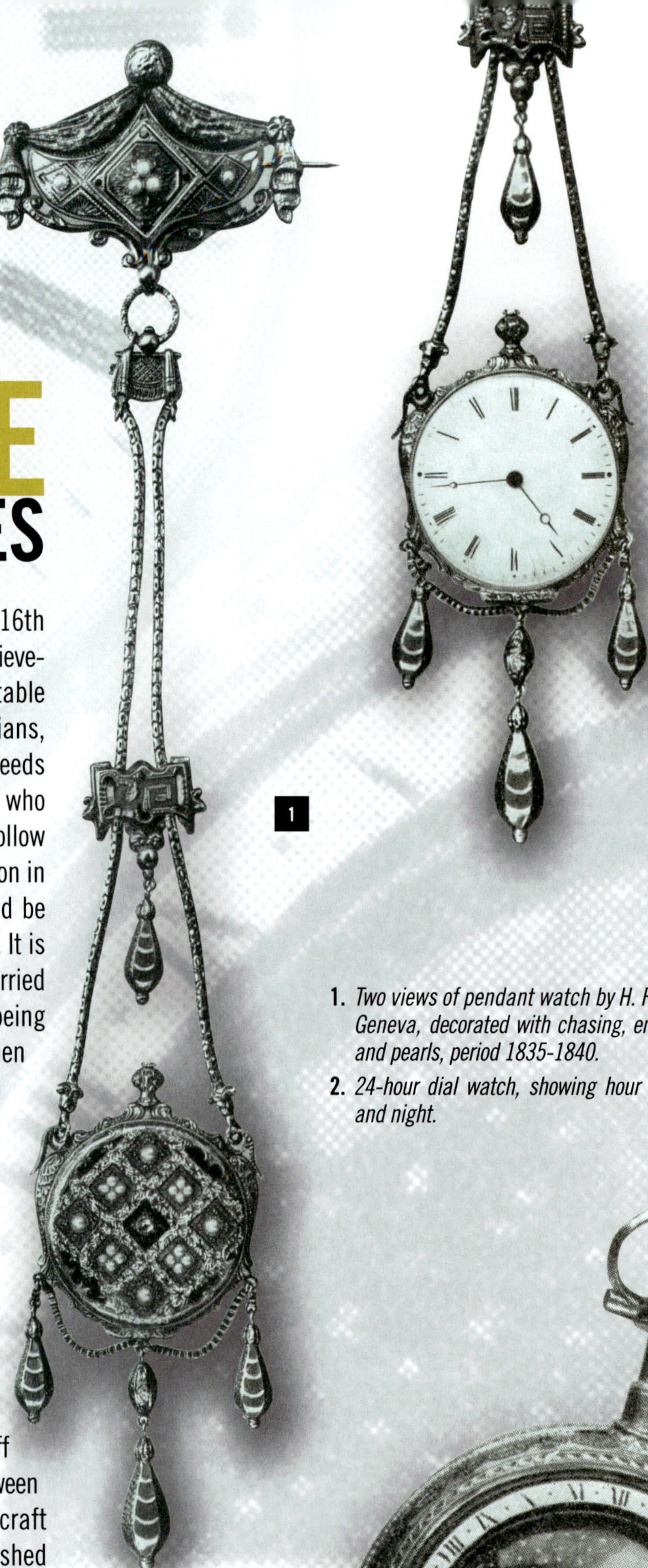

1

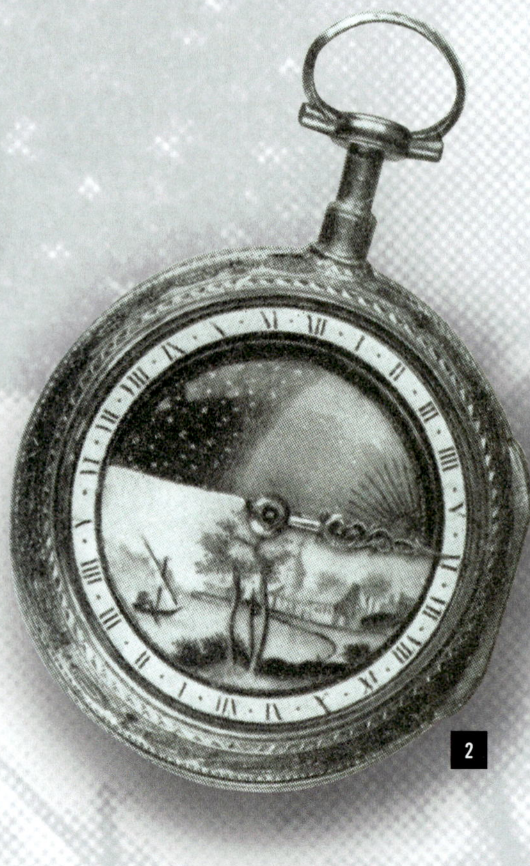

2

1. *Two views of pendant watch by H. Robert, Geneva, decorated with chasing, enamels and pearls, period 1835-1840.*
2. *24-hour dial watch, showing hour of day and night.*

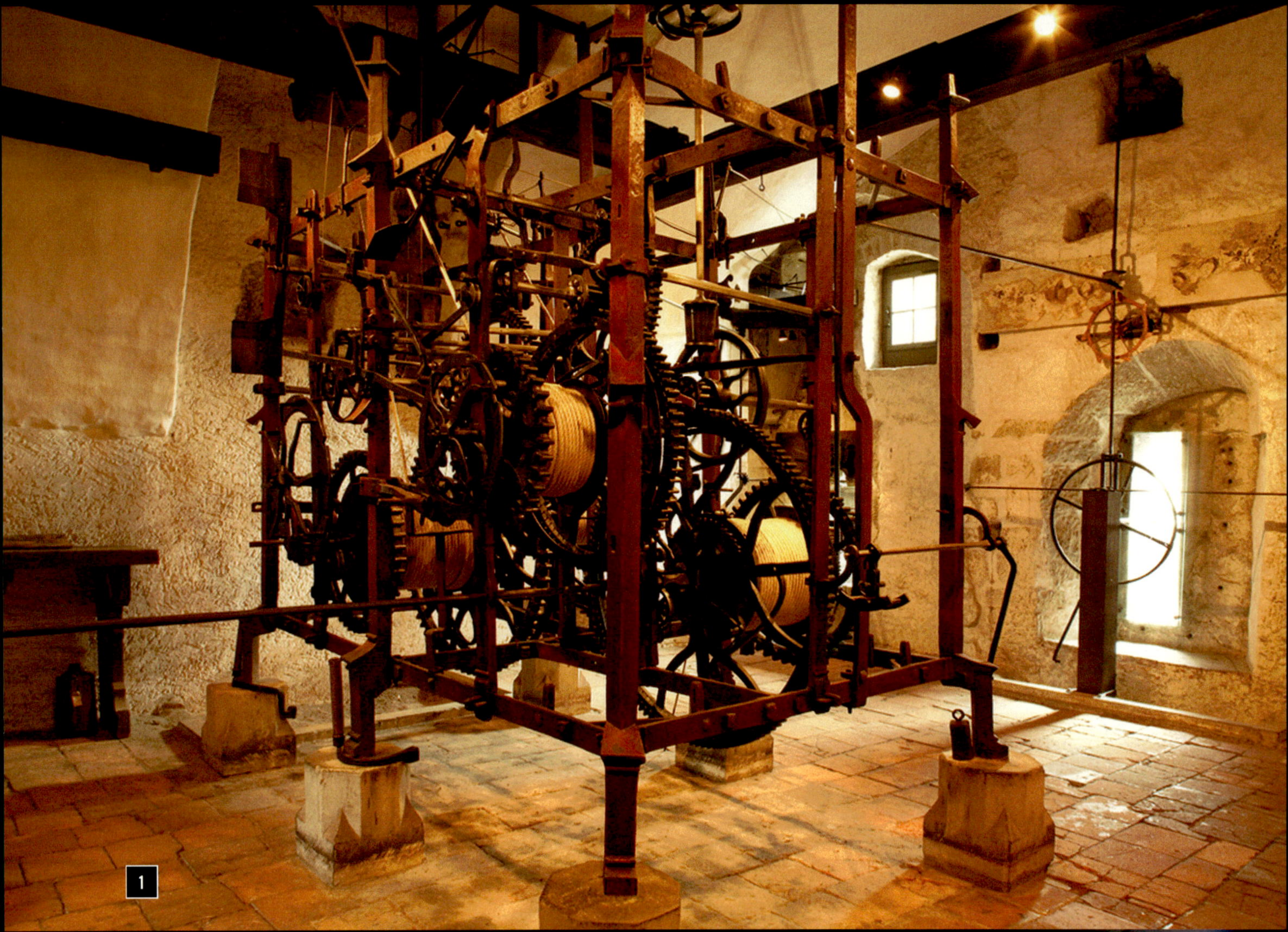

1

AN EVER-INCREASING NUMBER OF FUNCTIONS

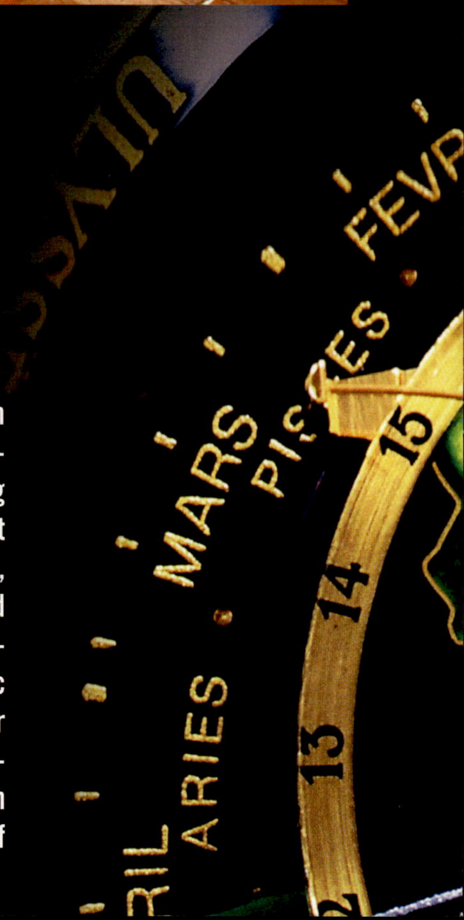

It was also during this period that horological complications became increasingly important. In addition to indicating hours, less frequently minutes and (in exceptional pieces) seconds, timepieces began to feature functions such as mechanisms striking in passing or on request, along with an alarm or tactile reading of the hours that was useful at night when the wearer did not necessarily wish to light a candle. Calendar and astronomical functions were also in vogue, especially since the introduction of the Gregorian calendar. The knowledge of the era enabled horologers to make instruments that would make a significant contribution to spreading astronomical principles such as moonphases, the position of the stars, the equation of time, Zodiac positions—a range of functions that were often added to the basic day and month calendar indications. Many of these historical timepieces often combined useful calendar and astronomical functions. These creations, which were obviously intended for a wealthy clientele often to be found in the entourage of various royal courts, remain an inestimably precious source of inspiration for contemporary grand complication watches. In parallel with this epic technological saga, one simply cannot ignore the decorative wealth of these ancient timekeepers. All the craftsmen's guilds lavished their talents on these models, including painters, engravers, cabinet-makers, goldsmiths and enamellers—whose work on both the movements and the exteriors significantly contributed to transforming these pieces into genuine works of art. Enameling became an art in its own right, as confirmed by the reproductions of paintings by the great masters such as Rembrandt, Raphaël, Perugino and Leonardo da Vinci on various timepieces of this era. These artistic crafts thus established a traditional hold on mechanical watchmaking that has endured right through to the modern age, though considerable efforts must now be made to save them from extinction, due to insufficient demand. Three centuries after they were made, these timepieces are some of the few mechanical objects that continue to run smoothly, not to mention their decorative beauty. In simple terms, one can say that over a period of two centuries, watchmakers succeeded with extremely limited means in creating masterpieces that had a profound influence on the lives of their contemporaries and continue to elicit boundless admiration to this day.

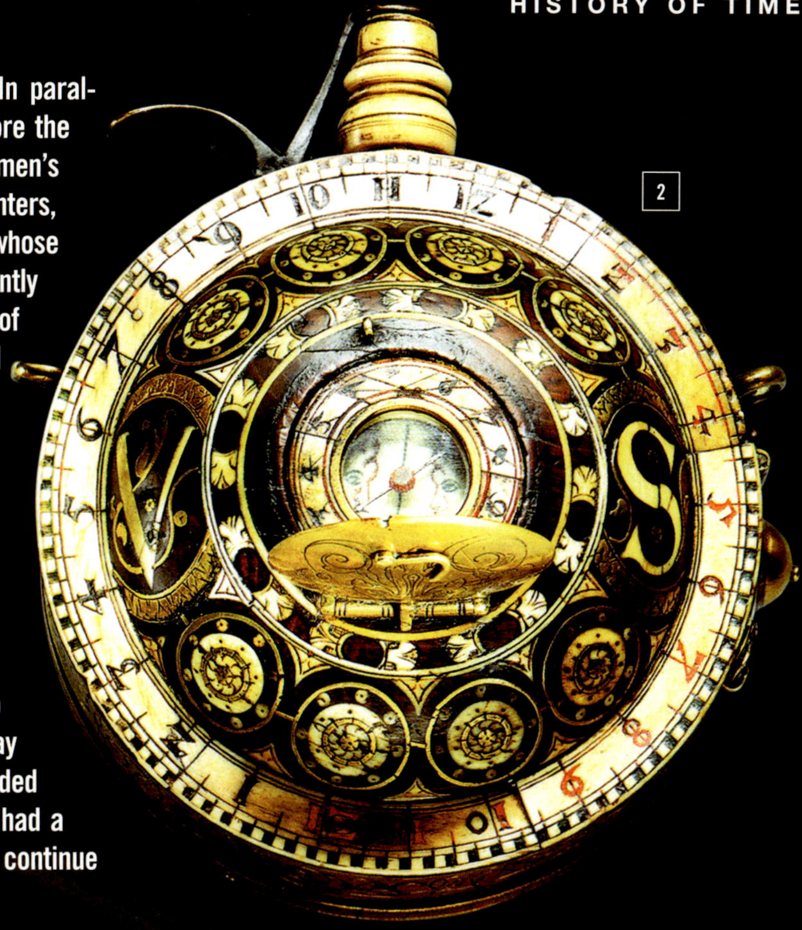

2

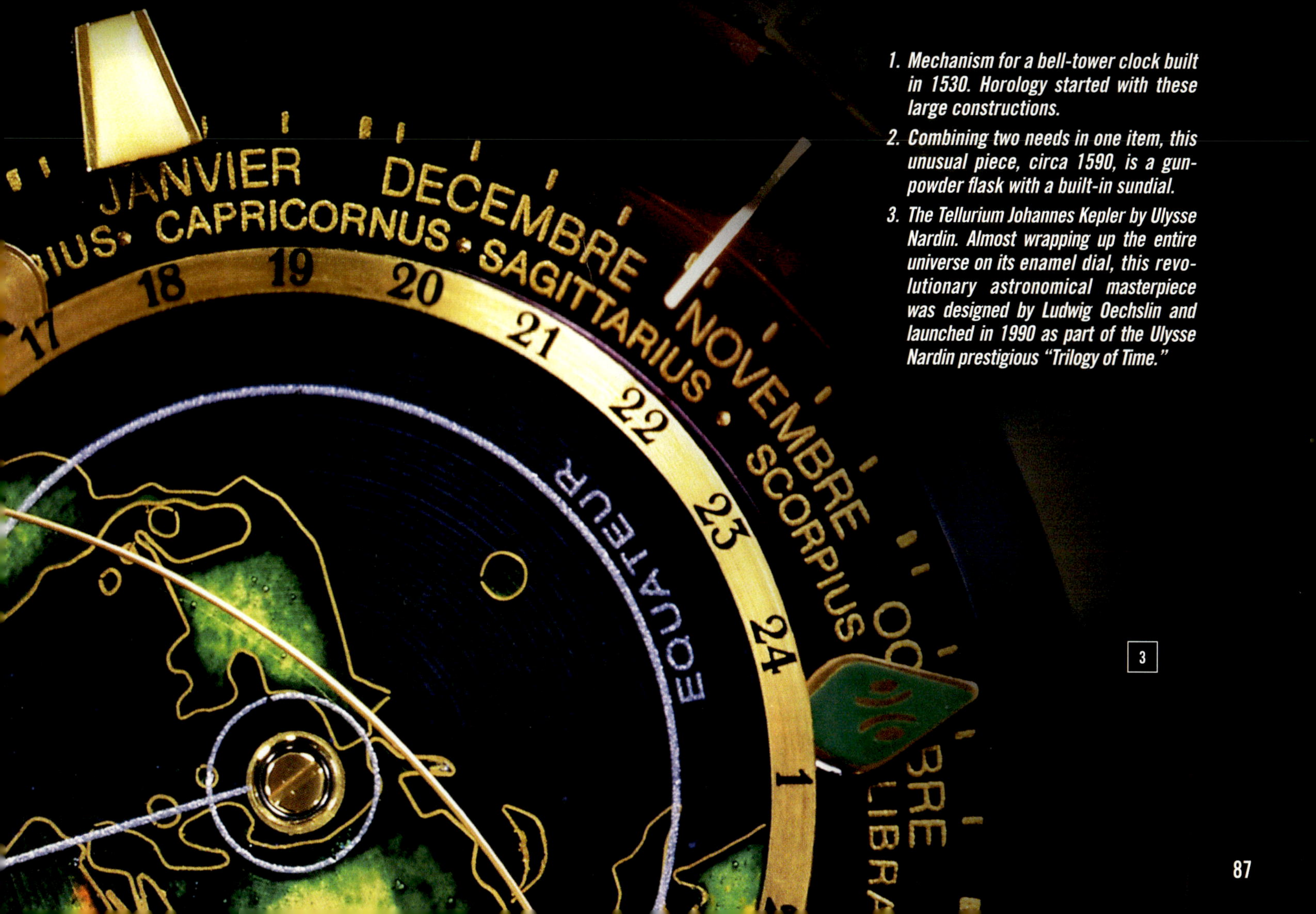

3

1. Mechanism for a bell-tower clock built in 1530. Horology started with these large constructions.

2. Combining two needs in one item, this unusual piece, circa 1590, is a gunpowder flask with a built-in sundial.

3. The Tellurium Johannes Kepler by Ulysse Nardin. Almost wrapping up the entire universe on its enamel dial, this revolutionary astronomical masterpiece was designed by Ludwig Oechslin and launched in 1990 as part of the Ulysse Nardin prestigious "Trilogy of Time."

RUSSIA, AN 18TH-CENTURY EL DORADO

As previously hinted, Imperial families paid rapt attention to the work of the master-watchmakers and displayed an immoderate love of their products. The Emperor Rodolphe II (1552-1612), for example, had his own private museum known as the Cabinet of Curiosities, and which housed a number of table clocks and mechanical celestial globes. A number of horologers did indeed devise and create complicated models with the aim of pleasing the Emperor, who was widely renowned for his knowledge of the field. Nor was he the only monarch of his time to take a keen interest in horology. To embellish his palaces, the founder of the Romanoff dynasty, Michael I of Russia (1596-1645), had over 20,000 clocks imported. He also enlisted the help of the finest specialists of the time in building monumental clocks to play religious hymns.

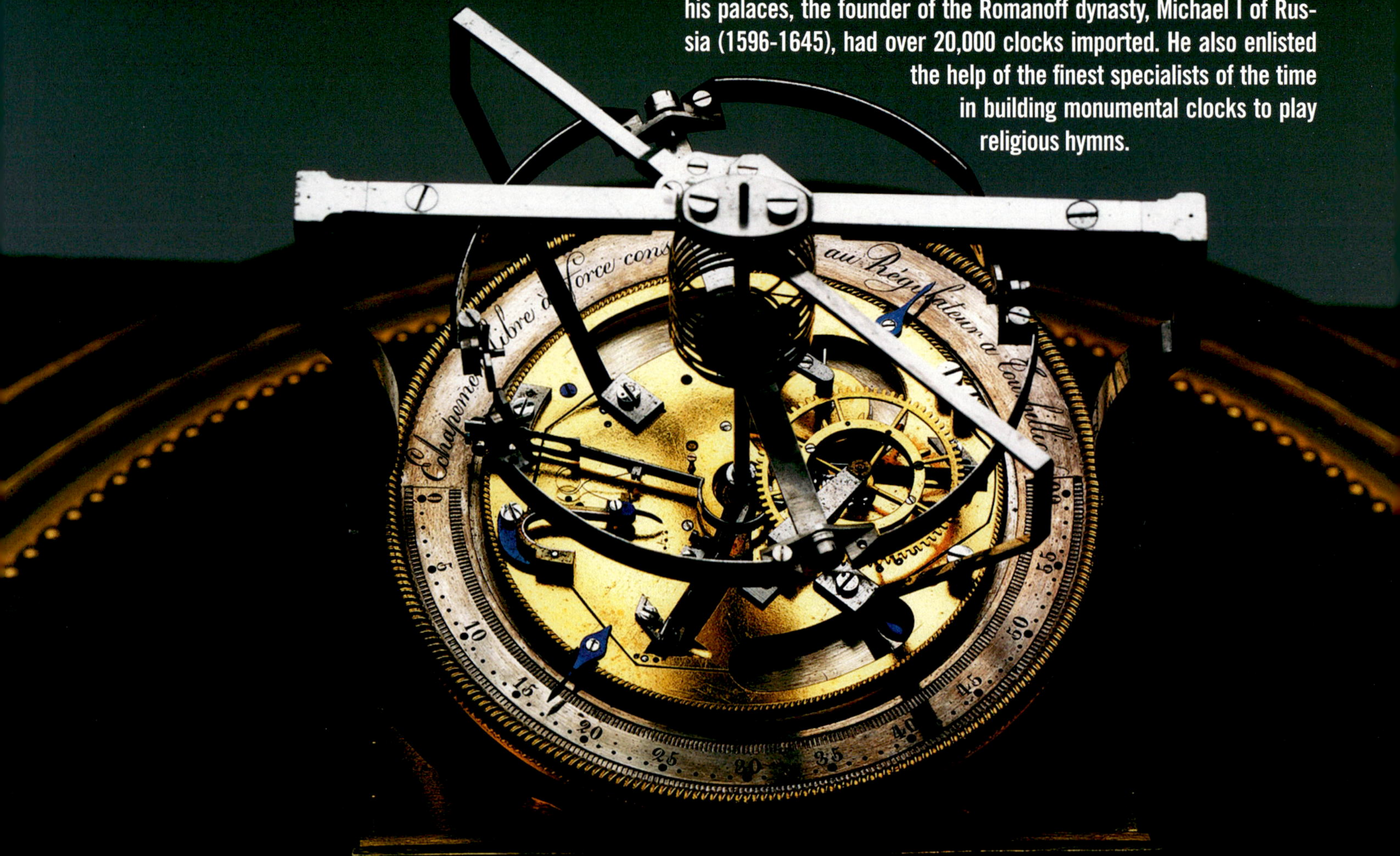

This pendulum presents two inventions patented by Abraham-Louis Breguet: the constant-force escapement and the tourbillon regulator.

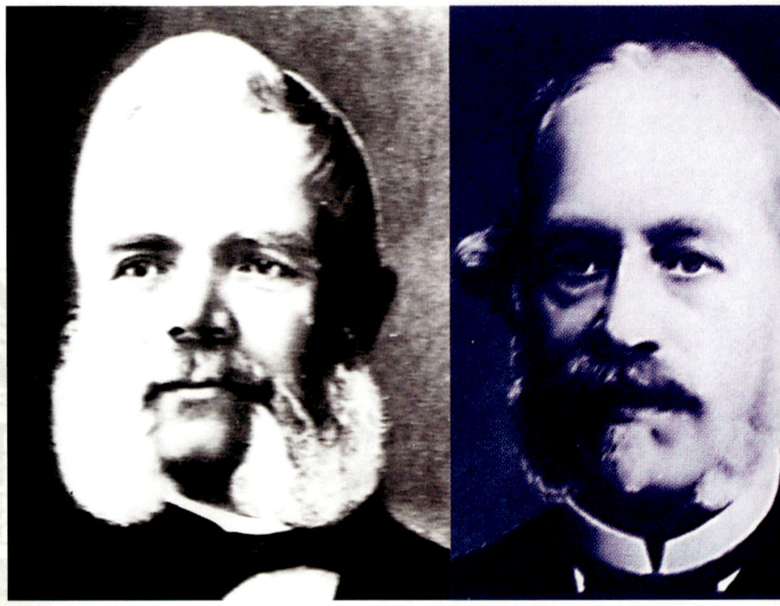

1

A century later, Catherine the Great of Russia (1729-1796) went a step further by setting up horological workshops on the spot. The first manufacture was thus established in 1773 thanks to two Geneva-born brothers, heralding a period of intensive exchanges between Russia and the watch industry. During the 18th and 19th centuries, Russia was a prime market for master-watchmakers, who were in turn expected to deploy the full measure of their talent. Abraham-Louis Breguet worked intensively for the imperial court of Russia, hence his official title as Horologer to His Majesty and to the Imperial Navy. His reputation was indeed such that his name became synonymous with the word "chronometer" in Russia. Meanwhile, Louis Audemars also earned the title of "Horologer to the Imperial Court." From 1848 onwards, Patek Philippe began developing business ties with the imperial court and the Russian nobility. Other companies such as Tissot, Louis Brandt (later to become Omega) and Zenith followed suit, until the advent of Bolshevism put a halt to this heyday.

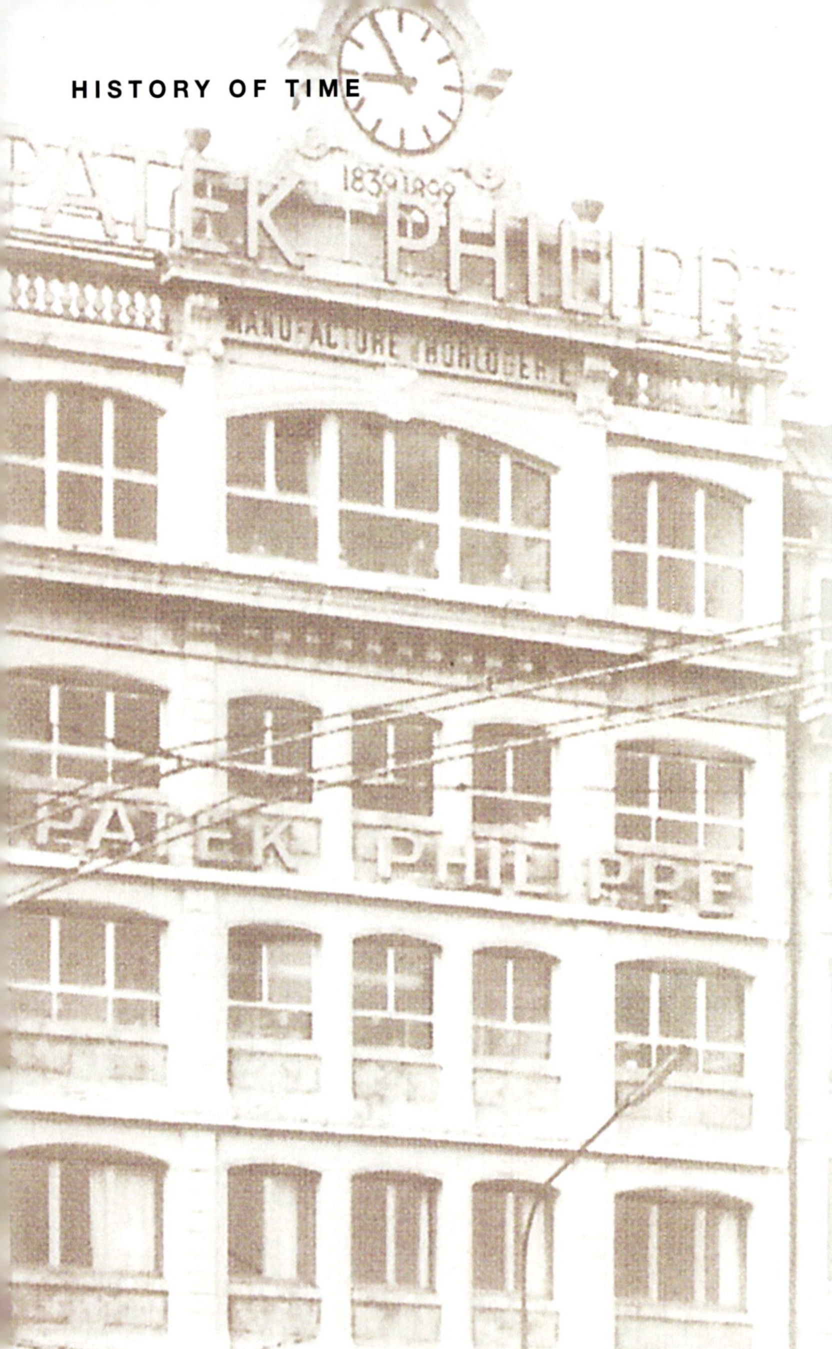

2

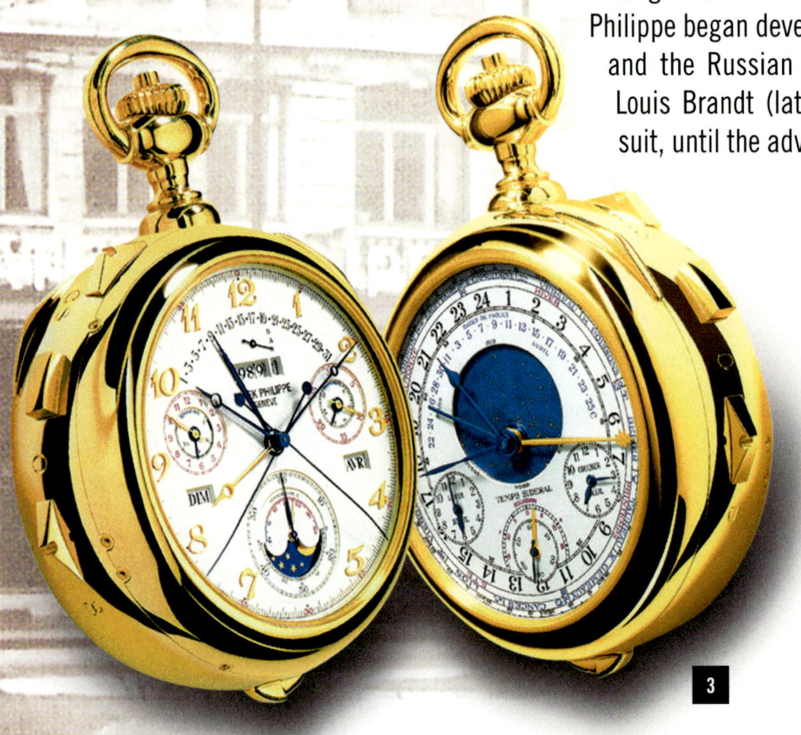

3

1. *Founder of Patek in 1839. Antoine Norbert de Patek (1812-1877) partnered in 1845 with friend and genius watchmaker, Jean Adrien Philippe (1815-1894) to create Patek Philippe, one of the most influential Houses in watchmaking history.*
2. *Patek Philippe's headquarters at 41 Rue du Rhône.*
3. *Patek Philippe created the most complicated watch ever made, the Calibre 89, which includes 33 complications.*

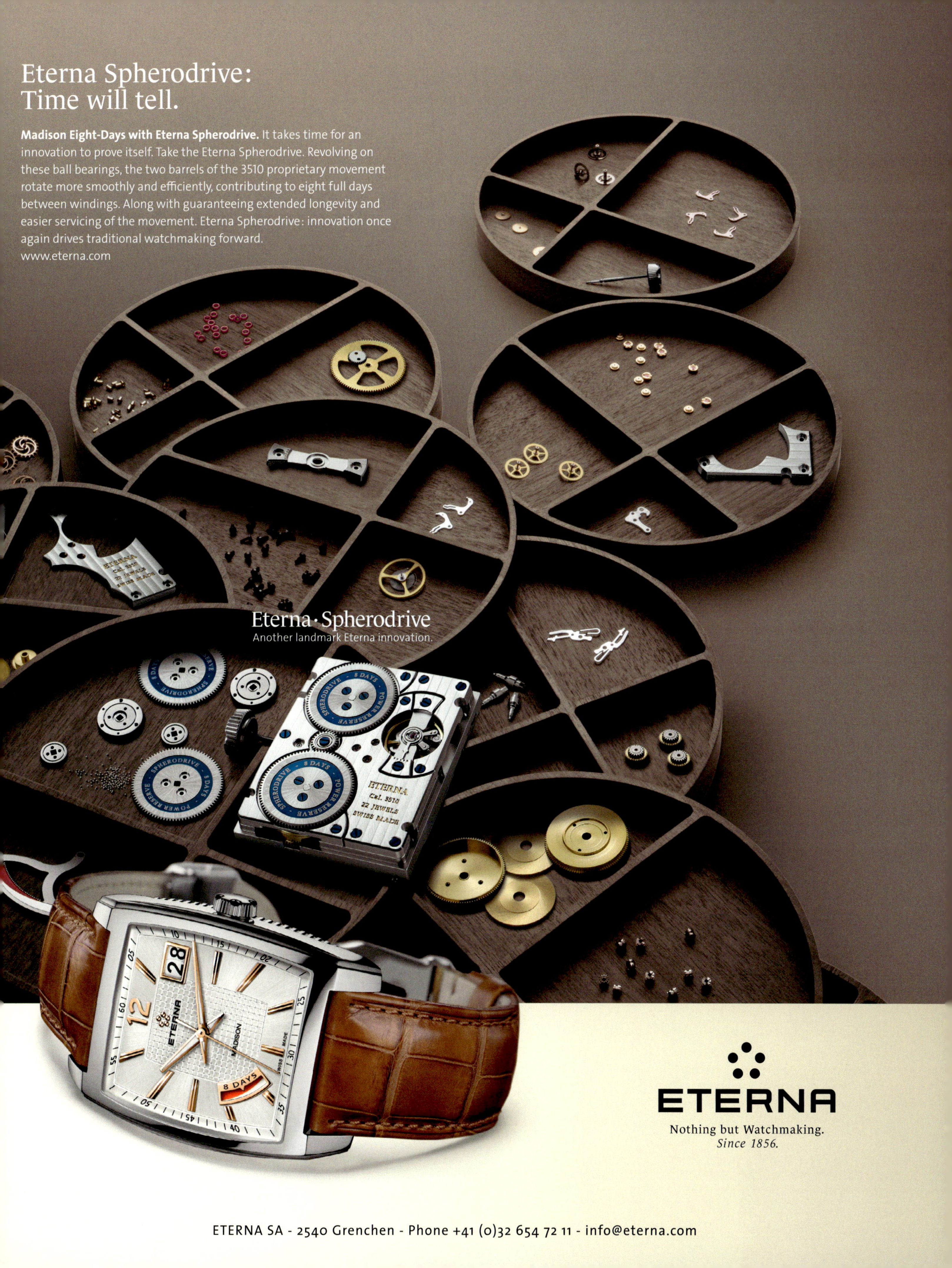
Eterna Spherodrive:
Time will tell.
Madison Eight-Days with Eterna Spherodrive. It takes time for an innovation to prove itself. Take the Eterna Spherodrive. Revolving on these ball bearings, the two barrels of the 3510 proprietary movement rotate more smoothly and efficiently, contributing to eight full days between windings. Along with guaranteeing extended longevity and easier servicing of the movement. Eterna Spherodrive: innovation once again drives traditional watchmaking forward.
www.eterna.com
Eterna·Spherodrive
Another landmark Eterna innovation.
ETERNA
Cal. 3510
22 JEWELS
SWISS MADE
ETERNA
MADISON
8 DAYS
ETERNA
Nothing but Watchmaking.
Since 1856.
ETERNA SA - 2540 Grenchen - Phone +41 (0)32 654 72 11 - info@eterna.com

ABRAHAM-LOUIS BREGUET, THE MOST INVENTIVE HOROLOGER’EVER

A Swiss watchmaker settled in Paris and among other distinctions a member of the French Bureau of Longitudes, Horologer to the French Royal Navy and a member of the French Academy of Science, Abraham-Louis Breguet is probably one of the most inventive watchmakers of all time. His long list of inventions includes the gong-spring for repeater watches, perfecting the lever escapement, the "pare-chute" anti-shock device, and the tourbillon escapement, for which a patent was filed in 1801. He was also much in demand at the royal court, and everyone has heard of the famous "Marie-Antoinette" watch, the most complicated watch of the era, which has had a long and eventful history. This exceptional model ordered for the queen from Abraham-Louis Breguet, and which neither would see in their lifetime, was bequeathed to the Islamic Art Museum in Jerusalem by the daughter of Sir David Salomons, its last owner and a fervent devotee of Breguet watches. However, the Marie-Antoinette was stolen in 1983 at the same time as the entire Salomons collection, under mysterious circumstances that have never been elucidated. The late Nicolas G. Hayek, in his capacity as Chairman of the Swatch Group and CEO of Breguet (acquired in 1999), simply could not let things stand. He decided to bring this legendary timepiece back to life by commissioning an exact replica to be crafted in the company's workshops. It took three and a half years of relentless work, based on the rare available photographs and written records, to reconstitute the Marie-Antoinette, which was presented in 2008 shortly before the original reappeared in circumstances just as obscure as those of its disappearance. The stuff of legends…

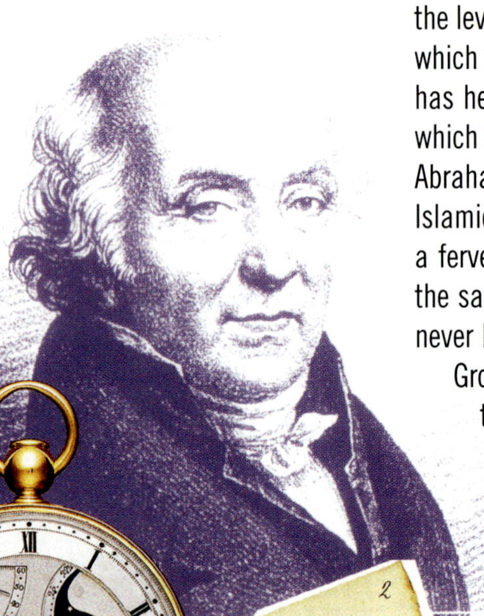

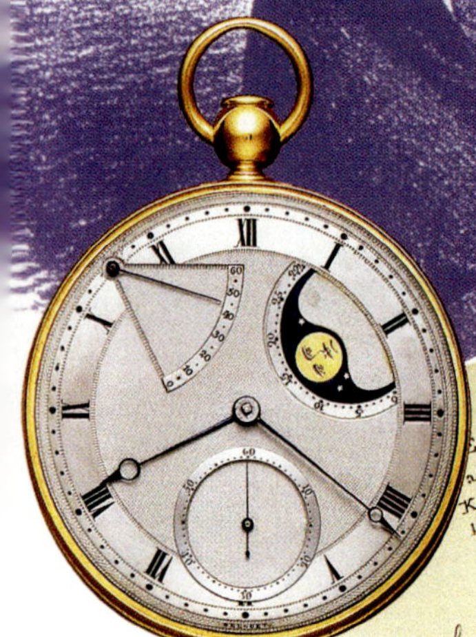

1

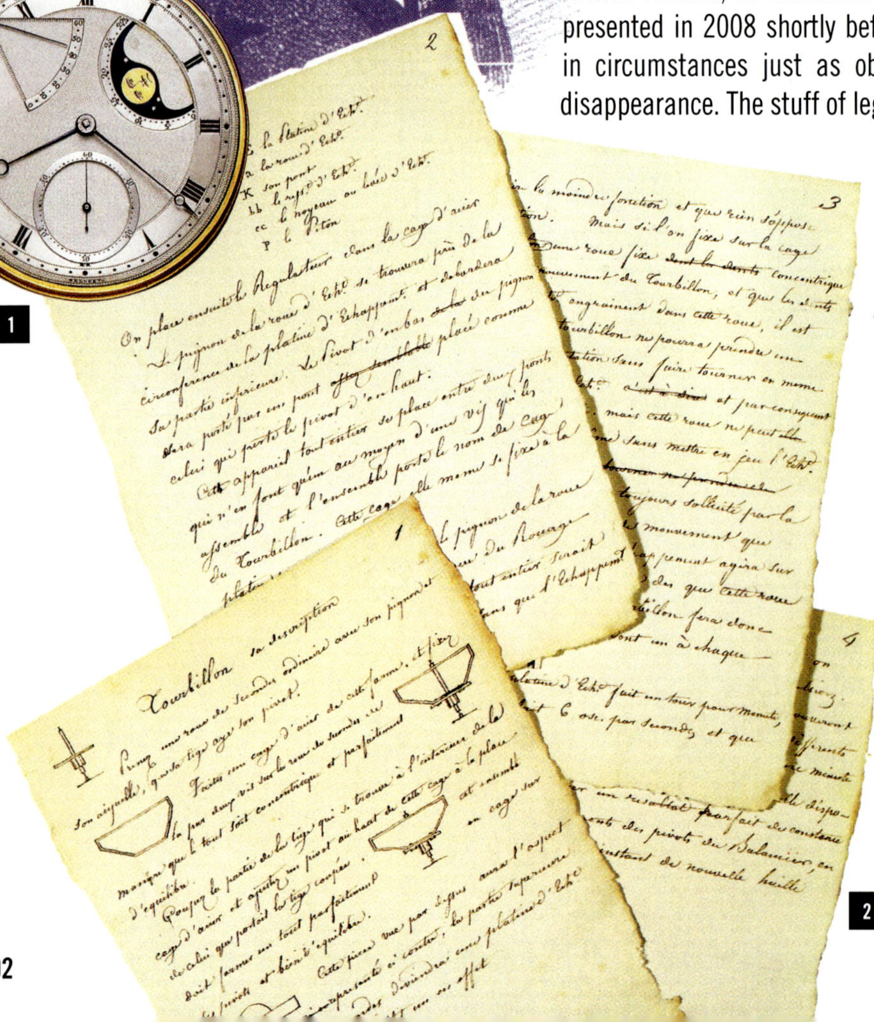

2

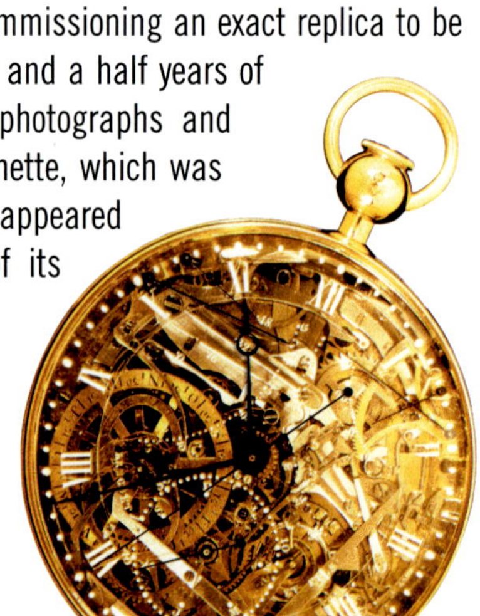

3

1. *The gold hand-worked "Lépine" watch provided the inspiration for Breguet to create the pocket watch . This "perpetual watch" with automatic rewind features a minute repeater and a calendar. Technical and aesthetic details of the timepiece, including a silver dial with spring development, a free lever escapement, and a flexible suspension, exemplify the masterpieces which have built the reputation of the House of Breguet. The watch came with a gold key for time adjustment. The piece was sold in 1791 to the Duke of La Force, General and Peer of France.*
2. *Notes written by Abraham-Louis Breguet about the development of his "Tourbillon" invention.*
3. *This unique piece was commissioned from Abraham-Louis Breguet for Queen Marie Antoinette. The order was placed in 1783, but the watch was not delivered until 1827. Neither the queen nor the watchmaker would see the finished product.*

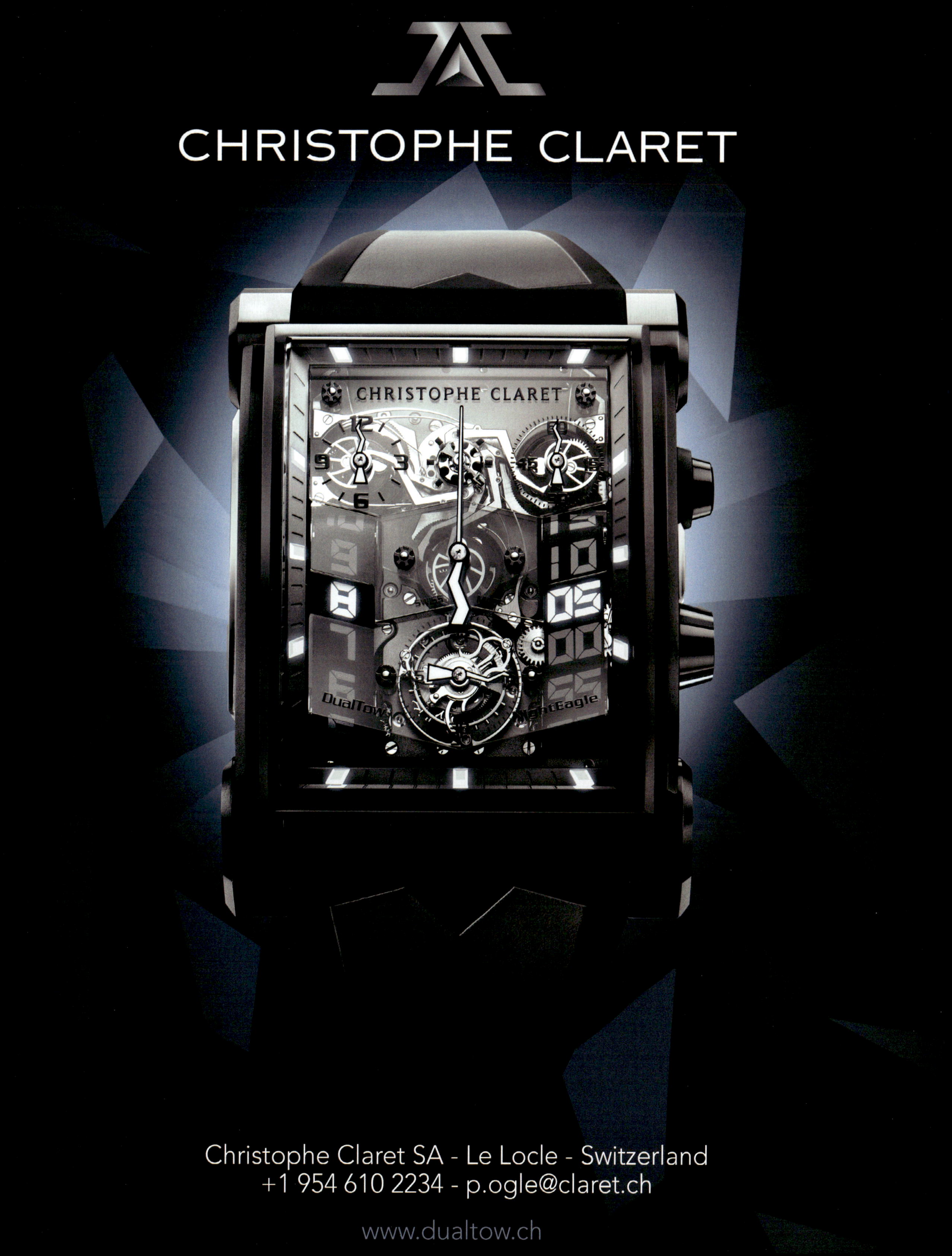
CHRISTOPHE CLARET
CHRISTOPHE CLARET
DualTow
Christophe Claret SA - Le Locle - Switzerland
+1 954 610 2234 - p.ogle@claret.ch
www.dualtow.ch

Abraham-Louis Breguet had another fervent admirer in Napoleon Bonaparte. Before setting off on his Egyptian campaign in 1798, Bonaparte purchased several Breguet models including a repeater watch. Upon his return from a disastrous campaign, Bonaparte came to see Breguet with his watch in hand, in order to prove to him that the timepiece had not survived the hard knocks of military life. He imperiously demanded a new model, a request to which Breguet naturally responded with all due haste and which would set the seal on a longstanding cooperation between the House of Breguet and the imperial family. From then on, various family members steadily built up a huge collection of Breguet watches that was subsequently further enriched by Napoleon III. Today, Jérome de Witt, founder of the DeWitt watch brand and a direct descendant of Napoleon's brother Jérôme de Westphalie, is the proud owner of some of the treasures from this collection. For a long period of time, watches developed in the wake of royal families. Their orders and their patronage procured unhoped-for prosperity for a number of master-watchmakers who were thus able to produce some truly exceptional watches.

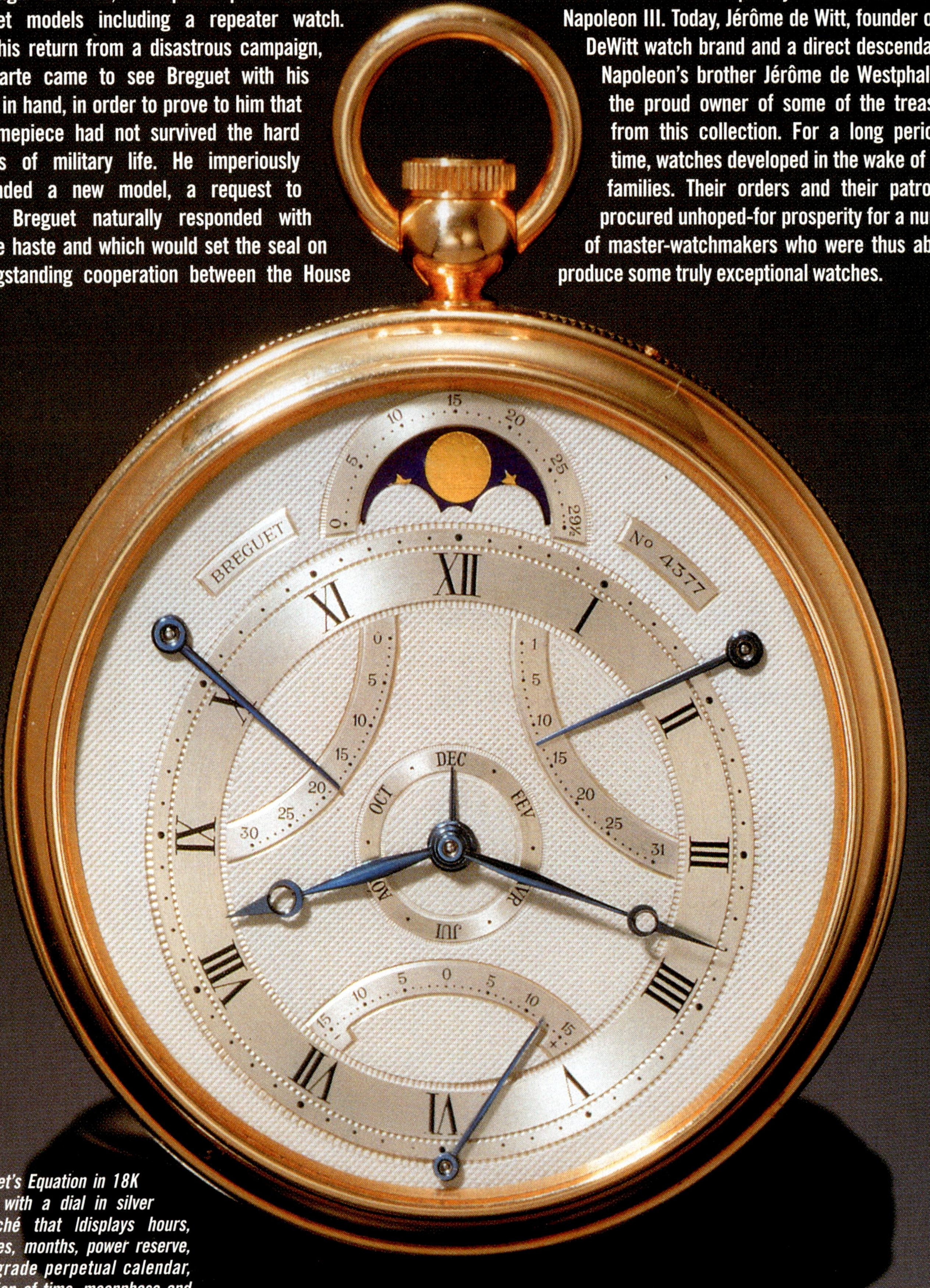

Breguet's Equation in 18K gold, with a dial in silver guilloché that ldisplays hours, minutes, months, power reserve, retrograde perpetual calendar, equation of time, moonphase and the age of the moon.

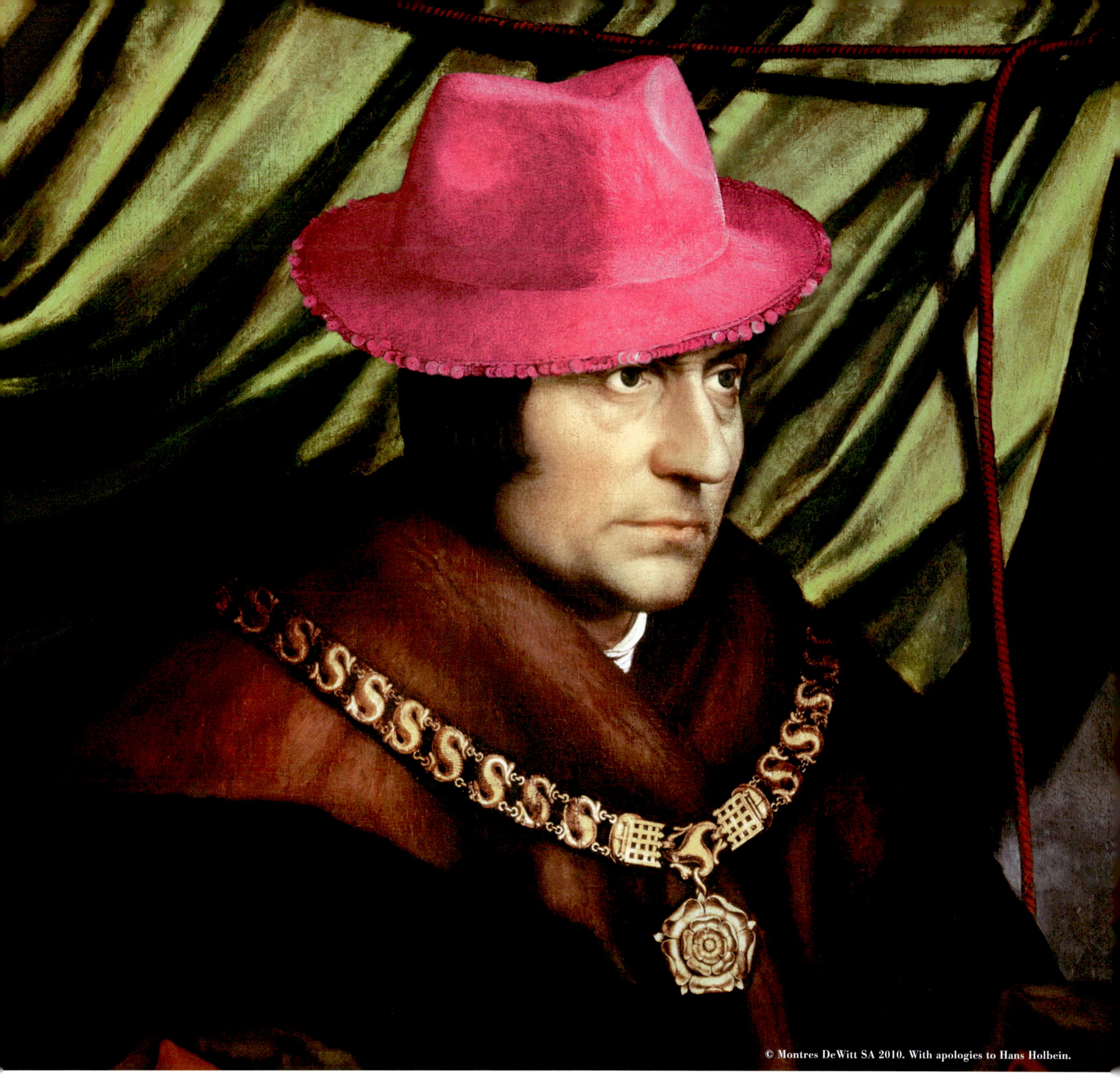
© Montres DeWitt SA 2010. With apologies to Hans Holbein.

JESUITS BRING HOROLOGY TO CHINA

China also fell within the ambit of these developments, since modern horology first came to the country when the Portuguese arrived in Macao and set up a trading post with the Middle Empire that included a thriving trade in clocks. The Jesuits, and particularly Friar Matteo Ricci (1522-1610), did a great deal to promote this expansion, particularly with respect to the Chinese imperial court that fell under the spell of these musical machines that sounded the time. European production was so greatly appreciated that the Emperor K'angh-hi in turn decided to set up several horological workshops in the country.

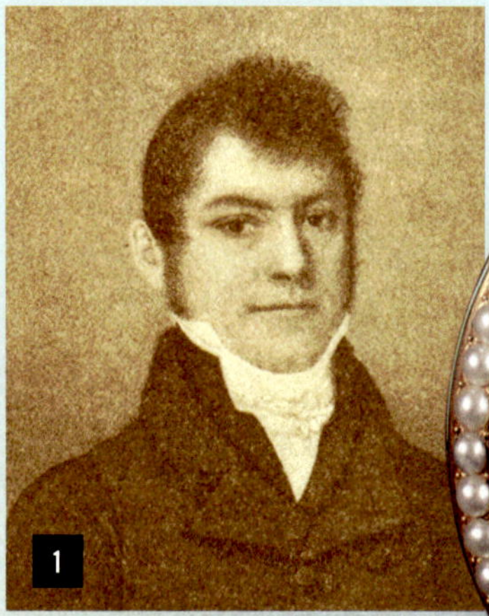

1

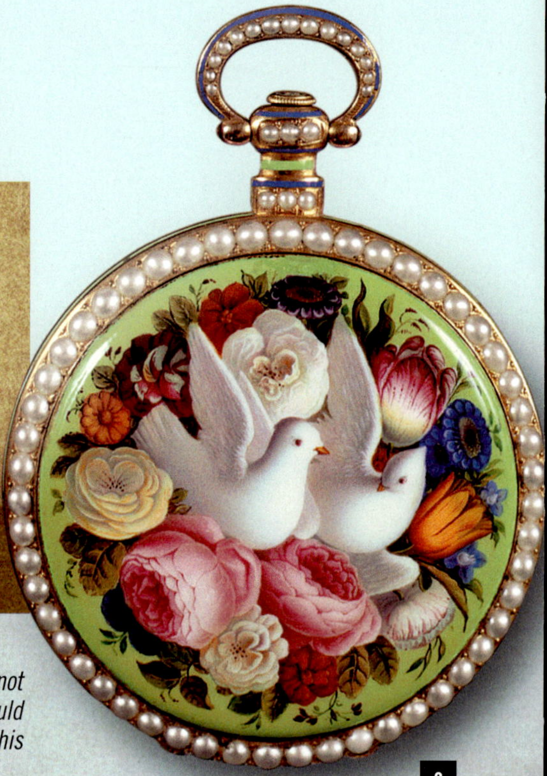

2

1. *"I left Whampoa at 9 o'clock in the morning and arrived in Canton at 1 o'clock in the afternoon. One cannot imagine the number of boats on this river," wrote Edouard Bovet when he came to China in 1818. He would stay until 1830 and significantly contribute to the growth of Swiss horology in China, especially with his "Chinese watches."*
2. *A Chinese watch, decorated and set with pearls.*
3. *In the 16th century, horology landed in China. The trading posts in Macao and Canton (pictured, now Guangzhou) rapidly became busy markets for European watches.*

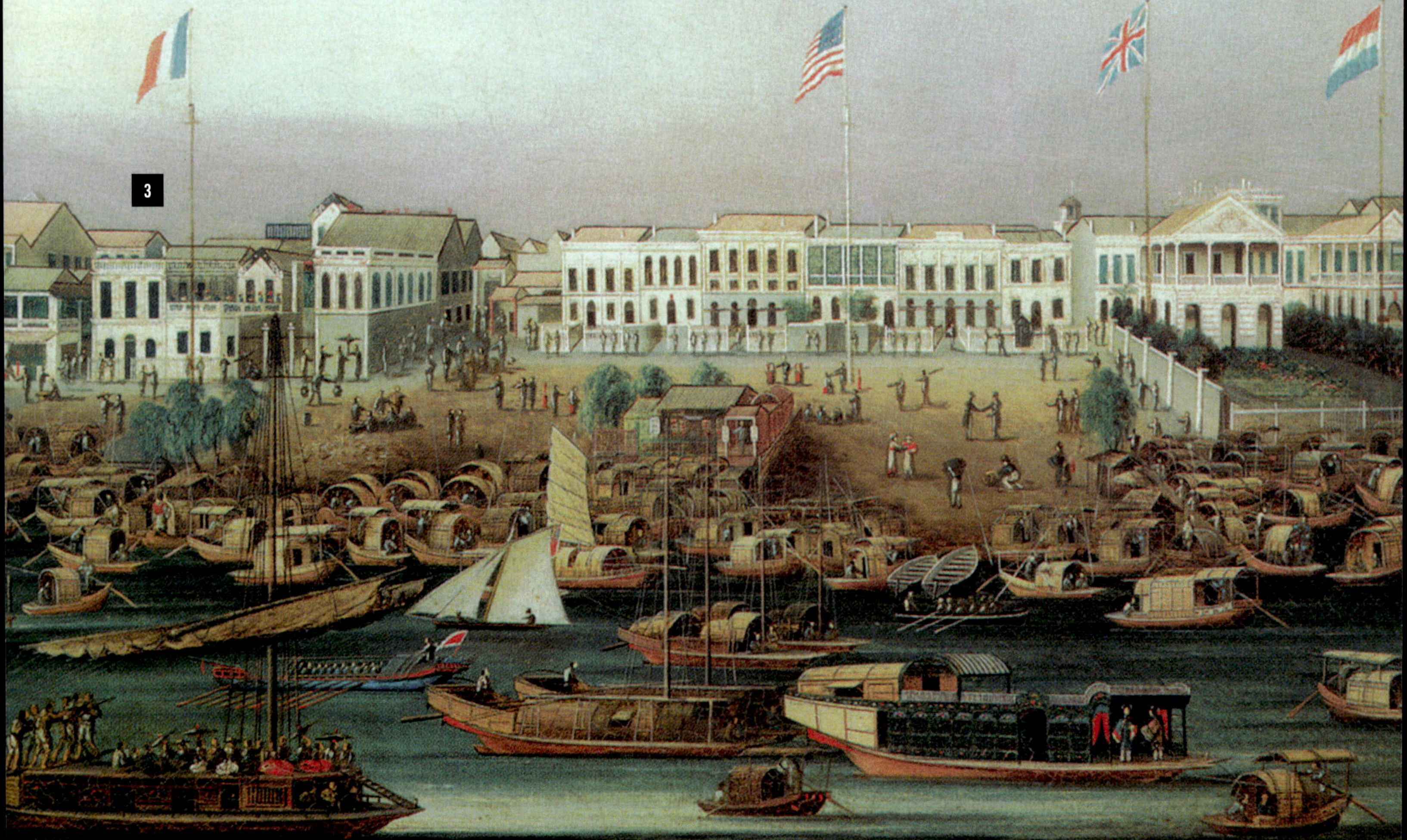

3

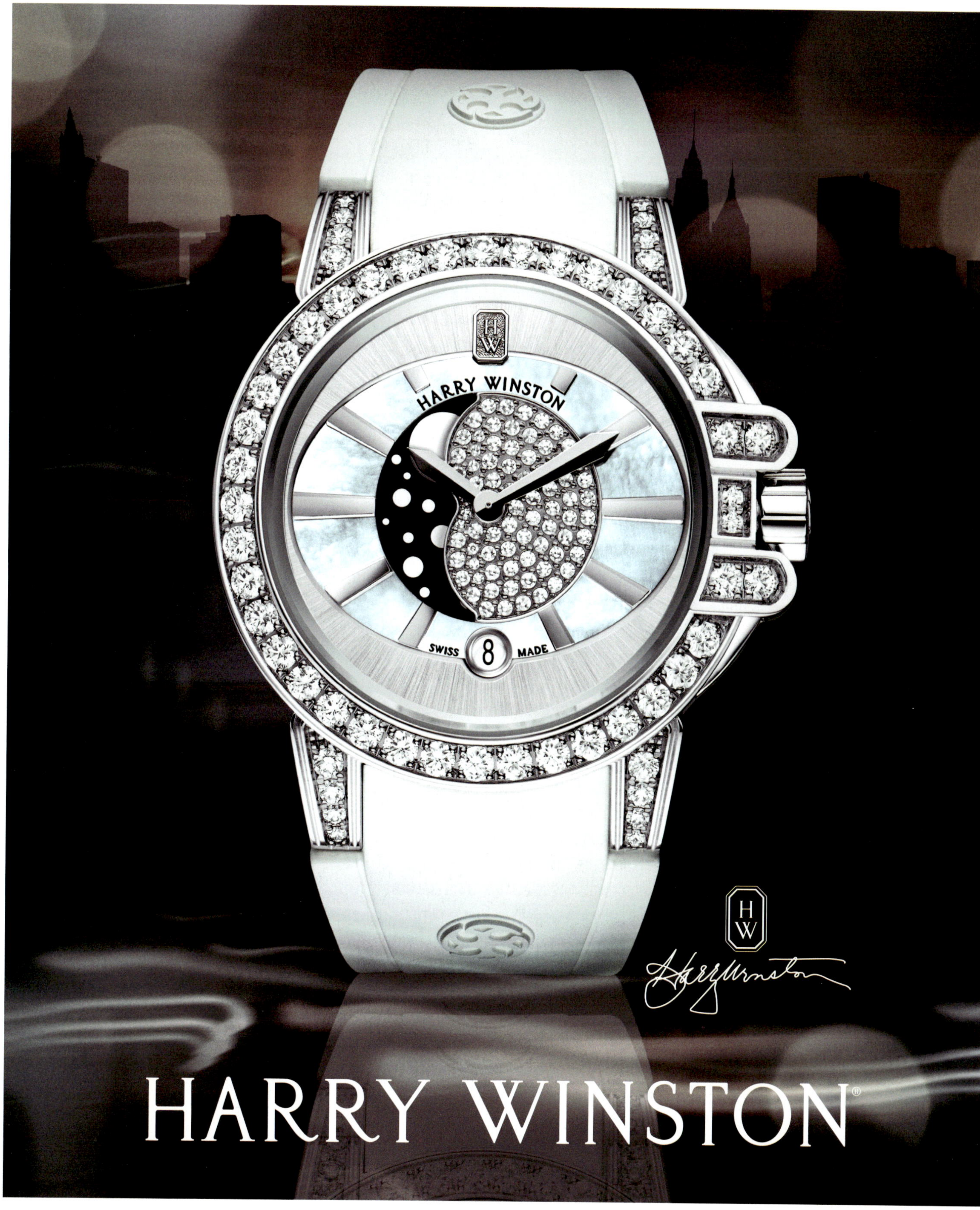
HARRY WINSTON
SWISS
8
MADE
HARRY WINSTON®

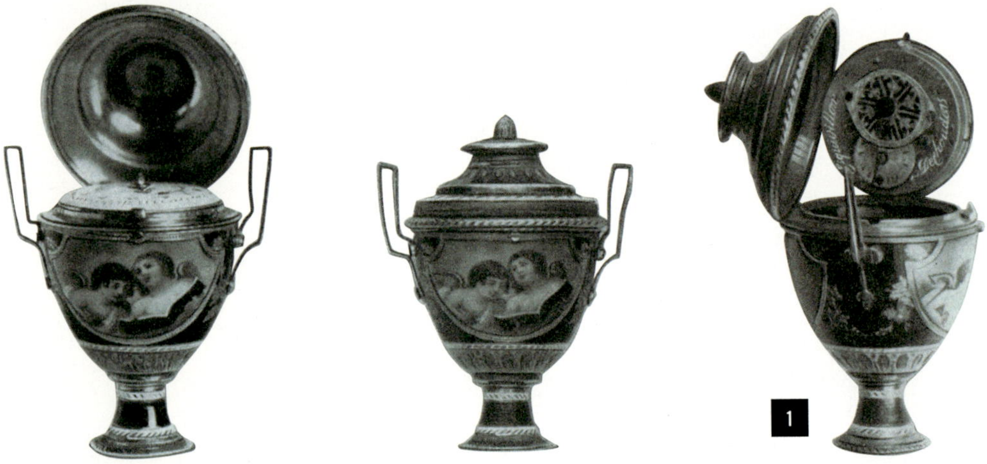

1

THE BEGINNINGS OF THE WRISTWATCH

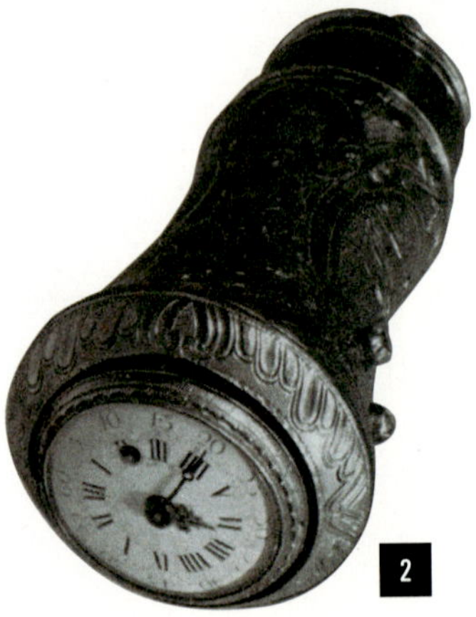

2

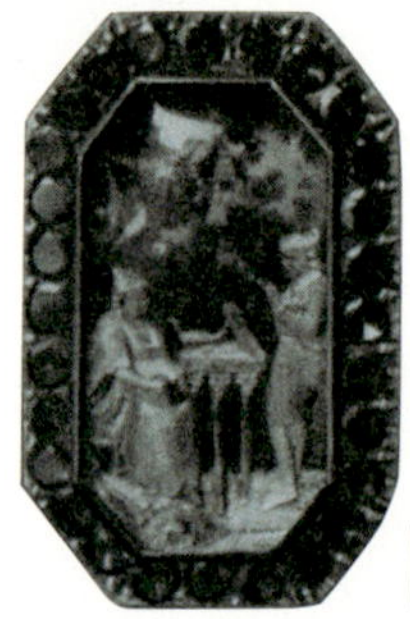

4

In the early 1570s, the Earl of Leicester, the favorite and Master of the Horse under Elizabeth I of England, gave the queen a round diamond-encrusted watch suspended from an armlet. Historians see this piece of jewelry as the forerunner of the wristwatch. Other historical references include the story that the French philosopher Blaise Pascal (1623-1662) wore his watch on his wrist; that a Parisian watchmaker produced wristwatches and ring-watches in the 1880s; while the 1790 company registers for the Maison Jaquet Droz mention "a watch secured by a bracelet."

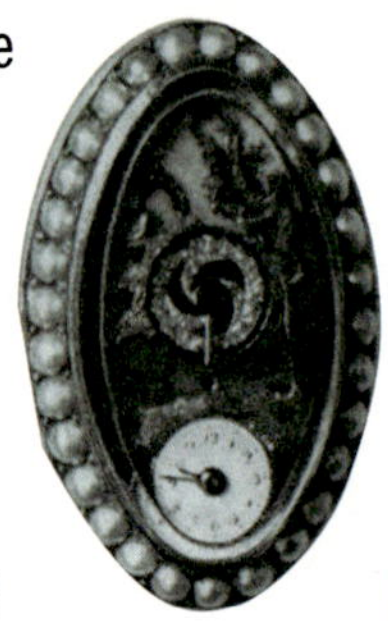

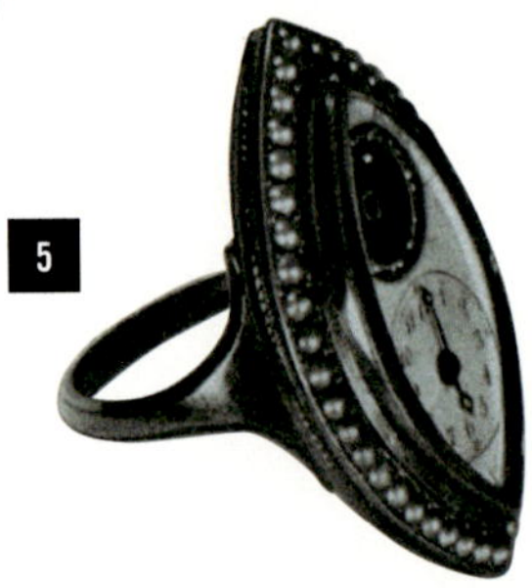

5

While there is no shortage among collectors of ring-watches from several different eras, the oldest wristwatches preserved until now date back to the early 19th century, a period when the sleeves of women's clothes were becoming shorter. The ring-watches were then generally rectangular with an off-set dial revealing the balance-wheel or featuring tiny automatons. It was this type of watch that was fixed to fabric straps or jewelry bracelets intended for high society ladies. The models introduced during this period notably include one by Abraham-Louis Breguet. In 1810, in response to an order placed by Caroline Murat, Queen of Naples, Breguet designed an oblong repeater watch with an off-set chapter ring and a thermometer, fitted with a wristlet composed of hair interwoven with gold thread.

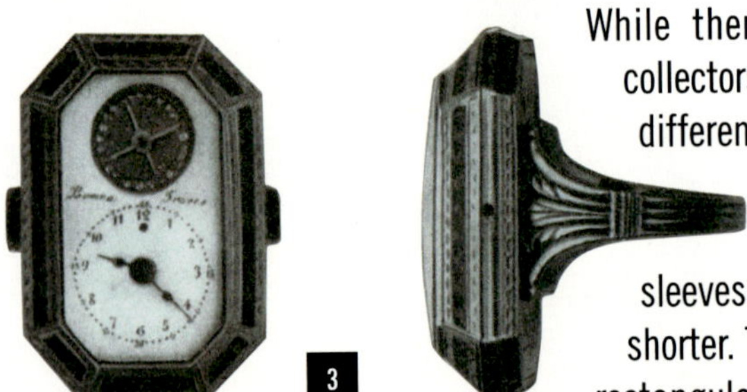

3

Novelty watches of the 19th century.

1. *Urn-shaped watch by Esquivillon & Dehoudens.*
2. *A watch in head of a cane, by Dupont.*
3. *Two views of watch set in a ring, by Bonna Fréres, Geneva.*
4. *Ring watch with visible balance.*
5. *Two rings with automatons.*

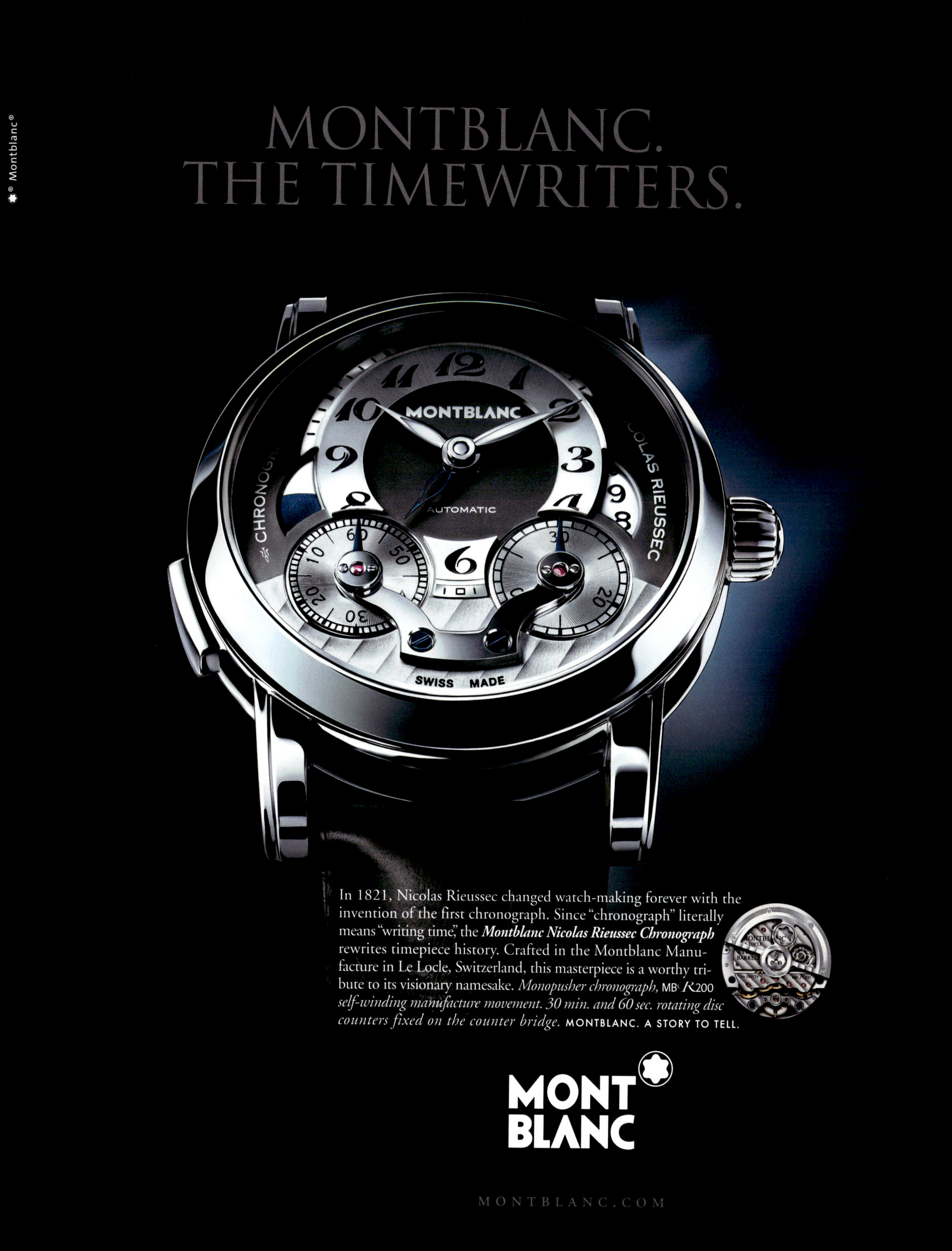
® Montblanc®
MONTBLANC.
THE TIMEWRITERS.
MONTBLANC
AUTOMATIC
NICOLAS RIEUSSEC
CHRONOGRAPH
SWISS MADE
In 1821, Nicolas Rieussec changed watch-making forever with the invention of the first chronograph. Since "chronograph" literally means "writing time," the ***Montblanc Nicolas Rieussec Chronograph*** rewrites timepiece history. Crafted in the Montblanc Manufacture in Le Locle, Switzerland, this masterpiece is a worthy tribute to its visionary namesake. *Monopusher chronograph,* MB R200 *self-winding manufacture movement. 30 min. and 60 sec. rotating disc counters fixed on the counter bridge.* MONTBLANC. A STORY TO TELL.
MONT BLANC
MONTBLANC.COM

Throughout the 19th century, particular attention was devoted to the ornamental quality of watches. Sizeable wristbands provide scope for creative expression by jewelers, engravers, chasers, enamellers and gem-setters. The time function was of secondary importance given the diminutive size of the watches, which could often be removed from the wristlet and worn as sautoir necklaces. It was not until the 1880s that the dial regained its importance, when wristwatches began to be series-produced based on standardized components, and still exclusively intended for women. The only known exception is the order for 2,000 wrist chronographs placed with Girard-Perregaux by the German Navy in 1880.

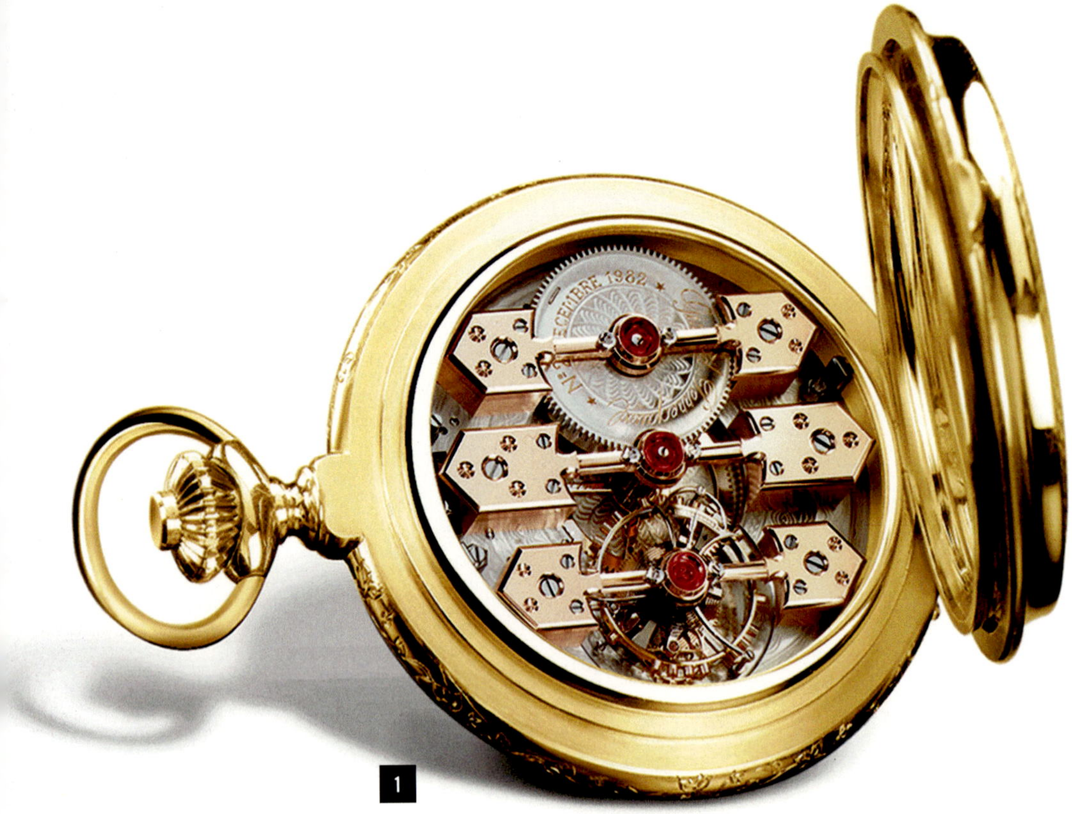

1

1. *Tourbillon under three gold bridges (Girard-Perregaux).*
2. *In 1856 Constant Girard and Marie Perregaux got married and unified the firm Girard-Perregaux.*
3. *Abraham-Louis Perrelet is held as the inventor of the first automatic watch in 1770. His invention meant that, at last, watches could be constantly rewound by means of natural movement. Two hundred years later, the watch's automatic-winding mechanism is still functioning accurately.*

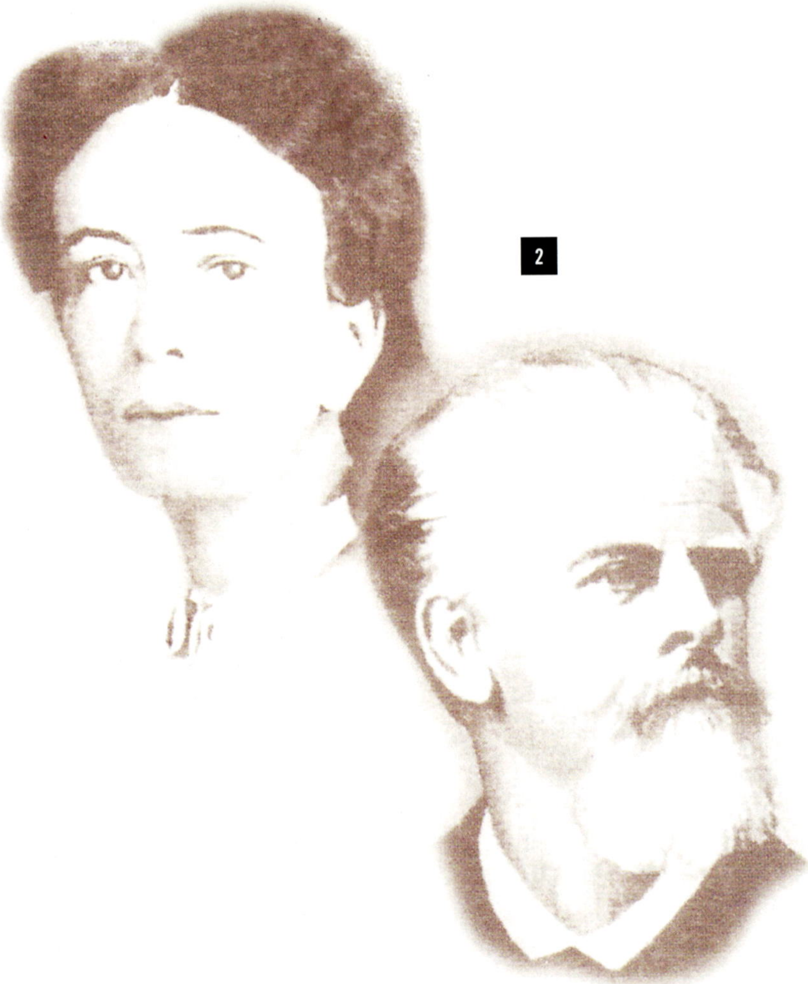

2

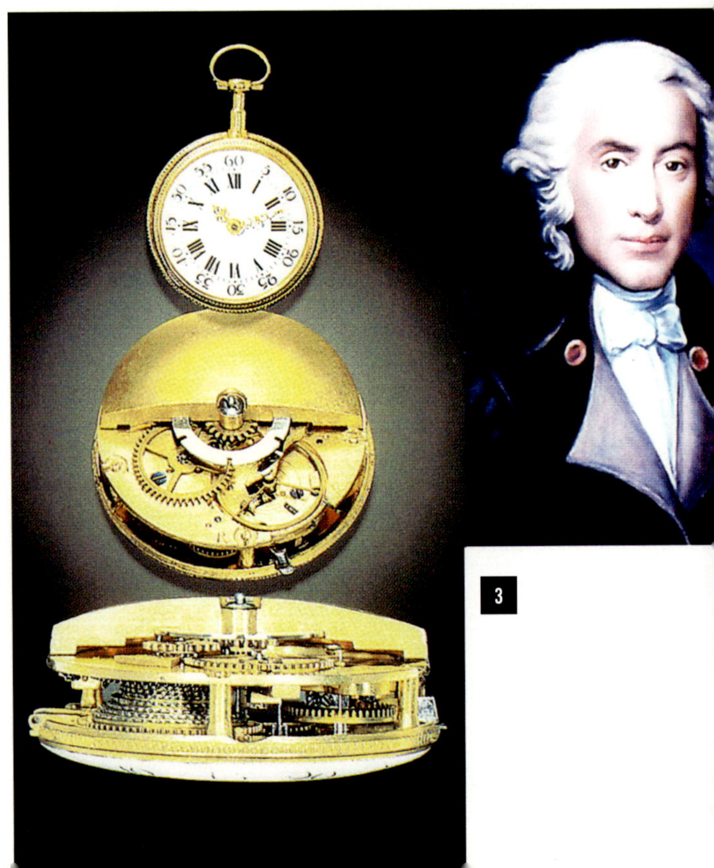

3

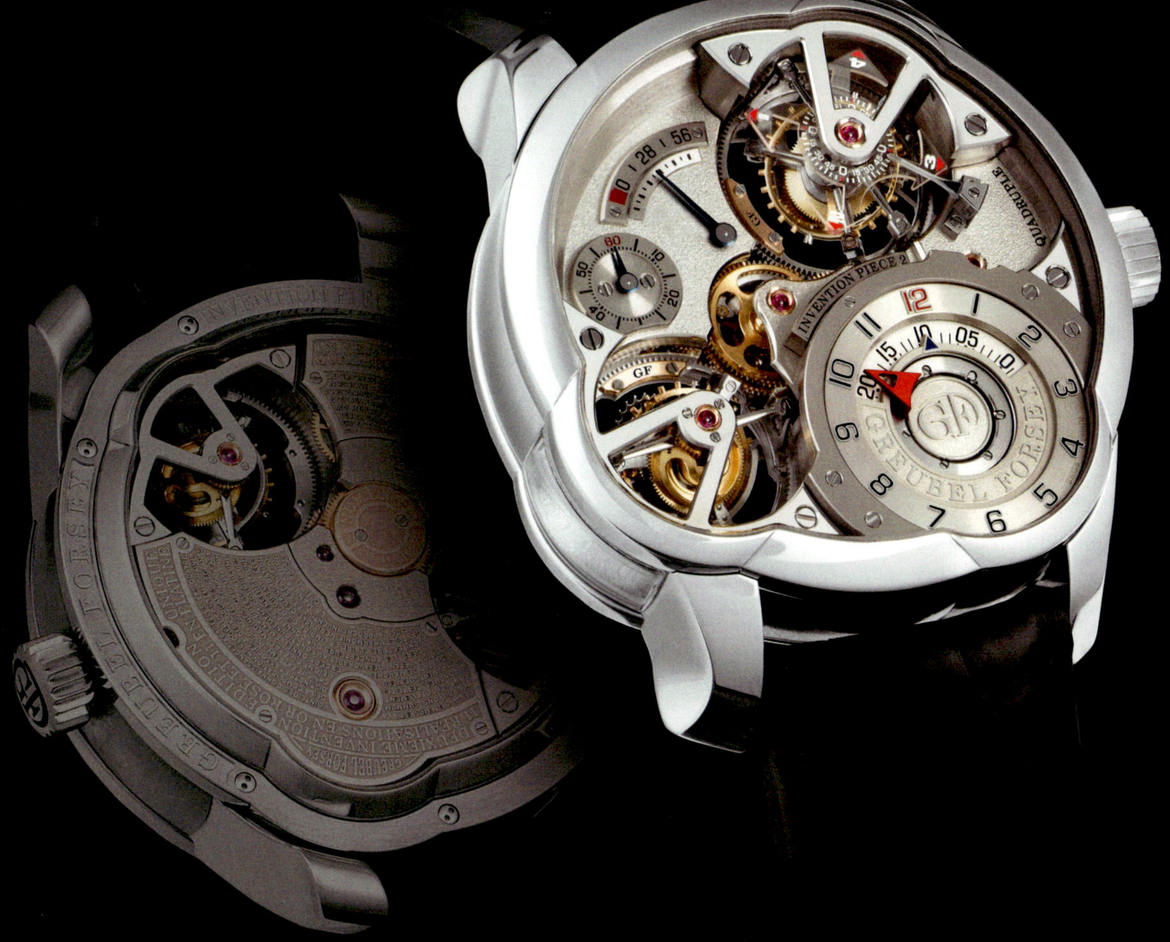
INVENTION PIECE 2
QUADRUPLE
GREUBEL FORSEY

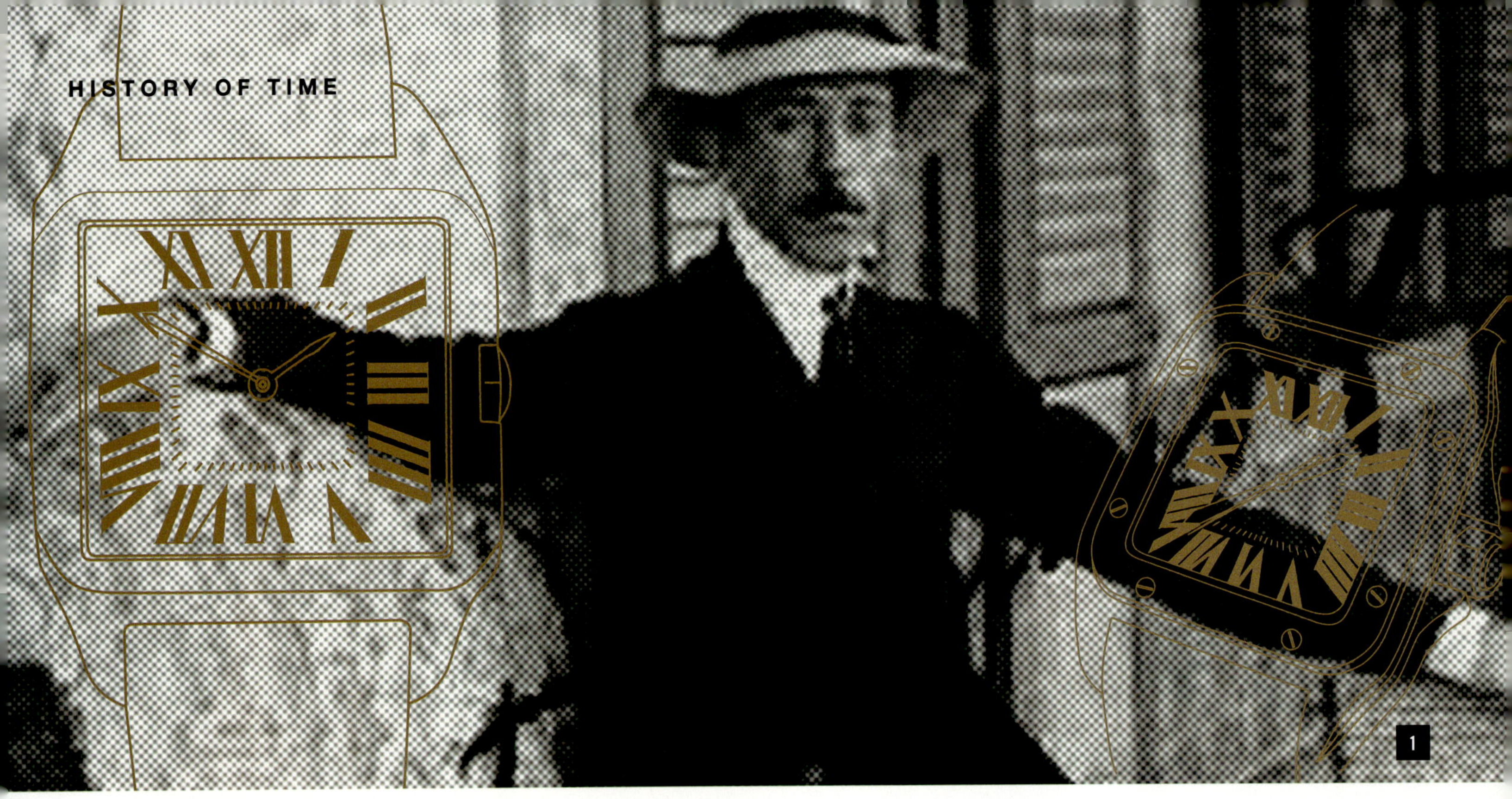

CARTIER CREATES THE SANTOS IN 1904

Thanks to the promulgation of intellectual property legislation, the first wristwatch patents were filed at the turn of the century, particularly in Switzerland from 1889 onwards. At the same time, various advertisements began to appear in trade magazines. An increasing number of manufacturers wagered on this new watchmaking development, even though it was not so much a technical revolution as a complete break with the aesthetic codes and customs of the era. Nonetheless, some countries continued to resist the trend, as was confirmed by the attempt made by Gallet et Cie to send models to its New York agent, who soon afterwards returned them due to lack of demand.

Despite such mixed results, watchmakers persevered, and Longines began supplying ladies' wristwatches to Baume et Cie, renamed Baume & Mercier in 1896; Omega began series production in 1902 and diversified its range by offering men's models in 1905. That same year, Hans Wilsdorf became aware that, when worn on the wrist, watches were indeed liable to become fashionable objects. He therefore began having large quantities of high-quality watches made by Herman Aegler, a watchmaker in Biel, and selling them from London throughout the British Empire and in the Far East. A year earlier, in 1904, Cartier had created a model for the aviator Santos Dumont, featuring a perfect aesthetic design that would become one of the all-time wristwatch classics.

1. *In 1904, Cartier created for the aviator Santos Dumont a wristwatch that would become a classic.*
2. *Swiss peasant's watch with silver inner case and outer case in tortoise-shell.*
3. *Movement with helicoidal gearing, by Ferdinand Melly, Geneva, 1837.*
4. *"Boston lever" movement, made for the American market by the Cortébert factory, late 19th century.*
5. *Movement with bars of peculiar forms, by G. Favre-Jacot, Le Locle.*
6. *Ebauche of independent center seconds watch by Ch.-E. Tissot & Fils, Le Locle, 1853.*

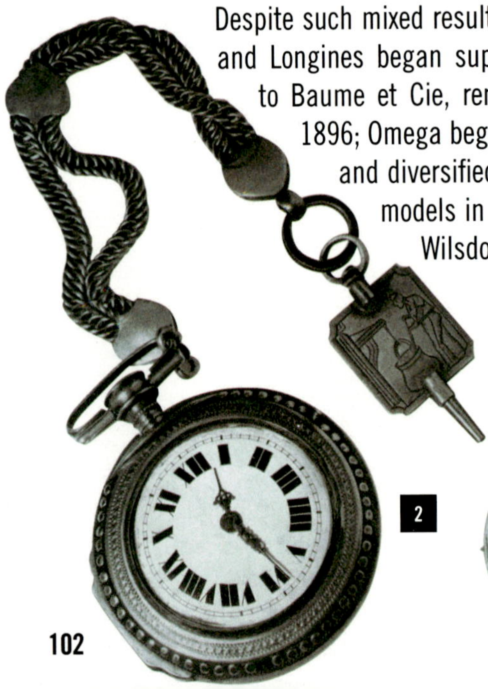

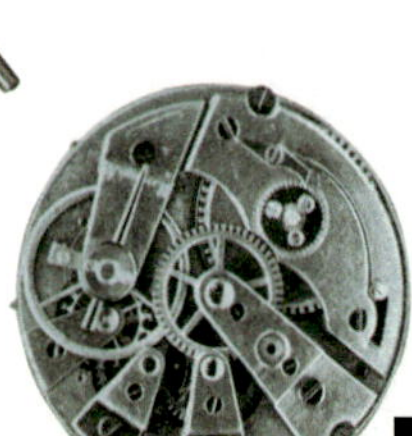

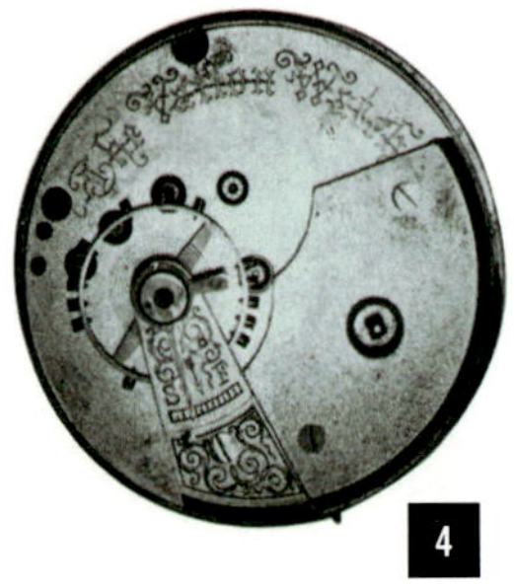

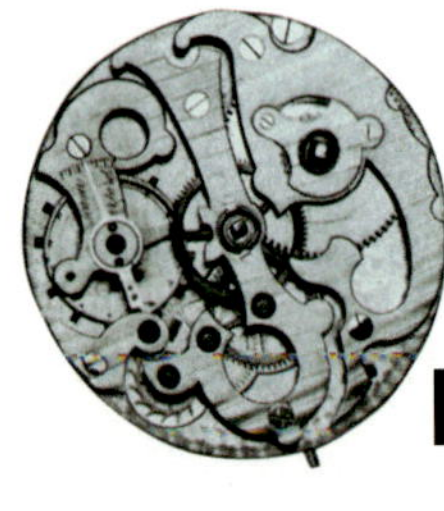

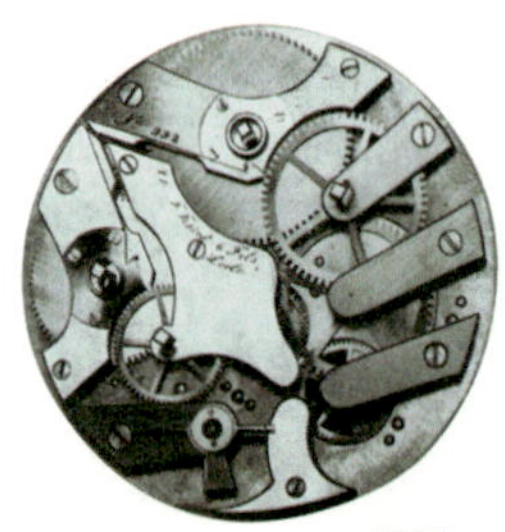

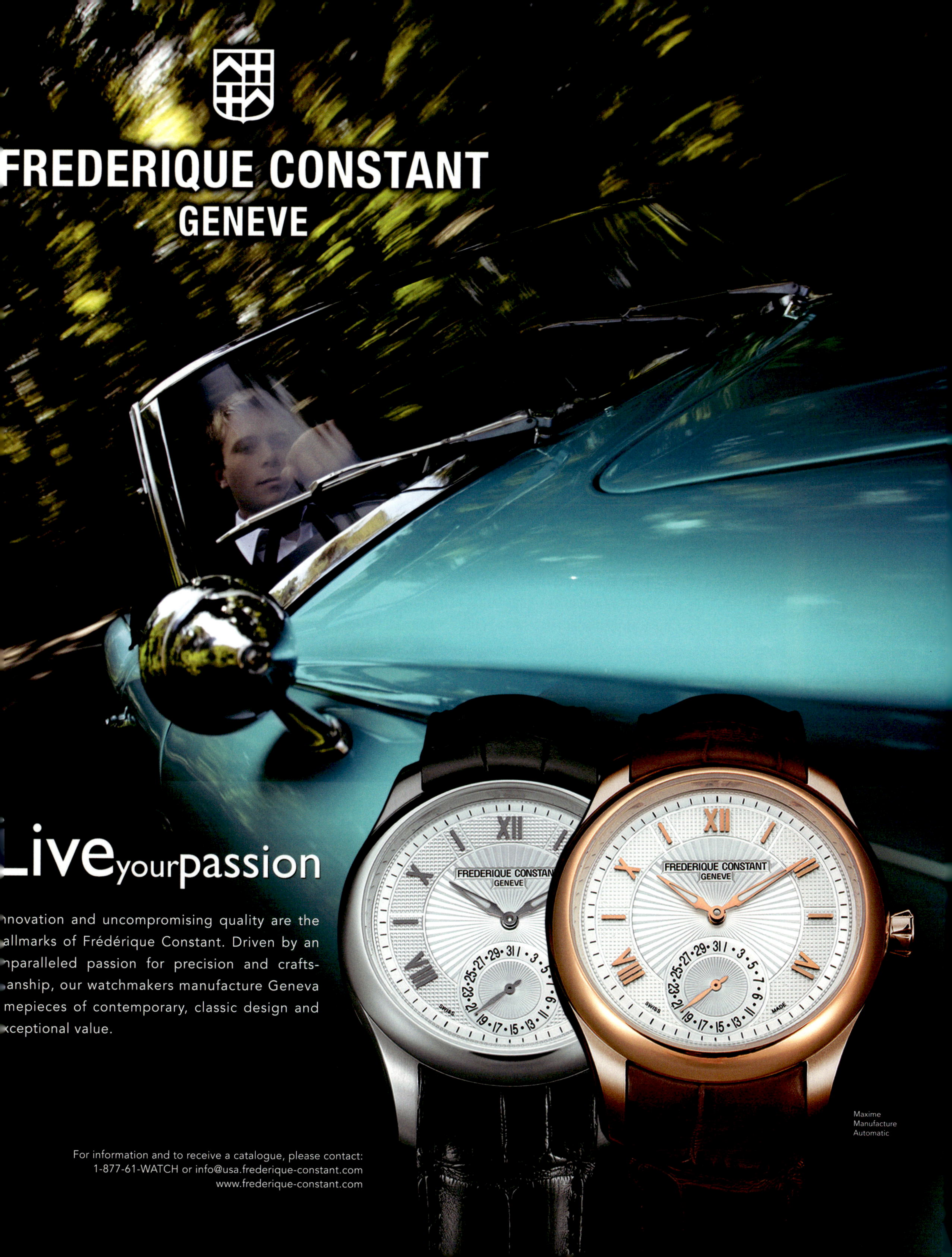
FREDERIQUE CONSTANT
GENEVE
Live your passion
nnovation and uncompromising quality are the allmarks of Frédérique Constant. Driven by an nparalleled passion for precision and crafts- anship, our watchmakers manufacture Geneva mepieces of contemporary, classic design and xceptional value.
For information and to receive a catalogue, please contact:
1-877-61-WATCH or info@usa.frederique-constant.com
www.frederique-constant.com
Maxime
Manufacture
Automatic

BIRTH OF THE SWISS MANUFACTURES

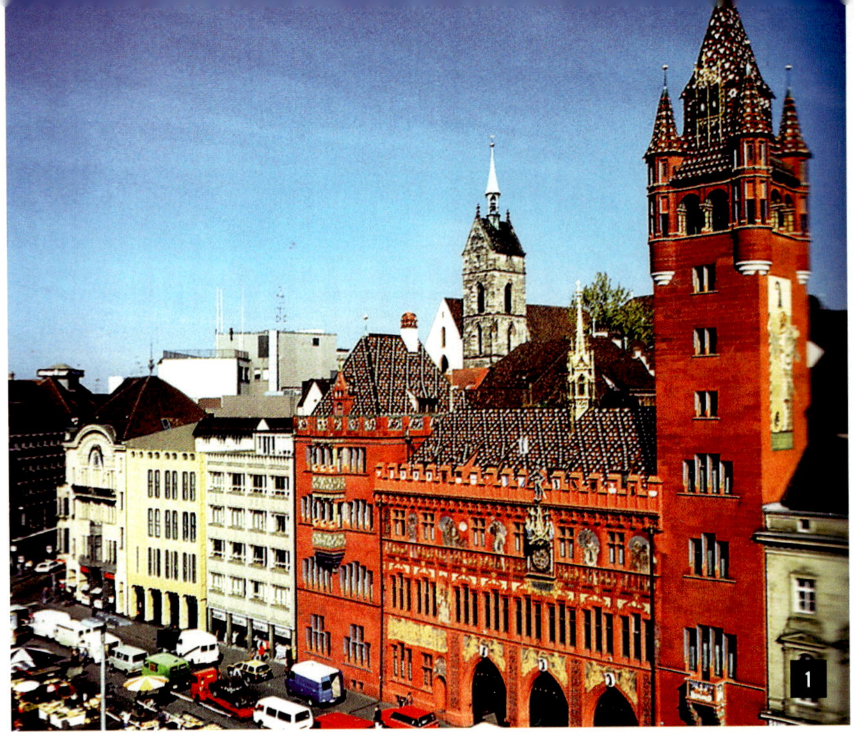

The revocation of the Edict of Nantes by Louis XIV in 1685 undoubtedly played a pivotal role in the development of horology in Switzerland. Within a very short period of time, this decision forced over 200,000 Protestants into exile, many of whom came to Switzerland where they contributed to establishing a "mountain-based industry that would one day dominate the world," as it has been described by the historian David S. Landes. From the mid-19th century onwards, Swiss watchmaking experienced a period of industrialization thanks to the arrival of electrical energy, a development favorable to mechanized production methods. Other factors would contribute to its development, including a high birth rate that swelled the workforce in the secondary sector, along with various free-trade exchanges that facilitated the circulation of products representing areas in which Switzerland enjoyed acknowledged expertise and was technically well ahead of the competition.

1. *The unique medieval architecture of the Basel Town Hall is the theater of the annual Fasnacht Carnival, three days of high-spirited and colorful celebration.*
2. *Advertisement for the Ami-LeCoultre Piguet watch "La Merveilleuse," which featured 22 complications.*

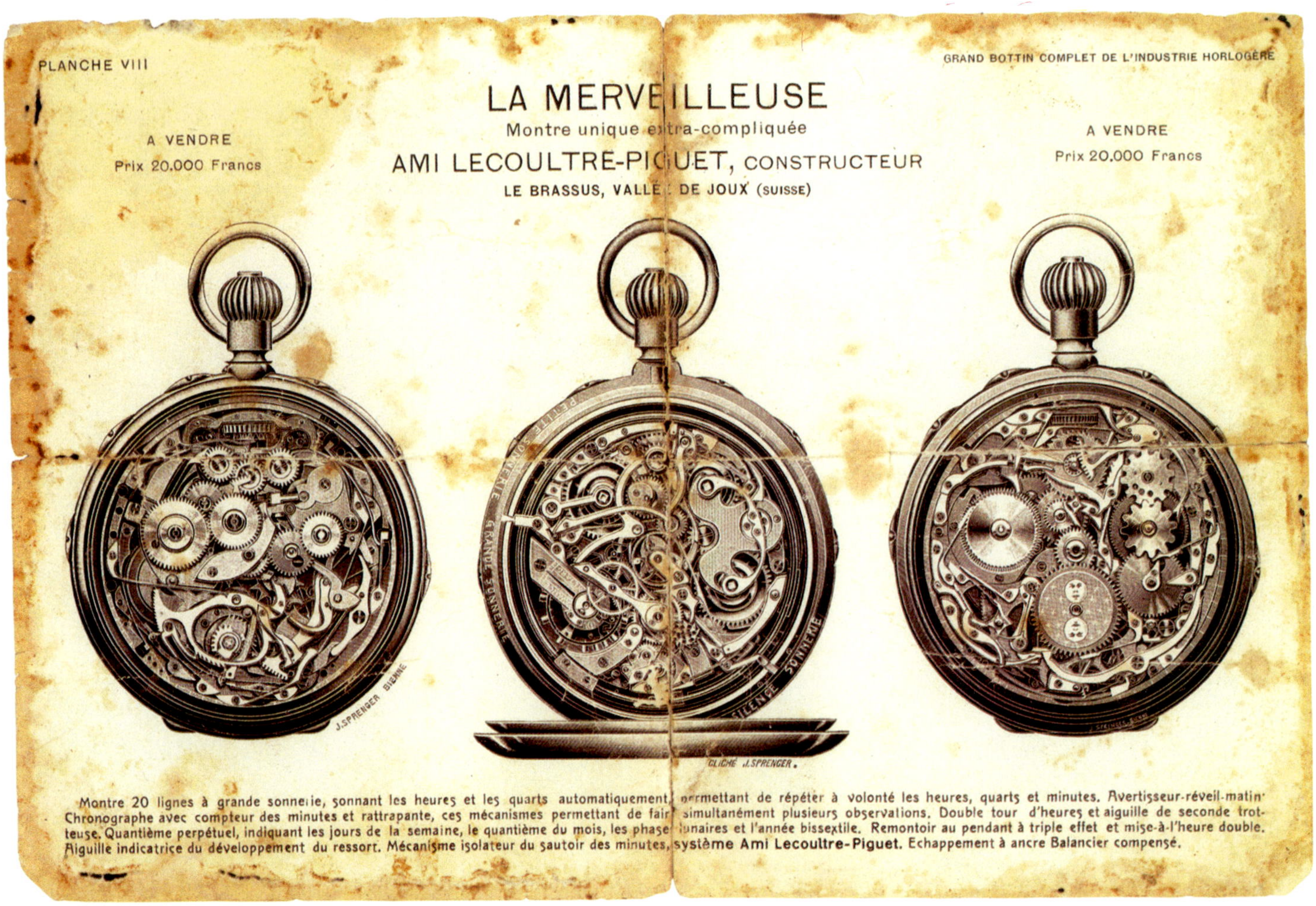

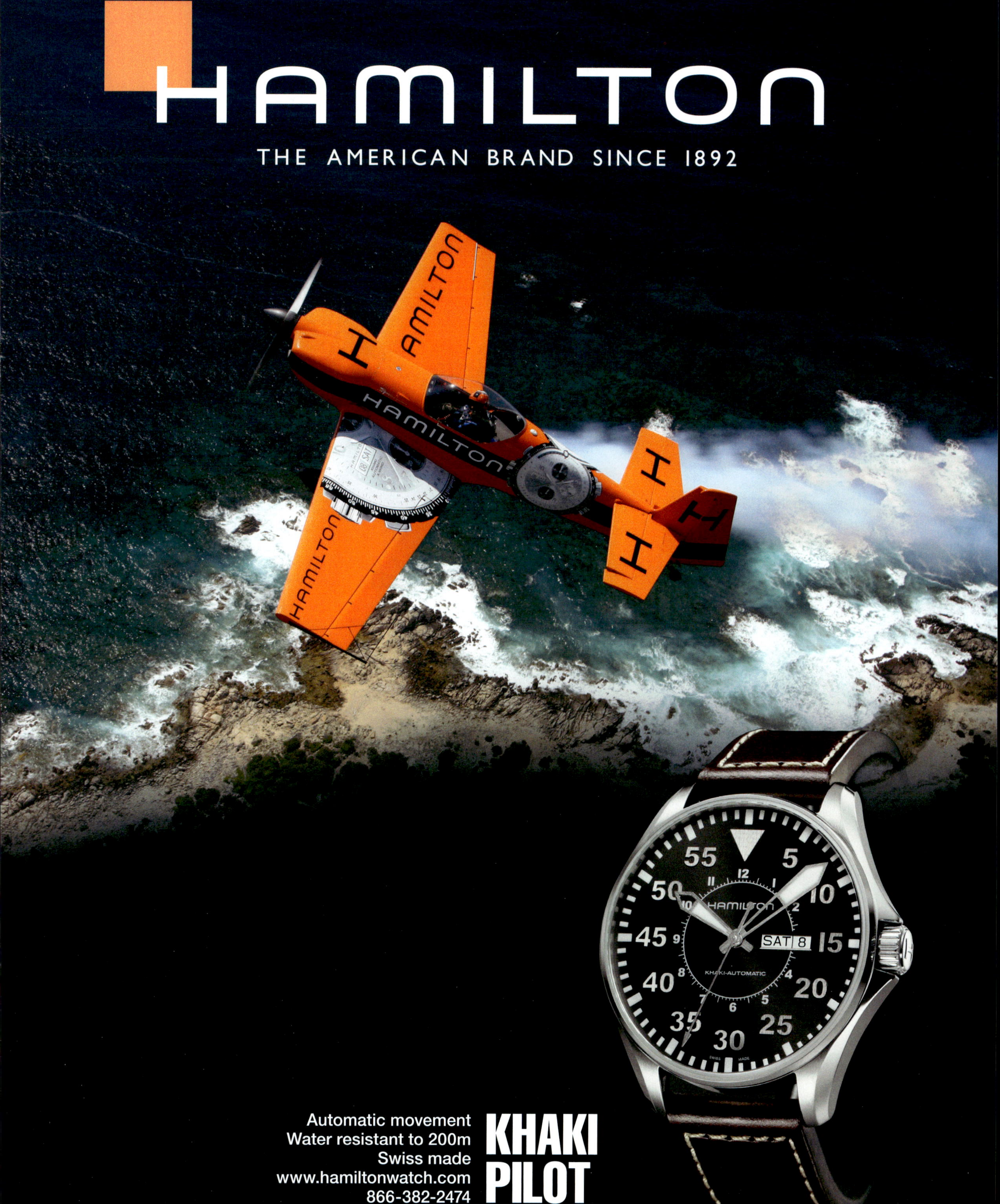

HAMILTON
THE AMERICAN BRAND SINCE 1892
Automatic movement
Water resistant to 200m
Swiss made
www.hamiltonwatch.com
866-382-2474
KHAKI
PILOT

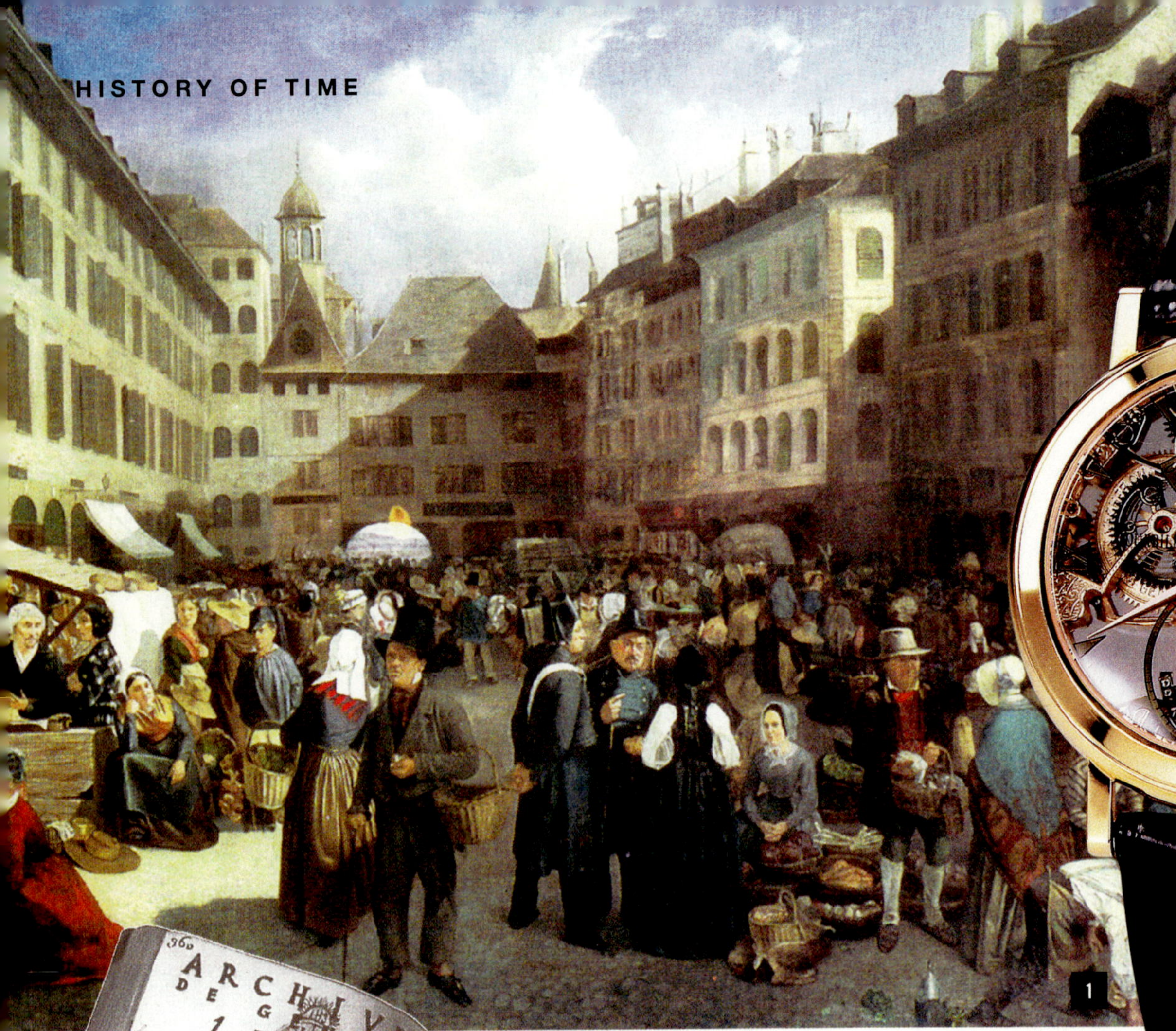

1

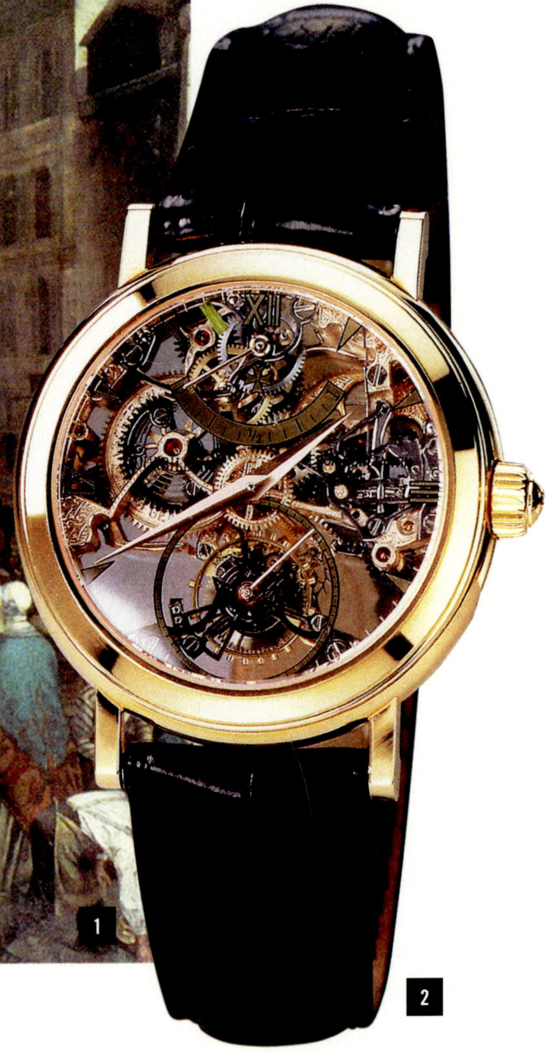

2

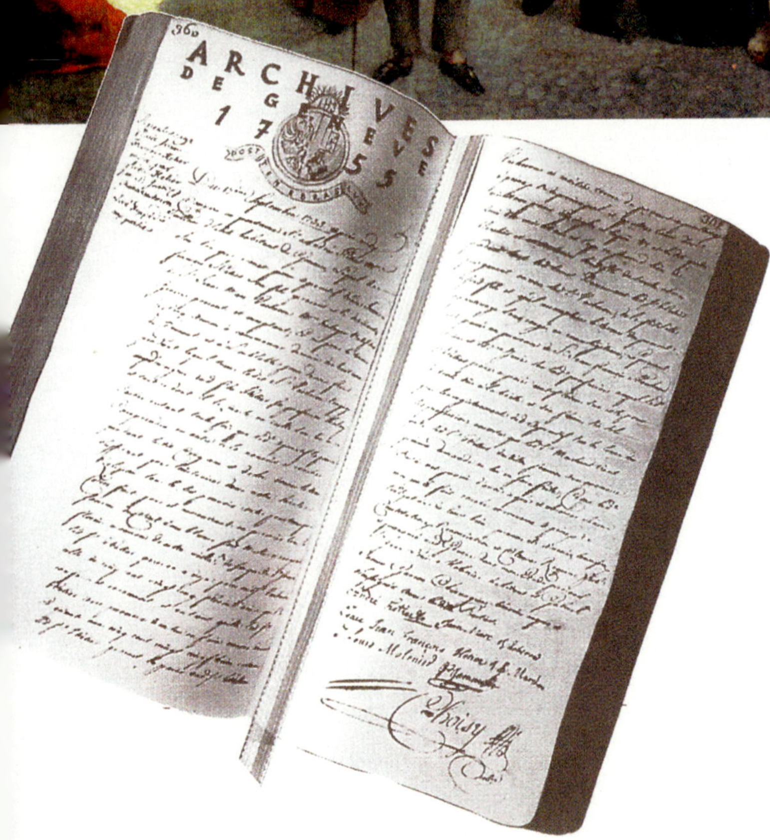

3

From 1870 onwards, production evolved along parallel paths: on the one hand, through a horizontally organized sector in which mass-produced components were assembled and sold by établisseurs or finishers; and on the other, a number of manufactures (industrial entities capable of making all parts of a watch) that progressively integrated the entire production process in order to create their own movements that they sold under their own name. In 1907, the seven largest manufactures employed around 10 percent of the workers in the sector. Among them were Longines, Omega, and Zenith, which are still going strong today. It was a spectacular boom period for the Swiss watch industry, with the number of jobs rising from 40,000 to over 62,000 between 1870 and 1914. Productivity followed exactly the same trend, with 82 watches produced per worker in 1888, compared with almost 320 thirty years later. These figures were naturally matched by strong growth in exports, with four times the number of units sold abroad in the space of 32 years.

1. *Place du Molard, Geneva's commercial center, as depicted by H-G Lacombe in 1843.*
2. *Documentary evidence of Vacheron Constantin's trade activities in 1755.*
3. *The Skeleton Tourbillon in rose gold by Vacheron Constantin features a movement with twin series-coupled barrels. Its regulating unit, escapement and balance wheel are mounted in a tourbillon carriage which rotates over one minute. The sapphire dial is inscribed with Roman numerals and features a power reserve indicator at 12. Vacheron Constantin's skeleton tourbillon is part of a limited series of only 300 to be produced.*

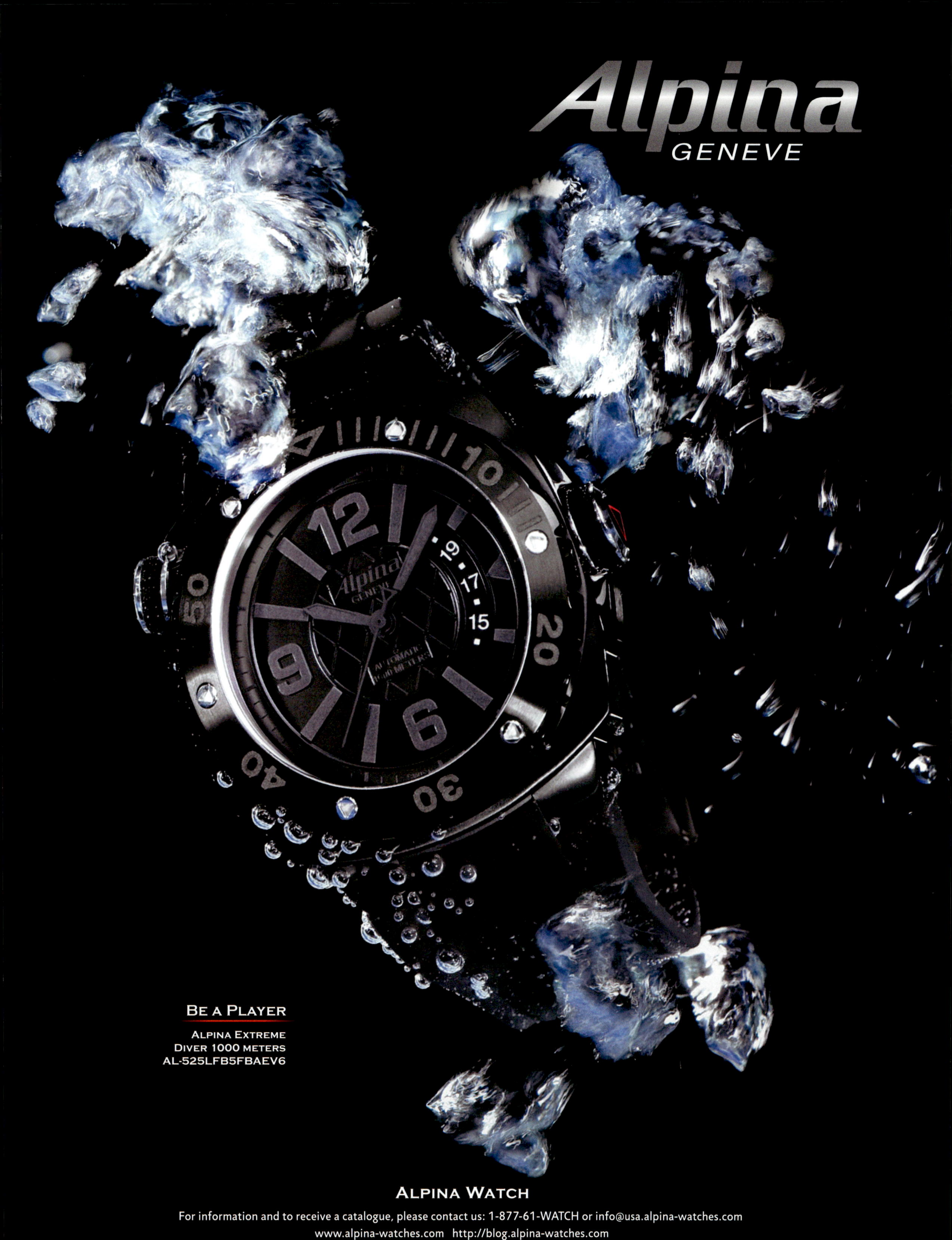
Alpina
GENEVE
BE A PLAYER
ALPINA EXTREME
DIVER 1000 METERS
AL-525LFB5FBAEV6
ALPINA WATCH
For information and to receive a catalogue, please contact us: 1-877-61-WATCH or info@usa.alpina-watches.com
www.alpina-watches.com http://blog.alpina-watches.com

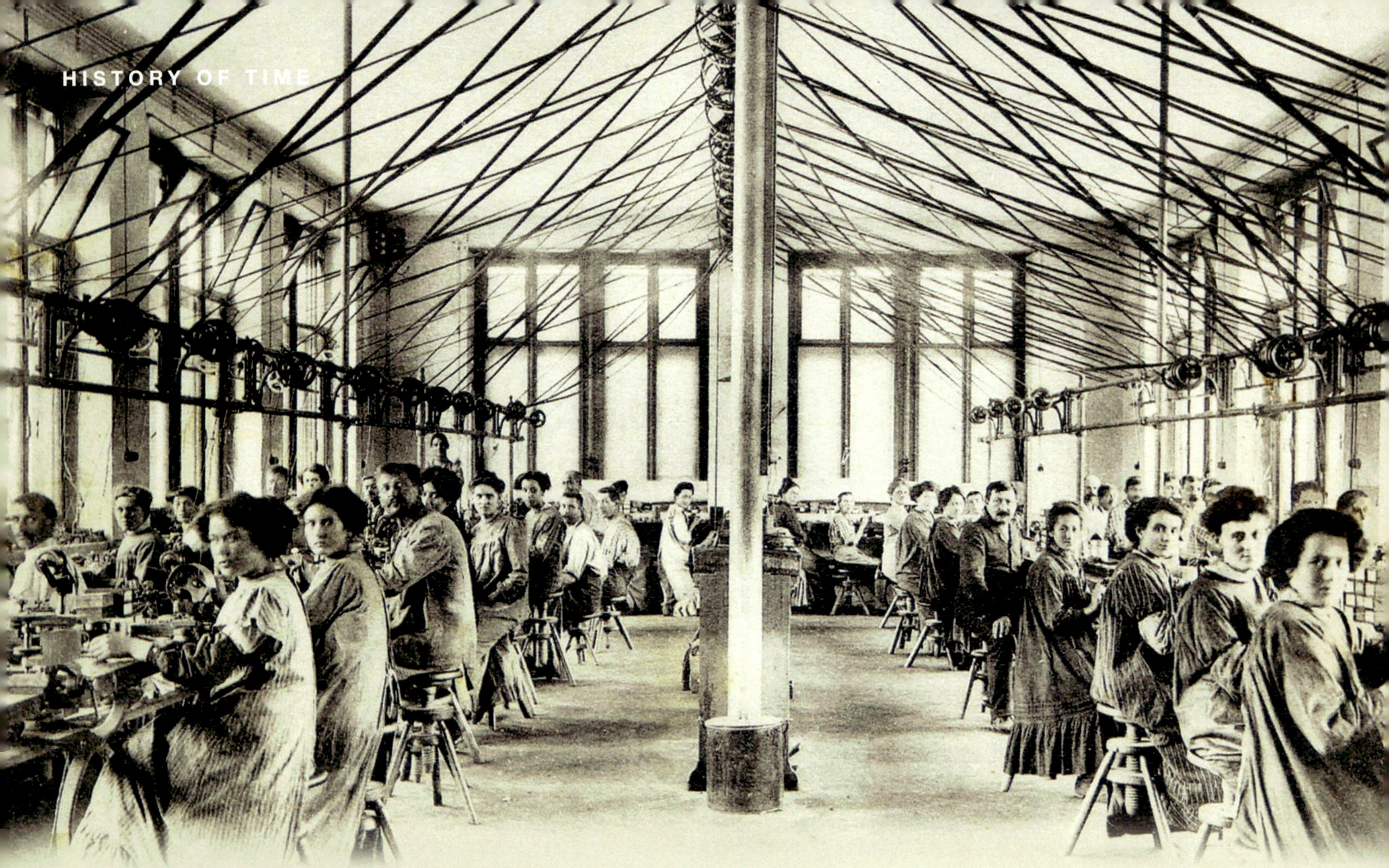

THE FIRST WATCH CRISIS, BETWEEN THE TWO WORLD WARS

The period between the two world wars brought a major crisis for the Swiss watch industry. The successive closures of the Russian market following the Bolshevik revolution, and of Germany's market due to the massive currency depreciation, combined with a renewed surge of protectionism on the main export markets, decimated the industry. Between 1920 and 1921, Swiss watch and movement exports experienced a brutal 43 percent drop. The industry was forced to slash jobs and sell off stocks at cut-rate prices, and still sustained a number of bankruptcies. Initially, trade professionals tried to handle the situation themselves, but the State had to be called to the rescue in order to avoid the collapse of an entire sector of the Swiss economy. This government intervention led to the establishment of the *Statut de l'horlogerie*, which was an original attempt to force the market to adjust under state patronage and supervision.

After a number of endeavors, the solution adopted involved regrouping several companies within four trust companies placed under the supervision of a holding company, the Société Générale de l'Horlogerie Suisse SA. Due to insufficient funding, the Société had to appeal to the Federal government, which granted support just as it had done for Swiss farmers a few years previously. While these structures subsequently evolved, the principle was not challenged before the crisis that hit the industry in the 1970s and completely redesigned the face of the entire sector. The cartel-type agreements, which are now prohibited, enabled Swiss watchmaking to avoid complete disaster. The *Statut de l'horlogerie* lasted around 40 years, until federal laws were relaxed in the late 1960s in order to establish a single definition of "Swiss Made."

In the mid-19th century, Swiss horology underwent a period of industrialization that gave rise to the first manufactures.

THE QUARTZ TIDAL WAVE

After living through the prosperous 30 "glorious" post-war years, which saw exports rise from 500 million Swiss francs in 1945 to over 3 billion in 1974, the Swiss watch industry was once again hit by a new slump that proved to be one of the most serious in its entire history. Between 1970 and 1976, the sector lost 40 percent of its jobs. Several factors contributed to this crisis, including the successive petrol crises and the rise of the Swiss franc against other major currencies, especially the dollar. Between 1970 and 1974 the franc rose 58 percent against the US dollar, which severely affected its competitiveness on international markets—a downturn that bore no relation to the quality of Swiss products.

Last but not least, Swiss watchmaking had been lulled into a sense of complacency by cartel-type agreements that guaranteed prices, and had completely missed out on the quartz revolution, even though this cheaper technology had in fact been originally been developed in Switzerland. Rather than a long-term product, the watch had become a mass consumer trend item that was easily interchangeable and even disposable due to its price—and above all far more reliable. The piezo-electric properties of these watches, with their built-in quartz crystal electronic circuit vibrating at a regular rate of 30,000 Hz, were naturally far more accurate than mechanical watches and boasted a mere one-second variation in rate every six years! Their failure to grasp the importance of this new technology was to severely penalize Swiss companies, of which the number was cut in half in the space of ten years, plummeting from 1,618 in 1970 to 861 in 1980.

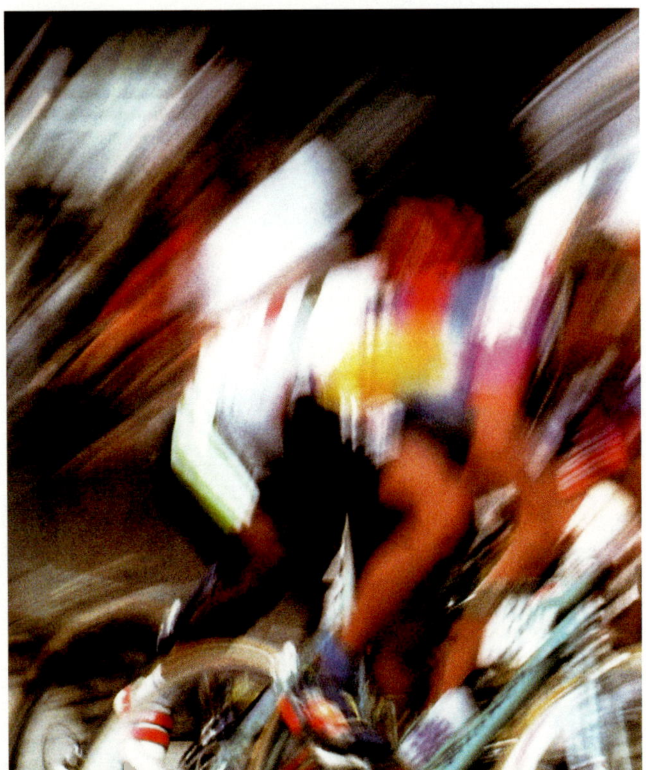

1

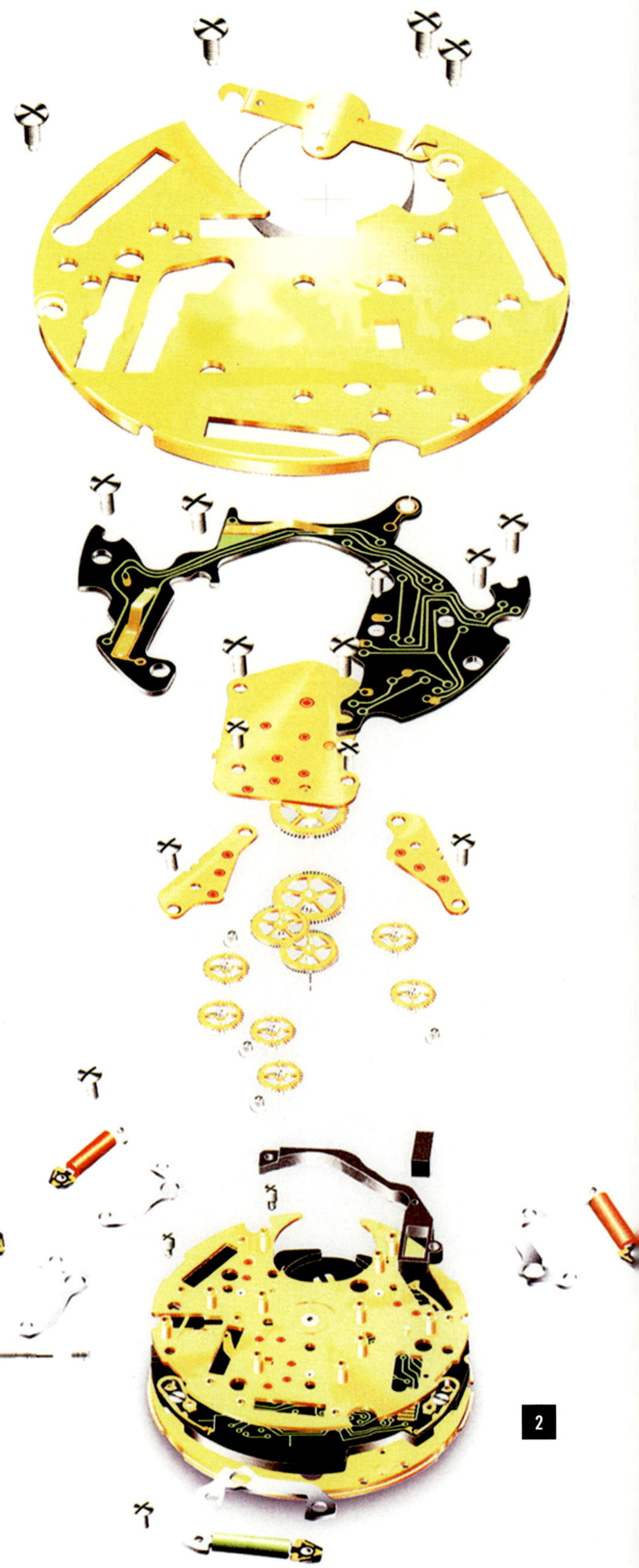

2

1. *The precision of quartz movements gave them precedence in such endeavors as timing athletic events.*
2. *Exploded view of a quartz movement.*

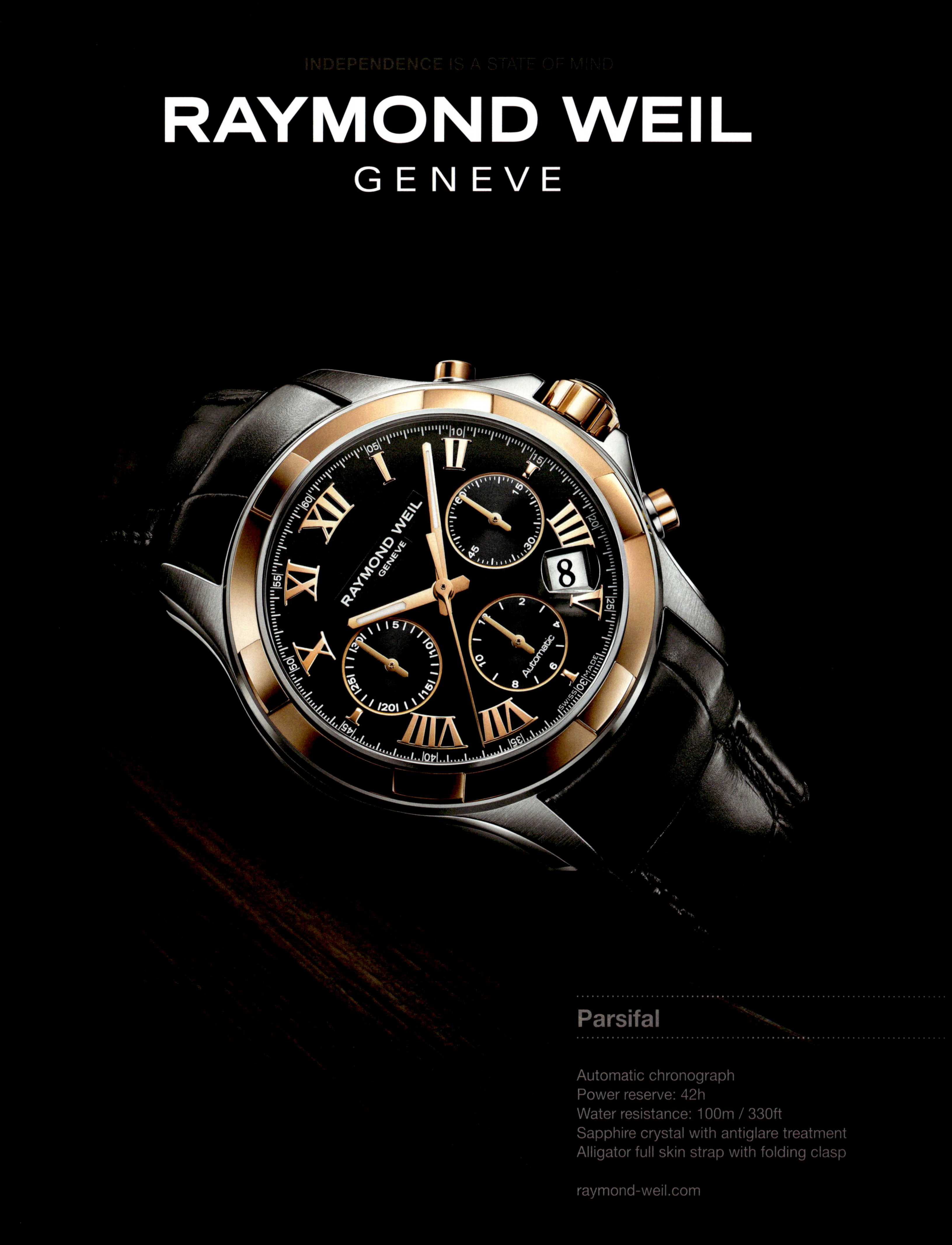
INDEPENDENCE IS A STATE OF MIND
RAYMOND WEIL
GENEVE
RAYMOND WEIL
GENEVE
Automatic
SWISS MADE
Parsifal
Automatic chronograph
Power reserve: 42h
Water resistance: 100m / 330ft
Sapphire crystal with antiglare treatment
Alligator full skin strap with folding clasp
raymond-weil.com

"SWISS MADE" WORKS WONDERS

Nonetheless, Swiss watchmaking had not given up the ghost—far from it. Though the 1970s watch crisis had severely affected the mechanical watch, this was the field that would ultimately save it. After regaining the ground that had been lost to quartz thanks to the Swatch, an electronic timepiece bearing the "Swiss Made" label synonymous with quality, industry professionals were able to restore the pedigree of high-end watchmaking, an area in which they had consistently accomplished great feats. Constantly pushing the technological limits of time measurement, and making no concessions in terms of quality, Swiss watch companies succeeded in establishing a virtual global monopoly on prestigious mechanical timepieces, whose origin alone is a guarantee of know-how and fine craftsmanship. Venturing onto markets the world over, they have found growth areas in emerging countries and in the creation of wealth that has been accelerating in recent years.

Thus, over the past decade and despite the difficulties encountered on the markets since the most recent financial downturn sparked by the sub-prime crisis in the fall of 2008, the brand has enjoyed almost unprecedented levels of success. Watch exports reached a record 17.03 billion Swiss francs in 2008, a 53 percent increase over the previous five years, before dropping back to 13.2 billion in 2009. Many watch companies are making up for lost ground, recording 20 percent year-on-year increases in the first ten months of 2010. In parallel, the average price of mechanical watches has risen 14 percent since 2004, to $2,365.

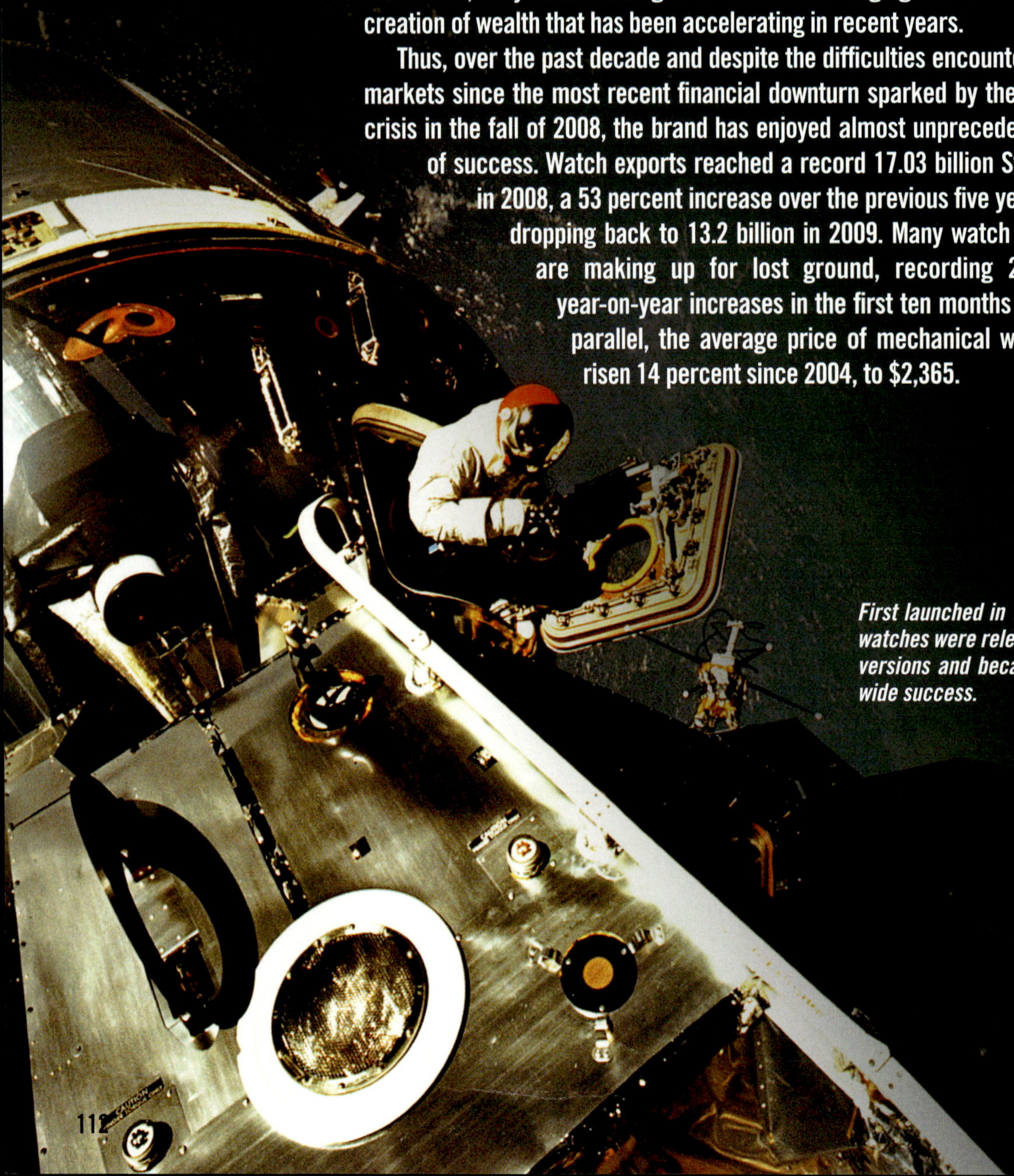

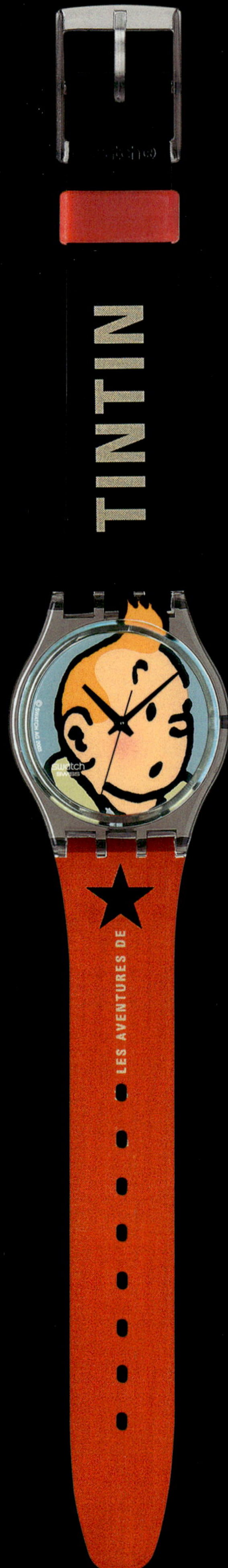

First launched in 1983, Swatch watches were released in many versions and became a worldwide success.

1

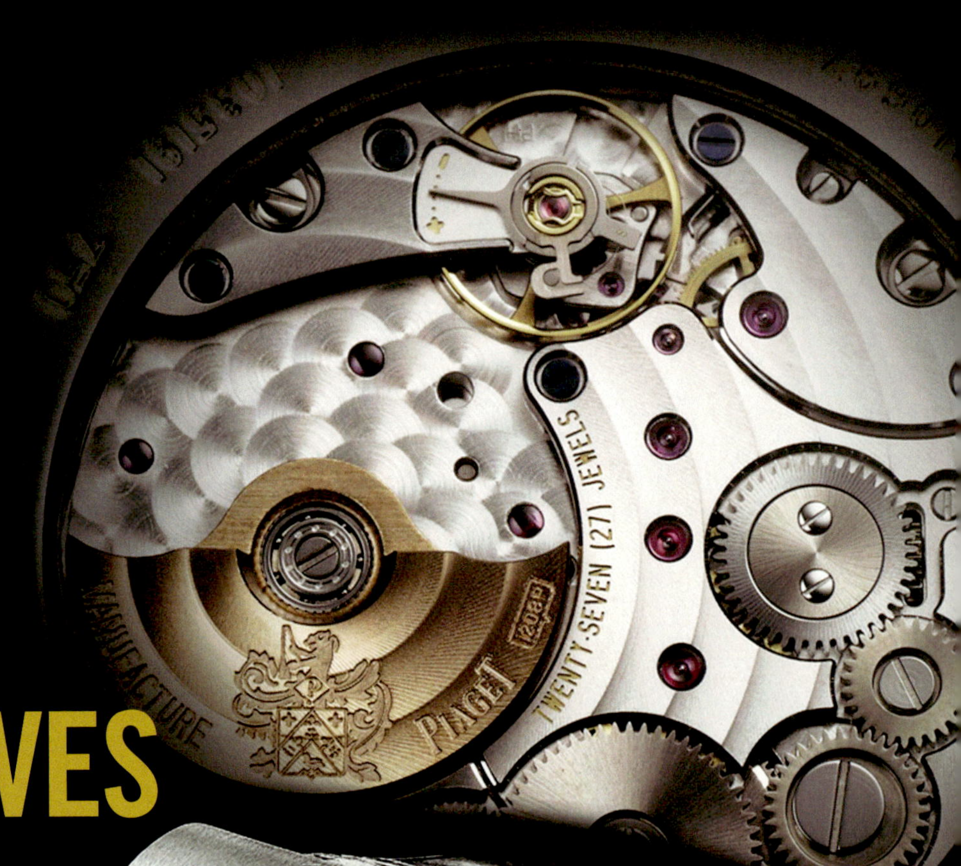

THE WORLD OF SUPERLATIVES

This supremacy of Swiss watches on the world markets is now evidenced by timepieces covering the entire watchmaking spectrum, with a special focus on mechanical models that single-handedly account for almost two-thirds of the industry's total exports in terms of value. And one must admit that Swiss watchmakers continue to accomplish great things in this field, even though it is often said that nothing significant has been invented since Breguet.

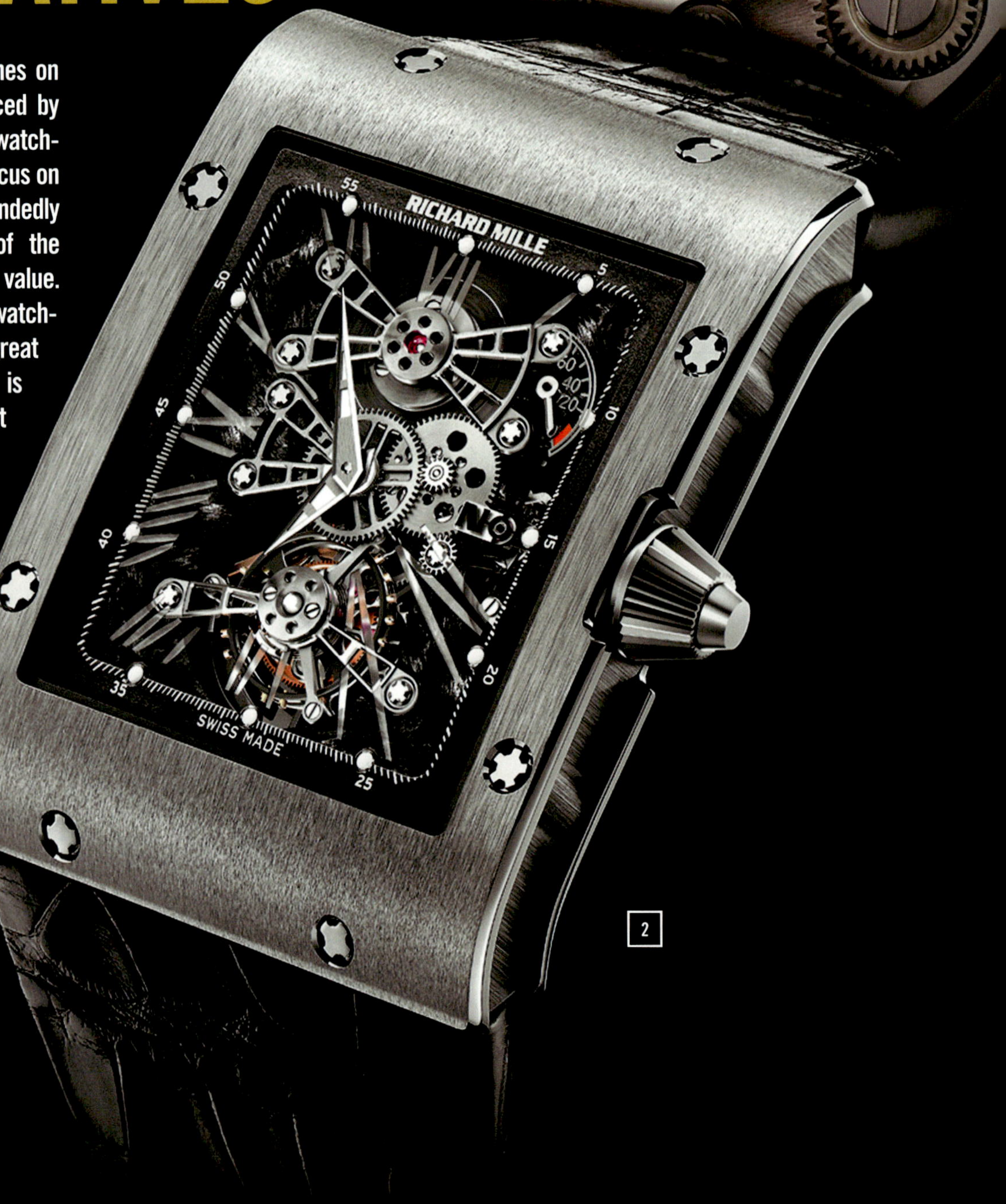

2

1. 1208P movement (Piaget)
2. RM 027 (Richard Mille)

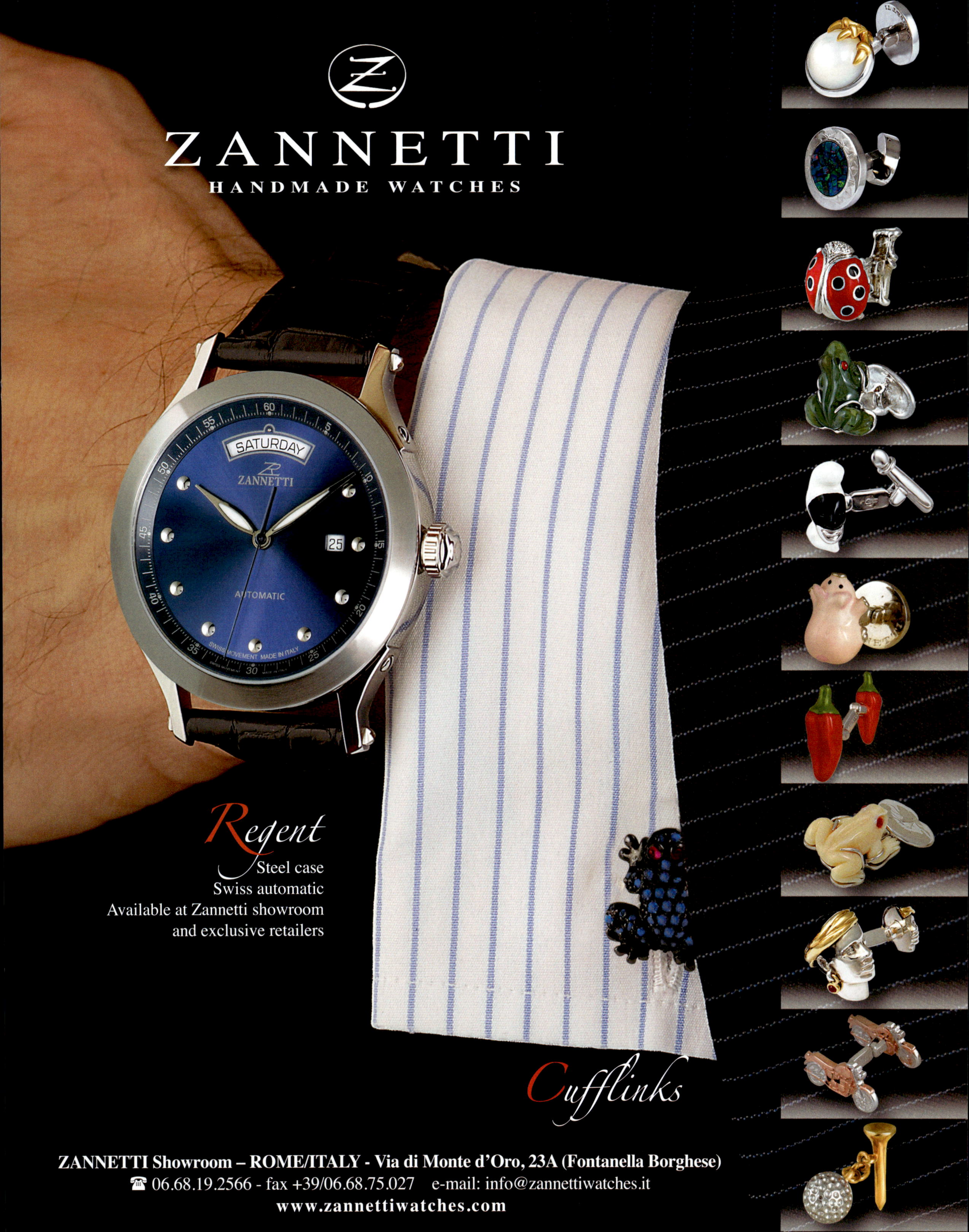
ZANNETTI
HANDMADE WATCHES
SATURDAY
ZANNETTI
AUTOMATIC
SWISS MOVEMENT MADE IN ITALY
Regent
Steel case
Swiss automatic
Available at Zannetti showroom
and exclusive retailers
Cufflinks
ZANNETTI Showroom – ROME/ITALY - Via di Monte d'Oro, 23A (Fontanella Borghese)
☎ 06.68.19.2566 - fax +39/06.68.75.027 e-mail: info@zannettiwatches.it
www.zannettiwatches.com

After several years of vying with each other in the field of complications, the various brands have broken new ground in the use of original alloys and new materials formerly reserved for the aeronautical or automotive industries, while continuing to cultivate the artistic crafts that play a crucial role in high-end watches.

1. Pendulum (TAG Heuer)
2. Freak Diavolo (Ulysse Nardin)
3. Hybris Mechanica à Gyrotourbillon (Jaeger-LeCoultre)

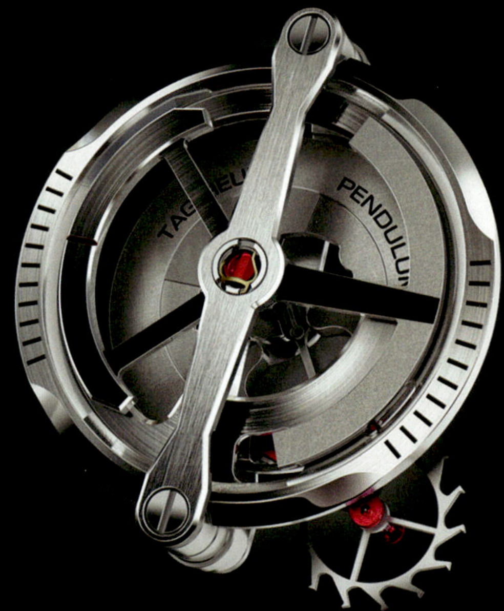

1

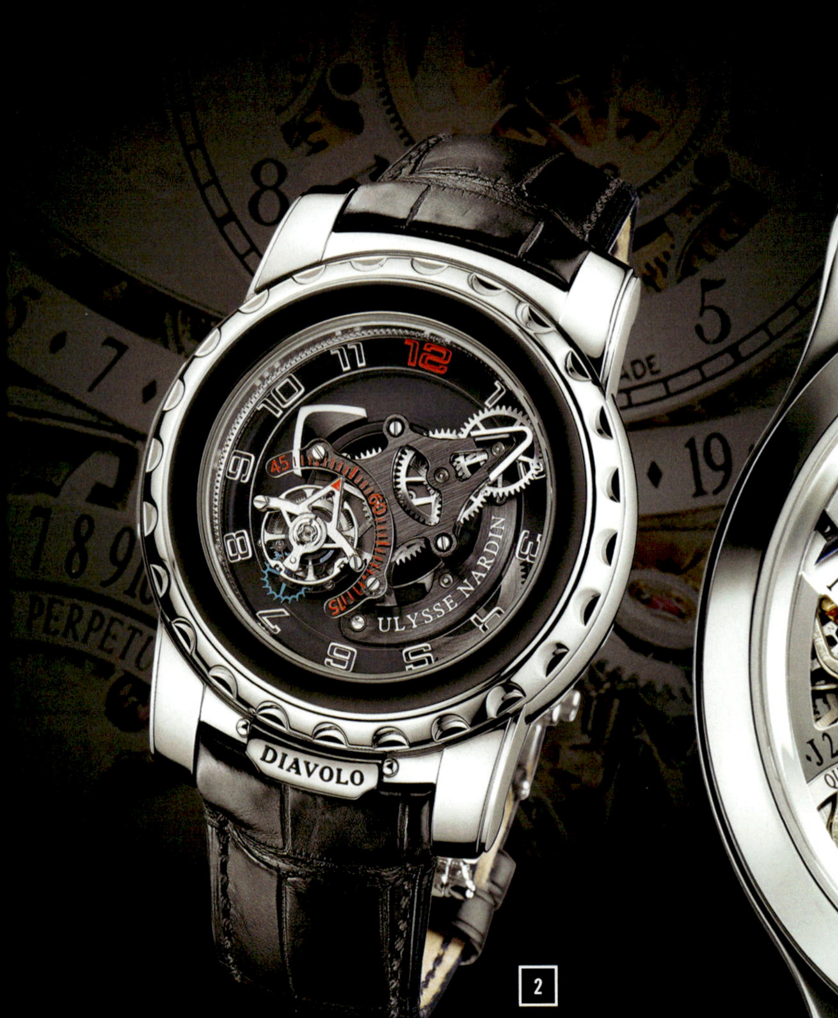

2

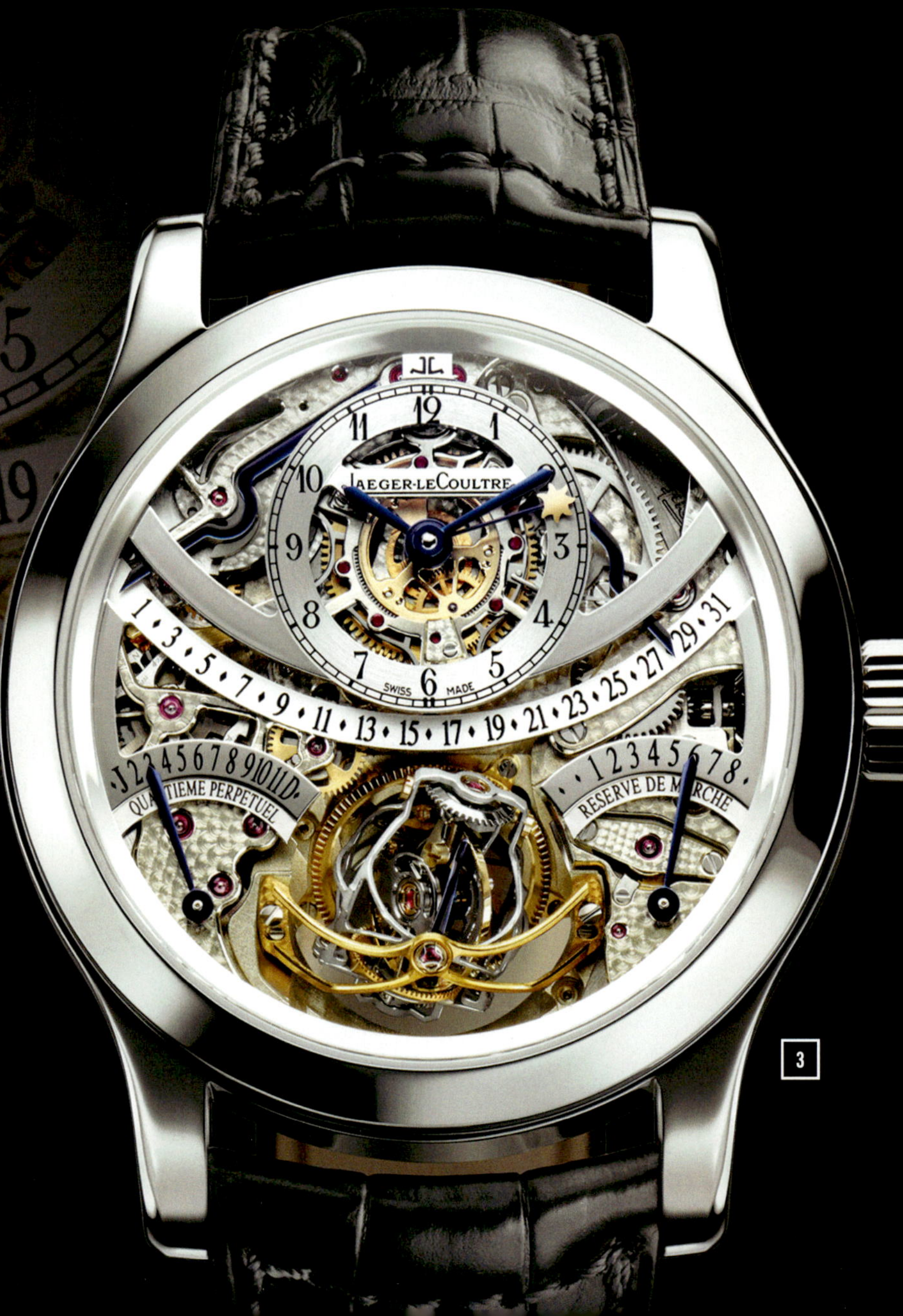

3

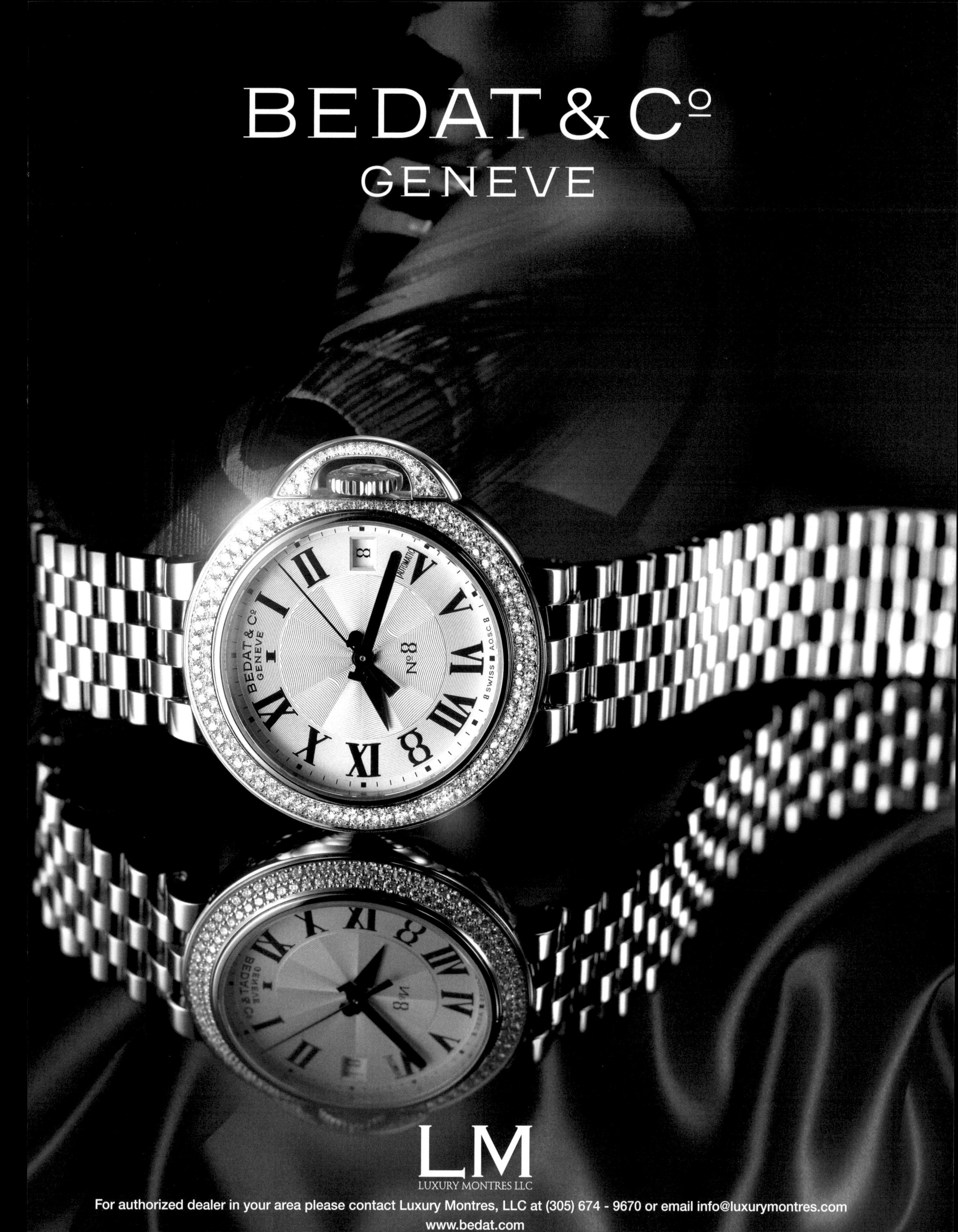
BEDAT & Cº
GENEVE
LM
LUXURY MONTRES LLC
For authorized dealer in your area please contact Luxury Montres, LLC at (305) 674 - 9670 or email info@luxurymontres.com
www.bedat.com

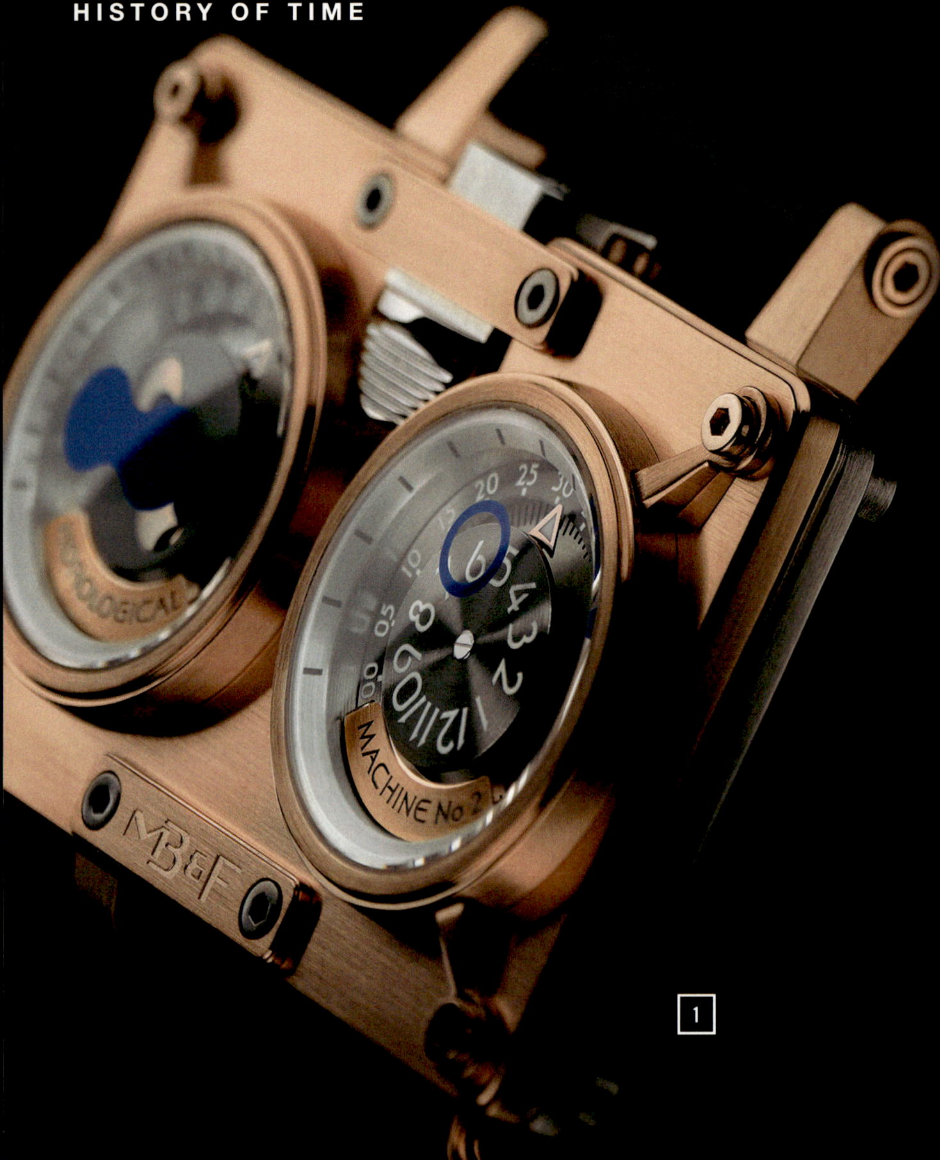

1

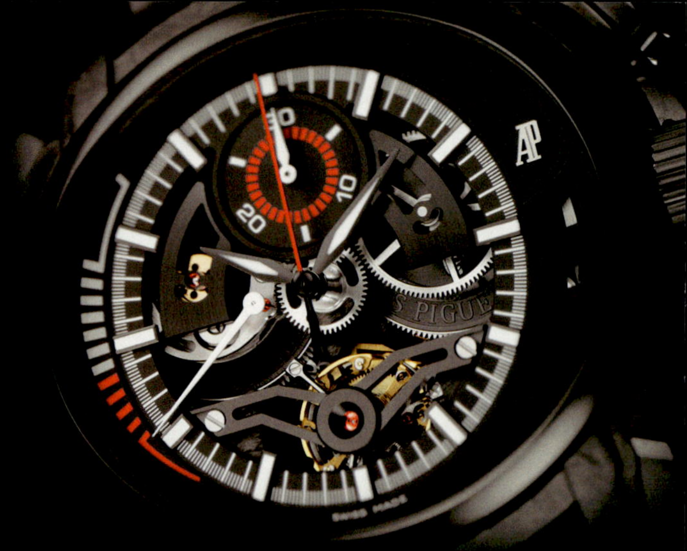

2

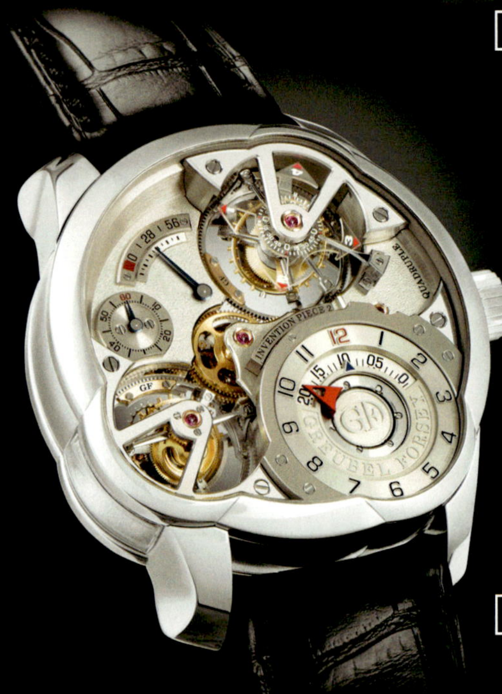

3

In this respect, while making no attempt to provide an exhaustive account, the list of impressive accomplishments must necessarily include the Hybris Mechanica watch trilogy by Jaeger-LeCoultre, which brings together 55 different functions; the Freak by Ulysse Nardin, one of the first watches to run without lubricants thanks to silicon-based technologies; the Métiers d'Art Les Masques collection from Vacheron Constantin featuring masterpieces of engraving work; the mastery of forged carbon developed by Audemars Piguet; the TAG Heuer concept watches including the recent Pendulum, the first timepiece to replace the balance-spring with magnetic fields; the first one-minute karussel wristwatch ever made, introduced by Blancpain; the Horological Machines by MB&F, which are revolutionizing horological architecture; the Greubel Forsey collections stemming from intensive research into tourbillon technology; the 1200P self-winding movement by Piaget, the thinnest in its category at just 2.35mm thick; along with the T-Touch by Tissot, the first ever tactile watch; and of course the countless interpretations of the Swatch, the now legendary watch stemming from avant-garde technology and without which the Swiss watch industry would doubtless not be what it now is.

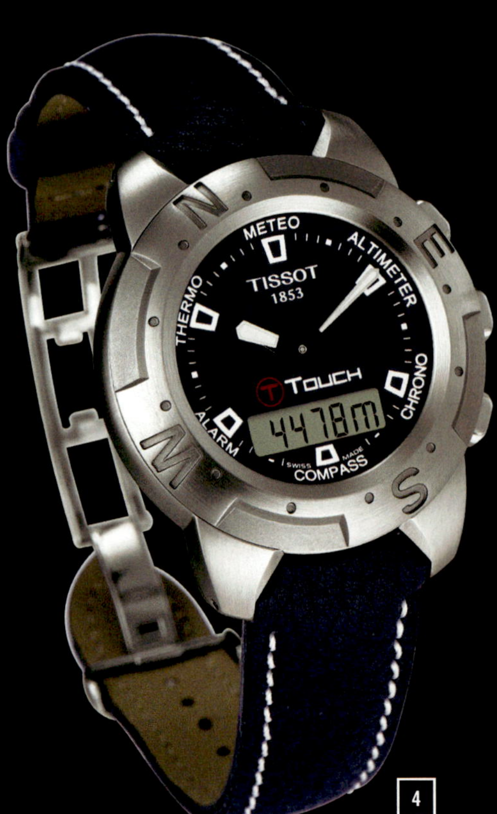

4

1. Horological Machine Nº 2 (MB&F)
2. Millenary Carbon One (Audemars Piguet)
3. Quadruple Tourbillon Edition IP2 (Greubel Forsey)
4. T-Touch (Tissot)

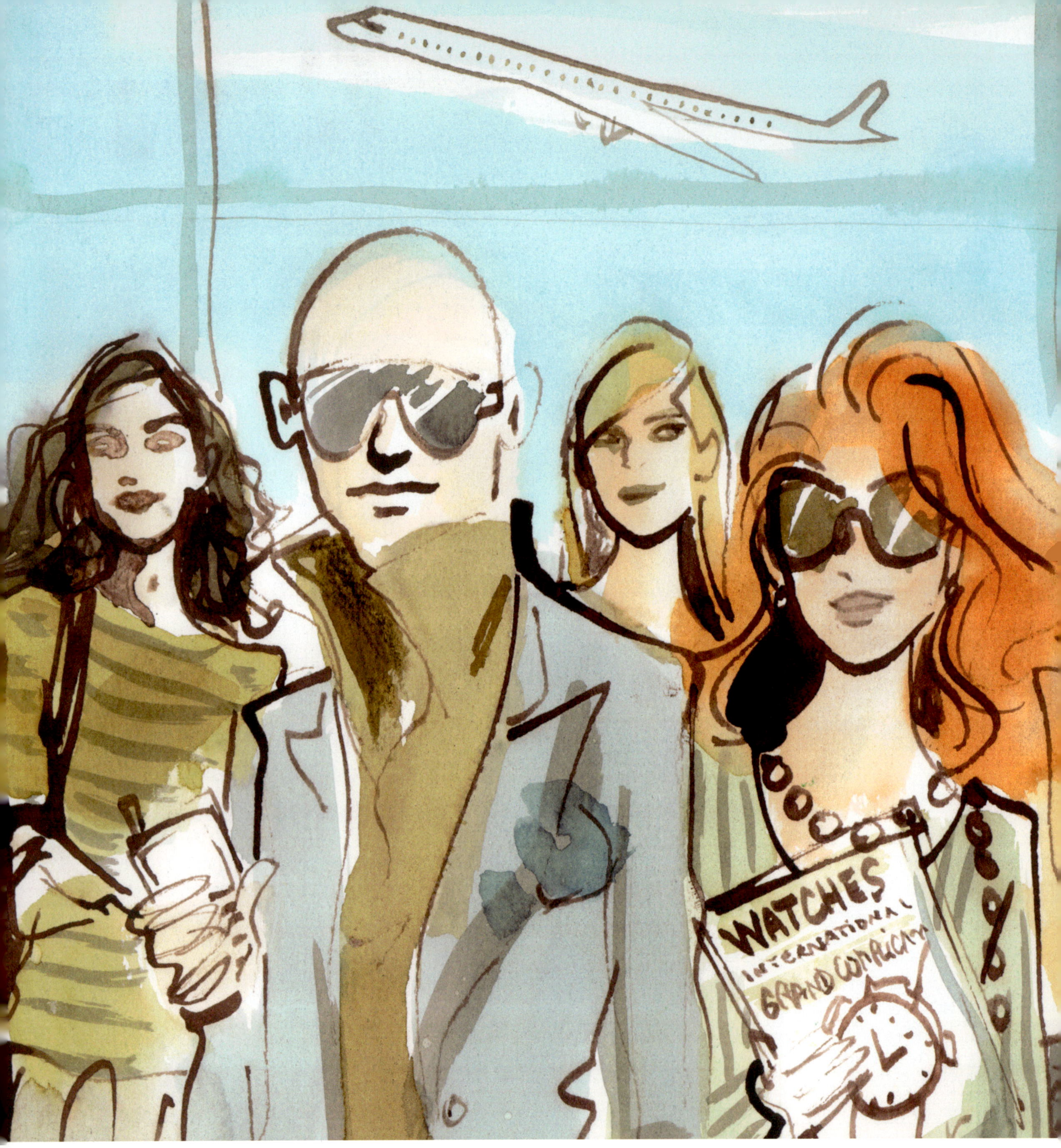
WATCHES
INTERNATIONAL

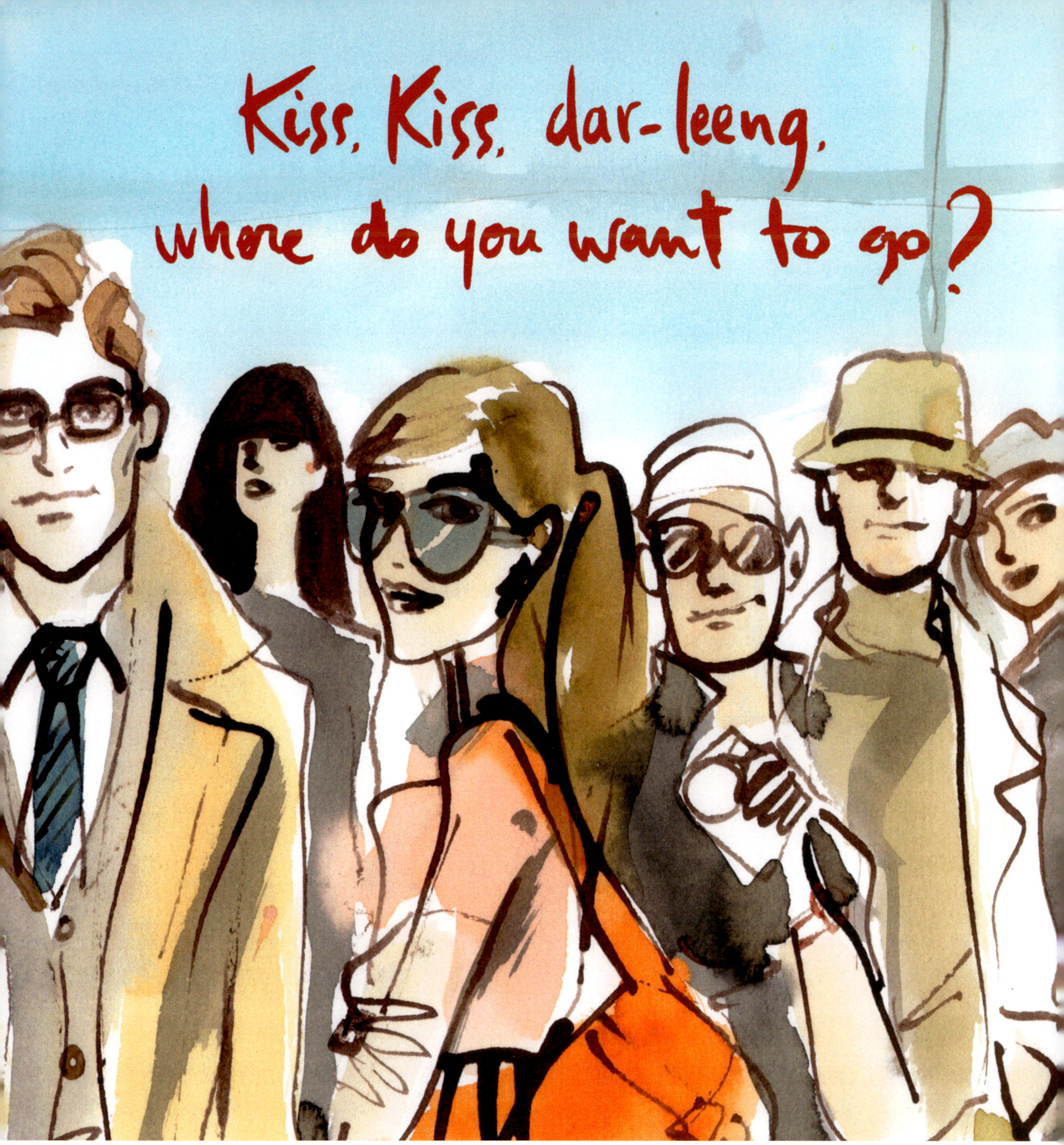

the Frenchway travel | we do it... with passion

A. LANGE & SÖHNE
GLASHÜTTE I/SA

THE SOUND OF PROGRESS

A. Lange & Söhne became the first non-Swiss brand to earn L'Aiguille d'Or when the German watchmaker won the coveted award in 2009 for its Zeitwerk at the annual Grand Prix d'Horlogerie de Genève.

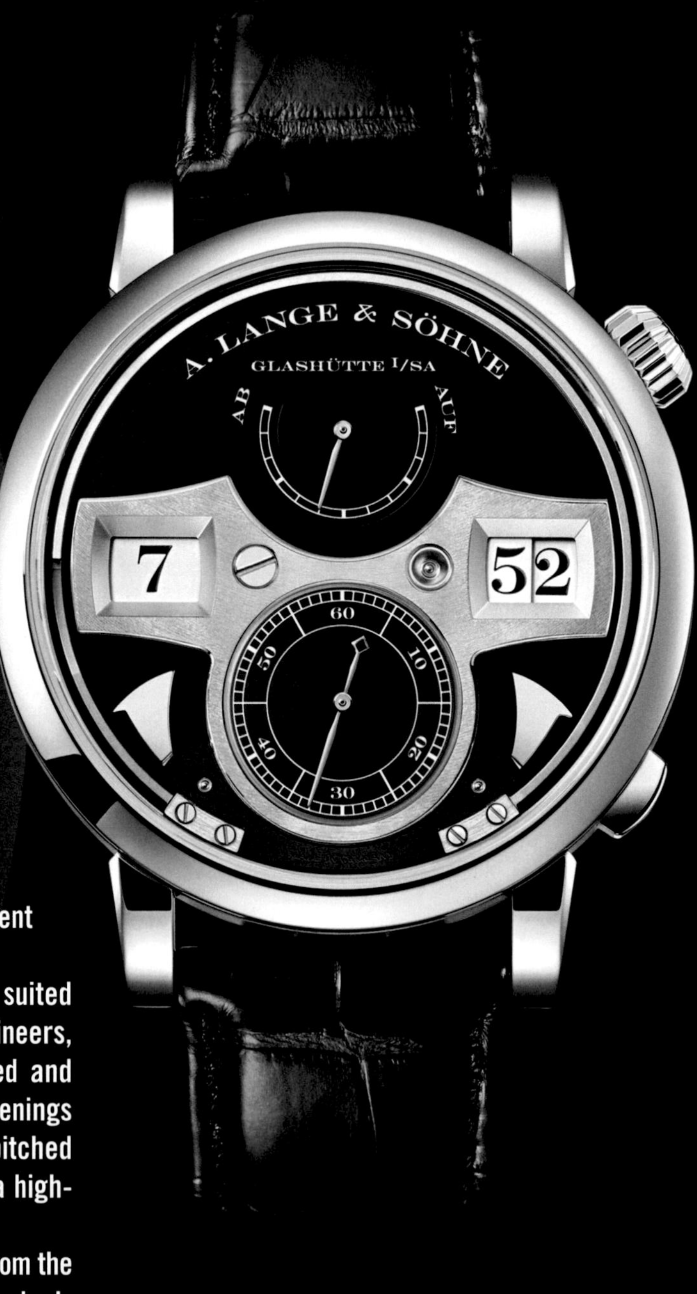

The mechanical model's novel design, which features both jumping hours and minutes, breaks ground once again in 2011 as the Glashütte-based firm unveils its first-ever chiming movement in the Zeitwerk Striking Time.

As it happens, the movement in the original Zeitwerk is well suited to incorporate a striking mechanism. According to the brand engineers, the jumping displays generate excess energy that is recovered and then used by two black hammers that are visible through openings on the dial. The hammer on the left strikes the hours on a low-pitched gong, while the hammer opposite strikes the quarter-hours on a high-pitched gong.

The Striking Time retains the visually captivating digital display from the award-winning Zeitwerk, which is governed by Lange's patented constant-force escapement. The latest incarnation, however, comes in a larger case, which has expanded from 41.9mm to 44.2mm and now includes a silencer button integrated on the case middle.

The Zeitwerk Striking Time's manufacture movement, generously decorated according to the highest standards of tradition, comes in a white-gold case with a black dial, or as a limited edition platinum version offered in a numbered series of 100 pieces.

With its resounding tone, the Striking Time rings out like a clarion call guiding Lange's bold charge into the future.

The first-ever repeater offered by Lange, the Zeitwerk Striking Time audibly indicates the quarter-hours and hours with hammers that can be seen at work through the solid silver dial.

Part of Lange's elite Pour le Mérite collection, the Richard Lange Tourbillon features separate displays for the minutes, hours and seconds. The section between 8 and 10 o'clock on the hour's chapter ring pivots into place when needed and is hidden the rest of the time.

A. Lange & Söhne vividly demonstrates its unerring command over watchmaking's rich past and bright future with the debuts of the Richard Lange Tourbillon Pour le Mérite and Zeitwerk Striking Time.

A. Lange & Söhne's Pour le Mérite collection takes its name from a civilian order founded in 1842 that recognized individuals for significant achievements in the arts and sciences. Drawing on the reputation of the order, the watches granted membership to the ranks of this select group represent some of the firm's greatest achievements.

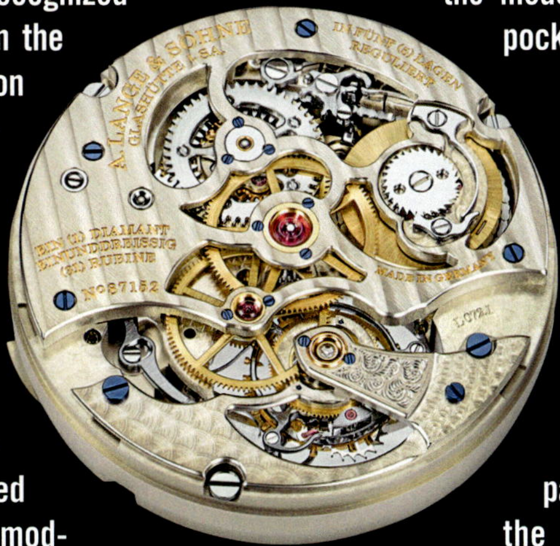

Launched in 1994, the Pour le Mérite collection is restricted to timepieces that feature Lange's modern version of the classic fusée-and-chain transmission system. In the past, Lange has awarded this prestigious distinction to only three models: the Tourbillon, Tourbograph and Richard Lange. Issued in limited numbers, each model has become prized by collectors.

Given that, it's easy to understand why Lange's announcement that it would welcome a fourth member to the Pour le Mérite collection in 2011 generated such excitement among horolophiles. The Richard Lange Tourbillon Pour le Mérite represents the latest addition to this elite circle.

Inspiration for the watch is tied to Johann Heinrich Seyffert, a noted German watchmaker of the early 19th century whose chronometers were valued for their high degree of precision. The Richard Lange Tourbillon Pour le Mérite re-imagines for the modern age an exceptional regulator-style pocket watch that Seyffert created in 1807.

The decentralized minutes, hours and seconds are displayed as intersecting circles on the solid silver dial. In particular, the attention to detail revealed by the seconds display elevates the watch to a rarefied level of horological refinement. Its open-worked design offers a view of the tourbillon oscillating below that is partially obscured by a small section of the hour display. To remedy this, Lange created a mechanical solution that pivots the overlapping section into place only when it is needed to indicate the hours between 8 and 10 o'clock. At other times, the section is tucked away out of sight, allowing a clear look at the tourbillon.

With this fascinating twist, the Richard Lange Tourbillon Pour le Mérite proves it is worthy of the noble company it keeps.

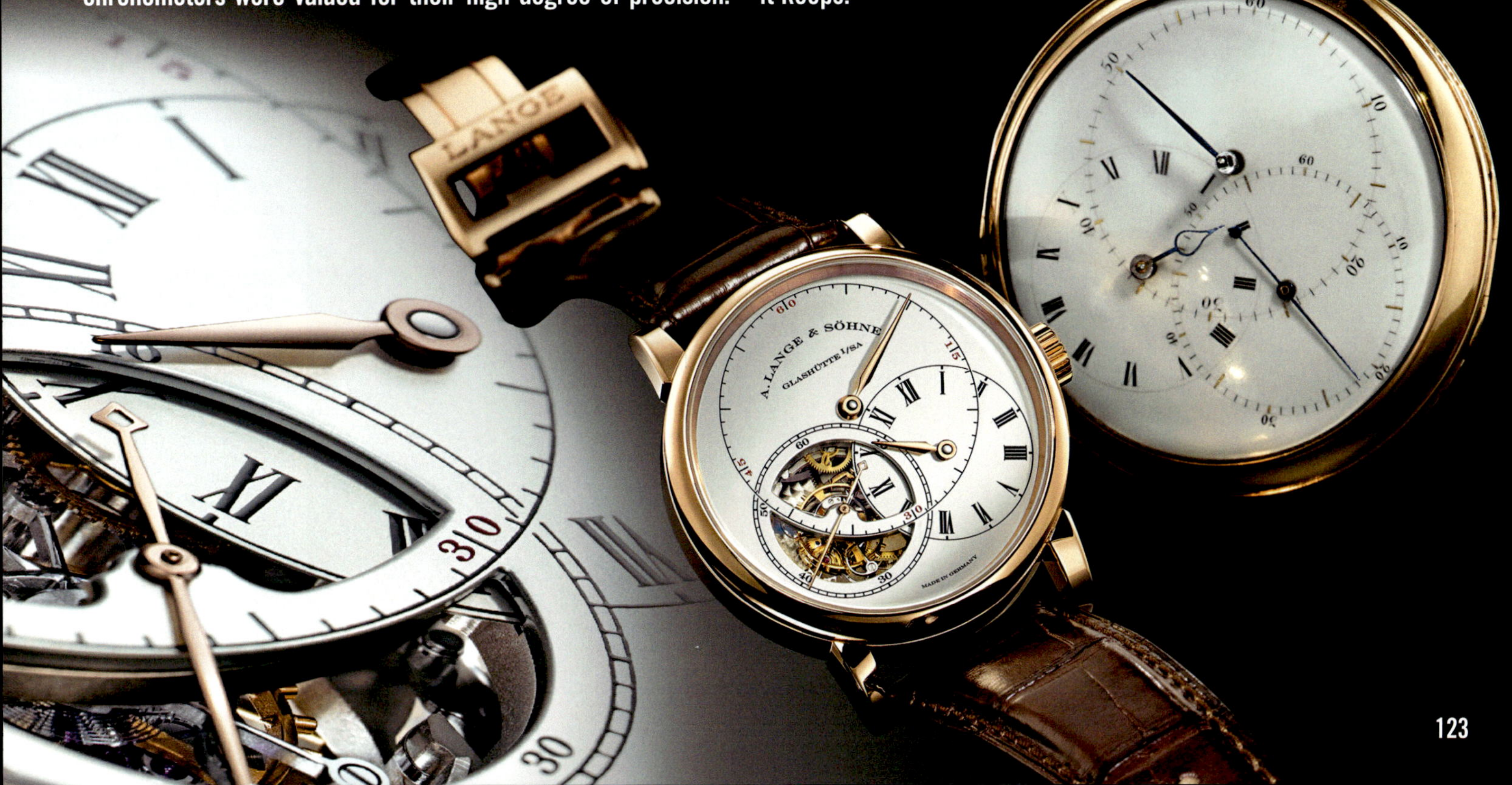

1815 — REF. 233.026

Movement: manual-winding Lange L051.1 caliber; 55-hour power reserve; 21 jewels; 21,600 vph; 188 components; decorated and assembled by hand; precision-adjusted in five positions; three-quarter plate made of untreated German silver; balance cock engraved by hand; five screwed gold chatons; shock-resistant Glucydur screw balance; Nivarox balance spring; whiplash precision index adjuster with patented beat adjustment mechanism.

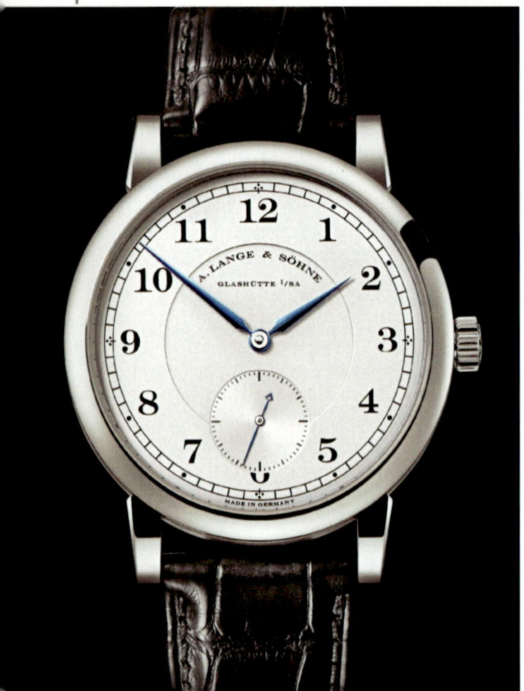

Functions: hours, minutes; small seconds.
Case: white gold; Ø 40mm, thickness: 8.9mm; crown for winding the watch and setting the time; sapphire crystal caseback.
Dial: solid silver; blued steel hands.
Strap: black crocodile; solid gold Lange prong buckle.
Also available: other dial and case combinations.

DATOGRAPH — REF. 403.032

Movement: manual-winding Lange L951.1 caliber; 36-hour power reserve; 40 jewels; 18,000 vph; 405 components; decorated and assembled by hand; precision-adjusted in five positions; plates and bridges made of untreated German silver; balance cock engraved by hand; four screwed gold chatons; shock-resistant Glucydur screw balance; Nivarox 1 hairspring; whiplash precision index adjuster with patented beat adjustment mechanism.

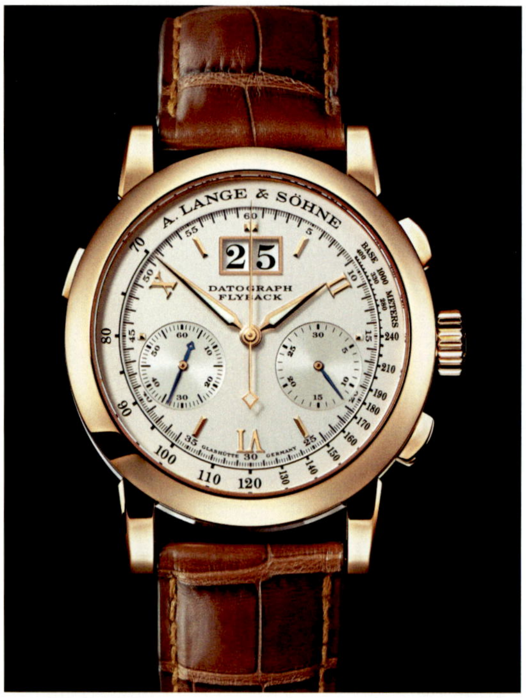

Functions: hours, minutes; small seconds with stop seconds; large date; chronograph: 30-minute counter, flyback and precisely jumping minutes counter.
Case: pink gold; Ø 39mm; crown for winding the watch and setting the time; two pushpieces for chronograph; one pushpiece for rapid correction of the outsize date; antireflective sapphire crystal caseback.
Dial: solid silver and black; pink-gold hands.
Strap: hand-stitched crocodile; solid pink-gold Lange prong buckle.
Also available: other dial and case combinations.

LANGE 1 — REF. 101.021

Movement: manual-winding Lange L901.0 caliber; 72-hour power reserve; 53 jewels; 21,600 vph; 365 components; decorated and assembled by hand; precision-adjusted in five positions; twin mainspring barrels; patented two-disc large date mechanism; stop seconds mechanism; three-quarter plate made of cross-laminated untreated German silver, damascened with Glashütte ribbing; balance cock engraved by hand; screwed gold chatons; shock-resistant Glucydur screw balance; Nivarox 1 balance spring; whiplash precision index adjuster with patented beat adjustment mechanism.

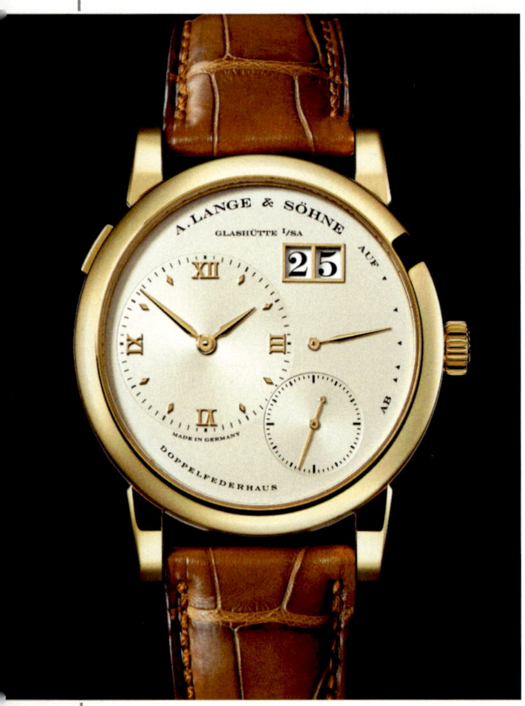

Functions: hours, minutes; small seconds with stop seconds.
Case: 18K yellow gold; Ø 38.5mm, thickness: 10mm; antireflective sapphire crystal caseback.
Dial: solid silver and champagne; yellow-gold hands.
Strap: hand-stitched crocodile; 18K yellow-gold Lange prong buckle.
Also available: other dial and case combinations.

LANGE 1 DAYMATIC — REF. 320.025

Movement: automatic-winding Lange L021.1 caliber; 50-hour power reserve; 67 jewels; 21,600 vph; 426 components; decorated and assembled by hand; precision-adjusted in five positions; central rotor with centrifugal mass in platinum; balance cock engraved by hand; seven screwed gold chatons; shock-resistant Glucydur balance with eccentric poising weights; superior quality balance spring manufactured in-house; whiplash precision index adjuster with patented beat adjustment mechanism.

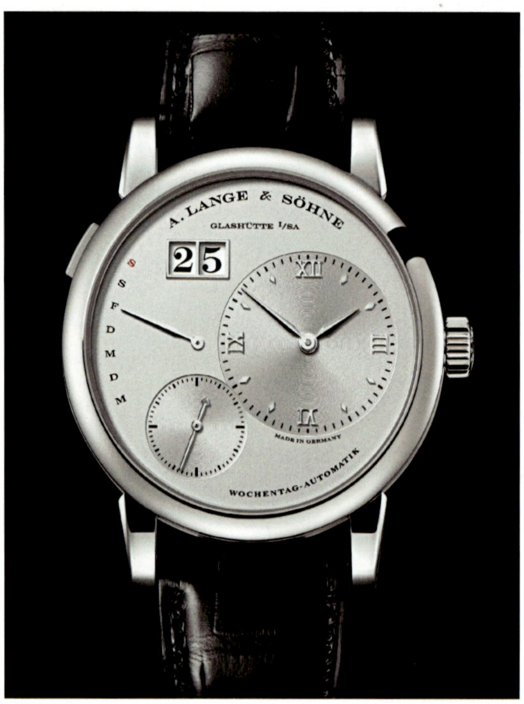

Functions: hours, minutes; small seconds with stop seconds; patented large date; retrograde display.
Case: white gold; Ø 39.5mm, thickness: 10.4mm; crown for winding the watch and setting the time; pushpieces for correcting the date and day displays; sapphire crystal caseback.
Dial: solid silver and argenté; white-gold hands.
Strap: hand-stitched crocodile; solid white-gold Lange prong buckle.
Also available: other dial and case combinations.

LANGE 1 TIME ZONE — REF. 116.032

Movement: manual-winding Lange L031.1 caliber; 72-hour power reserve; 54 jewels; 21,600 vph; 417 components; decorated and assembled by hand; precision-adjusted in five positions; twin mainspring barrel; plates and bridges made of untreated German silver; balance cock and intermediate-wheel cock engraved by hand; four screwed gold chatons; shock-resistant Glucydur screw balance; Nivarox balance spring; whiplash precision index adjuster with patented beat adjustment mechanism.
Functions: hours, minutes, small seconds with stop seconds; large date; home time; separate day/night indicators for main and second time zones with city ring.
Case: rose gold; Ø 41.9mm, thickness: 11mm; crown for winding the watch and setting the time; pushpiece for switching the large date; pushpiece for advancing the city ring; synchronized with the hour hand of the time zone display and the day/night indicator for time zone; antireflective sapphire crystal caseback.
Dial: solid silver and rhodié; blued-steel hands.
Strap: hand-stitched crocodile; rose-gold Lange prong buckle.
Also available: other dial and case combinations.

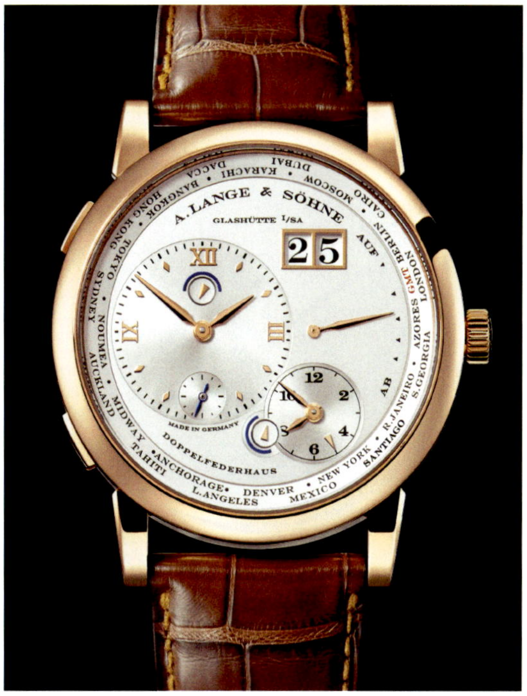

SAXONIA ANNUAL CALENDAR — REF. 330.026

Movement: automatic-winding Lange L085.1 SAX-0-MAT caliber; 46-hour power reserve; 43 jewels; 21,600 vph; 476 components; decorated and assembled by hand; precision-adjusted in five positions; three-quarter plate made of untreated German silver with integrated three-quarter rotor in 21K gold and centrifugal mass in platinum; reversing and reduction gear with four ball bearings; balance cock engraved by hand; shock-resistant Glucydur screw balance; Nivarox balance spring; whiplash precision index adjuster with patented beat adjustment mechanism.
Functions: hours, minutes; small seconds with stop seconds; zero-reset function; large date; annual calendar; day; month; moonphase.
Case: white gold; Ø 38.5mm, thickness: 9.8mm; crown for winding the watch and setting the time; sapphire crystal caseback.
Dial: solid silver and argenté; blued-steel hands.
Strap: hand-stitched crocodile; solid white-gold Lange prong buckle.
Also available: other dial and case combinations.

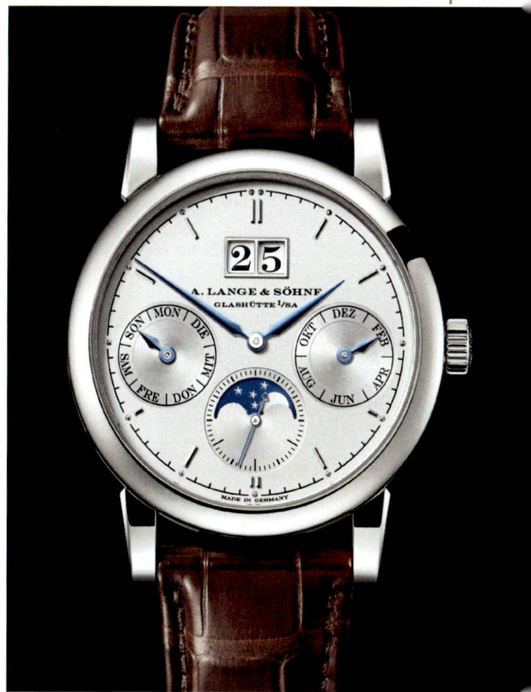

LANGE ZEITWERK — REF. 140.029

Movement: manual-winding Lange L043.1 caliber; 36-hour power reserve; 66 jewels; 18,000 vph; 388 components; decorated and assembled by hand; precision-adjusted in five positions; three-quarter plate made of untreated German silver; balance cock engraved by hand; constant-force escapement; shock-resistant Glucydur balance with eccentric poising weights; superior-quality balance spring manufactured in-house with patent-pending attachment system (balance spring clamp); whiplash precision index adjuster with patented beat adjustment mechanism.
Functions: jumping hours and minutes; small seconds with stop seconds.
Case: white gold; Ø 41.9mm, thickness: 12.6mm; crown for winding the watch and setting the time; sapphire crystal caseback.
Dial: solid silver and black; rhodium-gold hands; German silver and rhodium time bridge.
Strap: hand-stitched crocodile; solid white-gold Lange prong buckle.
Also available: other dial and case combinations.

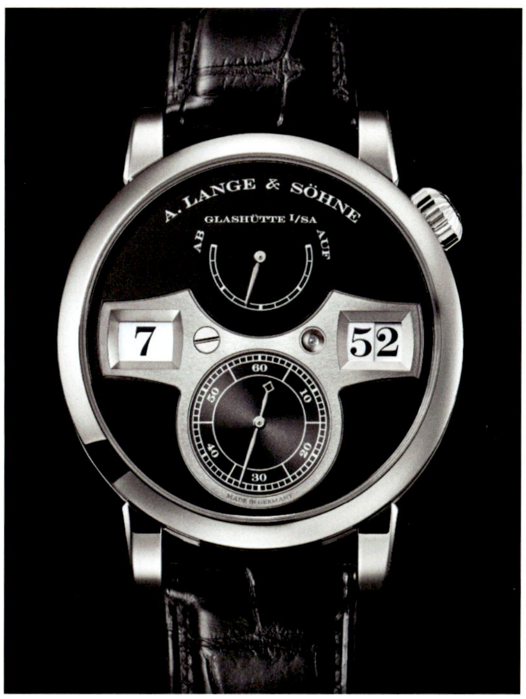

A. LANGE GRAND 1 "LUMINOUS" — REF. 115.028

Movement: manual-winding Lange L901.2 caliber; 72-hour power reserve; Ø 30.4mm, thickness: 5.9mm; 53 jewels; 21,600 vph; 365 components; decorated and assembled by hand; twin barrel.
Functions: hours, minutes; small seconds with stop seconds; large date; power reserve indicator.
Case: 18K white gold; Ø 41.9mm, thickness: 11mm; antireflective bezel with sapphire crystal; antireflective sapphire crystal caseback; water resistant to 3atm.
Dial: solid silver with SuperLumiNova; gold-coated hands with SuperLumiNova; pushpiece date corrector at 10.
Strap: black alligator with gray stitching; 18K white-gold Lange prong buckle.
Also available: other dial and case combinations.

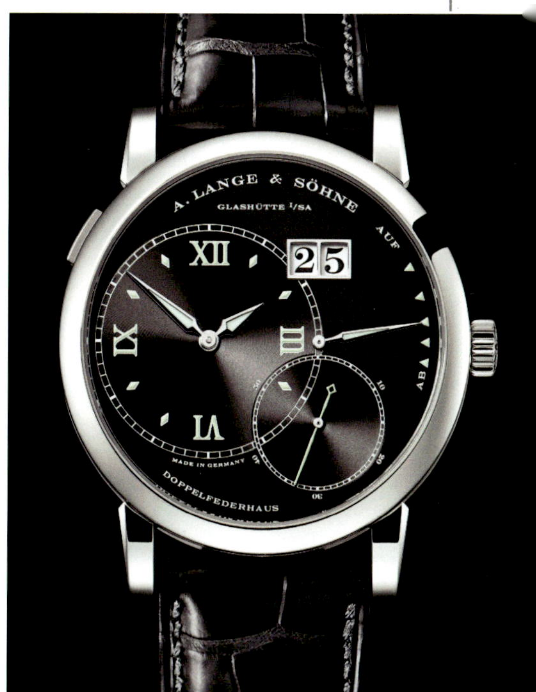

LANGE ZEITWERK "LUMINOUS" REF. 140.035

Movement: manual-winding Lange L043.1 caliber; 36-hour power reserve; Ø 33.6mm, thickness: 9.3mm; 68 jewels; 18,000 vph; 388 components; decorated and assembled by hand; precision-adjusted in five positions; three-quarter plate made of untreated German silver; balance cock engraved by hand; constant-force escapement; shock-resistant Glucydur balance with eccentric poising weights; superior-quality balance spring manufactured in-house with patent-pending attachment system (balance spring clamp); whiplash precision index adjuster with patented beat adjustment mechanism.
Functions: jumping hours and minutes; small seconds with stop seconds.
Case: platinum; Ø 41.9mm, thickness: 12.6mm; crown for winding the watch and setting the time; sapphire crystal caseback.
Dial: coated sapphire crystal; luminous numerals; German silver, PVD-coated time bridge; rhodium-gold hands.
Strap: black hand-stitched crocodile; solid platinum Lange prong buckle.
Note: limited to 100 pieces.
Also available: other dial and case combinations.

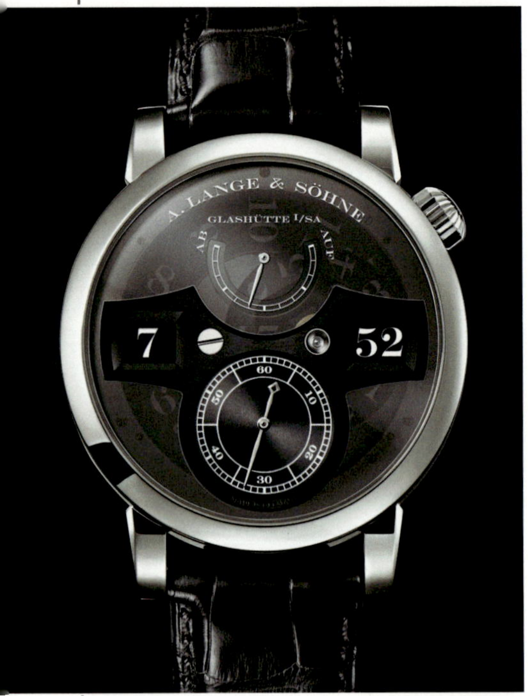

1815 CHRONOGRAPH REF. 402.032

Movement: manual-winding Lange L951.5 caliber; 60-hour power reserve; 40 jewels; 18,000 vph; 306 components.
Functions: hours, minutes; small seconds with stop seconds; chronograph: flyback, jumping minutes and 30-minute counter.
Case: 18K pink gold; Ø 39.5mm, thickness: 10.85mm; antireflective sapphire crystal bezel; antireflective sapphire crystal caseback; water resistant to 3atm.
Dial: solid silver and black; blued-steel hands; chronograph pushpiece at 2 and 4.
Strap: brown hand-stitched crocodile; solid pink-gold Lange prong buckle.
Also available: other dial and case combinations.

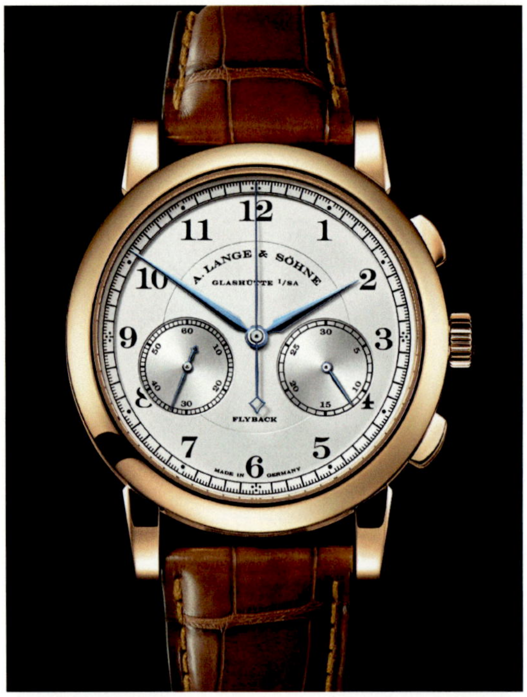

DOUBLE SPLIT REF. 404.032

Movement: manual-winding Lange L001.1 caliber; Ø 30.6mm, thickness: 9.45mm; 38-hour power reserve; 40 jewels; 21,600 vph; 465 components.
Functions: hours, minutes; small seconds with stop seconds; chronograph: jumping minutes counter; 30-minute rattrapante flyback; power reserve indicator.
Case: 18K pink gold; Ø 43.2mm, thickness: 15.3mm; antireflective sapphire crystal bezel; antireflective sapphire crystal caseback; water resistant to 3atm.
Dial: solid silver, chronograph pushpiece at 2 and 4; date pushpiece at 10; two silvered base and black subsidiary dials; applied 18K 4N pink-gold Roman numerals; luminous tachometer scale at 3, 9 and 12; 18K 4N pink-gold hour, minute, seconds, power reserve and chronograph hands with SuperLumiNova; blued steel chronograph rattrapante hands with SuperLumiNova.
Strap: reddish-brown hand-stitched alligator; 18K 5N pink-gold Lange prong buckle.

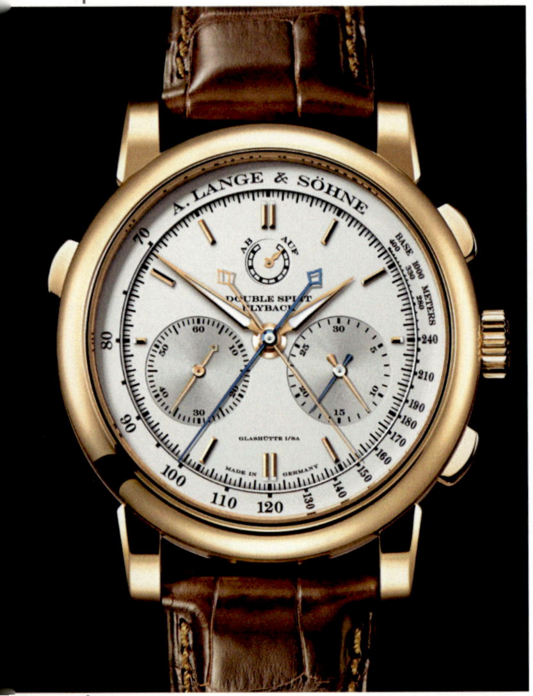

RICHARD LANGE REF. 232.025

Movement: manual-winding Lange L041.2 caliber; 38-hour power reserve; 26 jewels; 21,600 vph; 199 components; decorated and assembled by hand; precision-adjusted in five positions; plates and bridges made of untreated German silver; balance cock engraved by hand; shock-resistant Glucydur balance with off-center poising weights; superior-quality balance spring manufactured in-house with patent-pending attachment system (balance spring clamp); whiplash precision index adjuster with patented beat adjustment mechanism.
Functions: hours, minutes; sweep seconds.
Case: platinum; Ø 40.5mm, thickness: 11mm; antireflective sapphire crystal caseback.
Dial: solid silver; rhodium-gold hands; blued-steel seconds hand.
Strap: hand-stitched black crocodile with precious metal; platinum Lange prong buckle.
Also available: other dial and case combinations.

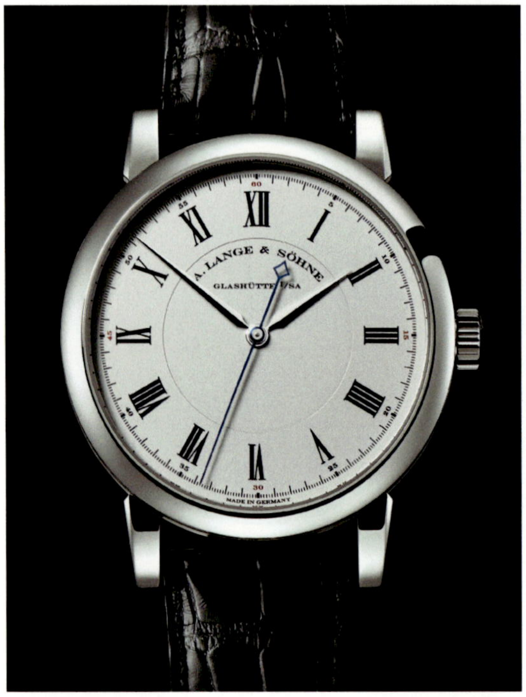

SAXONIA AUTOMATIK REF. 380.026

Movement: automatic-winding Lange L086.1 caliber; 72-hour power reserve; Ø 30.4mm, thickness: 3.7mm; 31 jewels; 21,600 vph; 209 components; decorated and assembled by hand; precision-adjusted in five positions; plate made of untreated German silver; balance cock engraved by hand; shock-resistant Glucydur screw balance; superior-quality balance spring manufactured in-house; whiplash precision index adjuster with patented beat adjustment mechanism.
Functions: hours, minutes; subsidary seconds with stop seconds.
Case: white gold; Ø 38.5mm, thickness: 7.8mm; crown for winding the watch and setting the time; sapphire crystal caseback.
Dial: solid silver, argenté; rhodium-gold hand.
Strap: black hand-stitched crocodile; white-gold Lange prong buckle.
Also available: pink-gold case with chestnut crocodile strap (ref. 380.032).

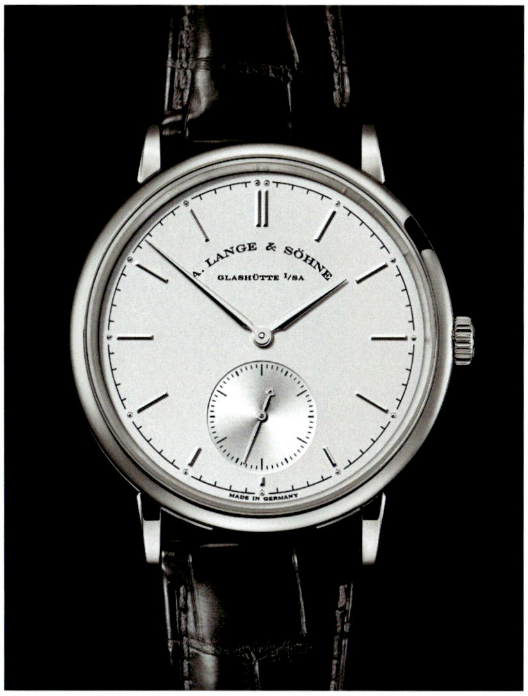

RICHARD LANGE TOURBILLON "POUR LE MÉRITE" REF. 760.032

Movement: manual-winding Lange L072.1 caliber; 36-hour power reserve; Ø 33.6mm, thickness: 7.6mm; 32 jewels; 21,600 vph; 351 components; fusée-and chain transmission; decorated and assembled by hand; precision-adjusted in five positions; three-quarter plate made of untreated German silver; fourth-wheel bridge engraved by hand; shock-resistant Glucydur screw balance with eccentric poising weights; superior-quality balance spring manufactured in-house with patent-pending attachment system (balance spring clamp); whiplash precision index adjuster with patented beat adjustment mechanism.
Functions: hours, minutes; subsidary seconds; one-minute tourbillon with patented stop seconds; pivoting dial segment.
Case: pink gold; Ø 41.9mm, thickness: 12.2mm; crown for winding the watch and setting the time; sapphire crystal caseback.
Dial: solid silver, argenté; pink-gold seconds hand; blued-steel hands.
Strap: red-brown hand-stitched crocodile; solid pink-gold Lange prong buckle.

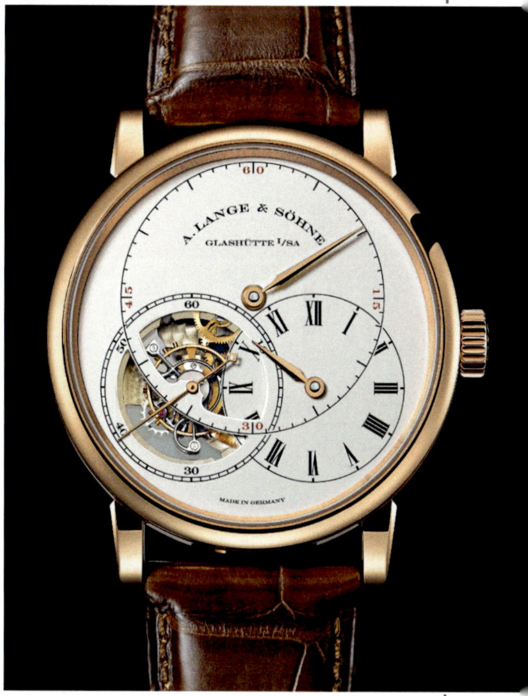

LANGE ZEITWERK STRIKING TIME REF. 145.029

Movement: manual-winding Lange L043.2 caliber; 36-hour power reserve; Ø 36mm, thickness: 10mm; 78 jewels; 18,000 vph; 528 components; decorated and assembled by hand; precision-adjusted in five positions; three-quarter plate made of untreated German silver; balance cock engraved by hand; shock-resistant Glucydur screw balance with eccentric poising weights; superior-quality balance spring manufactured in-house with patent-pending attachment system (balance spring clamp); whiplash precision index adjuster with patented beat adjustment mechanism.
Functions: jumping hours and minutes; subsidary seconds with stop seconds; power reserve indicator; acoustic signal at quarter-hours and full hours.
Case: white gold; Ø 44.2mm, thickness: 13.8mm; crown for winding the watch and setting the time; pushpiece for enabling and disabling the acoustic signal; sapphire crystal caseback.
Dial: solid silver and black; German silver and rhodium time bridge; rhodium-gold hand.
Strap: black hand-stitched crocodile; white-gold Lange prong buckle.
Also available: platinum case (ref. 145.025).

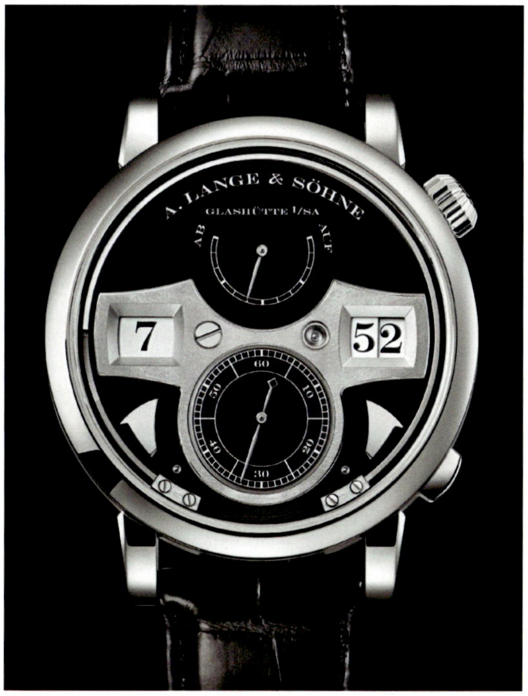

SAXONIA DUAL TIME REF. 385.026

Movement: automatic-winding Lange L086.2 caliber; 72-hour power reserve; Ø 30.4mm, thickness: 4.6mm; 31 jewels; 21,600 vph; 268 components; decorated and assembled by hand; precision-adjusted in five positions; plate made of untreated German silver; balance cock engraved by hand; shock-resistant Glucydur screw balance; superior-quality balance spring manufactured in-house; whiplash precision index adjuster with patented beat adjustment mechanism.
Functions: hours, minutes; subsidary seconds with stop seconds; second time zone with additional hour hand; 24-hour display and day/night indication.
Case: white gold; Ø 40mm, thickness: 9.1mm; crown for winding the watch and setting the time; one push piece each for stepping the time forward and backward in one-hour increments; sapphire crystal caseback.
Dial: solid silver, argenté; rhodium-gold hands; blued steel second time zone and 24-hour hand.
Strap: black hand-stitched crocodile; white-gold Lange prong buckle.
Also available: pink-gold case with chestnut crocodile strap (ref. 385.032).

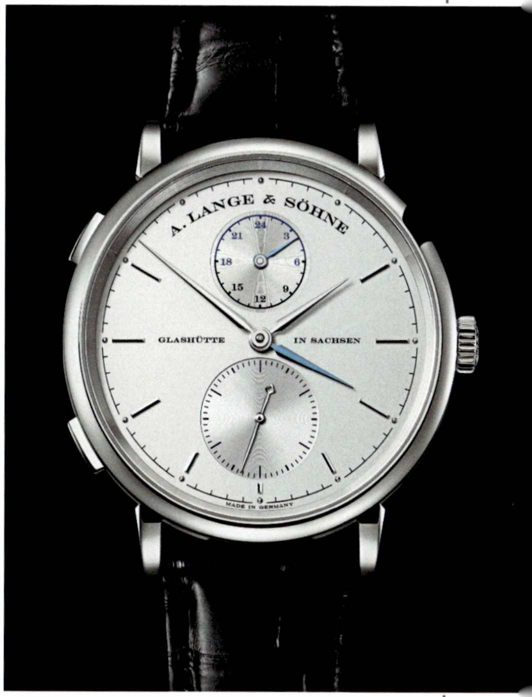

Alpina GENEVE

RACING
AHEAD OF THE PACK

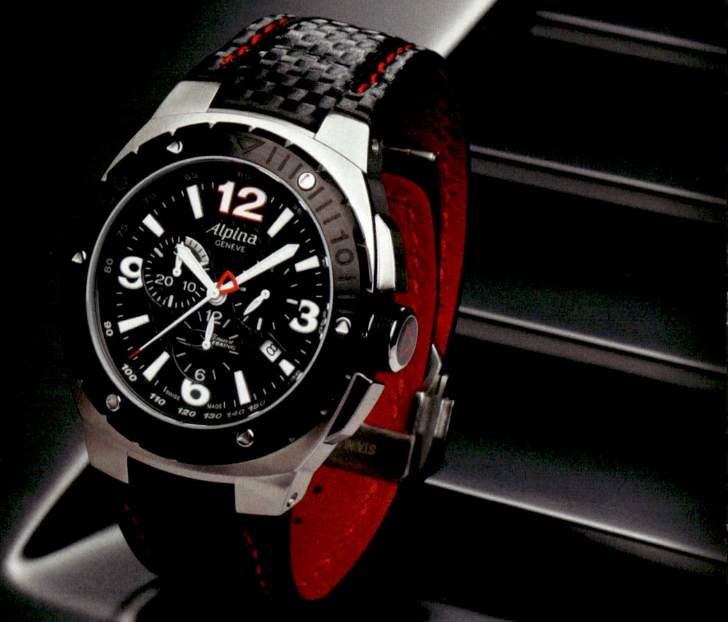

A successful independent watchmaker for more than a century, Alpina celebrated its 125-year anniversary in 2006 with the opening of a new, state-of-the-art workshop located just outside the city of Geneva.

The occasion marked the start of a new chapter in the company's rich history and signalled Alpina's intention of harnessing the brand's heritage of innovation. Indeed, its modern facility in Plan-les-Ouates enables the firm to dream, create and refine a new generation of mechanical wristwatches made entirely in-house.

Understandably, Alpina's workshop plays a key role in its success. By using the latest computer-controlled milling and drilling tools, the company's technicians are able to ensure the precision of the components the firm makes for the manufacture calibers at the heart of its finest watches.

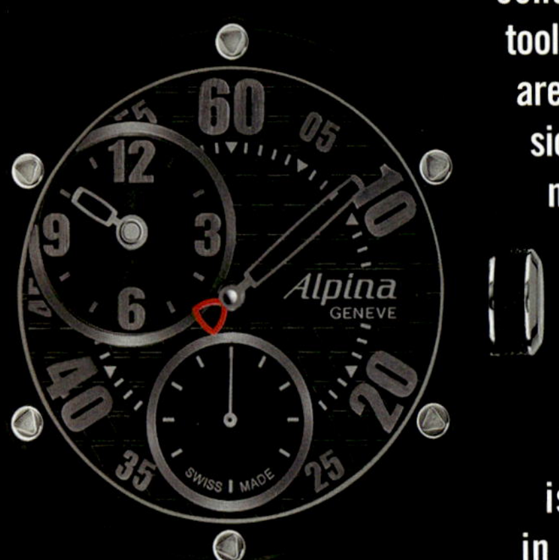

Beyond impeccable accuracy, another benefit realized by this streamlined process is a significant reduction in production costs. In turn, this allows Alpina to offer quality, Swiss-made timepieces that embody the notion of "accessible luxury."

The facility is also outfitted with machines designed specifically to test a watch's durability by subjecting it to real-life stresses like shocks and knocks. Alpina also employs the latest equipment to certify a watch's water resistance, a key characteristic of the entire collection.

This steadfast dedication to technical advancement, in tandem with rigorous quality control standards, is fuelling Alpina's ongoing global expansion. Alpina focuses this vast array of technological expertise to create three distinct collections of sports watches: Adventure, Racing and Club.

The first line projects an outgoing personality thanks to its rugged construction, which is designed to endure severe exposure to the elements. One of the most popular Adventure models, the Extreme Regulator features a classic regulator display in a bold 48mm case. The stylish Extreme Diver, meanwhile, is water resistant to an impressive 1,000 meters, making it equally at home swimming with the sharks in the ocean or the boardroom.

Alpina's Racing collection is attuned to those who demand the best from themselves and those around them. The company evokes one of the world's most arduous endurance races with its 12 Hours of Sebring. This limited edition is presented in a black, PVD-coated 47mm case equipped with an automatic chronograph movement that features a second time zone function.

Alpina imbues its growing collection of sports watches with the spirit of competition, using cutting-edge production methods and rigorous quality control standards to ensure an elite level of performance.

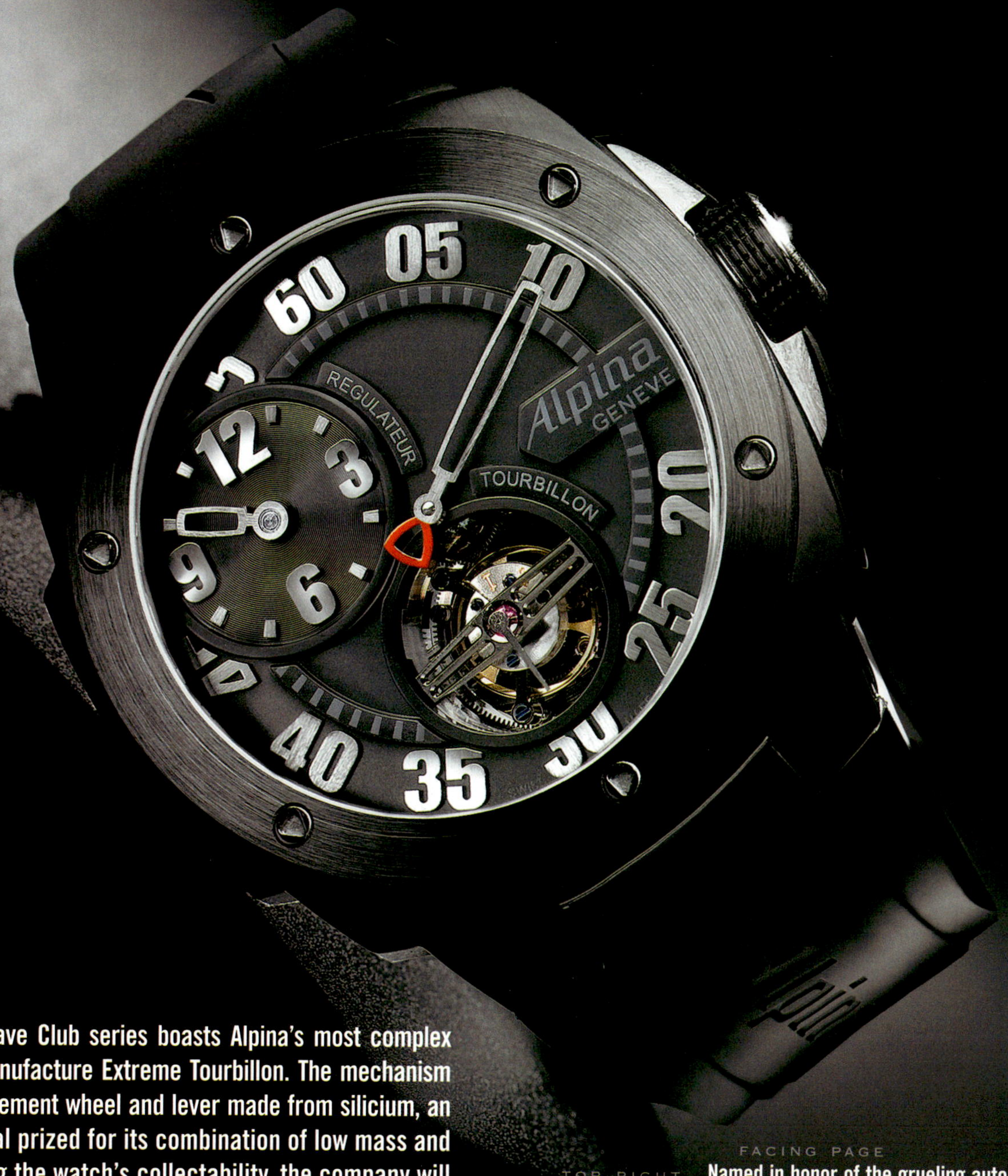

Finally, the suave Club series boasts Alpina's most complex timepiece, the Manufacture Extreme Tourbillon. The mechanism features an escapement wheel and lever made from silicium, an advanced material prized for its combination of low mass and strength. Ensuring the watch's collectability, the company will limit production to 18 pieces each in titanium, rose gold and titanium with black DLC coating.

While each line exhibits its own individual character, Alpina CEO Peter Stas says they all share a similar provocative appeal. "We design our watches for people who want to be players in their own life, and not spectators," he says. "An Alpina watch is made with passion for people who know how to live."

FACING PAGE

TOP RIGHT Named in honor of the grueling automotive endurance race, Alpina's 12 Hours of Sebring watch includes a chronograph movement enhanced with a second time zone function.

BOTTOM LEFT The Extreme Regulator depicts time using a regulator-style display and is presented in a 48mm stainless steel case fitted with a black, PVD-coated bezel.

THIS PAGE

Alpina's Manufacture Extreme Tourbillon is powered by the brand's own AL-980 automatic tourbillon movement, which possesses a silicium escapement wheel and lever.

EXTREME TOURBILLON MANUFACTURE — REF. AL-980BBT5FBAE6

Movement: automatic-winding AL-980 caliber; Tourbillon Regulator; 48-hour power reserve; 188 components; 33 jewels; 28,800 vph; Incabloc anti-shock system; Glucydur balance; Nivarox No. 1 balance spring; one-minute tourbillon; openworked cage bridges; bridges decorated with perlage and Côtes de Genève; anglage finishing; black PVD-coated rotor decorated with Côtes de Genève; silicium escapement wheel and silicium lever; movement individually numbered.

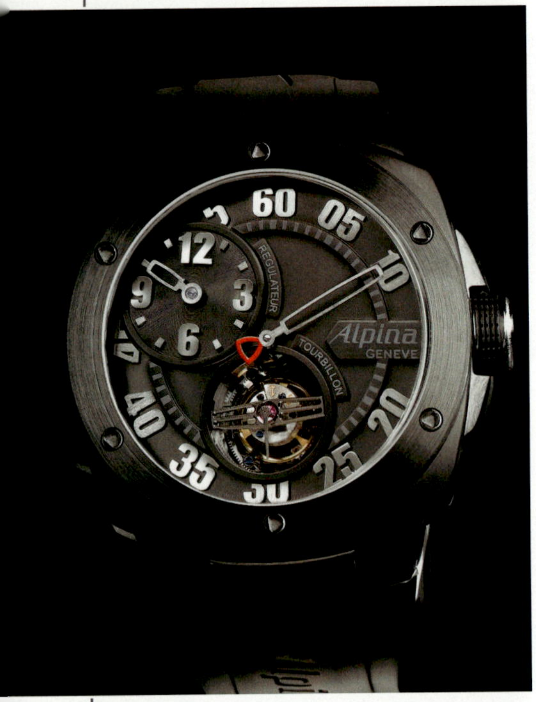

Functions: hours, minutes; subdial at 10 displaying the hour; open cage holding the tourbillon at 6.
Case: black DLC titanium; Ø 48mm; three-part case secured by 12 triangular screws; black ceramic bezel and caseback; ABS-coated screw-down crown with red Alpina triangle pattern; transparent sapphire crystal casback; each case is individually numbered; water resistant to 10atm.
Dial: black; applied fine-brushed stainless steel indexes; brushed black-steel skeleton hands.
Strap: black rubber; optional deployment buckle.
Suggested price: $47,500
Note: limited edition of 18 pieces.
Also available: rose gold.

12 HOURS OF SEBRING AUTOMATIC GMT CHRONOGRAPH — REF. AL-750LBR5FBAR6

Movement: automatic-winding AL-750 caliber; 42-hour power reserve; 28,800 vph; 26 jewels; bridges decorated with perlage; anglage finishing; black Alpina rotor decorated with Côtes de Genève.
Functions: hours, minutes, seconds; date; second time zone; world time; GMT; mechanical chronograph.
Case: black PVD-coated stainless steel; Ø 47mm; three-part case secured by six triangular stainless steel Alpina screws; fixed black PVD-coated bezel with luminescent digits; ABS-coated screw-down crown with red Alpina triangle; sapphire crystal; exhibition caseback with red engraving; water resistant to 10atm.

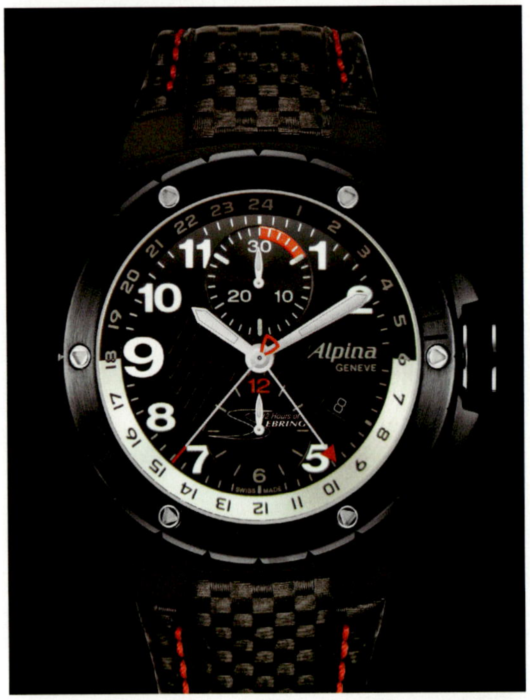

Dial: black with Alpina guilloché in the center; decorated Alpina triangle in the center; red elements and raised indexes; applied white luminescent Arabic numerals; white luminescent painted hands; black subdials for chronograph counters; exclusive 12 Hours of Sebring logo at 6.
Strap: black carbon; red lining and stitching; black PVD-coated Alpina deployment buckle.
Suggested price: $3,950
Note: limited edition of 158 pieces; delivered in exclusive gift box in black lacquered wood: black leather cover with famous Sebring Raceway-track printed on the top, red leather interior and special engravings on aluminum plaques, numbered in correspondence with the watch from 001/158 through 158/158.

12 HOURS OF SEBRING CHRONOGRAPH — REF. AL-352LBR5AR6

Movement: quartz chronograph.
Functions: hours, minutes, seconds; date; chronograph.
Case: brushed stainless steel; Ø 47mm; black PVD-coated stainless steel bezel; water resistant to 10atm.
Dial: black.
Strap: black carbon; hand-sewn red stitching.
Suggested price: $1,095
Also available: black PVD-coated stainless steel case and bezel (ref. AL-352LBR5F-BAR6).

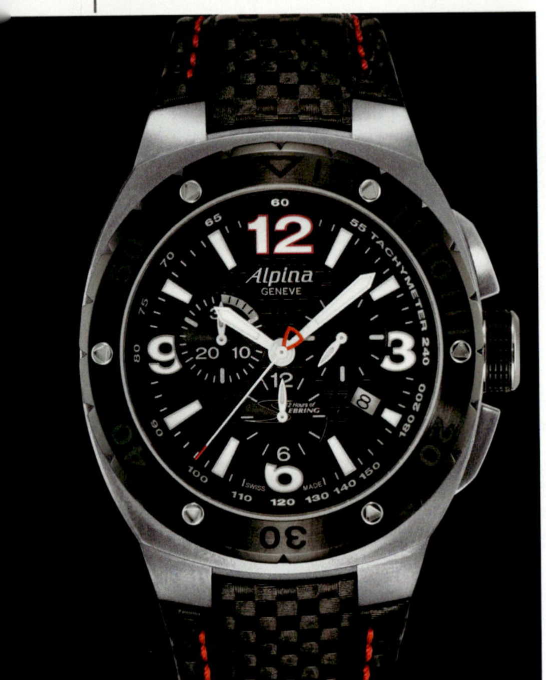

CLUB REGULATOR MANUFACTURE — REF. AL-950B4RC6

Movement: automatic-winding AL-950 caliber; Manufacture Regulator.
Functions: hours, minutes; off-set hour subdial and date visible in its own dial at 6.
Case: brushed stainless steel; Ø 44mm; water resistant to 10atm.
Dial: dark gray with Alpina guilloché in the center.
Strap: black crocodile calf.
Suggested price: $2,950

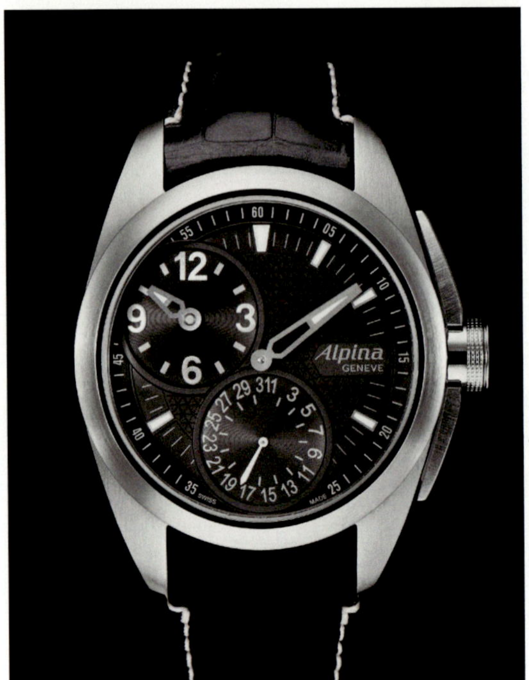

CLUB AUTOMATIC REF. AL-525B4FBRC6

Movement: automatic-winding AL-950 caliber; Manufacture Regulator.
Functions: hours, minutes, seconds; date.
Case: black PVD-coated stainless steel; Ø 44mm; ultra-hard scratch-proof sapphire crystal front and back; water resistant to 10atm.
Dial: black with Alpina guilloché in the center.
Strap: black crocodile calf.
Suggested price: $2,950
Also available: rose-gold-plated stainless steel case (ref. AL-525B4RC4).

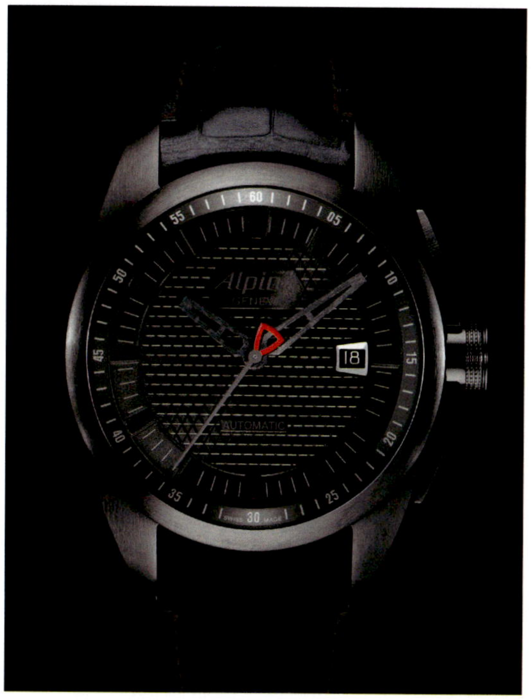

EXTREME DIVER 1000 METERS REF. AL-525LBCD5FBAEV6

Movement: automatic-winding AL-525 caliber.
Functions: hours, minutes, seconds; date; built in helium escape valve at 10.
Case: black PVD-coated stainless steel; Ø 48mm; unidirectional rotating bezel for measuring dive time; water resistant to 100atm.
Dial: black; blue luminous numerals.
Strap: rubber.
Suggested price: $3,190
Also available: black dial with orange numerals; black PVD-coated stainless steel case with black luminous numerals (ref. AL-525LFB-5FBAEV6).

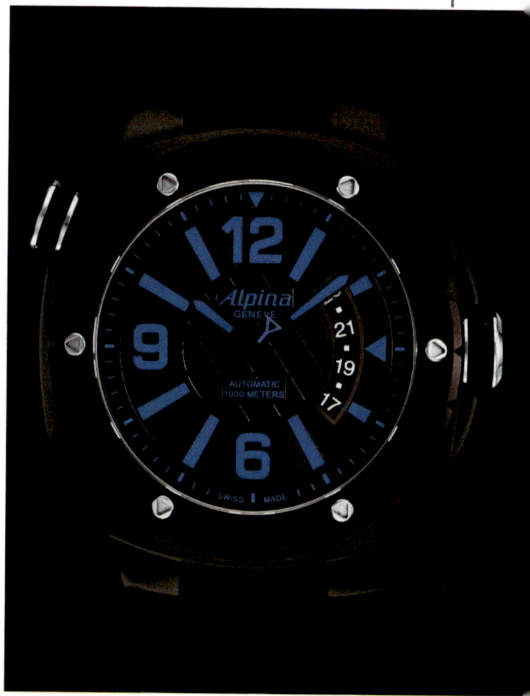

EXTREME REGULATOR REF. AL-650LBBB5FBAE6

Movement: manual-winding AL-650 caliber.
Functions: hours, minutes; off-set hour subdial; small seconds at 6.
Case: black PVD-coated stainless steel; Ø 48mm; black PVD-coated stainless steel bezel; water resistant to 10atm.
Dial: black with Alpina guilloché in the center.
Strap: rubber.
Suggested price: $2,750
Also available: rose-gold-plated stainless steel case with black PVD-coated stainless steel bezel (ref: AL-650BB5AE4).

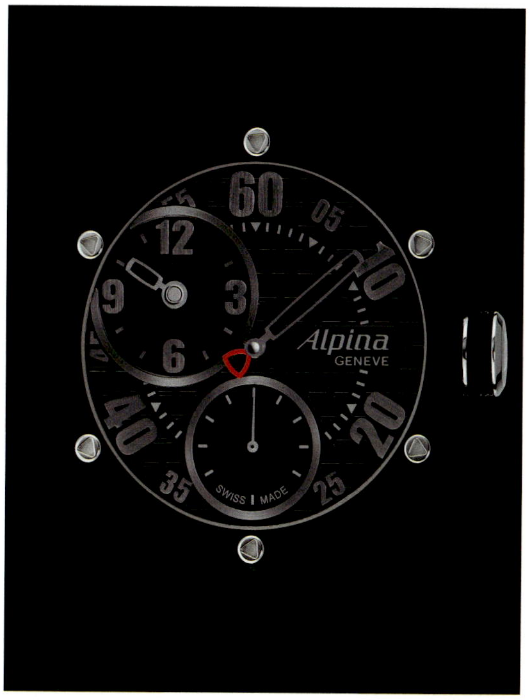

EXTREME REGULATOR FOR LADY REF. AL-650LSSS3AEDC6

Movement: automatic-winding AL-650 caliber.
Functions: hours, minutes; off-set hour subdial; small seconds at 6.
Case: white ceramic; Ø 42mm; stainless steel bezel set with diamonds.
Dial: white with Alpina guilloché in the center.
Strap: white rubber.
Suggested price: $4,950
Also available: white ceramic case with rose-gold-plated stainless steel bezel, with or without diamonds.

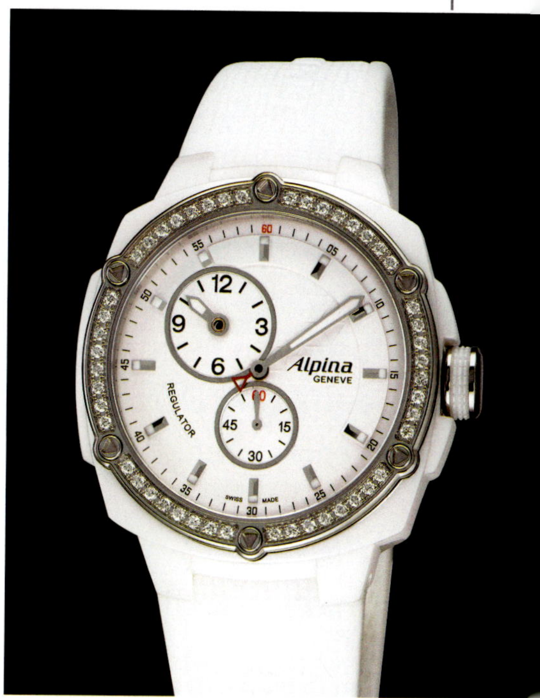

AP

AUDEMARS PIGUET

Le maître de l'horlogerie depuis 1875

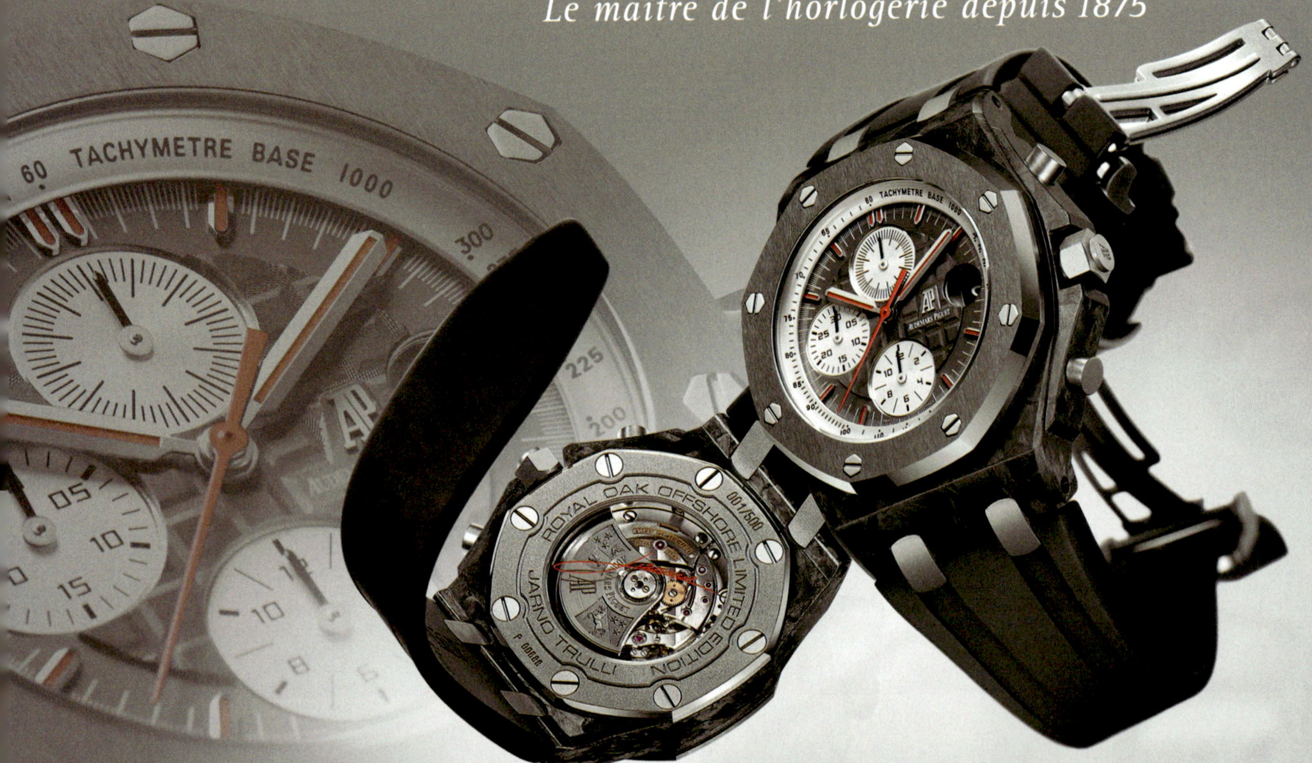

THE CROSSROADS OF AN AVANT-GARDE HERITAGE

Jules-Louis Audemars and Edward-Auguste Piguet, specialists in complicated watches, founded Audemars Piguet in the Vallée de Joux in 1875. One hundred and thirty-five years later, the company is still in the hands of the founders' descendants, and is indeed the oldest watch manufacturer that has always been a family business.

THIS PAGE ABOVE

Released in a limited edition of 500 pieces, the Royal Oak Offshore Jarno Trulli houses an automatic movement within a forged carbon case.

Today, Audemars Piguet works with over 1,000 employees spread throughout the world, of which about 750 are at the brand's three sites in Switzerland: SA de la Manufacture d'Horlogerie & Cie in Brassus, the brand's home village, Audemars Piguet (Renaud & Papi) in Le Locle, and Centror SA in Meyrin for production of the cases. A standard-bearer of the luxury watch market, the brand admirably combines innovation and ancestral savoir-faire, faithfully adhering to the watchwords of tradition, excellence and audacity.

Among its most daring feats is the 1972 launch of the famous Royal Oak. At the time, it was a real risk to produce a watch that was both high-end and sporty. The octagonal timepiece was the first of its kind and it redefined steel as a precious metal. 1992 saw the release of the Royal Oak Offshore, a collection devoted to extremes and that was to explore the possibilities of new materials at every opportunity. Regularly associated with competitive motor racing and the great Formula 1 drivers, the Royal Oak Offshore has now been released in a limited edition signed by the Italian champion Jarno Trulli, an Audemars Piguet ambassador since 2008.

The Millenary Carbon One takes advantage of high-tech materials and explores the possibilities of three-dimensional design, aiming for perfect symbiosis between the interior and exterior.

For lovers of haute horology, the Royal Oak Offshore welcomes a tourbillon movement with column-wheel chronograph in a rose-gold case, topped with a forged carbon bezel, while the rose-gold version of the Royal Oak possesses an extraordinary number of complications for a so-called "sporty" watch. The timepiece's automatic-winding caliber includes equation of time, sunrise and sunset, perpetual calendar and moonphase indications!

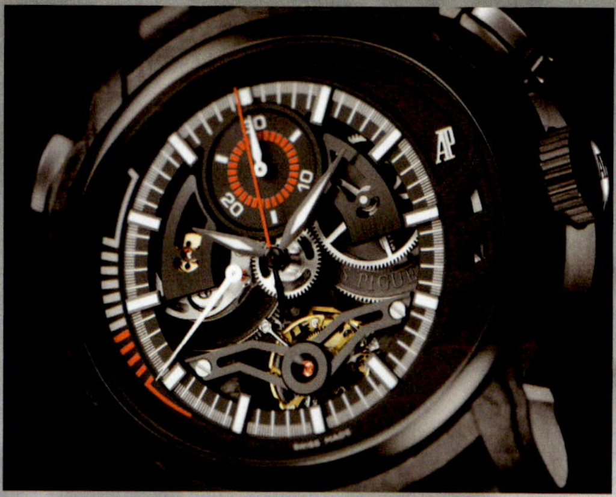

Since 2006, Audemars Piguet has produced its Oval Time concept in the Millenary case, inspired by the architecture of the Roman Coliseum. The collection consists of pieces with which the watchmaker explores the concept of three-dimensional design, searching for perfect symbiosis between the interior and the exterior. The Millenary Carbon One, equipped with a complex movement that includes a tourbillon and a column-wheel chronograph, is a recent example. The openworked dial reveals a modern movement that plays on the symmetries between the barrels, for example, and on redesigned shapes such as the tourbillon bridge. The piece also takes advantage of the availability of high-tech materials: blackened steel, aluminum and a very particular kind of carbon for the movement, and forged carbon, ceramic and blackened titanium for the case. Released in a limited edition of 120 pieces, the Millenary Carbon One sports a color scheme of black with red and white accents that recalls the automotive universe.

The Jules Audemars Collection is one of two collections dedicated to the brand's founders. The perpetual calendar movement making its debut in this collection is exceptionally thin, measuring just 4mm thick. The automatic caliber powering the timepiece boasts the world's thinnest central rotor (2.45mm thick). This rotor includes a gold segment to weigh it down, facilitating bi-directional winding and a better, more regular transmission of energy over a longer period. The choice of a central rotor, instead of an off-center mini-rotor, is justified by the additional space it allows for the barrel and the balance. This is important because the longer the diameter of the barrel, the more power can be held in reserve—and the greater the diameter of the balance, the more precise the watch. Like all movements from the Manufacture Audemars Piguet, the 2120/2802 movement benefits from haute horology finishing done by hand: beveling, circular graining and Côtes de Genève. The main plate presents five different diameters of finishing, and even the interior of the case is polished. The Jules Audemars Perpetual Calendar is available in a rose-gold case with a brown or silvered dial.

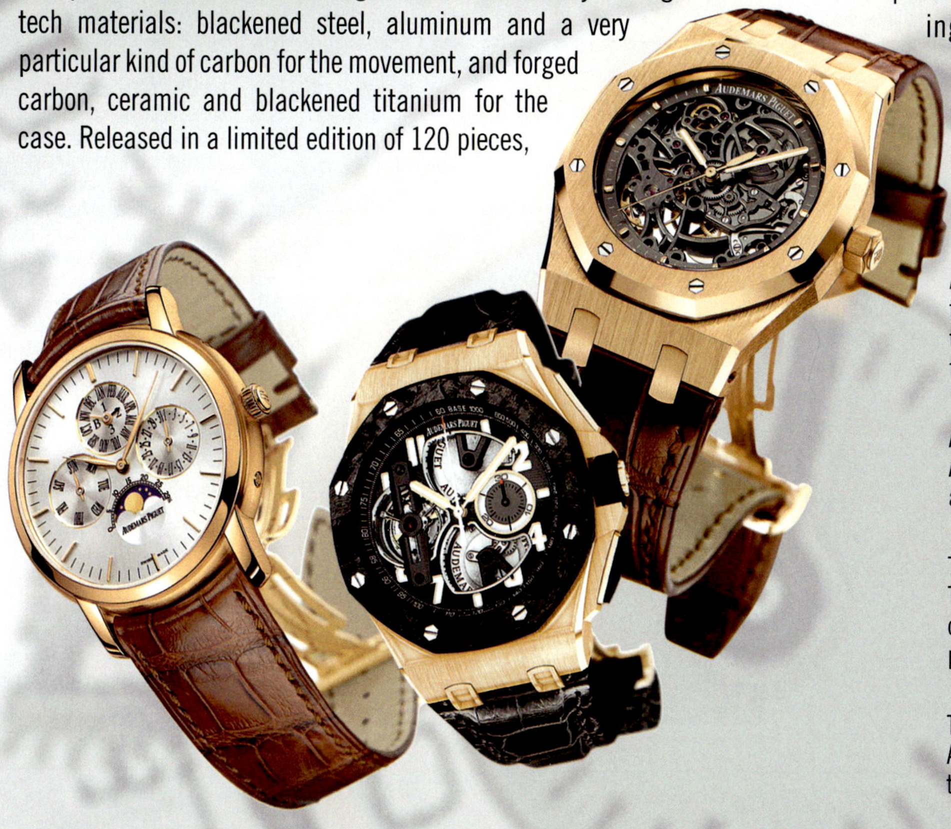

CENTER

Audemars Piguet's Millenary Carbon One includes a tourbillon and a chronograph, as well as an indication of its 240-hour power reserve, all housed in a forged carbon case with a black ceramic bezel.

BOTTOM LEFT

An extra-thin automatic movement powers the Jules Audemars Perpetual Calendar, which also possesses a moonphase display.

BOTTOM CENTER

The manual-winding movement of the Royal Oak Tourbillon Chronograph drives its two eponymous complications and boasts a full 237 hours of power reserve.

BOTTOM RIGHT

The Royal Oak Skeleton displays its skeletonized AP 3129 movement through a sapphire crystal on the front and back of the case.

ROYAL OAK SKELETON SELFWINDING — REF. 15305ST.OO.1220ST.01

Movement: automatic-winding 3129 caliber; poised balance with inertia blocks; bridges and mainplate hand-drawn with a file; polished angles; 22K gold decorated oscillating weight.
Functions: hours, minutes, seconds.
Case: stainless steel; 18K white-gold assembly screws; transparent sapphire crystal and caseback.
Dial: anthracite; 11 luminescent gold applied faceted hour markers; gold luminescent hands.
Bracelet: stainless steel; triple-blade AP folding clasp.
Suggested price: $31,100

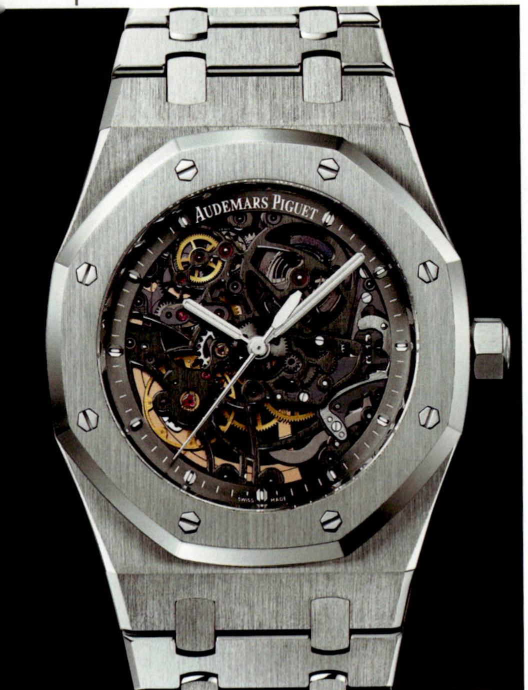

ROYAL OAK SELFWINDING WITH DATE — REF. 15300OR.OO.D002CR.01

Movement: automatic-winding 3120 caliber; poised balance with inertia blocks; rhodium-plated, Côtes de Genève decorative pattern and circular graining; 22K gold oscillating weight decorated with the Audemars and Piguet family crest.
Functions: hours, minutes, seconds; date.
Case: 18K pink gold; 18K white-gold assembly screws; antireflective sapphire crystal and caseback.
Dial: exclusive traditional guilloché Grande Tapisserie decorative pattern; luminescent hands; gold hour markers.
Strap: black alligator leather; 18K pink-gold AP folding clasp.
Suggested price: $25,300

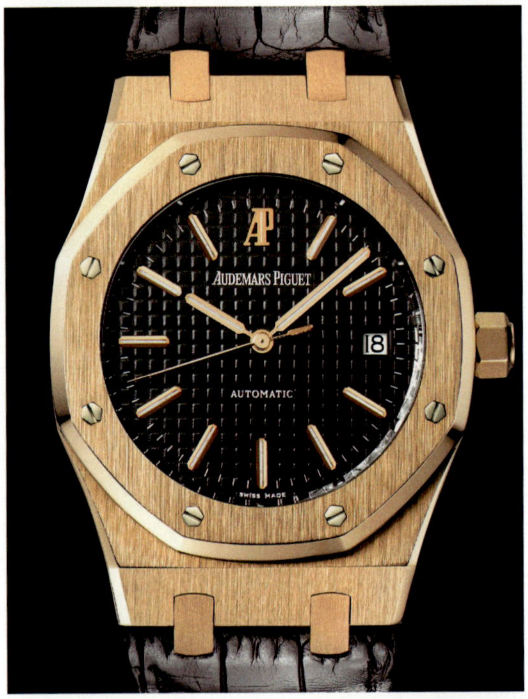

ROYAL OAK SELFWINDING CHRONOGRAPH — REF. 26300ST.OO.1110ST.07

Movement: automatic-winding 2385 caliber; 18K gold rotor; rhodium-plated, Côtes de Genève decorative pattern and circular graining.
Functions: hours, minutes; date; chronograph.
Case: stainless steel; 18K gold assembly screws; antireflective sapphire crystal.
Dial: exclusive traditional guilloché Grande Tapisserie decorative pattern; bi-color counters; applied gold luminescent hour markers; gold luminescent hands.
Bracelet: stainless steel.
Suggested price: $18,300

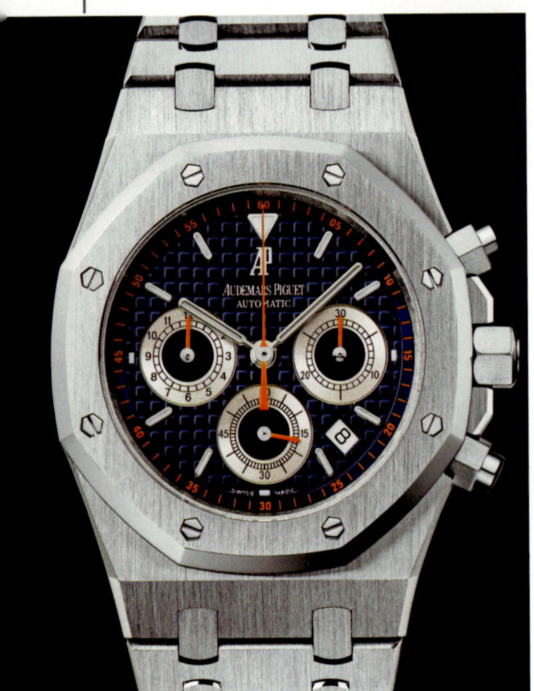

ROYAL OAK EQUATION OF TIME SELFWINDING PERPETUAL CALENDAR — REF. 26603OR.OO.D092CR.01

Movement: automatic-winding 2120/2808 caliber; 42-hour power reserve; poised balance with inertia blocks; 22K gold oscillating weight; rhodium-plated, Côtes de Genève decorative pattern and circular graining; distinctive feat: cams (sunrise and sunset times) and the flange (mean time of solar culmination) can be calibrated to most locations situated between the 56th parallel north and the 46th parallel south; the openworked oscillating weight may be personalized on request (the standard version has the AP letters).
Functions: hours, minutes, seconds; sunrise and sunset times; equation of time; perpetual calendar; astronomical moonphase.
Case: 18K pink gold; 18K gold assembly screws; antireflective sapphire crystal and caseback.
Dial: exclusive traditional guilloché Grande Tapisserie decorative pattern; applied gold luminescent hour markers; gold luminescent hands.
Strap: large-scale hand-sewn dark brown crocodile leather; 18K pink-gold AP folding clasp.
Suggested price: $100,600

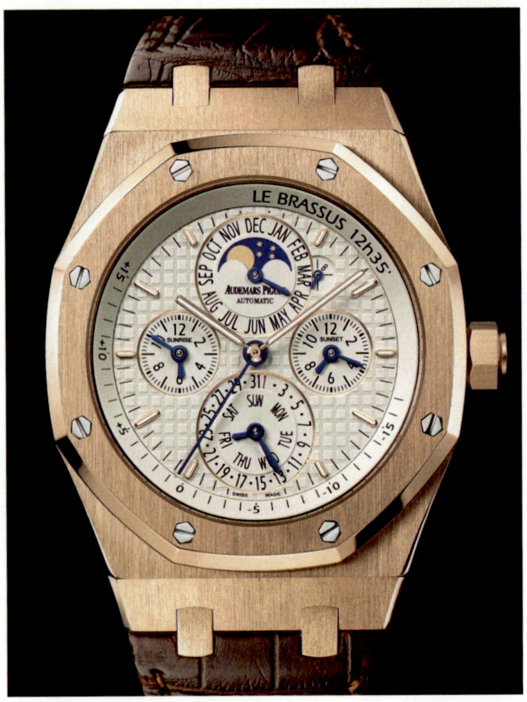

ROYAL OAK OFFSHORE SELFWINDING CHRONOGRAPH REF. 26400AU.OO.A002CA.01

Movement: automatic-winding 3126/3840 caliber; 22K gold oscillating weight; rhodium-plated, Côtes de Genève decorative pattern and circular graining.
Function: hours, minutes; date; chronograph.
Case: forged carbon; black ceramic bezel, crown and pushpieces; titanium pushpiece guards; titanium sapphire crystal caseback; water resistant to 10atm.
Dial: black with Mega Tapisserie pattern; black counters; applied white-gold hour markers with luminescent coating; black flange.
Strap: black rubber; titanium pin buckle.
Price: available upon request.

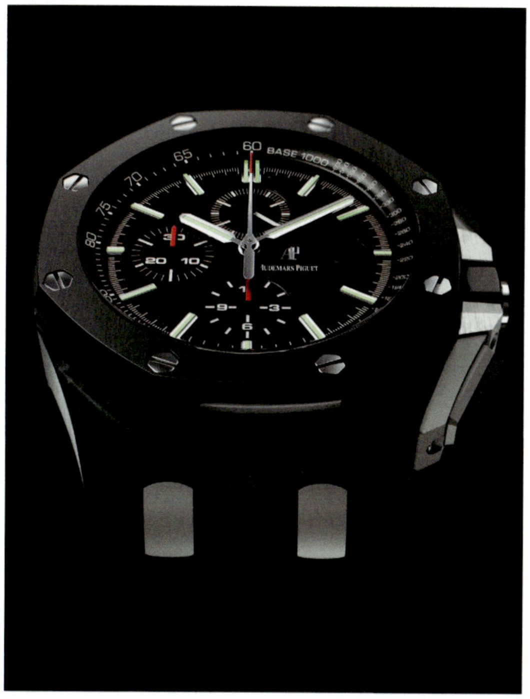

ROYAL OAK OFFSHORE HAND-WOUND TOURBILLON CHRONOGRAPH REF. 26288OF.OO.D002CR.01

Movement: manual-winding 2912 caliber; two barrels; tourbillon; 10-day power reserve; blackened steel bridges; circular-grained motifs; hand-drawn strokes; snailed and small circular-grained barrels bearing the Audemars Piguet signature.
Function: hours, minutes; chronograph.
Case: 18K pink gold; forged carbon bezel; black ceramic crown and pushers; assembly polished steel screws; antireflective sapphire crystal and caseback.
Dial: black; snailed and openworked at 6, 9 and 12; applied gold luminescent numerals and hands.
Strap: large-scale hand-sewn black crocodile leather; AP folding clasp in 18K gold.
Suggested price: $252,900

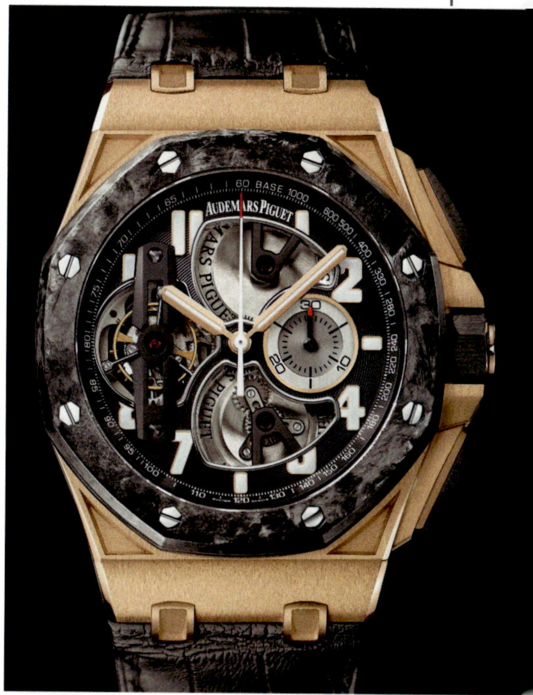

ROYAL OAK OFFSHORE SELFWINDING "DIVER" WRISTWATCH REF. 15703ST.OO.D002CA.01

Movement: automatic-winding 3120 caliber; poised balance with inertia blocks; 22K gold oscillating weight decorated with the Audemars and Piguet family crest; rhodium-plated, Côtes de Genève decorative pattern and circular graining.
Functions: hours, minutes; date; dive-time measurement.
Case: stainless steel; polished stainless steel assembly screws; antireflective sapphire crystal.
Dial: black with exclusive Mega Tapisserie decorative pattern; inner rotating ring with diving scale; applied white-gold luminescent hour markers and hands.
Strap: black rubber; oversized stainless steel pin buckle.
Suggested price: $15,200

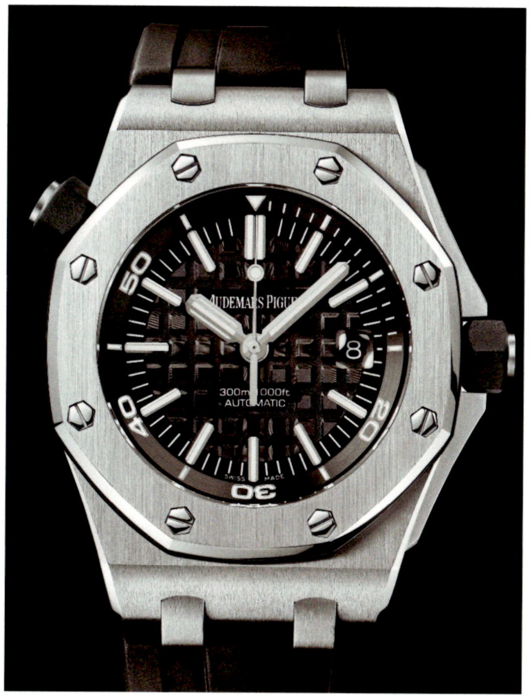

LADIES' ROYAL OAK OFFSHORE DIAMOND-SET SELFWINDING CHRONOGRAPH REF. 26048SK.ZZ.D010CA.01

Movement: automatic-winding 2385 caliber; 21K gold oscillating weight segment; rhodium-plated, Côtes de Genève decorative pattern and circular graining.
Functions: hours, minutes; date; chronograph.
Case: stainless steel; set with 32 brilliant-cut diamonds (Ø 2.2mm, 1.25 carats); stainless steel assembly screws; clad white rubber bezel, crown and pushpieces; antireflective sapphire crystal.
Dial: exclusive Mega Tapisserie decorative pattern; luminescent numerals and hands.
Strap: white rubber; stainless steel AP folding clasp.
Suggested price: $22,700

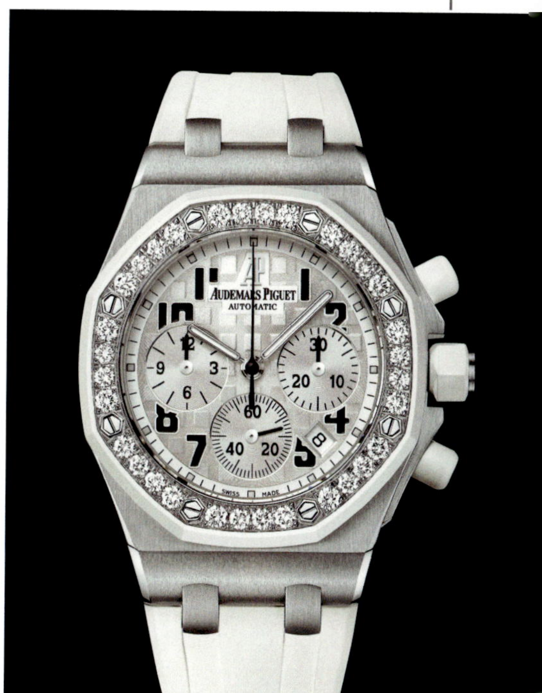

JULES AUDEMARS SELFWINDING ULTRA-THIN WRISTWATCH REF.15180OR.OO.A002CR.01

Movement: automatic-winding 2120 caliber; ultra-thin; 21K gold rotor segment; rhodium-plated, Côtes de Genève decorative pattern and circular graining.
Functions: hours, minutes.
Case: 18K pink gold; antireflective sapphire crystal and caseback.
Dial: black; applied pink-gold hour markers and hands.
Strap: large-scale hand-sewn crocodile leather; 18K gold pin buckle.
Suggested price: $19,400

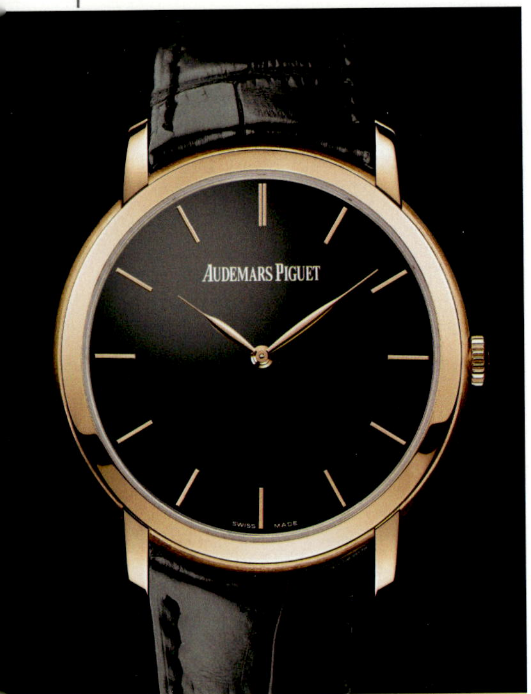

JULES AUDEMARS SMALL SECONDS REF. 77239BC.ZZ.A002CR.01

Movement: manual-winding proprietary 3090 caliber; all parts finely decorated; circular-grained mainplate; rhodium-plated bridges; beveled; snailed and adorned with Côtes de Genève.
Functions: hours, minutes; small seconds at 6.
Case: 18K white gold; gem-set bezel with 60 brilliant-cut diamonds (approx. 0.52 carat); sapphire crystal caseback.
Dial: silvered; applied pink-gold hour markers.
Strap: hand-sewn black crocodile leather with large square scales; secured by a white-gold pin buckle.
Price: available upon request.

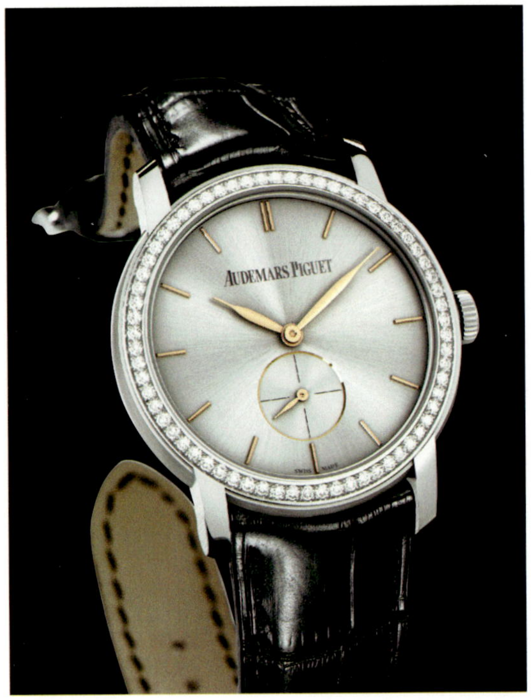

JULES AUDEMARS: DUAL TIME REF. 26380BC.OO.D002CR.01

Movement: automatic-winding 2329/2846 caliber; all parts finely decorated; mainplate beveled and circular-grained; bridges adorned with Côtes de Genève.
Functions: hours, minutes; date; dual time zone with day/night display; power reserve indication.
Case: 18K white gold.
Dial: silvered; applied pink-gold hour markers; pink-gold hour and minute hands.
Strap: hand-sewn black crocodile leather with large square scales; secured by an 18K white-gold AP folding clasp.
Price: available upon request.

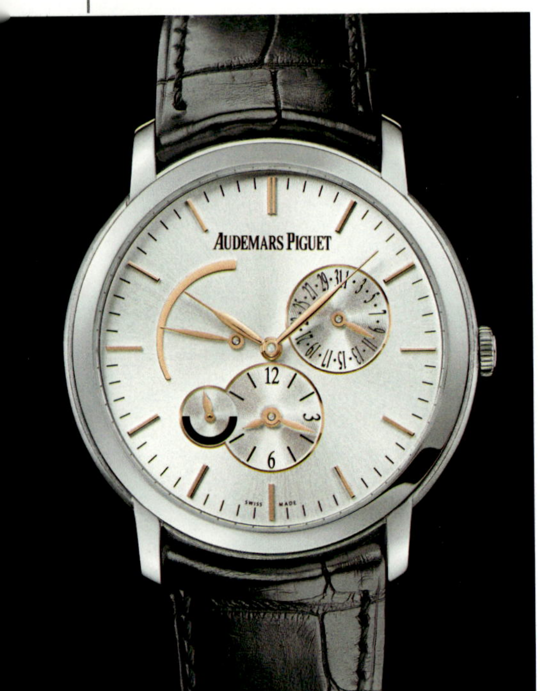

JULES AUDEMARS SELFWINDING PERPETUAL CALENDAR REF. 26390OR.OO.D088CR.01

Movement: automatic-winding 2120/2802 caliber; 21K gold rotor segment; rhodium-plated, Côtes de Genève decorative pattern and circular graining.
Functions: hours, minutes; perpetual calendar.
Case: 18K pink gold; antireflective sapphire crystal and caseback.
Dial: silvered; applied gold indexes; gold hands.
Strap: large-scale hand-sewn crocodile leather; 18K gold AP folding clasp.
Suggested price: $59,900
Also available: brown dial.

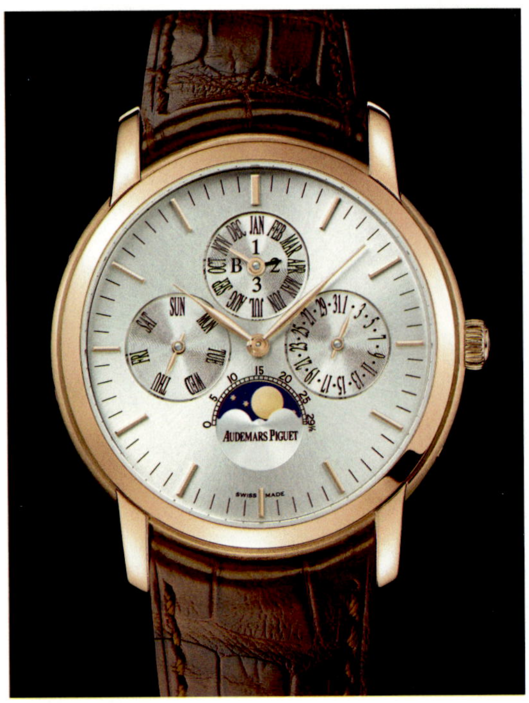

MILLENARY 4101 SELFWINDING WRISTWATCH REF. 15350OR.OO.D093CR.01

Movement: proprietary automatic-winding 4101 caliber; mainplate adorned with horizontal Côtes de Genève on the front and circular-grained on the back; rhodium-plated bridges, beveled, snailed and adorned with horizontal and circular Côtes de Genève and with circular graining: diamond-polished jewel sinks; diamond-polished countersinks and beveled wheel spokes; beveled screw rims and slots; AP monogram; Audemars and Piguet family crests engraved on the oscillating weight.
Functions: off-set hours and minutes at 3; off-set small seconds at 7.
Case: 18K pink gold; sapphire crystal caseback.
Dial: black and anthracite; applied pink-gold Roman numerals; pink-gold hands.
Strap: hand-sewn brown crocodile leather; large square scales; secured by a 18K pink-gold AP folding clasp.
Price: available upon request.
Also available: stainless steel.

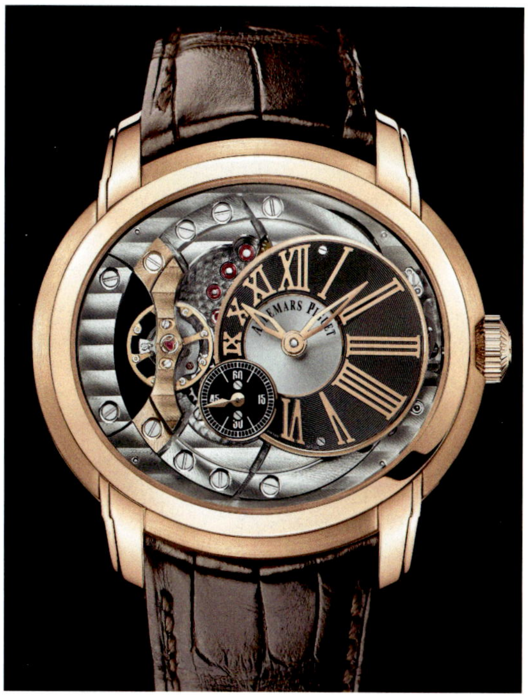

MILLENARY HAND-WOUND MINUTE REPEATER WITH AP ESCAPEMENT REF. 26371TI.OO.D002CR.01

Movement: Audemars Piguet 2910 caliber; finishing: all parts finely decorated, with hand-polished beveling, interior angles, snailing, hand-drawn file strokes, horizontal Côtes de Genève and circular graining on the mainplate.
Functions: offset hours and minutes at 3; offset small seconds at 7; minute repeater, repeater slide serving to activate the minute repeater at 7.
Case: titanium oval case; sapphire crystal caseback.
Dial: anthracite gray; applied pink-gold Roman numerals; silvered small seconds sub-dial.
Strap: hand-sewn black crocodile leather with large square scales; titanium AP folding clasp.
Note: limited edition of eight pieces.
Price: available upon request.

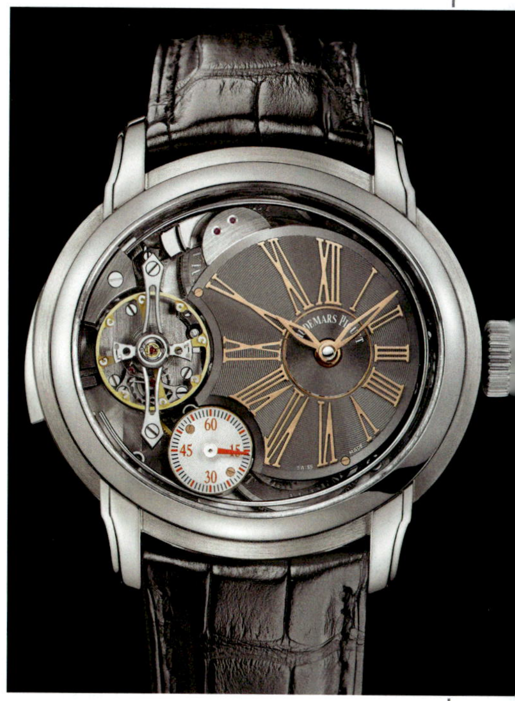

TRADITION SELFWINDING ULTRA-THIN WRISTWATCH REF. 15160PT.OO.A092CR.01

Movement: automatic-winding 2120 caliber; oscillating weight engraved with AP initials; 18K gold rotor; rhodium-plated, Côtes de Genève decorative pattern and circular graining.
Functions: hours, minutes.
Case: 950 platinum; antireflective sapphire crystal and caseback.
Dial: opaline; applied Roman numerals and cathédrale pink-gold hands.
Strap: large square-scale hand-sewn crocodile leather; 950 platinum AP folding clasp.
Suggested price: $52,400

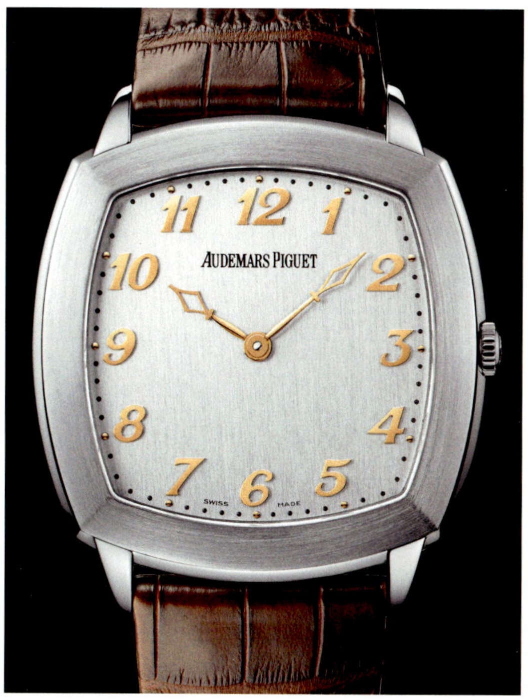

TRADITION MANUAL WINDING PERPETUAL CALENDAR REF. 26051PT.OO.D092CR.01

Movement: manual-winding 5020/2819 caliber; rhodium-plated, Côtes de Genève decorative pattern and circular graining.
Functions: hours, minutes; perpetual calendar; moonphase.
Case: 950 platinum; sapphire crystal and caseback.
Dial: opaline; applied Roman numerals and cathédrale pink-gold hands.
Strap: large square-scale hand-sewn alligator leather; platinum AP folding clasp.
Suggested price: $126,800

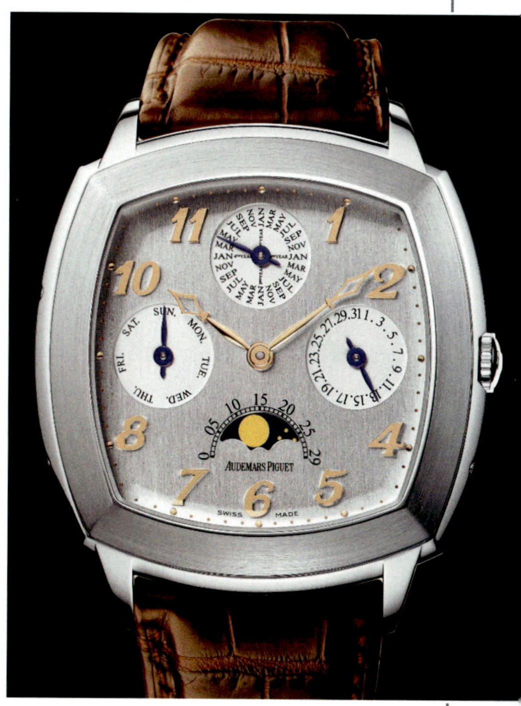

BEDAT & C°
GENEVE

OTHERWORLDLY ELEGANCE

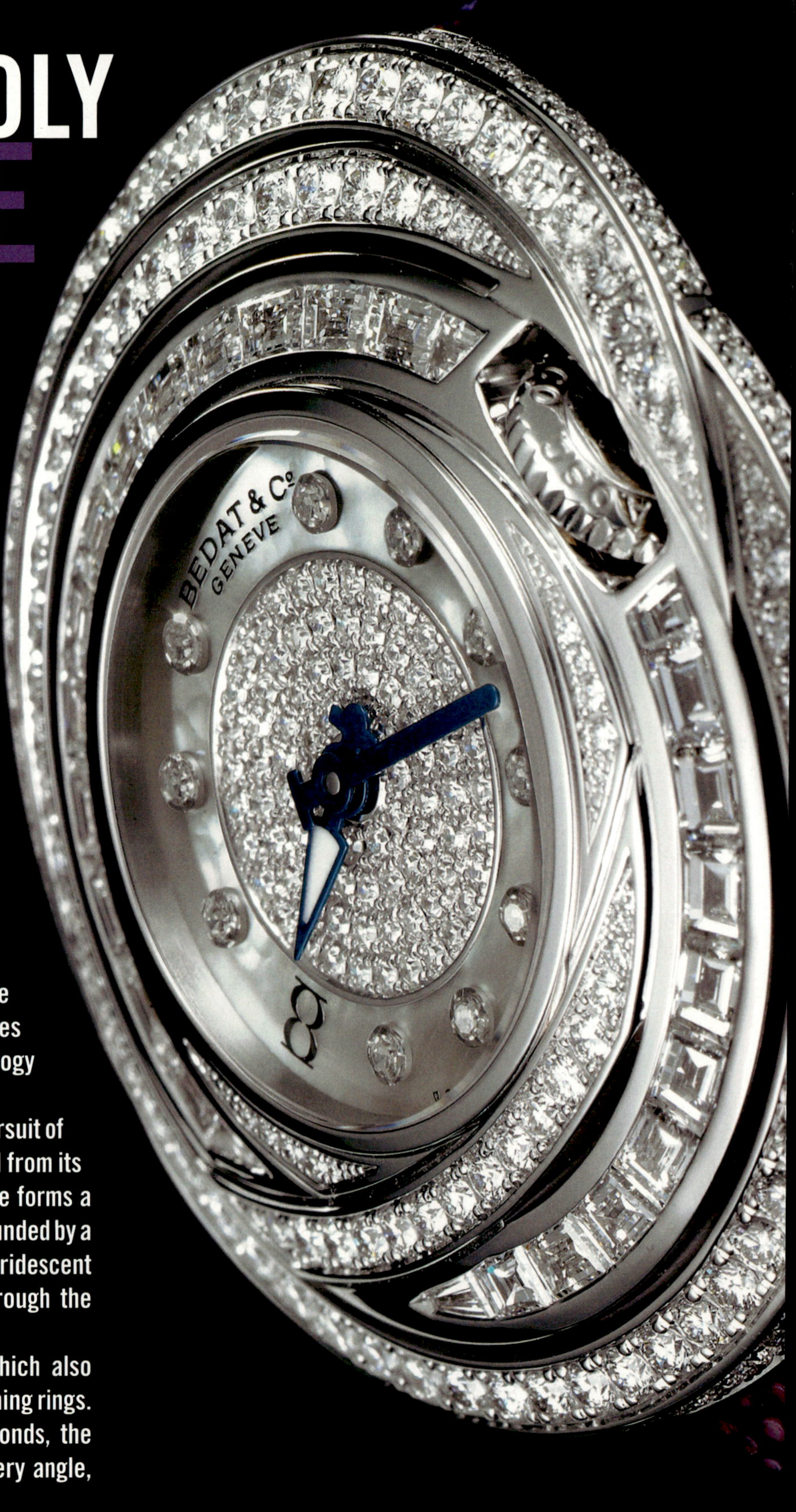

Fashion is quicksilver—ever changing. Style, however, is timeless. Bedat & Co. makes this distinction intuitively with designs that gently fold a modern spirit into Art Deco elegance to form its singular look.

Since the Geneva watchmaker's 1997 BaselWorld debut, Bedat & Co. has defined its vision of luxury with women's and men's timepieces that maintain the Swiss tradition of craftsmanship. In fact, each watch has earned the A.O.S.C. (Appellation d'Origine Suisse Certifiée), a guarantee that it was assembled in Switzerland using only Swiss-made components.

The firm enlivens its reverence for the past by exploring new design avenues that express a rare level of artistic sophistication. Bedat & Co. achieves this, in part, through a creative combination of horology and gemology.

The company eloquently articulates its endless pursuit of refinement through the 881, an haute joaillerie model from its No. 8 Extravaganza collection. A diamond-pavé circle forms a luminous planet at the heart of the dial, which is surrounded by a mother-of-pearl ring that blankets the tiny world in iridescent cloud cover. Sparkling diamond satellites burst through the gleaming haze to play the role of hour markers.

The dial anchors the 881's celestial design, which also includes a sizeable bezel made from several intertwining rings. Set with a mix of brilliant- and baguette-cut diamonds, the bezel emits a shimmering cascade of light from every angle, imbuing the design with a unique visual depth.

Art Deco style forms the foundation of the aesthetic identity that unites the Bedat & Co. collection, while the Geneva firm's strict adherence to Swiss watchmaking tradition ensures reliability.

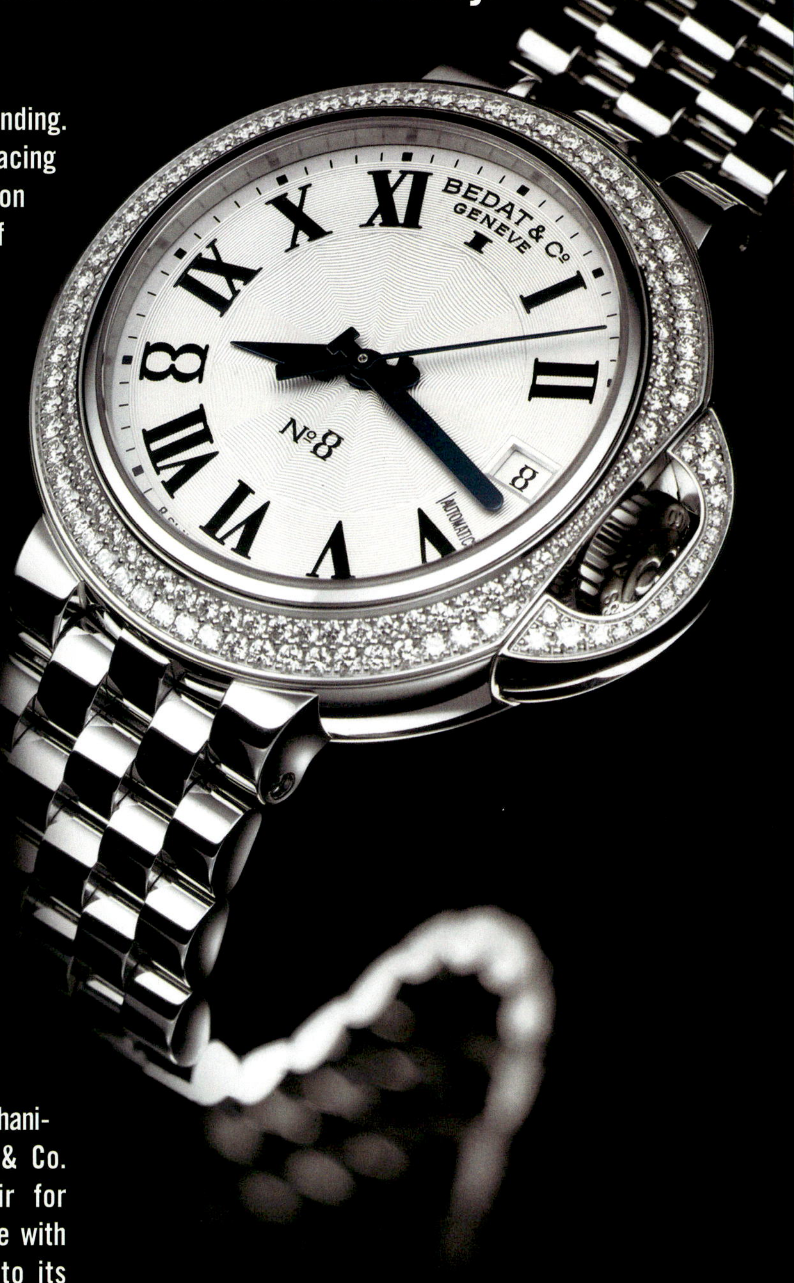

The Bedat & Co. logo is inextricably linked to the brand's founding. A stylized figure eight, the symbol is made from two opposite-facing B's that signify the company's founders: Simone Bédat and her son Christian. The logo appears on every watch, oftentimes in place of the hour marker at 8 o'clock.

That tradition holds true for the 828, a round women's model that takes its place alongside the 881 in the company's No. 8 collection. An automatic movement powers the 828's classic three-hand design as well as its date function, which is displayed through an opening on the guilloché dial.

Bedat & Co. presents the 828 in a stainless steel case that measures 36.5mm in diameter. The watch's circular outline extends slightly at 3 o'clock to accommodate the crown. For the jewelry version of this watch, both the bezel and crown protector can be set with 151 diamonds, which weigh approximately 1.5 carats.

Bedat & Co. switches from round to oval designs with its No. 2 collection. One of the line's highlights is certainly the 228, a model distinguished by two ellipse-shaped bezels. Insinuated one inside the other, these bezels can be set with 195 diamonds, framing the mother-of-pearl dial in rings of fiery brilliance.

The case, which is 36.5mm in diameter, houses a quartz movement and is water resistant to 164 feet (50 meters). The 228 is offered in rose gold or stainless steel and paired with either a matching bracelet or an alligator strap.

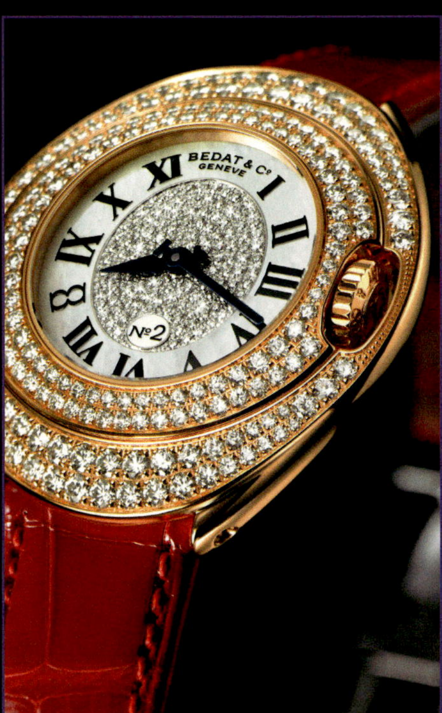

Round or oval, mechanical or quartz, Bedat & Co. demonstrates its flair for sophisticated elegance with the latest additions to its collection.

FACING PAGE

More than 300 diamonds adorn the 881, an haute joaillerie model presented in a 35mm white-gold case with a Swiss-made quartz movement.

THIS PAGE

ABOVE An automatic movement powers the 828, whose guilloché dial includes the Bedat & Co. logo in the 8 o'clock position.

LEFT The elliptical rose-gold loops that form the 228's dual-bezel design are set with 195 white brilliants, while the mother-of-pearl dial is paved with 126 diamonds.

NO. 2 **REF. 228.051.900**

Movement: quartz ETA.
Functions: hours, minutes.
Case: stainless steel; Ø 36.5mm; oval; external and internal diamond-set bezel; water resistant to 5atm.
Dial: mother-of-pearl.
Bracelet: stainless steel mille mailles; stainless steel folding clasp.
Suggested price: $19,950
Also available: rolled-edge hand-stitched alligator strap; stainless steel folding buckle.

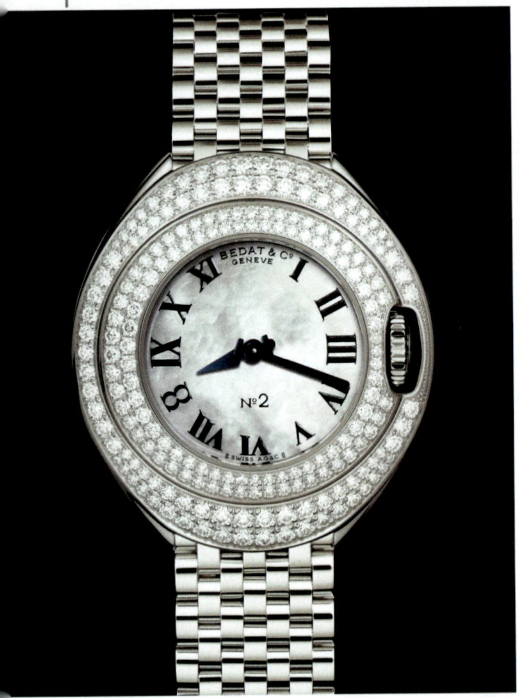

NO. 2 **REF. 228.450.989**

Movement: quartz ETA.
Functions: hours, minutes.
Case: 18K rose gold; Ø 36.5mm; oval; external and internal diamond-set bezel; water resistant to 5atm.
Dial: mother-of-pearl; diamond-set center.
Strap: rolled-edge hand-stitched alligator; 18K rose-gold cap with stainless steel folding buckle.
Suggested price: $32,950
Also available: 18K rose-gold mille mailles bracelet; stainless steel folding clasp.

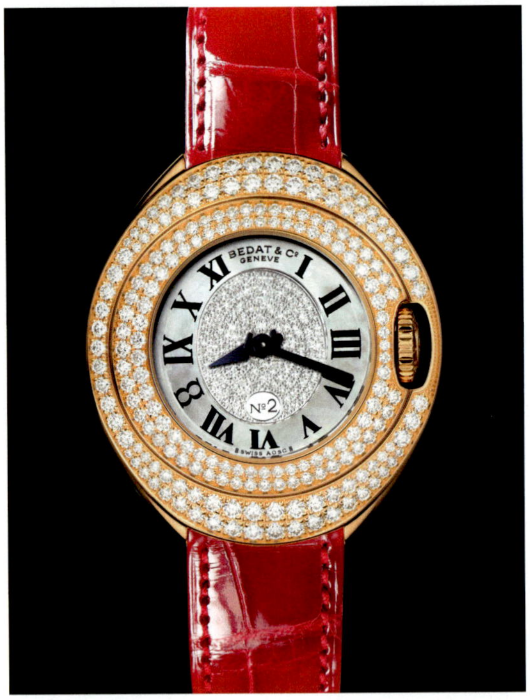

NO. 3 **REF. 304.031.109**

Movement: quartz ETA.
Functions: hours, minutes.
Case: stainless steel; 24.5x27.75mm; tonneau; diamond-set bezel; water resistant to 5atm.
Dial: white; stamped with wavy sunburst guilloché pattern; nine diamond hour markers.
Bracelet: stainless steel mille mailles; stainless steel folding clasp.
Suggested price: $7,800

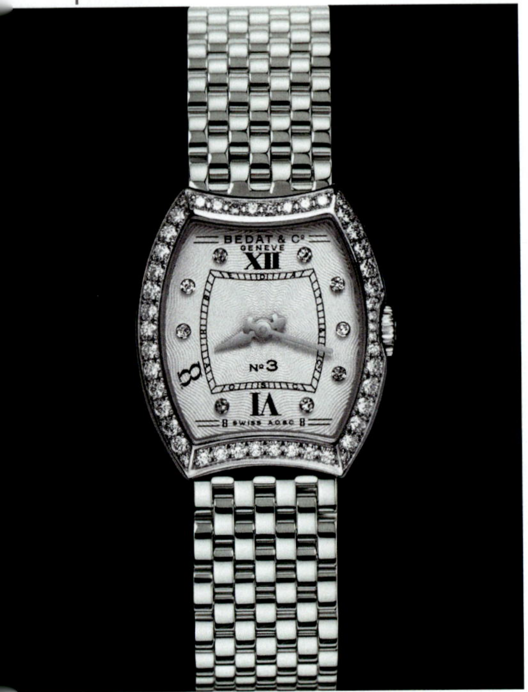

NO. 3 **REF. 384.031.600**

Movement: quartz ETA.
Functions: hours, minutes.
Case: stainless steel; elongated tonneau; diamond-set bezel; water resistant to 5atm.
Dial: silvered.
Bracelet: stainless steel mille mailles; stainless steel folding clasp.
Suggested price: $7,550

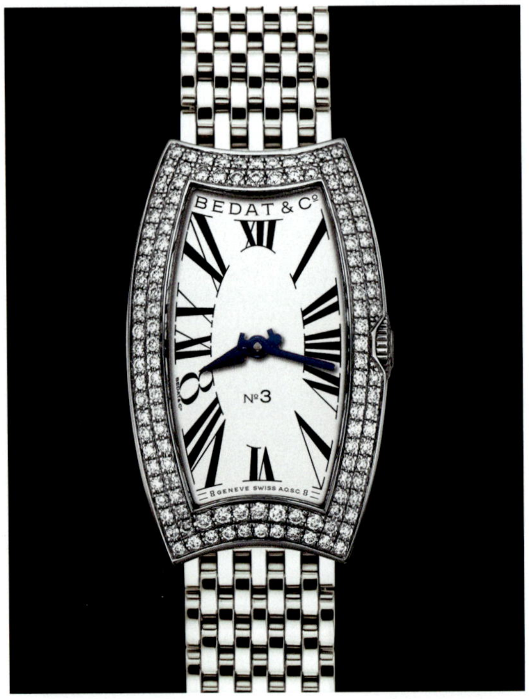

NO. 8 — REF. 828.041.600

Movement: automatic-winding.
Functions: hours, minutes, seconds; simple calendar.
Case: stainless steel; Ø 36.5mm; round; diamond-set bezel and crown protector; water resistant to 5atm.
Dial: opaline guilloché.
Bracelet: stainless steel mille mailles; stainless steel folding clasp.
Suggested price: $11,550
Also available: rolled-edge hand-stitched alligator strap; stainless steel folding buckle.

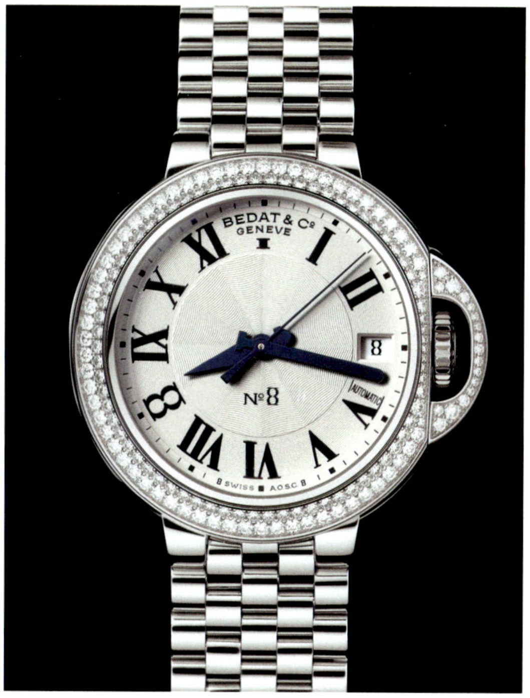

NO. 8 — REF. 828.011.600

Movement: automatic-winding.
Functions: hours, minutes; simple calendar.
Case: stainless steel; Ø 36.5mm; round; water resistant to 5atm.
Dial: opaline guilloché.
Bracelet: stainless steel mille mailles bracelet; folding clasp.
Suggested price: $4,250
Also available: rolled-edge hand-stitched alligator strap; stainless steel folding buckle.

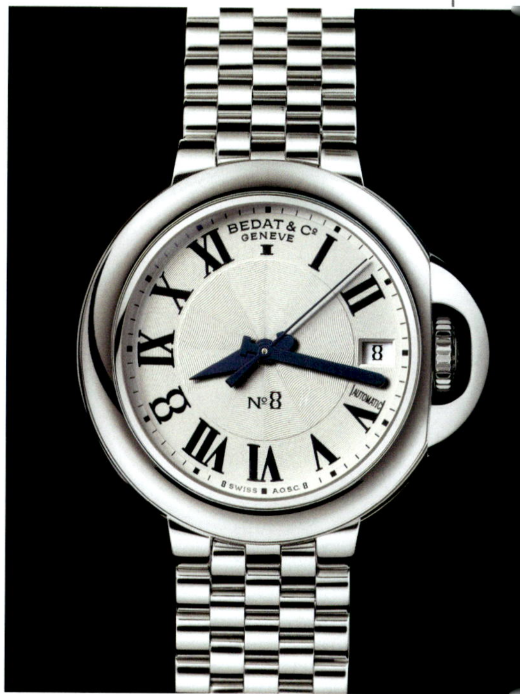

NO. 8 — REF. 828.444.600

Movement: automatic-winding.
Functions: hours, minutes, seconds; simple calendar.
Case: 18K rose gold; Ø 36.5mm; round; diamond-set bezel and crown protector; water resistant to 5atm.
Dial: opaline guilloché.
Bracelet: 18K rose-gold mille mailles, stainless steel folding clasp.
Suggested price: $33,750
Also available: rolled-edge hand-stitched alligator strap; 18K rose-gold cap, stainless steel buckle.

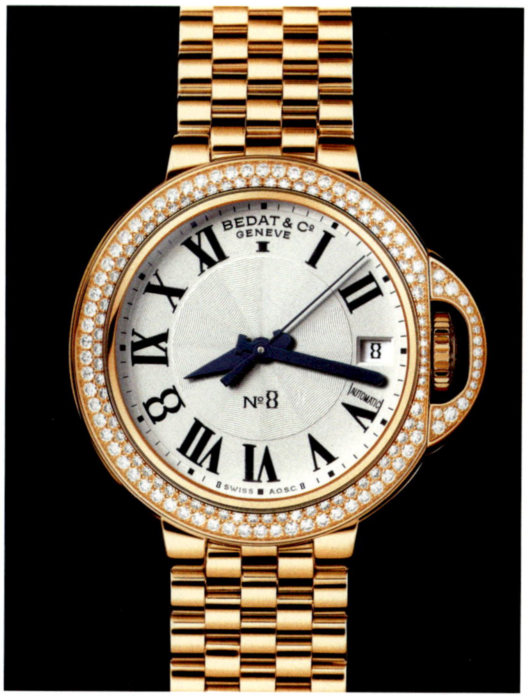

NO. 8 — REF. 828.440.909

Movement: automatic-winding.
Functions: hours, minutes, seconds.
Case: 18K rose gold; Ø 36.5mm; round case; diamond bezel and crown protector; water resistant to 5atm.
Dial: mother-of-pearl guilloché; six diamond hour markers.
Strap: rolled-edge hand-stitched alligator; 18K rose-gold cap; stainless steel folding buckle.
Suggested price: $21,750
Also available: stainless steel mille mailles bracelet; stainless steel folding clasp.

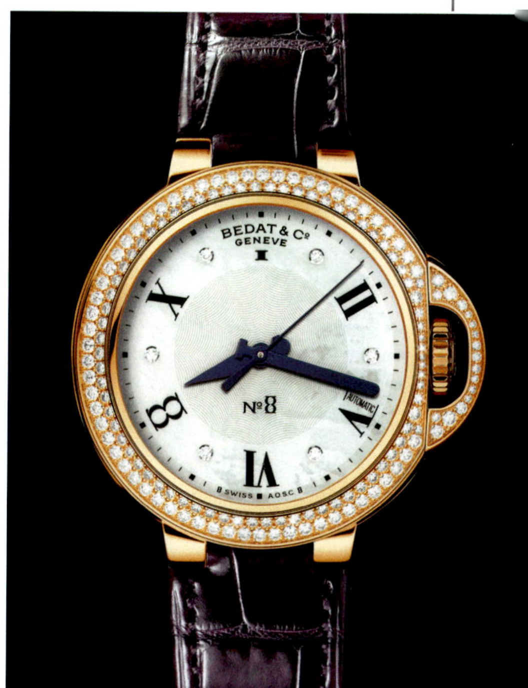

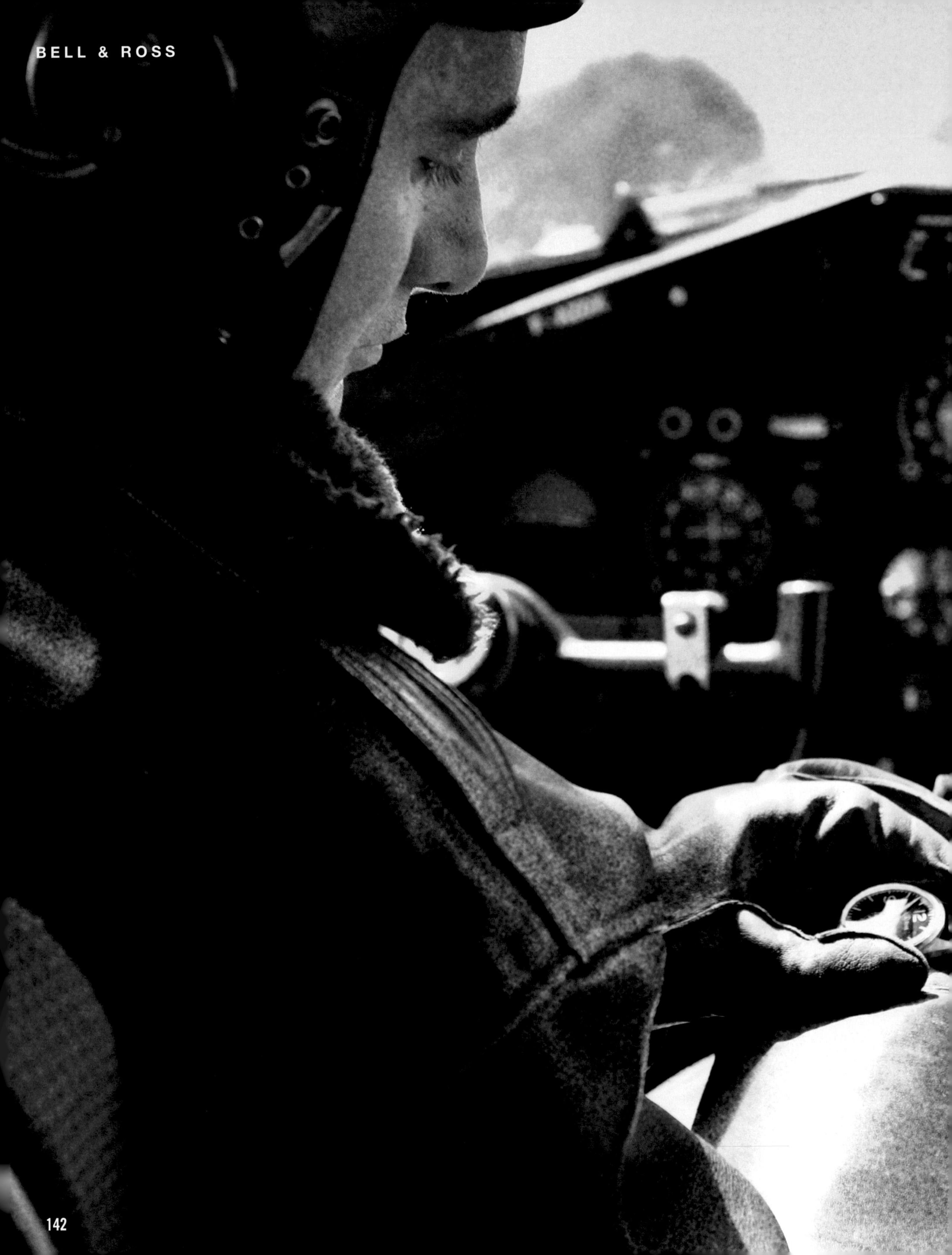

Bell & Ross

TIME INSTRUMENTS

FROM THE COCKPIT TO THE WRIST

Since its inception, Bell & Ross has been inspired by professional pilots, divers and military personnel. A team of watch designers and aircraft and space control specialists joined forces to create timepieces ideally suited for professional use. Their goal was to be part of the great Swiss watchmaking tradition, while meeting the demands of men and women facing extreme situations.

Today, Bell & Ross has become synonymous with superior and refined watchmaking, and many astronauts, pilots, divers and bomb disposal experts use Bell & Ross watches as tools for their missions.

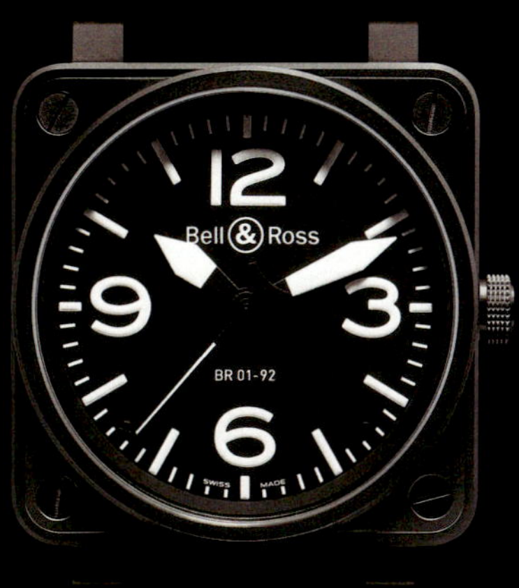

Bell & Ross's philosophy is that "function drives design": its four design principles are legibility, functionality, precision and reliability. A major source of inspiration for Bell & Ross designers is the precision and functionality of the instrument panel of a cockpit. The company's iconic watch, the BR 01, perfectly captures the function and design of the cockpit instrument, and its success stems from its unique design and beautiful simplicity. The wearer can look at his wrist and envision an airplane cockpit and the thrill of flying.

Panel instruments continue to be a source of inspiration for the creators of Bell & Ross watches. Some limited edition watches were inspired by other professional instruments, such as radar and the compass. These limited editions have become collectors' items because of their uniqueness and rarity.

After the success of the BR 01, Bell & Ross developed new watches that addressed the needs of deep-sea divers. The result is the BR 02 diving watch collection, the embodiment of perfection and precision for diving professionals. The cases are constructed to protect the exactness of a Swiss made movement, even as they withstand pressures of up to 1,000 meters under the sea. For sophisticated watch collectors, Bell & Ross engineers and designers used the company's founding principles to meet the challenge of building the ultimate timepiece: a tourbillon. The result is a limited edition collection of tourbillon watches that beautifully combine the complexity of a tourbillon mechanism with the functionality of a professional watch.

The story of Bell & Ross is the story of a passion for timepieces and an admiration for the world of extreme professionals. It is no wonder that one often finds the following phrase throughout the company's literature: "Because he wants to reach for the stars and explore the ocean depths, because he lives out his passions to the fullest, man has always measured himself against time, to turn a few seconds into a moment of eternity."

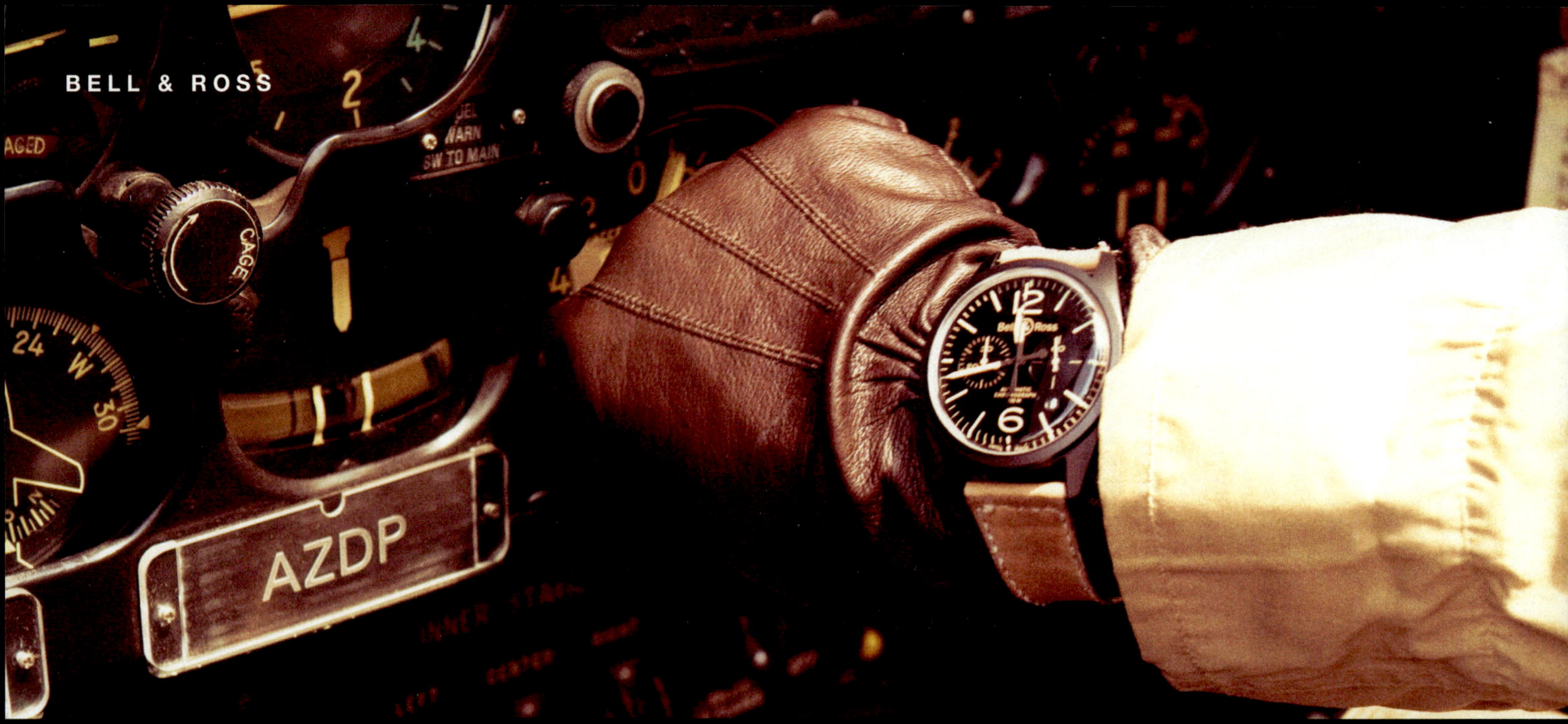

VINTAGE COLLECTION

Military pilots were the first professionals to consider the wristwatch as a tool to assist them in carrying out their missions. As a tribute to servicemen, particularly pilots, Bell & Ross created the Heritage collection. Its refined lines and style, both classical in its shape and modern in its design, evokes the era of the "Greatest Generation."

Bell & Ross created the Heritage collection by combining the design elements of the 1930s and '40s with the principles of cockpit legibility: a black matte finish to avoid disturbing light reflections, the sand color of the hands and numerals which reproduce the patina of vintage watches and the natural leather strap typical of period timepieces.

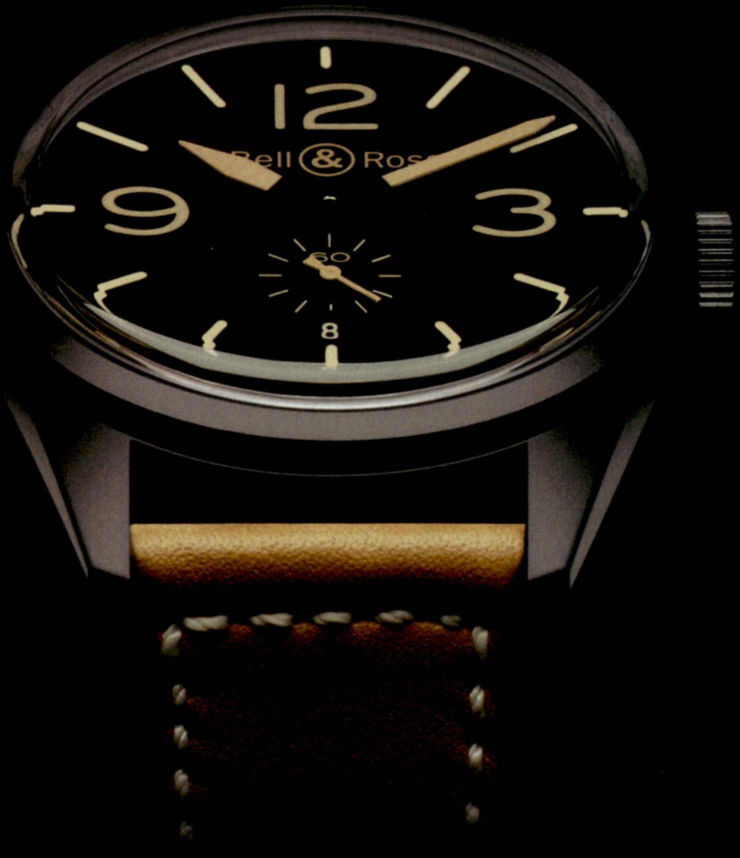

The Vintage BR 126 Heritage is powered by an automatic chronograph movement and housed within a carbon-finish steel case mounted on a natural leather strap. $4,200.

The Vintage BR 123 Heritage is also housed within a carbon-finish steel case and mounted on a natural leather strap. It is powered by an automatic movement. $2,900.

AVIATION COLLECTION

It all started with a simple idea: to turn a cockpit instrument panel clock into a wristwatch. To create the BR 01 aviation watch, our designers took their inspiration from aeronautical instrumentation, the ultimate reference point for readability, reliability and performance. Available with a variety of functions (chronograph, large date, power reserve, tourbillon...), case materials and finishes (steel, titanium, carbon, gold), and dial colors (white, black, orange, blue...), the BR 01 Instrument watch is no longer exclusively reserved for professional users. It has become an iconic watch, to the great delight of collectors of limited series and fine watches.

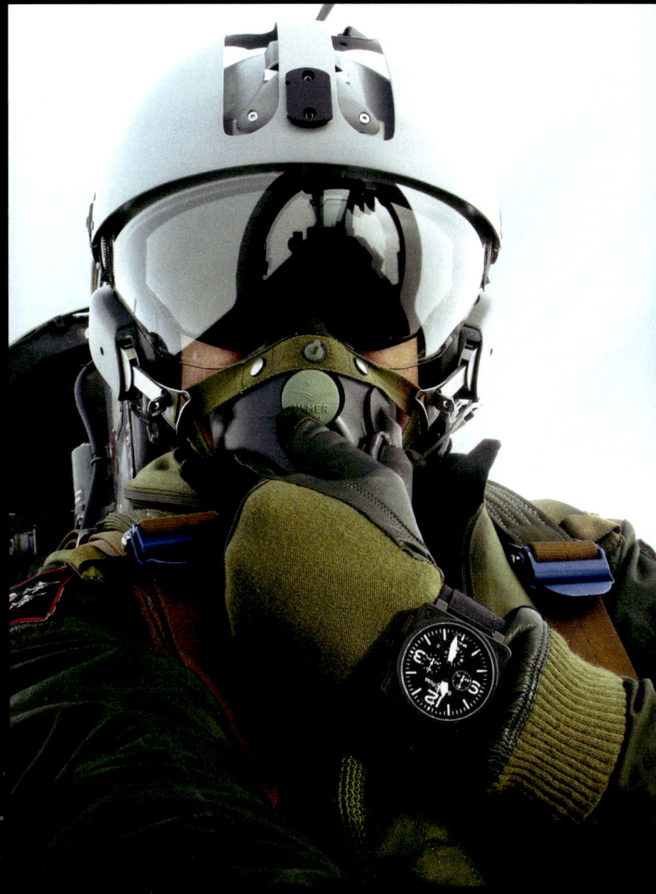

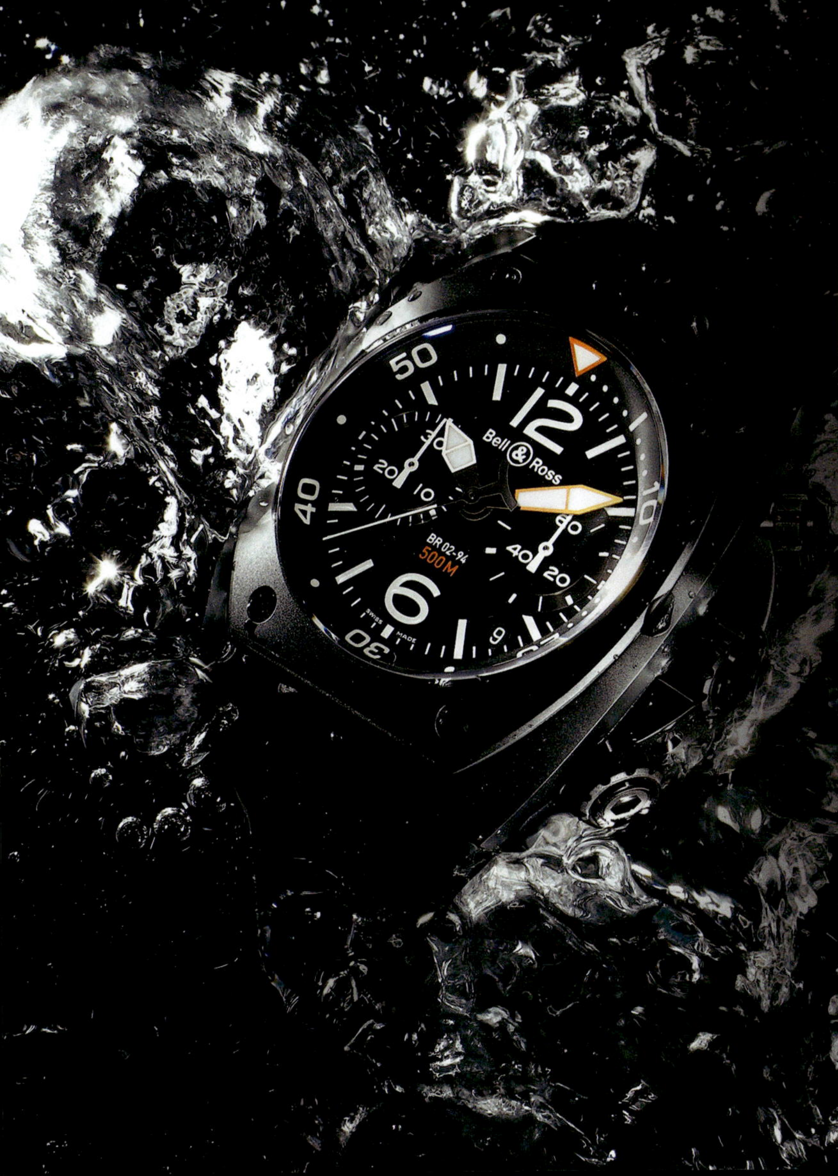

MARINE COLLECTION

Water resistant up to 1,000 meters, legible in the darkness of the deep, equipped with a decompression valve and a rotating bezel, unidirectional, notched and calibrated at 60 minutes, the BR 02 watch is a diving instrument perfectly adapted for professional use.

TOP

The Aviation BR 01-94 is clad in a carbon-finish steel case and powered by an automatic chronograph movement. $5,900.

LEFT

The Marine BR 02-94 houses an automatic chronograph movement within a carbon-finish steel case. $7,000.

VINTAGE BR 126 HERITAGE

Movement: automatic-winding ETA 2894.
Functions: hours, minutes, seconds; date; chronograph: 60-second and 30-minute counters.
Case: glass-bead-blasted 316 L stainless steel with vacuum carbon; Ø 41mm; black finish; antireflective sapphire crystal; water resistant to 10atm.
Dial: galvanic matte black; numerals, indexes and hands with a sand-colored photoluminescent coating to optimize nighttime reading.
Strap: natural leather.
Suggested price: $4,200

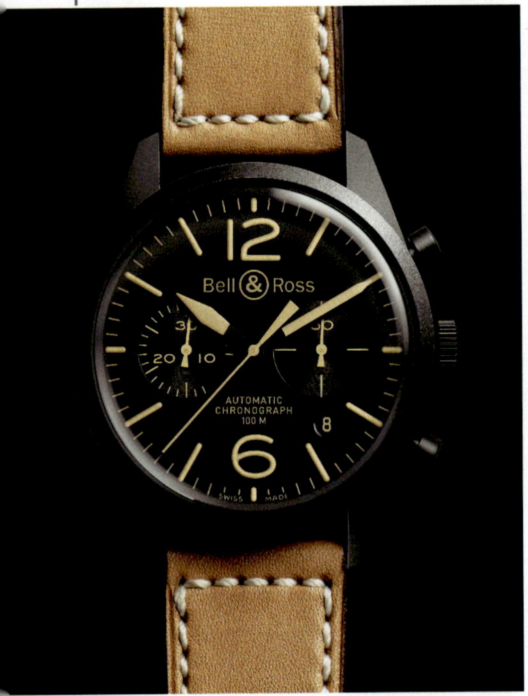

VINTAGE BR 123 ORIGINAL BLACK

Movement: automatic-winding ETA 2895.
Functions: hours, minutes; small seconds; date.
Case: satin-finished stainless steel; Ø 41mm; domed, antireflective sapphire crystal; water resistant to 10atm.
Dial: black; numerals, indexes and hands with photoluminescent coating to optimize nighttime reading.
Strap: black calfskin; satin-finished steel folding buckle.
Suggested price: $2,500

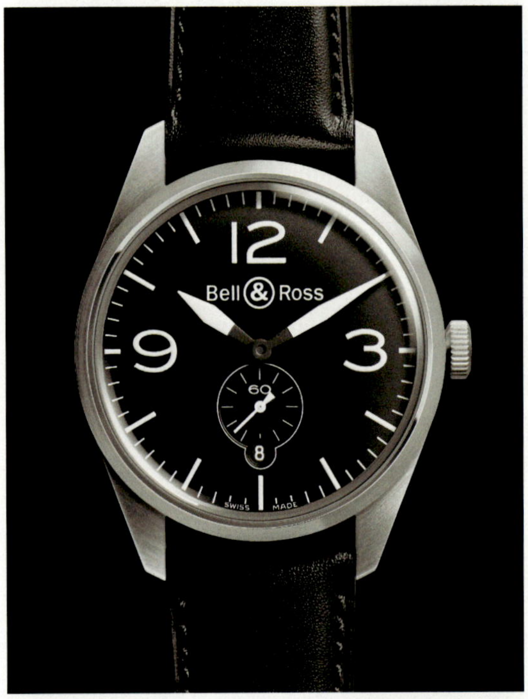

VINTAGE BR 123 CARBON BEIGE

Movement: automatic-winding ETA 2895.
Functions: hours, minutes; small seconds; date.
Case: shot-peened 316 L stainless steel with black PVD finish; Ø 41mm; antireflective sapphire crystal; screw-in caseback; water resistant to 10atm.
Dial: beige; numerals, indexes and hands with photoluminescent coating to optimize nighttime reading.
Strap: black leather; carbon finish tang buckle.
Suggested price: $2,900

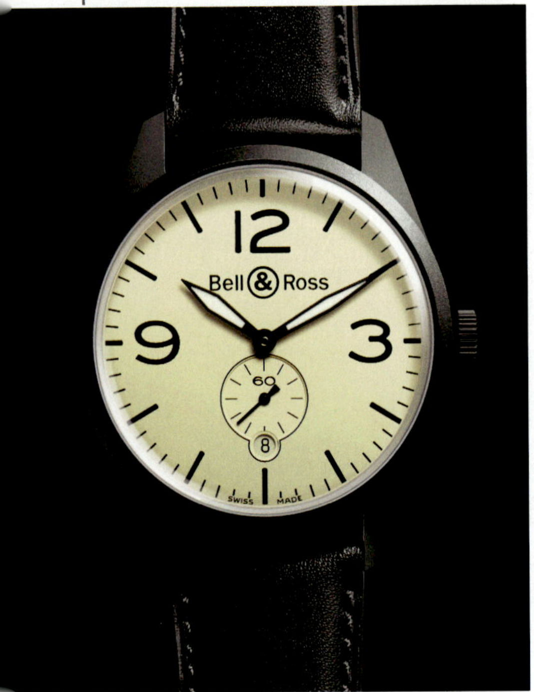

VINTAGE BR 126 OFFICER GREY

Movement: automatic-winding ETA 2894.
Functions: hours, minutes, seconds; date; chronograph: 60-second and 30-minute counters.
Case: polished stainless steel; Ø 41mm; domed, antireflective sapphire crystal; water resistant to 10atm.
Dial: silver; numerals, indexes and hands with photoluminescent coating to optimize nighttime reading; applied numerals and indexes.
Strap: gray alligator; polished steel folding buckle.
Suggested price: $4,000

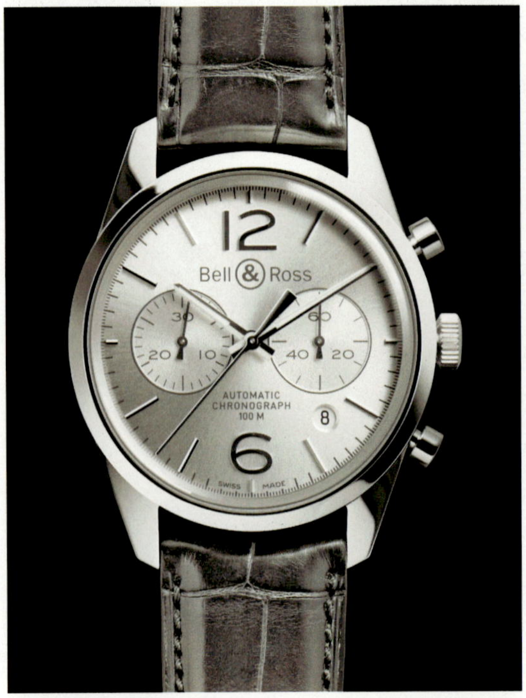

AVIATION BR 01-92 CARBON

Movement: automatic-winding ETA 2892.
Functions: hours, minutes, seconds.
Case: glass-bead blasted steel with black carbon powder coating; Ø 46mm; screw-in crown; antireflective sapphire crystal; water resistant to 10atm.
Dial: galvanic black; white numerals; indexes and hands with photoluminescent coating to optimize nighttime reading.
Strap: black rubber.
Suggested price: $4,000
Also available: satin finished 316 L stainless steel case; heavy-duty canvas strap.

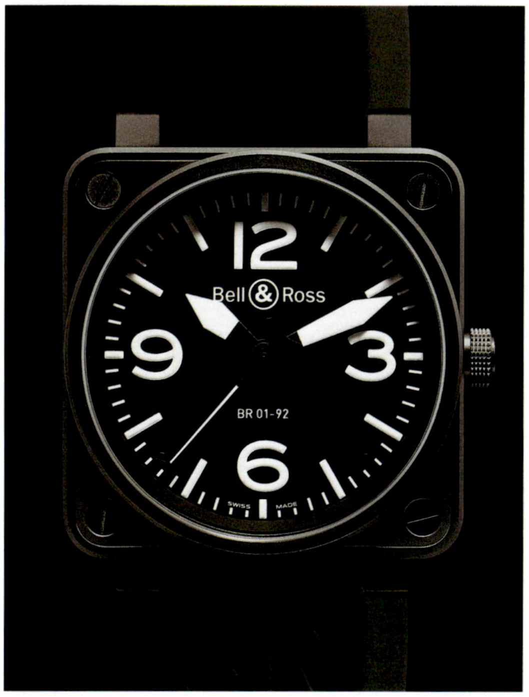

AVIATION BR 01-92 PINK GOLD / CARBON

Movement: automatic-winding ETA 2892.
Functions: hours, minutes, seconds.
Case: 18K pink gold with black PVD-finished steel; Ø 46mm; screw-in crown; antireflective sapphire crystal; water resistant to 10atm.
Dial: black; white numerals and indexes; indexes and hands with photoluminescent coating to optimize nighttime reading.
Strap: black rubber.
Suggested price: $8,900
Also available: leather or heavy-duty canvas strap.

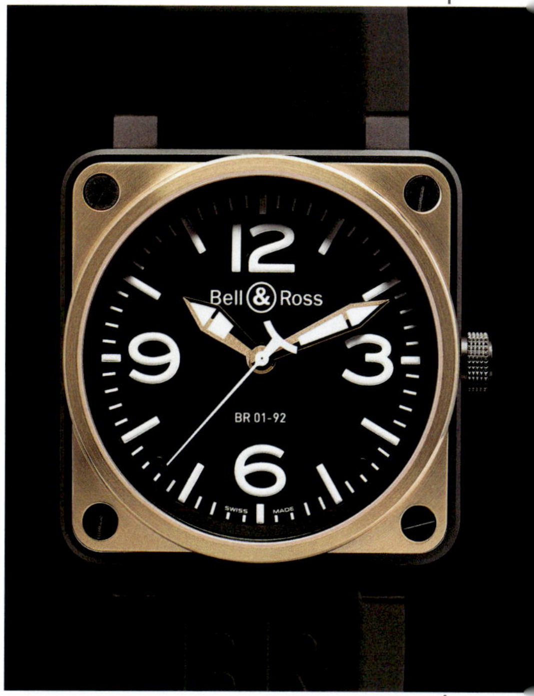

AVIATION BR 01-92 COMPASS

Movement: automatic-winding ETA 2892; disc display system.
Functions: hours, minutes.
Case: shot-peened 316 L stainless steel with black PVD finish; Ø 46mm; screw-in crown; antireflective sapphire crystal; water resistant to 10atm.
Dial: two concentric black discs; outside disc indicates the hours, inside disc indicates the minutes; numerals and indexes with photoluminescent coating to optimize nighttime reading.
Strap: black rubber.
Suggested price: $5,500
Also available: black leather strap; heavy-duty canvas strap.

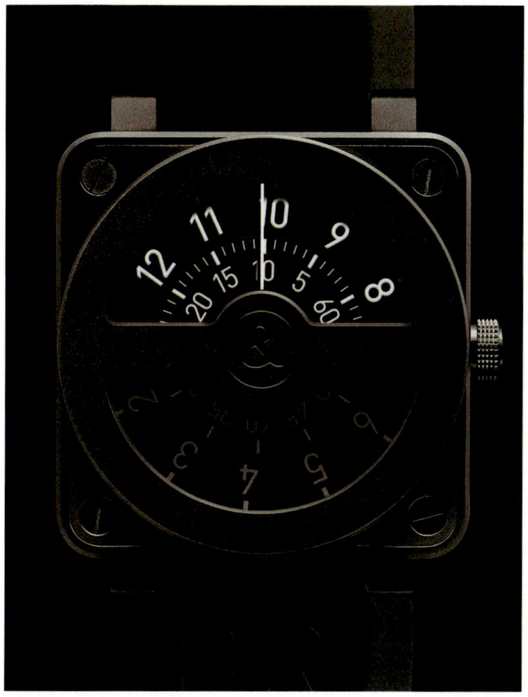

AVIATION BR 03-94 HERITAGE

Movement: automatic-winding ETA 2894.
Functions: hours, minutes, seconds; date; chronograph: 60-second and 30-minute counters.
Case: glass-bead-blasted 316 L stainless steel with black carbon powder finish; Ø 42mm; antireflective sapphire crystal; water resistant to 10atm.
Dial: black; numerals, indexes and hands with a sand-colored photoluminescent coating to optimize nighttime reading.
Strap: natural leather with embossed logo.
Suggested price: $5,500
Also available: black heavy-duty canvas strap.

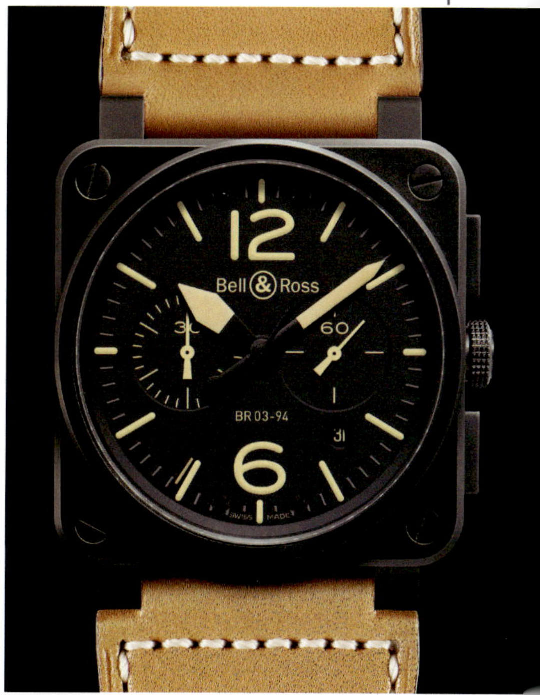

MARINE BR 02-92 PRO-DIAL 1000 M — CARBON

Movement: automatic-winding.
Functions: hours, minutes, seconds; date; decompression valve for deep-sea diving.
Case: glass-bead-blasted 316 L stainless steel with vacuum carbon black finish; Ø 44mm; unidirectional, cranted interior bezel graduated to 60 minutes with photoluminescent reference point; antireflective sapphire crystal; water resistant to 100atm.
Dial: black; large indexes with photoluminescent coating to optimize nighttime reading.
Strap: black rubber.
Suggested price: $4,500
Also available: heavy-duty canvas strap.

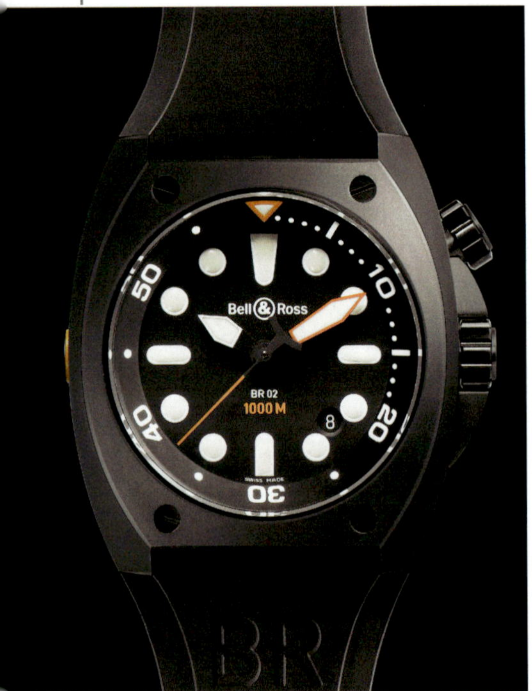

MARINE BR 02-94 CHRONOGRAPH 500 M — STEEL

Movement: automatic-winding.
Functions: hours, minutes, seconds; date; chronograph: 30-minute and 60-second counters; decompression valve for deep-sea diving.
Case: satin-polished stainless steel; Ø 44mm; unidirectional, cranted interior bezel graduated to 60 minutes with photoluminescent reference point; screw-in pushpieces, crowns and caseback; antireflective sapphire crystal; water resistant to 50atm.
Dial: black; numerals, indexes and hands with photoluminescent coating to optimize nighttime reading.
Strap: black rubber.
Suggested price: $6,500
Also available: glass-bead-blasted 316 L stainless steel case with vacuum carbon black finish; heavy-duty synthetic fabric strap.

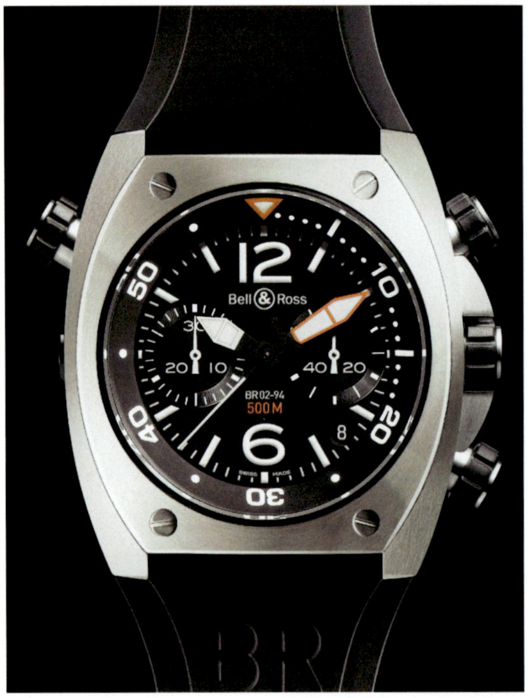

MARINE BR 02-92 300 M — PINK GOLD

Movement: automatic-winding.
Functions: hours, minutes, seconds; date; decompression valve for deep-sea diving.
Case: brushed solid 18K 5N pink gold; Ø 44mm; unidirectional, cranted interior bezel graduated to 60 minutes with photoluminescent reference point; screw-in crown; antireflective sapphire crystal; water resistant to 30atm.
Dial: carbon fiber; numerals and hands with photoluminescent coating to optimize nighttime reading; applied gold indexes.
Strap: black rubber.
Suggested price: $22,000
Also available: bicolor model: pink-gold and steel with vacuum carbon black finish case; heavy-duty canvas strap.

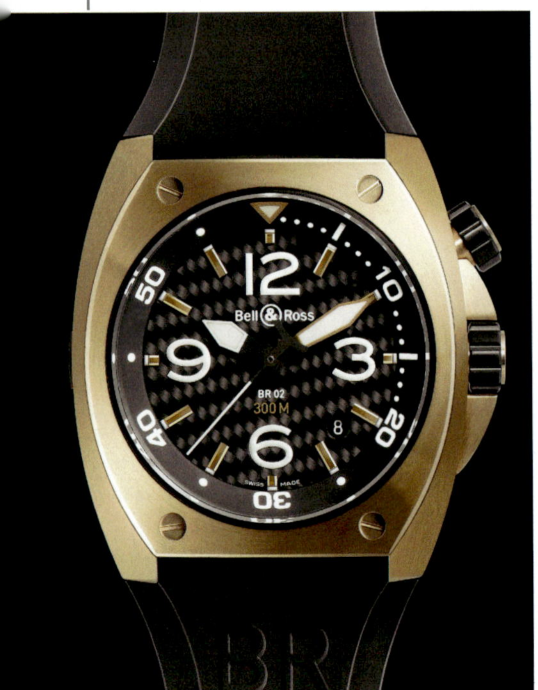

MARINE BR 02-94 CHRONOGRAPH 500 M — PINK GOLD/CARBON

Movement: automatic-winding.
Functions: hours, minutes, seconds; date; chronograph: 30-minute and 60-second counters; decompression valve for deep-sea diving.
Case: brushed solid 5N 18K pink gold; Ø 44mm; unidirectional, cranted interior bezel graduated to 60 minutes with photoluminescent reference point; screw-in pushpieces, crowns and caseback; antireflective sapphire crystal; water resistant to 30atm.
Dial: black; numerals and hands with photoluminescent coating to optimize nighttime reading; applied gold indexes.
Strap: black rubber.
Suggested price: $13,600
Also available: steel case with vacuum carbon black finish; heavy-duty canvas strap.

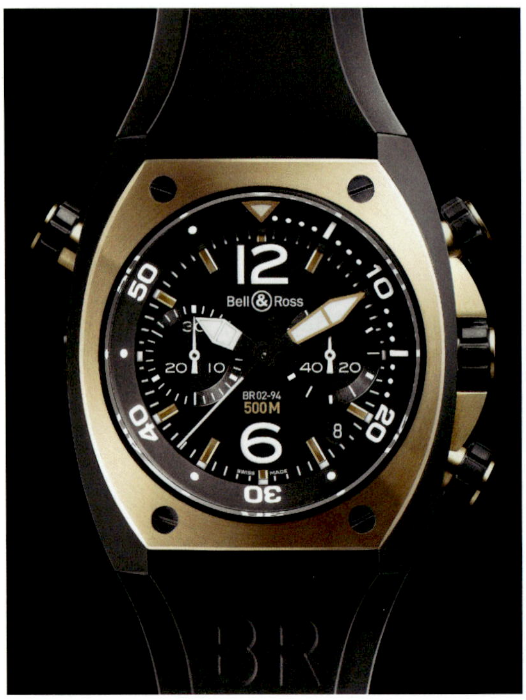

AVIATION BR 01 TOURBILLON PINK GOLD

Movement: manual-winding BR 01 tourbillon; 120-hour power reserve; carbon fiber mainplates and black-gold tourbillon carriage.
Functions: small hours at 12; central minutes; trust index at 3; power reserve indicator at 9.
Case: satin-polished pink gold; Ø 46mm; screw-in crown; antireflective sapphire crystal on both sides; water resistant to 10atm.
Dial: black carbon fiber; indexes and hands with photoluminescent coating to optimize nighttime reading.
Strap: black rubber.
Note: limited edition of 20 pieces.
Suggested price: $170,000
Also available: black alligator strap.

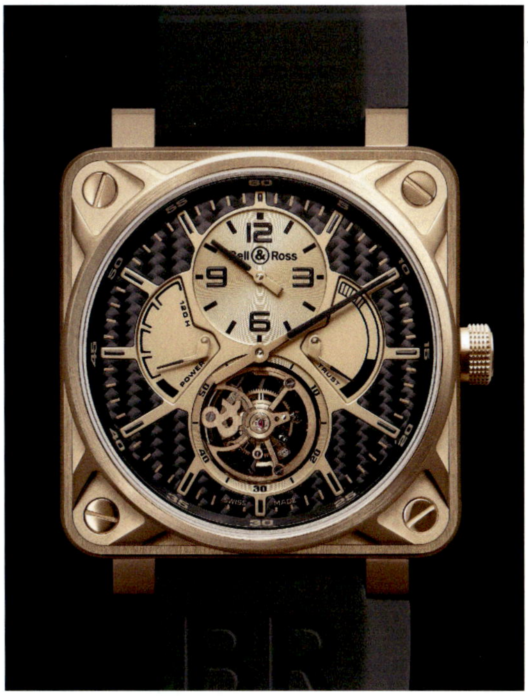

AVIATION BR 01 TOURBILLON

Movement: manual-winding BR 01 tourbillon; 120-hour power reserve; carbon fiber mainplates and black-gold tourbillon carriage.
Functions: small hours at 12; central minutes; trust index at 3; power reserve indicator at 9.
Case: glass-bead-blasted titanium with virtually unscratchable DLC coating (4,000 Vickers); Ø 46mm; screw-in crown; antireflective sapphire crystal on both sides; water resistant to 10atm.
Dial: black carbon fiber; indexes and hands with photoluminescent coating to optimize nighttime reading.
Strap: black rubber.
Note: limited edition of 60 pieces.
Suggested price: $140,000
Also available: black alligator strap.

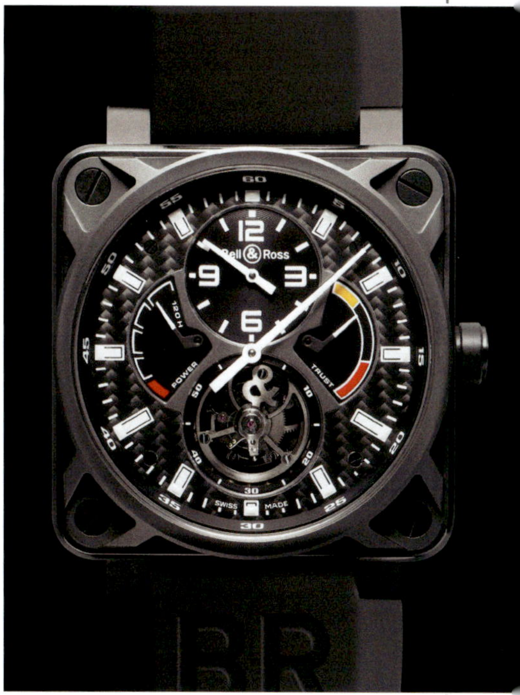

AVIATION BR 01 TOURBILLON PHANTOM

Movement: manual-winding BR 01 tourbillon; 120-hour power reserve; carbon fiber mainplates and black-gold tourbillon carriage.
Functions: small hours at 12; central minutes; trust index at 3; power reserve indicator at 9.
Case: glass-bead-blasted titanium with virtually unscratchable DLC coating (4,000 Vickers); Ø 46mm; screw-in crown; antireflective sapphire crystal on both sides; water resistant to 10atm.
Dial: black carbon fiber; indexes and hands with photoluminescent coating to optimize nighttime reading.
Strap: black rubber.
Note: limited edition of 18 pieces.
Suggested price: $150,000
Also available: black alligator strap.

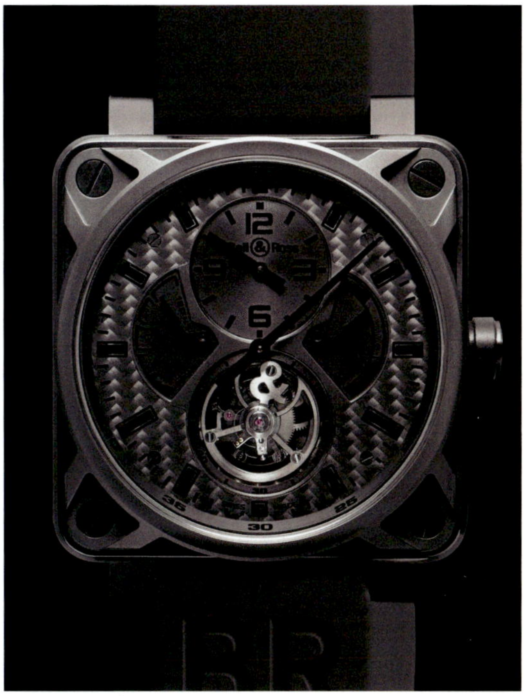

AVIATION BR 01 TOURBILLON AIRBORNE

Movement: manual-winding BR 01 tourbillon; 5-day power reserve; carbon fiber plates and bridges; black-gold tourbillon carriage.
Functions: tourbillon; trust index; regulator; power reserve indicator.
Case: titanium with DLC coating; Ø 46mm; titanium screw-in crown; antireflective sapphire crystal; sapphire caseback; water resistant to 10atm.
Dial: three-dimensional; black photoluminescent coating with mesh-like design.
Strap: shagreen.
Note: limited edition of 20 pieces.
Suggested price: $150,000

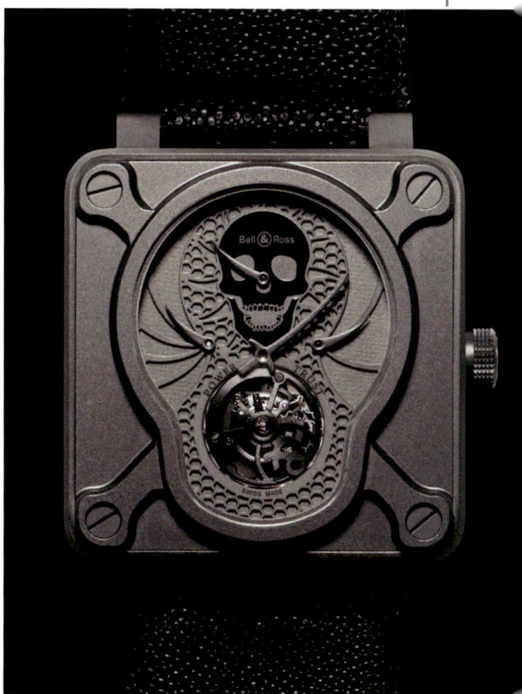

JB
1735
BLANCPAIN
MANUFACTURE DE HAUTE HORLOGERIE

CELEBRATING NEW BEGINNINGS

Located a few miles north of Lake Bienne, Villeret is a small village cradled in the craggy folds of the Swiss Jura Mountains where Jehan-Jacques Blancpain first started making watches in 1735.

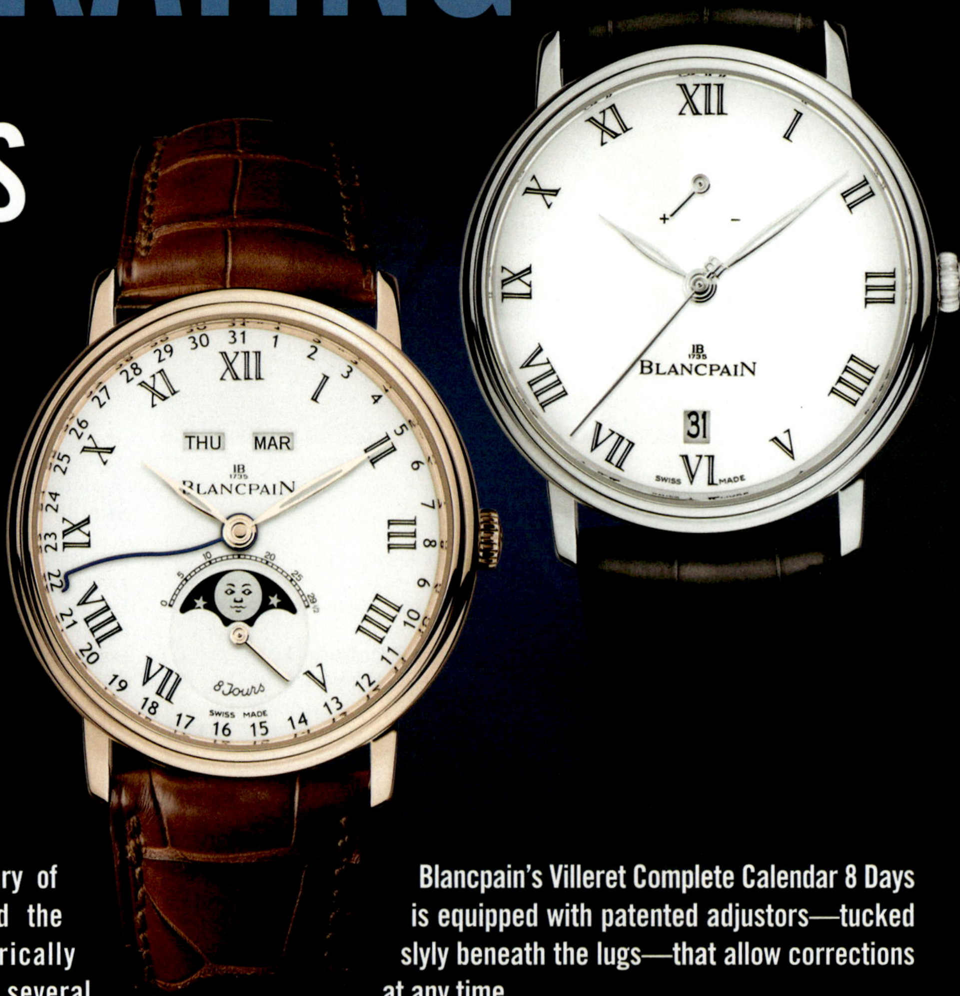

To celebrate the 275-year anniversary of this occasion, Blancpain revisited the collection named for this historically significant town in 2010 by welcoming several new additions to the Villeret family.

The renowned manufacture began with the Villeret Complete Calendar 8 Days. Like all the watches in this collection, the latest incarnation presents a style rooted firmly in a classic vein paired with a technical pedigree that is thoroughly modern. Its automatic movement boasts a trio of mainsprings that combine to imbue the timepiece with a power reserve notably more robust than similar models.

The watch bests its rivals once again with a patented innovation that improves its day-to-day functionality. While most complete calendar moonphase watches limit adjustments to certain times to avoid damaging the movement, Blancpain's Villeret Complete Calendar 8 Days is equipped with patented adjustors—tucked slyly beneath the lugs—that allow corrections at any time.

The wave of anniversary watches continues with the Villeret 8 Days Manual. A portrait of enchanting understatement, the white enamel dial is distilled to its essentials and embellished only with Roman numerals, date display and a power reserve indication whose extremes are marked simply by plus and minus symbols.

The Villeret 8 Days Manual's double-stepped case, a recurring visual theme throughout the Villeret collection for almost a generation, measures 42mm in diameter and is equipped with the company's manufacture 13R0 movement. Blancpain offers this model as a limited edition available in platinum or red gold.

Demonstrating a flair for handy invention, Blancpain offers a patented system on many of its watches to adjust the calendar function using a corrector hidden under the case's lug.

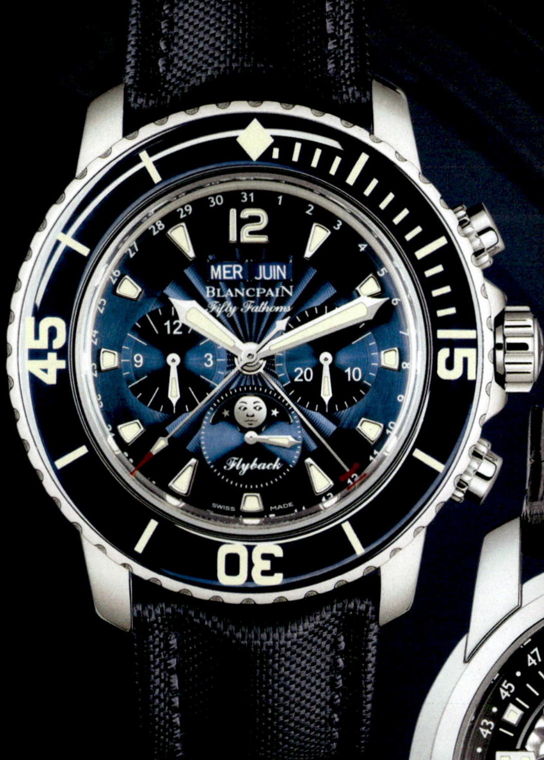

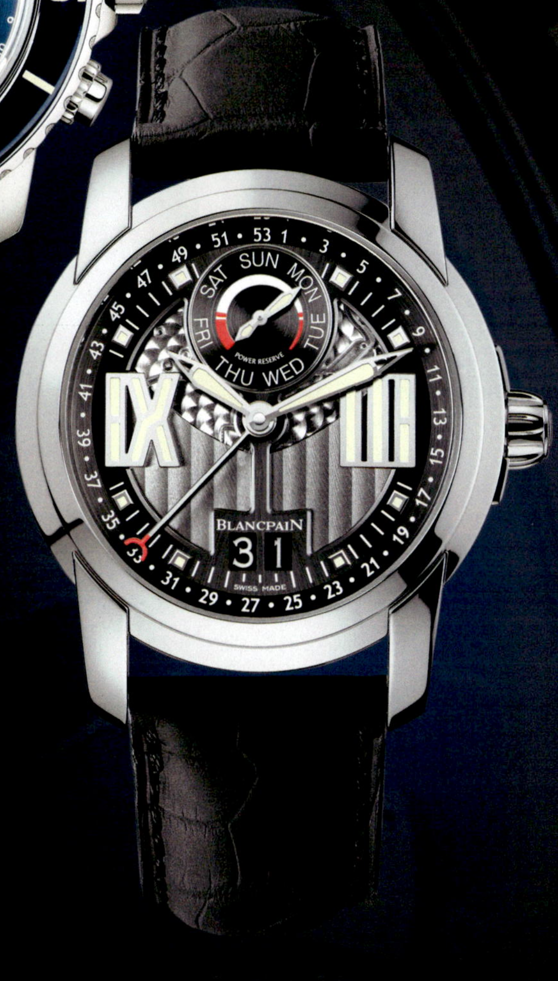

Blancpain takes one of its most popular designs into uncharted waters with the latest addition to its Fifty Fathoms collection. Already attuned to the rugged demands of water sports, Blancpain expands its capabilities with a moonphase, compete calendar and a column-wheel flyback chronograph.

Like many of Blancpain's calendar watches, adjustments to the Fifty Fathoms Complete Calendar Flyback Chronograph are not restricted to certain times. It also incorporates the same correctors hidden beneath the lug. This patented system, first unveiled in 2005, eliminates the need for an unsightly "dimple-style" corrector on the side of the case that requires a tool to manipulate. Instead, the corrector is concealed and can be operated by hand.

Water resistant to 30 bar, the 45mm stainless steel case is paired with a rich blue dial and a color-coordinated sapphire ring atop its unidirectional bezel.

Blancpain broadened the range of its L-Evolution collection a year after its 2009 debut with the addition of the Semainier Grande Date 8 Days.

Sharing the same bold look of its brethren, the watch's black Côtes de Genève dial opens at the top to reveal Blancpain's new côtes paraboliques decoration on the manufacture movement below. Large Roman numerals anchor the sides of the dial while a round display near the top indicates the day of the week, as well as the status of the power reserve. Along with two windows for the large date, the Semainier Grande Date 8 Days also includes a red-tipped hand that indicates the week of the year on a scale that runs along the dial's outer edge.

For this momentous anniversary, Blancpain welcomes a multitude of timepieces that not only honor its past, but also offer a clear vision of its future.

The Villeret Complete Calendar 8 Days is a limited edition model offered in a 32mm case cast in either platinum (75 pieces) or red gold (275 pieces).

The crisp design of the Villeret 8 Days Manual's white enamel dial features a subtle power reserve indicator as well as a date window.

The guilloché center of the Fifty Fathoms Complete Calendar Flyback Chronograph's blue dial features chronograph counters and a small seconds paired with a moonphase, as well as displays for the date, day of the week and month.

The L-Evolution Semainier Grande Date 8 Days adds an air of technical sophistication to the sporty collection by combining a display for week of the year, day of the week and power reserve indications for the exceptionally long eight-day power reserve.

CARROUSEL REPETITION MINUTES LE BRASSUS — REF. 0233-3634-55B

Movement: manual-winding 1736 caliber; Ø 32.8mm, thickness: 7.4mm; 60-hour power reserve; 48 jewels; 414 components; flying one-minute carrousel carriage.
Functions: hours, minutes; slide lever to operate minute repeater; cathedral gong.
Case: 18K red gold; Ø 45mm, thickness: 13.31mm; sapphire crystal caseback.
Dial: gray; skeletonized and open-worked, revealing BLANCPAIN movement.
Strap: dark brown Louisiana alligator leather.

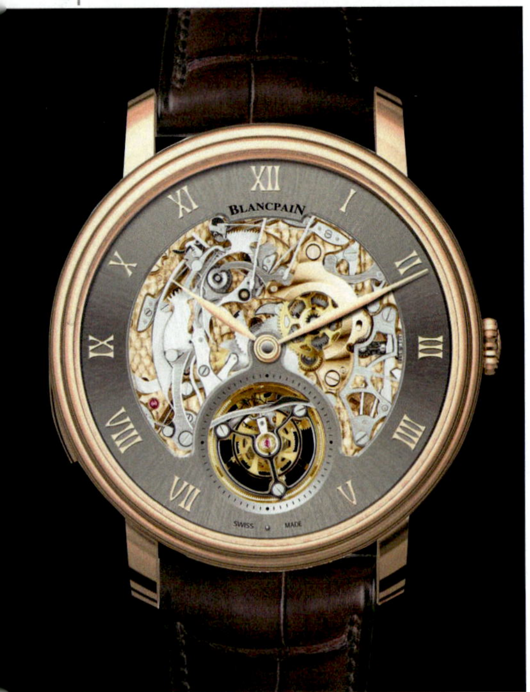

Note: limited to 10 pieces.
Suggested price: $365,500

TRIBUTE TO FIFTY FATHOMS "NO RADIATIONS" — REF. 5015B-1130-52

Movement: automatic-winding 1315 caliber; Ø 30.6mm, thickness: 4.57mm; 120-hour power reserve; 32 jewels; 222 components; soft iron antimagnetic cage.
Functions: hours, minutes, seconds; date at 3.
Case: stainless steel; Ø 45mm, thickness: 15.5mm; one-way rotating sapphire bezel; sapphire crystal caseback; water resistant to 3atm.
Dial: black; stainless steel hands.

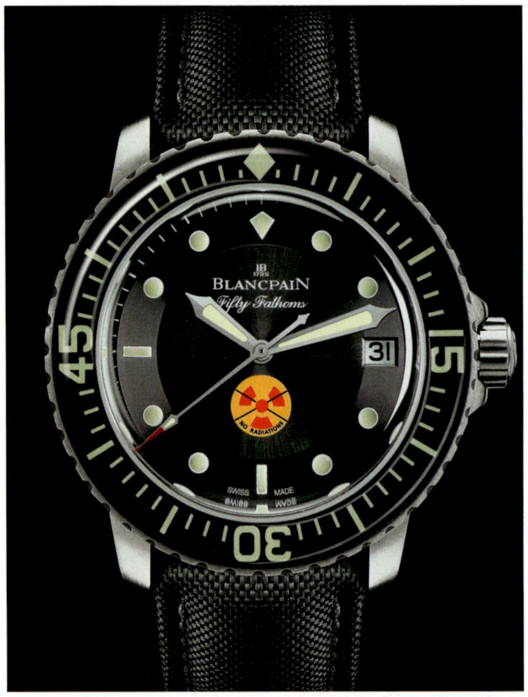

Strap: black snail canvas lined with rubber.
Note: limited to 500 pieces.
Suggested price: $14,600

L-EVOLUTION SEMAINIER GRANDE DATE 8 JOURS — REF. 8837-1134-53B

Movement: automatic-winding 37R8G caliber; Ø 32mm, thickness: 7.85mm; 192-hour power reserve; 46 jewels; 299 components.
Functions: hours, minutes, seconds; week; day; date at 6.
Case: stainless steel; Ø 43.5mm, thickness: 16.25mm; one-way rotating bezel; under-lug correctors; sapphire crystal caseback; water resistant to 10atm.
Dial: gray.

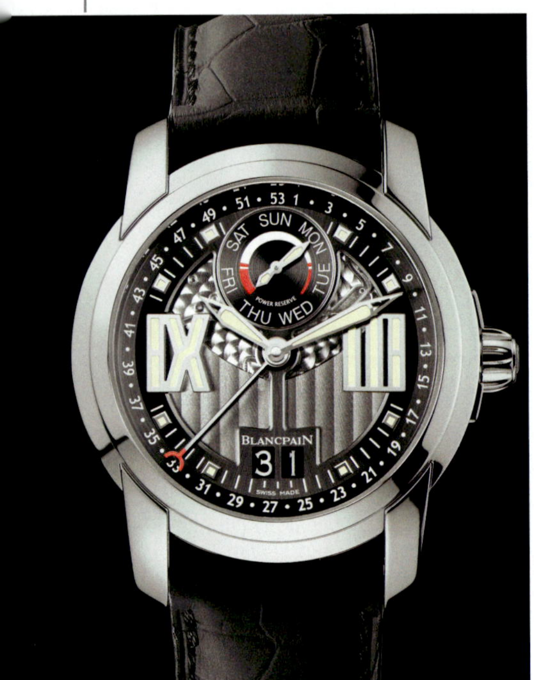

Strap: black Louisiana alligator leather.
Suggested price: $23,400
Also available: 18K red- or white-gold case with black dial (ref. 8837-3630-53B).

L-EVOLUTION TOURBILLON GMT — REF. 8825-3630-53B

Movement: automatic-winding 5025 caliber; Ø 32mm, thickness: 6.35mm; 192-hour power reserve; 33 jewels; 304 components.
Functions: hours, minutes, seconds; double-hand date display at 9; flying tourbillon at 12; GMT dual time zone.
Case: red gold; Ø 43.5mm, thickness: 13.45mm; sapphire crystal exhibition caseback; water resistant to 10atm.

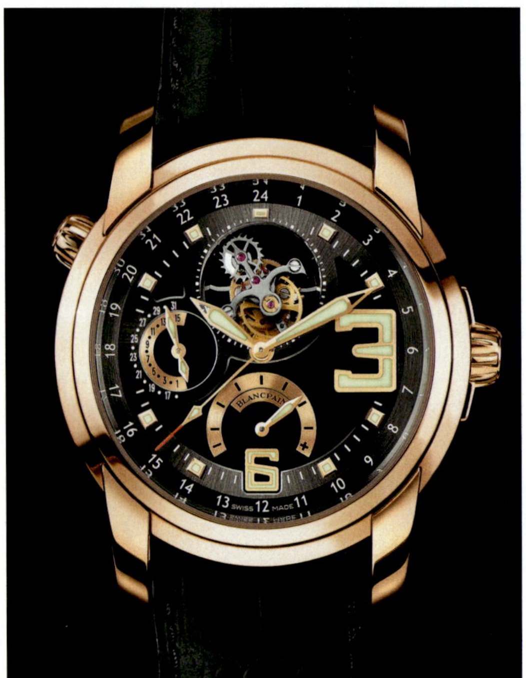

Dial: black; center provides distinct view of the dial baseplate adorned with Côtes de Genève; oversized 3 and 6 numerals.
Strap: Louisiana alligator leather.
Note: limited edition of 99 pieces.
Suggested price: $131,600
Also available: white gold.

VILLERET MONTRE DE POCHE DEMI-SAVONNETTE REF. 0151-3631-000A

Movement: manual-winding 151B caliber; Ø 36.1mm, thickness: 2.2mm; 40-hour power reserve; 20 jewels; 117 components.
Functions: hours, minutes; small seconds.
Case: rose gold; Ø 44.55mm, thickness: 8.94mm; sapphire crystal caseback.
Dial: gray; full fired enamel.
Suggested price: $58,500

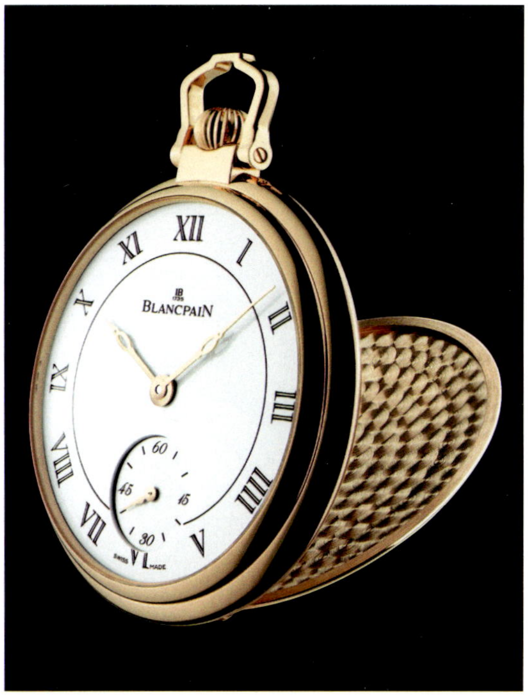

VILLERET 8 JOURS MANUELLE REF. 6613-3431-55B

Movement: manual-winding 13R0 caliber; Ø 30.6mm, thickness: 4.57mm; 192-hour power reserve; 28 jewels; 211 components.
Functions: hours, minutes; small seconds.
Case: platinum; Ø 42mm, thickness: 11.2mm; sapphire crystal caseback; water resistant to 3atm.
Dial: full fired enamel.
Strap: black Louisiana alligator leather.
Note: limited edition of 75 pieces.
Suggested price: $49,700
Also available: rose-gold case 6613-3631-55B, limited edition of 275 pieces.

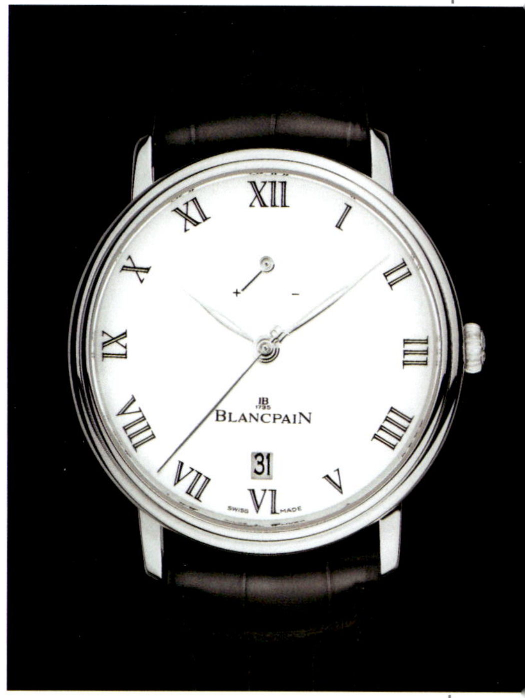

VILLERET COMPLETE CALENDAR 8 JOURS REF. 6639-3631-55B

Movement: automatic-winding 6639 caliber; Ø 32mm, thickness: 7.6mm; 192-hour power reserve; 36 jewels; 303 components.
Functions: hours, minutes; small seconds; complete calendar; moonphase.
Case: rose gold; Ø 42mm, thickness: 13.07mm; sapphire crystal caseback; water resistant to 3atm.
Dial: full fired enamel.
Strap: light brown Louisiana alligator leather.
Note: limited edition of 275 pieces.
Suggested price: $37,000
Also available: platimum case (ref. 6613-3631-55B).

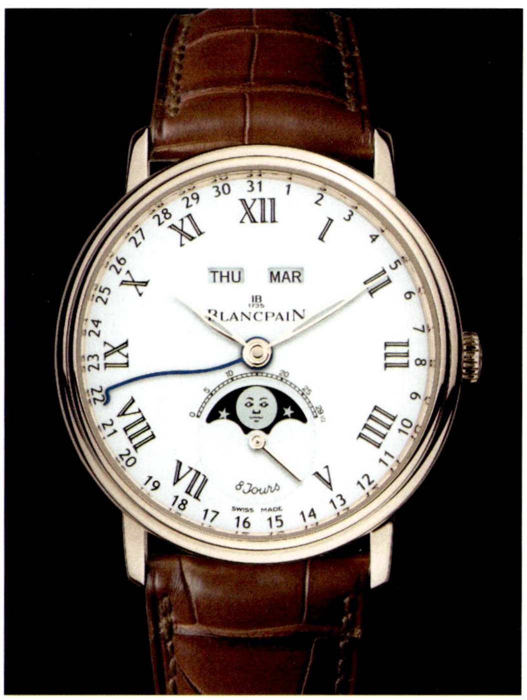

VILLERET PHASE DE LUNE DEMI-SAVONNETTE REF. 6664-3642-55B

Movement: automatic-winding 6654 caliber; Ø 32mm, thickness: 5.32mm; 72-hour power reserve; 28 jewels; 321 components.
Functions: hours, minutes; seconds; complete calendar; moonphase.
Case: rose gold; Ø 42mm, thickness: 13.07mm; under-lug correctors; sapphire crystal caseback; water resistant to 3atm.
Dial: opaline.
Strap: dark brown Louisiana alligator leather.
Suggested price: $26,200

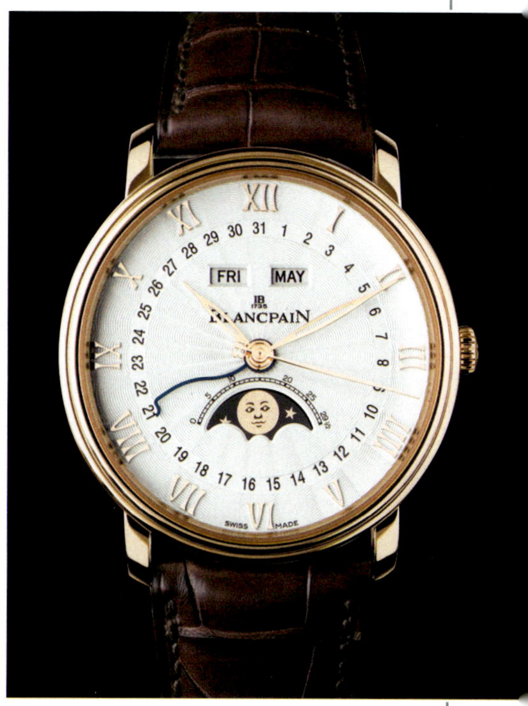

BOUCHERON

PARIS

CRAZY IN LOVE

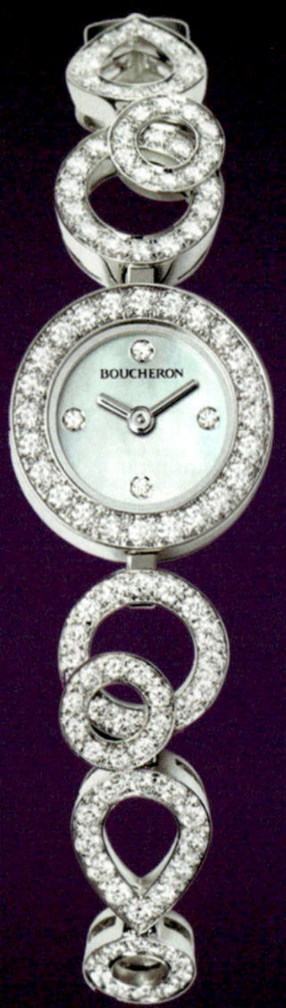

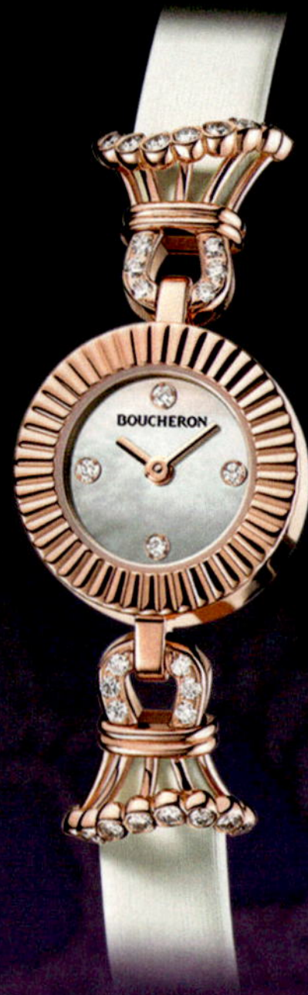

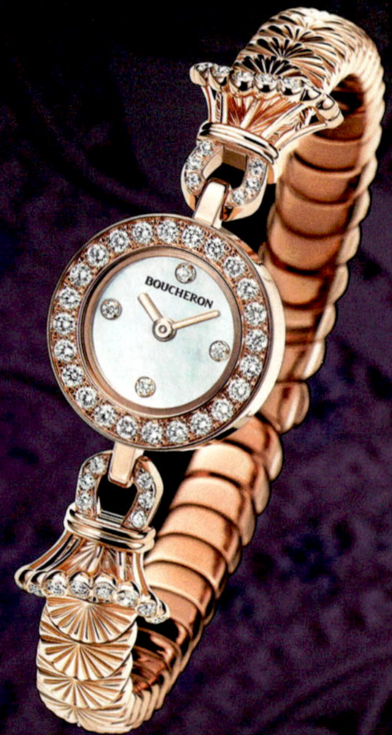

Known around the world for crafting jewelry watches that celebrate feminine sensuality and glamour, Boucheron's scintillating creations vividly reflect the individuality of the dynamic women who wear them.

A leader in petite ladies' wristwatches since the late 19th century, the legendary French jeweler offers an exceptional collection that artfully balances technical and aesthetic sophistication.

Boucheron's latest introductions burnish the House's reputation with sculptural bracelets and dainty dials adorned with exquisite gems. The Ava Déco leads the way. Its name, as well as its shapely profile and timeless beauty, are tributes to film star Ava Gardner, who began stealing hearts in the 1950s with her breakout role in director John Ford's *On The Beach*.

The Ava Déco's 18mm diamond-set case and its mother-of-pearl dial complete the visual motif carried out by the white-gold bracelet's sparkling round and teardrop-shaped links. Boucheron uses multiple white diamonds to decorate this curvaceous design.

The flowing feminine lines continue with Ma Jolie, a pink-gold model that underscores the consummate skills of the artisans responsible for the fine details that distinguish Boucheron's jewelry watches. Here, they forge golden corollas that are set with diamonds and used to connect the 18mm case to either a matching bracelet or a white brushed-satin strap. The bracelet is artfully constructed in a motif that evokes makeup brushes, the perfect symbol of the pampering inherent in any beauty ritual.

ABOVE

Diamond-tipped corollas connect the Ma Jolie's pink-gold case with a matching jewelry bracelet that features textured, overlapping links. To set the watch, a pushbutton is included on the caseback. The Ma Jolie watches are also available with satin straps.

Multiple diamonds decorate the Ava Déco's 18mm white-gold case and jewelry bracelet. A jewelry clasp secures the beguiling timekeeper to the wrist with a hidden fastener.

Boucheron draws inspiration from icons of femininity, grace and intelligence for its jeweled watches, which capture the essence of sensuality.

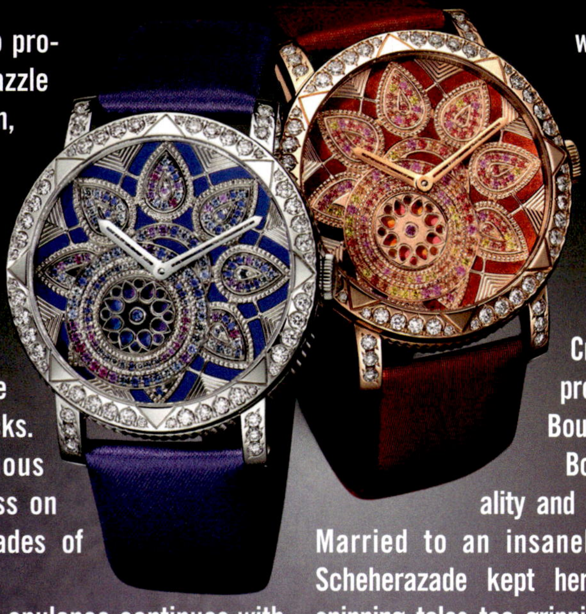

And because Boucheron likes to provide audacious timepieces that dazzle the senses of charismatic women, they have created a new character in its Crazy Jungle collection this year: Crazy Hathi, which means "elephant" in Hindi. This very rare and sacred talisman animal draws inspiration from Indian elephants, adorned with silk, carrying the Maharaja's treasures on their backs. In this timepiece, the prestigious animal carries a touch of madness on its carpet, unveiling different shades of color as the seconds slip by.

Boucheron's interest in sensual opulence continues with the Crazy Parade. An ostentatious peacock roosts on the watch's expansive dial, flaunting his plumage in a come-hither display intended to seduce his peahen's heart. The flirty feathers fill the dial with gorgeous colors and sharp details conjured by masters adept at the ancient decorative arts of engraving, enameling and gem-setting.

The champlevé grand feu enamel gives depth to the feathers' greens and blues, breathing life into the plumage of this proud Casanova. Boucheron artisans set a blue sapphire for the "eye" of each quill, using the gem again to create the peacock's chest. Impossible to fence in, the peacock's tail spills out from the dial and onto the white-gold bezel, where enamel and sapphires dance to the edge.

Beneath his proudly bejeweled chest beats the Seconde Folle (Crazy Second), a complication developed for Boucheron whose regular movement gives the impression that the peacock is strutting about an opulent courtyard. The Seconde Folle module is integrated into GP4000, an automatic movement manufactured by Girard-Perregaux that powers the Crazy Parade and Crazy Hathi. For a closer look at the precise machinations of the GP4000, Boucheron provides a clear caseback.

Boucheron spins a narrative of sensuality and opulence in the Crazy Shéhérazade. Married to an insanely jealous sultan, the legendary Scheherazade kept her head attached to her neck by spinning tales too gripping to interrupt, fictions that formed the *1,001 Arabian Nights*. Her courageous, wily spirit lives on in the watch that bears her name, whose diamond-adorned tourbillon's rhythm is as hypnotic as a perfectly told story. The timepiece's design draws inspiration from ancient Persian jewels, in an Oriental mosaic that is decorated with round golden beads, lapis lazuli or Sonora Sunrise and precious stones such as diamonds, multicolored sapphires, amethysts and aquamarine.

Only a house such as Boucheron—an innovator in the worlds of both jewelry and horology for nearly 152 years—could marshal the artistry and ingenuity needed to create models as rarefied, as sensual and as feminine as these.

ABOVE CENTER

Crazy Shéhérazade, powered by the GP400 automatic movement and equipped with a Seconde Folle module. Its dial and bezel are sculpted and composed like an oriental mosaic, available in white gold with pearled and engraved decorations, lapis lazuli, diamonds, multicolored sapphires, amethysts and aquamarine or in pink gold with Sonora Sunrise. Both of them have a Crazy Second module unveiling matching color discs underneath the golden mashrabiya.

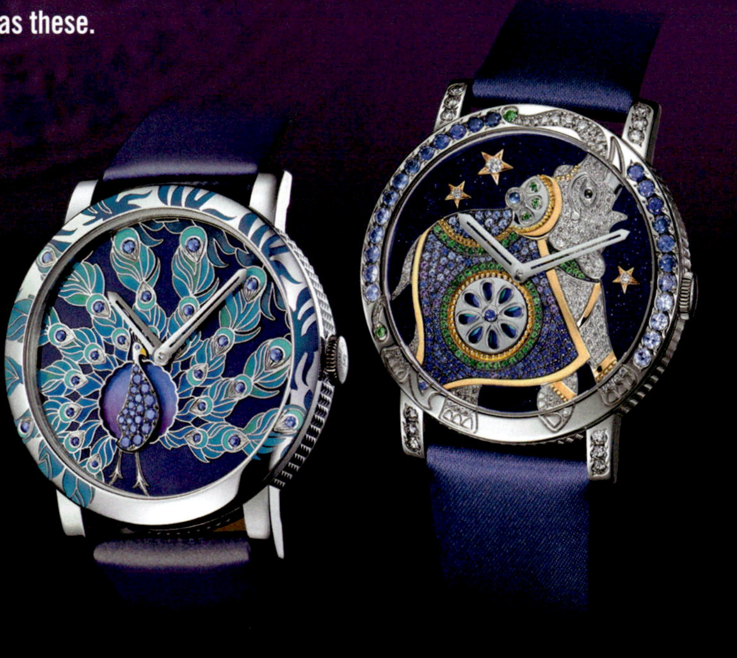

Crazy Parade with Grand Feu enameled peacock on the dial and bezel. Blue sapphires cover the bird's chest and plumage while the "Crazy Second" complication rotates below, making it appear as if the peacock is breathing.

The Crazy Hathi, in white gold, bears an elephant as talisman on the dial and bezel. The watch is set with diamonds, blue sapphires, tsavorites, amethysts and onyx; the sky is represented by aventurine glass with yellow-gold stars set with diamonds, and a Crazy Second module beats underneath the elephant's carpet.

PANAME AUTOMATIC CHRONOGRAPH IN STEEL AND DIAMONDS REF. WA010212

Movement: mechanical automatic-winding.
Functions: hours, minutes, seconds; date at 6; chronograph.
Case: polished stainless steel; Ø 42mm, thickness: 12.2mm; polished bezel set with 52 diamonds (~1.7 carats); fluted crown engraved with "26 Place Vendôme Paris"; polished middle case with rectangular pushbuttons and "Pointe de diamant" pattern; sapphire crystal with antireflective treatment on the inner side; brushed caseback with sapphire crystal; water resistant to 5atm.
Dial: silver; rhodium Arabic numerals; anthracite minute scale; two horizontal counters set with 72 diamonds; rhodium-plated hands; horizontal Boucheron mark at 12; "26 Place Vendôme" at 6.
Strap: white varanus; steel folding buckle with "Pointe de diamant" pattern and Boucheron mark.
Also available: steel anthracite dial and black strap.

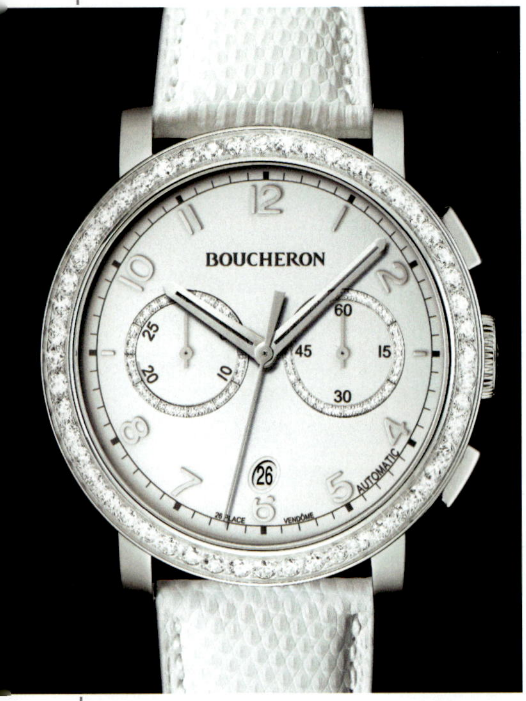

PANAME AUTOMATIC CHRONOGRAPH IN STEEL REF. WA010207

Movement: mechanical automatic-winding.
Functions: hours, minutes, seconds; date at 6; chronograph.
Case: polished stainless steel; Ø 42mm, thickness: 12.2mm; polished bezel with gadroons; fluted crown engraved with "26 Place Vendôme Paris"; sapphire crystal with antireflective treatment on the inner side; polished middle case with rectangular pushbuttons and "Pointe de diamant" pattern; sapphire crystal with antireflective treatment on the inner side; brushed caseback with sapphire crystal; water resistant to 5atm.
Dial: anthracite; rhodium Arabic numerals; white minute scale; two horizontal counters with rhodium outline and white graduation; rhodium-plated hands; horizontal Boucheron mark at 12; "26 Place Vendôme" at 6.
Strap: black alligator; steel folding buckle with "Pointe de diamant" pattern and Boucheron mark.
Also available: steel; silver dial with black alligator strap or white brushed-satin strap; pink gold, silver dial with brown alligator strap.

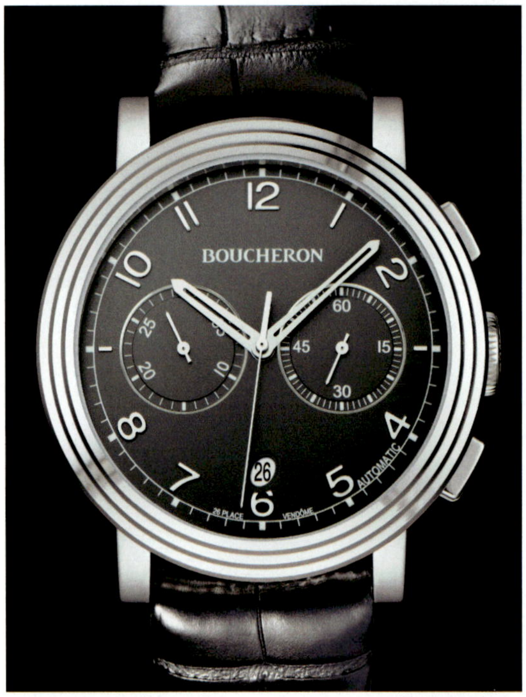

REFLET MEDIUM WATCH IN STEEL REF. WA009418

Movement: quartz.
Functions: hours, minutes.
Case: polished stainless steel; vertical gadroons; 34x21mm, thickness: 6.5mm; fluted crown engraved with "26 Place Vendôme Paris"; caseback with "Pointe de diamant" pattern; serial number with BOUCHERON historical stamp; sapphire crystal with antireflective treatment; water resistant to 3atm.
Dial: pink mother-of-pearl; Roman numerals (6 and 12); rhodium-plated hands; horizontal Boucheron mark at 12; "26 Place Vendôme" at 6.
Strap: interchangeable straps and bracelet available; sold with two straps chosen from the wide assortment.
Also available: white mother-of-pearl; Reflet Small with smaller case.

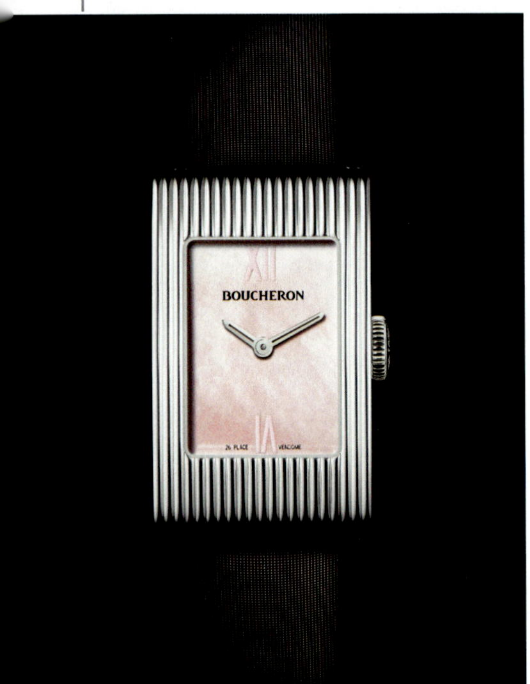

REFLET SMALL WATCH IN STEEL AND DIAMONDS REF. WA009503

Movement: quartz.
Functions: hours, minutes.
Case: polished stainless steel; vertical gadroons; set with 34 diamonds (~0.5 carat); 29.5x18mm, thickness: 6.4mm; fluted crown engraved with "26 Place Vendôme Paris"; caseback with "Pointe de diamant" pattern; serial number with BOUCHERON historical stamp; sapphire crystal with antireflective treatment; water resistant to 3atm.
Dial: silver; vertical gadroons pattern; four diamond indexes; rhodium-plated hands; horizontal Boucheron mark at 12; "26 Place Vendôme" at 6.
Strap: interchangeable straps and bracelet available; sold with two straps chosen from the wide assortment.
Also available: in steel non set, in yellow gold with or without diamonds; Reflet Medium with bigger case.

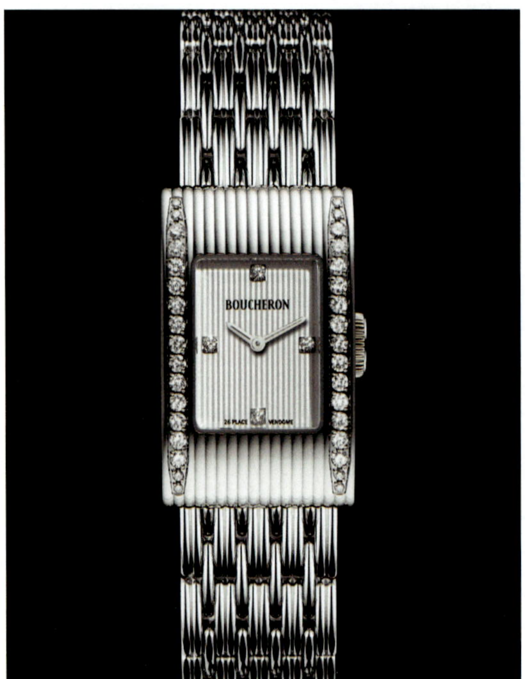

MA JOLIE - JEWELRY WATCH IN PINK GOLD & DIAMONDS REF. WA012501

Movement: quartz.
Functions: hours, minutes.
Case: 18K 5N pink gold; set with 24 diamonds (~0.5 carat); Ø 18mm, thickness: 6.8mm; pushbutton on the caseback for time setting; sapphire crystal with antireflective treatment; water resistant to 3atm.
Dial: white mother-of-pearl; four diamond indexes; 4N gold-plated hour and minute hands; horizontal Boucheron mark at 12.
Jewelry bracelet: 18K 5N pink gold; set with tie and powder puff made of golden thread with diamond bezel set on top (30 diamonds); links sculpted like little make-up brushes, secured jewelry clasp.
Also available: white brushed satin strap, 18K 5N pink-gold pin buckle.

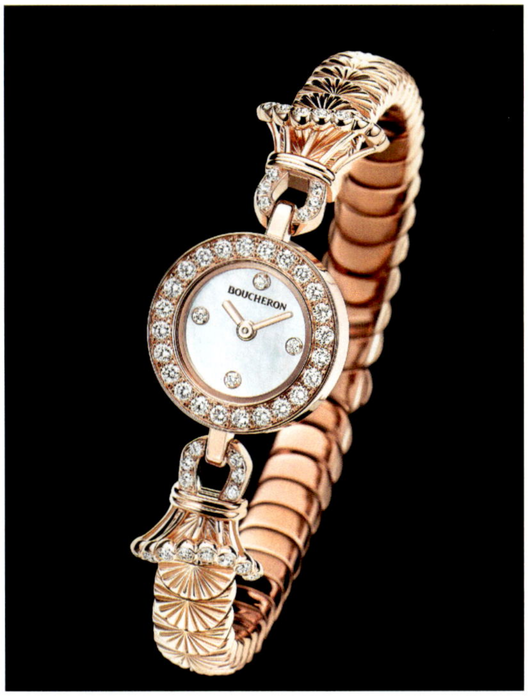

AVA DECO - JEWELRY WATCH IN WHITE GOLD & DIAMONDS REF. WA008503

Movement: quartz.
Functions: hours, minutes.
Case: 18K polished white gold; set with 24 diamonds (~0.5 carat); Ø 18mm, thickness: 6.8mm; pushbutton on the caseback for time setting; sapphire crystal with antireflective treatment; water resistant to 3atm.
Dial: white mother-of-pearl; four diamond indexes; nickel-plated hour and minute hands; horizontal Boucheron mark at 12.
Jewelry bracelet: 18K polished white gold; Ava Deco jewelry pattern, set with 104 diamonds; secured jewelry clasp set with diamonds.

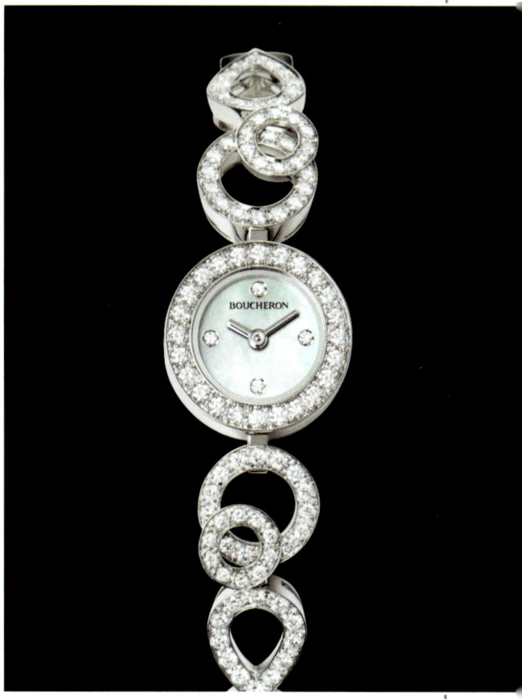

CRAZY PARADE IN WHITE GOLD - ENAMELED AND SET PEACOCK REF. WA010220

Movement: mechanical automatic-winding Girard-Perregaux manufacture GP4000 caliber; additional module Seconde Folle (Crazy Second); movement finishing personalized for Boucheron; oscillating weight shaped like the historical stamp of Boucheron.
Functions: hours, minutes and disc of seconds at 7.
Case: polished 18K white gold; Ø 42mm, thickness: 11.1mm; bezel set and covered with shaded blue opal Champlevé Enamel (Grand Feu); fluted crown engraved with "26 Place Vendôme Paris"; polished middle case with "Pointe de diamant" pattern; sapphire crystal with antireflective treatment; brushed caseback with sapphire crystal; water resistant to 5atm.
Dial: 18K white gold; engraved and set with blue sapphires; transparent purple, shaded blue opal and turquoise opaque Champlevé Enamel (Grand Feu); disc of seconds displaying blue and purple folding feathers of the parading peacock.
Strap: purple bronze leather; polished 18K white-gold buckle with "Pointe de diamant" pattern and Boucheron mark.
Also available: Crazy Jungle Collection featuring other animals.

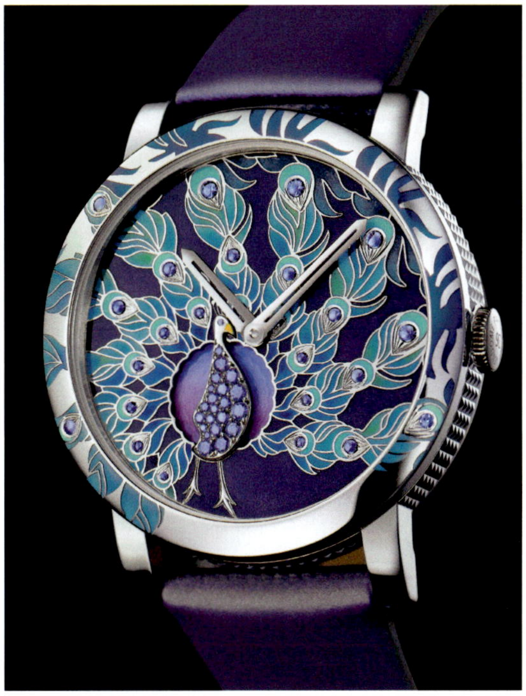

TOURBILLON SHEHERAZADE IN WHITE GOLD REF. WA010214

Movement: mechanical manual-winding flying tourbillon; Swiss escapement lever; bridges manually angled and shaped like the "B" of Boucheron.
Functions: hours, minutes; tourbillon.
Case: polished 18K white gold; polished middle case with "Pointe de diamant" pattern; Ø 42mm, thickness: 16.6mm; bezel set with diamonds and multi-colored sapphires; pearled crown set with a spinel cabochon; sapphire crystal with antireflective treatment; brushed caseback with sapphire crystal; water resistant to 5atm.
Dial: 18K 5N pink gold; covered with a mosaic of mother-of-pearl, diamonds, multi-colored sapphires, spinels, rubies and golden pearls; tourbillon carriage at 7; arms shaped like leaves, one leaf set with diamonds; additional module to off-center the hour and minute hands at 1.
Strap: red iridescent satin; polished 18K white-gold buckle with "Pointe de diamant" pattern and Boucheron mark.
Also available: blue version.

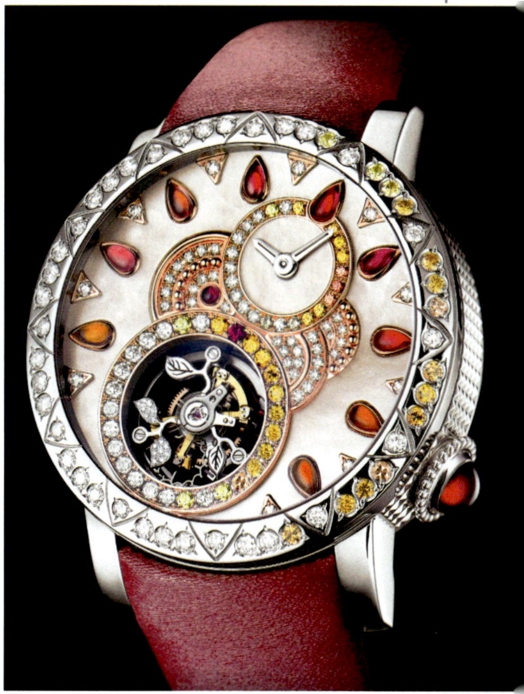

Breguet
Depuis 1775

HIGH-FLYING DESIGN

No complication expresses the art of watchmaking better than the repeater. More than just a technical challenge to assemble, it also demands an extraordinary level of artistry to fine-tune its ringing song.

Breguet once again proved its horological expertise in 2010 with the addition of an hour striker to its Reine de Naples collection. As its name suggests, this watch honors the Queen of Naples, Caroline Murat, who ordered the first wrist-worn timepiece from Breguet 200 years ago.

At the heart of the Reine de Naples Hour-Strike is a distinctive egg-shaped movement, whose ovoid form is echoed by the diamond-set white-gold case. When the caliber's repeater is engaged, it announces the hour automatically with two strikes repeated three times.

Decorated with a hammered texture, the white mother-of-pearl dial exposes the repeater's hammers at the top through two wing-like openings that are separated by a diamond solitaire. Below, two blued Breguet-shaped hands indicate the hours and minutes on the offset chapter ring.

Turning the watch over reveals the magnificent decoration applied to the automatic movement, which is shaped like a dove. Its wings are spread out in flight to show off the mechanism's construction and a number of its 54 jewels. To finish the look, Breguet's master artisans embellish the rotor with a detailed engraving of the dove's tail feathers.

In a nice visual twist, the bird slips the bonds of its cage as the tips of its feathers extend beyond the movement and onto the caseback ring where they are completed by an engraver's hand.

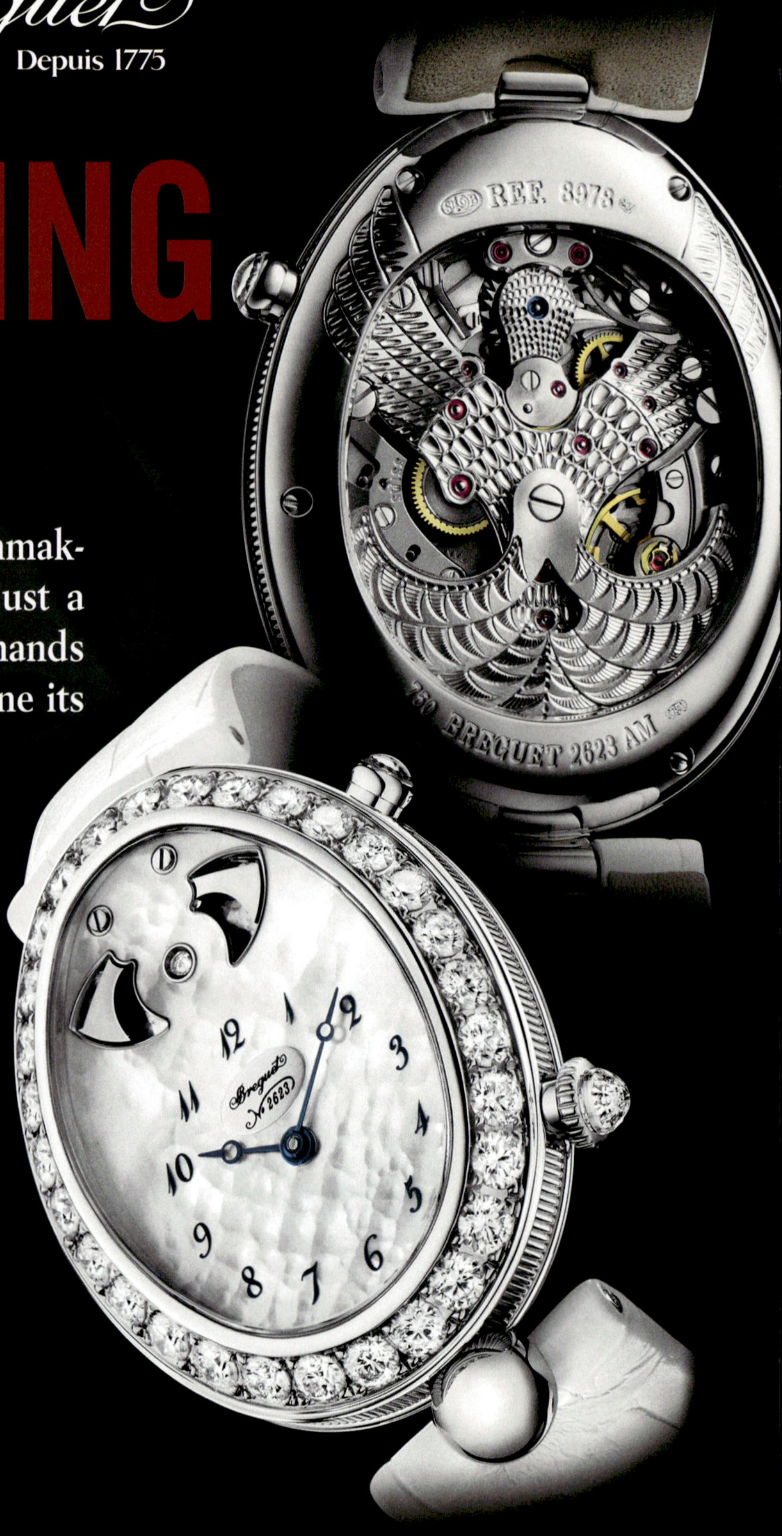

Caliber 78S0 is shaped like a dove in flight and features detailed hand engraving. The automatic movement's rotor is made to look like the bird's tail feathers.

The white-gold Reine de Naples Hour-Strike's egg-shaped bezel is set with 30 diamonds. The precious stones are also used on the mother-of-pearl dial between the repeater's hammers and on top of the crown.

Breguet spotlights its technical expertise with a silicon escapement in its Type XXII. The unique properties of the cutting-edge material allow the balance spring to achieve a remarkable 72,000 vibrations per hour.

Breguet celebrated aerial design of another kind last year with the latest version of its Type XXII, which is based on a chronograph the company created 60 years ago for the aviation wing of the French Navy.

The watchmaker updates the legendary original with a high-frequency silicon escapement equipped with a balance spring attuned to an incredible 72,000 vibrations per hour, a rate that results in a high level of precision. The integration of silicon makes this technical feat possible because it is lightweight, anti-magnetic and does not require lubrication like traditional escapements.

Unlike most watches with a flyback chronograph, the Type XXII sets itself apart with a rare design that features a red central chronograph seconds hand that completes its rotation once every 30 seconds. A retrograde display at the top of the dial indicates if the seconds hand is on its first or second revolution. Operating on a similar principle, the small seconds positioned at 9 o'clock also rotates once every 30 seconds.

Among the watch's other complications is a second time zone indicator at 6 o'clock. It is linked to the 24-hour indicator above, which can be used to determine if it is day or night in the second time zone. Breguet contains all of this technical expertise in a 44mm stainless steel case whose fluted caseband is topped with a rotating bezel.

With the craftsmanship and innovation of its Type XXII and Reine de Naples Hour-Strike, the company named for the father of modern horology more than lives up to its moniker.

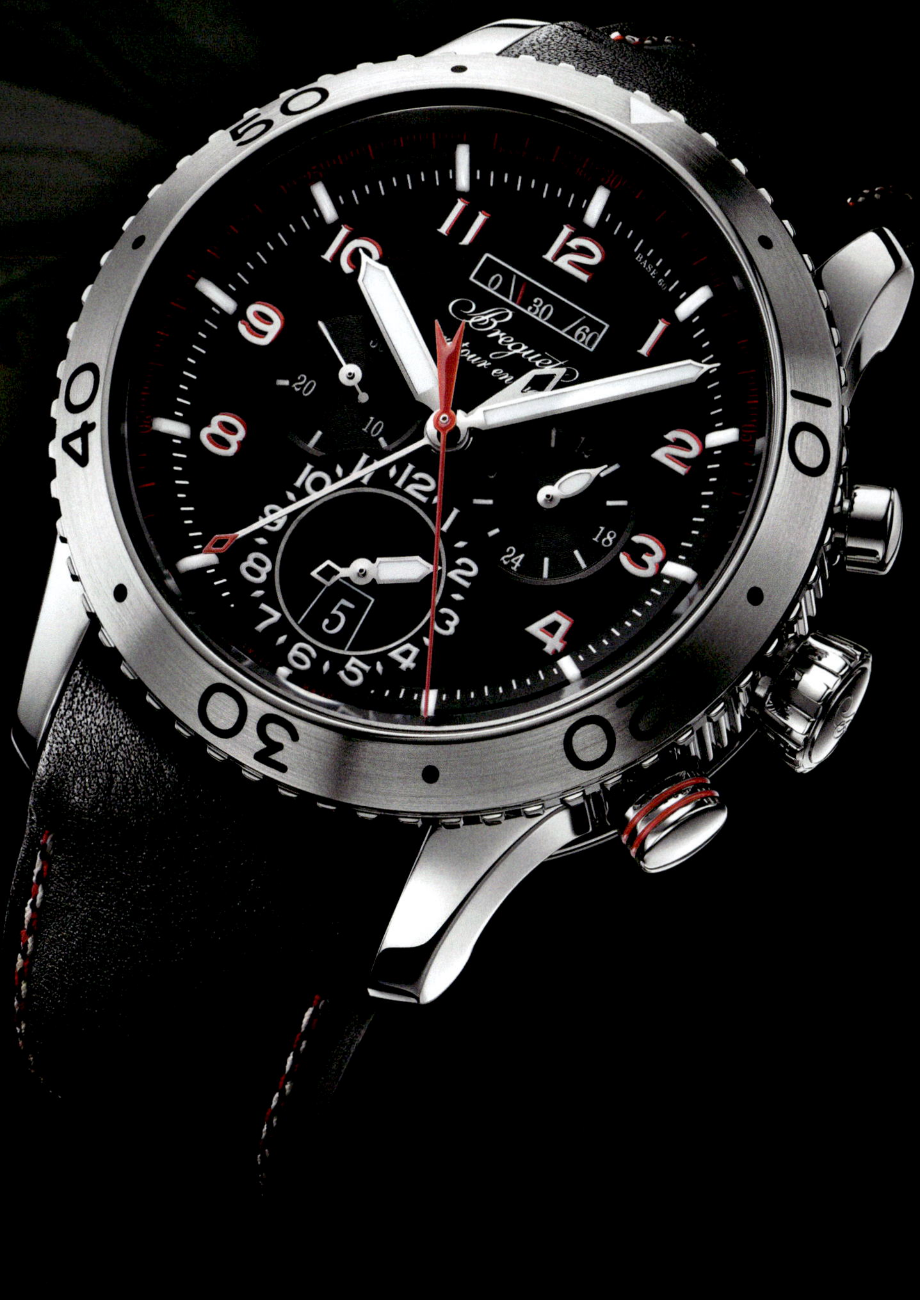

The Type XXII's 44mm stainless steel case houses an automatic flyback chronograph that features a second time zone function. The retrograde display near the center indicates whether the chronograph's red seconds hand has completed one or two 30-second revolutions.

TYPE XXII — REF. 3880ST

Movement: automatic-winding 589F caliber; 45-hour power reserve; 28 jewels; 10Hz BREGUET balance wheel with regulating screws; silicon balance-spring; 13 ¼‴; high-frequency silicon escapement; adjusted in five positions; numbered and signed BREGUET.
Functions: hours, minutes; small seconds on a 30-second basis at 9; date and second time zone indicator with luminous Arabic numerals at 6; 24-hour indicator at 3; 30- and 60-second indicator at 12; flyback.
Case: stainless steel; Ø 44mm; finely fluted caseband; twoway rotating bezel with 60-minute scale; screwlocked crown; round-ended horns; sapphire crystal caseback; water resistant to 10atm.
Dial: black oxidized; chapter ring with Arabic numerals; luminous hands and hour markers; red chronograph seconds hand on a 30-second basis at the center; 30-minute totalizer at the center; one diamond indicates the on/off setting of the hour-strike in an aperture at 12; two apertures on the dial at 11 and 1 leaving the hammers of the strikes visible; numbered and signed BREGUET.
Strap: black leather; two-tone crossed stitching.

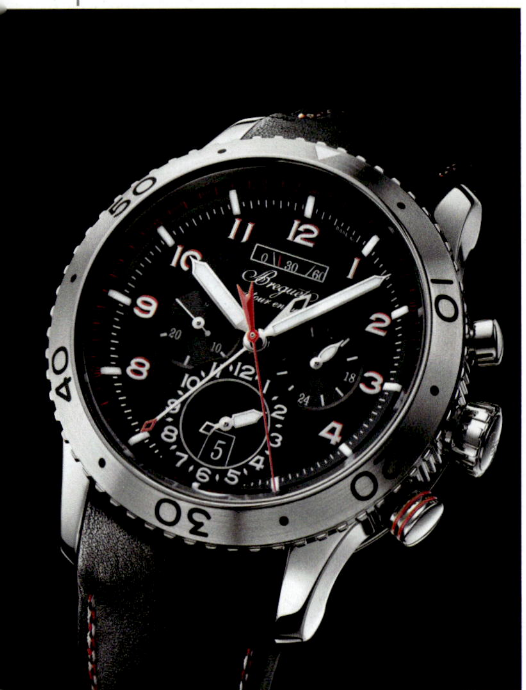

MARINE ROYALE — REF. 5847BB

Movement: automatic-winding 519R caliber; 45-hour power reserve; 36 jewels; 4Hz BREGUET balance wheel with regulating screws; 12‴; engine-turned 18K white-gold rotor; Swiss straight-line lever escapement; adjusted in five positions; numbered and signed BREGUET.
Functions: hours, minutes, seconds; date at 6; alarm power reserve indicator between 9 and 11; alarm on/off indicator at 12.
Case: 18K white gold; Ø 45mm; finely fluted caseband; rounded horns welded to case; screw-locked crown; one-way rotating bezel with luminous markers; alarm setting pushpieces at 4 sheathed in black rubber; wave-shaped ratchet at 3 to ensure the bezel's one-way rotation; rubber covered alarm on/off pushpieces at 8; manually engine-turned sapphire crystal caseback; water resistant to 3atm.
Dial: 18K silvered gold; chapter ring with applied blued Roman numerals and luminous dots; triangular hands at the center for setting alarm time; 18K blued-gold luminous, facetted, open-tipped BREGUET hands; wave patterns manually engraved on a rose engine; numbered and signed BREGUET.
Bracelet: 18K white gold.
Also available: 18K rose gold with a black rhodium dial, delivered with rubber and leather straps.

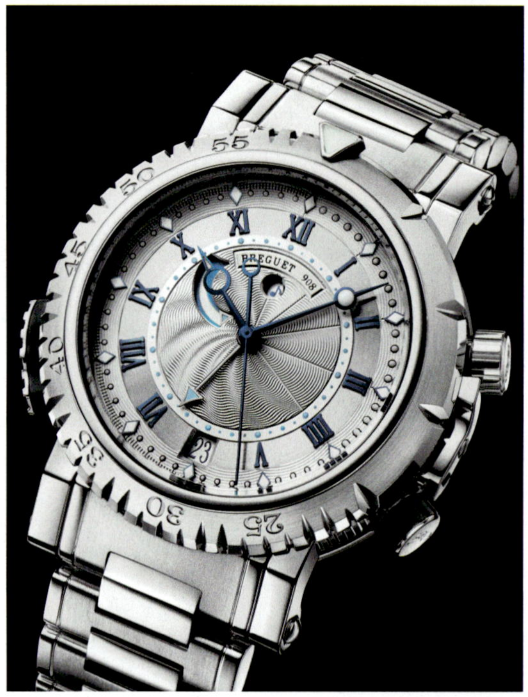

FUSEE TOURBILLON — REF. 7047PT

Movement: manual-winding 596 caliber; 50-hour power reserve; 43 jewels; 2.5Hz BREGUET balance wheel in titanium with four adjusting screws in gold; silicon balance-spring; 16‴; upper bridge of tourbillon carriage in titanium; torque regularity throughout the operation of the watch provided by fusee-and-chain transmission; BREGUET-shaped thin bar (barrette) in nonmagnetic stainless steel; Swiss straight-line lever escapement; high-frequency silicon escapement; adjusted in six positions; numbered and signed BREGUET.
Functions: hours, minutes; 60-second tourbillon at 1.
Case: 950 platinum; Ø 41mm; finely fluted caseband; rounded horns welded to case; screw pins securing the strap; sapphire crystal caseback; water resistant to 3atm.
Dial: silvered 18K gold; chapter ring with Roman numerals; polished steel open-tipped BREGUET hands; hand-engraved on a rose engine off-centered at 7; numbered and signed BREGUET.
Strap: black crocodile leather.

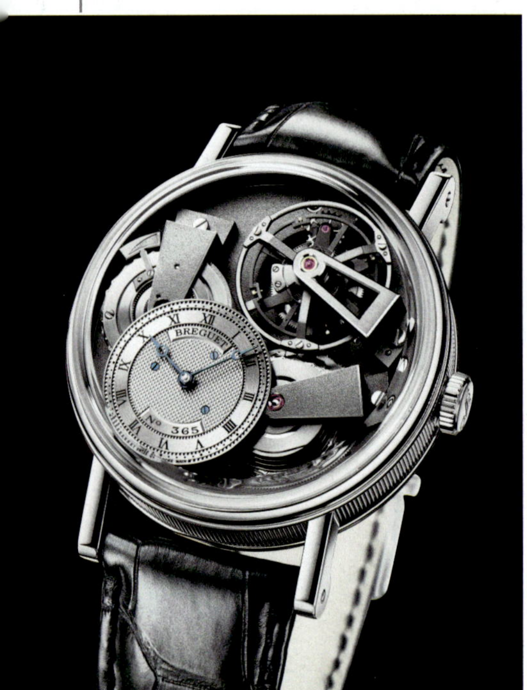

REVEIL MUSICAL — REF. 7800BA

Movement: automatic-winding 777M caliber; 55-hour power reserve; 4Hz frequency; 55 jewels; straight-line lever escapement; BREGUET balance wheel and overcoil.
Case: 18K yellow gold; Ø 48mm, thickness: 16.3mm; musical notes on the caseband; rounded horns welded to case; sapphire crystal caseback; water resistant to 3atm.
Dial: guilloché-rotating bridge with platinum effects; blued-steel hands.
Strap: brown leather; screw-in pin connection to case.
Suggested price: $63,400
Also available: white gold ($64,300).

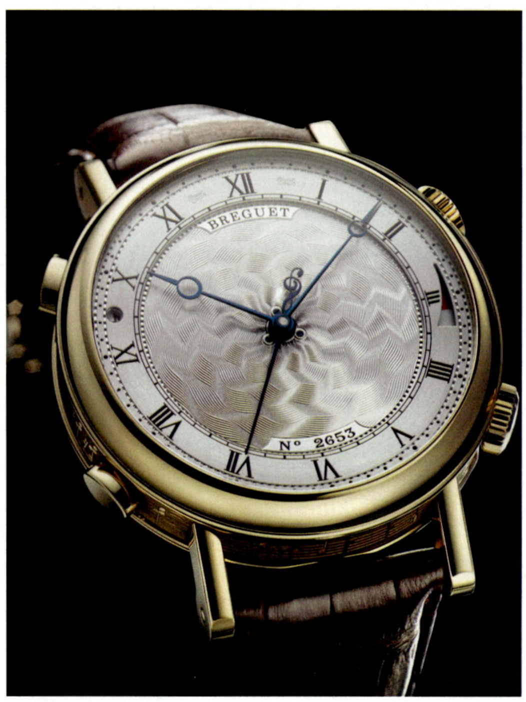

BREGUET TRADITION REF. 7057BB

Movement: manual-winding 507DR caliber; 50-hour power reserve indicator engraved on the front and back of the movement; 34 jewels; 3Hz BREGUET balance wheel with regulating screws; BREGUET balance-spring; 14 ½```; Swiss straight-line lever escapement; high frequency silicon escapement; adjusted in five positions; numbered and signed BREGUET.
Functions: hours, minutes, seconds.
Case: 18K white gold; Ø 40mm; finely fluted caseband; rounded horns welded to case; screw pins securing the strap; sapphire crystal caseback; water resistant to 3atm.
Dial: silvered 18K gold; chapter ring with Roman numerals; blued-steel open-tipped BREGUET hands; hand-engraved on a rose engine off-centered at 12; numbered and signed BREGUET.
Strap: blue crocodile leather; tang buckle.

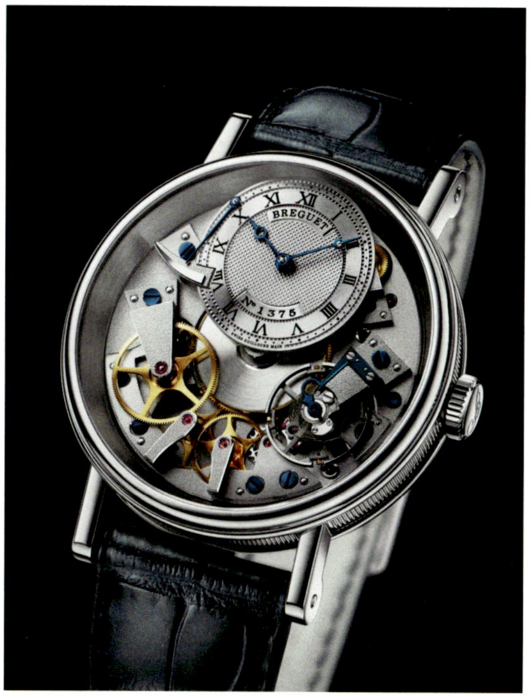

TRADITION 7027 REF. 7027BB

Movement: manual-winding 507DR caliber in anthracite gray alloy; 50-hour power reserve indicator engraved on front and back of movement; 3Hz frequency; 34 jewels; straight-line lever escapement; monometallic balance wheel; BREGUET overcoil; adjusted in five positions; numbered and signed BREGUET.
Case: 18K white gold; Ø 37mm; finely fluted caseband; rounded horns welded to case; sapphire crystal caseback; water resistant to 3atm.
Dial: black electroplated 18K gold; hand-engraved on rose engine; polished steel open-tipped BREGUET hands; individually numbered and signed BREGUET.
Strap: black leather; screw-in pin connection to case.
Suggested price: $24,850
Also available: pink gold.

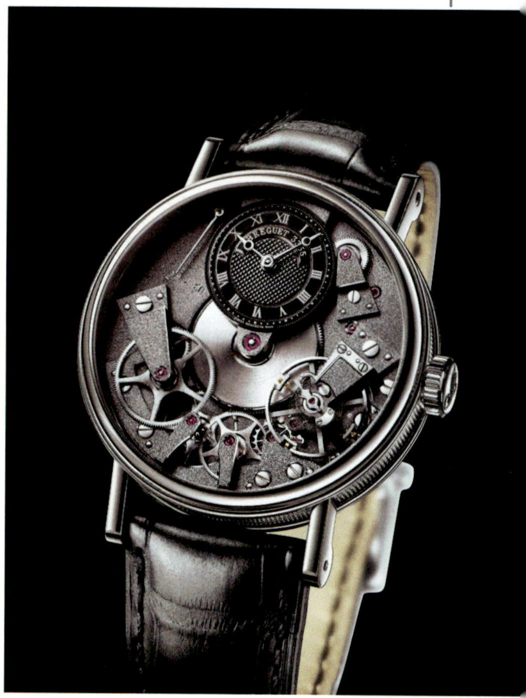

REINE DE NAPLES REF. 8967ST

Movement: automatic-winding 591C caliber; 38-hour power reserve; 4Hz frequency; 25 jewels; straight-line lever escapement; BREGUET balance wheel; flat, silicon balance spring.
Case: stainless steel; Ø 43.75x35.5mm, thickness: 9.45mm; sapphire crystal caseback; water resistant to 3atm.
Dial: mother-of-pearl; blued steel hands.
Strap: leather; screw-in pin connection to case.
Suggested price: $13,900
Also available: blue dial.

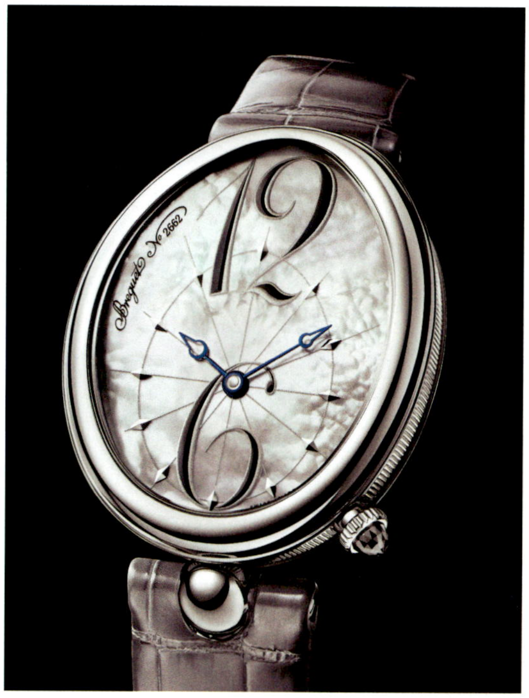

REINE DE NAPLES REF. 8978BB

Movement: automatic-winding 78SO caliber; 65-hour power reserve without strike, 50-hour power reserve when strike is on; 54 jewels; 3Hz BREGUET balance wheel with regulating screws; balance-spring; 13¼ x 9¾```; dove-shaped; hand-engraved 18K white-gold rotor; straight-line; Swiss lever escapement; numbered and signed BREGUET.
Functions: hours, minutes; minute repeater.
Case: 18K white gold; Ø 38.45x30.4mm, thickness: 11.6mm; egg-shaped; finely fluted caseband; bezel set with 30 diamonds (3 carats); crown set with a briolette diamond (approx. 0.26 carat); on/off pushpiece for striking mechanism at 2; crystal caseback; water resistant to 3atm.
Dial: natural white mother-of-pearl; chapter ring off-centered at 6; blue-steel open-tipped BREGUET hands; one diamond indicates the on/off setting of the hour-strike in an aperture at 12; two apertures on the dial at 11 and 1 leaving the hammers of the strikes visible; numbered and signed BREGUET.
Strap: white alligator leather; folding clasp set with 26 diamonds (approx. 0.14 carat).

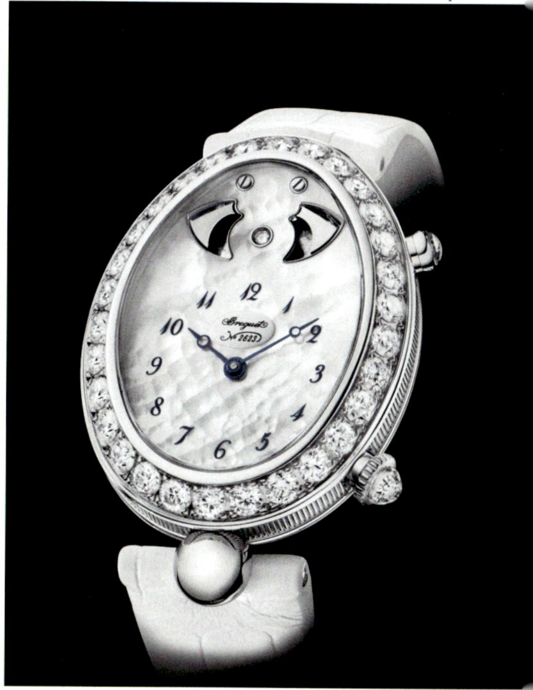

Buben & Zörweg's magnificent winding boxes come equipped with a computerized system of winders to power automatic watches by simulating a watch's movement when it is worn on the wrist.

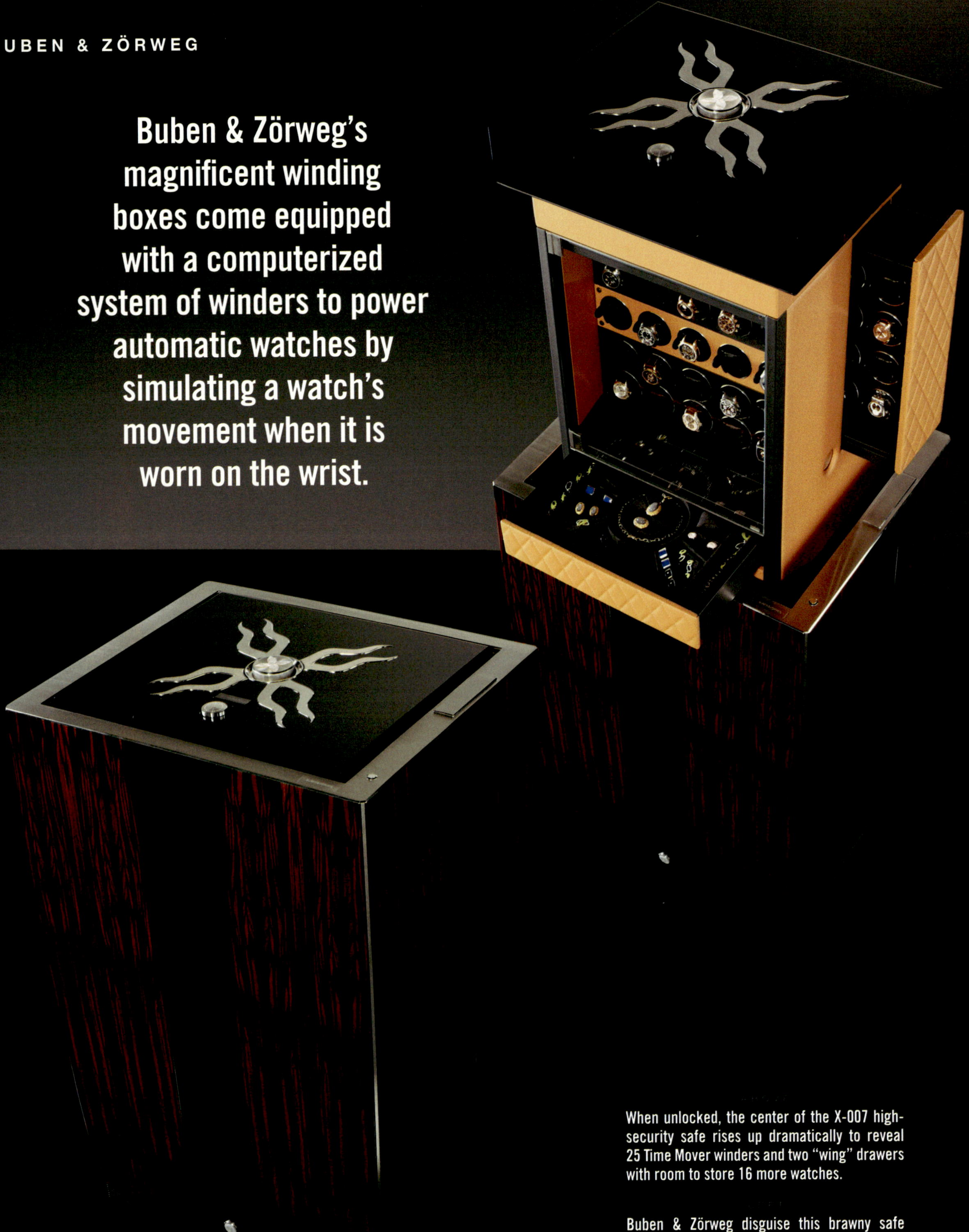

When unlocked, the center of the X-007 high-security safe rises up dramatically to reveal 25 Time Mover winders and two "wing" drawers with room to store 16 more watches.

Buben & Zörweg disguise this brawny safe with handsome details such as hand-stitched leather inside, macassar wood outside and an exquisite mother-of-pearl inlay on top.

BUBEN&ZORWEG

INSIDE THE BOX

For a collector who favors automatic movements, a winding box is essential gear. Especially if the goal is to spend more time wearing complicated timepieces and less time trying to remember how to reset them.

Designed for every level of horological enthusiast, Buben & Zörweg's advanced winding systems keep collections large and small powered up, protected and, above all, at the ready.

Each winder is crafted by hand using the finest materials and with the same attention to precision as their horological counterparts.

And just as there is a watch to fit every personality, Buben & Zörweg has spent the last 15 years ensuring there are as many options to wind them. The company has grown steadily by developing technology and refining details that make these exquisite winders such prized objects of both form and function.

At the heart of every Buben & Zörweg winder is the trademark Time Mover technology. This computerized system is designed to wind the mainspring by simulating the day-to-day movement of the watch when it is worn on the wrist. The system is easily configured to optimize the winding rate and capable of regulating everything from the frequency and direction of the watch's rotations, to a helpful sleep mode that prevents unnecessary wear to the mainspring due to excessive winding.

All of this technology is integrated seamlessly into intelligent designs that can be personalized with luxurious appointments such as various shades of hand-stitched Italian leather, gorgeously grained macassar and burled walnut woods, and adjustable LED lighting, as well as options for humidors, alarms and more.

The key to good camouflage is often the ability to hide in plain sight. Buben & Zörweg's X-007 epitomizes this notion, looking more like the latest chic design from the I Saloni furniture fair in Milan than a high-security safe.

Standing nearly four feet tall when closed, the X-007's hand-selected macassar panels project a refined style that is both masculine and modern. Hand-polished stainless steel outlines the top of the safe and includes a discreet panel to unlock the X-007.

When the security is properly disengaged, the center of the device rises up dramatically to a height of six and a half feet. When fully extended, the elegant interior reveals its secret cargo: 25 Time Mover winders, two "wing" drawers with space to store up to 16 more timepieces, and a front drawer for securing jewelry.

Don't be fooled by the attractive exterior and impressive presentation; this beauty is really a beast. Its patented construction includes walls made from Relastan, a trademarked material engineered to be substantially lighter than, but just as strong as other armor plating. The X-007 further protects with a compact locking mechanism by Paxos, a company whose reliable locks are trusted by banks and mints around the world.

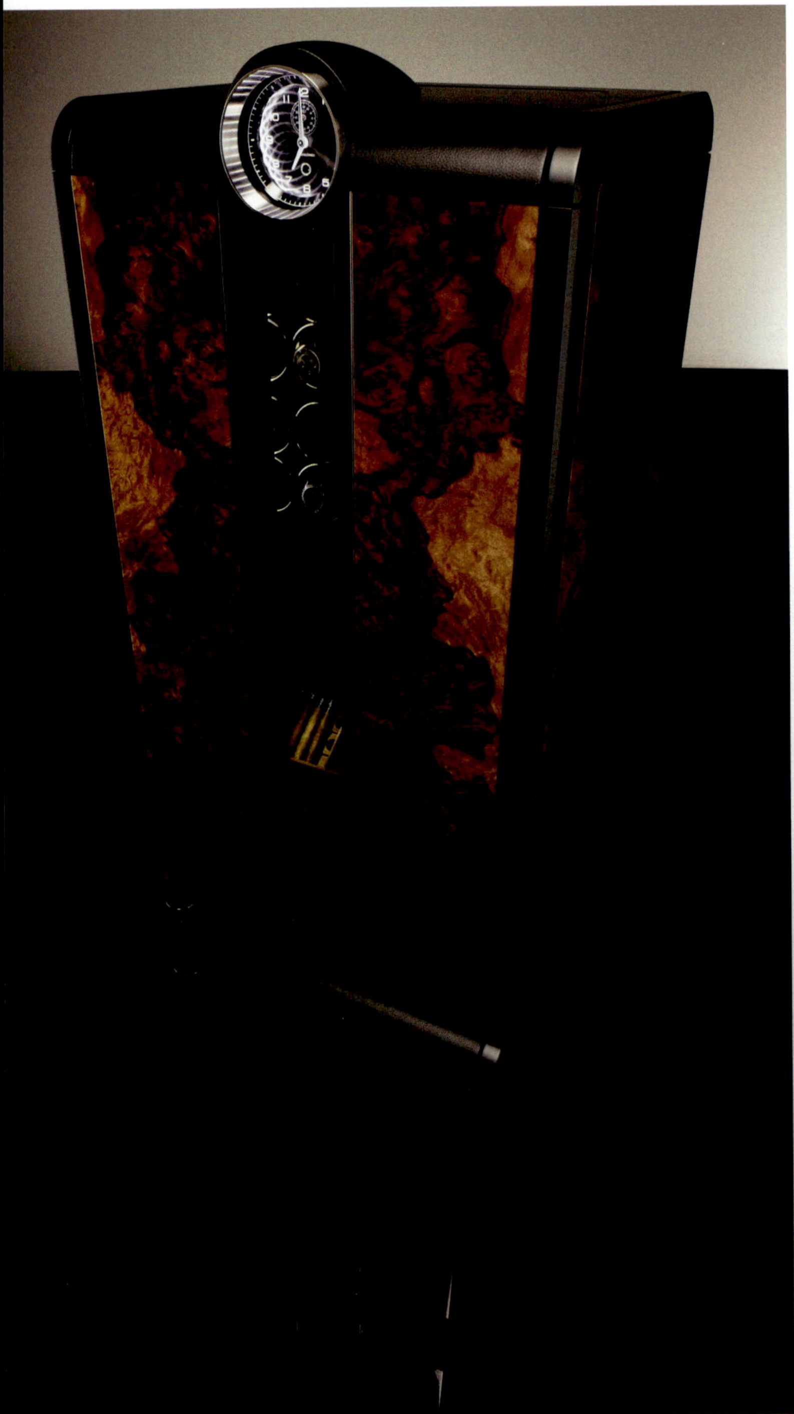

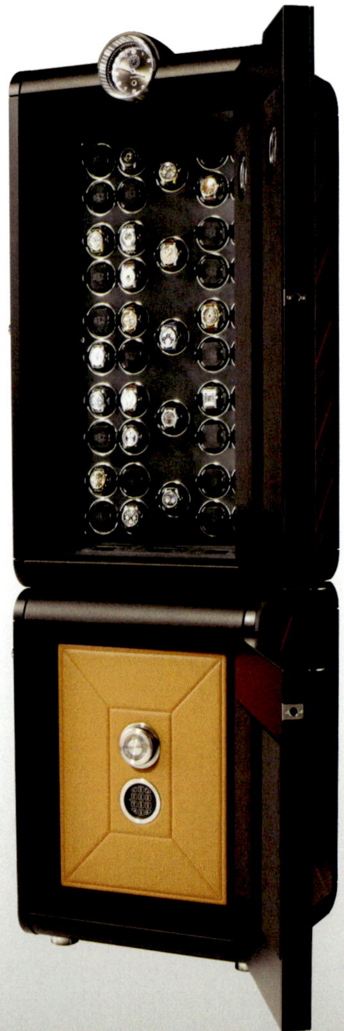

To accommodate more extensive collections, Buben & Zörweg offers two versions of its impressive Vanguard design.

From the outside, the Vanguard Collector and Vanguard Connoisseur look the same. Each cabinet measures just over six feet tall, is made using either macassar or burled walnut, and includes a German-made clock up top and a safe down below. Upholstered in leather and secured with a digital lock, the safe's door swings open to expose eight Time Mover winders along with three drawers to store additional watches and other valuables.

The detail that separates these designs is found behind the top door. Geared toward the avid horolophile, the Vanguard Collector's black velour interior is equipped with 45 Time Mover winders. For those with a weakness for both timepieces and cigars, the Vanguard Connoisseur combines 18 Time Mover winders with a humidor regulated by an electronic humidifier.

Buben & Zörweg goes to extremes with the company's Phantom and Solitaire Deluxe designs. At one end of the spectrum lies the Phantom, a winder so compact and contoured that it could be easily mistaken for a high-end bookshelf stereo. Made to accommodate either four or eight watches inside, the Phantom's exterior features macassar or carbon fiber at the ends and a transparent middle, which is where the case slides open when unlocked.

THIS PAGE

ABOVE Burled walnut gives this Vanguard Connoisseur a timeless look that conceals 18 watch winders, an adjustable humidor and a safe with eight additional watch winders.

ABOVE RIGHT The Vanguard Collector, shown here in macassar wood, includes 45 winders in the main section and eight more in the safe. A German-made clock is featured on top, while a thermometer and hygrometer are integrated inside.

FACING PAGE

TOP Clad in either macassar or carbon fiber, the Phantom can wind either four or eight watches simultaneously.

BOTTOM RIGHT Secured behind 16mm of bulletproof glass, the limited edition Solitaire Deluxe winds 48 watches (40 up top, eight in the safe). It also equipped with a humidor, stereo, alarm and the Buben & Zörweg Tourbillon clock.

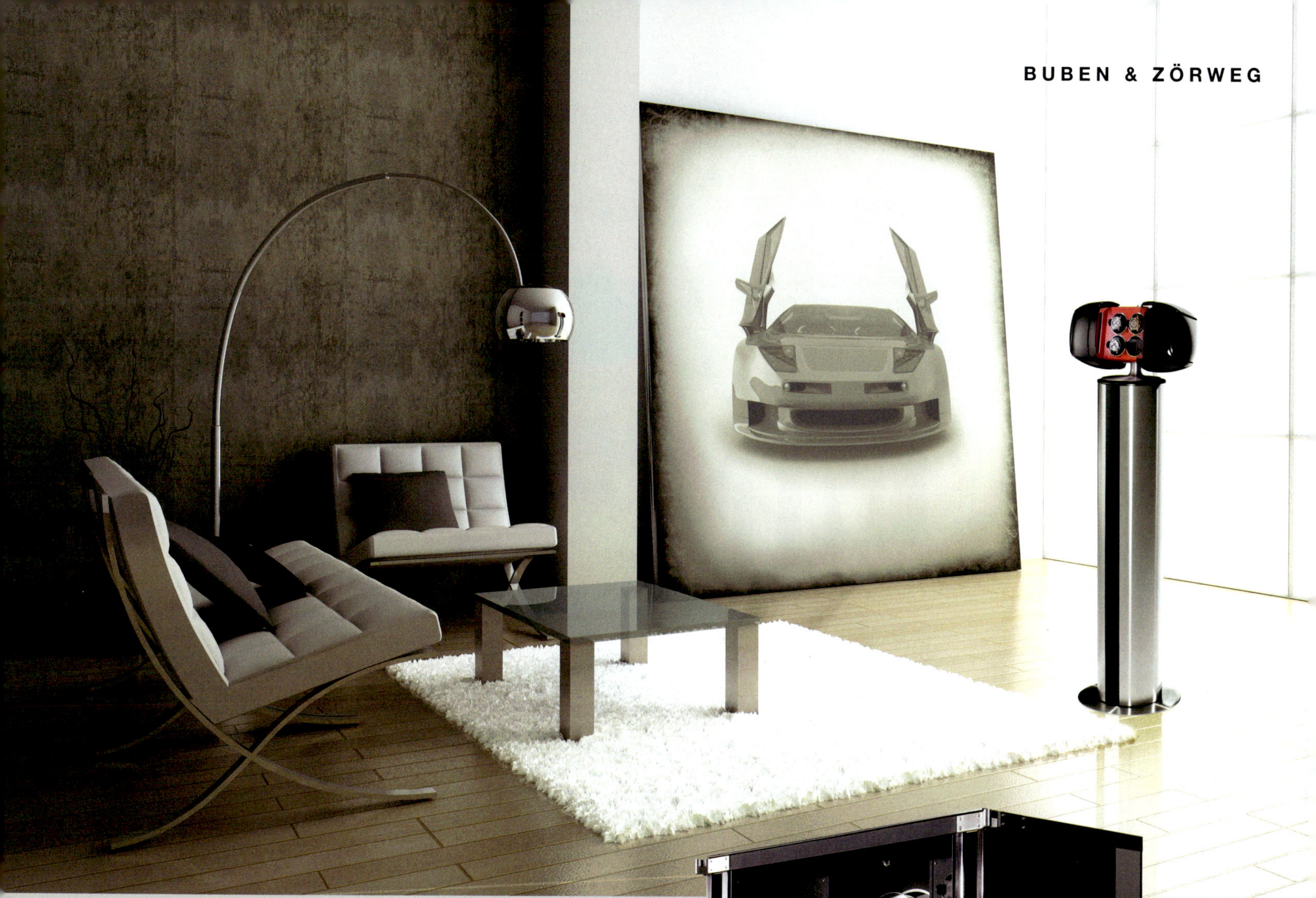

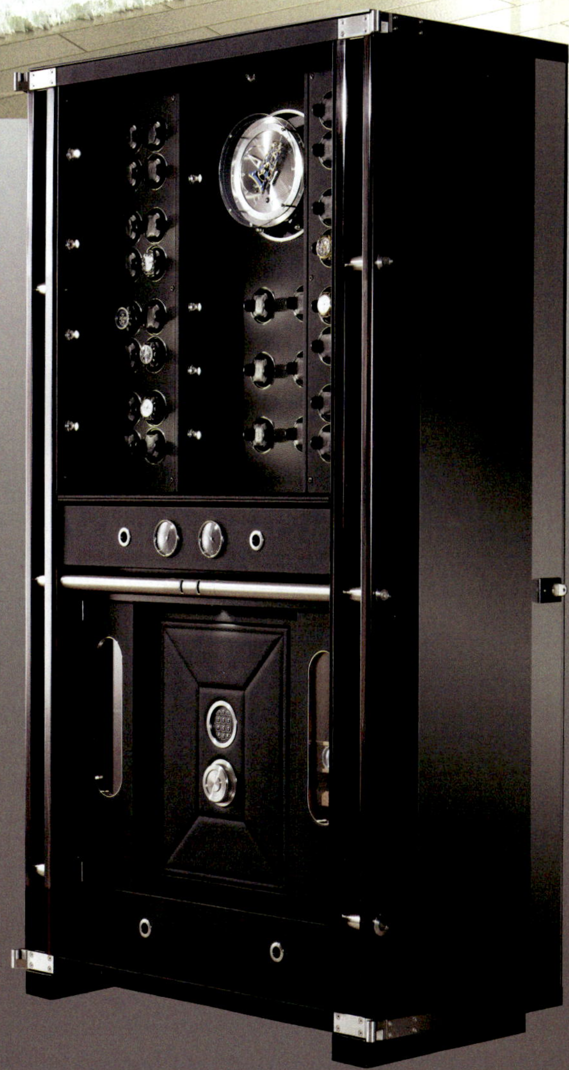

At the opposite end of the scale is the Solitaire Deluxe, a generously proportioned macassar cabinet that stands more than six feet tall and weighs in excess of 770 pounds.

Made in a limited edition of 75 numbered pieces, it represents the ultimate showcase for life's finer things. The top half houses 40 Time Mover winders, fine leather accents and the Buben & Zörweg Tourbillon, a German-made clock that indicates the date, power reserve and world time, and features a small seconds above the tourbillon mechanism.

The Solitaire Deluxe's lower half is divided between a bar compartment, an electronically controlled humidor and a safe with eight more Time Mover winders and drawers for additional storage. The cabinet comes equipped with adjustable LED lighting, an alarm system and a stereo. For an extra measure of security, the entire front of the cabinet is shielded behind a 16mm layer of bulletproof glass.

Like watch collectors, each Buben & Zörweg winder has a distinct personality. Despite their differences, however, they all share the company's dedication to exquisite craftsmanship, the finest materials and optimal security.

BVLGARI

A BRIGHT PROMISE

Bulgari expanded the historic Italian firm's legacy in 2010 when it christened the Manufacture du Sentier, a workshop that produces advanced movements for its Bulgari, Gérald Genta and Daniel Roth collections.

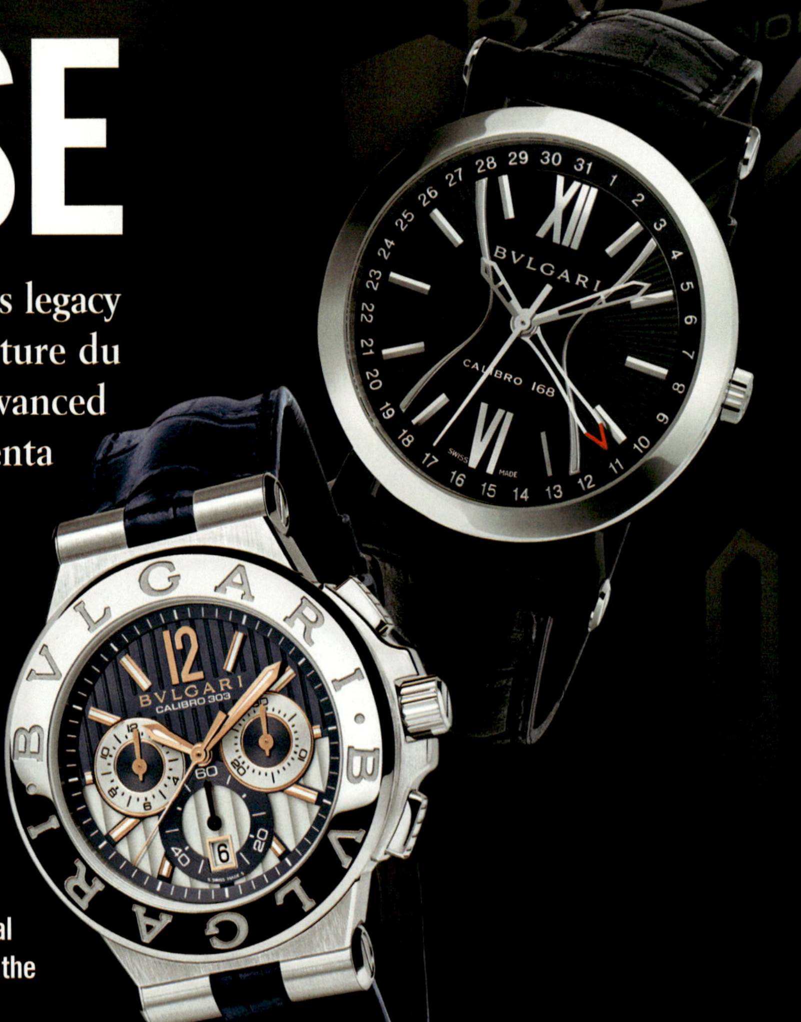

The first in-house creation to emerge from the Manufacture du Sentier is Calibre 168, an automatic movement introduced last year in the Sotirio Bulgari collection. The caliber provides the classic indications—hours, minutes and seconds—along with a jumping date. The complication uses a long central hand to indicate the date on a scale that runs along the dial's outer edge.

A bi-directional rotor powers Calibre 168, which can also be wound by hand. When the crown is engaged for manual winding, it triggers a disconnecting gear that prevents wear to the gear train, thereby enhancing the movement's longevity.

The movement achieves high marks in technical and aesthetic categories for its attention to detail. The construction utilizes nickel silver for the bridges and mainplate, which provide a robust platform for the movement. The mechanism itself exhibits classic finishing techniques, including traditional touches like Côtes de Genève and circular graining.

The Sotirio Bulgari is presented in a round 43mm case and offered in several different design configurations. One particularly beguiling example features a black dial adorned with a sunray pattern that radiates from a voluptuous hourglass figure at the center.

A fine example of form and function in balance, the Diagono Calibre 303 is the latest addition to Bulgari's Diagono collection, which debuted more than 20 years ago. The Diagono Calibre 303 features an automatic chronograph that uses the column wheel and vertical clutch construction preferred by many experienced collectors. Prized for its stability, this design prevents the chronograph's seconds hand from jumping when the timer is used, a drawback found among non-column-wheel chronographs. Bulgari showcases this peerless mechanism in action through the watch's sapphire crystal caseback.

The Sotirio Bulgari houses the first mechanical movement produced entirely in-house by Bulgari. Along with the hours, minutes and seconds, the watch also features a jumping date indication.

The Diagono Calibre 303's column-wheel chronograph can be read from the multi-layer blue dial, which is decorated with a Côtes de Genève motif.

Bulgari introduced its first-ever in-house movement—Caliber 168—last year, signaling a new direction that is destined to lead to a new generation of watches powered by cutting-edge horological complications.

The movement's 303 individual parts are housed within the Diagono's 42mm stainless steel case, which includes a generously proportioned white-gold bezel engraved with the company logo. The beautifully layered dial includes displays for the chronograph's minutes and hours, as well as a small seconds and date.

A second chronograph from the same collection, the Diagono X-Pro cuts a sportier profile with a bold, graphic design that features a black sapphire dial contrasted with white and red elements. The watch's black rubber strap attaches to a 45mm stainless steel case fitted with a titanium bezel coated partly in black Diamond-Like Carbon (DLC).

The Diagono X-Pro's automatic movement also provides a GMT function. An arrow-shaped hand indicates the time in a secondary time zone using a 24-hour counter that encircles the dial. Part of the counter is shaded to indicate whether it is day or night in the other location. As Bulgari marks the start of a new era with the opening of Manufacture du Sentier, the company is poised for big things to come on the horizon.

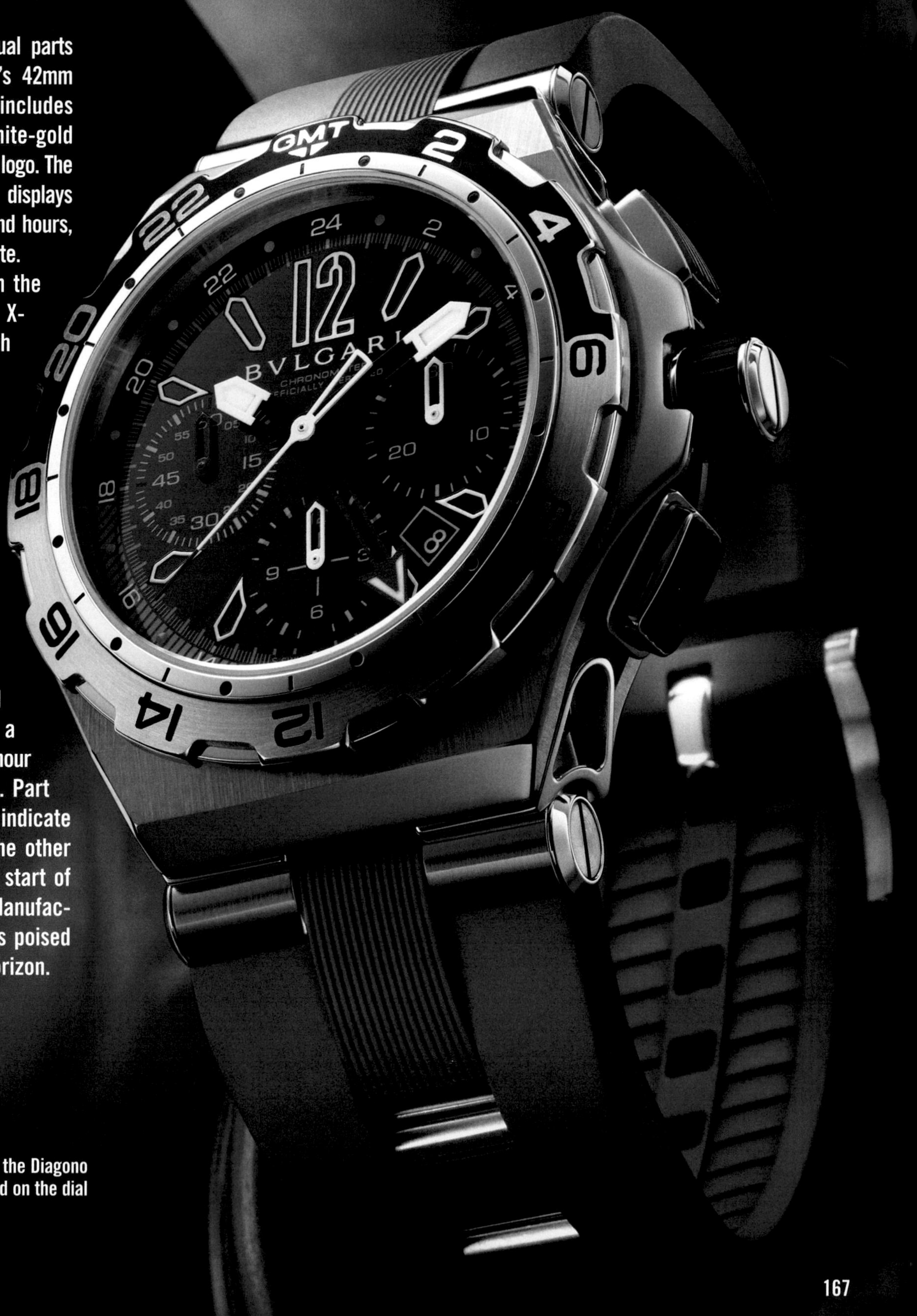

The certified chronometer that powers the Diagono X-Pro features a GMT function indicated on the dial by an arrow-shaped hand.

ENDURER CHRONOSPRINT — REF. BRE56BSLDCHS

Movement: automatic-winding DR1306 caliber; Ø 25.6mm, thickness: 6.1mm; 45-hour power reserve; 34 jewels; 28,800 vph; circular-grained Côtes de Genève finishing.
Functions: off-centered hour and minute hands; Chronosprint indicates hours and minutes by two hands mounted on a single arbor; large date at 12; pushbutton at 7:30, positioning the hands at 12 which starts chronograph.

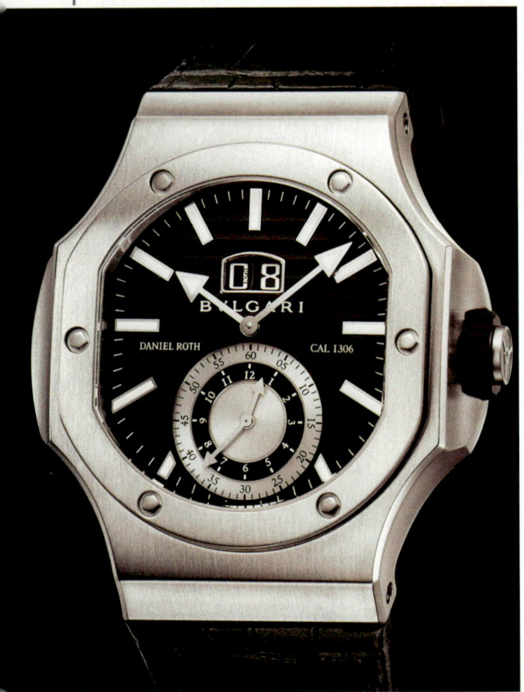

Case: brushed Staybrite steel; Ø 56.51mm, thickness: 14.55mm; polished finishing; ellipse-shaped; bezel set with six screws; DLC-treated steel Chronosprint pushbutton and crown; sapphire crystal; steel caseback with sapphire crystal; water resistant to 10atm.
Dial: black; satin-brushed.
Strap: alligator; steel pin buckle.
Suggested price: $14,300

DIAGONO X-PRO — REF.DP45BSTVDCH/GMT

Movement: automatic-winding BVL312 caliber; integrated chronograph with column-wheel; 48-hour power reserve; Ø 30mm, thickness: 8.33mm; 27 jewels; COSC-certified; 28,800 vph; uniderectional winding.
Function: hours, minutes; small seconds; date; three time zones; GMT; chronograph with 59-second, 29-minute and 11-hour counters.
Case: stainless steel, grade 5 titanium; black DLC and rubber; Ø 45mm; push and turn bidirectional stainless steel with PVD-treated rotating bezel with 24-hour scale (3 time zones); screw-down crown; mobile lugs; trasparent sapphire crystal caseback; water resistant to 10atm.

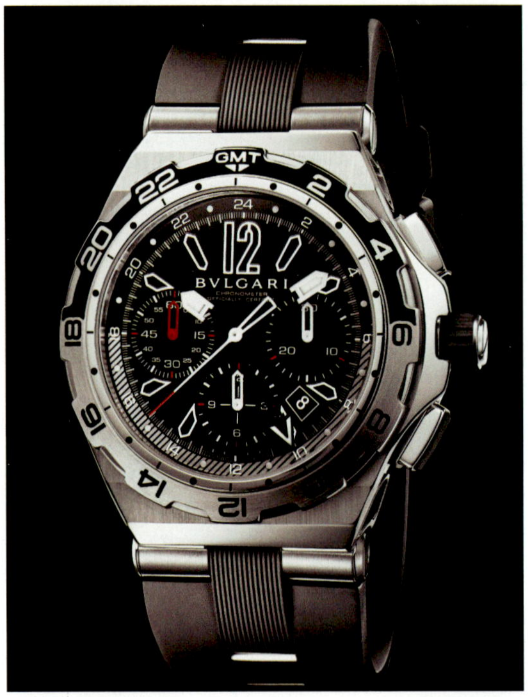

Dial: black; red stripe; Arabic numerals; stainless steel hands.
Strap: black rubber; titanium hook clasp.
Suggested price: $15,500

SOTIRIO BULGARI CALIBRO 168 — REF. SB43BSBLD

Movement: automatic-winding BVL 168 caliber; 42-hour power reserve; 168 parts; 11.5 lines; 863 parts; 25 jewels; 28,800 vph; bimetallic winding via bidirectional oscillating weight; three spokes Glucydur balance; micrometrical screws adjustment; barrel and gear train bridges; nickel silver mainplate and bridges; adorned circular-grained mainplates; circular grained lever bridge; Côtes de Genève bridge; beveled bridge rim; diamond-polished bridge bevel; snailed circular grained central date plate; nickel silver, dedicated Sotirio Bulgari cut-out, straight satin-brushed flange, sunburst satin-brushed heavy segment.

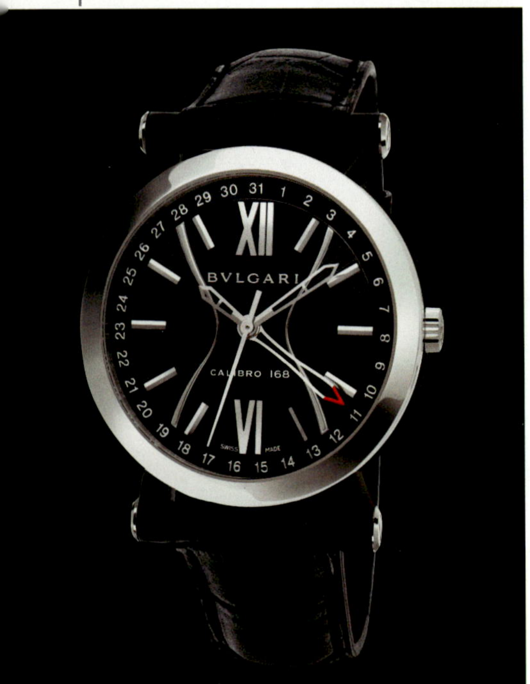

Functions: hours, minutes, seconds; instant-jump central date.
Case: steel with black DLC treatment; Ø 43mm.
Dial: black.
Strap: alligator; steel hook buckle.
Suggested price: $6,900

DIAGONO CALIBRO 303 — REF. DG42C3SWGLDCH

Movement: automatic-winding manufacture Calibre BVL 303; 40-hour power reserve; integrated column-wheel chronograph with vertical clutch; Ø 26.2mm, thickness: 5.5mm; 37 jewels; 21,600 vph; decorated with Côtes de Genève, perlage and satiné soleil finishes.
Functions: hours, minutes, seconds; date at 6; chronograph: minute counter at 3, seconds counter at 6; hour counter at 9.

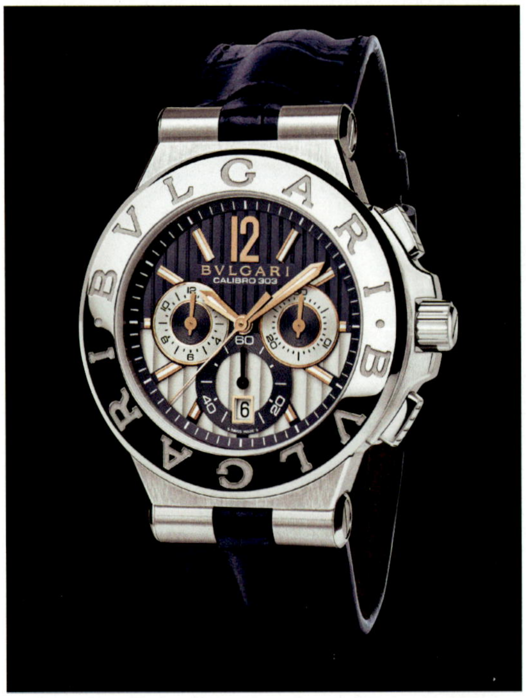

Case: stainless steel; Ø 42mm, thickness: 12.95mm; applied 18K white-gold bezel with transparent back; scratch-resistant sapphire crystal with antireflective treatment; satin-finished stainless steel caseback; water resistant to 10atm.
Dial: on three levels; vertical and satiné soleil finish; hand-applied faceted indexes; faceted hands with SuperLumiNova C1®.
Strap: blue alligator; 3-prong stainless steel folding buckle and safety system.
Suggested price: $10,900

OCTO BI-RETRO — REF. BG043BSCVDBR

Movement: automatic-winding GG7722 caliber; 45-hour power reserve; Ø 25.6mm, thickness: 5.53mm; 35 jewels; 28,800 vph; undirectional winding.
Functions: jumping hours; retrograde minutes; retrograde date.
Case: double finishing; sandblasted and polished stainless steel; Ø 43mm; ceramic bezel; beaded crown set with an onyx cabochon; transparent sapphire crystal caseback; water resistant to 10atm.
Dial: black and gray; cloisonné; Arabic numerals; stainless steel hands.
Strap: black rubber; stainless steel triple-blade folding clasp.
Suggested price: $18,200

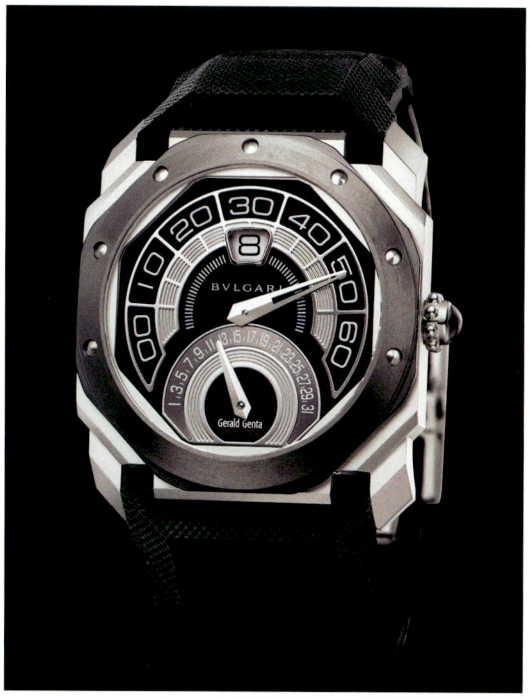

GEFICA BI-RETRO — REF. BGF47BBLDBR

Movement: automatic-winding GG1004 caliber; 45-hour power reserve; Ø 25.6mm, thickness: 5.6mm; 35 jewels; 28,800 vph.
Functions: jumping hours; retrograde minutes; seconds; retrograde date.
Case: sand-blasted bronze and satin-finished titanium; Ø 46mm, thickness: 19.3mm; titanium caseback with sapphire crystal; water resistant to 10atm.
Dial: black.
Strap: black alligator; three-blade titanium folding buckle.
Suggested price: $17,400

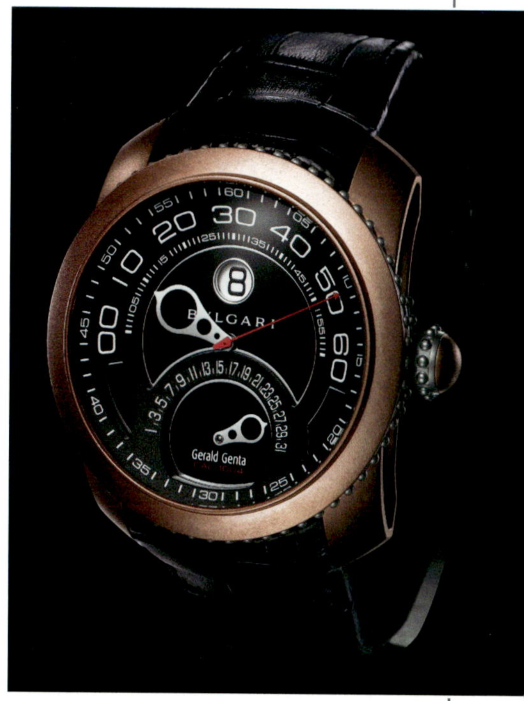

DANIEL ROTH GRANDE LUNE — REF. BRRP46C14GLDMP

Movement: manual-winding DR206 caliber; 42-hour power reserve; Ø 35.64mm, thickness: 2.3mm; 20 jewels; 21,600 vph.
Functions: hours, minutes; small seconds; date; moonphase.
Case: 18K rose gold; 44x41mm, thickness: 10.6mm; 18K rose-gold crown; sapphire crystal caseback; water resistant to 3atm.
Dial: white-lacquered and black gold satin-brushed; 18K rose-gold hands and hour markers; Roman numerals; three-arm second hand: minute hand, date and second subdials.
Strap: dark brown alligator; rose-gold three-blade folding buckle
Suggested price: $33,000

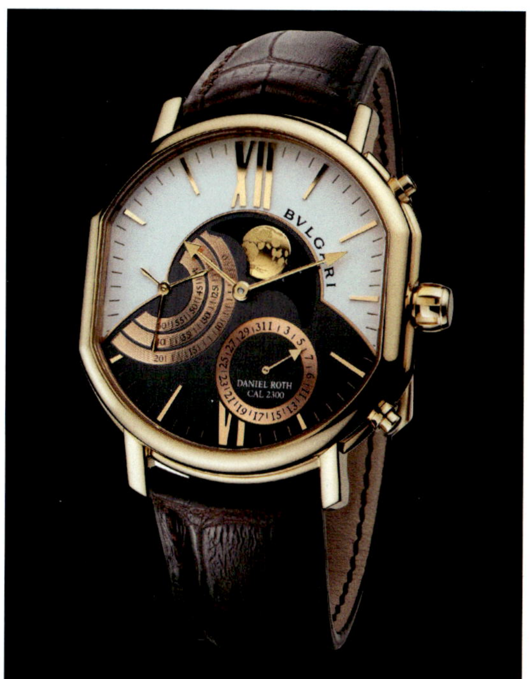

DANIEL ROTH PAPILLON CHRONOGRAPHE — REF. BRRP46C14GLCHP

Movement: automatic-winding DR2319 caliber; 38-hour power reserve; Ø 25.6mm, thickness: 8.55mm; 38 jewels; 21,600 vph.
Functions: hours, seconds; papillon minutes display with two rotating hands; date; chronograph: 59-second counter, 29-minute counter, 11-hour counter.
Case: 18K rose gold; 46x43mm, thickness: 15mm; 18K rose-gold crown; 18K rose-gold caseback with sapphire crystal; water resistant to 3atm.
Dial: multi-level white laquered anthracite; 18K rose-gold counters.
Strap: brown alligator; rose-gold three-blade folding buckle.
Suggested price: $49,500

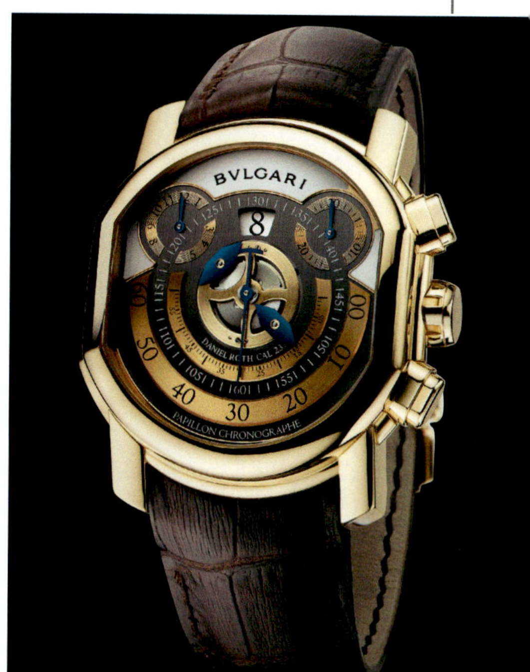

Carl F. Bucherer

FINE SWISS WATCHMAKING

INTELLIGENT DESIGN

Already one of Switzerland's oldest family-run watch brands, Carl F. Bucherer joined another elite group in 2008 when the Lucerne-based firm introduced its first manufacture movement.

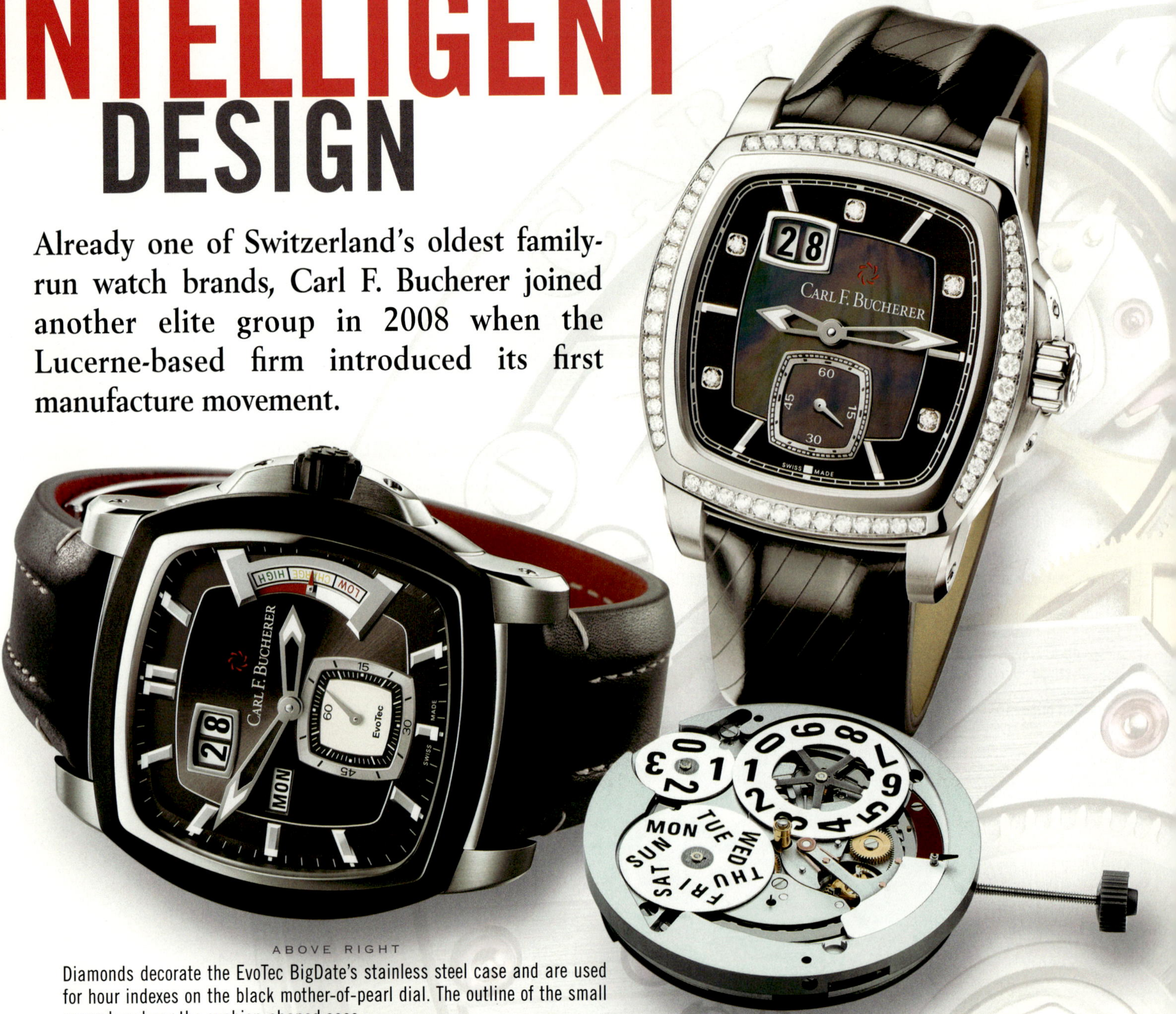

ABOVE RIGHT

Diamonds decorate the EvoTec BigDate's stainless steel case and are used for hour indexes on the black mother-of-pearl dial. The outline of the small seconds echoes the cushion-shaped case.

ABOVE

The stainless steel Patravi EvoTec PowerReserve displays how much power the movement has left on the curved gauge located between 2 and 4 o'clock.

RIGHT

Carl F. Bucherer's manufacture CFB A1002 movement, featured in the Patravi EvoTec PowerReserve, incorporates a moveable finger to ensure smooth and precise date changes.

The brand adheres to a philosophy it calls Evolution Technology, a comprehensive approach to watchmaking dedicated to creating the simplest and most reliable mechanism possible.

The CFB A1000's debut gave the brand more control over its future and reaffirmed the independent streak Carl Friedrich Bucherer instilled in the company in 1919 when he unveiled his first collection.

With a third generation at the helm today, Carl F. Bucherer is not just rethinking the way it produces watches, but also reimagining the way it designs them. The company calls its philosophy EvoTec, short for Evolution Technology, a comprehensive approach to watchmaking that emphasizes practicality and simplicity.

That concept guided the development of the Patravi EvoTec PowerReserve. Released in 2010, this model is equipped with CFB A1002, a manufacture caliber researched and produced by Carl F. Bucherer's workshop in Sainte-Croix.

Instead of following what came before to create the watch's automatic movement, the brand developed a new system from the ground up, using cutting-edge technology to create the simplest and most reliable mechanism possible.

The CFB A1002 powers the Patravi EvoTec PowerReserve's large date, as well as its signature power gauge between 2 and 4 o'clock. The latter uses a moveable finger to ensure smooth advancement of the autonomous rings that display the date. The company presents the model in a stainless steel, cushion-shaped case accompanied by either a rubber or steel bezel. The Patravi EvoTec PowerReserve is also offered in a rose-gold case.

For women who appreciate the allure of sophisticated watches and chic design, Carl F. Bucherer answered the call in 2009 with its first EvoTec model for ladies, the Patravi EvoTec BigDate.

The delicate curves of its cushion-shaped case project feminine charm from the wrist, while inside, its manufacture caliber is powered by a newly developed oscillating weight. Unlike a full-size rotor anchored to the center of a movement, the peripheral rotor powering all Patravi EvoTec models is housed on the exterior edge of the movement.

While not readily apparent at first glance, its design includes patented technologies that protect the rotor from shocks and simplify its fine-tuned adjustments. According to the brand, these innovations make the CFB A1000 "the first-ever reliably functioning peripheral rotor."

The peripheral rotor adds an aesthetic benefit as well. Its small size exposes much of the movement and its traditional finishing, which can be enjoyed through the sapphire crystal caseback.

The company continues to tempt women who prefer watches with brains and beauty with the Patravi ChronoDate Ladies. Its automatic movement combines a big date display with a chronograph and is featured in a 40mm stainless steel case with a diamond-set bezel.

Diamonds are also used to decorate the bezel found on the Patravi AutoDate, a modern classic that marries the convenience of an automatic movement with the timeless look of an all-stainless steel model. To accommodate different tastes, Carl F. Bucherer offers it in a case that is either 27mm or 34mm in diameter.

Much like the brand that created them, each of these watches exhibits its own distinct personality. The one constant that unites them all is Carl F. Bucherer's dedication to intelligent design.

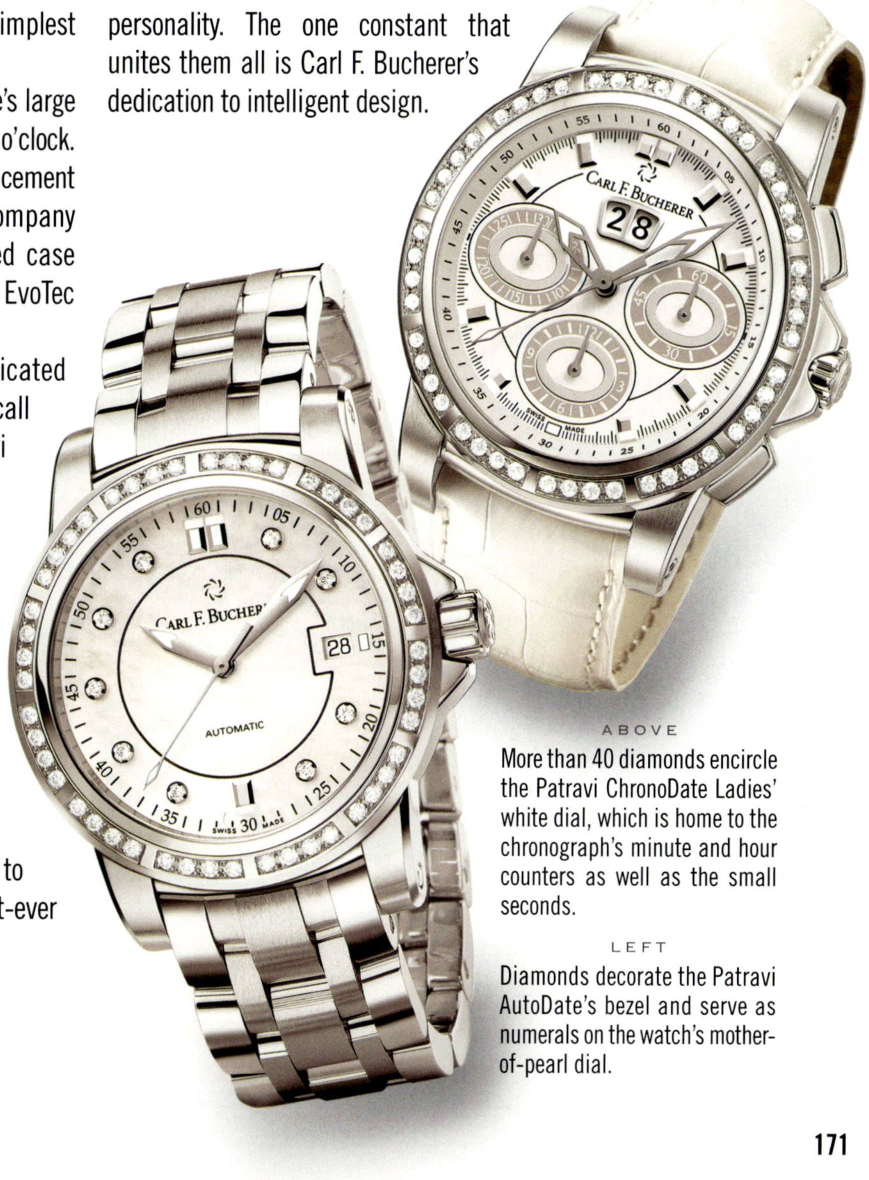

ABOVE

More than 40 diamonds encircle the Patravi ChronoDate Ladies' white dial, which is home to the chronograph's minute and hour counters as well as the small seconds.

LEFT

Diamonds decorate the Patravi AutoDate's bezel and serve as numerals on the watch's mother-of-pearl dial.

PATRAVI EVOTEC BIG DATE — REF. 00.10628.08.23.11

Movement: automatic-winding CFB A1003 caliber; Ø 32mm, thickness: 6.3mm; 55-hour power reserve; 33 jewels; 21,600 vph; peripheral rotor; dynamic shock absorber (DSA); patented Central Dual Adjusting System (CDAS), requiring adjustments only once.
Functions: hours, minutes; small seconds; large date.
Case: stainless steel with 56 TW VVS diamonds (1.1 carats); 38.54x39.25mm, thickness: 12.9mm; screw down crown; antireflective sapphire crystal on both sides; sapphire crystal caseback; water resistant to 5atm.
Dial: white; 11 polished index markers.
Strap: water snake; stainless steel folding clasp.
Suggested price: $20,000
Also available: python leather strap with stainless steel folding clasp.

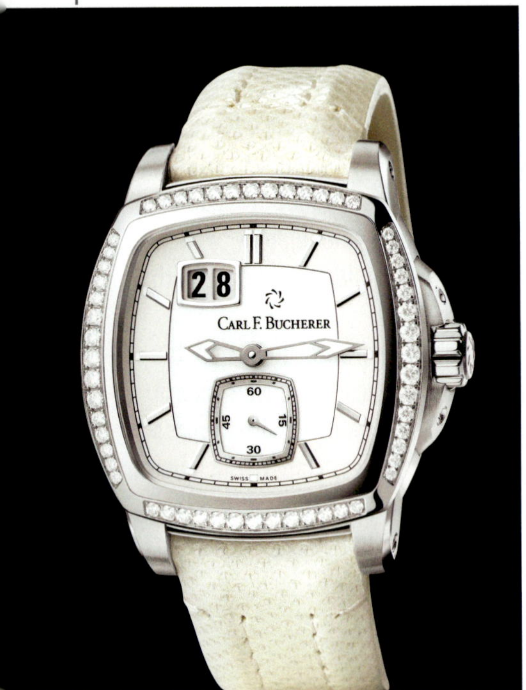

PATRAVI AUTO DATE — REF. 00.10617. 08.77.01

Movement: automatic-winding CFB 1950 caliber; 38-hour power reserve; 25 jewels.
Functions: hours, minutes, seconds; date at 3.
Case: stainless steel; Ø 38mm; sapphire crystal; sapphire crystal caseback; screw-down crown; water resistant to 5atm.
Dial: white mother-of-pearl; nine FC TW VVS diamonds, two index markers.
Strap: square-scale alligator leather in pearl white; stainless steel folding clasp.
Suggested price: $4,400
Also available: stainless steel bracelet ($4,800); diamond-set bezel on a python strap ($9,500); diamond-set bezel on a stainless steel bracelet ($9,900).

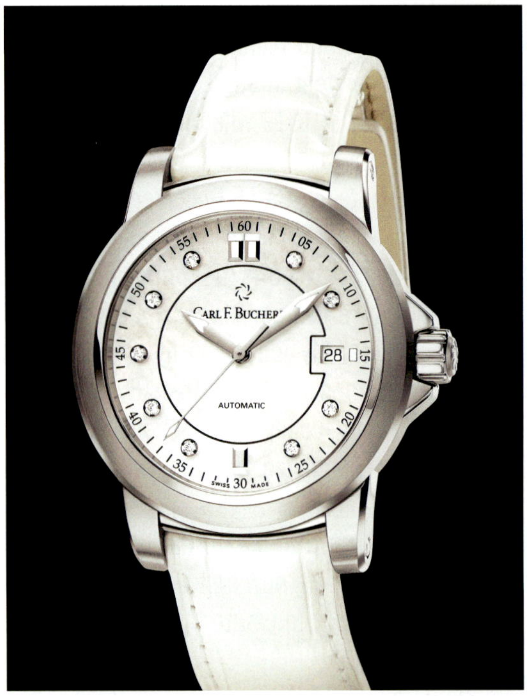

PATRAVI EVOTEC POWER RESERVE — REF. 00.10627.15.93.01

Movement: automatic-winding CFB A1002 caliber; Ø 32mm, thickness: 6.3mm; 55-hour power reserve; 33 jewels; peripheral mounted and bidirectional winding mechanism; dynamic shock absorber (DSA); patented Central Dual Adjusting System (CDAS), requiring adjustments only once.
Functions: hours, minutes; small seconds; large date; day.
Case: 18K rose gold; 43.75x44.5mm, thickness: 13.95mm; rubber bezel; screw-down crown; domed, antireflective sapphire crystal; sapphire crystal caseback; water resistant to 5atm.
Dial: brown; nine polished index markers; red power reserve indicator between 2 and 4, when watch is fully wound, background is in white, as it winds down, background is in Carl F. Bucherer red.
Strap: calfskin leather; 18K rose-gold folding clasp.
Suggested price: $37,900
Also available: stainless steel, black calfskin strap with stainless steel folding clasp ($15,900).

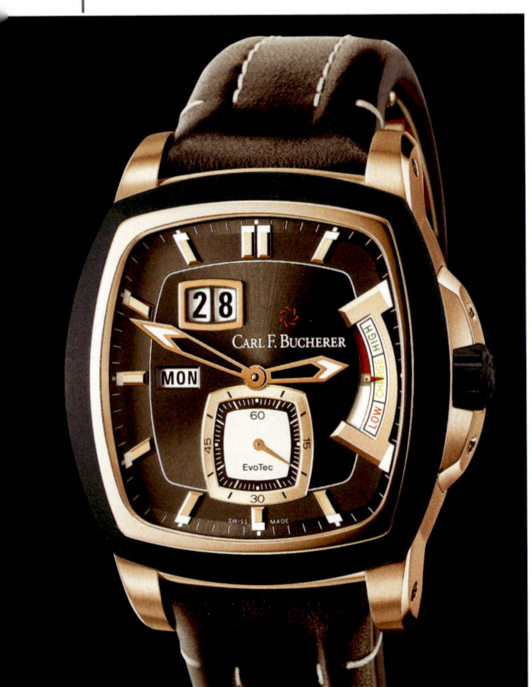

PATRAVI EVOTEC DAY DATE — REF. 00.10628.08.33.21

Movement: automatic-winding CFB A1001 caliber; Ø 32mm, thickness: 6.3mm; 55-hour power reserve; 33 jewels; peripheral rotor; dynamic shock absorber (DSA); patented Central Dual Adjusting System (CDAS), requiring adjustments only once.
Functions: hours, minutes; small seconds; large date; day.
Case: stainless steel; 44x44.5mm, thickness: 14mm; screw-down crown; anti-reflective sapphire crystal on both sides; sapphire crystal caseback; water resistant to 5atm.
Dial: black; 12 polished index markers.
Bracelet: stainless steel.
Suggested price: $14,800
Also available: stainless steel, black dial; black calfskin strap ($13,900).

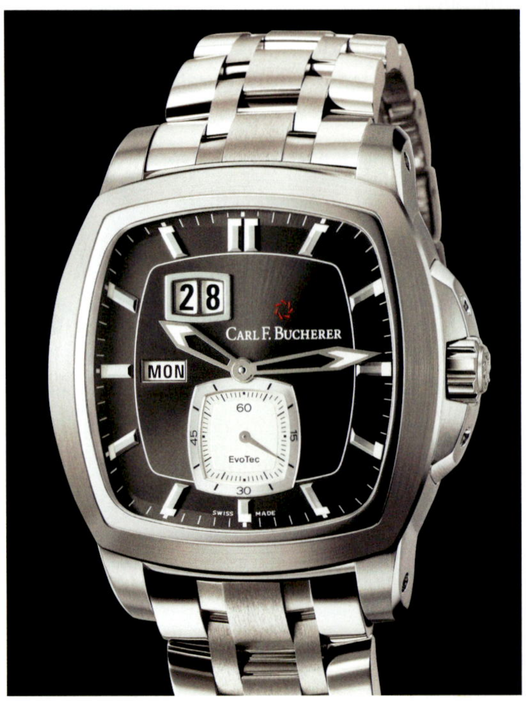

PATRAVI TRAVELTEC GMT — REF. 00.10620.08.53.21

Movement: automatic-winding CFB 1901 caliber; 42-hour power reserve; Ø 28.6mm, thickness: 7.3mm; 39 jewels; COSC-certified chronometer.
Functions: hours, minutes; small seconds; date at 4:20; GMT; 30-minute totalizer at 9, 12-hour totalizer at 6; chronograph pushbuttons at 2 and 4; second time zone ring, adjustable for East and West movement via bi-directional secured monopusher at 10; third time zone ring, adjustable from main crown at position C.
Case: stainless steel; Ø 46.6mm, thickness: 16mm; 70 components; screw-down crown; antireflective sapphire crystal; switch mechanism; single pushbutton mechanism visible through aperture in the side of the watchcase; water resistant to 5atm.
Dial: blue; polished index markers.
Bracelet: stainless steel.
Suggested price: $11,400
Also available: calfskin strap with a stainless steel folding clasp ($10,900); 18K rose gold on a strap ($44,000); 18K rose gold on a bracelet ($63,500); various dial color combinations.

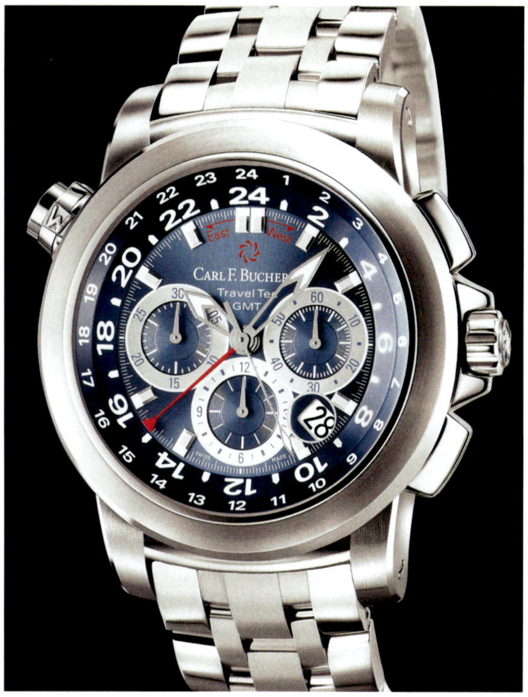

PATRAVI CHRONODATE ANNUAL — REF. 00.10619.03.93.01

Movement: automatic-winding CFB 1957.1 caliber; Ø 30mm, thickness: 7.3mm; 42-hour power reserve; 49 jewels; COSC-certified chronometer.
Functions: hours, minutes; small seconds; chronograph; big date; annual calendar.
Case: 18K rose gold; Ø 42mm, thickness: 14.1mm; screw-down crown; antireflective sapphire crystal; water resistant to 5atm.
Dial: chocolate brown; polished index markers.
Strap: hand-stitched Louisiana alligator leather; 18K rose-gold folding clasp.
Suggested price: $24,500
Also available: 18K rose gold on a bracelet ($42,000); various dial color combinations.

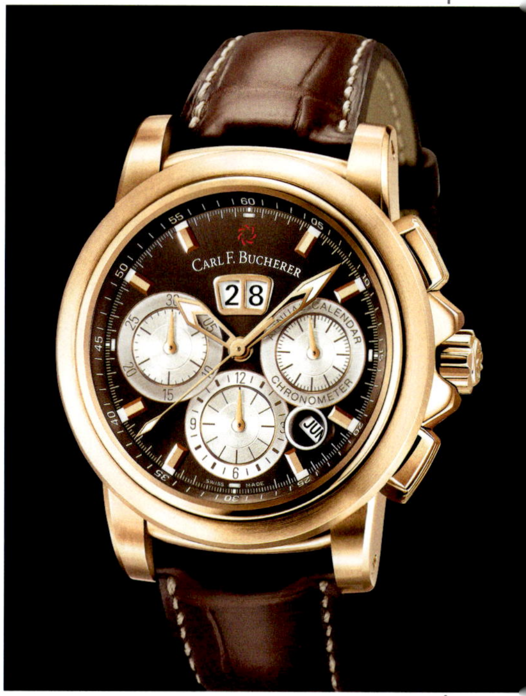

PATRAVI T-GRAPH — REF. 00.10615.08.33.01

Movement: automatic-winding CFB 1960 caliber; Ø 30mm, thickness: 7.3mm; 42-hour power reserve; 47 jewels.
Functions: hours, minutes; small seconds; chronograph; big date; bi-directional.
Case: stainless steel; ergonomic tonneau shape; 39x42mm; screw-down crown; antireflective sapphire crystal; water resistant to 5atm.
Dial: black; polished index markers.
Strap: black calfskin; stainless steel folding clasp.
Suggested price: $7,500
Also available: stainless steel bracelet ($8,000); 18K rose gold on a strap ($25,900) or 18K rose-gold bracelet ($43,500); various dial color combinations.

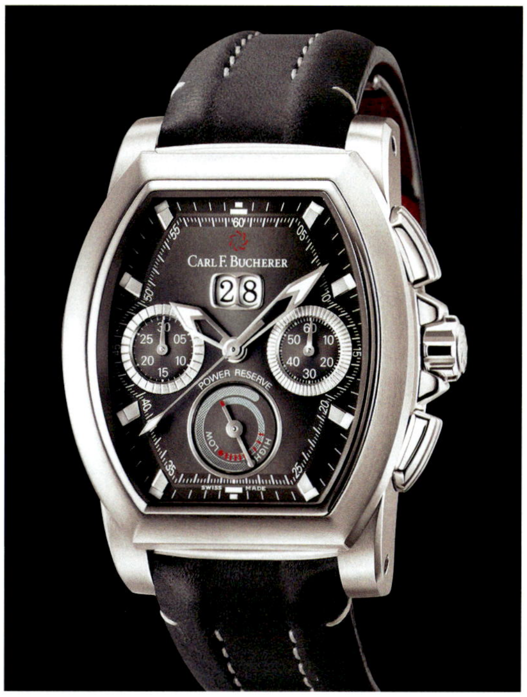

LADIES CHRONO DATE — REF. 00.10611.08.23.12

Movement: automatic-winding CFB 1956 caliber; Ø 30mm, thickness: 7.3mm; 42-hour power reserve; 49 jewels.
Functions: hours, minutes; small seconds; large date at 12; three chronograph counters.
Case: stainless steel; 48 TW VVS diamonds (0.8 carat); Ø 40mm, thickness: 13.5mm; screw-down crown; antireflective sapphire crystal on one side; sapphire crystal caseback; water resistant to 5atm.
Dial: white; nine polished index markers.
Strap: Louisiana alligator leather; stainless steel folding clasp.
Suggested price: $13,000
Also available: stainless steel bracelet ($13,300); no diamonds, on a strap ($6,900); stainless steel bracelet ($7,200); various straps and diamond combinations.

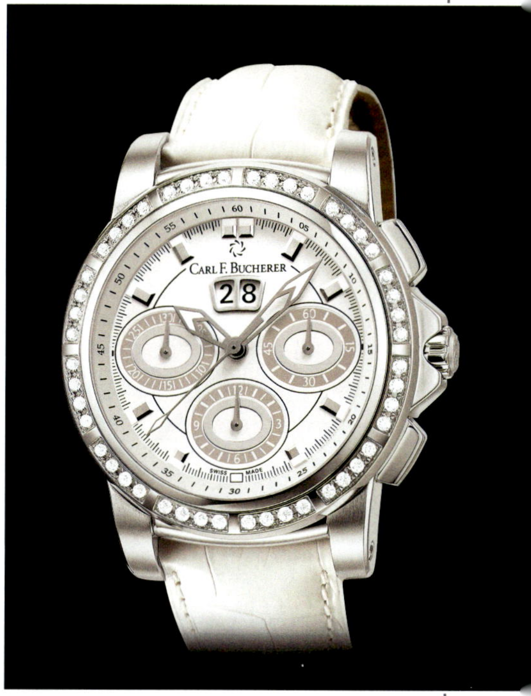

Cartier

REDEFINING A CLASSIC

After creating one of the first wrist-worn timepieces in 1904, Cartier spent the next century refining the art form with watches that balanced the weight of tradition against the constant push of innovation.

The historic firm is poised to hold sway over haute horology for another century with its Fine Watchmaking Collection, a new generation of timepieces powered by movements developed exclusively by Cartier's workshops.

A remarkable ambassador for the collection, the Rotonde de Cartier Astrotourbillon turns heads with an orbiting tourbillon that doubles as a seconds hand. The mechanism compensates for gravity-induced errors to the escapement's rate just as any other tourbillon would. Rather than remaining fixed to one point, however, the mechanism revolves around the center of the tiered dial, tethered to the movement by an elongated carriage tucked neatly beneath a layer of guilloché. As the captivating tourbillon makes its rounds, its arrow-shaped balance bridge indicates the seconds.

In haute horology, there is often a temptation to create complication for the sake of complication. With its Astrotourbillon, Cartier shows that true horological greatness is not measured by the thickness of an instruction manual, but rather by its poetic economy. That is not to diminish the enormous feat of micro-engineering Cartier accomplishes by successfully launching its tourbillon into orbit, but only to point out that the supreme beauty of the creation transcends the techniques used to achieve it.

Cartier keeps the spotlight on the tourbillon with the firm's Calibre 9455 MC, which powers the Rotonde de Cartier Skeleton Flying Tourbillon.

Produced entirely at the company's manufacture in the Geneva suburb of Meyrin, the movement bears the Geneva Seal, an independent and legally sanctioned label that signifies a movement meets or exceeds strict benchmarks for everything from decoration to precision.

The skeletonized design exhibits a certain musical quality, in that oftentimes the notes that remain silent are just as important as those that are played. Here, the negative space of the skeletonized bridges and mainplate amplifies the Roman numeral's powerful angles, which are juxtaposed against the circle-in-a-circle motif evoked by the balance wheel ensconced within the round white-gold case.

The theme of cool restraint carries over to the Rotonde de Cartier Jumping Hours, which does away with hands altogether. Instead, the minimalist display indicates the minutes with an arrow on a rotating disc and the hours in a large aperture that frames Cartier's signature Roman numerals as they advance instantaneously every 60 minutes.

The Jumping Hours features Cartier's 9905 MC movement, which controls the forceful release of energy required to snap the hour disc into place swiftly and precisely. In contrast to the dial's stark elegance, the transparent caseback exhibits the ornate flourishes applied to the caliber by the company's artisan decorators.

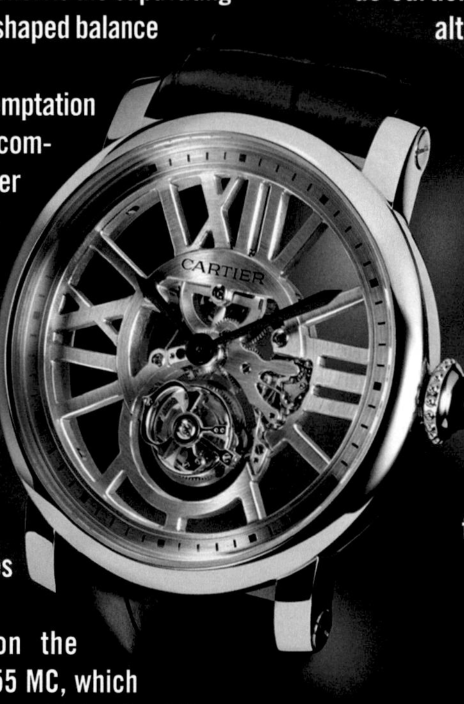

LEFT

Instead of a dial, the Rotonde de Cartier Skeleton Flying Tourbillon's mainplate and bridges are engraved extensively to form the chapter ring's Roman numerals.

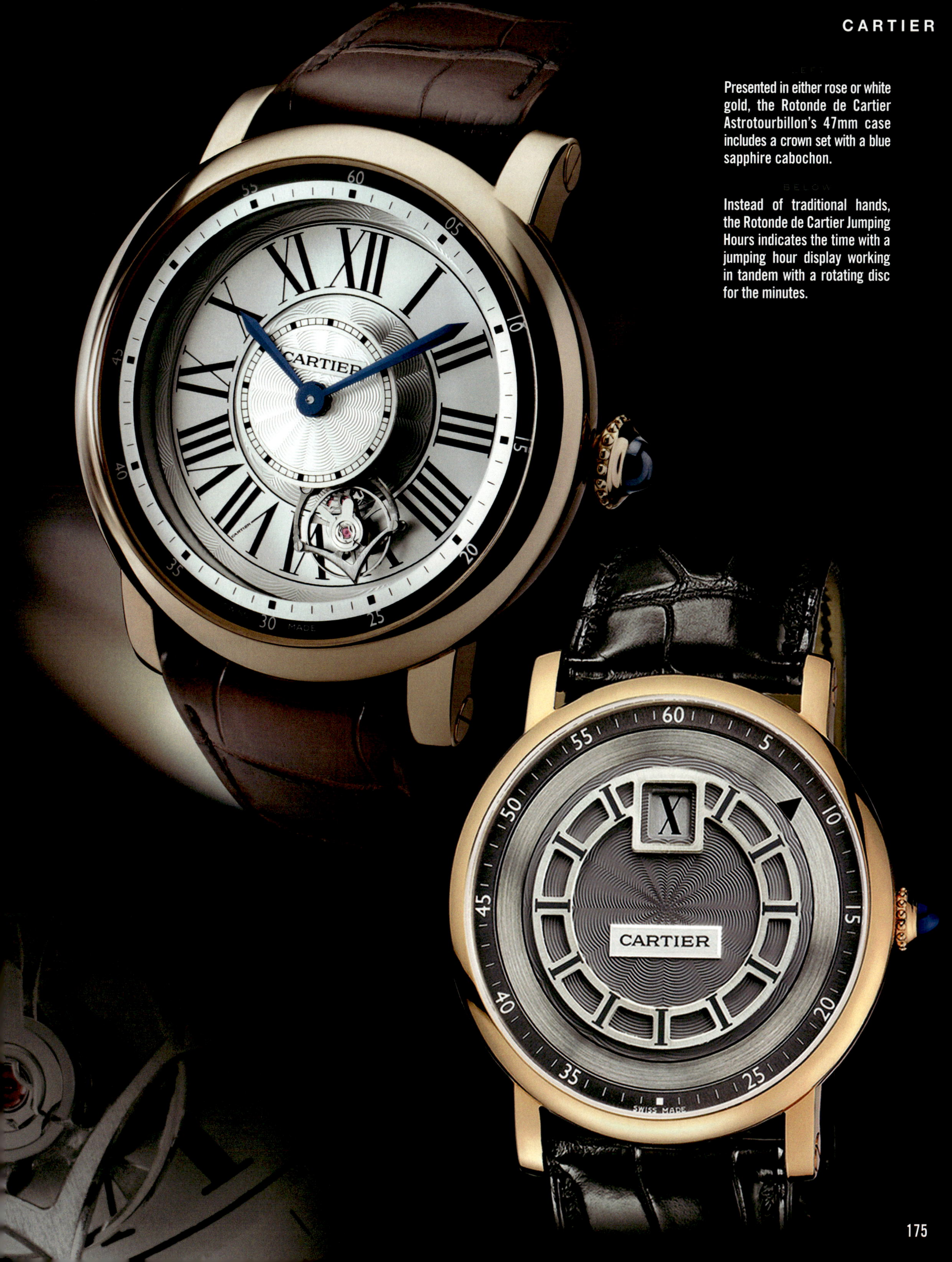

LEFT

Presented in either rose or white gold, the Rotonde de Cartier Astrotourbillon's 47mm case includes a crown set with a blue sapphire cabochon.

BELOW

Instead of traditional hands, the Rotonde de Cartier Jumping Hours indicates the time with a jumping hour display working in tandem with a rotating disc for the minutes.

In 1912, Cartier introduced a curved case whose sleek profile presaged by several years the Art Deco era that rose to prominence in Paris during the 1920s. The voluptuous contour of the new Tortue Perpetual Calendar recalls that distinctive profile from the brand's early years as a watchmaker.

The movement contained within this elegant barrel shape is a thoroughly modern invention and earns the distinction of being the first automatic perpetual calendar to emerge from Cartier's manufacture workshops.

To indicate the calendar, the company foregoes the usual arrangement of circular subsidiary dials in favor of something more dynamic. Cartier populates the surface of the dial with: a retrograde display for the day of the week; a ring that runs along the outer rim for the date; and a round display positioned at 12 o'clock from which the month and leap year are both read.

In place of a traditional dial, the Tortue Perpetual Calendar's partially skeletonized design uses the movement as decoration in a way that highlights the complexity required to mechanically account for the irregularity of the Gregorian calendar. Much like a pithy line penned by Hemingway or Twain, the Tortue Perpetual Calendar's elegance stems from the absence of superfluous gestures.

With the introduction of Calibre 1904, Cartier evokes the year Louis Cartier designed one of the world's first wristwatches at the behest of Brazilian aviator Alberto Santos-Dumont and thus launched the firm's historic legacy as a watchmaker.

The first automatic movement produced entirely by Cartier, Calibre 1904 entails several features designed with an eye toward chronometric precision, including a double barrel to ensure stability regardless of how much or little power is contained within the mainspring. The company's engineers enhanced the rotor itself, adding a system of ceramic ball bearings for resilience and a pawl system for faster winding.

Cartier's commitment to the ideals of the Swiss watchmaking tradition is evidenced by the attention to detail it lavishes on the movement's decoration. The application of Côtes de Genève to the rotor and bridges can be seen through the crystal caseback. Even more telling is the perlage used to decorate the mainplate, a section hidden from view to all but the technicians who will perform the watch's recommended service every five years.

The movement debuts in the Calibre de Cartier, a handsome watch that includes hours, minutes, small seconds and the date. Cartier presents the mechanism in a 42mm round case that is available in rose gold, stainless steel or a combination of the two.

Each of these timepieces is the spectacular result of Cartier's ongoing efforts to develop and produce its own movements in-house. If Cartier's early results are any indication, this is the start of something good.

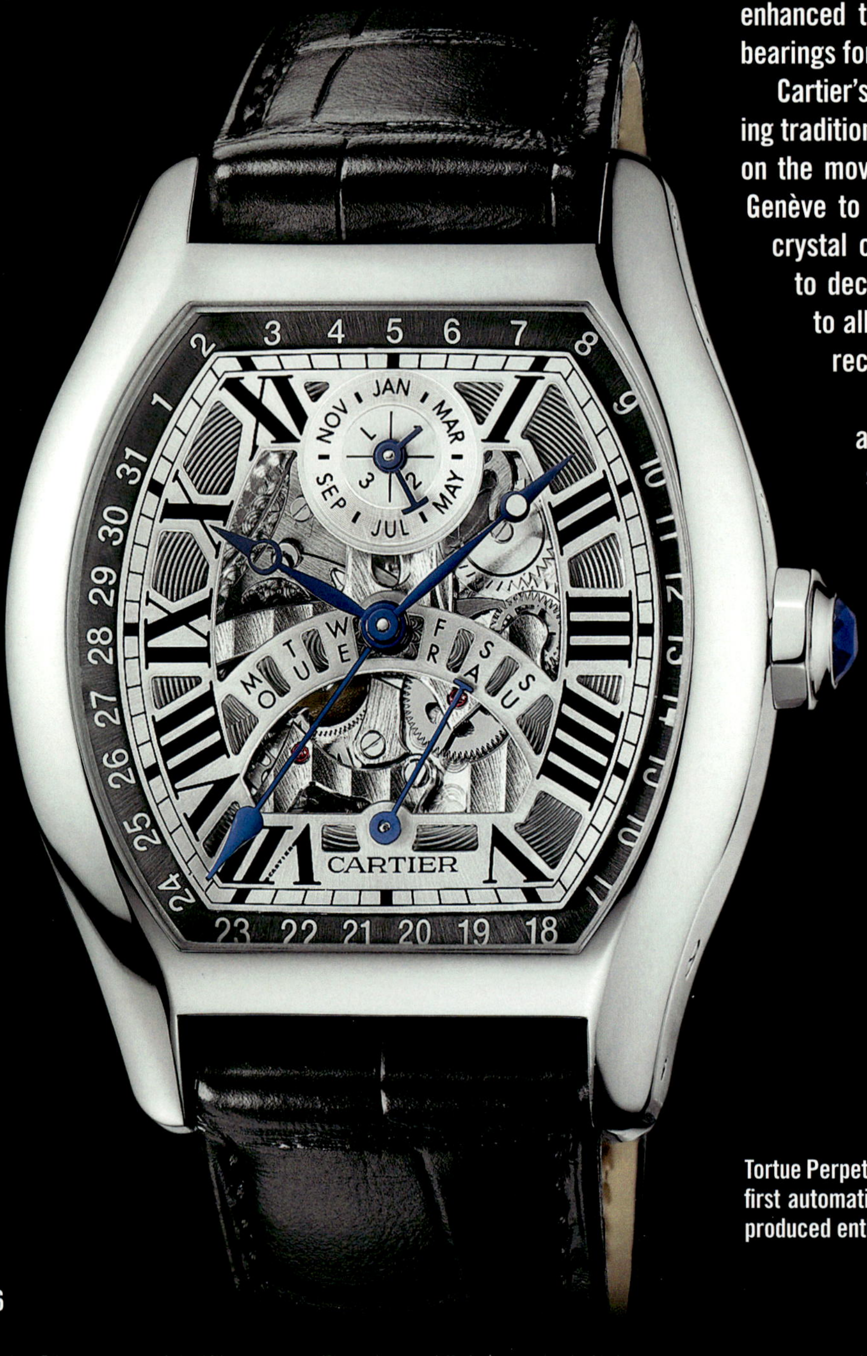

Tortue Perpetual Calendar is equipped with the first automatic perpetual calendar movement produced entirely in-house by Cartier.

Cartier equips a new generation of timepieces with an exceptional range of movements designed, produced, decorated and assembled at the firm's manufacture workshops in Geneva and La Chaux-de-Fonds.

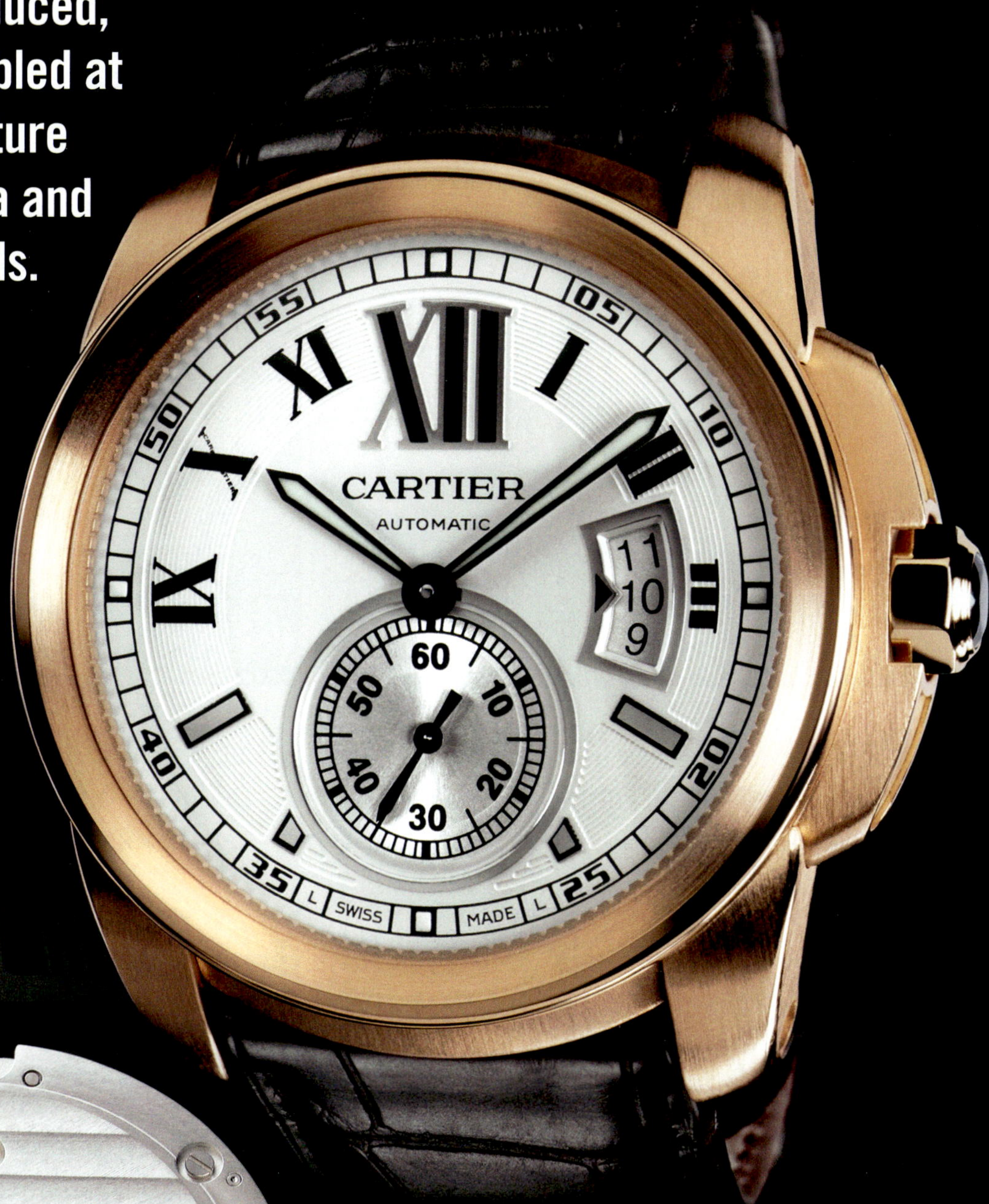

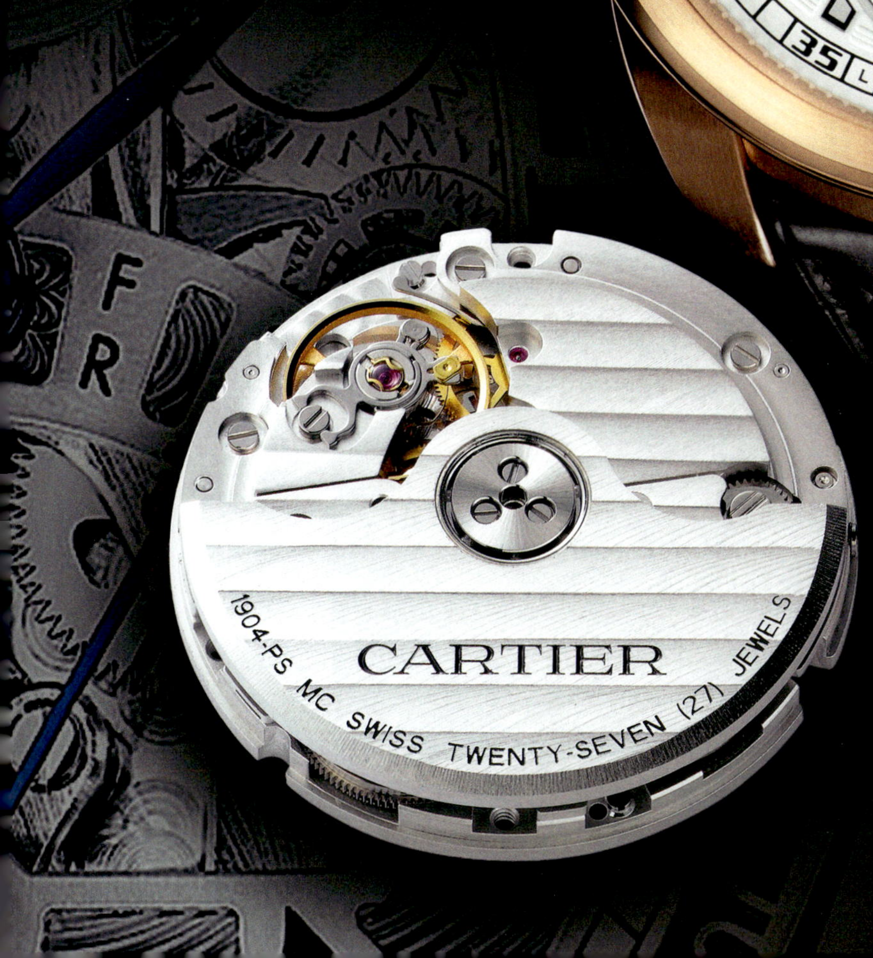

ABOVE

The 42mm rose-gold Calibre de Cartier is also available in steel with a white or black dial and on a black strap, and in steel and rose gold on a brown strap.

LEFT

Calibre de Cartier features Calibre 1904, an in-house movement named after the year Cartier introduced one of the world's first wrist-worn watches.

ROTONDE JUMPING HOURS REF. CRW1553751

Movement: manual-winding 9905 MC caliber; Cartier workshop-crafted.
Functions: jumping hours; trailing minutes with disc mechanism.
Case: 18K rose gold; Ø 42mm; circular-grained crown set with a sapphire cabochon; sapphire crystal; sapphire crystal caseback; water resistant to 3atm.
Dial: galvanic slate-colored guilloché; openwork satin-finish silvered grid sunburst motif; black transfer Roman numerals; slate-colored flange with sunburst finish.
Strap: black alligator skin; 18K rose-gold adjustable deployant buckle.
Price: available upon request.
Also available: white gold.

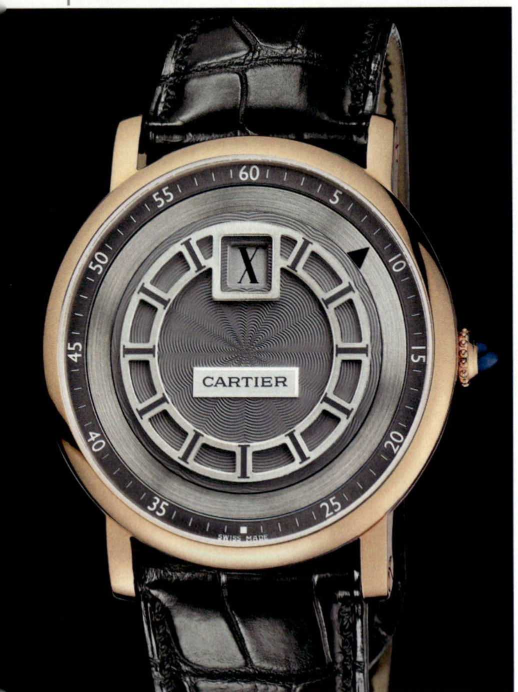

TORTUE PERPETUAL CALENDAR REF. CRW1580045

Movement: automatic-winding 9422 MC caliber; Cartier workshop-crafted.
Functions: hours, minutes; perpetual calendar; retrograde day display; month and leap year in a counter at 12.
Case: 18K rose gold; 18K rose-gold octagonal crown set with faceted sapphire; mineral crystal; sapphire crystal caseback; water resistant to 3atm.
Dial: white silvered guilloché; black transfer Roman numerals; apple-shaped hour and minute hands.
Strap: brown alligator skin; 18K rose-gold double-adjustable deployant buckle.
Price: available upon request.

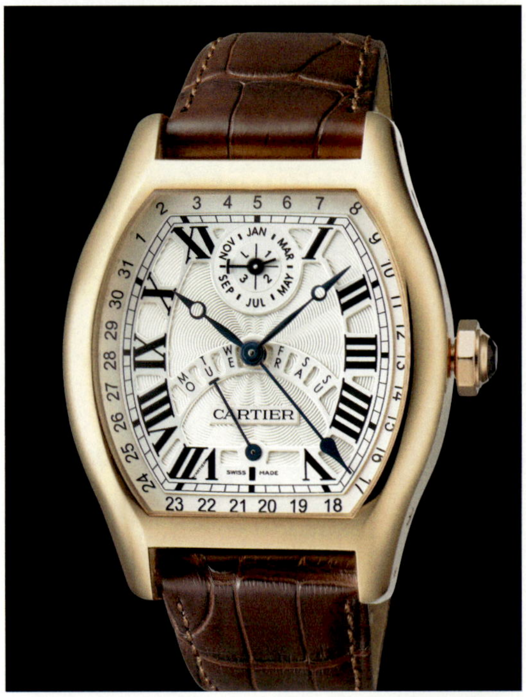

SANTOS-DUMONT SKELETON REF. CRW2020052

Movement: manual-winding 9612 MC caliber; Cartier workshop-crafted.
Functions: hours, minutes; skeleton bridges in the shape of Roman numerals.
Case: titanium and black ADLC coating; blackened titanium crown; black faceted spinel; sapphire crystal; sapphire crystal caseback; water resistant to 3atm.
Dial: skeleton; rhodium-plated brass sword-shaped hands.
Strap: black alligator skin; 18K white-gold and ADLC coating.
Price: available upon request.
Also available: white gold.

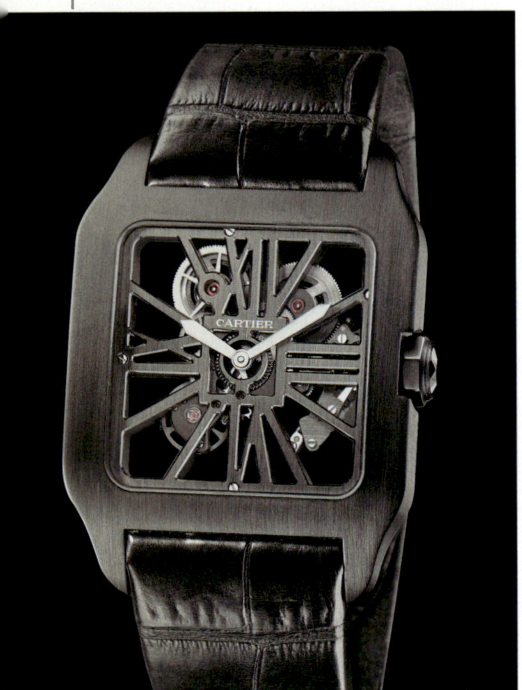

PASHA DE CARTIER SKELETON FLYING TOURBILLON REF. CRW3030021

Movement: manual-winding 9457 MC caliber; Cartier workshop-crafted; Geneva seal certified.
Functions: hours, minutes; flying tourbillon with display at seconds via C-shaped tourbillon carriage; skeleton bridge in shape of Arabic numerals.
Case: 18K white gold; Ø 42mm; 18K white-gold fluted crown with a sapphire cabochon; sapphire crystal; sapphire crystal caseback; water resistant to 3atm.
Dial: skeleton; blued-steel lozenge-shaped hands.
Strap: black alligator skin; 18K white-gold adjustable deployant buckle.
Price: available upon request.
Note: individually numbered and limited to 100 pieces.

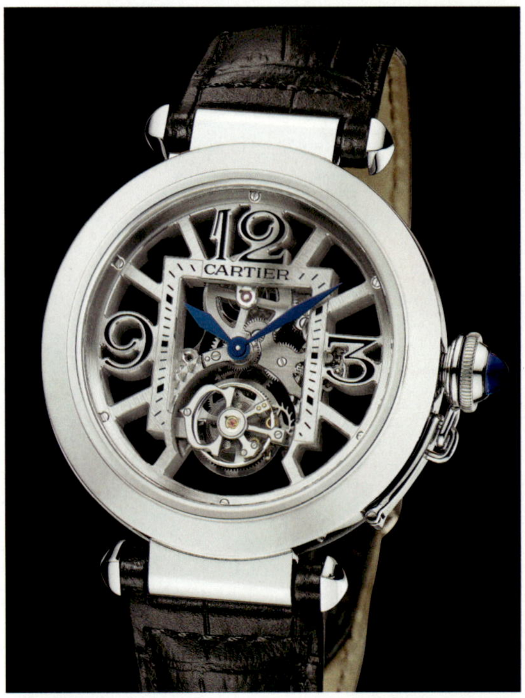

ROTONDE DE CARTIER 8 DAYS POWER RESERVE — REF. CRW1556203

Movement: manual-winding 9910 MC caliber; Cartier workshop-crafted; 5-day power reserve.
Functions: hours, minutes; small seconds; large date; power reserve indicator.
Case: 18K rose gold; beaded crown set with a sapphire cabochon; sapphire crystal; water resistant to 3atm.
Dial: silvered guilloché; 12 Roman numerals; apple-shaped blued-steel hands.
Strap: brown alligator; 18K rose-gold adjustable deployant buckle.
Price: available upon request.
Also available: white gold.

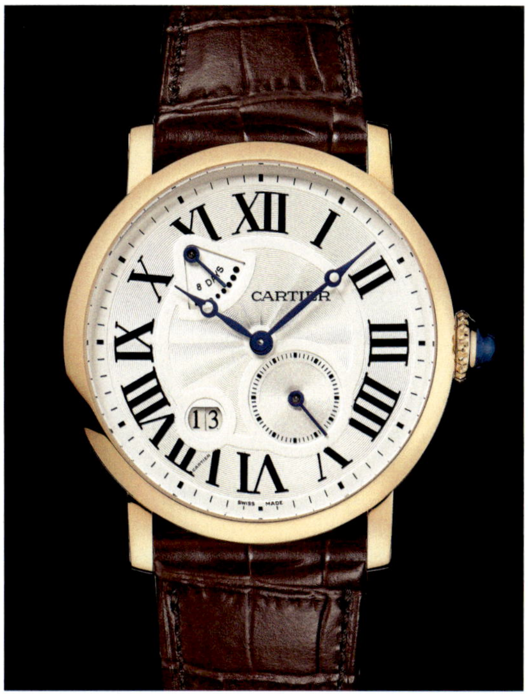

CALIBRE DE CARTIER — REF. CRW7100036

Movement: automatic-winding 1904-PS MC caliber; Cartier workshop-crafted.
Functions: hours, minutes; small seconds; date.
Case: 18K rose gold; Ø 42mm; 18K rose-gold bezel; stainless steel heptagonal crown set with a faceted spinel; sapphire crystal; water resistant up to 3atm.
Dial: silvered snailed opaline; outer rail-track minute circle with four luminescent spots; seven black transferred Roman numerals; small seconds counter with sunray satin finish; black oxidized steel and luminescent sword-shaped hands.
Bracelet: stainless steel and 18K rose gold.
Price: available upon request.
Also available: on a strap; stainless steel; 18K rose gold.

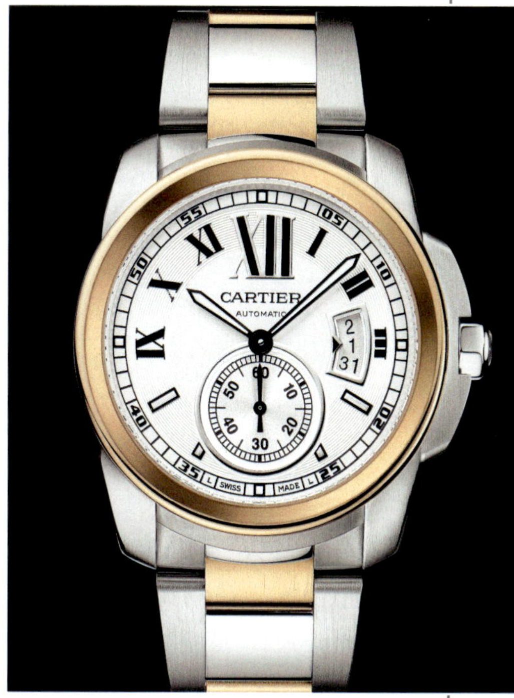

BALLON BLEU DE CARTIER CHRONOGRAPH — REF. CRW6920025

Movement: automatic-winding 8101 MC caliber.
Functions: hours, minutes, seconds; date at 9; chronograph counters at 3 and 6.
Case: stainless steel; Ø 44mm; stainless steel fluted crown set with a spinel; sapphire crystal; water resistant to 3atm.
Dial: 12 flinqué zones; nine white Roman numerals; rhodiumized steel sword-shaped hands.
Bracelet: stainless steel.
Price: available upon request.
Also available: stainless steel and gold with a white dial; stainless steel and 18K rose gold with a white dial; on a strap.

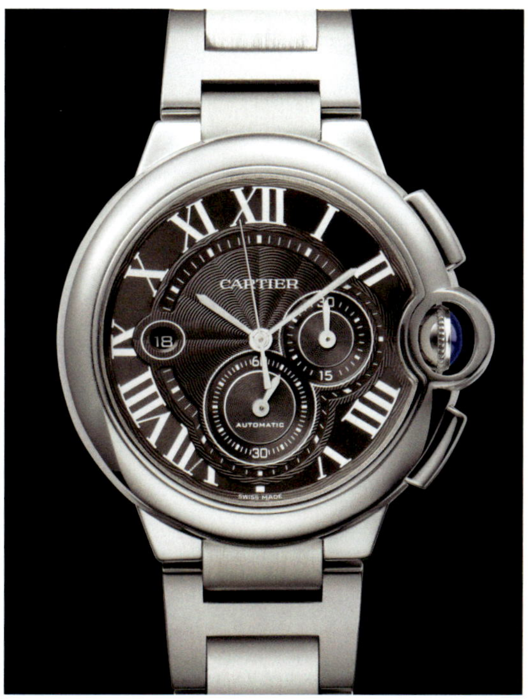

ROADSTER S CHRONOGRAPH — REF. CRW6206020

Movement: automatic-winding 8630 MC caliber.
Functions: hours, minutes, seconds; date; chronograph.
Case: stainless steel; stainless steel with black ADLC-coated bezel; stainless steel fluted crown; sapphire crystal; water resistant to 10atm.
Dial: silvered opaline; black matte varnished counters; 11 black transferred Roman numerals; black oxidized steel sword-shaped hands.
Strap: interchangeable black rubber strap; stainless steel double-adjustable deployant buckle.
Price: available upon request.
Also available: on a bracelet.

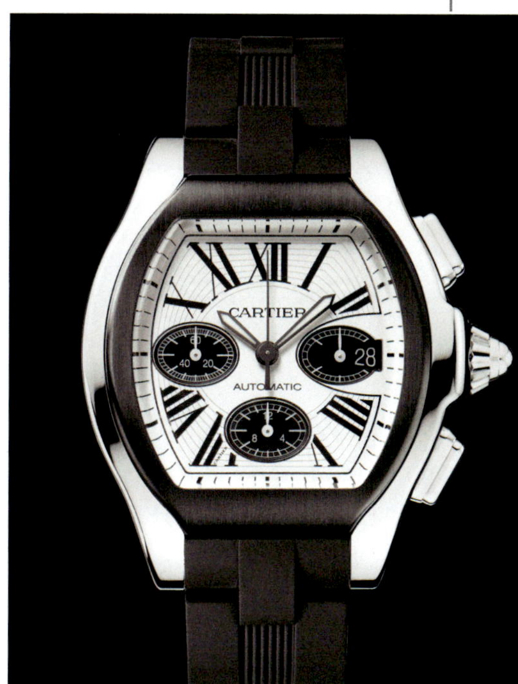

CARTIER D'ART COLLECTION TORTUE WITH JAGUAR MOTIF REF. CRHPI00412

Movement: manual-winding 9601 MC caliber; Cartier workshop-crafted.
Functions: hours, minutes.
Case: 18K yellow-gold Tortue XL case; jaguar motif; hand-engraved; champlevé Grand Feu enamel; octagonal crown set with a blue sapphire; sapphire crystal; water resistant to 3atm.
Dial: 18K yellow gold; jaguar motif; hand-engraved; champlevé Grand Feu enamel; 18K yellow-gold apple-shaped hands.

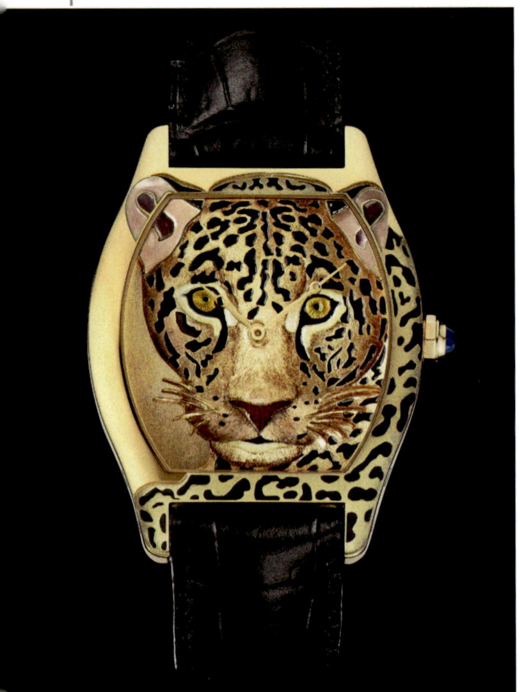

Strap: black semi-matte alligator; 18K yellow-gold adjustable deployant buckle.
Price: available upon request.
Note: limited and numbered to 80 pieces.

FELINE DE CARTIER REF. CRHPI00341

Movement: Cartier quartz 056 caliber; 5 jewels; time-setting tool in polished steel set with a titanium cabochon.
Functions: hours, minutes.
Case: 18K rhodiumized white gold; set with 655 round diamonds (7.01 carats); two emerald eyes (0.04 carat) and onyx nose (0.01 carat); water resistant to 3atm.
Dial: silvered sunray finished rhodiumized steel sword-shaped hands.

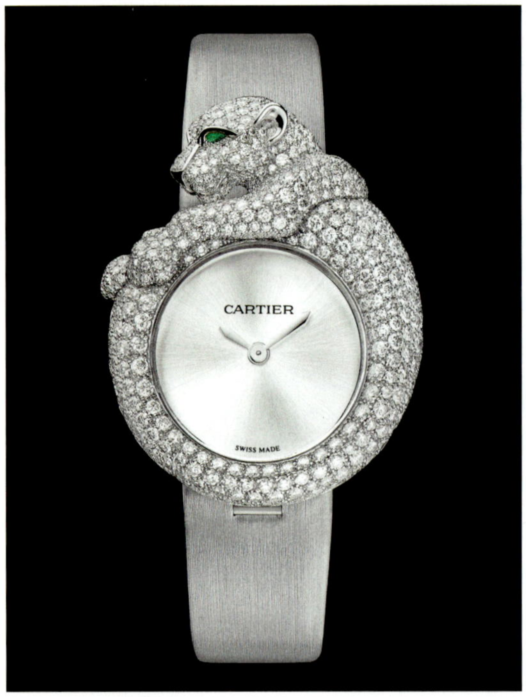

Bracelet: light gray toile brossée; 18K rhodiumized white-gold 14mm adjustable deployant buckle; set with round diamonds; comes with an additional dark gray toile brossée.
Price: available upon request.

BAIGNOIRE REF. WB520005

Movement: manual-winding 430 caliber; Cartier workshop-crafted.
Functions: hours, minutes.
Case: large model; 18K rose gold set with round diamonds; 44x32mm; 18K rose-gold octagonal crown set with a diamond; sapphire crystal; water resistant to 3atm.
Dial: silvered opaline; guilloché and lacquered; 12 black Roman numerals; sword-shaped blued steel hands.

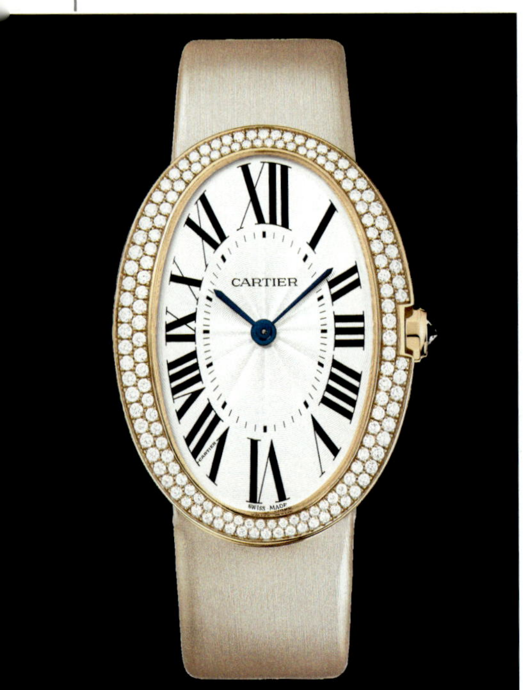

Strap: toile brossée; 18K rose-gold ardillon buckle.
Price: available upon request.
Also available: 18K yellow gold or 18K white gold; on a bracelet; in smaller size.

DELICE DE CARTIER REF. CRWG800006

Movement: Cartier quartz 157 caliber.
Functions: hours, minutes.
Case: large model; 18K rose gold; set with round diamonds (0.87 carat); beaded crown set with a diamond; sapphire crystal; water resistant to 3atm.
Dial: silvered lacquered; flinqué external decor; 12 black Roman numerals; blued-steel sword-shaped hands.

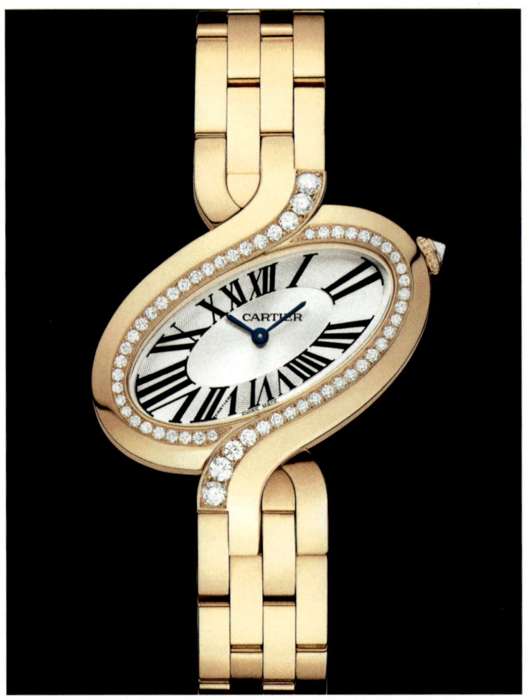

Bracelet: 18K rose gold.
Price: available upon request.
Also available: white gold; on a strap; without diamonds; in smaller size.

BALLON BLEU DE CARTIER — REF. CRWE9004Z3

Movement: automatic-winding Cartier 076 caliber.
Functions: hours, minutes, seconds.
Case: medium model; 18K yellow gold; Ø 36.5mm; set with round diamonds (1.22 carats); 18K yellow-gold fluted crown set with a cabochon sapphire; water resistant to 3atm.
Bracelet: 18K yellow gold.
Price: available upon request.
Also available: 18K white gold; 18K rose gold; stainless steel; stainless steel and 18K yellow gold; on a strap; without diamonds in Ø 28mm and Ø 42mm.

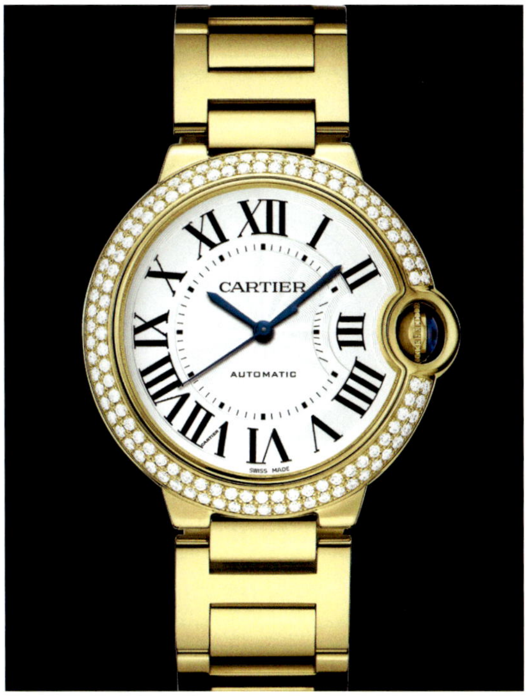

BALLON BLEU GOLD 11 DIAMONDS — REF. CRWE902026

Movement: automatic-winding 076 caliber.
Functions: hours, minutes.
Case: medium model; 18K rose gold; Ø 36.5mm; 18K rose-gold fluted crown set with a cabochon sapphire; sapphire crystal; water resistant to 3atm.
Dial: 12 zones flinqué; silvered lacquered sunray finish; set with 11 round diamonds (0.05 carat); one black Roman numeral; blue-steel sword-shaped hands.
Bracelet: 18K rose gold.
Price: available upon request.
Also available: in yellow gold; on a strap; in smaller size.

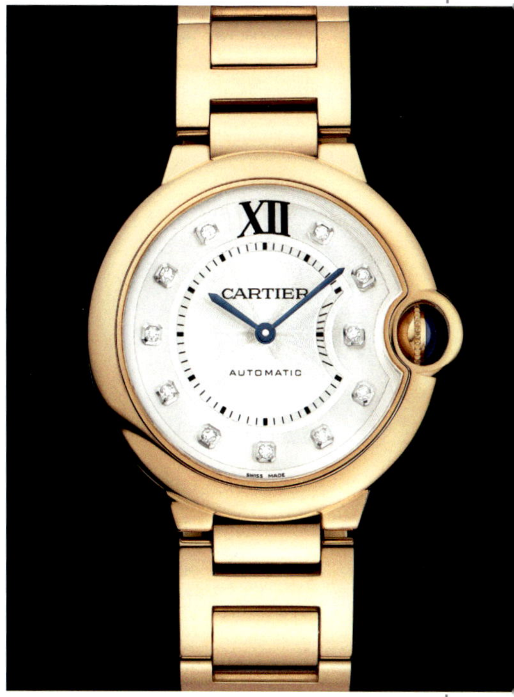

ROADSTER PINK DIAL — REF. CRW62017V3

Movement: quartz Cartier 688 caliber.
Functions: hours, minutes; date at 3.
Case: small model; stainless steel; stainless steel fluted crown; sapphire crystal; water resistant to 10atm.
Dial: pink lacquered; Roman numerals; luminescent sword-shaped black oxidized steel hands.
Bracelet: stainless steel, interchangeable with toile poudrée strap.
Price: available upon request.
Also available: with white dial.

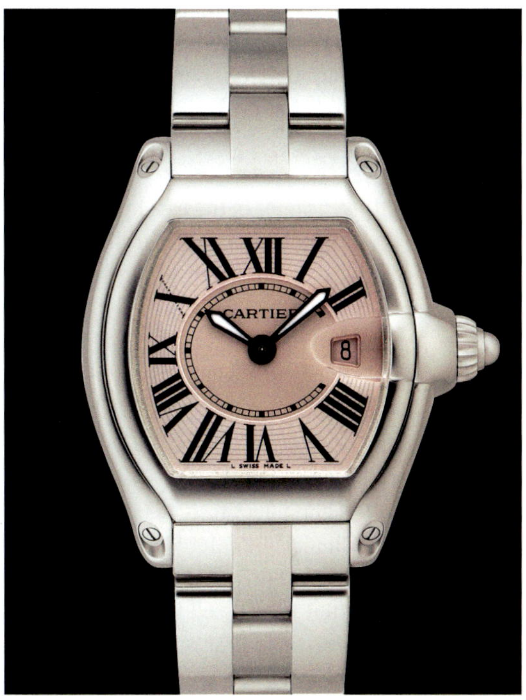

TANK SOLO — REF. CRW5200003

Movement: Cartier quartz 690 caliber.
Functions: hours, minutes.
Case: large model; stainless steel; circular-grained crown with blue spinel cabochon; sapphire crystal; water resistant to 3atm.
Dial: pale silvered opaline; blued-steel sword-shaped hands.
Strap: shiny black caiman; shiny black adjustable deployant buckle.
Price: available upon request.
Also available: smaller size; on a bracelet.

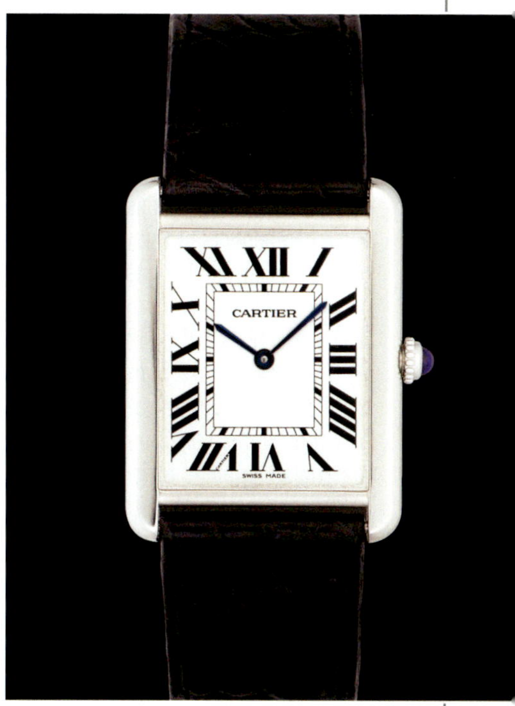

CHANEL

AUDACITY AND EXPERTISE

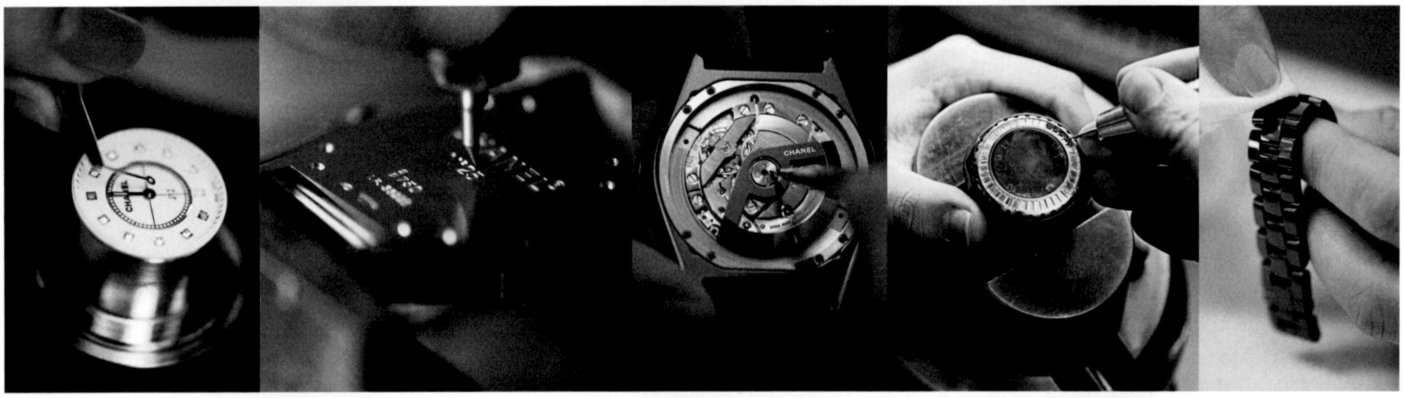

Inspired by Mademoiselle Chanel's creations, the brand's watches bring a new dimension to luxury watchmaking.

Gabrielle Chanel once said, "Fashion goes out of fashion, but style never." Simply inimitable, the CHANEL style was born from a subtle alchemy of highly original materials and colors charged with emotion. It became established through an extraordinary, avant-garde vision and endures thanks to its constant reinvention. Naturally, the spirit of Gabrielle Chanel is found in the watches' designs. The idea is to do away with the superfluous, go straight for the essentials and aim for simplicity while observing the CHANEL design codes. Technology is always used to enhance the quality of the products.

WATCHMAKER EXPERTISE

La Chaux-de-Fonds in Switzerland, located at an altitude of 1,000 meters above sea level, has 37,000 inhabitants, and the highest concentration of fine watchmakers and related activities worldwide. It was quite natural that the watchmaking facility of CHANEL was set up at La Chaux-de-Fonds, the birthplace of Swiss watchmaking. From conception to the final assembly process, CHANEL teams conceive, design, shape, mold, polish, assemble and fit all watch parts, including some components of the mechanical movements housed in the famous high-tech ceramic J12 cases.

MASTERING THE ART OF HIGH-TECH CERAMIC

The processes for producing ceramic, held in secret, protect the exclusivity of CHANEL watches and display a demanding level of know-how that unites earth, air, water and fire. Earth represents the natural materials combined to form the "powder" of which an exclusive mix is used to produce high-tech ceramic. Water is used for binding, forming and filtering these natural components. Air is used for drying and giving them form and structure. Fire is used for amalgamating them, bringing the material its immutable resistance and beauty, which has built the reputation of the J12 collection's cases and bracelets today. This chain of events would not be complete without the metal necessary for sculpting, piercing, grinding and beautifying the high-tech ceramic, nor without the secrets behind its polishing process.

THE J12: ICON OF THE 21ST CENTURY

Gabrielle Chanel subverted the types and functions of her creations, transforming their meaning and value. Cult objects destined to be legendary, such as the N° 5 perfume and 2.55 bag, were born out of this art of counterpoint. The J12 watch is part of this same philosophy of the twist in meaning and function so dear to Mademoiselle Chanel.

Inspired by the nautical world and born at the dawn of the third millennium, the J12 is an icon of 21st-century watchmaking. Ahead of its time, this watch metamorphoses ceramic, transforming it into a precious material, thus revolutionizing watchmaking codes and combining inalterable robustness with timeless Chanel elegance.

Intense black in 2000, followed by the first white model in 2003, the J12 associates night and day, masculine and feminine, strength and elegance, mystery and clarity to become a genuine mechanical talisman!

PREMIÈRE

Getting straight to the essential is one of the keys to the "code" of CHANEL. It is not surprising that the first watch launched by CHANEL in 1987 was baptized the "Première": it was both logical and fundamental to a new tradition. The shape of the Première reflects both a heritage and a message. Aesthetic heritage expresses itself as a reminder of the very characteristic geometry of Place Vendôme—a rectangle with cut-off corners—where its bronze column sits on the Parisian paving, indicating the passage of time like the hand of a sundial. A resemblance can also be found between the octagonal shape of the Première watchcase and the shape of the bottle stopper Gabrielle Chanel chose for her N° 5 perfume. A message of timelessness emerges from this silhouette with its power of indescribable seduction that pairs itself with gold or steel, diamonds or high-tech ceramic, pearls and interwoven leather, freeing itself from the test of time without ever tarnishing its honor. The Première's feminine lines are as much the lines of generations that unite, in complete simplicity, CHANEL tradition and its eternally renewed inventiveness.

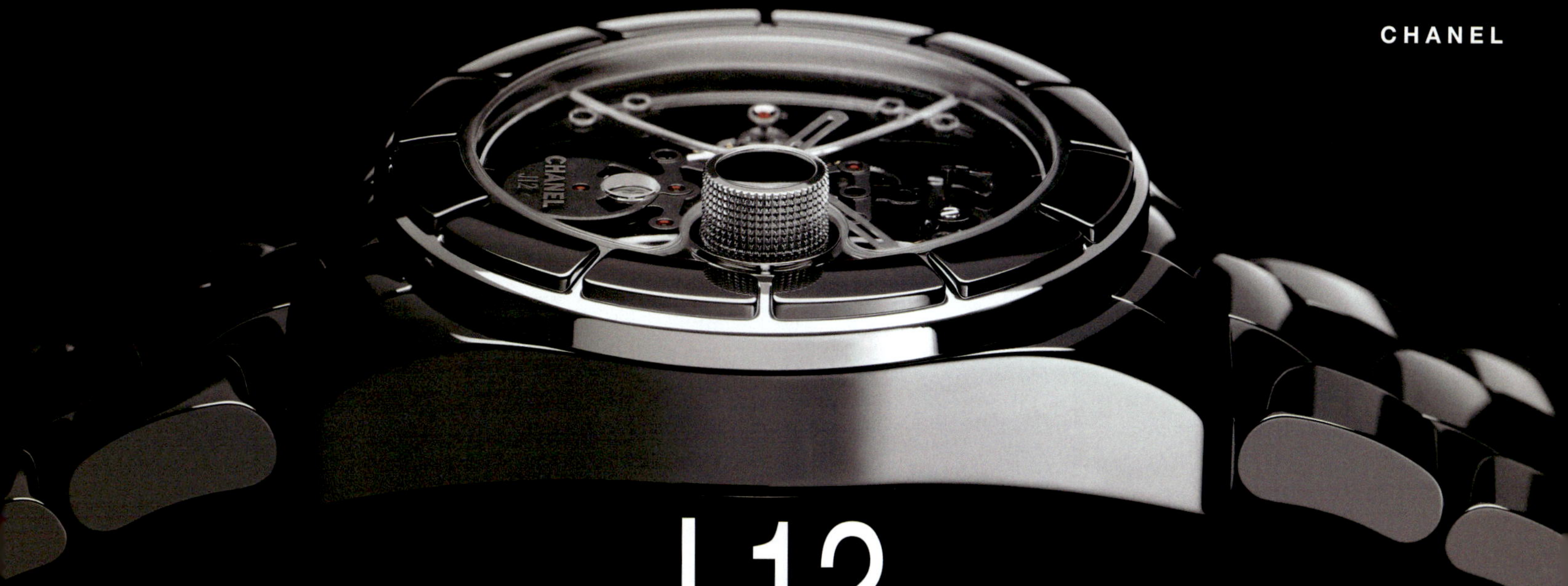

J 12
RÉTROGRADE MYSTÉRIEUSE

WHEN TECHNICAL PROWESS COMPLEMENTS AESTHETICS

CHANEL RMT-10 Calibre
R for Retrograde
M for Mysterious
T for Tourbillon

After introducing the first tourbillon featuring a highly innovative high-tech ceramic bottom plate, CHANEL confirmed its status as a pioneer of contemporary watchmaking by creating the J12 Rétrograde Mystérieuse. The Rétrograde Mystérieuse is a concentrated dose of innovation, bringing together complications and world premieres:

1. A tourbillon
2. A retractable vertical crown
3. A digital minutes display
4. A retrograde minute hand
5. A 10-day power reserve

This perfectly round watch, with a 47mm diameter, has been designed without a side crown to ensure optimum comfort on the wrist. The work on this complication was entrusted to one of the most state-of-the-art watchmaking design and construction workshops: the Giulio Papi team (APRP SA).

THE RÉTROGRADE MYSTÉRIEUSE

When the minute hand butts up against the crown built into the dial, it starts moving backwards around the dial until it is positioned on the other side of the dial: an entirely new retrograde design in the world of fine mechanical complications.

So that the watch continues to display the time while the minute hand reverses, a digital minute counter is displayed in a magnifying aperture at 6 o'clock: between minutes 11 and 19, the time is read with the classic hour hand and the figures that appear in this aperture. The watch remains totally accurate, further improved by its tourbillon.

The winding crown is retractable: when disconnected from its various functions (winding and setting the time), it is pushed in and remains locked in the down position.

Simple pressure brings it out of its housing, with no ill effect on the running of the watch, to restore its functions.

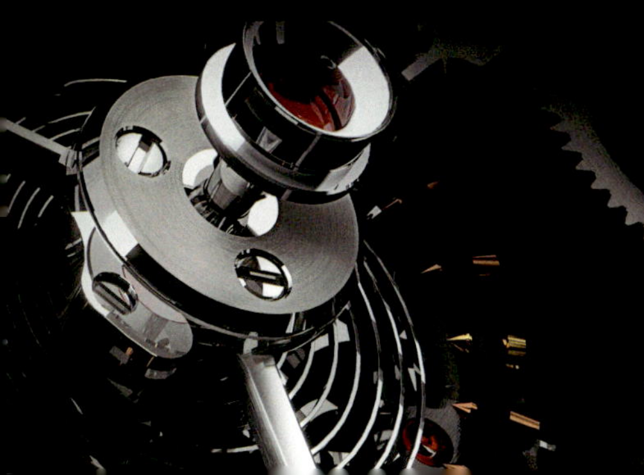

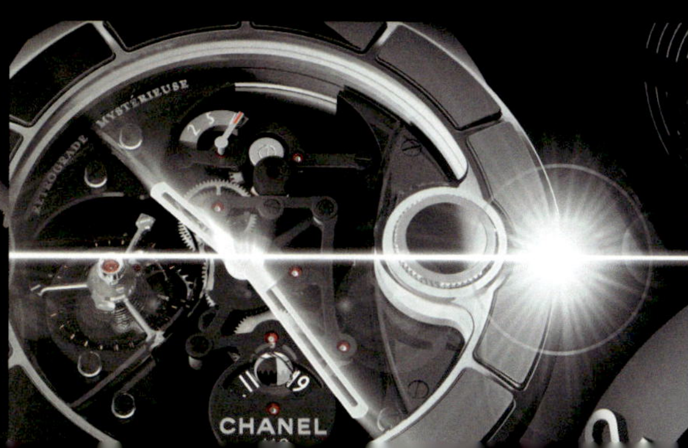

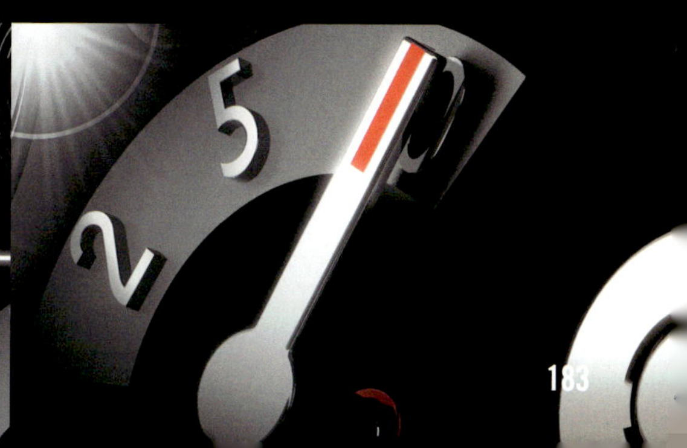

J12 HAUTE JOAILLERIE — REF. H2143

Movement: automatic-winding; 42-hour power reserve.
Functions: hours, minutes, seconds.
Case: 18K white gold; set with 52 baguette-cut diamonds (3.9 carats, F/G VVS1) and 22 baguette-cut cognac sapphires (1.2 carats); Ø 38mm; 18K white-gold bezel set with 46 baguette-cut diamonds (4.4 carats, F/G VVS1); water resistant to 5atm.
Dial: set with 57 baguette-cut diamonds (1.8 carats, F/G VVS1) and 84 baguette-cut cognac sapphires (2.1 carats).
Bracelet: 18K white gold; set with 270 baguette-cut diamonds (17.9 carats, F/G VVS1) and 232 baguette-cut cognac sapphires (11.2 carats); 18K white-gold triple-folding buckle; adjustable standard size.
Price: available upon request.
Note: limited edition of 12 pieces.
Also available: Ø 33mm case (high-precision quartz movement).

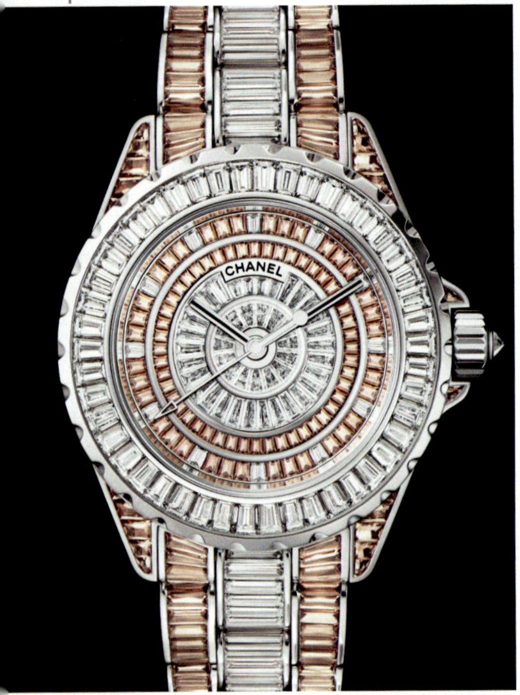

J12 CALIBRE 3125 — REF. H2129

Movement: automatic-winding CHANEL-manufactured AP 3125; 60-hour power reserve; black high-tech ceramic rotor; 22K rhodium-plated yellow gold mounted on high-tech ceramic ball bearings.
Functions: hours, minutes, seconds; date.
Case: black high-tech ceramic; Ø 42mm; 18K yellow-gold and black high-tech ceramic unidirectional bezel; sapphire crystal caseback; water resistant to 5atm.
Dial: lacquered black; 18K yellow-gold numerals.
Bracelet: black high-tech ceramic; 18K yellow-gold triple-folding buckle; adjustable standard size.
Suggested price: $25,000
Also available: black alligator strap.

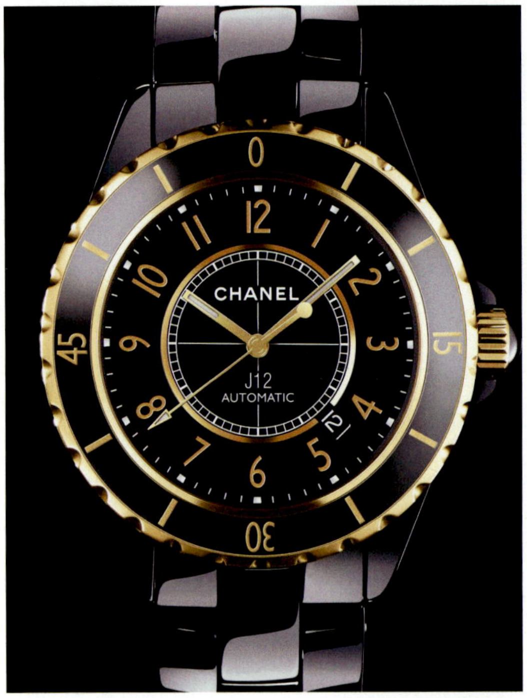

J12 JOAILLERIE — REF. H2029

Movement: automatic-winding; 42-hour power reserve.
Functions: hours, minutes, seconds.
Case: white high-tech ceramic; Ø 38mm; 18K white-gold bezel set with 46 baguette-cut diamonds (4.4 carats, F/G VVS1); water resistant to 10atm.
Dial: white high-tech ceramic center; set with 84 baguette-cut diamonds (2 carats, F/G VVS1) and 12 baguette-cut black high-tech ceramic indicators.
Bracelet: white high-tech ceramic; 18K white-gold triple-folding buckle; adjustable standard size.
Suggested price: $105,000
Also available: Ø 33mm case; Ø 42mm case.

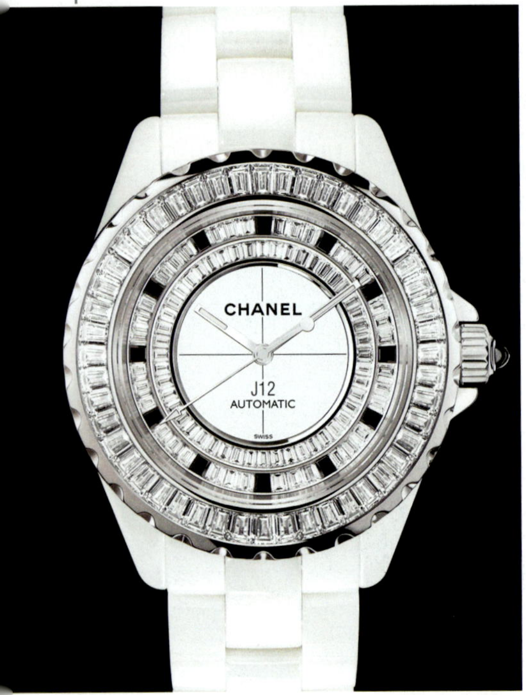

J12 JOAILLERIE — REF. H2311

Movement: automatic-winding; 42-hour power reserve.
Functions: hours, minutes, seconds; date.
Case: white high-tech ceramic; Ø 38mm; 18K pink-gold bezel set with 46 baguette-cut diamonds (4.4 carats, F/G VVS1); water resistant to 10atm.
Dial: lacquered white; eight diamond indicators.
Bracelet: white high-tech ceramic; 18K pink-gold triple-folding buckle; adjustable standard size.
Suggested price: $68,000
Note: limited edition of 100 pieces.
Also available: Ø 33mm case (high-precision quartz movement); black high-tech ceramic.

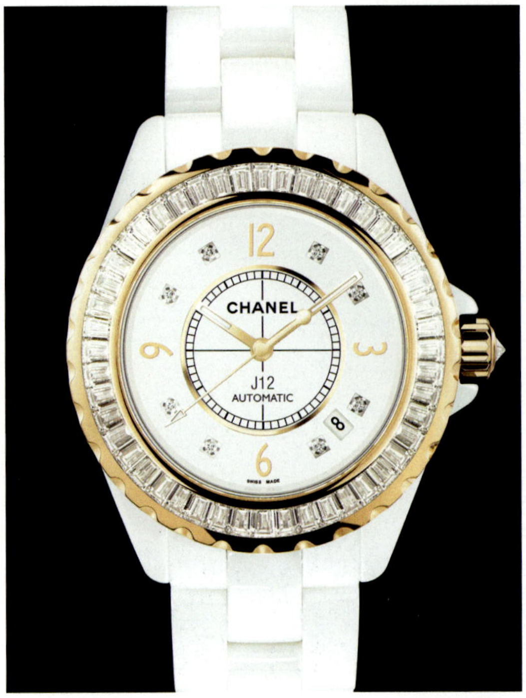

J12 DIAMONDS — REF. H2571

Movement: high-precision quartz movement.
Functions: hours, minutes, seconds.
Case: black high-tech ceramic and steel; Ø 29mm; bezel set with 40 brilliant-cut diamonds (0.9 carat, F/G VVS); water resistant to 5atm.
Dial: four rhodium-plated numerals set with eight diamond indicators (0.04 carat, F/G VVS).
Bracelet: black high-tech ceramic; steel triple-folding buckle; adjustable standard size.
Suggested price: $9,600
Also available: white high-tech ceramic.

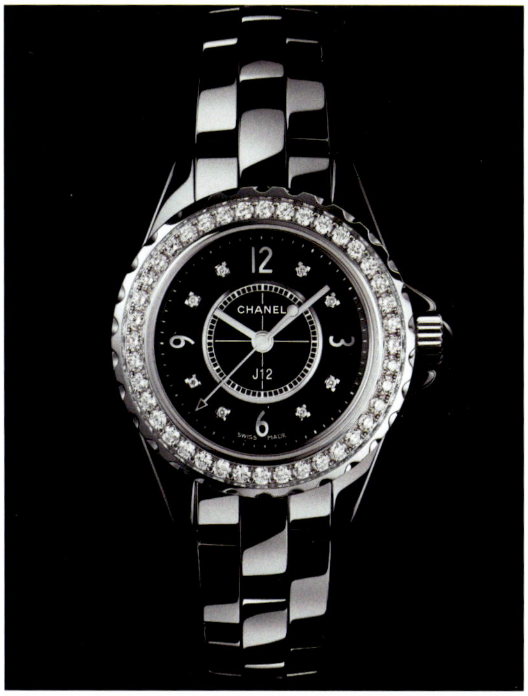

J12 DIAMOND DIAL — REF. H1757

Movement: automatic-winding; 42-hour power reserve.
Functions: hours, minutes, seconds; date.
Case: black high-tech ceramic and steel; Ø 38mm; water resistant to 20atm.
Dial: center pavé; set with 110 diamonds (0.27 carat, F/G VVS); 12 diamond indicators (0.09 carat F/G VVS).
Bracelet: black high-tech ceramic; steel triple-folding buckle; adjustable standard size.
Suggested price: $9,800
Also available: white high-tech ceramic; Ø 33mm case.

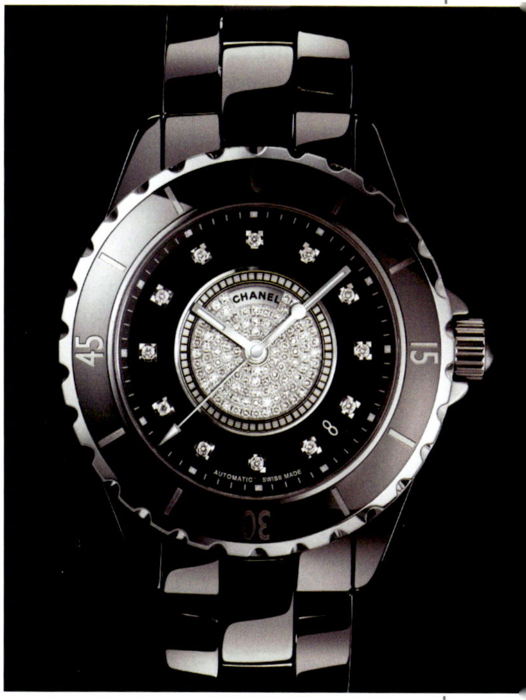

J12 DIAMONDS — REF. H0969

Movement: automatic-winding; 42-hour power reserve.
Functions: hours, minutes, seconds; date.
Case: white high-tech ceramic and steel; Ø 38mm; steel bezel set with 118 brilliant-cut diamonds (1.6 carats, F/G VVS); water resistant to 20atm.
Dial: white lacquered.
Bracelet: white high-tech ceramic; steel triple-folding buckle; adjustable standard size.
Suggested price: $13,300
Also available: black high-tech ceramic; Ø 33mm case.

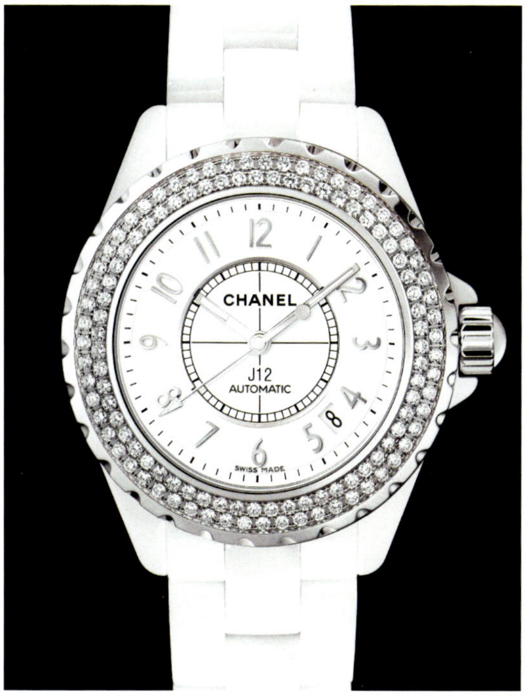

J12 MOTHER-OF-PEARL DIAL — REF. H2423

Movement: automatic-winding; 42-hour power reserve.
Functions: hours, minutes, seconds.
Case: white high-tech ceramic and steel; Ø 38mm; water resistant to 20atm.
Dial: mother-of-pearl; eight diamond indicators (0.05 carat F/G VVS).
Bracelet: white high-tech ceramic; steel triple-folding buckle; adjustable standard size.
Suggested price: $6,150
Also available: Ø 33mm case.

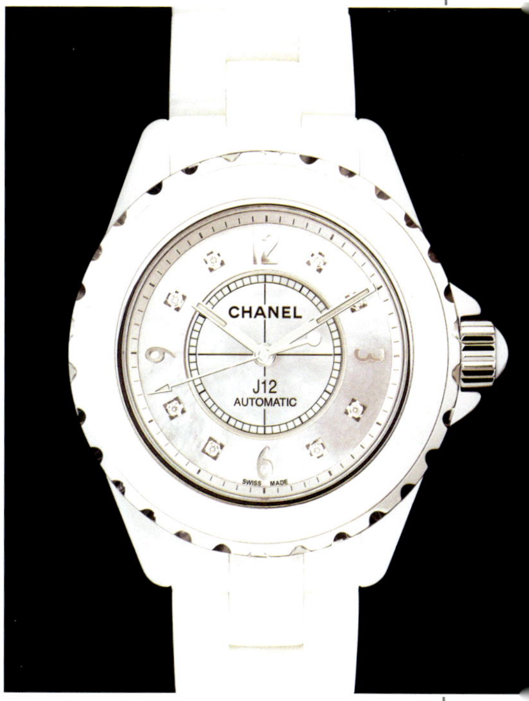

J12 GMT REF. H2012

Movement: automatic-winding; 42-hour power reserve.
Functions: hours, minutes, seconds; date; second time zone; GMT, read on the engraved 24-hour bezel.
Case: black high-tech ceramic and steel; Ø 42mm; water resistant to 10atm.
Dial: black lacquered.
Bracelet: black high-tech ceramic; steel triple-folding buckle; adjustable standard size.
Suggested price: $6,000
Also available: white high-tech ceramic (limited edition).

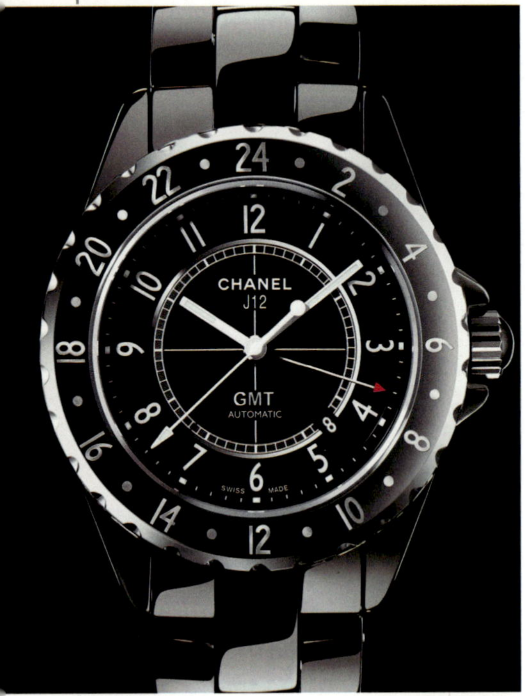

J12 REF. H0685

Movement: automatic-winding; 42-hour power reserve.
Functions: hours, minutes, seconds; date.
Case: black high-tech ceramic and steel; Ø 38mm; water resistant to 20atm.
Dial: black lacquered.
Bracelet: black high-tech ceramic; steel triple-folding buckle; adjustable standard size.
Suggested price: $4,700
Also available: Ø 33mm case; white high-tech ceramic.

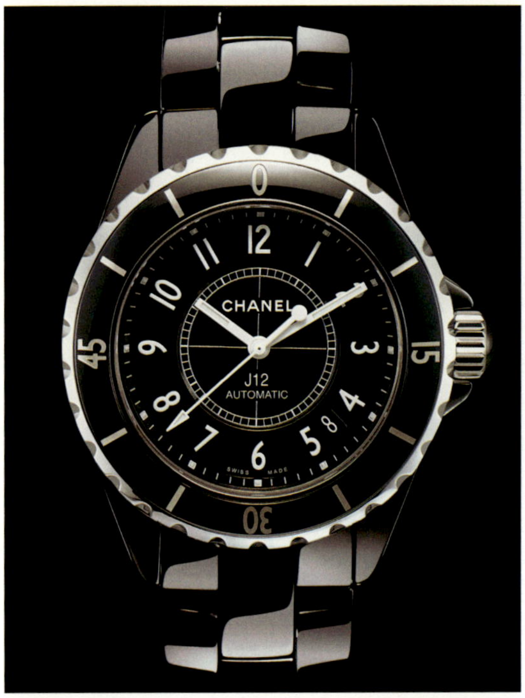

J12 CHRONOGRAPH REF. H1007

Movement: automatic-winding; 42-hour power reserve; COSC-certified chronograph.
Functions: hours, minutes; small seconds at 3; date; chronograph: center seconds, 12-hour and 30-minute counters.
Case: white high-tech ceramic and steel; Ø 41mm; water resistant to 20atm.
Dial: white lacquered.
Bracelet: white high-tech ceramic; steel triple-folding buckle; adjustable standard size.
Suggested price: $6,900
Also available: black high-tech ceramic.

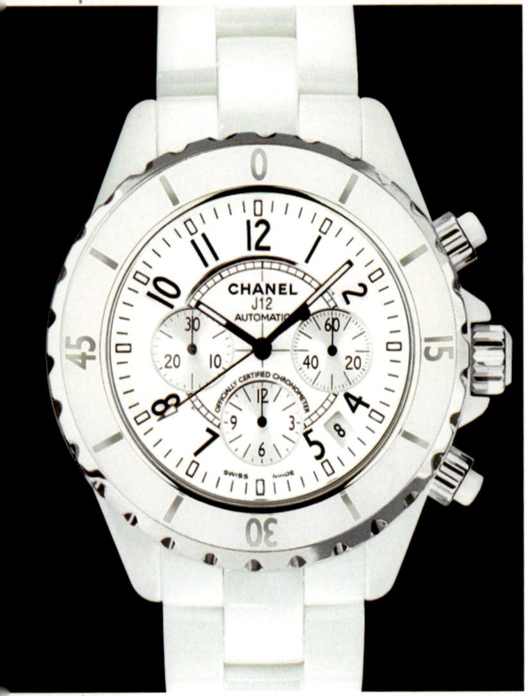

J12 REF. H0970

Movement: automatic-winding; 42-hour power reserve.
Functions: hours, minutes, seconds; date.
Case: white high-tech ceramic and steel; Ø 38mm; water resistant to 20atm.
Dial: white lacquered.
Bracelet: white high-tech ceramic; steel triple-folding buckle; adjustable standard size.
Suggested price: $4,700
Also available: Ø 33mm case; black high-tech ceramic.

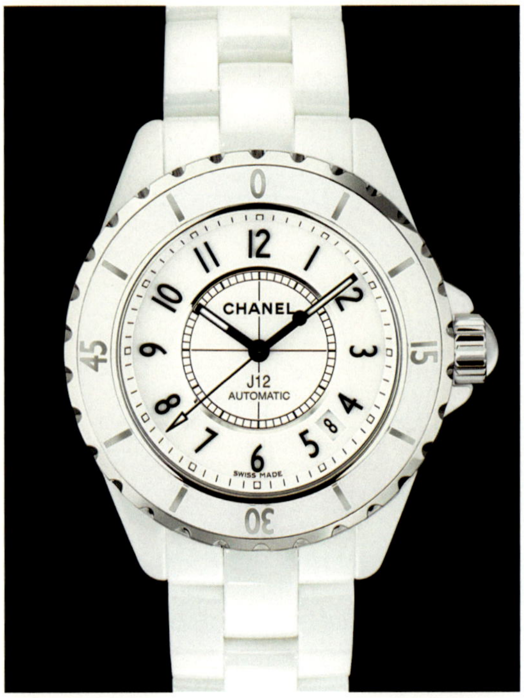

PREMIERE — REF. H2147

Movement: high-precision quartz movement; Ø 11mm.
Functions: hours, minutes.
Case: 18K white gold; set with 52 diamonds (0.26 carat, F/G VVS); water resistant to 3atm.
Dial: black lacquered.
Bracelet: 18K white gold and black high-tech ceramic; set with 202 diamonds (1.23 carats, F/G VVS); spring clasp; adjustable size.
Suggested price: $24,850
Also available: 18K white gold and white high-tech ceramic set with diamonds; steel version.

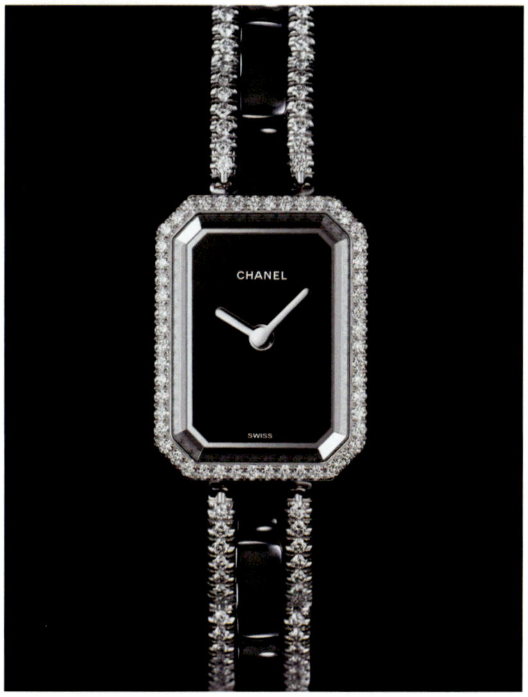

PREMIERE PEARLS — REF. H2032

Movement: high-precision quartz movement; Ø 11mm.
Functions: hours, minutes.
Case: 18K white gold; caseback set with 136 diamonds (0.7 carat, F/G VVS); water resistant to 3atm.
Dial: set with 34 baguette-cut diamonds (1.25 carats, F/G VVS).
Bracelet: 194 Akoya cultured pearls mounted on 18K white-gold threads; detachable 18K white-gold buckle set with 110 diamonds (0.55 carat, F/G VVS); bracelet ends set with 38 diamonds (0.2 carat, F/G VVS); adjustable size.
Suggested price: $52,000

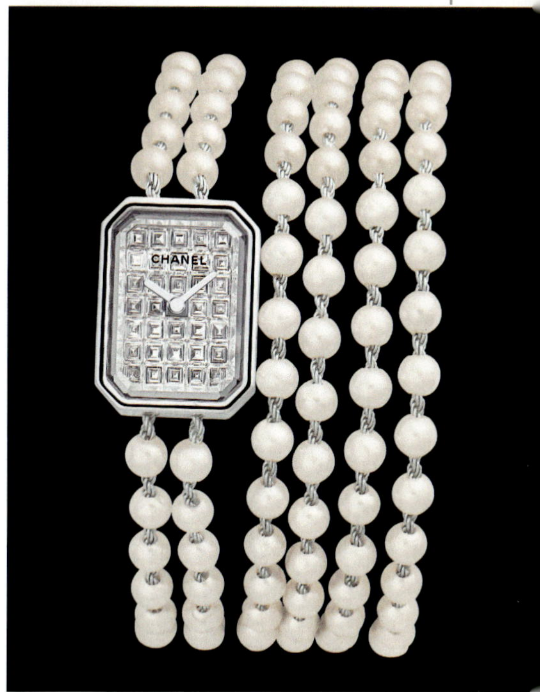

PREMIERE — REF. H2132

Movement: high-precision quartz movement; Ø 11mm.
Functions: hours, minutes.
Case: steel; set with 52 diamonds (0.26 carat, F/G VVS); water resistant to 3atm.
Dial: white lacquered.
Bracelet: steel and white high-tech ceramic; spring clasp.
Suggested price: $5,600
Also available: steel and black high-tech ceramic.

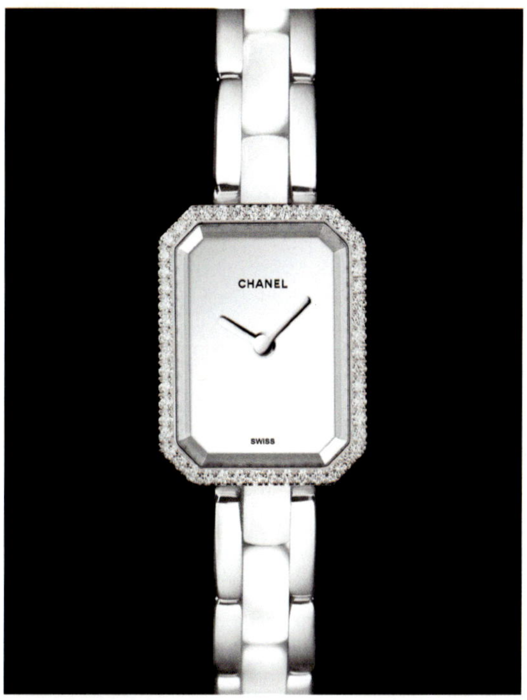

PREMIERE — REF. H2433

Movement: high-precision quartz movement; Ø 11mm.
Functions: hours, minutes.
Case: steel; set with 52 diamonds (0.26 carat, F/G VVS); water resistant to 3atm.
Dial: white mother-of-pearl; four diamond indicators.
Strap: white rubber; ardillon buckle.
Suggested price: $4,100
Also available: black rubber strap.

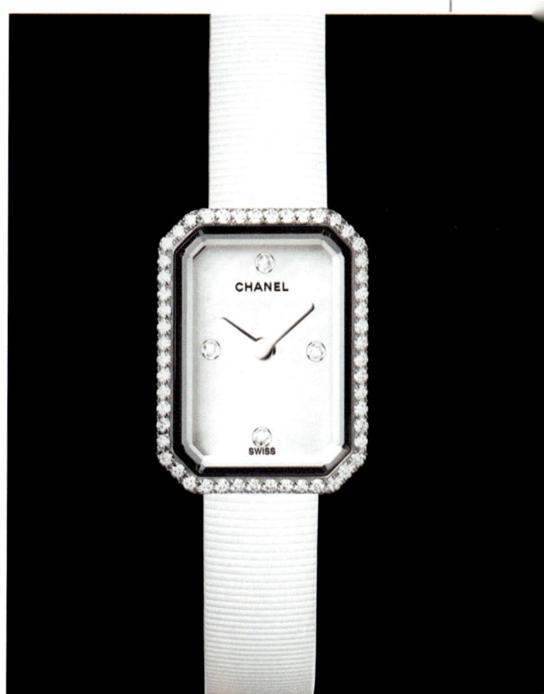

Chopard

MINGLED PASSIONS

It was in 1963 that the Scheufele family of watchmakers and jewelers bought Chopard, a Swiss watchmaking company founded in 1860. Karl and Karin, and later their children Karl-Friedrich and Caroline, would make the brand an active, internationally renowned company, especially in the creation of prestigious mechanical watches.

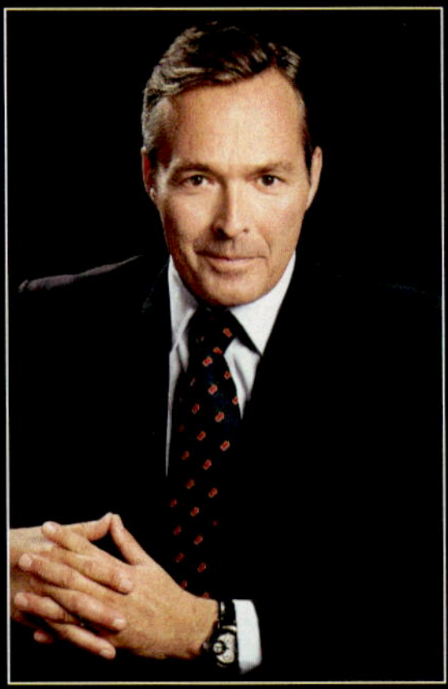

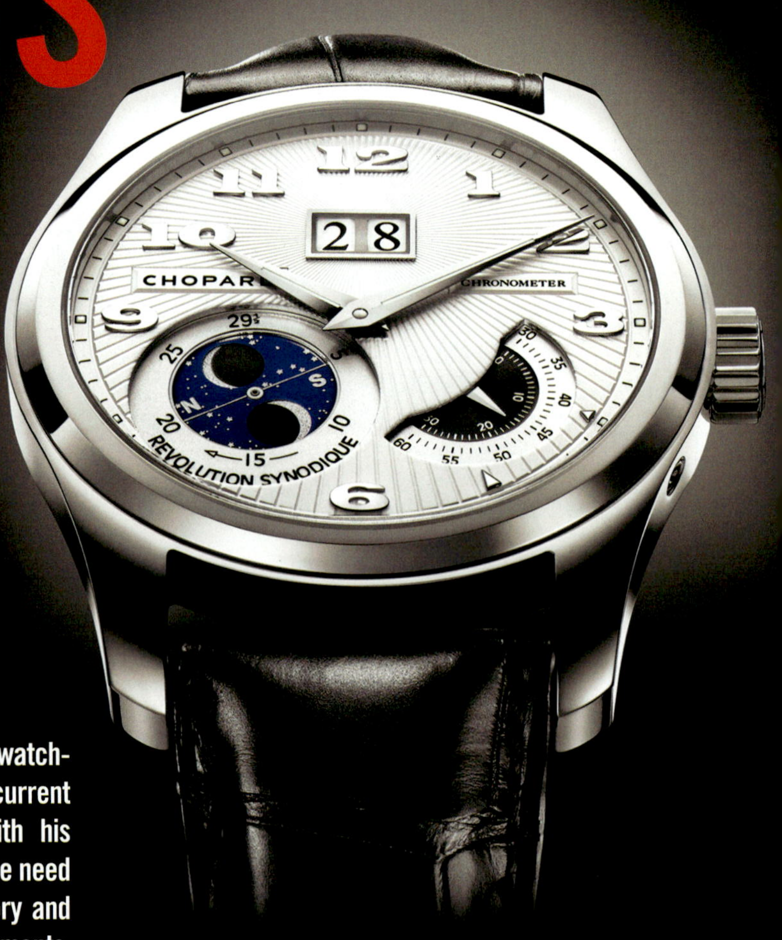

An aficionado of mechanical watchmaking, Karl-Friedrich, current co-president of Chopard (with his sister Caroline), was convinced of the need to reconnect with the brand's history and return to making its own movements. This idea was behind the creation of the Chopard Manufacture in Fleurier. This is where the House produces the L.U.C calibers, named for the founder of the brand, Louis-Ulysse Chopard. The project, launched in autumn of 1993, resulted in the presentation of Caliber 1.96 at the end of 1995. This automatic movement is characterized by a micro-rotor for maximum flexibility, bidirectional winding for reliability, a power reserve of 65 hours and a base that can welcome various complications. Today Chopard has ten exclusive calibers, of which some include new technologies developed by Chopard Technologies, its branch dedicated to research and development.

THIS PAGE

LEFT Karl-Friedrich Scheufele, co-president of Chopard, initiated the creation of Chopard Manufacture.

ABOVE The L.U.C. Lunar Big Date is a COSC-certified chronometer that displays the moonphase in both hemispheres with a lag of only one day every 122 years. The white-gold case with sapphire crystal caseback is available on a brown or black alligator leather strap or white-gold bracelet, and is released in a limited edition of 250 pieces.

FACING PAGE

BOTTOM RIGHT The Grand Prix de Monaco Historique.

" Our family history is the cornerstone of Chopard, laid by artisans and handed down from generation to generation. This know-how is infinitely precious."

—Karl-Friedrich Scheufele

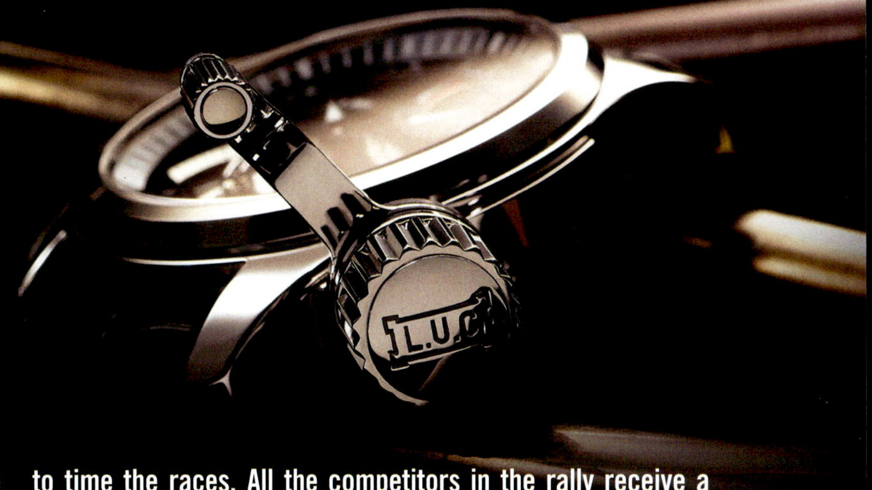

Completely crafted and decorated by hand, L.U.C watches are COSC-certified chronometers (except for the L.U.C XP, which does not have a seconds hand) and a significant number bear the prestigious Hallmark of Geneva. Two models have received the Fleurier Quality Foundation certification, a particularly thorough seal of approval with technical and aesthetic criteria jointly instituted by Chopard, Parmigiani Fleurier, Bovet Fleurier and Vaucher Manufacture Fleurier. Since July 2008, the Chopard family has also included Fleurier Ébauches. Using a more generalized approach, this arm of the company conceives and produces plans for movements at the industrial level, while maintaining the highest standards for materials and quality. The goal of all this activity is to increase Chopard's production of mechanical watches, especially in the sport segment of the market.

For Scheufele, automobile racing is the ultimate sport. Like his father and his grandfather before him, he is passionate about his collection of antique cars, his preference tending toward German and British cars from just before and after World War II (Bentley, Aston Martin, Porsche, Ferrari...and Mini Cooper). It was only natural that Chopard would get involved in Classic Racing and especially Mille Miglia, the legendary Italian racecourse created in 1927 and shut down in 1957, then relaunched for a rally in 1977 that would become an annual competition in 1994. Only vintage cars from the automakers that actually competed in the Mille Miglia between 1927 and 1957 are permitted to participate in the modern-day race. Scheufele personally competed in it for the first time in 1989 with the famous racecar driver Jacky Ickx in a Mercedes 300SL Gullwing, then returned in 1990 with his father as co-pilot before becoming a regular participant. Chopard's sponsorship of the event dates from 1988 and has inspired one of the brand's most admired watch collections. Each year Chopard releases new limited editions equipped with mechanical movements designed to time the races. All the competitors in the rally receive a personalized model, engraved with their competitor number.

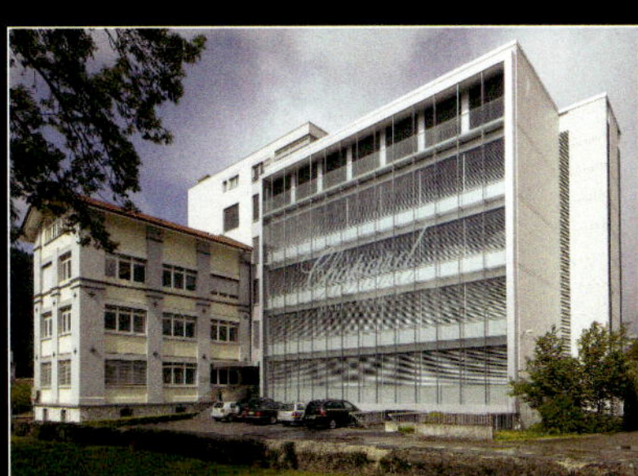

Chopard also supports the 1000 Millas Sport in Argentina, the Festa Milla Miglia in Japan, the California Mille in the United States and the highly prestigious Grand Prix de Monaco Historique. This last competition pits racecars from 1926 to 1978, in seven different categories, against each other on the F1 Grand Prix circuit. Organized in 1997 to commemorate the 700th anniversary of the Grimaldi dynasty, it was supposed to be a one-time-only event. However, the enthusiastic reception inspired the Automobile Club of Monaco to repeat the experiment and since then, the gathering of legendary cars has taken place every two years. Scheufele discovered the race in 2002 through his friend Ickx, and Chopard immediately became a partner and official timer of the event. The brand pays homage to the Grand Prix de Monaco Historique with classically inspired, refined sport watches, which are awarded to the winners in each category.

The list of Chopard's collections features not only the names Mille Miglia and Grand Prix de Monaco Hist orique, but also Classic Racing and Jacky Ickx, unmistakably marking the relationship between Chopard and the automotive world. For Scheufele, it is the most satisfying way to indulge in the two passions that drive him.

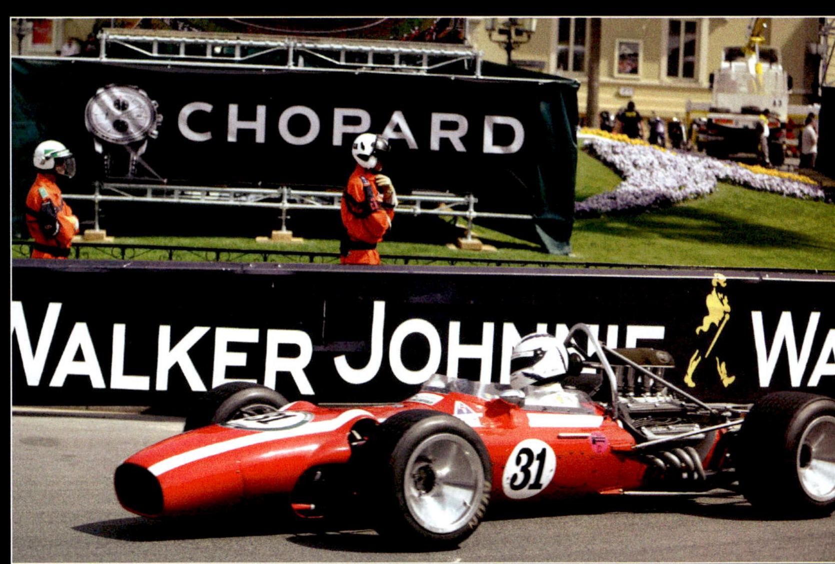

L.U.C TWIN REF. 161880-0001

Movement: automatic-winding L.U.C 4.96 caliber; 65-hour power reserve; L.U.C Twin technology (two stacked barrels); COSC-certified chronometer.
Functions: hours, minutes, seconds; date at 6.
Case: yellow gold; glare- and scratch-proof sapphire crystal; sapphire crystal caseback; water resistant to 3atm.
Dial: white guilloché.
Strap: leather; yellow-gold buckle.
Also available: white gold.

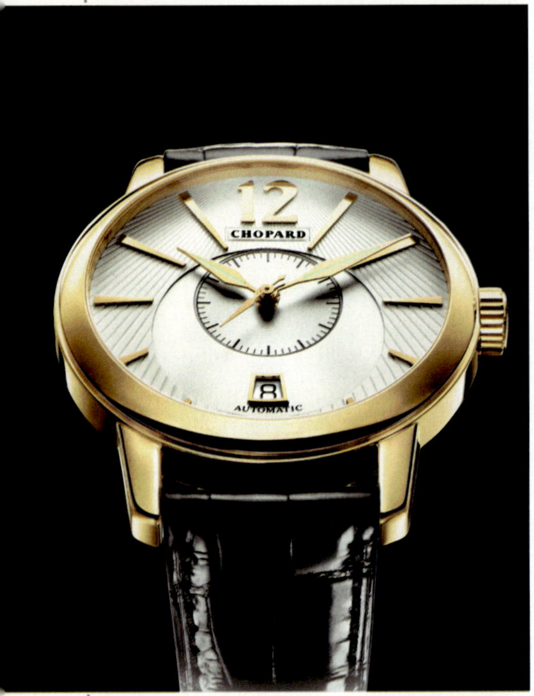

L.U.C LUNAR ONE REF. 161894-5001

Movement: manual-winding L.U.C 96QP caliber; 65-hour power reserve; bridges decorated with straight-line Côtes de Genève; COSC-certified chronometer; hallmarked with the Geneva Seal.
Functions: hours, minutes; small seconds; 24-hour display; perpetual calendar: date, day, month, year and moonphase.
Case: rose gold; glare- and scratch-proof sapphire crystal; sapphire crystal caseback; water resistant to 3atm.
Dial: solid gold, argenté; guilloché by hand with a wave pattern at the center; brushed hour ring; guilloché subdials; printed minute track with luminescent dots; applied faceted pink-gold markers and Roman numerals; luminescent pink-gold dauphine-style hour and minute hands.
Indications: month and 4-year cycle at 3; moonphase and small seconds at 6; day of the week and 24-hour at 9; large date display with a double window at 12.
Strap: hand-stitched crocodile leather; pink-gold fold-over clasp.
Note: limited edition of 250 numbered pieces.
Also available: white gold.

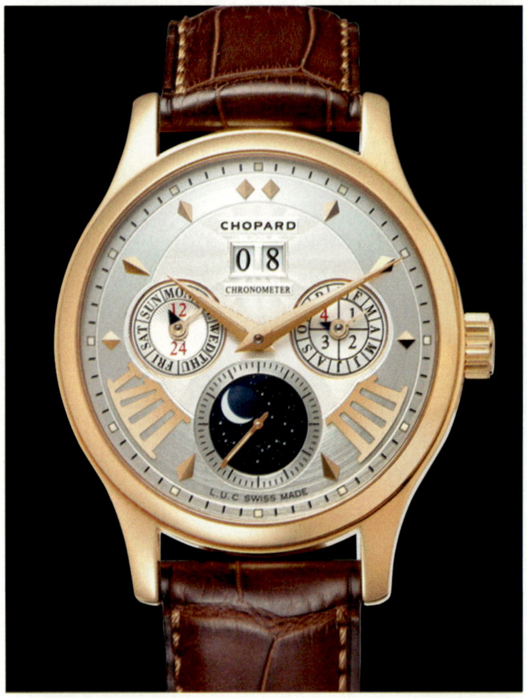

L.U.C CHRONO ONE REF. 161916-1002

Movement: automatic-winding L.U.C 11 CF caliber; 60-hour power reserve; 28,800 vph; "Variner" balance; COSC-certified chronometer.
Functions: hours, minutes; small seconds at 6; 30-minute counter at 3; date at 4:30; 12-hour counter at 9; flyback chronograph; stop seconds.
Case: white gold; glare- and scratch-proof sapphire crystal; sapphire crystal caseback; water resistant to 3atm.
Dial: black.
Strap: leather; white-gold folding clasp.
Also available: rose gold.

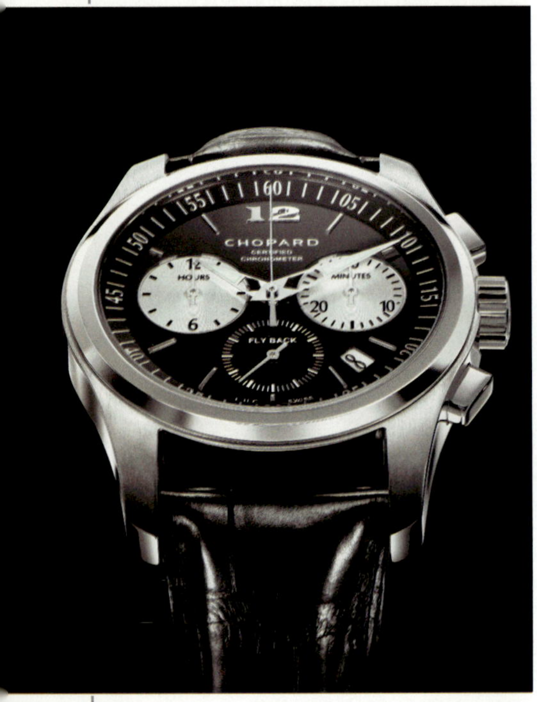

L.U.C EXTRA PLATE REF. 161902-1001

Movement: automatic-winding L.U.C 96HM caliber; 65- to 70-hour power reserve; equipped with two barrels; bridges decorated with Côtes de Genève.
Functions: hours, minutes; small seconds.
Case: white gold; antireflective sapphire crystal; water resistant to 3atm.
Dial: black; four Arabic numerals and applied baton hands; dauphine-style hour and minute hands.
Strap: crocodile leather; gold buckle.
Also available: yellow gold with white dial.

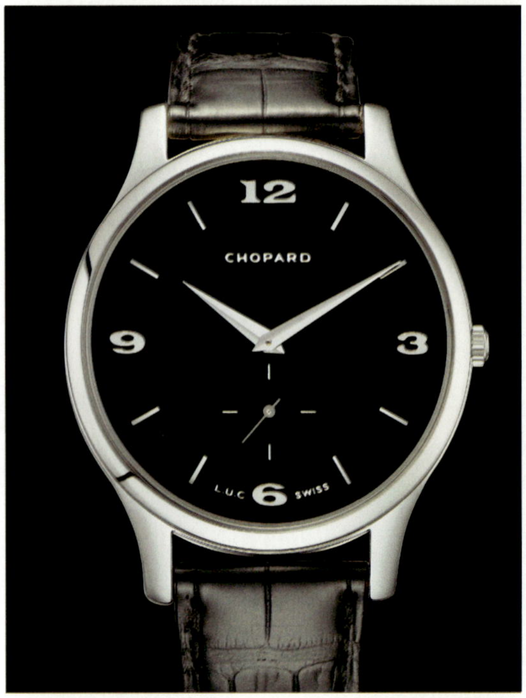

L.U.C TOURBILLON SL — REF. 168502-3001

Movement: manual-winding L.U.C 4TSL caliber; approx. 216-hour power reserve (9 days); 28,800 vph; L.U.C Quattro technology (4 barrels – 2 sets of 2 stacked barrels); "Variner" balance; COSC-certified chronometer.
Functions: hours, minutes; small seconds; power reserve indicator at 12; tourbillon at 6.
Case: titanium; glare- and scratch-proof sapphire crystal; sapphire crystal caseback; water resistant to 3atm.
Dial: black; contemporary dauphine-style hour and minute hands.
Strap: leather; titanium buckle.
Note: limited edition of 100 pieces.

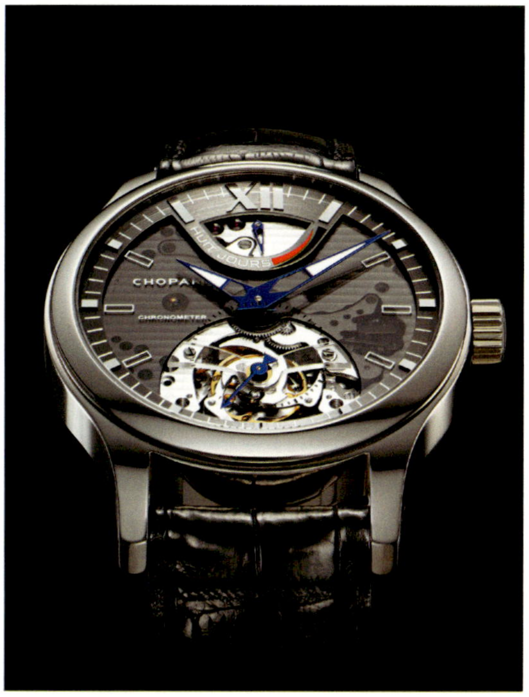

L.U.C PRO ONE GMT — REF. 168959-3001

Movement: automatic-winding L.U.C 96H24 Pro One caliber; 65-hour power reserve; two stacked barrels (L.U.C Twin® Technology); COSC-certified chronometer.
Functions: hours, minutes, seconds; date; fixed second time zone hand.
Case: steel; screw-down crown; antireflective sapphire crystal; antireflective caseback; water resistant to 30atm.
Dial: black; SuperLumiNova-coated arrow-style hands and hour markers for excellent nighttime readability.
Strap: hand-stitched crocodile leather strap; steel folding clasp.

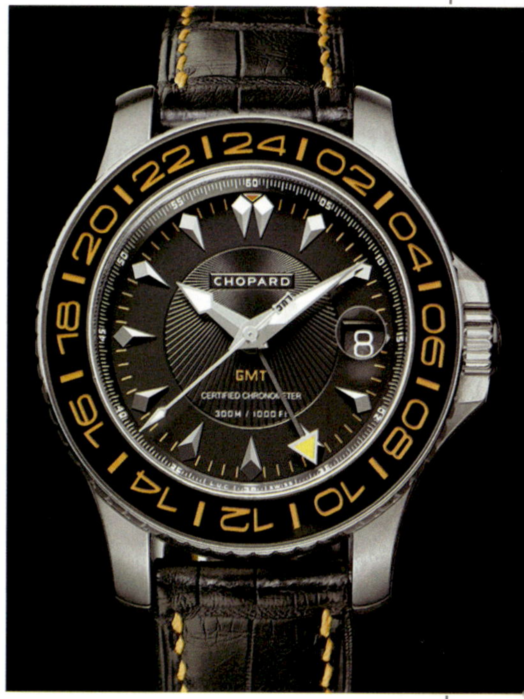

L.U.C 1937 — REF. 168527-3001

Movement: automatic-winding L.U.C 1.010 caliber; Ø 28.8mm, thickness: 4.95mm; 60-hour power reserve; 31 jewels; 28,800 vph; one barrel; COSC-certified chronometer.
Functions: hours, minutes, seconds; stop seconds.
Case: satin-brushed and polished stainless steel; Ø 42mm, thickness: 11.39mm; 6mm steel screw-down crown at 4 with L.U.C logo; multi-layered glare- and scratch-proof sapphire crystal; water resistant to 10atm.
Dial: rhodium-plated; applied Roman numerals; rhodium-plated dauphine-style hour and minute hands; red dauphine-style sweep seconds hand.
Strap: black hand-sewn alligator leather lined with brown alligator leather; steel fold-over clasp.
Note: limited edition of 1,937 pieces.

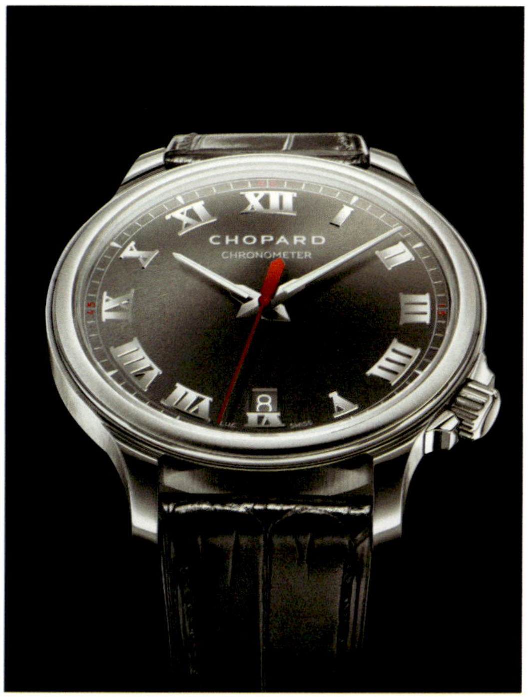

L.U.C ENGINE ONE TOURBILLON — REF. 168526-3001

Movement: manual-winding L.U.C 1TRM caliber; Ø 34x25.9mm, thickness: 5.6mm; 60-hour power reserve; 29 jewels; 28,800 vph; one barrel; COSC-certified chronometer.
Functions: hours, minutes; small seconds on the tourbillon at 6; power reserve at 12.
Case: brushed and polished titanium; 44.4x35.4mm, thickness: 10.9mm; titanium crown with L.U.C logo; engraved glare- and scratch-proof sapphire crystal; caseback secured with screws; water resistant to 5atm.
Dial: engraved Arabic numerals, tinted black under sapphire crystal; dauphine-style hour and minute hands; counter-type small seconds hand.
Strap: hand-sewn black alligator leather lined with brown alligator leather with gadroons; titanium buckle.
Note: limited edition of 150 pieces.

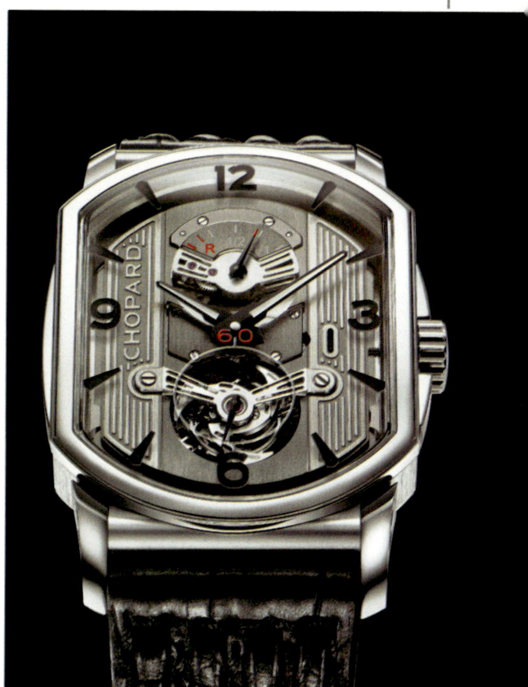

L.U.C LOUIS-ULYSSE – THE TRIBUTE REF. 161923-1001

Movement: manual-winding L.U.C EHG caliber; pocket movement; Ø 43.2mm, thickness: 5.5mm; 80-hour power reserve; 20 jewels; 21,600 vph; bridges adorned with Côtes de Genève; COSC-certified chronometer; hallmarked with the Geneva Seal.
Functions: hours, minutes; small seconds at 6.
Case: 18K white gold; Ø 49.6mm; 18K white-gold crown with L.U.C logo; glare- and scratch-proof sapphire crystal; water resistant to 3atm.
Dial: white lacquered ceramic; black dauphine-style hour and minute hands.
Strap: hand-sewn black alligator leather lined with brown alligator leather; 18K white-gold buckle.
Note: limited edition of 150 pieces.

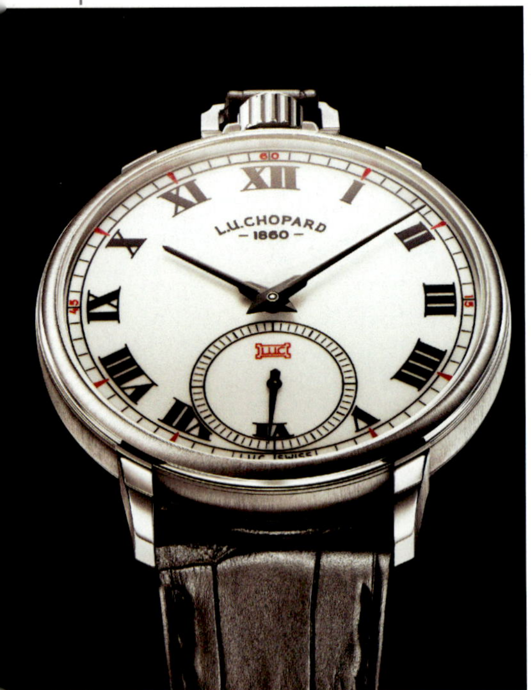

L.U.C 150 "ALL IN ONE" REF. 161925-1001

Movement: manual-winding L.U.C 4TQE caliber with tourbillon; Ø 33mm, thickness: 11.75mm; 189-hour power reserve; 42 jewels; 28,800 vph; four barrels; COSC-certified chronometer; hallmarked with the Geneva Seal.
Functions: hours, minutes; small seconds on the tourbillon at 6; perpetual calendar: date, day, week, month and leap year; equation of time; hour day/night indication; sunrise and sunset times in Geneva; astronomical orbital moonphase.
Case: 18K white gold; Ø 46mm, thickness: 18.5mm; gold crown with L.U.C logo; multi-layered glare- and scratch-proof sapphire crystals front and back; water resistant to 3atm.
Dial: hand-guilloché upper and lower dials; silver snailed hollowed counters; black applied Roman numerals; black dauphine-style hour and minute hands.
Strap: hand-sewn black half-glossy alligator leather lined with brown alligator leather; white-gold buckle.
Note: limited edition of 15 pieces.
Also available: rose gold.

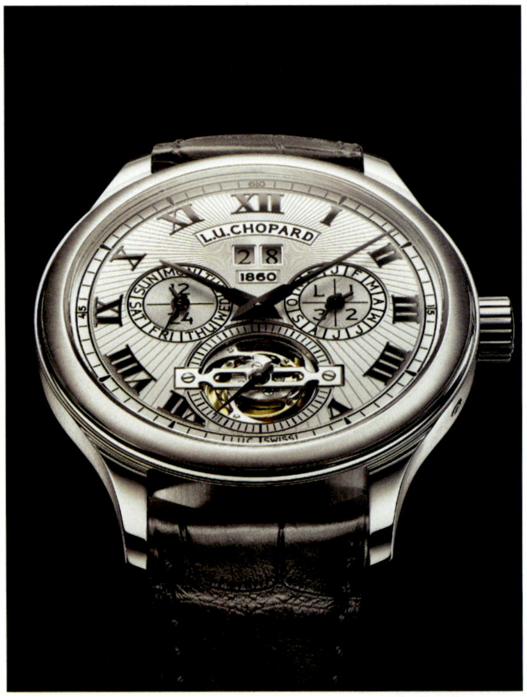

L.U.C TOURBILLON LADIES REF.134188-1003

Movement: automatic-winding L.U.C 4T (Quattro Technology) caliber; 216-hour power reserve; 28,800 vph; COSC-certified chronometer; hallmarked with the Geneva Seal.
Functions: hours, minutes; small seconds on the tourbillon at 6; power reserve indicator at 12.
Case: white gold; glare- and scratch-proof sapphire crystal; water resistant to 3atm.
Dial: mother-of-pearl set with diamonds.
Strap: alligator leather; white-gold buckle.
Note: limited edition of 100 pieces.

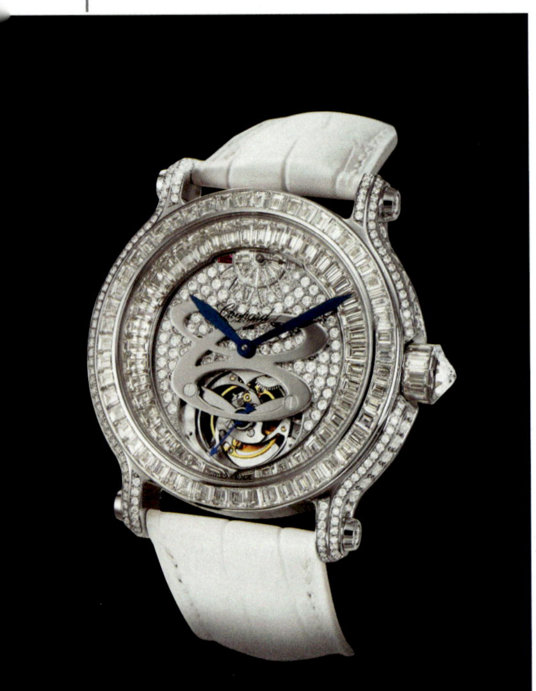

GRAND PRIX DE MONACO HISTORIQUE TIME ATTACK MF REF. 158518-3001

Movement: quartz movement; COSC-certified chronometer.
Functions: hours, minutes, seconds; date; timer; UTC time; chronograph; alarm; second time zone; alarm in the second time zone.
Case: stainless steel; cambered, glare- and scratch-proof sapphire crystal; water resistant to 5atm.
Dial: black dial; luminescent hands, numerals and indicators.
Bracelet: stainless steel.

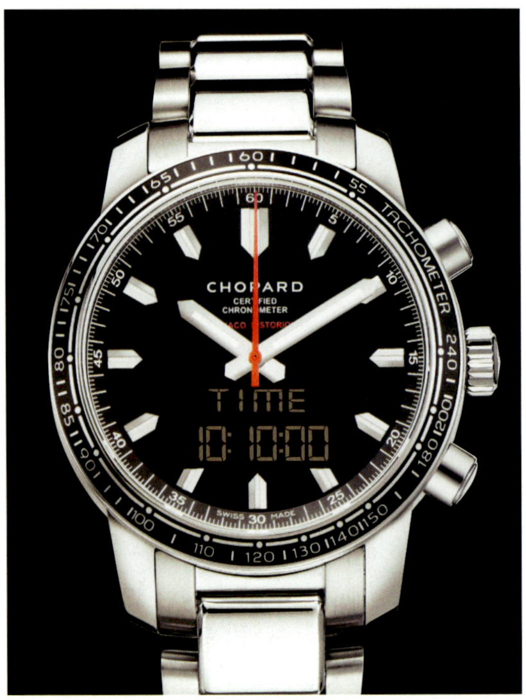

MILLE MIGLIA GT XL CHRONO — REF. 168459-3001

Movement: automatic-winding movement; 46-hour power reserve; 25 jewels; COSC-certified chronometer.
Functions: hours, minutes; small seconds; chronograph: 30-minute and 12-hour counters; tachometer; date at 3.
Case: stainless steel; screw-down crown; glare- and scratch-proof sapphire crystal; sapphire crystal caseback; water resistant to 10atm.
Dial: black; luminescent numerals and hands with SuperLumiNova.
Strap: rubber.
Also available: rose gold.

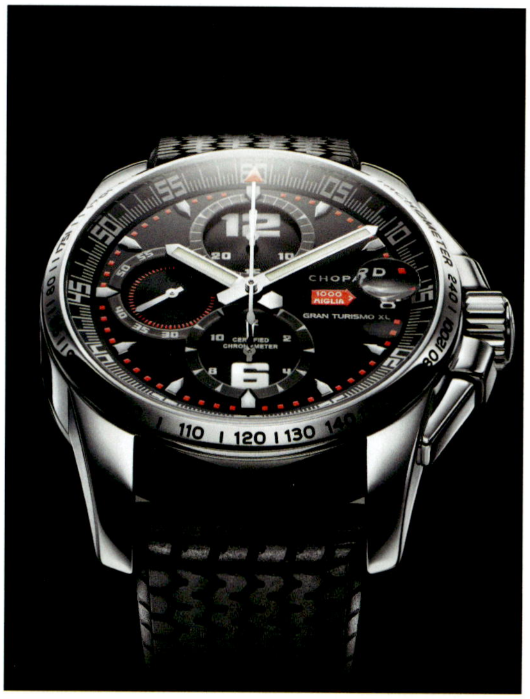

CLASSIC RACING – SUPERFAST CHRONO — REF. 161276-5003

Movement: automatic-winding ETA 2894-2; approx. 42-hour power reserve; 28,800 vph.
Functions: hours, minutes, seconds; date at 6; chronograph equipped with an hour counter at 6; minute counter at 9.
Case: rose gold; tachometric scale engraved on the bezel; glare- and scratch-proof sapphire crystal; water resistant to 10atm.
Dial: black and gray; luminescent numeral, hour markers and hands; central chronograph seconds hand with a red arrow tip.
Strap: black rubber; gold folding clasp.
Also available: steel.

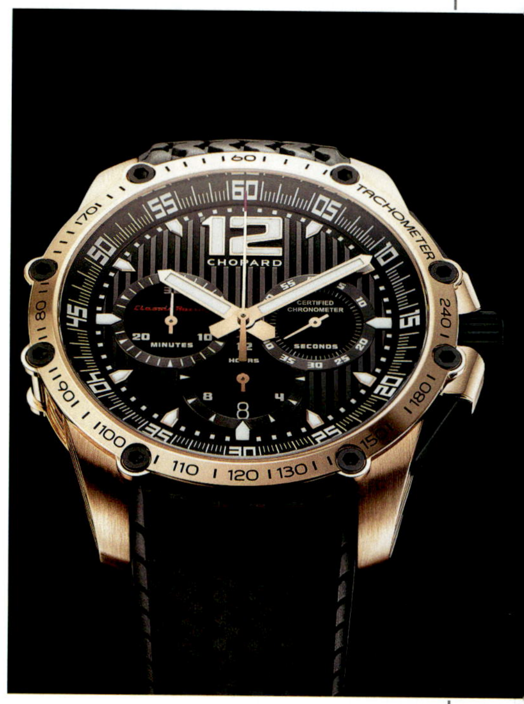

IMPERIALE — REF.384221-5004

Movement: quartz ETA movement.
Functions: hours, minutes, seconds; date.
Case: 18K rose gold; 18K rose-gold crown with amethyst cabochon; glare- and scratch-proof sapphire crystal; water resistant to 5atm.
Dial: silver; glaive-style hour and minute hands.
Bracelet: rose-gold bracelet; rose-gold buckle.

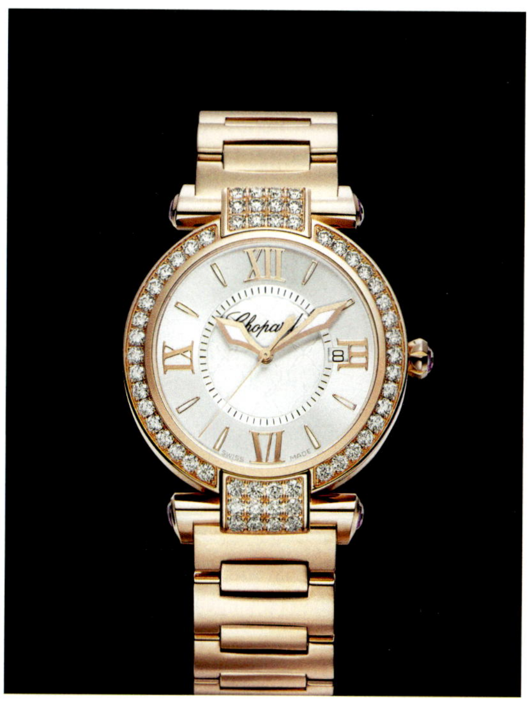

HAPPY SPORT — REF. 277472-5001

Movement: quartz ETA movement.
Functions: hours, minutes, seconds; date.
Case: 18K rose gold; rose-gold crown with sapphire cabochon; glare- and scratch-proof sapphire crystal; water resistant to 3atm.
Dial: brown; seven moving diamonds.
Bracelet: rose-gold bracelet; rose-gold buckle.
Also available: gold and steel.

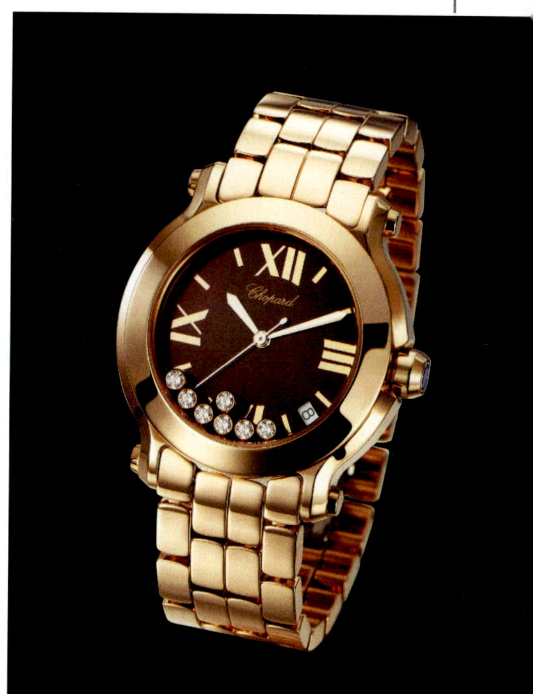

FROM THE SHADOWS TO THE LIMELIGHT

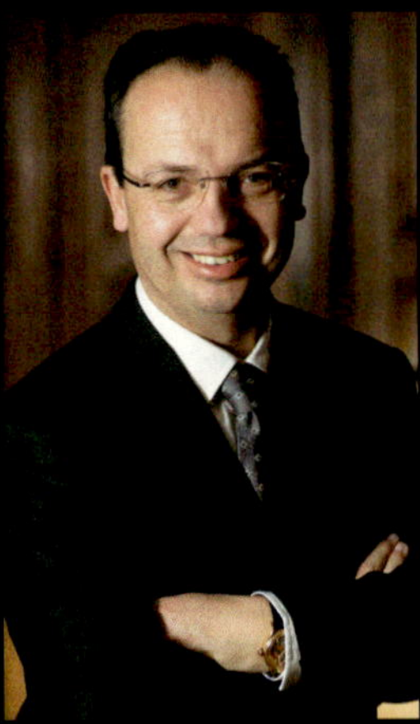

Christophe Claret's watchmaking adventure began a little over 20 years ago—it was in 1991, after buying up the shares of his former associates Giulio Papi and Dominique Renaud, that he founded the company that bears his name.

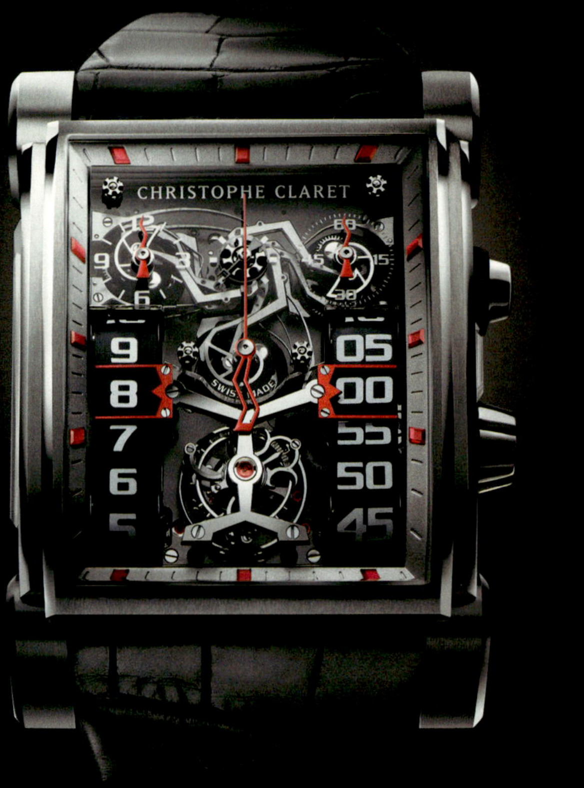

Working in the shadow of the most prestigious brands, he has created some of the most complicated and innovative movements on the market, from the minute repeater—the first complication developed by the watchmaker—to the tourbillon, as well as a perpetual calendar with roller-type display. Based on this experience, Christophe Claret launched his own brand in 2009. The first creation under his name was the DualTow, a single-pusher planetary chronograph with striking mechanism and tourbillon. The second, presented in Geneva in January 2011, has been christened Adagio. This minute repeater, large date and GMT model is a direct response to demand from collectors, and paves the way for a third model, to be unveiled at Baselworld 2011.

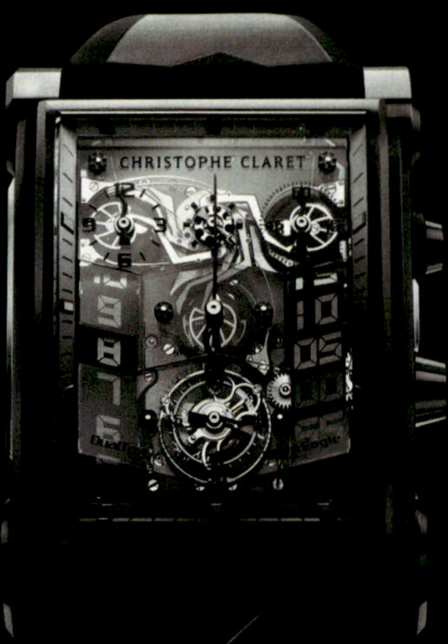

Claret, who hails from the region of Lyon, France, studied watchmaking in Geneva before beginning his career as a restorer of antique watches. In 1987, at the Basel-World Watch and Jewelry Show, the owner of a large Swiss watch company requested him to develop an exclusive minute repeater movement. To meet this order, he founded a company in 1989 that also featured two other talented watchmakers, Dominique Renaud and Giulio Papi—now at the head of Audemars Piguet (Renaud & Papi) in Le Locle. In 1992, feeling a need for independence, Christophe Claret bought up his partners' shares and renamed the company Christophe Claret SA.

ABOVE LEFT

After 20 years spent in the service of the most prestigious watch brands, Christophe Claret has launched his own brand.

ABOVE RIGHT

Originally created to celebrate the 20th anniversary of his company, the DualTow is the first model by the Christophe Claret brand.

FAR LEFT

DualTow NightEagle refers to the ultra-secret world of stealth aircraft such as the American F-117 Night Hawk, reflected in the watch's taut lines, sharp angles, tone-on-tone colors and transparency effects.

With the DualTow, many collectors, who had owned watches equipped with Christophe Claret movements without even knowing it, realized the full extent of the watchmaker's work and expertise.

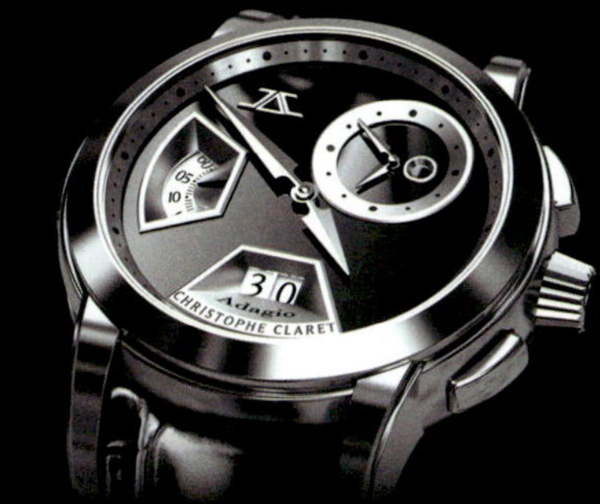

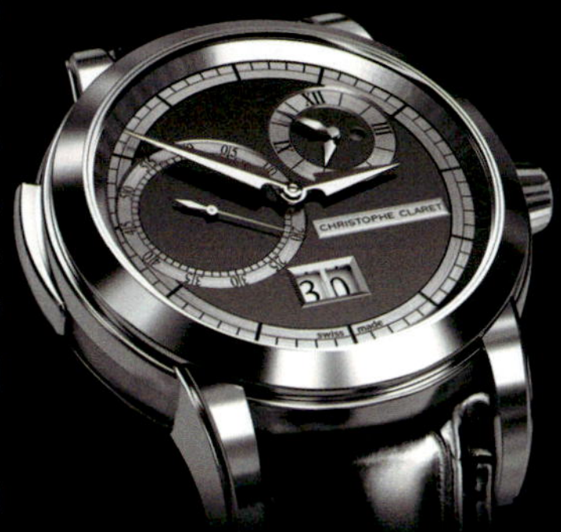

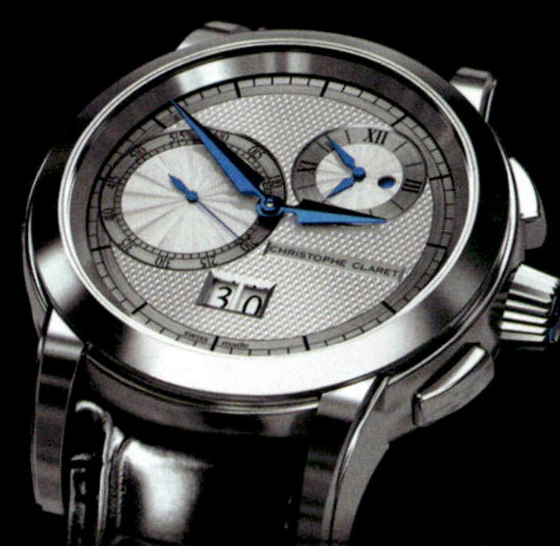

The following decade earned him steadily growing recognition and a high-end clientele. In 1999, Claret purchased a stately manor house on the heights above Le Locle. This marked the start of a new era: in two years, the company's clientele grew exponentially, and its personnel rocketed from 17 to 62. At the peak of the watch boom in 2008, it employed some 125 staff members. Due to lack of space, the Manufacture Christophe Claret first had a 500m² extension built in 2002, followed by a second of the same size in 2004. Equipped with impressive set of state-of-the-art machinery, the manufacture currently makes almost all its movement parts, as well as various watch exterior components.

2009 witnessed a second turning point: to celebrate the company's 20th anniversary, the watchmaker decided to create—just this once, he thought at the time—a model bearing his own name. Christened DualTow, this single-pusher planetary chronograph with striking mechanism and tourbillon embodied the full range of skills cultivated within the manufacture. From developing the movement to machining the sapphire bridges, almost all operations are performed in-house. The CC20A caliber powering it is a concentrated blend of innovations, starting with the single-pusher chronograph function that operates using three planetary gears, each of them featuring an identical structure. This mechanism is further enhanced by the addition of a striking mechanism that audibly signals the chronograph start, stop and reset operations. This unprecedented interpretation of the chronograph is protected by an exclusive patent. In due course, the DualTow collection will comprise 68 models, each of them uniquely personalized.

Hitherto little known to the public at large, the name of Christophe Claret suddenly became a talking point. As the watchmaker himself explains: "I have talked with a number of collectors from around the world, and many of them owned watches equipped with one of our movements, without knowing it. With the DualTow, they realized the full extent of our work and our expertise." This acclaim has been like a professional rebirth for Christophe Claret. Just a few months after the launch of the DualTow, he officially registered the brand bearing his name.

Christophe Claret watches did not in fact stem from a watchmaker's wish to create complete timepieces, but from connoisseurs' desire to get to know the watchmaker. "The Adagio model, the second from the brand, is intended for them," Claret confides. This minute repeater, large date and GMT model was presented in Geneva this January. Once again, the mechanism plays the starring role. The SLB88 caliber drives the hour and minute functions, as well as a patented large date at 6 o'clock and a dual time zone (hours and minutes) with day/night indication appearing in a subdial at 2 o'clock. Depending on the version, the small seconds appear in a subdial or an aperture at 9 o'clock.

But the best is definitely inside. A mechanism chimes on demand the hours, quarters and minutes on patented cathedral gong-rings. "They don't sound tinny, like some striking watches," says Christophe Claret. "We have developed a system to ensure they don't clash like cymbals." This concern for finishing detail is also reflected in the exterior. Three case and dial versions are available: a choice of case in white gold, rose gold or platinum; and dials that are hand-guilloché in silvered gold and rhodium-plated black or crafted from precious or semi-precious stones (lapis lazuli, black onyx, ruby, jade and opal). "Creating complete watches enables me to develop my creativity, to express the Claret spirit in all aspects of the model, and not merely in the movement," Claret explains. "As Michelangelo put it: 'Trifles make perfection, but perfection is no trifle.'"

TOP

This Adagio model features a dial in semi-precious stones, offering a choice between lapis lazuli, black onyx, ruby, jade or opal.

CENTER

This white-gold version of Christophe Claret's new Adagio model is adorned with a black rhodium-plated gold dial.

BOTTOM

An extremely classic version of the Adagio gives pride of place to the increasingly rare art of hand-crafted guilloché decoration.

DUALTOW — REF. MTR.CC20A.002

Movement: manual-winding CC20A caliber; 60-hour power reserve; 568 components; 65 jewels; 21,600 vph; eight ball bearings; twin barrels placed in parallel; one-minute tourbillon.
Functions: hours, minutes; single-pusher planetary-gear chronograph with mechanical striking mechanism sounding a cathedral gong for each change of function (start, stop, reset); tourbillon; power reserve display and operating mode indicator of the chronograph.

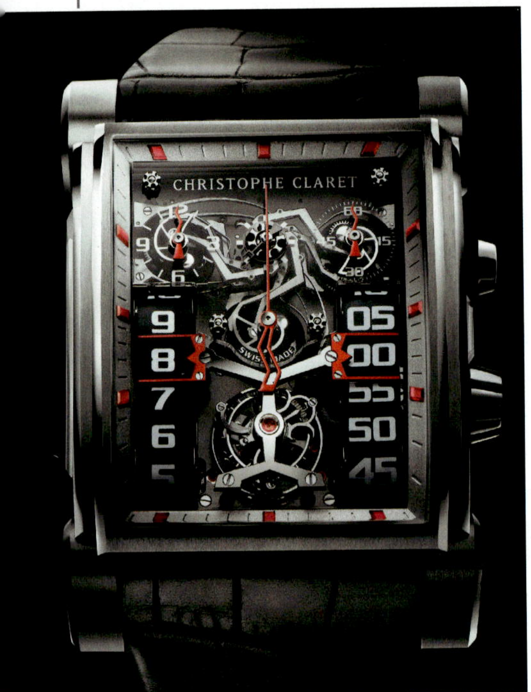

Case: white gold; rectangular and curved; 42.75x48.2mm, thickness: 15.85mm; crown fitted with locking device; flange features five second indexes for chronograph indications hand-cut from five different stones.
Dial: hour and minute display on belt; chronograph counters: 12 hours, 60 minutes, 60 seconds.
Strap: crocodile leather; triple-blade folding clasp; 10mm wrist extension.
Note: the DualTow model is a limited edition by movement and will feature only 68 unique and personalized configurations in all.
Suggested price: $515,000
Also available: pink gold and black PVD-coated titanium ($515,000); platinum ($567,000); leather strap with a rubber pattern and texture.

DUALTOW — REF. MTR.CC20A.012

Movement: manual-winding CC20A caliber; 60-hour power reserve; 568 components; 65 jewels; 21,600 vph; eight ball bearings; twin barrels placed in parallel; one-minute tourbillon.
Functions: hours, minutes; single-pusher planetary-gear chronograph with mechanical striking mechanism sounding a cathedral gong for each change of function (start, stop, reset); tourbillon; power reserve display and operating mode indicator of the chronograph.

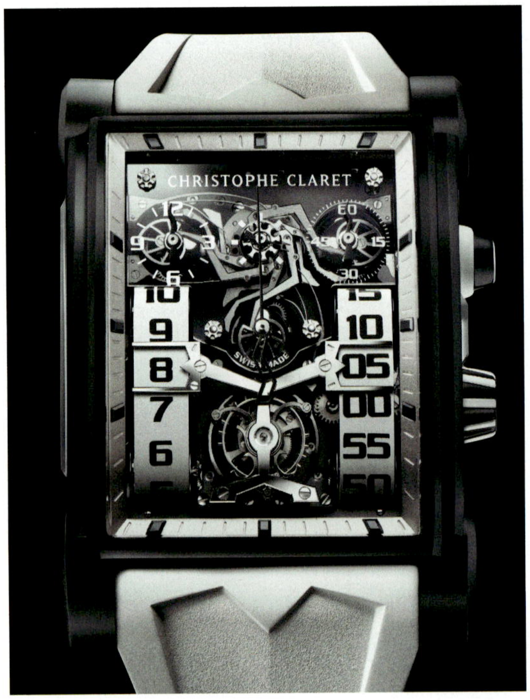

Case: black PVD-coated titanium; rectangular and curved; 42.75x48.2mm, thickness: 15.85mm; crown fitted with locking device; flange features five second indexes for chronograph indications hand-cut from five different stones.
Dial: hour and minute display on belt; chronograph counters: 12 hours, 60 minutes, 60 seconds.
Strap: leather with a rubber pattern and texture; triple-blade folding clasp; 10mm wrist extension.
Note: the DualTow model is a limited edition by movement and will feature only 68 unique and personalized configurations in all.
Suggested price: $515,000
Also available: pink gold and white gold ($515,000); platinum ($567,000); crocodile leather strap.

DUALTOW — REF. MTR.CC20A.016

Movement: manual-winding CC20A caliber; 60-hour power reserve; 568 components; 65 jewels; 21,600 vph; eight ball bearings; twin barrels placed in parallel; one-minute tourbillon.
Functions: hours, minutes; single-pusher planetary-gear chronograph with mechanical striking mechanism sounding a cathedral gong for each change of function (start, stop, reset); tourbillon; power reserve display and operaring mode indicator of the chronograph.

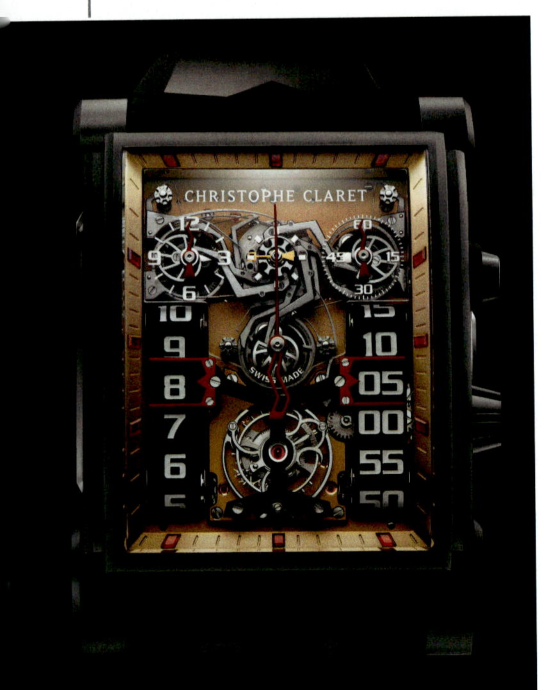

Case: black PVD-coated titanium; rectangular and curved; 42.75x48.2mm, thickness 15.85mm; crown fitted with locking device; flange features five second indexes for chronograph indications hand-cut from five different stones.
Dial: hour and minute display on belt; chronograph counters: 12 hours, 60 minutes, 60 seconds.
Strap: leather with a rubber pattern and texture; triple-blade folding clasp; 10mm wrist extension.
Note: the DualTow model is a limited edition by movement and will feature only 68 unique and personalized configurations in all.
Suggested price: $515,000
Also available: pink gold and white gold ($515,000); platinum ($567,000); crocodile leather strap.

DUALTOW - NIGHTEAGLE — REF. MTR.CC20A.009

Movement: manual-winding CC20A caliber; 60-hour power reserve; 574 parts; 65 jewels; 21,600 vph; eight ball bearings; twin barrels placed in parallel; one-minute tourbillon.
Functions: hours, minutes; small seconds on the tourbillon at 6; single-pusher planetary-gear chronograph with mechanical striking mechanism sounding a cathedral gong for each change of function (start, stop, reset); tourbillon; power reserve display and operating mode indicator of the chronograph. **Case:** black PVD-coated titanium; rectangular and curved; 42.75x48.2mm, thickness: 15.85mm; crown fitted with locking device; flange features five second indexes for chronograph indication in ceramic.

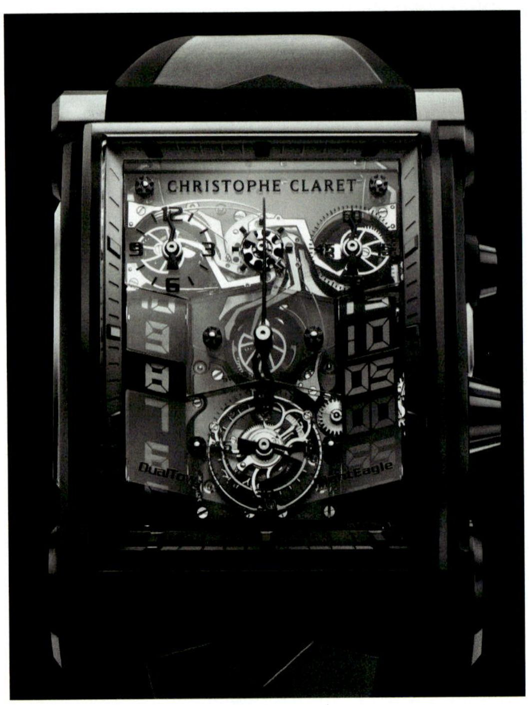

Dial: composed of three tinted sapphire crystals: the first serves as a bridge for the chronograph counters and is engraved with Christophe Claret, the second acts as a central bridge and carries the Swiss Made engraving, the third is the tourbillon bridge which is plated with the small seconds markings; hour and minute display on belt; chronograph counters: 12 hours, 60 minutes, 60 seconds.
Strap: leather with a rubber pattern and texture; triple-blade folding clasp; 10mm wrist extension.
Note: the DualTow model is a limited edition by movement and will feature only 68 unique and personalized configurations in all.
Suggested price: $567,000

ADAGIO — REF. MTR.SLB88.002

Movement: manual-winding SLB88 caliber; 48-hour power reserve; 455 components; 46 jewels; 18,000 vph.
Functions: hours, minutes; hour, quarter-hour, minute repeater featuring cathedral gongs; large date; GMT with day/night indication.
Case: white gold; Ø 44mm; crown fitted with locking device.
Dial: black onyx.
Strap: crocodile leather.
Note: each dial is a limited edition of eight pieces.
Suggested price: $282,000
Also available: rose gold ($282,000); platinum ($334,000); dial available in lapis lazuli, ruby, jade, opal, silver and black rhodium-plated gold and hand-guilloché.

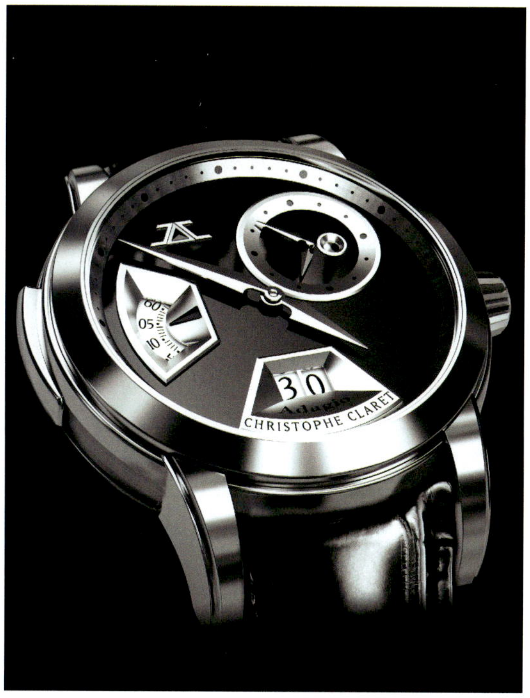

ADAGIO — REF. MTR.SLB88.007

Movement: manual-winding SLB88 caliber; 48-hour power reserve; 455 components; 46 jewels; 18,000 vph.
Functions: hours, minutes; hour, quarter-hour, minute repeater featuring cathedral gongs; large date; GMT with day/night indication.
Case: rose gold; Ø 44mm; crown fitted with locking device.
Dial: black onyx.
Strap: crocodile leather.
Note: each dial is a limited edition of eight pieces.
Suggested price: $282,000
Also available: white gold ($282,000); platinum ($334,000); dial available in lapis lazuli, ruby, jade, opal, silver and black rhodium-plated gold and hand-guilloché.

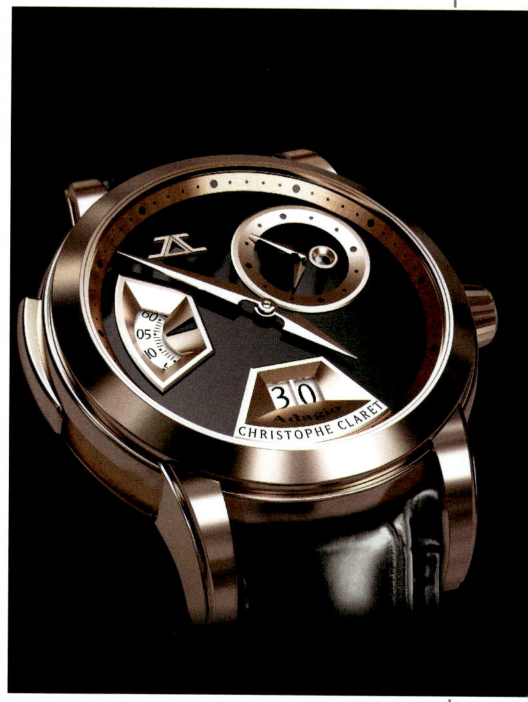

ADAGIO — REF. MTR.SLB88.016

Movement: manual-winding SLB88 caliber; 46-hour power reserve; 455 components; 46 jewels; 18,000 vph.
Functions: hours, minutes; hour, quarter-hour, minute repeater featuring cathedral gongs; large date; GMT with day/night indication.
Case: white gold; Ø 44mm; crown fitted with locking device.
Dial: hand-guilloché.
Strap: crocodile leather.
Note: each dial is a limited edition of eight pieces.
Suggested price: $282,000
Also available: rose gold ($282,000); platinum ($334,000); dial available in lapis lazuli, ruby, jade, opal, black onyx and silver and black rhodium-plated gold.

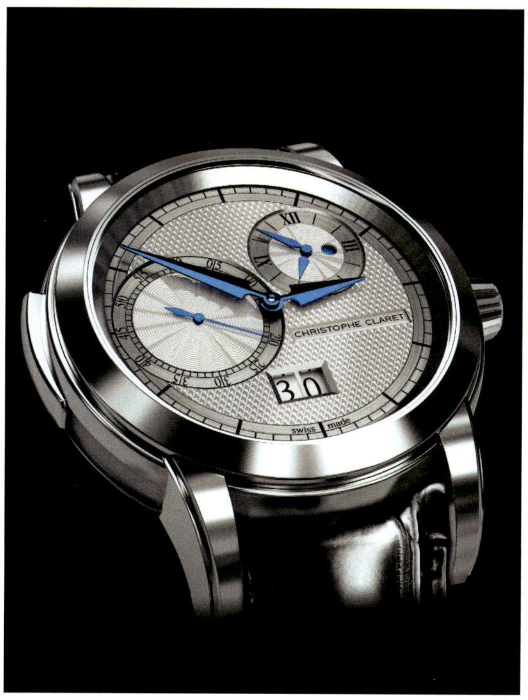

ADAGIO — REF. MTR.SLB88.050

Movement: manual-winding SLB88 caliber; 48-hour power reserve; 455 components; 46 jewels; 18,000 vph.
Functions: hours, minutes; hour, quarter-hour, minute repeater featuring cathedral gongs; large date; GMT with day/night indication.
Case: white gold; Ø 44mm; crown fitted with locking device.
Dial: silver and black rhodium-plated gold.
Strap: crocodile leather.
Note: each dial is a limited edition of eight pieces.
Suggested price: $282,000
Also available: rose gold ($282,000); platinum ($334,000); dial available in lapis lazuli, ruby, jade, opal, black onyx and hand-guilloché.

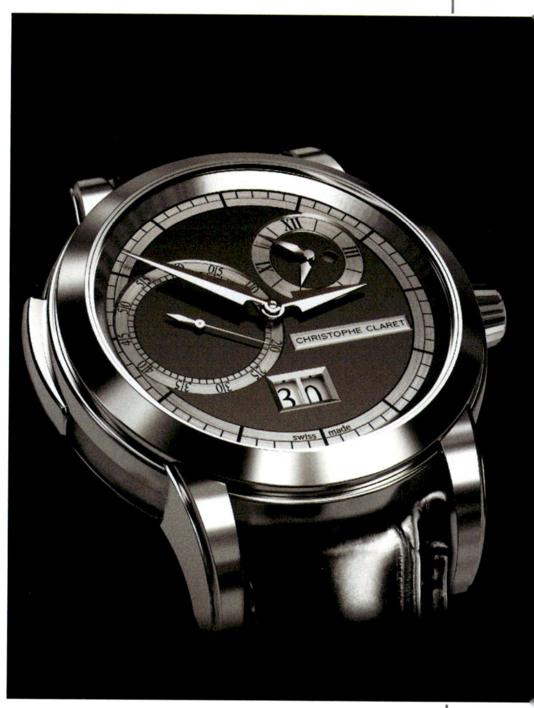

CLERC
GENEVE
1874

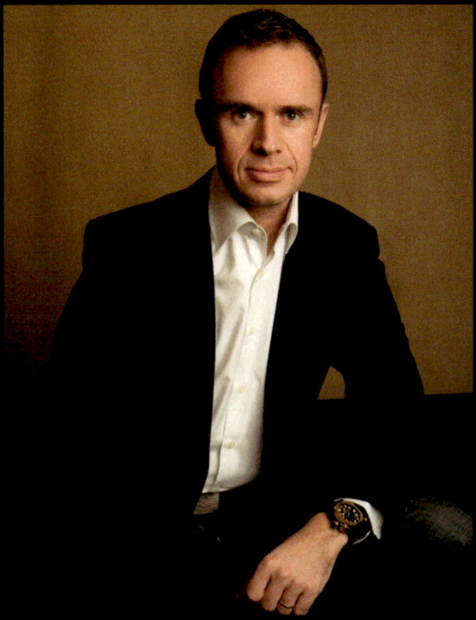

CONQUERING THE FUTURE

Clerc Genève is synonymous with escapism and adventure. Ever more efficient and technical, the Hydroscaph and Odyssey models are in the vanguard of refined and sophisticated collections.

Synonymous with a break from tradition, creations by Clerc Genève follow the dictates of a single rule: inventiveness. Each conceived as a unique work of art, Clerc watches yield no concessions in the drive to perfection. As Gérald Clerc loves to say, "I create timepieces the way I like them, without making any compromises." Creator of "futuristic haute horology," as he likes to define it, he is a cosmopolitan watchmaker with a keen interest in architecture. He is fascinated by the 1960s, a period brimming with optimism and confidence during which humankind threw itself wholeheartedly into the pursuit of progress—Gérald Clerc considers space exploration as the greatest adventure of all time. When this representative of the fourth generation took over Clerc Genève in 1997, he inherited not just expertise, but also a wealth of passion.

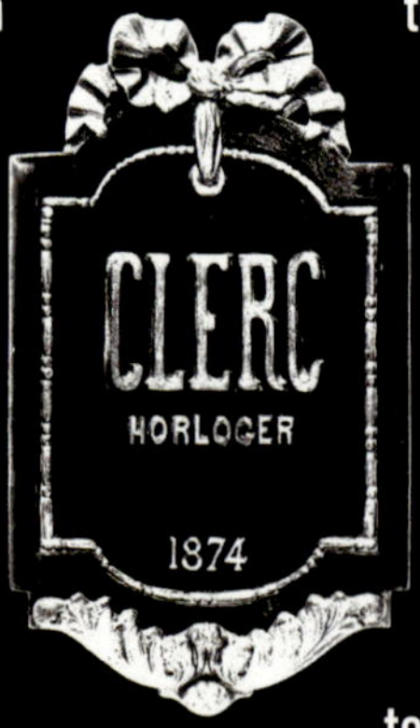

The Hydroscaph model, one of the brand's most iconic timepieces, has rapidly found a place for itself in the world of exclusive watchmaking. This sleekly sophisticated model, featuring a case so complex that it called for a whole new construction process to assemble its 103 components, offers an unprecedented vision of ocean-going fine watchmaking. Water resistant to 1,000 meters, this exceptional model is equipped with an automatic helium release valve, a 4mm-thick sapphire crystal and lateral reinforcements. Its exclusive self-winding movement drives the hour, minute and seconds hands, along with a power reserve display, large date and GMT, depending on the version. Nonetheless, the most striking new feature of this model lies in its rotating bezel mechanism: a retractable flap at 10 o'clock serves to pivot the bezel until the desired position. Once retracted, it is locked into place, thus avoiding any risk of accidentally modifying the settings while diving. The case features the brand's signature octagonal shape combining a perfect circle with a perfect square. Measuring 49.6mm in diameter and fitted with lugs that adjust perfectly to all wrist sizes and shapes, the Hydroscaph is one of the most sophisticated watches ever.

In 2009, Clerc Genève presented a grade 5 titanium version of the Hydroscaph, a model followed in 2010 by the steel sports series, the Hydroscaph Steel GMT. It comes with a choice of different case finishes—polished steel, blackened steel or two-tone steel and 18-karat red gold—framing a dial in various colors. On the all-steel model, the dual time zone hand and the indications linked to the power reserve are clothed in bright yellow or bright blue; on the blackened steel model, everything comes in shades of black and gray; and the two-tone model features gilded hands and black and white hour markers.

TOP LEFT

Gérald Clerc, representing the fourth generation of his family, is currently at the head of Clerc Genève.

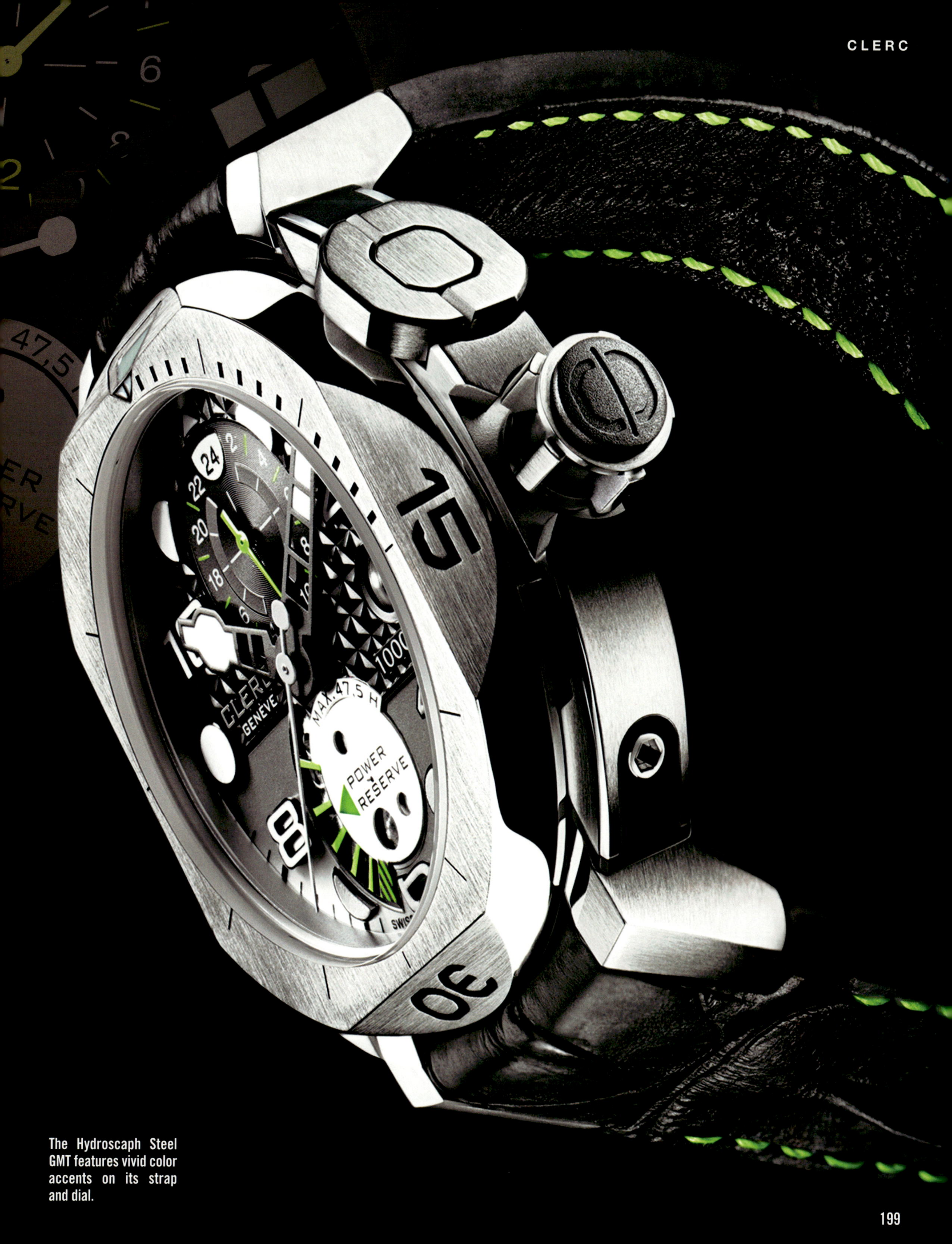

The Hydroscaph Steel GMT features vivid color accents on its strap and dial.

Another model presented in 2010 was an exclusive gold version of the Hydroscaph: the Hydroscaph Limited Edition Gold Tourbillon. This ultra-technical model is precious in more than one way. First of all because of its "motor": an exclusive hand-wound tourbillon movement housing two barrels that ensure a full 120-hour power reserve. This remarkable autonomy is truly exceptional for a diving watch, and definitely helps avoid the need to handle the crown in wet conditions. This exclusive Clerc 60-second tourbillon caliber, meeting the highest standards of Swiss watchmaking, powers the hour and minute hands, retrograde date at 1:30 and power reserve display at 5 o'clock. The dial is openworked in a highly contemporary style that hides nothing of its high-precision mechanisms. The hollowed vertical S-shaped tourbillon bridge echoes the equally hollowed hour and minute hands, while the numerals and hour markers are engraved on the inside of the antireflective sapphire crystal, thereby ensuring perfect readability.

The case of the brand's latest model, the Hydroscaph TI, is clothed in DLC-blackened grade 5 titanium, a coating that offers numerous advantages, including extreme hardness and enhanced thermal stability. The rotating bezel in brushed grade 5 titanium pivots in the same way as its predecessors. The dial is distinguished by its techno-luxury style. Each function has its own particular environment, swept over by broad and instantly recognizable hands and lending the watch a distinctly high-tech and yet ultra-readable face.

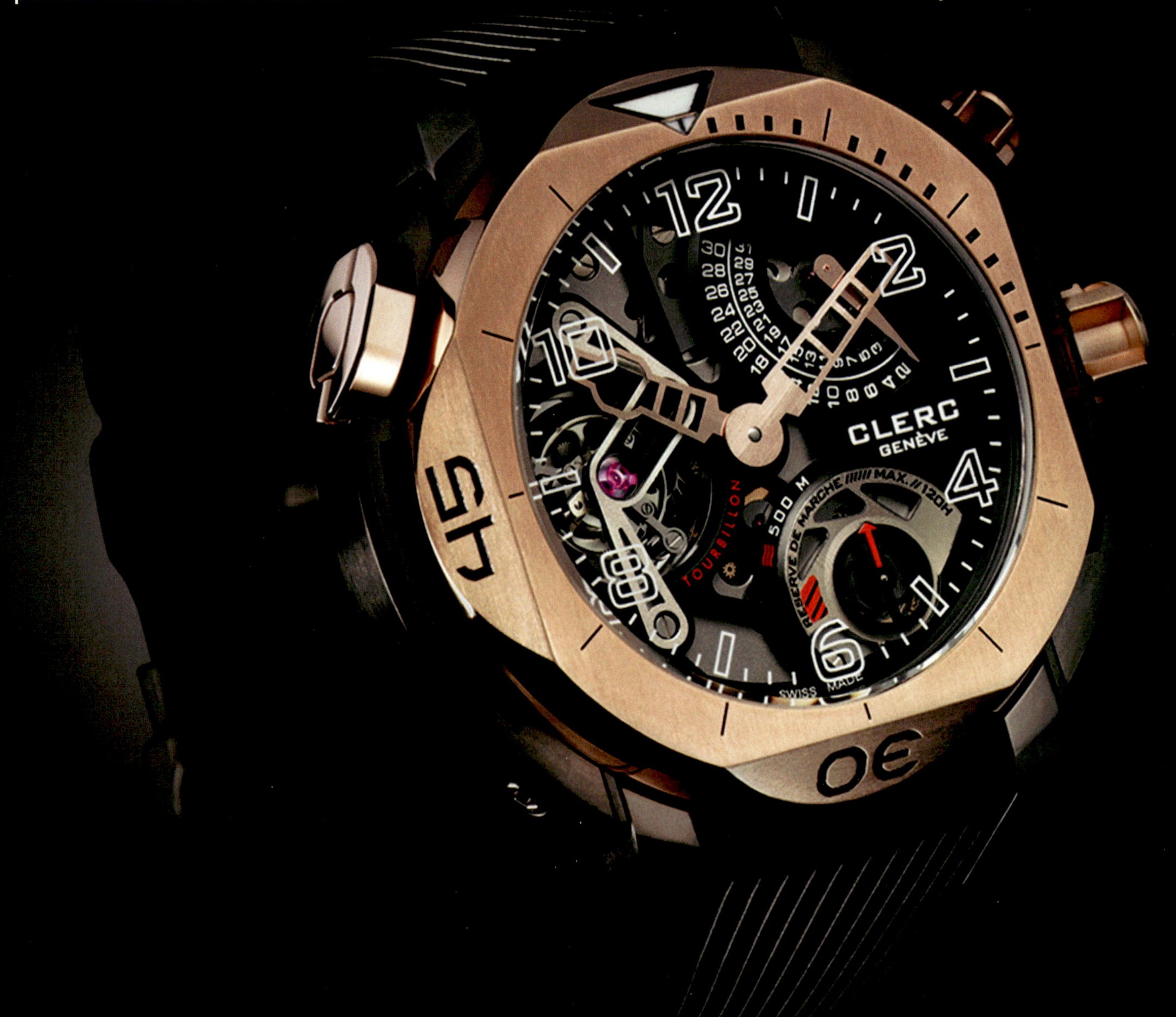

The Hydroscaph Limited Edition Gold Tourbillon, in a series of only 28 pieces, houses a precise one-minute tourbillon movement in a 49.6mm case in rose gold and black titanium.

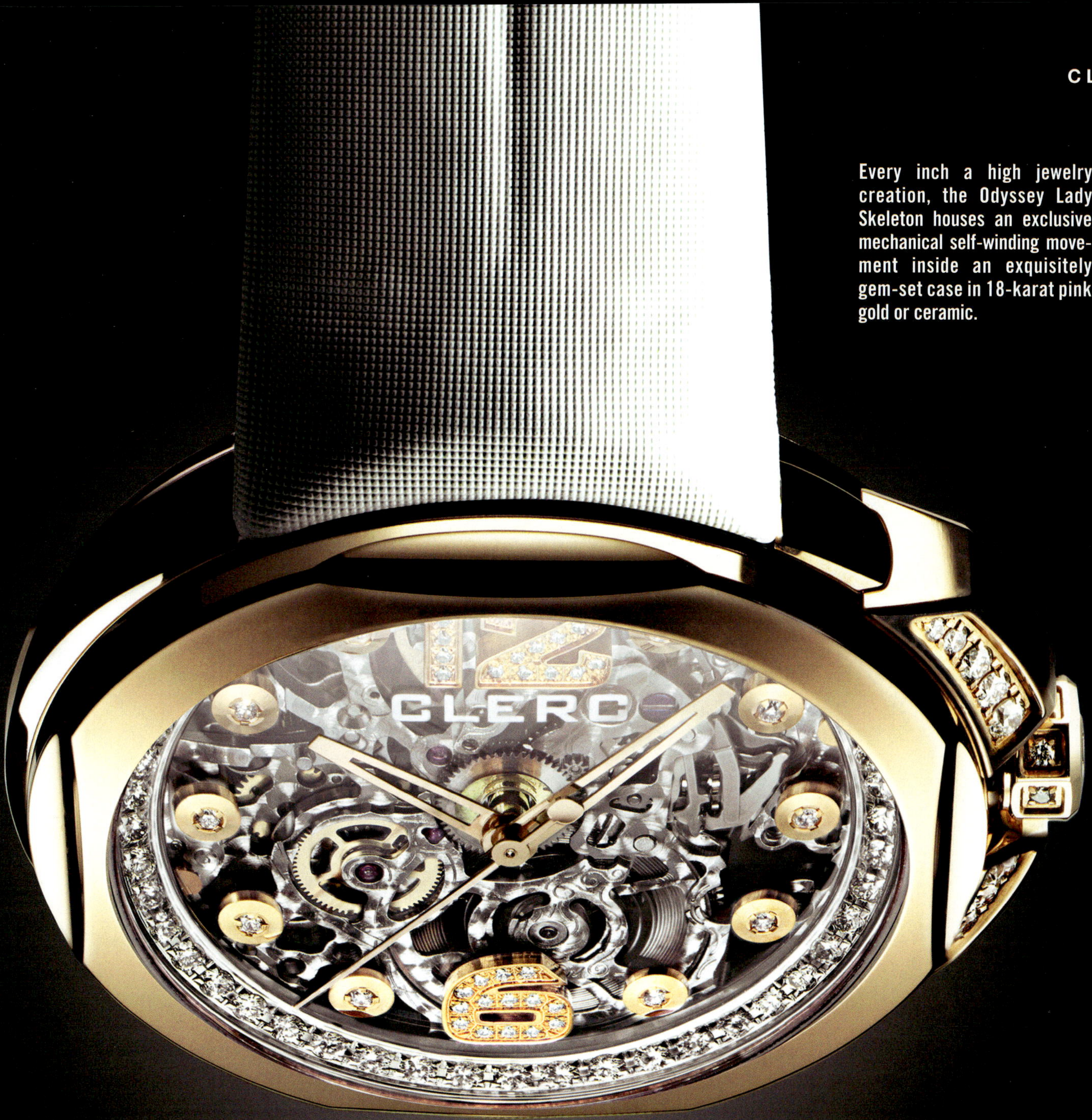

Every inch a high jewelry creation, the Odyssey Lady Skeleton houses an exclusive mechanical self-winding movement inside an exquisitely gem-set case in 18-karat pink gold or ceramic.

The Odyssey model, launched in 2008, is one of the star models from Clerc Genève. With materials inspired by space research—black titanium, ceramics, and carbon fiber—the Odyssey is clearly built for exploration and adventure. A sliding bridge-guard fixed to the case covers the crown, pushers and the mechanism activating the inner rotating bezel—forming a unique protection device that prevents any inadvertent handling. The exclusive mechanical hand-wound caliber, powered by two barrels supplying an exceptional 120-hour power reserve, offers hours, minutes and seconds functions, along with a retrograde date at 2 o'clock and a power reserve at 6 o'clock. "In designing the Odyssey, I was aiming for purity," says Gérald Clerc.

A watchmaker must also know how to speak the language of women. The Odyssey Lady Skeleton and the Odyssey Lady Galaxy, both released in 2010, are open invitations to all ladies eager to join in the adventure. The former is a superb high jewelry model equipped with an exclusive mechanical self-winding movement framed by a delicately gem-set 18-karat rose-gold or ceramic case. The Arabic numerals at 6 and 12 o'clock are also gem-set and give a unique depth effect to this transparent watch face, which offers a plunging view into the heart of the fine skeleton movement. The gear trains and bridges are visible through a transparent sapphire crystal cleverly fixed to an openworked baseplate, in a stunning expression of the horological art form. Meanwhile, the face of the Odyssey Lady Galaxy echoes the Milky Way with a spiral of diamonds swirling against a cloisonné mother-of-pearl or enamel backdrop. This exceptional feminine timepiece will appeal to dreamers who like to keep their heads in the stars.

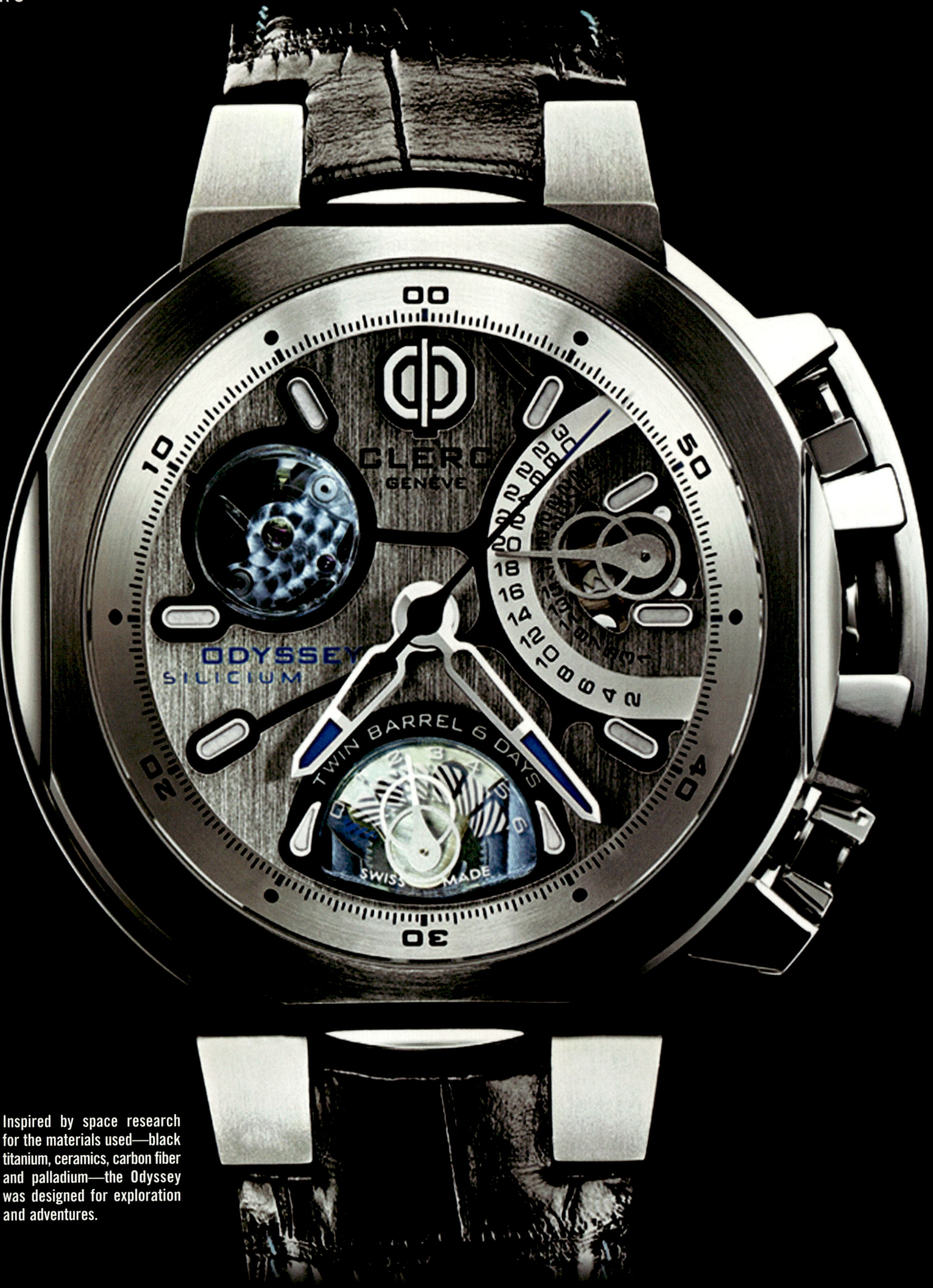

Inspired by space research for the materials used—black titanium, ceramics, carbon fiber and palladium—the Odyssey was designed for exploration and adventures.

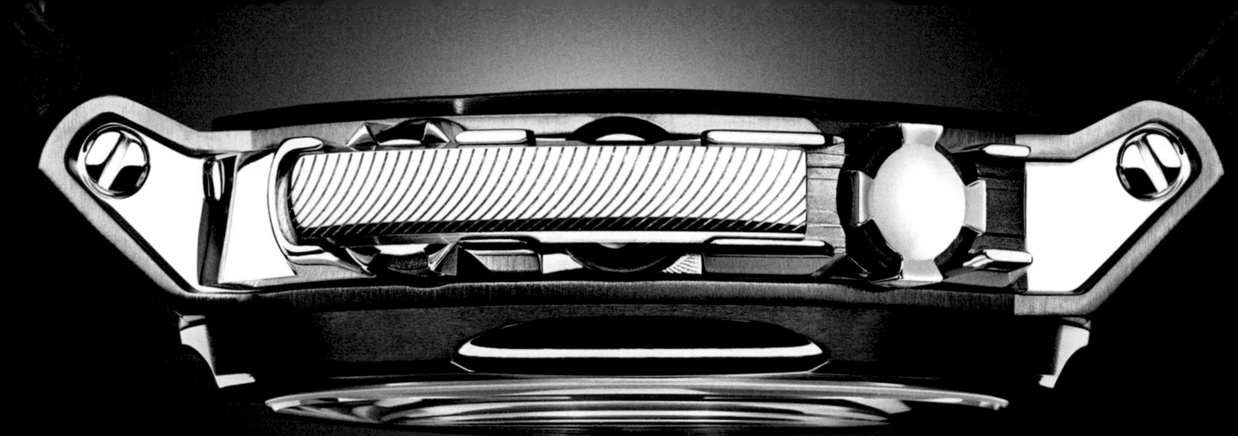

Clerc Genève rockets watchmaking into the 21st century with the new Odyssey S, a techno-luxury timepiece featuring space-age materials and a futuristic design.

Rocketing watchmaking into the 21st century, the new Odyssey S is a resolutely techno-luxury timepiece featuring space-age materials and a futuristic design with enhancements including a silicon heart. Antimagnetic, light, machinable to micro-level precision, resistant to both shocks and corrosion, and requiring no lubrication, this material proves absolutely ideal for these elements that are in constant motion year-round. The use of silicon stems from the latest breakthroughs in the field of fine watchmaking and is the exclusive preserve of a handful of manufacturers. This high-tech oscillating organ beats inside the exclusive new self-winding Clerc C201 movement—a refined version of Clerc Caliber C200—endowed with a seven-day power reserve.

On the new Odyssey S, the balance-spring and balance are visible through a dial opening at 10 o'clock, protected by a blue- or gray-tinted sapphire crystal, which also covers the power reserve indication at 6 o'clock. This model displays the hours, minutes, seconds and retrograde date at 2 o'clock and a countdown by a rotating inner bezel, all admirably staged on a new three-level dial evoking skeletonized bridges. The imposing 44mm case is water resistant to 100 meters and its base is made from grade 5 titanium, topped by 18-karat pink gold, grade 5 titanium or DLC blackened grade 5 titanium. This model is fitted with a vulcanized rubber or alligator leather strap.

Clerc watches are manufactured in Switzerland according to the most stringent watch industry quality criteria regarding the case production, the hand-finished movement or the dial details. Such famous brands as Rolex, Vacheron Constantin and Jaeger-LeCoultre have successively been associated with manufacturing watches for Clerc until the 1980s.

Over the generations, many celebrities have chosen Clerc because they were looking for a unique or custom-made object. These include royalty, such as Princess Grace of Monaco, heads of state such as Nikita Khrushchev, artists such as Maurice Chevalier, Salvador Dalí and Paco Rabanne, and more recently actors such as Michael Douglas, Jack Scalia and Goldie Hawn. For General de Gaulle, Clerc even made a clock shaped like a globe with a tiny subdial adorned with a sapphire in the location of Paris, and another embellished with a ruby indicating the time in Moscow. The French president presented it as a gift to Khrushchev.

Available in Asia, Europe, the Middle East and in the United States through a network of carefully selected retailers, Clerc creations are covered by a three-year international warranty. Better than any fine speeches, this approach is tangible proof of the extraordinarily superior quality of watches by Clerc Genève and is very much like the icing on the cake… A cake of which not all devotees of futuristic haute horology will be able to get a slice, since Gérald Clerc focuses exclusively on limited production creations.

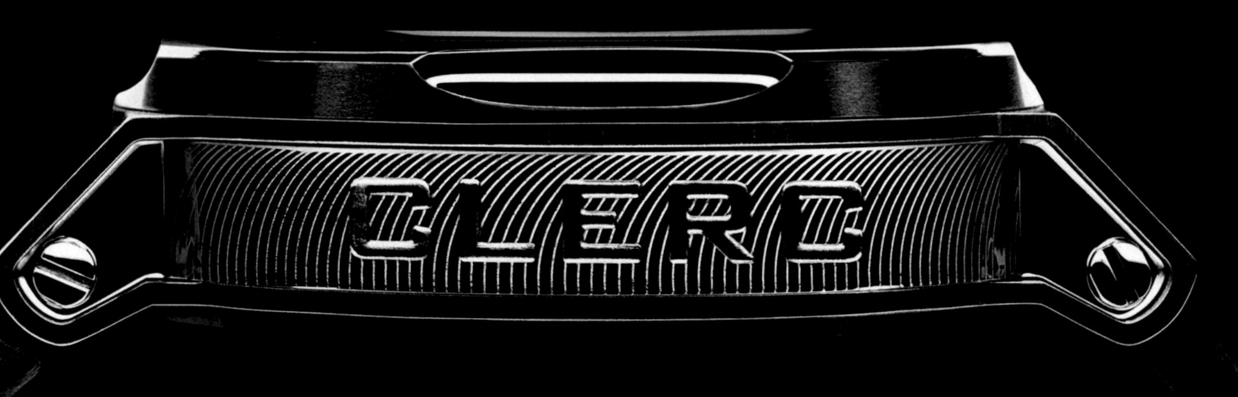

CONCORD

MAKING A DARING MOVE

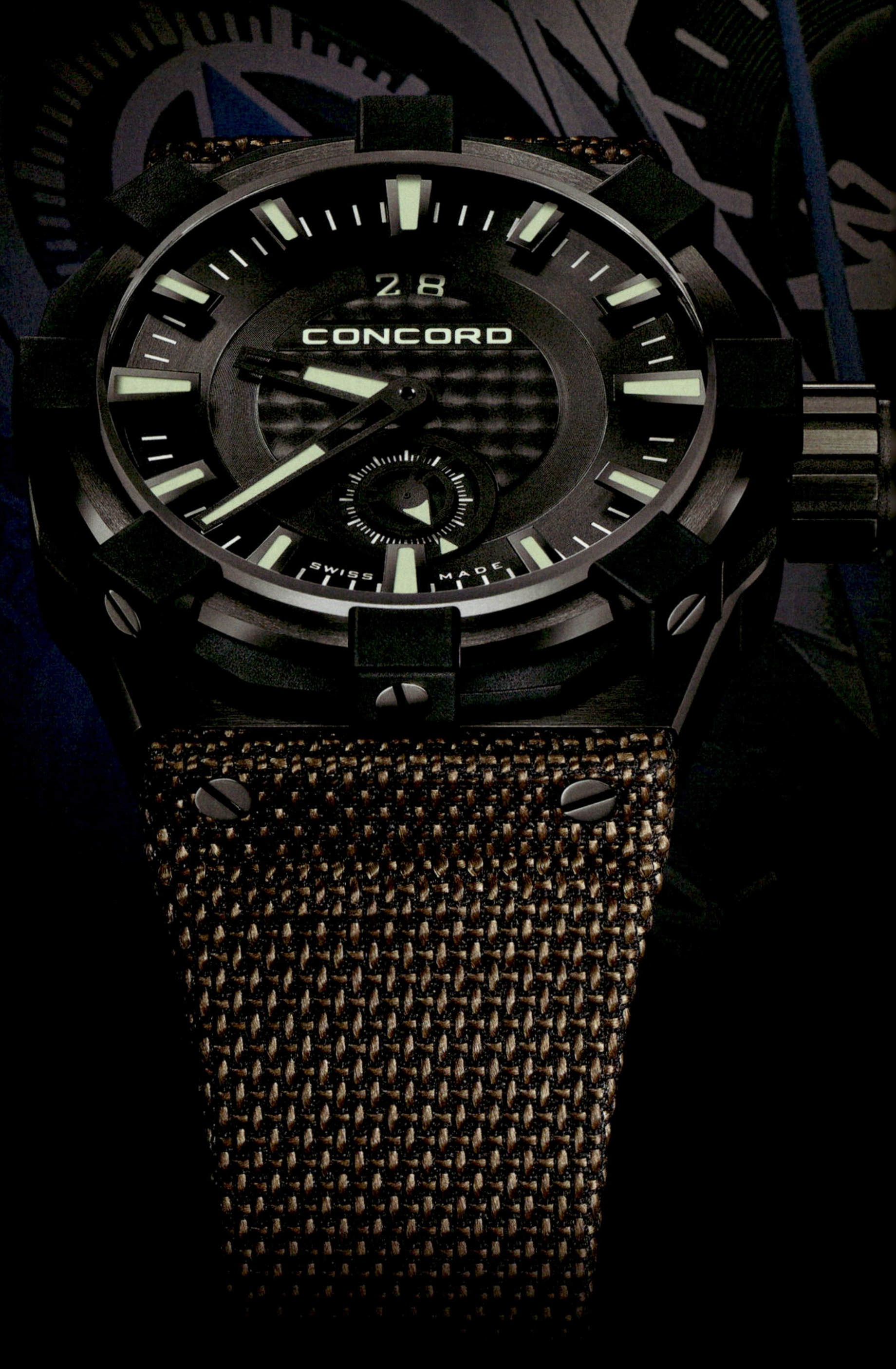

When Concord introduced the C1 collection in 2007, it marked the beginning of an exciting new chapter as the Swiss watchmaker embraced a strong visual identity and intensified its focus on innovation.

Since then, Concord has staked its claim to horology's cutting edge with a series of ambitious timepieces that push the boundaries of design and technology.

The company continued to build momentum in 2010 with the C1 Big Date Radar. The concept behind the watch is based on tradition—hours, minutes, small seconds and date. The execution, however, is anything but.

The multi-layer dial's combination of dark and luminous elements conjures a stealthy appeal enhanced by its subtle interplay of different textures. Circular graining at the center gives way to a grooved ring that resolves into the satin finish of the banked minute scale. The luminous hour markers extend over this shifting surface, adding a key element to the dynamic dial.

Inside the black PVD-treated case, a COSC-certified movement ensures precision timekeeping while displaying the date via two separate wheels and apertures. A woven technofiber strap completes the rugged look.

THIS PAGE

An unusually thick (3.3mm) sapphire crystal is fixed to the C1 Big Date Radar's 44mm stainless steel case by eight black rubber anchors. Coated in black PVD, the case is attached to a technofiber strap.

FACING PAGE

TOP LEFT The C1 MecaTech's COSC-certified chronograph movement is housed in a black PVD-coated 44mm case paired with a rose-gold bezel.

TOP RIGHT The C1 Vintage's case and strap are synthetically distressed to give the watch an appealing timeworn patina.

BOTTOM The one-of-a-kind C1 Eternal Gravity Tourbillon glitters with more than 20 carats of white diamonds on the case alone. The time display is pavé-set with 100 baguette-cut white diamonds, while 12 black diamonds mark the hours.

Concord completes its transformation from a bastion of tradition into a brand on the vanguard of high-end watchmaking with a growing collection of timepieces that blend mechanical precision with meticulous design.

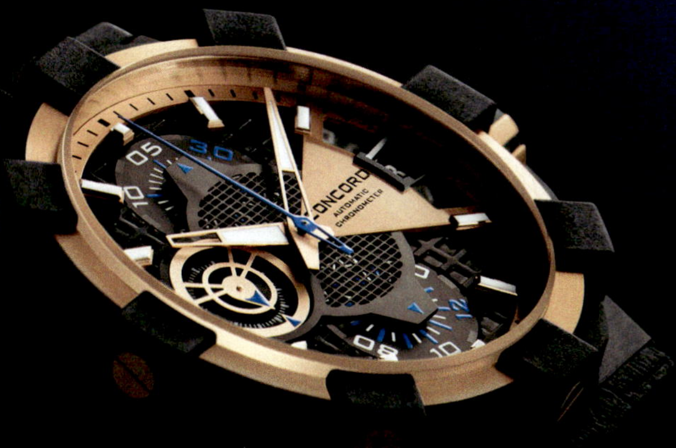

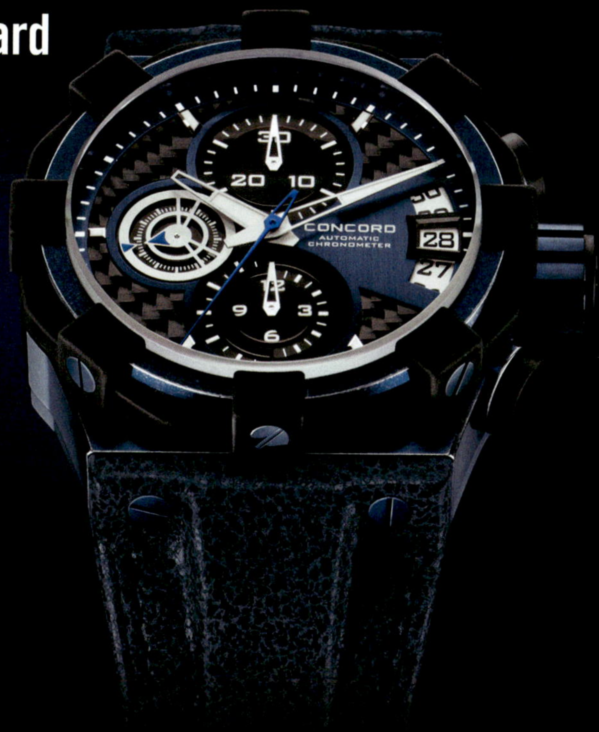

Concord recalls the radical chronograph design that helped redefine the brand with the C1 MecaTech. Unveiled last year, it maintains the original's instantly recognizable thick sapphire crystal and rotating seconds disc, but offers several bold variations on that theme. Underscoring the dial's pattern, black latticework added to the center of the dial includes two blue arrows for the chronograph's hour and minute displays.

Concord strikes a rough-and-tumble attitude with its C1 Vintage, a chronograph presented in a blue PVD-treated case that has been artificially distressed. Like a faded pair of jeans, the C1 Vintage projects just the right amount of scruffy style.

Concord realizes this timeworn patina by barrel-finishing the stainless steel case. According to the brand, this mechanical and chemical polishing process subjects the case to more than two hours of intense friction and vibration. Similarly, the blue leather strap is also put through a simulated aging process that creates an appealing mottled effect.

Despite its outward appearance, the C1 Vintage contains a contemporary automatic movement that is COSC-certified and equipped with a balance that operates at 4 Hz (28,000 vph).

While the Vintage provides a playful twist on the original C1 chronograph, the C1 Eternal Gravity revisits Concord's acclaimed C1 Tourbillon Gravity, which featured the world's first outboard-mounted vertical tourbillon. Introduced in 2008, the watch was named Design of the Year at the esteemed Grand Prix d'Horlogerie de Genève.

The C1 Eternal Gravity pays tribute to that award-winning design with a one-of-a-kind jewelry version that crackles with high-watt glamour. More than 200 baguette-cut white diamonds (weighing 20.17 carats) illuminate the watch's 48.5mm white-gold case alone. The dial combines 100 baguette-cut white diamonds with black diamonds for hour markers. A row of 34 carnelians form a semi-precious ring around the dial, which includes an indicator for the level of the power reserve and another for the status of the balance wheel's amplitude. This scintillating display offers the perfect expression of Concord's uncompromising nature.

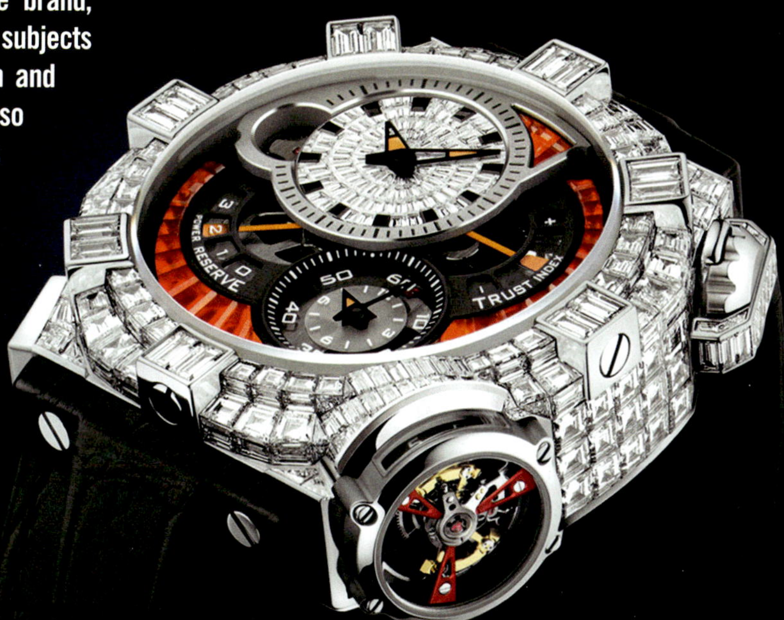

C1 BIG DATE RADAR — REF. 0320105

Movement: automatic-winding 3532 La Joux-Perret caliber; 11 ½'''; Ø 26.2mm, thickness: 4.9mm; 44-hour power reserve; 26 jewels; 28,800 vph; COSC-certified chronometer; black PVD rotor with openworked C1 logo.
Functions: hours, minutes; small seconds on permanent turning disc at 6; large date window at 12.
Case: black PVD-treated stainless steel; Ø 44mm, thickness: 12.95mm; black rubber-coated metal protective ring; fixed laterally by seven self-blocking screws; screw-down crown with embossed C1 logo; 3.3mm-thick sapphire crystal, antireflective on both sides; exhibition caseback embossed "Audace–Savoir-Faire–Avant-Garde"; water resistant to 20atm.
Dial: black engine-turned; black polished elevated hour markers with SuperLumiNova; dauphine-style hour and minute hands with SuperLumiNova, asymmetrically hollowed out.
Strap: khaki techno fiber; black PVD-treated stainless steel deployment buckle with embossed Concord cover.
Suggested price: $10,900

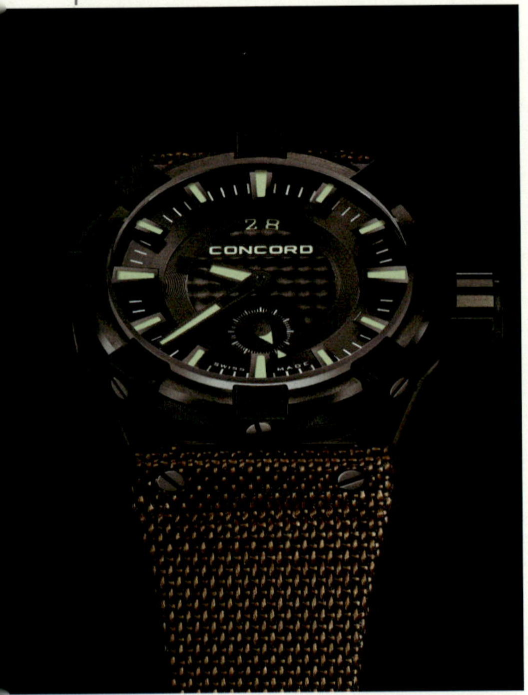

C1 VINTAGE — REF. 0320103

Movement: automatic-winding A07.211 Valgranges caliber; 16 ½'''; Ø 37.2mm, thickness: 7.9mm; 48-hour power reserve; 25 jewels; 28,800 vph; COSC-certified chronometer; black PVD rotor with openworked C1 logo.
Functions: hours, minutes; small seconds on permanent turning disc at 9; date window at 3; chronograph: central sweep seconds, 30-minute counter at 12, 12-hour counter at 6.
Case: blue PVD-treated worn stainless steel; Ø 44mm, thickness: 16.7mm; black rubber-coated metal protective ring; fixed laterally by seven self-blocking screws; screw-down crown with embossed C1 logo; 3.3mm-thick sapphire crystal, antireflective on both sides; exhibition caseback embossed "Audace–Savoir-Faire–Avant-Garde"; water resistant to 20atm.
Dial: three layers; black carbon fiber and galvanic blue; rhodium-plated hour markers with SuperLumiNova; dauphine-style hands, asymmetrically hollowed out; rhodium-lacquered with SuperLumiNova; chronograph seconds hand in blue.
Strap: blue vintage structured leather; black PVD-treated stainless steel deployment buckle with embossed Concord cover.
Suggested price: $13,900

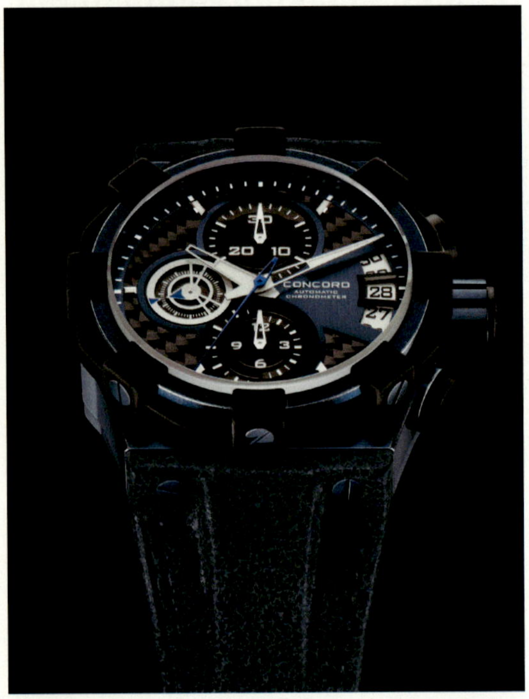

C1 MECATECH — REF. 0320097

Movement: automatic-winding A07.211 Valgranges caliber; 16 ½'''; Ø 37.2mm, thickness: 7.9mm; 48-hour power reserve; 25 jewels; 28,800 vph, COSC-certified chronometer; black PVD rotor with openworked C1 logo.
Functions: hours, minutes; small seconds on permanent turning disc at 9; date window at 3; chronograph: central sweep seconds, 30-minute counter at 12, 12-hour counter at 6.
Case: 18K 5N rose gold and black PVD-treated stainless steel; Ø 44mm, thickness: 16.7mm; black rubber-coated metal protective ring; fixed laterally by seven self-blocking screws; screw-down crown with embossed C1 logo; 3.3mm-thick sapphire crystal, antireflective on both sides; exhibition caseback embossed "Audace–Savoir-Faire–Avant-Garde"; water resistant to 20atm.
Dial: three layers; black ribbed guilloché and grid; 5N hour markers with SuperLumiNova; dauphine-style hands, asymmetrically hollowed out, 5N with SuperLumiNova; blue chronograph seconds hand.
Strap: black rubber-coated alligator; black PVD-treated stainless steel deployment buckle with embossed Concord cover.
Suggested price: $19,900

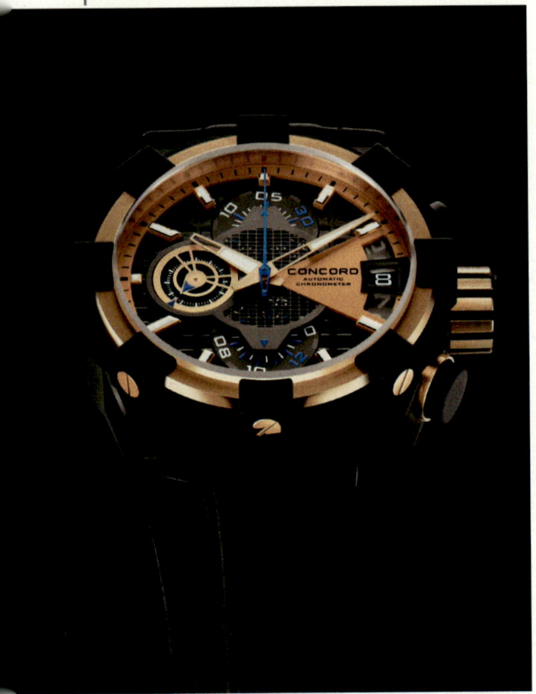

C1 WORLDTIMER 2010 — REF. 0320098

Movement: automatic-winding GMT Worldtimer Dubois-Dépraz 201 caliber; 11 ½'''; Ø 26.2mm, thickness: 5mm; 42-hour power reserve; 21 jewels; 28,800 vph.
Functions: hours, minutes, seconds; 24 time zones; cities at 9.
Case: stainless steel; Ø 47mm, thickness: 13.55mm; black rubber-coated metal protective ring; fixed laterally by seven self-blocking screws; screw-down crown with embossed C1 logo; 3.3mm-thick sapphire crystal, antireflective on both sides; caseback embossed "Audace–Savoir-Faire–Avant-Garde"; water resistant to 20atm.
Dial: black guilloché; wide gray opening for second time zone; rhodium-plated hour markers with SuperLumiNova; dauphine-style hands, asymmetrically hollowed out, rhodium-lacquered with SuperLumiNova.
Strap: black vulcanized rubber; stainless steel deployment buckle with embossed Concord cover.
Suggested price: $13,900

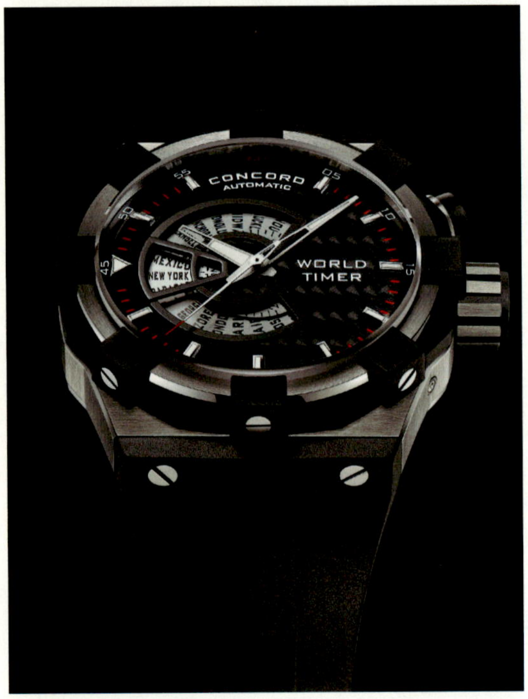

C1 HEART2HEART — REF. 0320092

Movement: automatic-winding A07.211 Valgranges caliber; 16 ½'''; Ø 37.2mm, thickness: 7.9mm; 48-hour power reserve; 25 jewels; 28,800 vph; COSC-certified chronometer; black PVD rotor with openworked C1 logo.
Functions: hours, minutes; small seconds on permanent turning disc at 9; date window at 3; chronograph: central sweep seconds, 30-minute counter at 12, 12-hour counter at 6.
Case: black PVD-treated stainless steel; Ø 44mm, thickness: 16.7mm; black rubber-coated metal protective ring; fixed laterally by seven self-blocking screws; screw-down crown with embossed C1 logo; 3.3mm-thick sapphire crystal, antireflective on both sides; exhibition caseback with Heart to Heart Foundation logo; water resistant to 20atm.
Dial: three layers; black carbon fiber; red seconds counter and date with number 21 in red; rhodium-plated hour markers with SuperLumiNova; dauphine-style hands, asymmetrically hollowed out, rhodium-lacquered with SuperLumiNova; red chronograph seconds hand.
Strap: black rubber-coated alligator with red stitching; black PVD-treated stainless steel deployment buckle with embossed Concord cover.
Note: limited edition.
Suggested price: $14,900

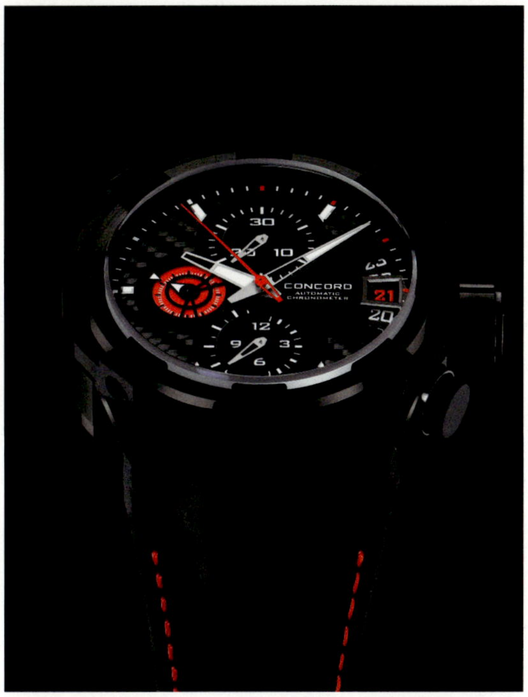

C1 RETROGRADE — REF. 0320054

Movement: automatic-winding 9094 Soprod caliber; 11 ½'''; Ø 25.6mm, thickness: 5.25mm; 42-hour power reserve; 30 jewels; 28,800 vph; black PVD rotor with openworked C1 logo.
Functions: hours, minutes, seconds; retrograde date at 3; day at 9; power reserve at 6.
Case: titanium; Ø 44mm, thickness: 13.15mm; black rubber-coated metal protective ring; fixed laterally by seven self-blocking screws; screw-down crown with embossed C1 logo; 3.3mm-thick sapphire crystal, antireflective on both sides; exhibition caseback embossed "Audace–Savoir-Faire–Avant-Garde"; water resistant to 20atm.
Dial: black ribbed guilloché; dark gray date disc; lacquered and sandblasted; rhodium-plated hour markers with SuperLumiNova; dauphine-style hands, asymmetrically hollowed out, rhodium-lacquered with SuperLumiNova.
Strap: black vulcanized rubber; DLC-treated stainless steel deployment buckle with embossed Concord cover.
Suggested price: $14,290

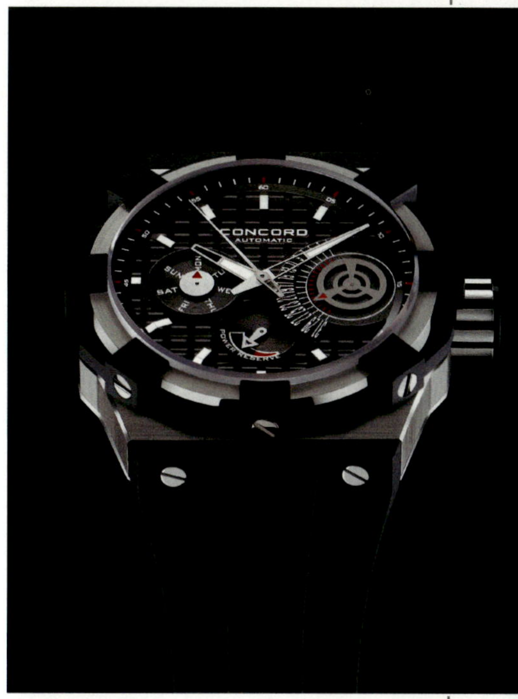

C1 BIG DATE PURE — REF. 0320044

Movement: automatic-winding 3532 La Joux-Perret caliber; 11 ½'''; Ø 26.2mm, thickness: 4.9mm; 44-hour power reserve; 26 jewels; 28,800 vph, COSC-certified chronometer; rhodium-treated rotor with openworked C1 logo.
Functions: hours, minutes; small seconds on permanent turning disc at 6; large date window at 12.
Case: stainless steel; Ø 44mm, thickness: 12.95mm; bezel set with 40 white diamonds (0.64 carat); white rubber-coated metal protective ring; fixed laterally by seven self-blocking screws; screw-down crown with embossed C1 logo; 3.3mm-thick sapphire crystal, antireflective on both sides; exhibition caseback embossed "Audace–Savoir-Faire–Avant-Garde"; water resistant to 20atm.
Dial: white and silver guilloché; hour markers set with ten diamonds (0.07 carat); dauphine-style hands, asymmetrically hollowed out, rhodium-lacquered with SuperLumiNova.
Strap: white vulcanized rubber; stainless steel deployment buckle with embossed Concord cover.
Suggested price: $15,300

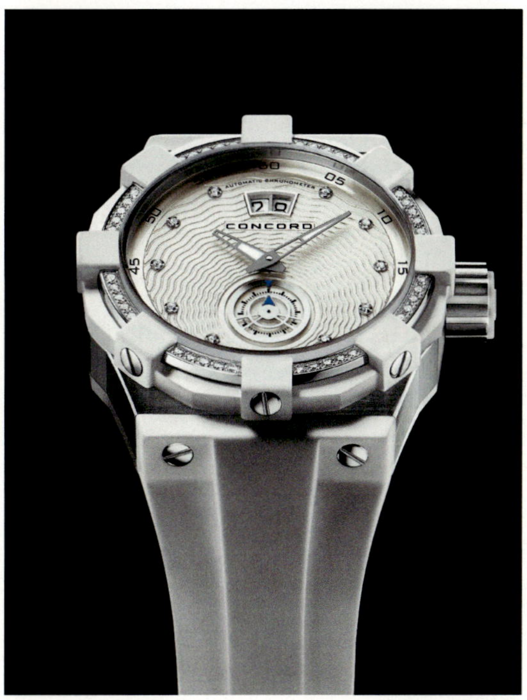

C1 DIAMOND GRAVITY — REF. 0320102

Movement: manual-winding C100 caliber; 16'''; chrono flyback tourbillon; Ø 36.2mm, thickness: 7.6mm; 84-hour power reserve; 38 jewels; 21,600 vph.
Functions: hours, minutes; seconds on tourbillon cage roll; external vertical tourbillon; power reserve indicator; trust index (indication of balance wheel amplitude); flyback chronograph with hours and minutes.
Case: titanium; Ø 48.5mm, thickness: 18.5mm; black rubber-coated metal protective ring; fixed laterally by seven self-blocking screws; 18K white-gold crown with rubber protector; 3.3mm-thick sapphire crystal, antireflective on both sides; exhibition caseback embossed "Audace–Savoir-Faire–Avant-Garde"; water resistant to 3atm.
Dial: skeleton; full pavé subdial set with 134 baguette-cut white diamonds (4.11 carats); hour markers set with 12 baguette-cut black diamonds (0.23 carat).
Strap: black vulcanized rubber; 18K white-gold deployment buckle with embossed Concord cover.
Suggested price: $390,000

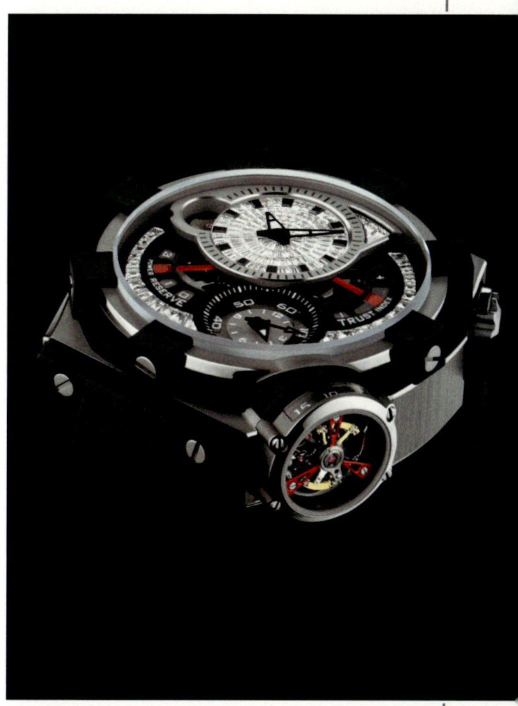

de GRISOGONO
GENEVE

INNOVATION RULES

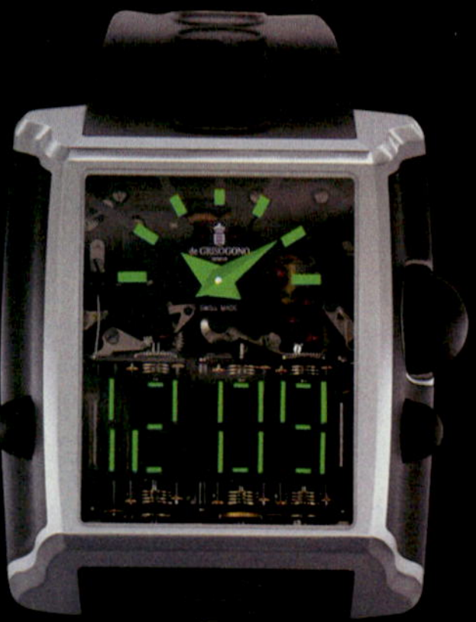

When Fawaz Gruosi first began creating jewelry in 1993, with no prospects and no business plan other than an instinctive desire to give free rein to his creativity, nobody would have dared to predict the incredible reputation de Grisogono has now earned. In the same way, when the Geneva-based company entered the field of fine watchmaking in 2000, it would have been hard to imagine that all timepieces bearing the de Grisogono signature would gain the credibility they now enjoy and that each would prove immensely successful. All of this is doubtless because, above and beyond producing appealing designs, the CEO and founder of de Grisogono has constantly targeted an innovative approach that excels by transcending existing watchmaking traditions.

"When you are seventeen you aren't really serious," wrote the French poet Arthur Rimbaud—a statement that this particular watch brand, which has just turned 17, both confirms and disproves. The latest creations from de Grisogono, which has a range of around 20 men's and ladies' watch collections, embody a subtle blend of aesthetic boldness and a rare capacity for innovation. Yet how can one still hope to surprise people when so much has already been done? What path should one take to innovate in a period when horological history already features such a large number of amazing inventions? While very few watch companies choose to explore new horizons, this youthful brand has consistently sought to offer a new take on watchmaking. Daring to introduce shapes that highlight functions, developing original complications, playing with time in order to better express the art of its measurement: such are just a few of the precepts that have guided the development of de Grisogono watches.

The Meccanico dG unveiled in 2009 is the kind of avant-garde watch that is not content with merely reinterpreting tried and tested principles and concepts. This concentrated blend of technologies draws its very essence from the finest watchmaking traditions, and projects them into the future. That is indeed undoubtedly where Fawaz Gruosi's true genius lies, since he has proved capable, not just of presenting one of the most complex mechanisms currently on the market, but of using it to power the world's first ever watch with a patented double analog and digital display mode driven by an entirely mechanical system. This feat called for an amazingly inventive mindset, as well a certain degree of recklessness required to venture into such unknown territory. The mechanism of the Meccanico dG is out of the ordinary in every imaginable way.

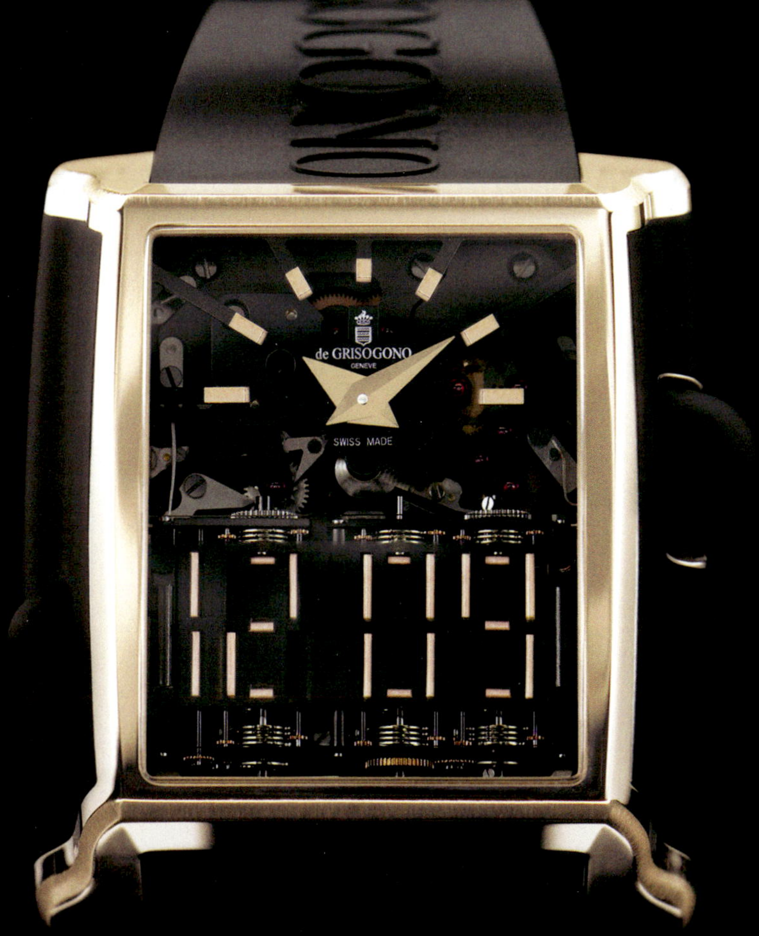

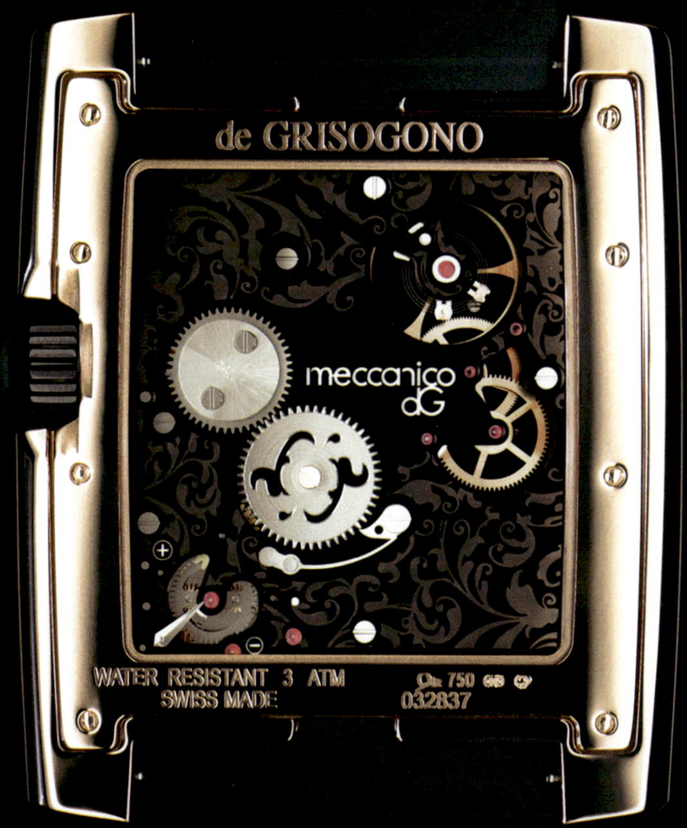

Consisting of a set of micro-systems equipped with highly sophisticated cam and gear mechanisms, the mechanical hand-wound movement of the Meccanico dG comprises no less than 651 parts. Each plays its role in handling the analog display of the hours and minutes in the upper part of the dial, as well as the mechanical digital dual timezone display in the lower section, along with tens of hours, single hours, tens of minutes and single minutes. The great originality of this patented movement, which is a fascinating nod to watchmaking history in its clever allusion to the quartz era, lies in the operation of the mobile micro-segments, driven by a system of 23 cams combined with gears and a trigger/synchronization device. This highly complex mechanism, produced in a 177-piece limited run, is clearly revealed through the transparent dial. The design is indeed a fine match for the technical side of this watch. The unusual nature of the movement driving the Meccanico dG is housed within a sleek, contemporary exterior. The generously sized curving case is available in rose gold, titanium, titanium and rubber, titanium and rose gold or titanium and platinum versions. These combinations of materials accentuate the innovative character of the design, reinforced by the vulcanized rubber surrounding the correctors and the crown guard, as well as the green-colored platelets adorning the hands, hour markers and digital numerals on certain versions.

FACING PAGE

The Meccanico dG, shown here in its titanium and rubber version, won the Public Prize at the 2009 Geneva Watchmaking Grand Prix.

THIS PAGE

LEFT Featuring a delightful blend of rose gold and rubber, the Meccanico dG combines sophisticated and elegant aesthetic elegance with an exceptional mechanism that is one of the most complex of its kind.

RIGHT Elegant from all angles, whether viewed from the front or back, the Meccanico dG takes refinement to its ultimate limits, adorned with the brand's emblematic curlicue motif.

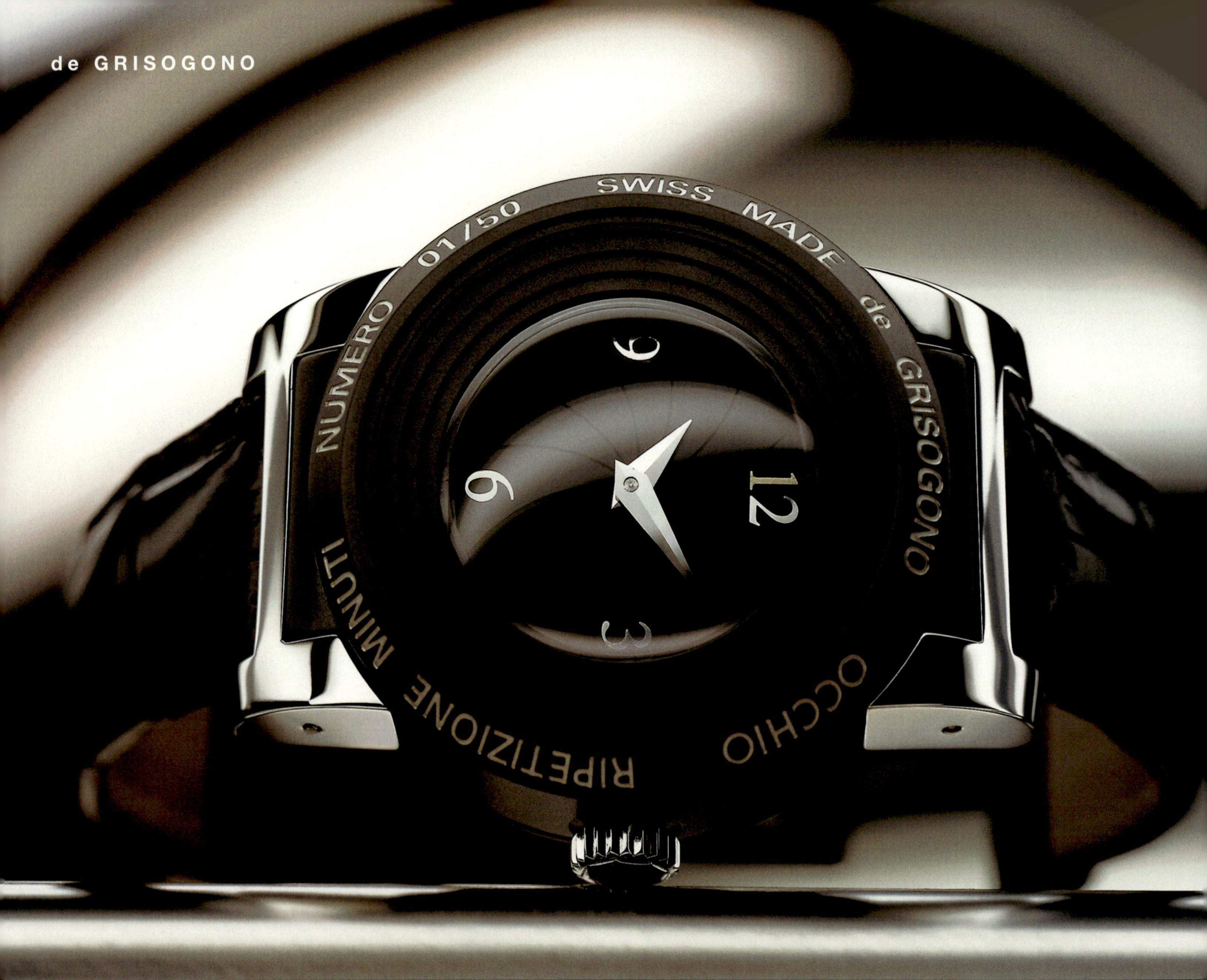

A few years earlier, in 2005, de Grisogono had already caused a sensation by introducing an extremely original innovation. The Occhio Ripetizione Minuti, endowed with a minute repeater and cathedral gong strike, features a truly unique display system. Developed on the basis of a reflex camera that captures a moment with an instant shutter opening, immortalizing it on film, the Instrumento Occhio is equipped with a aperture that reveals the movement while it is striking and then closes up to conceal the movement once more from prying eyes. The twelve mobile titanium aperture shutters open instantly when the minute repeater is activated, before closing again once the hours, quarter-hours and minutes have been struck on three gongs. This display system gives pride of place to aesthetic appeal, especially since the watch is entirely dedicated to ensuring maximum transparency. On the front, the strongly convex spherical sapphire crystal, not unlike a camera lens, affords an astonishingly clear view of the aperture and, when the latter is open, of the intricate motion of the racks, levers and springs. Meanwhile, the cambered sapphire crystal caseback enables one to admire the movement of the three hammers as well as the superb decorative finishing. de Grisogono now pays a sparkling tribute to this mechanical magic by presenting an even more radiant version of the Occhio Ripetizione Minuti. Whereas the watch has been characterized thus far by its extremely restrained, understated lines, it reveals a new facet of its personality with a setting of 154 baguette-cut diamonds totaling 18 carats and adorning the bezel, case sides and lugs. This garment of light plays on contrasts and highlights the originality of the mechanism driving this exceptional timepiece.

How can a watch company still hope to surprise people when so much has already been done—when horological history already features such a large number of amazing inventions? de Grisogono answers the question with astounding new models.

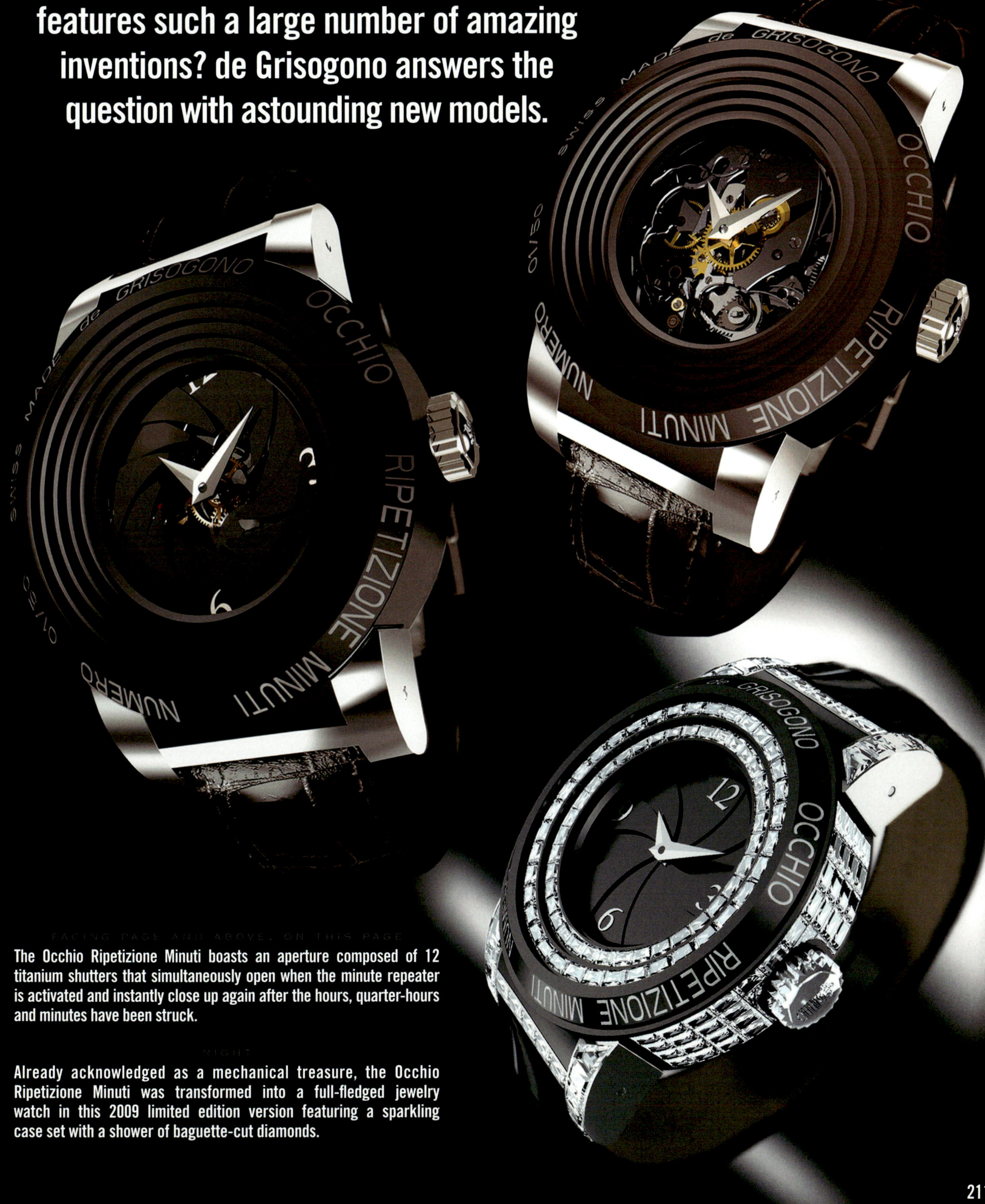

FACING PAGE AND ABOVE, ON THIS PAGE

The Occhio Ripetizione Minuti boasts an aperture composed of 12 titanium shutters that simultaneously open when the minute repeater is activated and instantly close up again after the hours, quarter-hours and minutes have been struck.

RIGHT

Already acknowledged as a mechanical treasure, the Occhio Ripetizione Minuti was transformed into a full-fledged jewelry watch in this 2009 limited edition version featuring a sparkling case set with a shower of baguette-cut diamonds.

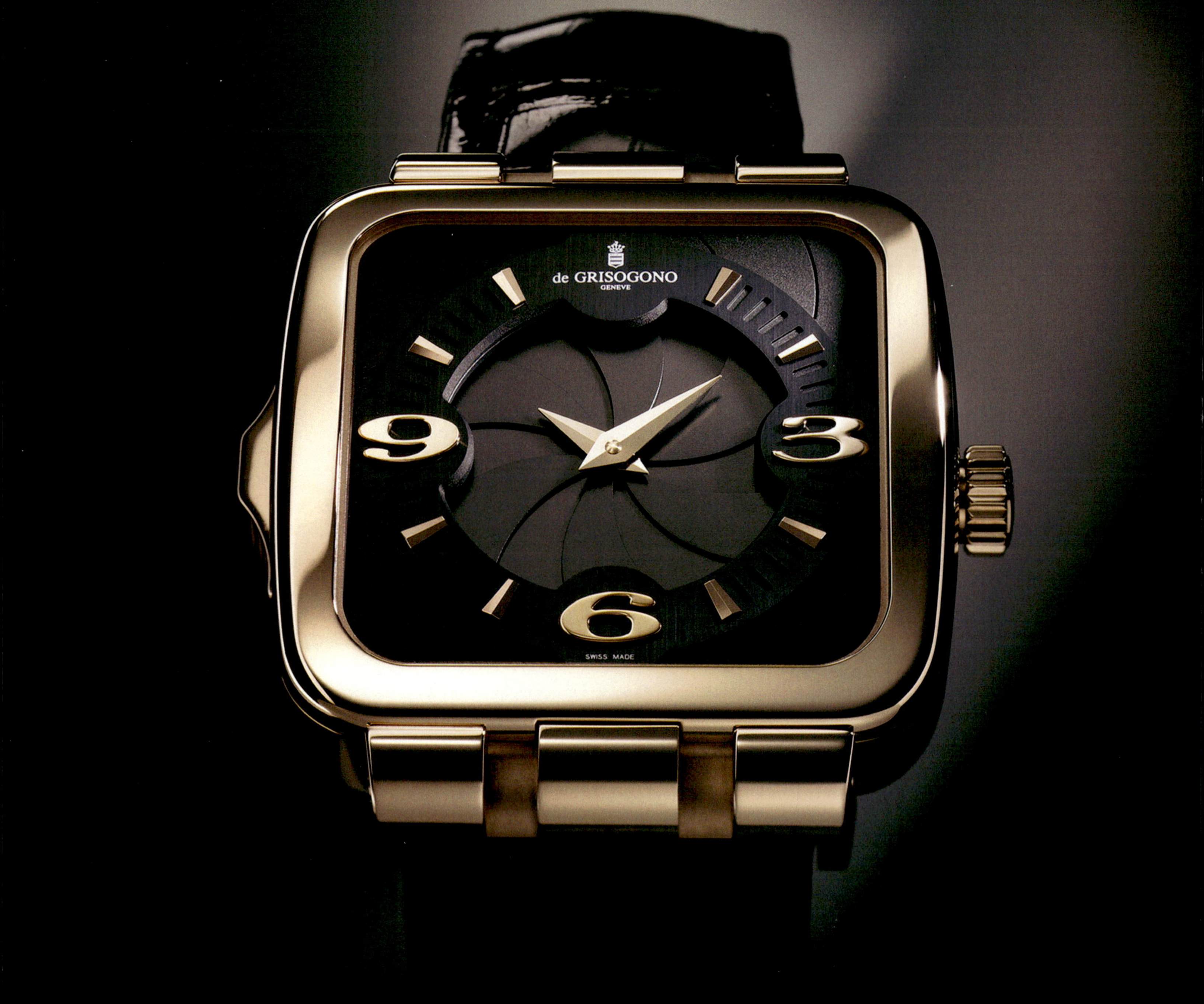

The Fuso Quadrato is entirely in tune with this innovative philosophy. With this model, de Grisogono offers an unprecedented dual timezone display that the user may choose to hide or reveal, as they wish, thanks to the brand's cherished aperture system. This technical feat sets the highly functional timepiece apart from other watches intended for travelers accustomed to juggling time zones. Activated by means of a slide positioned on the side of the case opposite the crown, the aperture composed of 12 titanium shutters opens to reveal not only the local hours and minutes in the center, but also a 12-hour display of the second time zone by means of a black hour hand with an open-tipped extension. Within this model embodying a perfect blend of technical and aesthetic aspects, the design of the rose- or white-gold case also plays a starring role. Square-shaped with rounded angles, it radiates sensuality while ensuring a perfect fit on the wrist thanks to a gentle curve along the 6-12 axis. The result is a further demonstration of the incredible inventiveness that de Grisogono has consistently evidenced over the past ten years, and of its now inescapable presence right up among the most innovative brands. Venturing off the beaten track, inventing, springing surprises. More than a mere aspiration, the brand has made this attitude a genuine art of living in the field of creative contemporary watchmaking.

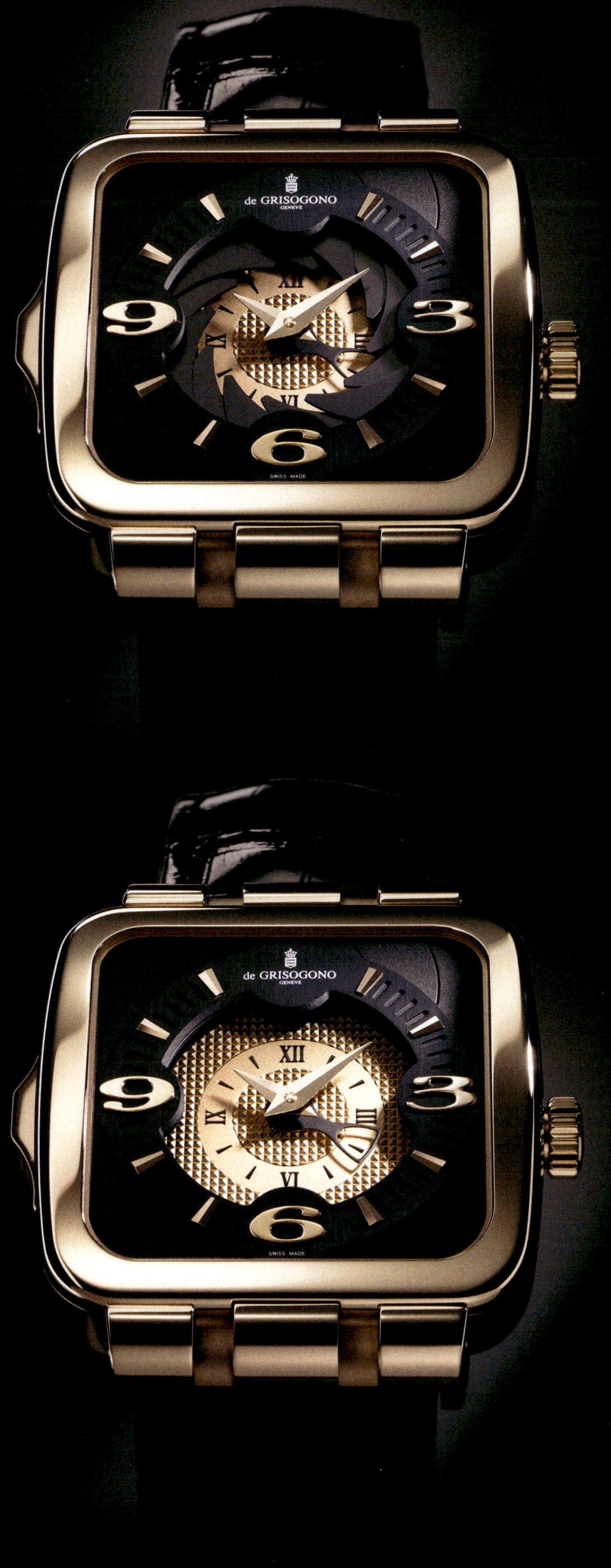

Activated by a slide on the side of the case exactly opposite the crown, the Fuso Quadrato's aperture, with 12 titanium shutters, can be opened to reveal the dual time zone or closed to show only local hours and minutes.

A SUBTLE BLEND OF TECHNOLOGY AND DESIGN

It has taken less than ten years for de Grisogono to become an acknowledged signature in the watch industry. This is a major accomplishment when one considers just how hard it is to earn a place within this particularly exclusive universe—and even more so to keep that place! Ever since the very first watch in its company history, presented in 2000 and named Instrumento N° Uno, the brand philosophy has steadily asserted itself with each new model. de Grisogono watches are all equipped with useful, practical and user-friendly horological complications clothed in exteriors with powerful identifying features. Every single model in the brand's twenty-odd men's and ladies' collections is recognizable at a glance as a watch created by Fawaz Gruosi, and therein lies the strength of a firm that has found a way to stand out from the crowd without ever doubting its own perspicacity. Nonetheless, the brand's lasting success cannot be exclusively ascribed to the aesthetic creativity characteristic of the timepieces launched by Gruosi. For several years now, de Grisogono has been able to rely on a state-of-the-art production facility. Located right near the company headquarters in Plan-les-Ouates, the three-floor 850m^2 watchmaking workshop dedicates its skills and expertise to expressing the exuberant creativity of de Grisogono's founder and CEO. Equipped with a research and development department with a six-strong staff, the workshop has successfully orchestrated all the projects that have come to life under the company name since it entered the watchmaking field in 2000. It has also registered several patents, including one relating to two opposite-facing analog displays, and another to a large date display. The company excels in the domain of enriching movements with additional movements. It is also known for its expertise in the PVD (Physical Vapor Deposition) treatment of the movements powering watches with transparent casebacks. In 2007, de Grisogono took an additional step in the area of in-house production by opening up a new unit devoted to the production of small series and prototypes. The acquisition of new computer digitally-controlled machinery now ensures enhanced flexibility and fast reaction times for this company that holds a place all its own in the world of haute horology.

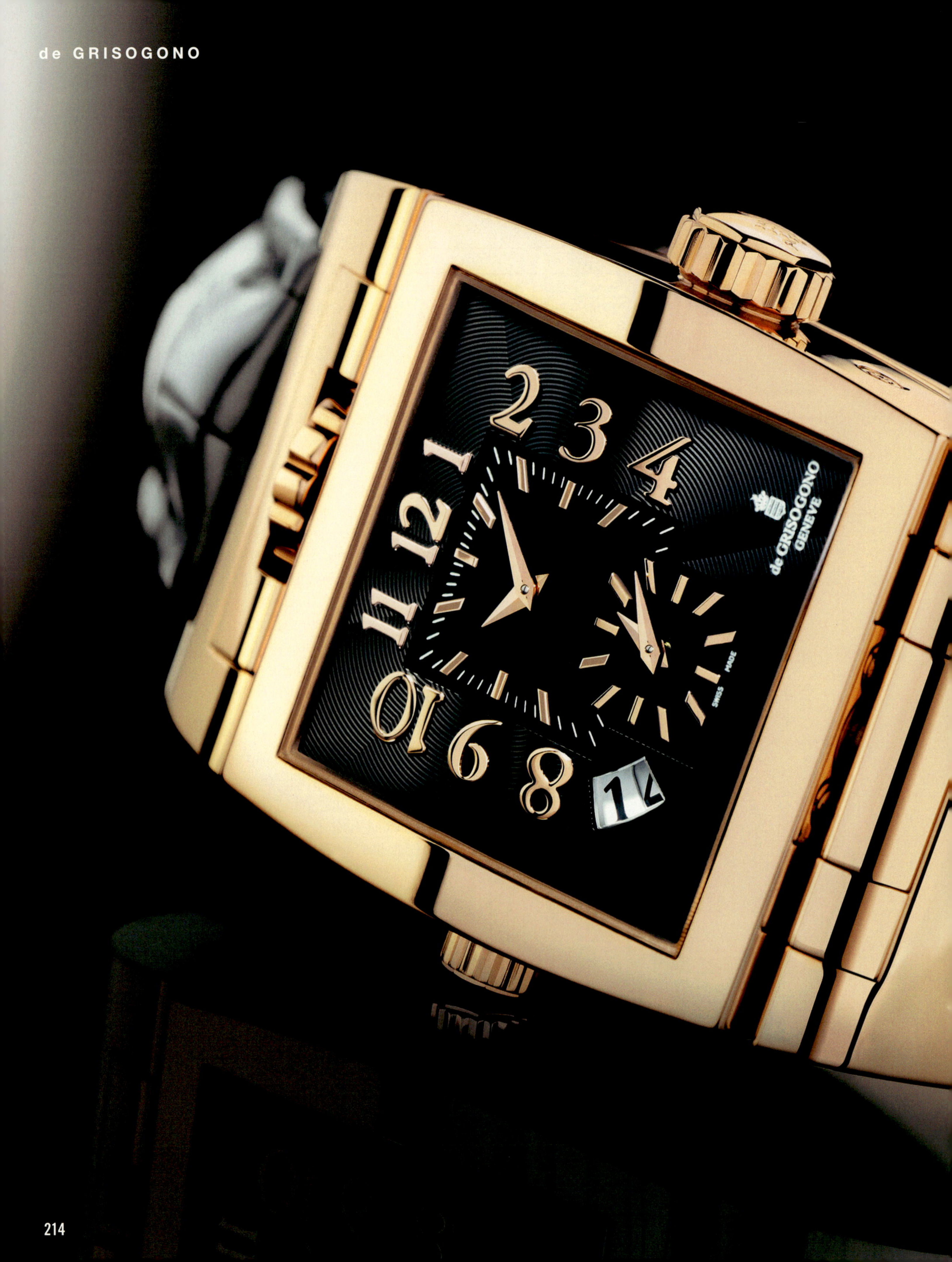
de GRISOGONO
GENEVE
SWISS MADE

INSTRUMENTO DOPPIO TRE: FORM AND FUNCTION

Two faces, two dials, three time zones… and a single mechanical movement! The celebrated de Grisogono magic is clearly at work in the Instrumento Doppio Tre watch unveiled in 2003. The case of this exclusive timepiece swivels in a matter of seconds. The first dial provides joint dual time zone and large date displays. The two time zones are read off of superimposed and overlapping dials surrounded by a square minute track. The second dial reveals a third time zone with an analog display of the hours and minutes. This extremely original arrangement of the useful functions is further accentuated by the way the dial is positioned beneath the rotor, while the hands cross right through the oscillating weight.

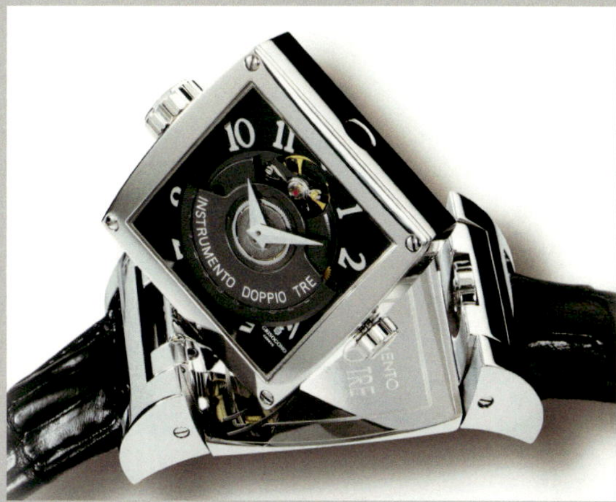

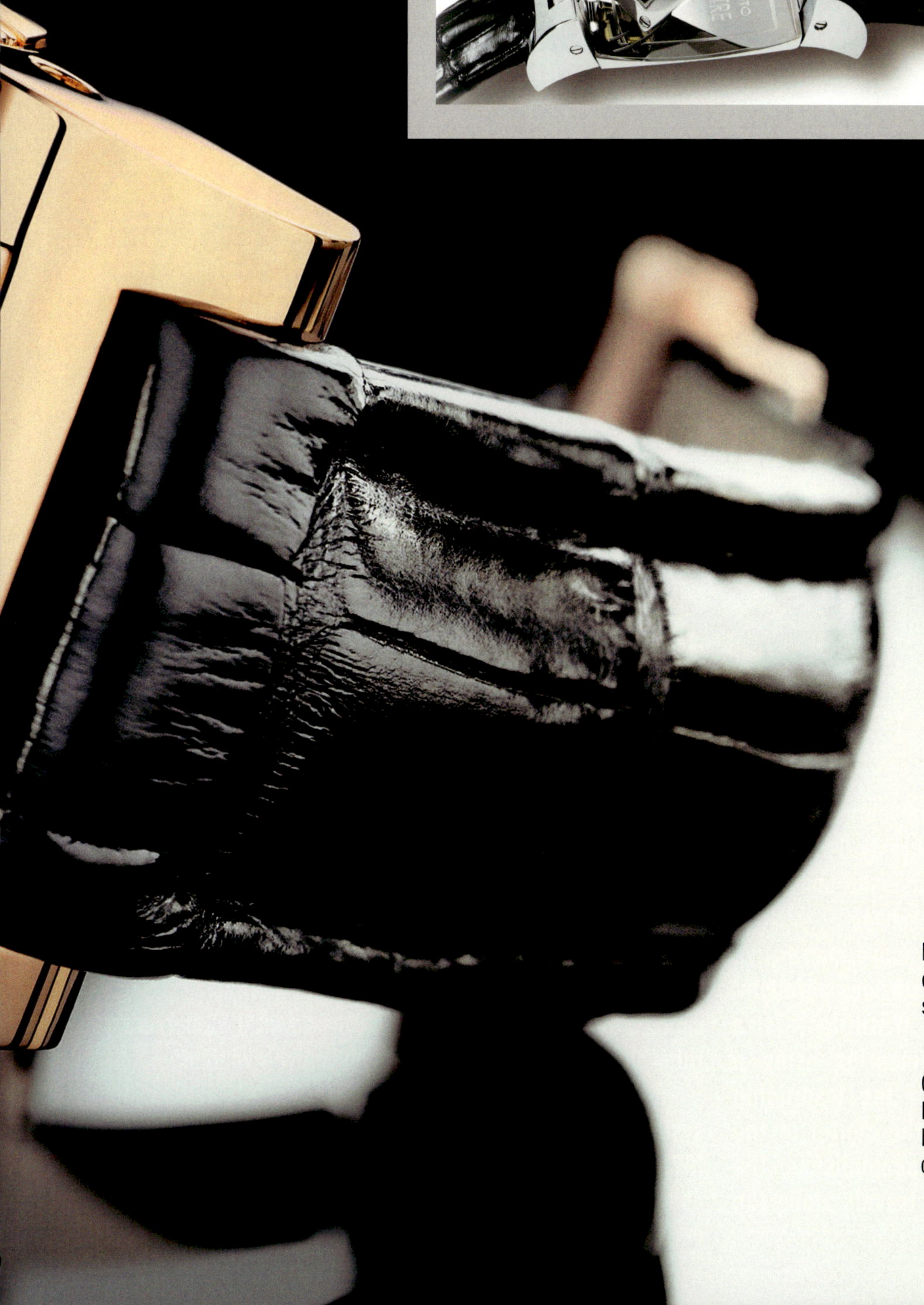

LEFT

In addition to displaying two time zones and a large date indication, the Doppio Tre has a case that swivels to reveal a third time zone display.

INSET

One of the most original features of the Doppio Tre lies in its dial placed beneath the rotor, as well as the hands crossing right through the oscillating weight of the automatic movement.

DEWITT

EXPLORING NEW HORIZONS

DeWitt began charting a bold new course in early 2010 with the introduction of the Twenty-8-Eight, a collection that features the first tourbillon produced in-house by the independent watchmaker.

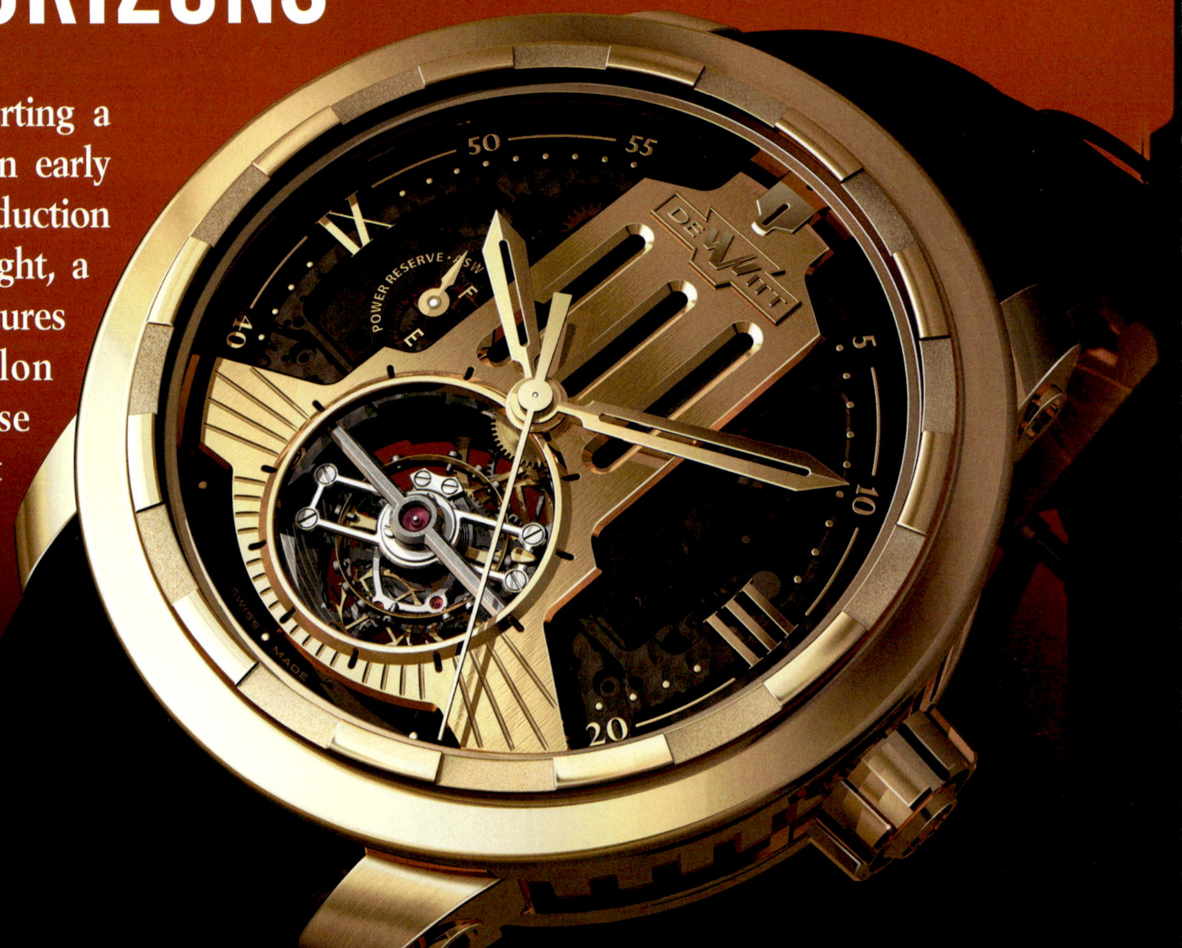

The Geneva firm took another step on that journey a few months later when it unveiled the Twenty-8-Eight Regulator A.S.W. Horizons, the first automatic tourbillon movement crafted entirely at the DeWitt workshops.

What makes this achievement all the more impressive is the explanation behind the watch's mysterious acronym. A.S.W.—for Automatic Sequential Winding—is a patented system that powers the mainspring using a peripheral oscillating rotor. Instead of the traditional half-moon-shaped weight anchored at the center of the movement, DeWitt's clever design accomplishes the same task with a U-shaped weight that travels along the movement's outer circumference.

The A.S.W. is not just visually pleasing; its function also represents a major milestone in micro-mechanics. The Twenty-8-Eight Regulator's peripheral rotor winds the mainspring until the reserve is 96 percent full. At that point, a lever disengages the pawl from winding the barrel and forces it to continue its movement in the air, without increasing the mainspring's torque. When the reserve runs down to 92 percent, the rotor engages and once again begins actively winding.

The underlying reason for this on-again, off-again winding system is to stabilize the mainspring at its optimal tension (92-96 percent). This clever solution ensures a constant and even flow of energy, thereby overcoming a challenge that has vexed movement designers through the ages.

With a new generation of timepieces like the Twenty-8-Eight Regulator A.S.W. Horizons, DeWitt combines its instantly recognizable design sensibility with a growing reputation for technical prowess.

No explanation is required to understand the A.S.W. system's visual benefits. A quick glance through the sapphire crystal caseback reveals all.

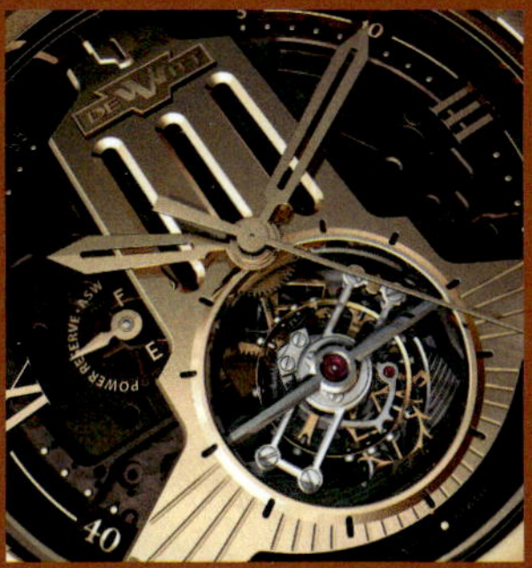

Unlike a traditional winding weight, the peripheral rotor's path and slim profile do not obscure the DW 8014's design. This is particularly important considering the appealing visual balance of the mechanism, which is finished with Côtes de Genève, satin-brushed surfaces and circular graining on the mainplate.

Creating a delightful visual continuity, the architectural shape of the movement's bridges echoes the design featured on the dial. That majestic rose-gold figure draws inspiration from Art Deco structures like the Empire State, GE and Chrysler buildings that began defining New York City's skyline during the great skyscraper race of the 1930s.

The design's four columns tower over the aperture that houses the tourbillon. The complex mechanism achieves an extraordinary level of precision thanks to its cutting-edge escapement, which is equipped with a patented Straumann Hairspring with Phillips curve.

Even more of the movement is visible through the transparent sapphire crystal dial, which is tinted brown, much like the strong coffee that so much of Gotham runs on. The dial also features a gauge at 9 o'clock that indicates the status of the movement's 72-hour power reserve.

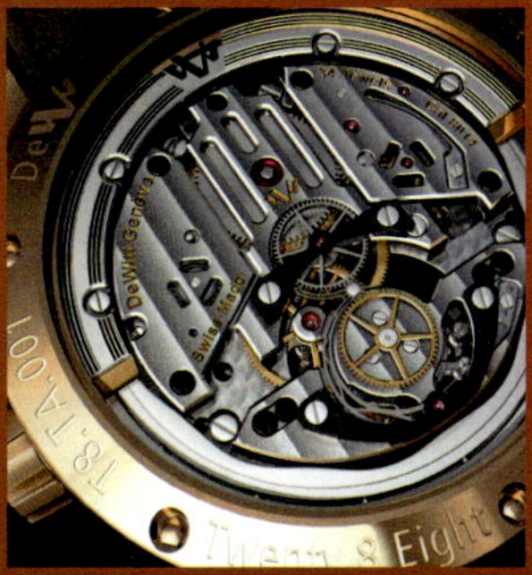

DeWitt presents the Twenty-8-Eight Regulator A.S.W. Horizons in a 46mm rose-gold case decorated with 48 of the brand's signature "imperial columns" on the case middle. The motif continues on the bezel, which features satin-finished sections between raised, polished columns.

As DeWitt expands its collection of in-house movements with proprietary calibers like the DW 8014, the Twenty-8-Eight Regulator A.S.W. Horizons provides the perfect view of what's on the horizon for the company.

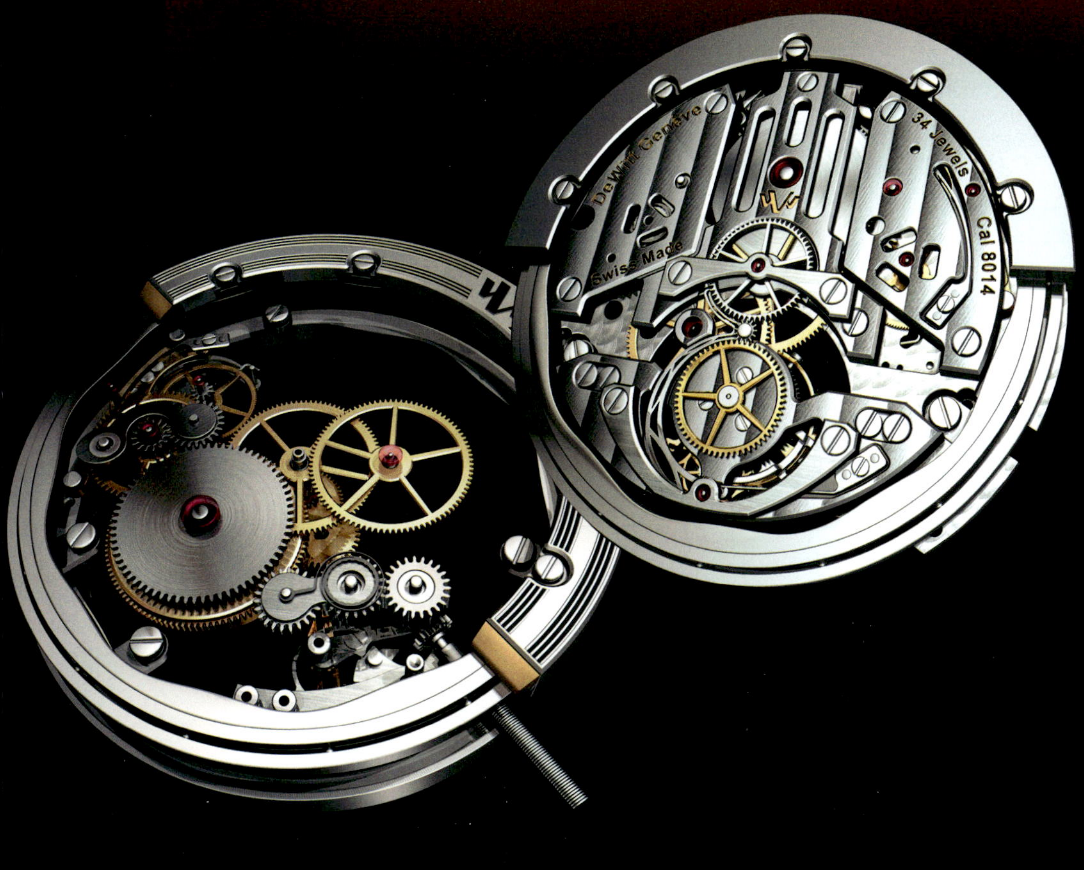

FACING PAGE

The four-column rose-gold figure on the dial takes inspiration from the Art Deco skyscrapers that began filling New York City's skyline in the 1930s.

ABOVE LEFT

The transparent dial of the Twenty-8-Eight Regulator A.S.W. Horizons is crafted from tinted sapphire crystal.

ABOVE RIGHT

The piece is presented in a 46mm rose-gold case and produced in a limited edition of 250 pieces.

FAR LEFT

Adorned with DeWitt's trademark "W," the DW 8014 movement's peripheral rotor is a key component in the firm's newly patented Automatic Sequential Winding system.

LEFT

DeWitt's first in-house automatic tourbillon movement, the DW 8014 features a decidedly architectural flair that is accentuated by Côtes de Genève finishing on the bridges.

ACADEMIA BLACKSTREAM CHRONOGRAPH — REF. AC.6005.37A.M090

Movement: automatic-winding DW6005 (ETA 7753) caliber; Ø 30mm; 48-hour power reserve; 27 jewels; 28,800 vph; three-armed Glucydur balance; flat balance spring.
Functions: hours, minutes; chronograph.
Case: grade 5 titanium, black PVD and black rubber; Ø 44mm, thickness: 13.35mm; adorned with DeWitt's imperial columns pattern on the flanks and bezel; grade 5 titanium crown (DeWitt design) adorned with a ring made in blackened titanium with "W" signature; sapphire crystal caseback secured with screws; water resistant to 3atm.

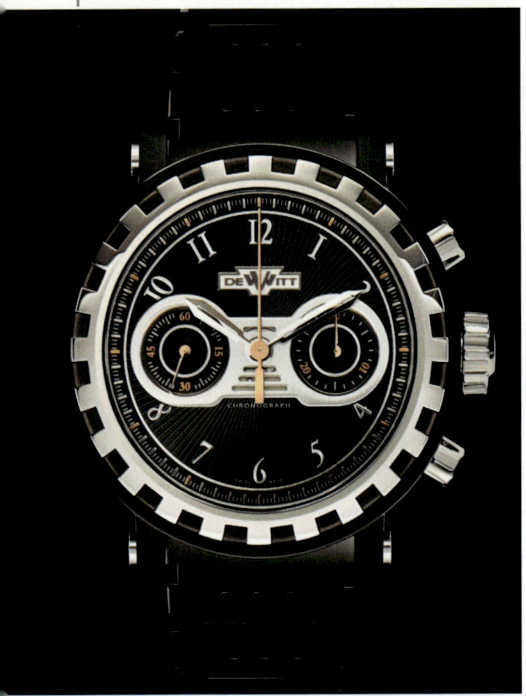

Dial: black velvet color tone; refined sunray pattern; applied rhodium-plated center and DeWitt signature; open-worked hour and minute hands in the shape of two-edged swords; thin and elegant central chronograph hand; small leaf-shaped counter hands.
Strap: matte black rubber with special DeWitt imperial columns pattern; blackened PVD grade 5 titanium triple-blade folding clasp; engraved "W" signature.
Note: limited production of 250 pieces.
Also available: matte black alligator leather strap.

ACADEMIA BLACKSTREAM TRIPLE COMPLICATION GMT3 — REF. AC.2041.37.M050

Movement: automatic-winding DW2041 (ETA 2893 with Agenhor module) caliber; Ø 26.2mm; 42-hour power reserve; 21 jewels; 28,800 vph; three-armed Glucydur balance; flat balance spring.
Functions: hours, minutes; GMT; day/night; dissociated date.
Case: grade 5 titanium, blackened PVD; Ø 44mm, thickness: 13.25mm; adorned with DeWitt's imperial columns pattern on the flanks and bezel; grade 5 titanium (DeWitt design) lockable crown adorned with ring made in blackened titanium with "W" signature; sapphire crystal caseback secured with screws; water resistant to 5atm.

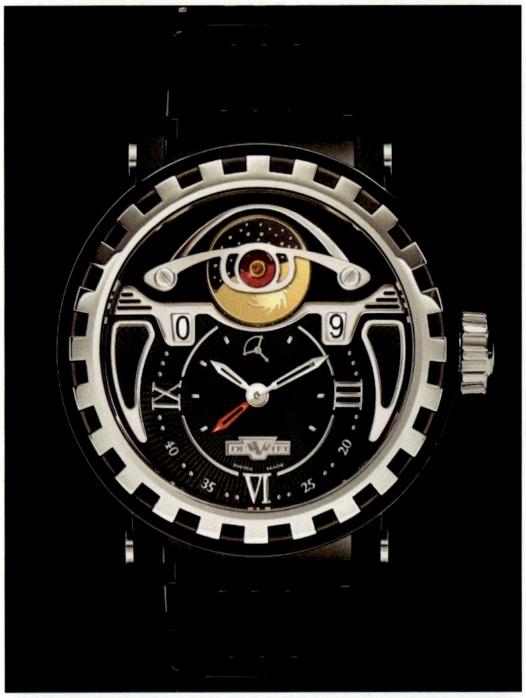

Dial: black velvet color tone; refined sunray pattern; applied rhodium-plated Roman numerals; two "radiator-grilles"; day/night display: yellow sun and blue starlit night sky; applied DeWitt signature at 6; open-worked hour and minute hands in the shape of two-edged swords; red open-worked second time zone hand in the shape of two-edged sword; small blue seconds hand, shaped like a navigation tool.
Strap: matte black rubber with special DeWitt imperial columns pattern; blackened PVD grade 5 titanium triple-blade folding clasp; engraved "W" signature.
Note: limited production of 250 pieces.
Also available: matte black alligator leather strap.

ACADEMIA TOURBILLON FORCE CONSTANTE A CHAINE — REF. AC.8050.53.M103

Movement: manual-winding DW8050 caliber; Ø 30.4mm; 72-hour power reserve; 27 jewels; 21,600 vph; 192 components; integrating a flying tourbillon mechanism with Constant Force; power reserve with chain-driven device, indicated on a worm screw; hand-beveled and decorated with Côtes de Genève; four-armed Glucydur balance; flat balance spring.
Functions: hours, minutes; power reserve.

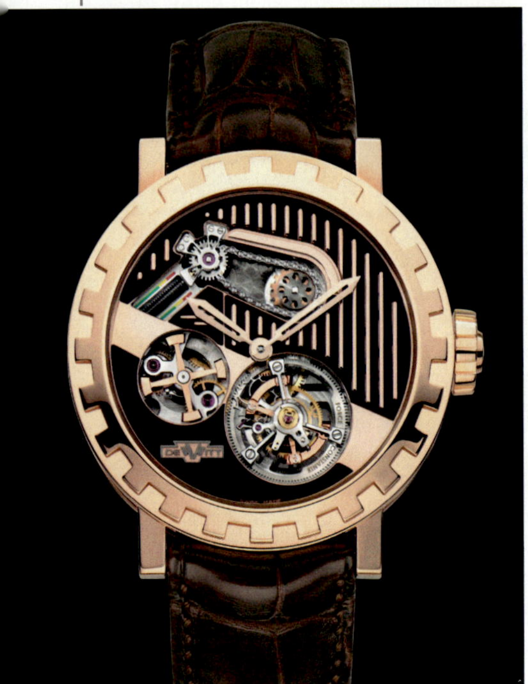

Case: 18K rose gold; Ø 43mm, thickness: 12.95mm; adorned with DeWitt's imperial columns; 18K rose-gold polished crown with "W" signature; sapphire crystal caseback secured with screws; water resistant to 3atm.
Dial: chocolate-colored background; decorated with elegant strips; large opening for the tourbillon cage and Constant Force system; open-worked hour and minute hands in the shape of two-edged swords.
Strap: matte chocolate brown alligator leather; 18K rose-gold triple-blade folding clasp; engraved "W" signature.
Note: limited production of 99 pieces.

TWENTY-8-EIGHT AUTOMATIC — REF. T8.AU.53.001

Movement: automatic-winding DWT8AU (ETA 2892) caliber; 42-hour power reserve; 21 jewels; 28,800 vph; three-armed Glucydur balance; flat balance spring.
Functions: hours, minutes, seconds.
Case: 18K rose gold; Ø 43mm, thickness: 10.28mm; adorned with DeWitt's imperial columns pattern on the flanks; 18K rose-gold polished crown adorned with a blackened titanium ring with "W" signature; sapphire crystal caseback secured with screws; water resistant to 3atm.

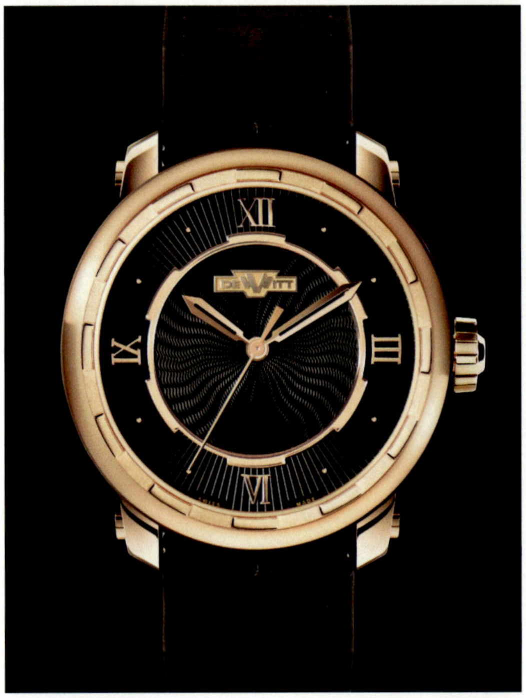

Dial: black velvet color; two-zone guilloché: internal with flame pattern and external with baguette pattern; circle applique with columns, Roman numerals and cabochons; open-worked hour and minute hands in the shape of two-edged swords.
Strap: matte black alligator leather; 18K rose-gold pin buckle; engraved "W" signature.
Note: limited edition of 500 pieces.

TWENTY-8-EIGHT TOURBILLON REF. T8.TH.53.001

Movement: manual-winding DW8028 caliber; Ø 14.6, thickness: 7.45mm; 72-hour power reserve; 19 jewels; 18,000 vph; 185 components; variable-inertia Glucydur balance; spiral with Breguet curve sequenced at 2.5 Hz.
Functions: hours, minutes; tourbillon.
Case: 18K rose gold; Ø 43mm, thickness: 10.28mm; adorned with DeWitt's imperial columns pattern on the flanks; 18K rose-gold polished crown adorned with a blackened titanium ring with "W" signature; sapphire crystal caseback secured with screws; water resistant to 3atm.
Dial: refined, hand-made guilloché tapestry in the center; miniature "W" pattern; three hand-engraved dotted circles on the periphery separating the hours, minutes and seconds indications; open-worked hour and minute hands in the shape of two-edged swords.
Strap: matte black alligator leather; 18K rose-gold triple-blade folding clasp; engraved "W" signature.
Note: limited edition of 250 pieces.

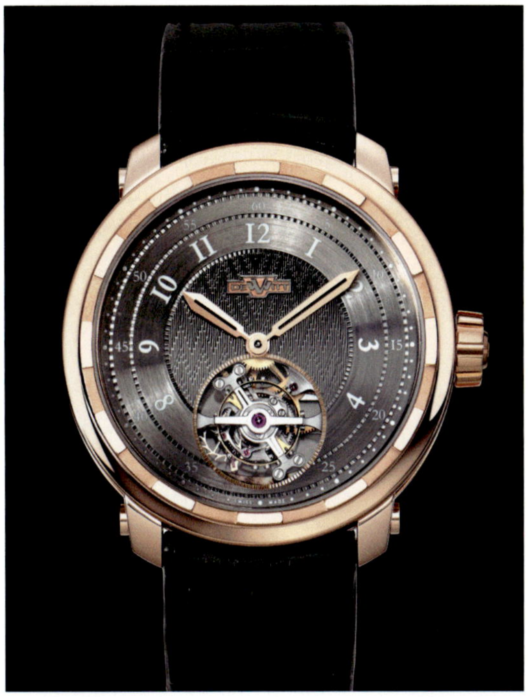

TWENTY-8-EIGHT REGULATOR A.S.W. HORIZONS REF. T8.TA.53.011

Movement: automatic sequential-winding (A.S.W.) device; driven by a peripheral oscillating rotor; dead-beat second is directly connected to the tourbillon cage; Ø 37mm, thickness: 6.38mm; 72-hour power reserve; 34 jewels; 18,000 vph; 320 components; variable-inertia Glucydur balance; Straumann Hairspring® spiral with Phillips curve sequenced at 2.5 Hz.
Functions: hours, minutes; dead-beat seconds; power reserve indicator.
Case: 18K rose gold; Ø 46mm, thickness: 12.88mm; adorned with DeWitt's imperial columns pattern on the flanks; 18K rose-gold polished crown adorned with a blackened titanium ring with "W" signature; sapphire crystal caseback secured with screws; water resistant to 3atm.
Dial: tinted sapphire with chocolate-brown tonalities; central appliqué and printed 5N color numerals; open-worked hour and minute hands in the shape of two-edged swords; thin and elegant dead-beat seconds hand; thin power reserve hand with 5N colored tip.
Strap: semi-matte dark brown alligator leather; 18K rose-gold triple-blade folding clasp; engraved "W" signature.
Note: limited edition of 250 pieces.

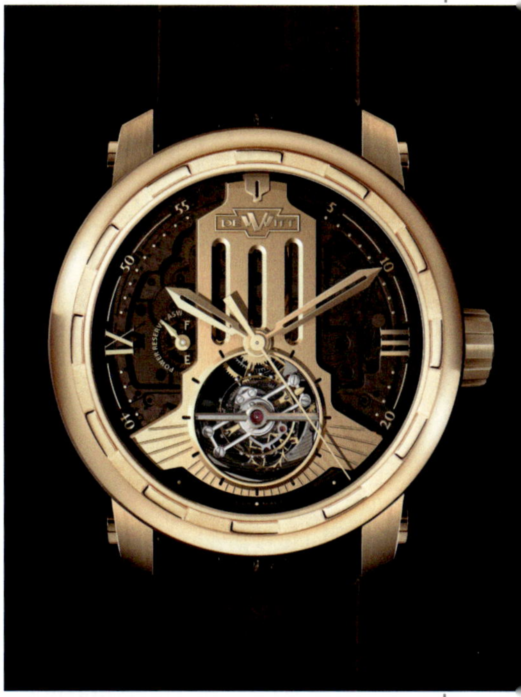

ACADEMIA REPETITION MINUTES TOURBILLON GMT ANTIPODE REF. AC.8900.38.M060

Movement: manual-winding DW8900 caliber; 72-hour power reserve; 46 jewels; 21,600 vph; four-armed Gyromaz balance; flat balance spring; black-gold Côtes de Genève.
Functions: hours, minutes; minute repeater; GMT; tourbillon.
Case: titanium grade 5 and white-gold PVD; Ø 45.5mm, thickness: 16.8mm; water resistant to 3atm.
Dial: tinted sapphire crystal.
Bracelet: titanium grade 5 and black PVD; integrated folding clasp.
Note: limited edition of 25 pieces.

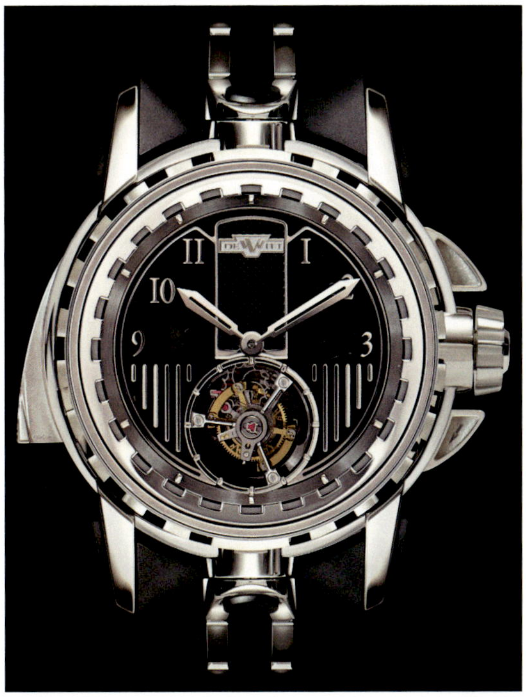

WX-1 REF. WX-1.36.M1100

Movement: manual-winding; made in black eloxed lithium-aluminium; 504-hour power reserve; 21,600 vph; vertical flying tourbillon; electronically driven pointed tool, or by hand; Glucydur balance; flat balance spring.
Functions: hours, minutes displayed by rotating discs; vertical flying tourbillon.
Case: 18K rose gold, titanium and aluminum; length: 72.51mm, width: 48.64mm; thickness: 21.17mm; inter-horn width: 24mm; sapphire crystal screw-on caseback; water resistant to 3atm.
Strap: black rubber; 18K rose-gold buckle.
Note: strictly limited edition to 33 pieces.

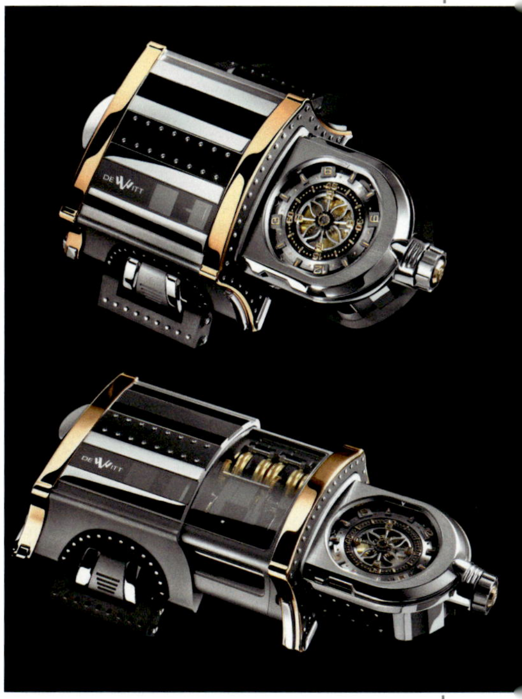

DIOR HORLOGERIE

OR THE HERITAGE OF THE ART OF HAUTE COUTURE

Designed in the Avenue Montaigne studios, the Dior Christal, La D de Dior and Chiffre Rouge timepieces are continually reinventing and reviving the same spirit of creativity, excellence and exceptionalness that has animated the fashion house since 1947.

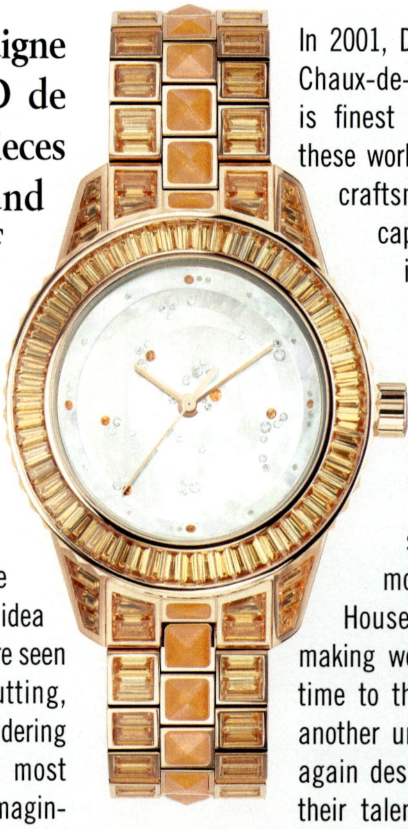

Time is precious in an Haute Couture house. The closer it gets to the day of the show, the more every second counts, the more every idea fuses together. And the more the seamstresses are seen making miracles—cutting, draping, sewing, embroidering and embellishing the most exceptional dresses imaginable. For Christian Dior in Paris, all the floors at 30 Avenue Montaigne live in step with the exciting and bustling rhythm of the design studio. Time is precious. In the real and in the figurative sense, since this house now creates haute horlogerie in the same spirit of creativity, excellence and exceptionalness that animates the elaboration of an haute couture dress. Dior Haute Horlogerie is in a permanent state of creation. The house's artistic directors are given free rein with their imaginations, making sketches and expressing their desires. Then, they pass the baton to expert Swiss watchmakers who translate their ideas into terms of feasibility.

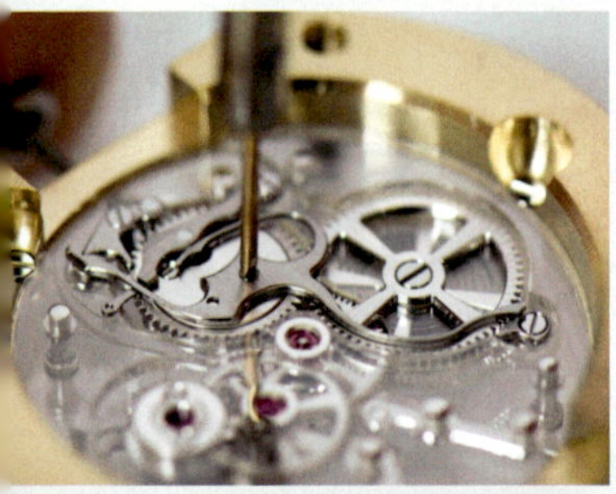

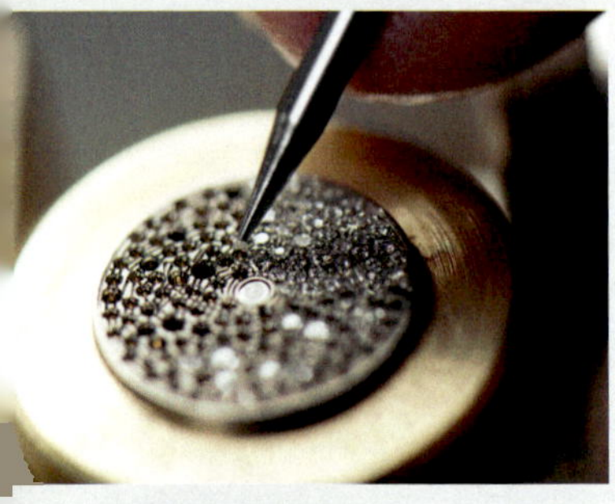

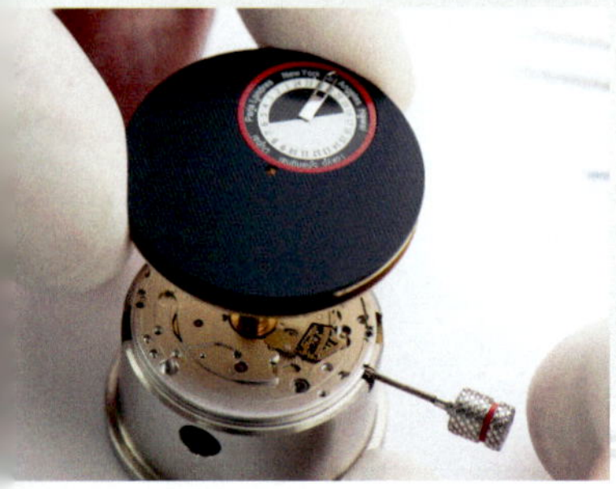

In 2001, Dior set up its own production unit at La Chaux-de-Fonds, the legendary cradle of all that is finest in Swiss timekeeping. Two years later, these workshops, including a team of watchmaking craftsman and development experts, proved their capacity to combine creation, tradition and innovation with the development of the La D de Dior. Victoire de Castellane had dreamed of a watch with a dual personality. On the one hand, she imagined a classic, almost masculine design in sparse, 1970s-inspired lines; on the other hand, a more vivacious style created by precious stones in seductive colors in the same mode as the high jewelry she designs for the House of Dior. The following year, the watchmaking workshops at La Chaux-de-Fonds set their time to the radical chic of Dior Homme. This was another universe with a whole other story, yet here again designers and technicians knew how to team their talents and know-how, producing the Chiffre Rouge timepiece that attracted the admiration of connoisseurs as soon as it was launched. Finally in 2005, another challenge, another innovation: John Galliano sought to transpose the ultra-femininity of his designs into the world of watchmaking.

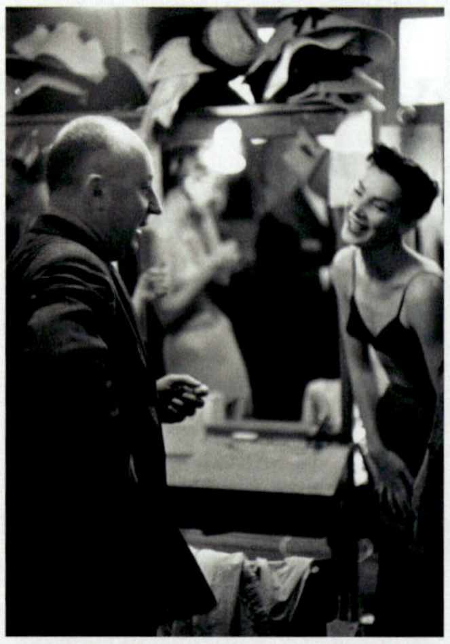

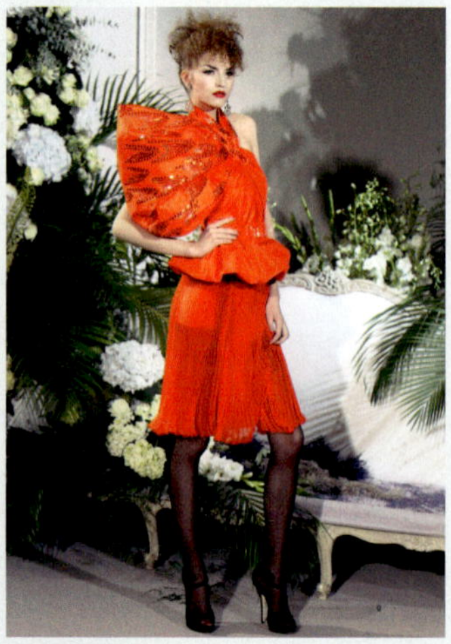

The floors at 30 Avenue Montaigne live in step with the exciting and bustling rhythm of the design studio.

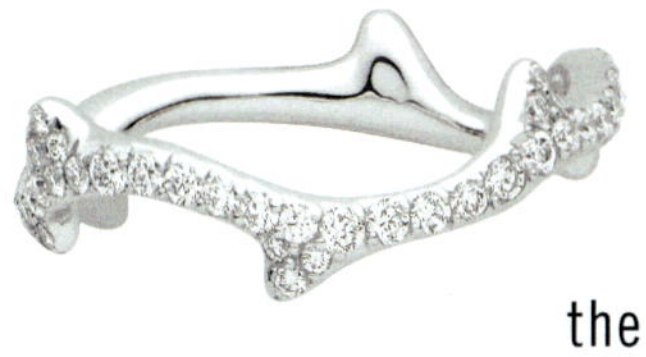

Famous for his fondness for fashion twists, the designer now launched a new take on sapphire crystal, the traditional material for a watch's glass, by using it to inlay the bezel and bracelet with inserts and pyramids. From the very outset, the couture allure of the Dior Christal wristwatch compelled recognition.

In 2008, its preciousness was accentuated even further with the launch of the Dior Christal Tourbillon fitted with one of the greatest watchmaking movements and enhanced by the unusual transparent design of the mechanism.

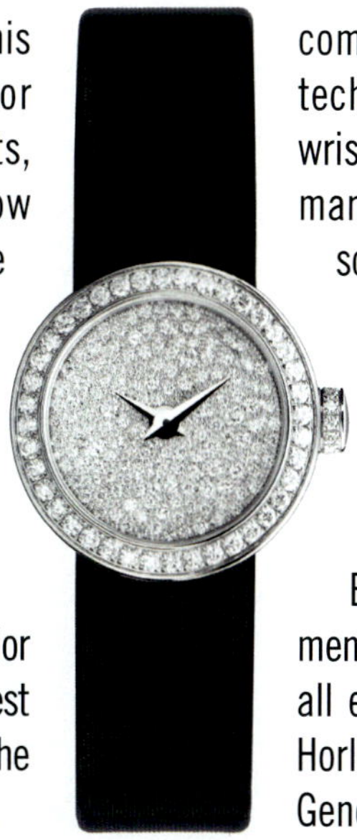

DIOR IN TIME: WITH THE GREAT WATCHMAKERS

Watchmaking innovation and savoir-faire in the service of creation and new ideas: in fact, it took Dior very little time to propose timepieces that renew traditional watchmaking. It's a question of style...and of haute couture as well as an haute horlogerie mindset, since both of these domains devoted to exceptional craftsmanship have more than one thing in common. As the show draws closer, the seamstresses of a fashion house can neither do nor know how to do absolutely everything, so Dior turns to outside specialized artisans for the feather work or the making of lace and embroidery. In the same way, when a designer imagines a watch requiring a specific technology, mechanism or effect not within the competence of the workshops at Chaux-de-Fonds, Dior Horlogerie never hesitates to call upon specialists' talents. This was notably the case for the launch of the Dior Christal "mystérieuse." John Galliano had wanted a completely transparent movement. This technology existed for clocks but not for wristwatches. At least, not until the Quinting manufacture proposed an electro-mechanical solution that met the challenge made by the House of Dior's designer.

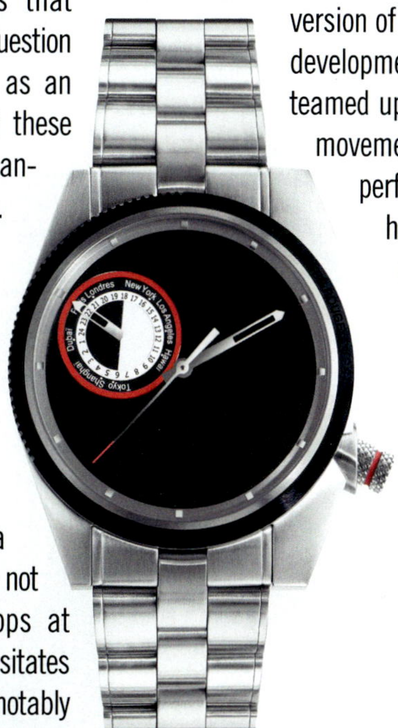

Time is stimulating and precious in all its forms of creation, yet paradoxically these are crafts that never count the hours it takes to achieve the sublime. Beautiful workmanship, exquisite embellishment and meticulous festooning or paving are all extremely important details. Therefore, Dior Horlogerie turned to the Maison Bunter in Geneva, recognized by the entire profession for the precious stone settings of its haute horlogerie. For the mechanisms, it called upon another choice partner, the Zenith manufacture, for the making of the "irreducible" movement in the Chiffre rouge limited series, for its hand-wound elite movement in the 42mm La D de Dior timepiece, as well as for the automatic version of the Dior Christal Diamonds. For the development of its tourbillon caliber, Dior also teamed up with the conceiver of the Concepto movement. All these mechanical feats perfectly illustrate the spirit of haute horlogerie inhabiting these treasures of precision that push back the boundaries of the impossible again and again. This is also the spirit of haute couture, a spirit constantly questioning itself, never hesitating to break with habit while tirelessly aiming for perfection.

FACING PAGE
TOP Dior Christal "Passage n°2"

THIS PAGE
TOP CENTER La Mini D de Dior
BOTTOM Chiffre Rouge T01

DIOR CHRISTAL DIAMONDS AND PYTHON — REF. CD114561A001

Movement: automatic Elite calibre by Zénith for Dior; 50-hour power reserve; oscillating weight with white mother-of-pearl.
Functions: hours, minutes, seconds.
Case: 18K white gold; Ø 38mm; bezel set with 79 baguette diamonds (3.09 carats); crown set with a rose-cut diamond (0.2 carat); horns set with 12 baguette diamonds (1.1 carats); transparent sapphire crystal caseback; water resistant to 5atm.
Dial: white mother-of-pearl marquetry; set with 290 diamonds (1.46 carats).
Strap: black python; 18K white-gold ardillon buckle with white mother-of-pearl.
Note: limited edition of 10 pieces.

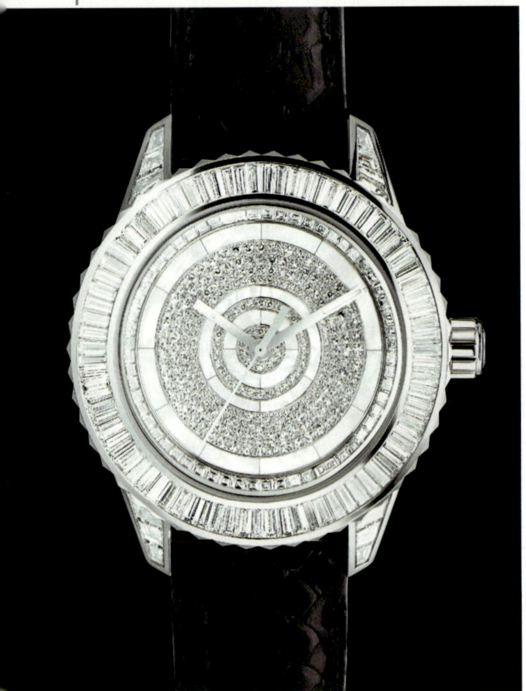

DIOR CHRISTAL TOURBILLON BLACK DIAMONDS — REF. CD115963A001

Movement: manual-winding Dior tourbillon calibre; 80-hour power reserve.
Functions: hours, minutes.
Case: 18K white gold; Ø 42mm; bezel set with 25 black baguette diamonds (1.68 carats); black sapphire crystal inserts; crown set with a rose-cut black diamond (0.34 carat); transparent sapphire crystal caseback; water resistant to 5atm.
Dial: transparent shaded gray sapphire crystal; set with 43 baguette black diamonds (0.96 carat).
Strap: hand made double-sided alligator; 18K white-gold ardillon buckle, set with 13 baguette black diamonds (1 carat).
Note: limited edition of 15 pieces.

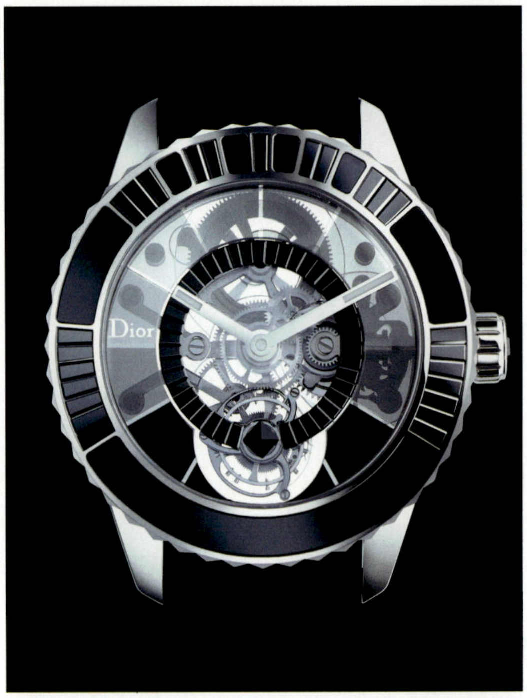

DIOR CHRISTAL GOLD & LACQUER — REF. CD114750A001

Movement: automatic-winding Dior calibre "8 Fuseaux Horaires"; 42-hour power reserve; oscillating weight with gold leaf.
Functions: hours, minutes, seconds; eight time zones; day-night indicator.
Case: 18K yellow gold; Ø 38mm; bezel set with black sapphire crystal; transparent sapphire crystal caseback; water resistant to 5atm.
Dial: lacquer; golden and white mother-of-pearl, gold leaf.
Hands: hour indicator on the eight time zone satellite; golden minute and black second hands.
Strap: black python; 18K yellow-gold ardillon buckle.
Note: limited edition of eight pieces.

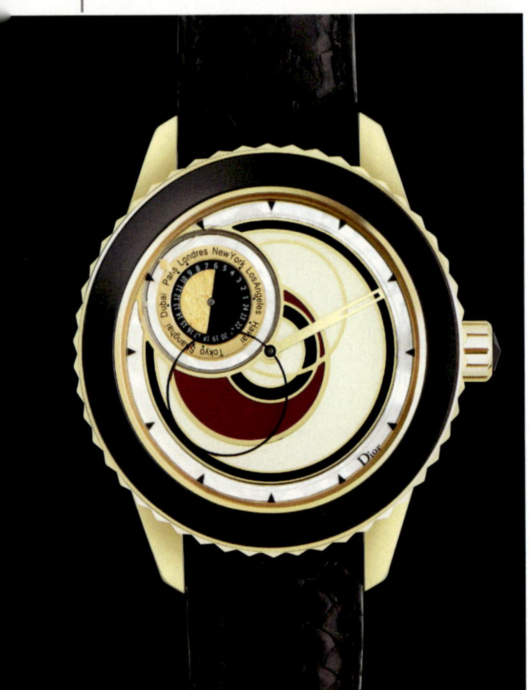

DIOR CHRISTAL MOTHER-OF-PEARL & DIAMONDS — REF. CD114710M001

Movement: automatic Dior calibre "8 Fuseaux Horaires"; 42-hour power reserve; golden oscillating weight.
Functions: hours, minutes, seconds; eight time zones; day-night indicator.
Case: stainless steel; Ø 38mm; bezel set with 120 diamonds (1.5 carats); transparent sapphire crystal caseback with white mother-of-pearl; water resistant to 5atm.
Dial: golden and white mother-of-pearl.
Hands: hour indicator on the eight time zone satellite; golden minute and white second hands.
Bracelet: stainless steel; set with three rows of white sapphire crystal inserts.
Note: limited edition of 100 pieces.

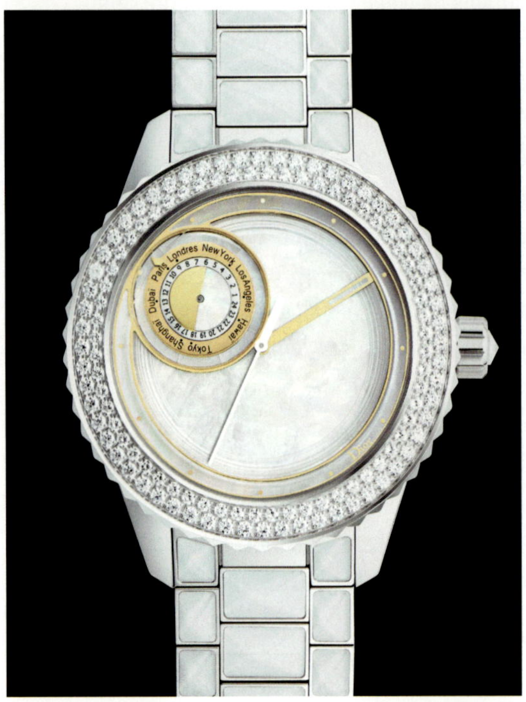

DIOR CHRISTAL MYSTERIEUSE REF. CD114411M001

Movement: electromechanical movement by Quinting Manufacture for Dior.
Functions: hours, minutes, seconds.
Case: stainless steel; Ø 38mm; bezel set with 58 diamonds (0.725 carat) and black sapphire crystal inserts; central ring set with 38 diamonds (0.19 carat); transparent sapphire crystal caseback; water resistant to 5atm.
Dial: six plates decorated with mother-of-pearl; white, black, golden and gray metallizations.
Bracelet: stainless steel; set with three rows of black sapphire crystal inserts.
Note: limited edition of 200 pieces.

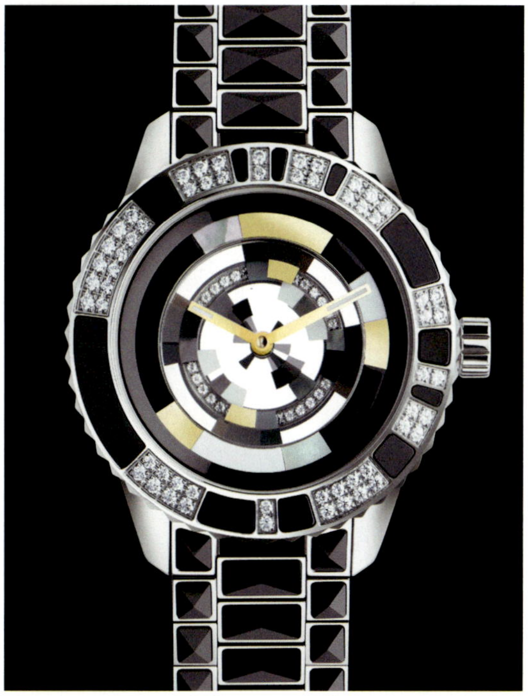

DIOR CHRISTAL AUTOMATIC BLACK REF. CD115511M001

Movement: ETA automatic; 42-hour power reserve; black lacquered oscillating weight.
Functions: hours, minutes, seconds; date.
Case: stainless steel; Ø 42mm; bezel set with 84 diamonds (1.05 carats) and black sapphire crystal inserts; transparent sapphire crystal caseback; water resistant to 5atm.
Dial: black, lacquered; set with 106 diamonds (0.42 carat).
Bracelet: stainless steel; set with three rows of black sapphire crystal inserts.

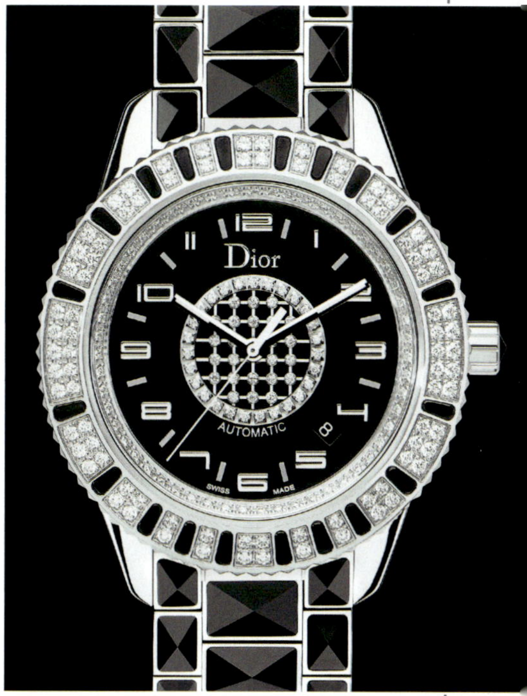

DIOR CHRISTAL RED REF. CD11311CA001

Movement: ETA quartz.
Functions: hours, minutes, seconds; date.
Case: stainless steel; Ø 33mm; bezel set with 97 diamonds (0.58 carat) and white sapphire crystal inserts; water resistant to 5atm.
Dial: white mother-of-pearl; silver sun-brushed.
Strap: red patent calf.

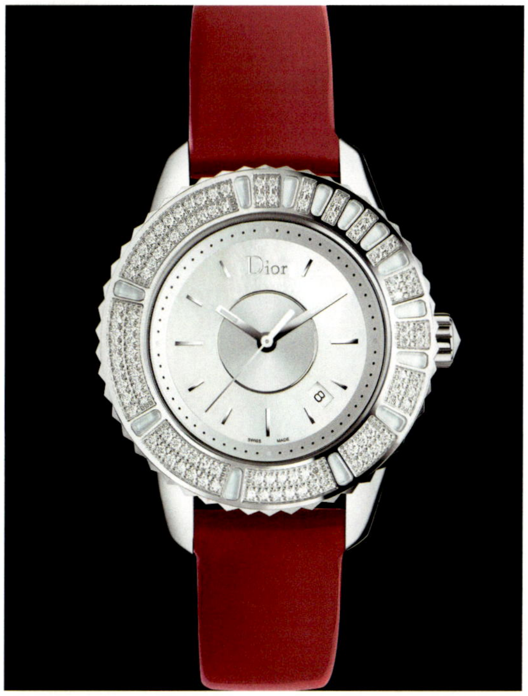

DIOR CHRISTAL BLACK REF. CD112119A001

Movement: ETA quartz.
Functions: hours, minutes, seconds.
Case: stainless steel; Ø 28mm; bezel set with 109 diamonds (0.54 carat) and a black sapphire crystal insert; water resistant to 5atm.
Dial: black, lacquered and sun-brushed.
Strap: black patent calf.

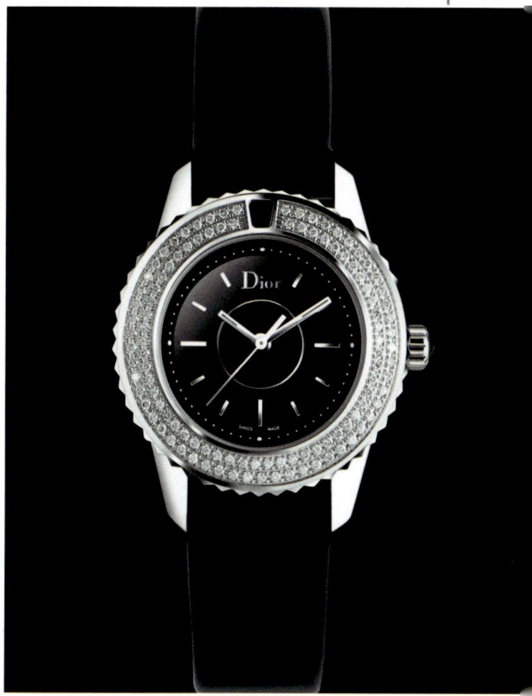

CHIFFRE ROUGE T01 — REF. CD085710M001

Movement: automatic Dior calibre "8 Fuseaux Horaires"; 42-hour power reserve; oscillating weight with guilloché pattern.
Functions: hours, minutes, seconds; eight time zones; day-night indicator.
Case: stainless steel; Ø 42mm; ceramic bezel; transparent black sapphire caseback; water resistant to 5atm.
Dial: black, sun-brushed with "piqué de coton" pattern.
Bracelet: stainless steel.
Note: limited edition to 100 pieces.

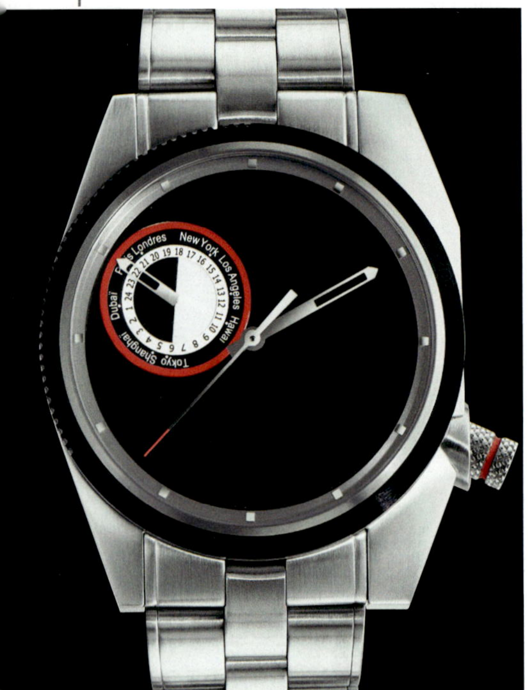

CHIFFRE ROUGE A05 — REF. CD084840R001

Movement: ETA automatic chronograph chronometer; COSC-certified; 42-hour power reserve.
Functions: chronograph; hours, minutes, seconds; date; tachymeter.
Case: stainless steel; Ø 41mm; molded with black rubber; translucent red mineral caseback; water resistant to 5atm.
Dial: black, sun-brushed with tachymeter scale.
Bracelet: stainless steel molded with black rubber.

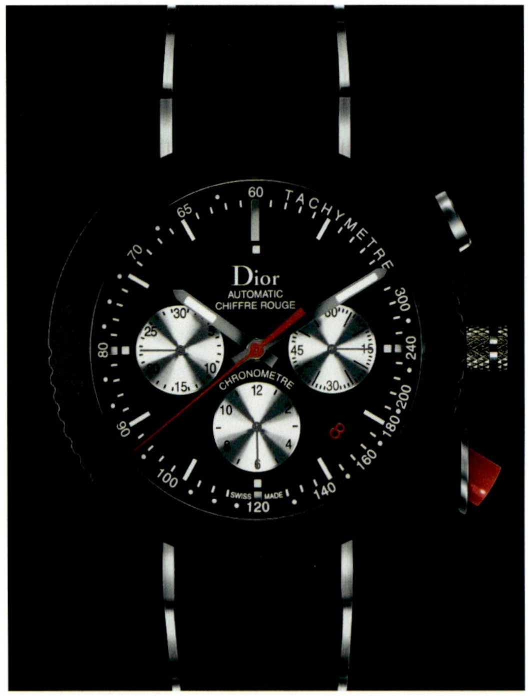

CHIFFRE ROUGE A03 — REF. CD084510A001

Movement: ETA automatic; 42-hour power reserve.
Functions: hours, minutes, seconds; date.
Case: stainless steel; Ø 36mm; translucent black sapphire caseback; water resistant to 5atm.
Dial: black sun-brushed.
Strap: black fabric; ardillon buckle.

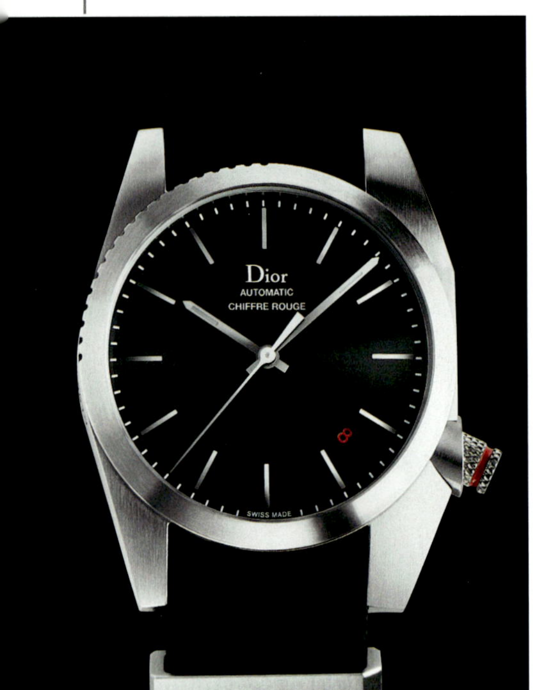

CHIFFRE ROUGE I02 — REF. CD084860A001

Movement: automatic chronograph chronometer, "Irréductible" calibre by Zénith for Dior; COSC-certified; 50-hour power reserve.
Functions: hours, minutes, seconds; date; chronograph.
Case: 18K white gold; Ø 38mm; crown and pushbutton set with 26 diamonds (0.23 carat); opalescent sapphire caseback set with 1 diamond (0.01 carat); water resistant to 5atm.
Dial: white lacquered; set with 4 baguette diamonds (0.12 carat).
Strap: double-sided black alligator; white-gold ardillon buckle.

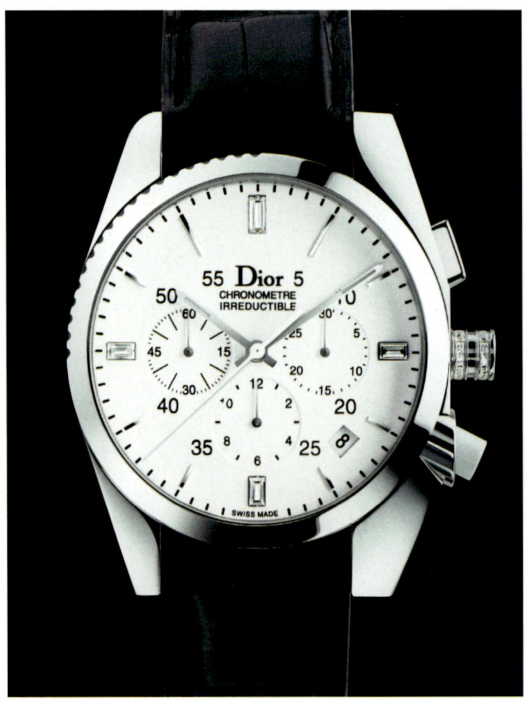

LA MINI D DE DIOR SNOW SET — REF. CD040160A001

Movement: ETA quartz.
Functions: hours, minutes.
Case: 18K white gold; Ø 19mm; bezel set with 40 diamonds (0.32 carat); crown set with 13 diamonds (0.03 carat); water resistant to 3atm.
Dial: 18K white gold; set with 145 diamonds (0.46 carat).
Strap: black satin; white-gold ardillon buckle, set with 29 diamonds (0.14 carat).

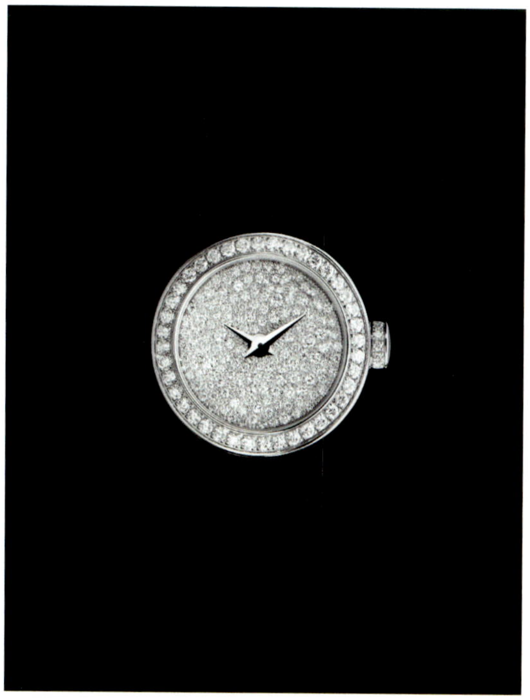

LA MINI D DE DIOR — REF. CD040110A006

Movement: ETA quartz.
Functions: hours, minutes.
Case: stainless steel; Ø 19mm; bezel set with 40 diamonds (0.32 carat); crown set with 13 diamonds (0.03 carat); water resistant to 3atm.
Dial: white mother-of-pearl.
Strap: black patent calf; ardillon buckle, set with 18 diamonds (0.11 carat).

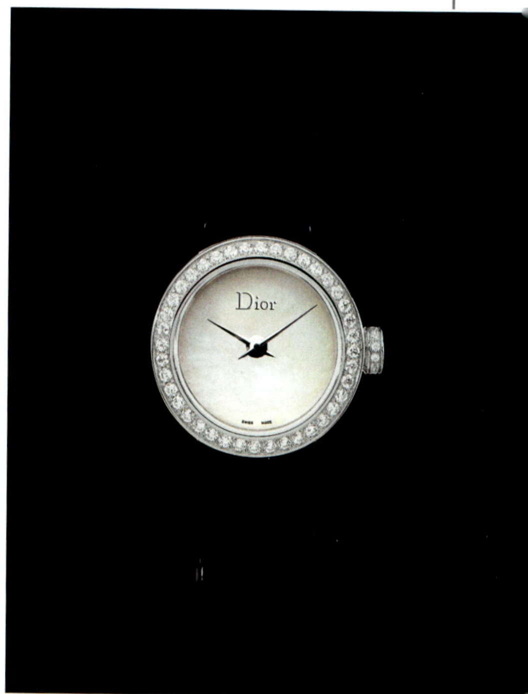

LA D DE DIOR 25MM — REF. CD040160A001

Movement: ETA quartz.
Functions: hours, minutes.
Case: stainless steel; Ø 25mm; bezel set with 50 diamonds (0.5 carat); crown set with 13 diamonds (0.03 carat); water resistant to 3atm.
Dial: silver; set with four diamonds (0.02 carat).
Bracelet: stainless steel.

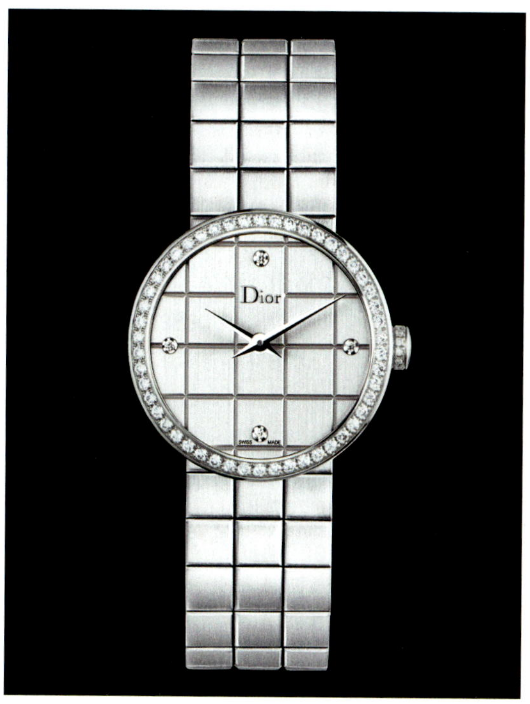

LA D DE DIOR OPAL — REF. CD043960A001

Movement: manual-winding Elite calibre by Zénith for Dior; 50-hour power reserve.
Functions: hours, minutes.
Case: 18K white gold; Ø 38mm; bezel set with 76 diamonds (0.76 carat); crown set with 18 diamonds (0.11 carat); transparent sapphire crystal caseback; water resistant to 3atm.
Dial: black opal (Australia).
Strap: black satin; 18K white-gold ardillon buckle, set with 64 diamonds (0.55 carat).
Note: limited edition of 5 pieces.

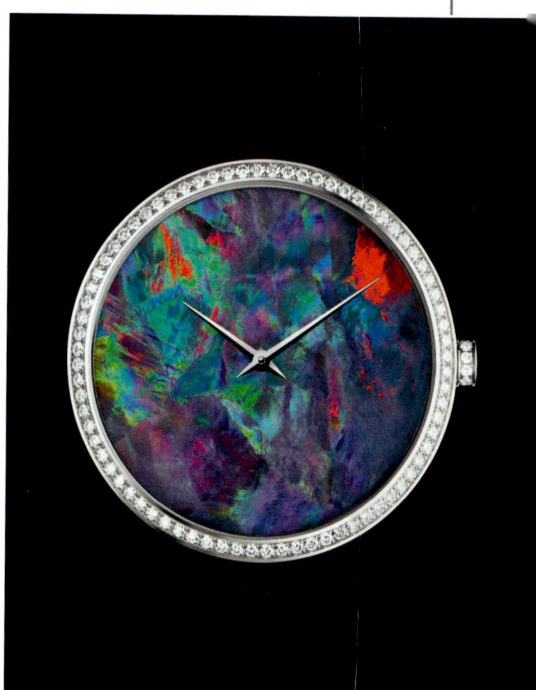

ETERNA

Nothing but Watchmaking.
Since 1856.

TIME ROLLS ON...

Eterna has always been a leader in horological development. For over 150 years, the Swiss brand has developed a reputation for coming up with new and exciting innovations that have advanced the industry as a whole, and the brand continues to delight watchmaking aficionados with innovations such as the Eterna Spherodrive, as well as variations on classic themes.

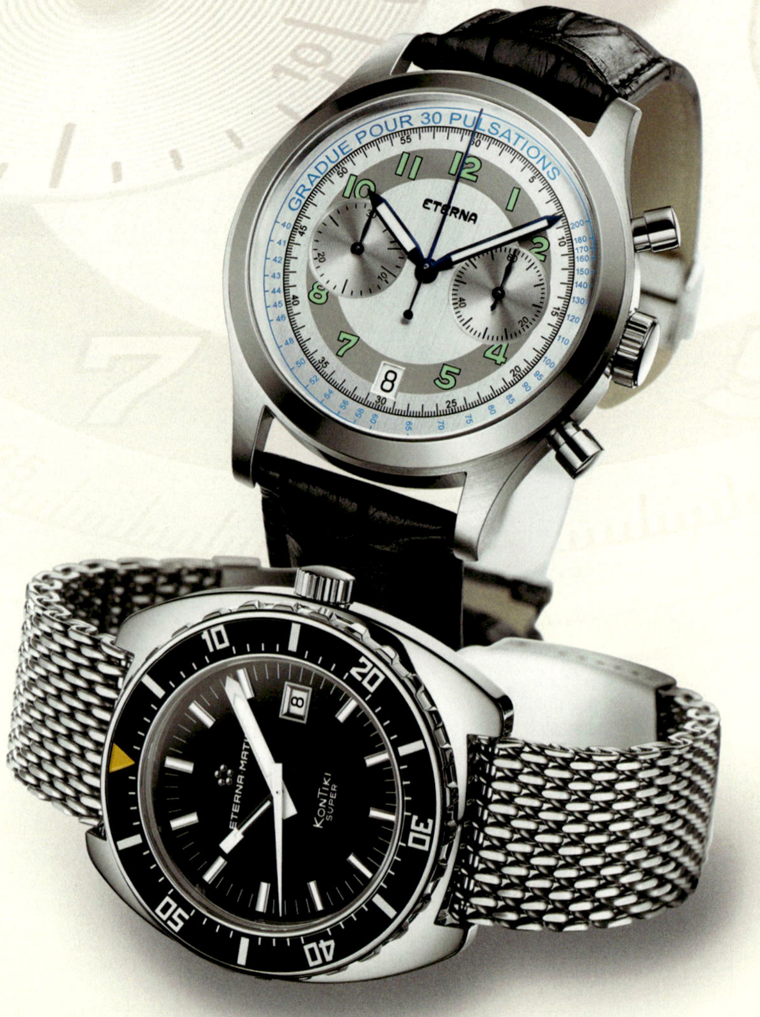

Its new Heritage Collection explores this rich legacy, starting with two of the Swiss brand's most iconic pieces: the Pulsometer Limited Edition 1942 and the Super KonTiki Limited Edition 1973. First designed in 1942 for medical professionals, the new iteration of the Pulsometer is available in a limited edition of 1,942 pieces, each one engraved with its edition number. The movement possesses a power reserve of 42 hours, and the round case measures 42mm across. The Heritage version of the Pulsometer is true to the original in many important respects, retaining its classic blue- and green-accented dial layout with a pulsometric scale, minute totalizer and small seconds subdial. Added for the contemporary Eterna fan is a date window at 6 o'clock.

The Super KonTiki takes its name from Thor Heyerdahl's celebrated rafting voyage, a journey on which Heyerdahl and his crew all wore their trusted Eterna watches. As one of Eterna's most successful designs, the KonTiki has been periodically redesigned and reissued to a faithful audience, and the Super KonTiki Limited Edition 1973 revisits a version of this classic piece from the 1970s. To commemorate this signal year, the watch is being released in a limited edition of 1,973 pieces, with each caseback bearing an engraved edition number and a KonTiki medallion. The watch's cambered rectangular case sports a retro rotating bezel, adorned with alternating Arabic numerals and hour markers.

Launched at BaselWorld to wide acclaim, the Madison Eight-Days combines a practical sophistication with revolutionary solutions to age-old conundrums. Its stainless steel case houses the Eterna 3510 Caliber, fitted with Eterna's brilliantly innovative Eterna Spherodrive, which mounts the spring barrel on ball bearings.

Subtle lateral decorations on the case are just one mark of the timepiece's attention to detail. The dial face, available in black, gray or silver variations, features a textured center, with a sunray pattern emanating out to the minute markers. The rhodium-plated or gold-colored seconds hand matches the hour markers, and the hour and minute hands are graced with a luminescent coating for nighttime readability. The watch's name bears witness to one of its most salient and useful qualities: a power reserve of eight days. This power reserve is indicated by a unique display between 7 and 8 o'clock, directly across the dial from the oversized date window. The unusual positions of these two functions highlight their unequaled usefulness for the practical traveler.

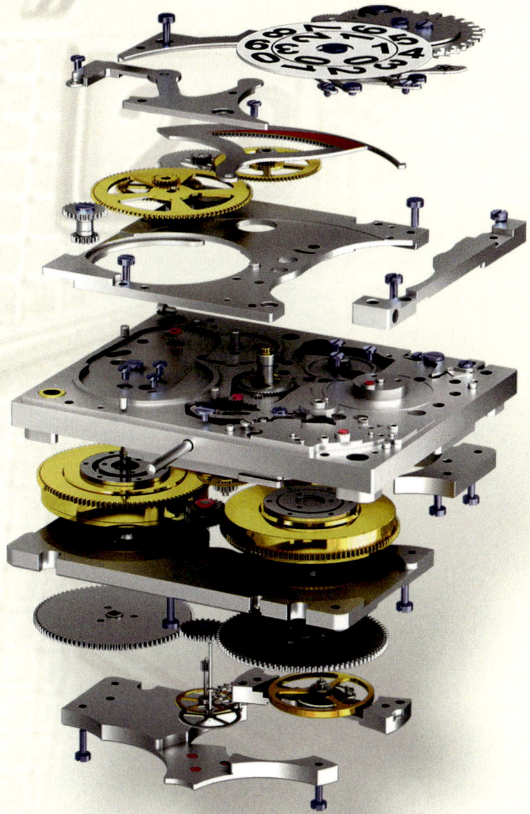

FACING PAGE

TOP RIGHT Powered by the automatic ETA 2894-2 movement, the Heritage Pulsometer Limited Edition 1942 is housed in a polished and brushed stainless steel case that provides water resistance to 50m (5 bar).

BOTTOM RIGHT Eterna's Heritage Super KonTiki Limited Edition 1973 pays homage to its namesake voyage with several touches, including water resistance to 200m (20 bar), power reserve of 38 hours, and a polished stainless steel mesh bracelet with diver's extension and safety clasp.

THIS PAGE

TOP RIGHT The Eterna Spherodrive, housed in the Eterna 3510 caliber, features a double ball bearing system, practically eliminating the friction usually endured by the barrel spring.

RIGHT The Madison Eight-Days is available with a silver, gray or black dial, on a brown, gray or black Louisiana alligator leather strap.

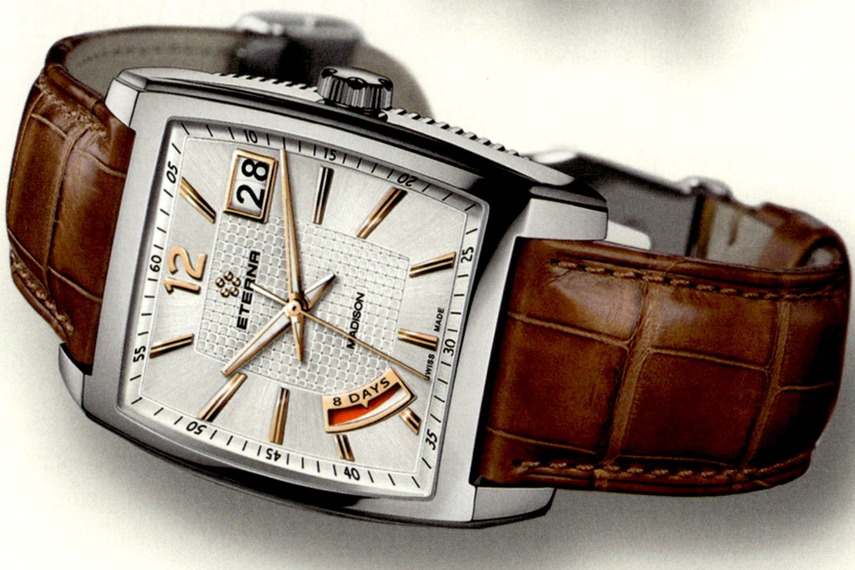

The major innovation driving the 3510 Caliber is the Eterna Spherodrive. Eterna's engineers solved the problem of friction by mounting the barrel spring on zirconium oxide ball bearings, eliminating the need for lubrication.

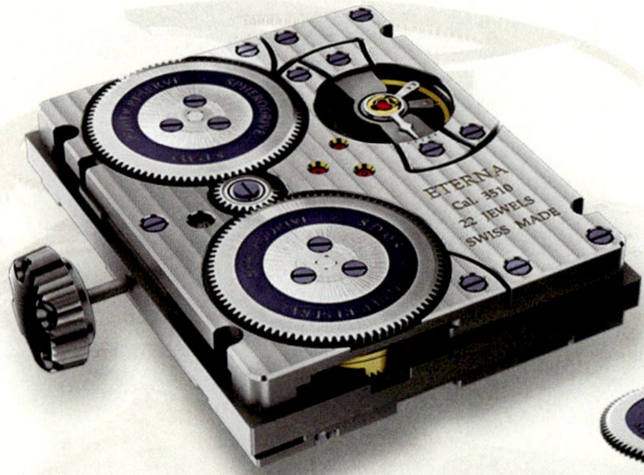

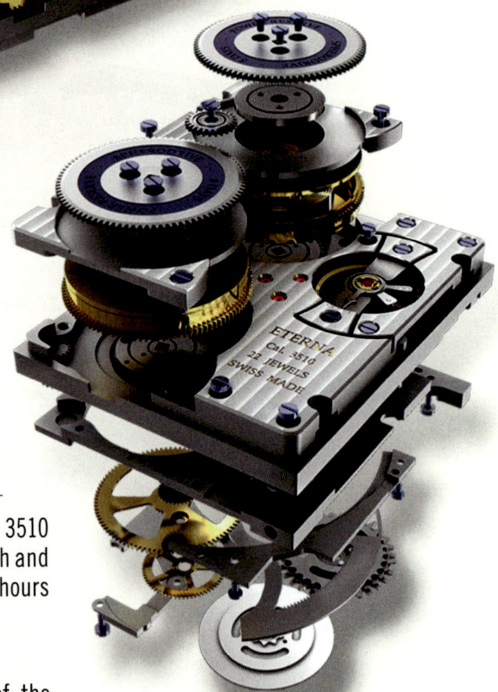

ABOVE AND RIGHT

The proprietary Eterna Caliber 3510 movement beats at 28,800 vph and provides an exceptional 192 hours of power reserve.

FAR RIGHT

The understated elegance of the Madison Eight-Days's stainless steel case is only enhanced by the sapphire crystal porthole in the caseback, revealing the workings of the Eterna 3510 Caliber inside.

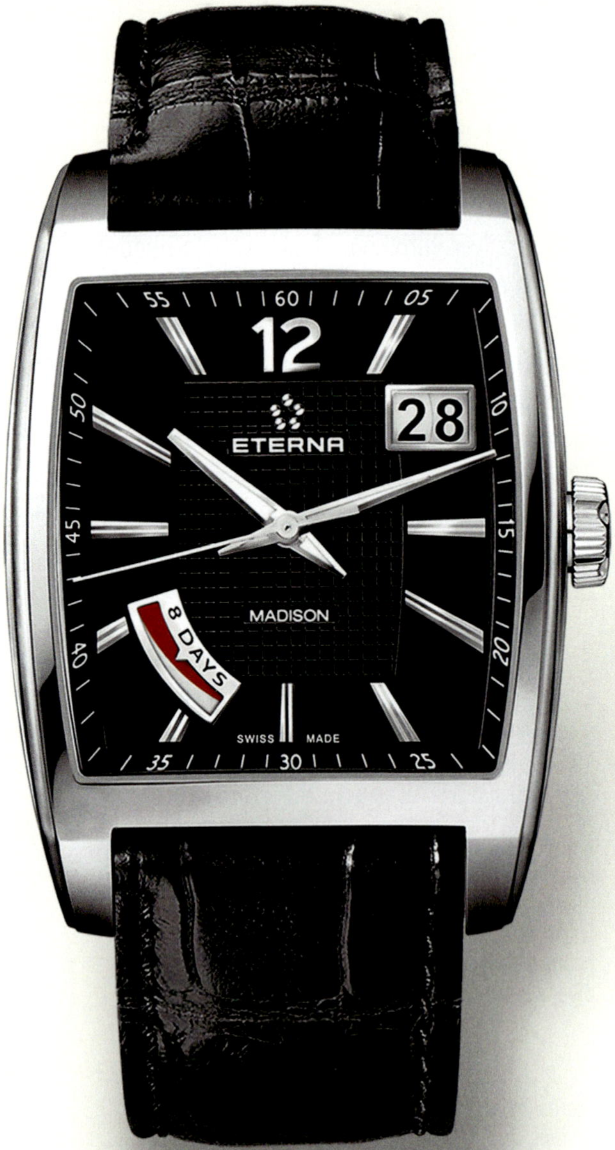

Within the Madison Eight-Days beats Eterna's 3510 Caliber, which possesses several spectacular innovations. The two series-coupled barrels provide all three hands of the watch with eight days of unparalleled smooth and regular operation, shown in the 192 hour gradations of the red and white power reserve indicator. To ensure the precise functioning of the movement, the Eterna 3510 includes an automatic cutoff of the balance wheel after eight days of nonstop functioning. The fast-acting date corrector at 10 o'clock can be used at any hour of the day or night, a perfect match for any traveler who finds himself regularly jetting from one time zone to another.

The major innovation driving the 3510 Caliber, however, is the Eterna Spherodrive. One eternal problem faced by watchmakers has been the pressure and friction endured by the balance spring, leading to wear and tear and necessitating lubrication and maintenance. Eterna's engineers solved this problem by completely rethinking the structure of the barrel spring, entirely obviating the need for lubrication by mounting the barrel spring on zirconium oxide ball bearings. This ultra-precise double ball bearing system is a great leap forward for the industry; not only does it create more stability for the spring barrel, but because the new system features a rolling motion, friction is almost totally eliminated as a force to be reckoned with. Because the Eterna Spherodrive has solved the friction problem, it requires much less maintenance than a traditional watch.

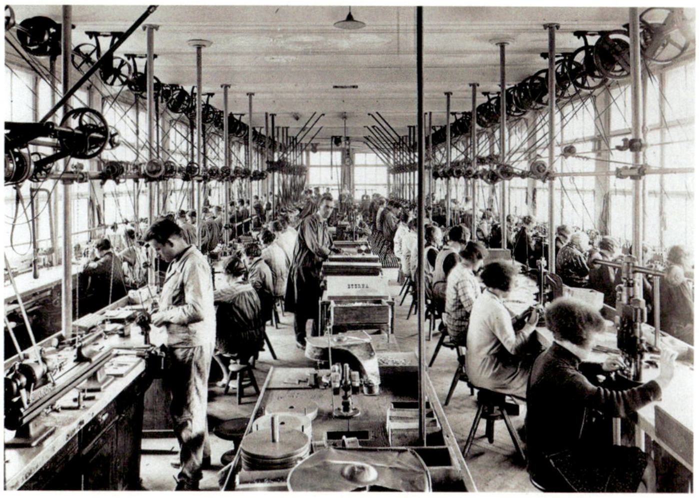

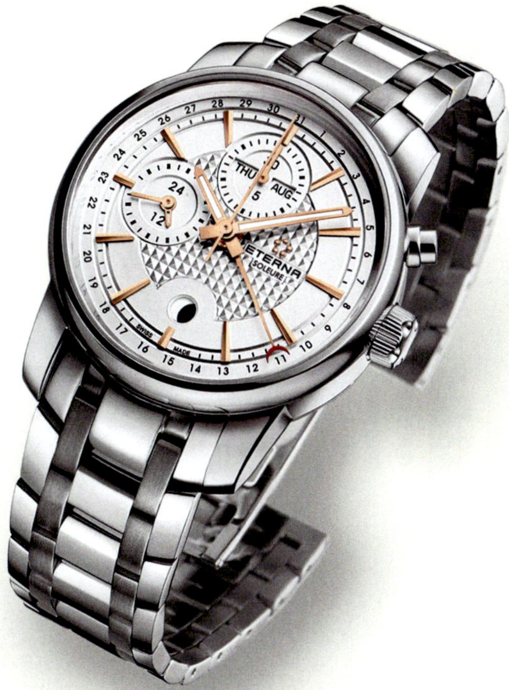

The latest movements—in both senses of the word—in the watch industry have always served as inspiration for Eterna's Soleure collection, which avails itself of the brand's inimitable alchemy to turn industry-wide trends into pieces that bear Eterna's unmistakable imprint. Named for the French name of the Swiss canton where Eterna was founded in 1865, Soleure is aimed at a younger, more fashion-forward crowd that includes increasing numbers of women. The Soleure Moonphase Chronograph is a shining example of why the collection has become Eterna's most accessible and popular. Sheathed in a polished stainless steel case with a 42mm diameter, its proprietary adaptation of ETA's Valjoux 7751 movement possesses 48 hours of power reserve. The chic dial, available in black or silver, shows off a center textured with a Clous de Paris motif, periodically interrupted by a 30-minute totalizer at 12 o'clock, an elegantly simple moonphase display at 6 o'clock, continuous seconds and 24-hour display at 9 o'clock. The sub-dial at 12 o'clock also features a date display that is completed by a fourth hand indicating the date printed on the rim of the dial. A variety of straps in Louisiana alligator leather or polished and satin-finished stainless steel finish off the look.

Women are also drawn to Eterna's Contessa line, the height of elegance and feminine determination. Eterna has always provided delightful horological options for women, mostly by concentrating on miniaturizing watches to sit as daintily as possible on the wrist. In 1950, Eterna released a record-breaking tiny self-winding movement, winning such glamorous fans as Gina Lollobrigida and Brigitte Bardot. The brand continues to develop its winning strategy with the sophisticated Contessa, crafted in stainless steel and set with Top Wesselton diamonds. The slightly concave Art Deco-inspired case boasts a diamond pavage, as well as diamond hour markers and a stone set in the crown for a final touch of luxury.

Combining a proven historical record with a feel for contemporary trends, Eterna never ceases to delight its following. From the tasteful elegance of the petite Contessa to the bold thinking behind the Eterna Spherodrive, Eterna proves its importance to the past, present and future of watchmaking.

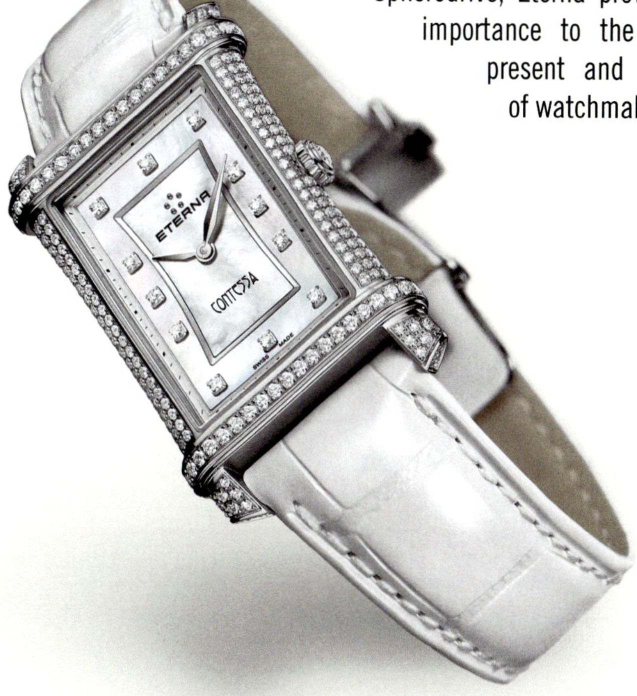

TOP LEFT

Eterna's engineers specialize in horological breakthroughs such as the Eterna Spherodrive, which solved several watchmaking puzzles in one fell swoop.

TOP RIGHT

The round stainless steel case of the Soleure Moonphase Chronograph offers water resistance to 50m (5 bar), and its dial features luminescent coating on the hour and minute hands, and the continuous seconds and 24-hour display at 9 o'clock.

RIGHT

Combining the strength of stainless steel and the delicate femininity of precious materials, the Contessa has a white mother-of-pearl dial to complement its gently curved form and choice of white or black Louisiana alligator leather straps.

FRANCK MULLER
GENEVE

Master of complications

IN FULL BLOOM

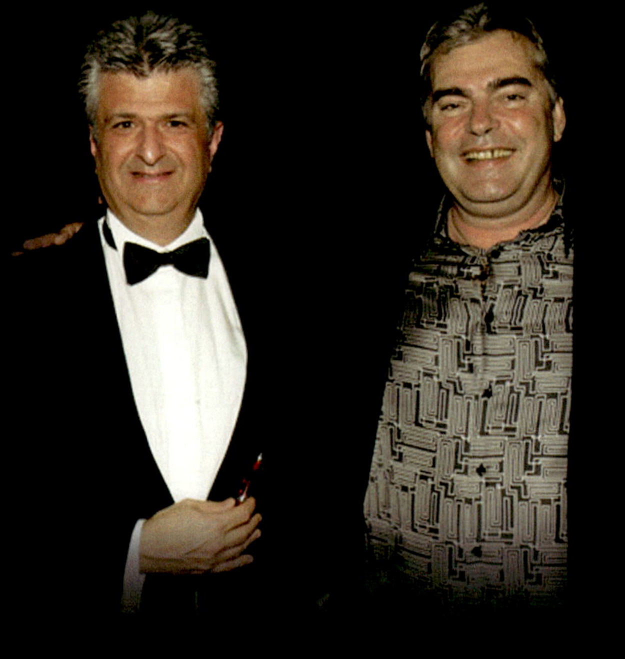

While working as an in-demand watch restorer in the early 1980s, Franck Muller decided to devote his energies to crafting wristwatch movements whose technical pedigree would rival that of the most complex pocket watches.

His journey began in 1983, when he introduced the first in an annual series of world premiere complications, each presented in a unique timepiece bearing his name. Each one an horological tour de force, his first creations included a tourbillon with jumping hours and an inverted tourbillon with a minute repeater and perpetual calendar.

Those early accomplishments culminated in 1992 with the unveiling of a wristwatch dubbed the most complicated in the world. The amazing timepiece integrated a grande and petite sonnerie, minute repeater, perpetual calendar, moonphase and an indicator that displayed the movement's internal temperature.

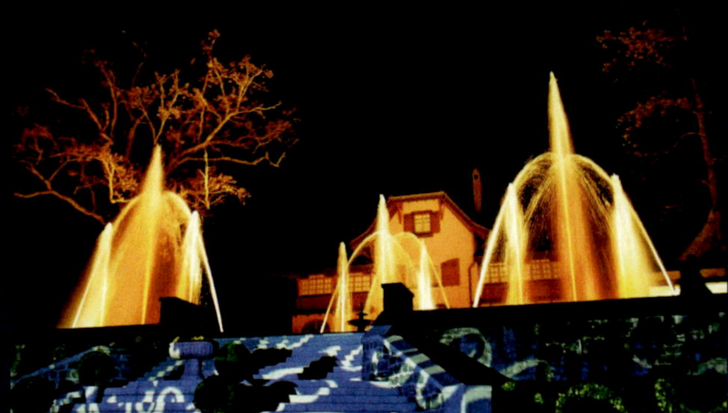

That same year, Muller started his eponymous company in Genthod, a village just outside the Swiss capital that overlooks Lake Geneva and offers a view of the snowcapped peak of Mont Blanc. After establishing its base of operations amid this picturesque backdrop, the company expanded rapidly, building a modern and growing industrial complex it calls Franck Muller Watchland.

Officially christened in 2001, the 38,000-square-foot site is dedicated to the art watchmaking. In one location, it unites all the trades necessary to produce a timepiece, from research to after-sales service. At the heart of the sprawling operation is the Franck Muller headquarters, which is housed in a Neo-Gothic mansion designed by Swiss architect Edmond Fatio in the early 1900s.

In less than 30 years, Muller has evolved from a rising star to a paragon of the watch world, earning both the respect of peers and the adoration of collectors.

Franck Muller intrigued connoisseurs of fine watchmaking in 1999 with the brand's Double Mystery. This innovative timepiece included a patented mechanism that showed the time using a pair of rotating discs instead of traditional hands.

More than a decade after its debut, the Double Mystery returns once again, this time with a new design that evokes the natural beauty of the shifting seasons. The Double Mystery Quatre Saisons offers a scintillating exhibition of Franck Muller's mastery of the traditional art of gem setting.

Franck Muller upholds its reputation for original complications and traditional artisanship with the Double Mystery Quatre Saisons, a gem-set beauty that tells time with rotating discs instead of hands.

This 42mm round ladies model features a striking bezel design that recreates the changing colors of the seasons with a progression of more than 200 colored round gemstones. Naturally, spring launches this sparkling parade around the case with a selection that includes emeralds and garnet tsavorites, followed by summer's orange and yellow sapphires; autumn's garnet pyropes and garnet spessartites; and winter's blue sapphires.

White diamonds cover the Double Mystery Quatre Saisons' dial except for the 12 colored gems used for the hour markers. Each rotating disc is adorned with a triangular colored stone to indicate the time, including a large gem for the hours and a small gem for the minutes.

A movement (FM 2892) crafted at the Franck Muller workshops in Genthod powers this creative display. The automatic caliber, which features a 42-hour power reserve, is displayed through the transparent caseback.

After weathering a generation of changing seasons, Franck Muller emerges in full bloom to continue surprising and delighting collectors with its beguiling creativity.

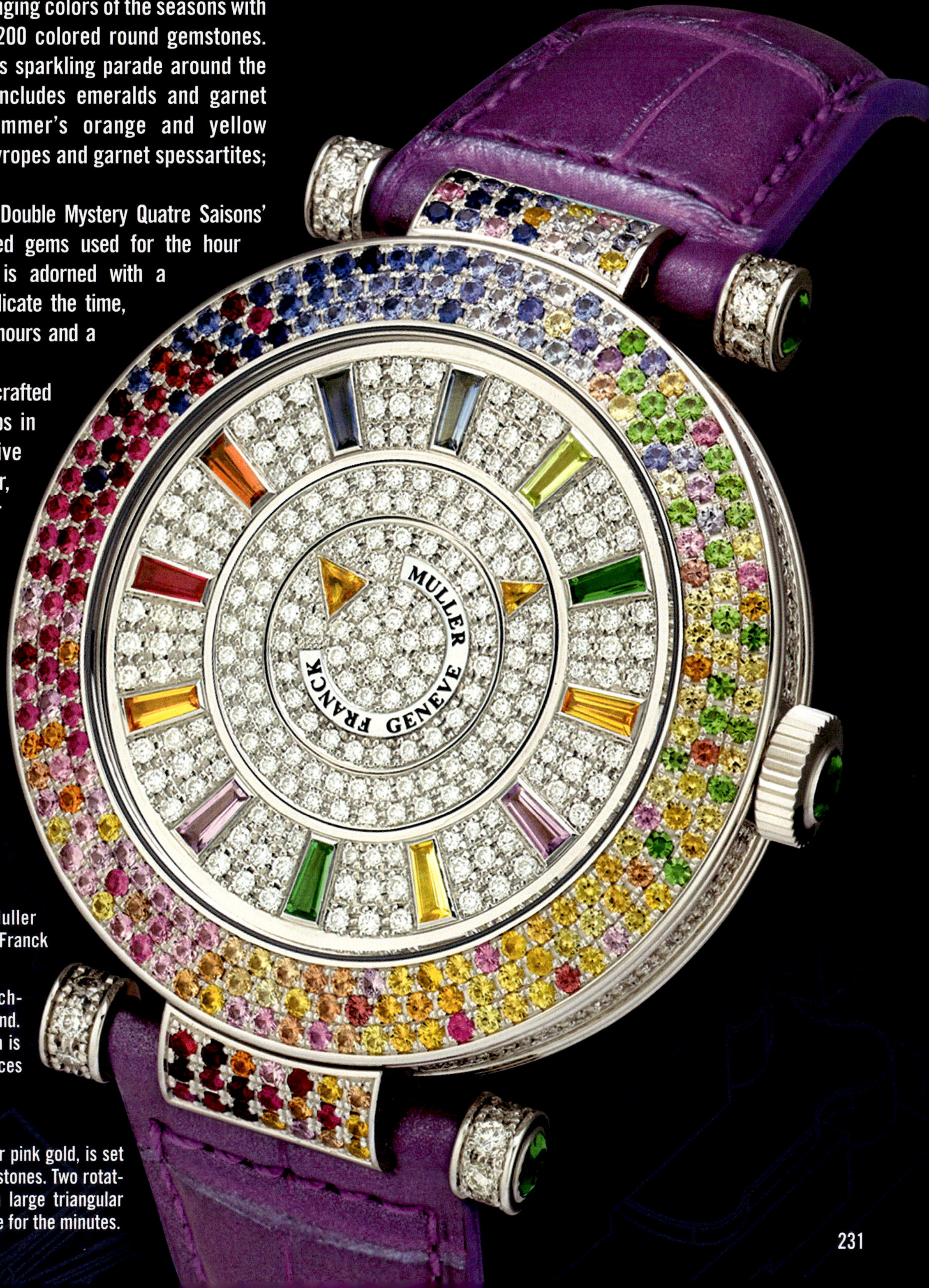

FACING PAGE

TOP Watchmaker Franck Muller and Vartan Sirmakes, CEO of the Franck Muller Group.

CENTER Franck Muller Watchland is located in Genthod, Switzerland. The sprawling site near Lake Geneva is responsible for producing timepieces from concept to completion.

THIS PAGE

The 42mm case, available in white or pink gold, is set with 338 diamonds and 273 colored stones. Two rotating discs indicate the time using a large triangular stone for the hours and a smaller one for the minutes.

TOURBILLON AETERNITAS MEGA IV — REF. 8888 T QP S

Movement: automatic-winding FM 3480 QPSE caliber; three-day power reserve; 34.4x41.4mm, thickness: 13.65mm; 99 jewels; 18,000 vph; 1,483 components; world first; Franck Muller exclusive.
Functions: hours, minutes; equation of time; secular calendar accurate for 999 years: day, month, retrograde date display; minute repeater: Westminster carillon on four hammers and four gongs; one-minute tourbillon; flyback chronograph; three time zones with 24-hour indication; moonphase.
Case: white gold; 42x61mm, thickness: 19.15mm; sapphire crystal; sapphire crystal caseback.
Dial: silver; sunray guilloché.
Strap: black alligator.
Price: available upon request.
Also available: platinum.

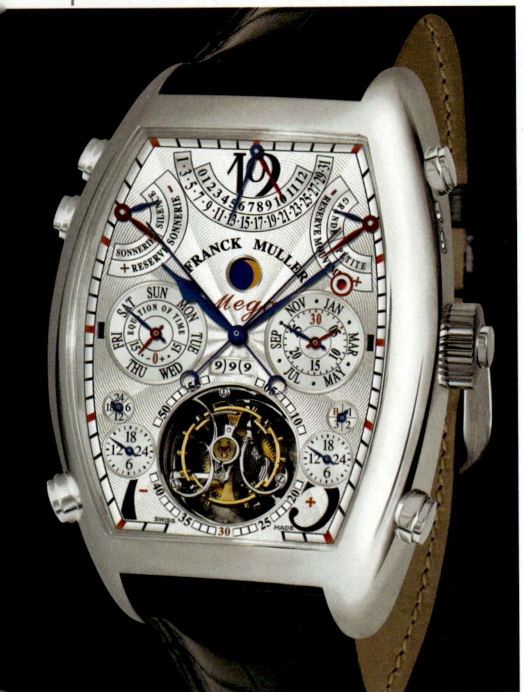

TOURBILLON 9850 EVOLUTION 3.1 — REF. 9850 T EV 3.1

Movement: manual-winding tri-axial tourbillon caliber; 24-hour power reserve; perpetual calendar; world first; Franck Muller exclusive.
Functions: hours, minutes; day, month, year, retrograde date display; tourbillon on three axes.
Case: white gold; sapphire crystal.
Dial: silver; sunray guilloché.
Strap: black alligator.
Price: available upon request.
Also available: platinum.

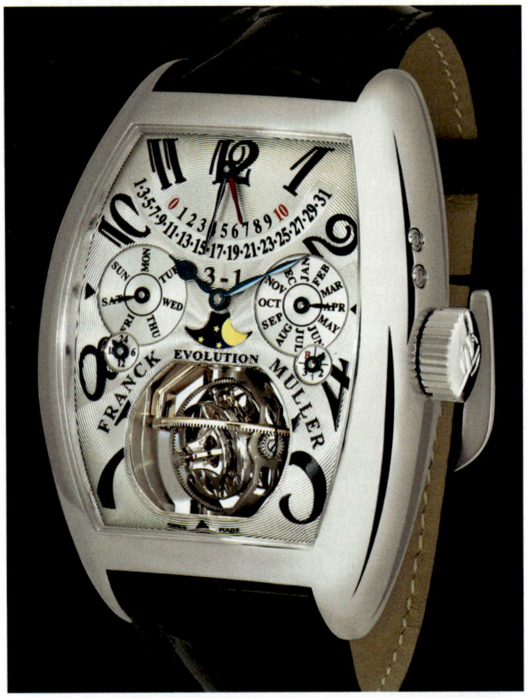

TOURBILLON CURVEX POWER RESERVE SQUELETTE — REF. 8888 T PR SQT

Movement: automatic-winding FM 3400 T caliber; eight-day power reserve; 34.4x41.4mm, thickness: 7.55mm; 42 jewels; 18,000 vph; 350 components; skeletonized; flying tourbillon; tourbillon cage on ball bearings; Franck Muller exclusive.
Functions: hours, minutes; flying tourbillon; power reserve indication at 12.
Case: white gold; sapphire crystal.
Strap: black alligator.
Price: available upon request.
Also available: platinum.

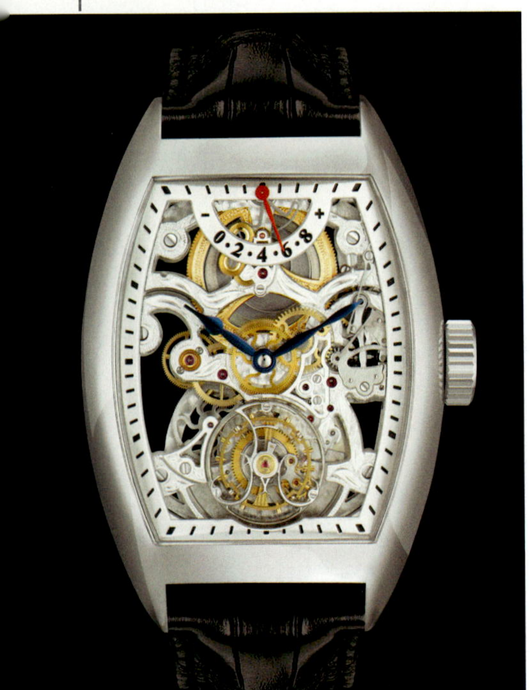

TOURBILLON SQUELETTE — REF. 7008 T SQT

Movement: manual-winding FM 2001R11 caliber; Ø 33.4mm, thickness: 5.3mm; 21 jewels; 18,000 vph; 193 components; skeletonized; flying tourbillon; Franck Muller exclusive.
Functions: hours, minutes; flying tourbillon.
Case: white gold; Ø 42mm, thickness: 12.4mm; sapphire crystal; water resistant to 3atm.
Strap: black alligator.
Price: available upon request.
Also available: platinum.

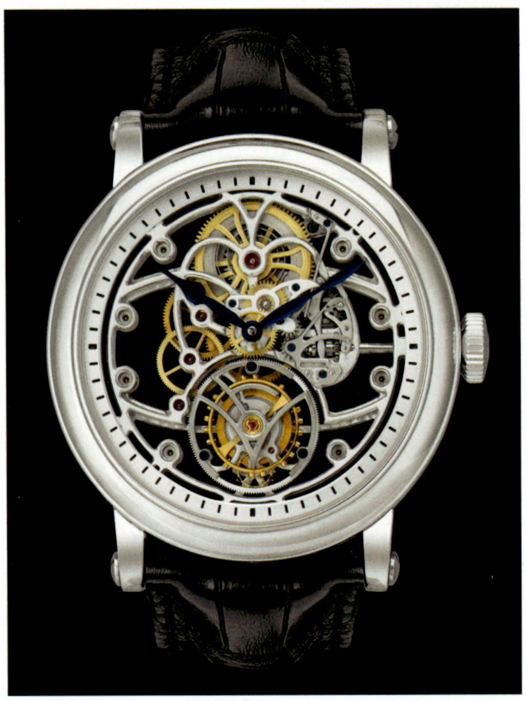

CONQUISTADOR GRANDPRIX, CHRONOGRAPH — REF. 9900 CC GP ERG

Movement: automatic-winding FM 7000 caliber; 48-hour power reserve; chronograph; platinum 950 oscillating mass.
Functions: hours, minutes; small seconds; date at 6; chronograph: 30-minute counter at 3, 60-second counter at 9.
Case: titanium and ergal; curved shape; sapphire crystal.
Dial: black; flame pattern; Arabic numerals painted in relief.
Strap: black alligator; red stitching.
Price: available upon request.

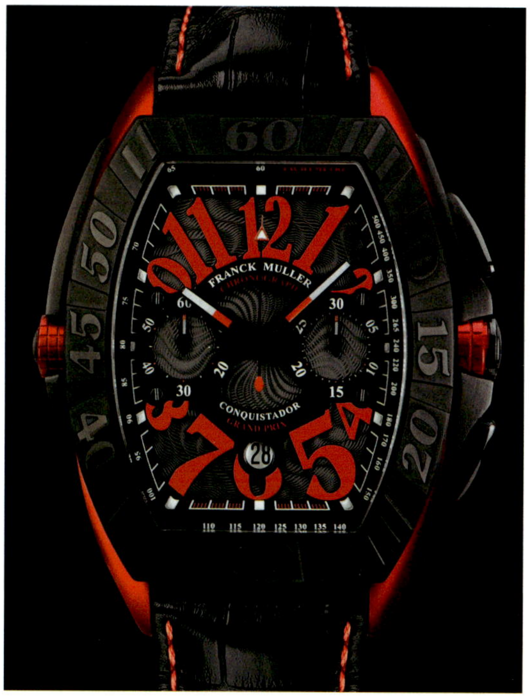

CONQUISTADOR SC GRANDPRIX — REF. 9900 SC GP 5N

Movement: automatic-winding FM 0800 caliber; oscillating mass in 950 platinum.
Functions: hours, minutes, seconds; date at 6.
Case: titanium and red gold; curved shape; sapphire crystal; water resistant to 3atm.
Dial: black; flame pattern; Arabic numerals painted in relief.
Strap: black alligator.
Price: available upon request.
Also available: red gold; leather strap.

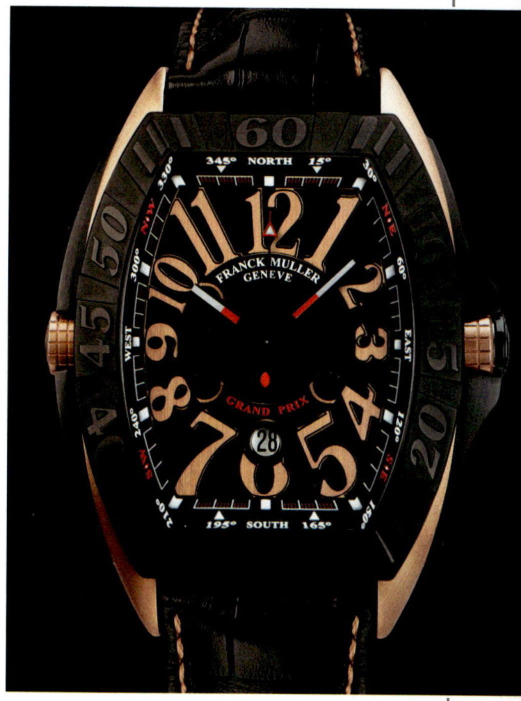

INFINITY REKA SAFARI — REF. 3740 QZ SAF D CD

Movement: quartz.
Functions: hours, minutes.
Case: diamond-pavé red gold; ultra-thin; sapphire crystal; water resistant to 3atm.
Dial: full-set diamond pavé; zebra-print.
Strap: alligator.
Price: available upon request.
Also available: leather strap.

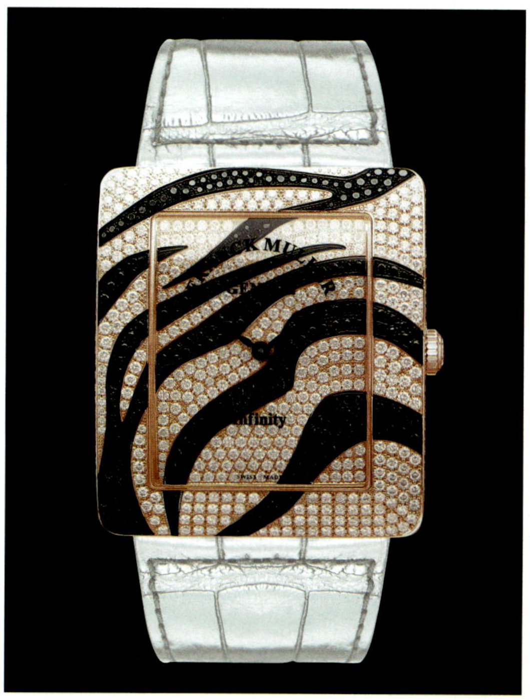

DOUBLE MYSTERY 42 D CD — REF. DBLE MIST. 42 D CD F

Movement: automatic-winding Double Mystery caliber; oscillating mass in 950 platinum; Franck Muller patent; Franck Muller exclusive.
Functions: hours, minutes; mysterious time indication via two rotating discs.
Case: white gold; Ø 42mm; sapphire crystal; water resistant to 3atm.
Dial: two rotating discs; full-set diamond pavé.
Bracelet: white gold; full-set diamond pavé.
Price: available upon request.
Also available: yellow or rose gold; leather strap; yellow-, rose- or white-gold bracelet without diamonds.

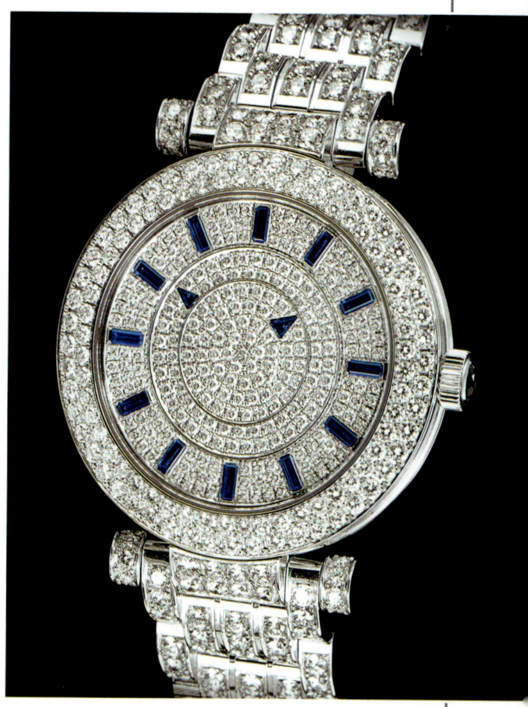

FREDERIQUE CONSTANT
GENEVE

SWISS SUCCESS STORY

More than 20 years after Frédérique Constant began making watches in Geneva, the family-owned company has evolved into one of Switzerland's most successful independent manufactures.

The firm has consistently posted an annual growth rate of at least 20 percent since 1998 and expanded production to more than 100,000 watches in 2010. Frédérique Constant announced sales figures from the first half of 2010 that were the best in the company's history. CEO Peter Stas attributes the surge to the brand's focus on "accessible luxury."

"The initial concept behind the brand was to create Swiss Made, high-quality and innovative watches at sensible prices," he said in a recent statement. "Still today, it is this mission that drives our passion."

To achieve this ambition, Frédérique Constant established its production facility in Plan-les-Ouates, Geneva, where it began producing many of its watch movements in-house in 2004. All aspects of watchmaking—from initial inspiration to final certification—are centralized there.

In less than a decade, the workshop has earned a reputation for innovation with the introduction of several cutting-edge movements, including the FC-980 and FC-985 featured in the Manufacture Tourbillon Silicium collection. Both calibers incorporate escapement wheels made from silicium (aka silicon).

This advanced material, used extensively in semiconductor production, is harder than steel but has a low mass, making it ideal for a number of watchmaking applications. Silicium's main advantage, however, is that it does not require lubrication. This means the silicium escape wheels Frédérique Constant uses in its Manufacture Tourbillon Silicium watches do not require re-oiling every four years like a standard mechanical timepiece.

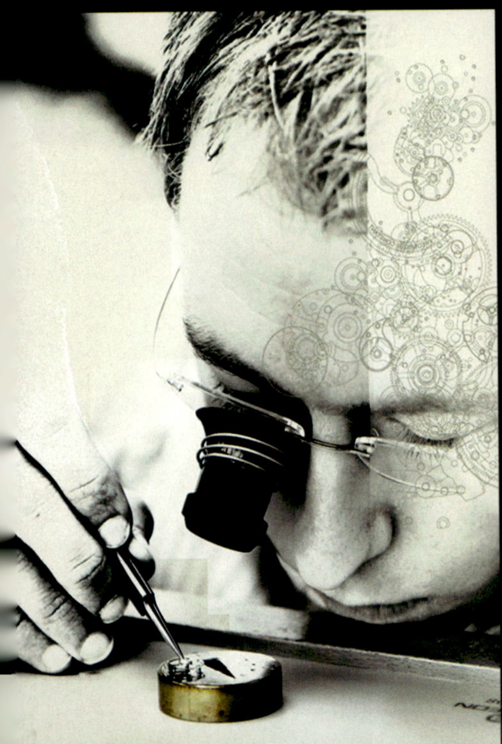

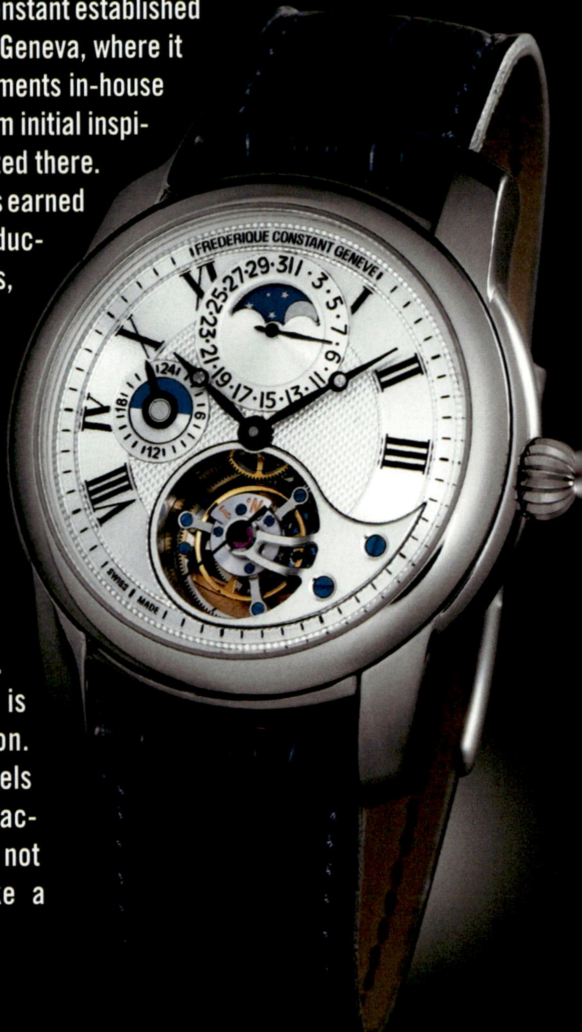

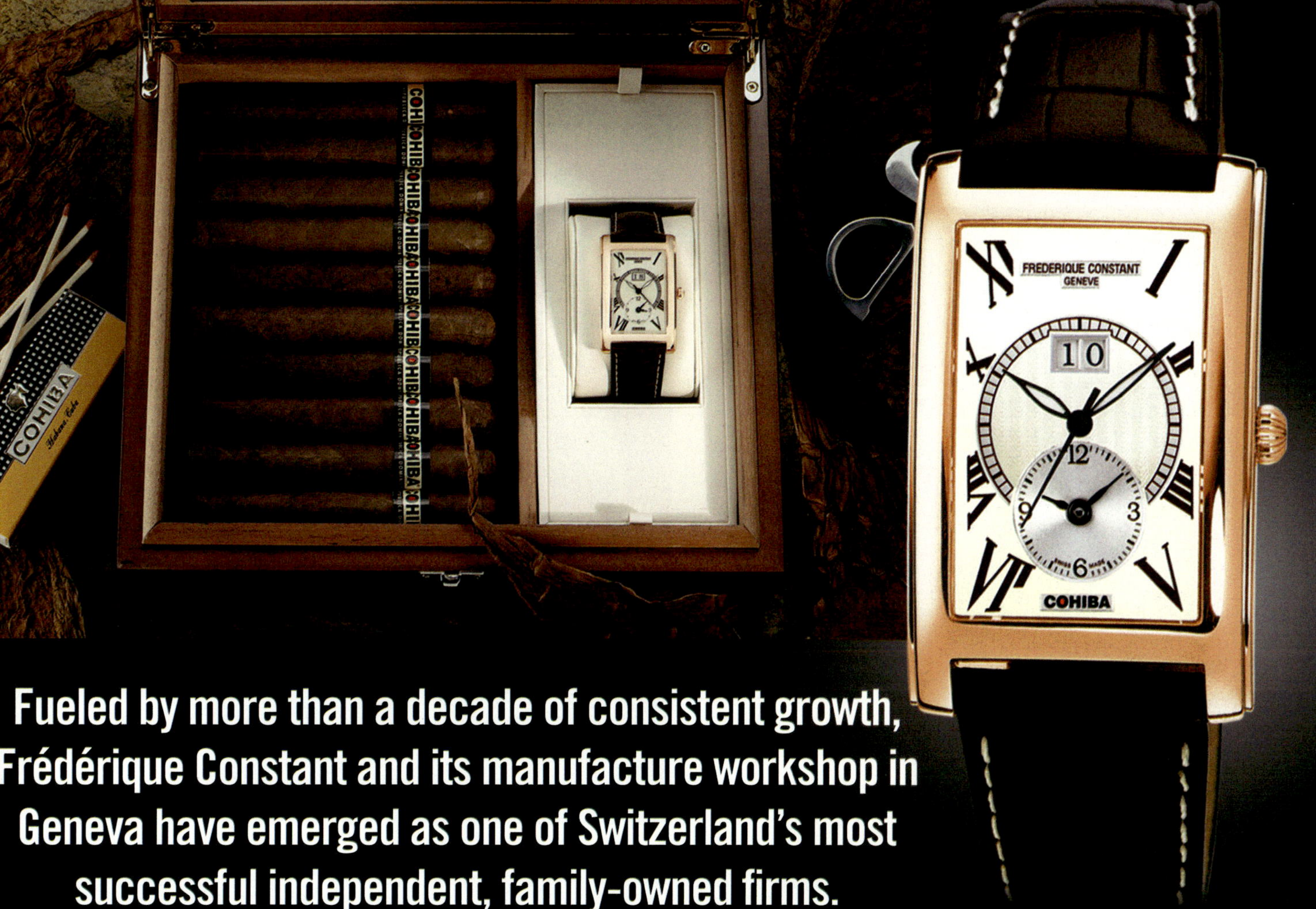

Fueled by more than a decade of consistent growth, Frédérique Constant and its manufacture workshop in Geneva have emerged as one of Switzerland's most successful independent, family-owned firms.

Another Frédérique Constant specialty is limited edition timepieces presented with exceptional accessories. The company recently unveiled several outstanding sets, including an automatic watch that pays tribute to the Runabout sports boat, which comes with a scale version of the classic watercraft from the 1920s. Another collection pairs an automatic chronograph with a mechanical stopwatch in homage to the Austin-Healey, a vintage British sports car popular in the '50s and '60s.

Last winter, the firm hosted an invitation-only event in New York City to unveil the Frédérique Constant for Cohiba Limited Edition. Available exclusively in the United States, the set highlights the shared tradition of handmade excellence that connects luxury watches and cigars.

For the collection, Frédérique Constant will produce 188 watches in stainless steel and an equal number that are plated with rose gold. Fitted with an ivory-colored dial, these numbered timepieces feature tobacco-colored Roman numerals and matching straps. The company presents the watch in an elegantly crafted wooden humidor accompanied by 25 Cohiba Crystal cigars.

In addition to hosting special events for clients, Frédérique Constant is also active in a number of charity events. Last fall, the company served as official sponsor of the Par Coeur Gala, an annual fete hosted by actress Eva Longoria.

Held at the Cambon Capucines Pavillon in Paris, the Par Coeur Gala raises funds and awareness for charity organizations dedicated to helping families and children around the world. "We are committed to celebrate and support those passionate charitable organizations that go the extra mile to improve the lives of less fortunate people worldwide," Stas said.

A skilled watchmaker patiently assembles one of the many manufacture movements produced entirely in-house at Frédérique Constant's workshops in Plan-les-Ouates, Geneva.

The limited edition white-gold Tourbillon Manufacture Silicium Moon Phase and Date features an innovative silicium escapement design created by Frédérique Constant.

The Frédérique Constant for Cohiba Limited Edition is produced in a numbered set of 376 pieces (188 each in stainless steel and rose-gold-plated) and is offered exclusively in the United States.

TOURBILLON MANUFACTURE SILICIUM — REF. FC-980MC4H9

Movement: automatic-winding FC-980 caliber; 42-hour power reserve; 33 jewels; 28,800 vph.
Functions: hours, minutes, seconds; Heart Beat; one-minute tourbillon; sun-moon indicator.
Case: 18K rose gold; Ø 42mm, thickness: 11mm; crown with two O-rings; convex sapphire crystal; water resistant to 3atm.
Dial: silver; guilloché center.
Strap: black alligator.
Suggested price: $49,000
Note: limited edition of 188 pieces.
Also available: white gold (limited edition of 88 pieces).

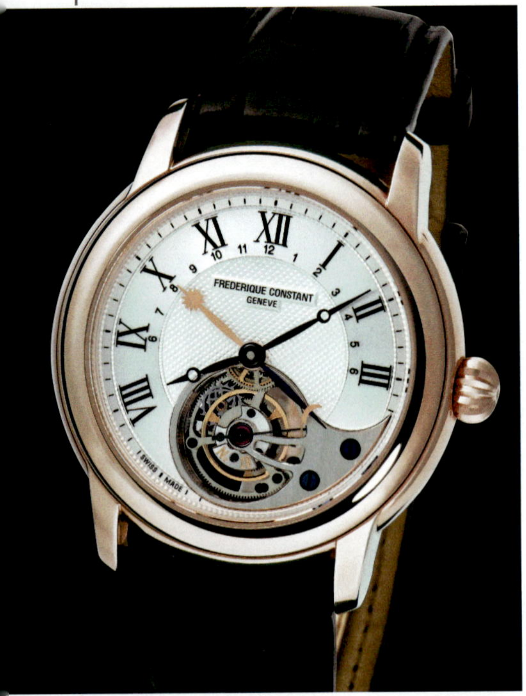

MAXIME MANUFACTURE AUTOMATIC — REF. FC-700MS5M6

Movement: automatic-winding FC-700 caliber; 42-hour power reserve; 26 jewels; 28,800 vph.
Functions: hours, minutes; date.
Case: stainless steel; Ø 42mm, thickness: 10mm; screw-in crown; convex sapphire crystal; water resistant to 5atm.
Dial: silver; guilloché center.
Strap: black alligator.
Suggested price: $2,550
Also available: rose gold; two-tone; stainless steel bracelet.

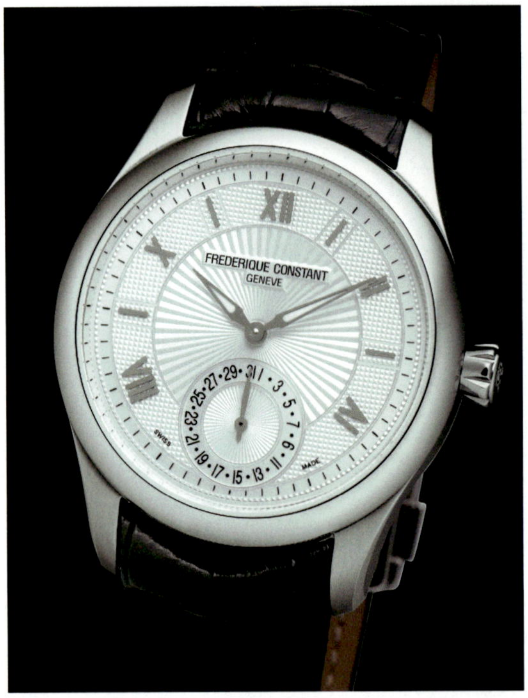

MAXIME MANUFACTURE LADY — REF. FC-700MPWD3MD6

Movement: automatic-winding FC-700 caliber; 42-hour power reserve; 26 jewels; 28,800 vph.
Functions: hours, minutes; date.
Case: diamond-set stainless steel; Ø 39mm, thickness: 11.3mm; crown with two O-rings; convex sapphire crystal; water resistant to 5atm.
Dial: mother-of-pearl; silver guilloché center.
Strap: gray galuchat (also comes with gray satin strap).
Suggested price: $4,250
Also available: stainless steel without diamonds; stainless steel with 18K rose-gold top ring.

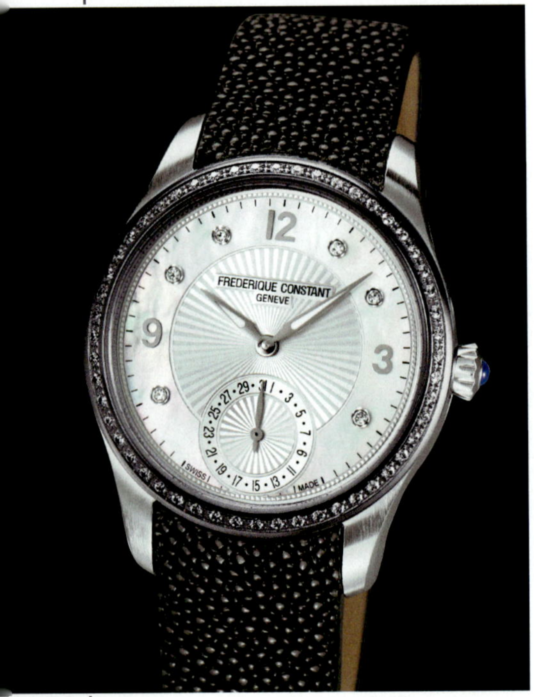

JUNIOR AUTOMATIC — REF. FC-303S4B26

Movement: automatic-winding FC-303 caliber; 42-hour power reserve; 25 jewels; 28,800 vph.
Functions: hours, minutes, seconds; date.
Case: stainless steel; Ø 38.5mm, thickness: 10.3mm; crown with two O-rings; convex sapphire crystal; water resistant to 6atm.
Dial: silver; luminous indexes.
Strap: brown leather.
Suggested price: $725
Also available: black dial; stainless steel bracelet.

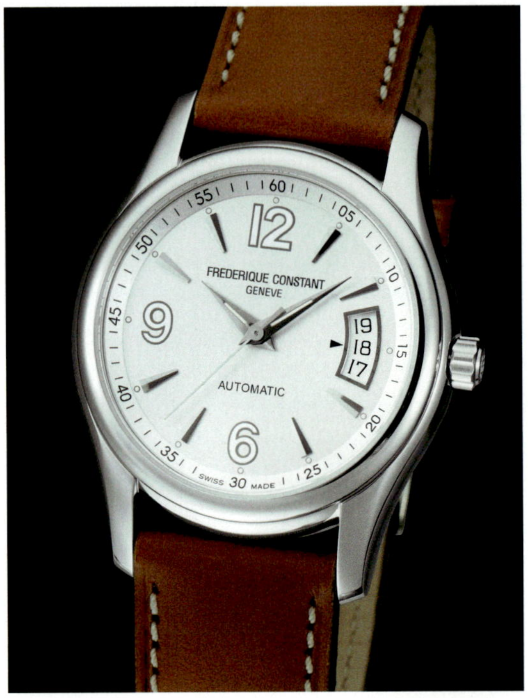

LADY CHOCOLATE DOUBLE HEART BEAT — REF. FC-310CDHB2PD4

Movement: automatic-winding FC-310 caliber; 42-hour power reserve; 25 jewels; 28,800 vph.
Functions: hours, minutes, seconds; Heart Beat.
Case: rose-gold-plated diamond-set stainless steel; Ø 34mm, thickness: 10mm; crown with two O-rings; convex sapphire crystal; water resistant to 6atm.
Dial: chocolate brown mother-of-pearl.
Strap: chocolate brown satin.
Suggested price: $4,150
Also available: stainless steel; white or vanilla dial; metal bracelet.

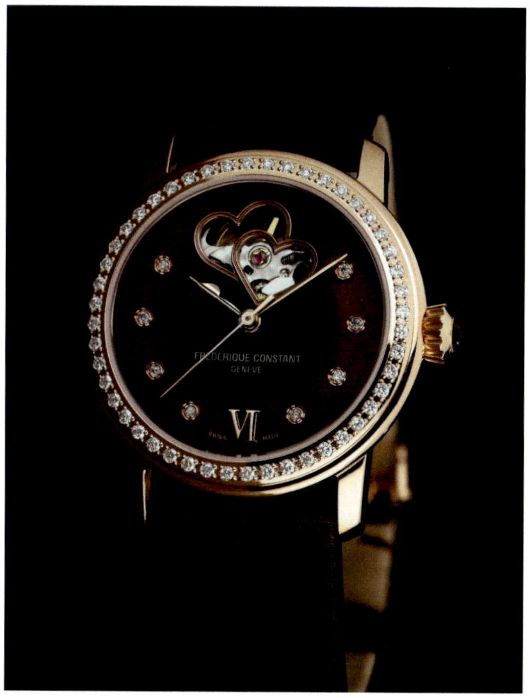

HEALEY AUTOMATIC CHRONOGRAPH — REF. FC-392CH6B4

Movement: automatic-winding FC-392 caliber; 42-hour power reserve; 25 jewels; 28,800 vph.
Functions: hours, minutes, seconds; date; chronograph.
Case: rose-gold-plated stainless steel; Ø 43mm, thickness: 8mm; screw-in crown; convex sapphire crystal; water resistant to 10atm.
Dial: chocolate brown; Healey logo.
Strap: chocolate brown racing leather.
Suggested price: $2,950
Note: limited edition of 1,888 pieces.
Also available: stainless steel with silver dial (limited edition of 1,888 pieces).

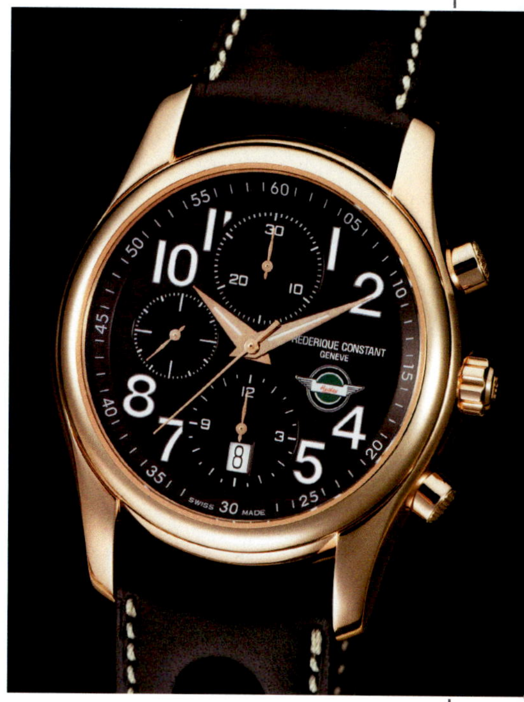

COHIBA — REF. FC-325CW4C24

Movement: automatic-winding FC-325 caliber; 38-hour power reserve; 21 jewels; 28,800 vph.
Functions: hours, minutes, seconds; large date; second time zone.
Case: rose-gold-plated stainless steel; 47x30.7mm, thickness: 10.9mm; crown with two O-rings; convex sapphire crystal; water resistant to 6atm.
Dial: ivory-colored; Côtes de Genève in center.
Strap: Havana brown leather.
Suggested price: $1,750
Note: limited edition of 188 pieces (United States only).
Also available: stainless steel (limited edition of 188 pieces) (United States only).

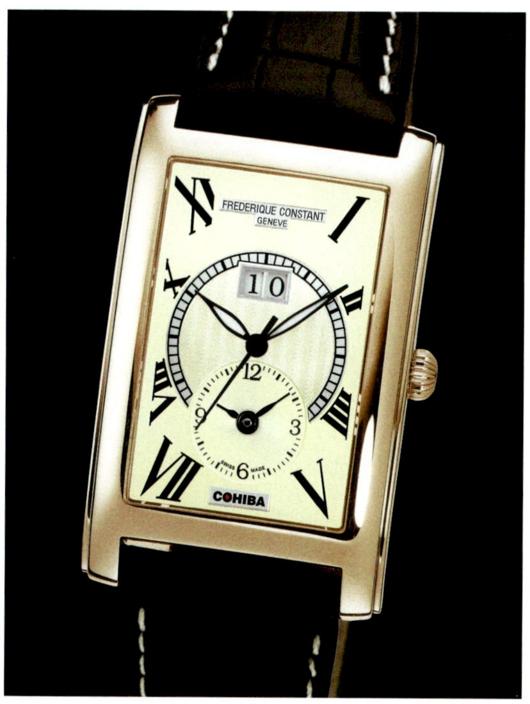

CHOPIN — REF. FC-303CH4P5

Movement: automatic-winding FC-303 caliber; 38-hour power reserve; 25 jewels; 28,800 vph.
Functions: hours, minutes, seconds; date.
Case: yellow-gold-plated stainless steel; Ø 40mm, thickness: 10mm; crown with two O-rings; convex sapphire crystal; water resistant to 6atm.
Dial: silver; guilloché center.
Strap: black leather.
Suggested price: $1,595
Note: limited edition of 1,810 pieces.
Also available: stainless steel (limited edition of 1,810 pieces).

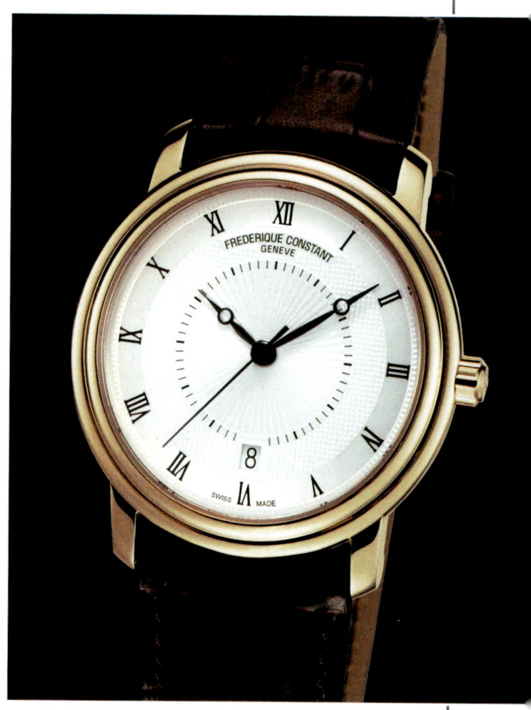

CUSTOMIZING TIME SINCE 1967

THE JOURNEY OF TIME

A timepiece is an extension of self. Beyond expressing your personal style, the right watch will also carry you through the rigors of your day with accuracy and distinction.

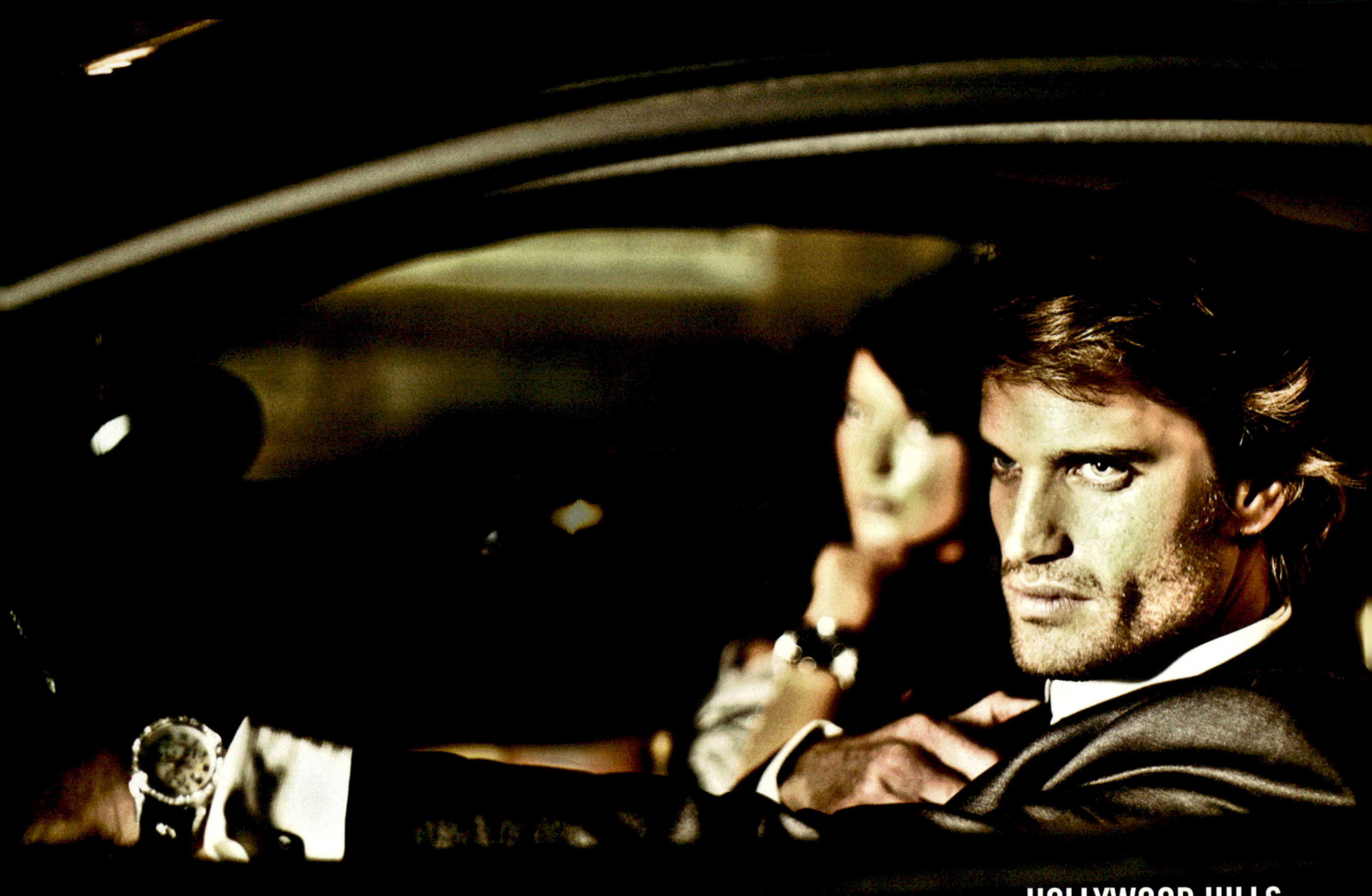

No matter where you are in the world, a Giantto timepiece is there to remind you that the most valuable thing that exists is time. With its daring approach to luxury and avant-garde design, Giantto typifies a lifestyle dedicated to the relentless quest for distinctive luxury.

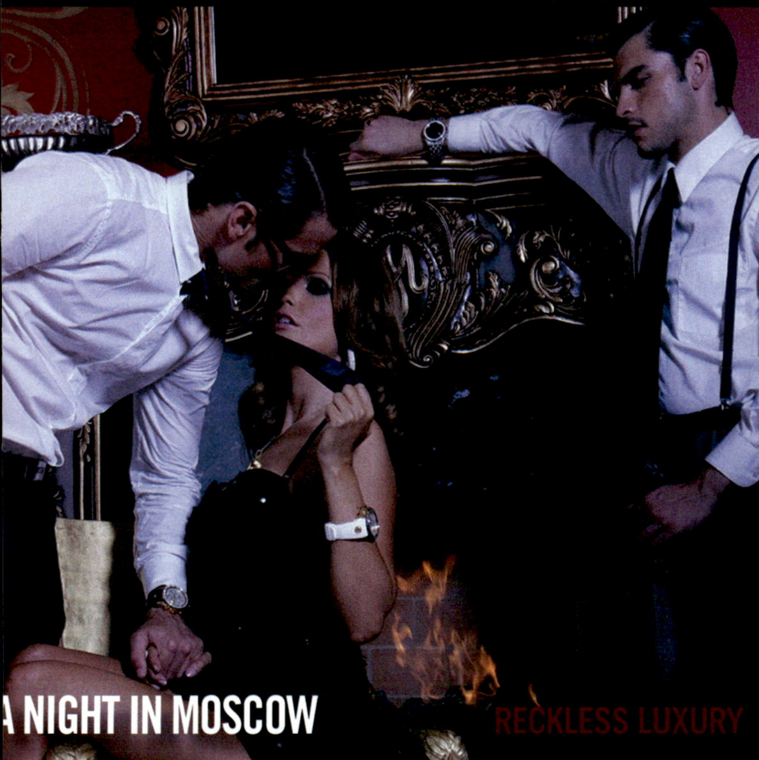

Giantto is not for the faint of heart. The collection projects a worldly elegance that is at home shimmering in the twilight breeze that blows through the Hollywood Hills, or glinting in the firelight of a sizzling Moscow rendezvous.

The spirit of Giantto captures the feeling that comes from living in the moment. The company's timepieces personify this attitude through a heady mix of oversized details, captivating jewelry accents and a sporty confidence. The bold combination delivers a healthy measure of flash tempered with finesse.

A father and son team recently founded the Los Angeles-based firm. The elder is an Old World artisan whose expert hands have spent decades crafting exquisite jewelry. His progeny is a businessman whose fresh style is attuned to the now. Together, the duo's diverse experiences mesh seamlessly to create compelling timepieces that balance traditional artistry with a modern sensibility.

For many, a Giantto watch is more than a meticulous symphony of gears and pinions designed to keep time. Rather, it is a precious totem, one that neatly reflects their passionate nature and desire for authentic beauty. Each precious member of the Giantto family of watches beats to this intensely personal rhythm.

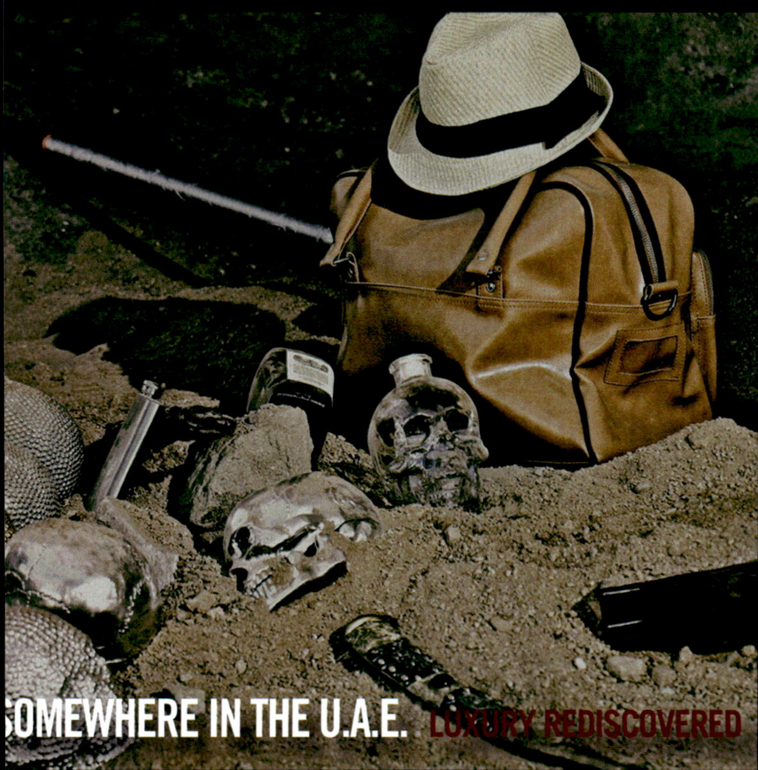

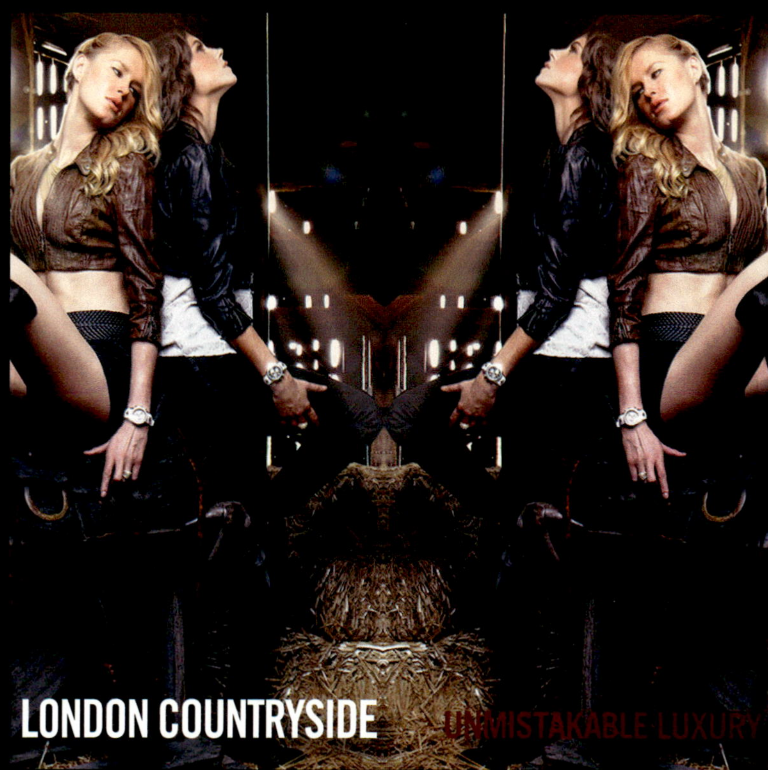

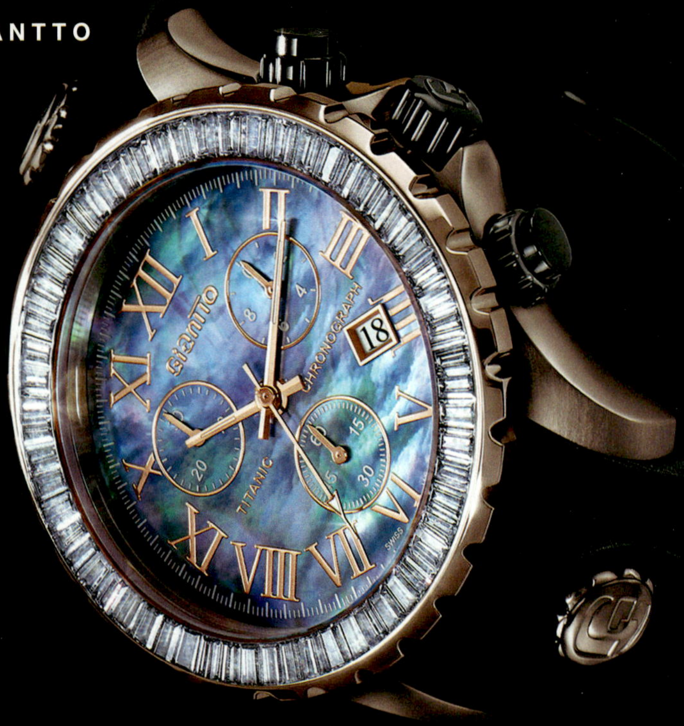

T4 The rose-gold and black IP T4 chronograph includes a bezel set with sapphire-cut gems that frame the mother-of-pearl dial.

Easily adaptable to any style or situation, all the watches in the T3 and T4 collections feature an interchangeable bezel. This enables the wearer to quickly customize the look of the watch. With a simple twist, the original bezel can be removed and replaced with one customized with an array of diamonds or semi-precious stones.

Along with this visual versatility, another Giantto brand signature found throughout the collection is the "G-button." Engraved with the company logo, this instantly recognizable metal stud decorates both of the watch's silicon straps.

The Giantto collection offers a range of case sizes for men, including the 47mm T3 and T4 timepieces, plus the T7 line, which boasts a diameter of 50mm. The t3 and t4 watches for women are offered in 38mm-diameter cases.

In addition to its production models, Giantto also offers a number of limited edition timepieces. Prized by collectors, these watches typically feature a combination of precious metals and diamonds.

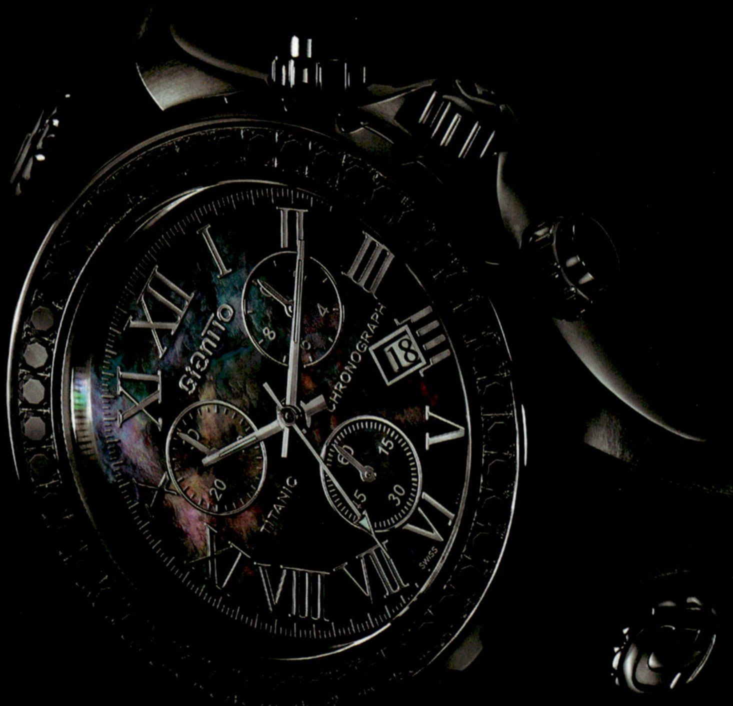

T4 Presented in a striking black design, the T4 features a matching mother-of-pearl dial, diamond-set bezel and case.

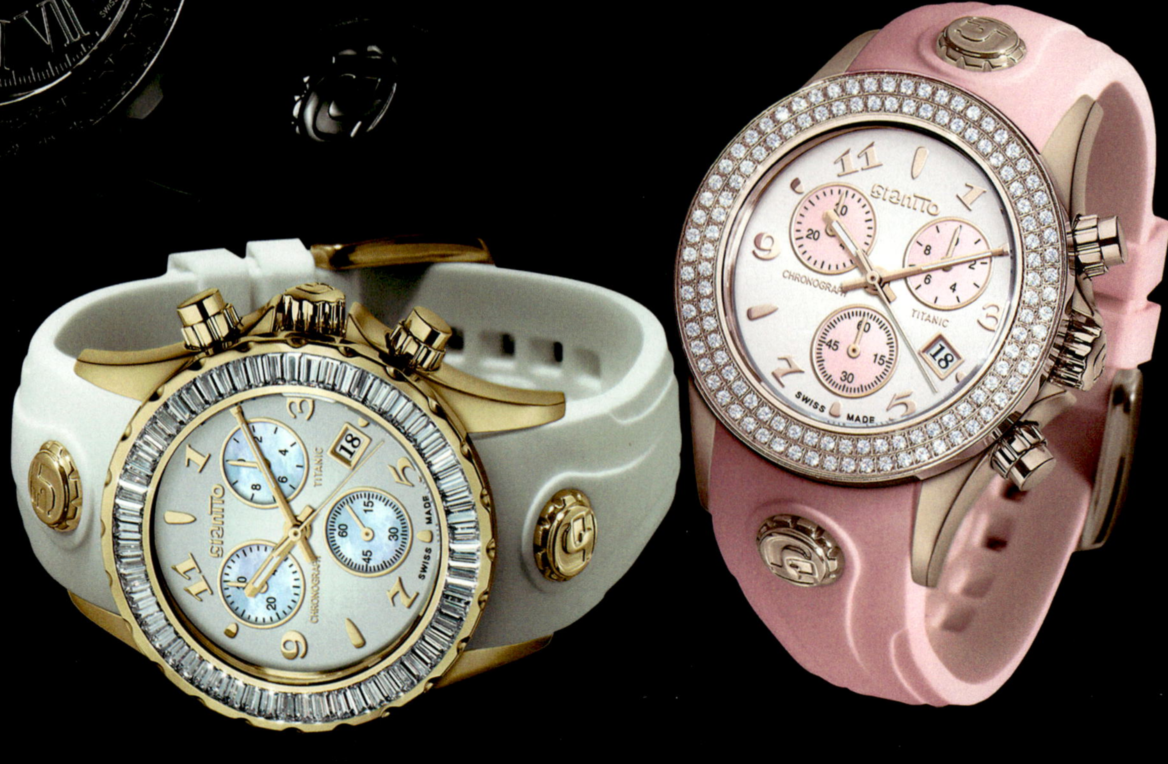

T4 Giantto pairs a yellow-gold IP case and gem-set bezel with a white silicone strap for the ladies t4 chronograph.

T4 This all-pink version of the t4 features two rows of diamonds on the bezel, plus mother-of-pearl subsidiary dials for the chronograph counters and small seconds.

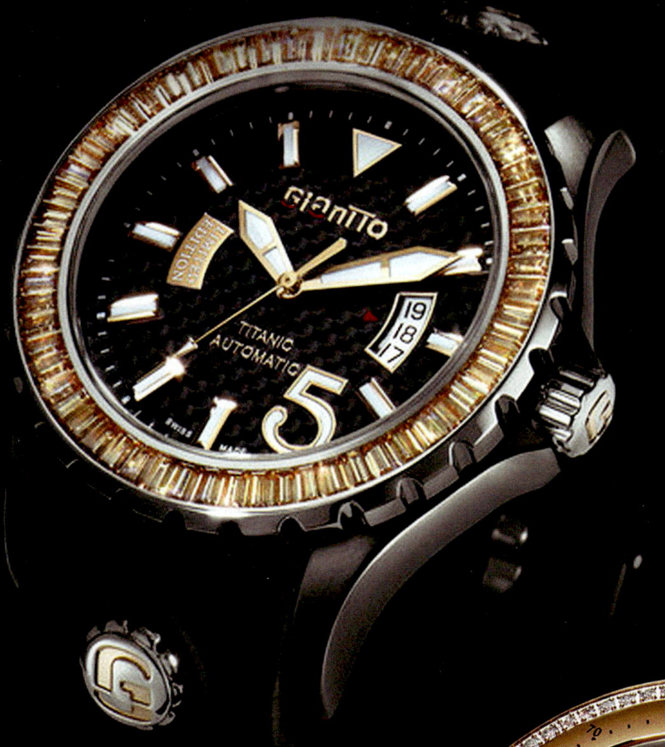

With its handmade, custom, and over-the-top designs, Giantto truly sets itself apart from other watchmakers. This attention to individuality, aided by Giantto's proximity to the entertainment industry, has attracted the attention of a large number of celebrities, including stars of film, music, sports and more. The company's A-List clientele includes such boldface names as Kim Kardashian, Nikki Hilton, Hulk Hogan, Jamie Foxx and world champion boxer Manny Pacquiao.

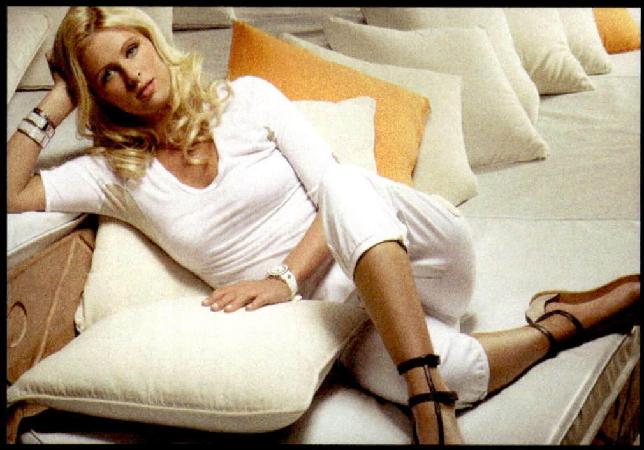

Nicky Hilton wears the ladies' t4.

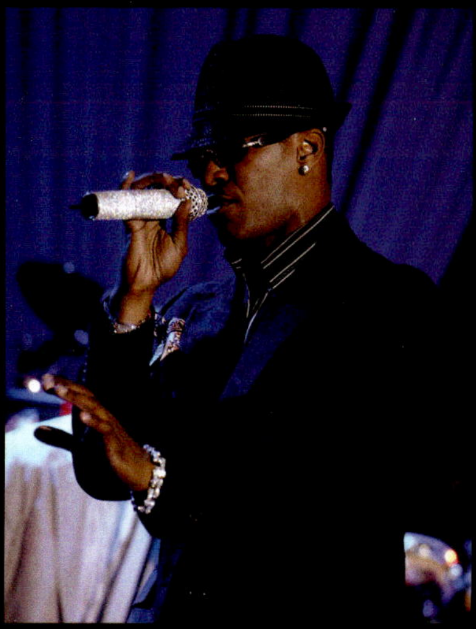

Singer-actor Jamie Foxx croons into Giantto's "million-dollar microphone."

T5 This limited edition T5 sports a carbon fiber dial, an automatic movement and a bezel set with baguette-cut gems.

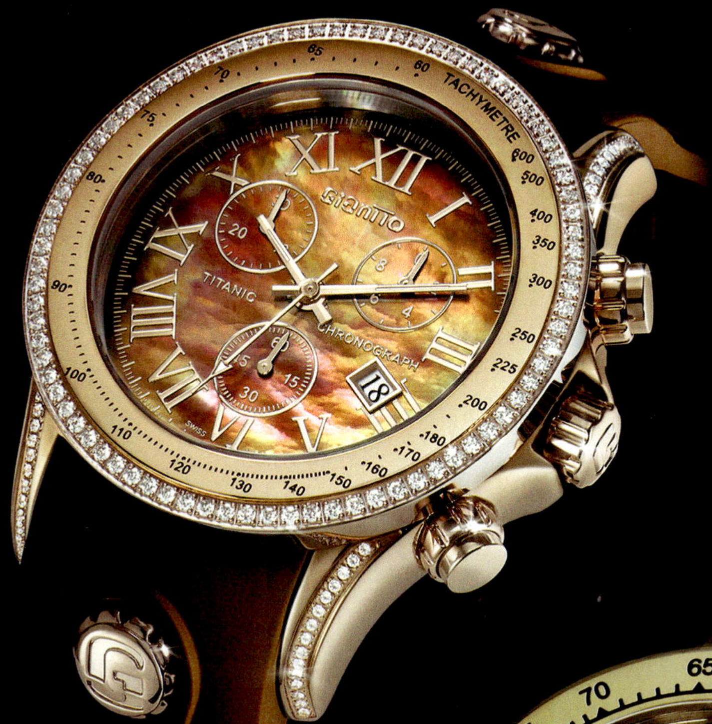

T4 Razor-set diamonds line the bezel and lugs of this rose-gold IP T4, which is equipped with a Swiss Made chronograph.

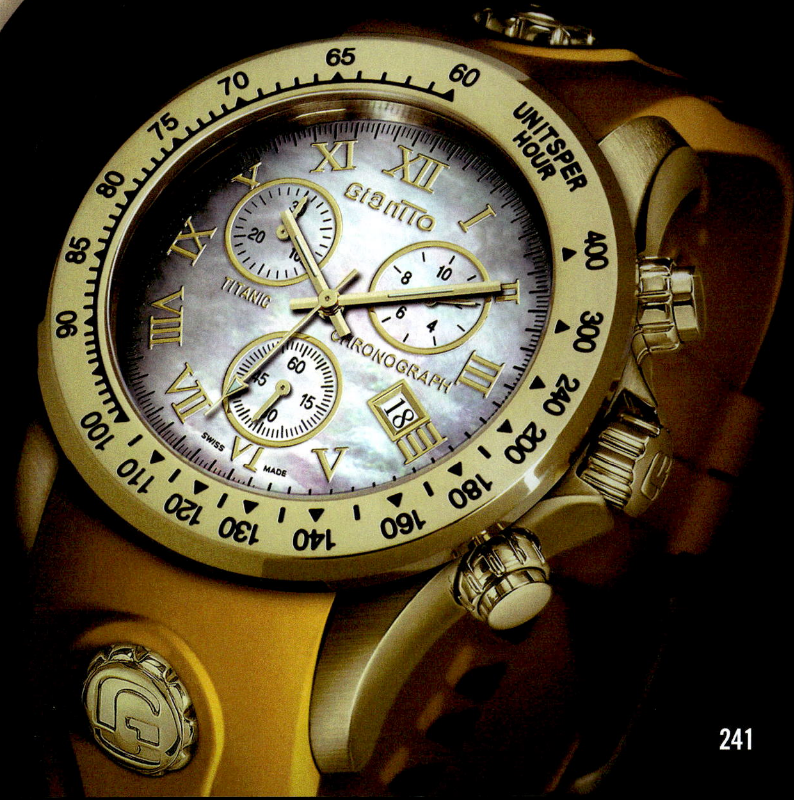

T4 The T4 includes a tachometer scale for measuring speed and a Swiss Made chronograph for timing events. Its yellow-gold IP case is water resistant to 10atm.

GP

GIRARD-PERREGAUX

AN EYE ON THE SKY

A relentless drive to honor watchmaking tradition by advancing both its art and science has propelled Girard-Perregaux's success for more than two centuries as the Swiss manufacture continues its never-ending pursuit of horological excellence through its dedication to inventive design and groundbreaking research.

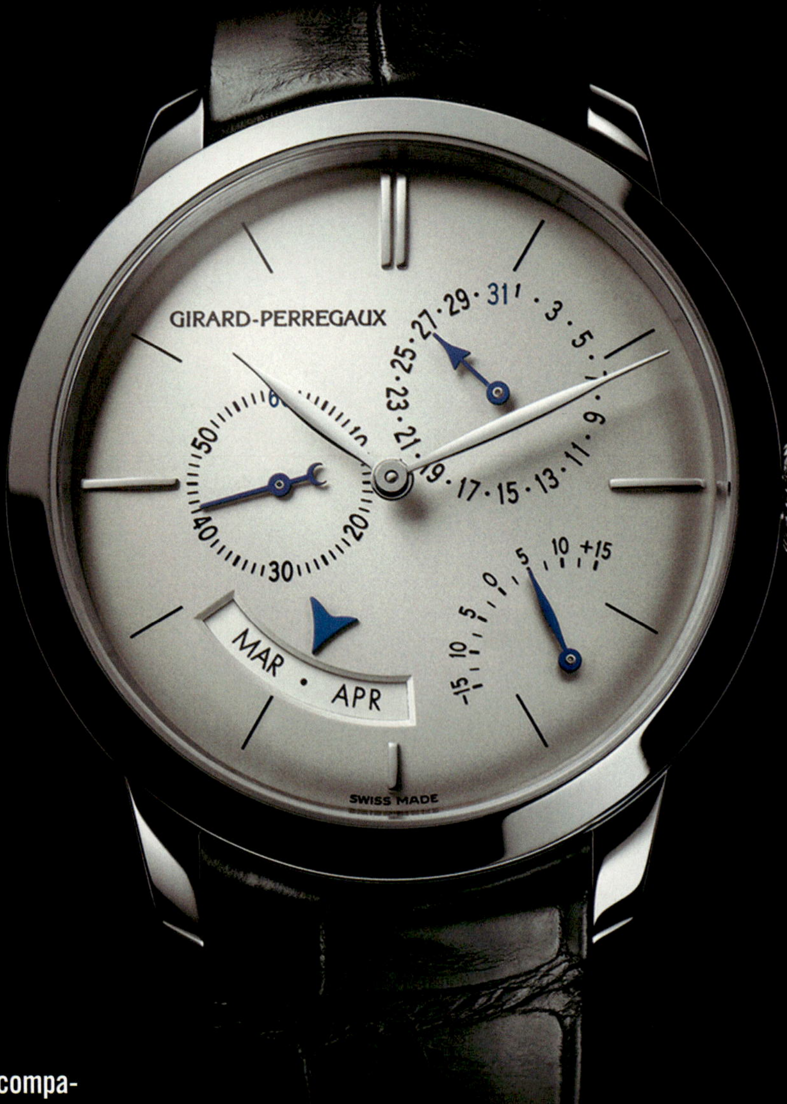

ABOVE

The company now offers the Girard-Perregaux 1966 Annual Calendar and Equation of Time's 40mm case in white gold. Made up of nearly 300 components, its movement displays the date and month as well as calculating the difference between solar and legal time.

That commitment served the La Chaux-de-Fonds-based company well in the 1860s when it debuted its now iconic design for a tourbillon with three gold bridges in a pocket watch created by Constant Girard. A more recent example of the brand's pioneering spirit came a century later in 1966, when its research team developed the first high-frequency movement to oscillate at a rate of 36,000 vibrations per hour, a leap beyond the highest frequency at the time, which was 21,600 vph. In fact, the sophisticated caliber's increased precision was such a significant achievement that the Neuchâtel Observatory awarded it the *Prix du Centenaire* later that year.

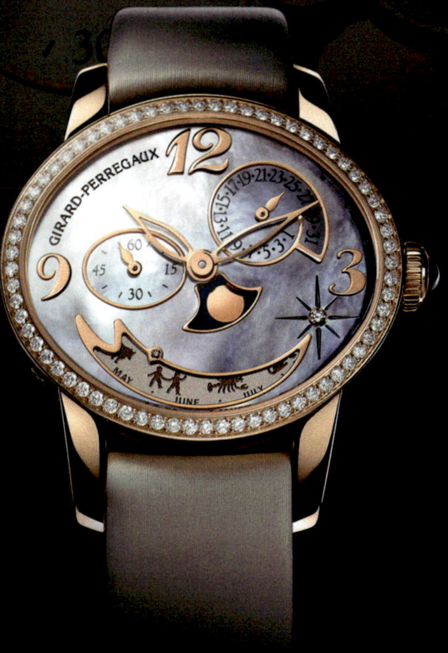

LEFT

The mother-of-pearl dial found in the Cat's Eye Annual and Zodiac Calendars combines lunar, astronomical and earthly time. Nearly 70 white diamonds adorn the pink-gold case's oval bezel.

RIGHT

Many of Girard-Perregaux's workshops are housed in this Art Nouveau building, which was designed by architect Léon Boillot and built in La Chaux-de-Fonds, Switzerland in 1905.

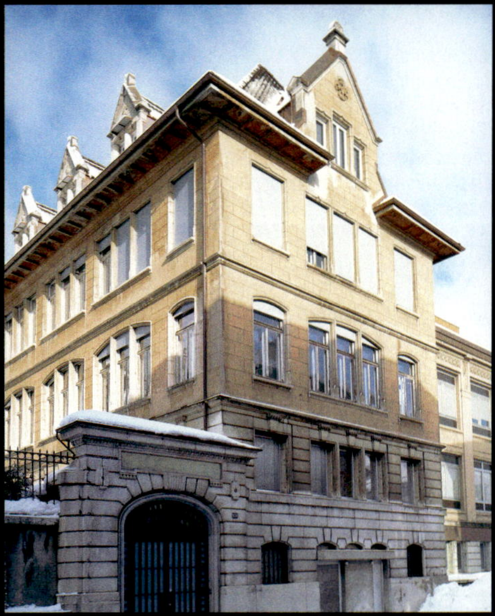

To honor that era of innovation, the company recently introduced the Girard-Perregaux 1966 collection. The latest addition to that line is a new white-gold version of the Girard-Perregaux 1966 Annual Calendar and Equation of Time.

Its elegantly thin case houses the brand's automatic movement, a sophisticated mechanism that combines the practical and esoteric. For everyday use, the calendar displays the date and month, needing only an annual adjustment during non-leap years. For moments of celestial contemplation, the equation of time calculates the difference between solar and legal time and displays it on the scale found between 4 and 5 o'clock. Solar time varies day-to-day (approximately +/- 15 minutes) because of the Earth's elliptical orbit, while legal time represents the standard 24-hour day.

Despite the watch's high level of complication, the overall design remains a paragon of refined understatement expressed by baton indexes and blued steel hands all framed within a tasteful 40mm white-gold case.

Girard-Perregaux's exploration of celestial themes extends to its Cat's Eye Annual and Zodiac Calendars. Designed to captivate both the hearts and minds of women, this timekeeper displays not only the time, date, month and phases of the moon, but also astrological signs. Like a constellation of 68 scintillating stars, the diamonds set on the ovoid case's bezel encircle the mother-of-pearl dial, whose swirling iridescence provides an otherworldly background where lunar, astronomical and earthly time all come together in a harmonic convergence that is visually intoxicating.

An opening near the center reveals the moon's waxing and waning while the signs of the Zodiac and the months streak across the dial in a nearby opening shaped like the tail of a comet. The cosmic cues continue with the date indicator, whose coiled form evokes the shape of a spiral galaxy. Even the small seconds offers galactic implications with its elliptical outline subtly suggesting the Earth's orbit around the Sun.

A transparent caseback lifts the curtain on the mechanical magic behind the Cat's Eye Annual and Zodiac Calendars, offering a glimpse at the intricate arrangement of gears and pinions that make up the company's automatic caliber GP033M0. Much like the aforementioned Girard-Perregaux 1966 model, the Cat's Eye calendar requires a single correction in February, except during leap years. When fully wound, its movement provides nearly two full days of power.

Led today by the Macaluso family, Girard-Perregaux continues to build upon its rich heritage of design and innovation with new timepieces like the Girard-Perregaux 1966 Annual Calendar and Equation of Time and the Cat's Eye Annual and Zodiac Calendars that are emblematic of its holistic approach to watchmaking.

The swirling iridescence of the mother-of-pearl dial of the Cat's Eye and Annual Calendars provides an otherworldly background for lunar, astronomical and earthly time to join in an intoxicating harmonic convergence.

TOURBILLON BI-AXIAL — REF. 99810-53-000-BA6A

Movement: manual-winding GPE0201 caliber; 15 1/3'''; 72-hour power reserve; 28 jewels; 21,600 vph.
Functions: hours, minutes; bi-axial tourbillon.
Case: 18K white gold; Ø 45mm, thickness: 18.5mm; sapphire crystal caseback secured by six screws; water resistant to 3atm (100 feet).
Strap: black large-scale alligator leather, hand-stitched; 18K white-gold folding buckle.
Note: limited and numbered edition of 33 pieces.
Also available: 18K 5N pink-gold version.

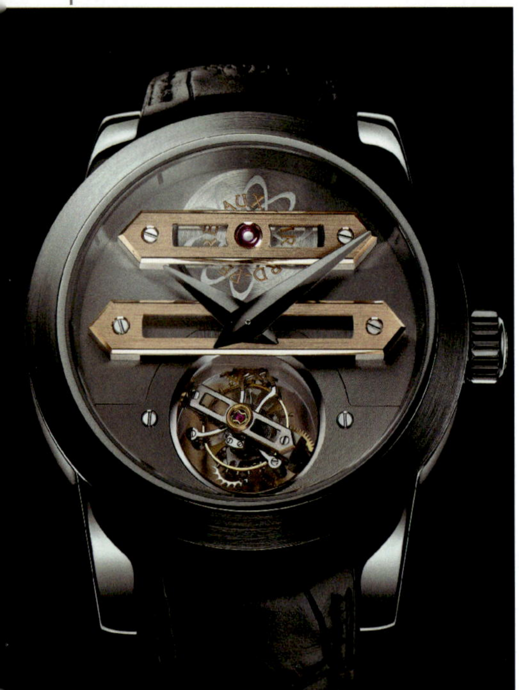

VINTAGE 1945 TOURBILLON WITH THREE GOLD BRIDGES — REF. 99880-52-000-BA6A

Movement: automatic-winding GP9600C caliber; 28.6x30.3mm; 48-hour power reserve; 30 jewels; 21,600 vph; tourbillon with three gold bridges.
Functions: hours, minutes; small seconds on the tourbillon.
Case: 18K 5N pink gold; 36.1x35.25mm, thickness: 11.4mm; sapphire crystal caseback secured by four screws; water resistant to 3atm (100 feet).
Strap: black large-scale alligator leather, hand-stitched; 18K pink-gold folding buckle.
Note: limited and numbered edition of 50 pieces.

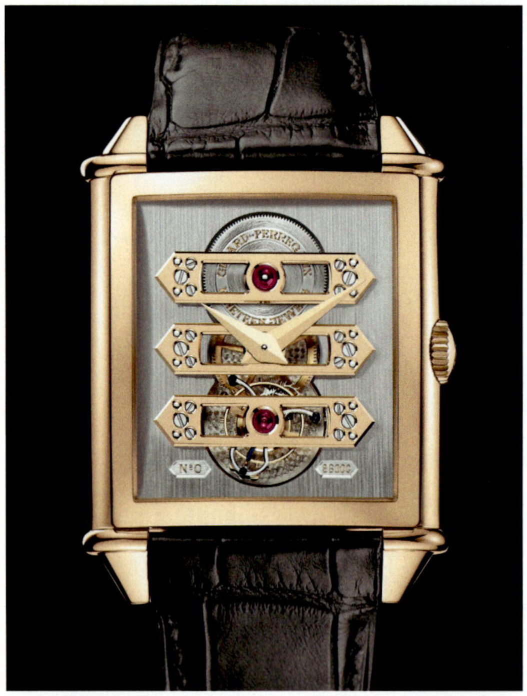

VINTAGE 1945 XXL OFF-CENTERED HOURS AND MINUTES — REF. 25845-52-741-BA6A

Movement: automatic-winding GP01900 caliber; 11 ½'''; 46-hour power reserve; 29 jewels; 28,800 vph.
Functions: hours, minutes; small seconds; date; power reserve indicator.
Case: 18K 5N pink gold; 36x37mm, thickness: 12.9mm; sapphire crystal caseback secured by four screws; water resistant to 3atm (100 feet).
Dial: handcrafted Grand Feu enamel.
Strap: black large-scale alligator leather, hand-stitched; 5N 18K pink-gold folding buckle.
Also available: 18K white-gold version.

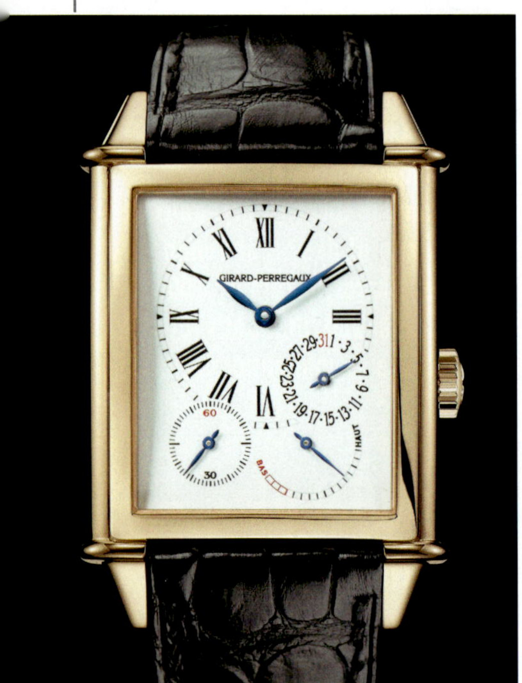

VINTAGE 1945 SMALL SECOND — REF. 25835-52-161-BACA

Movement: automatic-winding GP03300 caliber; 11 ½'''; 46-hour power reserve; 28 jewels; 28,800 vph.
Functions: hours, minutes; small seconds; date.
Case: 18K 5N pink gold; 32x32mm; sapphire crystal caseback secured by four screws; water resistant to 3atm (100 feet).
Dial: wave guilloché patterns, curved; applied Arabic numerals and indexes.
Strap: brown large-scale alligator leather, hand-stitched; 18K pink-gold folding buckle.
Also available: stainless steel version.

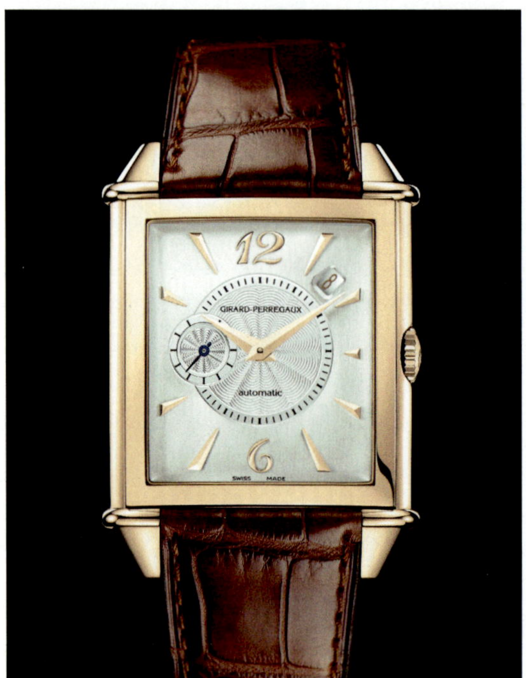

WW.TC SMALL SECOND — REF. 49865-11-151-BA6A

Movement: automatic-winding GP03300 caliber; 11 ½'''; 46-hour power reserve; 32 jewels; 28,800 vph.
Functions: hours, minutes; small seconds; world time with day/night indicator.
Case: fine-brushed stainless steel; Ø 41mm, thickness: 11mm; polished stainless steel fixed bezel; sapphire crystal caseback secured by six screws; water resistant to 5atm (165 feet).
Dial: satin-brushed silver; three applied Arabic numerals; eight luminescent hour markers.
Strap: black large-scale alligator leather, hand-stitched; stainless steel folding buckle.
Also available: stainless steel case with anthracite gray dial; 18K 5N pink-gold case.

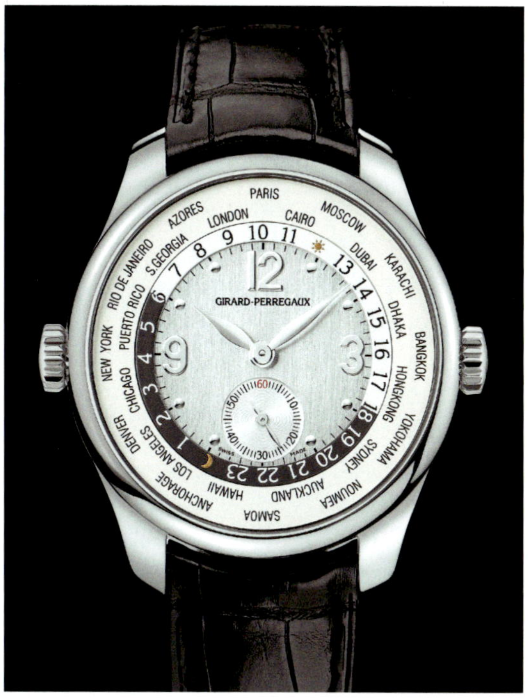

WW.TC LADY JEWELLERY — REF. 49870D53PB01-BK7A

Movement: automatic-winding GP033G0 caliber; 11 ½'''; 46-hour power reserve; 26 jewels; 28,800 vph.
Functions: hours, minutes; world time with day/night indicator.
Case: 18K white gold set with 274 white round diamonds (4.12 carats); Ø 41mm, thickness: 11mm; crown set with two diamonds (0.4 carat); sapphire crystal caseback secured by six screws; water resistant to 5atm (165 feet).
Dial: set with 245 white round diamonds (1.47 carats); 12 black diamond hour markers.
Strap: white large-scale alligator leather, hand-stitched; 18K white-gold folding buckle set with 18 diamonds (0.2 carat).

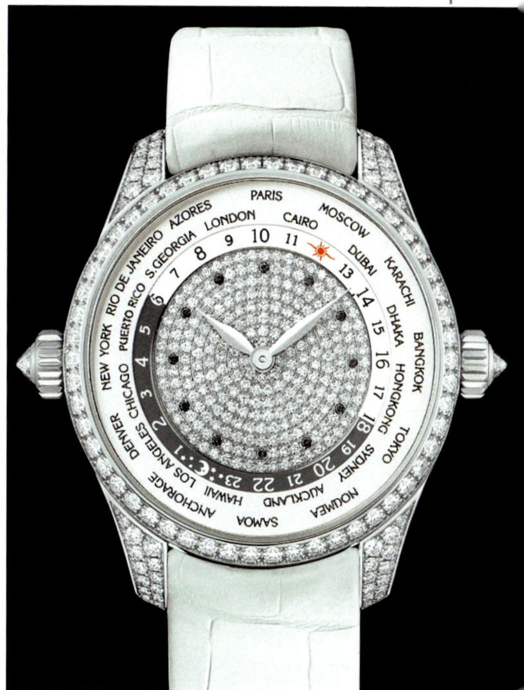

GIRARD-PERREGAUX 1966 PERPETUAL CALENDAR — REF. 90535-52-131-BK6A

Movement: automatic-winding GP033Q0 caliber; 11 ½'''; 46-hour power reserve; 26 jewels; 28,800 vph.
Functions: hours, minutes; perpetual calendar; moonphase indicator.
Case: 18K 5N pink gold; Ø 40mm, thickness: 10.74mm; press-in sapphire crystal; water resistant to 3atm (100 feet).
Dial: silvered opaline; applied markers; leaf-shaped hour and minute hands.
Strap: black large-scale alligator leather, hand-stitched; 18K 5N pink-gold folding buckle.
Also available: 18K white-gold version.

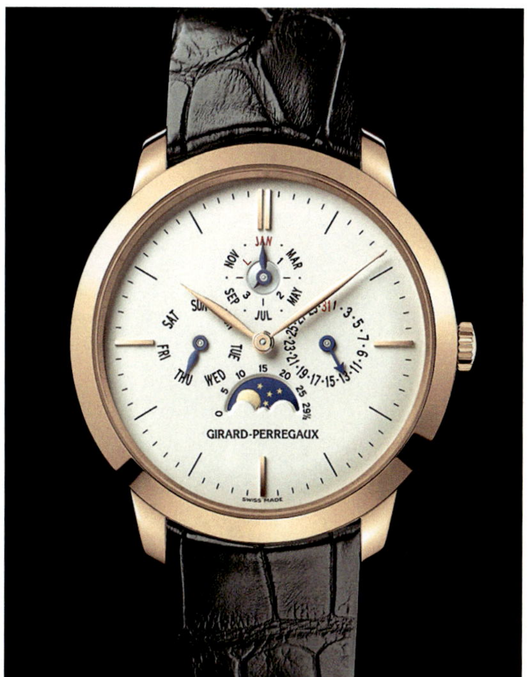

GIRARD-PERREGAUX 1966 CHRONOGRAPH — REF. 49539-52-151-BK6A

Movement: automatic-winding GP030C0 caliber; 10 ½'''; 36-hour power reserve; 38 jewels; 28,800 vph.
Functions: hours, minutes; small seconds; column-wheel chronograph.
Case: 18K 5N pink gold; Ø 40mm, thickness: 12.5mm; press-in sapphire crystal; water resistant to 3atm (100 feet).
Dial: silvered opaline.
Strap: black large-scale alligator leather, hand-stitched; 18K 5N pink-gold folding buckle.
Also available: 18K white-gold version.

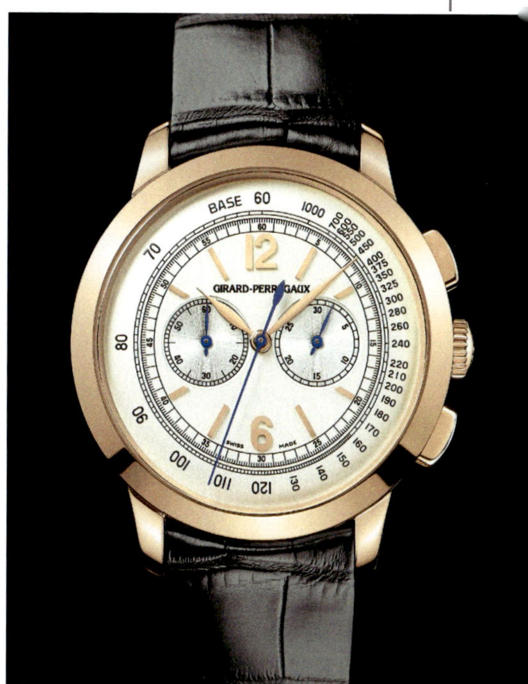

GRAHAM LONDON

PRECISION WITH PERSONALITY

English clockmaker and astronomer George Graham refined the precision of timekeeping in the 18th century with the invention of several devices, most notably the cylinder escapement in clocks that still bears his name.

The company that adopted his name in 1995 is doing more than keeping Graham's name alive, it's also carrying on his legacy of innovation with its Tourbillograph. Introduced in 2009, this complex Swiss Made mechanism combines a shock-resistant tourbillon and a column-wheel chronograph—two complications, ironically, that remained undiscovered in Graham's lifetime. Graham not only combines an automatic-winding function with the tourbillon and chronograph, but it does so at a much more approachable price point than any other tourbillon-making brand.

Graham collaborated closely with its movement maker, La Joux-Perret, to develop the Tourbillograph movement from scratch, earning a pair of patents for the movement and tourbillon. Among the movement's technical achievements is its chronograph-level accuracy, which is aided by the inclusion of a large balance wheel to increase amplitude.

In 2010, Graham showcased this sophisticated automatic caliber in the limited edition Tourbillograph Trackmaster Black. The dial opening that frames the tourbillon is strategically positioned on the dial to balance the chronograph's minutes indication nearby.

The surface of its 47mm stainless steel case takes its dark tone from a coating deposited using PVD. The shade extends to the chronograph pushers, which are adorned with Clous de Paris finishing. More than just decorative, this hobnail pattern also prevents fingers from slipping off the pushers by improving their grip.

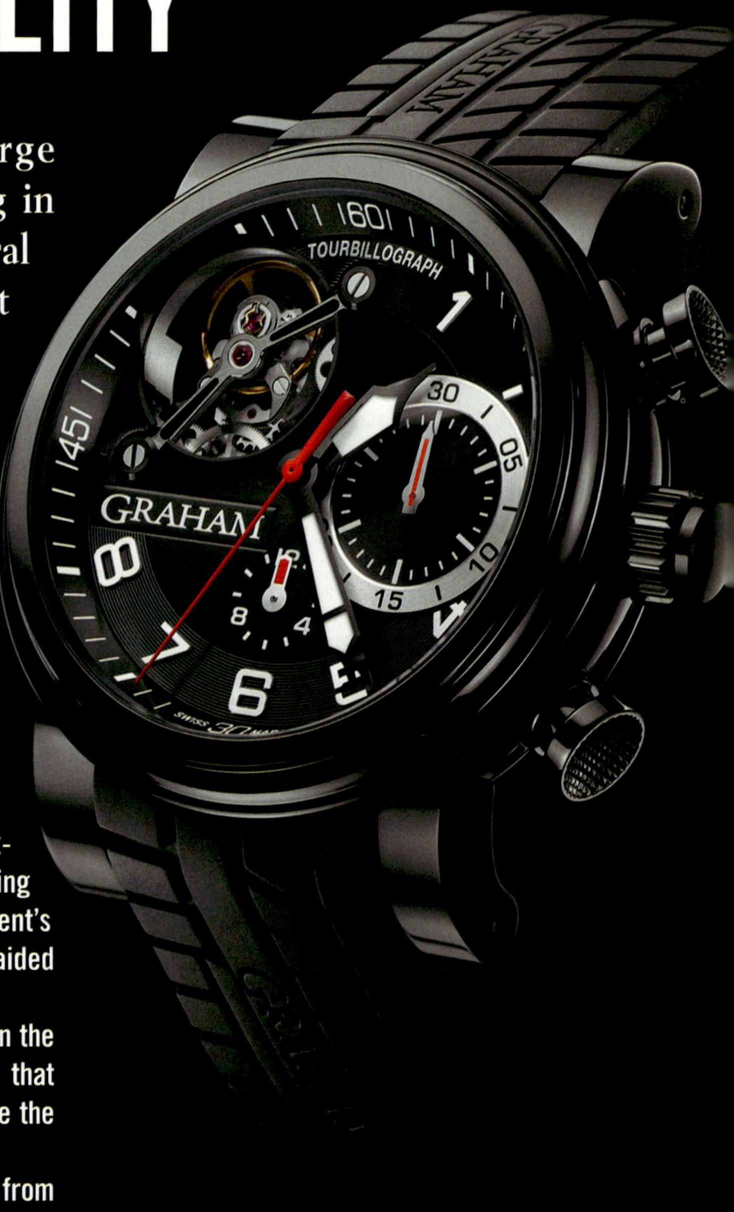

The Tourbillograph Trackmaster Black is equipped with a technically advanced tourbillon that is extremely shock-resistant as well as a classic column wheel chronograph.

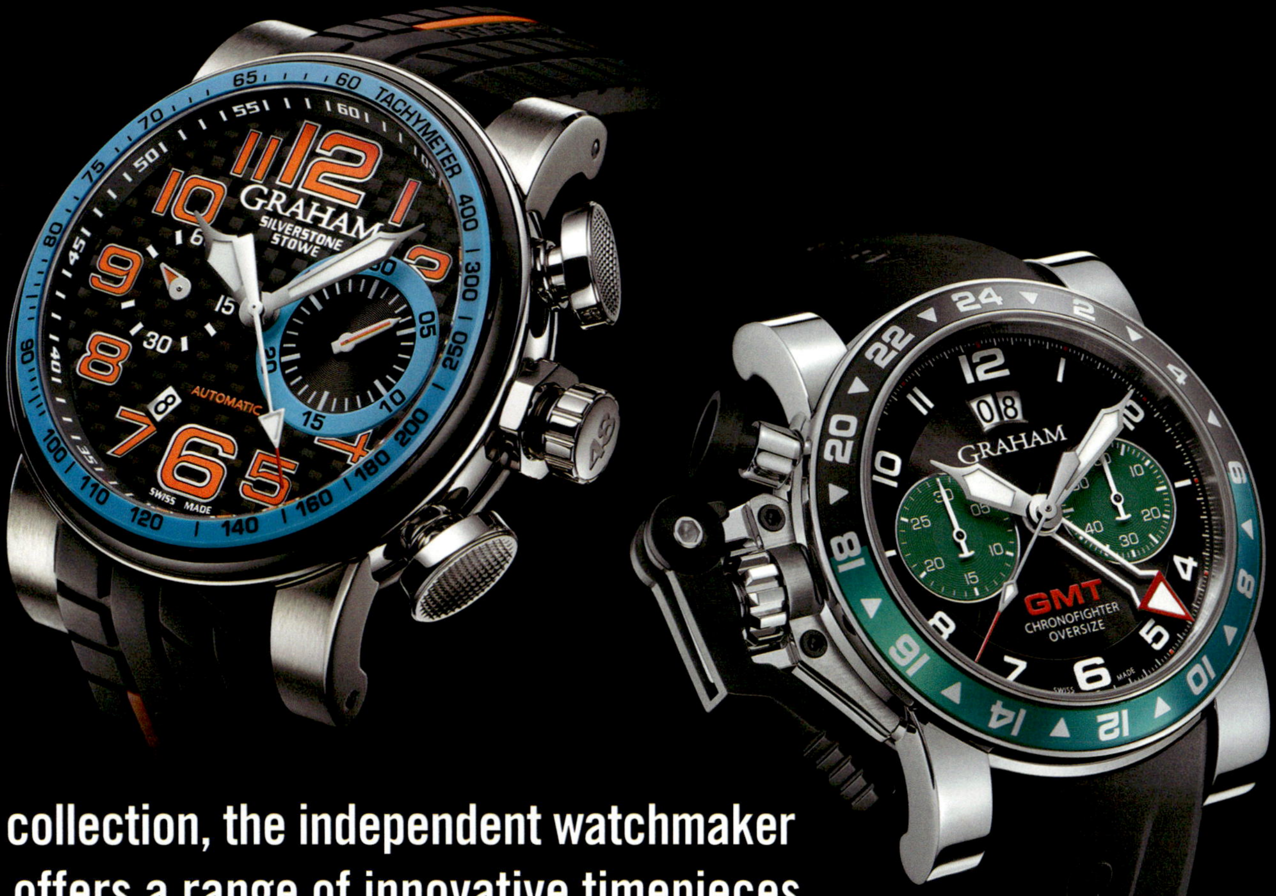

With its collection, the independent watchmaker Graham offers a range of innovative timepieces that draw inspiration from its namesake, the 18th-century English clockmaker George Graham.

The La Chaux-de-Fonds-based watchmaker presents the Tourbillograph Trackmaster Black on a rubber strap molded with a tire-tread motif. Graham will produce 100 pieces with a silver dial and an equal number with a black dial.

The chronograph is Graham's trademark. With the Silverstone Stowe Gulf Blue and the Chronofighter Oversize GMT, the brand shows off two daring designs that spotlight the popular stopwatch function.

The Silverstone collection is named after the historic racetrack north of London that became the site of the first Formula 1 race in 1950. The line includes three different models, each named after one of the racetrack's treacherous turns—Woodcote, Luffield and Stowe.

Bold colors enliven the Silverstone Stowe Gulf Blue's carbon-fiber dial and its bezel, which includes a tachometer scale to calculate speed. Poised on the side of the 48mm stainless steel case, two oversized pushers control the column-wheel chronograph's counters.

From roaring across terra firma, Graham shifts to barnstorming the blue yonder with its Chronofighter series. The generous proportions that distinguish this collection owe a debt to pilots, who require a precision instrument that is easy to both read and operate.

The Chronofighter Oversize GMT fits the bill nicely with color-coordinated chronograph counters activated by the collection's signature trigger-style stop/start button, which serves double duty as a crown protector.

To indicate the second time zone, the watch includes a skeletonized hand and a 24-hour scale on a scratch-proof crystal bezel. The scale also operates as a day/night display, using the black section to indicate night and the colored area for day.

With all of its timepieces, Graham achieves a hard-fought balance of form and function that deftly combines eye-catching designs with innovative technical prowess.

TOP LEFT

The 48mm stainless steel Silverstone Stowe Gulf Blue uses oversized pushers to activate and reset the chronograph's counters on the watch's carbon-fiber dial.

TOP RIGHT

The large curved trigger on the left side of the Chronofighter Oversize GMT's 47mm stainless steel case ensures easy activation of the chronograph.

CHRONOFIGHTER OVERSIZE GMT BLUE STEEL & GOLD — REF. 20VGG.B26A

Movement: automatic-winding G1733 caliber; bi-compax chronograph; 48-hour power reserve; 27 jewels; 28,800 vph, Incabloc shock absorber.
Functions: hours, minutes, seconds; chronograph counters: 60 seconds and 30 minutes; GMT/second time zone; large date with double disc at 12.
Case: steel; Ø 47mm; 18K red-gold crown; sapphire bezel, blue bezel with GMT scale; steel with black PVD left-hand fast-action start/stop trigger and reset pusher; domed sapphire crystal and sapphire crystal caseback with antireflective coating on both sides; water resistant to 10atm.
Dial: black; blue counters; white SuperLumiNova hands and numerals; white skeleton GMT hand with white SuperLumiNova tip and red counters.
Strap: integrated blue crocodile or rubber; black rubber, calf or crocodile.
Suggested price: $16,500
Also available: steel or gold case.

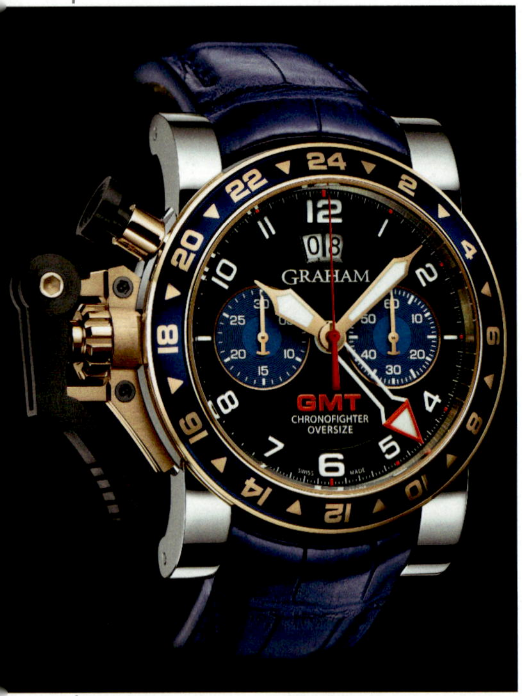

CHRONOFIGHTER OVERSIZE DIVER TURBO TECH — REF. 20VEV.B15A

Movement: automatic-winding G1734 caliber; bi-compax chronograph; 48-hour power reserve; 27 jewels; 28,800 vph, Incabloc shock absorber.
Functions: hours, minutes, seconds; chronograph counters: 60 seconds and 30 minutes; date at 7; Helium valve.
Case: steel; Ø 47mm; black PVD-coated steel bezel, rotating rim to measure decompression time; steel with black PVD left-hand fast-action start/stop trigger; reset pusher with Clous de Paris high grip pattern; domed sapphire crystal with antireflective coating on both sides; stainless steel caseback with Royal Marine crown-symbol; water resistant to 33atm.
Dial: black; yellow contour; black 30-minute counter with silver ring; black and yellow 60-second counter with silver ring; white SuperLumiNova hands and indexes.
Strap: integrated black rubber.
Suggested price: $9,300
Also available: steel; steel with black PVD.

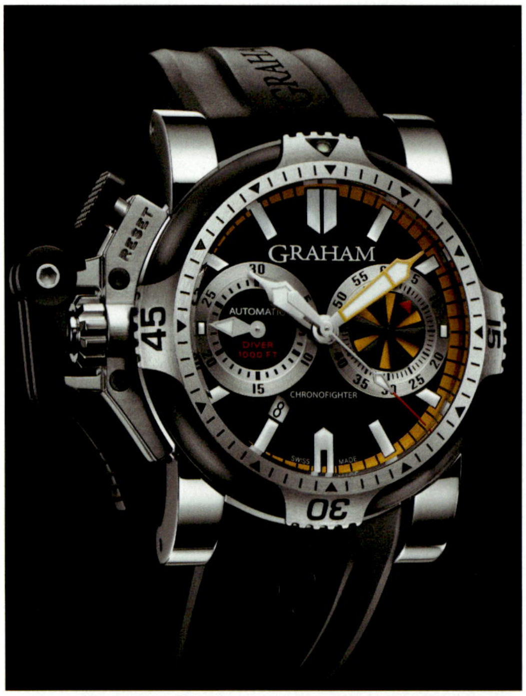

SILVERSTONE STOWE GMT GREEN — REF. 2BLCB.B07A

Movement: automatic-winding G1721 caliber; bi-compax chronograph; 48-hour power reserve; 28 jewels; 28,800 vph; Incabloc shock absorber.
Functions: hours, minutes, seconds; chronograph counters: 60 seconds and 30 minutes; large date with double disc at 6; flyback; GMT/second time zone.
Case: steel with black PVD-coating; Ø 48mm; black carbon bezel; green rim with GMT; steel with black PVD right-hand control pushers with Clous de Paris high grip pattern; domed sapphire crystal; antireflective coating on both sides; sapphire crystal caseback with limited edition serial number engraved; water resistant to 10atm.
Dial: black carbon; black carbon seconds counter; black snailed minutes counter with green ring; black tachometer scale on external ring; white SuperLumiNova hands and numerals; black GMT hand with white SuperLumiNova tip and red contour.
Strap: integrated black tire-tread rubber; green inset.
Note: limited edition of 250 pieces.
Suggested price: $9,900
Also available: red version.

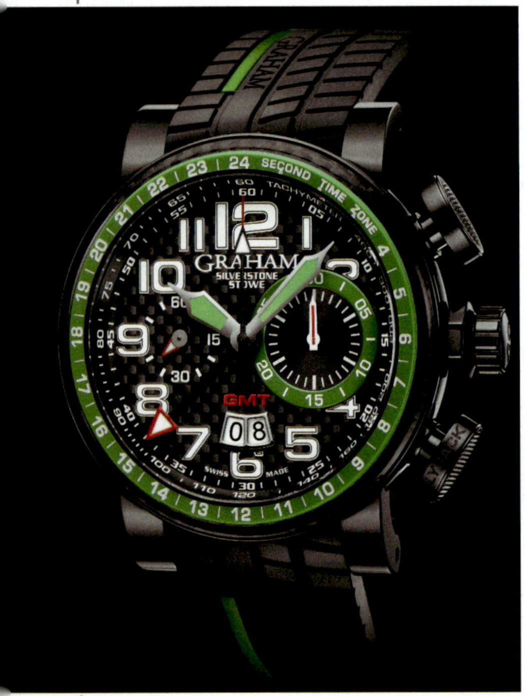

SILVERSTONE STOWE RACING BLUE — REF. 2BLDC.B13A

Movement: automatic-winding G1742 caliber; bi-compax column-wheel chronograph; 48-hour power reserve; 27 jewels; 28,800 vph; Incabloc shock absorber.
Functions: hours, minutes, seconds; column-wheel chronograph counters: 60 seconds and 30 minutes; date at 7.
Case: steel; Ø 48mm; faceted horns; black ceramic bezel, blue rim with tachometer scale; steel right-hand control pushers with Clous de Paris high grip pattern; domed sapphire crystal; sapphire crystal caseback; antireflective coating on both sides; water resistant to 10atm.
Dial: black carbon; black carbon seconds counter; black snailed minutes counter with blue ring; white SuperLumiNova hands; orange SuperLumiNova numerals.
Strap: integrated black tire-tread rubber with orange inset.
Suggested price: $6,900
Also available: steel; gold.

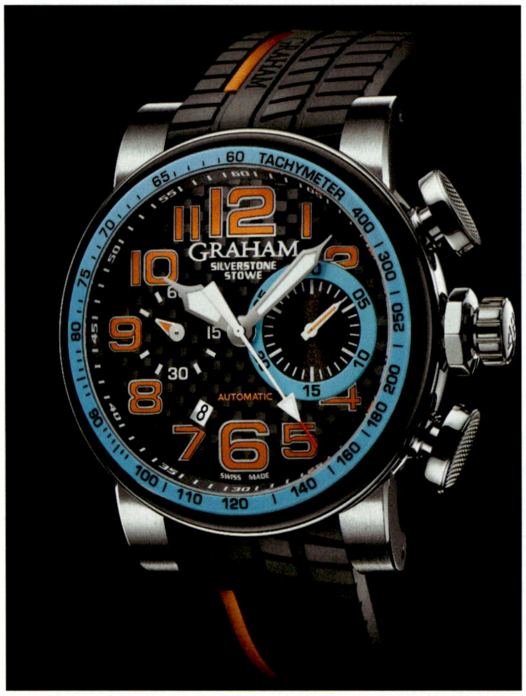

MERCEDES GP TRACKMASTER — REF. 2MEAS.B01A

Movement: automatic-winding G1734 caliber; bi-compax chronograph; 48-hour power reserve; 27 jewels; 28,800 vph; Incabloc shock absorber.
Functions: hours, minutes, seconds; chronograph counters: 60 seconds and 30 minutes; date at 7.
Case: steel; Ø 47mm; steel bezel with Clous de Paris; steel right-hand start/stop and reset pushers with Clous de Paris high grip pattern; domed sapphire crystal; antireflective coating on both sides; sapphire crystal caseback with Mercedes GP Petronas logo printed; water resistant to 10atm.
Dial: black carbon; black snailed minutes counter with silver rim and silver arrows for minute scale; black snailed seconds counter with internal Mercedes GP Petronas green rim and external silver rim; black external rim with minute scale; silver brass hands, numerals and indexes; white Mercedes GP inscription at 5.
Strap: integrated black tire-tread rubber.
Suggested price: $6,300
Also available: varnished silver dial.

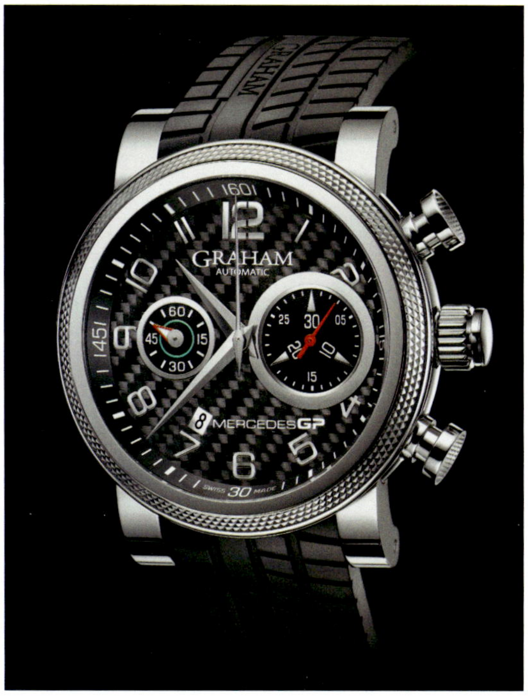

SWORDFISH ALL BLACK PVD — REF. 2SWAB.B35L

Movement: automatic-winding G1710 caliber; bi-compax chronograph; 48-hour power reserve; 34 jewels; 28,800 vph; Incabloc shock absorber.
Functions: hours, minutes, seconds; chronograph counters: 60 seconds and 30 minutes.
Case: steel with black PVD coating; Ø 46mm; steel bezel with black PVD coating; two steel portholes with black PVD coating at 3 and 9; steel with black PVD left-hand control pushers with black PVD-coating and Clous de Paris high grip pattern; flat sapphire crystal with antireflective coating on both sides; steel caseback with black PVD-coating and Royal Marine crown symbol; water resistant to 10atm.
Dial: black; black counters; gray SuperLumiNova minutes hand and numerals; black skeleton hour hand; seconds hand, hour and minute counters' hands with red tip; rectangular red sweep seconds hand.
Strap: black rubber.
Suggested price: $9,000
Also available: right-hand control pushers.

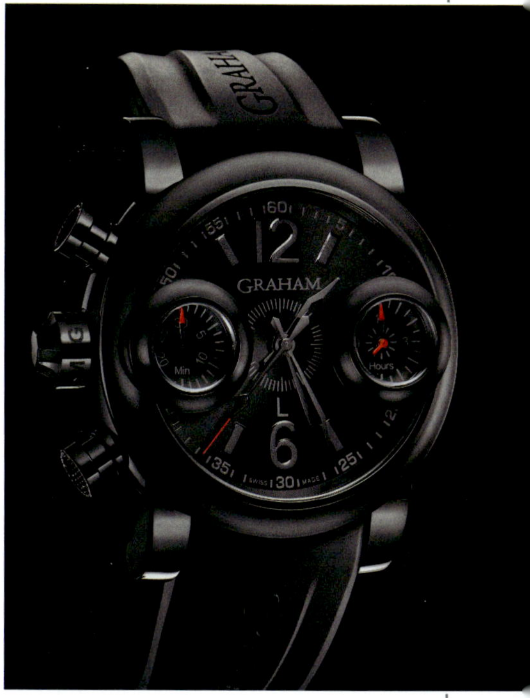

CHRONOFIGHTER RAC BLACK FIGHTER — REF. 2CRBS.B02A

Movement: automatic-winding G1742 caliber; bi-compax chronograph; 48-hour power reserve; 27 jewels; 28,800 vph; Incabloc shock absorber.
Functions: hours, minutes, seconds; column-wheel chronograph counters: 60 seconds and 30 minutes; date at 7.
Case: steel; Ø 43mm; steel bezel; left-hand fast-action start/stop trigger and reset pusher; domed sapphire crystal and sapphire crystal caseback with antireflective coating on both sides; water resistant to 10atm.
Dial: black; black counters; white SuperLumiNova hands, numerals and indexes.
Strap: bomber brown calf.
Suggest price: $7,950
Also available: black rubber, calf or crocodile; black and orange or brown calf; brown crocodile; steel bracelet.

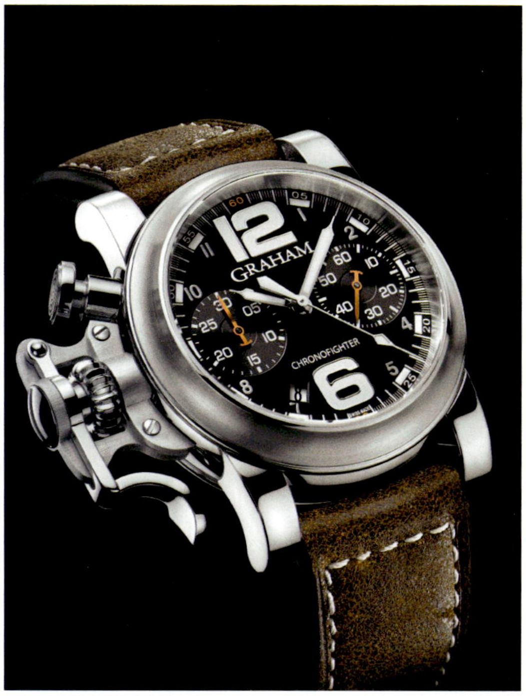

TOURBILLOGRAPH TRACKMASTER CHROMIUM — REF. 2TWTS.S03A

Movement: caliber G1781, automatic bi-compax column wheel chronograph-tourbillon; 48-hour power reserve; 34 jewels; 28,800 vph; Incabloc shock absorber; movement finished with perlages, stripes, manually chamfered and polished edges; column wheel with polished segments on base cog wheel with black low-friction coating; skeletonised black chromium rotor with 925 sterling silver ocillating weight; tourbillon cage: 48 components: 0.485g; off-center construction at 11; completely transparent tourbillon; two patents; black PVD-coated double bridge construction.
Functions: hours, minutes, seconds; column-wheel chronograph counters: 60 seconds and 30 minutes. **Case:** steel; Ø 47mm; steel bezel with Clous de Paris; steel right-hand start/stop and reset pushers with Clous de Paris high grip pattern; domed sapphire crystal and sapphire crystal caseback with engraved name and limited edition serial number; antireflective coating on both sides; water resistant to 10atm. **Dial:** silver; external black minute scale rim; silver hour counter; silver snailed minute counter with black rim; white SuperLuminova hands and indexes. **Strap:** integrated black tire-tread rubber; ceramic folding buckle. **Note:** limited edition of 100 pieces.
Suggested price: $39,750
Also available: black crocodile strap.

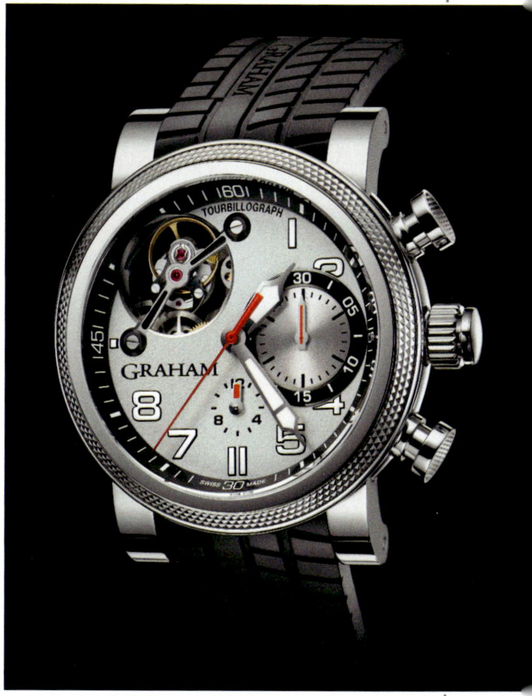

GREUBEL FORSEY
INVENTEURS HORLOGERS

STRIKING GOLD

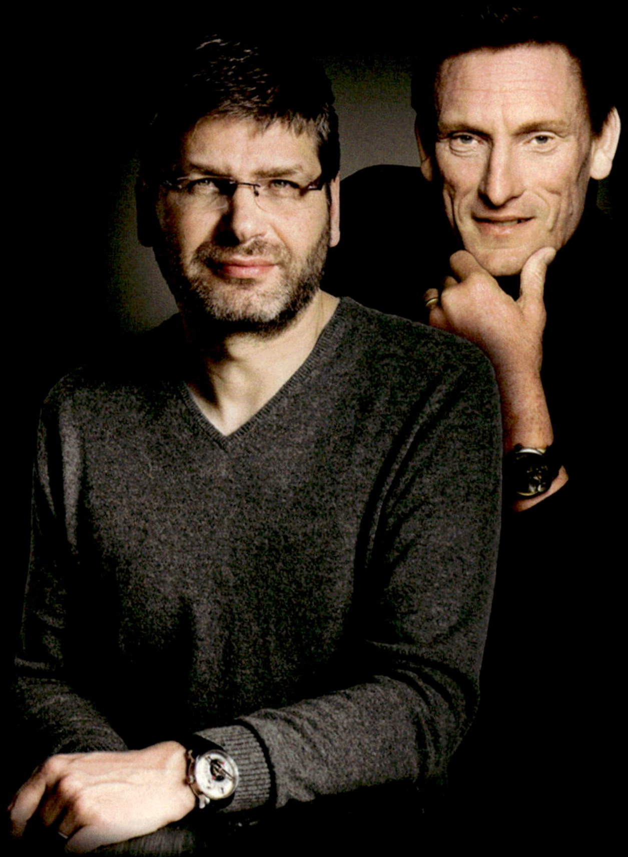

Greubel Forsey earned its second major award in as many years at the 2010 Grand Prix d'Horlogerie de Genève, as the young brand's Double Tourbillon 30° Edition Historique was honored with L'Aiguille d'Or (the Golden Hand).

Awarded to the watch judged to be the best from all of the competition's categories, l'Aiguille d'Or is the most prestigious prize bestowed by the Grand Prix.

The accolade provides a celebratory coda for the Double Tourbillon 30° Contemporaine line, which Greubel Forsey stopped producing at the end of 2010. The Double Tourbillon 30° mechanism has been an important part of the brand from the beginning and was featured in the first watch Robert Greubel and Stephen Forsey introduced in 2004, when the inventor-watchmakers launched Greubel Forsey. Since then, the ranks of the Double Tourbillon 30° collection have swelled to include several interpretations: Vision, Secret, IP1, Historique and Technique, the latter earning the "Best Complicated Watch" prize at the 2009 Geneva Grand Prix.

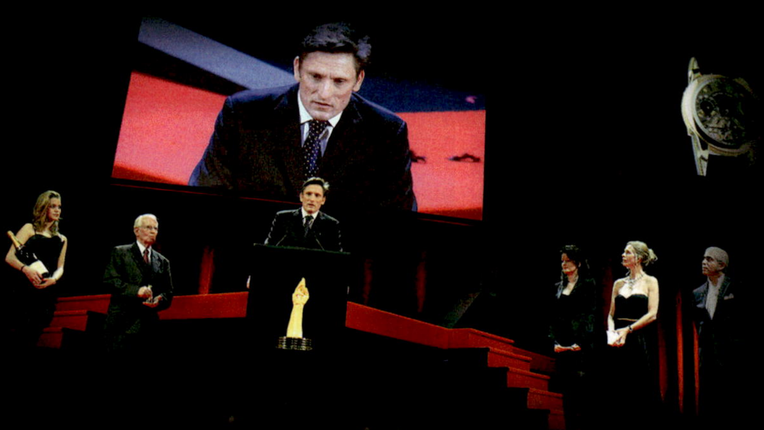

The vital role that the original model played in the brand's rapid ascension cannot be overstated. In a field crowded with horological legends, the watch's remarkable complication thrust the then-new brand into the spotlight. More importantly, it also convinced discerning enthusiasts of Greubel Forsey's legitimacy. Collectors with an affinity for technicity recognized the significance of the complication, which combines a tourbillon positioned at a 30° inclination rotating once in 60 seconds inside a second tourbillon carriage with a four-minute rotation. The groundbreaking arrangement maximizes chronometric performance by averaging out errors induced by the force of gravity on the balance. The Double Tourbillon 30° was the first of many inventions to emerge from Greubel Forsey's atelier in La Chaux-de-Fonds in just seven years.

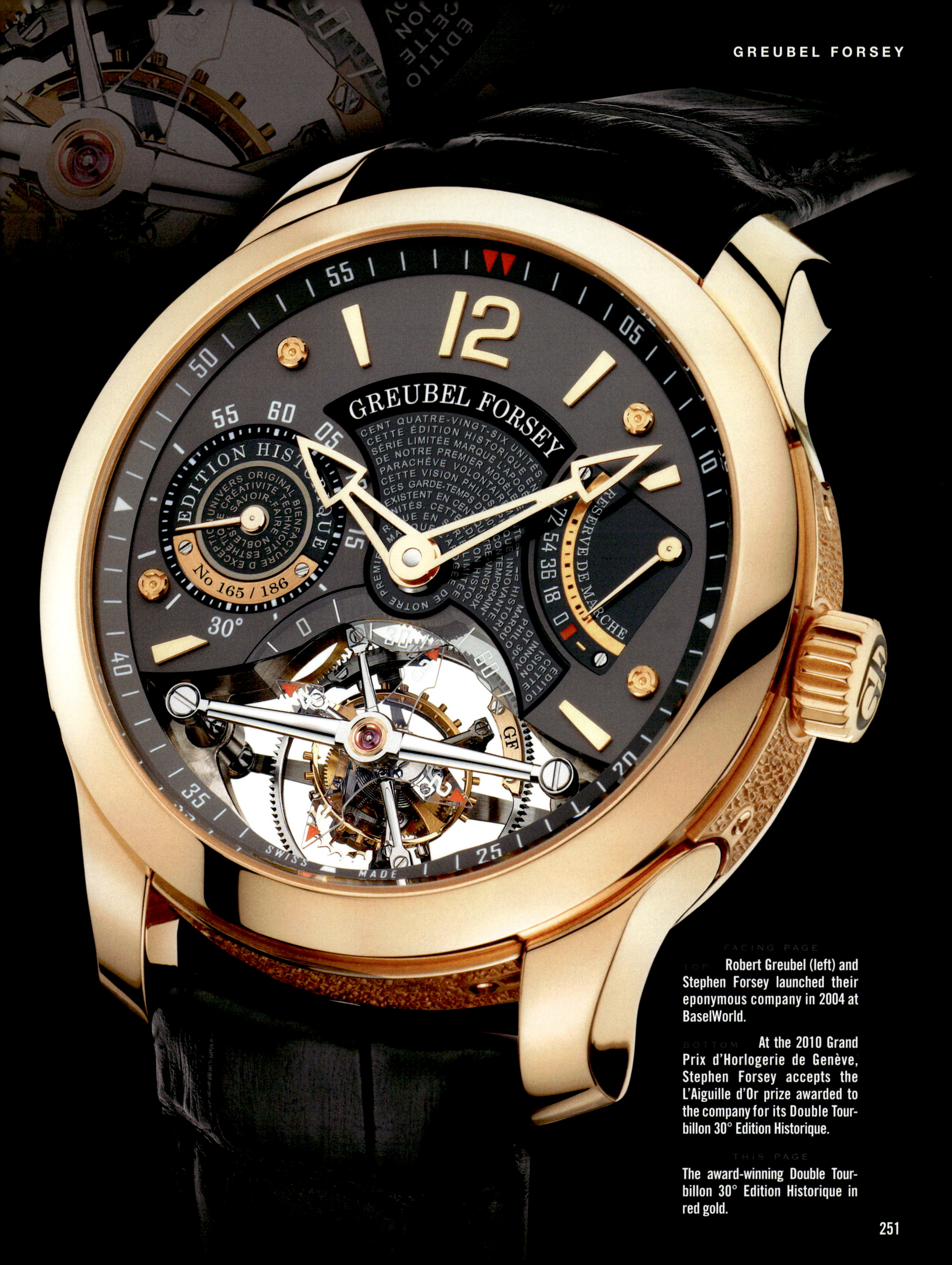

FACING PAGE

TOP Robert Greubel (left) and Stephen Forsey launched their eponymous company in 2004 at BaselWorld.

BOTTOM At the 2010 Grand Prix d'Horlogerie de Genève, Stephen Forsey accepts the L'Aiguille d'Or prize awarded to the company for its Double Tourbillon 30° Edition Historique.

THIS PAGE

The award-winning Double Tourbillon 30° Edition Historique in red gold.

To the delight of horological aficionados, Greubel Forsey develops and produces mechanical solutions whose raison d'être is to improve the performance of mechanical watches with completely original inventions.

A year after the brand's debut, Greubel Forsey unveiled the Quadruple Tourbillion prototype. Its patented design combines two double tourbillons linked by a spherical differential to elevate the level of precision achieved by the movement.

Greubel Forsey continued to indulge its passion for innovative tourbillon movements in 2006 with the prototype of the Tourbillon 24 Secondes. Unlike the previous multi-tourbillon movements, this timepiece features a single tourbillon inclined at 25° with a rapid rotation enabling a high rate of accuracy for a single tourbillon cage.

Along with these impressive complications, Greubel Forsey also pioneered a number of solutions conceived to enhance the performance of the mechanical wristwatch movement. One of the most recent, the Différentiel d'Egalité, is a device created to provide a more constant supply of energy from the mainspring to the escapement.

While these complex creations appear anything but straightforward, the philosophy that led to their invention was unfailingly simple: respect the past by not repeating it. "Robert Greubel and I both agree that there is still much to be invented in the horological universe," says Stephen Forsey. "We take a fresh approach to the time-honored tradition of watchmaking by refusing to accept that everything has been invented and adhering to a rigorous analytical approach to each complication in order to explore new avenues."

The same meticulous attention given to the timepieces' technical details is also used to craft the magnificent visual features of Greubel Forsey's handsomely appointed dials and cases, including two asymmetrical case designs equipped with curved sapphire crystal windows integrated into the case band.

The exceptional hand-finishing of the movement serves as a major point of pride for the company. Greubel Forsey's trademark aesthetics include a frosted finish on the bridges and mainplates, mirror-like black polishing and myriad of hand-beveled parts.

The extraordinary level of mechanical complexity and decorative beauty requires a great deal of time to execute. As a result, Greubel Forsey timepieces are produced in extremely limited quantities of just over 100 timepieces a year.

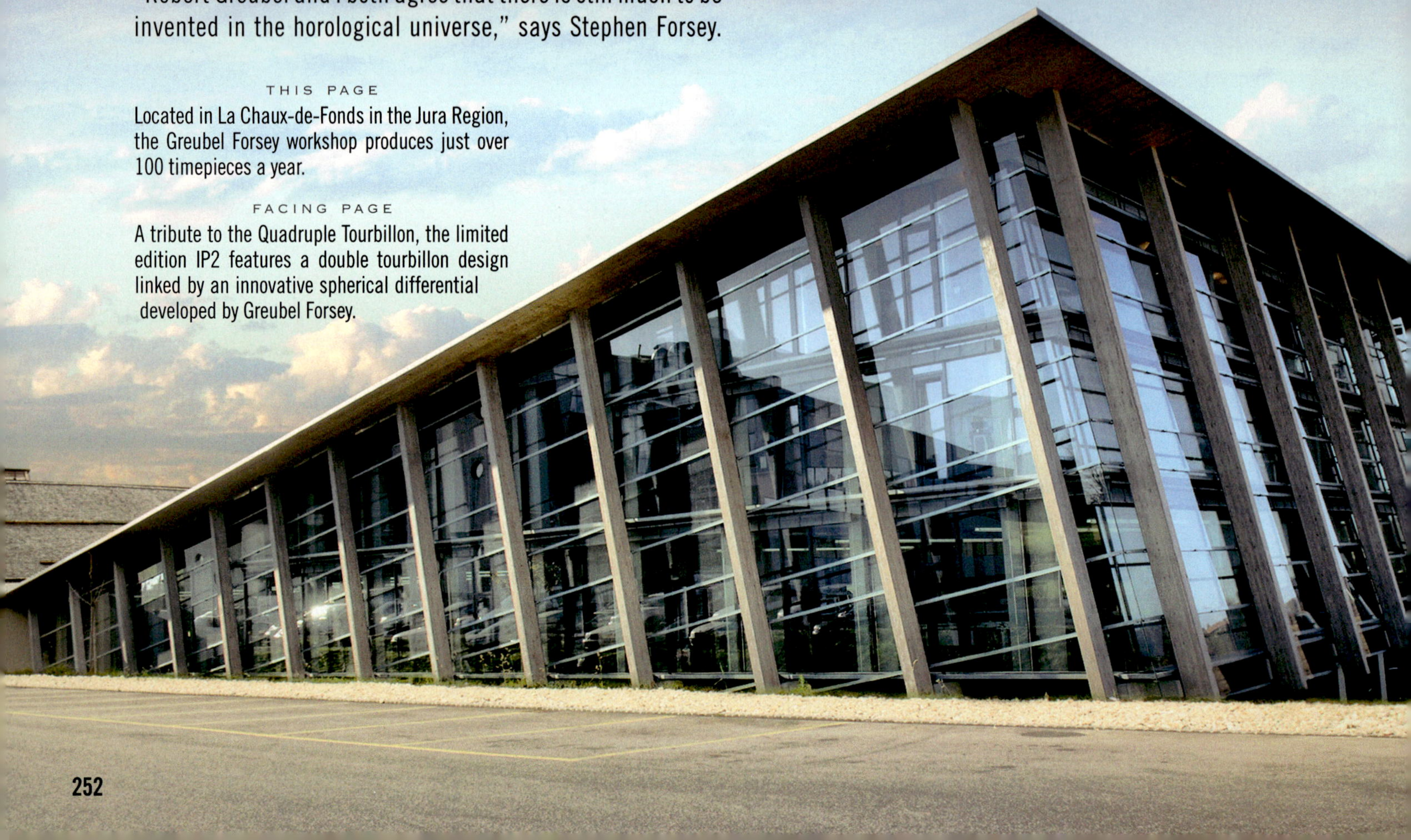

THIS PAGE
Located in La Chaux-de-Fonds in the Jura Region, the Greubel Forsey workshop produces just over 100 timepieces a year.

FACING PAGE
A tribute to the Quadruple Tourbillon, the limited edition IP2 features a double tourbillon design linked by an innovative spherical differential developed by Greubel Forsey.

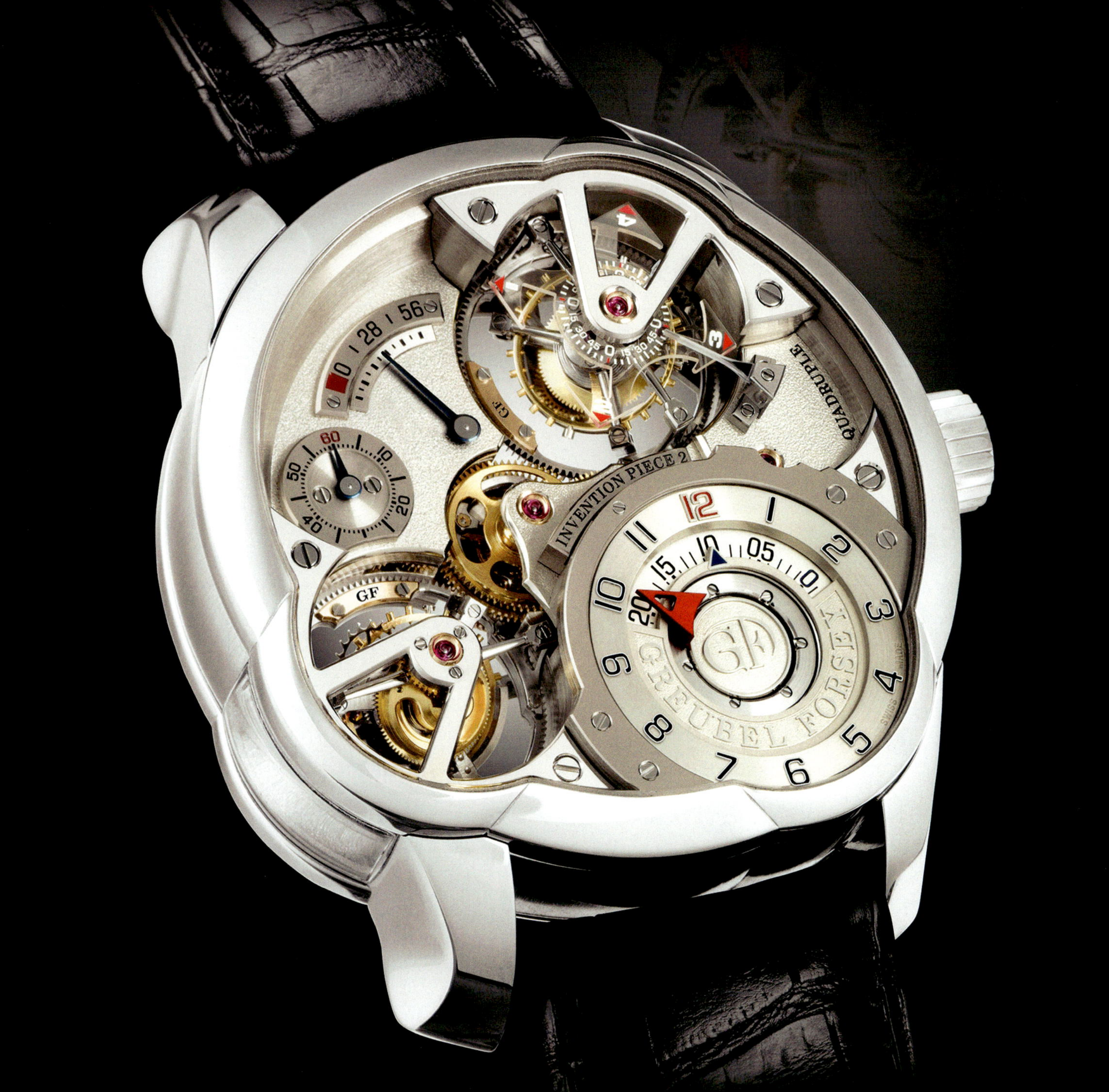

In 2007, Greubel Forsey initiated the "Invention Piece (IP)," a line of unique edition watches designed to pay homage to the company's horological mechanisms and complications. The Invention Piece collection honoured the Double Tourbillon 30° with IP1 in 2007 and the Tourbillon 24 Seconds in 2009 with IP3.

At the 2011 Salon International de la Haute Horlogerie (SIHH) in Geneva, Greubel Forsey added to the collection with IP2, a unique edition tribute to their Quadruple Tourbillon.

The open architecture of IP2 highlights all angles of the two double tourbillons, and the spherical differential used to connect them, by fully exposing their exquisitely choreographed mechanical ballet.

In juxtaposition with its mechanical sophistication, IP2 uses the muted tone of the movement's frosted finish as a background for the small seconds and the 56-hour power reserve indicator. The latter at 11 o'clock articulates the status of the triple mainspring barrels, which are positioned at 5 o'clock. Concealing the barrels, the time display indicates the hours with a revolving red triangle and the minutes on a rotating disc.

As with all Invention Pieces, production of IP2 will be extremely limited. Greubel Forsey will manufacture a unique edition of just 11 pieces each in platinum and red gold.

Present from the beginning, the dedication to performance, refinement and exclusivity are brand hallmarks today and emblematic of the holistic watchmaking philosophy developed by Greubel Forsey.

FROM A TO ZEPHYR

Few contemporary elite watchmakers design both jewelry and timepieces. One notable exception is Guy Ellia. The avant-garde designer whose innovations create some of the most complicated watches in the industry considers horology his main passion, yet his bejeweled background is evident in every watch he designs—right down to the beautiful mechanical movements that are as stunning as they are precise.

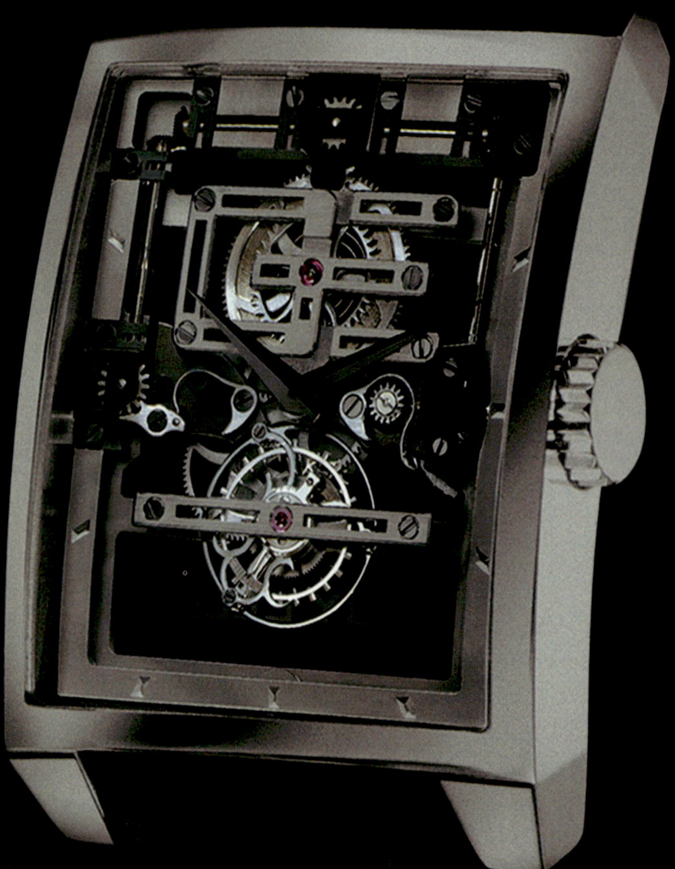

As a diamond dealer and jewelry designer, Guy Ellia launched his first innovative line of timepieces in 1999, which immediately rocketed him into the realm of watchmaking royalty. Collaborating with such prestigious movement designers as Parmigiani, Piguet and, most recently, Christophe Claret, Guy Ellia's extraordinary creative vision continuously emerges in surprising ways through his watch designs. Ellia's Répétition Minute Zephyr, introduced in Basel three years ago, is a marvel of form and function. The watch's transparency and extraordinarily high complications—yet ethereal with dreamlike visage—made it an instant classic for men.

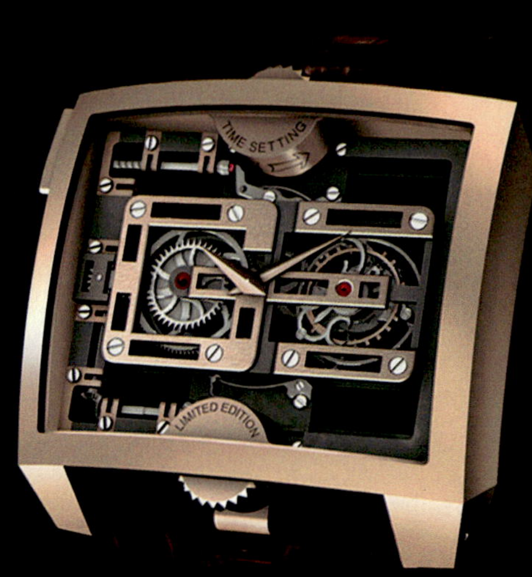

ABOVE The Tourbillon Magistère Titanium is powered by the manual-winding Christophe Claret caliber TGE 97, which possesses a titanium mainplate and bridges.

RIGHT Housed in a bi-convex red-gold case, the Tourbillon Magistère II is also available in white gold.

The inner workings of a Guy Ellia watch often take center stage, making the watch itself into a jewel.

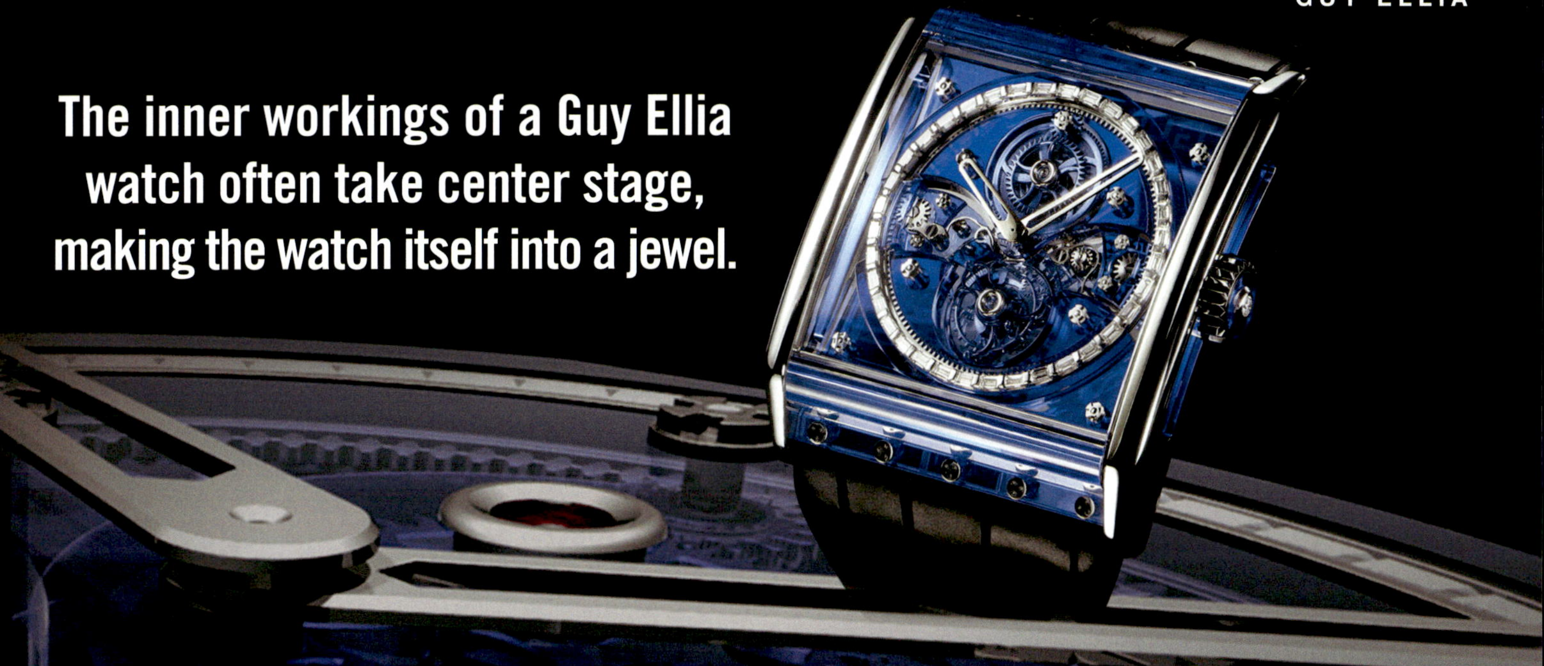

"Creation is a delicate thing," says Ellia. "Watch designs must be trendy, yet timeless. Each year, we must show something different; but luxury watches must be perfect. There is a constant need to create new and better technology." Because of the level of complication in Ellia's designs, his watches can take five or six years to develop.

In his offices on the glamorous rue de la Paix in Paris, Ellia's relaxed demeanor belies his opulent luxury businesses. Dressed in jeans, his striking white hair casually wind-tousled, Ellia exudes a blend of understated elegance, bohemian charm and quintessential French intellectualism. It is this combination of characteristics that identifies Ellia and informs his designs.

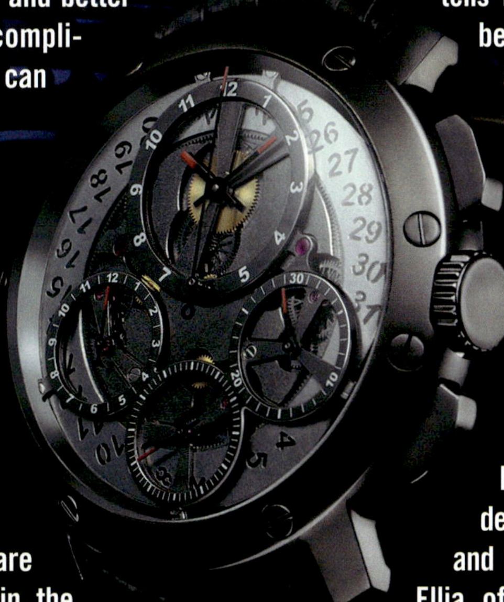

While Ellia declares that "watches are one of the most difficult businesses in the luxury world," he also concedes that haute timepieces seem to be one of the few niches relatively impervious to financial hardship: a watch is often the only accessory a man will allow himself; without a watch encircling her wrist, a woman still feels naked. In an era when watches are no longer necessities, the timepiece a person chooses to wear tells much more about that person than ever before. Men and women who favor Guy Ellia are hip, yet refined, savvy and individualistic—more likely to start their own trends than to join in on someone else's.

Incredibly selective when it comes to choosing retailers, Guy Ellia is enjoying ever-increasing attention around the globe. In the popular film *L'Emmerdeur*, which was released in December 2008, the lead character sports a Guy Ellia watch. Some of the biggest names in French cinema are said to own Ellia designs, including Jean Reno, Gérard Darmon and Gérard Lanvin. With his latest designs, Guy Ellia offers watches that transcend time.

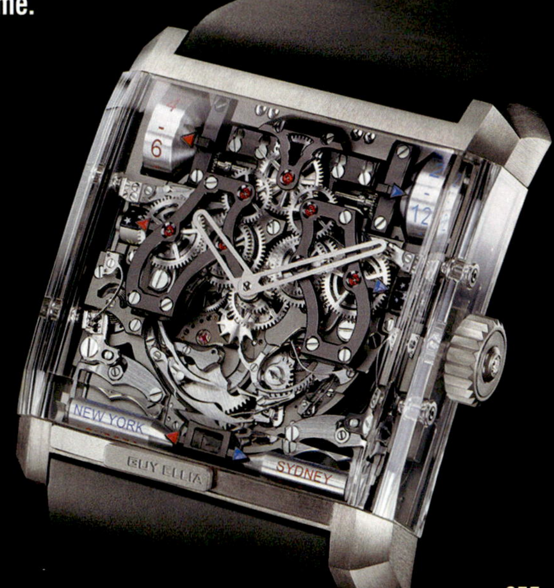

TOP The dial of the Tourbillon Zephyr offers glimpses of the manual-winding Christophe Claret GES 97 caliber that powers it.

CENTER The Jumbo Chrono displays the day at 2 o'clock via a unique coloration system.

RIGHT Also available in pink gold and titanium, Guy Ellia's Répétition Minute Zephyr is pictured in a sapphire crystal case that measures a bold 53.6x43.7mm.

REPETITION MINUTE ZEPHYR

Movement: manual-winding Christophe Claret GEC 88 caliber; 41.2x38.2mm, thickness: 9.41mm; 48-hour power reserve; 72 jewels; 18,000 vph; 720 components; flat balance-spring; gear wheels with different platings; five-position adjustment.
Functions: hours, minutes; power reserve indicator; minute repeater; five time zones with day/night indicators.
Case: sapphire crystal block; convex; 53.6x43.7mm, thickness: 14.8mm; sapphire and 18K gold crown set with a Ø 2.2mm diamond; water resistant to 3atm.
Strap: rubber; width case/buckle: 33/24mm; 18K solid white-gold folding buckle (17.27g).
Note: limited edition of 20 numbered pieces.
Also available: pink gold and titanium; alligator strap.

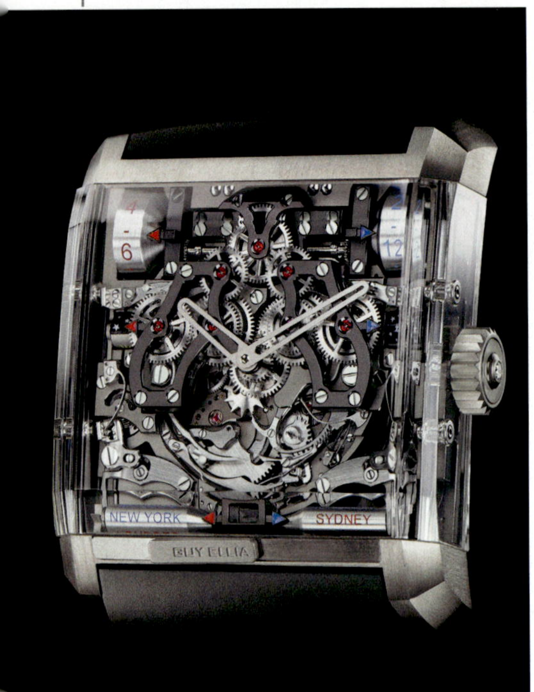

TOURBILLON ZEPHYR

Movement: manual-winding Christophe Claret GES 97 caliber; 37x37mm, thickness: 6.21mm; 110-hour power reserve; 17 jewels; 21,600 vph; 233 components; flat balance-spring; winding ring set with 36 baguette-cut diamonds (1.04 carats) or guilloché; one-minute tourbillon; entirely hand-chamfered cage; bottom plate and bridges in blue sapphire; five-position adjustment.
Functions: hours, minutes; tourbillon.
Case: 18K gold sides; convex; 54x45.3mm, thickness: 15.4mm; crown set with a Ø 1mm diamond; sapphire crystal with thermal counter-shock marking; transparent caseback, hearth engraving; water resistant to 3atm.
Strap: alligator; width case/buckle: 37/22mm; 18K solid gold folding buckle (15.64g).
Note: limited edition of 12 numbered pieces.
Also available: white gold.

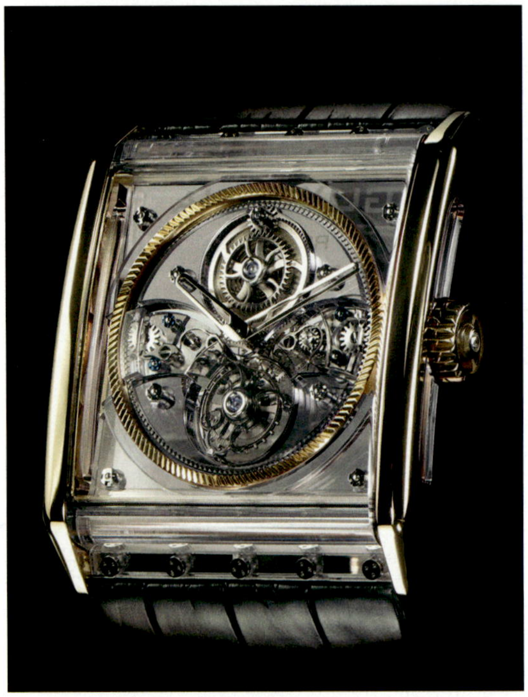

TOURBILLON MAGISTERE TITANIUM

Movement: manual-winding Christophe Claret TGE 97 caliber; 37.4x29.9mm, thickness: 5.4mm; 110-hour power reserve; 20 jewels; 21,600 vph; flat balance-spring; mysterious winding; one-minute tourbillon; skeletonized barrel and ratchet-wheel; entirely hand-chamfered cage; titanium bottom plate and bridges.
Functions: hours, minutes.
Case: titanium (18.2g); biconvex; 43.5x36mm, thickness: 10.9mm; sapphire crystal with thermal counter-shock marking; water resistant to 3atm.
Strap: alligator; width case/buckle: 24/20mm; 18K solid white-gold folding buckle (9.65g) and titanium hood.

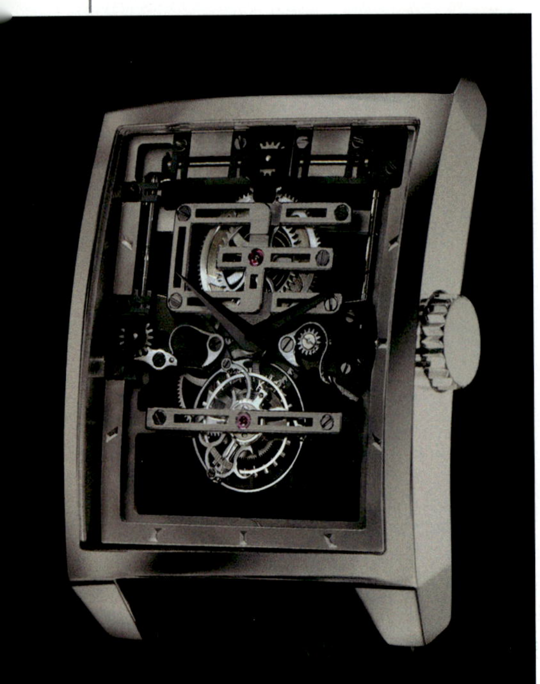

TOURBILLON MAGISTERE II

Movement: manual-winding Christophe Claret MGE-97 caliber; 38.4x30.9mm, thickness: 5.71mm; 90-hour power reserve; 33 jewels; 21,600 vph; 266 components; flat balance-spring; mysterious winding; one-minute tourbillon; skeleton ratchet and wheels with curved arms and wolf-teeth; entirely hand-chamfered cage; barrel bridges and tourbillon in 18K gold.
Functions: hours, minutes.
Case: 18K 5N red gold (97.54g); biconvex; 44.2x36.7mm, thickness: 15mm; sapphire crystal with antireflective treatment; transparent caseback; water resistant to 3atm.
Strap: alligator; 18K 5N red-gold folding buckle (14.61g).
Note: limited edition of 12 numbered pieces.
Also available: white gold.

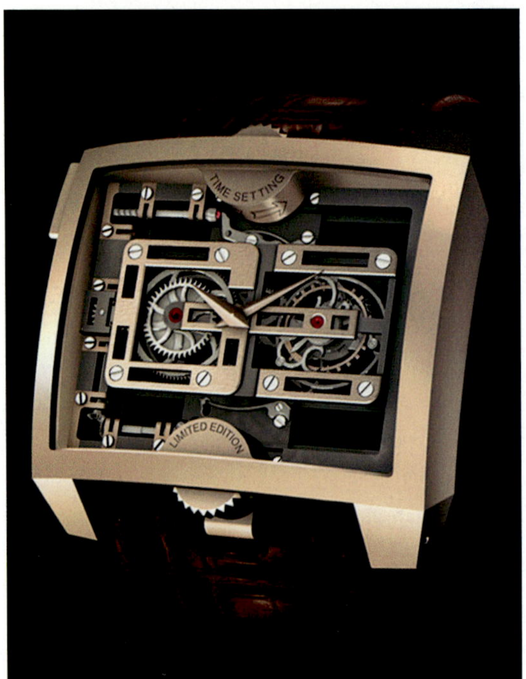

JUMBO CHRONO

Movement: automatic-winding Frédéric Piguet PGE 1185 caliber; Ø 26.2mm, thickness: 5.5mm; column-wheel chronograph; 45-hour power reserve; five-position adjustment; Côtes de Genève-finished bridges with rhodium plating; GUY ELLIA logo engraved on rotor with rhodium plating.
Functions: hours, minutes at 12; small seconds at 6; day by coloration at 2; 30-minute counter at 4; 12-hour counter at 8; central chronograph sweep seconds.
Case: 18K black-gold (87g); Ø 50mm, thickness: 11.5mm; sapphire crystal with thermal counter-shock marking; water resistant to 3atm.
Strap: alligator; width case/buckle: 26/20mm; 18K black-gold folding buckle (16g).
Also available: set black-gold bezel; full-set black gold; white gold; set white-gold bezel; full-set white gold; pink gold; set pink-gold bezel; full-set pink gold.

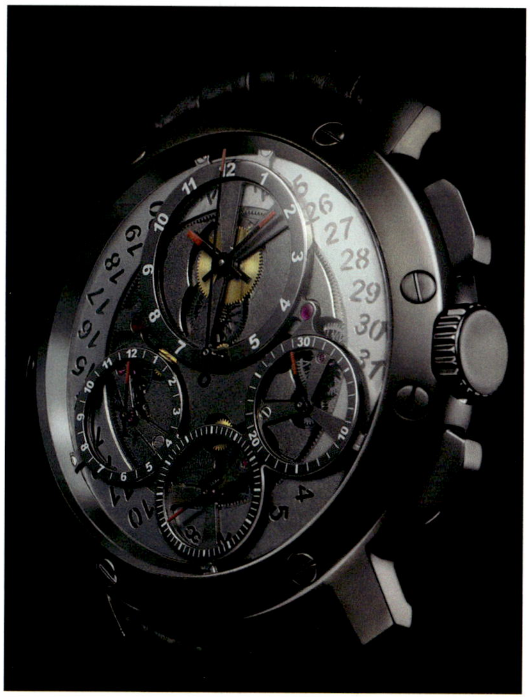

TIME SPACE QUANTIEME PERPETUEL

Movement: manual-winding Frédéric Piguet PGE 5615 D caliber; Ø 35.64mm, thickness: 4.7mm; 43-hour power reserve; 20 jewels; 21,600 vph; five-position adjustment; Côtes de Genève-finished bridges with black PVD treatment; GE logo engraved on stippled plate with black PVD treatment; watch box with an integrated specific automatic winder.
Functions: hours, minutes; day; date; month; moonphase; leap years.
Case: 18K black gold (32.87g); Ø 46.8mm, thickness: 7.75mm; white sapphire case middle ring; sapphire crystal with thermal counter-shock marking; water resistant to 3atm.
Strap: alligator; width case/buckle: 26/18mm; 18K black-gold pin buckle (4.73g).
Also available: set black-gold bezel; full-set black gold; white gold; set white-gold bezel; full-set white gold; pink gold; set pink-gold bezel; full-set pink gold.

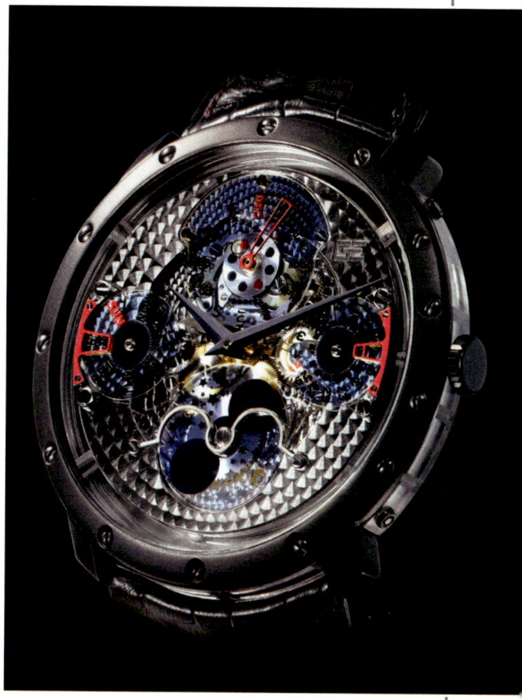

TIME SPACE

Movement: manual-winding Frédéric Piguet PGE 15 caliber; Ø 35.64mm, thickness: 1.9mm; 43-hour power reserve; 20 jewels; 21,600 vph; five-position adjustment; Côtes de Genève-finished bridges with black PVD treatment; GE logo engraved on stippled plate with black PVD treatment.
Functions: hours, minutes.
Case: 18K pink gold (33.5g); Ø 46.8mm, thickness: 4.9mm; sapphire crystal with thermal counter-shock marking; water resistant to 3atm.
Strap: alligator; width case/buckle: 26/18mm; 18K white-gold pin buckle (4.73g).
Also available: set pink-gold bezel; full-set pink gold; white gold; set white-gold bezel; full-set white gold; black gold; set black-gold bezel; full-set black gold.

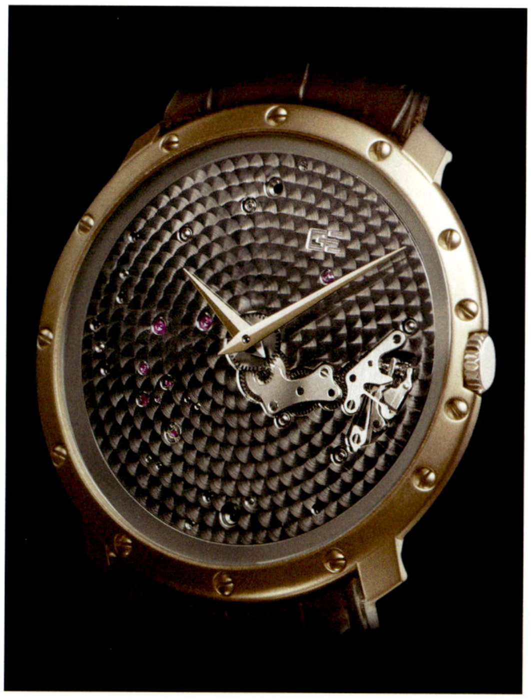

CIRCLE

Movement: Frédéric Piguet PGE 820 caliber; Ø 18.8mm, thickness: 1.95mm.
Functions: hours, minutes.
Case: 18K polished white gold (83.86g); Ø 52mm, thickness: 7mm; bezel set with 124 diamonds (diamonds: Ø 1.5mm); sapphire crystal with thermal counter-shock marking; crown set with one Ø 2.8mm diamond; mirror-polished caseback set with a Ø 0.95mm diamond on the "i" of ELLIA; water resistant to 3atm.
Dial: 18K white-gold mirror; markers set with 168 brilliants (1 carat); dauphine-shaped 18K white-gold hands.
Strap: alligator; 18K solid white-gold pin buckle set with 86 diamonds (0.384 carat); pin set with one Ø 0.9mm diamond; width case/buckle: 31.6/20mm.
Also available: set case, matte white-gold bezel; full-set white gold; matte black, glossy black, opaline or matte gold dial; shiny black, mirror-polished gold, gold outline or polished copper outline hour markers.

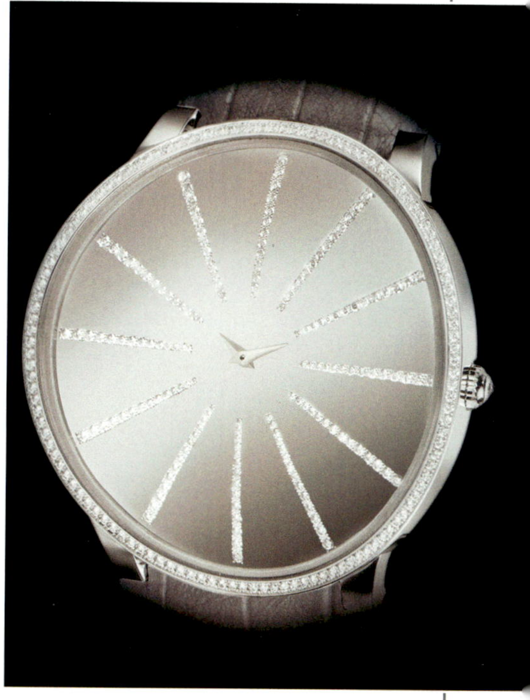

H. Moser & Cie.

THE MOON AND TIDES

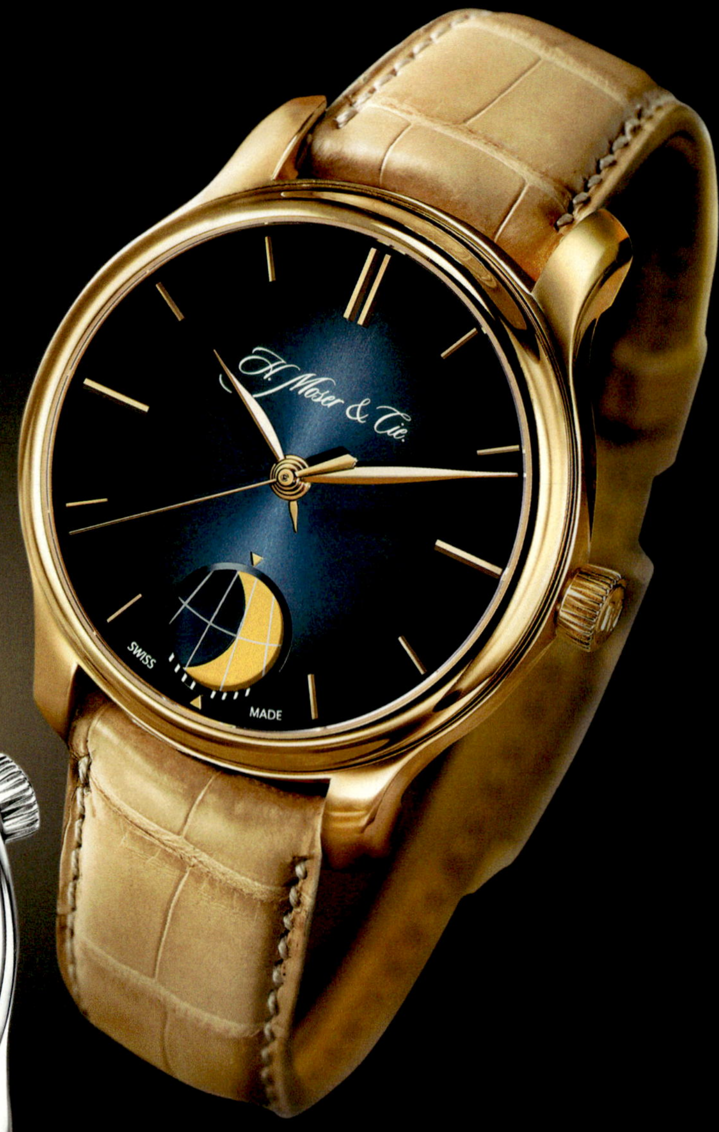

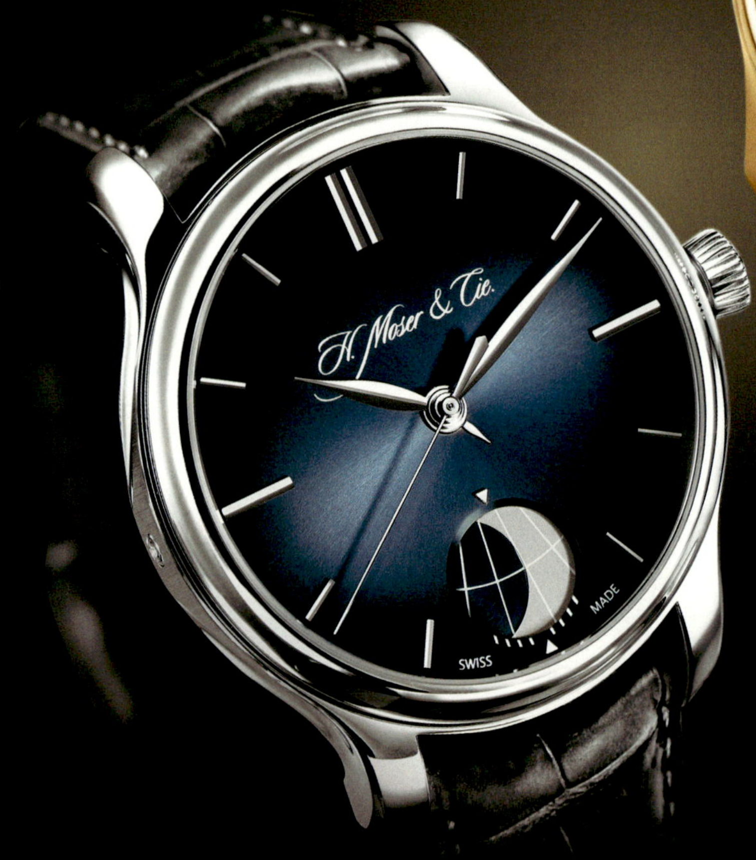

When Heinrich Moser returned to Schaffhausen in the mid-1800s, he harnessed the river tides with a dam to power his growing industrial empire. More than a century later, H. Moser & Cie seeks dominion over the moon with a groundbreaking lunar indication.

The Perpetual Moon set a new benchmark for moonphase watches with a movement that will reflect the true length of the lunar cycle to within one day, after more than a century of continuous use.

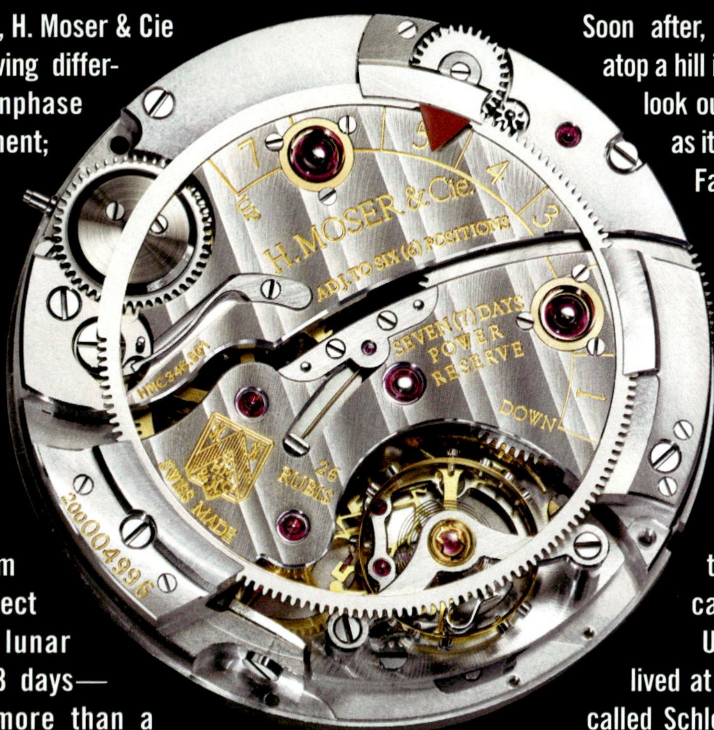

With its Perpetual Moon, H. Moser & Cie underscores the growing differences among moonphase watches. All require adjustment; however, depending on the complexity of the movement, that frequency can range from as often as once a year for a large percentage of watches, to roughly once every century for an elite class of "astronomical" moonphases.

H. Moser & Cie surpasses both with a mechanism designed to accurately reflect the true length of the lunar cycle—approximately 29.53 days—to within one day, after more than a century of continuous use.

The watchmaker's attention to precision is also reflected in the savvy way the movement connects the hour indicator directly to the moonphase so it can be set to the minute.

Glistening with light caught in the grooves of its sunray brushing, the deep blue dial takes on personalities as different as day and night depending on the case metal. In rose gold it emits a cheerful glow much like its yellow moon. For the platinum case, a pale gray moon rises through the dial opening at 6 o'clock.

On the flip side, a sapphire crystal shows off the movement's traditional finishing along with the Perpetual Moon's power reserve indicator. The number of days remaining is engraved directly on the movement, with an added gear ring and triangular hand indicating the appropriate number.

After leaving Schaffhausen as a young man in 1827, watchmaker Heinrich Moser made his reputation crafting timepieces with Swiss Made movements that are still prized throughout Russia and Asia. Moser was a wealthy man in his early 40s when he left St. Petersburg and returned to Schaffhausen with his family in 1848.

Soon after, he began building his home atop a hill in Schaffhausen, where he could look out and see the Rhine River bend as it rushed toward the nearby Rhine Falls. More than a decade later, the vantage point would also afford Moser a view of one of his biggest successes, the hydroelectric plant he built on the river near Schaffhausen's Old Town area. Completed in 1864, it helped power Moser's growing concerns, which encompassed factories that made wagons, railway cars and more.

Until his death in 1874, Moser lived at his family's manor, which was called Schloss Charlottenfels in honor of his first wife Charlotte, who died in a carriage accident just two years after the family moved to Schaffhausen.

In November 2010, H. Moser & Cie opened Charlottenfels to the public and began scheduling appointments for tours of the home and its grounds. The museum's main focus is on original furniture and artifacts collected by Heinrich Moser and his son, Henri. Horolophiles will especially appreciate the vintage watchmaking tools in the atelier as well as an exhibition of historical watches and wall clocks owned by Heinrich and Henri Moser. The timepieces displayed by the museum are on loan from Moser Group AG and Dr. Jürgen Lange.

A tour of Charlottenfels opens a window not only into Moser's life, but also the fascinating story behind how Schaffhausen's industrial revolution fostered its reputation for fine watchmaking.

H. Moser & Cie. offers the Perpetual Moon in a 40.8mm case made of rose gold or platinum. The dark blue dial includes a window for reading the astronomical moonphase.

A seven-day power reserve indicator is engraved on the movement that powers the Perpetual Moon.

MAYU MARRONE — REF. 321.503-015

Movement: manual-winding HMC 321.503 caliber; 80-hour power reserve; bevel wheels; Straumann hairspring with stabilized Breguet overcoil; interchangeable escapement module.
Functions: hours, minutes; small seconds with stop function.
Case: 18K rose gold; Ø 38.8mm, thickness: 9.3mm; power reserve display on movement side; antireflective sapphire crystal caseback.
Dial: light brown; applied faceted diamond-polished indexes; pocket-watch seconds hand.
Strap: brown crocodile leather; solid rose-gold clasp.
Suggested price: $12,000

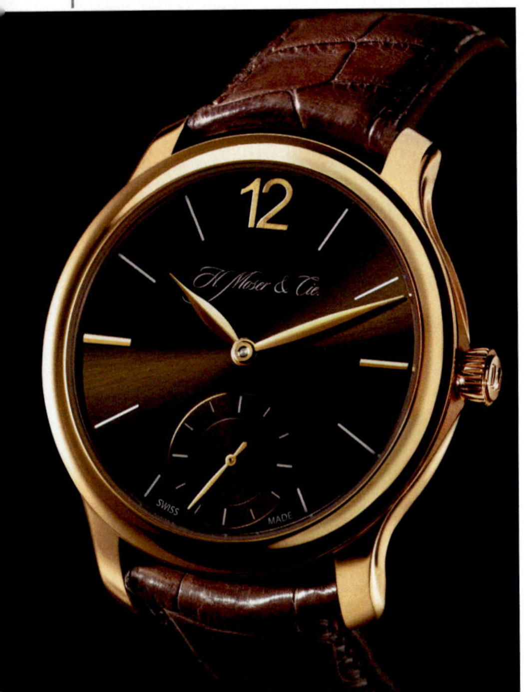

MAYU MARRONE — REF. 321.503-016

Movement: manual-winding HMC 321.503 caliber; 80-hour power reserve; bevel wheels; Straumann hairspring with stabilized Breguet overcoil; interchangeable escapement module.
Functions: hours, minutes; small seconds with stop function.
Case: white gold; Ø 38.8mm, thickness: 9.3mm; power reserve display on movement side; antireflective sapphire crystal caseback.
Dial: dark brown; applied faceted diamond-polished indexes; pocket-watch seconds hand.
Strap: brown crocodile leather; solid white-gold clasp.
Suggested price: $12,000

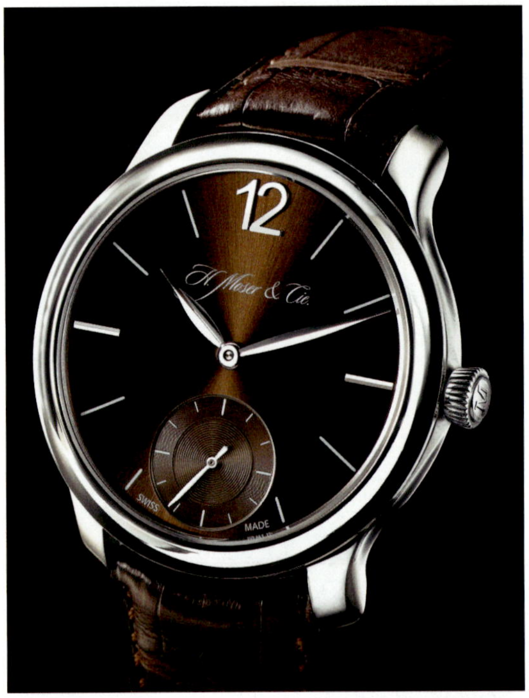

MONARD — REF. 343.505-017

Movement: manual-winding HMC 343.505 caliber; 7-day power reserve; bevel wheels; dual barrel; Straumann hairspring with stabilized Breguet overcoil; interchangeable escapement module.
Functions: hours, minutes; small seconds with stop function.
Case: 18K rose gold; Ø 40.8mm, thickness: 10.85mm; power reserve display on movement side; antireflective sapphire crystal caseback.
Dial: black lacquered.
Strap: black crocodile leather; solid rose-gold clasp.
Suggested price: $15,800

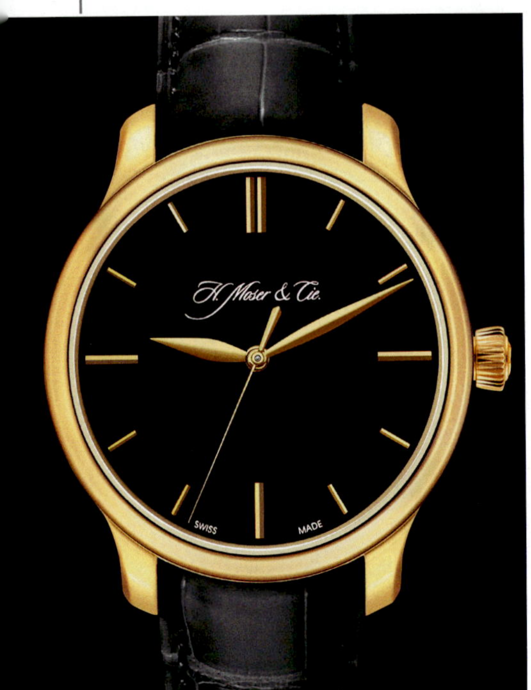

MONARD FUME — REF. 343.505-016

Movement: manual-winding HMC 343.505 caliber; 7-day power reserve; bevel wheels; dual barrel; Straumann double hairspring; interchangeable escapement module.
Functions: hours, minutes; seconds with stop function.
Case: palladium; Ø 40.8mm, height: 10.85mm; power reserve display on movement side; antireflective sapphire crystal caseback.
Dial: fumé; fine sun-pattern ground finish.
Strap: black crocodile leather; solid palladium clasp.
Suggested price: $21,100

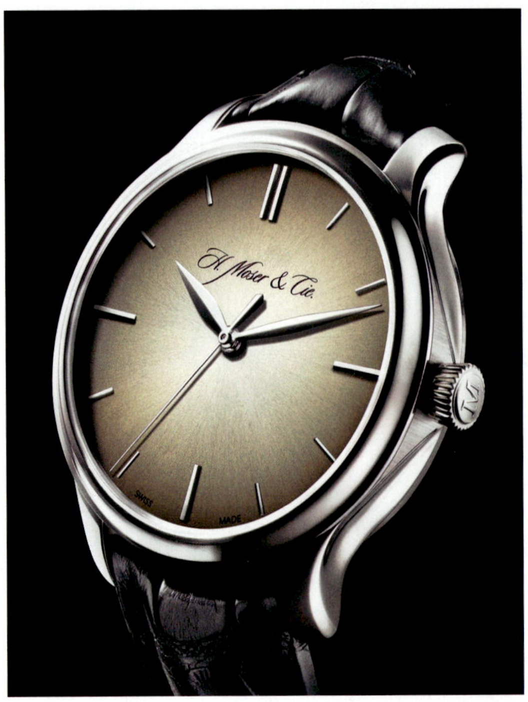

HENRY DOUBLE HAIRSPRING — REF. 324.607-006

Movement: manual-winding rectangular shaped HMC 324.006 caliber; 4-day power reserve; bevel wheels; large volume barrel; Straumann double hairspring; interchangeable escapement module.
Function: hours, minutes; small seconds with stop function.
Case: platinum tonneau; Ø 44.1x38.6mm, thickness: 10.4mm; power reserve display on movement side; antireflective sapphire crystal caseback.
Dial: ardoise; sun pattern ground finish; Moser pocket-watch seconds hand.
Strap: crocodile leather; solid platinum clasp.
Suggested price: $27,500

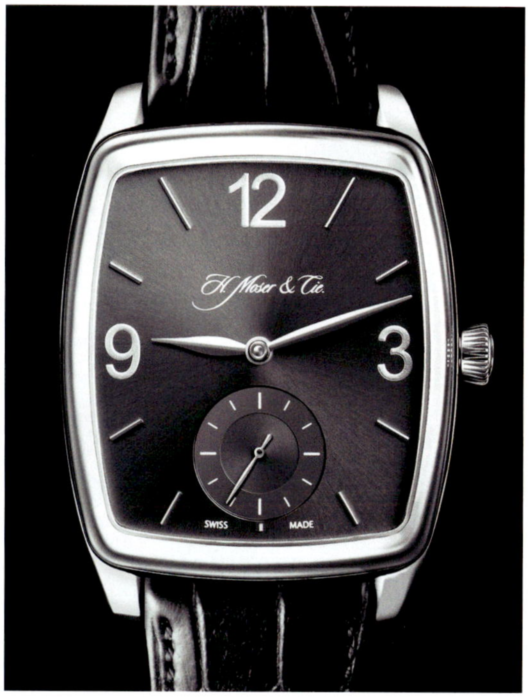

MONARD DATE — REF. 342.502-003

Movement: manual-winding HMC 342.502 caliber; 7-day power reserve; bevel wheels; dual barrel; Straumann hairspring with stabilized Breguet overcoil; interchangeable escapement module.
Functions: hours, minutes; seconds with stop function; large date; calendar adjustable forwards and backwards via crown.
Case: 18K rose gold; Ø 40.8mm, thickness: 10.85mm; double pull crown mechanism; power reserve display on movement side; antireflective sapphire crystal caseback.
Dial: silver-plated; sun-pattern ground finish.
Strap: black crocodile leather; solid rose-gold clasp.
Suggested price: $20,700

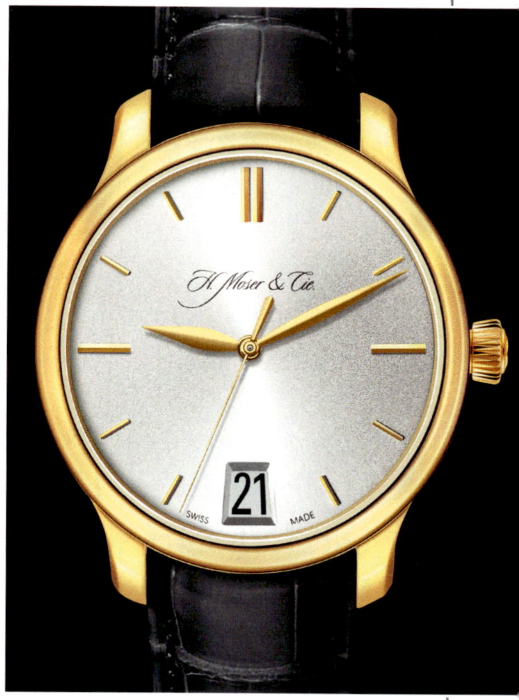

MOSER PERPETUAL 1 — REF. 341.501-004

Movement: manual-winding HMC 341.501 caliber; 7-day power reserve; bevel wheels; dual barrel; Straumann hairspring with stabilized Breguet overcoil; interchangeable escapement module.
Functions: hours, minutes; small seconds with stop function; date; month; power reserve indication; perpetual flash calendar display; calendar adjustable forwards and backwards via crown independently of movement.
Case: 18K rose gold; Ø 40.8mm, thickness: 11.05mm; double pull crown mechanism.
Dial: silver-plated; sun-pattern ground finish.
Strap: black crocodile leather; solid rose-gold clasp.
Suggested price: $34,700

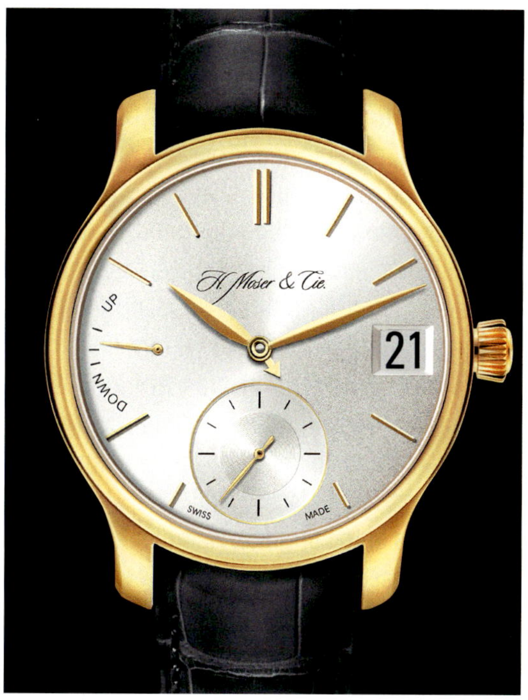

PERPETUAL MOON — REF. 348.901-015

Movement: manual-winding HMC 348.901 caliber; 7-day power reserve; bevel wheels; dual barrel; Straumann hairspring with stabilized Breguet overcoil; interchangeable escapement module.
Functions: hours, minutes; small seconds with stop function; perpetual moonphase function with one day left after 1027 years.
Case: platinum; Ø 40.8mm, thickness: 11.05mm.
Dial: blue fumé.
Strap: black crocodile leather; solid platinum clasp.
Suggested price: $36,000

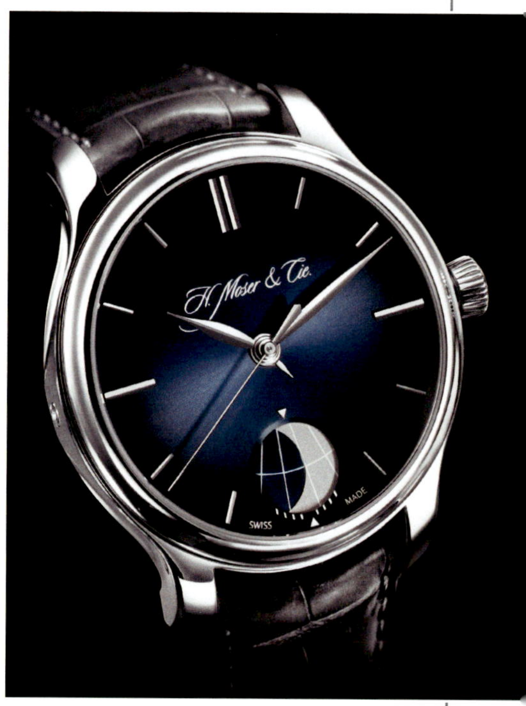

HAMILTON

THE AMERICAN BRAND SINCE 1892

NAVIGATING CROSSWINDS

Few watch brands can claim an American pedigree as distinctive as Hamilton's. Rooted in Pennsylvania Dutch country since the late 1800s, the company and the country came of age together in the 20th century.

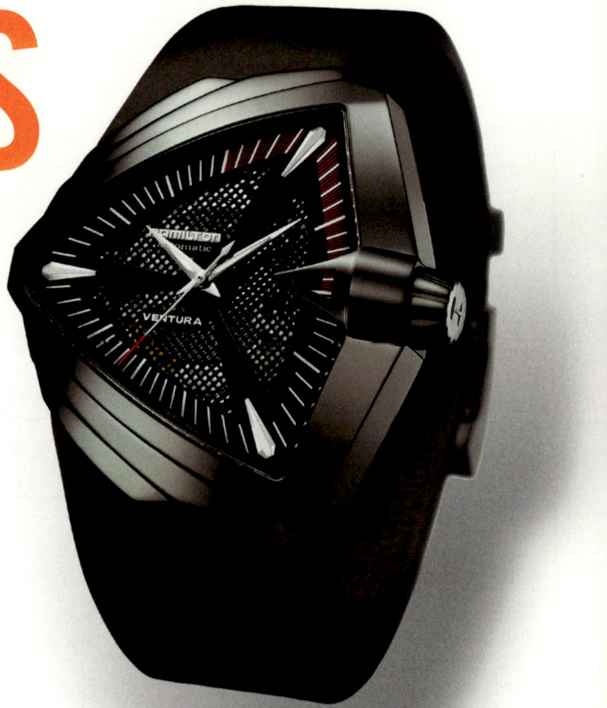

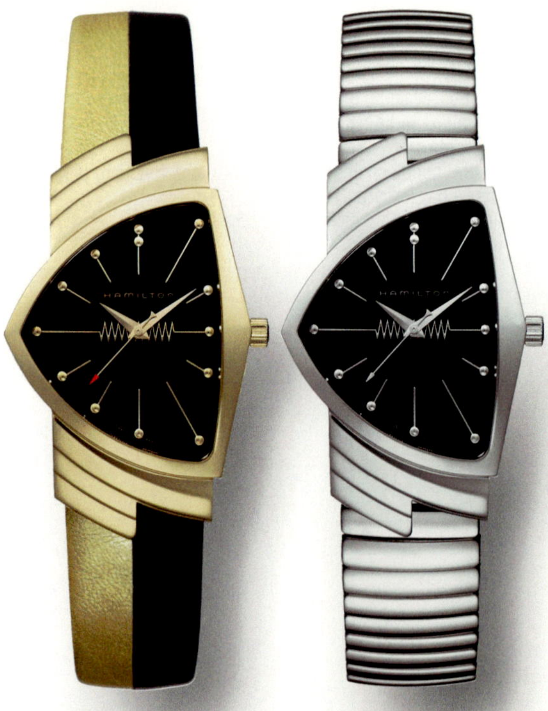

TOP RIGHT

Part of the Elvis Presley Anniversary Collection, the limited edition Ventura XXL updates the look of the original Ventura with a larger profile, perforated dial and rubber strap.

ABOVE

Offered on a two-tone leather strap, the Ventura's shield-shaped case calls to mind the tailfin of a '57 Chevy (left); Elvis Presley wore a similar Ventura in *Blue Hawaii.* This replica was issued to mark what would have been the artist's 75th birthday (right).

From the pockets of rail men to the wrists of World War II soldiers, many trusted their lives to the Hamilton Watch Company's reputation for accuracy. But it was the brand's personality that caught people's eyes in 1961 when Elvis Presley wore its Ventura model in *Blue Hawaii.*

To honor what would have been the King's 75th birthday in 2010, Hamilton created vintage and modern versions of this classic design for its limited edition Elvis Anniversary Collection.

The first pays tribute to the original Ventura, the world's first electrical, battery-powered watch. Introduced in 1957, the watch's technical achievement was enhanced by a dynamic look that combined a sweeping angle reminiscent of the tailfin from a golden-age hot rod and the elegant minimalism of designer George Nelson's iconic "Ball" wall clock.

For fans of the original, Hamilton offers a quartz-powered replica in stainless steel or steel with a yellow gold PVD coating. The case can be paired with bracelet or a daring two-tone leather strap. For those who prefer a more contemporary mien, Hamilton presents the Ventura XXL. Not only does it exceed the dimensions of the original, it also welcomes a stylish new gunmetal finish and an automatic movement.

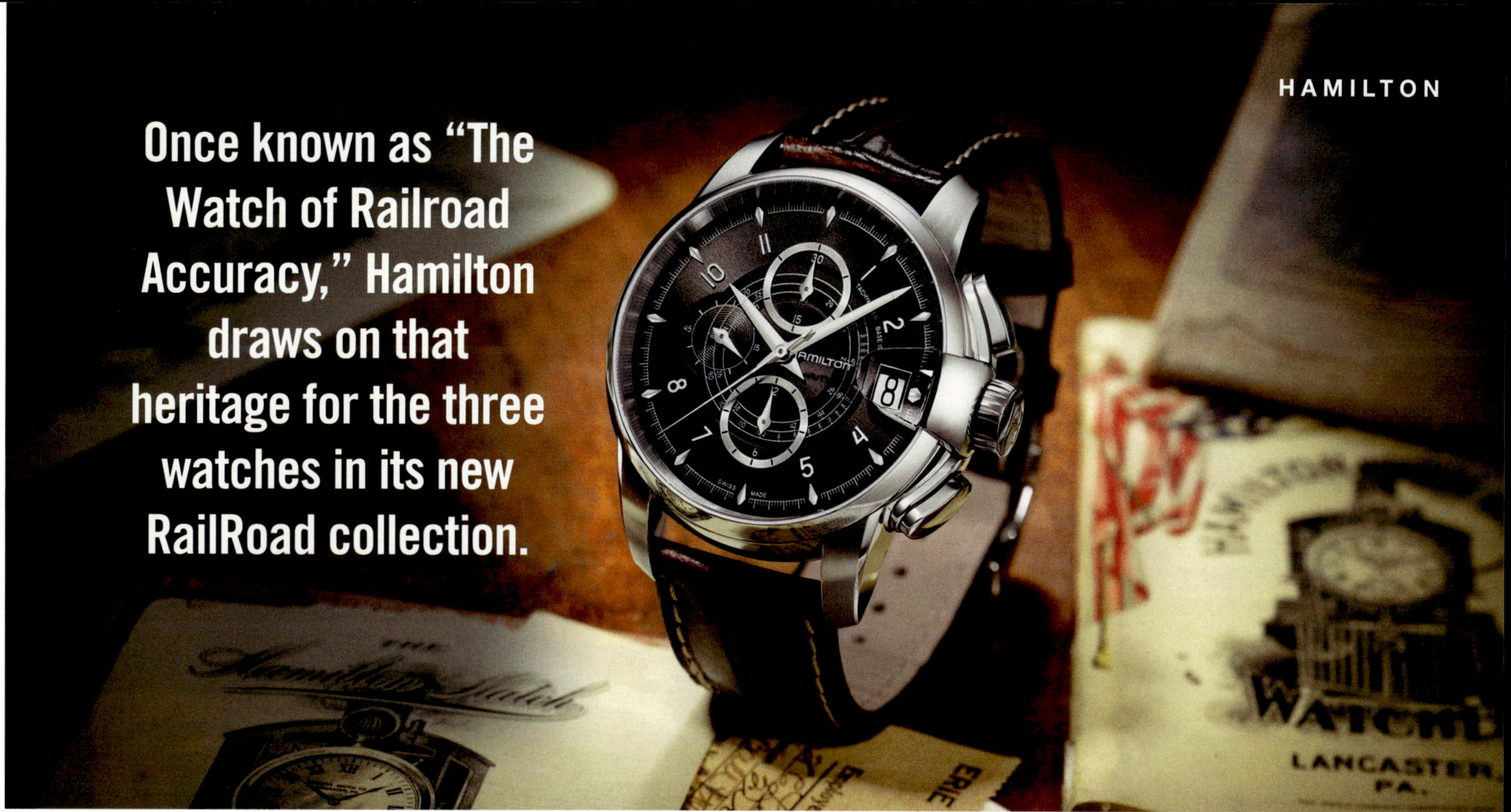

Once known as "The Watch of Railroad Accuracy," Hamilton draws on that heritage for the three watches in its new RailRoad collection.

At the start of the 20th century, railroads were vital lifelines that spurred America's rapid industrialization. Pennsylvania was home to thousands of miles of track, making it an important crossroads, one that stretched from the Atlantic Ocean to the Mississippi River and from Canada to Kentucky.

Born into this humming hub in 1892, Hamilton pocket watches were frequent travelers on the rails, where they enjoyed great popularity among conductors who valued the watch's reliability. In fact, for a time the brand was known as "The Watch of Railroad Accuracy."

The company draws on that heritage for its new RailRoad series, a collection that includes three different models. The first is a 38mm stainless steel version with an automatic movement. A second automatic model is distinguished by a larger (44mm) stainless steel case and the addition of a small seconds. Hamilton also offers a 46mm version in a black PVD-treated case equipped with a chronograph.

Switching from rails to contrails, Hamilton spotlights the world of aviation with several watches in its Khaki collection. More than just stylish accoutrements inspired by captains of the sky, many of these models possess specialized instruments normally reserved for the cockpit.

A prime example is the Khaki X-Wind Automatic. Powered by the Swiss-made Valjoux 7750 chronograph, the watch also features a sophisticated system of rotating bezels that calculate the correction required for a plane to stay on course while flying through a crosswind.

After more than a century, Hamilton has proven adept at doing just that, safely navigating challenging conditions as it soars to new heights.

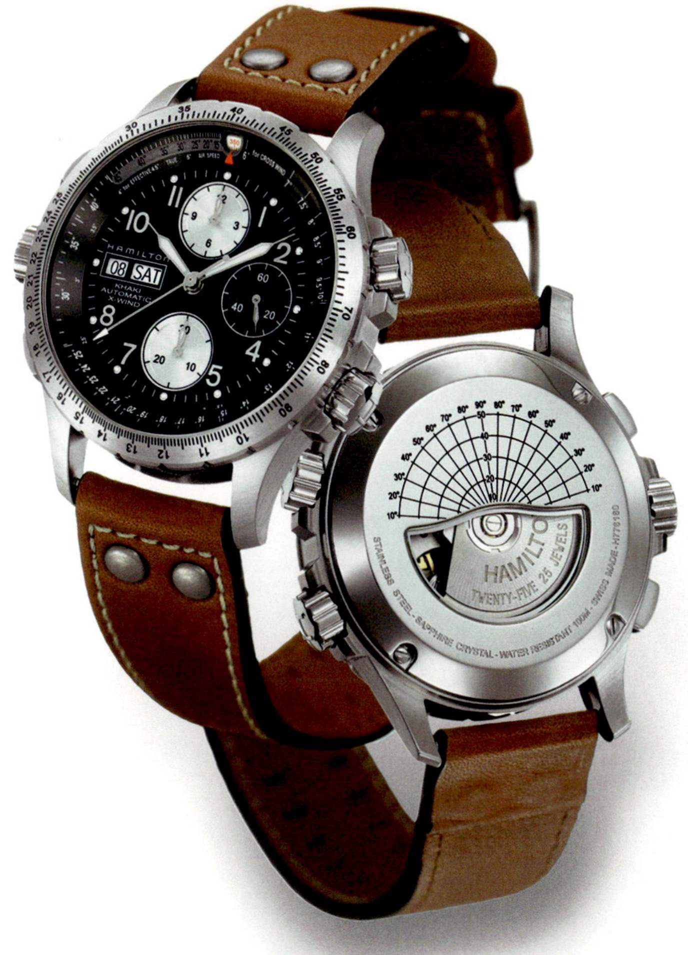

ABOVE

The 46mm RailRoad Auto Chrono evokes its connection to the rails with a tachometer ring on the inner dial made to look like train tracks.

BELOW

The 44mm stainless steel Khaki X-Wind Automatic includes an automatic chronograph movement, plus rotating bezels that calculate the correction required for a plane to stay on course while flying through a crosswind.

JAZZMASTER TRAVELER 2 — REF. H32625555

Movement: Swiss ETA Auto 2893-2 caliber; 21 jewels.
Functions: hours, minutes; sweep seconds; date; second time zone on a 24-hour scale.
Case: stainless steel; Ø 42mm; two screw-down crowns; sapphire crystal; transparent caseback secured by five screws; water resistant to 20atm.
Dial: silver; SuperLumiNova hands.
Strap: genuine brown ostrich leather.

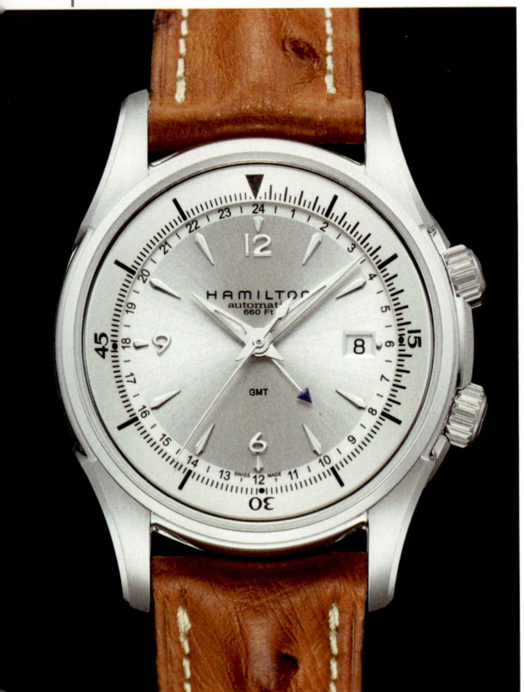

VENTURA AUTO XXL — REF. H24615331

Movement: Swiss ETA Auto 2824-2 caliber; 25 jewels.
Functions: hours, minutes; sweep seconds.
Case: gun PVD on stainless steel; sapphire crystal; transparent caseback; water resistant to 5atm.
Dial: black transparent.
Strap: black rubber.

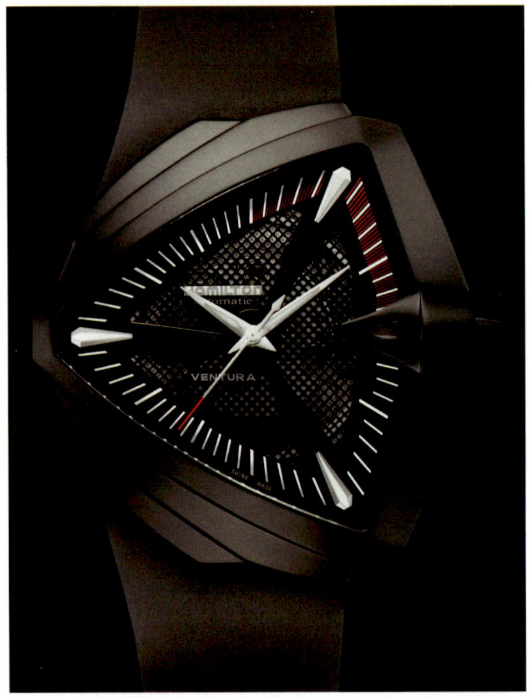

KHAKI OFFICER 44MM SMALL SECOND — REF. H70655733

Movement: Swiss ETA Auto 2895-2 caliber; 27 jewels.
Functions: hours, minutes; small seconds counter at 6; date at 3.
Case: stainless steel; Ø 44mm; sapphire crystal; transparent caseback; water resistant to 10atm.
Dial: black; SuperLumiNova hands.
Strap: beige nubuck leather.

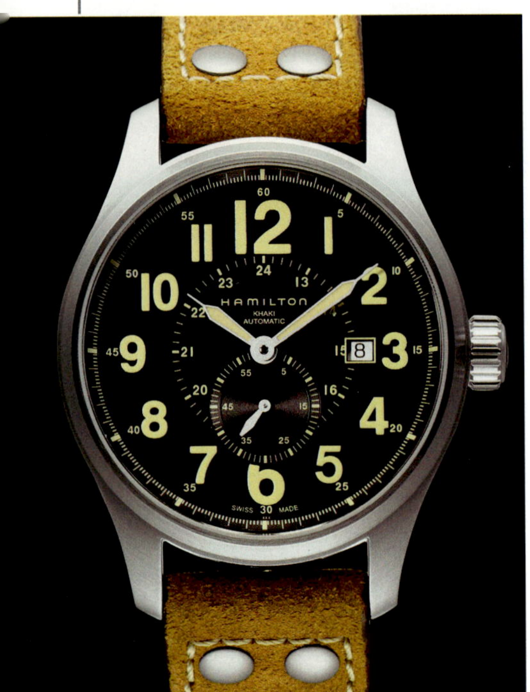

CUSHION AUTO CHRONO — REF. H36516535

Movement: Swiss ETA Auto Chrono 7750 caliber; 25 jewels.
Functions: hours, minutes; seconds; chronograph: counters at 6, 9 and 12; date between 4 and 5.
Case: stainless steel; Ø 44mm; sapphire crystal; transparent caseback; water resistant to 10atm.
Dial: black.
Strap: genuine brown leather.

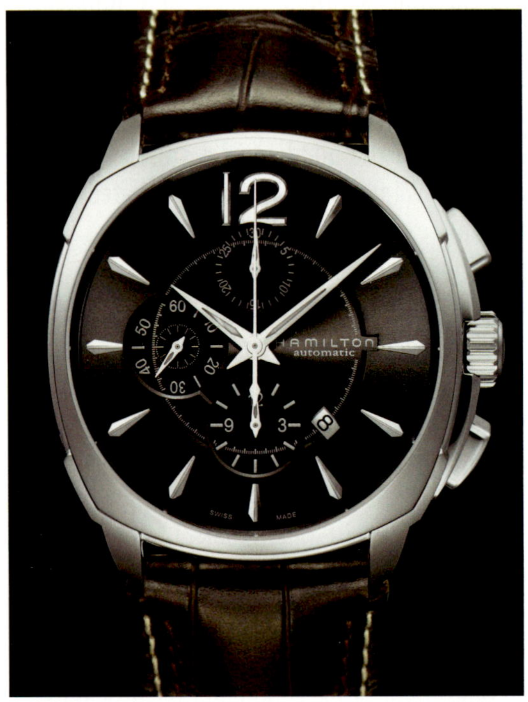

KHAKI X-WIND — REF. H77696793

Movement: Swiss ETA Auto Chrono 7750 caliber; 25 jewels.
Functions: hours, minutes, seconds; integrated drift angle calculator; day-date at 9.
Case: black PVD and rose-gold-plated stainless steel; Ø 44mm; three rotating bezels; three crowns; two pushers; sapphire crystal; transparent caseback.
Dial: black carbon fiber; three chrono counters.
Strap: genuine black leather with carbon fiber effect.

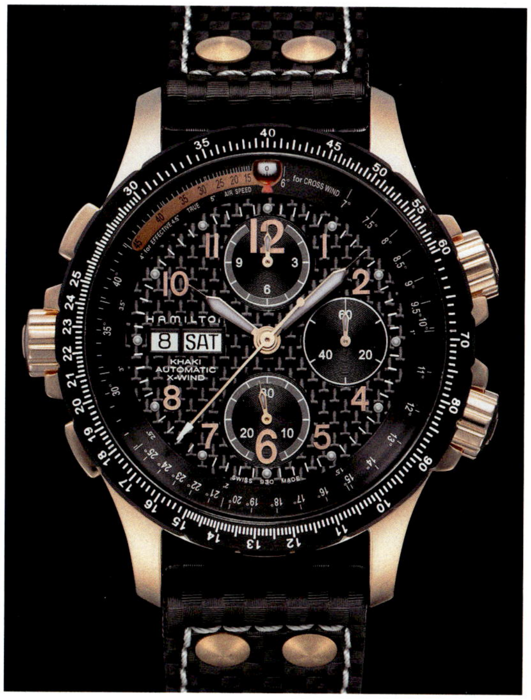

KHAKI PILOT 46MM — REF. H64715885

Movement: Swiss ETA Auto 2836-2 caliber; 25 jewels.
Functions: hours, minutes, seconds; versized outer second counter; inner hour counter; day-date at 3.
Case: stainless steel; Ø 46mm; screw-down crown; sapphire crystal; transparent caseback secured by four screws; water resistant to 20atm.
Dial: gray; SuperLumiNova hands.
Strap: genuine brown leather.

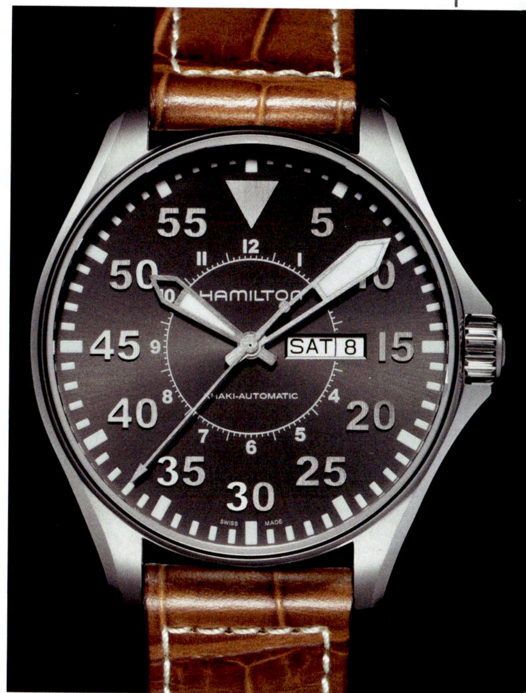

PULSOMATIC — REF. H52515139

Movement: Swiss ETA Auto H1970 caliber; world's first automatic digital watch with 120-day power reserve; 8 jewels.
Functions: hours, minutes; date.
Case: stainless steel; 38.5x48mm; sapphire crystal; transparent caseback; water resistant to 5atm.
Dial: black with LCD display.
Bracelet: stainless steel.

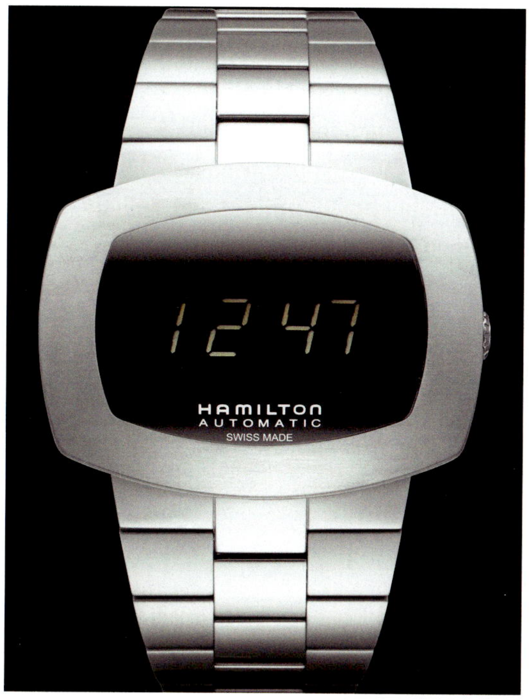

RAIL ROAD AUTO ETA — REF. H40415115

Movement: Swiss 2824 caliber; 25 jewels.
Functions: hours, minutes; sweep seconds; date.
Case: stainless steel; Ø 38mm; sapphire crystal; transparent caseback; water resistant to 10atm.
Dial: silver; SuperLumiNova hands; magnifier and date at 3.
Bracelet: stainless steel.

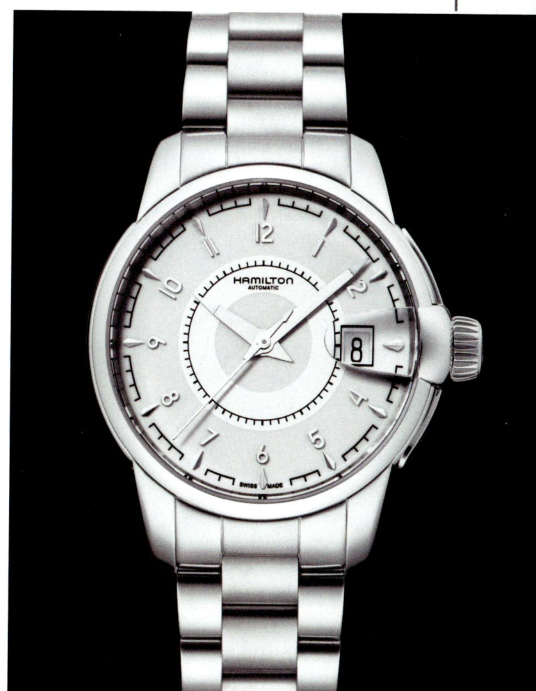

HARRY WINSTON

WEALTH OF

Already one of the world's most famous jewelers, Harry Winston took high-end watchmaking by storm in 2001 when it introduced the first watch in its ongoing Opus series.

To create these limited edition timepieces every year, the company partners with independent watchmaking luminaries, the ranks of which have included such talents as François-Paul Journe, Christophe Claret, and Greubel Forsey. For the series' tenth installment—Opus X—Harry Winston joined with Jean-François Mojon, whose Le Locle-based company, Chronode, specializes in high-complication movements.

The design is revolutionary in every sense. Rather than a stationary dial, the Opus X features a quartet of indications that orbit around a point fixed at the dial's center. The displays maintain their readability by rotating individually as they saunter gracefully around the case's circular confines.

The Opus X includes disassociated displays to indicate the hours and minutes, each encircled by its own opaque black ring with raised silver-colored numerals. Nestled between these timers, an X-shaped pointer rotates once a minute as it displays the seconds. A small circle monogrammed with the Harry Winston initials completes the constellation. A yellow arrow protrudes from this disc to indicate a second time zone on the 24-hour scale that runs along the dial's outer edge.

To showcase the ever-popular "whirlwind" complication, Harry Winston launched the Histoire de Tourbillon collection in 2009. Last year, the company introduced the second timepiece in that family with the Histoire de Tourbillon 2, a limited numbered edition of 20 pieces.

The futuristic design combines a bi-axial flying tourbillon with independent hours and minutes in a white-gold case that stretches 48.5mm in diameter. The tourbillon's exceptional construction gives it the appearance of being suspended in mid-air, while the absence of an upper bridge exposes the mechanism's smallest details. The tourbillon's titanium outer carriage also doubles as a seconds indicator, pointing out the current increment on a scale that spans 0 to 120.

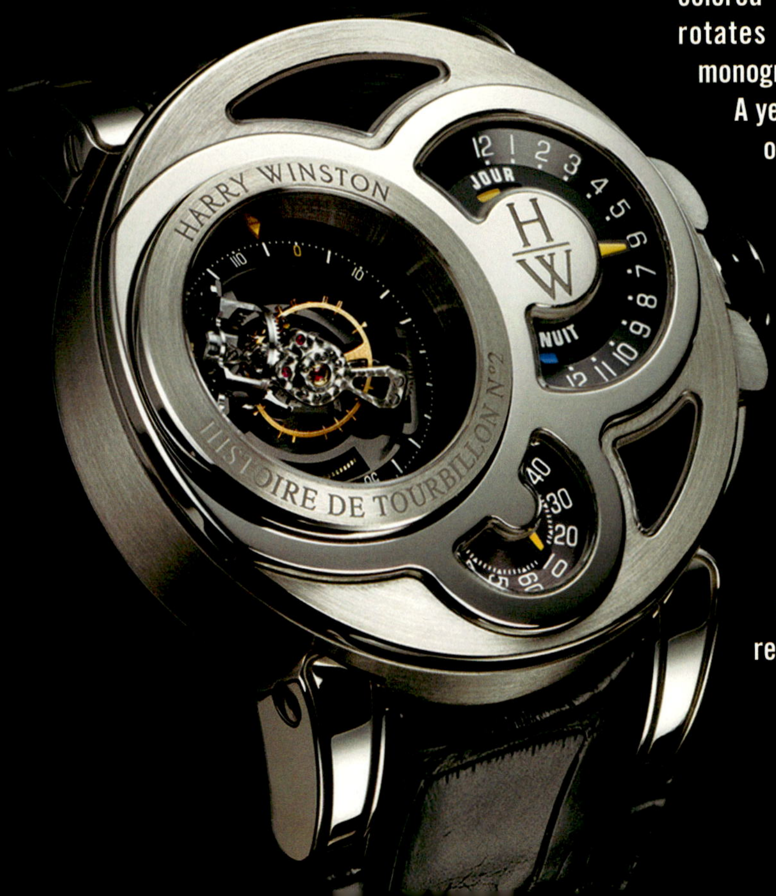

The opening on the left side of its white-gold case contains the Histoire de Tourbillon 2's bi-axial flying tourbillon, a complex mechanism comprised of 95 individual parts.

For more than two decades, Harry Winston's collection of refined timepieces has celebrated both mechanical and aesthetic sophistication with superlative examples of bold innovation and unmatched beauty.

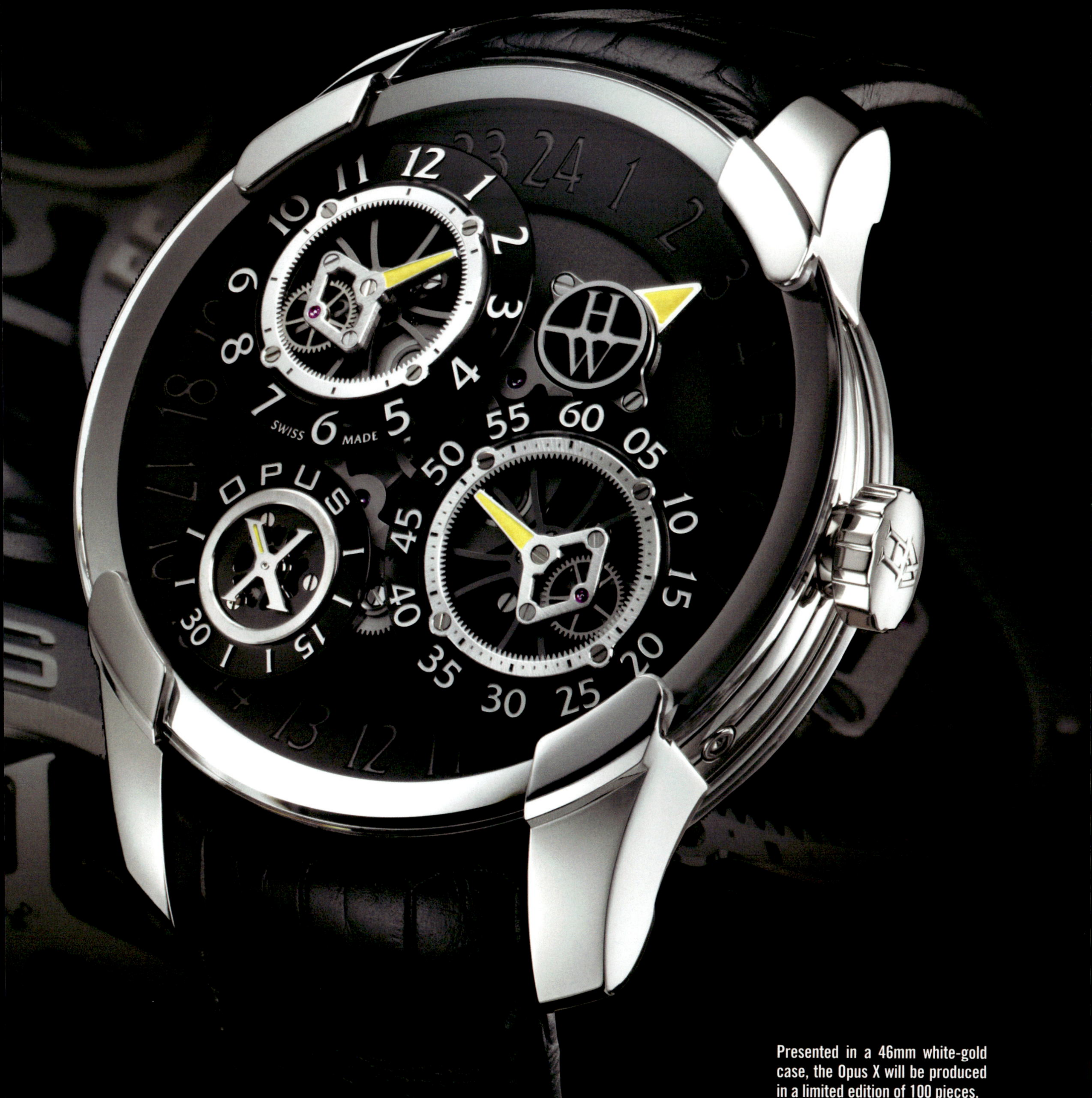

Presented in a 46mm white-gold case, the Opus X will be produced in a limited edition of 100 pieces.

The tourbillon remains the focus in the Ocean Tourbillon GMT, where the complication appears in the form of a single-axis design topped by a seconds hand. Harry Winston integrates the gravity-compensating mechanism into an automatic movement that also includes a second time zone function.

The Ocean Tourbillon GMT's Côtes de Genève dial features two displays, one positioned at 3 o'clock for the reference time and a second for the time in the destination city. An opening near the GMT display highlights one of 24 cities, each a representative of the world's different time zones.

Harry Winston added a new material to the watchmaking lexicon in 2004 when it unveiled a case made from Zalium. This zirconium-based alloy—used primarily in aeronautical engineering—underscored the pioneering spirit that defines the timepieces introduced under the Project Z rubric.

Not only is Project Z6 the latest addition to this limited edition series, but it is also the first Harry Winston watch to include a 24-hour alarm complication. Made from more than 300 components, the watch's mechanical movement includes a hammer, which can be seen ringing the alarm's monobloc bell through an opening on the dial.

The dial features two intersecting displays, one on the upper left for the current time and another on the lower right for the alarm time. The watchmaker presents a timepiece made from Zalium for women with the Lady Z. Three indications are arranged on the sunburst guilloché dial, including one for the hours and minutes, a moonphase and a small seconds display.

Reflecting Harry Winston's inestimable reputation as a jeweler, the watch's Zalium case and silvered dial are set with brilliant-cut white diamonds. All told, the Lady Z features 149 gems that weigh a total of 4.5 carats.

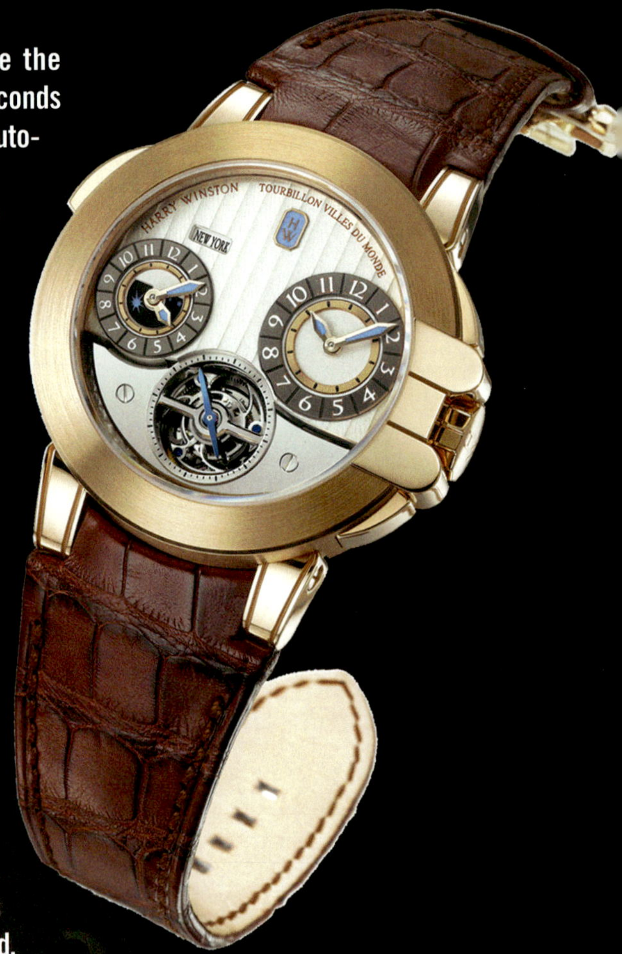

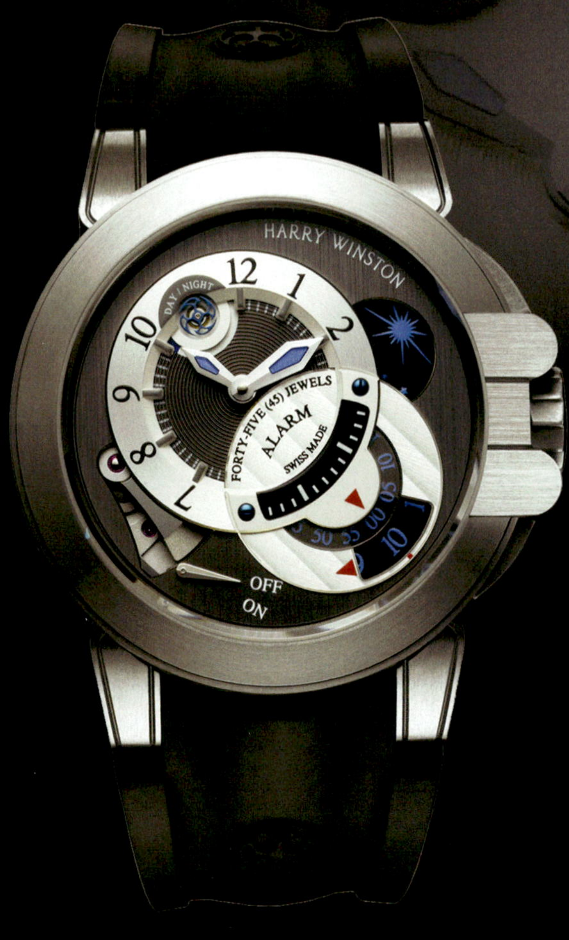

The tides and moon mingle in blissful harmony with the Ocean Lady Moon Phase. The watch's signature complication takes center stage on the dial with an artful arrangement of mother-of-pearl and diamonds.

Harry Winston presents the Ocean Lady Moon Phase in a 36mm case offered in either white or rose gold. The watch is paired with a rubber strap that provides a comfortable fit while adding a sporty undercurrent to the design's bejeweled elegance, which encompasses 285 diamonds.

ABOVE

The limited edition Ocean Tourbillon GMT comes in a rose- or white-gold case that can be set with diamonds.

LEFT

Harry Winston's first alarm watch, Project Z6 features a 44mm case made from Zalium, a material available exclusively from the company.

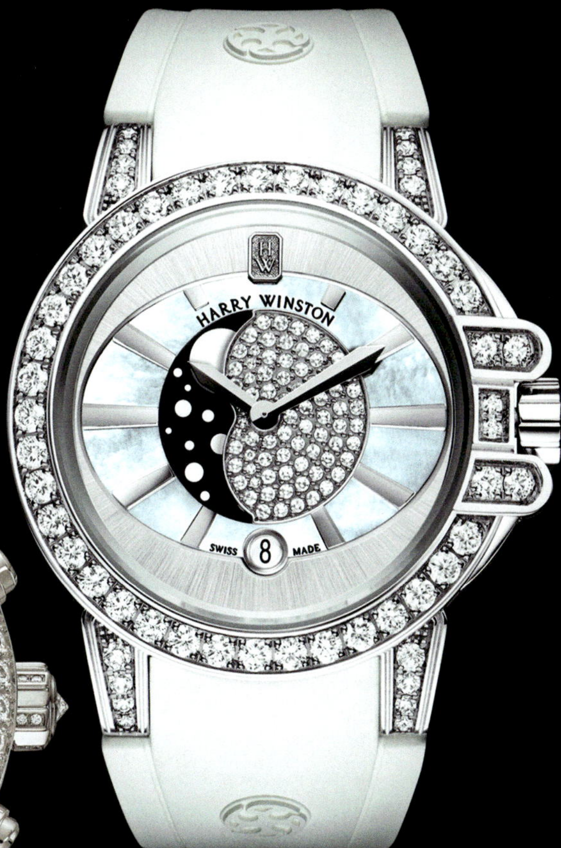

LEFT

A quartz movement powers the Ocean Lady Moon Phase, which is offered in a 36mm case that is water resistant to 100 meters.

FAR LEFT

Harry Winston uses more than 300 brilliant-cut diamonds to create the 39mm white-gold Premier Large Chronograph.

BELOW

The Lady Z's 36mm case is set with 56 diamonds that frame the silvered sunburst guilloché dial.

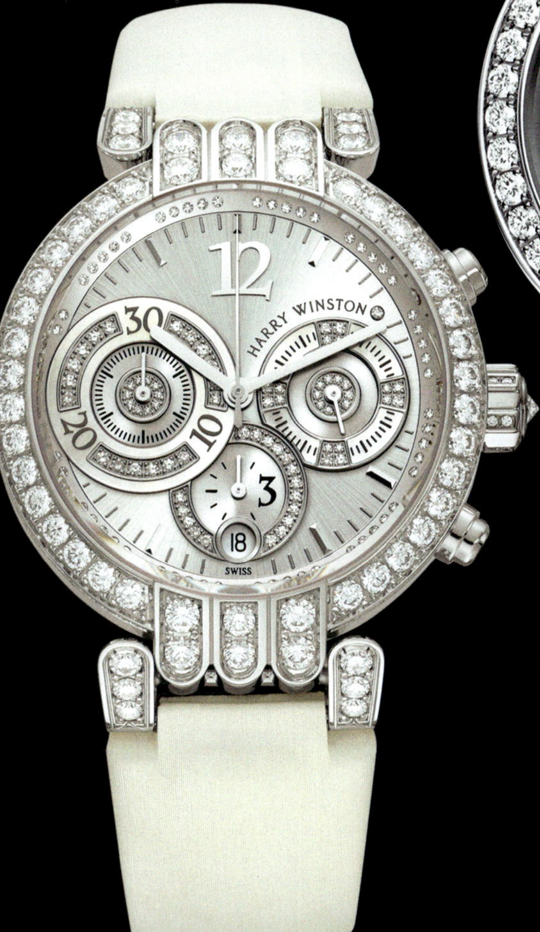

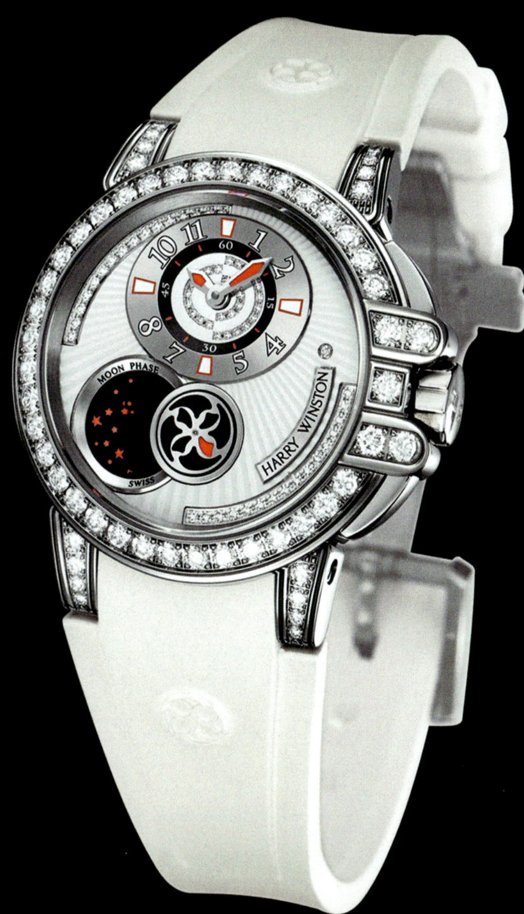

The seductive relationship between horology and gemology continues with the Premier Large Chronograph. It is among the newest members of the Premier collection, which was one of the first watch lines introduced by Harry Winston.

The classic timer complication appears here in a 39mm white-gold case set with more than 140 brilliant-cut diamonds. This sparkling skin encases an automatic movement endowed with a 42-hour power reserve.

The push and pull between the Premier Large Chronograph's subdials creates a delicious visual tension on the dial that resolves nicely into a dynamic design punctuated emphatically by a wealth of gems.

Whether they draw on the company's jewelry expertise, its passion for groundbreaking haute horology or both, all Harry Winston Timepieces offer up an uncompromisingly original expression of time.

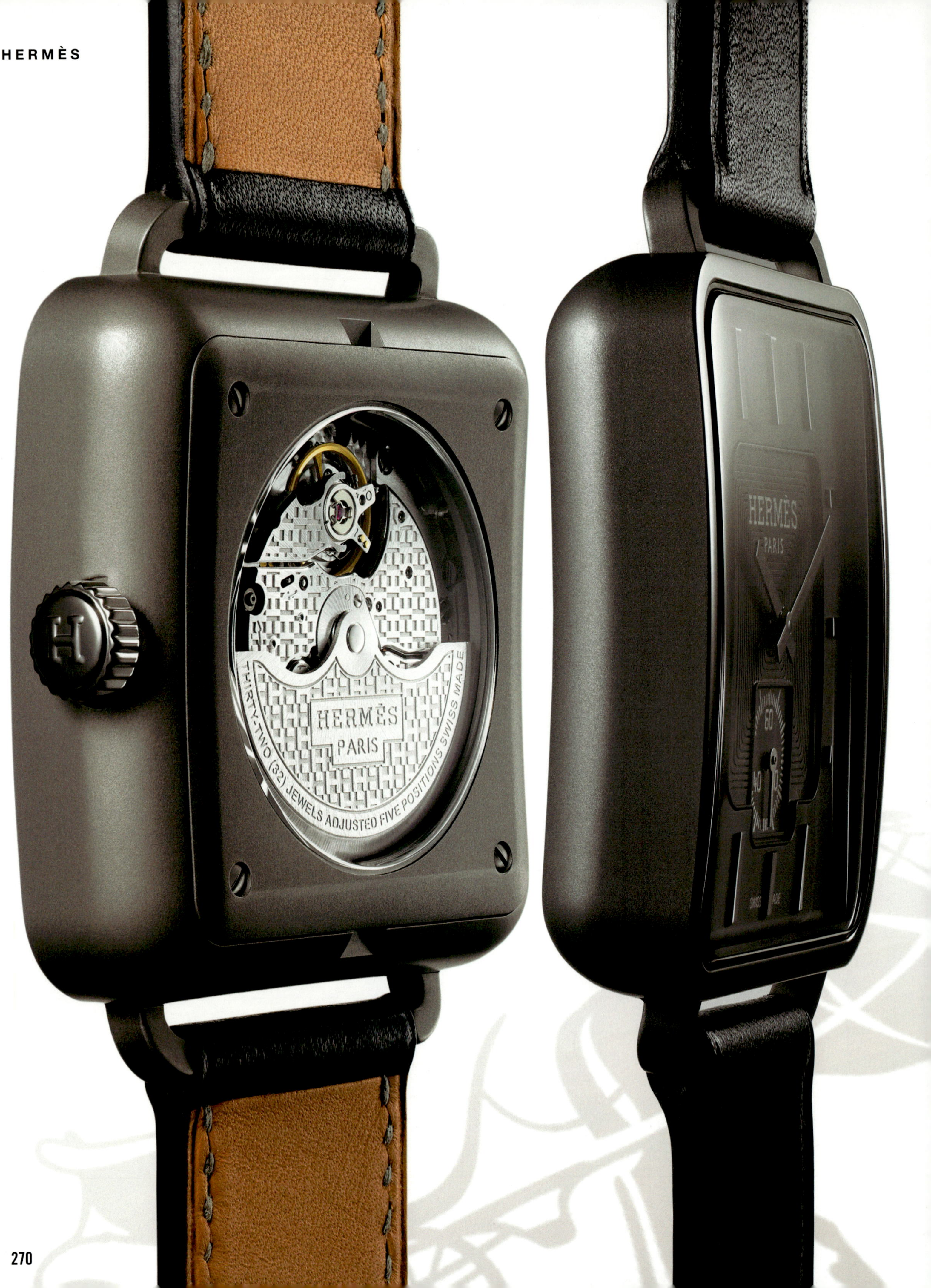
HERMÈS
PARIS
THIRTY-TWO (32) JEWELS ADJUSTED FIVE POSITIONS SWISS MADE
HERMÈS
PARIS
60

HERMÈS
PARIS

SQUARING THE CIRCLE

Whether Hermès is making saddles, bags, scarves or watches, one thing the family-run firm has done well for six generations is change with the times, without letting the times change it. The first Hermès watches entered the scene in 1928, and 50 years later, the company signaled its commitment to watchmaking with the establishment of La Montre Hermès.

FACING PAGE

LEFT The titanium case's outline is reiterated on the anthracite-colored dial, where it is used for the small seconds and the guilloché section below the hour and minute hands.

RIGHT The rounded corners on top of the case give way to a graceful dome below. The titanium's surprisingly soft finish is the result of a microbead blasting treatment.

In 2010, the brand showcased that intuitive adaptability with the introduction of the Carré H, a wristwatch whose richly detailed geometric design stems from a collaborative effort by Hermès Artistic Director Pierre-Alexis Dumas and designer-architect Marc Berthier.

Coincidently, the collaboration was fated years earlier by Dumas's father, Jean-Louis, during his nearly 30-year tenure as the company's CEO. It was he who originally asked Berthier to come up with ideas for a timepiece suited for a "traveling dandy."

Berthier's subsequent sketches remained at Hermès until 2006, when Pierre-Alexis discovered them. "I was…immediately struck by his sketch of a square shape," he recalled during a recent interview in which he and Berthier discussed the Carré H.

Intrigued and inspired by what he saw, Dumas arranged to meet Berthier. The two quickly developed a rapport and were soon at work on what Berthier described as "a genuine architect's watch." One, Dumas said, "is born of a love of geometry."

The Carré H evolved at the Hermès watch workshop in Biel, Switzerland, where Hermès La Montre Artistic Director Philippe Delhotal oversaw its journey into production.

The *carré* ("square") looms large in the firm's legend. After all, it is the shape of the coveted Hermès scarf, a timeless expression of refinement articulated succinctly by a silk square.

For the Carré H, Hermès translates the scarf's balanced proportions to the wrist for a titanium case that measures 36.5x36.5mm. The elegant simplicity of four equal lines and angles is part of the square's appeal and also what makes it such a challenge for designers. "To compose these forms," Berthier explained, "you have to look for harmony in purity and perfection in details."

The Carré H delivers on both counts, employing a minimalist aesthetic while creating dynamic visual interplay by nesting squares within squares. "That's why people will not tire of the design of this watch," Dumas said, "because it is full of subtle features."

The uncluttered dial exudes a quiet confidence amplified by the small details. "The hands are the same width as the hour marker bars and are lined up exactly in such a way as to extend them," Berthier said. "Everything is calculated to within a tenth of a millimeter. Achieving this degree of perfection meant reworking the composition on the square countless times."

The *carré* looms large in the firm's legend, as it is the shape of the coveted Hermès scarf, a timeless expression of refinement articulated in silk.

The final result is a square case that is not entirely square. Instead of sharp angles, the Carré H bends softly at the corners to produce a shape that echoes throughout, serving as a template for the small seconds and the fine guilloché grooves that radiate from the center of the anthracite-colored dial.

Not only do the rounded edges temper the taut lines of the hands and hour markers on the dial, they extend below to form a graceful dome for the case. Dumas described its profile as "supple, accurate, and anthropomorphic," adding: "The counter-curve on the wrist makes it extremely light to wear and eliminates any stiffness. It is the epitome of contemporary classicism."

"The Carré H is an extremely contemporary design," Berthier said. "I designed it before today's nomadic objects such as cell phones and laptops, which used to have sharp-sided shells and cases and now feature softened angles."

The shape provides ample room for the watch's automatic movement. Produced in the Swiss Jura region by Sowind, the precise mechanism reveals its ornate decoration through Carré H's transparent caseback. Assembled on a circular-grained baseplate, the caliber's bridges and rotor are embellished with an alternating pattern of interlocking H's.

Much like a gifted artisan in Hermès's famed leather atelier works a hide into a buttery suppleness, the Carré H's titanium case is blasted with microbeads to achieve a velvety texture that is soft to the touch.

"On the upper part of the case, the edge is meticulously polished, making the light bounce off it as it does off the edge of leathers polished with wax at Hermès," Dumas said. "This is where the link between the treatment of metal and leather is expressed. It's our House signature."

With its black, saddle-stitched calfskin strap, the Carré H subtly evokes the tailored masculinity of the horse harnesses to which Hermès's early legacy was hitched. In a final nod to the brand's historic equine roots, the strap attaches to the case using a stirrup-like loop instead of lugs.

Unveiled in 2010, Hermès will produce 173 examples of the Carré H, one for each year since the family started the brand in 1837.

As Hermès continues its global expansion, the brand's progress is ensured by a core belief that tradition should not be blindly followed, but rather shaken to life by change.

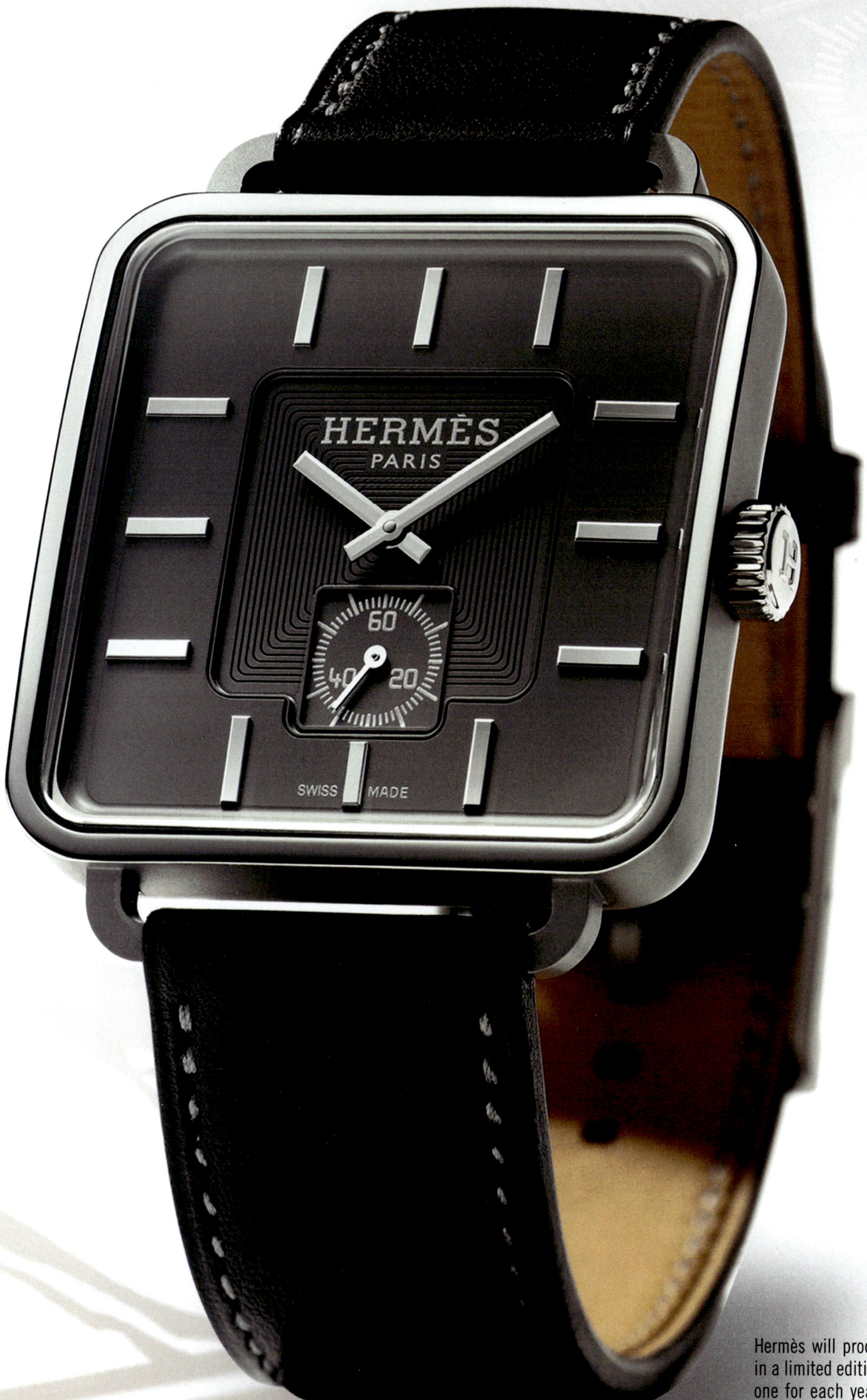

Hermès will produce the Carré H in a limited edition of 173 pieces, one for each year of the family-run firm's existence.

HEURE H PM — REF. 036717WW00

Movement: quartz.
Functions: hours, minutes.
Case: steel; 21x21mm; antireflective sapphire crystal; water resistant to 3atm.
Dial: white; varnished; dark gray transfer; stamped sunburst motif.
Strap: natural Barenia.
Suggested price: $2,000
Also available: other straps and sizes.

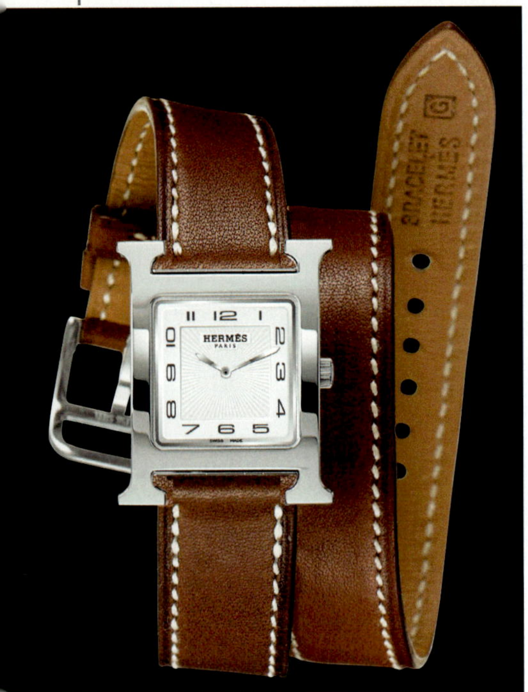

CARRE H — REF. 028030WV89

Movement: automatic-winding 3200 Sowind caliber; 10 ½'''; 44-hour power reserve; 28,800 vph.
Functions: hours, minutes; small seconds at 6.
Case: micro bead-blasted titanium with polished upper surface; water resistant to 3atm.
Dial: charcoal gray.
Strap: black Barenia calfskin; micro bead-blasted titanium pin buckle.
Suggested price: $16,225

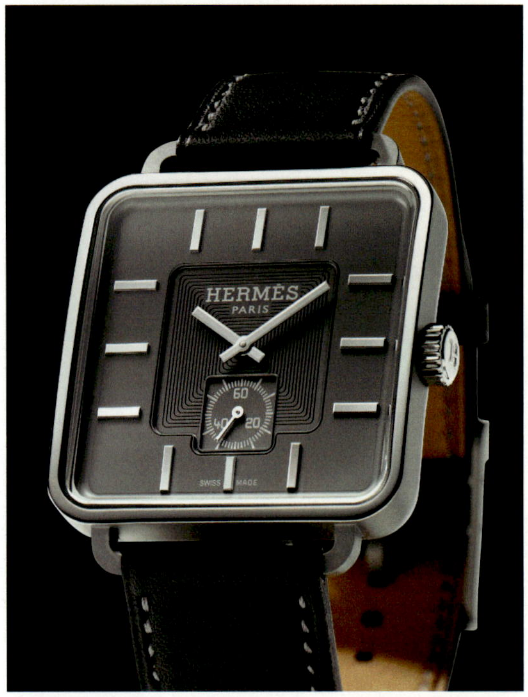

ARCEAU CHRONO COLORS — REF. 036249WW00

Movement: automatic-winding; 42-hour power reserve.
Functions: hours, minutes; small seconds; date; chronograph: central seconds counter, 60-second counter, 30-minute counter at 9, 12-hour counter at 6.
Case: steel; Ø 43mm; sapphire crystal; water resistant to 5atm.
Dial: white; varnished; dark gray transfer; rhodium-plated hour and minute hands; large orange seconds and counter hands.
Strap: white Epsom calf.
Suggested price: $5,700
Also available: other straps.

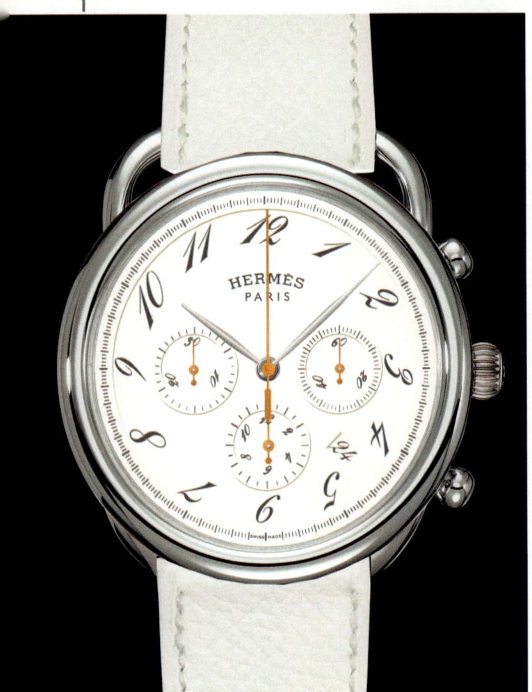

ARCEAU GRAND MOON — REF. 036756WW00

Movement: automatic-winding Dubois-Dépraz 9313 caliber; large moonphase; 42-hour power reserve.
Functions: hours, minutes, seconds; date and large moonphase at 6; day display at 11; month display at 1.
Case: steel; Ø 43mm; sapphire crystal; water resistant to 3atm.
Dial: opaline silver; stamped herringbone motif and rhodium-plated hour markers.
Strap: Havana alligator.
Suggested price: $6,800
Also available: other straps.

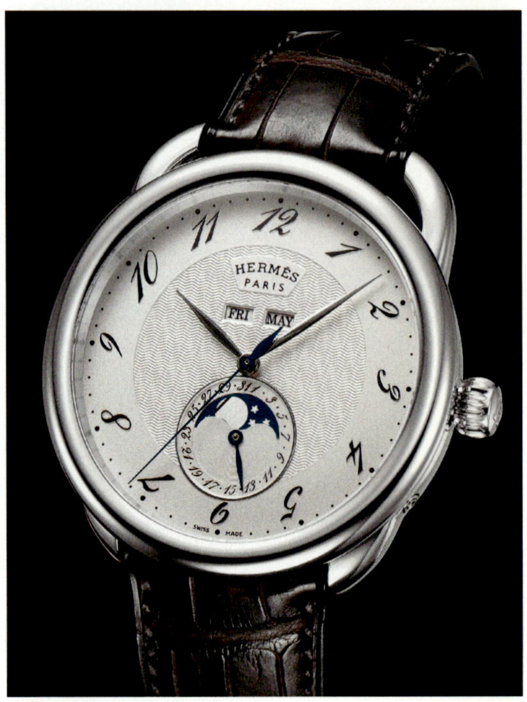

CAPE COD SIMPLE CALENDAR REF. 036308WW00

Movement: automatic-winding in both directions; 42-hour power reserve; circular-grained and snailed bridges; oscillating weight adorned with Côtes de Genève motif.
Functions: hours, minutes, seconds; date at 3.
Case: steel; 36.5x35.4mm; sapphire crystal; water resistant to 5atm.
Dial: opaline silver.
Strap: Havana alligator.
Suggested price: $4,700
Also available: other straps.

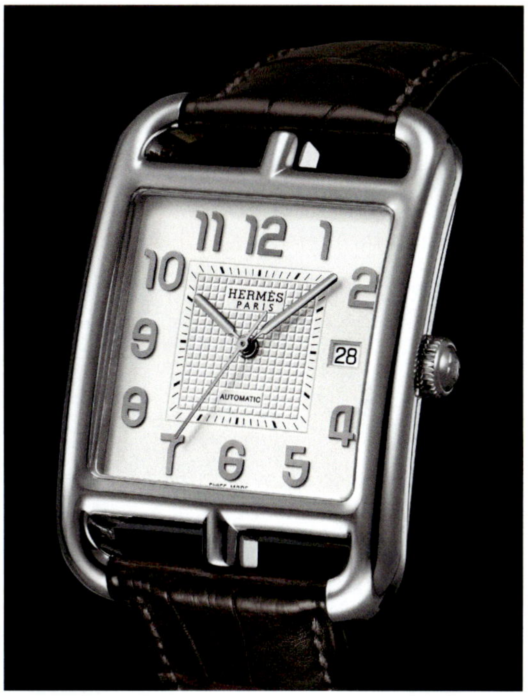

CAPE COD ROSE GOLD WITH DIAMONDS REF. 035236WW00

Movement: quartz.
Functions: hours, minutes.
Case: 750 rose gold; set with 52 brilliant-cut diamonds; 26.5x28mm; antireflective sapphire crystal; water resistant to 3atm.
Dial: natural white mother-of-pearl.
Strap: smooth Etruscan brown alligator leather; 750 rose-gold pin buckle.
Suggested price: $17,200
Also available: other straps.

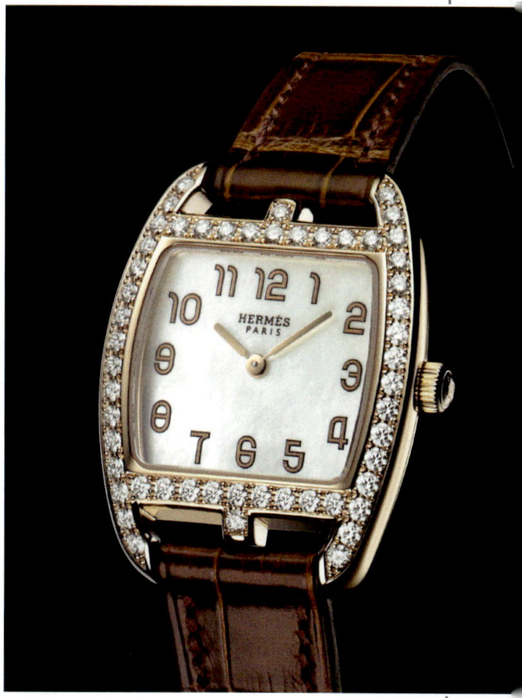

CLIPPER CHRONO MECANIQUE PLONGEE REF. 036058WW00

Movement: automatic-winding chronograph; 46-hour power reserve.
Functions: hours, minutes; small seconds at 12; simple calendar at 3; chronograph: central seconds counter, hour counter at 6, minute counter at 12.
Case: steel; Ø 44mm; sapphire crystal; titanium caseback; water resistant to 20atm.
Dial: blue.
Strap: blue rubber.
Suggested price: $6,350
Also available: other straps.

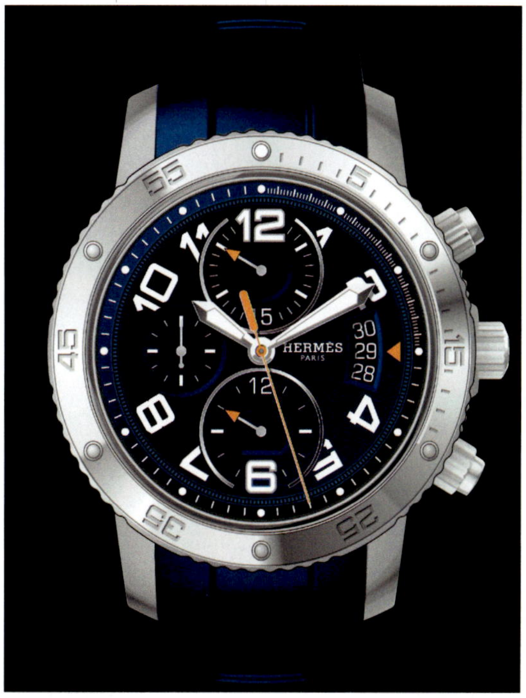

DRESSAGE PERPETUAL CALENDAR REF. 034669WW00

Movement: manual-winding Hermès H1935 caliber; Ø 27mm; 55-hour power reserve; 393 components; 32 jewels; 28,800 vph; hand-chamfered and polished bridges and mechanisms; exclusive Hermès decorative motif.
Functions: hours, minutes, seconds; retrograde perpetual calendar; month at 3; day at 9; retrograde date on a 225 degree segment; year at 12; moonphase.
Case: 750 rose gold (70 grams); Ø 40mm; screw-down crown; transparent sapphire crystal and caseback; water resistant to 5atm.
Dial: dark gray.
Strap: matte Havana alligator; 18K 750 rose-gold buckle.
Note: limited edition of 24 in white gold and 24 in rose gold.
Suggested price: $64,850
Also available: gold version.

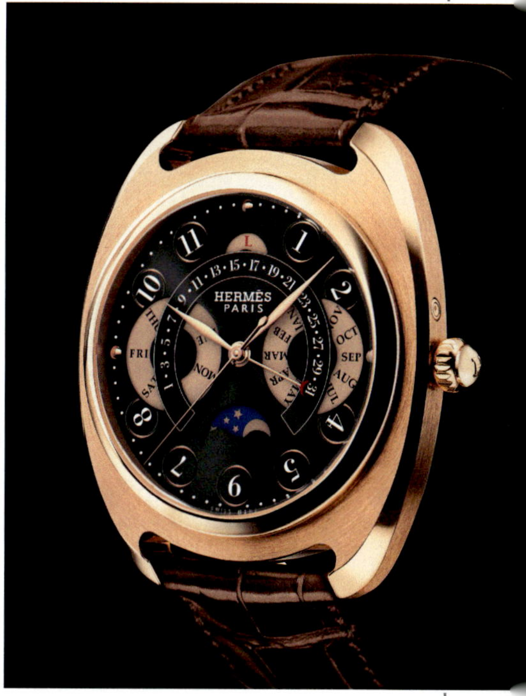

HUBLOT
GENEVE

AMERICAN BANG

America welcomed its first two boutiques from Hublot last year as the Swiss luxury watch brand, renowned for its Big Bang collection, continues to expand its universe of signature stores. Both U.S. boutiques are located in affluent Florida beach communities where surf and sand provide a suitably breathtaking backdrop for Hublot's dynamic timepieces.

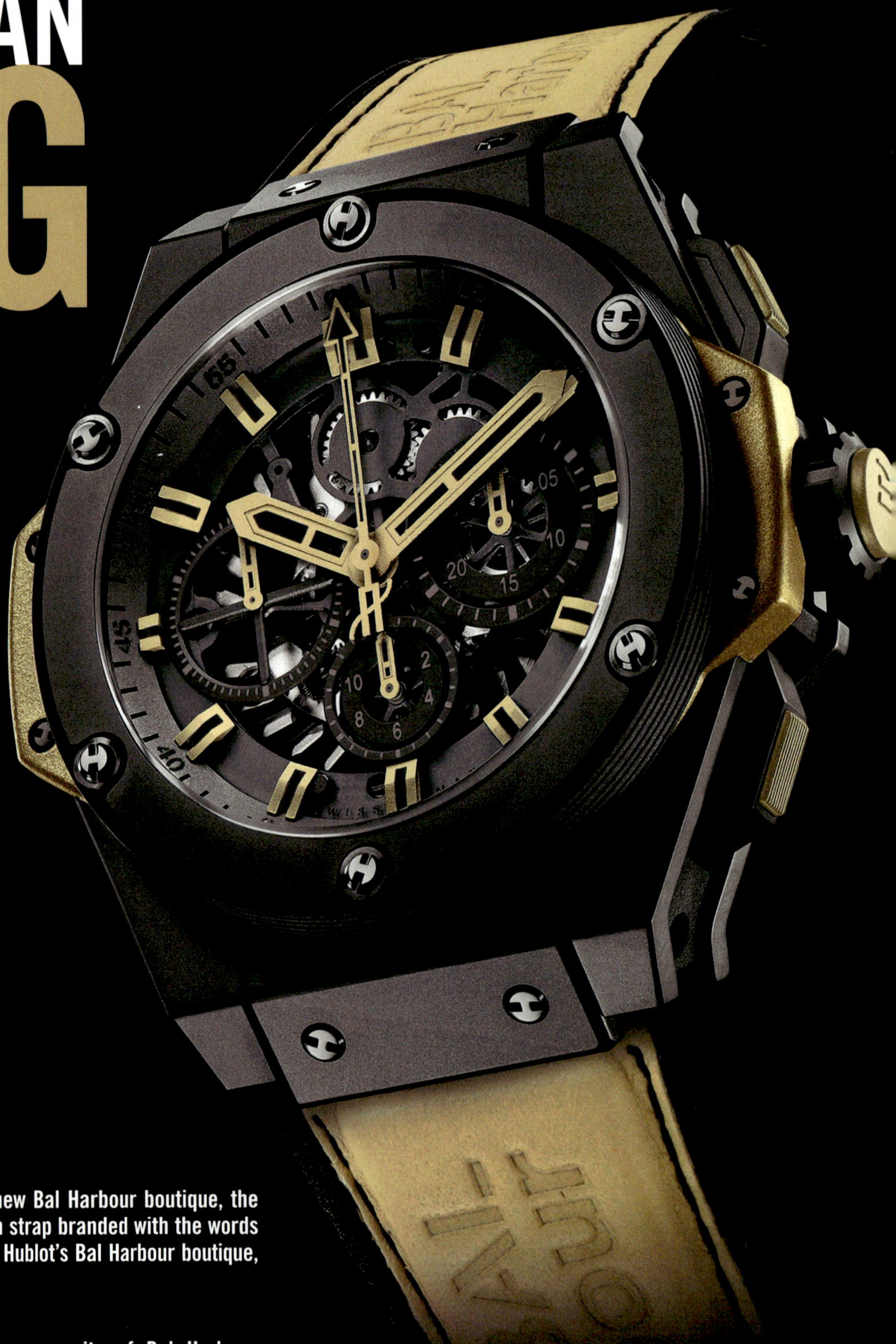

RIGHT

Created to commemorate the opening of Hublot's new Bal Harbour boutique, the King Power "Aero All Black" is paired with a calfskin strap branded with the words "Bal Harbour Limited Edition." Available exclusively at Hublot's Bal Harbour boutique, this model is offered in a limited edition of 25 pieces.

FACING PAGE

Hublot opened its first U.S. store in the beach community of Bal Harbour, Florida. The store's modern interior showcases the brand's collection as well as timepieces from its Vendôme Collection, which is available only at Hublot boutiques and select retailers.

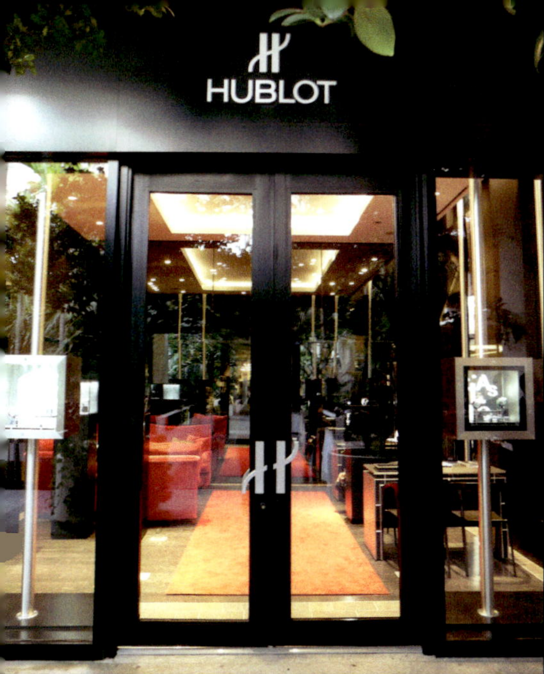

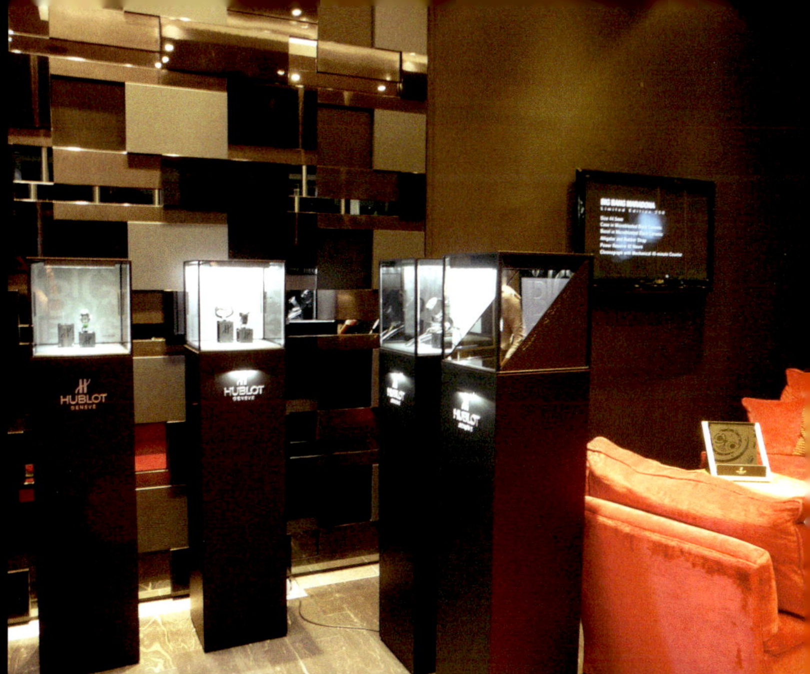

At all of Hublot's boutiques, guests can view a selection of timepieces from its new Vendôme Collection, which is exclusive to the brand's own boutiques and just a few select retailers worldwide.

The first store debuted in Bal Harbour at the open-air Bal Harbour Shops. It was soon followed by a location in Boca Raton in the upscale outdoor Mizner Park shopping center. Both feature modern interiors that subtly allude to Hublot's trademark fusion of unexpected materials; the decor of each includes elements in carbon, metal, leather and rubber.

"The two spaces reflect the brand's DNA of innovation and tradition, luxury and design, past and present, all combined within its vision of fusion," Hublot CEO Jean-Claude Biver said in a statement. "It is an important step for us as it aims to further our relationship with U.S. clients by providing the best service as well as a more in-depth and rounded Hublot experience."

At all of Hublot's boutiques, including those in Florida, guests can view the latest additions to the brand's existing lines alongside a selection of timepieces from Hublot's new Vendôme Collection. This line of special edition watches is only available at the brand's boutiques and a few select retailers worldwide. These exclusive models are clearly distinguished by the Vendôme Collection logo which is stamped on the dial and engraved on the caseback of each watch.

Hublot previewed timepieces from the collection last fall at the opening of its first store in Singapore. During the event, the brand introduced three exclusive collections: the Classic Fusion All Black Blue, Tutti Frutti Mirror and King Power Foudroyante All Black Blue.

Hublot was scheduled to officially unveil the entire Vendôme Collection in December 2010 at the christening of the Hublot Place Vendôme Boutique in Paris. The store was designed by Peter Marino, an award-winning architect renowned for creating dramatic retail spaces around the world for leading luxury brands.

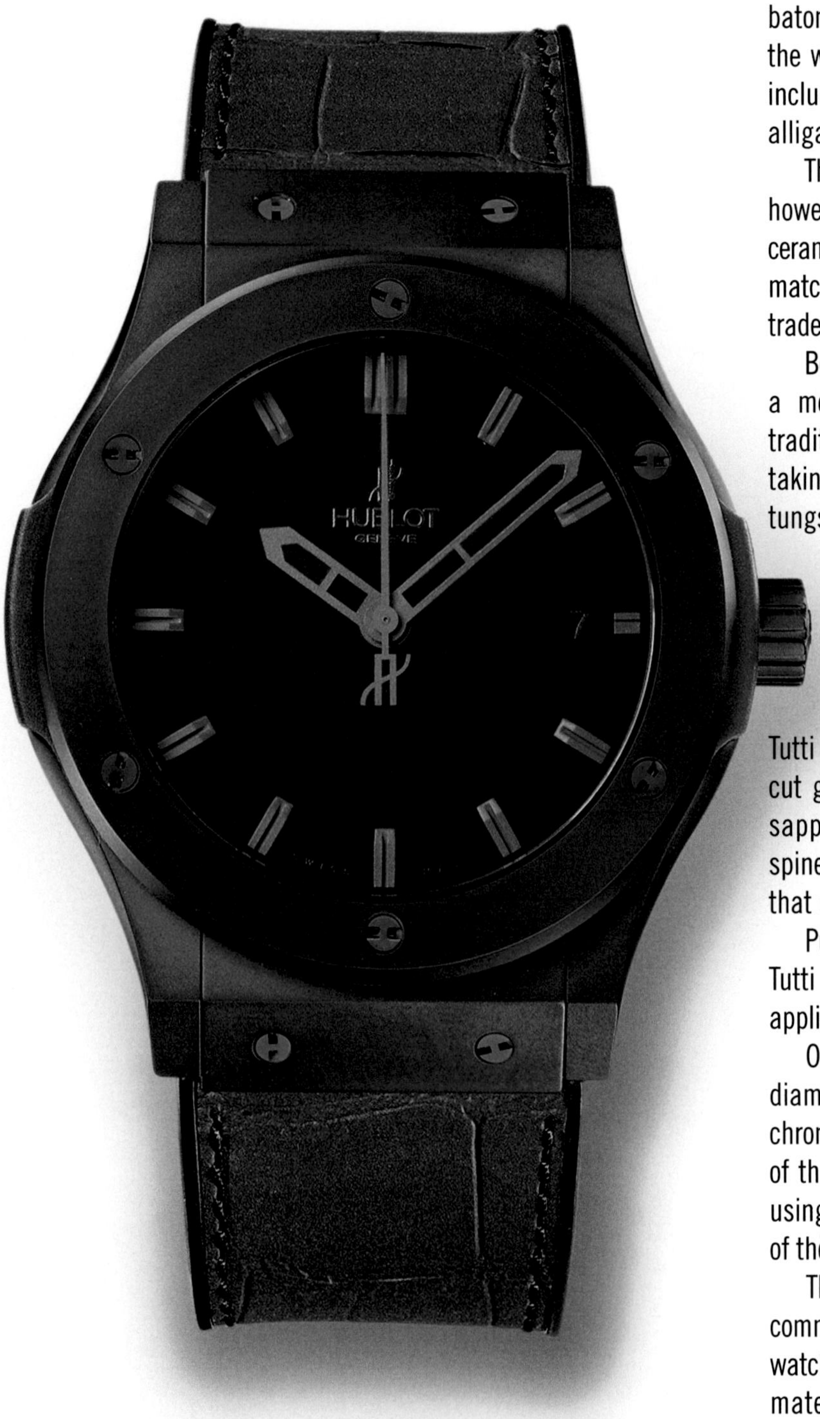

ABOVE

Part of Hublot's Vendôme Collection, the Classic Fusion All Black Blue is presented in a 45mm black ceramic case with a matching bezel. Its automatic movement features a 42-hour power reserve.

The Classic Fusion All Black Blue takes its place among the Vendôme Collection's exceptional examples of horology.

As its name suggests, this timepiece exhibits a traditional bent thanks to its clean dial design, which combines dark blue baton indexes on a matte black background. Hublot reiterates the watch's namesake color combination in a number of places, including blue hands with black luminescent markings and a blue alligator-skin strap with a comfortable black-rubber lining.

The Classic Fusion All Black Blue parts ways with tradition, however, in terms of size and material with a 45mm-diameter ceramic case that is more at home in watchmaking's modern era. The matching black ceramic bezel is secured to the case with Hublot's trademark H-shaped screws, which are coated with black PVD.

Beneath the dial beats the automatic Hublot Calibre HUB1112, a movement whose details reflect centuries of watchmaking tradition, including satin-finished bridges that have been painstakingly beveled and polished by hand. The automatic caliber's tungsten-carbide rotor powers the Classic Fusion All Black Blue's 42-hour power reserve.

Hublot covers the spectrum for women with the Big Bang Tutti Frutti Mirror, the second model from its Vendôme Collection. Like the brand's popular Tutti Frutti model, Hublot offers six color-coordinated versions of the Big Bang Tutti Frutti Mirror. Each variant features a different baguette-cut gemstone set around its bezel, including amethyst (purple), sapphire (pink or orange), tsavorite (green), topaz (blue) and spinel (red). Each design integrates a strap and case elements that match the bezel.

Putting its own twist on the Tutti Frutti tradition, the Big Bang Tutti Frutti Mirror is presented with a special mirrored dial with applied indexes and numerals that match the watch's color scheme.

Offered in Hublot's stainless steel Big Bang case (41mm in diameter), the Tutti Frutti Mirror is equipped with an automatic chronograph movement. Controlled by two pushpieces on the side of the case, the chronograph allows the wearer to time an event using the minute and hour indicators found on the lower left side of the dial.

The debut of the Vendôme Collection continues Hublot's commitment to the "Art of Fusion"—Hublot was the first Swiss watch luxury brand to fuse precious metals with more unconventional materials such as rubber. When Biver took the reins of the company in 2004, he defined the brand's personality with the "Big Bang," the multiple award-winning chronograph that marked the start of the brand's success and its impressive growth. Today, the Vendôme joins collections such as Big Bang, King Power and Classic Fusion housing complications such as the tourbillon, minute repeater, split second, jumping second, retrograde date and GMT (to name just a few), continuing to forge a link between tradition and 21st-century creativity.

THIS PAGE

Hublot offers six versions of the Tutti Frutti Mirror as part of its Vendôme Collection. Each stainless steel model includes a bezel set with 48 baguette-cut gemstones and color-coordinated accents.

CENTER

Red spinels encircle the mirrored dial of this Tutti Frutti Mirror, whose 41mm case is accompanied by a red alligator strap that includes a form-fitting rubber lining.

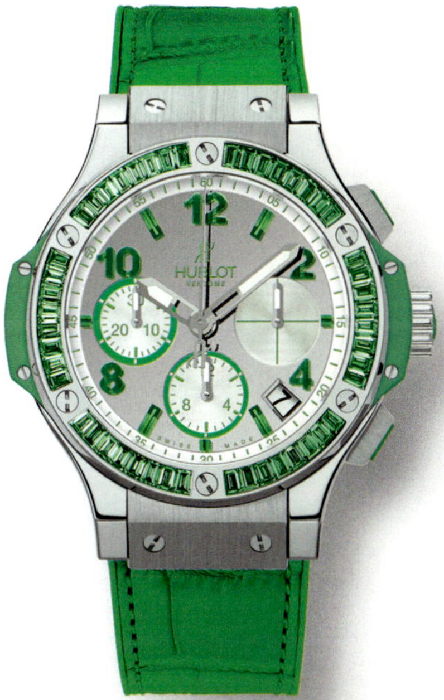

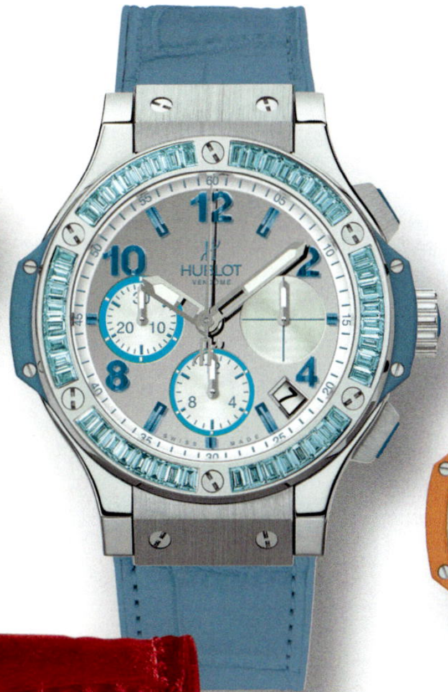

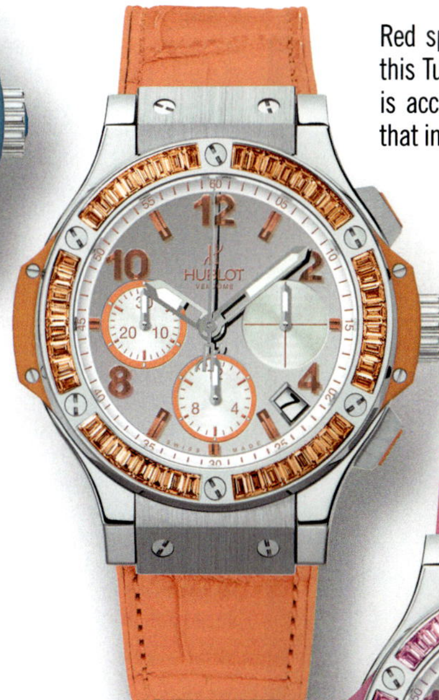

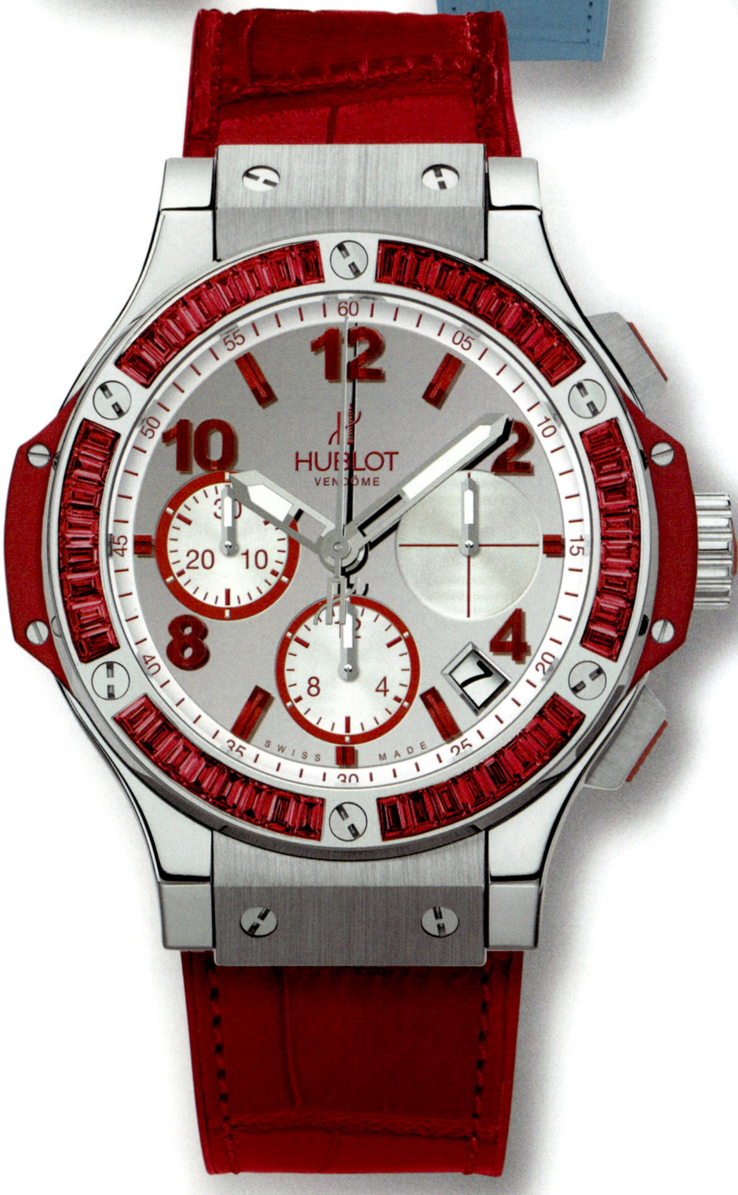

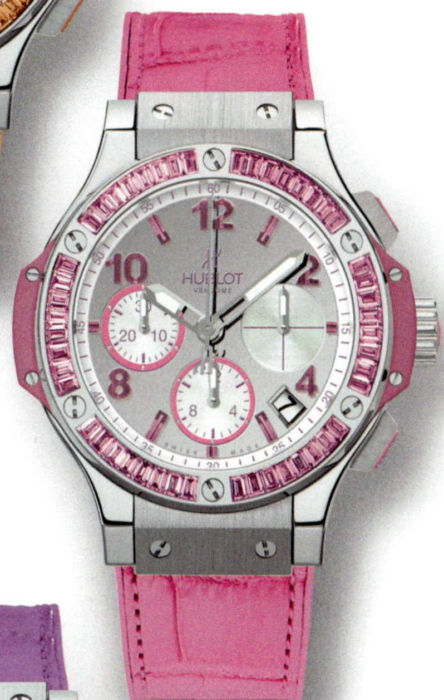

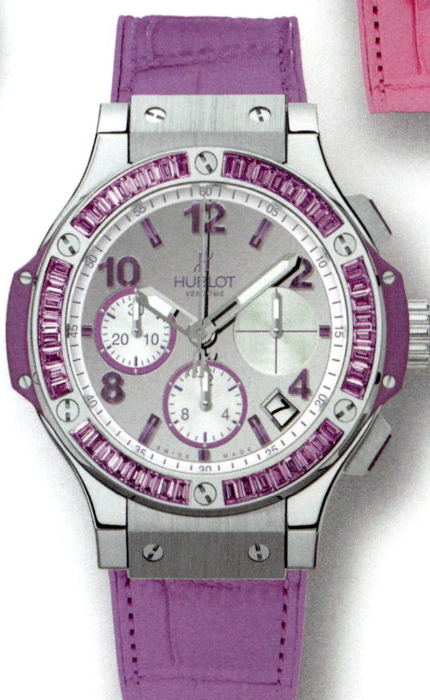

KING POWER F1TM MONZA — REF. 710.CI.0123.NR.MZA10

Movement: HUB 4400 automatic-winding skeleton chronograph; 42-hour power reserve; 252 components; 27 jewels; microblasted black chrome bridges and mainplate; Glucydur hairspring escapement.
Functions: hours, minutes, seconds; chronograph; date.
Case: King Power; Ø 48mm; microblasted black ceramic; microblasted black ceramic bezel with black rubber molding and six H-shaped black PVD-coated titanium screws; FORMULA 1 MONZA engraving in red; black PVD-coated titanium crown and pushpieces with black rubber inserts; solid red-tinted crystal world first; microblasted black ceramic caseback; water resistant to 10atm.
Dial: multi-piece with sapphire base; matte black counters; red indexes with white SuperLumiNova; microblasted red hands with white SuperLumiNova; red and white minute track; metal-plated F1 logo at 9.
Strap: adjustable black rubber and Nomex with red stitching; microblasted black ceramic clasp with black PVD-coated steel.
Note: limited to 200 pieces.
Suggested price: $26,900

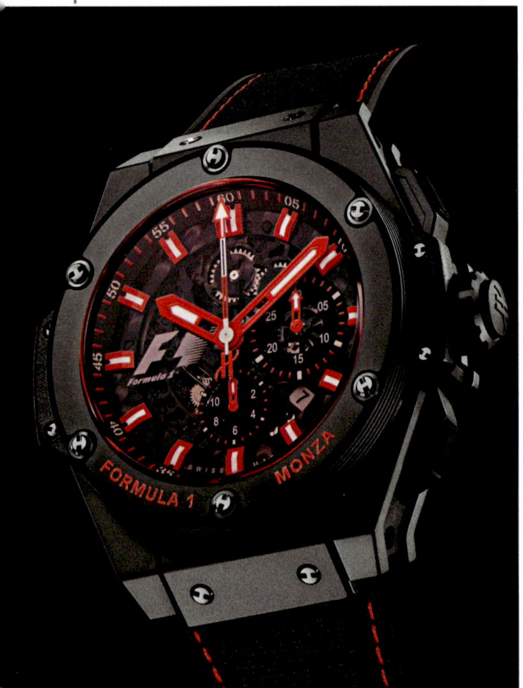

KING POWER F1 — REF. 703.ZM.1123.NR.FM010

Movement: HUB 4100 automatic-winding chronograph; 42-hour power reserve; 252 components; 27 jewels; microblasted, beveled and polished bridges; sandblasted and rhodium-plated mainplate; reinforced spring barrel; Glucydur hairspring escapement.
Functions: hours, minutes, seconds; chronograph; date.
Case: King Power; Ø 48mm; satin-finished zirconium; zirconium and ceramic bezel, disc brake decoration with six H-shaped black PVD-coated titanium screws; black PVD-coated titanium crown with black rubber inserts; black PVD-coated titanium pushpieces with red rubber inserts, marked START and RESET; antireflective sapphire crystal; satin-finished zirconium caseback; water resistant to 10atm.
Dial: multi-piece; black nickel indexes with black SuperLumiNova; microblasted, satin-finished and rhodium-plated hands with SuperLumiNova; F1 logo at 12.
Strap: black rubber with Hublot and F1 logo inside and black Nomex outside; titanium folding clasp with black PVD-coated steel.
Note: limited to 500 pieces.
Suggested price: $16,900

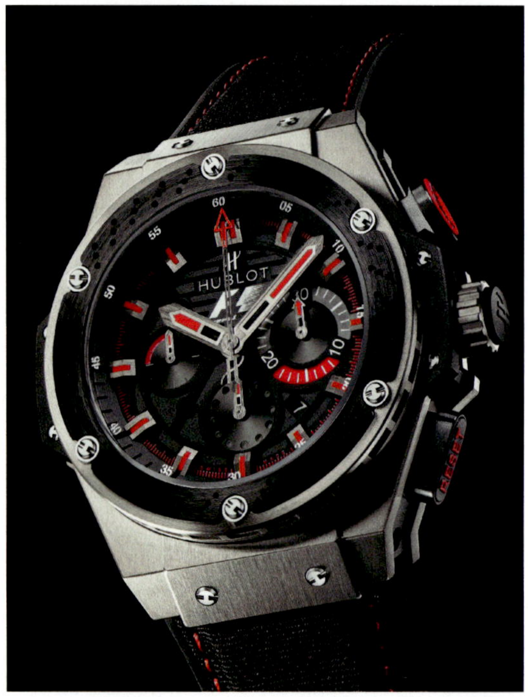

KING POWER UNICO ALL BLACK — REF. 701.CI.0110.RX

Movement: HUB 1240 UNICO automatic-winding flyback chronograph; 72-hour power reserve; microblasted beveled bridges with black galvanic treatment; microblasted mainplate with black galvanic treatment; reinforced barrel spring; Swiss pallet escapement with silicium pallet fork and escapement wheel.
Functions: hours, minutes, seconds; flyback chronograph; date.
Case: King Power; Ø 48mm; microblasted black ceramic; microblasted black ceramic bezel with black rubber molding and six H-shaped black PVD-coated titanium screws; black PVD-coated titanium crown and pushpieces with rubber inserts; antireflective sapphire crystal; black microblasted ceramic caseback; water resistant to 10atm.
Dial: multi-piece with sapphire base; matte black microblasted additional counters and flange; applied indexes with black nickel treatment and black SuperLumiNova; satin-finished black nickel hands with black luminescent coating.
Strap: articulated black rubber; microblasted black ceramic PVD-coated steel deployant buckle.
Note: limited to 500 pieces.
Suggested price: $18,900

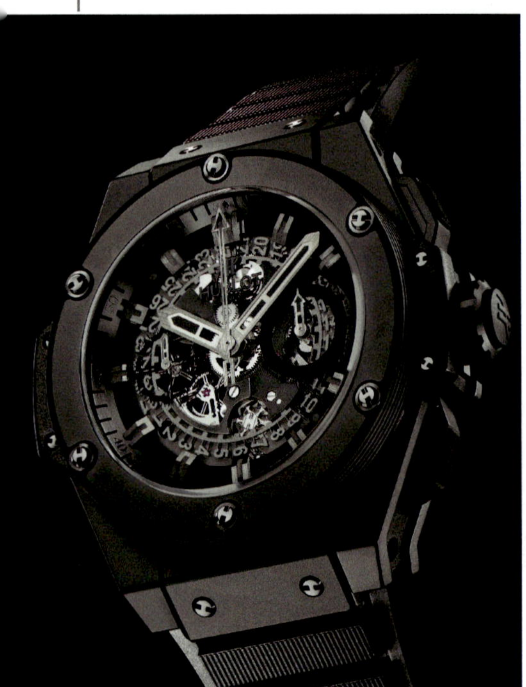

HUBLOT CALIBRE HUB1240

Movement: automatic-winding ceramic ball bearing; Pellaton type 2-way winding; Ø 30.4mm, thickness: 8.05mm; 70-hour power reserve; 330 components; 36 jewels; column-wheel chronograph mechanism integrated on the dial side; bi-compax; two pushpieces; double horizontal clutch; no jumper in the chronograph mechanism; removable platform escapement.
Functions: hours, minutes, seconds at 9; date; 60-second and 60-minute chronograph; flyback; semi-instant calendar; second stop device.

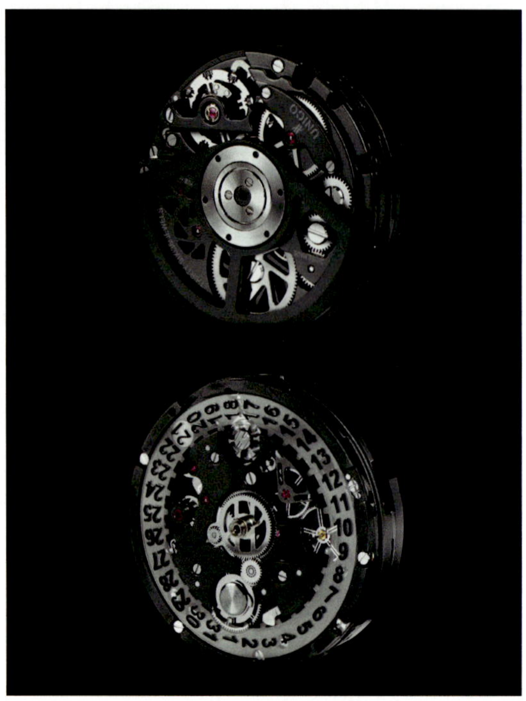

KING POWER TOURBILLON MANUFACTURE REF. 705.CI.0007.RX

Movement: HUB 6002 manual-winding tourbillon; 120-hour power reserve; microblasted angled and polished bridges and mainplate with black galvanic treatment; Glucydur hairspring escapement.
Functions: off-centered hour and minute indicators at 12; seconds via tourbillon cage at 6.
Case: King Power; Ø 48mm; microblasted black ceramic; microblasted black ceramic bezel with black rubber molding and six H-shaped black PVD-coated titanium screws; black PVD-coated titanium crown with black rubber inserts; antireflective sapphire crystal; microblasted black ceramic caseback; water resistant to 3atm.
Dial: multi-piece; polished black nickel hour and minute hands with black SuperLumiNova.
Strap: adjustable articulated black rubber; microblasted black ceramic and black PVD-coated steel deployant buckle.
Note: limited to 30 pieces.
Suggested price: $160,000

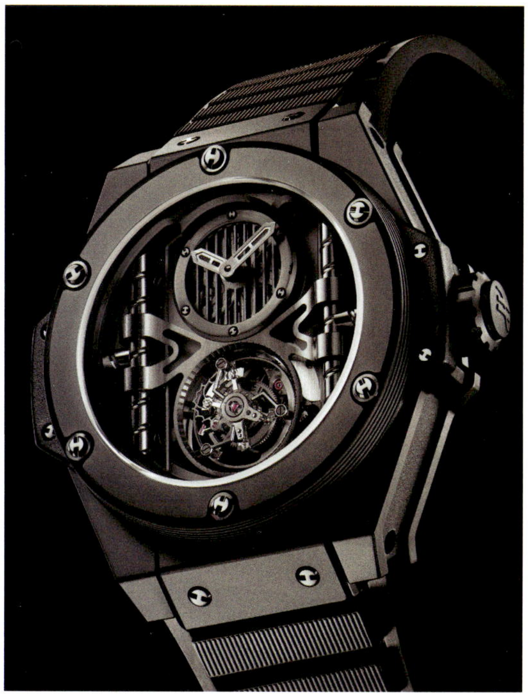

KING POWER GOLD TOURBILLON GMT REF. 706.OM.1180.RX

Movement: HUB 6121 manual-winding tourbillon GMT retrograde date; Ø 35.6mm, thickness: 6.9mm; 90-hour power reserve; 278 components; 30 jewels; 21,600 vph; microblasted black chrome mainplate.
Functions: hours, minutes; GMT dial at 1 in red and blue; tourbillon cage at 5; retrograde date at 9.
Case: King Power; Ø 48mm; King Gold; microblasted black ceramic bezel with black rubber molding and six H-shaped black PVD-coated titanium screws; King Gold crown and pushpieces with black rubber inserts; antireflective sapphire crystal; King Gold caseback; water resistant to 3atm.
Dial: multi-piece; microblasted gold-dusted matte-black counters and flange; gold-plated applied indexes with black SuperLumiNova transfers; gold-plated hands with black SuperLumiNova.
Strap: adjustable articulated black rubber; King Gold folding buckle with gold PVD-coated steel.
Note: limited to 28 pieces.
Suggested price: $175,000

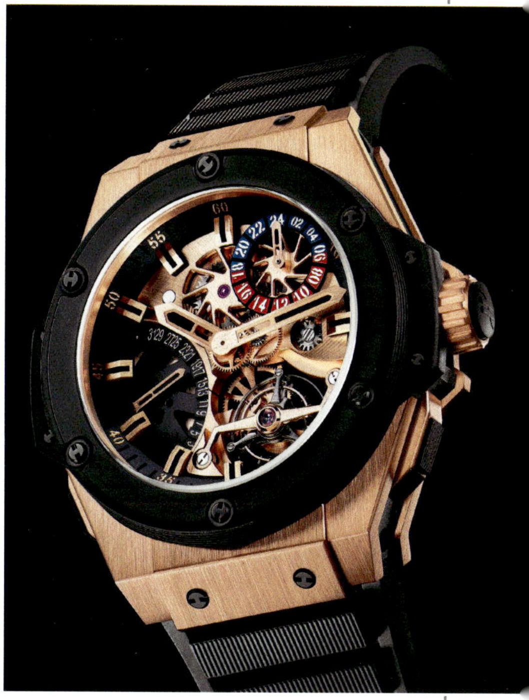

BIG BANG MINUTE REPEATER TOURBILLON GOLD REF. 304.PX.1180.LR

Movement: HUB 8000 manual-winding skeleton minute repeater tourbillon; 120-hour power reserve; 308 components; 44 jewels; 21,600 vph.
Functions: hours, minutes; minute repeater; tourbillon.
Case: Big Bang; Ø 44.5mm; 5N red gold; 5N red-gold bezel with six H-shaped titanium screws; 5N red-gold crown with black rubber inserts; antireflective sapphire crystal; open, 5N red-gold caseback; water resistant to 3atm.
Dial: skeleton with applied 5N red gold; 5N red-gold indexes; plated, polished skeleton 5N red-gold hands.
Strap: adjustable black rubber and semi-matte alligator; 5N red-gold clasp with black PVD coating.
Note: limited to 10 pieces.
Suggested price: $290,000

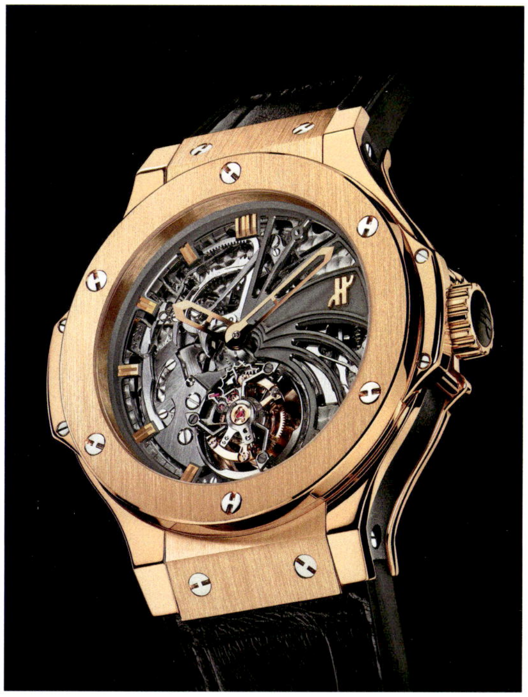

BIG BANG EARL GRAY GOLD HEMATITE REF. 341.PT.5010.LR.1912

Movement: HUB 4300 automatic-winding chronograph; 42-hour power reserve; 278 components; 37 jewels; Glucydur hairspring escapement.
Functions: hours, minutes, seconds; date; chronograph.
Case: Big Bang; Ø 41mm; 5N gold; 5N gold bezel with six H-shaped titanium screws, sunken, polished and locked; set with 48 baguette cut hematites; 5N gold crown with gray rubber inserts; polished and satin-finished end pieces; antireflective sapphire crystal; antireflective sapphire 5N gold caseback; water resistant to 10atm.
Dial: tantalum gray; satin-finished applied 5N gilt numerals; faceted, diamond-set, 5N gilt hands with white SuperLumiNova.
Strap: adjustable black rubber and semi-matte alligator; 5N gold clasp with black PVD coating.
Note: limited to 10 pieces.
Suggested price: $36,700

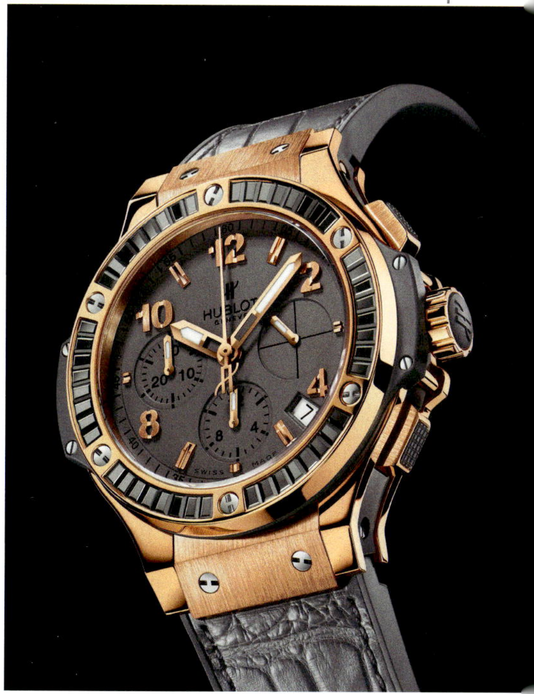

IWC

INTERNATIONAL WATCH CO. SCHAFFHAUSEN
SWITZERLAND, SINCE 1868

ROCK THE BOAT

The ample outline and boundless versatility of the Portuguese case has proven to be a prolific muse for IWC watchmakers, as the company pairs this nuanced case with a rich selection of movements.

The Portuguese began its modern expedition in 1993, when IWC reintroduced the case's noble profile to commemorate the Schaffhausen watchmaker's 125-year anniversary. Since then, the imposing round case has hosted a number of IWC-manufactured movements, including automatics, perpetual calendars and tourbillons. During a recent two-year stretch, the company staked out extreme ends of the mechanical spectrum with the Portuguese Hand-Wound in 2008 and the Portuguese Grande Complication in 2010, the latter appearing for the first time ever in the popular case.

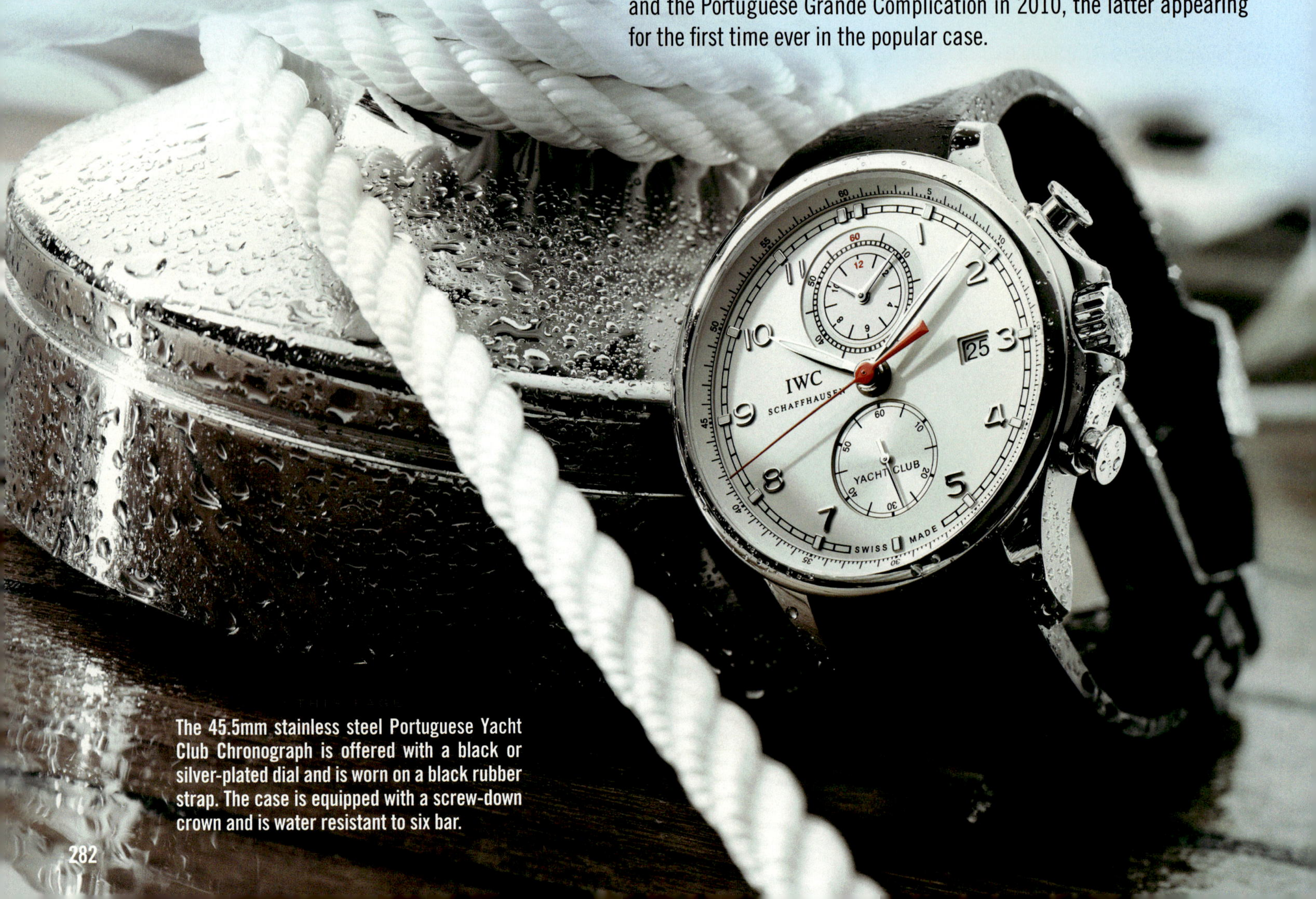

The 45.5mm stainless steel Portuguese Yacht Club Chronograph is offered with a black or silver-plated dial and is worn on a black rubber strap. The case is equipped with a screw-down crown and is water resistant to six bar.

Since the Portuguese was reintroduced in 1993, IWC has used the imposing case to showcase some of the finest movements manufactured at the company's Schaffhausen workshop.

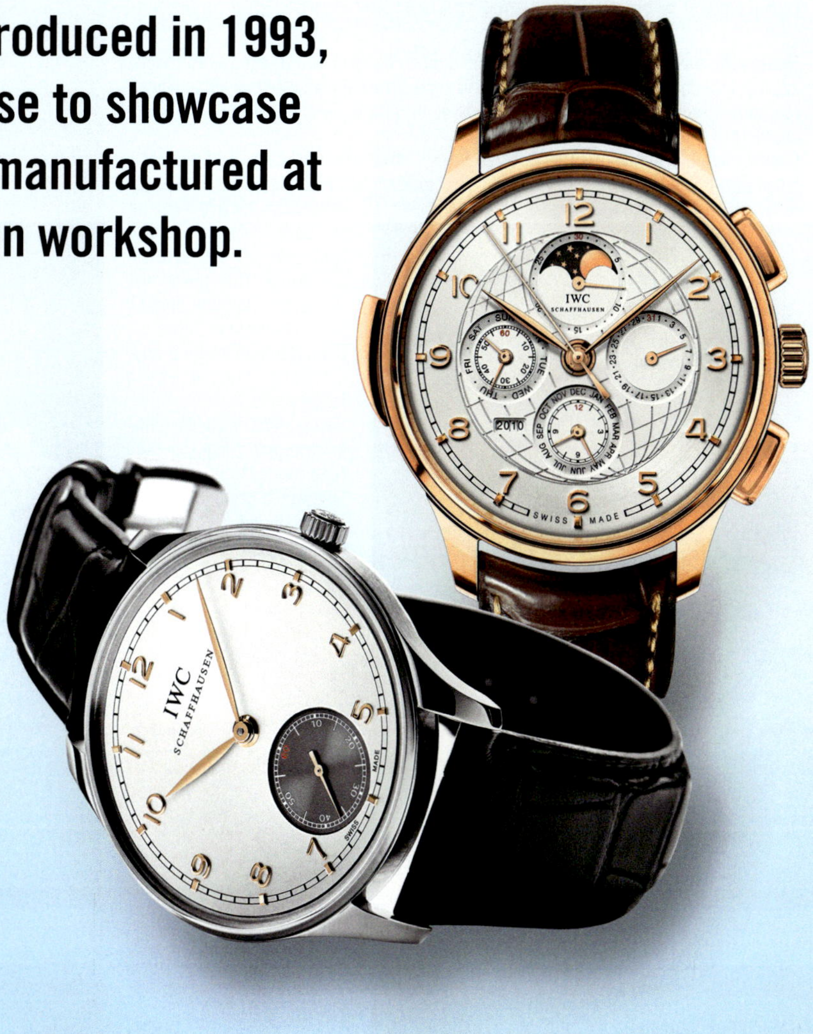

The Grande Complication was not the only new addition to the Portuguese family last year. IWC also took the Yacht Club out of dry dock for its maiden voyage in the case. After its 1967 debut, the Yacht Club rose to become one of IWC's best-selling watches before sailing out of sight in the '80s. Designed with an eye toward seaworthiness, the rugged watch was beloved for its resistance to both water and sudden knocks.

The new Portuguese Yacht Club Chronograph maintains a close link to that past, offering water resistance to six bar along with a stable and precise IWC manufacture movement. And yet, this new union manages to chart its own course by effectively aligning the Yacht Club's athletic essence with the Portuguese's elegance. The result is a watch that skillfully navigates the crosscurrent between nautical instrument and handsome accoutrement.

A grand complication is the highest expression of the watchmaking art. It combines at least three functions, typically one each from the ranks of astronomic, acoustic and timer complications.

These ultra-complicated watches are a specialty at IWC, which created the first grand complication pocket watch in 1890. A century later the company celebrated the achievement's centennial by presenting the first grand complication wristwatch.

For 20 years, IWC has offered that signature Grande Complication in a case made exclusively for the watch. That changed in 2010 when the brand also began offering the Grande Complication in a red-gold Portuguese case.

This model features a newly designed silver-plated dial embellished with an engraving of the globe and its longitude and latitude lines. The dial's intuitive arrangement allows for the quick reading of the watch's perpetual calendar, perpetual moonphase and chronograph displays.

The Portuguese Grande Complication also features a minute repeater. Historically, repeater watches are not highly water resistant because sealing the case tightly against infiltration prevents the air movement necessary for the repeater to achieve the proper volume and tone. IWC overcame this challenge with a complex case design that is water resistant to three bar without diminishing the repeater's mellifluous call.

Casting a mirror image of the Portuguese Grand Complication, the unassuming Portuguese Hand-Wound finds its charm in the timeless elegance of its refinement. It expresses a deep connection to the past, resembling the look of the first Portuguese watch, which IWC created in 1939 at the behest of a pair of watch importers from Portugal. The brand now offers two versions of the stainless steel Portuguese Hand-Wound, one with a black dial and the other silver-plated.

By announcing 2010 as the Year of the Portuguese, IWC raised expectations high. Without a doubt, the Schaffhausen manufacture exceeded the mark with a collection that reveals the many personalities of the Portuguese.

ABOVE

The 44mm stainless steel Portuguese Hand-Wound is offered with either a black dial and silver-plated small seconds or silver-plated dial and gray small seconds.

TOP RIGHT

IWC will make the 45mm red-gold Portuguese Grande Complication in a limited series of 50 pieces every year. In tribute to Portugal's historic naval prowess, a captain's sextant is engraved on the caseback.

IWC DA VINCI PERPETUAL CALENDAR EDITION KURT KLAUS REF. IW376205

Movement: automatic-winding IWC 89360 caliber; 68-hour power reserve; 40 jewels; 28,800 vph; double-pin winding device and seconds-stopping system; column wheel.
Functions: hours, minutes; small seconds at 9; date at 6; chronograph with three counters.
Case: rose-gold; tonneau-shaped; three-piece; 44x43mm, thickness: 14.4mm; polished and brushed finish; screw-down crown; rocking pushers; domed sapphire crystal, antireflective coating on both sides; caseback fastened by six screws, displaying the movement through a sapphire crystal; water resistant to 3atm.
Dial: black; extra-long hour markers; simple baton hands.
Strap: black crocodile leather; rose-gold clasp.
Note: limited to 1,000 pieces.
Suggested price: $36,400
Also available: stainless steel (limited to 1,000 pieces).

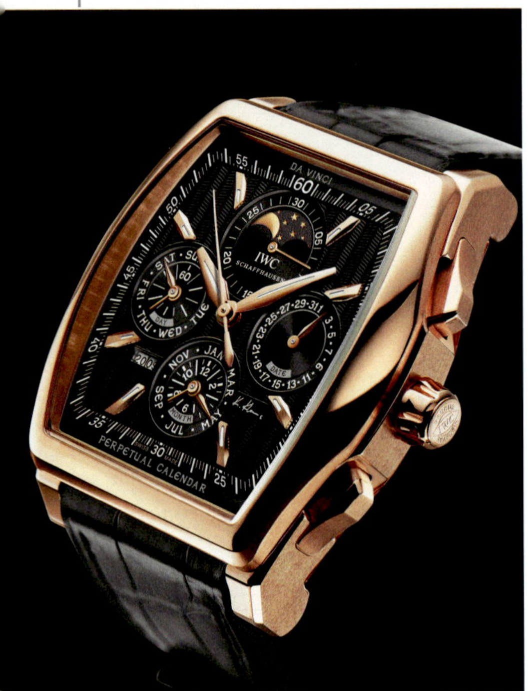

IWC DEEP TWO REF. IW354701

Movement: automatic-winding 30110 caliber; 21-hour power reserve; 40 jewels; 28,800 vph.
Functions: hours, minutes; central seconds hand with stop function; date at 3; mechanical depth gauge from 6 to 12.
Case: stainless steel; external mechanical rotating bezel; sapphire crystal, antireflective coating on both sides; screw-in caseback.
Dial: rhodium-plated black dial; white luminescent indexes; depth gauge.
Bracelet: stainless steel.
Suggested price: $14,900-$15,900
Also available: black rubber strap.

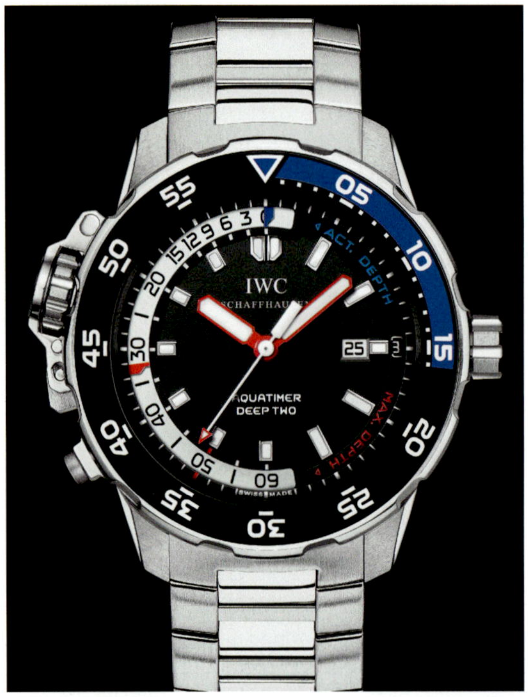

IWC AQUATIMER AUTOMATIC 2000 REF. IW356802

Movement: automatic-winding 30110 caliber; 21-hour power reserve; 40 jewels; 28,800 vph.
Functions: hours, minutes; central seconds with stop function; date at 3.
Case: stainless steel; external mechanical rotating bezel; sapphire crystal, antireflective coating on both sides; screw-in caseback.
Dial: rhodium-plated black dial; white luminescent indexes.
Strap: black rubber.
Suggested price: $4,400-$5,400
Also available: stainless steel bracelet; white dial on black rubber strap or stainless steel bracelet.

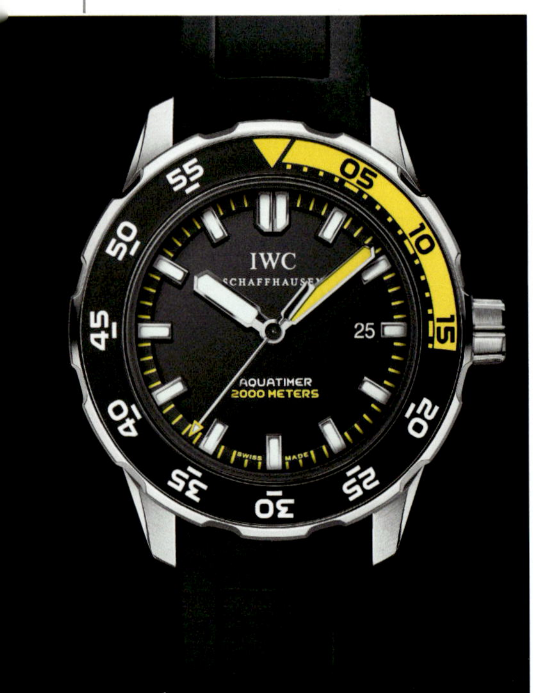

IWC DA VINCI PERPETUAL CALENDAR DIGITAL DATE-MONTH REF. IW376101

Movement: automatic-winding 89800 caliber; 68-hour power reserve; 52 jewels; 28,800 vph.
Functions: hours, minutes; small seconds with stop function at 6; chronograph; perpetual calendar; large month display at 3; large date at 9; combined hour and minute counters at 12.
Case: platinum; sapphire crystal, antireflective coating on both sides; exhibition caseback.
Dial: rhodium-plated silver dial.
Strap: black crocodile leather.
Note: limited to 500 pieces.
Suggested price: $44,300-$70,000
Also available: rose gold on brown crocodile leather strap.

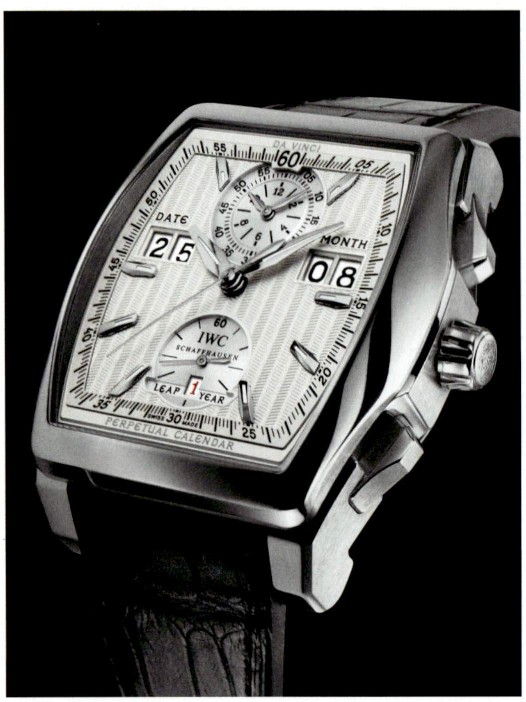

IWC INGENIEUR AUTOMATIC MISSION EARTH REF. IW323601

Movement: automatic-winding IWC 80110 caliber; 44-hour power reserve; 28 jewels; 28,800 vph.
Functions: hours, minutes; central seconds hand with stop function; date at 3.
Case: stainless steel; sapphire crystal, antireflective coating on both sides.
Dial: rhodium-plated black dial; Arabic numerals and indexes.
Strap: black rubber.
Suggested price: $6,900
Also available: stainless steel bracelet.

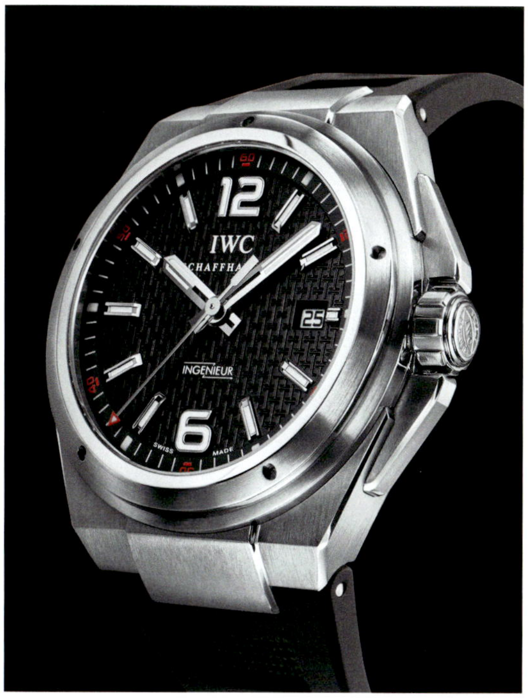

IWC INGENIEUR AUTOMATIC: VINTAGE COLLECTION REF. IW323301

Movement: 80111 caliber with Pellaton automatic-winding system; 44-hour power reserve; 28 jewels; 28,800 vph.
Functions: hours, minutes, seconds; date at 3.
Case: stainless steel; Ø 42.5mm, thickness: 14.5mm; screw-down crown; crossed out antireflective sapphire crystal; sapphire crystal caseback; water resistant to 12atm.
Dial: rhodium-plated black dial; dot-and-line markers (the dots are luminescent); dauphine hands.
Strap: black crocodile leather; stainless steel clasp.
Suggested price: $7,300-$38,000
Also available: platinum (limited to 500 pieces); rose gold; white gold.

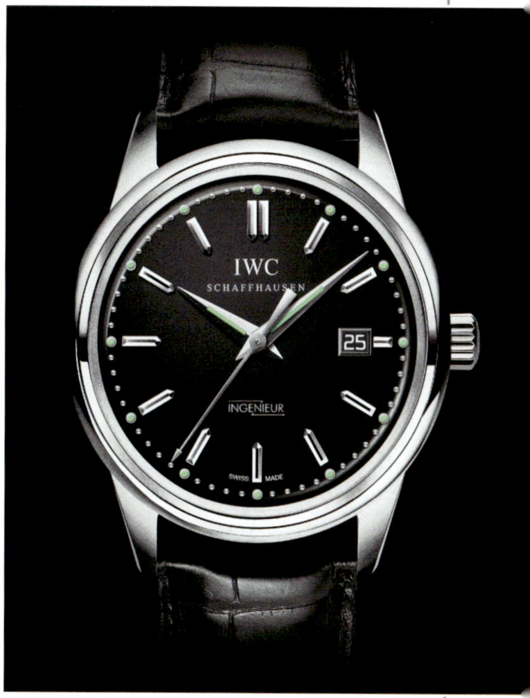

IWC PORTOFINO HAND-WOUND: VINTAGE COLLECTION REF. IW544801

Movement: manual-winding 98800 caliber; 46-hour power reserve; 18 jewels; 18,800 vph; Breguet spring.
Functions: hours, minutes; small seconds at 6; moonphase at 12.
Case: stainless steel; Ø 46mm, thickness: 11mm; crossed out antireflective sapphire crystal; sapphire crystal caseback; water resistant to 3atm.
Dial: black; elongated Roman numerals.
Strap: black crocodile leather; stainless steel clasp.
Suggested price: $10,900-$44,000
Also available: platinum (limited to 500 pieces); rose gold; white gold.

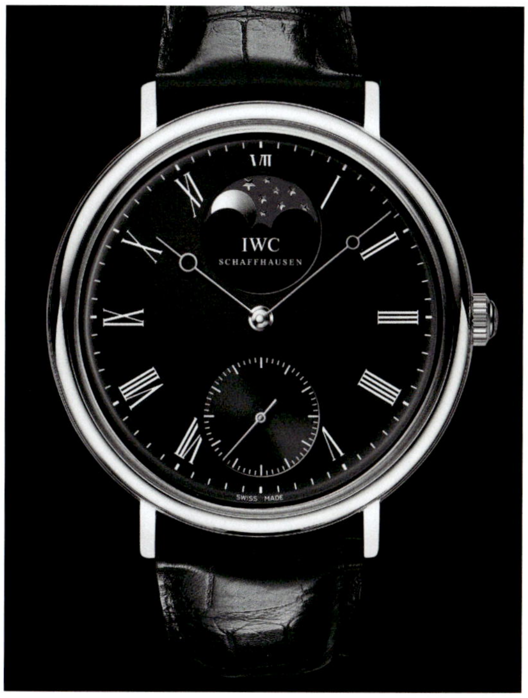

IWC PILOT'S WATCH HAND-WOUND: VINTAGE COLLECTION REF. IW325401

Movement: manual-winding 98300 caliber; 46-hour power reserve; 18 jewels; 18,000 vph.
Functions: hours, minutes; small seconds at 6.
Case: stainless steel; Ø 44mm, thickness: 12mm; rotating bezel with pointer; antireflective sapphire crystal; sapphire crystal caseback; water resistant to 6atm.
Dial: black; classic IWC cockpit-style design; luminescent hands and numerals.
Strap: brown buffalo strap; stainless steel clasp.
Suggested price: $8,900-$41,600
Also available: platinum (limited to 500 pieces); rose gold; white gold.

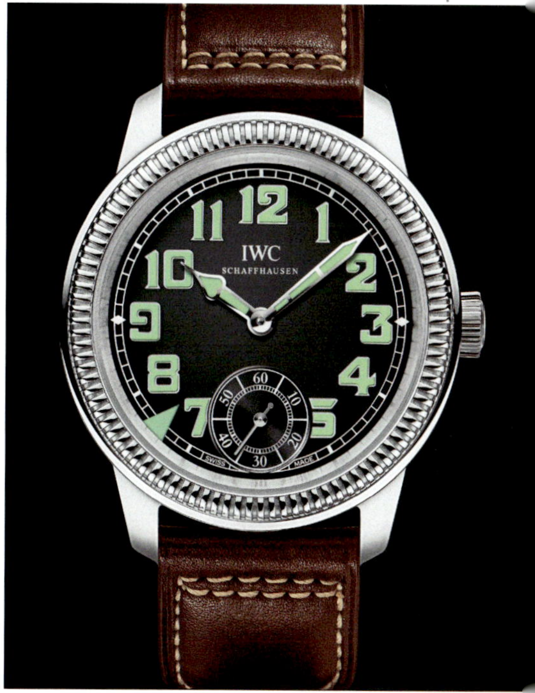

IWC PILOT'S WATCH CHRONO-AUTOMATIC — REF. IW371701

Movement: automatic-winding IWC 79320 caliber; 44-hour power reserve; 25 jewels; 28,800 vph.
Functions: hours, minutes; small seconds hand with stop function; day and date; stopwatch.
Case: stainless steel; three-piece; Ø 42mm, thickness: 14.7mm; soft iron for protection against magnetic fields; domed, antireflective sapphire crystal resistant against pressure drop.

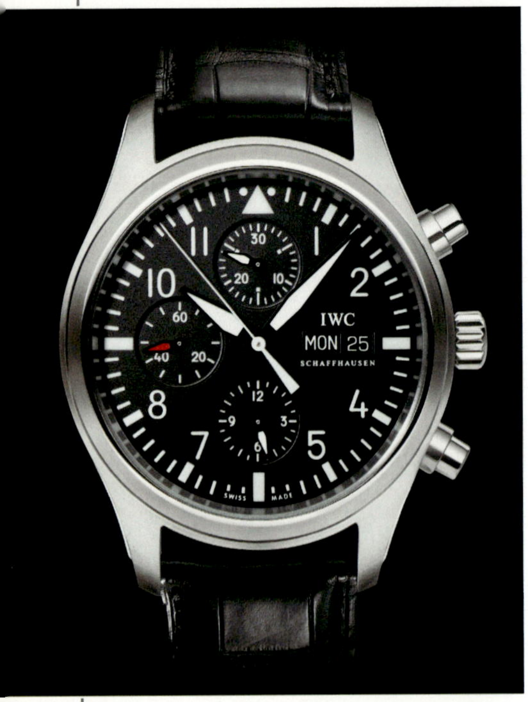

Dial: black; applied Arabic numerals; chapter ring; propeller-like hands; day and date at 3; stopwatch at 6, 9 and 12.
Strap: black hand-stitched crocodile leather; stainless steel fold-over clasp.
Suggested price: $4,400-$14,500
Also available: stainless steel bracelet equipped with folding clasp and special IWC bracelet system that allows for quick adjustment; rose gold on a brown hand-stitched crocodile leather strap with rose-gold fold-over clasp.

IWC BIG PILOT'S WATCH — REF. IW500401

Movement: automatic-winding IWC 51110 caliber; 7-day power reserve; 44 jewels; 21,600 vph; Breguet spring.
Functions: hours, minutes; power reserve display at 3; date at 6; central seconds hand with stop function.
Case: stainless steel; three-piece; Ø 46.2mm, thickness: 15.8mm; soft iron for protection against magnetic fields; domed antireflective sapphire crystal resistant against pressure drop.

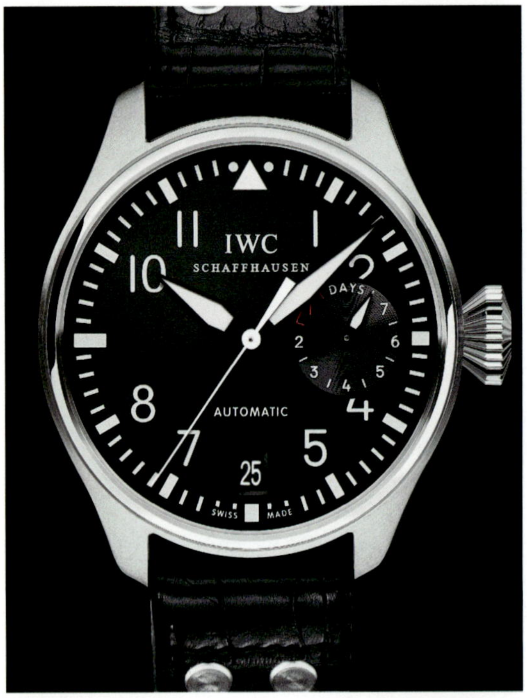

Dial: black; applied Arabic numerals; propeller-like hands.
Strap: black hand-stitched crocodile leather; stainless steel fold-over clasp.
Suggested price: $13,500-$26,500
Also available: 18K gold on a dark brown hand-stitched crocodile leather strap.

IWC PORTUGUESE AUTOMATIC — REF. IW500106

Movement: IWC 51010 caliber with Pellaton automatic-winding system; 7-day power reserve; 44 jewels; 21,600 vph; Breguet spring; 18K yellow-gold medallion rotor.
Functions: hours, minutes; small seconds hand with stop function at 9; power reserve display at 3; date display at 6.
Case: 18K white-gold; three-piece; Ø 42.3mm, thickness: 13.9mm; domed antireflective sapphire crystal.

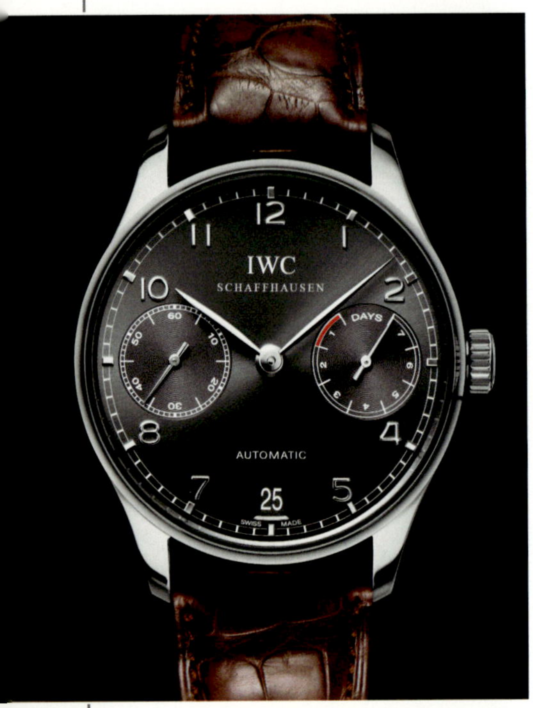

Dial: rhodium-plated; ardoise; railway-style minute chapter ring; applied gilded Arabic numerals; recessed subdials for the minutes and seconds counters.
Strap: dark brown crocodile leather, hand-stitched; white-gold fold-over clasp.
Suggested price: $10,900-$20,500
Also available: rose gold on a brown hand-stitched crocodile leather strap; in stainless steel on a blue or black hand-stitched crocodile strap.

PILOT'S WATCH DOUBLE CHRONOGRAPH EDITION TOP GUN — REF. IW379901

Movement: automatic-winding IWC 79230 caliber (integral chronograph modified for the split-second feature) with a seconds-stopping system; 44-hour power reserve; 29 jewels; 28,800 vph.
Functions: hours, minutes, seconds; day and oversized date at 3; split second chronograph with three counters: hours at 6, small seconds at 9, minutes at 12.
Case: black ceramic and natural titanium; two-piece; Ø 46mm, thickness: 17.8mm; matte finish; screw-down crown and pushers with case protection (the one for the split-second chronograph at 10 in titanium); additional ductile iron inside for the deviation of magnetic fields; very thick curved sapphire crystal, antireflective coating on both sides; highly depressurization-resistant; titanium screw-on caseback in titanium with Top Gun logo; water resistant to 6atm.

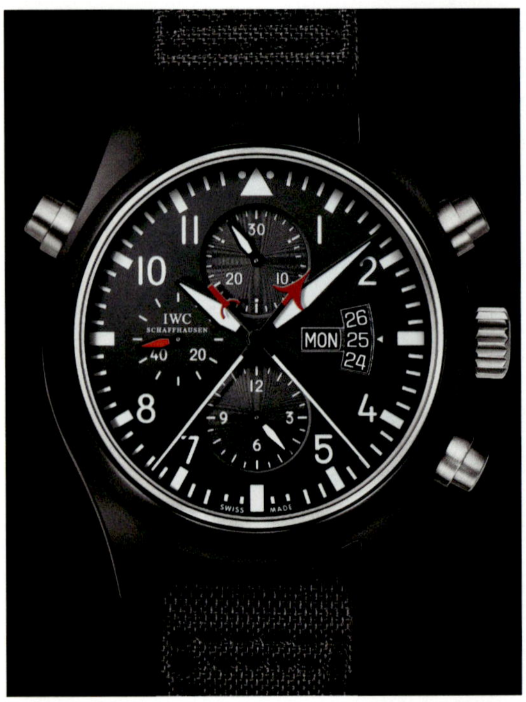

Strap: black fabric; brushed titanium clasp.
Suggested price: $10,900

IWC DA VINCI AUTOMATIC: VINTAGE COLLECTION — REF. IW546101

Movement: 80111 caliber with Pellaton automatic-winding system; 44-hour power reserve; 28 jewels; 28,800 vph.
Functions: hours, minutes, seconds; date at 3.
Case: stainless steel; Ø 41mm, thickness: 13.5mm; screw-down crown; antireflective sapphire crystal; sapphire crystal caseback; water resistant to 3atm.
Dial: black dial with extra-long markers and simple baton hands.
Strap: black crocodile leather; stainless steel clasp.
Also available: platinum (limited to 500 pieces); rose gold; white gold.
Suggested price: $7,300-$38,000

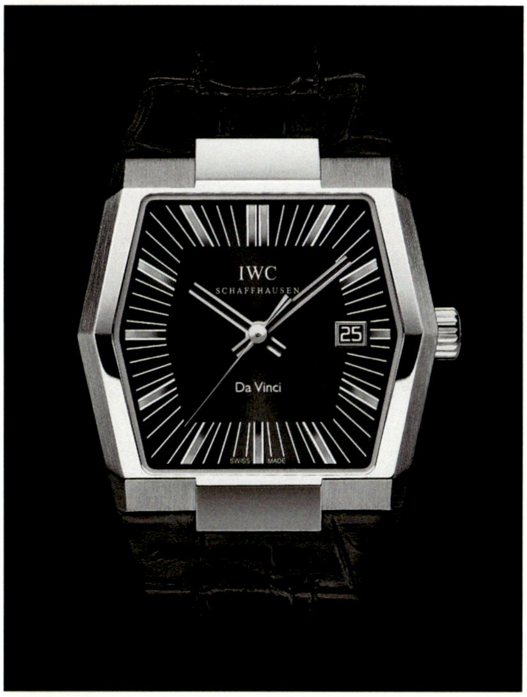

PILOT'S WATCH MARK XVI — REF. IW325501

Movement: automatic-winding IWC 30110 caliber; 42-hour power reserve; 21 jewels; 28,800 vph.
Functions: hours, minutes, seconds; date at 3.
Case: stainless steel; three-piece; Ø 39mm, thickness: 11.5mm; soft iron for protection against magnetic fields; domed antireflective sapphire crystal resistant against pressure drop.
Dial: black; Arabic numerals; propeller-like hands.
Strap: black crocodile leather, hand-stitched; stainless steel fold-over clasp.
Suggested price: $3,500-$4,900
Also available: stainless steel bracelet with special IWC system enabling quick adjustment.

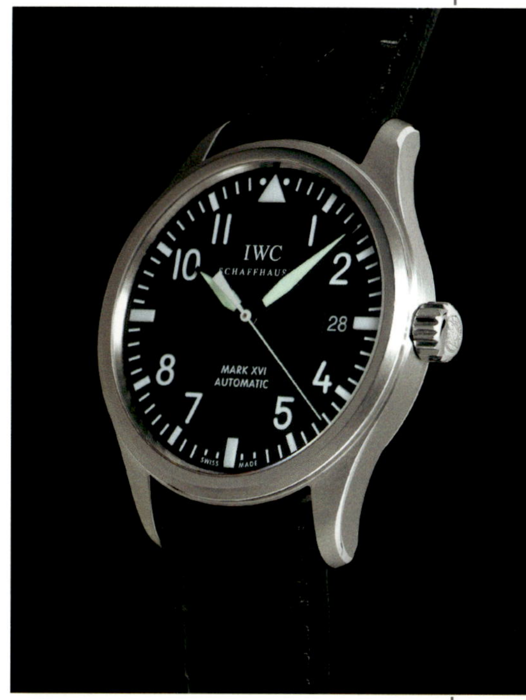

IWC PORTUGUESE HAND-WOUND: VINTAGE COLLECTION — REF. IW544501

Movement: manual-winding 98295 caliber; 46-hour power reserve; 18 jewels; 18,000 vph; Breguet spring.
Functions: hours, minutes; small seconds at 6.
Case: stainless steel; Ø 44mm, thickness: 10mm; crossed out antireflective sapphire crystal; sapphire crystal caseback; water resistant to 3atm.
Dial: rhodium-plated black; silvered indexes; railway-style minute chapter ring; applied gilded Arabic numerals.
Strap: black leather.
Suggested price: $9,900-$41,500
Also available: platinum (limited to 500 pieces); rose gold; white gold.

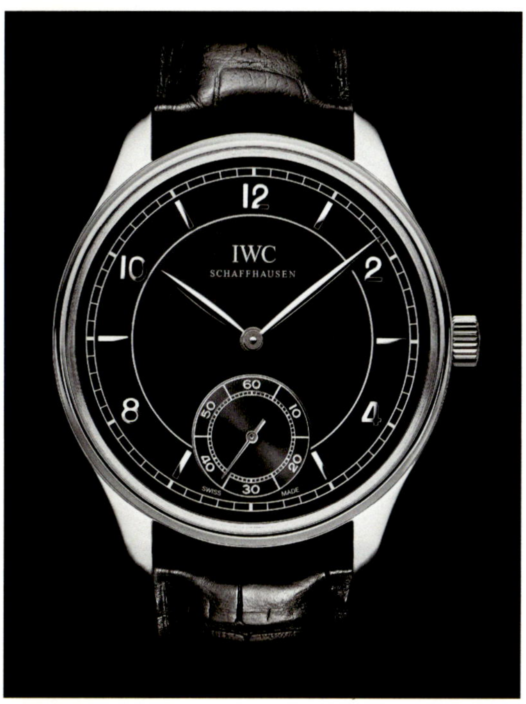

IWC PORTUGUESE GRANDE COMPLICATION — REF. IW377402

Movement: automatic-winding 79091 caliber with chronograph; 44-hour power reserve; 657 components; 75 jewels; 28,800 vph; Breguet spring.
Functions: perpetual calendar: day, date, month, complete year in four digits; perpetual moonphase; minute repeater: hours, quarter-hours, minutes; small hacking seconds; stopwatch: hours, minutes, seconds.
Case: 18K red gold; Ø 45mm, thickness: 16.5mm; antireflective sapphire crystal coating on both sides; special back engraving; water resistant to 3atm.
Dial: silver-plated.
Strap: dark brown alligator leather; 18K red-gold folding clasp.
Note: limited edition of 50 pieces per year.
Suggested price: $217,000

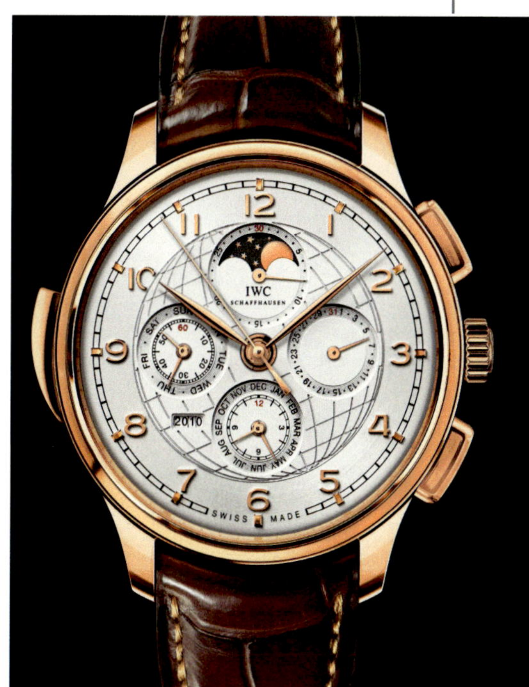

PORTUGUESE TOURBILLON MYSTERE RETROGRADE REF. IW504402

Movement: 51900 caliber with Pellaton automatic-winding system; 7-day power reserve; 81 parts; 44 jewels; 19,800 vph; Breguet spring; 18K yellow-gold medallion rotor.
Functions: hours, minutes; retrograde date; flying one-minute tourbillon.
Case: 18K red gold; Ø 44.2mm, thickness: 15.5mm; domed sapphire crystal with antireflective coating on both sides; exhibition sapphire crystal caseback; water resistant to 3atm.
Dial: silver-plated.
Strap: dark brown alligator leather; 18K red-gold folding clasp.
Suggested price: $102,000
Note: limited edition of 250 in platinum and 500 in 18K red gold.
Also available: platinum case with black crocodile strap.

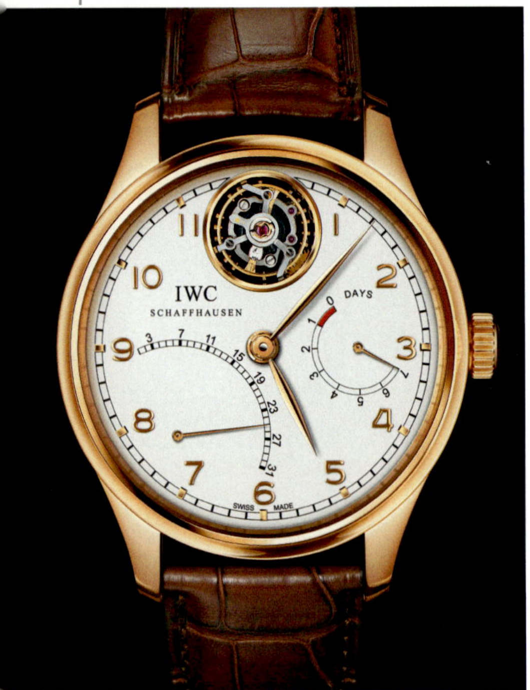

PORTUGUESE TOURBILLON HAND-WOUND REF. IW544705

Movement: manual-winding 98900 caliber; pocket watch; 54-hour power reserve; 21 jewels; 28,800 vph; three-quarter bridge.
Functions: hours, minutes; small seconds at 6; flying minute tourbillon at 9.
Case: 18K red gold; Ø 43.1mm, thickness: 11mm; domed antireflective sapphire crystal coating on both sides; exhibition sapphire caseback; water resistant to 3atm.
Dial: black.
Strap: black alligator leather; 18K red-gold folding clasp.
Suggested price: $53,500
Note: limited edition of 500 pieces in 18K red gold.

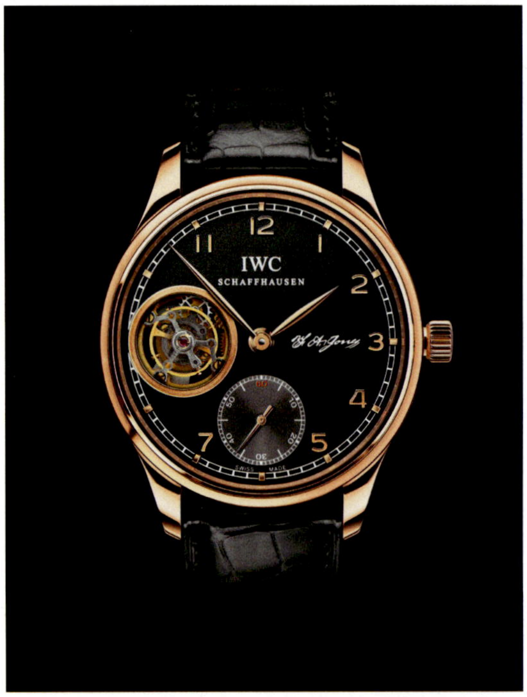

PORTUGUESE MINUTE REPEATER REF. IW544905

Movement: manual-winding 98950 caliber; Ø 44mm; 46-hour power reserve; 52 jewels; 18,800 vph; Glucydur® beryllium alloy balance with high-precision adjustment cam on balance arms; three-quarter bridge; Breguet spring.
Functions: hours, minutes; small hacking seconds; minute repeater: hours, quarter-hours and minutes.
Case: 18K red gold; Ø 44mm, thickness: 14mm; antireflective sapphire crystal coating on both sides; exhibition sapphire caseback.
Dial: silver-plated.
Strap: brown alligator leather; 18K red-gold folding clasp.
Suggested price: $86,900
Note: limited edition of 500 pieces each in platinum and 18K red gold.
Also available: platinum case on black crocodile strap.

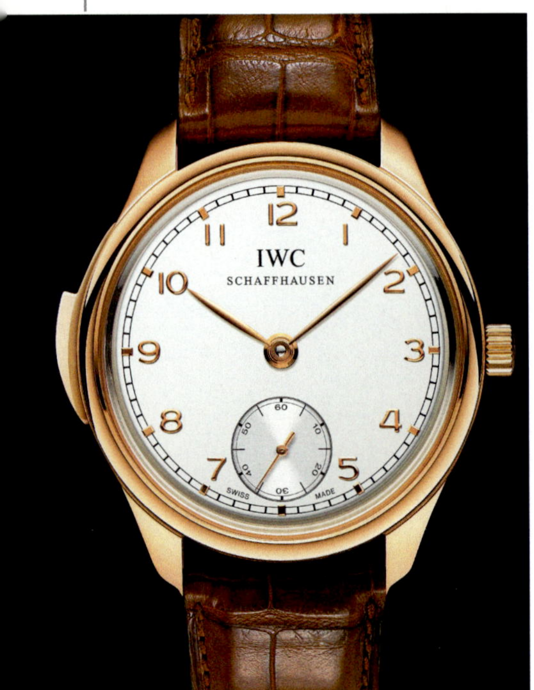

PORTUGUESE PERPETUAL CALENDAR REF. IW502121

Movement: IWC 51614 caliber with Pellaton automatic-winding system; 7-day power reserve, 62 jewels; 21,600 vph; Breguet spring; 18K yellow-gold medallion rotor.
Functions: hours, minutes; small hacking seconds; perpetual calendar: date, day, month, four-digit year display; perpetual moonphase.
Case: 18K white gold; Ø 44.2mm, thickness: 15.5mm; polished and brushed finish; antireflective sapphire crystal coating on both sides; exhibition sapphire caseback; water resistant to 3atm.
Dial: midnight blue; subdial decorated with circular beads; applied gilded Arabic numerals.
Strap: black alligator leather; 18K white-gold fold-over clasp.
Suggested price: $32,500-$39,300
Also available: red gold with black dial on brown crocodile strap.

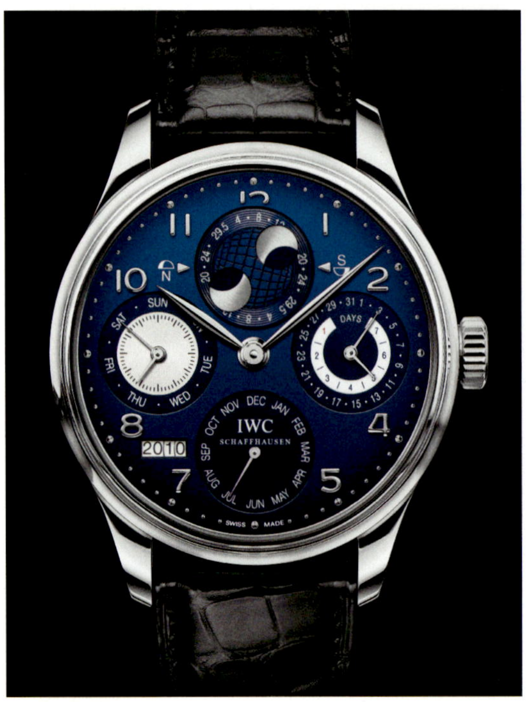

PORTUGUESE PERPETUAL CALENDAR — REF. IW502302

Movement: IWC 51613 caliber with Pellaton automatic-winding system; 7-day power reserve; 62 jewels; 21,600 vph; Breguet spring; 18K yellow-gold medallion rotor.
Functions: hours, minutes; small hacking seconds; perpetual calendar: date, day, month, four-digit year display; perpetual moonphase.
Case: 18K red gold; Ø 44.2mm, thickness: 15.5mm; polished and brushed finish; antireflective sapphire crystal coating on both sides; exhibition sapphire caseback; water resistant to 3atm.
Dial: silver-plated; subdial decorated with circular beads; applied gilded Arabic numerals.
Strap: dark brown alligator leather; 18K red-gold fold-over clasp.
Suggested price: $30,500-$35,000
Also available: 18K white-gold case with slate-colored dial on dark brown crocodile strap.

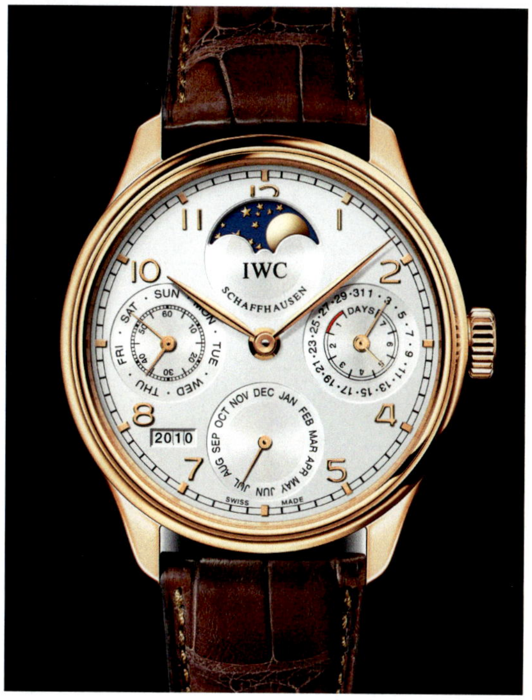

PORTUGUESE YACHT CLUB CHRONOGRAPH — REF. IW390206

Movement: automatic-winding IWC 89360 caliber; 68-hour power reserve; 40 jewels; 28,800 vph.
Functions: hours, minutes; small hacking seconds; date; chronograph: hours, minutes, and seconds; hour and minute counters combined in a single totalizer at 12; flyback.
Case: stainless steel; Ø 45.4mm, thickness: 14.5mm; screw-down crown; domed antireflective sapphire crystal coating on both sides; exhibition sapphire caseback; water resistant to 6atm.
Dial: silver-plated.
Strap: black rubber; stainless steel fold-over clasp.
Suggested price: $12,600-$23,100
Also available: red gold on black rubber strap; stainless steel with black dial on black rubber strap.

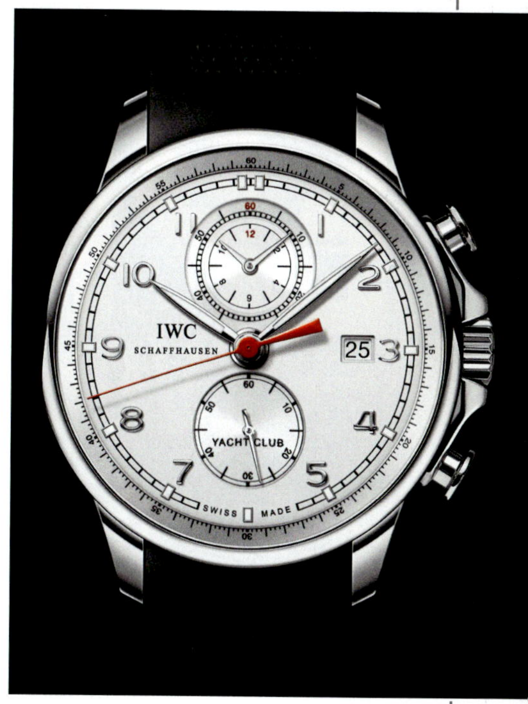

PORTUGUESE CHRONOGRAPH — REF. IW371480

Movement: automatic-winding 79350 caliber with chronograph; 44-hour power reserve; 31 jewels; 28,800 vph.
Functions: hours, minutes; small hacking seconds; stopwatch: minutes and seconds.
Case: 18K red gold; Ø 40.9mm, thickness: 12.3mm; screw-down crown; domed antireflective sapphire crystal coating on both sides; water resistant to 3atm.
Dial: silver-plated.
Strap: dark brown alligator leather; 18K red-gold pin buckle.
Suggested price: $14,300
Also available: stainless steel with black and white dials; red gold with black dial; white gold with slate dial.

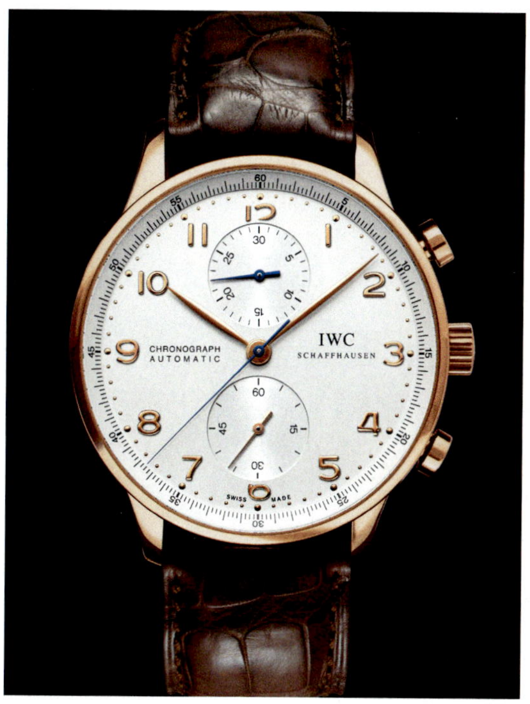

DA VINCI CHRONOGRAPH CERAMIC — REF. IW376601

Movement: automatic-winding 89360 caliber with chronograph; 68-hour power reserve; 40 jewels; 28,800 vph.
Functions: hours, minutes; small hacking seconds; date; stopwatch: hours, minutes and seconds; hour and minute counters combined in a single totalizer at 12; flyback.
Case: grade 5 titanium; Ø 44x52.8mm, thickness: 15.1mm; screw-down crown; domed antireflective sapphire crystal coating on both sides; exhibition sapphire caseback; water resistant to 3atm.
Dial: black, tonneau shaped.
Strap: black calfskin.
Suggested price: $16,600

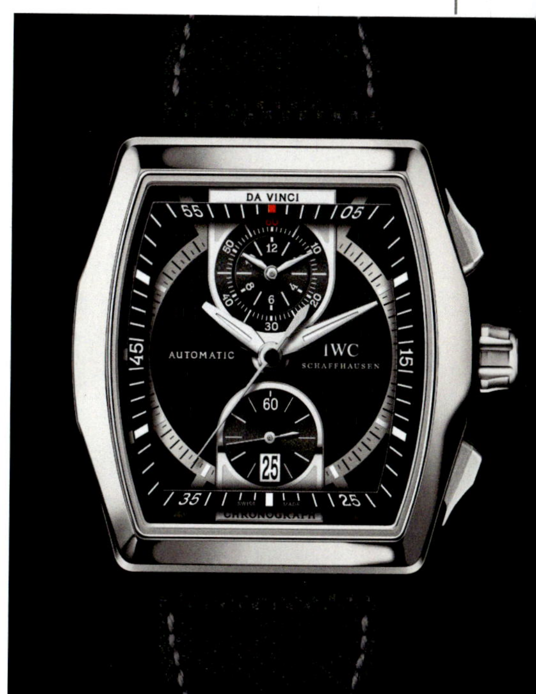

JACOB & CO

EPIC EVOLUTION

Since Jacob & Co introduced the Epic Automatic Chronograph at Basel in 2008, the collection has evolved technically and blossomed aesthetically into one of the renowned luxury brand's most successful and recognizable designs.

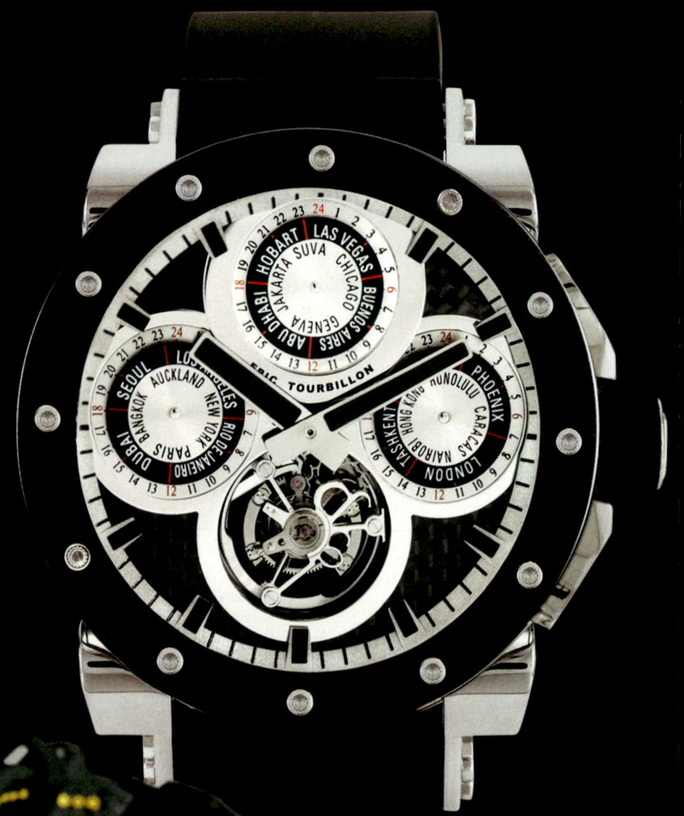

To account for different tastes, the company offers the Epic Automatic Chronograph in either a rectangular case (Epic I) that measures 51x47mm, or a round case (Epic II) that is 47mm in diameter. It also recently added more compact versions of these watches in a series it calls Epic V.2. Regardless of their case differences, all of these watches share the same bold, graphic design and superb chronograph function.

The Epic Tourbillon represents a bold new direction for the Epic line, combining a tourbillon movement with the ability to display multiple time zones. In fact, the mechanism powering the watch is the same manual-winding movement used for the company's popular Rainbow Tourbillon.

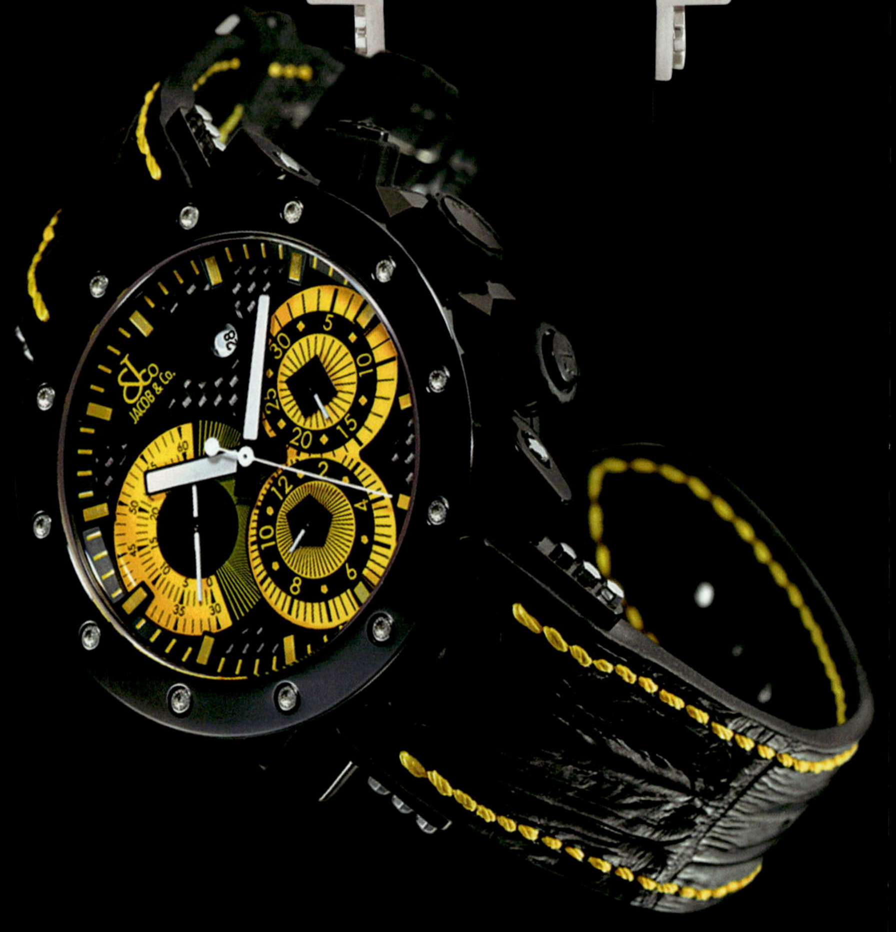

TOP

The stainless steel 47mm Epic Tourbillon frames its multi-layered dial with a black ceramic bezel.

BOTTOM

The Epic Automatic Chronograph takes full advantage of Jacob & Co's signature bold geometric forms and striking color accents.

Much like the larger-than-life personalities such as Tom Cruise and Madonna frequently spotted wearing Jacob & Co timepieces, the firm's finely crafted creations are impossible to miss.

The complexity of the caliber is evident from the watch's carbon fiber dial, which boasts three subsidiary displays for the multiple time zone function. Each indicates the time in eight different cities for a total of 24 time zones. That figure does not include the centrally fixed hour and minute hands, which are set by the wearer to indicate their reference time.

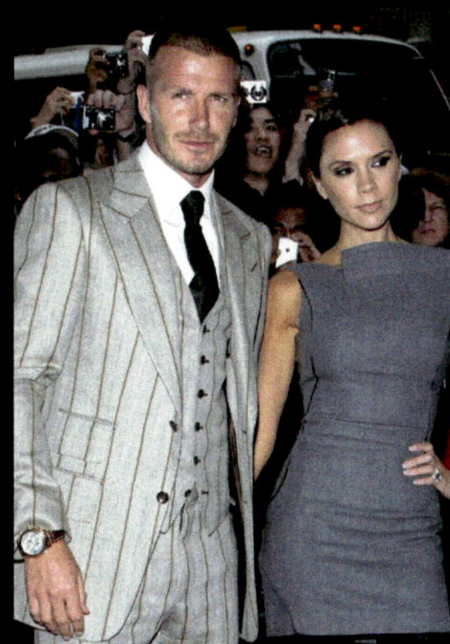

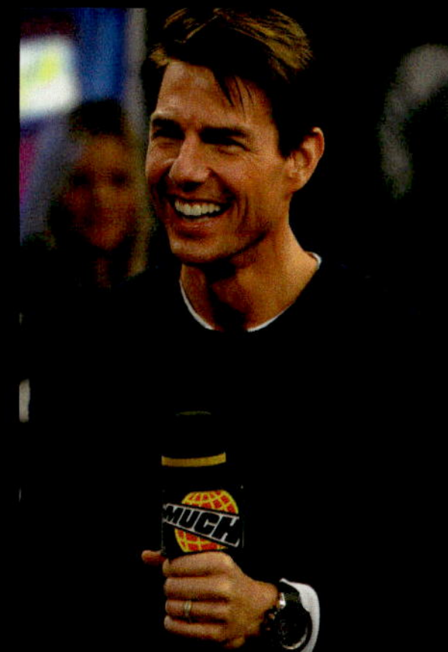

Below the time zone displays, an opening on the dial reveals the rapid oscillations (21,600 vph) of the escapement, which regulates the release of energy from the movement's mainspring. When fully wound, it provides five days of reserve power.

Jacob & Co recently unveiled its Crystal collection, an extensive range of eclectic designs for women that draws on the firm's more than 25 years of experience in the realms of both watchmaking and jewelry design.

Despite the aesthetic variations, there are several common denominators that unite all the Crystal watches, which are powered by a quartz movement and presented in a 44mm case made from either rose gold or stainless steel. Another shared trait is the liberal use of diamonds to decorate everything from bezels to dials to crowns.

A number of the visual motifs found in the Crystal collection have roots in the brand's celebrated Five Time Zone collection, including skulls rendered in colored diamond pavé, as well as a world map with enamel and diamond accents emblematic of the World Is Yours design.

Other distinctive models from the Crystal collection feature mother-of-pearl dials that provide an irresistibly iridescent backdrop for everything from an arrangement of overlapping hearts to a swirling pinwheel.

Yet another design harnesses the dark and mysterious gleam of black aventurine to create a dramatic setting for a quartet of diamond-set Roman numerals positioned like compass points around the dial. Nearly 500 white diamonds (more than 6 carats) elegantly enrobe the watch's stainless steel case.

Indeed, the playful *joie de vivre* expressed by the Crystal collection runs like a thread through all the timepieces created by Jacob & Co.

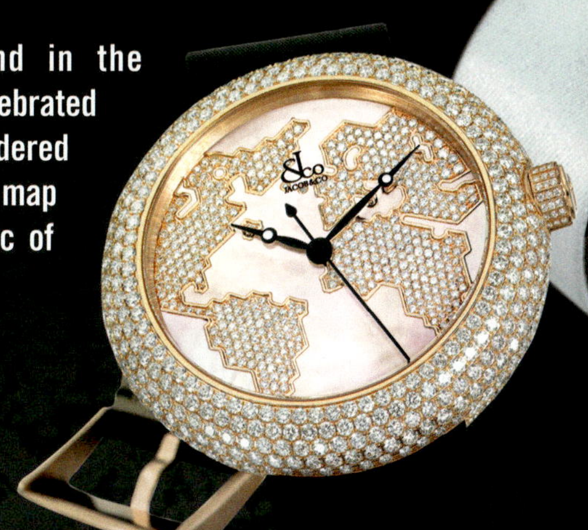

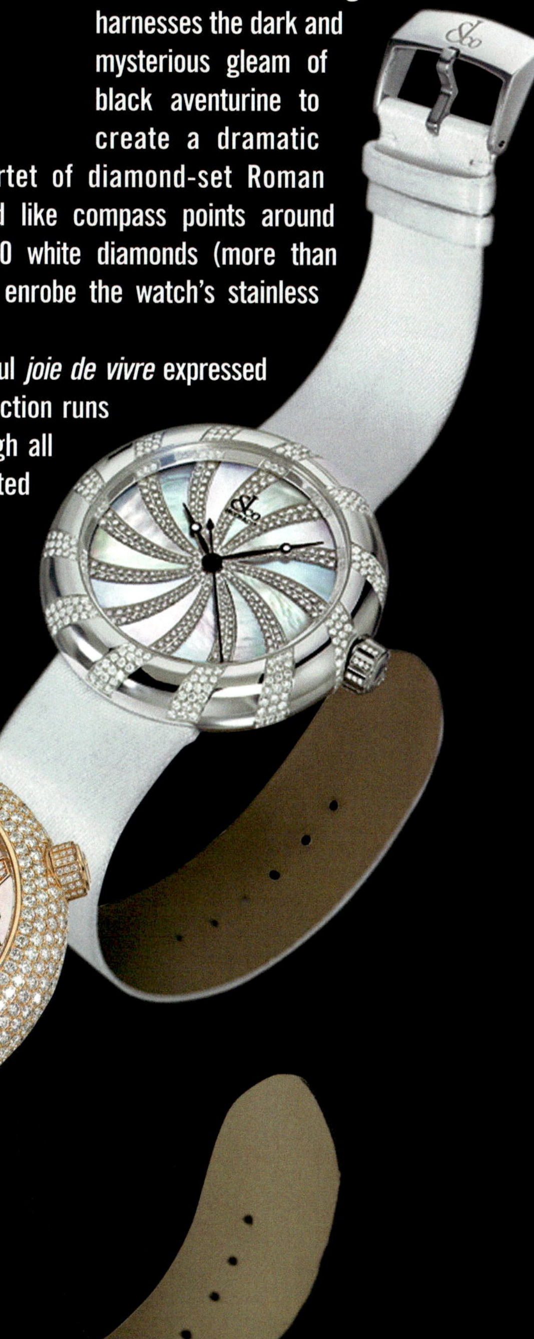

TOP

LEFT David Beckham accompanied by his rose-gold H24 and his wife Victoria.

RIGHT Tom Cruise sporting his stainless steel Epic II Automatic Chronograph.

RIGHT

One Crystal design features a diamond-set world map on a mother-of-pearl dial.

FAR RIGHT

A swirling diamond pinwheel design epitomizes the playfulness of Jacob & Co's Crystal collection.

EPIC TOURBILLON REF. ET3

Movement: manual-winding tourbillon; 120-hour power reserve; 27 jewels; 21,600 vph.
Functions: hours, minutes; tourbillon; 12- and 24-hour time zones.
Case: black PVD and stainless steel; Ø 47mm; ceramic bezel.
Dial: six-layer multi-tiered dial; signature Jacob & Co geometric subdials and hands.
Strap: rubber.
Suggested price: $200,000
Also available: 18K rose gold.

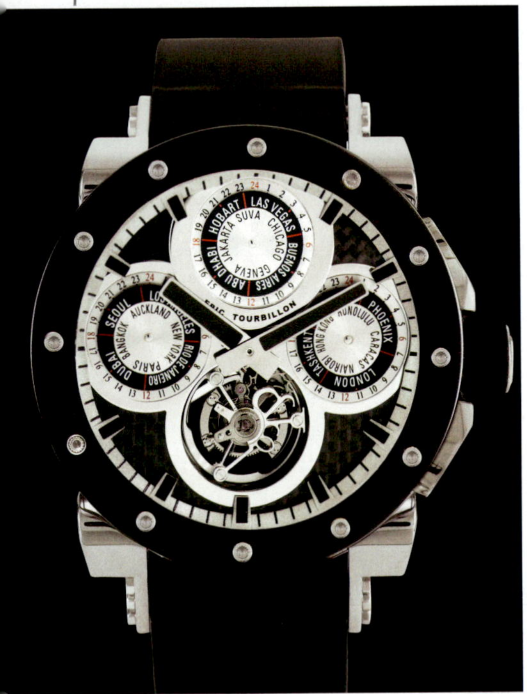

EPIC TOURBILLON REF. ET2

Movement: manual-winding tourbillon; 120-hour power reserve; 27 jewels; 21,600 vph.
Functions: hours, minutes; tourbillon; 12- and 24-hour time zones.
Case: black PVD; Ø 47mm; ceramic bezel.
Dial: six-layer multi-tiered dial; signature Jacob & Co geometric subdials and hands.
Strap: rubber.
Suggested price: $200,000
Also available: 18K rose gold; stainless steel.

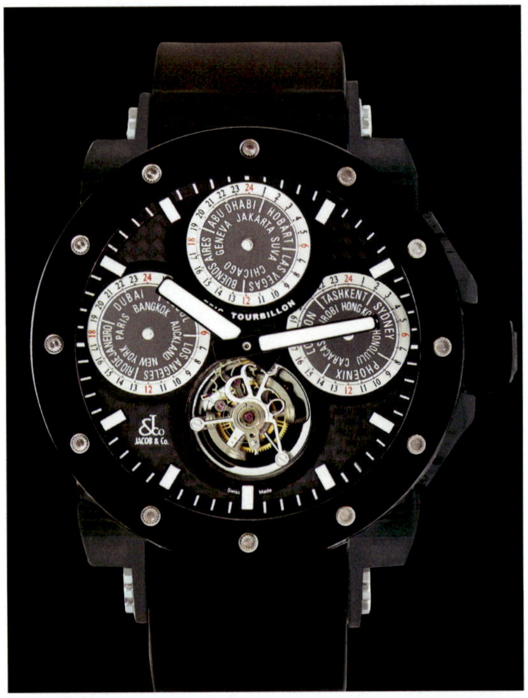

EPIC II REF. E3RGR

Movement: automatic-winding Jacob & Co 2121 chronograph; 48-hour power reserve; 27 jewels; 28,800 vph; Incabloc shock-absorption system.
Functions: hours, minutes, seconds; chronograph: 30-minute counter, 12-hour counter; date; early seconds.
Case: 18K rose gold; Ø 47mm; rubber bezel.
Dial: six-layer multi-tiered dial; signature Jacob & Co geometric subdials and hands.
Strap: rubber.
Suggested price: $27,000
Also available: black PVD; stainless steel.

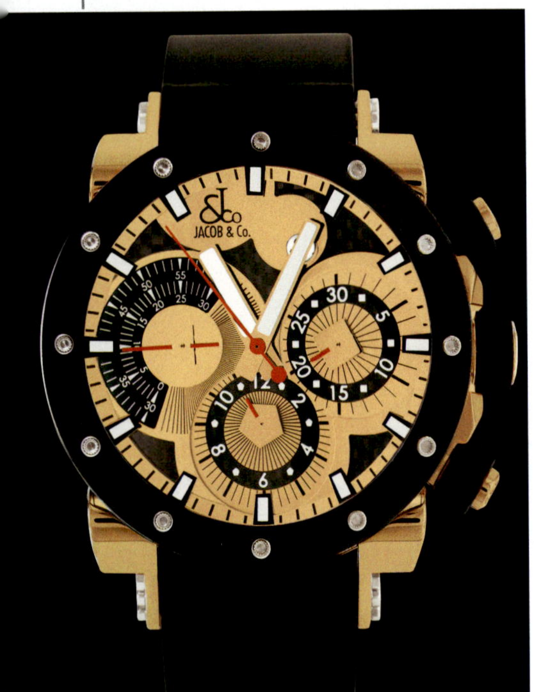

EPIC II REF. E15

Movement: automatic-winding Jacob & Co 2121 chronograph; 48-hour power reserve; 27 jewels; 28,800 vph; Incabloc shock-absorption system.
Functions: hours, minutes, seconds; chronograph: 30-minute counter, 12-hour counter; date; early seconds.
Case: black PVD; Ø 47mm; ceramic bezel.
Dial: six-layer multi-tiered dial; signature Jacob & Co red geometric subdials and markers.
Strap: alligator with red stitching.
Suggested price: $16,800
Also available: yellow geometric subdials and markers.

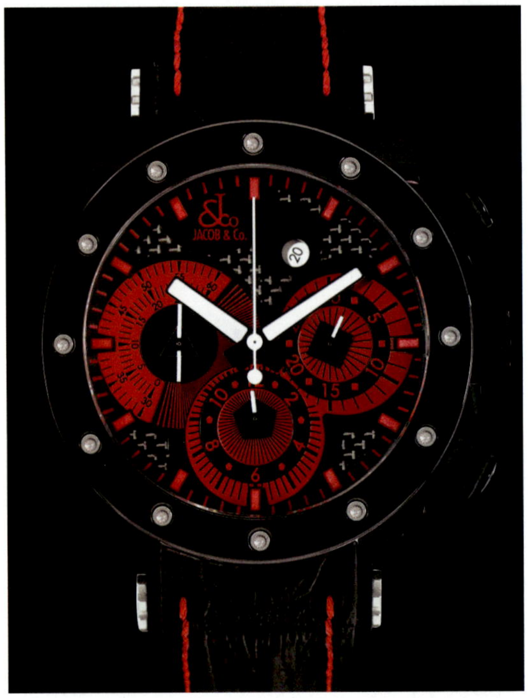

EPIC II — REF. E14

Movement: automatic-winding Jacob & Co 2121 chronograph; 48-hour power reserve; 27 jewels; 28,800 vph; Incabloc shock-absorption system.
Functions: hours, minutes, seconds; chronograph: 30-minute counter, 12-hour counter; date; early seconds.
Case: black PVD; Ø 47mm; ceramic bezel.
Dial: six-layer multi-tiered dial; signature Jacob & Co yellow geometric subdials and markers.
Strap: alligator with yellow stitching.
Suggested price: $16,800
Also available: red geometric subdials and markers.

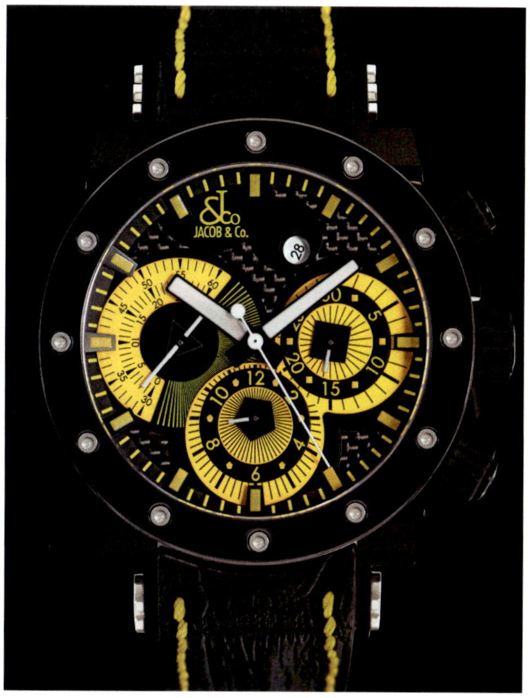

EPIC I V.2 — REF. Q2B

Movement: automatic-winding Jacob & Co 2121 chronograph; 48-hour power reserve; 27 jewels; 28,000 vph; Incabloc shock-absorption system.
Functions: hours, minutes, seconds; chronograph: 30-minute counter, 12-hour counter; date; early seconds.
Case: black PVD; 47.5x41mm, thickness: 17mm.
Dial: six-layer multi-tiered dial; signature Jacob & Co geometric subdials and hands.
Strap: rubber.
Suggested price: $12,000
Also available: 18K rose gold and stainless steel versions.

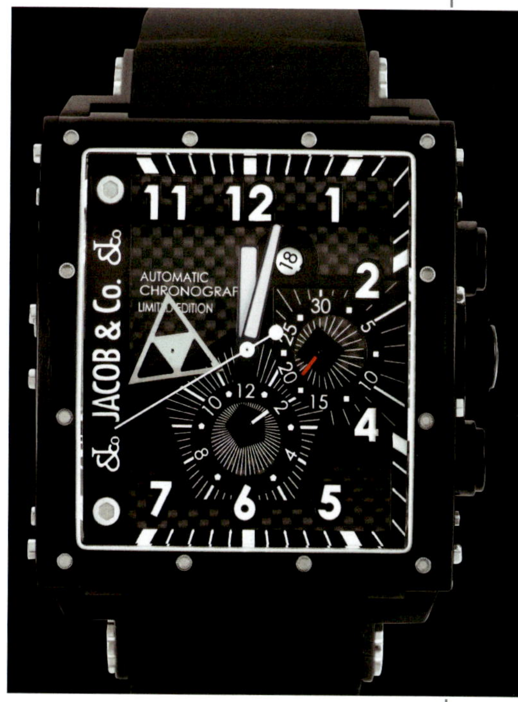

EPIC I V.2 — REF. Q8

Movement: automatic-winding Jacob & Co 2121 chronograph; 27 jewels; 28,000 vph; Incabloc shock-absorption system.
Functions: hours, minutes, seconds; chronograph: 30-minute counter, 12-hour counter; date; early seconds.
Case: 18K rose gold; 47.5x41mm, thickness: 17mm.
Dial: six-layer multi-tiered dial; signature Jacob & Co geometric subdials and hands.
Strap: rubber.
Suggested price: $25,000
Also available: black PVD; stainless steel.

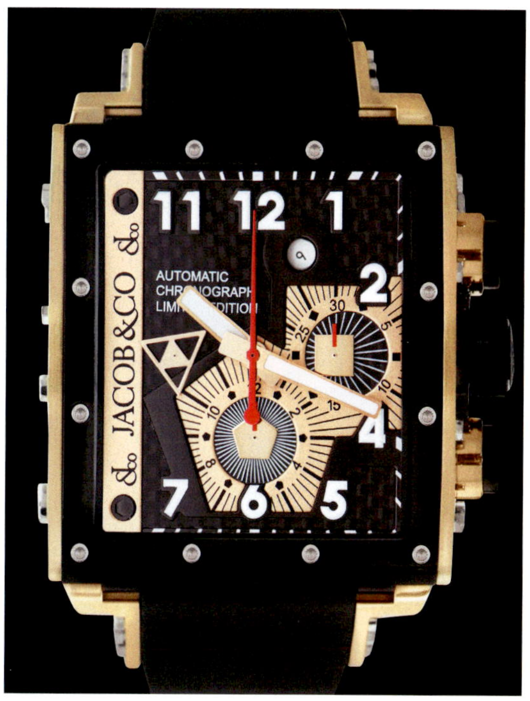

QUENTTIN — REF. QUENRG

Movement: vertical Jacob & Co movement; 31-day power reserve; winding escapement with Swiss anchor mounted in tourbillon cage; cage suspended without roller bearings and positioned vertically; winding via integrated key, external hand key or motorized in the box.
Functions: hours, minutes; power reserve made by vertical discs assembled coaxially.
Case: 18K rose gold; 56x47mm, thickness: 21.5mm; carbon fiber applications on case sides.
Strap: rubber.
Suggested price: $440,000
Also available: 18K white gold or magnesium with carbon fiber applications on case sides.

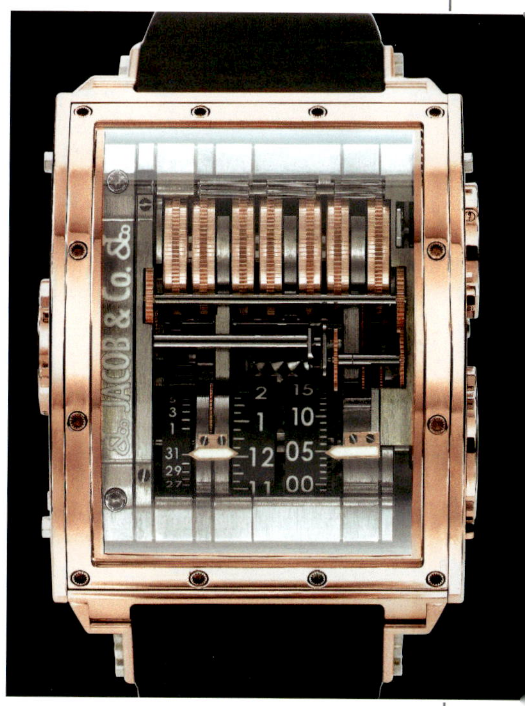

H24 — REF. H24CRFG

Movement: automatic-winding Jacob & Co Caliber ETA A07.11.
Functions: hours, minutes; sweep seconds; date; five time zones.
Case: 18K rose gold; Ø 47.5mm, thickness: 15.95mm.
Dial: black carbon fiber with ivory-colored discs and date indicator; rose-gold leaf shaped hands; Roman numerals on the main dial.
Strap: alligator.
Suggested price: $58,000
Also available: stainless steel.

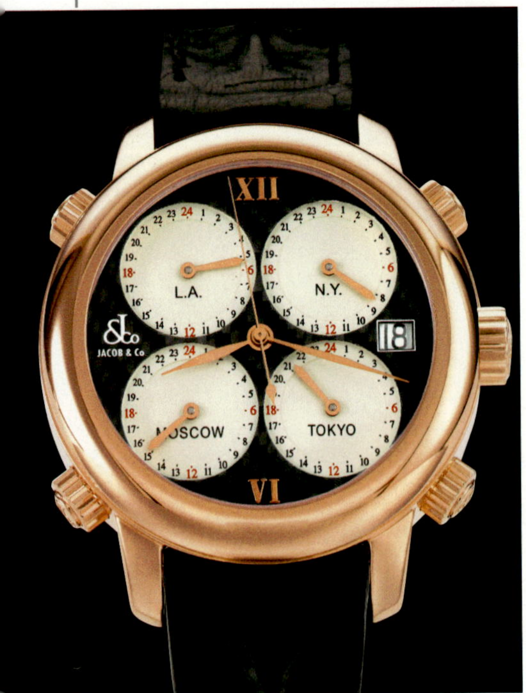

NAPOLEON QUADRA — REF. QUADRG

Movement: manual-winding Jacob & Co. Caliber 8082; four 60-second tourbillon escapements; 652 components; 78 jewels; sapphire bridges.
Functions: hours, minutes; tourbillon; four time zones.
Case: 18K rose gold; Ø 55.5mm, thickness: 10.05mm; exhibition caseback.
Dial: transparent sapphire disc revealing four skeletonized tourbillon escapements and four time zone apertures.
Strap: alligator.
Suggested price: $580,000
Also available: black PVD; 18K white gold.

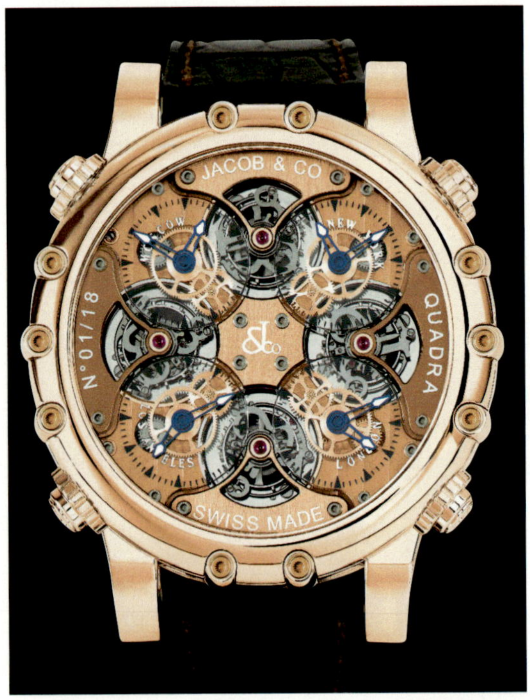

NAPOLEON — REF. NT3WG

Movement: manual-winding Jacob & Co Caliber 8005; 652 components; 19 jewels; sapphire bridges.
Functions: hours, minutes; tourbillon.
Case: 18K white gold; Ø 46mm, thickness: 6.5mm; sapphire crystal caseback.
Dial: transparent sapphire disc revealing skeletonized tourbillon cage featuring Jacob & Co logo.
Strap: alligator.
Suggested price: $195,000
Also available: 18K rose gold; with 0.4-carat diamond bridge.

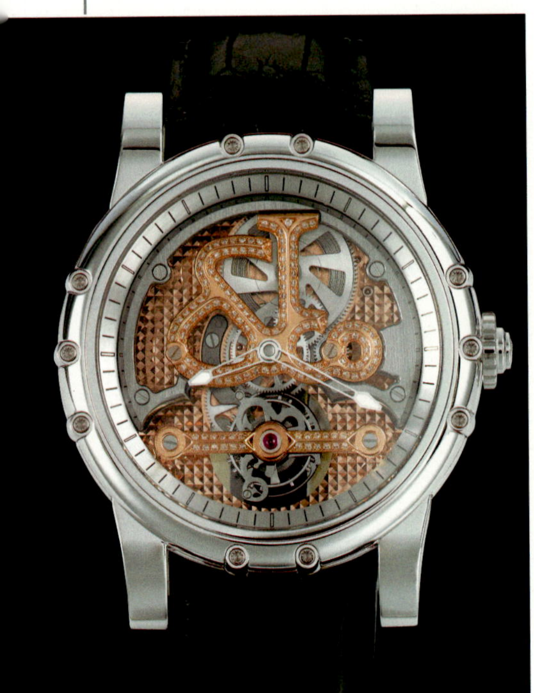

RUBY BAGUETTE RAINBOW TOURBILLON — REF. RUBY1

Movement: manual-winding Caliber 1 tourbillon; 120-hour power reserve; 21,600 vph; 24 jewels.
Functions: hours, minutes; 24 time zones; tourbillon; GMT.
Case: 18K white gold; set with 294 baguette rubies (33.54 total carats including the buckle); Ø 47.5mm, thickness: 14.95mm.
Dial: set with 204 baguette rubies (5.98 total carats).
Strap: alligator; buckle set with baguette-cut rubies.
Suggested price: $1,500,000

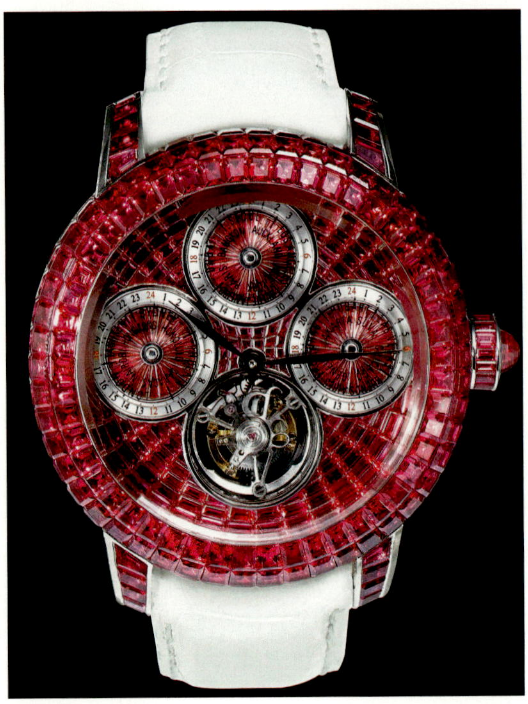

BLACK BAGUETTE RAINBOW TOURBILLON — REF. R15WG

Movement: manual-winding tourbillon; 120-hour power reserve; 24 jewels; 21,600 vph.
Functions: hours, minutes; 24 time zones; tourbillon; GMT.
Case: 18K white gold; set with black baguette diamonds (25.53 carats); Ø 47.5mm, thickness: 14.95mm.
Dial: set with black baguette diamonds (5.46 carats); white discs; steel leaf-shaped hands with gunmetal treatment.
Strap: alligator; buckle set with black baguette diamonds (2.22 carats).
Suggested price: $1,100,000

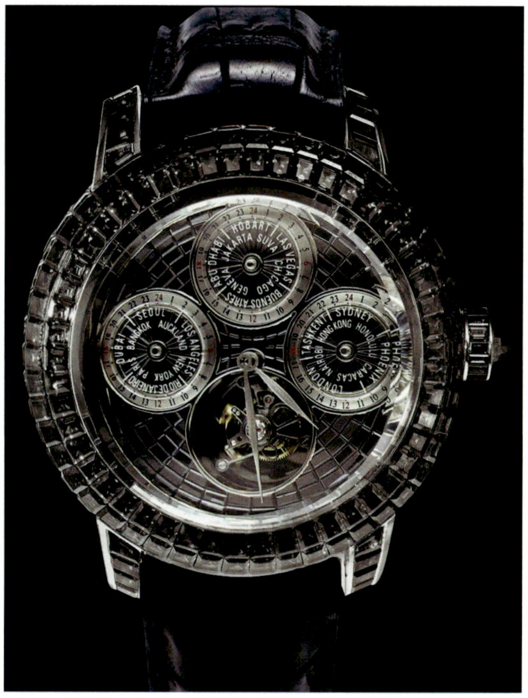

RAINBOW TOURBILLON — REF. R1WGDC

Movement: manual-winding tourbillon; 120-hour power reserve; 24 jewels; 21,600 vph.
Functions: hours, minutes; 12- and 24-hour time zones; tourbillon.
Case: 18K white gold; set with white diamonds (13.12 carats); Ø 47.5mm; exhibition caseback with multi-row Rainbow Tourbillon movement.
Dial: multi-colored timers painted and embossed with a special guilloché; steel leaf-shaped hands with gunmetal treatment.
Strap: alligator.
Suggested price: $300,000
Also available: 18K rose gold.

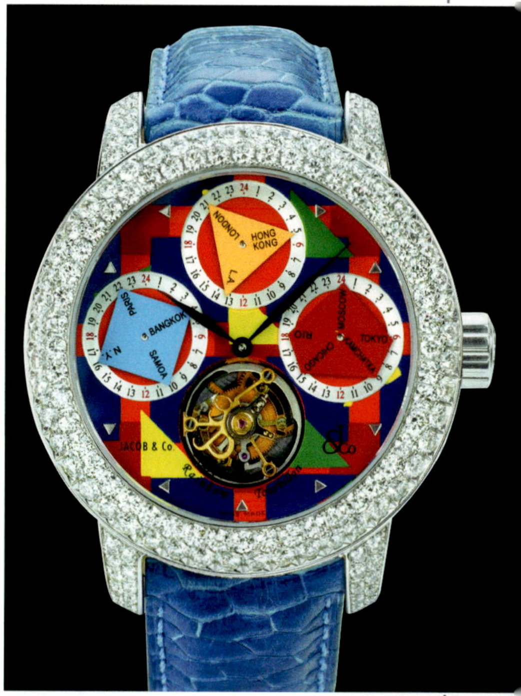

PANGEA TOURBILLON — REF. PANGWG

Movement: Jacob & Co Caliber 2901 tourbillon; 50-hour power reserve; 18 jewels; 28,800 vph.
Functions: hours, minutes; tourbillon.
Case: 18K white gold; Ø 46mm.
Dial: Côtes de Genève; tourbillon cage featuring Jacob & Co logo.
Strap: alligator.
Suggested price: $180,000

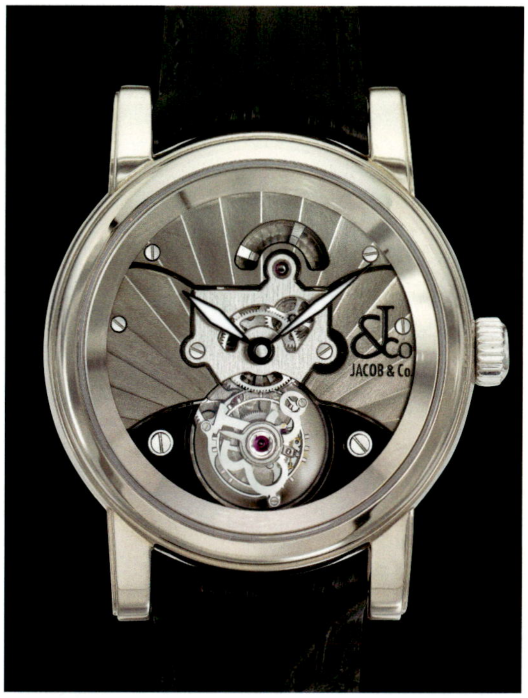

GMT — REF. GMT7RG

Movement: automatic-winding Jacob & Co ETA A07.111; 46-hour power reserve; 24 jewels; 28,800 vph.
Functions: hours, minutes; sweep seconds; date; five time zones.
Case: 18K rose gold; Ø 47.5mm; sapphire crystal caseback.
Dial: rose gold; painted and embossed with special guilloché; black accents; rose discs; steel leaf-shaped hands; Roman numerals on main dial.
Strap: alligator.
Suggested price: $59,000
Also available: yellow gold and stainless steel.

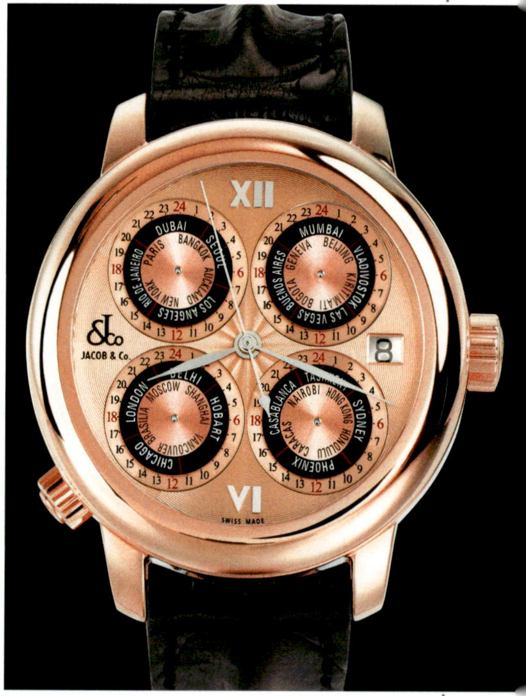

MANHATTAN — REF. MANWGBB

Movement: quartz ETA, E01-701; 5 jewels.
Functions: hours, minutes.
Case: 18K white gold; unique square case with no crown; set with 364 baguette-cut diamonds (17.5 total carats).
Dial: 3-dimensional; analog display; set with 403 round diamonds (1.81 carats); 20 baguette-cut diamonds in the center (0.9 carat).
Strap: alligator; buckle set with baguette diamonds (0.62 carat).
Suggested price: $660,000

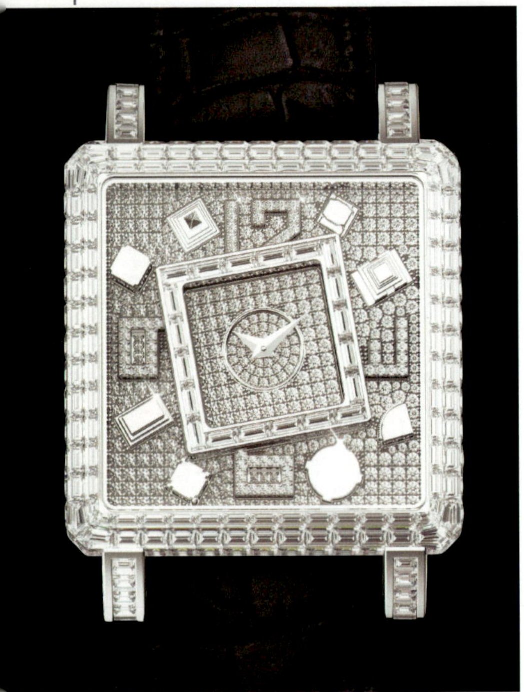

CRYSTAL — REF. CR47SRWRRG-F

Movement: quartz ETA 956.102; 7 jewels.
Functions: hours, minutes, seconds.
Case: 18K rose gold; set with pavé diamonds (6.75 carats); Ø 44mm.
Dial: mother-of-pearl; world map design set with pavé diamonds (1.19 carats).
Strap: alligator.
Suggested price: $45,000

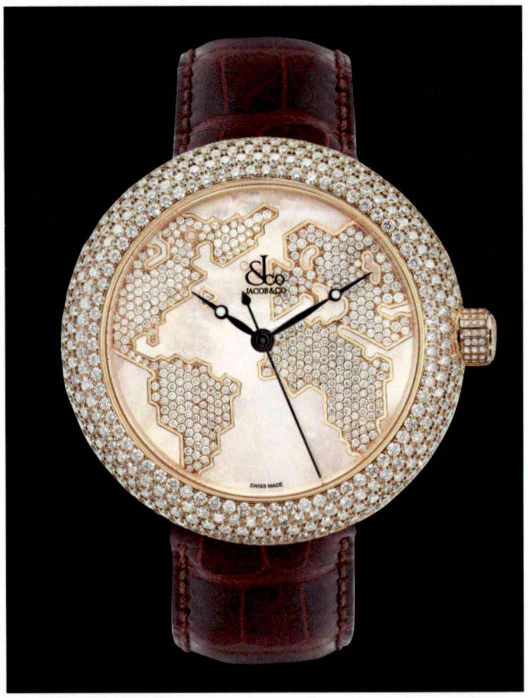

CRYSTAL — REF. CR47B-F

Movement: quartz ETA 956.102; 7 jewels.
Functions: hours, minutes, seconds.
Case: stainless steel; set with pavé diamonds (6.75 carats); Ø 44mm.
Dial: blue aventurine; world map design set with pavé diamonds (1.19 carats).
Strap: alligator.
Suggested price: $29,000

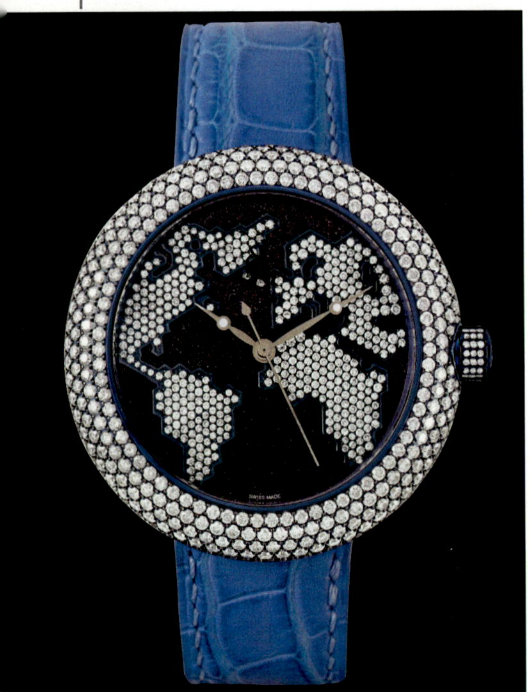

CRYSTAL — REF. CR5

Movement: quartz ETA 956.102; 7 jewels.
Functions: hours, minutes, seconds.
Case: stainless steel; set with pavé diamonds (1.67 carats); Ø 44mm.
Dial: mother-of-pearl; pinwheel design set with pavé diamonds (1.09 carats).
Strap: alligator.
Suggested price: $26,000

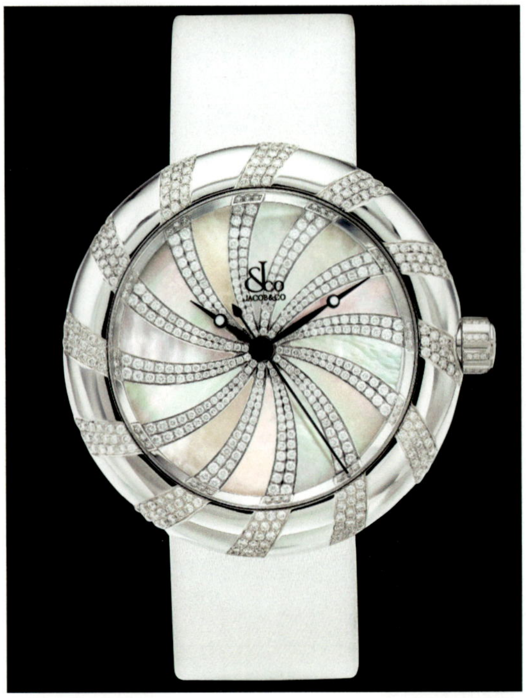

CRYSTAL — REF. CR9RG-F

Movement: quartz ETA 956.102; 7 jewels.
Functions: hours, minutes, seconds.
Case: 18K rose gold; set with pavé diamonds (7.3 carats); Ø 44mm.
Dial: set with pavé diamonds (2.9 carats).
Strap: alligator.
Suggested price: $45,000

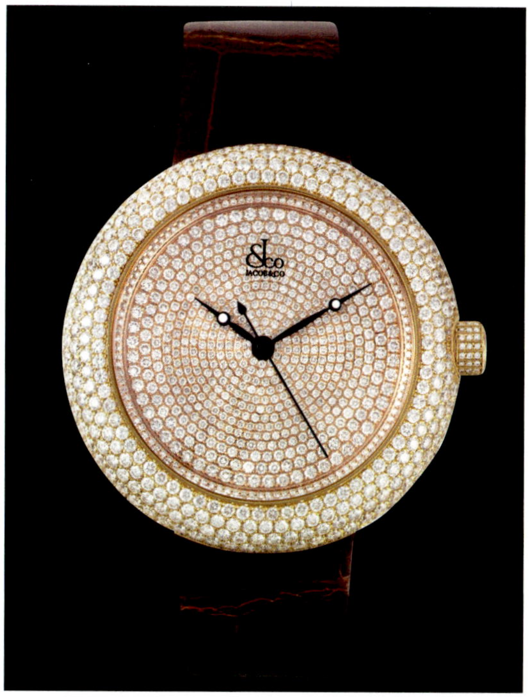

ROYAL — REF. ROYAL1RG

Movement: automatic ETA 2004-1; 20 jewels.
Functions: hours, minutes, seconds.
Case: 18K rose gold; set with 342 baguette diamonds (21.26 carats); Ø 42mm, thickness: 10.54mm.
Strap: alligator.
Suggested price: $380,000

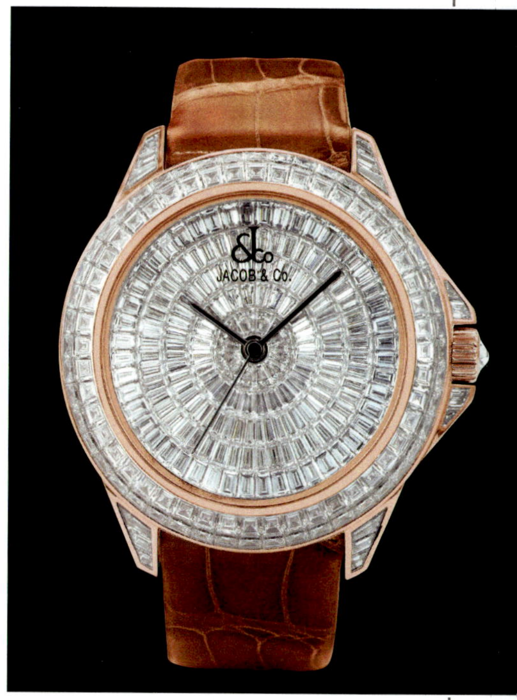

RUBY CRYSTAL TOURBILLON — REF. CRY20

Movement: Jacob & Co 7 Caliber; sapphire bridges; Ø 32.6mm, thickness: 5.2mm; set with baguette diamonds (1.6 carats); crafted, assembled, and decorated by hand to the highest of Jacob & Co quality standards; skeleton movement.
Functions: hours, minutes; tourbillon.
Case: 18K white gold; set with 264 baguette-cut rubies; Ø 47mm, thickness: 14mm.
Dial: transparent; skeleton tourbillon movement.
Strap: alligator; 18K white-gold clasp set with 30 baguette-cut rubies.
Suggested price: $1,800,000

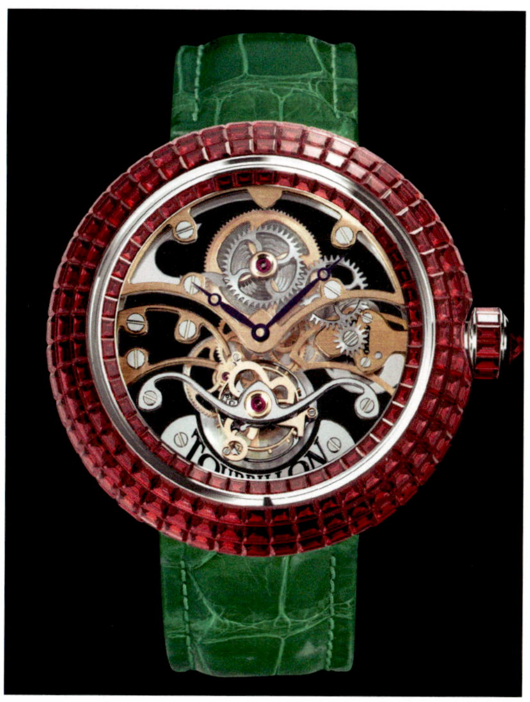

CRYSTAL TOURBILLON — REF. CRYSTAL TOUR

Movement: Jacob & Co 7 Caliber movement; skeleton; Ø 32.6mm, thickness: 5.2mm; set with baguette diamonds (1.6 carats); sapphire bridges; crafted, assembled, and decorated by hand to the highest Jacob & Co quality standards.
Functions: hours, minutes; tourbillon.
Case: 18K white gold; Ø 47mm (with crown guard), thickness: 14mm; baguette diamonds (17.48 carats); sapphire crystal caseback.
Dial: transparent; skeleton tourbillon movement.
Strap: alligator; buckle set with baguette diamonds (2.22 carats).
Suggested price: $900,000
Note: limited edition of 18 pieces.

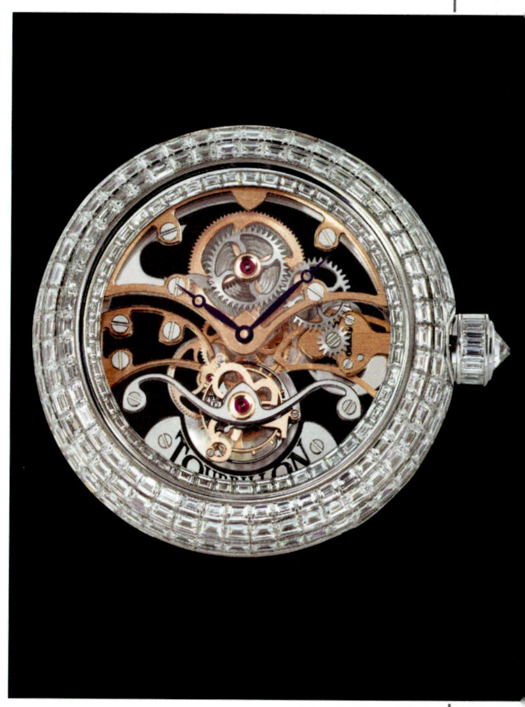

JAEGER-LECOULTRE

JUST LIKE HEAVEN

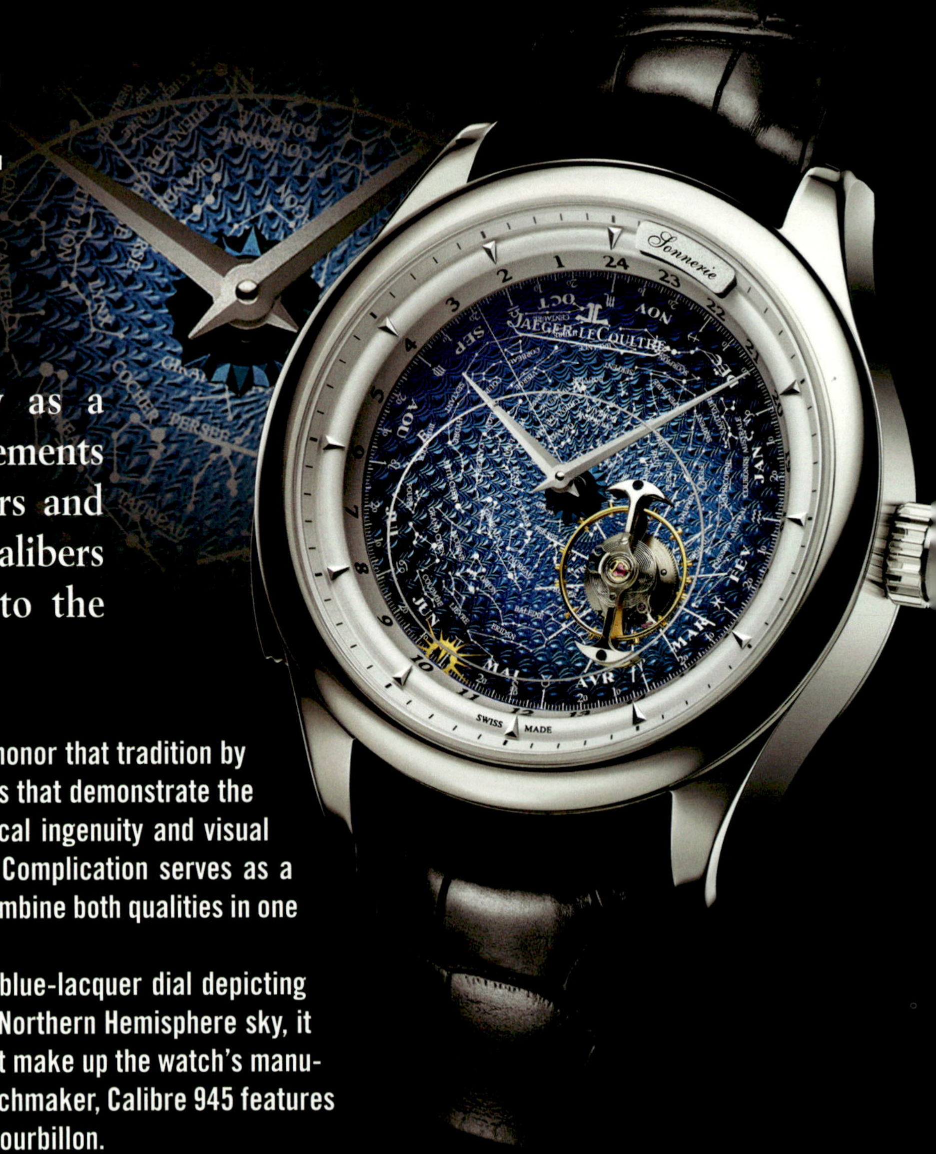

Jaeger-LeCoultre's rich history as a maker of innovative watch movements encompasses more than 175 years and includes a number of historic calibers that range from the ultra-thin to the über-complicated.

The manufacture's Le Sentier workshops honor that tradition by building on it with a new wave of timepieces that demonstrate the company's profound capacity for mechanical ingenuity and visual creativity. The Master Grande Tradition Grande Complication serves as a prime example of Jaeger-LeCoultre's ability to combine both qualities in one amazing timepiece.

The round case not only frames a gorgeous blue-lacquer dial depicting a chart of the stars as they appear overhead in Northern Hemisphere sky, it also accommodates the more than 500 parts that make up the watch's manually wound movement. Assembled by a single watchmaker, Calibre 945 features a Zodiac calendar, minute repeater and a flying tourbillon.

What makes this particular tourbillon mechanism unique is that it is the first flying tourbillon to be used as an hour hand to indicate the sidereal time. Unlike a solar day, which uses the sun as a reference and lasts an average of 24 hours, a sidereal day uses fixed stars as a reference and is nearly four minutes shorter.

In a tech-savvy twist, Jaeger-LeCoultre fashions the tourbillon's anchor and escape wheel from silicium. Lightweight and able to operate without lubrication, the material improves the mechanism's efficiency and precision.

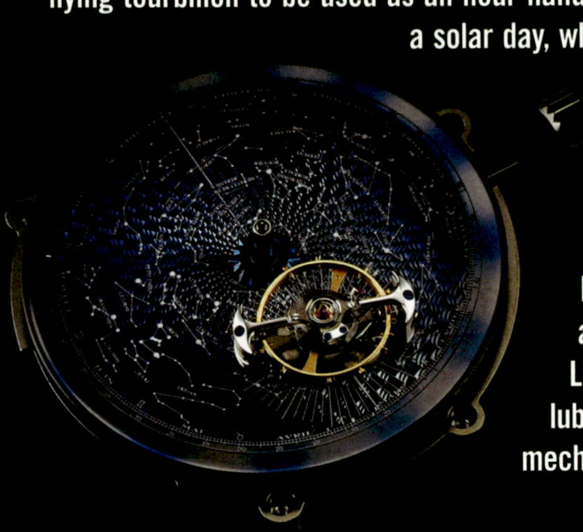

Offered in a limited edition of 75 pieces, the white-gold Master Grande Tradition Grande Complication combines a flying tourbillon, Zodiac calendar and minute repeater.

The flying tourbillon acts as an hour hand that indicates sidereal time—a unit of measurement used by astronomers to track the stars.

Jaeger-LeCoultre presents a trio of timepieces powered by technically advanced movements that reflect the firm's rich heritage of mechanical innovation, which dates back to 1833.

Advanced technology also enhances the performance of the Master Grande Tradition Grande Complication's minute repeater. It features the "trébuchet hammer," a proprietary design that strikes the gongs with a great deal more force than the hammers found in other repeaters, producing a more resonant tone.

A perennial challenge for makers of complicated movements is the loss of accuracy caused when energy from the mainspring is diverted from the escapement to power a secondary function.

To remedy this vexing limitation, Jaeger-LeCoultre devised a dual-wing movement that combines two independent mechanisms in one movement. Introduced in 2007, this novel design features two mainsprings—one dedicated to powering the escapement and the other devoted to various complications.

With its new Duomètre à Quantième Lunaire, Jaeger-LeCoultre proudly flaunts this arrangement through two wing-like apertures. Above, a small display on the right shows the hours and minutes. The seconds can be read two ways: from the scale along the edge of the dial, or from the small display at 6 o'clock, which features a jumping seconds that measures to one-sixth of a second.

The subsidiary dial on the left neatly incorporates several indications, including the date, the age of the moon and the phases of the moon in both the northern and southern hemispheres.

Jaeger-LeCoultre enriches the legacy of one of its most historic designs with the Reverso Squadra Chronograph GMT Palermo Open. The firm's signature swiveling case is rendered here for the first time with sections of vulcanized black rubber. To underscore the watch's technical look, it is paired with a masculine strap made from textile fused with a rubber core.

The case—available in stainless steel or rose gold—is equipped with a Jaeger-LeCoultre-manufactured automatic movement. The mechanism combines a column-wheel chronograph, date and a GMT. The latter is displayed on a 24-hour counter positioned at 6 o'clock on the black dial.

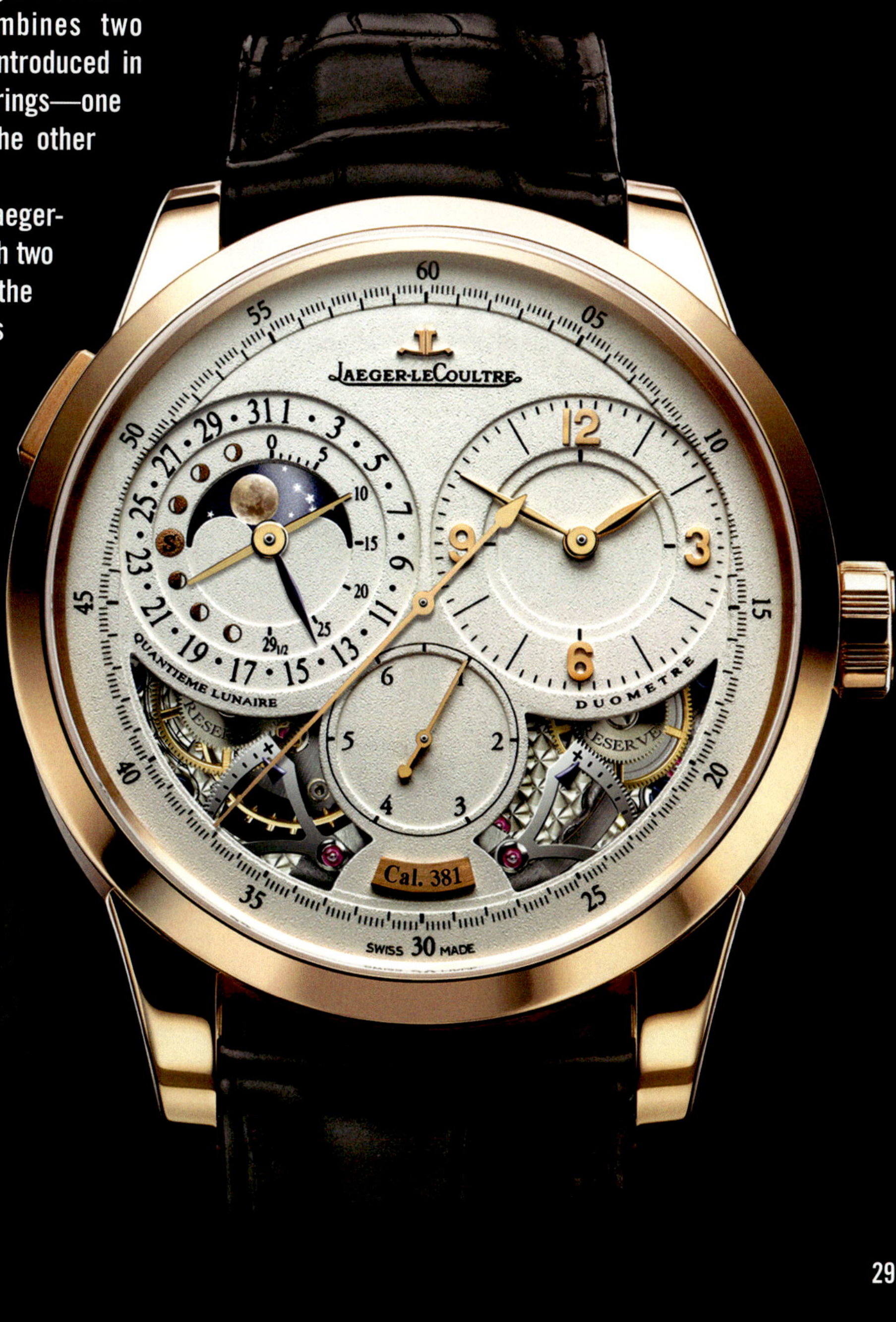

The Duomètre à Quantième Lunaire includes three subdials that display the time, foudroyante seconds, date, the age of the moon, and the moonphase in both the north and south hemispheres.

AMVOX 5 WORLD CHRONOGRAPH — REF. 193.L4.71

Movement: automatic-winding Jaeger-LeCoultre 752 caliber; 65-hour power reserve; 279 components; 41 jewels; 28,800 vph; two barrels.
Functions: hours, minutes; date; world time indication simultaneously indicating the time in all 24 time zones; chronograph: hour counter; 60-second counter, 30-minute counter; movement operating indicator.
Case: 18K pink-gold and ceramic; Ø 44mm; water resistant to 5atm.
Dial: black; baton hands.
Strap: black calfskin leather; double folding buckle.
Suggested price: $26,150
Note: limited to 200 pieces.

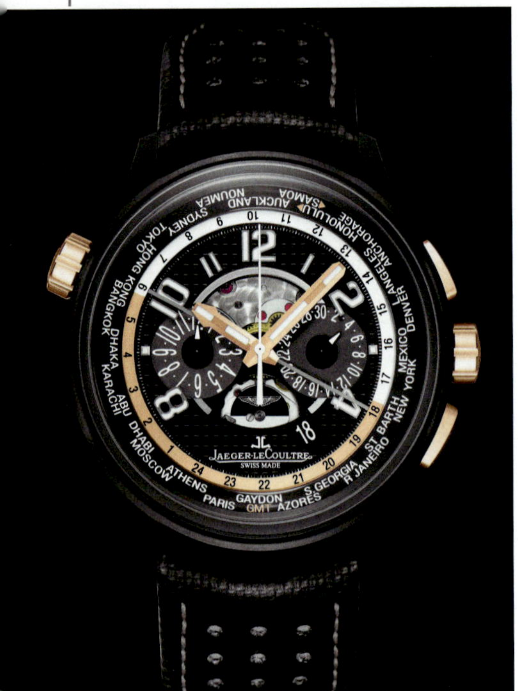

MASTER COMPRESSOR EXTREME WITH ALARM — REF. 177.84.70

Movement: automatic-winding Jaeger-LeCoultre 912 caliber; 45-hour power reserve; 315 components; 28,800 vph; two barrels.
Functions: hours, minutes, seconds; date; world time indication simultaneously indicating the time in all 24 time zones; alarm with double hour and minute display; alarm function on/off selector.
Case: stainless steel and titanium; Ø 46.3mm; water resistant to 10atm.
Dial: black; luminescent numerals and hour markers; trapèze hands.
Strap: black alligator leather with white stitching; double folding buckle.
Suggested price: $13,600
Also available: black rubber strap.

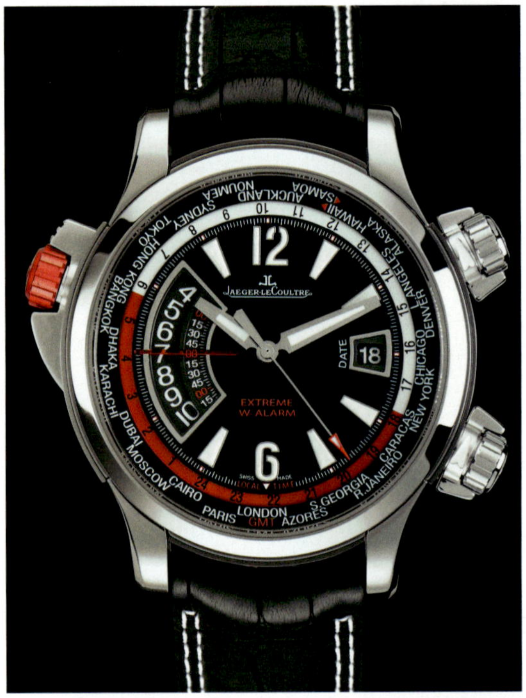

MASTER COMPRESSOR DIVING AUTOMATIC NAVY SEALS — REF. 201.87.70

Movement: automatic-winding Jaeger-LeCoultre 899 caliber; 43-hour power reserve; 219 components; 32 jewels; 28,800 vph; one barrel.
Functions: hours, minutes, seconds; date; diving bezel.
Case: stainless steel; Ø 42mm; water resistant to 30atm.
Dial: black galvanic; trapèze-shaped skeletonized hands.
Strap: black articulated rubber.
Suggested price: $10,000
Note: limited to 1500 pieces.
Also available: black leather strap.

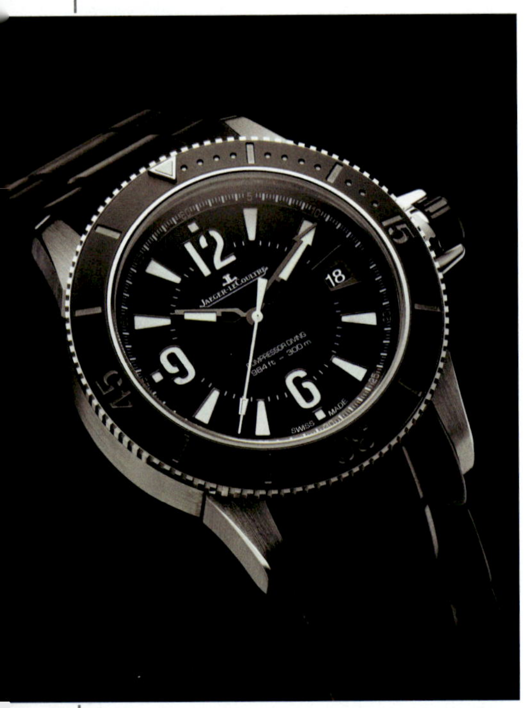

REVERSO SQUADRA WORLD CHRONO POLO FIELDS — REF. 702.J6.7P

Movement: automatic-winding Jaeger-LeCoultre 753 caliber; 65-hour power reserve; 366 components; 44 jewels; 28,800 vph; two barrels.
Functions: front: hours, minutes, seconds; large date; chronograph: hour counter, 30-minute counter; day/night indicator; back: world time GEO.
Case: ceramic and titanium; 52.9x36.5mm; water resistant to 5atm.
Dial: front: black guilloché center; transferred numerals; back: black; baton hands.
Strap: black articulated rubber.
Suggested price: $24,100

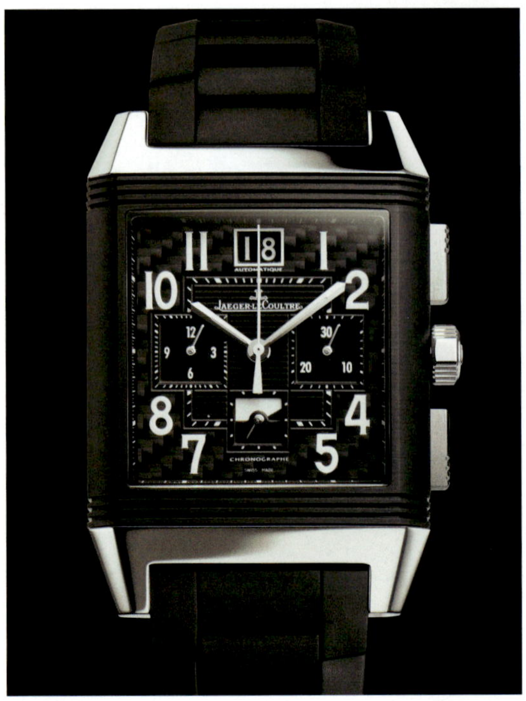

MASTER CHRONOGRAPH — REF. 153.84.20

Movement: automatic-winding Jaeger-LeCoultre 751 A/I caliber; 65-hour power reserve; 277 components; 28,800 vph; two barrels.
Functions: hours, minutes; small seconds; date; chronograph: hour-counter, central seconds, 30-minute counter.
Case: stainless steel; Ø 40mm; water resistant to 5atm.
Dial: silver sunray-brushed; Alpha hands.
Strap: black alligator leather; double folding buckle.
Suggested price: $9,850
Also available: 18K pink gold (ref. 153.24.20).

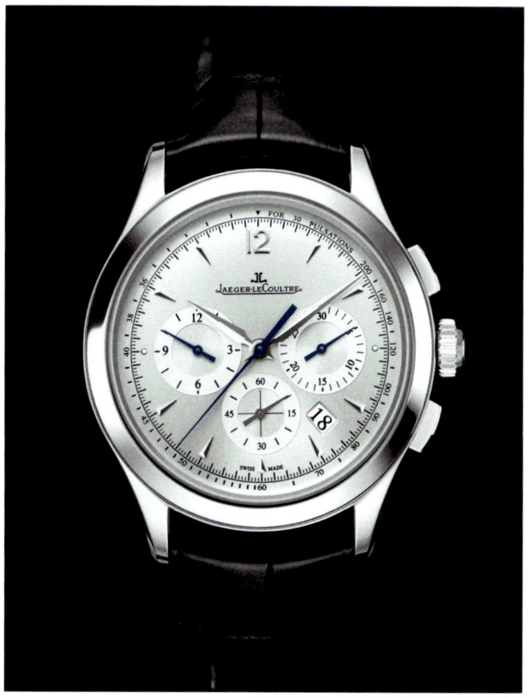

MASTER MEMOVOX — REF. 141.24.30

Movement: automatic-winding Jaeger-LeCoultre 956 caliber; 45-hour power reserve; 268 components; 23 jewels; 28,800 vph.
Functions: hours, minutes, seconds; date at 3; alarm.
Case: 18K pink gold; Ø 40mm, thickness: 14.2mm; solid caseback stamped with Master Control logo; water resistant to 5atm.
Dial: silvered; 18K pink-gold numerals and hour markers; 18K pink-gold Alpha hands.
Strap: black alligator leather; double folding buckle.
Suggested price: $20,350
Also available: stainless steel (ref. 141.84.30)

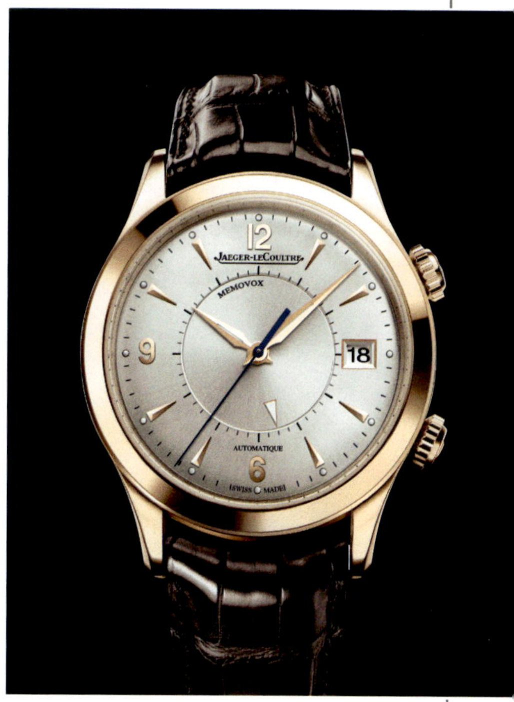

MASTER CALENDAR — REF. 151.84.2A

Movement: automatic-winding Jaeger-LeCoultre 924 caliber; 43-hour power reserve; 339 components; 41 jewels; 28,800 vph; one barrel.
Functions: hours, minutes, seconds; date; day; month; moonphase; power reserve indicator.
Case: stainless steel; Ø 40mm; sapphire crystal caseback; water resistant to 5atm.
Dial: silvered sunray-brushed; stainless steel Alpha hands.
Strap: brown alligator leather; double folding buckle.
Suggested price: $9,100
Also available: pink-gold case; stainless steel bracelet.

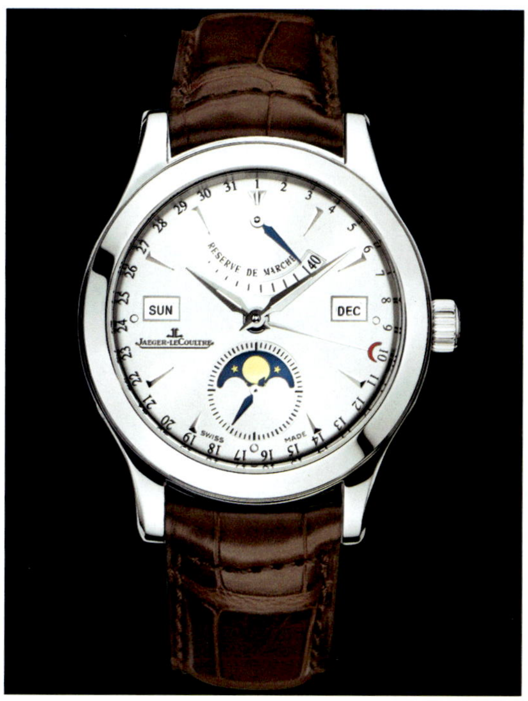

MASTER GRANDE ULTRA THIN — REF. 135.24.20

Movement: automatic-winding Jaeger-LeCoultre 896 caliber; 43-hour power reserve; 242 components; 34 jewels; 28,800 vph; one barrel.
Functions: hours, minutes; small seconds.
Case: 18K pink gold; Ø 40mm; sapphire crystal caseback; water resistant to 5atm.
Dial: beige; frosted minute scale; gilt numerals and hour markers; dauphine-style hands.
Strap: dark brown alligator leather.
Suggested price: $13,000
Also available: stainless steel case; stainless steel bracelet (ref. 135.84.70).

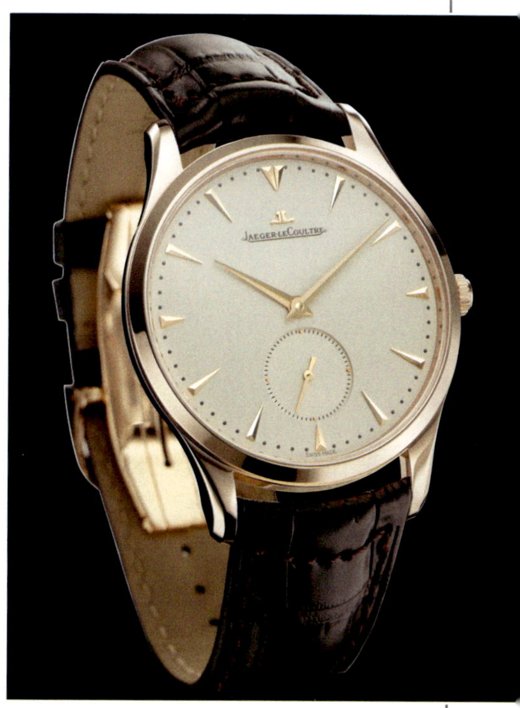

REVERSO DUETTO CLASSIQUE — REF. 256.24.02

Movement: manual-winding Jaeger-LeCoultre 865 caliber; 48-hour power reserve; 130 components; 21,600 vph.
Functions: hours, minutes (identical front and back).
Case: 18K pink gold; 38.5x23.05mm; set with 65 Top Wesselton WS F-G diamonds (0.72 carat); water resistant to 3atm.
Dial: silvered with radical guilloché; black transferred floral numerals.
Strap: dark brown alligator leather; double folding buckle.
Suggested price: $15,950

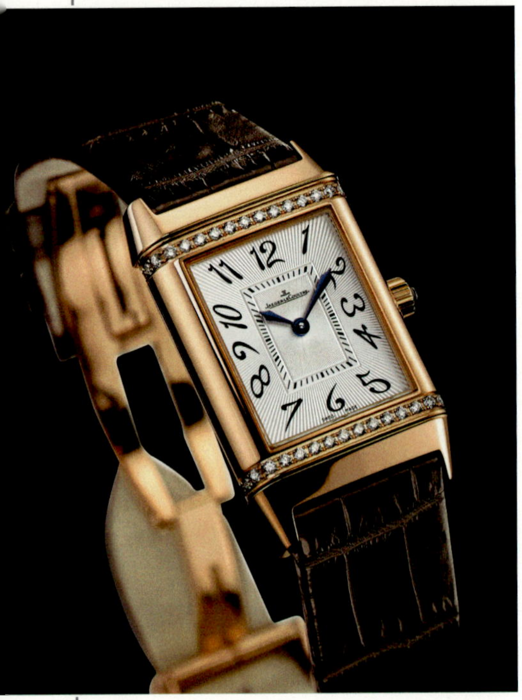

REVERSO SQUADRA LADY — REF. 703.84.93

Movement: quartz Jaeger-LeCoultre 657 caliber; 4 jewels.
Functions: hours, minutes.
Case: stainless steel; 42x28.8mm; set with 36 Top Wesselton WS F-G diamonds (0.55 carat); water resistant to 5atm.
Dial: mother-of-pearl marquetry effect; silvered floral numerals; stainless steel baton hands.
Strap: purple alligator leather.
Suggested price: $7,600

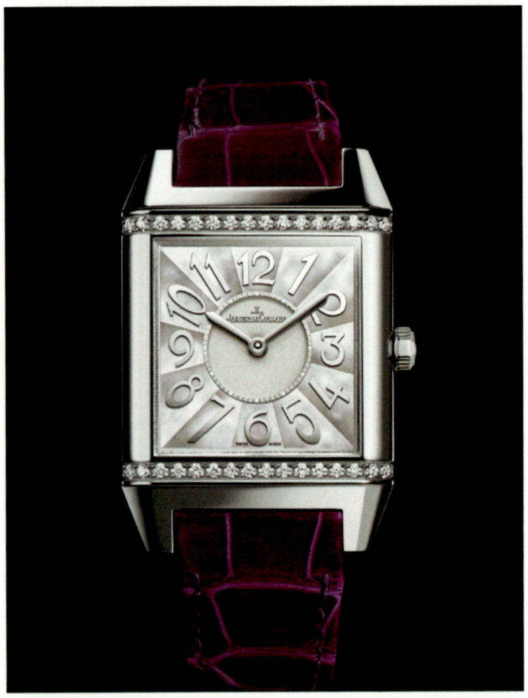

REVERSO GRANDE GMT — REF. 302.84.20

Movement: manual-winding Jaeger-LeCoultre 878 caliber; 8-day power reserve; 276 components; 35 jewels; 28,800 vph; two barrels.
Functions: front: hours, minutes, seconds; large date; day/night indicator; back: power reserve; second time zone; 24-hour display; GMT.
Case: stainless steel; 46.5x29.25mm; water resistant to 3atm.
Dial: front: silvered guilloché; black transfered numerals; baton hands; back: black brilliant dial; white transfered numerals; fan-shaped hands.
Strap: light brown alligator leather; double folding buckle.
Suggested price: $11,850

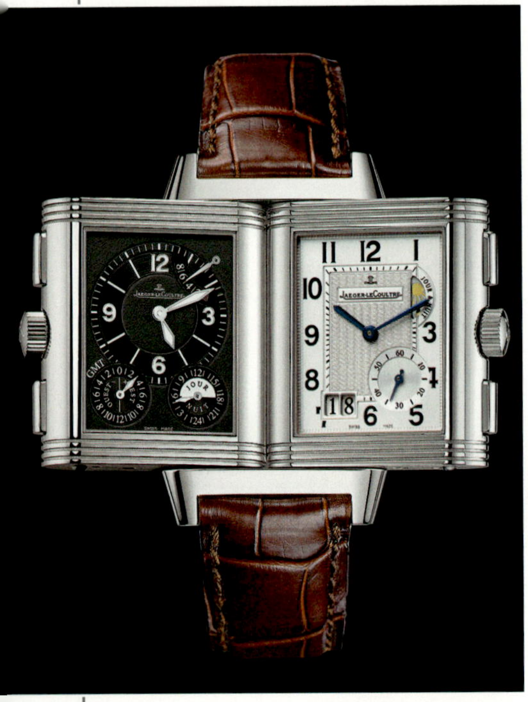

GRANDE REVERSO 976 — REF. 373.84.20

Movement: manual-winding Jaeger-LeCoultre 976 caliber; 48-hour power reserve; 151 components; 19 jewels; 28,800 vph; one barrel.
Functions: hours, minutes; small seconds.
Case: stainless steel; 48.5x30mm; sapphire caseback; water resistant to 3atm.
Dial: white vertical guilloché and Clou de Paris; black transferred numerals; baton hands.
Strap: dark brown alligator leather; double folding buckle.
Suggested price: $6,250

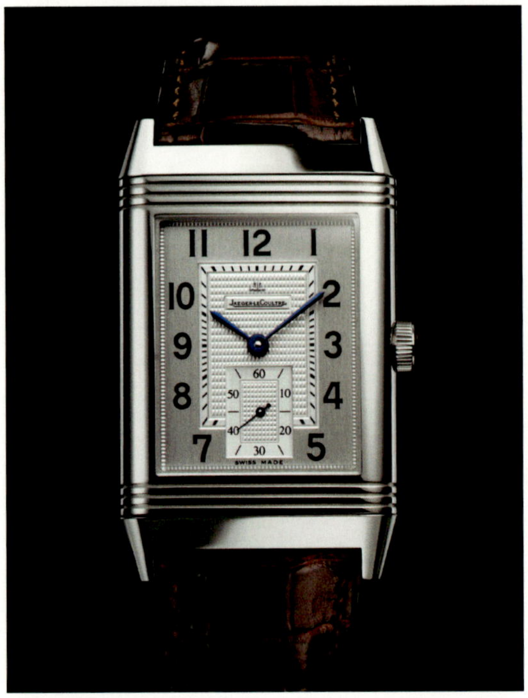

DUOMETRE A QUANTIEME LUNAIRE — REF. 604.24.20

Movement: manual-winding Jaeger-LeCoultre 381 caliber; Ø 33.7mm; 50-hour power reserve; 369 components; 40 jewels; 21,600 vph; two barrels.
Functions: hours, minutes, seconds; date; jumping second; moonphase (north and south).
Case: 18K pink gold; Ø 42mm, thickness: 13.5mm; polished and satin-brushed finishing; cambered, sapphire crystal caseback, hardness: N° 9; water resistant to 5atm.
Dial: beige; leaf-shaped, brass, gold-plated hour and minute hands; baton, pear-shaped counterweight, gold-plated seconds hand; welded lugs.
Strap: chocolate brown alligator leather; 18K gold folding clasp.
Suggested price: $35,100
Also available: yellow-gold case (ref. 604.04.20); limited edition of 300 pieces.

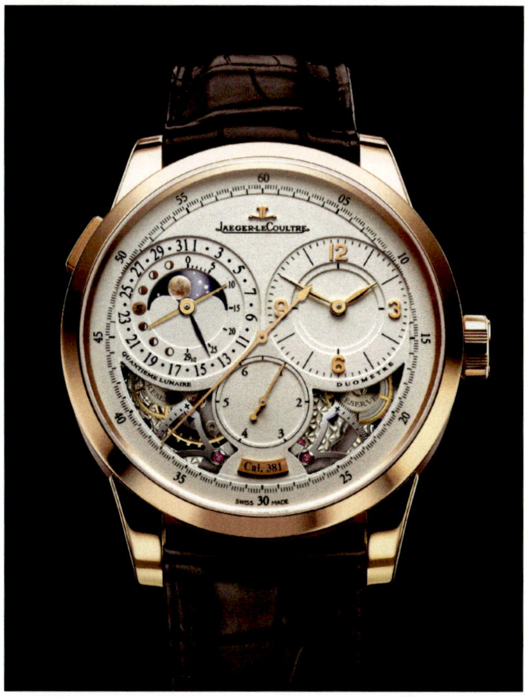

MASTER TOURBILLON — REF. 165.24.20

Movement: automatic-winding Jaeger-LeCoultre 978 caliber; 48-hour power reserve; 302 components; 33 jewels; 28,800 vph; one barrel.
Functions: hours, minutes, seconds; date; second time zone; 24-hour display; tourbillon.
Case: 18K pink gold; Ø 41.5mm; sapphire crystal caseback; water resistant to 5atm.
Dial: silvered sunray-brushed; gilt numerals and hour markers; Alpha hands.
Strap: dark brown alligator leather; double folding buckle.
Suggested price: $58,200

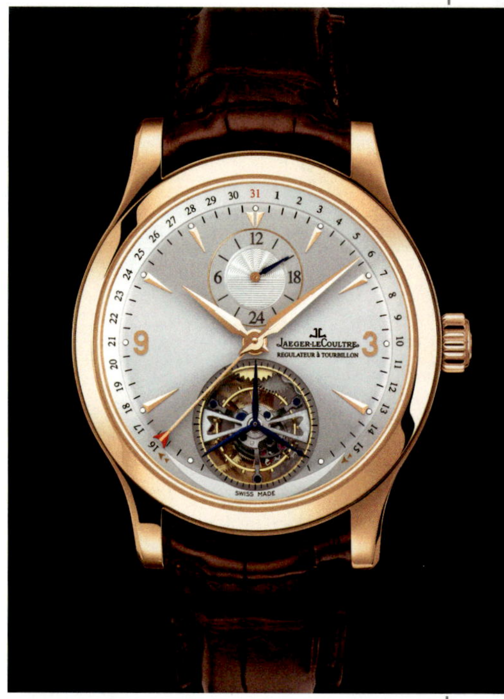

REVERSO GYRO 2 — REF. 233.64.20

Movement: manual-winding Jaeger-LeCoultre 174 caliber; 50-hour power reserve; 371 components; 28,800 vph.
Functions: front: hours, minutes, seconds; 24-hour display; spherical tourbillon; back: movement operation indicator.
Case: platinum; 55x36mm; water resistant to 3atm.
Strap: black alligator leather.
Suggested price: $350,000
Note: limited to 75 pieces.

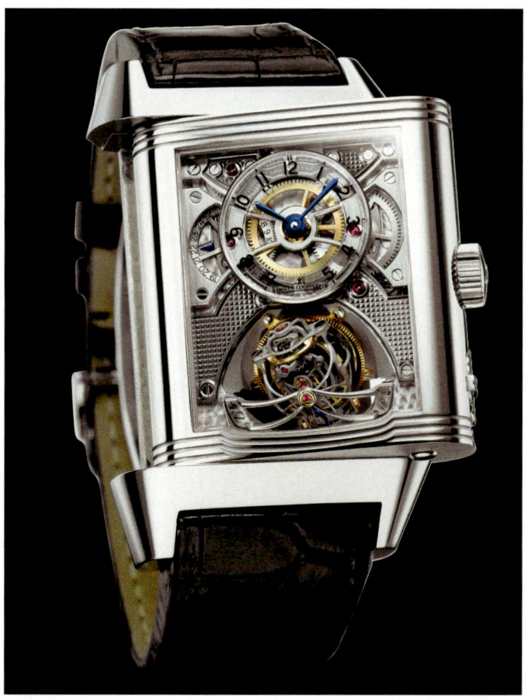

HYBRIS MECHANICA 55 GRANDE SONNERIE — REF. 603.34.20

Movement: automatic-winding Jaeger-LeCoultre 182 caliber; two barrels of 50-hour power reserve.
Functions: jumping hours; minutes on 60-minute counter; Westminster chimer; three striking modes: grande sonnerie, petite sonnerie, silent minute repeater; flying tourbillon.
Case: white gold; Ø 44mm; water resistant to 5atm.
Dial: white; leaf-shaped hands.
Strap: black alligator leather.
Suggested price: $1,340,000
Note: limited edition of 30 pieces.

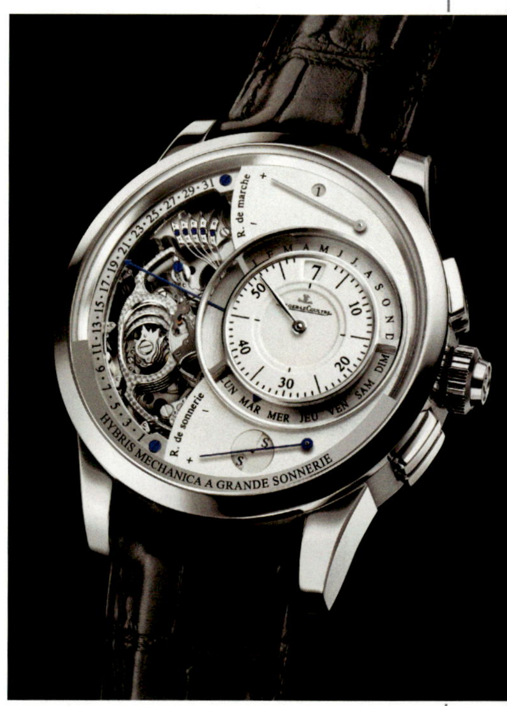

LONGINES

LONGINES DOLCEVITA

Contemporary elegance created through a combination of steel and gold

The Longines DolceVita collection was created in 1997 and has enjoyed immense success ever since. It embodies the brand's vision of contemporary elegance. With their typical harmonious rectangular case, the various models in this collection are based on the delights of the Italian way of life—*la dolce vita.*

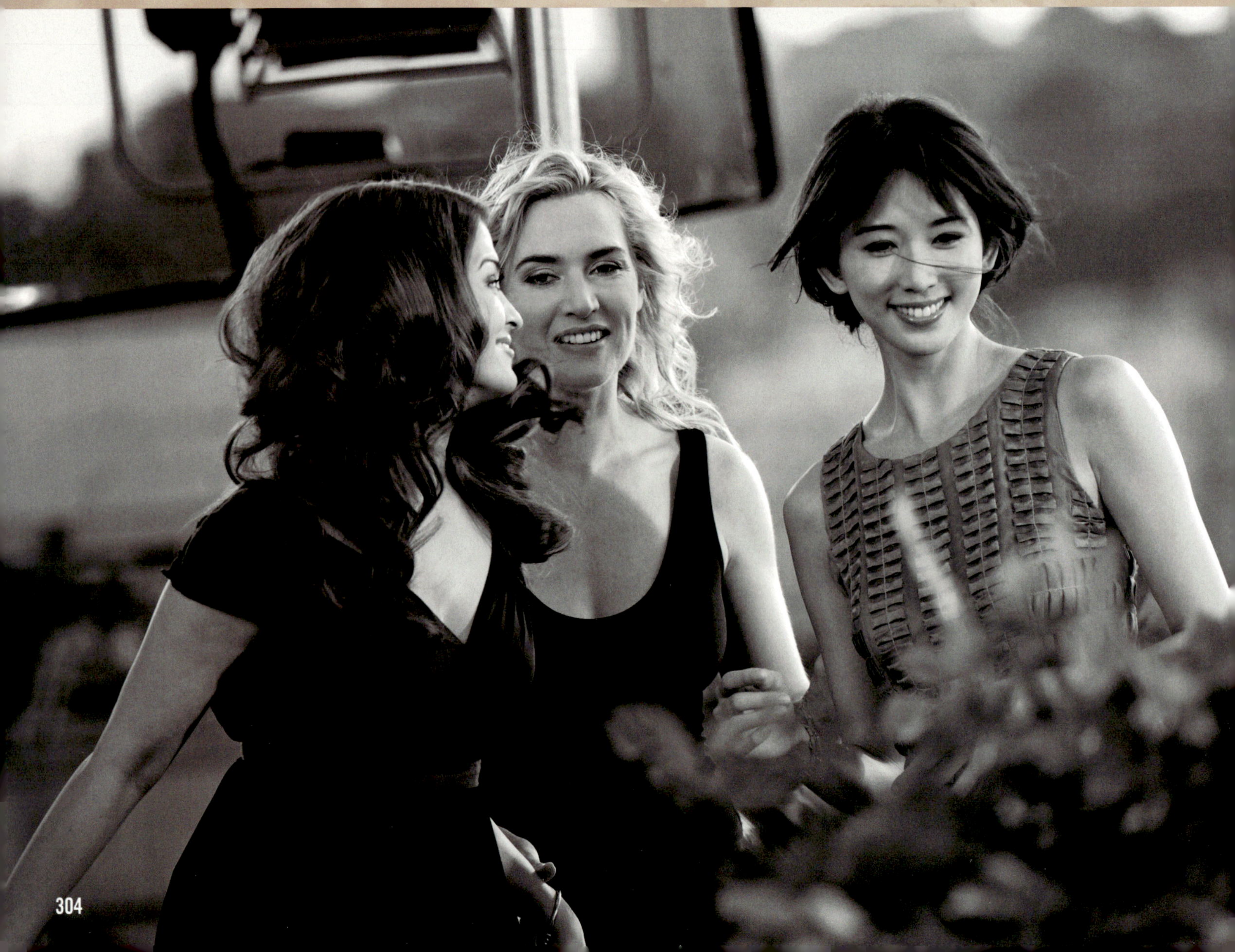

Longines has created a new version of horological elegance by combining steel with yellow or rose gold. British film star Kate Winslet, who won the 2009 Oscar for Best Actress, Bollywood icon Aishwarya Rai Bachchan and Asian star Chi Ling Lin can be seen wearing this work of art.

The Longines DolceVita collection embodies the brand's vision of contemporary elegance. Created in 1997, this collection has been immensely successful all around the world and today adorns the wrists of many women who appreciate refinement. The models in the collection typically have a rectangular case that offers great potential for variation. Now Longines has decided to create a new version of contemporary elegance by using different colors of gold to enhance the brilliance of the steel. This new model, which will enchant all female customers, is available in steel with yellow gold or steel with rose gold. It offers a new dimension to the elegance of Longines' products.

The new additions to the DolceVita collection that combine steel with yellow or rose gold are available in three sizes, to suit all tastes and requirements. They feature either a white dial with Arabic numerals and indexes, a silvered "flinqué" dial with blue Roman numerals or a white mother-of-pearl dial set with diamonds. The versions in steel and rose gold also have a white mother-of-pearl dial with Arabic numerals. Like the rectangular case that combines steel with gold, the bracelet on which these new models are mounted brings together the brilliance of steel and the gentle warmth of gold. Certain models are set with diamonds. All models are fitted with a quartz movement.

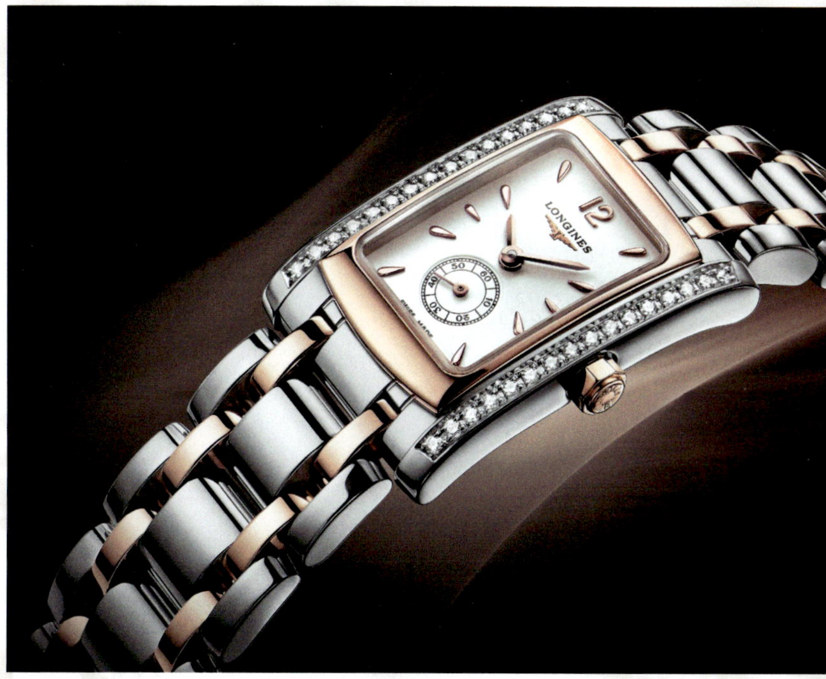

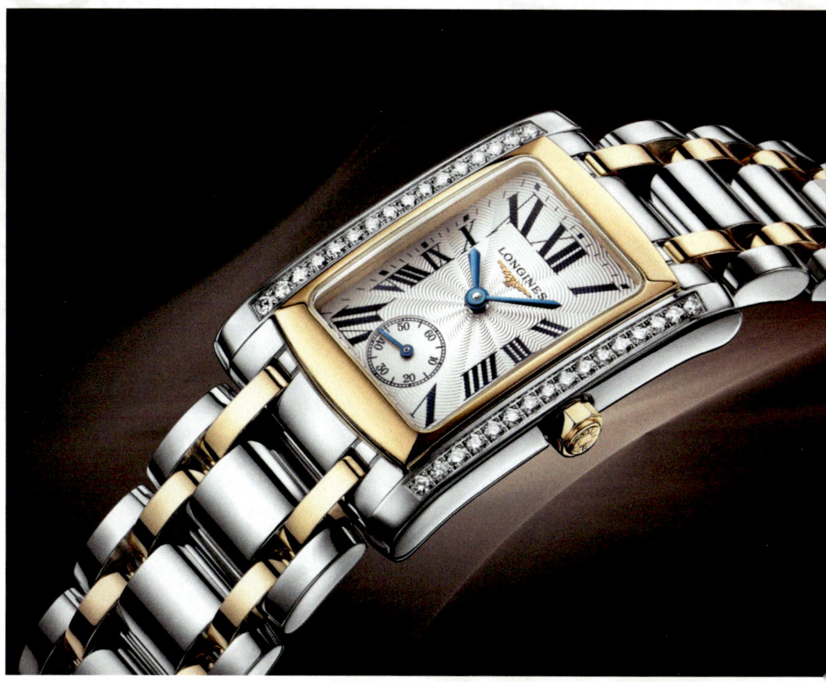

TOP

This quartz watch in steel and rose gold is set with 32 diamonds (0.269 carat, Top Wesselton VVS) whose sparkle emphasises the rectangular form and harmonious proportions of the case. The white dial features ten indexes and an Arabic numeral 12 and has rose-gold hands to indicate the hours and minutes, as well as a small seconds at 6 o'clock. This elegant, contemporary model is mounted on a steel and rose-gold bracelet. Water resistant to 3 bar (30m /~100ft).

RIGHT

This quartz watch in steel and yellow gold is set with 32 diamonds (0.384 carat, Top Wesselton VVS) whose sparkle emphasises the rectangular form and harmonious proportions of the case. The silvered "flinqué" dial features blue Roman numerals and hands that indicate the hours and minutes, as well as small seconds at 6 o'clock. The watch is beautifully combined with a steel and yellow-gold bracelet to match the case. Water resistant to 3 bar (30m /~100ft).

Travelling through Italy, the attentive tourist will be aware of the charms of a Mediterranean country full of subtle perfumes. Offering a dreamlike walk through the remains of an illustrious empire, or precious moments of relaxation on the beach, or a quiet rest on a sunny terrace in a village square, this country enjoys a way of life that is unique—*la dolce vita*. With the Longines DolceVita collection, launched in 1997, the brand offers a horological vision of this gentle way of life. A new version that combines steel with yellow or rose gold has now been added to the collection. The British film star Kate Winslet, who won an Oscar for Best Actress in 2009, the Bollywood icon Aishwarya Rai Bachchan and the Asian star Chi Ling Lin can all be seen wearing a model in the Longines DolceVita collection.

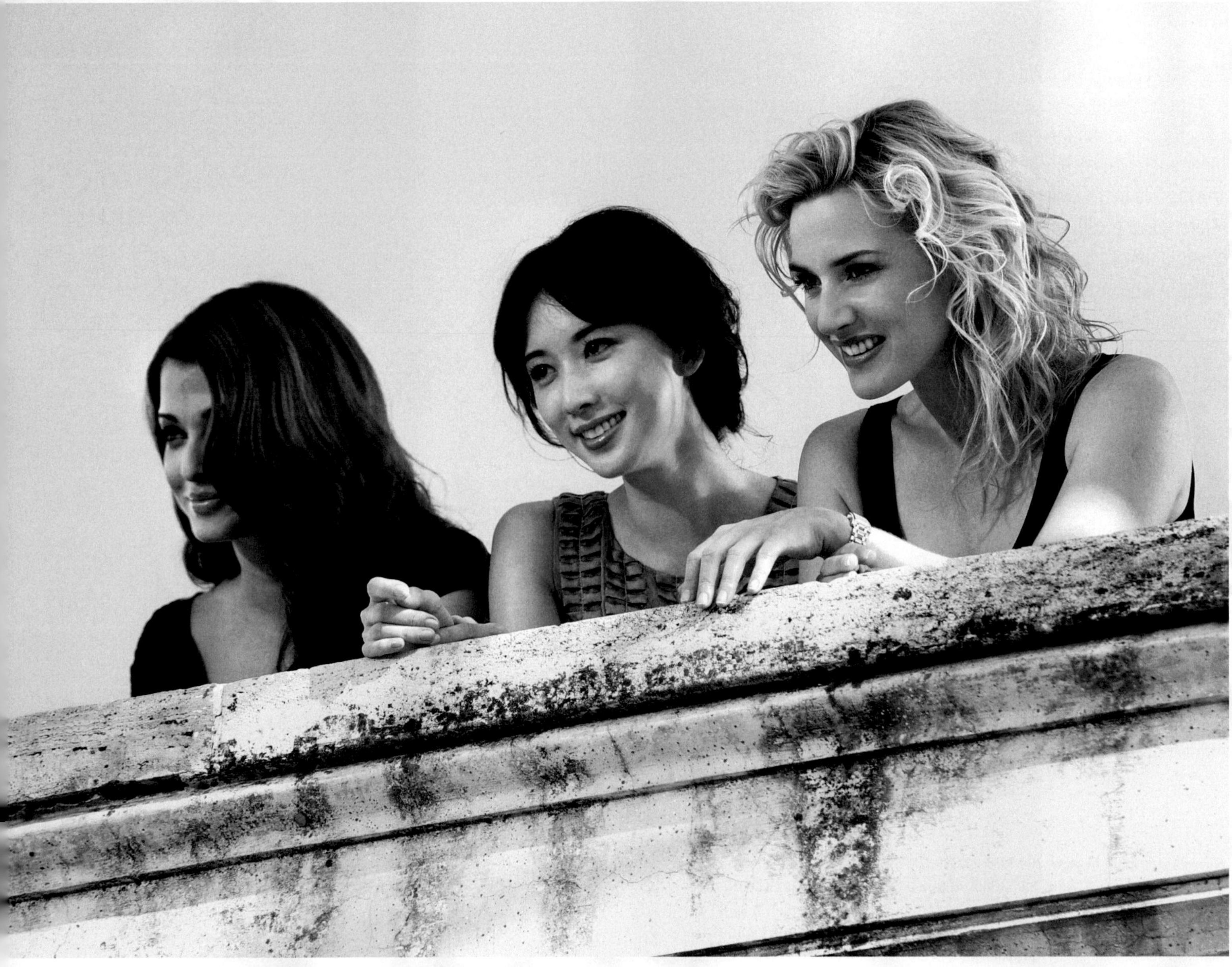

FACING PAGE

Longines has given a fresh new look to its exemplary series of contemporary, elegant designs within the Longines DolceVita collection, by using different colors of gold in order to enhance the brilliance of the stainless steel with which they are combined. This quartz watch in steel and yellow gold is characterised by a rectangular case with pleasing proportions. The white mother-of-pearl dial features 12 diamond indexes (0.055 carat, Top Wesselton) and the blued hands show the hours and minutes. This elegant, contemporary model is mounted on a steel and yellow-gold bracelet. Water resistant to 3 bar (30m /~100ft).

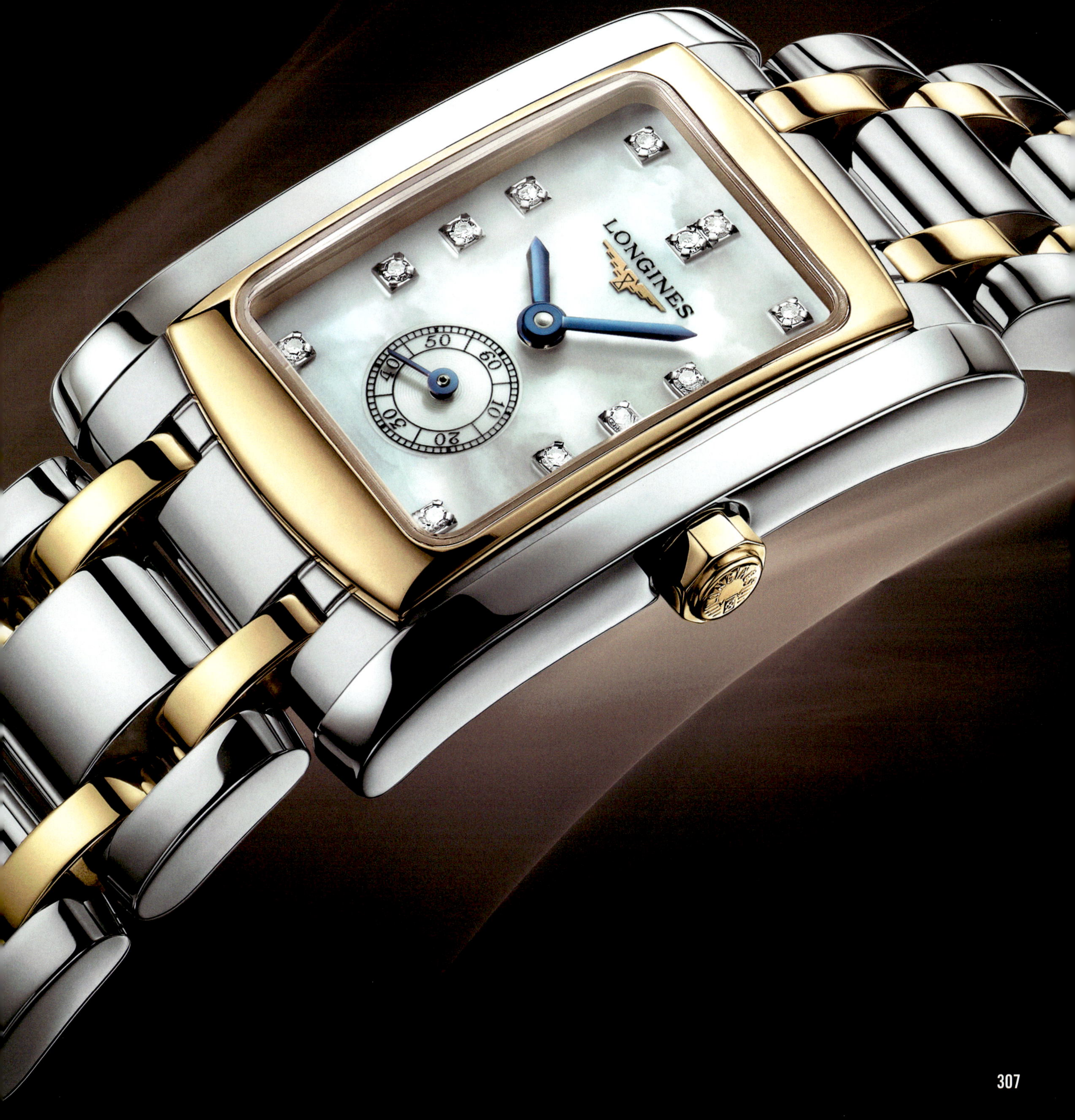
LONGINES
50
60
40
10
30
20

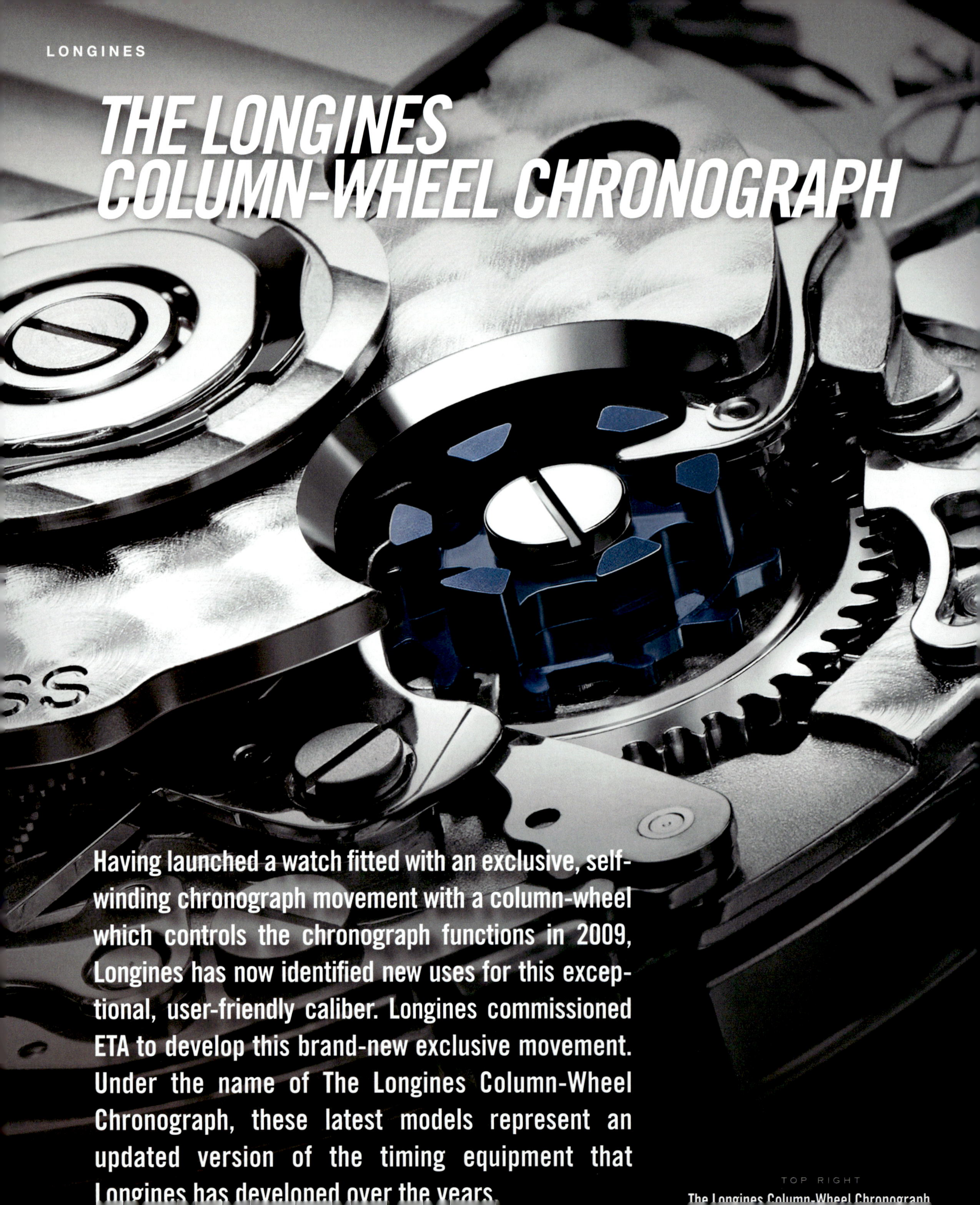

THE LONGINES COLUMN-WHEEL CHRONOGRAPH

Having launched a watch fitted with an exclusive, self-winding chronograph movement with a column-wheel which controls the chronograph functions in 2009, Longines has now identified new uses for this exceptional, user-friendly caliber. Longines commissioned ETA to develop this brand-new exclusive movement. Under the name of The Longines Column-Wheel Chronograph, these latest models represent an updated version of the timing equipment that Longines has developed over the years.

TOP RIGHT
The Longines Column-Wheel Chronograph

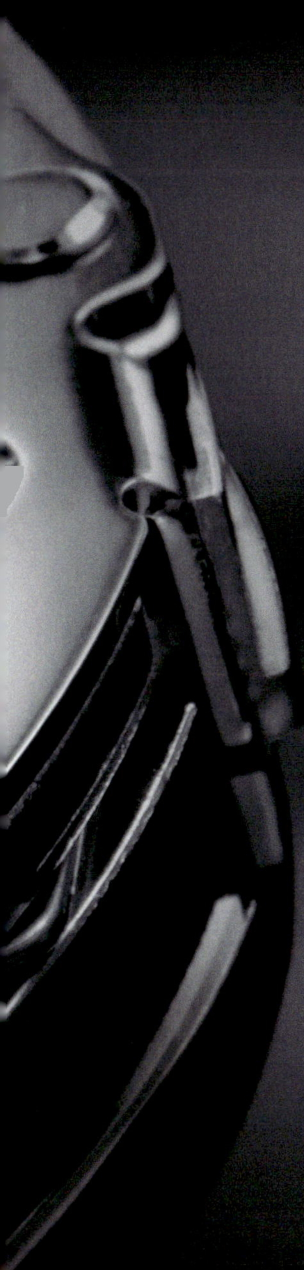

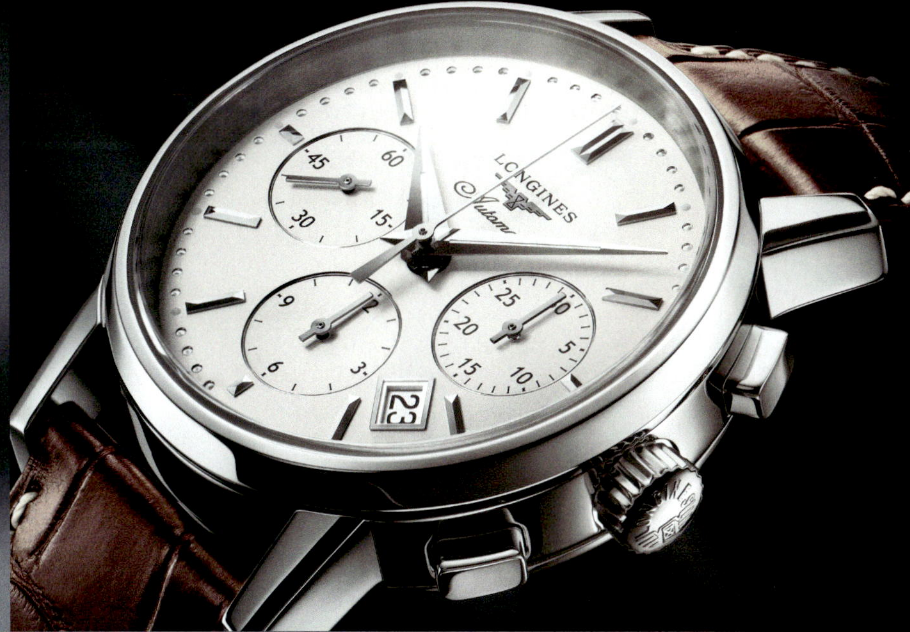

Longines commissioned ETA to develop a brand-new exclusive self-winding movement with a column-wheel for a wrist chronograph. The reference number given to the new caliber was L688.2. As part of the continual program of reviving the mechanical watch that was started at the beginning of the 21st century, this new creation meets the requirements of changing demand with regard to watches as well as the growing popularity of mechanical chronographs and the fascination for traditional horological devices. Column-wheel chronographs correspond to the new taste in watches. As part of the line of timing instruments created by Longines, this caliber constitutes the present-day embodiment of the far-reaching experience in mechanical timekeeping that is the heritage of the famous Swiss watchmaker.

Fitted with 27 jewels, the L688.2 movement is a self-winding caliber with a diameter of 30mm and a height of 7.9mm. The purpose of its column-wheel is to control the chronograph functions (start, stop, return to zero). This system, and in particular the column-wheel that was designed by ETA's engineers, is exceptionally user-friendly for a mechanical chronograph, requiring only the finest touch to start and stop the mechanism and to reset the hands at zero. The blued steel column-wheel is surrounded by the fascinating beauty of a movement which is in fact an updated version of a traditional technical system. In addition to its refined design, the L688.2 caliber reveals a construction designed to meet the demands of timing. Longines has so far created several timepieces as a tribute to this high-tech movement. The combination of these timing features and the re-issue of an elegant, traditional or sporty design results in several The Longines Column-Wheel Chronograph models that are contemporary watches steeped in the great tradition of mechanical timing.

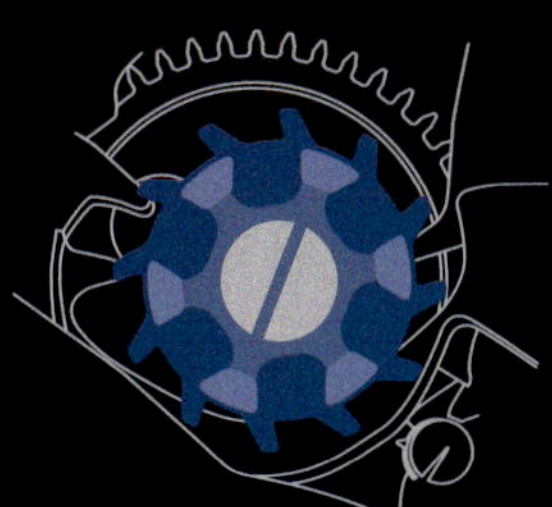

Calibre L688
Exclusive Longines Movement

Longines, maker of column-wheel chronograph movements since 1878.

LONGINES DOLCEVITA REF. L5.155.5.19.7

Movement: quartz caliber L178.2.
Functions: hours, minutes; small seconds.
Case: stainless steel and rose gold; 19.8x24.5mm; set with 32 Top Wesselton VVS diamonds (0.269 carat); sapphire crystal; water resistant to 3atm.
Dial: white; ten hour markers and one rose-gold Arabic numeral; rose-gold hands.
Bracelet: stainless steel and rose gold with folding safety clasp and pushpieces.

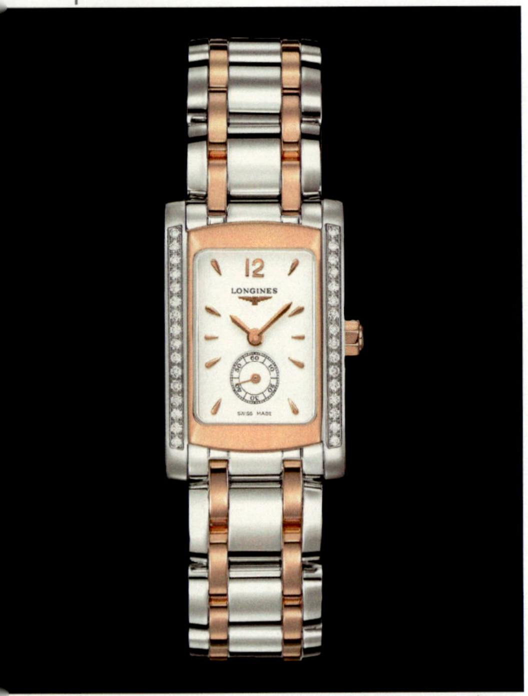

LONGINES PRIMALUNA REF. L8.110.5.79.6

Movement: quartz caliber L250.2.
Functions: hours, minutes, seconds; date.
Case: stainless steel and rose gold; Ø 26.5mm; set with 44 Top Wesselton VVS diamonds (0.299 carat); antireflective sapphire crystal; water resistant to 3atm.
Dial: silvered with flinqué decoration; eleven blue Roman numerals; blued-steel hands.
Bracelet: stainless steel and rose gold with folding safety clasp and pushpieces.

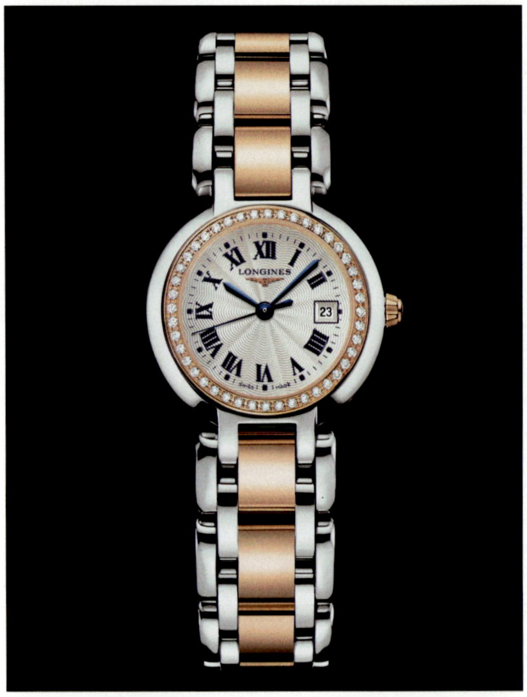

LA GRANDE CLASSIQUE DE LONGINES REF. L4.241.0.11.6

Movement: quartz caliber L209.
Functions: hours, minutes.
Case: stainless steel; Ø 24mm, thickness: 4.4mm; set with 48 Top Wesselton VVS diamonds (0.403 carat); sapphire crystal; water resistant to 3atm.
Dial: white; twelve black Roman numerals; blackened steel hands.
Bracelet: stainless steel with triple-folding safety clasp and pushpieces.

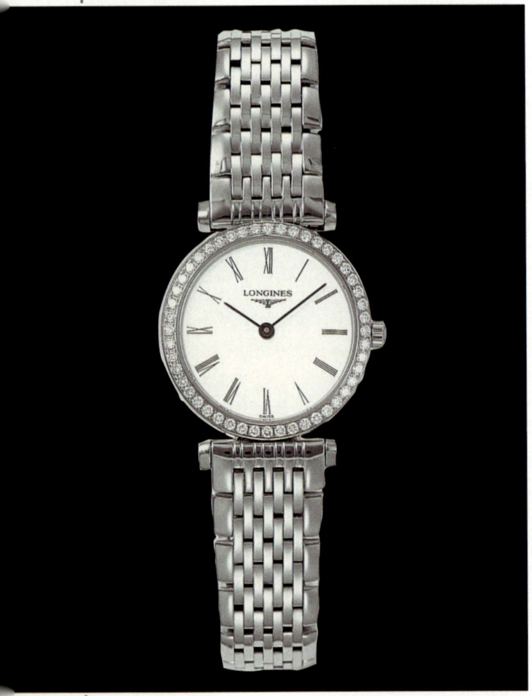

LA GRANDE CLASSIQUE DE LONGINES "TONNEAU" REF. L4.205.4.11.6

Movement: quartz caliber L209.
Functions: hours, minutes.
Case: stainless steel, ultra-thin; 22.2x24.5mm; sapphire crystal; water resistant to 3atm.
Dial: white; black Roman numerals; blackened steel hands.
Bracelet: stainless steel with triple-folding safety clasp and pushpieces.

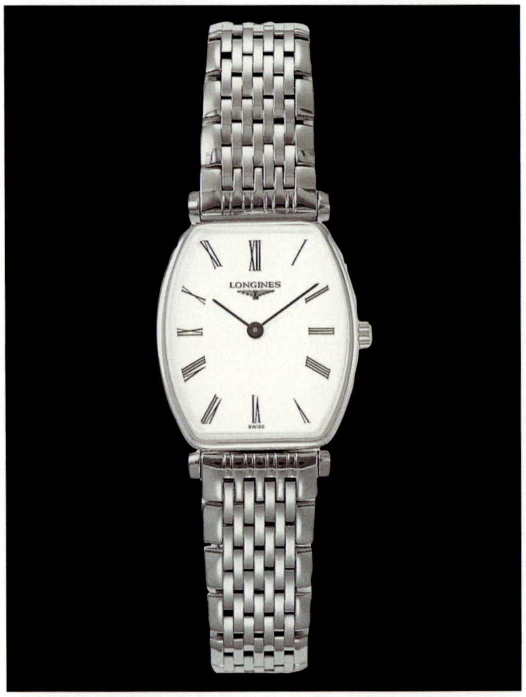

THE LONGINES MASTER COLLECTION — REF. L2.673.4.78.3

Movement: automatic-winding caliber L678; 13¼ lines; 48-hour power reserve; 25 jewels; 28,800 vph.
Functions: hours, minutes; small seconds and 24-hour indicator at 9; date; day and month at 12; moonphase at 6; chronograph: center 60-second hand, 12-hour counter at 6 and 30-minute counter at 12.
Case: stainless steel; Ø 40mm; antireflective sapphire crystal; sapphire crystal caseback; water resistant to 3atm.
Dial: silver-finished stamped "barleycorn"; nine Arabic numerals; blued-steel hands; black-painted minute track, 31-day calendar.
Strap: dark brown alligator; triple-folding safety clasp.

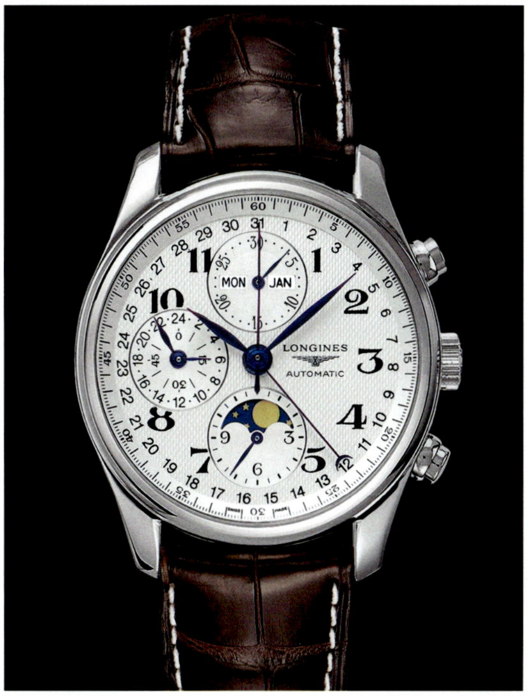

THE LONGINES MASTER COLLECTION — REF. L2.717.4.78.3

Movement: automatic-winding caliber L698; 16½ lines; 46-hour power reserve; 25 jewels, 28,800 vph.
Functions: hours, minutes; four retrograde functions: day, date, seconds and second time zone on a 24-hour scale.
Case: stainless steel; Ø 44mm; antireflective sapphire crystal; transparent sapphire crystal caseback; water resistant to 3atm.
Dial: silver-finished stamped "barleycorn"; eleven Arabic numerals; six blued-steel hands; black-painted minute track.
Strap: dark brown alligator; triple-folding safety clasp.

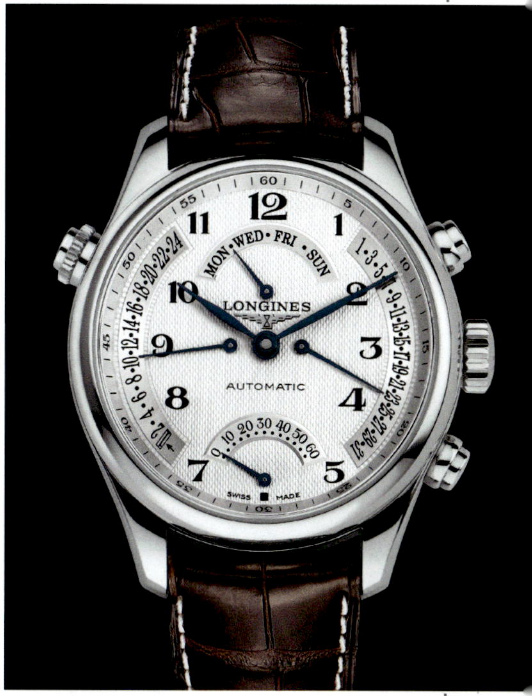

LONGINES EVIDENZA — REF. L2.643.4.73.4

Movement: automatic-winding caliber L650; 12½ lines; 42-hour power reserve; 37 jewels, 28,800 vph.
Functions: hours, minutes, seconds; date; chronograph: central 60-second hand, 30-minute counter at 9, 12-hour counter at 6.
Case: stainless steel; 34.9x40mm; antireflective sapphire crystal; water resistant to 3atm.
Dial: silvered "flinqué"; twelve blue-painted Arabic numerals; blued-steel hands.
Strap: dark brown alligator; triple-folding safety clasp.

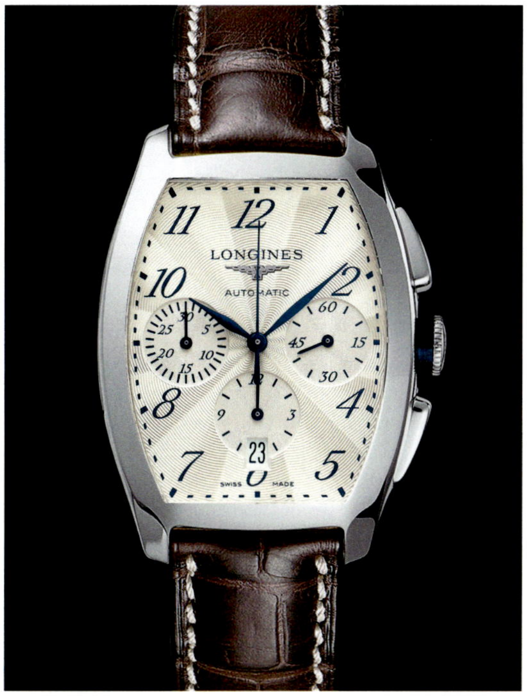

THE LONGINES COLUMN-WHEEL CHRONOGRAPH — REF. L2.733.4.72.2

Movement: automatic-winding caliber L688.2; column-wheel chronograph; 13¼ lines; 54-hour power reserve; 27 jewels, 28,800 vph.
Functions: hours, minutes, seconds; date; chronograph: central sweep seconds, 30-minute counter at 3, 12-hour counter at 6.
Case: stainless steel; Ø 39mm; antireflective sapphire crystal; transparent sapphire crystal caseback; water resistant to 3atm.
Dial: silvered; thirteen applied rhodium-plated hour-markers with SuperLumiNova; rhodium-plated dauphine-style hands with SuperLumiNova.
Strap: dark brown alligator with buckle.

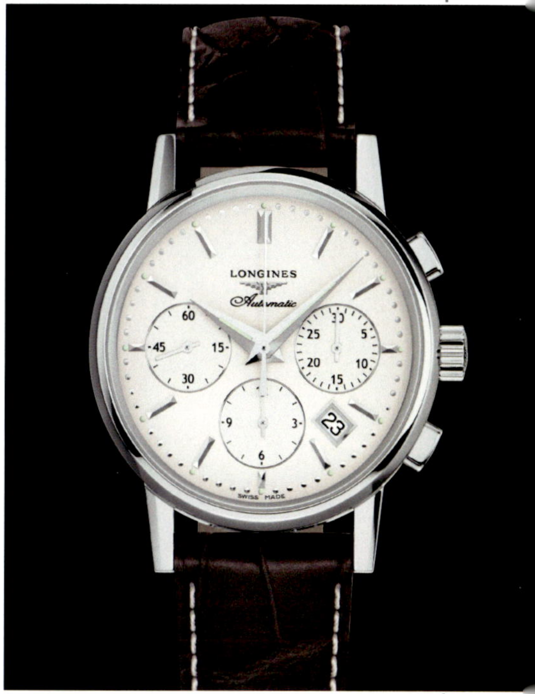

CONQUEST — REF. L3.661.4.56.7

Movement: automatic-winding caliber L667; 13¼ lines; 48-hour power reserve; 25 jewels; 28,800 vph.
Functions: hours, minutes; small seconds at 9; date at 3; chronograph: center seconds hand, 12-hour counter at 6, 30-minute counter at 12.
Case: stainless steel; Ø 41mm; black ceramic bezel and cabochon; screw-in crown with crown protection; screw-down caseback; antireflective sapphire crystal; water resistant to 3atm.
Dial: black lacquered; silver "large 12" Arabic numeral; eleven indexes; polished, rhodium-plated hands.
Bracelet: stainless steel; black central ceramic links with triple-folding safety clasp.

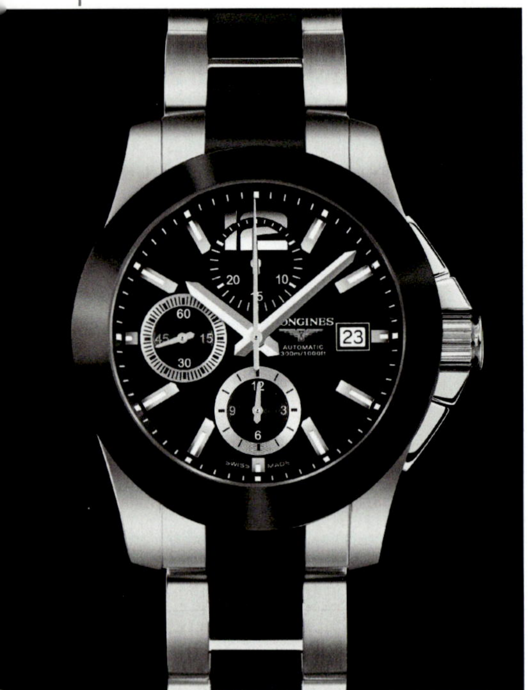

LONGINES ADMIRAL — REF. L3.667.4.56.7

Movement: automatic-winding caliber L705; 16½ lines; 46-hour power reserve; 27 jewels; 28,800 vph.
Functions: hours, minutes; small seconds at 9; date at 6; chronograph: center seconds, 30-minute counter at 3.
Case: stainless steel; Ø 42mm; black ceramic bezel with tachometer; screw-in ceramic crown and ceramic pushpieces with protective shoulder; antireflective sapphire crystal; screw-in caseback; water resistant to 10atm.
Dial: black; "large 12" Arabic numeral with SuperLumiNova coating; eight applied, polished rhodium-plated hour markers with SuperLumi Nova; polished, rhodium-plated hands with SuperLumiNova.
Bracelet: stainless steel with central links in black ceramic; triple-folding safety clasp.
Also available: gray version.

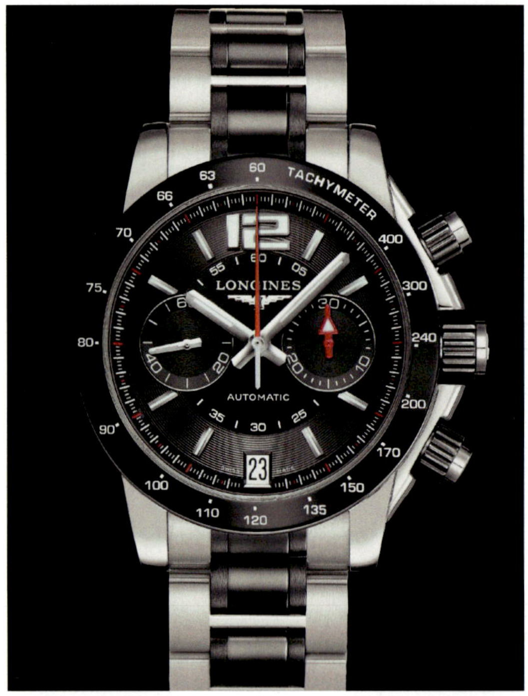

FLAGSHIP HERITAGE — REF. L4.795.4.78.2

Movement: automatic-winding caliber L615.2; 11½ lines; 42-hour power reserve; 27 jewels; 28,800 vph.
Functions: hours, minutes; small seconds and date at 6.
Case: stainless steel; Ø 38.5mm; antireflective sapphire crystal; water resistant to 3atm.
Dial: stainless steel; eleven golden indexes; golden dauphine-style hands with SuperLumiNova.
Strap: brown alligator with buckle.

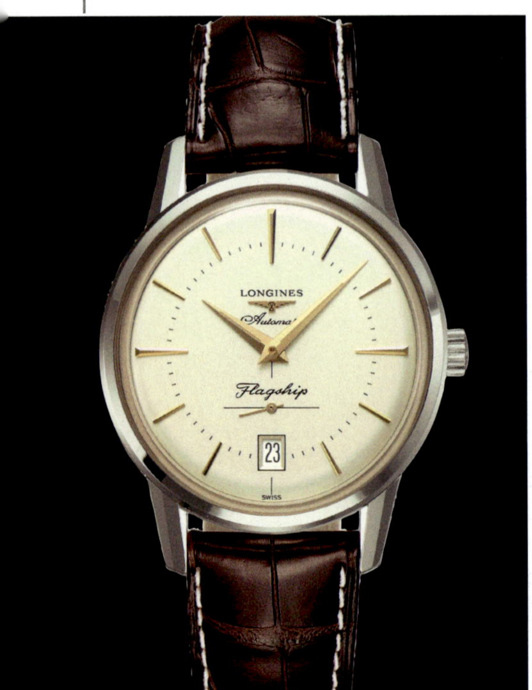

THE LONGINES LEGEND DIVER WATCH — REF. L3.674.4.50.0

Movement: automatic-winding caliber L633; 11½ lines; 38-hour power reserve; 25 jewels; 28,800 vph.
Functions: hours, minutes, seconds; date at 3.
Case: stainless steel; Ø 42mm; internal turning diving bezel; two screw-in crowns; antireflective sapphire crystal; screw-down caseback with embossed diver symbol; water resistant to 30atm.
Dial: black lacquered with SuperLumiNova; rhodium-plated hands with SuperLumiNova.
Strap: black synthetic fabric; buckle.

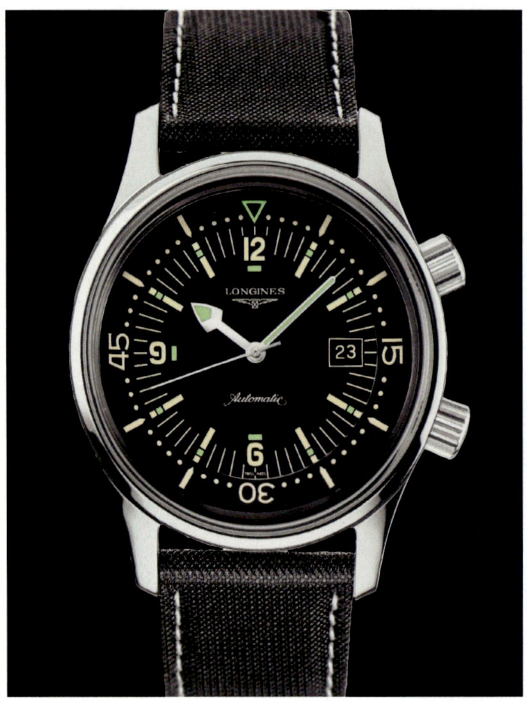

LONGINES HERITAGE 1951 REF. L2.745.4.53.4

Movement: automatic-winding caliber L683; 13¼ lines; 48-hour power reserve; 27 jewels; 28,800 vph.
Functions: hours, minutes; small seconds at 9; date at 4:30; chronograph: central sweep seconds, 30-minute counter at 3, 12-hour counter at 6.
Case: stainless steel, Ø 41mm; antireflective sapphire crystal; water resistant to 3atm.
Dial: silvered; white printed Arabic numerals with SuperLumiNova; white railway track minute ring and second ring; rhodium-plated "baton skeleton" hands.
Strap: black alligator with buckle.

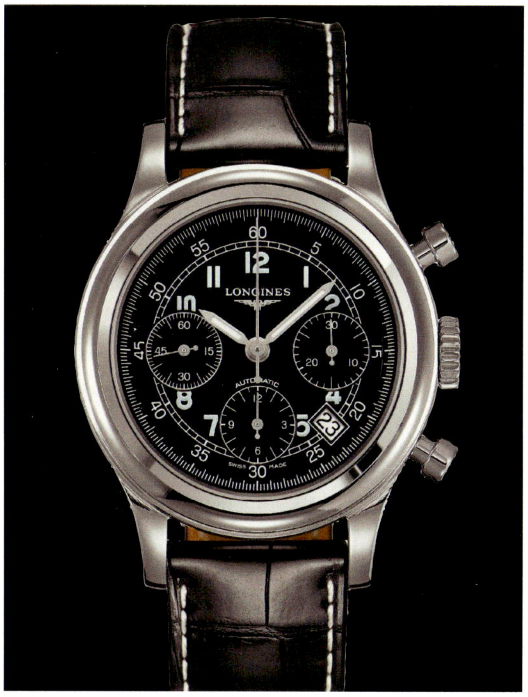

LONGINES HERITAGE 1954 REF. L2.747.4.72.2

Movement: automatic-winding caliber L674; 13¼ lines; 48-hour power reserve; 25 jewels; 28,800 vph.
Functions: hours, minutes; small seconds at 9; date at 3; day; date; tachometer and telemeter scales; chronograph: central sweep seconds, 12-hour counter at 6, 30-minute counter at 12.
Case: stainless steel; Ø 40mm; antireflective sapphire crystal; water resistant to 5atm.
Dial: silvered; eight applied hour markers; railway track minute ring and second ring; blued-steel hands.
Strap: brown alligator with buckle.

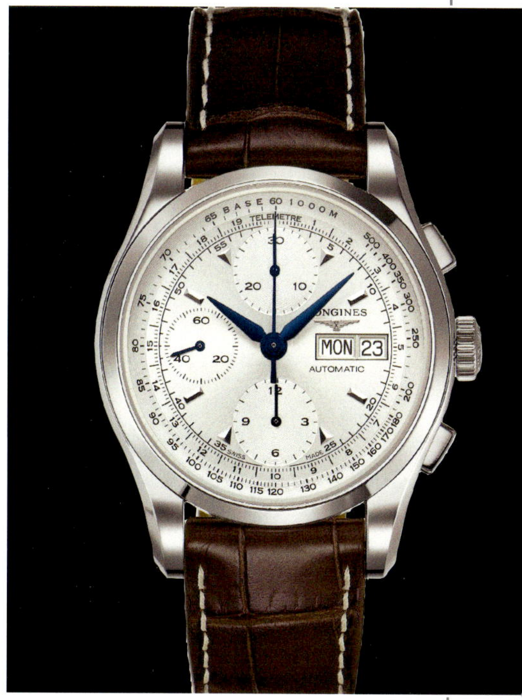

THE LONGINES WEEMS SECOND-SETTING WATCH REF. L2.713.8.13.0

Movement: automatic-winding caliber L699; 16½ lines; 46-hour power reserve; 24 jewels; 28,800 vph.
Functions: hours, minutes, seconds; rotating central dial for synchronisation to the second with a radio time signal.
Case: polished 18K rose gold; Ø 47.5mm; engraved and numbered (not limited edition) caseback with opening to reveal transparent antireflective sapphire crystal; water resistant to 3atm.
Dial: white lacquer; black-painted external railway track minute ring; twelve black painted Arabic numerals; opaline silvered rotating center dial; black-painted railway track minute ring; blued-steel Breguet design hands.
Strap: brown alligator; "Charleston" clasp and extension.

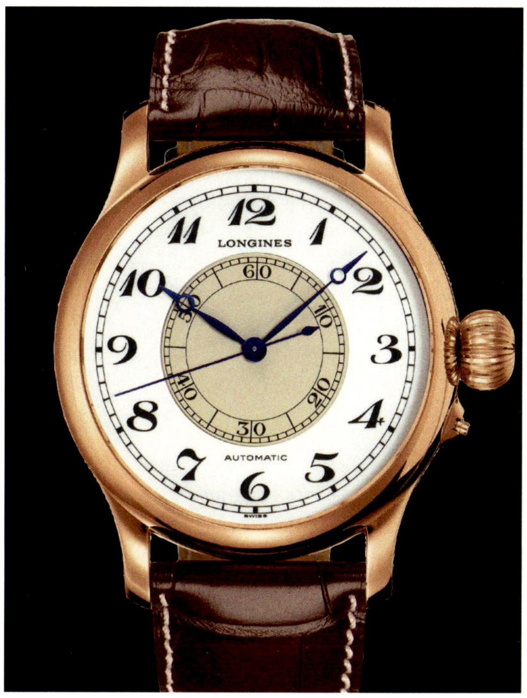

LONGINES LINDBERGH'S ATLANTIC VOYAGE WATCH REF. L2.730.4.11.0

Movement: automatic-winding caliber L705; 16½ lines; 46-hour power reserve; 27 jewels; 28,800 vph.
Functions: hours, minutes, seconds; chronograph: 30-minute counter at 3, 60-minute counter at 9.
Case: stainless steel; Ø 47.5mm; engraved and numbered (not limited edition) caseback with opening to reveal transparent antireflective sapphire crystal; water resistant to 30atm.
Dial: silvered; ten black Arabic numerals; black tachometer, 500-600 kph; blued-steel Breguet hour and minute hands; blued-steel counter-weight line pear flyback hand; blued-steel arrow 30-minute counter hand; blued-steel counter-weight stick pear small seconds hand.
Strap: brown alligator; triple-folding safety clasp.

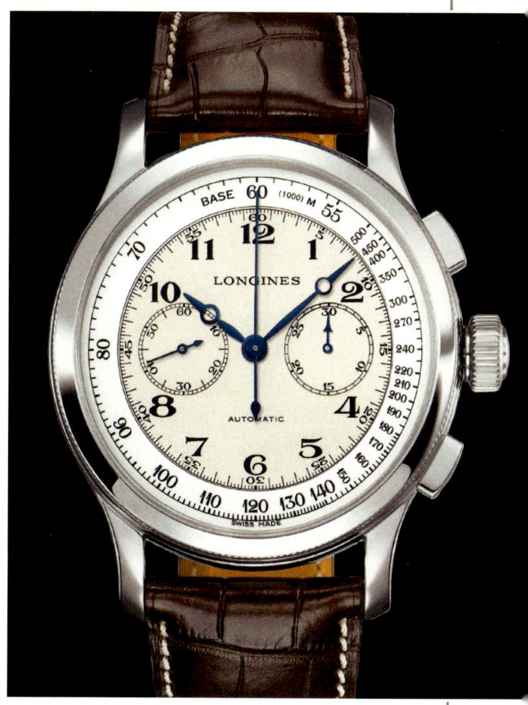

LOUIS VUITTON

REDEFINING TIME

Louis Vuitton quickly made its mark in haute horology by applying to watchmaking the same uncompromising craftsmanship and artistry that has made the French firm a luxury icon for more than 150 years.

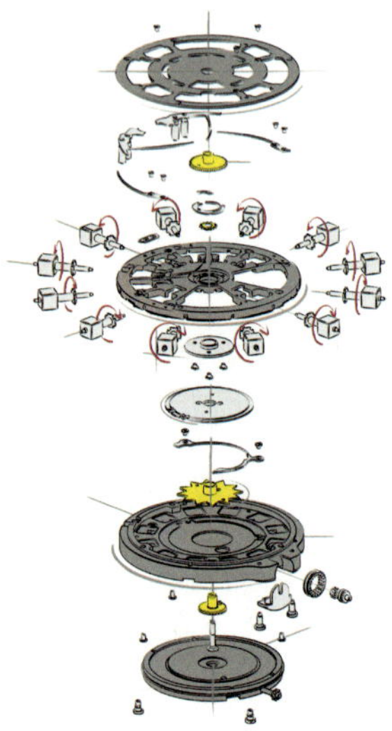

The company began its foray into the watchmaking world in 2002 with the introduction of its first Tambour model. Since then, the collection has grown to encompass a range of complicated timepieces that includes a regatta-style chronograph, a tourbillon and another that indicates the direction north for both hemispheres.

The primary inspiration behind of all its timepieces is the yearning to explore inherent in human nature, explains Hamdi Chatti, vice president of watches and jewelry at Louis Vuitton. "Above all, Tambour is a travel instrument, both beautiful and useful. With the GMT and the Régate, the desire to travel is there, always combined with the idea of movement, of getting away from it all, of all the values that turn daily life into pleasure."

Signaling its reverence for Swiss watchmaking's tradition of precision and elegance, Louis Vuitton established its atelier in La Chaux-de-Fonds, a bastion of horological knowledge for centuries. The facility plays an essential role that enables the company to not only maintain its rigorous standards of quality, but also develop new innovations.

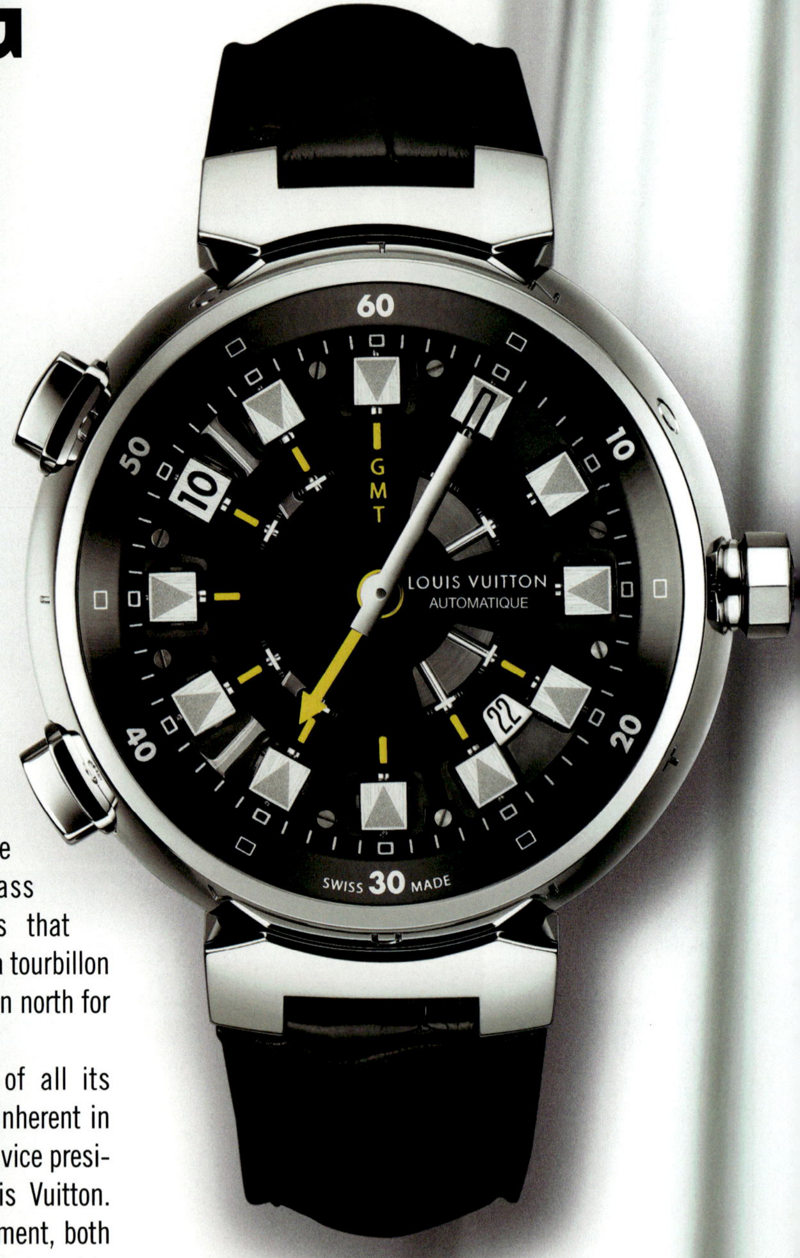

ABOVE

The Tambour Spin Time GMT XL's 44mm white-gold case houses an original jumping hour function that eliminates the need for an hour hand.

LEFT

In place of hour markers, Louis Vuitton uses a complex system of rotating cubes to display the current hour. The bright yellow arrow indicates the watch's second time zone function.

Louis Vuitton embraced Swiss watchmaking tradition in 2002 when it launched the Tambour collection and began designing its own complicated movements at its workshops in La Chaux-de-Fonds.

In fact, the firm recently introduced a patented crown stem lifting system it calls Level Up. Created to improve the crown's operation, its design is based on an automotive transfer case, a device that distributes power from the transmission to the front and rear axles in a four-wheel drive vehicle. "The development of movements designed by the Louis Vuitton watchmaking workshops is the very essence of our watchmaking future," Chatti says.

In a stunning demonstration of technical brio, Louis Vuitton welcomed the Tambour Spin Time GMT XL to its collection in 2010. Its movement incorporates an imaginative jumping hour display that replaces the traditional hour markers with 12 rotating cubes, thereby eliminating the need for an hour hand altogether.

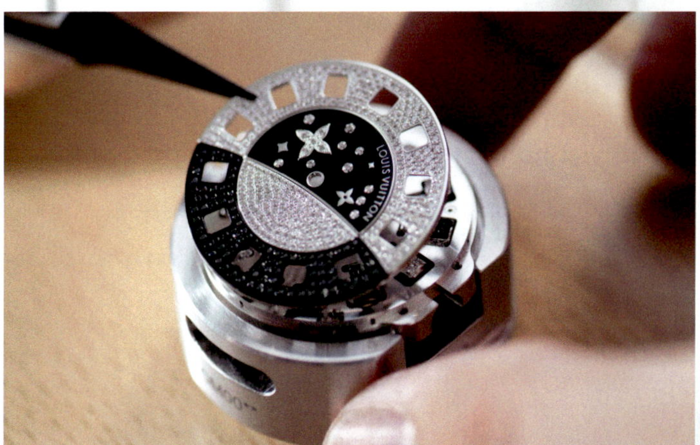

To indicate the hour, a single cube is turned to reveal an engraved number while the other 11 display Louis Vuitton's signature "V." When the minute hand completes its 60-minute rotation around the dial, the cubes representing the outgoing and incoming hours turn simultaneously. The Tambour Spin Time GMT XL's black dial is perforated at the center to reveal the rotating pinions that execute this clever maneuver.

In place of the missing hour hand, the watch includes a vivid yellow arrow fixed at the center of the dial that indicates a second time zone. A pusher on the side of the 44mm white-gold case quickly and easily adjusts this GMT hand.

Louis Vuitton demonstrates its signature élan with a jewelry version of the Tambour Spin Time that combines mechanical prowess and natural beauty in an exquisite display of feminine glamour.

The sparkling design shines a spotlight on the delicate touch used by the firm's gem-setting artisans, who pave the Tambour Spin Time's dial and lugs with rows of black and white diamonds. This opulent display also plays a starring role in the watch's signature jumping hour function. The rotating hour cylinders blend seamlessly into the diamond-set dial, except for the one indicating the current hour. Instead, it flashes a quartet of diamonds that contrast with the surrounding background.

Louis Vuitton is quickly carving out a new identity with a growing watch collection that stands on its own.

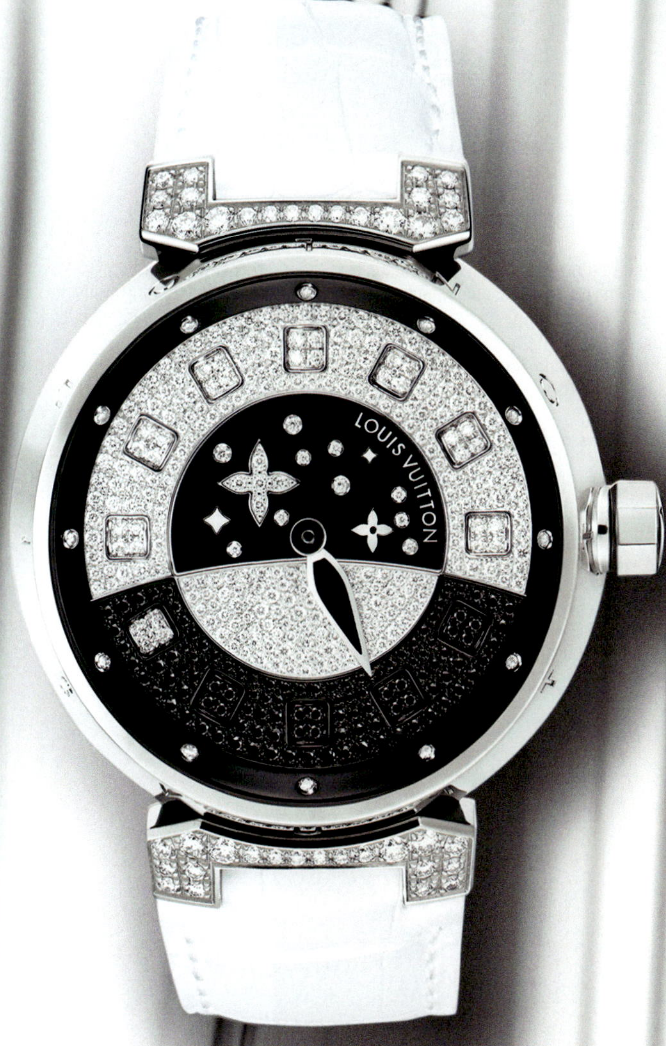

A jewelry version of the Tambour Spin Time is set with black and white diamonds and includes a black lacquer center decorated with flowers that evoke the Louis Vuitton monogram.

TAMBOUR SPIN TIME AUTOMATIC GMT

Movement: automatic-winding LV119 caliber; 40-hour power reserve.
Functions: hours, minutes; date; GMT; spin time function: hours appear on the rotating cylinders.
Case: 18K white gold; Ø 44mm; transparent caseback; water resistant to 10atm.
Dial: black.
Strap: black alligator; 18K white-gold buckle.

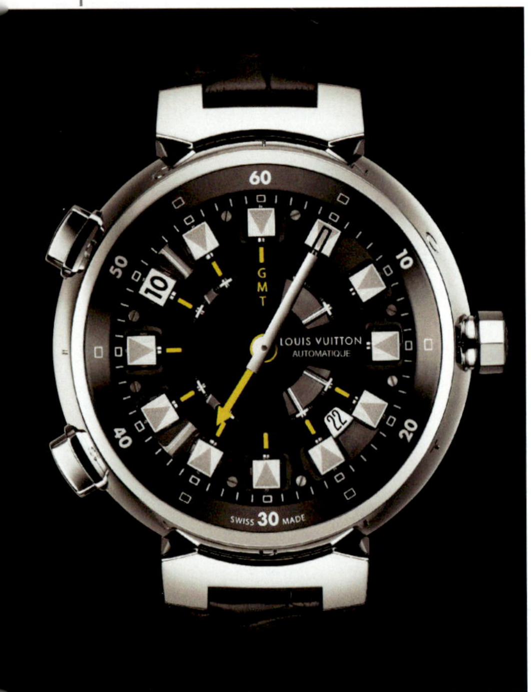

TAMBOUR TOURBILLON MONOGRAM

Movement: automatic-winding LV103 caliber; 90-hour power reserve.
Functions: hours, minutes; tourbillon.
Case: 18K pink gold; Ø 41.5mm; water resistant to 10atm.
Dial: skeletonized.
Strap: khaki stingray.
Note: personalized upon request.

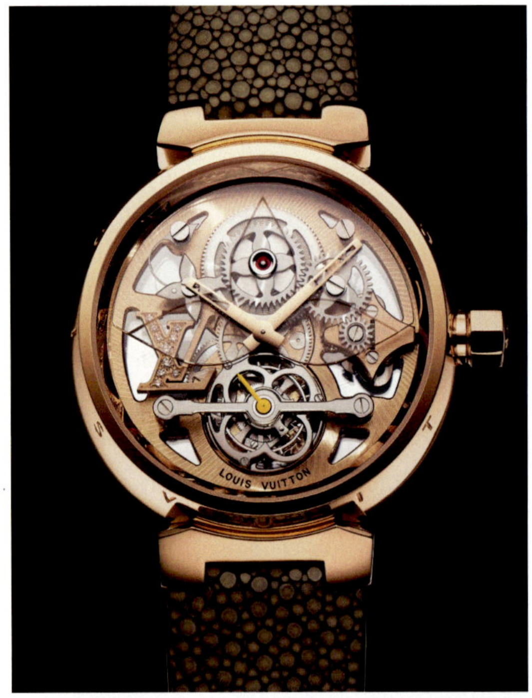

TAMBOUR SPIN TIME DIAMONDS

Movement: automatic-winding LV96 caliber; 40-hour power reserve.
Functions: hours, minutes; spin time function: hours appear on the rotating cylinders.
Case: 18K white gold; Ø 39.5mm; horns set with diamonds; transparent caseback; water resistant to 10atm.
Dial: black and white diamond-pavé dial.
Strap: white alligator; 18K white-gold buckle.

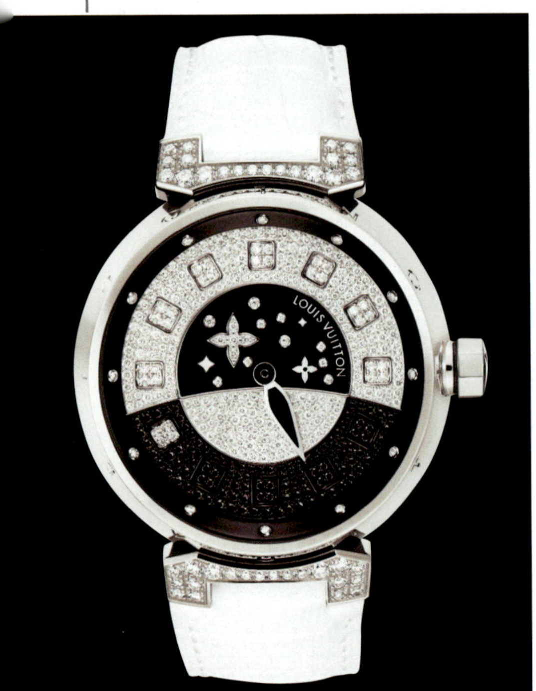

TAMBOUR LV 277 FOREVER AUTOMATIC CHRONOGRAPH

Movement: automatic-winding LV277 caliber; 50-hour power reserve.
Functions: hours, minutes, seconds; date; chronograph.
Case: 18K white gold; Ø 41.5mm; diamond-pavé case, horns and crown; transparent caseback; water resistant to 10atm.
Dial: diamond-pavé.
Strap: black alligator.

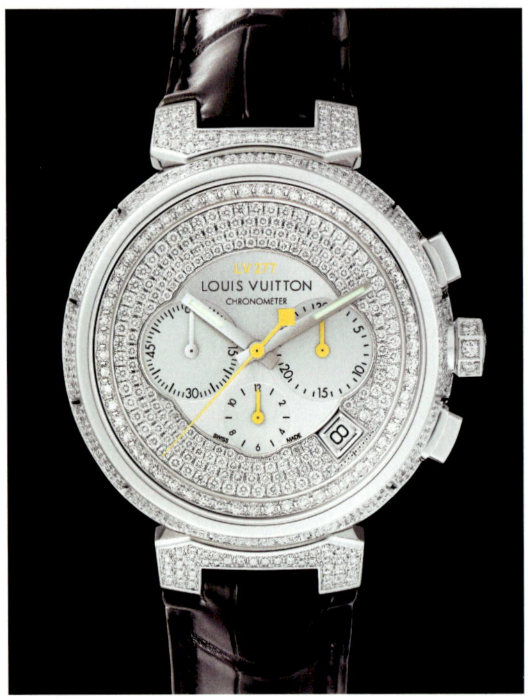

TAMBOUR LV277 AUTOMATIC CHRONOGRAPH

Movement: automatic-winding LV277 caliber; 50-hour power reserve.
Functions: hours, minutes, seconds; date; chronograph.
Case: steel; Ø 41.5mm; transparent caseback; water resistant to 10atm.
Dial: brown and black.
Strap: brown alligator.

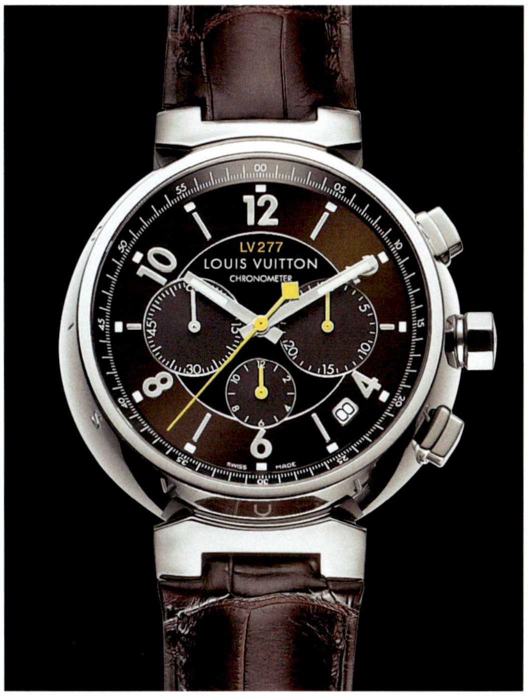

TAMBOUR ORIENTATION AUTOMATIC

Movement: automatic-winding LV122 caliber; 42-hour power reserve.
Functions: hours, minutes, seconds; date; orientation function: north direction indication; sunstone indicating the solar time.
Case: steel; Ø 44mm; transparent caseback; water resistant to 10atm.
Dial: brown and black engraved dial; Tahitian mother-of-pearl counters.
Strap: brown alligator.

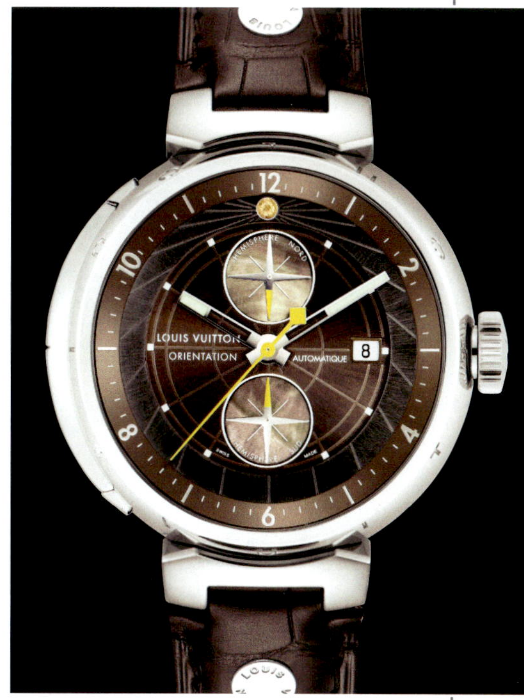

TAMBOUR AUTOMATIC CHRONOGRAPH

Movement: automatic-winding ETA 2894.2; 42-hour power reserve.
Functions: hours, minutes, seconds; chronograph.
Case: steel; Ø 41.5mm; water resistant to 10atm.
Dial: brown.
Strap: brown alligator.

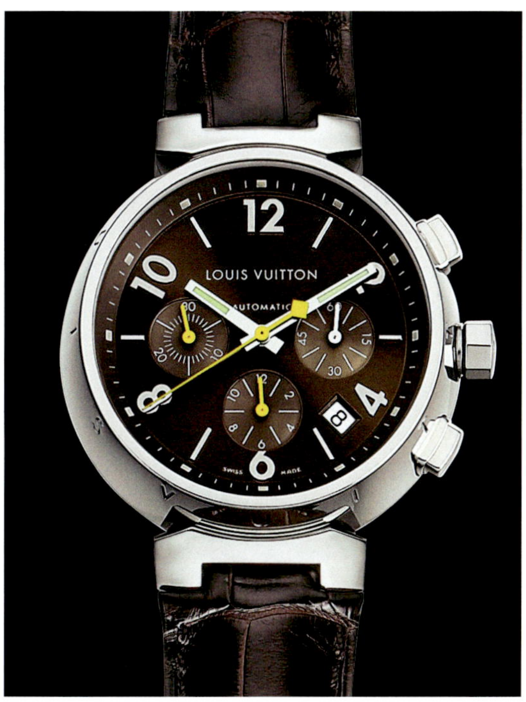

TAMBOUR AUTOMATIC GMT - YELLOW GOLD

Movement: automatic-winding ETA 2893.2; 42-hour power reserve.
Functions: hours, minutes, seconds; GMT: two time zones.
Case: 18K yellow gold; Ø 41.5mm; water resistant to 10atm.
Dial: two-tone brown and black; Monogram tapestry in the center.
Strap: brown alligator; 18K yellow-gold buckle.

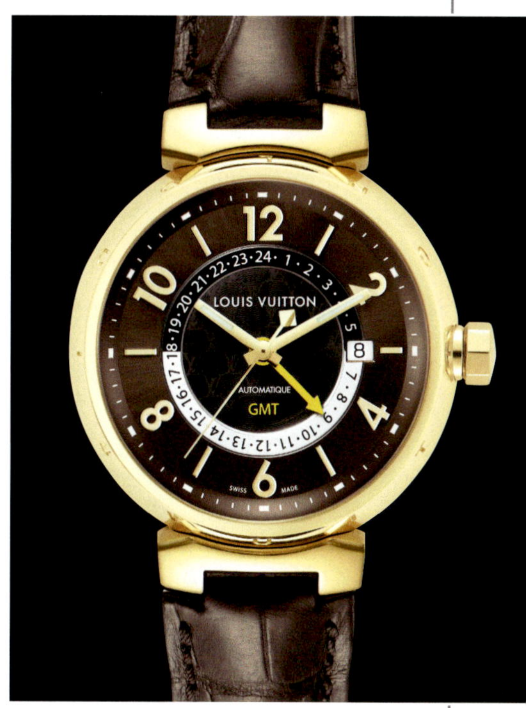

TAMBOUR IN BLACK LV277 AUTOMATIC CHRONOGRAPH

Movement: automatic-winding LV277 caliber; 50-hour power reserve.
Functions: hours, minutes, seconds; date; chronograph.
Case: Black Force steel and pink gold; Ø 44mm; transparent caseback; water resistant to 10atm.
Dial: black.
Strap: black Damier rubber.

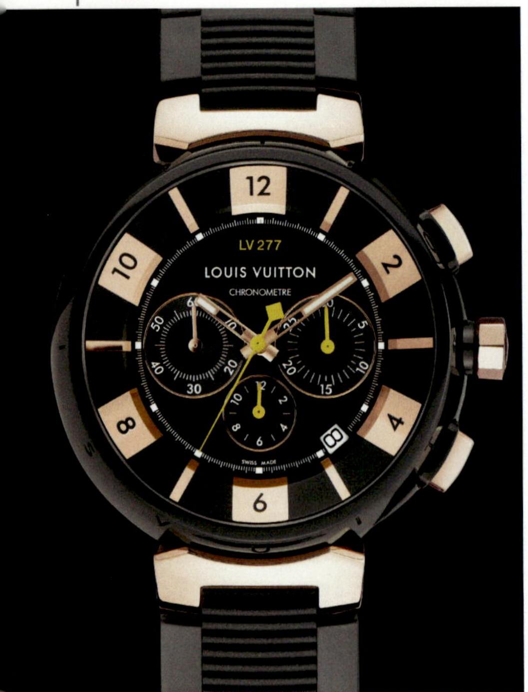

TAMBOUR DIVING II GREY

Movement: automatic-winding ETA 2895.2; 42-hour power reserve.
Functions: hours, minutes; small seconds; diving function: unidirectional turning bezel to measure diving time.
Case: steel; Ø 44mm; water resistant to 30atm.
Dial: grey; sunray effect.
Strap: black rubber.

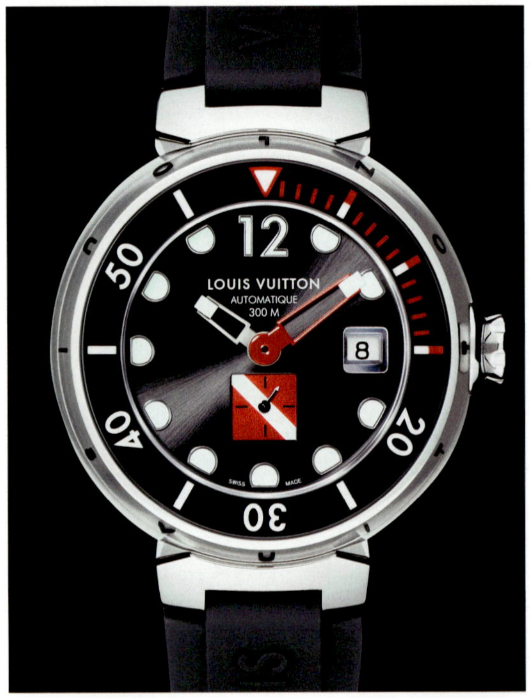

TAMBOUR IN BLACK DIAMONDS

Movement: quartz ETA 955.402.
Functions: hours, minutes, seconds.
Case: Black Force steel; Ø 39.5mm; case and horns set with diamonds; water resistant to 10atm.
Dial: black; diamond-pavé indexes.
Strap: black Monogram rubber.

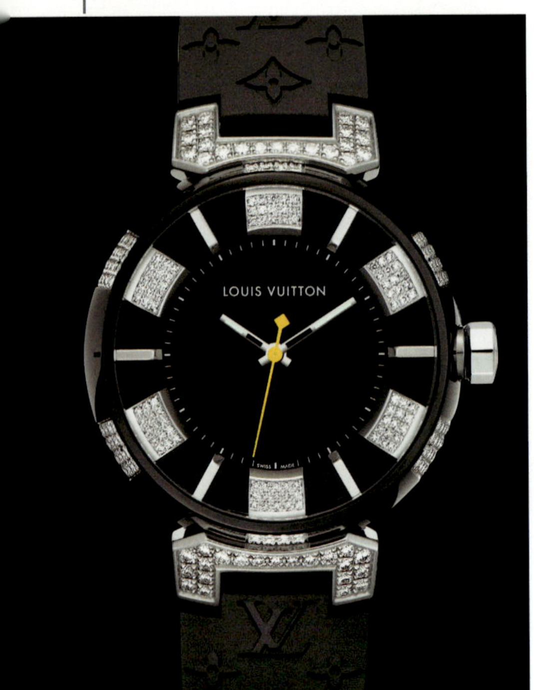

TAMBOUR REGATTA NAVY AUTOMATIC CHRONOGRAPH

Movement: automatic-winding LV171 caliber (Dubois-Dépraz manufacture); 42-hour power reserve.
Functions: hours, minutes; chronograph; countdown; flyback.
Case: steel; Ø 44mm; water resistant to 10atm.
Dial: blue.
Strap: black sewn rubber.

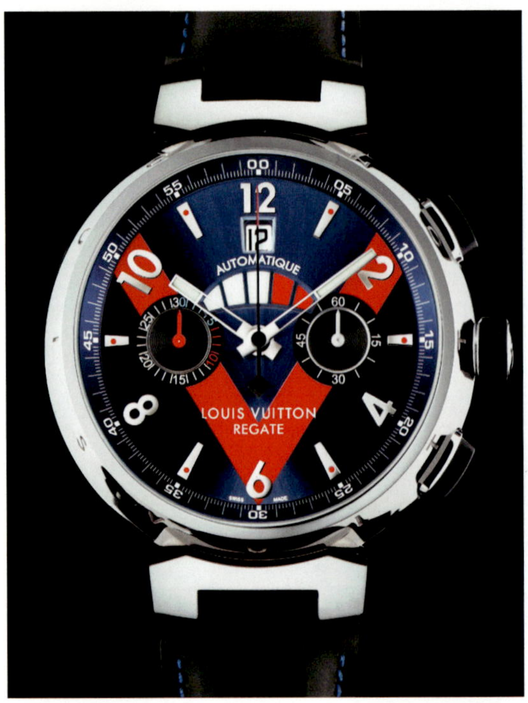

TAMBOUR LOVELY CUP DIAMONDS

Movement: quartz ETA 251.272.
Functions: hours, minutes; small seconds; chronograph.
Case: steel; Ø 39.5mm; diamond-pavé horns; water resistant to 10atm.
Dial: black; diamond indexes.
Strap: black Monogram rubber.

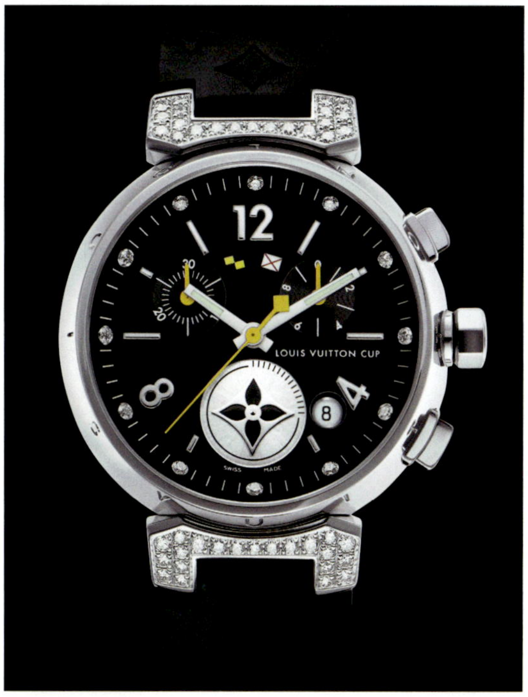

TAMBOUR DISC DIAMONDS

Movement: quartz ETA 955.432.
Functions: hours, minutes.
Case: steel; Ø 34mm; diamond-pavé horns; water resistant to 10atm.
Dial: diamond-pavé Amarante dial and indexes; Monogram pattern visible throughout the lacquer.
Strap: Amarante Monogram vernis leather.

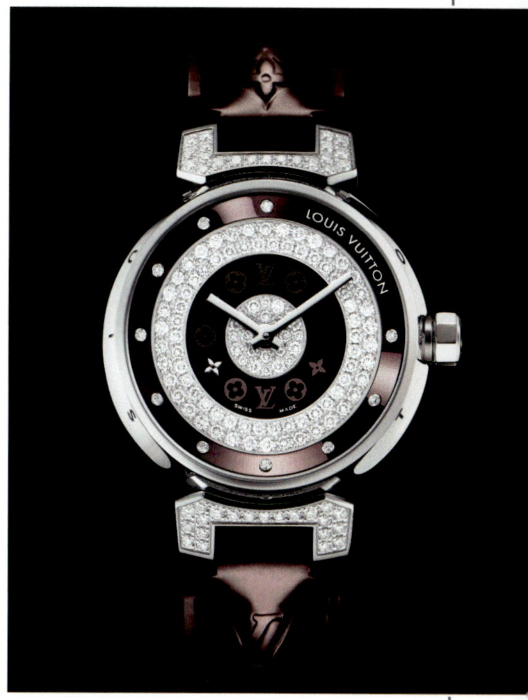

TAMBOUR LOVELY CUP

Movement: quartz ETA 251.471.
Functions: hours, minutes; small seconds; chronograph.
Case: steel; Ø 34mm; water resistant to 10atm.
Dial: white mother-of-pearl.
Strap: white Monogram rubber.

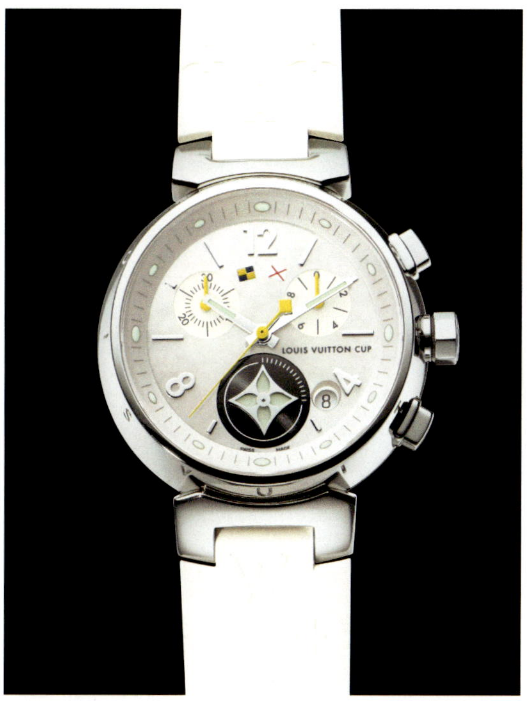

TAMBOUR BLUSH

Movement: quartz ETA 255.461.
Functions: hours, minutes, seconds; date.
Case: steel; Ø 34mm; water resistant to 10atm.
Dial: pink Blush.
Strap: pink alligator.

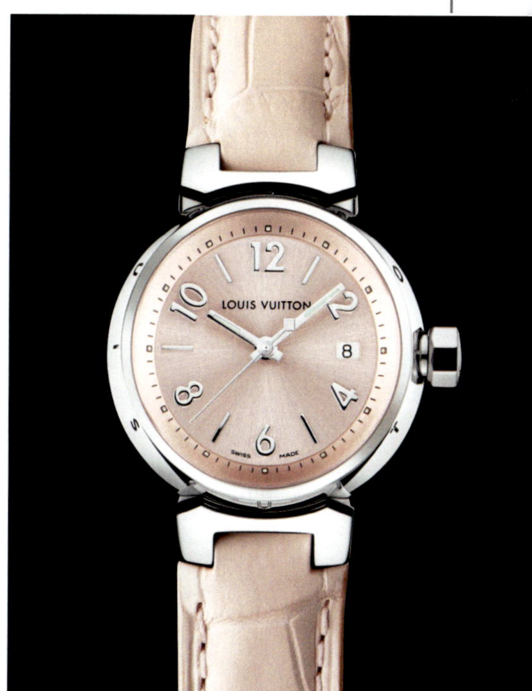

MONT BLANC

TRANSFORMATIVE DESIGN

How long does it take to upend centuries of Swiss watchmaking tradition by transforming what has come before into something utterly new? For Montblanc, the answer is 15 seconds.

That is the approximate time it takes the Montblanc Metamorphosis to physically change its dial from one that displays the time using regulator-style hours and retrograde minutes into one dedicated exclusively to the chronograph function.

Undoubtedly, the transformation needs to be seen to fully appreciate the technical complexity at work here, but imagine the hour display at 12 o'clock as curtains that part and disappear to reveal the chronograph's hour counter. A similar process unfolds at 6 o'clock, where the date display splits to uncover the chronograph's minute counter, which then rises up like a dais.

This unprecedented design is the result of a vision shared by watch specialists Johnny Girardin and Franck Orny. They realized the concept behind the Metamorphosis working with Montblanc through the company's new TimeWriter program, which fosters young talent by helping select individuals develop and introduce their ambitious projects.

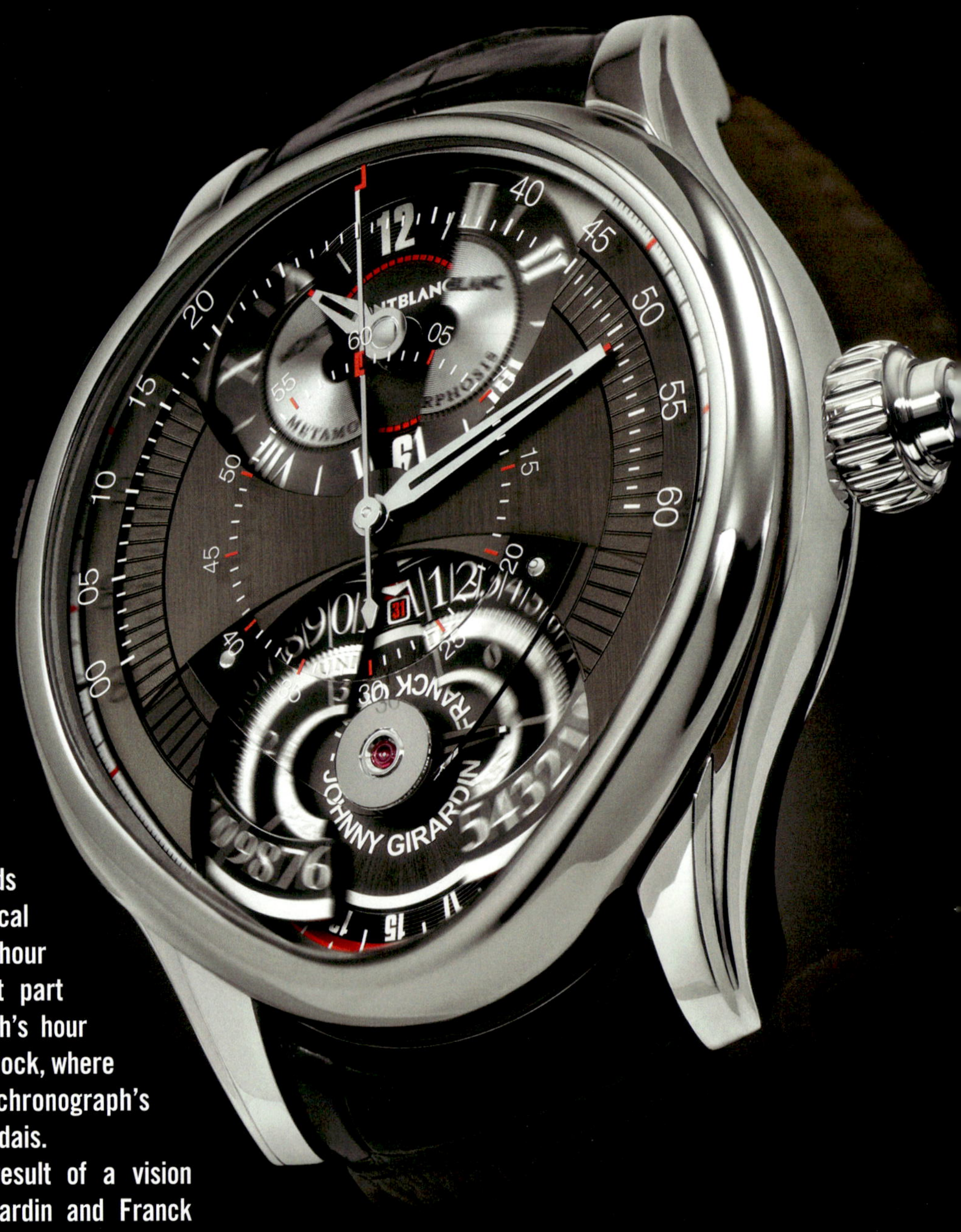

This extraordinary masterpiece is the first of its kind. The Metamorphosis is the first watch to have two different faces with completely different functions. Push the slide on the left-hand side and the transformation begins, from a watch displaying time and date, to a chronograph. The image above shows the watch in transition.

Montblanc expands its popular TimeWalker collection with the addition of two models clad in Diamond-Like Carbon and accented with the warmth of rose gold.

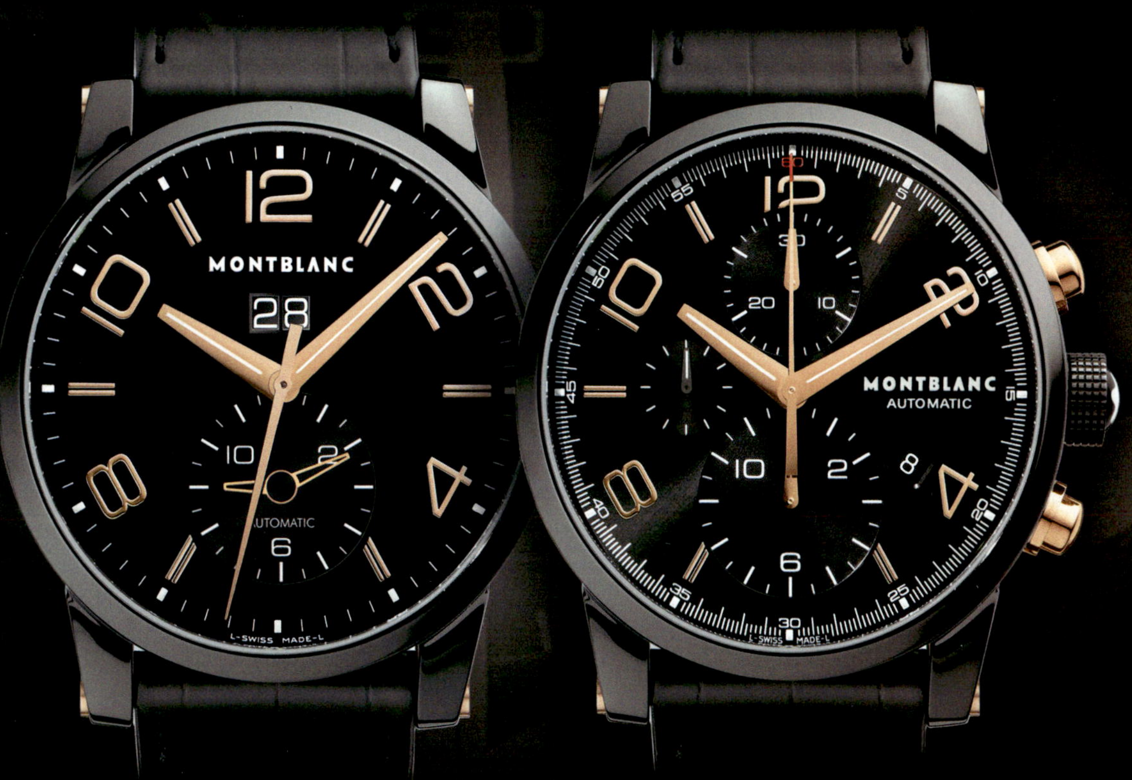

The TimeWalker Dual Carbon Dual Time indicates its second time zone function in a subsidiary dial decorated with a circular grooved texture.

Montblanc pairs rose gold with an advanced diamond-like carbon coating for its TimeWalker Dual Carbon Chronograph.

To create the Montblanc Metamorphosis, Girardin and Orny adapted their concept to Montblanc's MBM Calibre 16.29, adding 315 parts to the movement and bringing the watch's total number of components to a remarkable 567.

Presented in the teardrop-shaped case typical of the brand's Villeret 1858 collection, the Montblanc Metamorphosis is a limited edition that will be produced in an exclusive run of 28 pieces in white gold.

Montblanc's TimeWalker collection was back in black for 2010, with the addition of two models clad in Diamond-Like Carbon (DLC), a dark coating approximately 13 times harder than steel and extremely resistant to corrosion.

Its stability, coupled with its aesthetic appeal, has fueled DLC's growing popularity in case construction over the past several years. To further enhance the strength of conventional DLC, Montblanc developed a process it calls Dual Carbon that substantially increases its hardness. The brand debuts this new coating on chronograph and dual time models from its TimeWalker collection.

For the TimeWalker Dual Carbon Chronograph, Montblanc contrasts the case's lustrous DLC coating with rose-gold accents, including the chronograph's pushers and the screws that secure the wristband to the case's skeletonized lugs.

Equipped with an automatic movement capable of storing 46 hours of reserve power, the timepiece's chronograph measures intervals of up to 12 hours using the minute and hour counters positioned at the top and bottom of the dial respectively.

The TimeWalker Dual Carbon Dual Time is the second timepiece to feature Montblanc's proprietary DLC coating. As with the aforementioned chronograph, rose gold provides warm accents to the dial in the form of hands, indexes and Arabic numerals.

The large date and second time zone displays play prominent roles on the watch's smooth black dial, where their offset arrangement adds a nice visual balance. By using a secondary chapter ring for the second time zone, Montblanc provides a highly legible alternative to other dual time watches that relegate the function to a centrally fixed hour hand.

These latest flourishes to the Montblanc collection extend the hot streak of innovation maintained by the company's Le Locle workshops over the past several years.

VILLERET 1858 GRAND EXOTOURBILLON CHRONOGRAPHE REF. 106164

Movement: manual-winding MBM 16.60 caliber; monopusher chronograph with tourbillon at 12; approx. 55-hour power reserve; 32 jewels; 18,000 vph (2.5 Hz).
Functions: hours, minutes, seconds; chronograph minutes and seconds; home time; tourbillon; day/night indication.
Case: 18K white gold; Ø 47mm, thickness: 16.67mm; crown with mother-of-pearl and Montblanc logo; cambered sapphire crystal; screwed, domed, sapphire crystal caseback; hinged cuvette case with patented release mechanism; water resistant to 3atm.
Dial: 18K solid gold; ruthenium hand guilloché; 18K gold hands.
Strap: black hand-stitched alligator; 18K white-gold prong buckle.
Note: limited to 8 pieces.
Suggested price: $249,600
Also available: 18K red gold; limited to 8 pieces (ref.106165, $236,100).

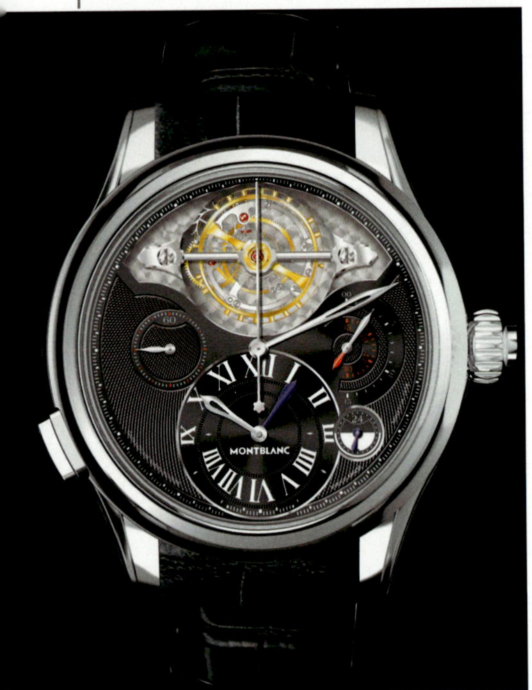

VILLERET 1858 VINTAGE CHRONOGRAPHE COLIMACON REF. 106167

Movement: manual-winding MBM 16.29 caliber; monopusher chronograph; approx. 55-hour power reserve; 22 jewels; 18,000 vph (2.5 Hz); telemeter and tachometer scale.
Functions: hours, minutes, seconds; chronograph minutes and seconds.
Case: 18K red gold; Ø 43.5mm; crown with mother-of-pearl and Montblanc logo; cambered sapphire crystal; screwed sapphire crystal caseback; water resistant to 3atm.
Dial: 18K gold; Grand Feu enamel.
Strap: brown hand-stitched alligator; 18K red-gold prong buckle.
Note: limited to 58 pieces.
Suggested price: $49,900
Also available: 18K white gold; limited to 58 pieces (ref.106166, $52,600).

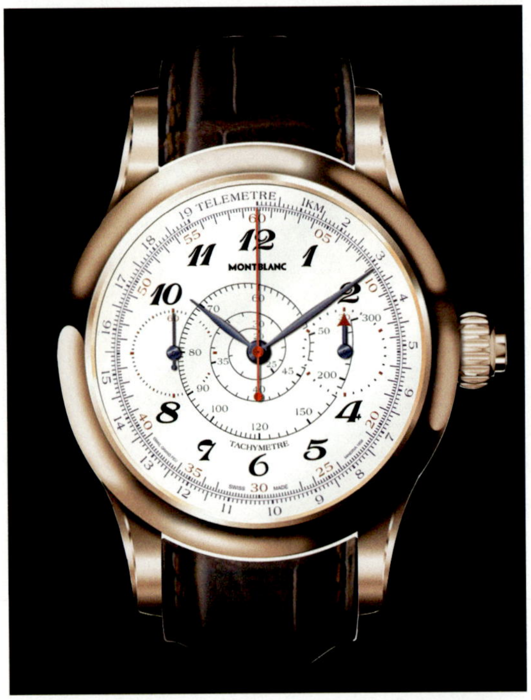

VILLERET 1858 GRAND CHRONOGRAPHE METAMORPHOSIS REF. 106168

Movement: manual-winding MBM 16.29 caliber; monopusher chronograph; approx. 55-hour power reserve; 67 jewels; 18,000 vph (2.5 Hz).
Functions: hours, retrograde minutes, seconds; date; chronograph.
Case: 18K white gold; Ø 47mm, thickness: 14.8mm; crown with mother-of-pearl and Montblanc logo; cambered sapphire crystal; sapphire crystal caseback.
Dial: titanium and stainless steel; peraluman date hand; brass hour and minute hands; steel chronograph elapsed second hand.
Strap: black hand-stitched alligator; 18K white-gold prong buckle.
Note: limited to 10 pieces.
Suggested price: $297,000

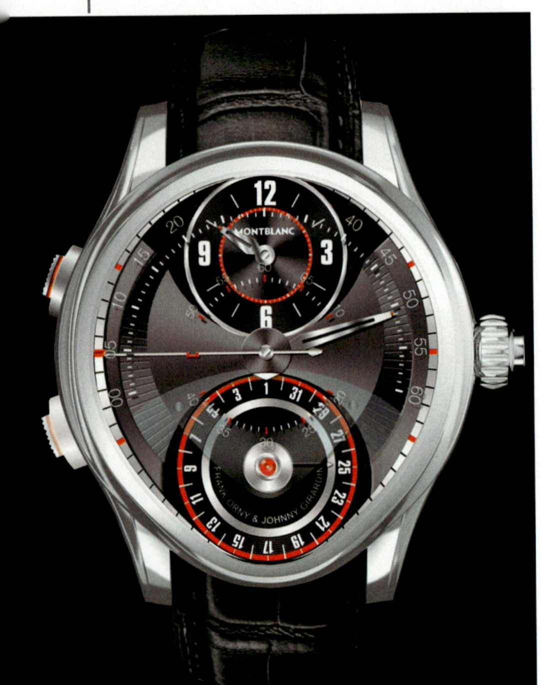

NICOLAS RIEUSSEC OPEN DATE SILICON ESCAPEMENT REF. 105920

Movement: manual-winding MB R120 caliber; monopusher chronograph; column-wheel control and vertical disc clutch; Ø 31mm, thickness: 7.6mm; approx. 72-hour power reserve; 31 jewels; 28,800 vph; 259 parts; large balance wheel with screws; escape wheel and lever in silicon; flat hairspring; rhodium-plated and circular-grained plates; rhodium-plated bridges with Côtes de Genéve; wheel train with special toothing.
Functions: off-center hours, minutes; date; power reserve display on caseback; 30-minute and 60-second counters with rotating discs; date by discs.
Case: 18K red gold (124g); Ø 43mm, thickness: 14.8mm; fixed bezel; 18K red-gold crown with mother-of-pearl and Montblanc logo, non-screw crown with one O-ring; domed sapphire crystal with double antireflective coating; sapphire crystal caseback; water resistant to 3atm.
Dial: silver-colored; black numerals on appliqué hour circle; blue feuille and baton hands; 22/20mm distance between horns and clasp.
Strap: brown hand-stitched alligator; 18K red-gold double-folding clasp.
Note: limited to 50 pieces.
Suggested price: $37,800

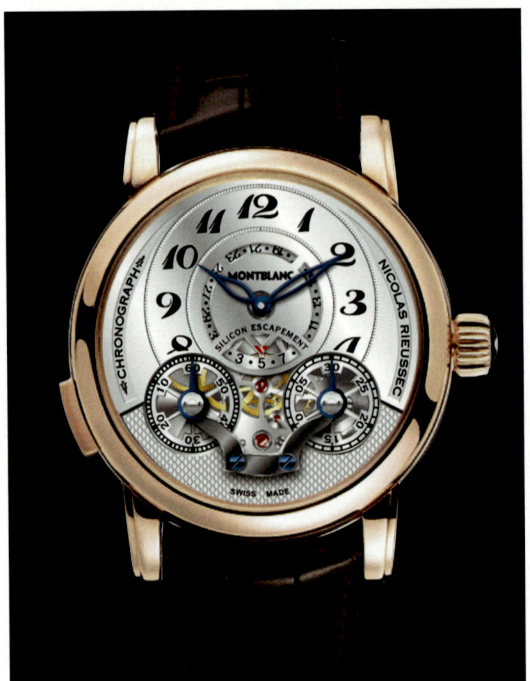

NICOLAS RIEUSSEC MONOPUSHER CHRONOGRAPH AUTOMATIC REF. 104273

Movement: automatic-winding MB R200 caliber; monopusher chronograph; approx. 72-hour power reserve; 40 jewels; 28,800 vph.
Functions: off-center hours and minutes; home time; chronograph: 30-minute and 60-second counters with turning discs; date display.
Case: stainless steel; Ø 43mm, thickness: 14.8mm; fixed bezel; non-screw crown with one O-ring; domed sapphire crystal with double antireflective coating; sapphire crystal caseback.
Dial: silver-colored; black numerals on appliqué hour circle; feuille and baton hands; 22/20mm distance between horns and clasp; water resistant to 3atm.
Strap: brown alligator; double-folding clasp.
Suggested price: $9,200
Also available: 18K white gold, set with 144 Top Wesselton diamonds (1.656 carats) with black alligator strap (ref. 104707, $43,200); 18K red gold, beige dial with brown alligator strap (ref. 104271, $30,350).

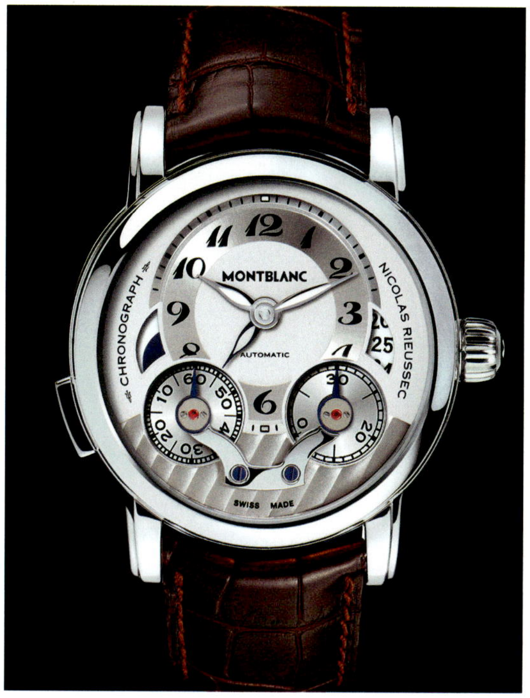

STAR 4810 CHRONOGRAPH AUTOMATIC REF. 105856

Movement: automatic-winding MB 4810/501 caliber; approx. 46-hour power reserve; 25 jewels; 28,800 vph.
Functions: hours, minutes; sweep seconds; date; chronograph: 12-hour and 30-minute counters; central chronograph hand.
Case: stainless steel; Ø 44mm, thickness: 14.5mm; fixed bezel; non-screw crown with one O-ring; domed sapphire crystal with double antireflective coating; sapphire crystal caseback; water resistant to 3atm.
Dial: silver-colored guilloché; red-gold-plated indexes; red-gold-plated regate and baton luminescent hands; 22/20mm distance between horns and clasp.
Strap: black alligator; triple-folding clasp.
Suggested price: $3,825

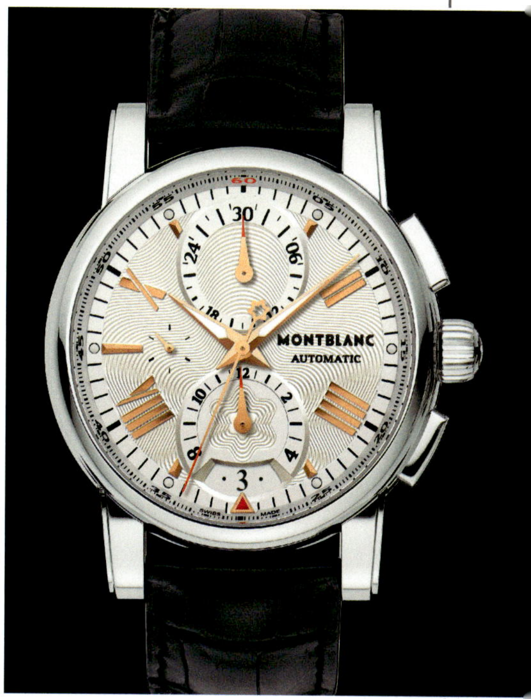

STAR 4810 AUTOMATIC REF. 105858

Movement: automatic-winding MB 4810/401 caliber; approx. 42-hour power reserve; 21 jewels; 28,800 vph.
Functions: hours, minutes; sweep seconds; date.
Case: stainless steel; Ø 41.5mm, thickness: 11.6mm; fixed bezel; non-screw crown with one O-ring; domed sapphire crystal with double antireflective coating; sapphire crystal caseback; water resistant to 3atm.
Dial: silver-colored guilloché; red-gold-plated indexes; red-gold-plated regate and baton luminescent hands; 21/20mm distance between horns and clasp.
Strap: black alligator; triple-folding clasp.
Suggested price: $2,360

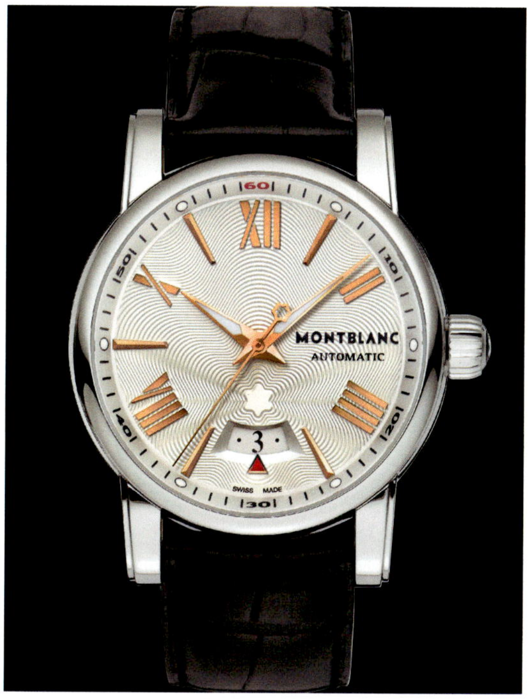

STAR DATE AUTOMATIC REF. 105896

Movement: automatic-winding MB 4810/401 caliber; approx. 42-hour power reserve; 21 jewels; 28,800 vph.
Functions: hours, minutes, seconds; date.
Case: stainless steel; Ø 39mm, thickness: 9mm; fixed bezel; non-screw crown with one O-ring; domed sapphire crystal with double antireflective coating; sapphire crystal caseback fixed with six screws; water resistant to 3atm.
Dial: silver guilloché; red-gold-plated indexes and numerals; red-gold-plated feuille and baton hands; 19/17mm distance between horns and clasp.
Strap: brown alligator; triple-folding clasp.
Suggested price: $2,160
Also available: black guilloché dial with black alligator strap (ref. 105895, $2,160); silver-colored guilloché dial with stainless steel bracelet (ref. 105961, $2,375).

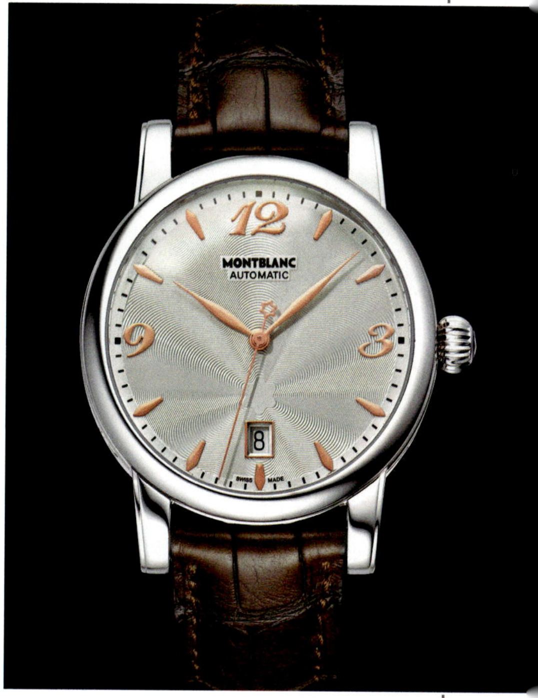

SPORT DLC CHRONOGRAPH AUTOMATIC REF. 104279

Movement: automatic-winding MB 4810/501 caliber; approx. 46-hour power reserve; 25 jewels; 28,800 vph.
Functions: hours, minutes; sweep seconds; date display with magnifying glass; chronograph: 12-hour and 30-minute counters, central chronograph hand.
Case: black DLC-coated stainless steel; Ø 44mm, thickness: 14.9mm; unidirectional turning bezel; screw-down crown with two O-rings; flat sapphire crystal with antireflective coating; screwed black DLC-coated stainless steel caseback; water resistant to 20atm.
Dial: black; luminescent indexes; black luminescent hands; 22/20mm distance between horns and clasp.
Strap: black alligator; triple-folding clasp.
Suggested price: $5,350

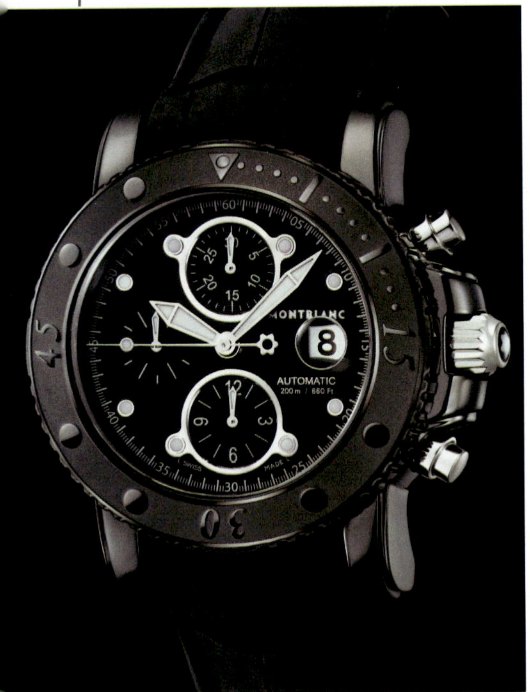

TIMEWALKER CHRONOGRAPH AUTOMATIC – U.S. SPECIAL EDITION REF. 106582

Movement: automatic-winding MB 4810/502 caliber chronograph; 46-hour power reserve; 27 jewels; 28,800 vph.
Functions: hours, minutes; continuous second; date; chronograph: 12-hour, 30-minute counters, central chronograph hand.
Case: stainless steel; Ø 43mm, thickness: 14.3mm; non-screw crown with one O-ring; domed sapphire crystal with antireflective coating; sapphire crystal caseback; water resistant to 3atm.
Dial: black; red-gold-plated luminescent hands; 22/20mm distance between horns and clasp.
Strap: black calfskin with stitching; stainless steel pin buckle.
Suggested price: $3,600
Also available: silver-colored matte dial with brown calfskin strap(ref.106592, $3,600).

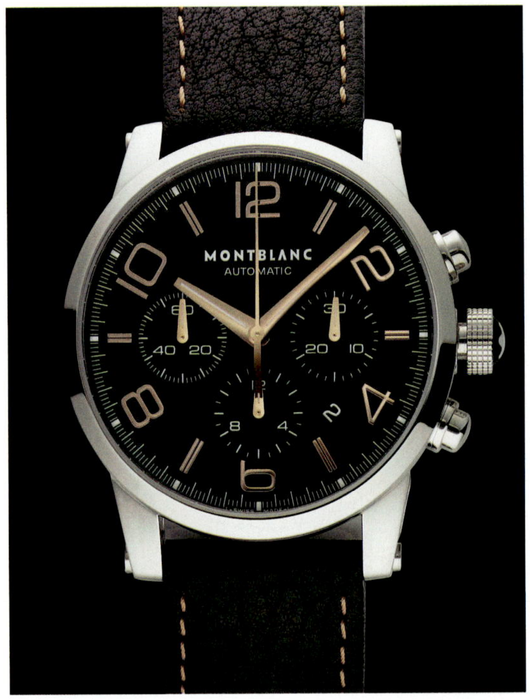

TIMEWALKER DUAL CARBON CHRONOGRAPH AUTOMATIC REF. 105805

Movement: automatic-winding MB 4810/502 caliber; approx. 46-hour power reserve; 27 jewels; 28,800 vph.
Functions: hours, minutes; sweep seconds; date; chronograph: 12-hour and 30-minute counters, central chronograph hand.
Case: black DLC-coated stainless steel; Ø 43mm, thickness: 14.4mm; non-screw crown with one O-ring; 18K red-gold pushers; domed sapphire crystal with double antireflective coating; sapphire crystal caseback; water resistant to 3atm.
Dial: black; red-gold-plated hands and numerals; luminescent hands and indexes; 22/20mm distance between horns and clasp.
Strap: black alligator with stitching; black DLC-coated stainless steel pin buckle.
Suggested price: $6,400

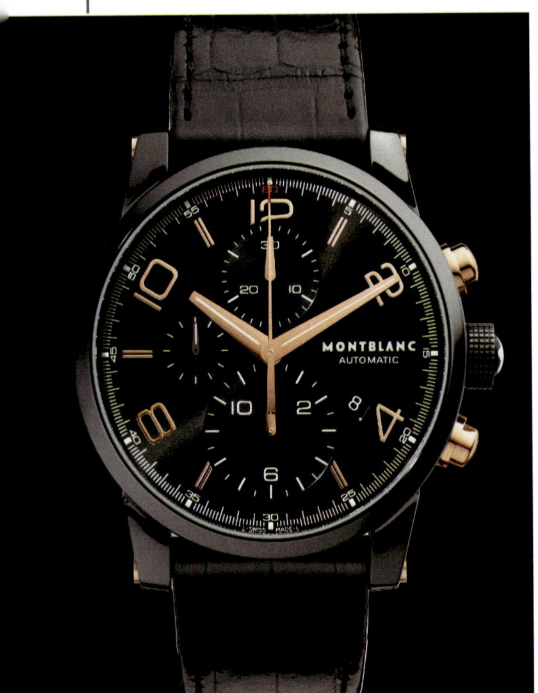

TIMEWALKER DUAL CARBON DUAL TIME AUTOMATIC REF. 106066

Movement: automatic-winding MB 4810/911 caliber; approx. 42-hour power reserve; 21 jewels; 28,800 vph.
Functions: hours, minutes, seconds; date; second time zone.
Case: black DLC-coated stainless steel; Ø 42mm, thickness: 12mm; non-screw crown with one O-ring and Montblanc logo in mother-of-pearl; domed sapphire crystal with double antireflective coating; sapphire crystal caseback; water resistant to 3atm.
Dial: black; red-gold-plated hands and numerals; luminescent hands and indexes; 22/20mm distance between horns and clasp.
Strap: black alligator with stitching; black DLC-coated stainless steel pin buckle.
Suggested price: $5,900

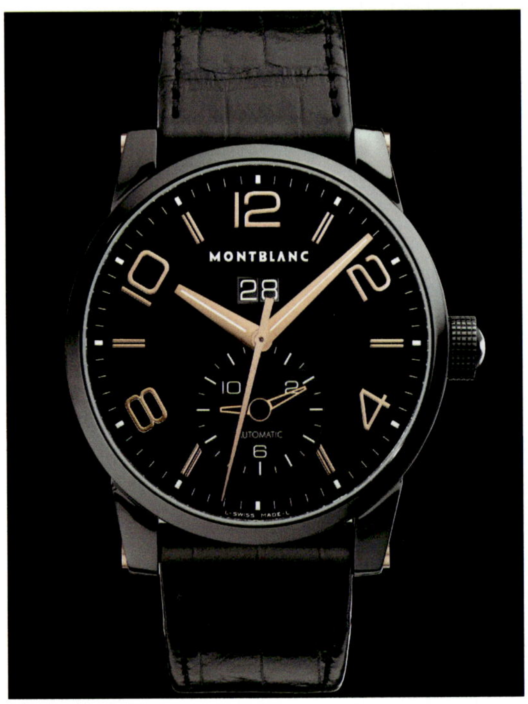

TIMEWALKER AUTOMATIC REF. 105962

Movement: automatic-winding MB 4810/409 caliber; approx. 42-hour power reserve; 25 jewels; 28,800 vph.
Functions: hours, minutes, seconds; date.
Case: stainless steel; Ø 39mm, thickness: 10.4mm; non-screw crown with one O-ring; domed sapphire crystal with double antireflective coating; screwed stainless steel caseback; water resistant to 3atm.
Dial: black; rhodium-plated hands and indexes; 20/18mm distance between horns and clasp.
Bracelet: stainless steel; triple-folding clasp.
Suggested price: $2,860
Also available: silver matte dial with black alligator strap (ref. 105813, $2,590); black dial with black alligator strap (ref. 105812, $2,590).

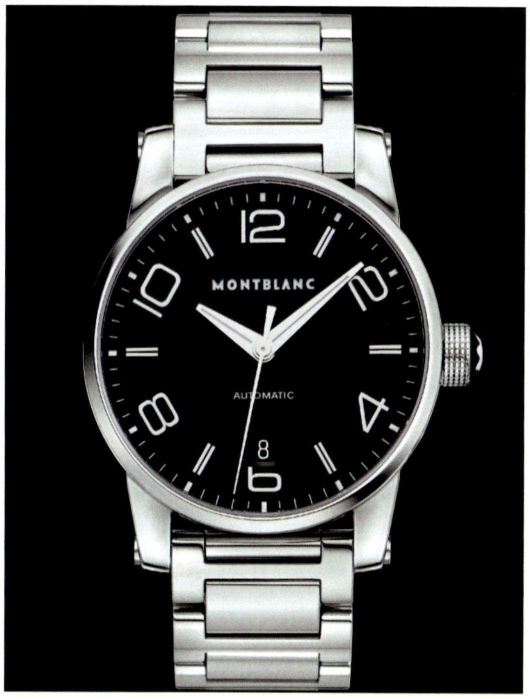

STAR DATE AUTOMATIC REF. 105893

Movement: quartz MB 4810/101 caliber; battery: 395/1.5V; 7 jewels.
Functions: hours, minutes, seconds; date; battery end-of-life indicator.
Case: stainless steel; Ø 39mm, thickness: 9mm; fixed bezel; non-screw crown with one O-ring; domed sapphire crystal with antireflective coating; stainless steel caseback; water resistant to 3atm.
Dial: black lacquer; silver-colored indexes and numerals; rhodium-plated feuille and baton hands; 19/17mm distance between horns and clasp.
Strap: black calfskin; stainless steel pin buckle.
Suggested price: $1,335
Also available: silver lacquer dial with brown calfskin strap (ref. 105894, $1,335); black lacquer dial with stainless steel bracelet (ref. 105913, $1,740).

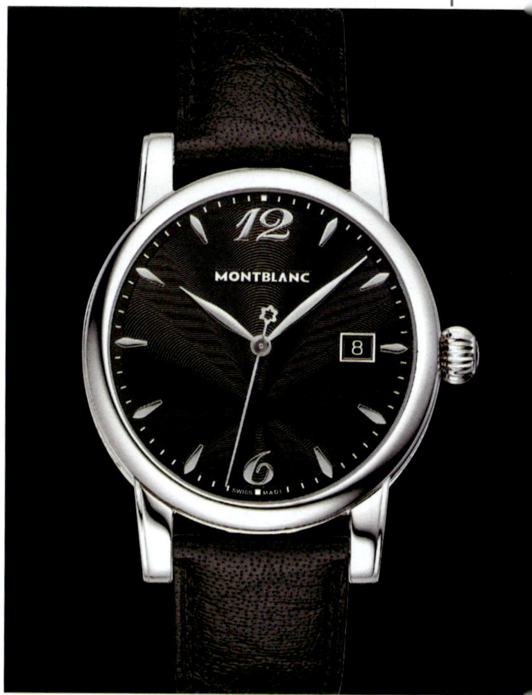

STAR MAGIE D'ETOILES REF. 105898

Movement: quartz MB 4810/103 caliber; battery: 397/1.5V; 7 jewels.
Functions: hours, minutes, seconds; date; battery end-of-life indicator.
Case: 18K white gold (68.4g); set with 20 Top Wesselton diamonds (0.15 carat); Ø 36mm, thickness: 11.6mm; non-screw crown with one O-ring, 18K white gold with Montblanc diamond (0.055 carat); domed sapphire crystal with double antireflective coating; 18K white-gold caseback.
Dial: black mother-of-pearl; set with 34 Top Wesselton VVS diamonds (0.064 carat); flange set with 80 Top Wesselton diamonds (0.17 carat); rhodium-plated feuille and baton hands; 19/17mm distance between horns and clasp.
Strap: black satin strap; 18K white-gold pin buckle.
Note: limited to 10 pieces.
Suggested price: $27,000
Also available: white mother-of-pearl dial with white satin strap; limited to 15 pieces (ref. 105897, $27,000).

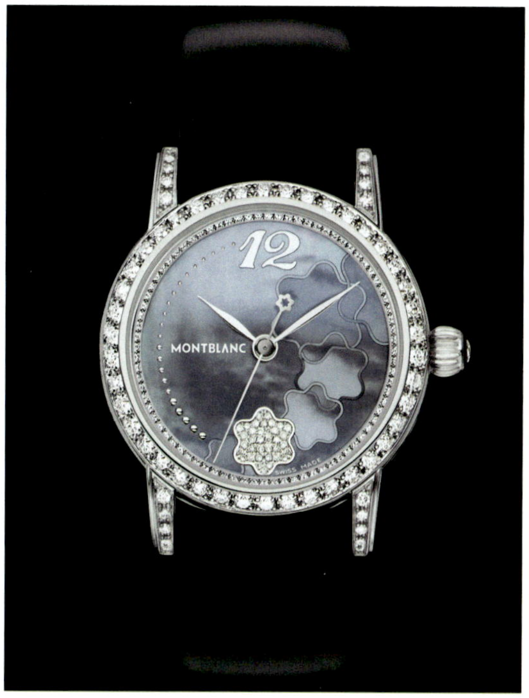

PROFILE LADY ELEGANCE REF. 104288

Movement: quartz MB 4810/110 caliber; battery: 317/1.5V; 5 jewels.
Functions: hours, minutes.
Case: 18K red gold (38.4g); set with 29 Top Wesselton VVS Diamonds (0.14 carat); 23x35mm, thickness: 8.3mm; non-screw crown with one O-ring; domed sapphire crystal with antireflective coating; 18K red-gold caseback; water resistant to 3atm.
Dial: white mother-of-pearl; crossover Roman numerals in diamonds at 3, 6 and 9; seven diamonds at 12 (0.068 carat) and Montblanc diamond (0.1 carat); red-gold-plated baton hands; 18/16mm distance between horns and clasp.
Strap: white satin; 18K red-gold pin buckle.
Suggested price: $13,360
Also available: black mother-of-pearl dial with black satin strap (ref. 104289, $13,360).

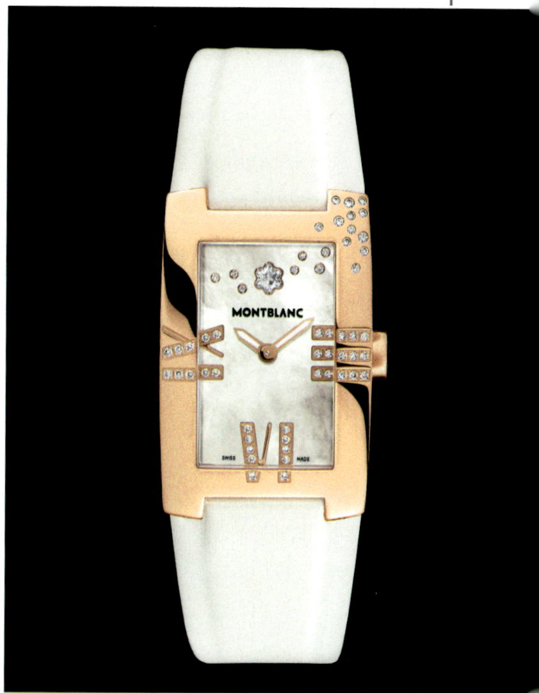

PANERAI

UNDER THE TUSCAN STARS

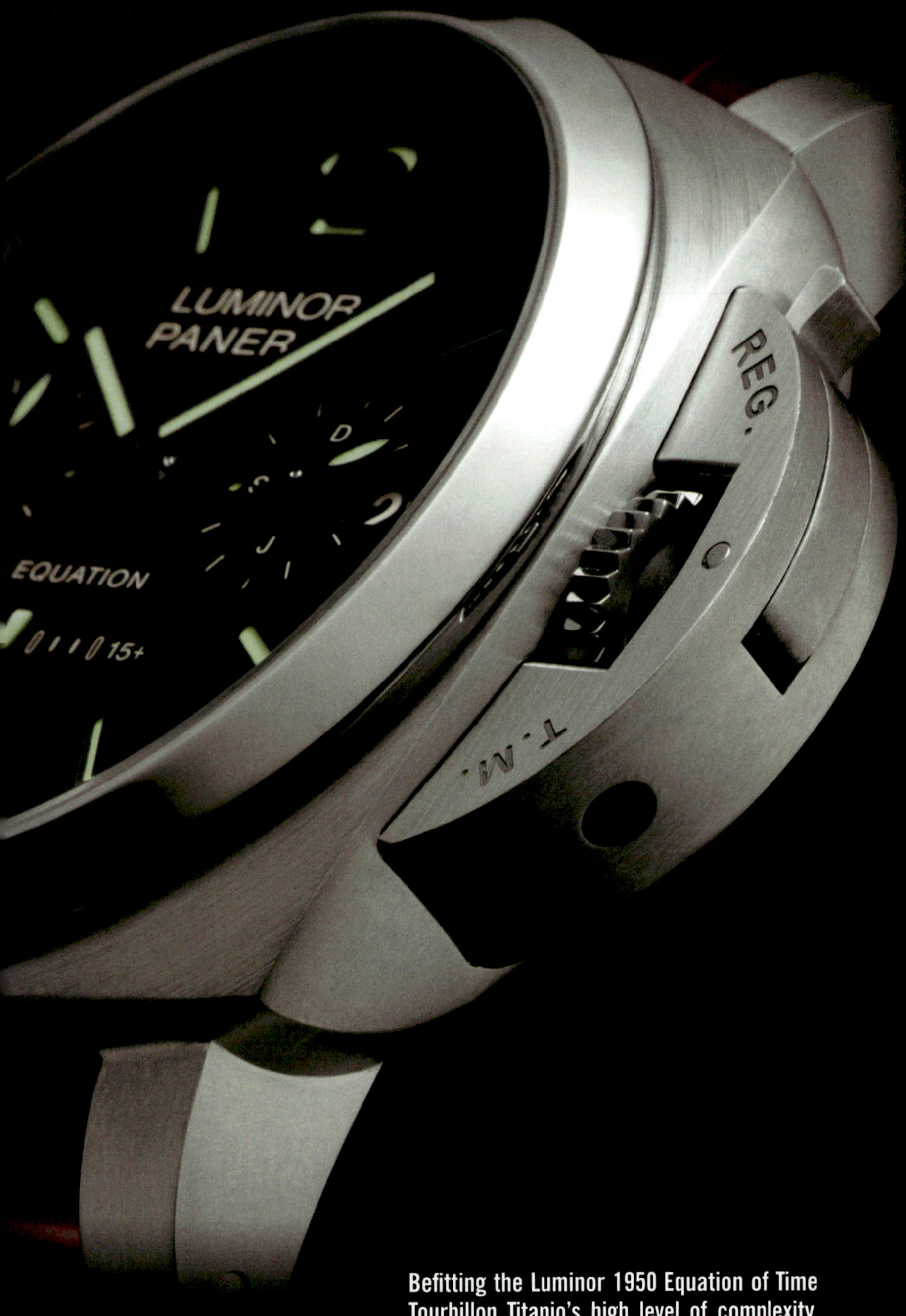

Befitting the Luminor 1950 Equation of Time Tourbillon Titanio's high level of complexity, Panerai will only produce 30 pieces in titanium or, by request, pink gold.

While living in Florence in 1610, Galileo Galilei built one of the first telescopes and within a few months revolutionized astronomy when he discovered four of the largest moons orbiting Jupiter and observed the phases of Venus.

Precisely 250 years later, not far from where Galileo lived as a boy, Giovanni Panerai founded Officine Panerai, the city's first watch workshop. Panerai introduced its most sophisticated timepiece ever in 2010 to celebrate these shared Tuscan roots and honor Galileo's contributions to both astronomy and horology—he designed an escapement for a pendulum clock shortly before his death in 1642.

The Luminor 1950 Equation of Time Tourbillon Titanio, powered by a new movement manufactured by Panerai, combines several celestial complications, including an equation of time indication, sunrise and sunset times, and an exquisitely detailed star chart.

To elevate this already impressive achievement, Panerai designed the movement so that it can be calibrated to reflect the celestial conditions for a specific city chosen by the client when the watch is purchased. This enables the watch to accurately indicate the length of the day for a particular location, which varies between +16.24 and -14.22 minutes throughout the year due to the earth's elliptical orbit and the tilt of its axis. The location also informs the star chart found on the movement side, which depicts the movement of the constellations in the ever-changing night sky above the chosen city.

Panerai celebrates its Tuscan roots with the Luminor 1950 Equation of Time Tourbillon Titanio, an ultra-complicated timepiece made to honor fellow Florence native Galileo Galilei, the father of modern science.

Along with these celestial complications, the Luminor 1950 Equation of Time Tourbillon Titanio also features a tourbillon. Patented in 1801, this mechanism is designed to counteract gravity's negative effects on a watch's escapement. Viewable from the back, the tourbillon is concealed from the front beneath the dial. The only evidence of its existence is an inconspicuous dot at 9 o'clock that spins once every 30 seconds to indicate the tourbillon's progress.

Panerai performs a tasteful horological striptease with its Radiomir Tourbillon GMT Ceramica, peeling away much of the dial to bare the inner workings of the timepiece's manufacture movement.

A fine lattice supports the luminescent hour markers and numerals, as well as the day/night indication and small seconds positioned on opposite sides of the dial. Below the watch's various indications, the mesh offers a prime view of the three barrels that, when fully wound, give the watch six days of autonomy.

The open-worked dial also highlights the technical intricacy of the tourbillon as it rotates once every 30 seconds, a rate quicker than the 60 seconds typical of a large percentage of the "whirlwind" mechanisms.

The movement is cased in zirconium oxide ceramic, a material whose hardness makes it resistant to both scratches and corrosion. To form the robust case, Panerai's workshops begin with a solid mass of black ceramic. Next, a computer-controlled milling machine shapes the block into its recognizable cushion shape. Like the original Radiomir, which was created for the Royal Italian Navy, the Radiomir Tourbillon GMT Ceramica is water resistant and certified to 100 meters (approximately 328 feet).

This skeleton design, together with the ultra-complicated Luminor 1950 Equation of Time Tourbillon Titanio, stake out opposite ends of the spectrum and show how far Panerai has come since it began creating movements in-house in 2002.

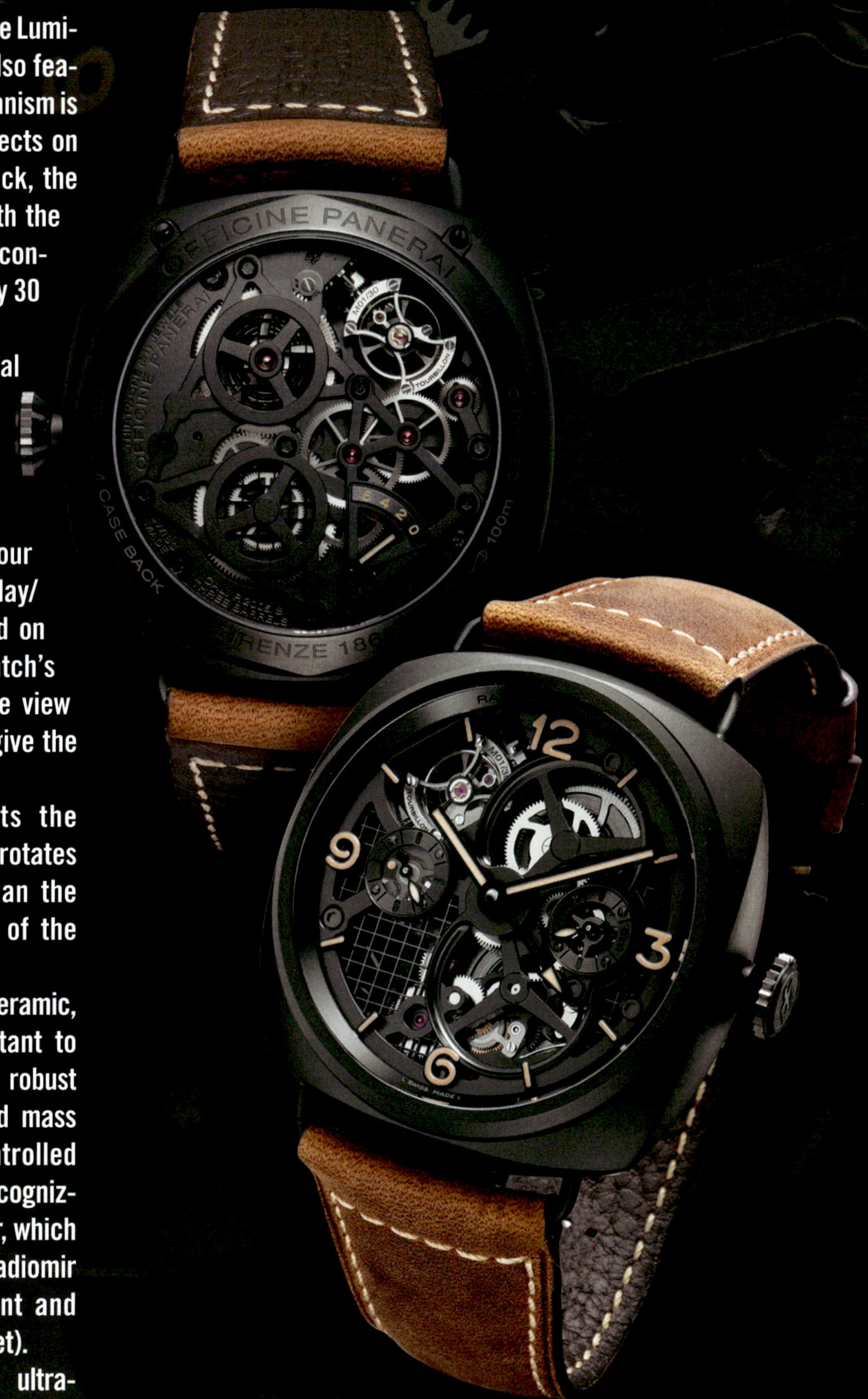

Offered in a limited edition of 30 pieces, the Radiomir Tourbillon GMT Ceramica combines a 48mm black ceramic case and an exquisite open-worked design.

LUMINOR 1950 MARINA 3 DAYS AUTOMATIC — REF. PAM00312

Movement: automatic-winding Panerai P.9000; 3-day power reserve.
Functions: hours, minutes; small seconds at 9; date at 3.
Case: brushed 316L steel; Ø 44mm; trademark crown-protection device; antireflective sapphire crystal; sapphire crystal caseback; water resistant to 300 meters.
Dial: black; sandwich-style; luminescent markers and Arabic numerals.
Strap: black PANERAI-personalized alligator leather; second strap supplied with strap-changing tool.
Suggested price: $7,400
Also available: brushed 316L steel on PANERAI-personalized steel bracelet (PAM00328, $8,600); polished 316L steel with black dial and patina-finished luminescent Arabic numerals on PANERAI-personalized black calf strap (PAM00359, $7,400); brushed and polished titanium with brown dial and PANERAI-personalized alligator strap (PAM00351, $8,000); brushed and polished titanium with brown dial on PANERAI-personalized titanium bracelet (PAM00352, $9,300).

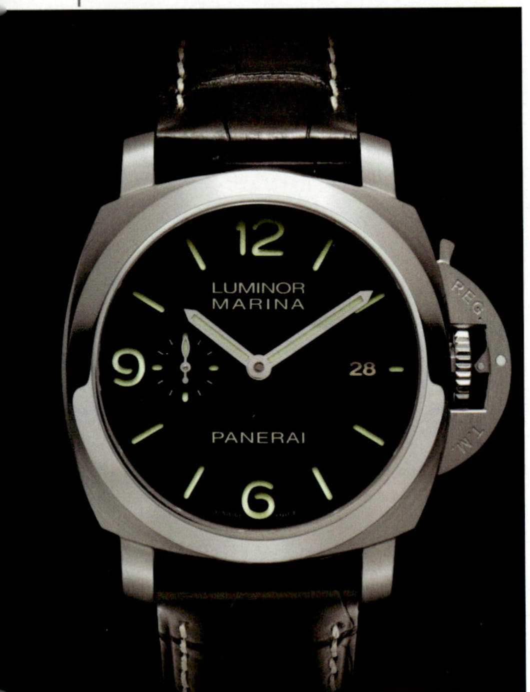

LUMINOR 1950 SUBMERSIBLE 3 DAYS AUTOMATIC — REF. PAM00305

Movement: automatic-winding Panerai P.9000; 3-day power reserve.
Functions: hours, minutes; small seconds at 9; date at 3; calculation of immersion time.
Case: brushed titanium; Ø 47mm; trademark crown-protection device; unidirectional bezel with graduated scale to calculate immersion time and ratchet click at 1-minute intervals; antireflective sapphire crystal; sapphire crystal caseback; water resistant to 300 meters.
Dial: black; applied luminescent dots and hour markers.
Strap: PANERAI-personalized rubber; second strap supplied with strap-changing tool.
Suggested price: $9,600

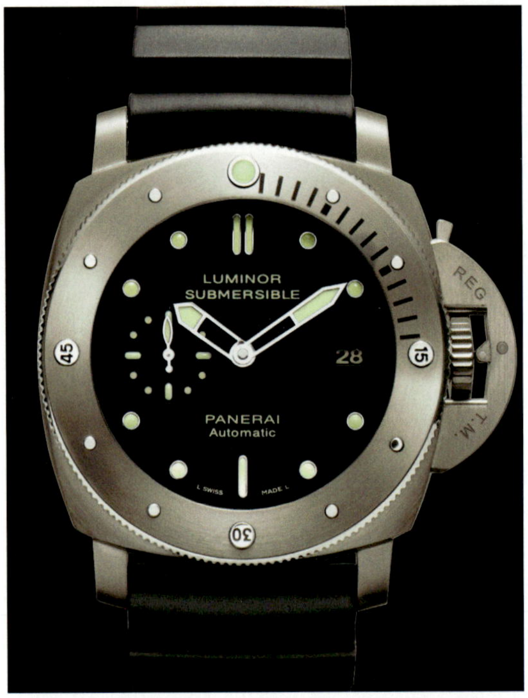

LUMINOR 1950 3 DAYS GMT AUTOMATIC — REF. PAM00329

Movement: automatic-winding Panerai P.9001; 3-day power reserve.
Functions: hours, minutes; small seconds at 9; date at 3; seconds reset; second time zone.
Case: brushed 316L steel; Ø 44mm; trademark crown-protection device; power reserve indicator on caseback; antireflective sapphire crystal; sapphire crystal caseback; water resistant to 300 meters.
Dial: black; sandwich style; luminescent markers and Arabic numerals; second time zone GMT hand.
Bracelet: PANERAI-personalized steel with bracelet removal tool.
Suggested price: $9,950
Also available: brushed 316 steel on brown PANERAI-personalized alligator leather strap (PAM00320, $8,900).

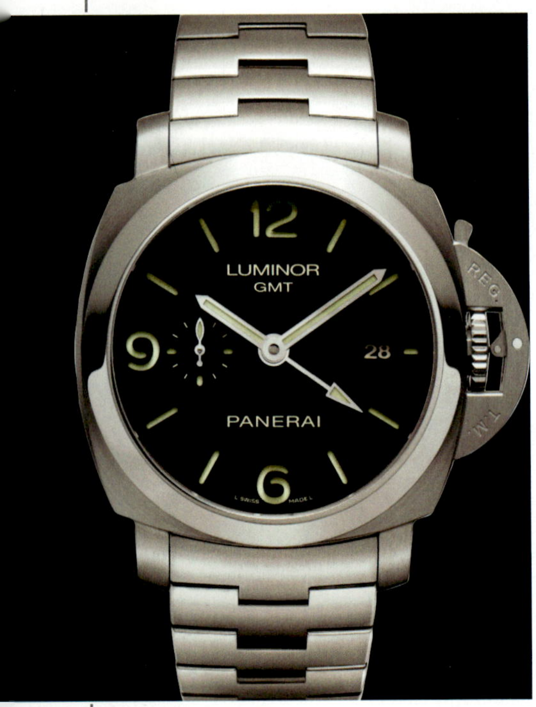

LUMINOR 1950 3 DAYS GMT POWER RESERVE AUTOMATIC — REF. PAM00321

Movement: automatic-winding Panerai P.9002; 3-day power reserve.
Functions: hours, minutes; small seconds at 9; date at 3; power reserve indicator at 4; seconds reset; second time zone.
Case: brushed and polished 316L steel; Ø 44mm; trademark crown-protection device; antireflective sapphire crystal; sapphire crystal caseback; water resistant to 300 meters.
Dial: black; sandwich style; luminescent markers and Arabic numerals; second time zone GMT hand.
Strap: black PANERAI-personalized alligator leather; second strap supplied with strap-changing tool.
Suggested price: $9,000
Also available: brushed and polished 316L steel on PANERAI-personalized steel bracelet (PAM00347, $10,100).

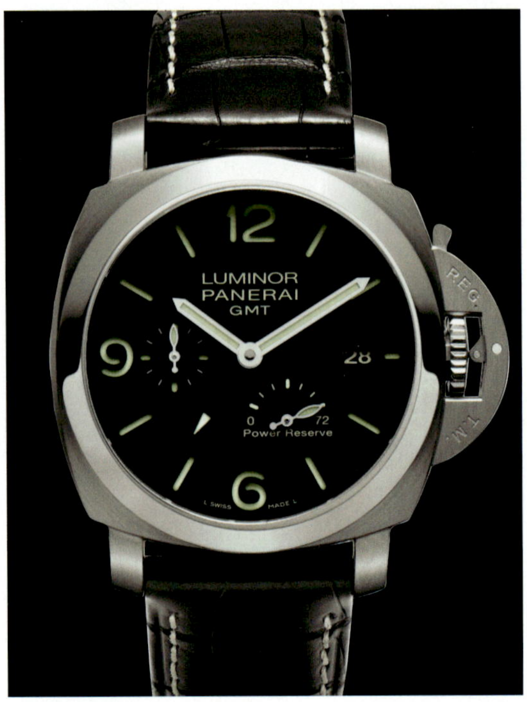

LUMINOR 1950 8 DAYS GMT — REF. PAM00233

Movement: manual-winding Panerai P.2002; 8-day power reserve; 247 components; three barrels.
Functions: hours, minutes; small seconds and 24-hour indicator at 9; date at 3; linear power reserve indicator at 6; seconds reset; second time zone.
Case: brushed 316L steel; Ø 44mm; trademark crown-protection device; antireflective sapphire crystal; sapphire crystal caseback; water resistant to 100 meters.
Dial: black; sandwich style; luminescent markers and Arabic numerals; second time zone hand.
Strap: black PANERAI-personalized vintage calf leather; second strap supplied with strap-changing tool.
Suggested price: $14,700
Also available: brushed and polished 18K rose gold on brown PANERAI-personalized alligator strap (PAM00289, $30,200).

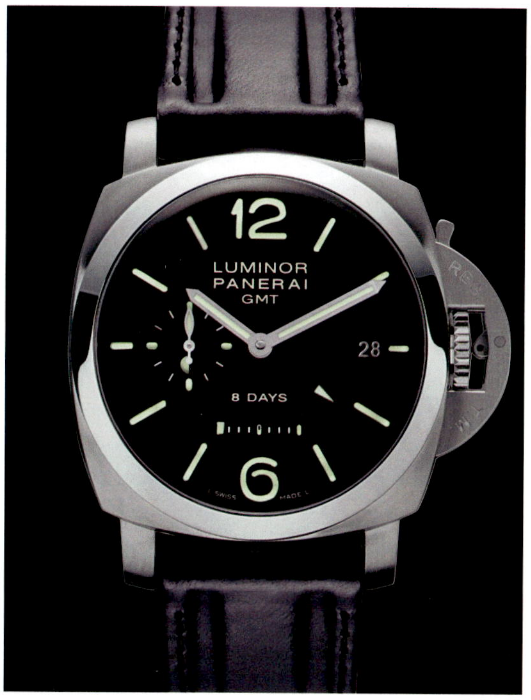

RADIOMIR 8 DAYS TITANIO — REF. PAM00346

Movement: manual-winding Panerai P.2002; 8-day power reserve; 247 components; three barrels.
Functions: hours, minutes; small seconds; date at 3; seconds reset.
Case: brushed titanium; Ø 45mm; power reserve visible through caseback; OP-personalized screw-down crown and patented removable wire loop strap attachments; antireflective sapphire crystal; sapphire crystal caseback; water resistant to 100 meters.
Dial: brown; sandwich-style; luminescent markers and Arabic numerals.
Strap: brown PANERAI-personalized alligator leather; second strap supplied with strap-changing tool.
Suggested price: $13,400
Also available: polished 316L steel with black dial featuring linear power reserve indicator on black PANERAI-personalized alligator strap (PAM00268, $11,900).

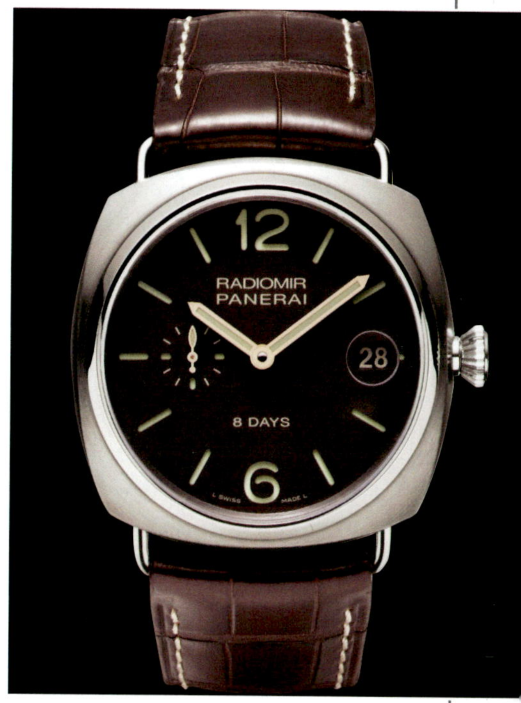

RADIOMIR 10 DAYS GMT AUTOMATIC — REF. PAM00323

Movement: automatic-winding Panerai P.2003; 10-day power reserve; 269 components; three barrels.
Functions: hours, minutes; small seconds and day/night indication at 9; date at 3; second time zone; seconds reset; circular power reserve indicator at 6.
Case: polished 316L steel; Ø 47mm; OP-personalized screw-down crown and patented wire-loop strap attachments; antireflective sapphire crystal; sapphire crystal caseback; water resistant to 100 meters.
Dial: black; sandwich style; luminescent markers and Arabic numerals.
Strap: PANERAI-personalized alligator leather.
Suggested price: $14,800

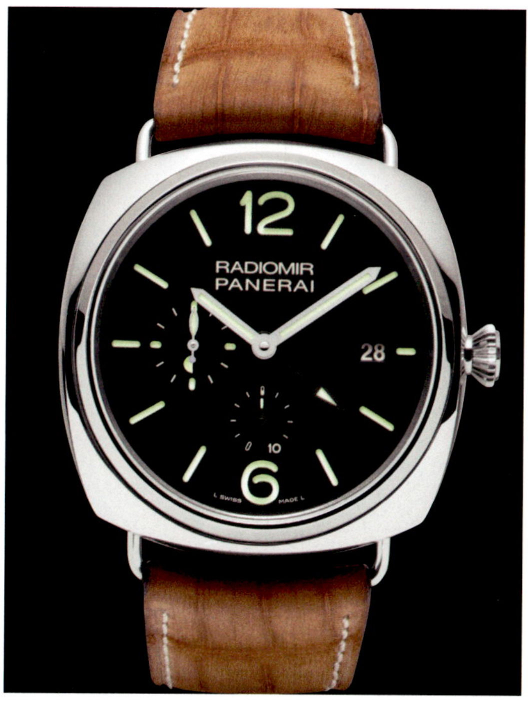

LUMINOR 1950 10 DAYS GMT CERAMICA — REF. PAM00335

Movement: automatic-winding Panerai P.2003; 10-day power reserve; 296 components; three barrels.
Functions: hours, minutes; small seconds and 24-hour indicator at 9; date at 3; linear power reserve indicator at 6; seconds reset; second time zone.
Case: black ceramic; Ø 44mm; trademark crown-protection device; antireflective sapphire crystal; sapphire crystal caseback; water resistant to 100 meters.
Dial: black; sandwich style; luminescent markers and Arabic numerals; second time zone GMT hand.
Strap: black PANERAI-personalized leather; second strap supplied with strap-changing tool.
Suggested price: $19,300
Also available: brushed 316L steel with black dial on brown PANERAI-personalized alligator strap (PAM00270, $17,300).

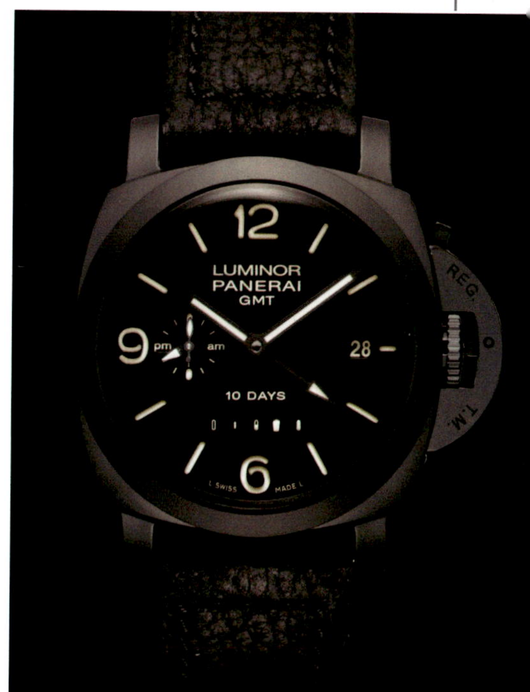

LUMINOR 1950 CHRONO MONOPULSANTE 8 DAYS GMT TITANIO REF. PAM00311

Movement: manual-winding Panerai P.2004; 8-day power reserve; 321 components; three barrels.
Functions: hours, minutes; small seconds and 24-hour indicator at 9; date at 3; linear power reserve indicator at 6; second time zone; GMT; single button chronograph with two counters.
Case: brushed titanium; Ø 44mm; trademark crown-protection device; antireflective sapphire crystal; sapphire crystal caseback; water resistant to 100 meters.
Dial: brown; sandwich style; luminescent markers and Arabic numerals; second time zone GMT hand; central chronograph hand.
Strap: brown PANERAI-personalized alligator strap; second strap supplied with strap changing tool.
Suggested price: $21,100
Also available: brushed 316L steel with black dial and black PANERAI-personalized alligator strap ($18,400, PAM00275).

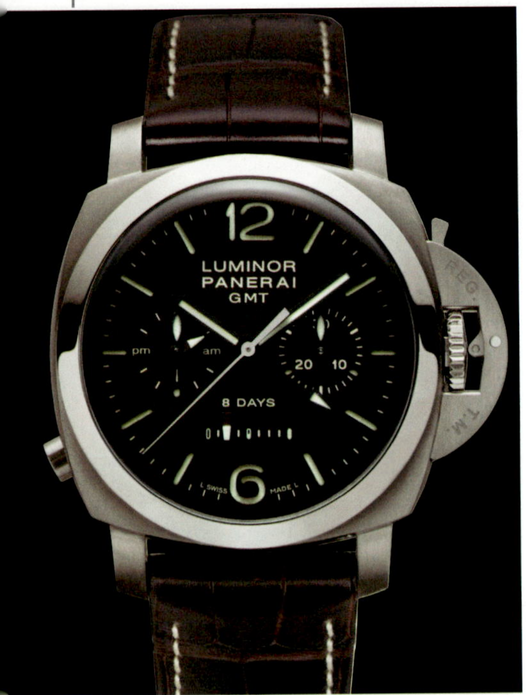

LUMINOR 1950 CHRONO MONOPULSANTE 8 DAYS GMT CERAMICA REF. PAM00317

Movement: manual-winding Panerai P.2004; 8-day power reserve; 321 components; three barrels.
Functions: hours, minutes; small seconds and 24-hour indicator at 9; date at 3; linear power reserve indicator at 6; second time zone; GMT; single button chronograph with two counters.
Case: black ceramic; Ø 44mm; trademark crown-protection device; antireflective sapphire crystal; sapphire crystal caseback; water resistant to 100 meters.
Dial: black; sandwich style; luminescent markers and Arabic numerals; second time zone GMT hand; central chronograph hand.
Strap: black PANERAI-personalized leather; bridges and buckles treated with special hard black coating; second strap supplied with strap-changing tool.
Suggested price: $25,600
Also available: brushed 316L steel with black dial and PANERAI-personalized black alligator strap ($18,400, PAM00275).

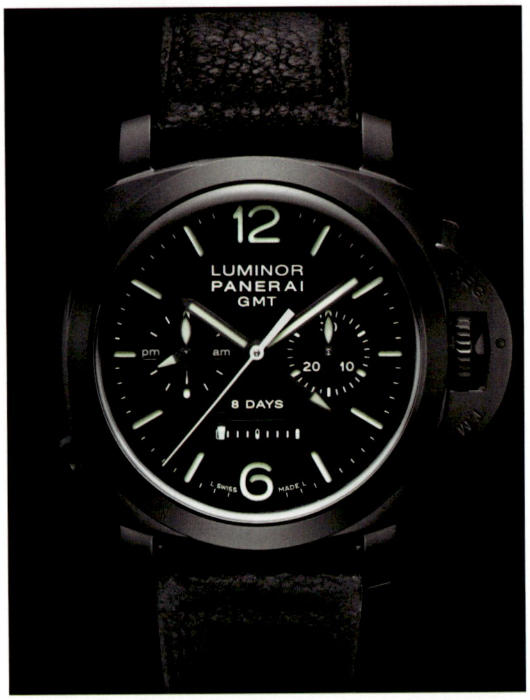

LUMINOR 1950 8 DAYS RATTRAPANTE ORO ROSA REF. PAM00319

Movement: manual-winding Panerai P.2006/3; 8-day power reserve; 356 components; three barrels.
Functions: hours, minutes; small seconds at 9; split-seconds chronograph with central chronograph hand and two counters: minutes at 3, seconds at 9; linear power reserve indicator at 6.
Case: brushed and polished 18K pink gold; Ø 47mm; trademark crown-protection device; antireflective sapphire crystal; sapphire crystal caseback; water resistant to 100 meters.
Dial: brown; sandwich style; luminescent markers and Arabic numerals.
Strap: brown PANERAI-personalized alligator leather; second strap supplied with strap-changing tool.
Note: limited edition of 300 pieces.
Suggested price: $43,000

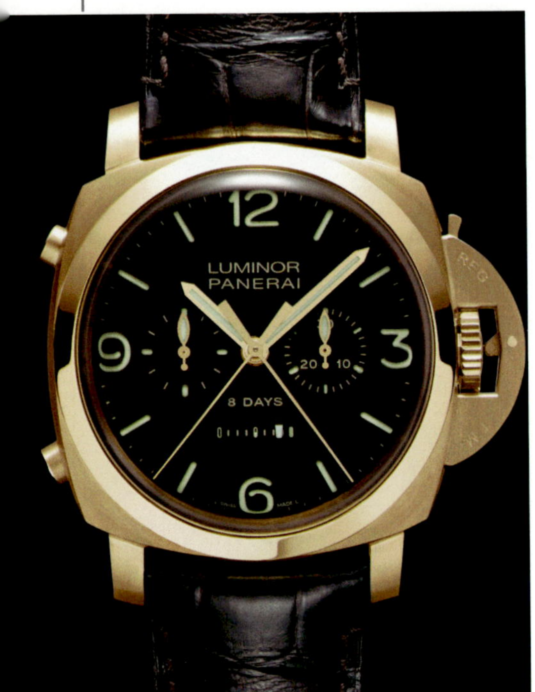

RADIOMIR ORO ROSA REF. PAM00336

Movement: manual-winding Panerai P. 999; 60-hour power reserve; swan's neck regulator; 154 components.
Functions: hours, minutes; small seconds at 9.
Case: brushed and polished 18K pink gold; Ø 42mm; OP-personalized screw-down winding crown and patented removable wire-loop strap attachments; antireflective sapphire crystal; sapphire crystal caseback; water resistant to 100 meters.
Dial: brown; sandwich style; luminescent markers and Arabic numerals.
Strap: PANERAI-personalized alligator strap; polished 18K pink-gold buckle.
Note: limited edition of 500 pieces.
Suggested price: $17,000
Also available: brushed titanium with black sandwich-style dial and black PANERAI-personalized alligator strap (PAM00338, $7,900).

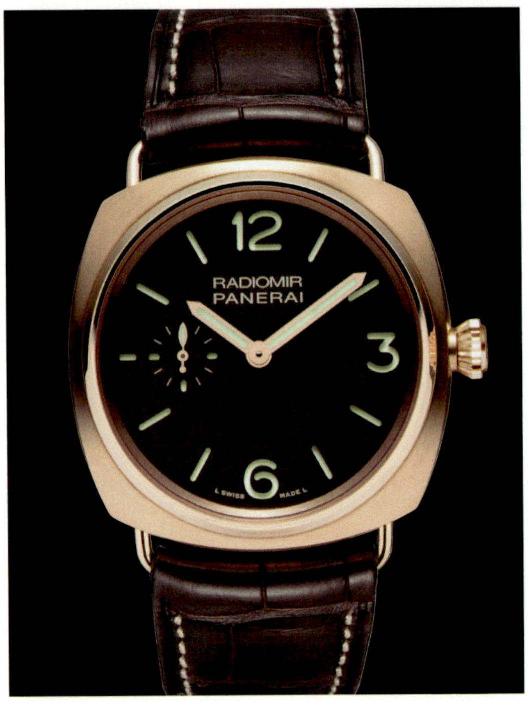

RADIOMIR REF. PAM00337

Movement: manual-winding Panerai P. 999; 60-hour power reserve; 154 components.
Functions: hours, minutes; small seconds at 9.
Case: polished 316L steel; Ø 42mm; OP-personalized screw-down winding crown and patented removable wire-loop strap attachments; antireflective sapphire crystal; sapphire crystal caseback; water resistant to 100 meters.
Dial: black; sandwich style; luminescent markers and Arabic numerals.
Strap: PANERAI-personalized alligator leather; polished steel buckle.
Suggested price: $7,200
Also available: brushed titanium with black sandwich-style dial and black PANERAI-personalized alligator strap (PAM00338, $7,900).

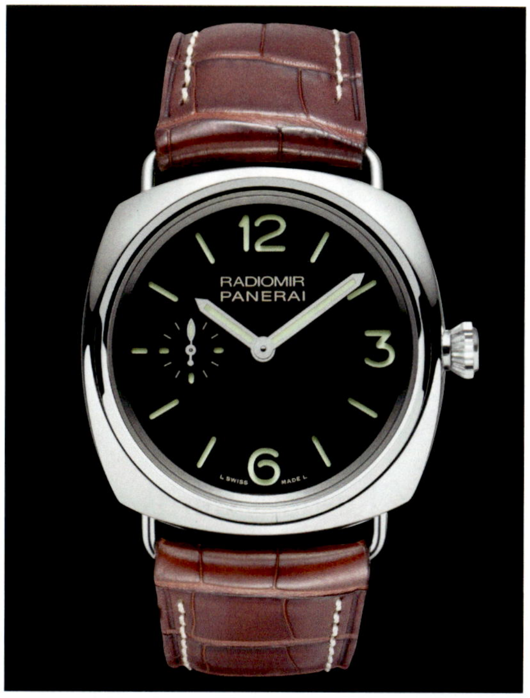

RADIOMIR TOURBILLON GMT PLATINO REF. PAM00316

Movement: manual-winding Panerai P.2005; 239 components; three barrels.
Functions: hours, minutes; small seconds and tourbillon indicator at 9; 24-hour indicator at 3; second time zone.
Case: platinum; Ø 48mm; OP-personalized screw-down winding crown and patented wire-loop strap attachments; antireflective sapphire crystal; sapphire crystal caseback revealing tourbillon and power reserve indicator; water resistant to 100 meters.
Dial: black; sandwich style; knurled platinum ring around outer edge; luminescent markers and Arabic numerals; second time zone GMT hand.
Strap: black PANERAI-personalized alligator leather; polished 18K white-gold buckle.
Suggested price: $137,000
Also available: brushed and polished titanium with brown sandwich-style dial and brown PANERAI-personalized alligator leather strap (PAM00315, $122,700); 18K pink gold with brown sandwich-style dial and brown PANERAI-personalized alligator leather strap (PAM00330, $133,000).

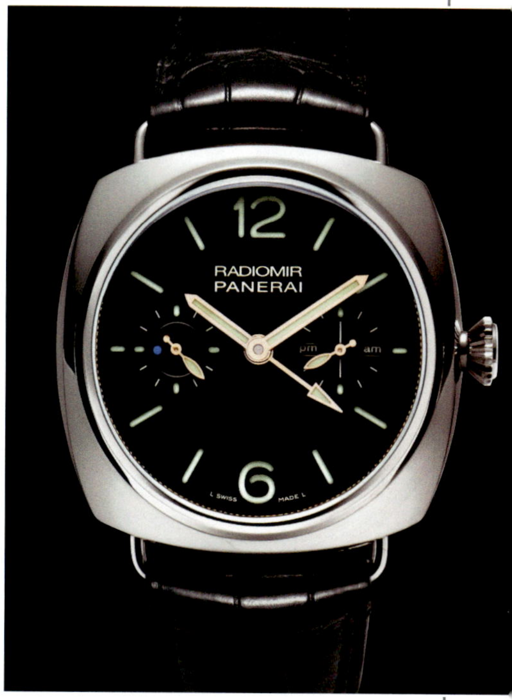

LUMINOR MARINA 1950 3 DAYS AUTOMATIC COMPOSITE REF. PAM00386

Movement: automatic-winding Panerai P.9000; 3-day power reserve.
Functions: hours, minutes; small seconds at 9; date at 3.
Case: Panerai Composite®; Ø 44mm; trademark crown-protecting device; antireflective sapphire crystal; sapphire crystal caseback; water resistant to 300 meters.
Dial: brown; sandwich style; luminescent markers and Arabic numerals.
Strap: PANERAI-personalized leather; large Panerai Composite® buckle; supplied with a second interchangeable strap and a steel screwdriver.
Price: available upon request.
Also available: brushed 316L steel on PANERAI-personalized steel bracelet (PAM00328, $8,600.00); polished 316L steel, black dial with patina-finished luminescent Arabic numbers on PANERAI-personalized black calf strap (PAM00359, $7,400); titanium, brown dial on PANERAI-personalized brown alligator strap (PAM00351, $8,000); titanium, brown dial on PANERAI-personalized titanium bracelet (PAM00352, $9,300).

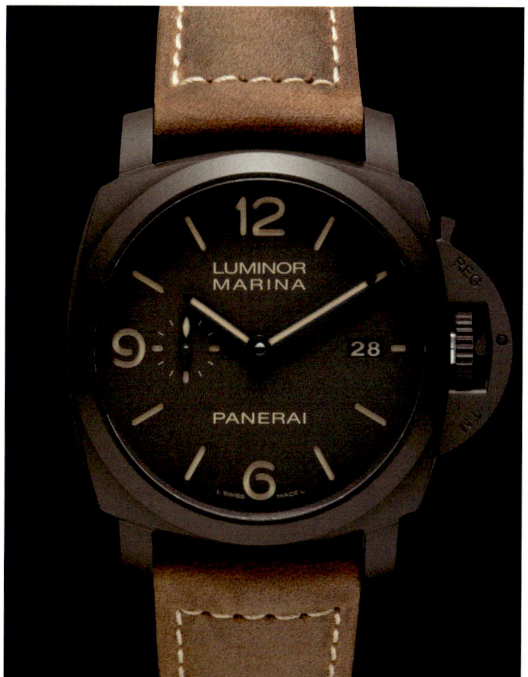

LUMINOR 1950 3 DAYS REF. PAM00372

Movement: manual-winding Panerai P.3000; 3-day power reserve.
Functions: hours, minutes.
Case: polished 316L steel; Ø 47mm; trademark crown-protecting device; sapphire crystal caseback; water resistant to 100 meters.
Dial: black; sandwich style; luminescent markers and Arabic numerals covered by 3mm-thick Plexiglas®.
Strap: PANERAI-personalized leather; large buckle; supplied with a second interchangeable strap and strap changing tool.
Price: available upon request.

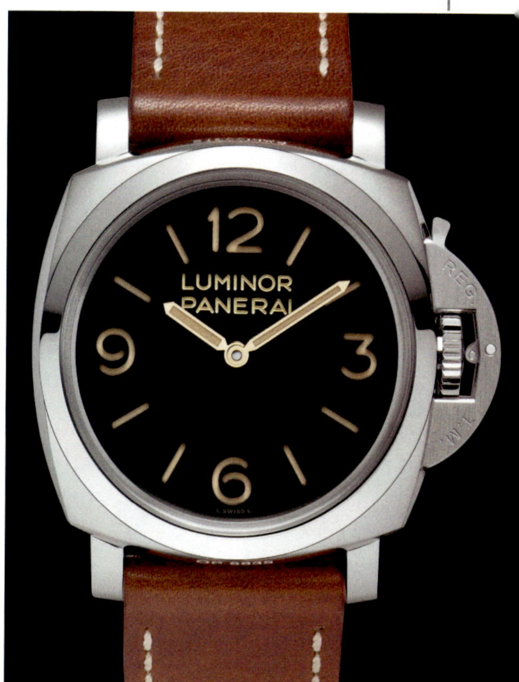

PARMIGIANI

COMPLEX TIME SIGNATURES

Restless spirits who heed adventure's irresistible call quickly realize that if you get far enough away, you'll soon be on your way back home. Parmigiani Fleurier captures this paradox of wanderlust elegantly with its Tonda Hémisphères.

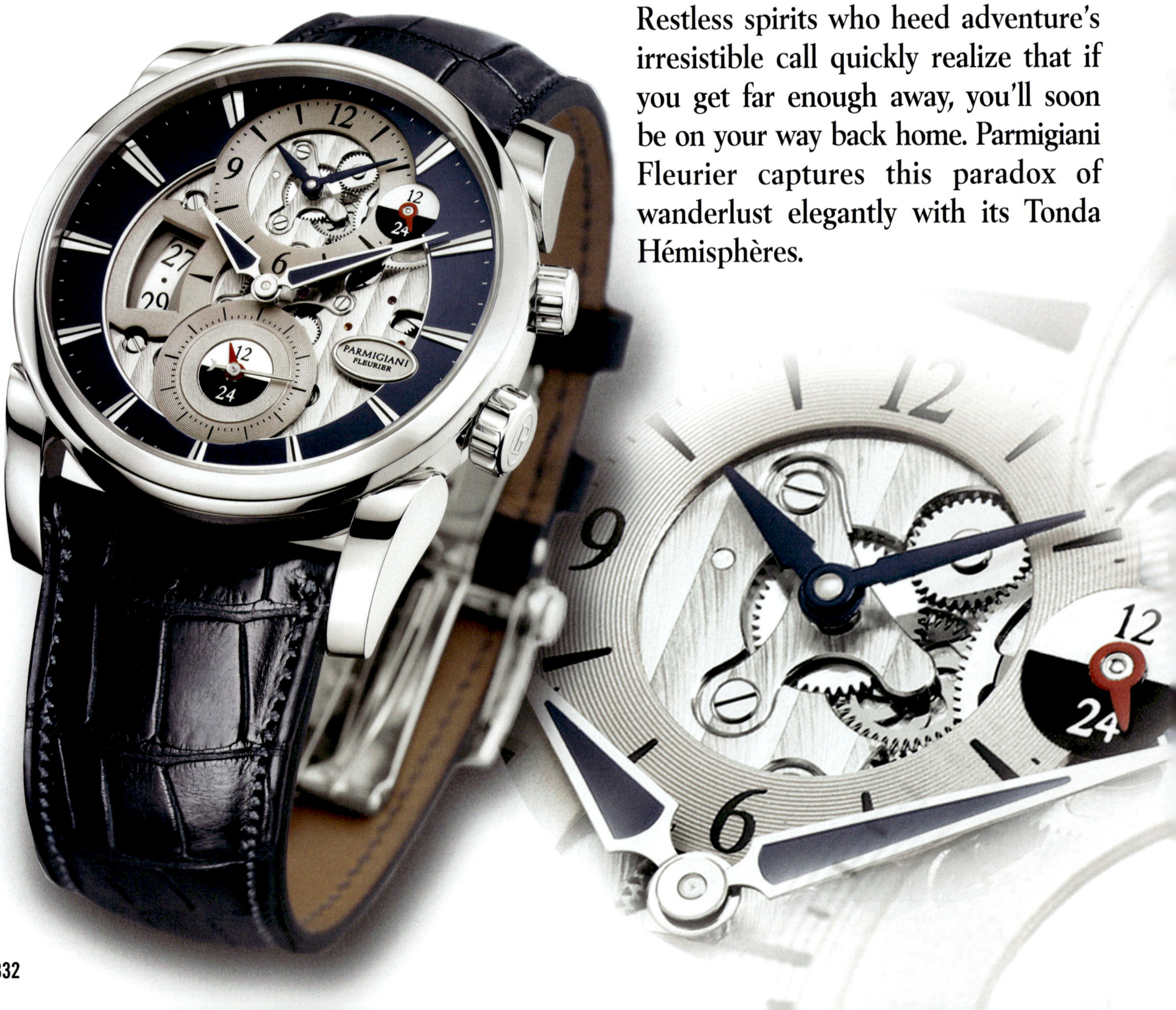

Parmigiani's Tonda Hémisphères features an in-house caliber with a second time zone function that can be set to the minute, unlike similar models that can only be set to the hour.

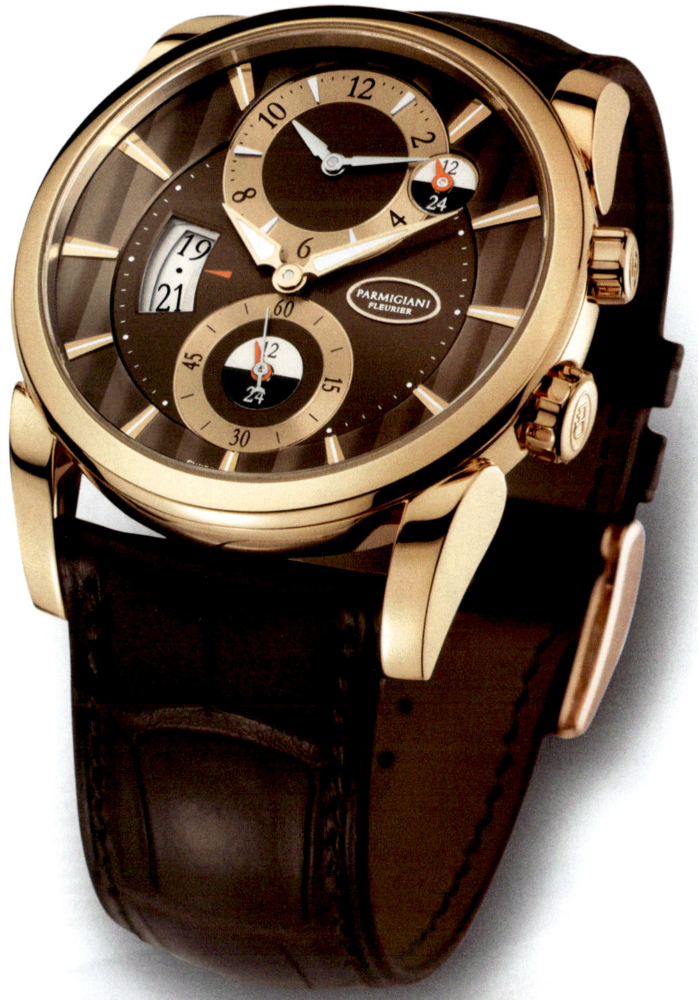

The design reflects this poetic observation visually by indicating two different time zones using separate displays that follow divergent paths around the dial before connecting at the 12. While it does not allow the traveler to be in two locations simultaneously, it does enable him to stay on time in two places—even if they are at opposite ends of the globe.

Parmigiani originally introduced the Tonda Hémisphères in 2008. Two years later, the Fleurier-based manufacture updates the timepiece's look by welcoming a new, partially skeletonized dial.

The open-worked design offers a tantalizing look at the series of gears below the second time zone and the nearby day/night indicator at the top of the dial. It also reveals the traditional Côtes de Genève decoration applied to the automatic movement by the sure-handed artisans who ply their time-honored trade at the firm's expansive workshops in Switzerland's Three Lakes region.

This latest addition to the Tonda Hémisphères family also boasts a vibrant new color scheme that uses royal blue for the grooved ring that forms the dial's perimeter, as well as the matching hour and minute hands fixed at the center of the dial. The blue hue continues outside the 42mm stainless steel case with a handsome alligator strap, hand-stitched exclusively for Parmigiani by the legendary leather craftsmen at Hermès.

To elevate the Tonda Hémisphères beyond the rank of mere travel companion, Parmigiani equips the watch with the firm's own in-house caliber. Unlike most watches with a second time zone function, the company's engineers have devised a movement that allows the secondary time to be set independently.

To accomplish this, the watch includes two separate crowns on the side of the case. The top crown sets the second time zone and the one below adjusts both the reference time and the date.

Not only is the design intuitive to operate, it also offers more flexibility. By allowing this autonomous calibration, the second time zone can be set to the minute. This represents a major leap forward when compared to the preponderance of second time zone watches that rely on movements that can only be set to the hour.

In other words, the Tonda Hémisphères' second time zone easily accommodates locations that stray from standard time zone increments like India or Nepal, which deviate by 30 and 45 minutes respectively. What makes this adaptability all the more impressive is that the watch handles these unusual time signatures as simply as adjusting the time on a standard watch.

To ease the burden of travelers as they weather wicked bouts of jet lag, Parmigiani includes a day/night indicator for each time display, which eliminates the mental math sometimes necessary to determine if the sun is coming or going.

With its simplicity and adaptability, Parmigiani's Tonda Hémisphères makes it easy to find the time wherever you may roam.

FACING PAGE

LEFT The partially skeletonized dial reveals the inner workings of Calibre PF 337, an automatic movement produced exclusively at Parmigiani's workshops in Fleurier, Switzerland.

RIGHT The 42mm stainless steel Tonda Hémisphères displays the reference time centrally, along with a subsidiary chapter ring at the top for a second time zone that can be set to the minute.

THIS PAGE

The two crowns seen on this rose-gold version of the Tonda Hémisphères are used to set the reference and second time zone displays independently.

KALPAGRAPH REF. PFC128-1001200

Movement: automatic-winding Parmigiani manufacture PF 334.
Functions: hours, minutes; small seconds at 3; date; ¼-second chronograph: central seconds hand, 30-minute counter, 12-hour counter.
Case: 18K rose gold; 53.4x39.2mm, thickness: 12.8mm; tonneau-shape; Ø 7mm crown; antireflective sapphire crystal; sapphire crystal caseback engraved with individual number; water resistant to 3atm.

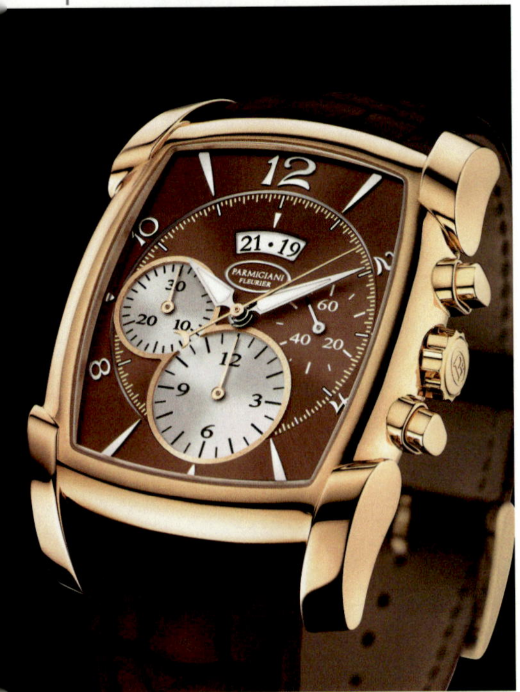

Dial: azured-finish counters; velvet-finish center; satin-finished sunray outer; applied indexes; delta-shaped hands with luminescent coating.
Strap: Hermès alligator; rose-gold and palladium ardillon buckle, polished finish.
Suggested price: $28,300

KALPAGRAPH REF. PFC128-1202600

Movement: automatic-winding Parmigiani manufacture PF 334.
Functions: hours, minutes; small seconds at 3; date; ¼-second chronograph: central seconds hand, 30-minute counter, 12-hour counter.
Case: 18K white gold; 53.4x39.2mm, thickness: 12.8mm; tonneau-shape; Ø 7mm crown; antireflective sapphire crystal; sapphire crystal caseback engraved with individual number; water resistant to 3atm.

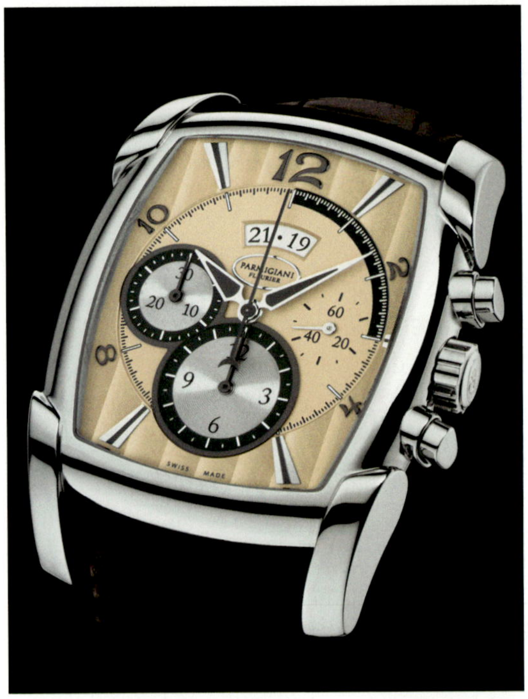

Dial: Côtes de Genève outer; velvet-finish center; counters with azured finish centers; delta-shaped hands with luminescent coating.
Strap: Hermès alligator; rose-gold and palladium ardillon buckle, polished finish.
Suggested price: $29,800

TONDA 42 HEMISPHERES REF. PFC231-0001800

Movement: automatic-winding Parmigiani manufacture PF 337.
Functions: hours, minutes; small seconds and day/night indication at 6; date at 9; second time zone hours and minutes at 12; second time zone day/night at 1:30.
Case: stainless steel; three-piece; Ø 42mm, thickness: 11.15mm; polished finish; Ø 5.5mm crown; antireflective sapphire crystal; sapphire crystal caseback engraved with individual number; water resistant to 3atm.

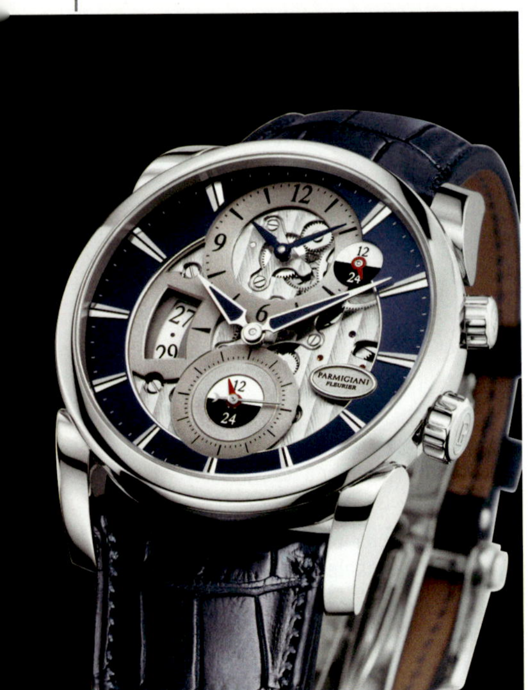

Dial: circular satin finish; opaline counter center; azure-finish rims; applied diamond-faceted hour markers.
Strap: Hermès alligator; ardillon buckle, polished finish.
Suggested price: $24,000

TONDA 42 HEMISPHERES REF. PFC231-1000100

Movement: automatic-winding Parmigiani manufacture PF 337.
Functions: hours, minutes; small seconds and day/night indication at 6; date at 9; second time zone hours and minutes at 12; second time zone day/night at 1:30.
Case: 18K rose gold; three-piece; Ø 42mm, thickness: 11.15mm; polished finish; Ø 5.5mm crown; antireflective sapphire crystal; sapphire crystal caseback engraved with individual number; water resistant to 3atm.

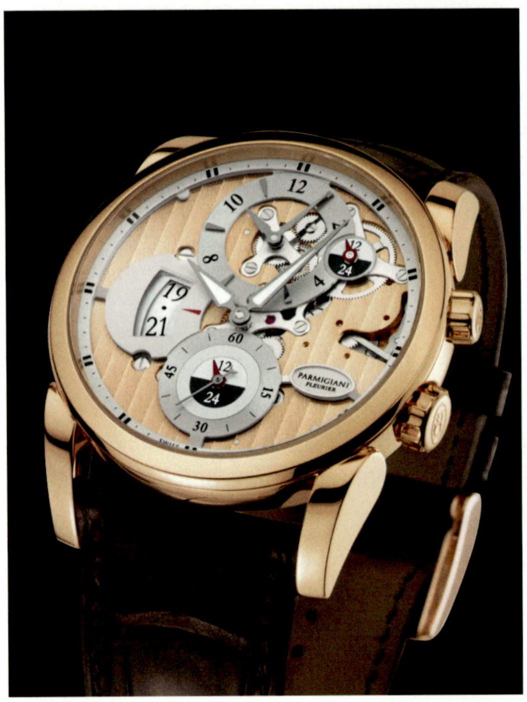

Dial: circular satin finish; opaline counter center; azure-finish rims; applied diamond-faceted hour markers.
Strap: Hermès alligator; ardillon buckle, polished finish.
Suggested price: $35,600

TONDA 1950 — REF. PFC267-1200400

Movement: automatic-winding Parmigiani manufacture PF 701; 42-hour power reserve; 13 ¼‴; Ø 30mm, thickness: 2.6mm; 29 jewels; 21,600 vph; one barrel; Côtes de Genève decoration; hand-beveled bridges; oscillating micro-weight made from 950 platinum.
Functions: hours, minutes; small seconds at 6.
Case: 18K rose gold; three-piece; Ø 39mm, thickness: 7.8mm; polished finish; Ø 5mm crown; antireflective sapphire crystal; sapphire crystal caseback engraved with individual number; water resistant to 3atm.
Dial: graphite and grained white; applied diamond-polished opaline background delta-shaped hands with luminescent coating.
Strap: alligator; rose-gold ardillon buckle, polished finish.
Suggested price: $20,500

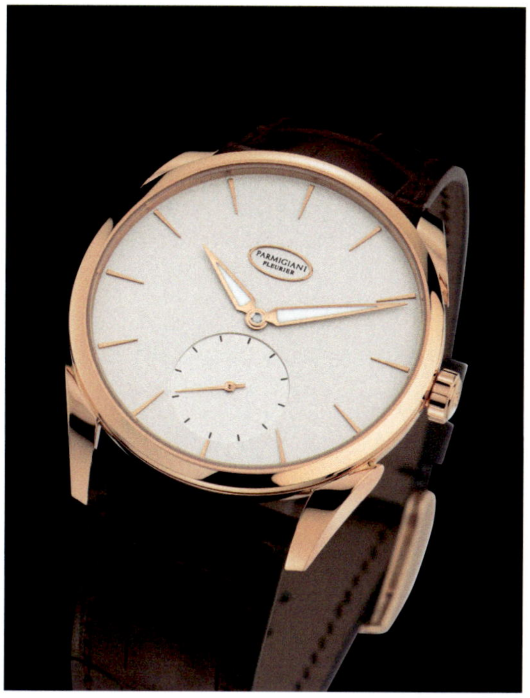

KALPARISMA AUTOMATIC — REF. PFC125-1043300

Movement: automatic-winding Parmigiani manufacture PF 332.
Functions: hours, minutes; small seconds at 6.
Case: 18K rose gold; 37.5x31.2mm, thickness: 8.4mm; Ø 5.5mm crown; polished finish; antireflective sapphire crystal; sapphire crystal caseback engraved with individual number.
Dial: white mother-of-pearl; delta-shaped hands with luminescent coating; applied indexes; star-shaped small seconds.
Bracelet: Kalpa type; rose gold; polished finish folding buckle.
Suggested price: $40,600

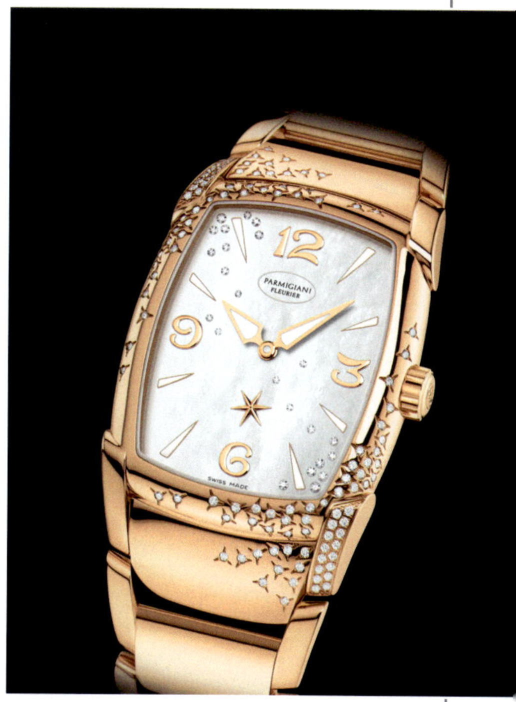

PERSHING 002 CHRONOGRAPH — REF. PFC528-1263501

Movement: automatic-winding Parmigiani manufacture PF 334.
Functions: hours, minutes; small seconds at 3; date; ¼-second chronograph: large seconds, 30-minute counter, 12-hour counter.
Case: 18K white gold; Ø 42mm, thickness: 13.1mm; polished and satin-finished; bezel set with 42 brilliant-cut Top Wesselton VVS diamonds (1.2 carats) and 14 brilliant-cut sapphires (0.7 carat); unidirectional turning bezel; Ø 7mm crown; metal pushers; antireflective sapphire crystal; caseback engraved with Pershing boat and individual number; water resistant to 10atm.
Dial: blue tinted mother-of-pearl dial; ring overlaid on circular azure finish counters; applied indexes; delta-shaped hands with luminescent coating; polished starfish seconds hand with engraved tentacles; center seconds in the form of an octopus.
Strap: Hermès white Epsom calf; folding buckle with safety clasp.
Suggested price: $47,900

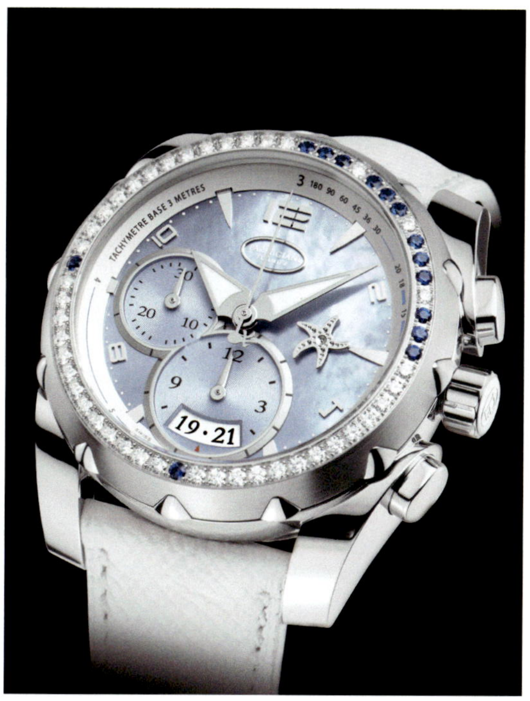

PERSHING 005 CHRONOGRAPH — REF. PFC528-1010301

Movement: automatic-winding Parmigiani manufacture PF 334.
Functions: hours, minutes; small seconds at 3; date; ¼-second chronograph: large seconds, 30-minute counter, 12-hour counter.
Case: 18K rose gold; Ø 45mm, thickness: 14.2mm; polished and satin-finished; unidirectional turning bezel; Ø 8mm crown; metal pushpieces; antireflective sapphire crystal; caseback engraved with Pershing boat and individual number; water resistant to 20atm.
Dial: Côtes de Genève; ring overlaid on counters; circular azure finish counters; applied indexes; delta-shaped hands with luminescent coating.
Strap: Hermès alligator; rose-gold ardillon buckle, polished finish.
Suggested price: $43,800

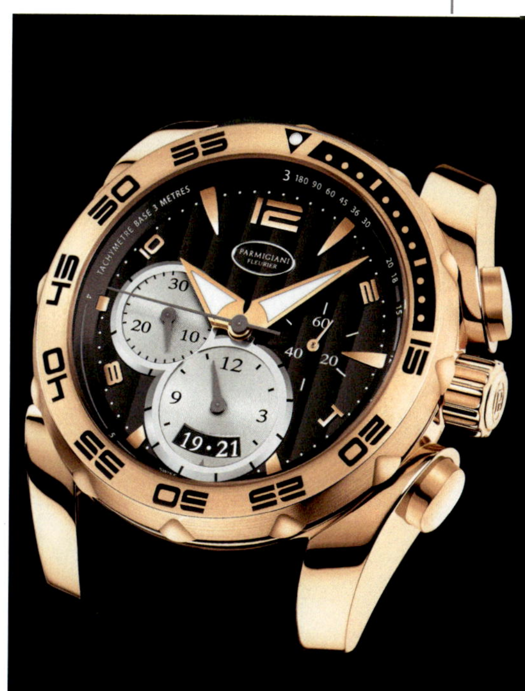

TORIC QUAESTOR SKELETON REF. PFH437-1002800

Movement: manual-winding Parmigiani manufacture PF 355; 72-hour power reserve; 13'''; Ø 29.3mm; 35 jewels; 21,600 vph; minute repeater with two cathedral gongs with chime rhythm regulator flywheel; device for disengaging time setting while the chime is sounding; Côtes de Genève rhodium-plated bridges; hand-polished beveling and backing; steel circular-grained lengthwise.
Functions: hours, minutes, seconds; minute repeater.

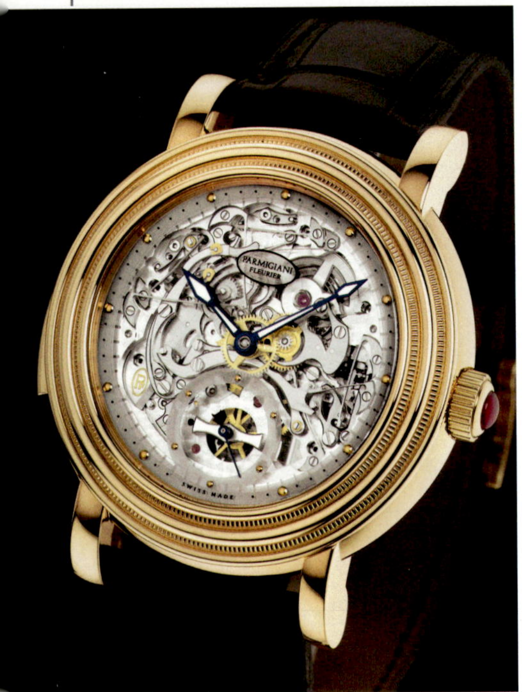

Case: 18K rose gold; Ø 46mm, thickness: 13.2mm; polished finish; double knurled bezel; Ø 7mm crown, genuine ruby cabochon; sapphire crystal caseback engraved with individual number; water resistant to 3atm.
Dial: sapphire base; dulled areas; transferred black minute track and logo; blued steel javelin-shaped hour and minute hands with SuperLumiNova; blued steel seconds counter hand.
Strap: Hermès brown alligator; knurled rose-gold ardillon buckle, polished finish.
Suggested price: $448,700

KALPA XL TOURBILLON REF. PFH150-1000200

Movement: manual-winding Parmigiani manufacture PF 501.
Functions: hours, minutes, seconds; power reserve indicator; tourbillon.
Case: 18K rose gold; 44.7x37.2mm, thickness: 11.5mm; polished finish; Ø 7mm crown; antireflective sapphire crystal; sapphire crystal caseback engraved with individual number.
Dial: open-worked center; Côtes de Genève on the outer area; delta-shaped skeleton hands; applied rose-gold indexes.
Strap: Hermès alligator; ardillon buckle, polished finished.
Suggested price: $204,300

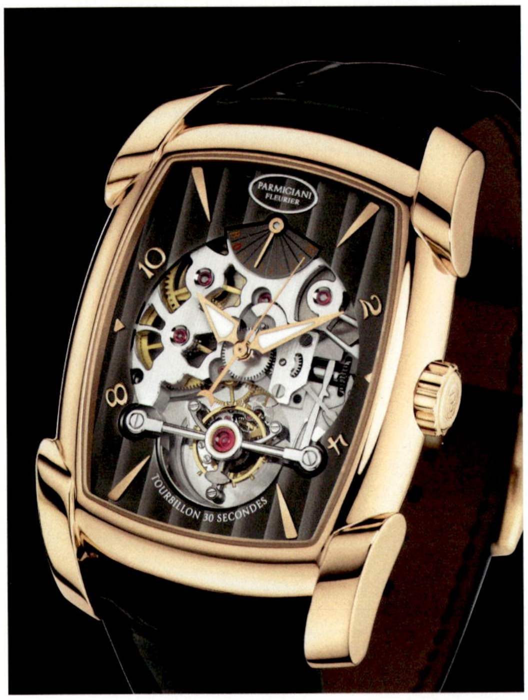

TONDAGRAPH 43 TOURBILLON REF. PFH236-1000300

Movement: manual-winding Parmigiani manufacture PF 354.
Functions: hours, minutes; small seconds at 9; tourbillon; ¼-second chronograph: large seconds hand, 30-minute counter at 3.
Case: 18K rose gold; Ø 43mm, thickness: 13.3mm; polished finish; Ø 7mm crown; antireflective sapphire crystal; sapphire crystal caseback engraved with individual number; water resistant to 3atm.
Dial: Côtes de Genève center opaline ring; applied indexes; delta-shaped hands with luminescent coating.
Strap: Hermès alligator; folding buckle, polished finish.
Suggested price: $238,100

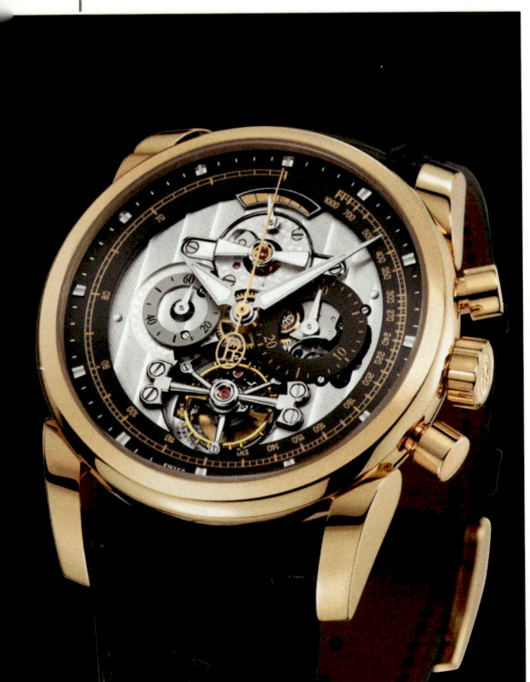

PERSHING OPENWORKED TOURBILLON REF. PFH552-1010300

Movement: manual-winding Parmigiani manufacture PF 511; one-week power reserve; PVD mainplate and bridges; 30-second tourbillon; colored skeleton.
Functions: hours, minutes, seconds; power reserve indicator; tourbillon.
Case: 18K rose gold and palladium; Ø 45mm, thickness: 14.2mm; polished and satin-finished; unidirectional turning bezel; Ø 8mm crown; antireflective sapphire crystal; sapphire crystal caseback; water resistant to 20atm.
Dial: open-worked sapphire dial; rhodium-plated applied indexes; delta-shaped hands with luminescent coating.
Strap: Hermès alligator; safety folding buckle, polished finish.
Note: delivered with extra rubber strap.
Suggested price: $230,400

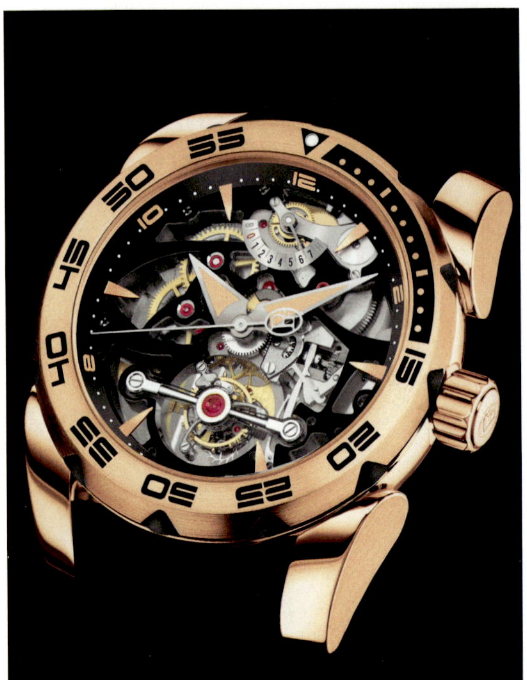

TONDA 42 RETROGRADE PERPETUAL CALENDAR — REF. PFC227-1200300

Movement: automatic-winding Parmigiani manufacture PF 333.
Functions: hours, minutes, seconds; precision moonphase; perpetual calendar: retrograde date, leap year, day and month window.
Case: 18K white gold; Ø 42mm, thickness: 11.15mm; polished finish; Ø 7mm crown; antireflective sapphire crystal; sapphire crystal caseback engraved with individual number; water resistant to 30atm.
Dial: cut-out; velvet date ring; applied indexes; delta-shaped hands with luminescent coating.
Strap: Hermès alligator; ardillon buckle, polished finish.
Suggested price: $65,200

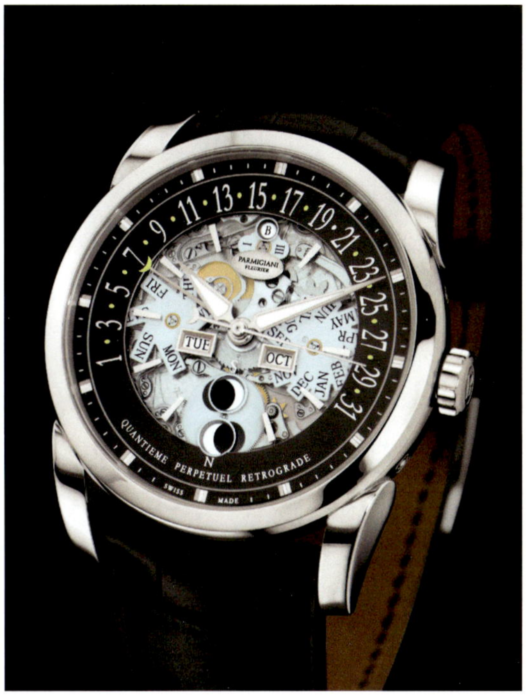

BUGATTI SUPER SPORT — REF. PFP-3651201400

Movement: manual-winding Parmigiani manufacture PF 372; 10-day power reserve; 15.96x25x37.01mm; 40 jewels; 21,600 vph; two-plane movement; gold black-colored plates and bridges; two series-coupled barrels; Côtes de Genève; perlage, polished and beveled angles.
Functions: hours, minutes; power reserve indicator.
Case: 18K white gold; 36x50.7mm, thickness: 22.7mm; polished and satin finished; single dynamometric crown for the time setting and winding; six antireflective sapphire crystals; metallized front and top crystal on the outer edge; sapphire crystal caseback engraved with individual number; water resistant to 1atm.
Dial: black carbon face; applied polished and satin-finished EB marker; applied shaped and polished indexes at 3 and 6; Bugatti nail motifs; delta-shaped hands and luminescent coating.
Strap: Hermès alligator; 18K white-gold deployant buckle.
Note: special edition of 30 pieces.
Suggested price: $285,000

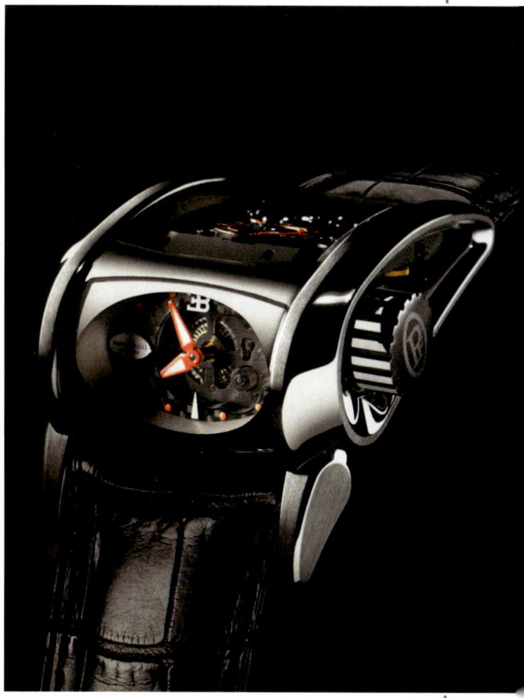

TORIC WESTMINSTER GRAND DATE — LIMITED EDITION

Movement: manual-winding Parmigiani manufacture PF 256.
Functions: hours, minutes; large date; tourbillon; sounds the hours, quarter-hours and minutes with four cathedral gongs in the Westminster chime.
Case: platinum; Ø 46mm, thickness: 17.38mm; polished finish; double knurled bezel; Ø 7mm crown, genuine blue sapphire cabochon; antireflective sapphire crystal; sapphire crystal caseback engraved with individual number; water resistant to 1atm.
Dial: engraved or enameled; javelot-shaped hands.
Strap: Hermès alligator; ardillon buckle, polished finish.
Price: available upon request.
Also available: bezel set with 60-baguette cut Top Wesselton VVS diamonds (5 carats).

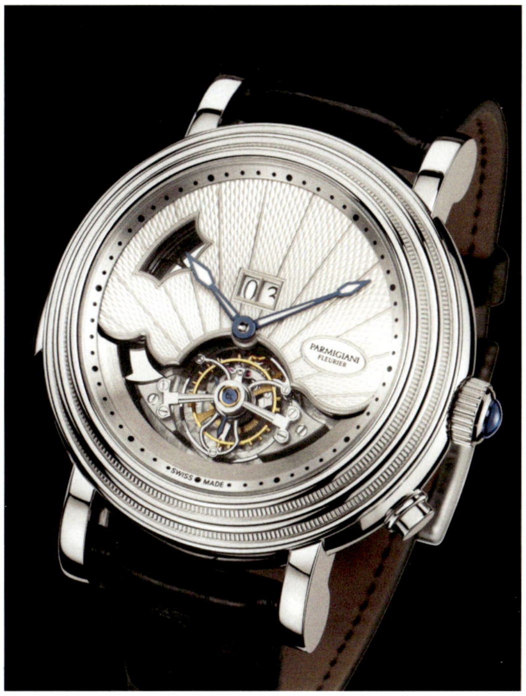

TORIC TECNICA CHRONO — REF. PFH435-2005300-HA1441

Movement: manual-winding Parmigiani manufacture PF 352 tourbillon; 48-hour power reserve; 13´´´; Ø 29.3mm; 47 jewels; 21,600 vph; bridges engraved by hand according to the theme; hand-polished beveling and backing; steel circular-grained lengthwise.
Functions: hours, minutes; seconds; date; tourbillon; chronograph; minute repeater with two cathedral chimes. **Case:** 950 platinum; Ø 44mm, thickness: 16mm; polished finish; double knurled bezel; Ø 7mm crown, genuine blue sapphire cabochon; sapphire crystal hinged double caseback with enameled cloisonné, set with diamonds according to the theme, engraved with individual number; water resistant to 30atm.
Dial: 18K gold base; engraved according to the theme; transferred black minute track; counters and logo; transferred blue ring; blued steel javelin-shaped hour and minute hands with super SuperLumi-Nova; blued steel counter and chronograph hands.
Strap: black Hermès alligator skin; 750 white-gold ardillon buckle, engraved with a transparent light green-blue enameling, polished finish.
Price: available upon request.

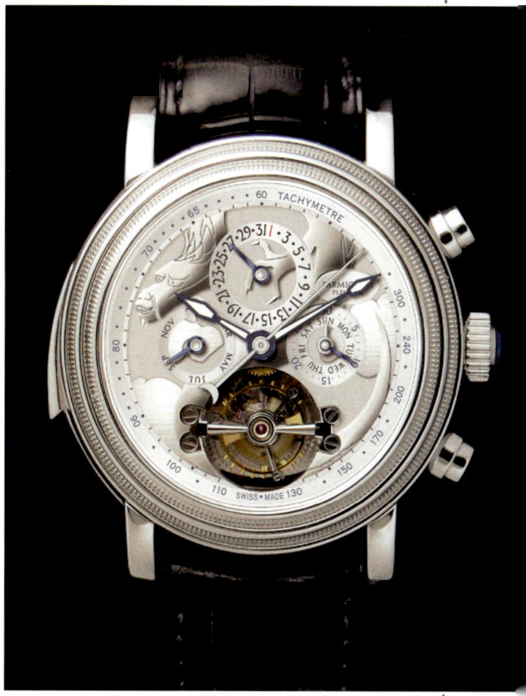

PATEK PHILIPPE
GENEVE

ALL IN THE TIMING

Patek Philippe made history in the early 1920s when the Geneva-based company offered the first split-seconds chronograph wristwatch. That made-to-order model heralded a now-famous line of chronographs from the independent firm.

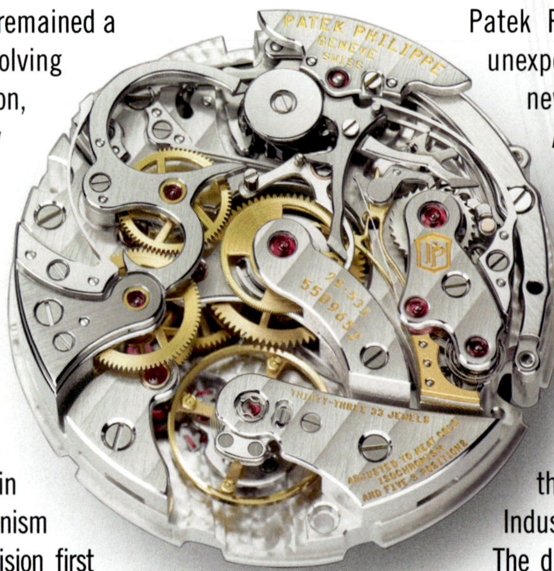

The classic timer function has remained a constant at Patek Philippe, evolving through decades of innovation, from pre-war pieces treasured today by collectors to a growing number of movements produced entirely at the company's workshop.

One of its latest inventions, the CH 29-535 PS, is the first hand-wound chronograph movement manufactured by the firm in-house. Heir to a legend, this new column-wheel caliber will begin replacing the CH 27-70, a mechanism whose exquisite decoration and precision first caught watch enthusiasts' attention in 1986.

The decision to replace the beloved design came after five years of research, which yielded six patented advances that enabled the CH 29-535 PS to surpass its predecessor. The overriding principle driving each innovation was improved user convenience, a key aspect of the Patek Philippe Seal, a set of strict technical and aesthetic specifications to which all movements must adhere.

Beyond these proprietary enhancements, the CH 29-535 PS also incorporates an instantaneous 30-minute chronograph counter. Instead of moving constantly when the chronograph is activated, the hand jumps forward to the next minute marker, which provides a more concise reading.

Patek Philippe demonstrated its flair for the unexpected by introducing this important new movement in a model for women. Appropriately christened the Ladies First Chronograph (Ref. 7071), it is the first wristwatch chronograph by Patek Philippe to debut in a model for women.

If not for the modern movement inside, the refined Art Deco elegance of the rose-gold cushion-shaped case and guilloché dial would look at home on display at the 1925 International Exposition of Modern Industrial and Decorative Art in Paris.

The dial—available in black or white—features a chapter ring with baton markers and Roman numerals at the north and south positions. Ovoid-shaped subsidiary dials indicate the seconds on the left and the chronograph's minutes on the right.

A railroad track-style scale spans the dial's circumference and is easily read thanks to a seconds hand that extends out to the very edge. Beyond that, more than 130 round white diamonds cover the flange to form a sparkling frame that accentuates the case's rounded corners.

The crystal caseback provides a panoramic view of the chronograph's column-wheel, as well as the decorative finishing applied by Patek Philippe artisans, including Côtes de Genève stripes on the bridges and perlage on the mainplate.

Patek Philippe expands its legendary collection of chronographs with a new generation developed and manufactured entirely in-house. Its latest, a manual column-wheel chronograph, makes its debut in a model for women.

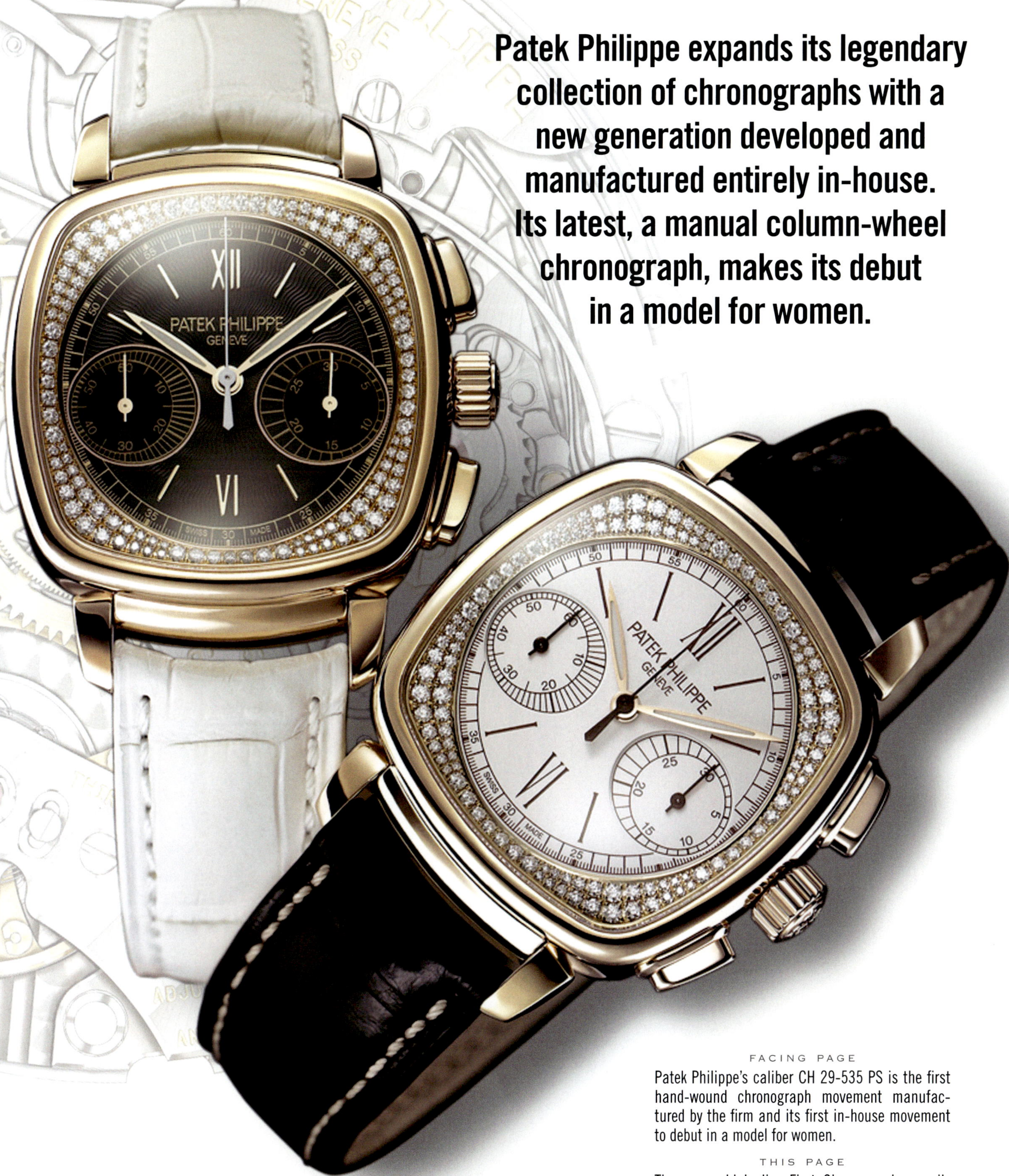

FACING PAGE

Patek Philippe's caliber CH 29-535 PS is the first hand-wound chronograph movement manufactured by the firm and its first in-house movement to debut in a model for women.

THIS PAGE

The rose-gold Ladies First Chronograph—available with a black or white dial—features a flange set with more than half a carat of round white diamonds.

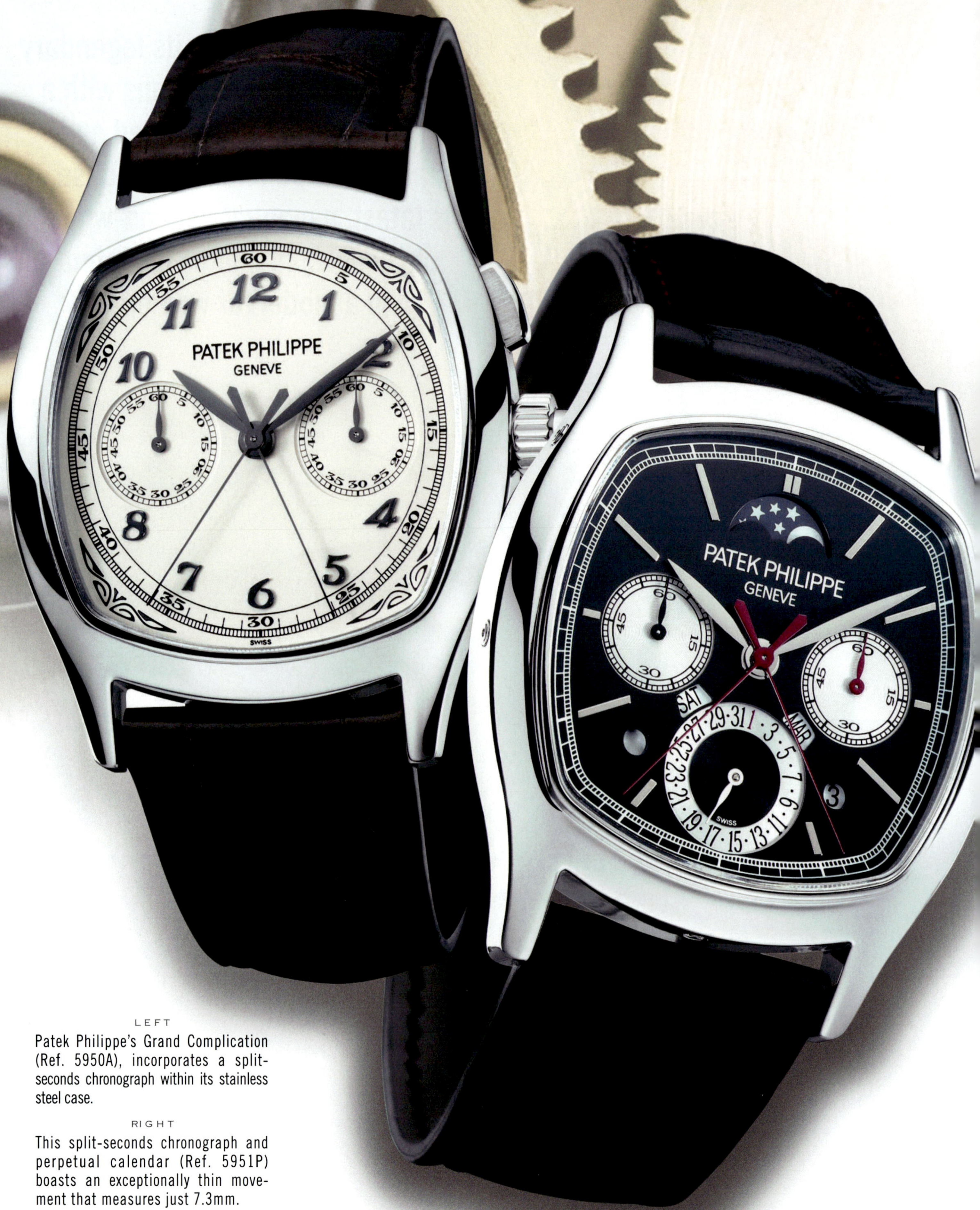

LEFT

Patek Philippe's Grand Complication (Ref. 5950A), incorporates a split-seconds chronograph within its stainless steel case.

RIGHT

This split-seconds chronograph and perpetual calendar (Ref. 5951P) boasts an exceptionally thin movement that measures just 7.3mm.

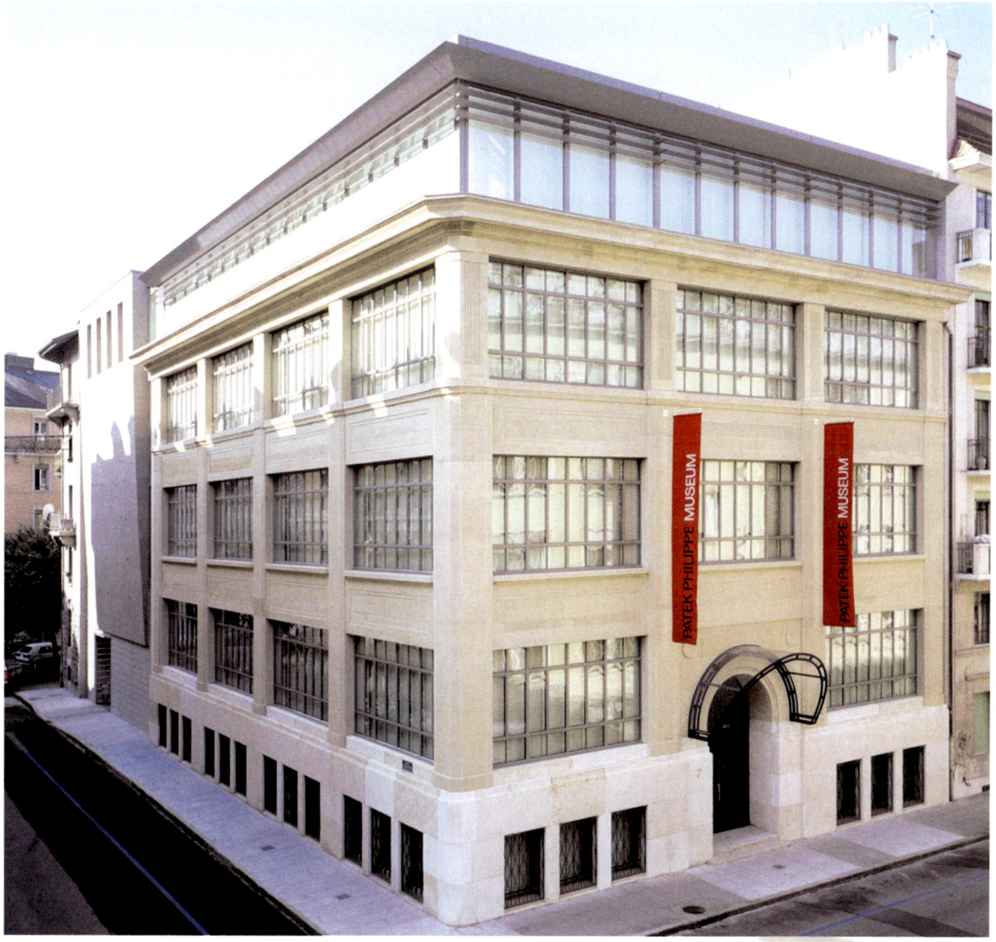

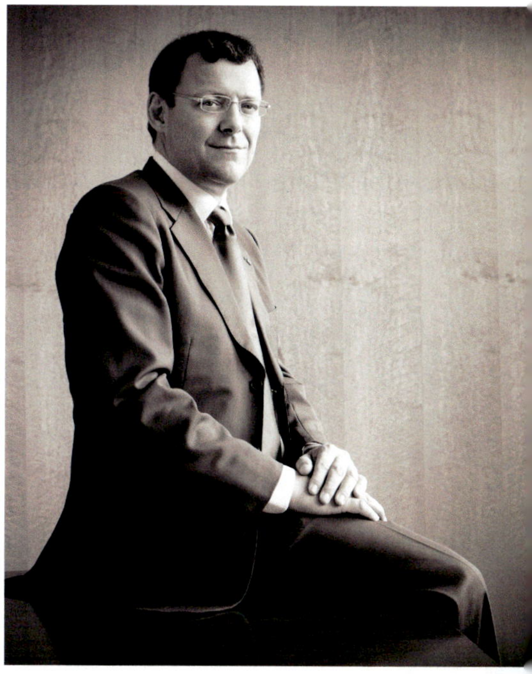

ABOVE
Thierry Stern, President of Patek Philippe.

LEFT
Located in Geneva, the Patek Philippe Museum celebrates its ten-year anniversary in 2011. Its extensive exhibit of timepieces includes selections taken from the company's entire history.

Patek Philippe keeps the focus on historic in-house chronographs with the Grand Complication (Ref. 5950A). This timepiece for men features CHR 27-525 PS, the first chronograph movement developed and manufactured entirely by the company. At the time of its 2005 introduction, the movement set the record for thinnest split-seconds column-wheel movement.

The caliber allows for the timing of events that begin together, but end at different times. A pusher on the side of the case sets the chronograph's seconds hand in motion. When a second button (integrated into the crown) is pushed, the seconds hand splits; one half stops while the other continues. Once the time is read, the crown button is pushed a second time, causing the stationary hand to catch up to the one in motion.

Patek Philippe encases its movement in a stainless steel cushion shape that measures 37x44.6mm. Pairing a round display with the watch's rounded square case creates triangular sections at the corners of the dial, which the firm covers with black, lacquer-filled engravings. These curvilinear arabesques not only give the design a decidedly Art Nouveau slant, but are also repeated on the movement and visible through the caseback.

Another exceptional model recently introduced is the thinnest split-seconds chronograph ever made with a perpetual calendar (Ref. 5951P). The movement's base, the CHR 27-525 PS caliber, was quite thin, and once Patek Philippe's craftsmen had added a calendar module with indications for date, day, month, leap year cycle and moonphase, it still measured a remarkably slim 7.3mm. The movement's diameter is just 27.3mm, which makes its slender profile an even greater horological feat. With roots that date back more than 170 years, Patek Philippe has made its share of horological history. To honor that rich heritage and share its passion for the art of watchmaking, the company inaugurated the Patek Philippe Museum in 2001.

Located between the Rhône and Arve rivers in the Plainpalais section of Geneva, the museum is housed in a beautifully restored Art Deco building that has welcomed more than 100,000 guests since it opened. The Patek Philippe Museum encompass several floors and more than five centuries of European horology. One floor contains more than 400 antique watchmaking tools from the early 1900s that illustrate how the watchmaking process has evolved.

Two additional floors are dedicated exclusively to timepieces. One is home to an extensive collection of more than 1,000 pieces, including an extremely early German drum-watch made around 1530. The other retraces Patek Philippe's entire history with pieces that span 1839 to the present day, including Caliber 89—the most complicated timepiece ever made. In 2009, Patek Philippe welcomed as president Thierry Stern, a member of a watchmaking dynasty's fourth generation and the son of Philippe Stern, who inspired the Museum. With these changes, and its continued devotion to watchmaking innovation, Patek Philippe strikes a balance between its reverence for the past and its passion for the future.

PATEK PHILIPPE CHRONOGRAPH REF. 5170J

Movement: manual-winding CH 29-535 PS caliber; column-wheel chronograph; Ø 29.6mm, thickness: 5.35mm; 65-hour power reserve; 269 components; 33 jewels; 28,800 vph; four-arm Gyromax balance, four poising weights; Breguet balance spring.
Functions: hours, minutes; chronograph: sweep seconds, 30-minute counter between 3 and 4, seconds subdial between 8 and 9; chronograph start and stop at 2; chronograph reset at 4.
Case: 18K yellow gold; Ø 39mm, thickness: 10.9mm; two-position crown: push: to wind the watch; pull: to set the time and stop seconds; sapphire crystal, screw-down sapphire crystal caseback; water resistant to 3atm.

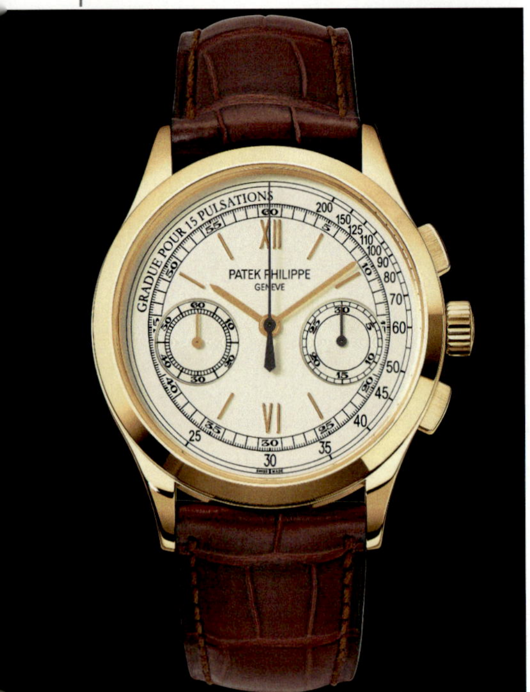

Dial: silvery opaline; Pulsimeter scale calibrated to 15 beats and railway-track minute scale, transfer-printed in black along the periphery; six applied baton-style 18K yellow-gold hour markers; two applied 18K yellow-gold Roman numerals at 12 and 6; 18K yellow-gold baton-style hour and minute hands; black oxidized counterbalanced arrow-style chronograph hand; white off-center subdials with circular guilloché patterns: seconds subdials between 3 and 4: 18K yellow-gold baton-style hands; 30-minute counter between 3 and 4: 18K yellow-gold black nickel-plated baton-style hands.
Strap: hand-stitched matte brown alligator skin with rectangular scales; 18K yellow-gold fold-over clasp.

ANNUAL CALENDAR CHRONOGRAPH REF. 5960P

Movement: automatic-winding CH 28-520 IRM QA 24H caliber; column-wheel chronograph Annual Calendar; Ø 33mm, thickness: 7.68mm; 55-hour power reserve; 456 components; 40 jewels; 28,800 vph; four-arm Gyromax balance, four poising weights; Breguet balance spring.
Functions: hours, minutes; chronograph: sweep chronograph seconds hand; power reserve indicator at 12; combined monocounter dial at 6: 60-minute counter (counts the elapsed minutes on two concentric scales from 0 to 30 in blue and from 30 to 60 in black), 12-hour counter; day of week between 10 and 11; date at 12 in a polished white-gold frame; month between 1 and 2; day/night indicator at 6.

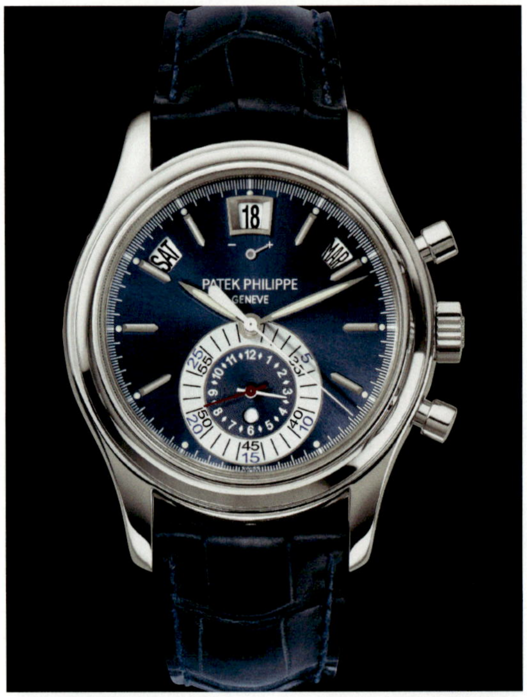

Case: 950 platinum; Ø 40.5mm, thickness: 13.55mm; cambered sapphire crystal; sapphire crystal caseback; water resistant to 3atm.
Dial: two-tone: matte blue sunburst and silvered; 18K white-gold eight hour markers; 11 SuperLumiNova luminescent dots; 18K white-gold leaf-shaped hour and minute hands with SuperLumiNova luminescent coating; rhodium-plated steel baton-style chronograph hand with counterweight; rhodium-plated 18K white-gold power reserve indicator with baton-style hand; subsidiary dial with circular guilloché pattern with a matte blue center and silvery periphery; white-lacquered brass baton-style hour-counter hand with counterweight; red-lacquered brass baton-style minute counter hand with counterweight.
Strap: hand-stitched large-scaled blue alligator strap; platinum fold-over clasp.

SPLIT-SECONDS MONOPUSHER CHRONOGRAPH WITH PERPETUAL CALENDAR REF. 5951P

Movement: manual-winding CHR 27-525 PS Q caliber; split-seconds monopusher chronograph with column-wheel control, chronograph and rattrapante hand; Ø 27.3mm, thickness: 7.3mm; 48-hour power reserve; 400 components; 27 jewels; 21,600 vph; two-arm Gyromax balance, eight poising weights; Breguet balance spring. **Functions:** hours, minute; chronograph: sweep chronograph and rattrapante hands; subdial: seconds subdial at 9, 60-minute counter at 3, date at 6; perpetual calendar with day, month, leap year, and day/night indication in apertures and analog date; moonphase.
Case: 950 platinum; Ø 37mm, thickness: 12.35mm; interchangeable solid platinum and sapphire crystal caseback; satin-finished frame with fold-filled engravings in the corners; water resistant to 3atm.

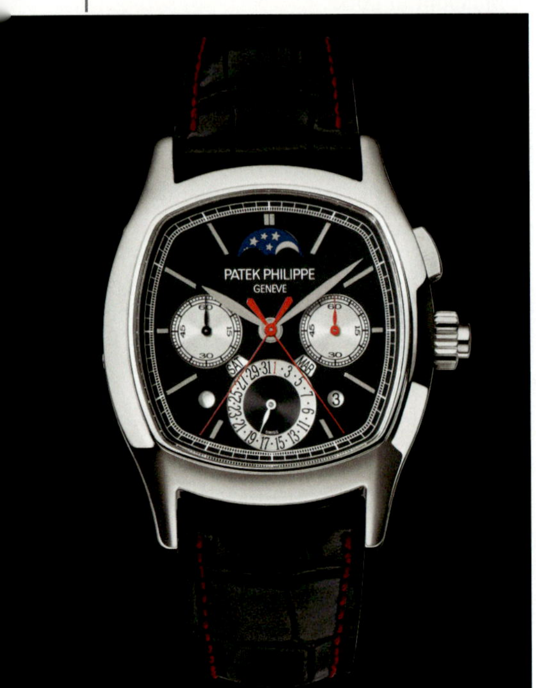

Dial: black; transfer-printed railway track minute scale along entire periphery; 12 applied 18K white-gold baton-style hour markers; 18K white-gold leaf-shaped hour and minute hands; red painted arrow-style counterbalanced sweep chronograph and rattrapante hands; rhodium-plated subdials with circular guilloché patterns: seconds subdial at 9: 18K white-gold and painted black leaf-shaped seconds hand; 60-minute counter at 3: 18K white-gold and painted red leaf-shaped minute-counter hand; date at 6 on two-tone dial, rhodium-plated on the outside ring and black in the center: 18K white-gold and painted white leaf-shaped hand.
Strap: hand-stitched alligator with large rectangular scales, matte black with red stitching; platinum prong buckle.

SPLIT-SECONDS MONOPUSHER CHRONOGRAPH REF. 5950A

Movement: manual-winding CHR 27-525 PS caliber; split-seconds monopusher chronograph with column-wheel control, chronograph hand, 60-minute counter, subsidiary seconds; Ø 27.3mm, thickness: 5.25mm; 48-hour power reserve; 252 components; 27 jewels; 21,600 vph; two-arm Gyromax balance, eight poising weights; Breguet balance spring.
Functions: hours, minutes; chronograph: sweep seconds and rattrapante hands; subsidiary dials: seconds subdial at 9, continuously running 60-minute counter at 3; chronograph start, stop and reset with in-crown pushpiece; rattrapante function with pushpiece between 1 and 2.

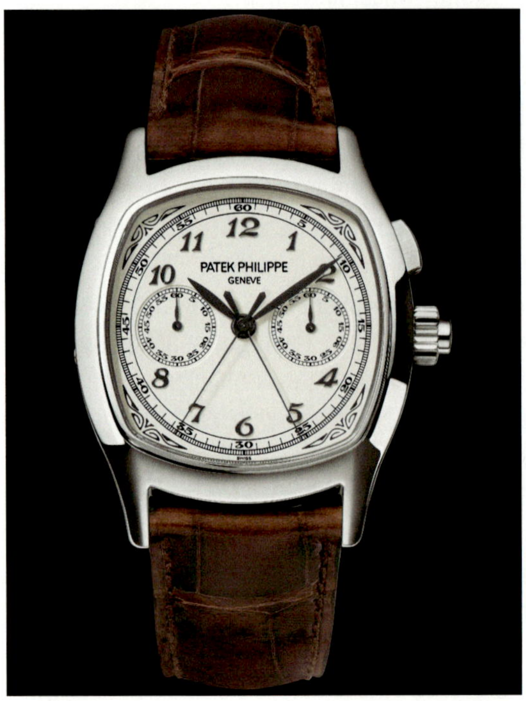

Case: stainless steel; Ø 37mm, thickness: 10.15mm; cambered sapphire crystal caseback; interchangeable solid stainless steel and sapphire crystal snap caseback; satin-finished frame with fold-filled engravings in the corners; water resistant to 3atm.
Dial: silvery opaline; black lacquered corner engravings; transfer-printed railway-track minute scale along the periphery; 10 applied 18K white-gold and black oxidized Breguet numerals; 18K yellow-gold and black oxidized leaf-shaped hour and minute markers; black oxidized counterbalanced chronograph and rattrapante arrow-style hands; circular guilloché patterns on subdials: seconds subdial at 9: 18K yellow-gold and black oxidized leaf-shaped hands; 60-minute counter at 3: 18K yellow-gold and black oxidized leaf-shaped hand.
Strap: hand-stitched shiny brown alligator skin with rectangular scales; 18K white-gold prong buckle with black-lacquered engraving.

NAUTILUS CHRONOGRAPH REF. 5980R

Movement: automatic-winding CH 28-520 C caliber; column-wheel chronograph; Ø 30mm, thickness: 6.63mm; 55-hour power reserve; 327 components; 35 jewels; 28,800 vph; four-arm Gyromax balance, four poising weights; Breguet balance spring.
Functions: hours, minutes; chronograph: sweep chronograph seconds hand; dual subsidiary counter dial at 6: 60-minute counter (counts the elapsed minutes on two concentric scales from 0 to 30 in black and from 30 to 60 in red), 12-hour counter; quick-action date at 3 based on a patent granted to Patek Philippe in 1991 (date-change in less than a tenth of a second).
Case: 18K rose gold; Ø 44mm, thickness: 12.16mm; screw-down crown; sapphire crystal caseback; vertical satin finish bezel; water resistant to 20atm.
Dial: gradation from brown in the middle to dark brown at the periphery, horizontal embossed pattern; nine applied 18K rose-gold baton markers with SuperLumiNova luminescent coating; 18K rose-gold baton-style hour and minute hands with SuperLumiNova luminescent coating; sandblasted and gold-plated steel chronograph/seconds hand; two-zone monocounter with brown circular guilloché center and silvery periphery, separated by a gold thread; white lacquered brass baton-style counterbalanced hour-counter hand; red lacquered brass arrow-shaped counterbalanced minute-counter hand.
Strap: hand-stitched large-scale alligator skin; 18K rose-gold fold-over clasp.

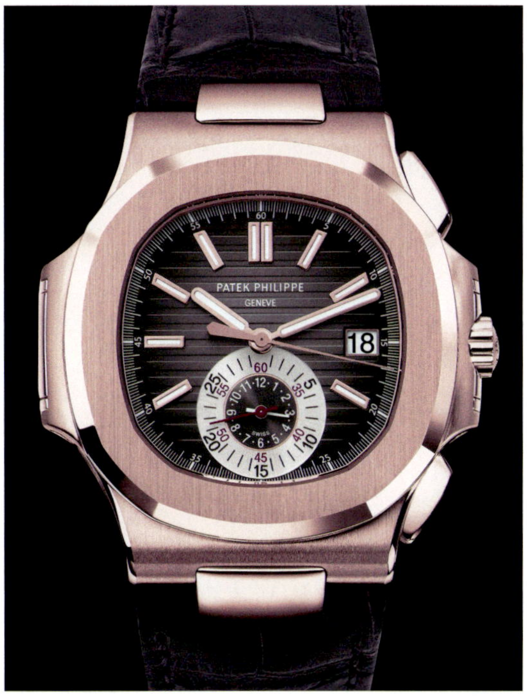

NAUTILUS CHRONOGRAPH REF. 5980/1A

Movement: automatic-winding CH 28-520 C caliber; column-wheel chronograph; Ø 30mm, thickness: 6.63mm; 55-hour power reserve; 327 components; 35 jewels; 28,800 vph; four-arm Gyromax balance, four poising weights; Breguet balance spring.
Functions: hours, minute; chronograph: sweep chronograph seconds hand; dual subsidiary counter dial at 6: 60-minute counter (counts the elapsed minutes on two concentric scales from 0 to 30 in black and from 30 to 60 in red), 12-hour counter; quick-action date at 3 based on a patent granted to Patek Philippe in 1991 (date-change in less than a tenth of a second).
Case: stainless steel; Ø 44mm, thickness: 12.16mm; sapphire crystal caseback; screw-down crown; vertical satin finish bezel; water resistant to 20atm.
Dial: gradation from charcoal gray in the center to black at the periphery, horizontal embossed pattern; nine applied 18K white-gold baton markers with SuperLumiNova luminescent coating; 18K white-gold baton-style hour and minute hands with SuperLumiNova luminescent coating; sandblasted and rhodium-plated steel chronograph hand; two-zone monocounter with brown circular guilloché center and silvery periphery, separated by a gold thread; white lacquered brass baton-style counterbalanced hour-counter hand; red lacquered brass arrow-shaped counterbalanced minute-counter hand.
Bracelet: stainless steel, middle links polished, outer links satin-finished; stainless steel fold-over clasp.

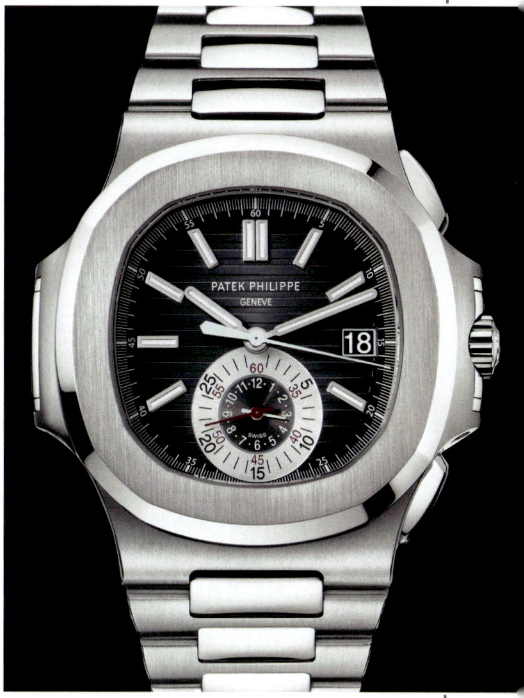

CALIBER 27-525 PS Q

Movement: manual-winding; Ø 27.3mm, thickness 7.3mm; 48-hour power reserve; 27 jewels; 21,600 vph; two-arm Gyromax with eight poising weights; Breguet balance spring.
Functions: split-seconds chronograph with column-wheel control; chronograph and rattrapante hands; 60-minute counter, seconds subdial; perpetual calendar with day, month, leap year, and day/night indication in apertures and analog date; moon-phase.

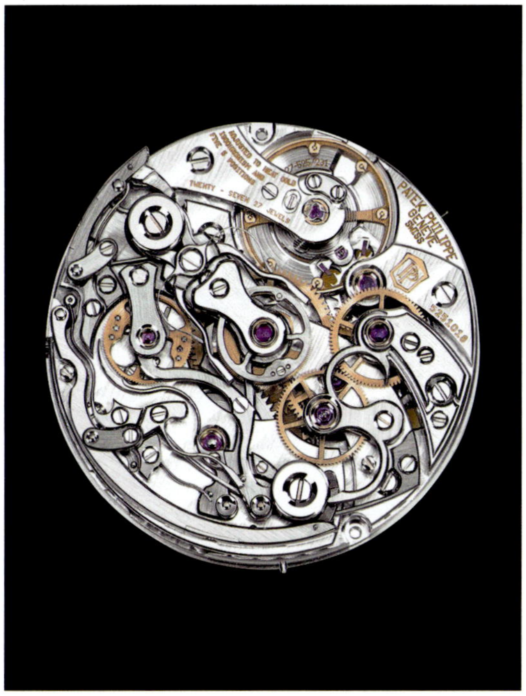

CALIBER 28-520 C

Movement: 55-hour power reserve; Ø 30mm; 35 jewels, 327 components; 13 bridges; 28,800 vph; Breguet balance spring.
Functions: chronograph with 60-minute and 12-hour monocounter; date.

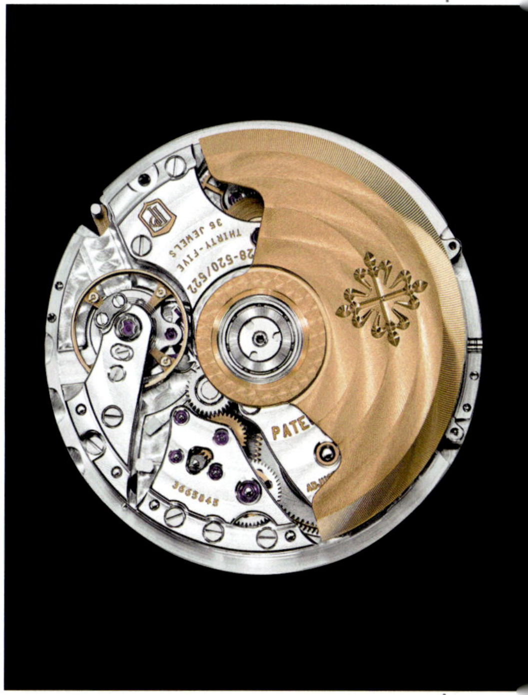

SEDUCTION OF REDUCTION

A pioneer in the realm of ultra-thin movements, Piaget introduced the world's thinnest automatic in 1960. Fifty years later, the Swiss manufacture celebrates its record-breaking achievement by repeating it.

The story begins with Calibre 12P, a groundbreaking design from 1960 that demonstrated Piaget's expertise in micro-mechanics and heralded a procession of ever-thinner movements to come. To honor the 12P's golden anniversary in 2010, the company presented two worthy heirs, Calibre 1200P and Calibre 1208P. At just 2.35mm thick, they are both thin enough for Piaget to reclaim the title for world's thinnest automatic movement.

To showcase both of these mechanisms, Piaget introduced a new version of its Altiplano, the signature case it uses for many of the brand's ultra-thin timepieces. The newly redesigned Altiplano measures 43mm in diameter.

The expansion creates more room for calibers 1200P and 1208P to spread out laterally. As a result of this wider design, engineers were also able to reduce the Altiplano's overall height to 5.25mm. According to the brand, this makes the 43mm Altiplano the thinnest in its category.

Calibre 1200P makes its debut in the Altiplano Anniversary Edition. Its understated design distills a wristwatch to its essentials, creating a harmonious design to which nothing need be added and from which nothing need be removed. The dial embodies this simple elegance with baton hour markers arranged on a ring of guilloché.

Piaget will issue the Altiplano Anniversary Edition in a limited and numbered series that includes 235 made in white gold with a black dial and an equal number in pink gold with a blue dial. The production run of 235 pieces is of course a sly reference to the movement's record-setting measurement.

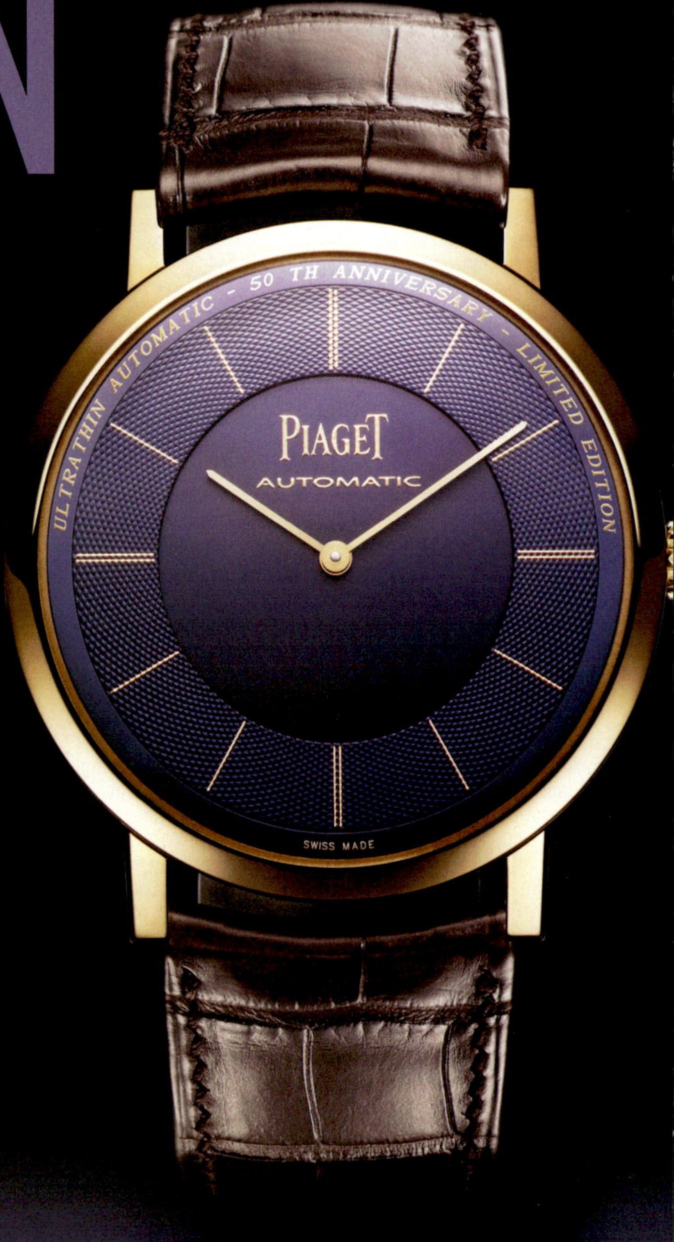

ABOVE

This pink-gold version of the Altiplano Anniversary Edition commemorates the 50th anniversary of the historic Calibre 12P, and features a platinum micro-rotor engraved with the Piaget coat of arms.

FACING PAGE

Now offered as part of Piaget's general collection, the white-gold Altiplano 43mm features baton hands and hour markers along with small seconds at 4 o'clock.

To honor the golden anniversary of the 12P, Piaget's groundbreaking movement, the company released Calibre 1200P and Calibre 1208P. Both movements, measuring just 2.35mm, qualify for the title of world's thinnest.

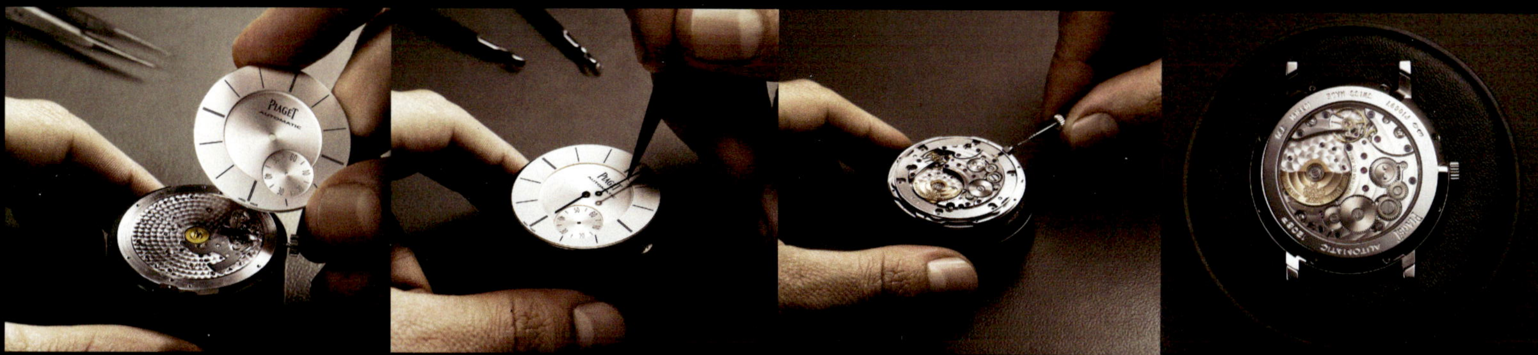

Because the new Altiplano case is so exceptional, Piaget is now offering the 43mm case as part of the brand's general collection. The first member of this new line, the Altiplano 43mm, is powered by Calibre 1208P. Much like the anniversary caliber, this highly decorated movement reflects hours of traditional hand finishing, including beveled bridges adorned with Côtes de Genève, circular sunray-brushed wheels, tapering lugs, slender bezel and a visually refined dial. The small seconds display at 4 o'clock adds visual interest to the dial and makes the extreme thinness of the movement even more impressive.

To replenish the watch's 40-hour power reserve, Piaget includes a pink-gold micro-rotor engraved with the brand's coat of arms. For its inaugural year, Piaget will offer the Altiplano 43mm in white or pink gold with a silver dial.

Its classic styling may recall a more elegant time, but this is far from a vintage or retro piece. The extreme technical sophistication of its mechanics and its timeless style make the Altiplano nothing less than a modern classic.

With new ultra-thin models like the Altiplano Anniversary Edition and Altiplano 43mm, Piaget demonstrates the firm's remarkable ability to create seduction by reduction.

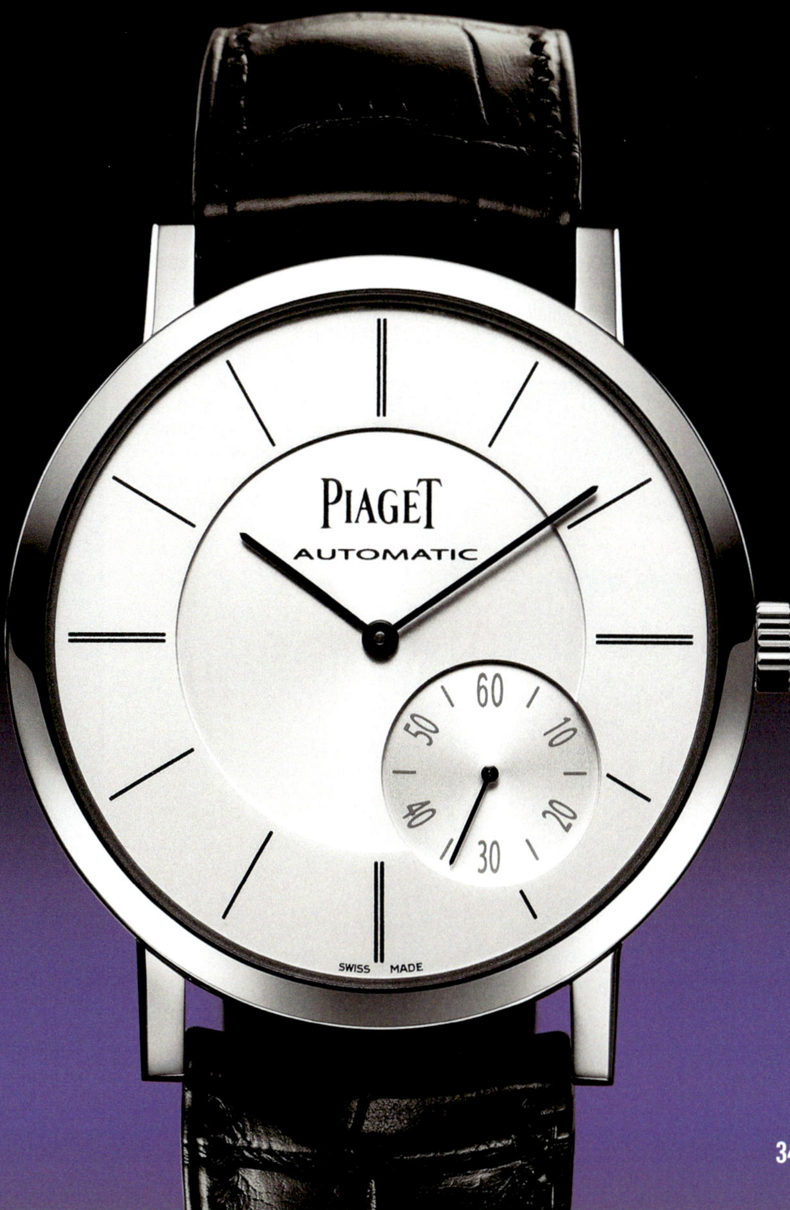

PIAGET EMPERADOR — REF. GOA33070

Movement: automatic-winding Piaget 551P; Ø 20.5mm, thickness: 4.95mm; approx. 40-hour power reserve; 27 jewels; 21,600 vph; circular Côtes de Genève; beveled hand-drawn bridges; blued screws.
Functions: hours, minutes; small seconds at 10; power reserve indicator at 6.
Case: 18K pink gold.
Dial: silvered sunburst; applied 18K pink-gold hour-markers and the Piaget coat of arms.
Strap: brown alligator leather; 18K pink-gold pin buckle.

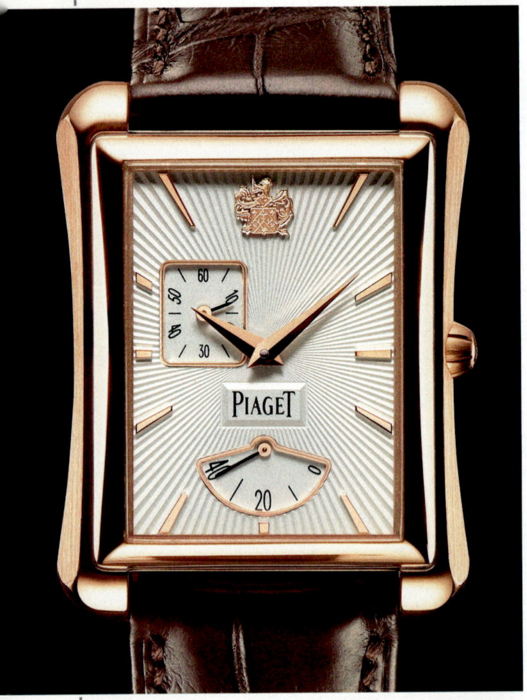

PIAGET EMPERADOR SKELETON TOURBILLON — REF. GOA29108

Movement: manual-winding Piaget 600P skeleton tourbillon; Ø 28.64mm, thickness: 3.5mm; 40-hour power reserve; 24 jewels; 21,600 vph; circular Côtes de Genève; beveled hand-drawn bridges; blued screws.
Functions: hours, minutes, seconds; power reserve at 6.
Case: white gold; 32x41mm; sapphire crystal caseback; water resistant to 3atm.
Dial: skeleton.
Strap: black alligator leather; 18K white-gold folding clasp.

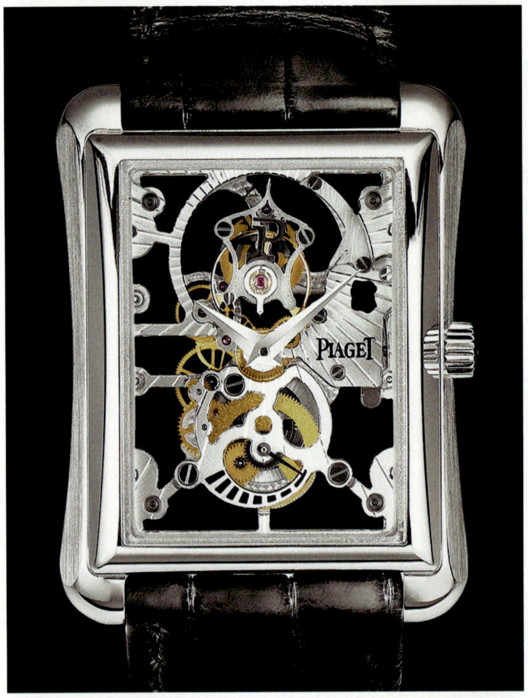

PIAGET EMPERADOR COUSSIN PERPETUAL CALENDAR — REF. GOA33019

Movement: automatic-winding Piaget 855P perpetual calendar; Ø 28.4mm, thickness: 5.6mm; approx. 72-hour power reserve; 38 jewels; 21,600 vph; circular Côtes de Genève; circular-grained plate; bridges beveled and drawn with a file; blued screws; oscillating weight engraved with the Piaget coat of arms.
Functions: hours, minutes; small seconds at 4; month/leap year at 12; retrograde date indicator at 3; dual time at 8; retrograde day indicator at 9.
Case: 18K pink gold; sapphire crystal caseback.
Dial: blue; three satin-finished counters; applied 18K pink-gold hour markers.
Strap: brown alligator leather; 18K pink-gold pin buckle.

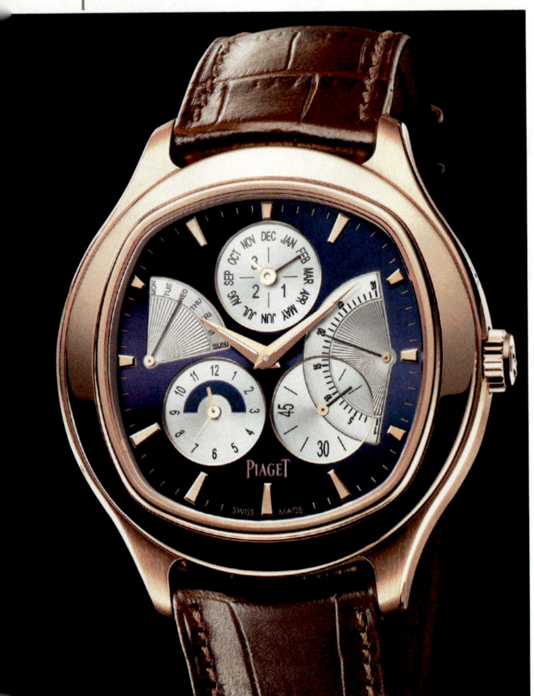

PIAGET EMPERADOR COUSSIN MOON PHASE — REF. GOA34021

Movement: automatic-winding Piaget 860P; Ø 28.4mm, thickness: 6.15mm; 72-hour power reserve; 25 jewels; 21,600 vph; circular Côtes de Genève; circular-grained mainplate; beveled bridges; blued screws.
Functions: hours, minutes; moonphase.
Case: 18K white gold; XL model; sapphire crystal caseback.
Dial: slate-gray; applied 18K white-gold hour markers; sunburst satin-brushed; silvered center; large 18K white-gold moon at 6.
Strap: black alligator leather; 18K white-gold folding clasp.

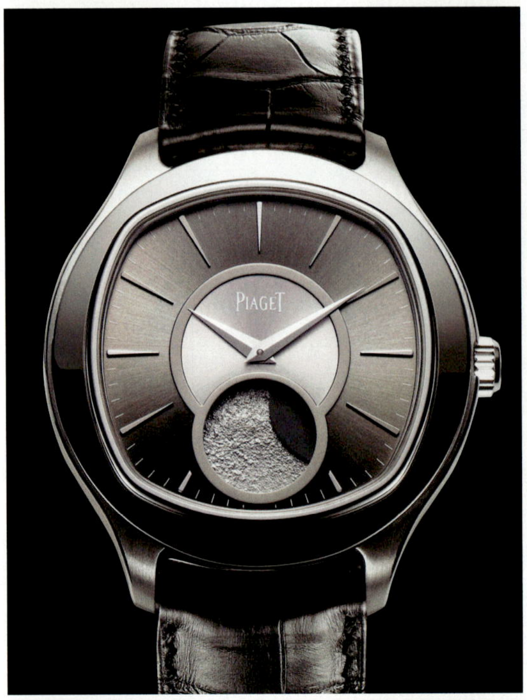

PIAGET EMPERADOR COUSSIN REF. G0A32016

Movement: automatic-winding Piaget 850P; Ø 26.8mm, thickness: 4mm; approx. 72-hour power reserve; 30 jewels; 21,600 vph; circular Côtes de Genève; circular-grained plate; beveled bridges; blued screws.
Functions: hours, minutes; small seconds at 4; date at 12; dual time at 8 with day/night indicator.
Case: 18K white gold; sapphire crystal caseback.
Dial: silvered; sunburst guilloché; polished white-gold counters; applied white-gold indexes.
Strap: black alligator leather; 18K white-gold folding clasp.

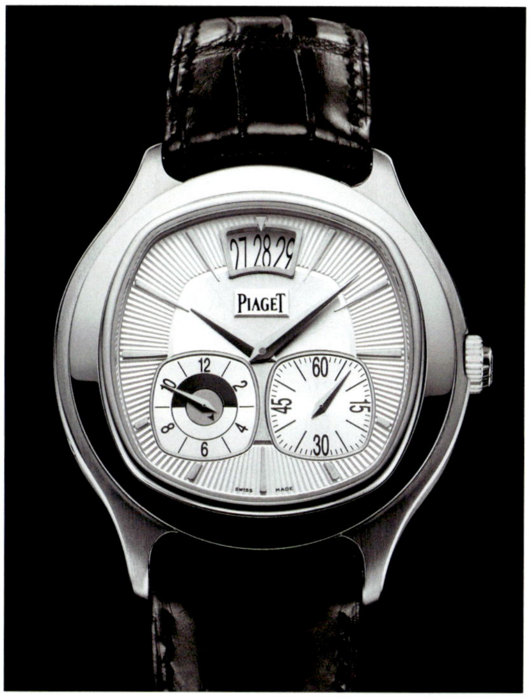

PIAGET EMPERADOR COUSSIN REGULATOR REF. G0A34025

Movement: manual-winding Piaget 835P; Ø 26.8mm, thickness: 3.9mm; approx. 60-hour power reserve; 27 jewels, 21,600 vph; circular Côtes de Genève; circular-grained mainplate; beveled bridges; blued screws.
Functions: hours, minutes; retrograde seconds at 12; hour subdial at 6; central minute hand.
Case: 18K pink gold; sapphire crystal caseback.
Dial: blue; applied 18K pink-gold hour and minute markers.
Strap: blue alligator leather; 18K pink-gold folding clasp.

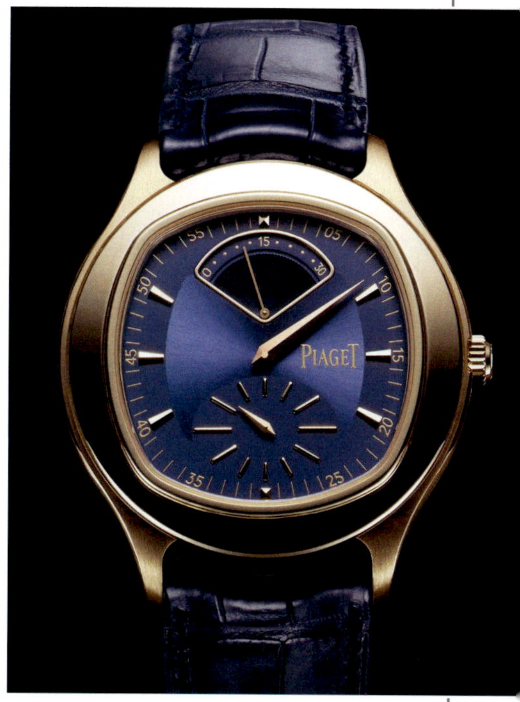

PIAGET RECTANGLE A L'ANCIENNE REF. G0A33061

Movement: automatic-winding Piaget 561P; Ø 20.5mm, thickness: 5.1mm; approx. 40-hour power reserve; 29 jewels; 21,600 vph; circular Côtes de Genève; circular-grained plates; beveled bridges; blued screws.
Functions: hours, minutes; retrograde seconds at 12; large date; power reserve at 6.
Case: 18K white gold.
Dial: polished 18K white gold; silvered; Grains d'orge guilloché center; applied silver index.
Strap: black alligator leather; 18K white-gold ardillon buckle.

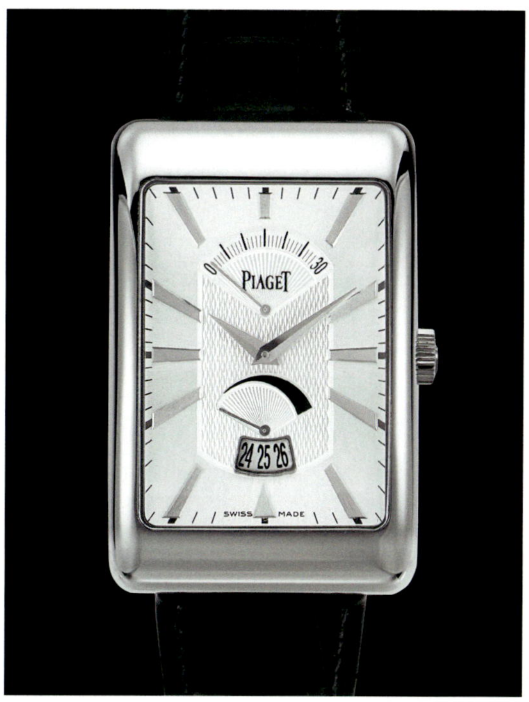

PIAGET PROTOCOLE XXL REF. G0A32005

Movement: manual-winding Piaget 830P; Ø 26.8mm, thickness: 2.5mm; approx. 60-hour power reserve; 19 jewels; 21,600 vph; circular Côtes de Genève; circular-grained mainplate; beveled and drawn-out bridges; blued screws.
Functions: hours, minutes.
Case: 18K pink gold; large model; vertical guilloché motifs and alternating polished and satin-brushed surfaces; sapphire crystal caseback.
Dial: silvered; applied 18K pink-gold hour markers.
Strap: brown alligator leather; 18K pink-gold folding clasp.

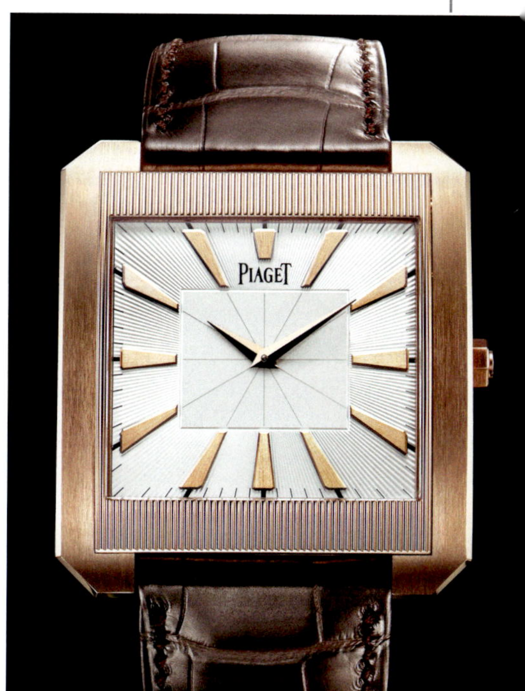

PIAGET ALTIPLANO 38MM — REF. GOA29112

Movement: manual-winding, ultra-thin Piaget 430P; Ø 20.5mm, thickness: 2.15mm; 18 jewels; 21,600 vph; circular Côtes de Genève; circular-grained plate; bridges beveled and drawn with a file; blued screws.
Functions: hours, minutes.
Case: 18K white gold; Ø 38mm.
Dial: silvered; black baton hour markers; baton hands.
Strap: black alligator leather; 18K white-gold pin buckle.

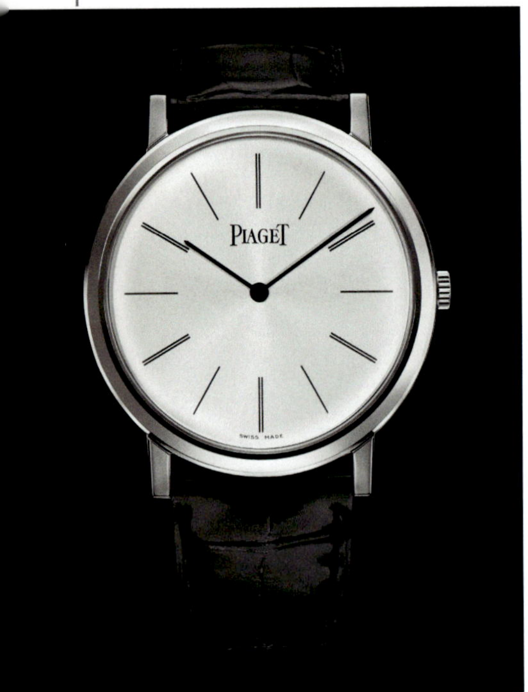

PIAGET ALTIPLANO 43MM — REF. GOA35130

Movement: automatic-winding, ultra-thin Piaget 1208P; Ø 29.9mm, thickness: 2.35mm; approx. 40-hour power reserve; 27 jewels; 21,600 vph; circular Côtes de Genève; circular-grained plate; beveled bridges; 22K pink-gold oscillating weight engraved with Piaget coat of arms.
Functions: hours, minutes; small seconds at 4.
Case: 18K white gold; Ø 43mm.
Dial: silvered; black baton hour markers; baton hands.
Strap: black alligator leather; 18K white-gold pin buckle.

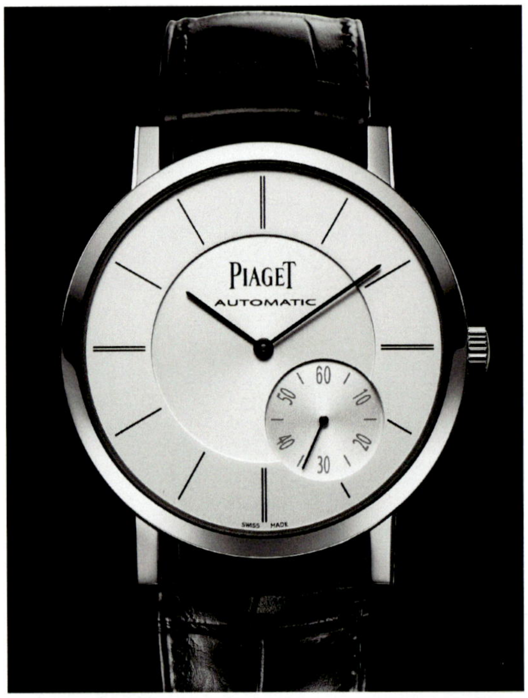

PIAGET ALTIPLANO SKELETON — REF. GOA33115

Movement: manual-winding Piaget 838P skeleton; Ø 26.8mm, thickness: 2.7 mm; approx. 60-hour power reserve; 19 jewels; 21,600 vph; circular Côtes de Genève; sunburst guilloché; circular-grained bottom plate; beveled hand-drawn bridges; blued screws.
Functions: hours, minutes; small seconds at 10.
Case: 18K white gold.
Dial: silvered flange; gray hour markers.
Strap: black alligator leather; 18K white-gold pin buckle.

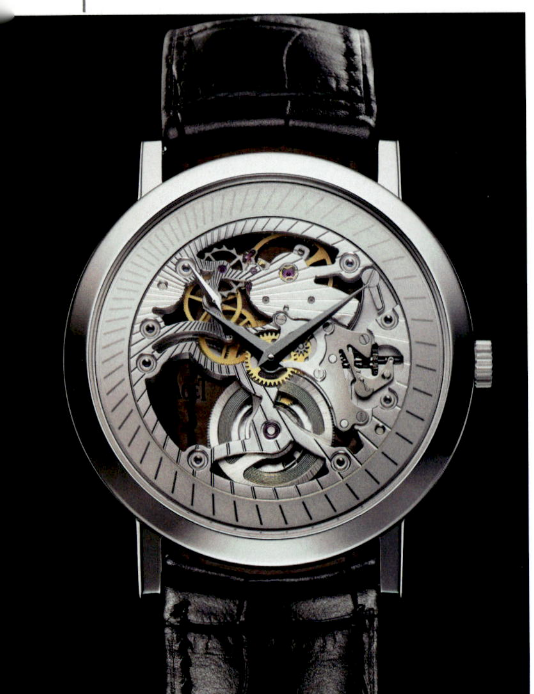

PIAGET ALTIPLANO 34MM — REF. GOA31107

Movement: manual-winding, ultra-thin Piaget 450P; thickness: 2.1mm; approx. 40-hour power reserve; 18 jewels; 21,600 vph; circular Côtes de Genève finishing; rhodium-plated beveled bridges.
Functions: hours, minutes; small seconds.
Case: 18K pink gold; medium model; Ø 34mm; set with 72 brilliant-cut diamonds (approx. 0.5 carat).
Dial: white mother-of-pearl; stylized gilded Arabic numerals; small seconds at 10, ringed with 28 brilliant-cut diamonds (approx. 0.1 carat).
Strap: white satin; 18K pink-gold pin buckle.
Also available: white-gold version.

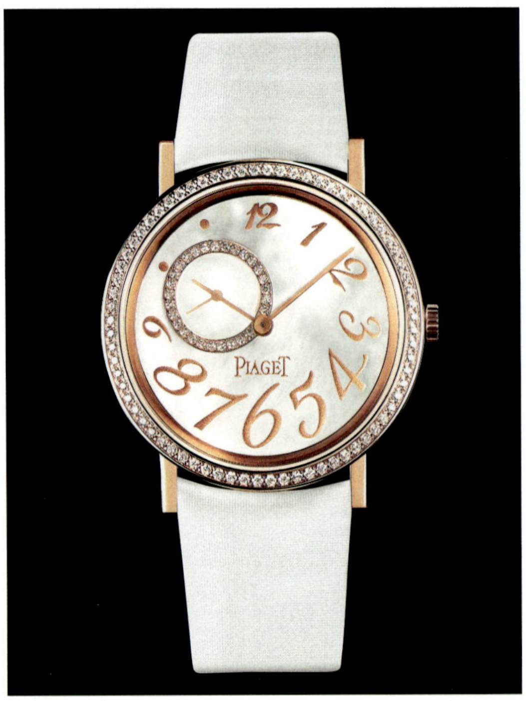

PIAGET POLO FORTYFIVE CHRONOGRAPH REF. GOA34002

Movement: automatic-winding Piaget 880P chronograph; Ø 26.8mm, thickness: 5.6mm; approx. 50-hour power reserve (double barrel); 35 jewels; 28,800 vph; circular Côtes de Genève; circular-grained mainplate; beveled bridges; blued screws.
Functions: hours, minutes; small seconds at 6; dual 24-hour time zone at 9; flyback chronograph function: 30-minute counter at 3.
Case: titanium; large model; titanium bezel with alternating satin-brushed surfaces and polished steel gadroons; titanium and rubber screw-down crown; sapphire crystal caseback; water resistant to 10atm.
Dial: black; luminescent hour markers.
Strap: rubber with steel inserts; steel triple-folding safety clasp with summer and winter positions.

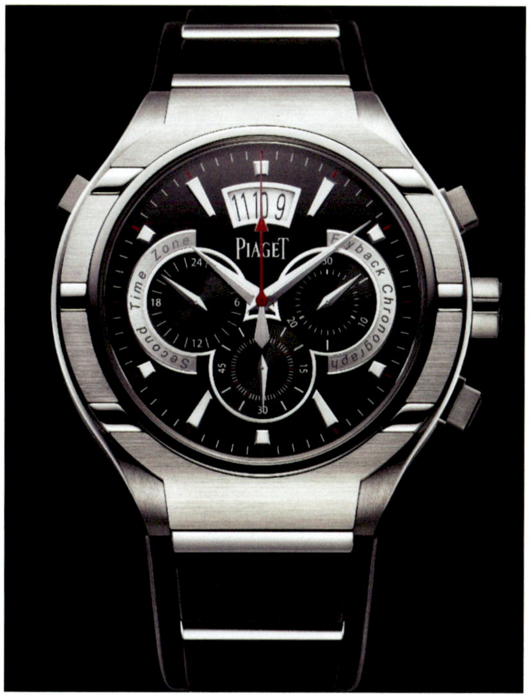

PIAGET POLO FORTYFIVE LADY REF. GOA35013

Movement: Piaget 15P quartz.
Functions: hours, minutes, seconds; date at 6.
Case: 18K pink gold; Ø 38mm; bezel set with 50 brilliant-cut diamonds (approx. 0.7 carat); polished gadroons; water resistant to 5atm.
Dial: white; set with eight brilliant-cut diamonds (approx. 0.05 carat); applied luminescent Arabic numerals and hour markers.
Strap: white rubber; 18K pink-gold inserts; 18K pink-gold pin buckle.

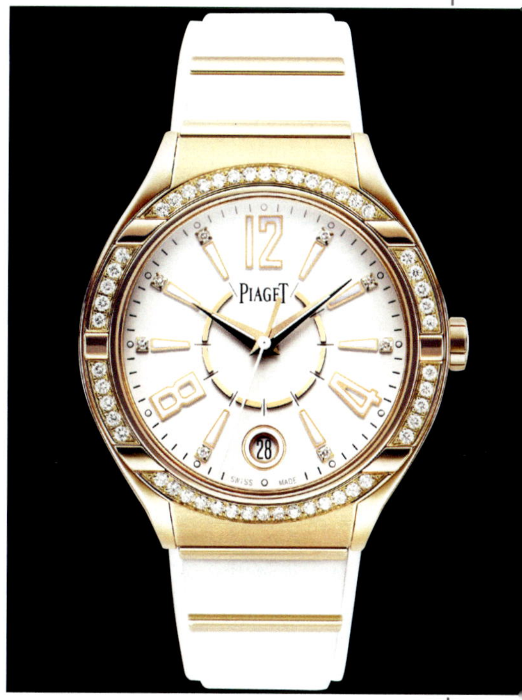

PIAGET POLO AUTOMATIC REF. GOA31149

Movement: automatic-winding Piaget 800P; Ø 26.8mm, thickness: 4mm; approx. 72-hour power reserve; 25 jewels; 21,600 vph; circular Côtes de Genève; circular-grained plate; bridges beveled and drawn with a file.
Functions: hours, minutes, seconds; date at 6.
Case: 18K pink gold; sapphire crystal caseback.
Dial: silvered; applied 18K pink-gold Arabic numerals and hour markers.
Strap: brown alligator leather; 18K pink-gold folding clasp.

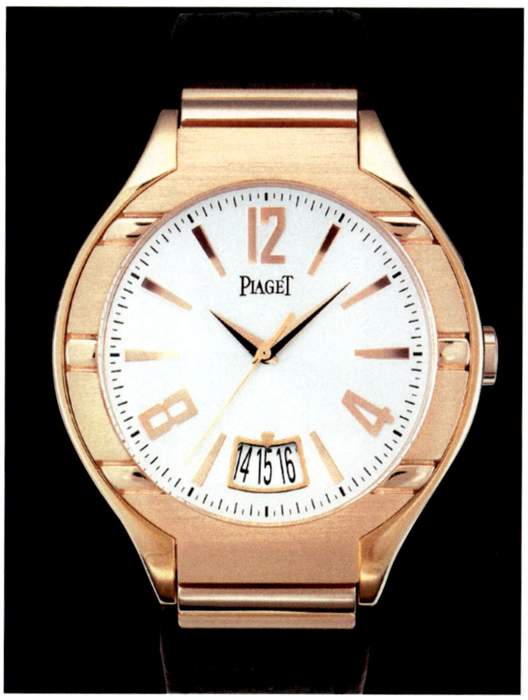

PIAGET POLO TOURBILLON RELATIF REF. GOA31123

Movement: manual-winding Piaget 608P tourbillon; Ø 25.6mm, thickness: 3.28mm; approx. 72-hour power reserve; 27 jewels; 21,600 vph; circular Côtes de Genève; bridges beveled and drawn with a file; blued screws.
Functions: hours, minutes, seconds; flying tourbillon: the minute hand, which has its center of rotation at the center of the watch, performs one complete rotation per hour; the 0.2g tourbillon carriage with three titanium bridges, suspended on the minute hand, spins once per minute on its own axis.
Case: 18K white gold.
Dial: silvered; applied white-gold Arabic numerals and hour markers.
Strap: black alligator leather; 18K white-gold folding clasp.
Also available: diamond-set version.

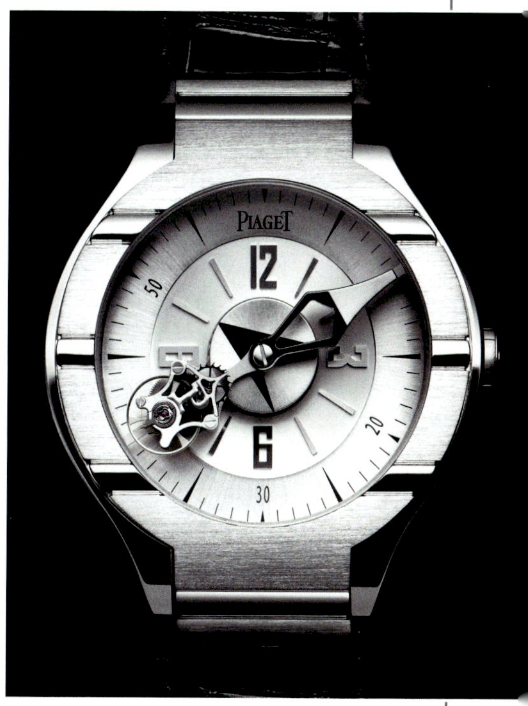

LIMELIGHT MAGIC HOUR — REF. G0A35099

Movement: Piaget 56P quartz.
Functions: hours, minutes.
Case: 18K white gold; set with 302 brilliant-cut diamonds (approx. 4.9 carats).
Note: an invisible mechanism developed in-house endows this timepiece with the unique power to be three watches in one: when positioned horizontally, the ellipse provides a generous dial opening; with a touch, the oval swivels to take on a slant; with another 45° turn, diamond-set numerals are revealed.
Dial: silvered; set with 20 brilliant-cut diamonds (approx. 0.03 carat).
Strap: black satin; 18K white-gold pin buckle.

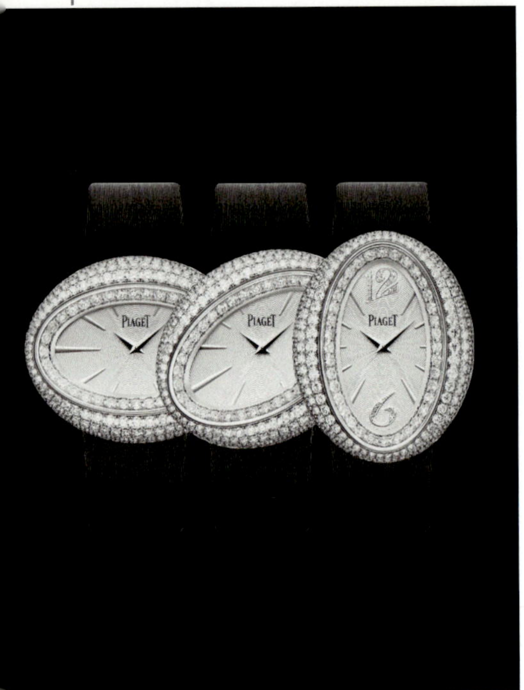

LIMELIGHT TWICE — REF. G0A34137

ONE WATCH, TWO DIALS: two quartz 56P movements; total of 332 brilliant-cut diamonds (approx. 6 carats), on black satin strap with reversible integrated clasp.

FIRST DIAL:
Case: 18K white gold; 52 brilliant-cut diamonds (approx. 1.2 carats).
Dial: silver colored; black Roman numerals.
Clasp: 18K white gold.

SECOND DIAL:
Case: 18K white gold; sunburst motif; set with 226 brilliant-cut diamonds (approx. 4.6 carats).
Dial: black.
Clasp: 18K white gold; set with 54 brilliant-cut diamonds (approx. 0.2 carat).

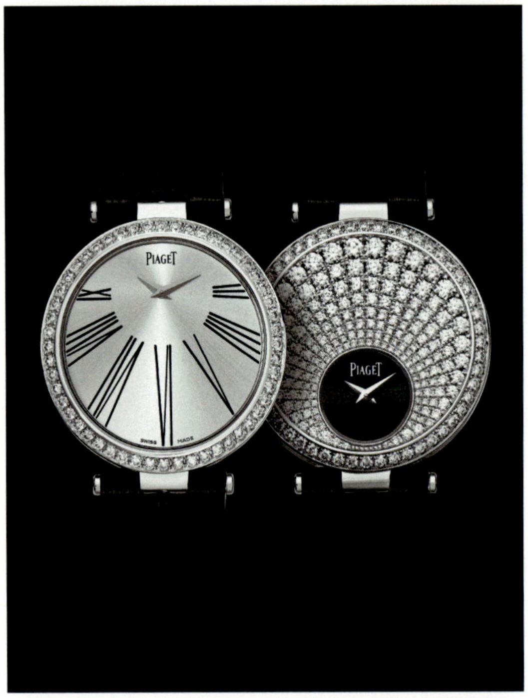

LIMELIGHT JAZZ PARTY — REF. G0A35157

Movement: Piaget 56P quartz; Ø 26.2mm, thickness: 2.5mm; 7 jewels.
Functions: hours, minutes.
Case: 18K white gold; set with 124 brilliant-cut diamonds (approx. 2.5 carats).
Dial: 18K white gold; set with 335 brilliant-cut diamonds (approx. 2.0 carats).
Bracelet: 18K white gold; set with 522 brilliant-cut diamonds (approx. 16.3 carats).

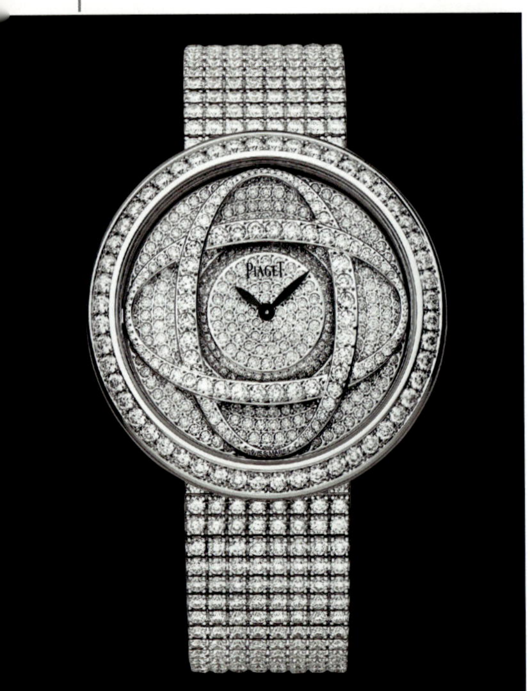

LIMELIGHT FRINGES INSPIRATION — REF. G0A34063

Movement: Piaget 56P quartz; Ø 26.2mm, thickness: 2.5mm; 7 jewels.
Functions: hours, minutes.
Case: 18K pink gold; set with 102 brilliant-cut diamonds (approx. 3.1 carats).
Dial: silvered; three brilliant-cut diamond indexes (approx. 0.02 carat).
Strap: brown satin; clasp set with 34 brilliant-cut diamonds (approx. 0.3 carat).

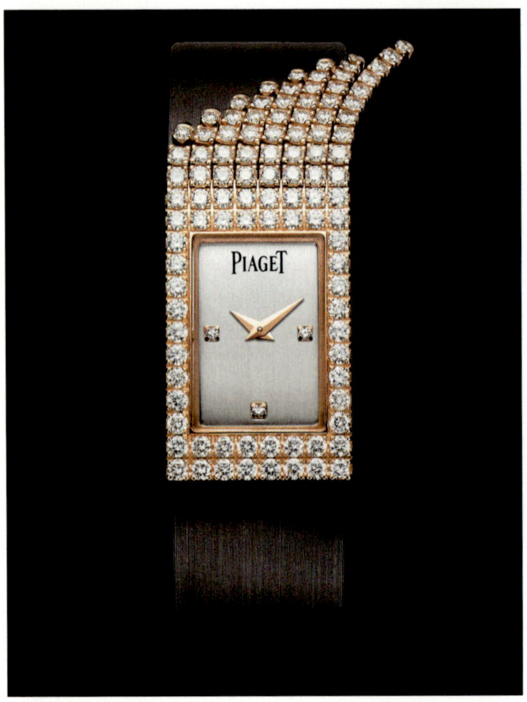

PIAGET TRADITION REF. G0A10800

Movement: manual-winding Piaget 430P; Ø 20.5mm, thickness: 2.15mm; 40-hour power reserve; 18 jewels; 21,600 vph; circular Côtes de Genève; circulargrained plate; beveled hand-drawn bridges; blued screws.
Functions: hours, minutes.
Case: 18K white gold; set with 50 brilliant-cut diamonds (approx. 0.8 carat).
Dial: silvered; 12 brilliant-cut diamond indexes (approx. 0.1 carat).
Bracelet: 18K white-gold; integrated clasp.

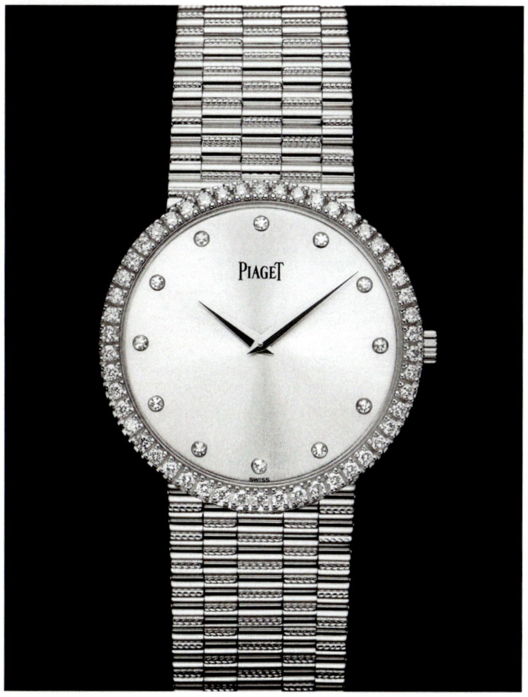

PIAGET DANCER REF. G0A34055

Movement: manual-winding, ultra-thin Piaget 430P; Ø 20.5mm, thickness: 2.15mm; 40-hour power reserve; 18 jewels; 21,600 vph; circular Côtes de Genève; circular-grained plate; beveled hand-drawn bridges; blued screws.
Functions: hours, minutes.
Case: 18K pink gold.
Dial: silvered; applied 18K pink-gold and black indexes.
Bracelet: 18K pink gold; integrated clasp.

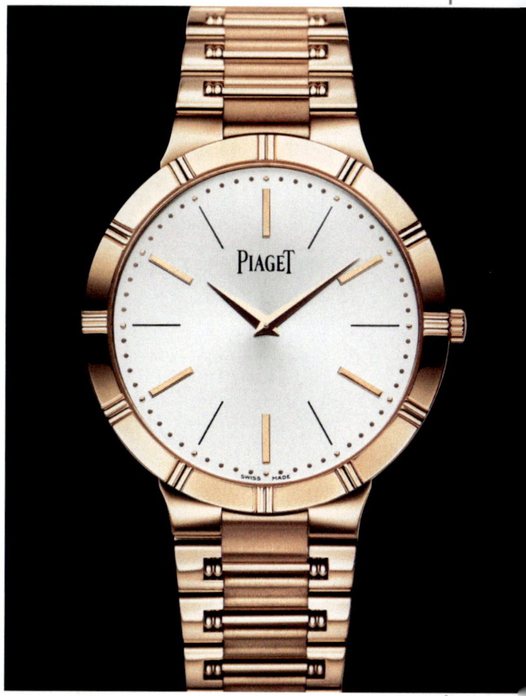

PIAGET POLO REF. G0A33223

Movement: automatic-winding Piaget 504P; Ø 24.6mm, thickness: 3.55mm; 40-hour power reserve; 26 jewels; 21,600 vph; circular Côtes de Genève; circular-grained plate; beveled bridges; blued screws.
Functions: hours, minutes, seconds; date at 6.
Case: 18K white gold; set with 34 brilliant-cut diamonds (approx.1.3 carats); polished gadroons.
Dial: silvered; date underlined with polished 18K white gold; white-gold Arabic numerals; applied index set with 41 brilliant-cut diamonds (0.1 carat).
Bracelet: 18K white gold; integrated folding clasp.

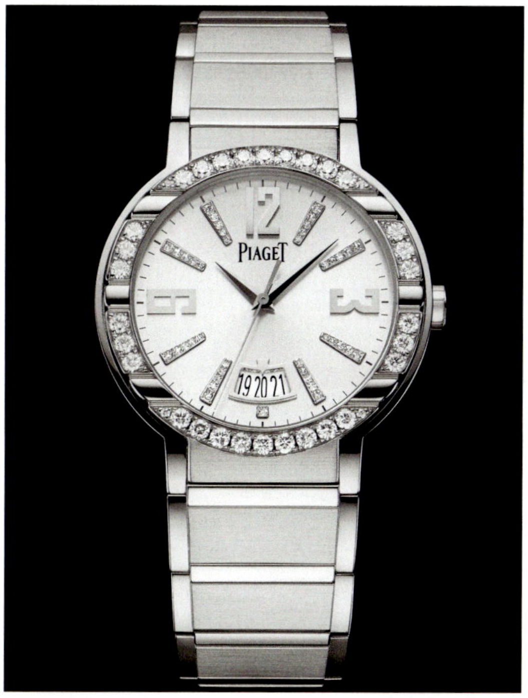

LIMELIGHT TONNEAU XL SHAPE REF. G0A32094

Movement: Piaget 690P quartz.
Functions: hours, minutes.
Case: 18K pink gold; set with 38 brilliant-cut diamonds (approx. 0.9 carats); crown set with one brilliant-cut diamond (approx. 0.1 carat).
Dial: white mother-of-pearl; applied pink-gold Arabic numerals (12 and 6); copper-colored numerals and indexes.
Bracelet: 18K pink gold; integrated folding clasp.

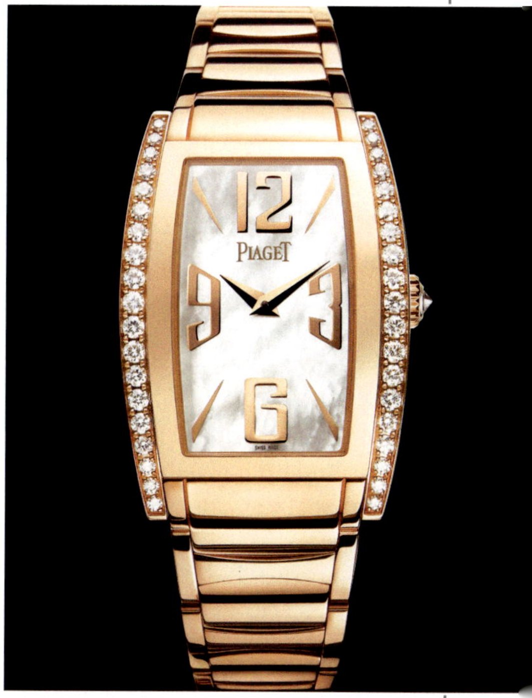

PORSCHE DESIGN
TIMEPIECES
P'6000

A DESIGN LEGACY

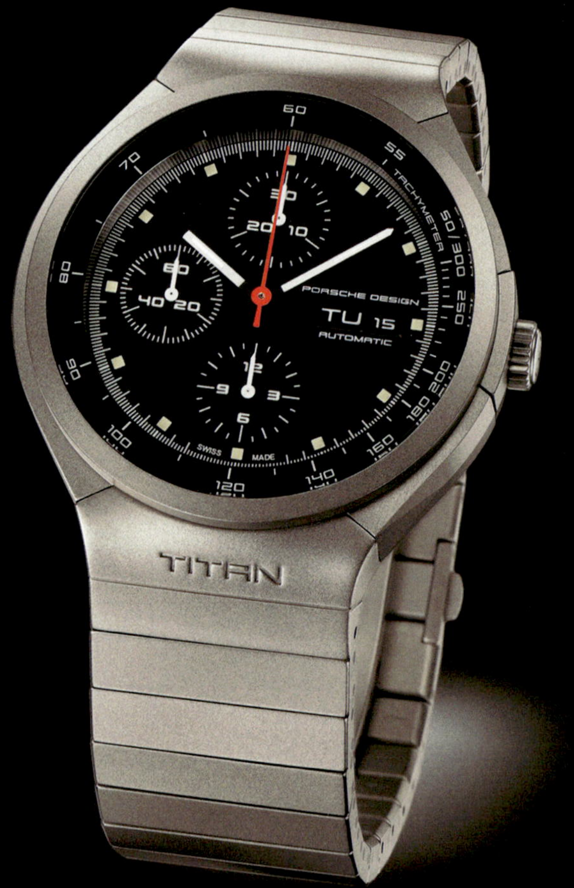

The Porsche Design Studio is organized around one simple principle: form follows function. This approach leads to watches whose every aspect serves a purpose, no matter how small.

The emphasis on functionality springs from the automotive roots of Porsche Design. Professor Ferdinand Alexander Porsche is the son of the man who first brought Porsche into sports cars, and the distinguishing characteristics of highly functional but luxurious automobiles leave their traces all over the timepieces produced by the brand. Porsche Design is now turning to tending its legacy, using its new Heritage collection to revive the glories of the past. The inaugural piece in the collection is the P'6530 Titanium Chronograph. The watch's shot-blasted titanium case includes integrated pushpieces, an engraved edition number on the caseback and a printed tachometric scale on the face's sapphire crystal.

The 1980 first titanium chronograph was the first watch crafted entirely in titanium upon its original release thirty years ago. This reissue remains faithful to the ideas of the original, particularly in its clarity and purity of form. The one change is that the case has been enlarged to encompass a diameter of 44mm, a size more in tune with today's taste for bigger statement watches.

The P'6530 comes in a limited edition of 911 pieces, each one powered by an automatic Valjoux 7750 chronograph movement. Its sleek black dial shows off the horological functions and more besides—a 30-minute counter at 12 o'clock, day and date at 3 o'clock, 12-hour counter at 6 o'clock and small seconds at 9 o'clock. An orange center hand indicates chronograph seconds.

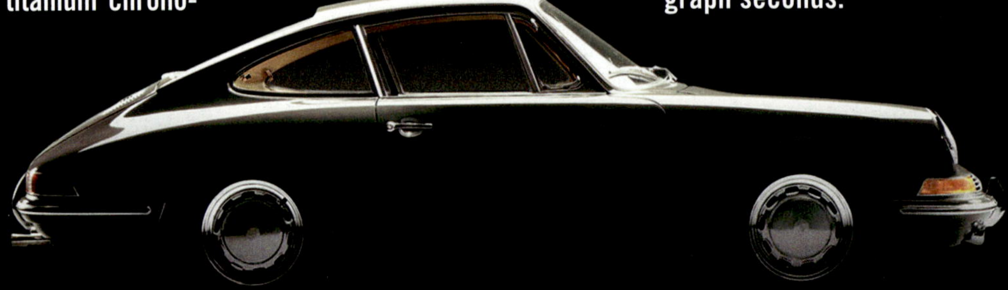

"When you think about the function of something, its design sometimes emerges of its own accord."

— Professor Ferdinand Alexander Porsche

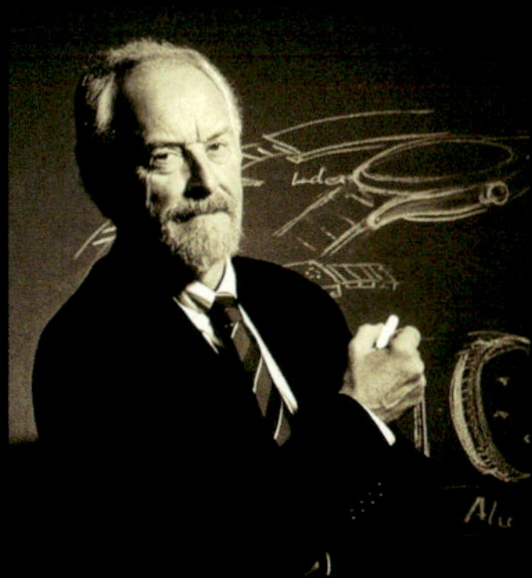

Porsche Design is also focused firmly on the future, with the P'6780 Diver, a new diving watch (the brand's second) that is water resistant to 1,000m (100 bar). The time of the dive is measured via the bezel that rotates counter-clockwise around the perimeter of the dial and bears inscriptions for the minutes. The real revolutionary leap forward, however, lies in the design of the case: a circular stainless steel container houses the dial and the movement, but it is not strapped directly to the wrist, as one would find in other watches. Instead, the container is attached by a hinge to a shot-blasted titanium bridge structure, which in turn is mounted on the strap. This incredibly useful and innovative hinged container can be raised to set the crown, but even more practical is that when it is snapped back into place, neither the crown nor the rotating bezel can be inadvertently turned, thus ensuring that the diver will not accidentally change the diving time or damage the watch. This secure system is completely unique to the P'6780. In another practical touch, the strap has a special extension, allowing it to fit over a diving suit without opening the folding clasp.

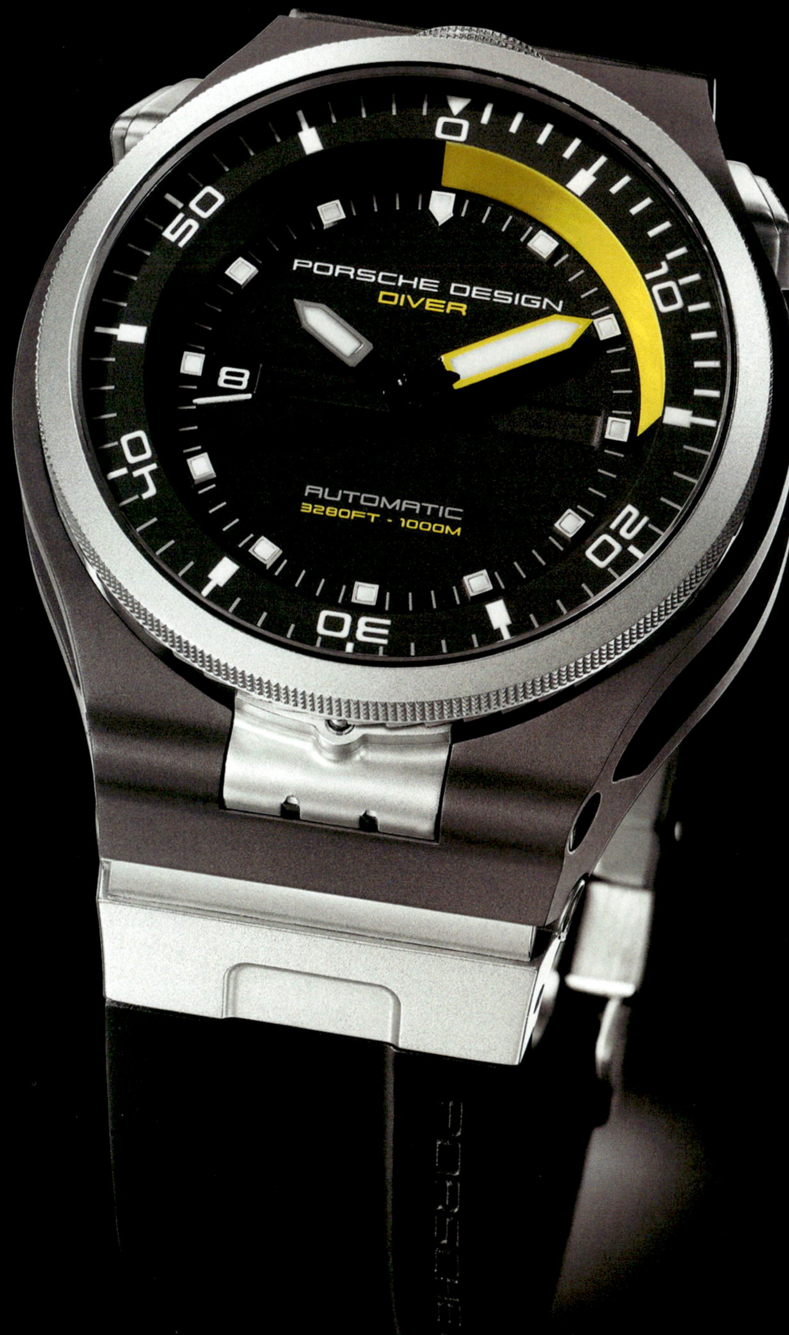

FACING PAGE

Released in a limited edition of 911 pieces, each P'6530 Titanium Chronograph comes with an informational booklet on its history.

CENTER The Porsche 911, which has strongly influenced Porsche Design Timepieces, is a modern classic developed in 1963 by Prof. Porsche, founder of Porsche Design

THIS PAGE

TOP LEFT Professor Ferdinand Alexander Porsche, founder of Porsche Design, aspired to create products that could act as "companions through life."

RIGHT The P'6780 Diver is powered by an automatic movement that possesses 42 hours of power reserve and beats at 28,800 vph.

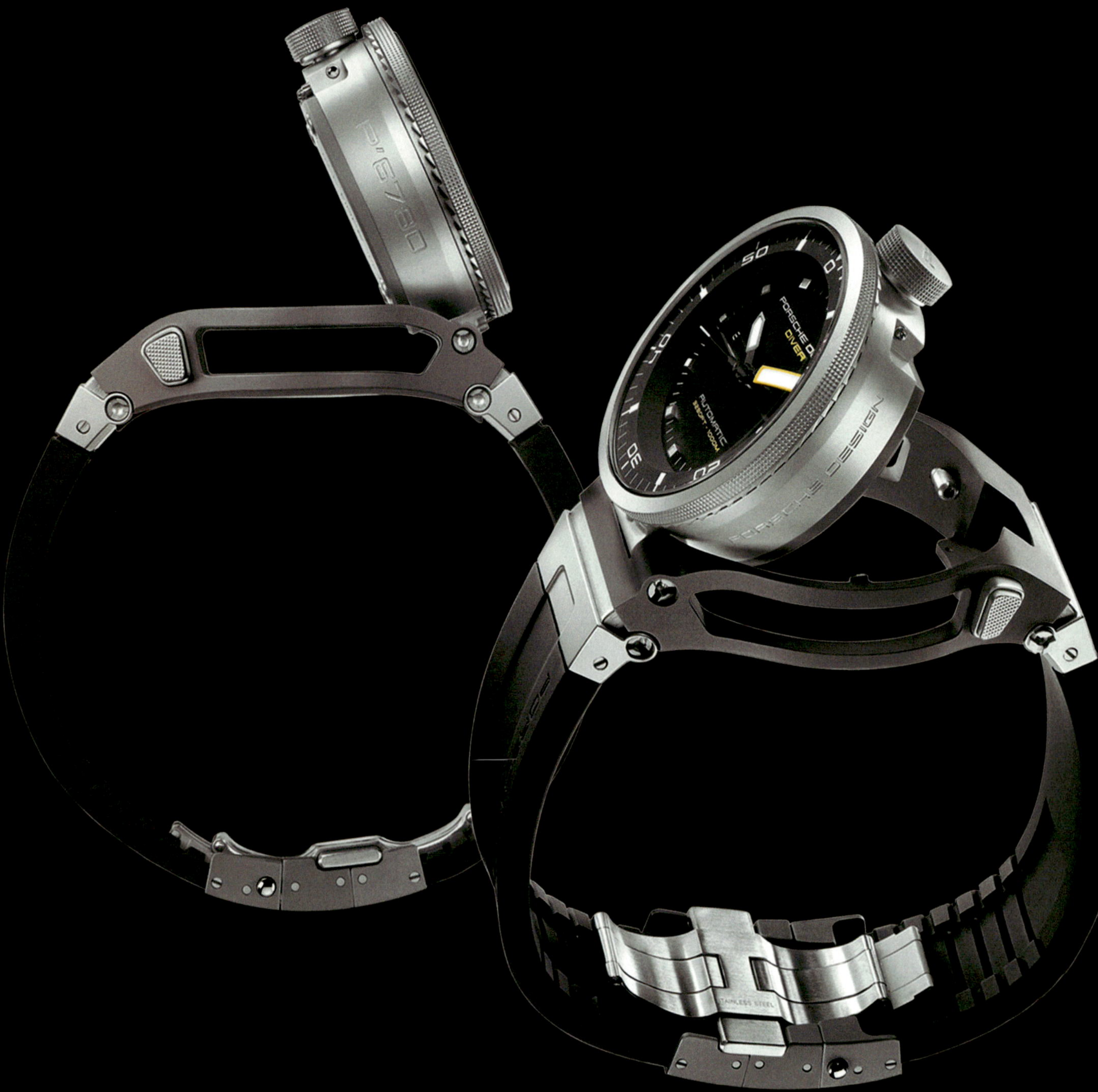

The color scheme of the watch is a testament to its legacy: the stainless steel container is an effective complement to the anthracite gray of the titanium bridge structure, eschewing any superfluous aesthetic bells and whistles and echoing other Porsche Design creations. The only significant color accent—a yellow arc that stretches across the first 15 minutes of the diving scale—stands out all the more for being the singular touch of color. Every choice made in the conception and production of the watch follows the Porsche Design philosophy, best expressed by Prof. Porsche himself: "When you think about the function of something, its design sometimes emerges of its own accord." The use of titanium also hearkens back to another Porsche Design achievement: the Ocean 2000 watch, created in 1983. Designed for the divers of the German Navy, the anti-magnetic titanium watch was conceived to avoid setting off undersea mines as they were being disarmed.

Useful synergies often arise when horological feats and automotive savoir-faire mingle. For example, the Porsche Carrera GT, a high-powered sports car, exerted a strong influence on the legendary P'6910 Indicator, and now it works its magic on the P'6930 Chronograph, in ways both visible and hidden. The two ridged push-pieces on the side are inspired by the pedals of the Carrera GT, and the COSC-certified automatic Valjoux 7750 movement boasts an energy-optimized rotor system with an aesthetic foundation in the wheel rim of the Carrera GT. Even the strap bears aspects of automotive design, with a tire-tread interior that allows air to circulate next to the skin. The dial itself combines a large amount of information with the always-crucial instant readability. A 30-minute counter is positioned at 12 o'clock, day and date are at 3 o'clock, a 12-hour counter is at 6 o'clock, and small seconds tick away at 9 o'clock. All of these indications—and, of course, the time—are immediately readable, thanks to the clarity of the dial design. The hour and minute hands are partially skeletonized, so as not to block any of the other functions on the dial, and the solid portions are treated with luminescent coating, as are the numerals and hour indexes on the dial, whose honeycomb texture is another nod to the automotive roots of Porsche Design.

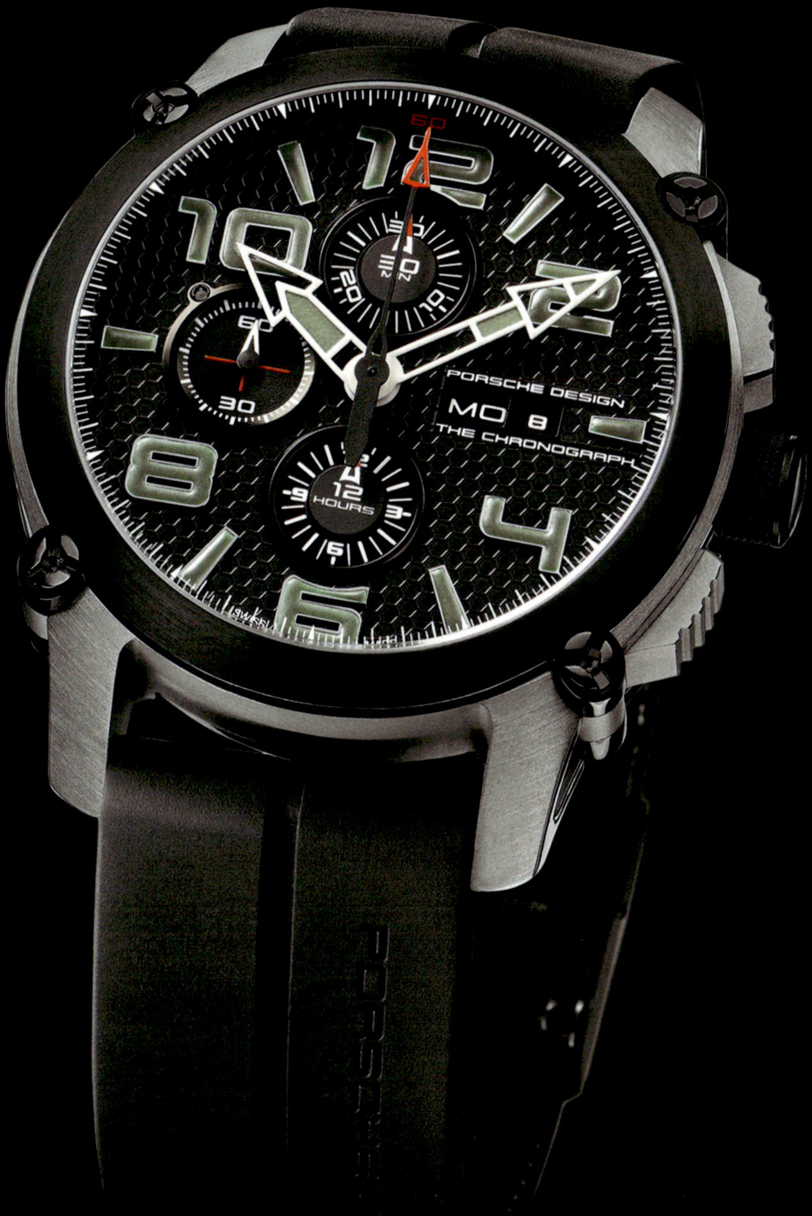

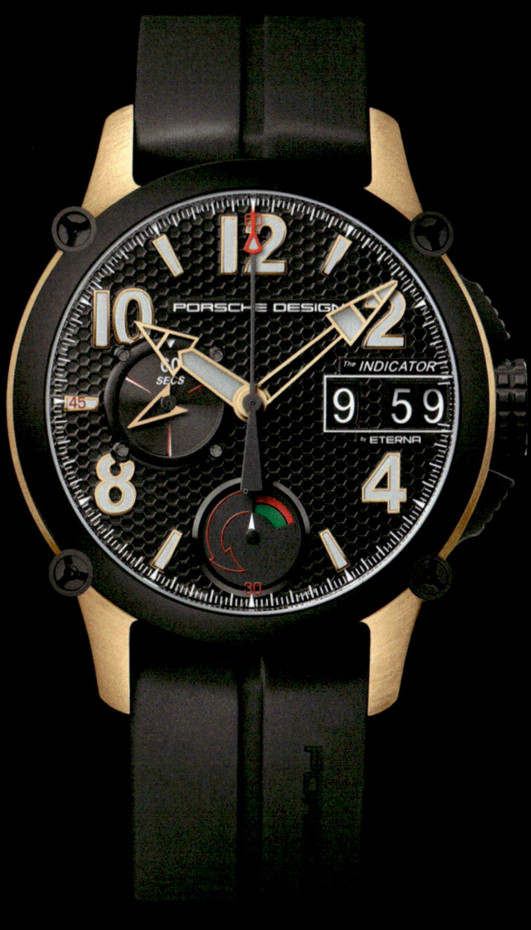

FACING PAGE

The P'6780 Diver does not need a screw-down crown or a helium release valve, thanks to its unorthodox design. The unique hinged case of Porsche Design's P'6780 Diver protects the crown, and the rotating bezel that measures diving time, from inadvertent manipulation.

THIS PAGE

ABOVE The P'6930 Chronograph is available in an all-black PVD-treated version and a version that is only partially treated with black PVD coating.

LEFT The exterior of the P'6910 indicator is modeled on the Porsche Carrera GT design.

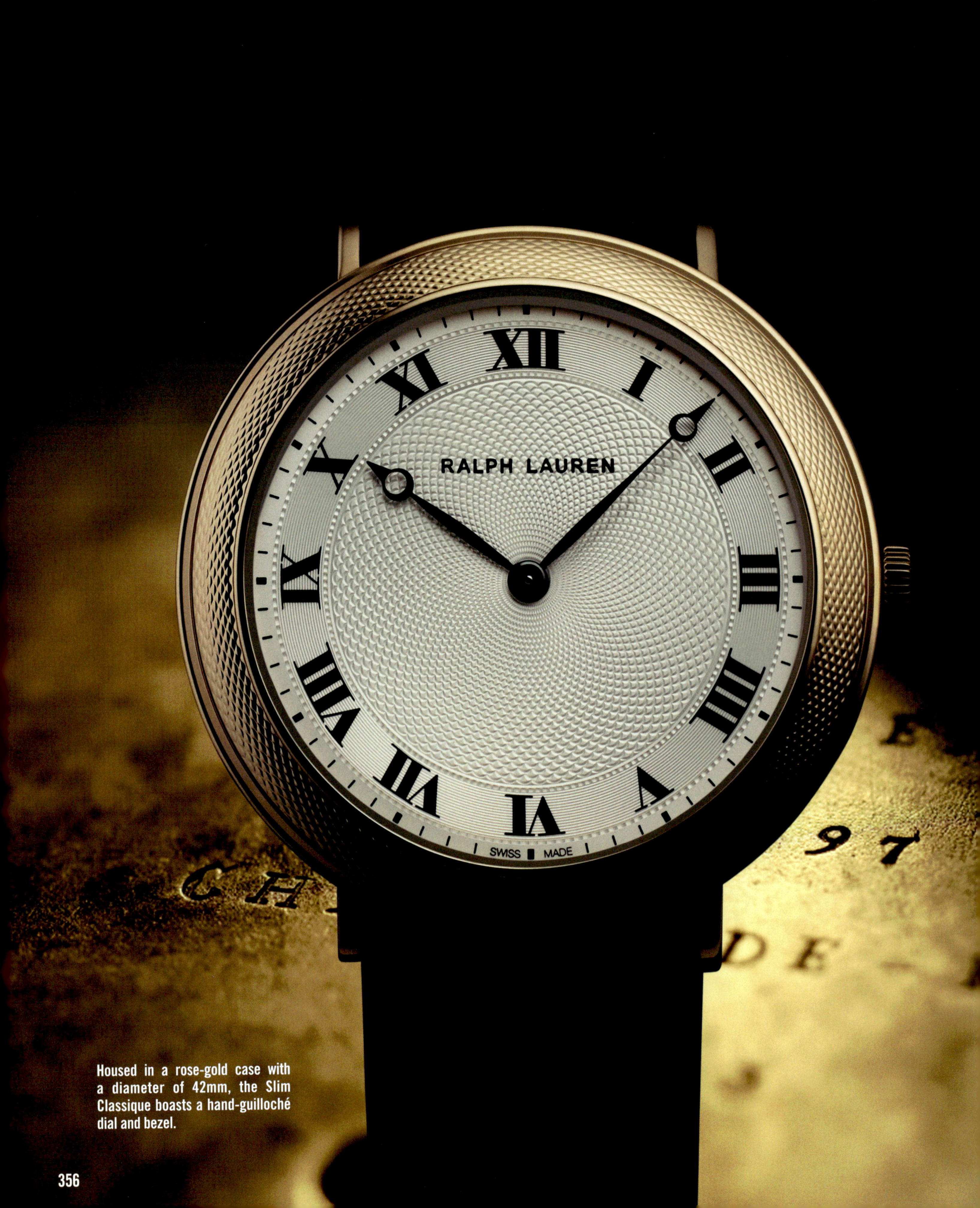

Housed in a rose-gold case with a diameter of 42mm, the Slim Classique boasts a hand-guilloché dial and bezel.

A GENUINE HOROLOGICAL PEDIGREE

Launched in 2009, Ralph Lauren watches are released in three collections that are unmistakably imprinted with the brand's identity. They are created with a care for horological authenticity that is rare for a brand primarily known for its work in the fashion world. Noble materials, manufacture-made mechanical movements and finishings worthy of the best of the horological world add to their timeless charm. The Slim Classique Collection pays tribute to the guilloché tradition as it is still practiced by a few artisan engravers.

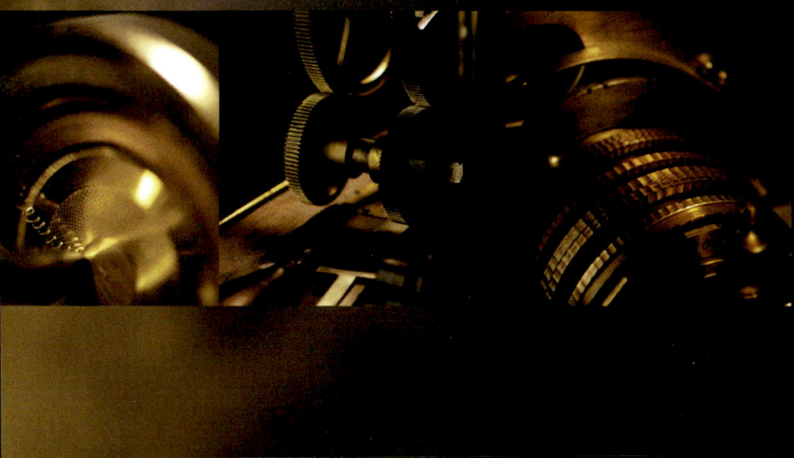

Slim Classique, as its name indicates, is a collection of round watches with ultra-thin measurements—just 5.35mm thick—that evoke Ralph Lauren's signature timeless style. Available in white gold, rose gold or platinum with a 42mm diameter, or in white gold or rose gold in a new 38mm diameter case, the elegant models are mounted on straps in black alligator leather or on satin straps (in black, red, navy blue or violet). In keeping with the brand's characteristic glamorous sensibility, Ralph Lauren has chosen to enhance the line with jeweled versions in white gold, set with either one or two rows of brilliant-cut diamonds, or a row of baguette-cut diamonds. When the piece bears two rows of brilliant-cut diamonds, the rows are slightly staggered, providing a smooth surface that allows the gems to best reflect the light and show off their brilliance. The baguette-cut gems are set using the closed-set method that folds the metal around the edges of the stones, integrating them into the setting. The silvered opalescent dial is swept over by Breguet-style hands, and the numerals are always of the Roman variety. The wearer can also have a personal message engraved on the polished back of the case within which beats the RL430 caliber, a manual-winding movement from the Piaget manufacture that has been personalized for Ralph Lauren. The movement is one of the thinnest in the world, measuring just 2.1mm thick.

The main distinction of the Slim Classique Collection is that the bezels that are not set with precious stones bear a barleycorn guilloché pattern. This motif, which appears on the dials of all the Slim Classique Collection watches, is particularly difficult to trace on the bezel because of its convex surface. In the dial centers, compositions in concentric lines lend each piece a gracefully sophisticated note. Eighty waves spiral in from the exterior to the interior of the circle, where their delicacy is such that they are invisible to the naked eye. The guilloché decoration is completed by markings that line the path of the Roman numerals.

On the Slim Classique watches, the guillochage is done by hand. The execution, of a rare beauty, is easily recognizable by an experienced eye. It is in no way comparable with stamped metal, a pale imitation of guilloché that consists of a high-pressure impression of a pattern on a decorative plate. This method flattens the crystalline structure of the metal and dulls the surface, while authentic guilloché reveals the grain of the metal, leaving it intact. The guilloché lines reflect the light with incomparable brilliance that cannot be achieved by any other method.

Born in the 17th century, the art of guilloché finishing first appeared in horology in the 18th, and it was particularly fashionable in the 19th and beginning of the 20th, up until the 1940s. Having fallen into disuse with the arrival of industrial techniques, it is currently experiencing a resurgence of popularity, particularly in pieces from high-end brands such as Ralph Lauren. However, artisans who have mastered this art are few and far between. Though at one time there were over a thousand specialists in the Swiss Jura alone, that number has shrunk to just a few today.

Guilloché finishing consists of a decoration composed of hollow-engraved and overlapping lines. By varying the spacing and the interlacing, it is possible to obtain an infinite quantity of designs, from strictly geometrical to daringly fanciful. There are two techniques, depending on whether one uses a "straight-line" machine or a rose engine lathe, which traces the curved lines needed for Ralph Lauren's preferred barleycorn motif, for example. With the left hand, the artisan turns a crank, while the right hand wields an engraving tool on wheels. The engine's roses serve as guides for the long and difficult work, and the result depends on the speed of the rotation and the amount of pressure applied. Patience and concentration are necessary to assure a perfect regularity in the line and an equal depth for each groove, whose width generally varies from 0.1mm to 0.5mm, and depth measures less a hair's breadth: three or four one-hundredths of a millimeter. The artisan watches over the progress being made with the help of a powerful magnifying glass or a small binocular microscope. Of course, the least instant of inattention can bring all previous work to naught. The pieces are made one at a time, and even though it is done with a machine, we refer to hand-guilloché work because the quality wholly depends on the artisan's hands. In using the machine, dexterity, precision and sensitivity count for everything. The value of a hand-guilloché piece is naturally much higher than that of an industrially stamped piece.

Guilloché finishing machines are now almost as rare as the artisans who work them; none have been produced since the middle of the last century. The rose engine lathe used for the barleycorn motif on the dials and bezels of the Slim Classique watches dates back to 1897. By preserving the art of guilloché finishing, Ralph Lauren breathes new life into one of the most beautiful decorative techniques of traditional horology.

The brand's founder, Ralph Lauren himself, has always been fascinated by beautiful watches, and he possesses an impressive private collection. He had always wanted to enter the world of haute horology, but waited until he could create models that would respond in every way to his requirements for design and expertise. Slim Classique, Stirrup and Sporting form a collection that "represents everything I expect in terms of quality, authenticity and aesthetics," explains the designer. Each line translates the essence of the brand into the language of luxury, glamour and timelessness. The watches are produced in Switzerland with the greatest respect for watchmaking tradition.

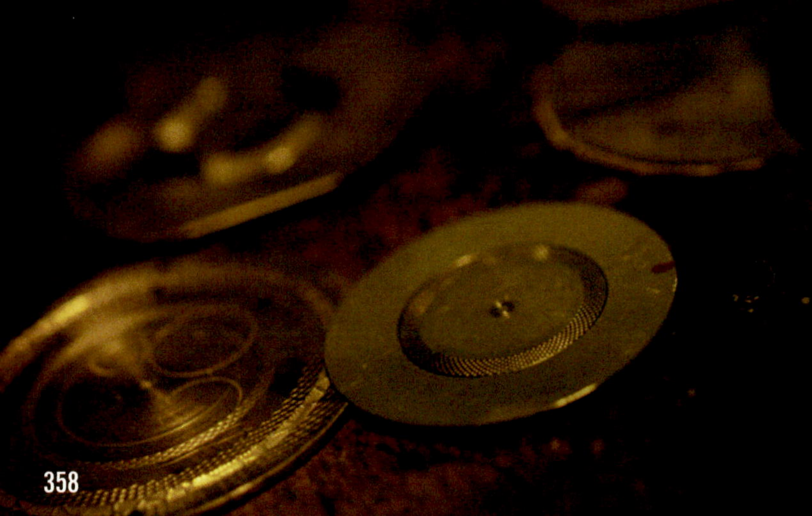

THIS PAGE

The guilloché finishing on the Slim Classique was executed on a rose engine built in 1897.

FACING PAGE

LEFT Some versions of the Slim Classique sport a double alternating row of diamonds. This version, in a 42mm white-gold case, is mounted on a black alligator strap.

RIGHT Here pictured is the Slim Classique in a 38mm white-gold case with one row of brilliant-cut diamonds, presented on a red satin strap and powered by an ultra-thin movement from the manufacture of Piaget that provides 40 hours of power reserve.

The brand's founder, Ralph Lauren himself, has always been fascinated by beautiful watches, and he possesses an impressive private collection.

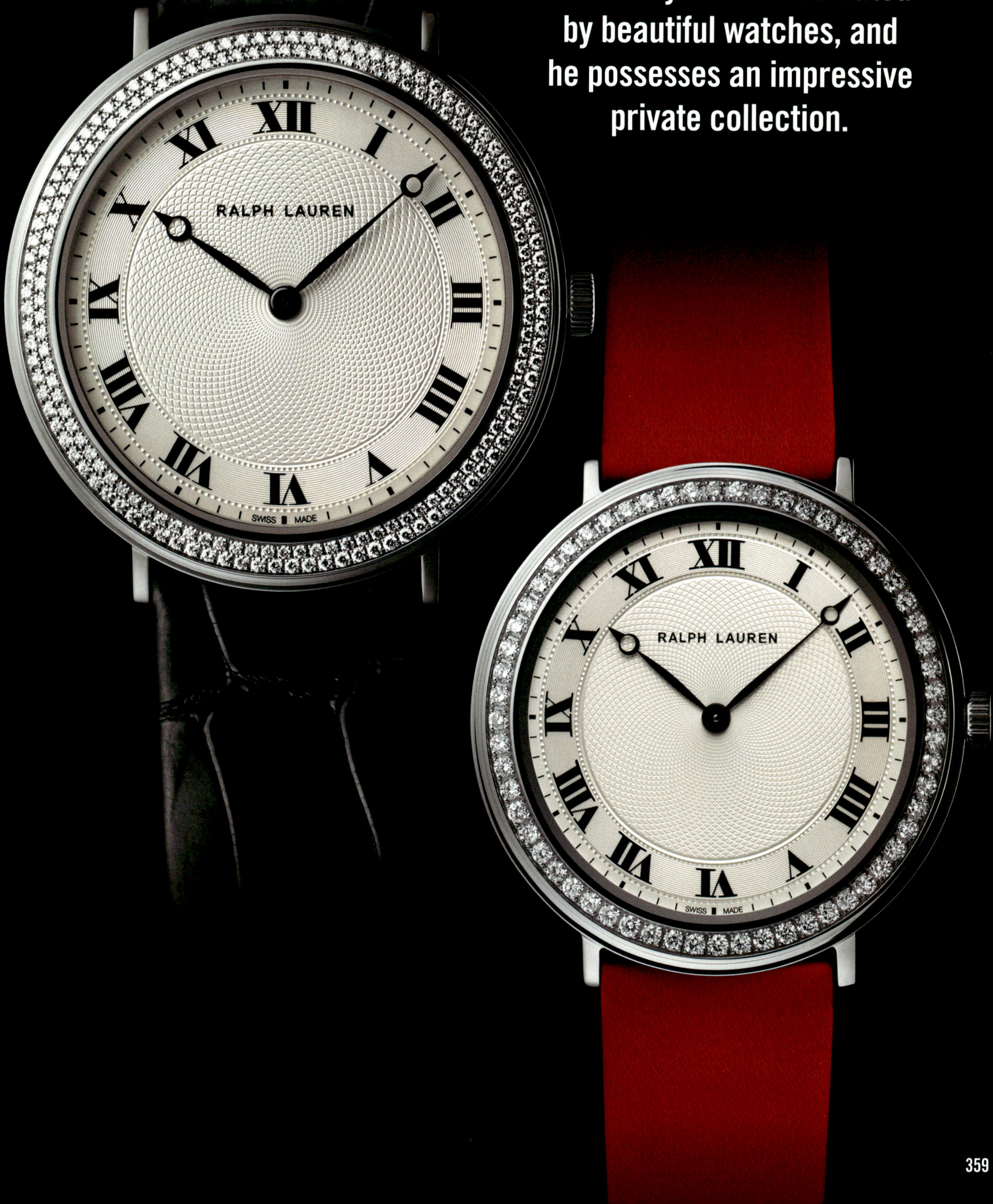

RAYMOND WEIL

GENEVE

FAMILY VALUES

Raymond Weil founded his Geneva workshop more than 30 years ago and built it into a globally recognized luxury watch brand based on the foundations of family and independence.

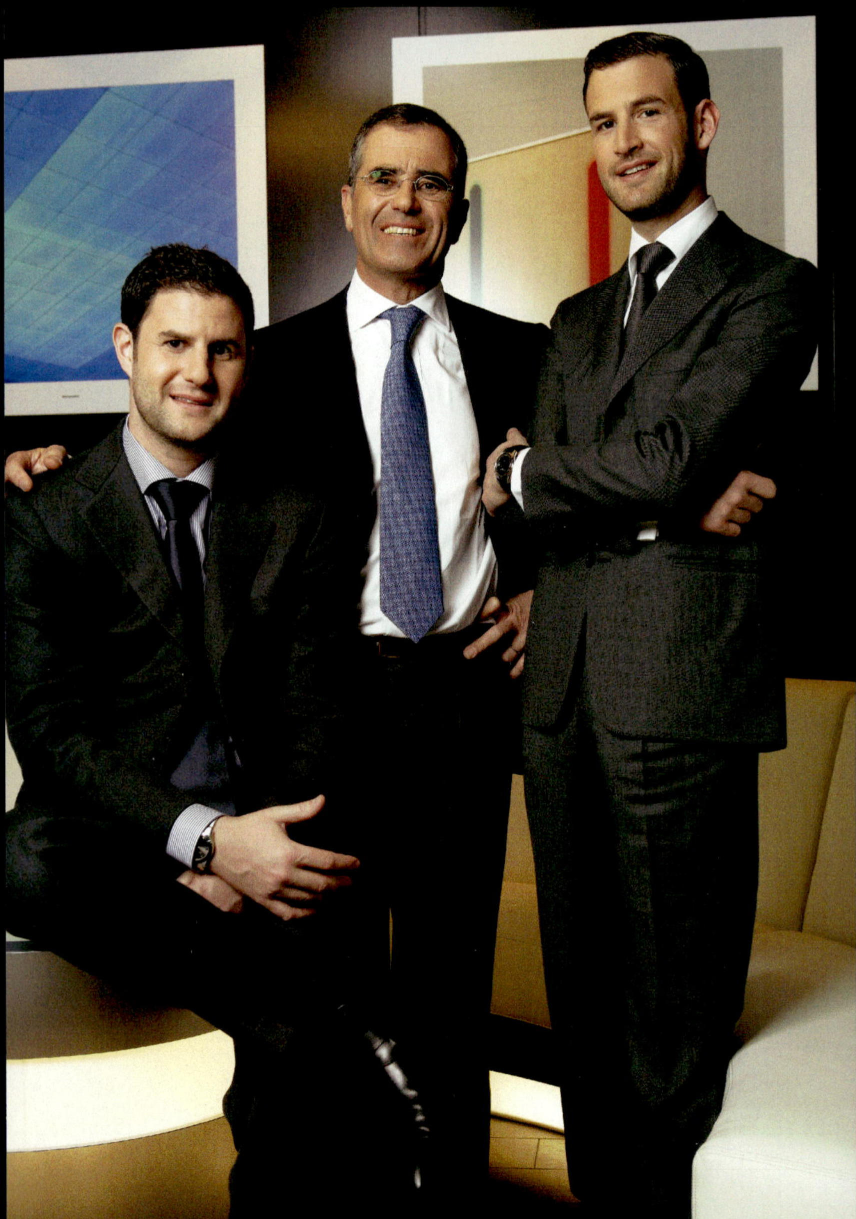

The firm that bears his name remains in family hands and is today led by CEO and President Olivier Bernheim, who is Weil's son-in-law. The founder's grandsons also occupy key positions within the company, with Elie Bernheim and Pierre Bernheim serving as directors.

The company's tireless devotion to refining its timeless style and developing progressively complex movements has fueled its successful trajectory and helped it establish footholds in the emerging Chinese and Indian markets.

A critical turning point came in 1999 when the firm launched a department dedicated to research and development. This expansion further enhanced the company's independence by enabling it to fully control the design process. Equally important, it also allowed Raymond Weil to keep pace with, and respond to, the furious pace of aesthetic and mechanical evolution that continues to define the modern watchmaking era.

The firm's investment in R&D paid handsome dividends in the years that followed with the introduction of its own GMT function, as well as a patented system for women's watches that permits quick bracelet changes.

From left to right: Elie Bernheim, Olivier Bernheim and Pierre Bernheim.

Part of the collection celebrating the Parsifal's 20-year anniversary, this chronograph model is featured with a stainless steel case and a rose-gold bezel with matching accents.

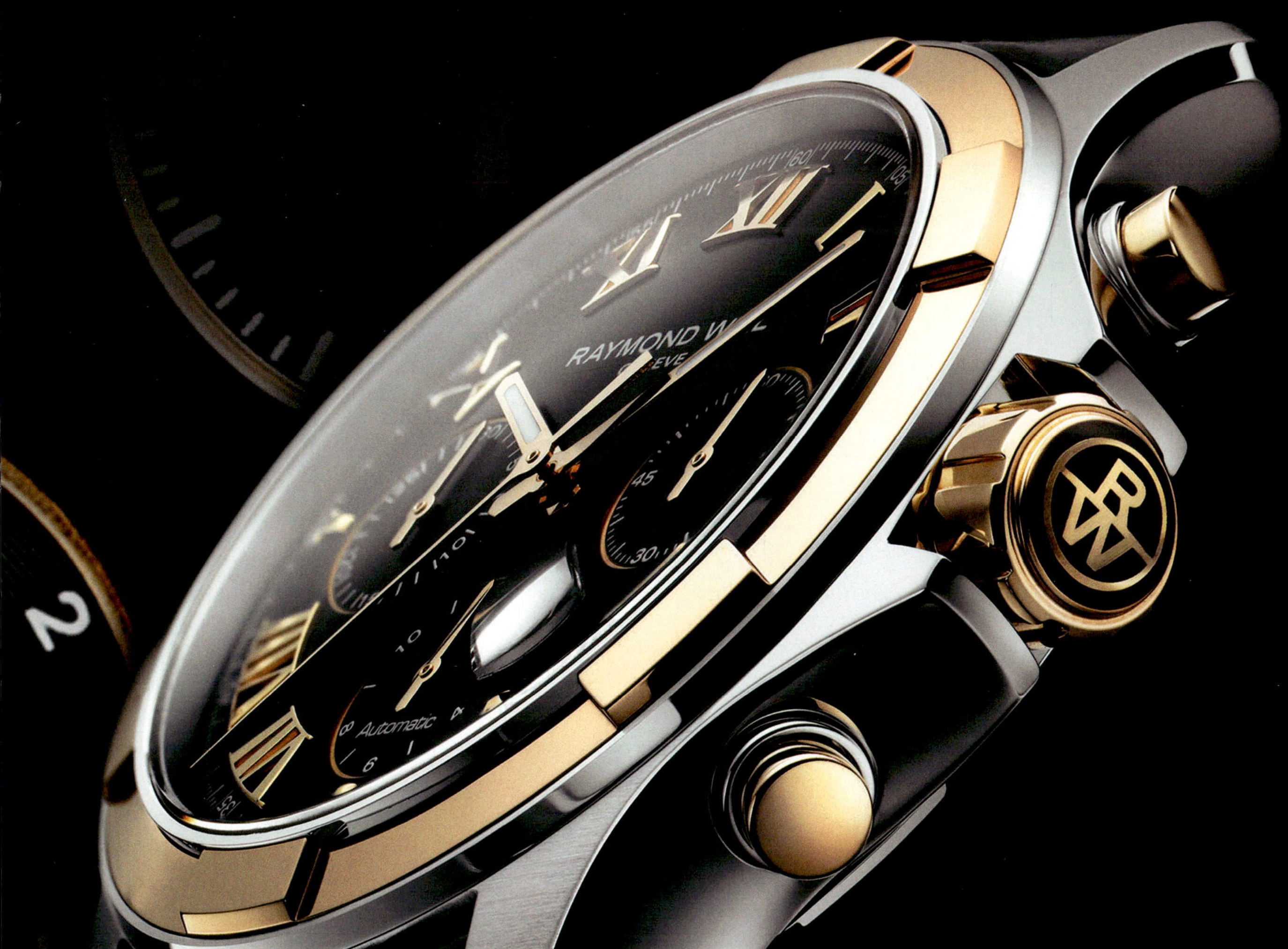

Among the brand's major triumphs since its inception has been the 1990 introduction of the flagship Parsifal collection for men and women. These timepieces combine complicated movements, sleek designs and precious elements to form a tightly knit family of watches emblematic of the brand's core values.

Raymond Weil celebrated the 20-year anniversary of this emblematic model in 2010 with the debut of a new Parsifal collection. While staying true to the spirit of the watch's four previous incarnations, the Parsifal anniversary collection re-imagines the watch's signature elegance with a contemporary flair.

The latest additions include two men's models and one for women. The first design for gentlemen is an automatic that features chronograph and date functions. It is offered in 41mm case that comes in stainless steel, rose gold, or a combination of the two.

An automatic movement powers the second men's model, which is available in a 39mm case. The Roman numerals used for the chapter ring are interrupted at 3 o'clock for a date display with a magnifier integrated into the sapphire crystal. Raymond Weil presents three versions of this design: yellow gold and stainless steel with a white dial; rose gold and stainless steel with a black dial; and an attractive all stainless steel model with a gray dial.

THIS PAGE

The Parsifal, named after Wagner's last opera, integrates a magnifying glass into its sapphire crystal above the date display at 3 o'clock.

FACING PAGE

The newly developed Maestro collection includes three different models that share the same 39.5mm stainless steel case and blued, Breguet-style hands.

For women, the brand introduces a feminine model equipped with a quartz movement housed in a stainless steel case that is available with or without gold and diamond accents.

The Parsifal name may sound familiar to those with an affinity for German opera. Indeed, Raymond Weil named the watch in honor of the last opera completed by the late 19th-century composer Richard Wagner.

He based his three-act musical drama on a 13th-century epic poem about the Arthurian knight Percival's quest for the Holy Grail. Taking 25 years to complete the work, Wagner finally staged Parsifal in 1882 at the annual music festival in Bayreuth, Germany.

According to the brand: "The Parsifal collection exalts the chivalrous spirit of its hero through humanistic values of nobility, courage, loyalty, purity and spirituality; a timeless vision relevant more than ever today."

The Parsifal is one of the many Raymond Weil collections that reference the arts. The Nabucco collection for men, for example, takes its names from an opera by Giuseppe Verdi, while the Don Giovanni Così Grande family of timepieces owes its moniker to an opera by Wolfgang Amadeus Mozart.

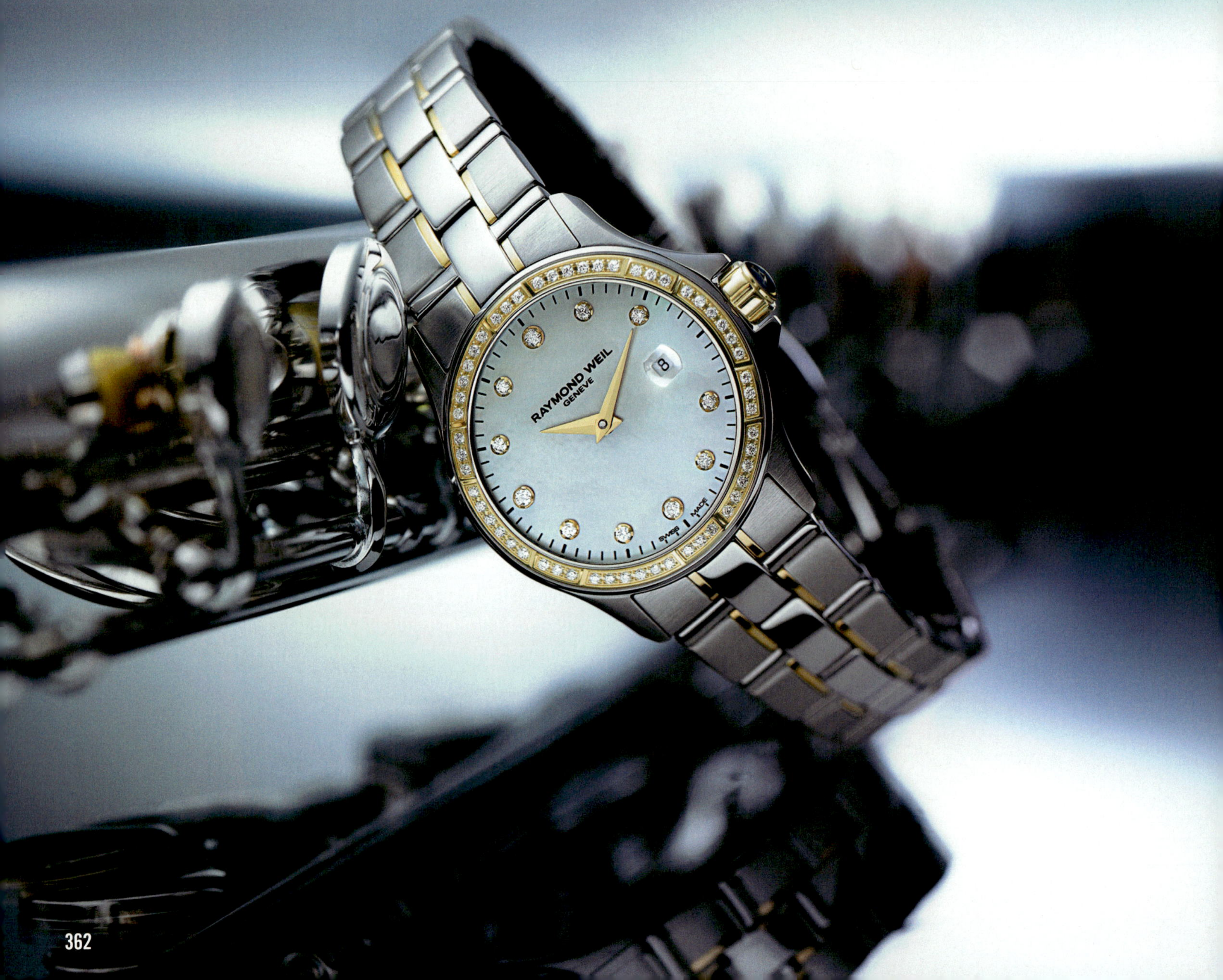

developing complicated movements featured in attractively priced timepieces with broad appeal, such as the Maestro collection.

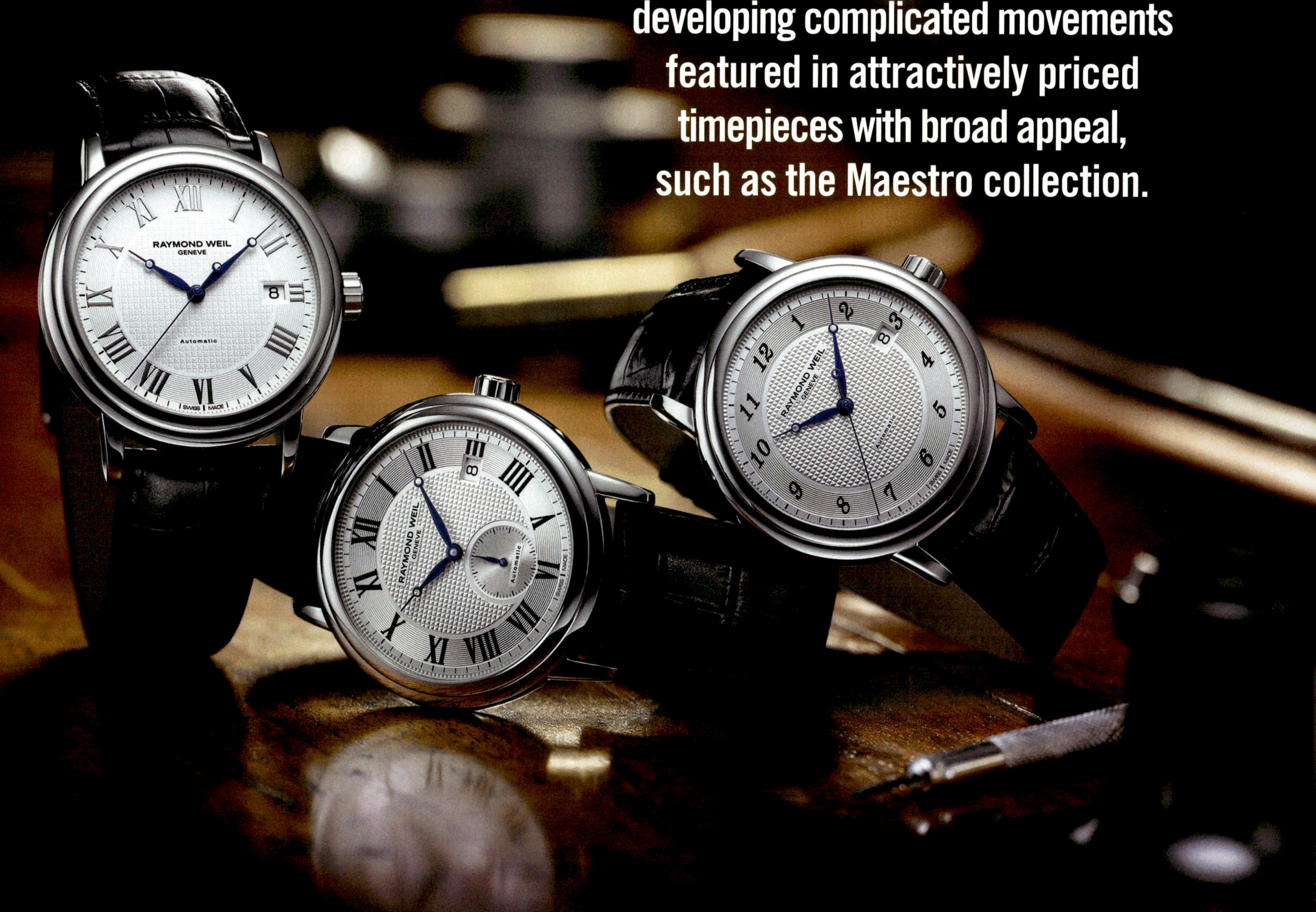

From its earliest days, the watch brand has been a dynamic supporter of the arts. Several years ago, Raymond Weil began sponsoring the RW Club International Photography Prize, which is today acclaimed as one of the world's most prestigious photography competitions.

Raymond Weil conducts a symphony of chic style and watchmaking history with the Maestro Tradition, the latest collection to emerge from the firm's Geneva workshops. The new line contains three models that offer variations on the same classic theme.

While each member of the trio shares the same 39.5mm stainless steel case, its polished profile is used to frame three different looks.

The first includes a dial decorated with a square relief pattern fenced in by a snailed chapter ring with Roman numerals indicated by blued, Breguet-style hands. The next version swaps the Roman numerals for Arabic and features the classic Clous de Paris decoration on the dial. Both models are equipped with an automatic movement (RW4200) that delivers 38 hours of reserve power.

A different automatic movement (RW4250) powers the final iteration of the Maestro, which introduces a small seconds indicator to the dial's Clous de Paris pattern.

With its Maestro Tradition and anniversary Parsifal collections, Raymond Weil harnesses its spirit of independence to create dynamic timepieces that demonstrate its commitment to mechanical and creative sophistication.

NEVER COMPROMISE PASSION, INTENSITY, TIME OR MONEY!

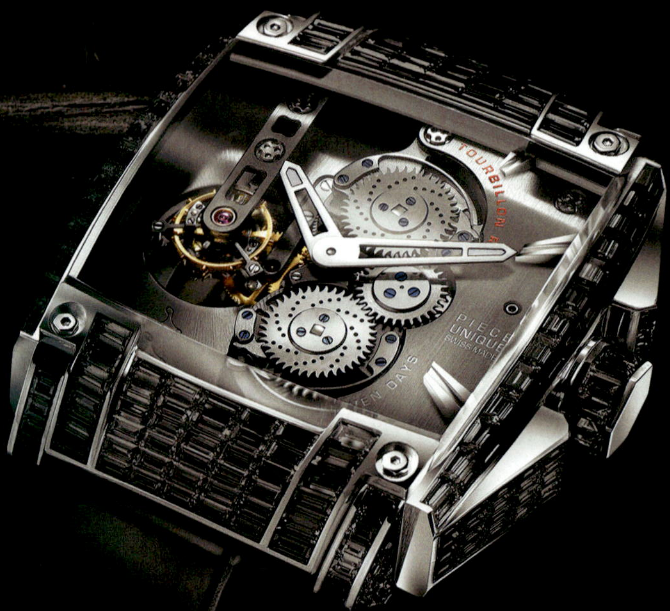

HISTORY: REBELLION WRITING AN ORIGINAL PASSION PLAY

Once upon a time there were two young boys, childhood friends who were passionate about cars and construction toys. The boys grew up to be men, but their passions remained the same.

The Rebellion adventure began in 2007 with some pretty unusual ideas, sketches drawn on the back of an envelope and plenty of heated debate. The brand was launched a year later, and although there were inevitable growing pains, the passion was never in doubt. Collectors looking for something a bit different very quickly grew interested in the brand.

In 2009 Rebellion consolidated by appointing prestigious partners such as Laurent Besse for the conception of two new movements and Eric Giroud for the design of a new version of the original case. BaselWorld 2009 was an unqualified success, with the establishment of the brand's first markets and points of sale throughout the world.

The tenacity and stubbornness of Rebellion's founders had triumphed, and the same character traits can be found in the world of endurance car racing of Le Mans, another shared passion to which Rebellion is completely committed through the Swiss team, Rebellion Racing.

THE BRAND

Launched in 2008, Rebellion is a young and daring independent Swiss high-end watch brand, based in Lonay, on the shores of Lake Leman. Rebellion's timepieces are crafted in extremely limited quantities, with precision-engineered cases and exclusive movements. All of Rebellion's research, development and production takes place in Switzerland, where the very highest standards are both demanded and obtained. Rebellion blends highly sophisticated technical know-how, including high-tech precision lasers, with an uncompromising approach to quality. Their timepieces are for those who demand a very exclusive, high quality, high-tech wristwatch.

Inspiring deep emotion, Rebellion's exclusive and ageless watches provide a sophisticated and powerful contemporary identity for today's dynamic generation. Rebellion is geared toward the fiercest of individualists.

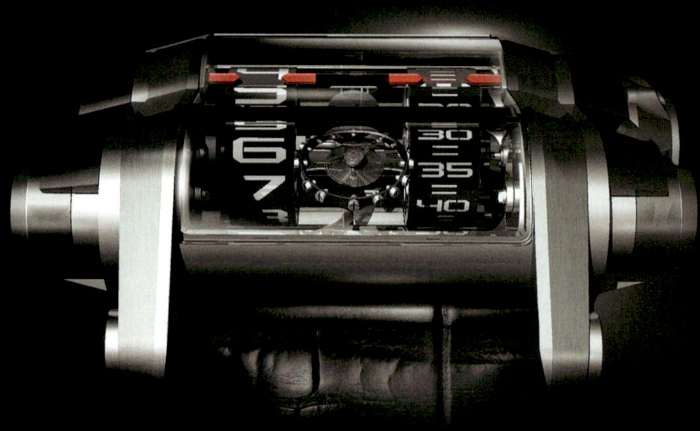

Rebellion Racing offers an ideal platform for its watchmaking partner to enhance its exposure worldwide with the media opportunities provided by the *Le Mans Series* and *24 hours of Le Mans*.

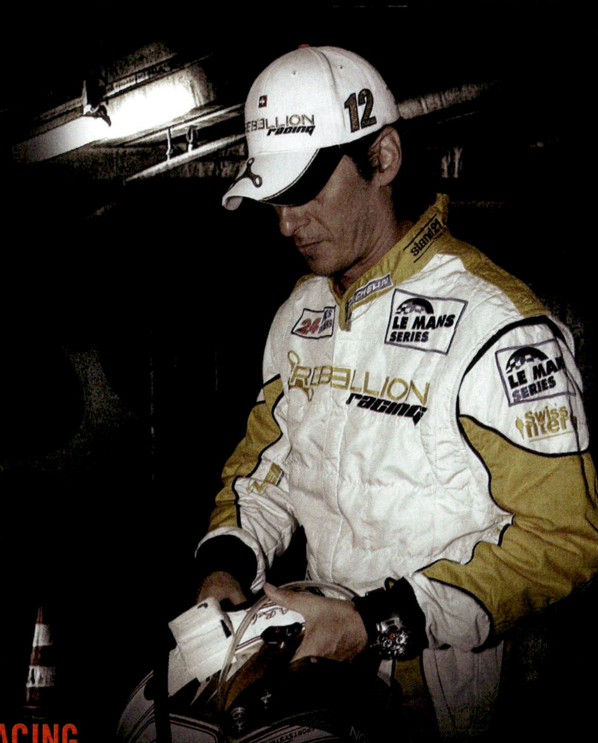

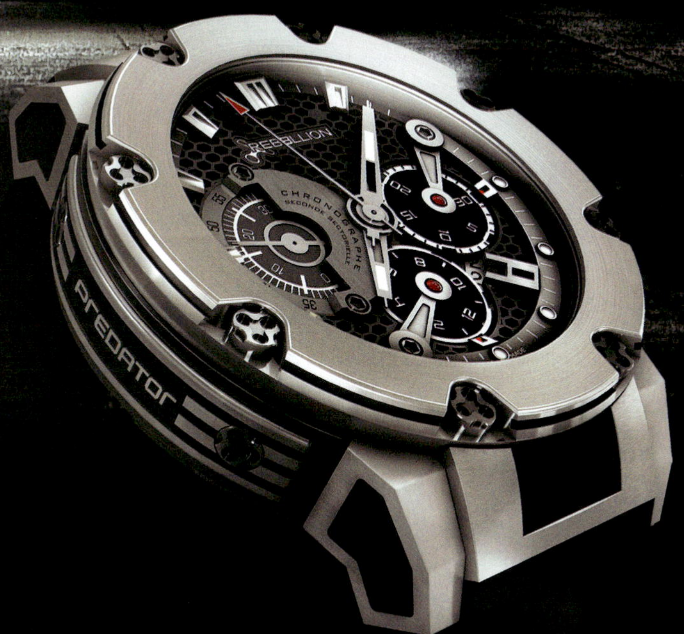

REBELLION RACING

Over the last few seasons, Rebellion Racing has grown and evolved. With strong results on the track for both its reputation and image, the prestigious watchmaking brand Rebellion has decided to increase its involvement with the Swiss team.

Rebellion Racing provides the ideal platform to allow its main partner to further accelerate its global development with maximized exposure, focused on the *Le Mans Series* and *24 hours of Le Mans*, with two Lola LMP1 coupes.

For 2011, the Lola LMP1 coupes of Rebellion Racing will be powered by Toyota engines, in a technological partnership with Rebellion Timepieces. Using the latest technology for all materials, components and manufacturing has amply displayed the synergistic possibilities of Rebellion Timepieces' association with a race engine. An exceptional watch and a prototype of the *24 Hours of Le Mans* share the values of technology, performance and reliability.

Rebellion Racing drivers for the 2010 season: Andrea Bellicchi, Neel Jani, Nicolas Prost, Jean-Christophe Boullion, Guy Smith and Marco Andretti. With hugely talented and highly experienced pilots, Rebellion Racing once again demonstrates its ambition for success.

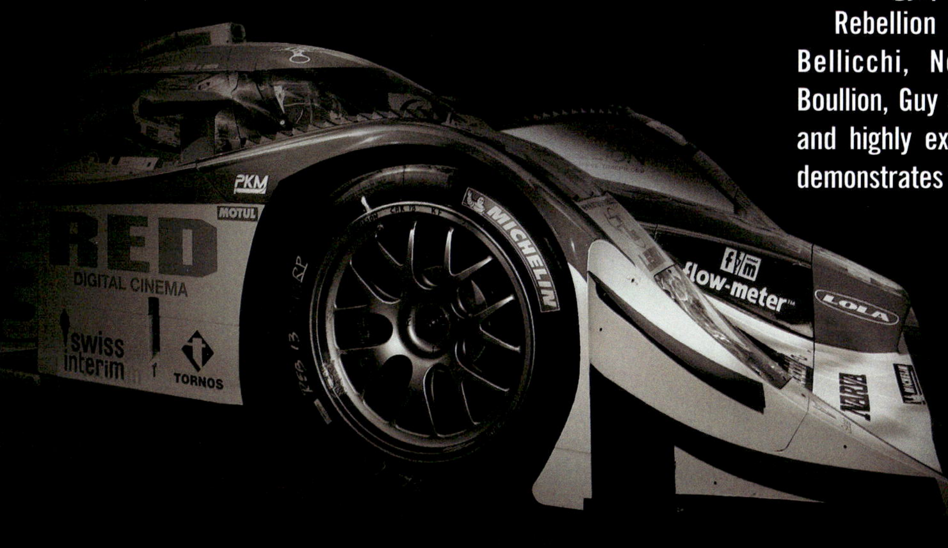

The Full Black Diamond version of the REB-5 Tourbillon Diamonds is a one-of-a-kind piece.

Rebellion's T-1000 Time Machine possesses 1,000 hours of power reserve.

The Predator Chronographe boasts a multi-layered dial.

REB-5 TOURBILLON RED GOLD — REF. REB5TFG

Movement: manual-winding REB-5 caliber; tourbillon with 1-minute rotation; 38.25x36.7mm; 7-day power reserve; 45 components; 23 jewels; 21,600 vph; galvanic black-gold plates; gold-plated wheels; blue- and black-gold screws, wolf-teeth barrels.
Functions: hours, minutes, seconds.
Case: red gold; 46x56.7mm, thickness: 19.6mm; modular construction; beveled edges; antireflective sapphire crystal caseback; water resistant to 10atm.
Strap: natural rubber; double folding buckle in metal matching case.
Note: limited to 12 pieces.
Suggested price: $189,000
Also available: white gold.

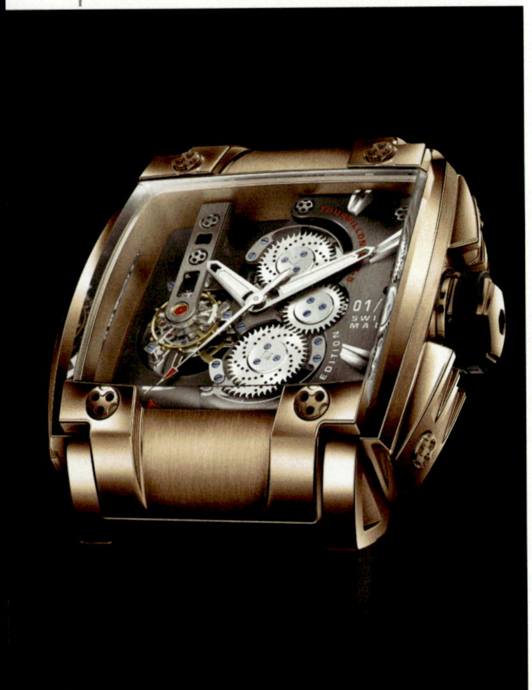

REB-7 REGULATOR STAINLESS STEEL — REF. REB7RSS

Movement: automatic-winding regulator REB-7 caliber; Ø 30mm, thickness: 6mm; 42-hour power reserve; 45 components; 23 jewels; 28,800 vph; galvanic black-gold plates; black-gold date ring; gold-plated wheels.
Functions: hours, minutes, seconds; large date at 6; hours in sub-dial at 12.
Case: stainless steel; 46x56.7mm, thickness: 19.6mm; modular construction; beveled edges; antireflective sapphire crystal caseback; water resistant to 10atm.
Strap: natural rubber; double folding buckle in matching case metal.
Note: limited to 36 pieces.
Suggested price: $23,500
Also available: red gold.

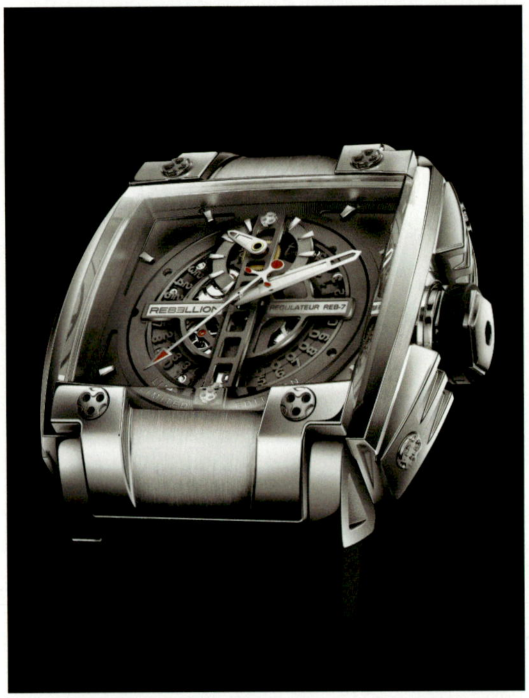

RE-1 CHRONOGRAPH STAINLESS STEEL — REF. RE1SS

Movement: automatic-winding RE-1 caliber; 13 ¼'''; 50-hour power reserve; 45 components; 28,800 vph.
Functions: hours, minutes, seconds; date; chronograph with hour and minute counters; start/stop at 2, return-to-zero at 4.
Case: stainless steel; 46x56.7mm, thickness: 19.6mm; modular construction; beveled edges; antireflective sapphire crystal caseback; water resistant to 5atm.
Strap: natural rubber; double folding buckle.
Suggested price: $19,000
Also available: red gold.

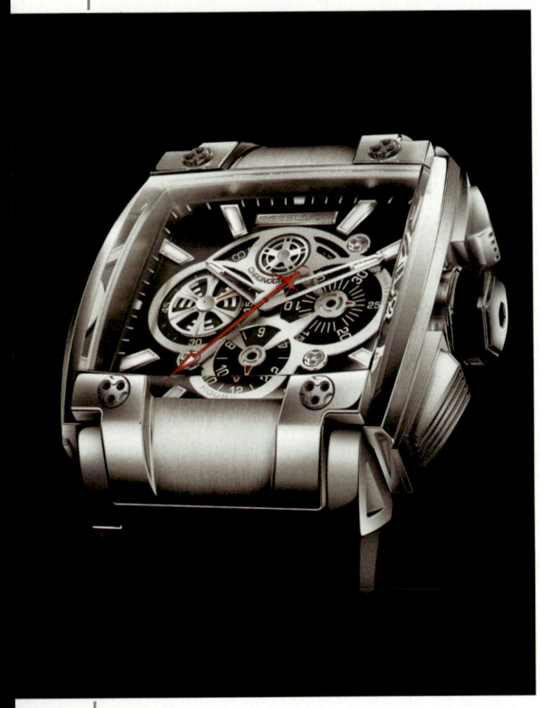

PREDATOR 3-HANDS STEEL-STEEL — REF. RE8THDSS

Movement: automatic-winding RE-1 caliber; 50-hour power reserve; 28,800 vph.
Functions: hours, minutes; sectorial seconds; date at 4:30.
Case: steel-steel; Ø 48mm; steel crown; water resistant to 5atm.
Dial: black DLC honeycomb; steel indexes with SuperLumiNova.
Strap: black rubber; deployment buckle.
Suggested price: $15,000
Also available: steel-ceramic, red gold-red gold and red gold-ceramic.

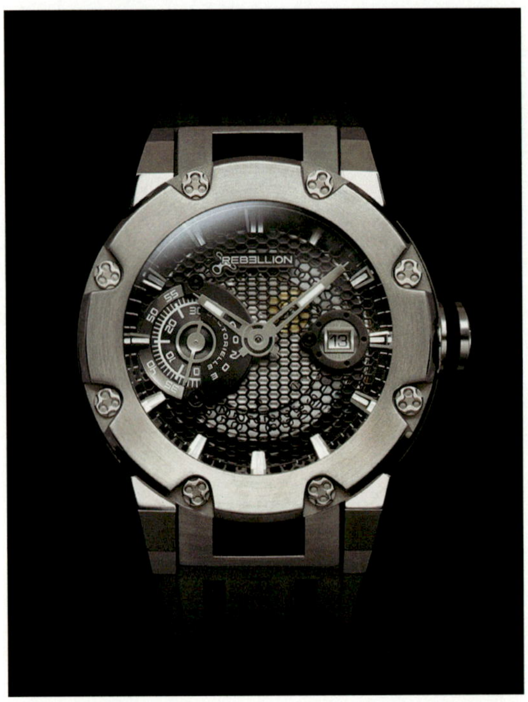

PREDATOR CHRONOGRAPH STEEL-STEEL — REF. RE1CSSSS

Movement: automatic-winding RE-1 caliber; 50-hour power reserve; 28,800 vph.
Functions: hours, minutes; sectorial seconds; date at 4:30; chronograph with hour and minute counters.
Case: steel-steel; Ø 48mm; steel crown; water resistant to 5atm.
Dial: black DLC honeycomb; steel indexes with SuperLumiNova.
Strap: black rubber; deployment buckle.
Suggested price: $18,000
Also available: steel-ceramic, red gold-red gold and red gold-ceramic.

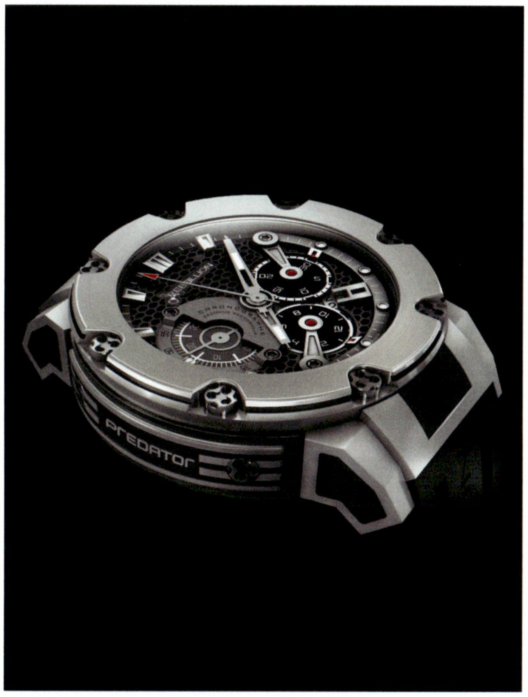

PREDATOR CHRONOGRAPH 24H (LE MANS 2010) — REF. RE1C24TIT

Movement: automatic-winding RE-1 caliber; 50-hour power reserve; 28,800 vph; chronometer with endurance racecar-inspired design.
Functions: hours, minutes; sectorial seconds at 9; 30-minute counter at 3; date at 4:30; 24-hour counter at 6; 60-second chronograph counter at 9.
Case: racing-grade titanium; Ø 48mm; modular construction; carbon fiber bezel with pilot's name engraved; steel crown with rubber band; engraved limited edition plate screwed to the side of the case; sapphire crystal caseback secured by six torx screws; water resistant to 10atm.
Dial: black DLC honeycomb; steel indexes with SuperLumiNova; steel diamond-cut hour, minute and chronograph hands with SuperLumiNova.
Strap: black rubber; patented deployment buckle allowing watch to be worn over racing suit.
Note: limited to 24 pieces.
Suggested price: $25,500

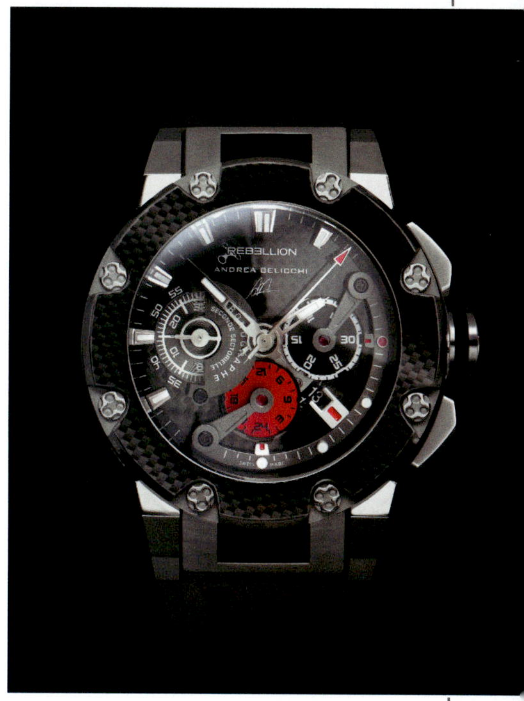

PREDATOR CHRONOGRAPH MONO-PUSHER STEEL-STEEL — REF. RE9MPCSC

Movement: automatic-winding RE-1 caliber; 50-hour power reserve.
Functions: hours, minutes; sectorial seconds; chronograph with minute and second counters.
Case: steel-steel; Ø 48mm; water resistant to 5atm.
Dial: black DLC honeycomb.
Strap: black rubber; deployment buckle.
Suggested price: $20,500
Also available: steel-ceramic, red gold-red gold and red gold-ceramic.

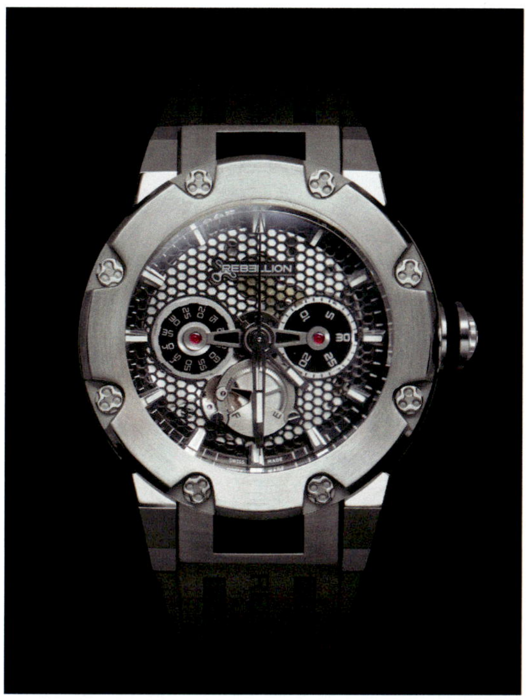

T-1000 — REF. T1000TIT

Movement: manual-winding REB T-1000 caliber; aluminum; 1,000-hour power reserve; 693 components; 14 jewels; 22 rubies; 18,000 vph.
Functions: hours, minutes.
Case: titanium; 46.7x46.9mm, thickness: 19.5mm; crown with patented pushbutton clutch system; water resistant to 5atm.
Strap: black alligator leather; patented folding clasp with micrometric pushbutton regulation.
Note: limited to 100 pieces.
Suggested price: $105,000

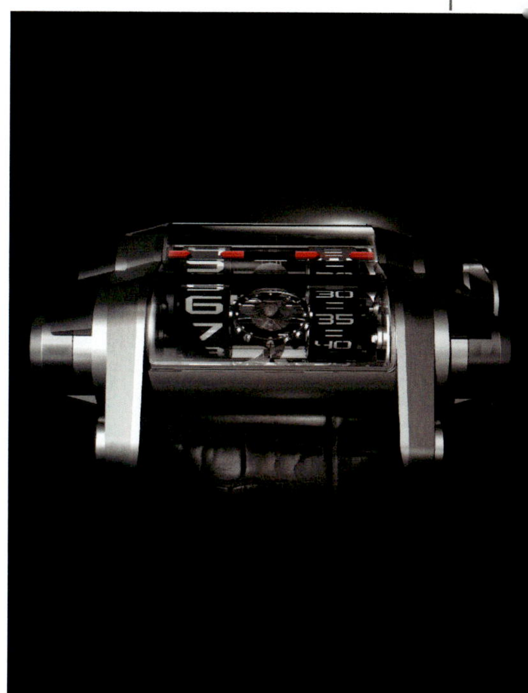

RICHARD MILLE

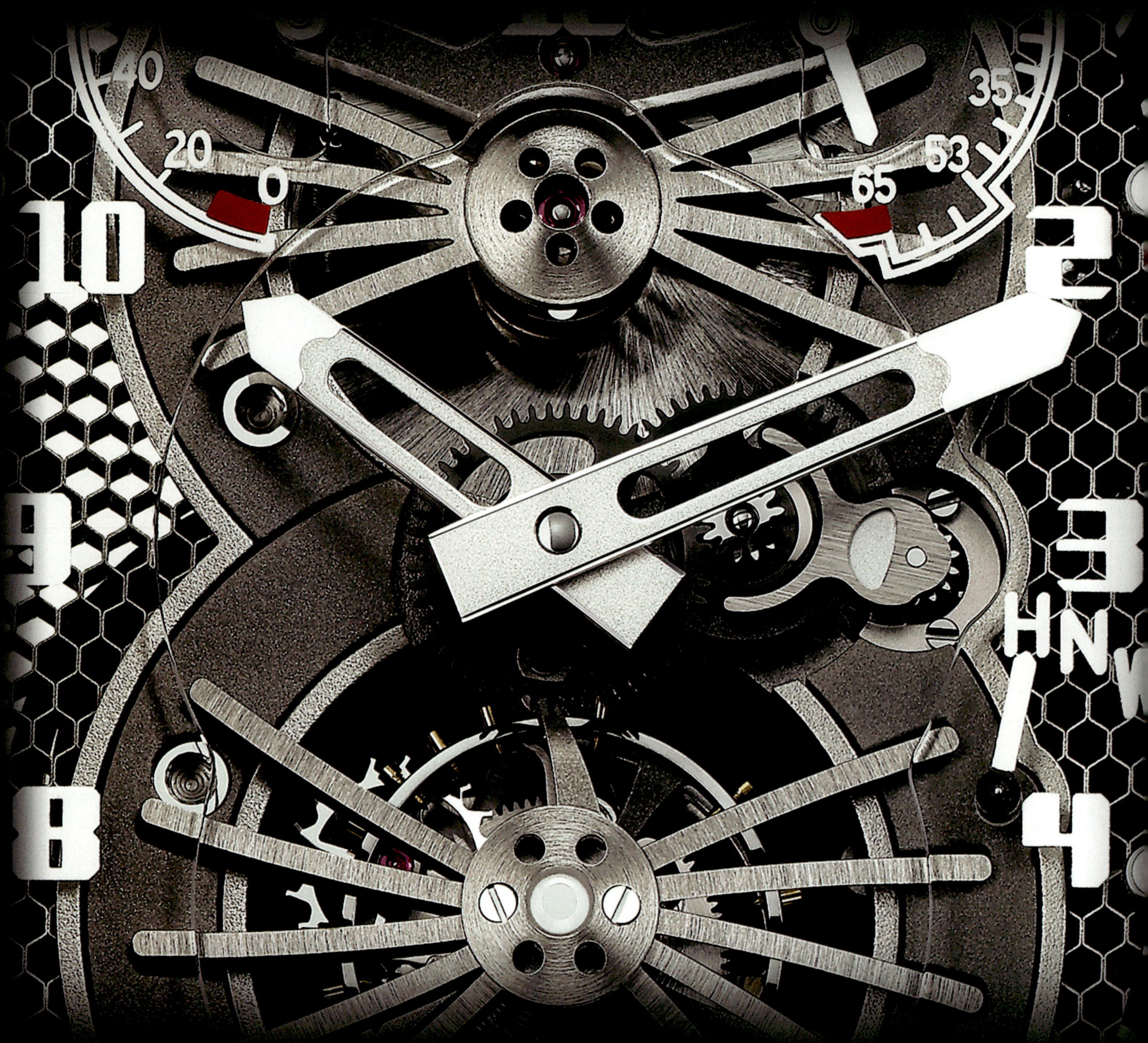

HIGH-TECH INSPIRATION

"I have always been fascinated and curious about new technologies, materials and ideas that break the mold of the status quo and push forward into innovative areas of development. This freedom is the driving force and objective behind everything I do."

—*Richard Mille*

The strength of Richard Mille's timekeeping creations lies in his horological vision, in which mechanically inspired disciplines are redefined for application to a new philosophy of watchmaking.

THE LIMITLESS POSSIBILITIES OF RICHARD MILLE WATCHES

The last ten years have seen the brand present record-breaking advances in horology with new materials, concepts, technology and solutions never before seen in watchmaking. In that decade, we have become so used to titanium in high-end watchmaking as well as carbon nanofiber, naked mechanical structures, super light materials, torque and function indicators, cross-over technology from F1 and the aerospace industries and dozens of other developments that we forget what the watch world was like before Mille entered the scene. There is a reason why journalists back in 2000 talked of a rupture created by Richard Mille in the then-existing world of watchmaking—a revolution before and after Mille.

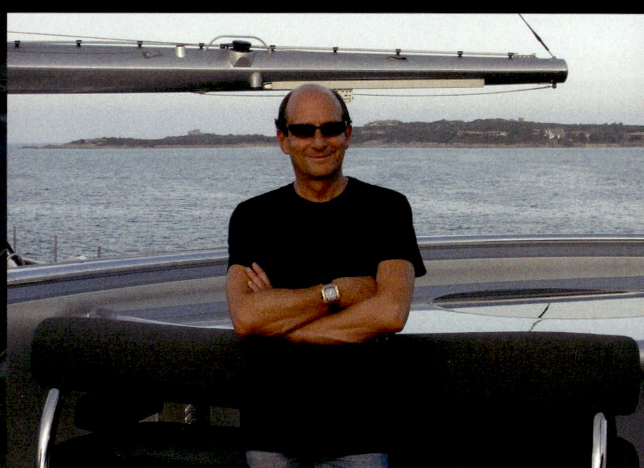

Creating watches that extend the limits of watchmaking are second nature to a man like Mille. His uncanny ability to transform the very essence of classical watchmaking tradition and fuse it with futuristic materials and techniques constitutes only a small part of the brand's acknowledged success. The real strength of these timekeeping creations lies in his special vision of watchmaking, combining catalytic and creative impulses where principles from other mechanically inspired disciplines—such as F1 motor sports, the marine world of racing yachts and the aerospace industry—are redefined for application to a new philosophy of watchmaking. This is a world governed by connections made by lateral thinking, with fascinating results: a new definition of horology for the future.

The discussions about his watches will never leave you cold—the timepieces embody far too much passion and vision for a merely neutral response. Mille says, "I was always astonished at how the industry was using 21st-century materials and techniques such as Cadcam to make 19th-century watches. Many of these products are fantastic, and I respect them. But in my opinion, if we are going to use today's material and technology, then we have to make contemporary watches." He consequently set out to do just that by elevating the industrial techniques of stamping and CNC (computer numerical control) machining to brand-new forms of modern art. For instance, the signature tonneau shape of his watch cases require a staggering 28 stamping operations even before the actual cutting and shaping can begin. Nonetheless, this does not mean that Richard Mille rejects the past; in fact, quite the contrary is true. "My watches have more hand-finishing than you will find in the majority of high-end watches," Mille explains. You can see it in the hand-beveling of screws and the black polish on my tourbillons. Even my watch hands are hand-finished! At the same time, you will also see a wide use of advanced techniques. This is exactly how F1 cars are created. A modern engine is created using Cadcam but many parts of it will always be hand-finished, polished and adjusted." Achieving the highest performance possible, in Mille's view, is only possible by uniting the best of both worlds.

The fact that he had to focus on creating legitimacy for his products make it doubly important that his watches reflect an extreme dedication to quality. Without a 200-year-old name, a watchmaker must provide other factors to prove itself to collectors and lovers of fine watchmaking. Mille firmly believes that the timing was just right for him when the high-end luxury market shifted its focus: "Twenty years ago, a brand name in itself was the only thing that defined status. Today such status is accorded almost solely by the actual product. People will buy something if it is the very best, even if the brand is not known. This has opened up avenues for me." Above all, it is his deepest desire to advance technology and luxury beyond existing confines that has brought Mille to the lofty ranks of high-end watchmaking.

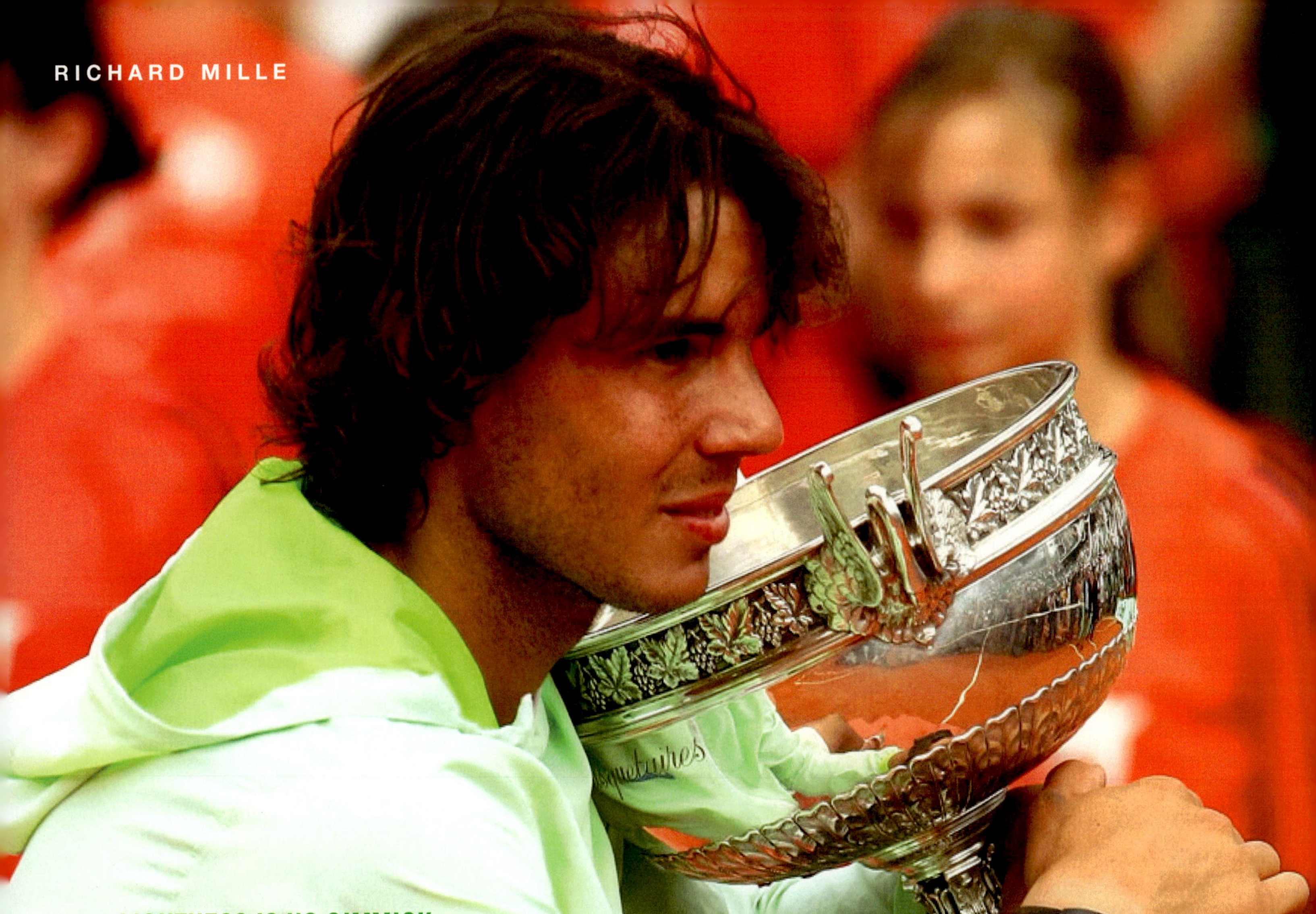

LIGHTNESS IS NO GIMMICK

The limited series RM 027, weighing only 18 grams and presented in 2010, was originally created for Rafael Nadal and worn by him during all his tournaments in 2010. This model was the third study in "the lightness of luxury." Previous models were the RM 006 and RM 009 Felipe Massa creations, the previous record breakers for the lightest mechanical tourbillons in the industry. Mille says, "I never make gimmick watches; there is always a reason behind everything I create. Both Felipe and Rafael came to me with requests for light watches...Why? Because at high speeds on the track, or on the tennis courts, every bit of weight on your arm is greatly magnified by the G forces at play during such activities. If you are a sportsman at the top of your field, even a small adjustment required for the weight of a heavy watch on your wrist will affect your reaction time—and could therefore mean the difference between winning or losing. That's why I have spent so much money and time researching these kinds of concepts. Now it is accepted that a light watch can cost as much as a heavy watch. After all, who is going to say, 'My car weighs five tons, so it should cost more than a car that weighs one ton?' Everybody is fighting against weight today. And to fight against weight costs a fortune. Just look at satellites and F1 cars where every gram has to be accounted for; they have been busy with this subject for years already."

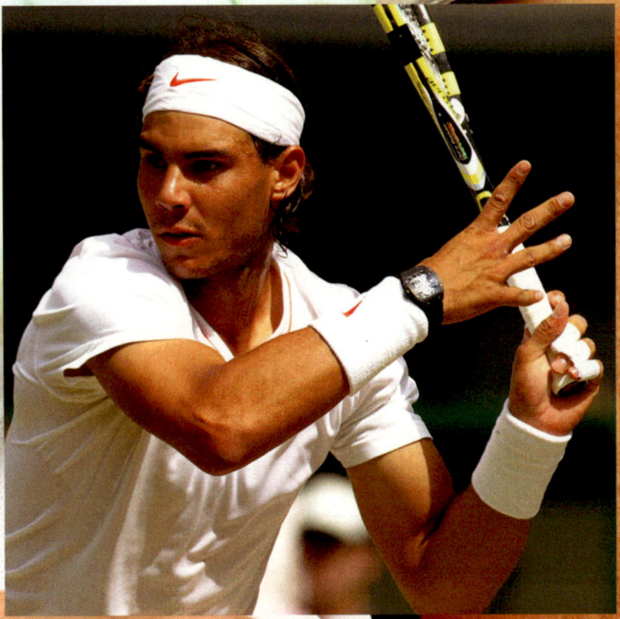

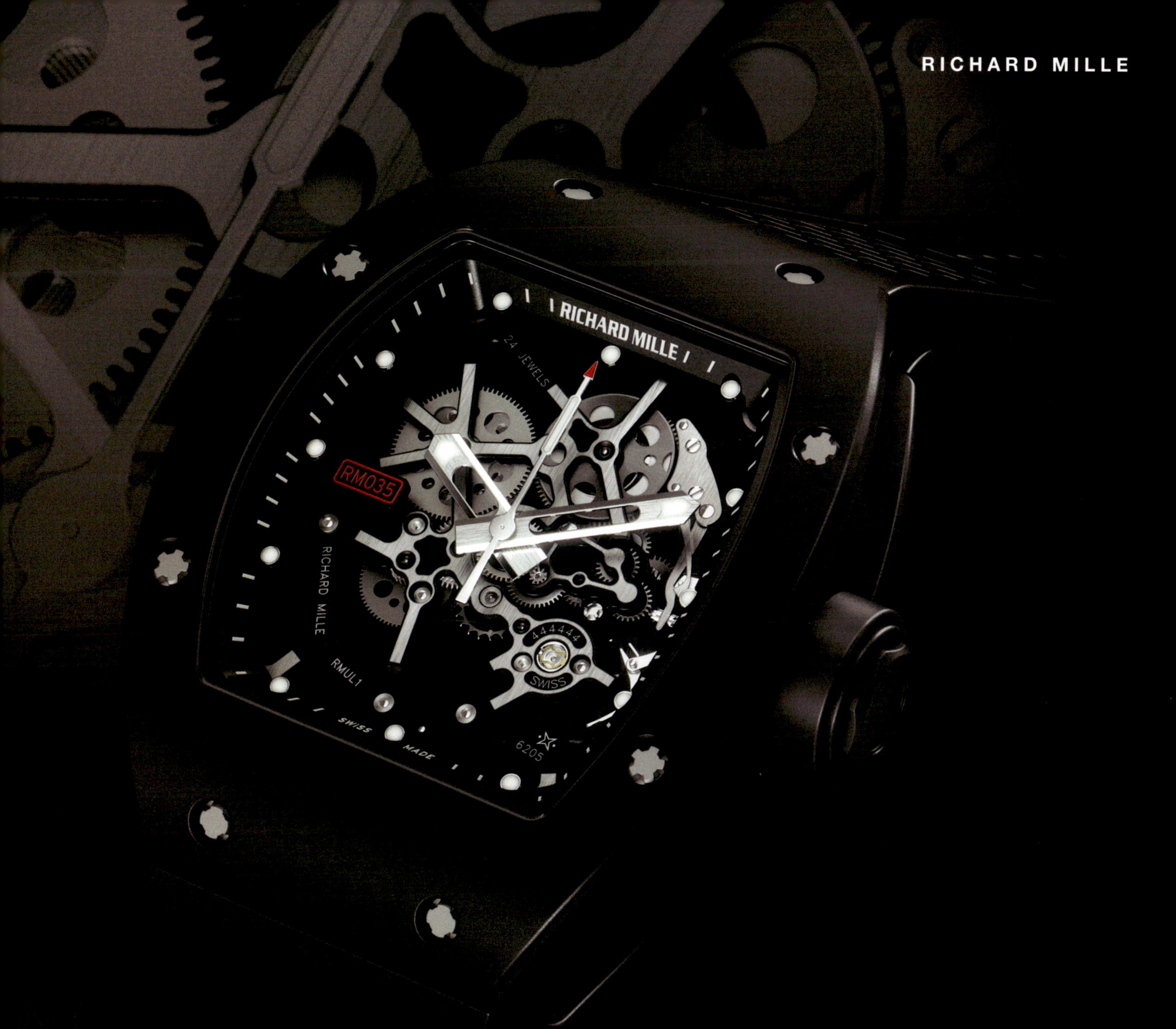

RM 035
RAFAEL NADAL CHRONOFIABLE®

Experimental concepts like those used in the creation of the RM 027 feed directly into other inspiration for other watches in the collection. This was a driving force behind the development of the new RM 035 Rafael Nadal Chronofiable®, a skeletonized manual-winding wristwatch, certified Chronofiable®. The Chronofiable® accelerated aging test simulates normal wearing conditions with an intensity factor of about eight over a period of 21 days (the equivalent of six months' effective wear), by the execution of a long series of tests. Chronofiable® testing starts with initial monitoring of the movement functions and an additional rate and the amplitude test, at two temperature levels (0°C and 50°C) followed by monitoring of the power reserve and the winding velocity. Then comes the toughest part: aging cycles consisting of linear and angular accelerations with more than 20,000 shocks ranging from 250 to 5500 m/s^2 as well as changes in temperature and humidity during these cycles. The Chronofiable® test assures that the RMUL1 caliber within the RM 035 has the ability to withstand many extreme conditions without experiencing any effects on its performance.

A TOUGH CONTENDER: RM 035

With one of the lightest skeletonized manual-winding movements ever created, the new RM 035 proves that lightness and strength go hand in hand. The case of the RM 035 is made of a special alloy of extremely rugged aluminum and magnesium, normally used in the automotive and aerospace industries. This alloy, combined with a plasma treatment, is known for its light weight, corrosion resistance and longevity.

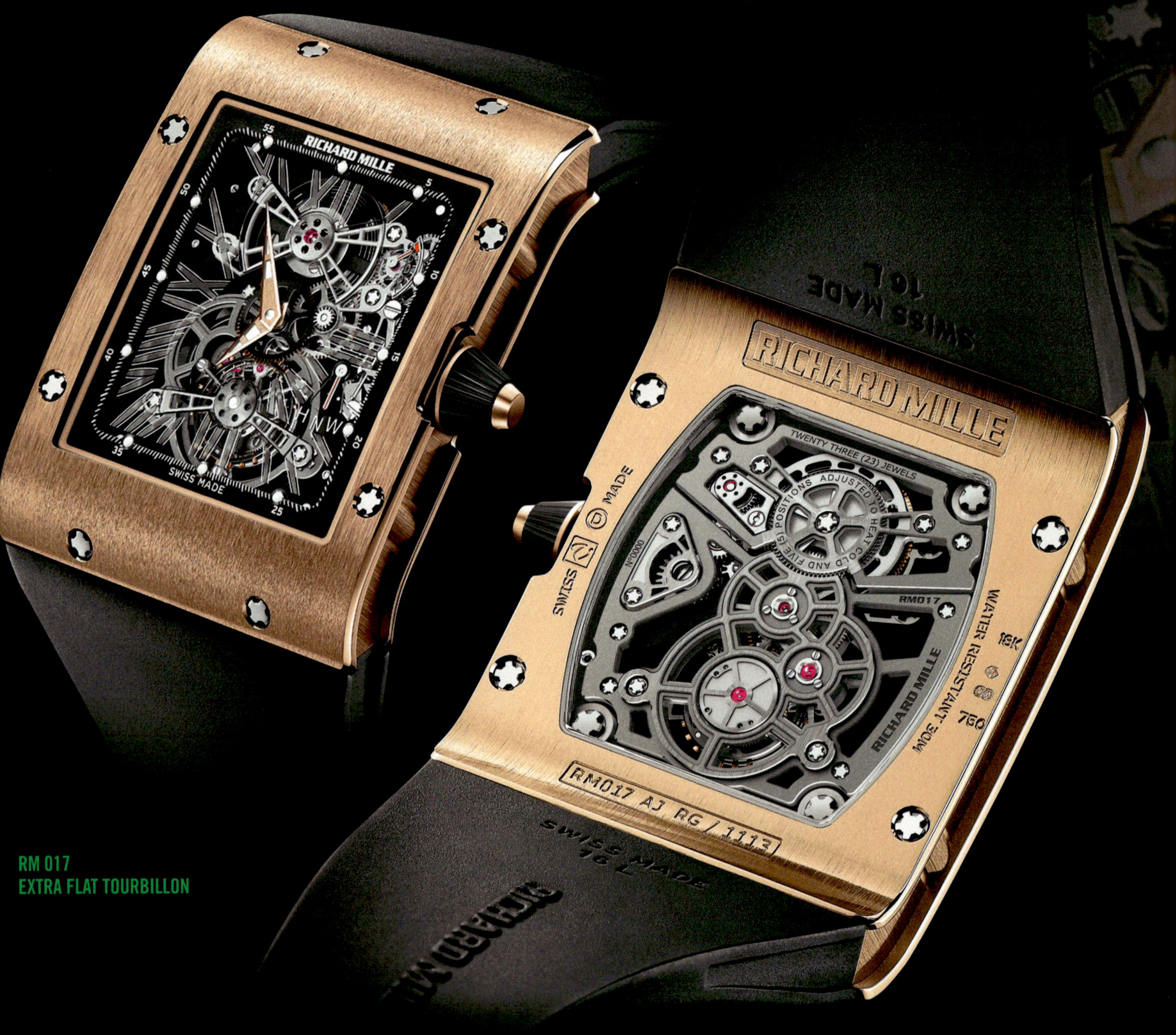

RM 017
EXTRA FLAT TOURBILLON

RM 017 EXTRA FLAT TOURBILLON

Mille relates, "You know it is funny; originally, when I started my brand, I wanted to make a rectangular model. But to fit all of the movement's mechanism inside, I had to enlarge it into a tonneau. In my first drawing of the RM 001, the watch was rectangular! So when the RM 016, the visual predecessor of the RM 017 tourbillon, was released, it was like coming home in a way." New for 2011, the RM 017 Extra Flat tourbillon continues the development of the highly successful rectangular models that proudly take their place alongside the uniquely curvaceous Richard Mille tonneau shape. With a total height comprising a mere 8.7mm, sporting a new extra-flat, manual-winding movement crafted in titanium, it is among the thinnest tourbillon constructions ever created. The RM 017's dimensions of 49.8x38mm retain a proportional harmony with the other cases in the collection, and perpetuates, of course, the same wrist-fitting curvature and tapering thickness towards 12 and 6 o'clock that every Richard Mille fan has come to admire.

TECHNICAL BUT ELEGANT

The RM 017 Extra Flat Tourbillon continues the visual lines set out by the rectangular watches of the Richard Mille collection. The movement, only 4.65mm thick, is made of components manufactured in grade 5 titanium and treated with a black PVD coating. As a consequence the whole assembly is extremely rigid, with precise surface flatness, an essential quality for the perfect functioning of the geartrain. A special pusher in the crown activates the functions for winding, neutral and hand-setting.

JEWELED MYSTERY— RM 026 TOURBILLON

For 2011, a new tourbillon using semi-precious and precious stones is being added to the Richard Mille collection, a welcome addition for everyone who values a unique combination at the highest level of watchmaking with high-quality jewelry. The new RM 026 is a combination of esoteric sensibility and technical horology. The design and inspiration of this new tourbillon are fully grounded in the eternal themes of nature, Gaia and the passage of time.

For the RM 026 Tourbillon, two creatures adorn its precious movement: two snakes, encrusted with rubies and emeralds respectively, writhe and search within the tourbillon movement, simultaneously holding it in place. Serpents in mythology have complex roles that can be either good or evil. In connection with the positive properties of black onyx, however, they take on a protective role, representing the potent guardians of temples and other sacred spaces. Thus, they are natural guardians of treasures or sacred sites that are intimate and need to be protected.

The mainplate of the watch has been created of pure black onyx, a variety of cryptocrystalline quartz chalcedony composed of siliceous dioxide (SiO). Onyx varieties with rectilinear black and white parallel stripes are actually a part of the agate family, whereas the fully black type is what one commonly calls true black onyx. This is a gemstone able to deflect and channel harmful energy towards the Earth, thus providing stability. Due to this ability, black onyx is considered a stone of protection against negative thoughts, as well being the stone of equilibrium and inspiration.

In keeping with the technical nature of all watches created by the brand, the RM 026 Tourbillon Serpent utilizes a newly developed power reserve indicator that makes use of a differential gearing system, directly connected to the winding barrel. Via a red line etched on its surface, the direct turning of the 48-hour power reserve barrel allows the wearer to easily note if the watch requires winding. An additional security system, a torque-limiting crown, prevents any chance of accidental over-winding, which could possibly cause damage to the winding stem or exert extreme pressure on the mainspring barrel.

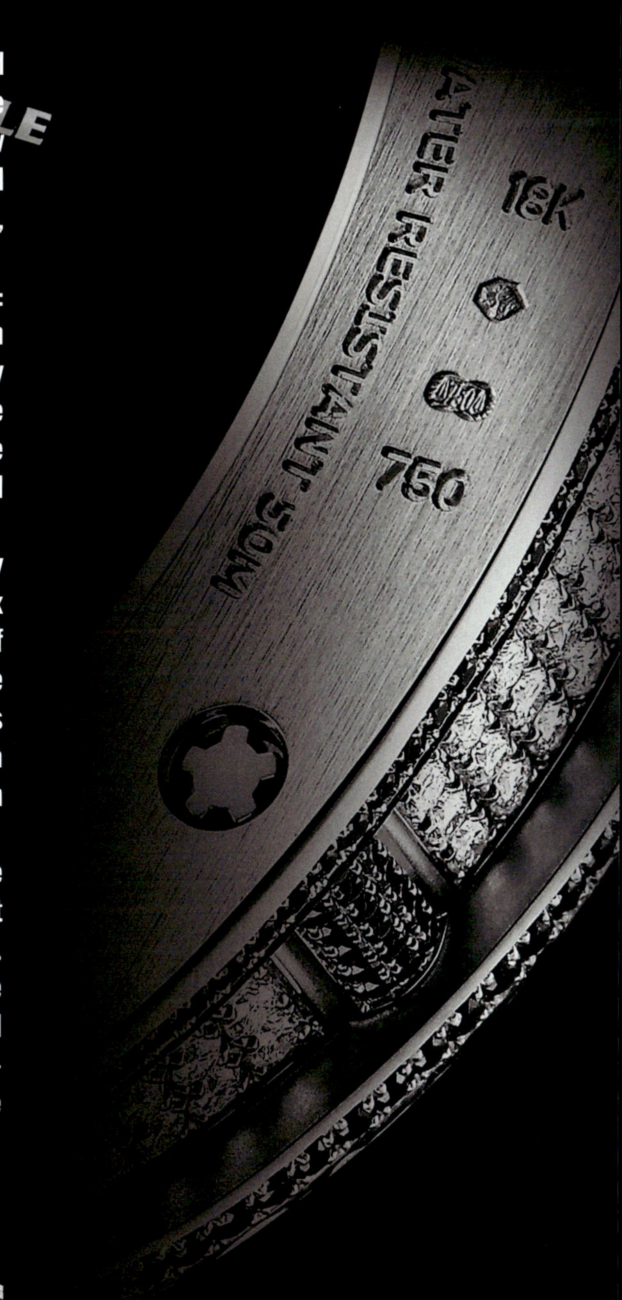

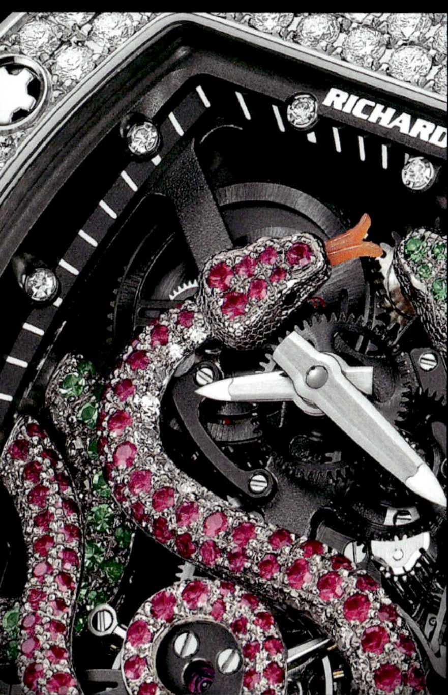

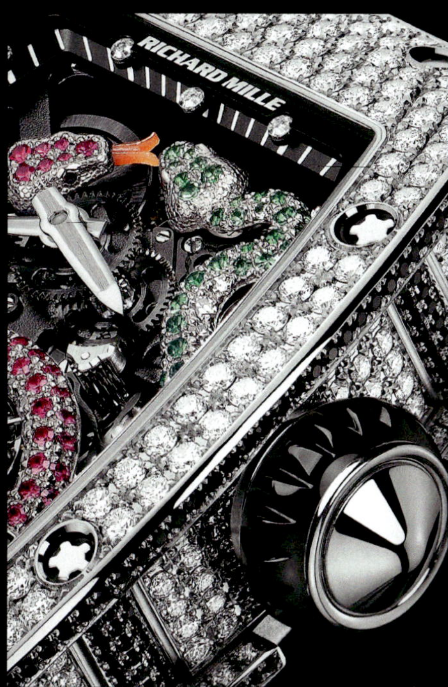

RM 026
TOURBILLON

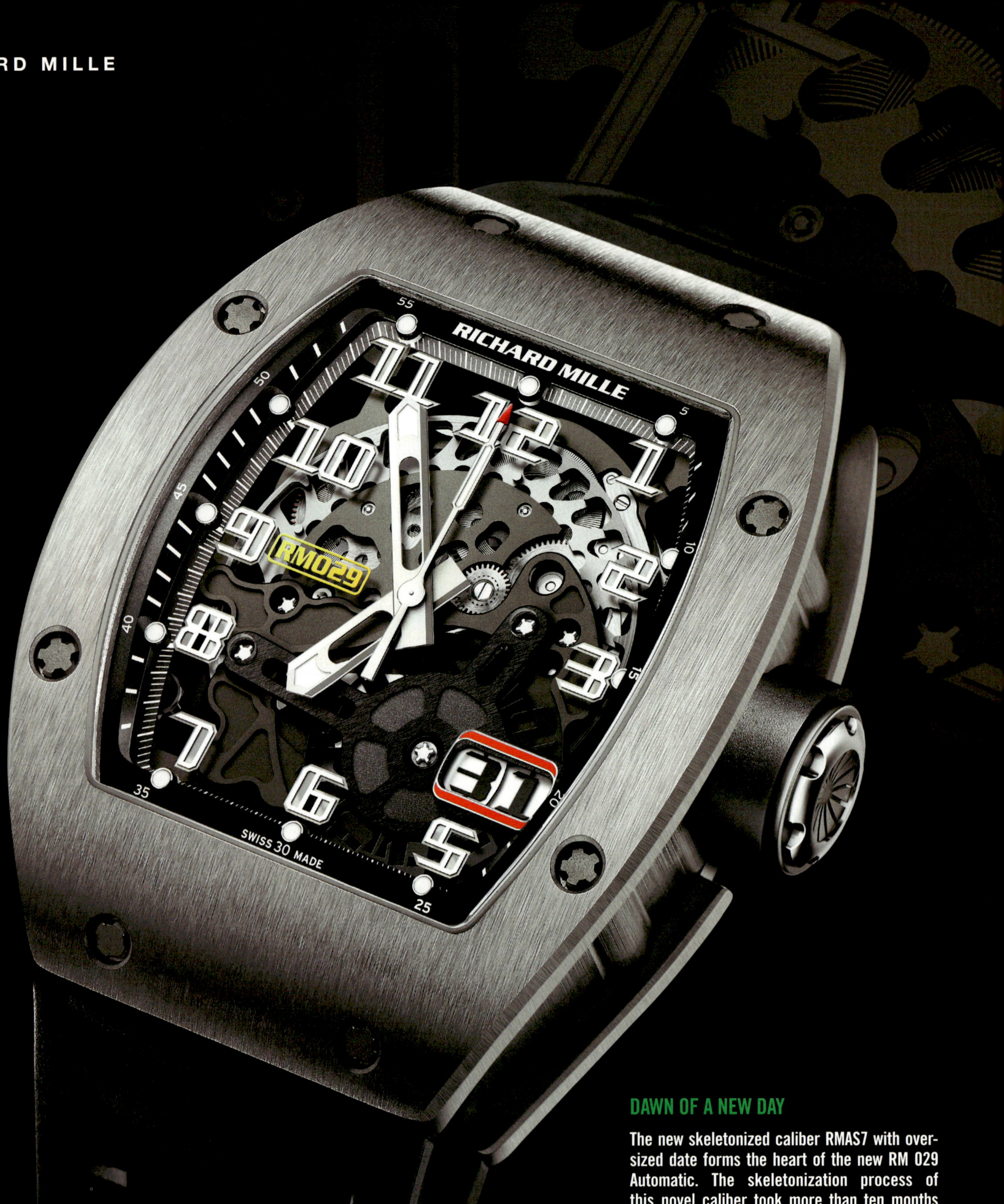

DAWN OF A NEW DAY

The new skeletonized caliber RMAS7 with oversized date forms the heart of the new RM 029 Automatic. The skeletonization process of this novel caliber took more than ten months to finalize, as there could be no compromise in the movement's strength or ability to withstand shocks. Within its case dimensions of 48x39.7mm (widest point) and 12.6mm thickness beats an automatic movement with oversize date mechanism inspired by the RM 011 and a rotor with variable geometry. This exclusive Richard Mille design allows the re-winding of the mainspring to be adapted most effectively to the user's activity level within sports or leisure environments.

RM 029
OVERSIZE DATE
AUTOMATIC

TECHNICAL HIGHLIGHT: RM 030 AUTOMATIC WITH DECLUTCHABLE ROTOR

Inside the case of the RM 030 beats the novel caliber RMAR1, representing a further advancement in the world of automatic wristwatch design. The rotor of the RM 030 turns in the normal manner through the physical movements of the wearer, thus providing energy to the winding barrel, which reaches its optimal point once it is fully wound. After this point, over-winding can easily occur and needs to be avoided. This is traditionally achieved through the use of a sliding flange that allows the spring to slip, thus avoiding the movement becoming over-wound. However, this traditional system allows the build-up of harmful debris inside the winding barrel, as the flange releases the excess energy of over-winding during longer periods, especially when a person is particularly active. This in turn can severely affect chronometric results. To avoid such adverse conditions, Richard Mille took four years to develop the concept and design of a rotor able to declutch automatically. With this system, the winding barrel is automatically disconnected from the rotor's winding mechanism at the moment when the spring is optimally wound. Additionally, this new mechanism is linked to the power reserve indicator to provide an optimal winding control. This allows both the movementand the winding rotor to work with the best ratio of constant torque/power to provide ultimate chronometric performance.

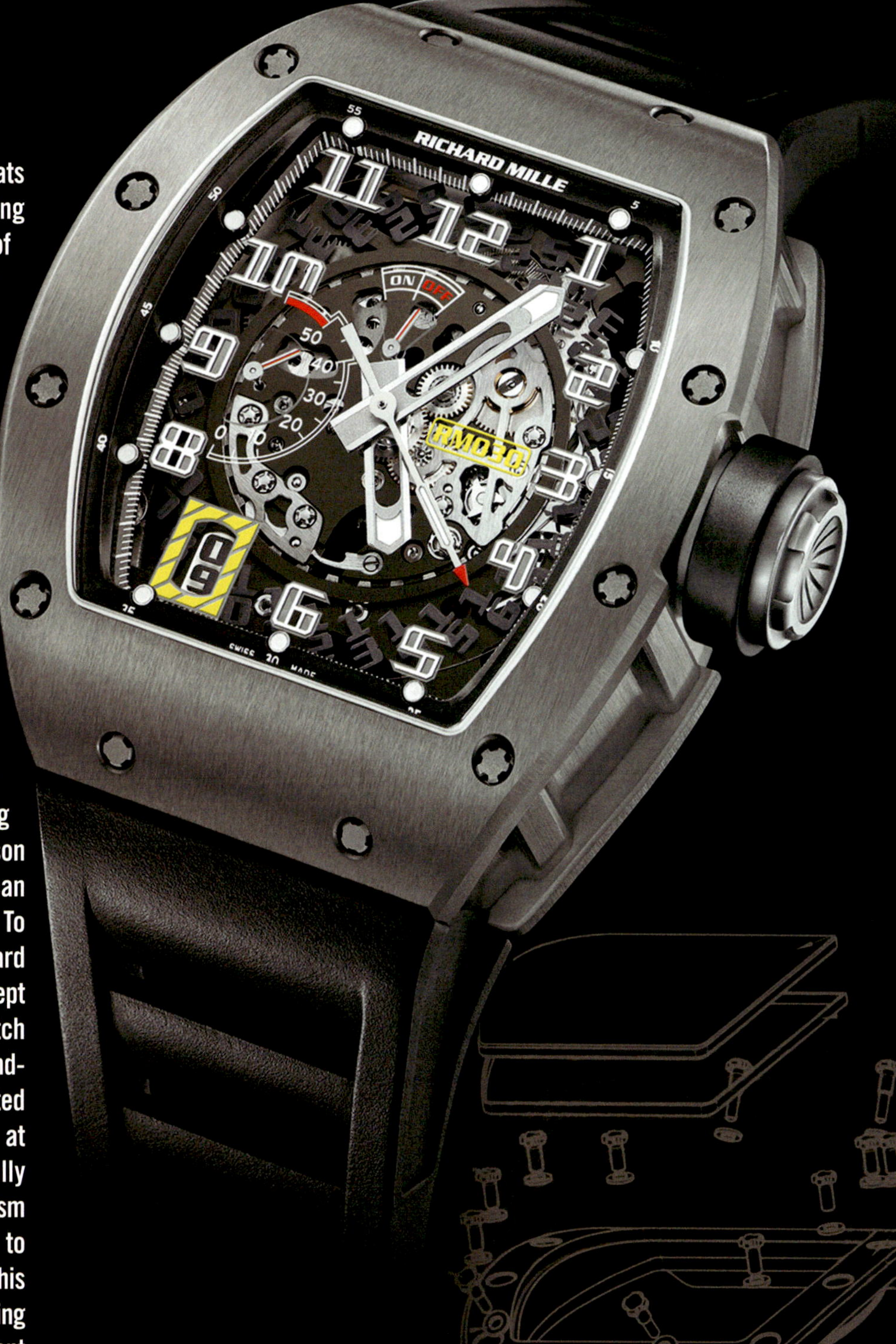

RM 030
DECLUTCHING ROTOR
AUTOMATIC

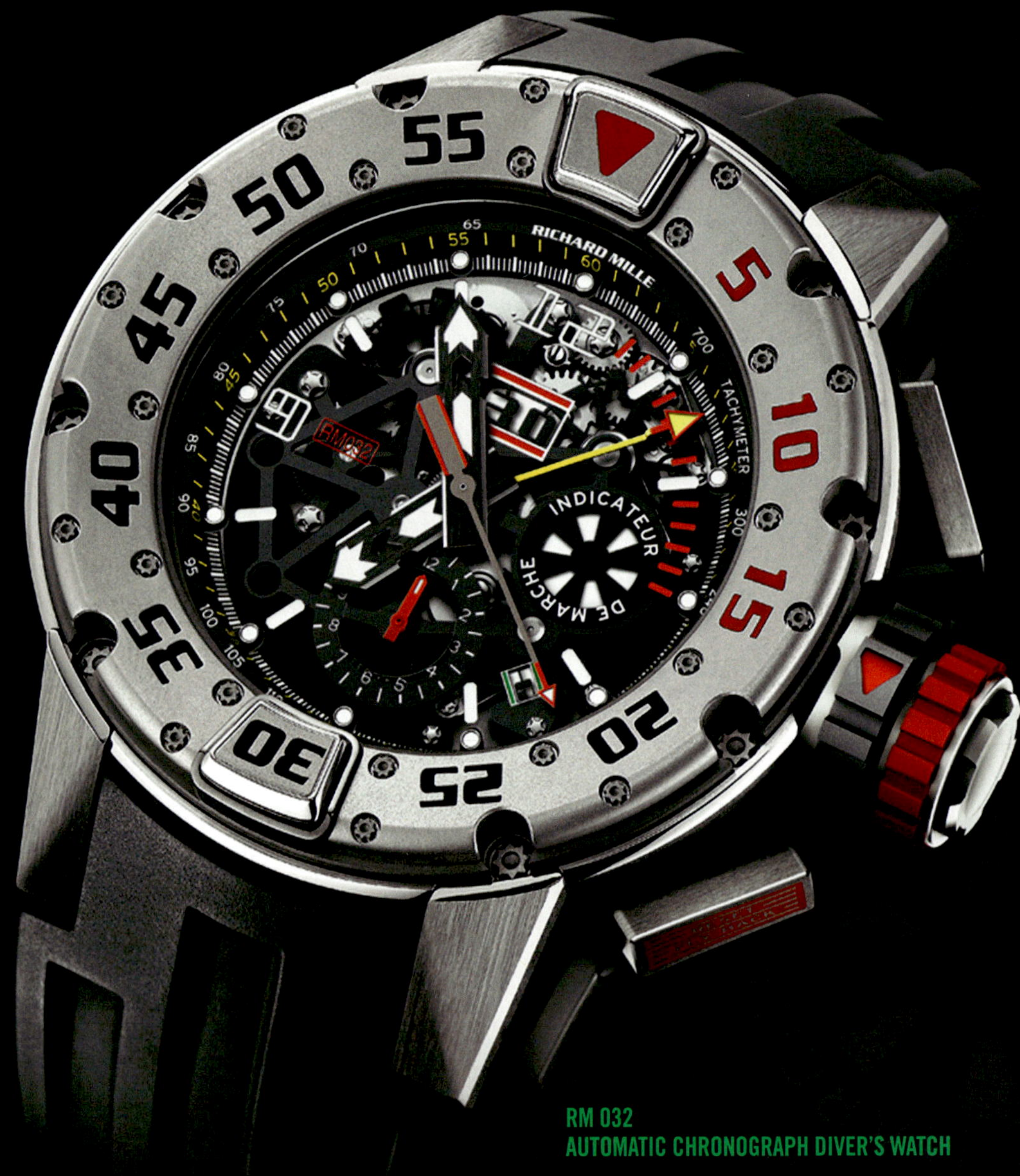

RM 032
AUTOMATIC CHRONOGRAPH DIVER'S WATCH

RM 032 AUTOMATIC CHRONOGRAPH DIVER'S WATCH

This newest Richard Mille creation for the depths of the sea offers the broadest variety of functions available within the Richard Mille divers' collection. The RM 032 offers hours, minutes, seconds, 60-minute countdown, 12-hour totalizer and flyback chronograph functions, combined with an annual calendar sporting an oversized date at 12 o'clock and a month indicator (with numerals from 1 to 12) between 4 and 5 o'clock. The digits for the date indicator are composed of two discs, with the digits cut out like positive stencils, offering great visual clarity combined with style. The annual calendar allows for the date change to be automatically calculated for months of 30 and 31 days; the only holdout is the month of February. The caliber RMAC2 is protected by a large case measuring 50x17.8mm, with water resistance of 30 atmospheres (300 meters) and a unidirectionally turning bezel following ISO 6425 norms in order to prevent miscalculations whilst diving. Built up of three layers connected with 22 screws, the bezel and the system attaching it to the watchcase makes it absolutely stable as well as impossible to inadvertently dislocate or loosen. For clearer visibility under murky conditions, starting at 12 o'clock, the five-minute markers of the first quarter are highlighted red. All of these details mark the RM 032 as a tool ready for the harsh environment of the sea. A new mechanism created by Richard Mille, the running indicator, is located at 3 o'clock. Thanks to both its geometry and 2-rpm rotational frequency, it is possible to check at a glance the correct functioning of the running movement under stressful environments. The running indicator disc is composed of successive SuperLumiNova and black sectors; as a result it can be easily seen, day or night.

RM 033 ULTRA FLAT AUTOMATIC

An ultra-flat movement is something most subtle and elegant in the world of horology since the expertise of the watchmaker resides in achieving something almost invisible. The constraints of producing this model are made even more challenging given the limited space available.

In the case of an automatic ultra-flat wristwatch like the RM 033, one of its secrets lies in the placement of the RMXP1 caliber's automatic micro-rotor to the side rather than the center of the movement, thus saving precious millimeters in total height. To provide perfect weight distribution for this off-center rotor to function optimally, it has been created to wind bi-directionally and manufactured from solid platinum, allowing for efficient winding as well as compact dimensions, and the spatial layout of the ultra-flat skeletonized movement. The round case design of the RM 033 measures 45.7mm in diameter and a mere 6.3mm in thickness, with the curving caseback and typical spline case screws that have become the trademark of the entire Richard Mille Watches collection.

For the creation of the RMXP1 caliber, the bottom plate bridges and balance cock are made of titanium. The manufacturing of these components in grade 5 titanium with black PVD coating allows the entire ultra-flat assembly to be given great rigidity, as well as precise surface flatness that is essential for the perfect functioning of the gear train as well as the stability of the movement.

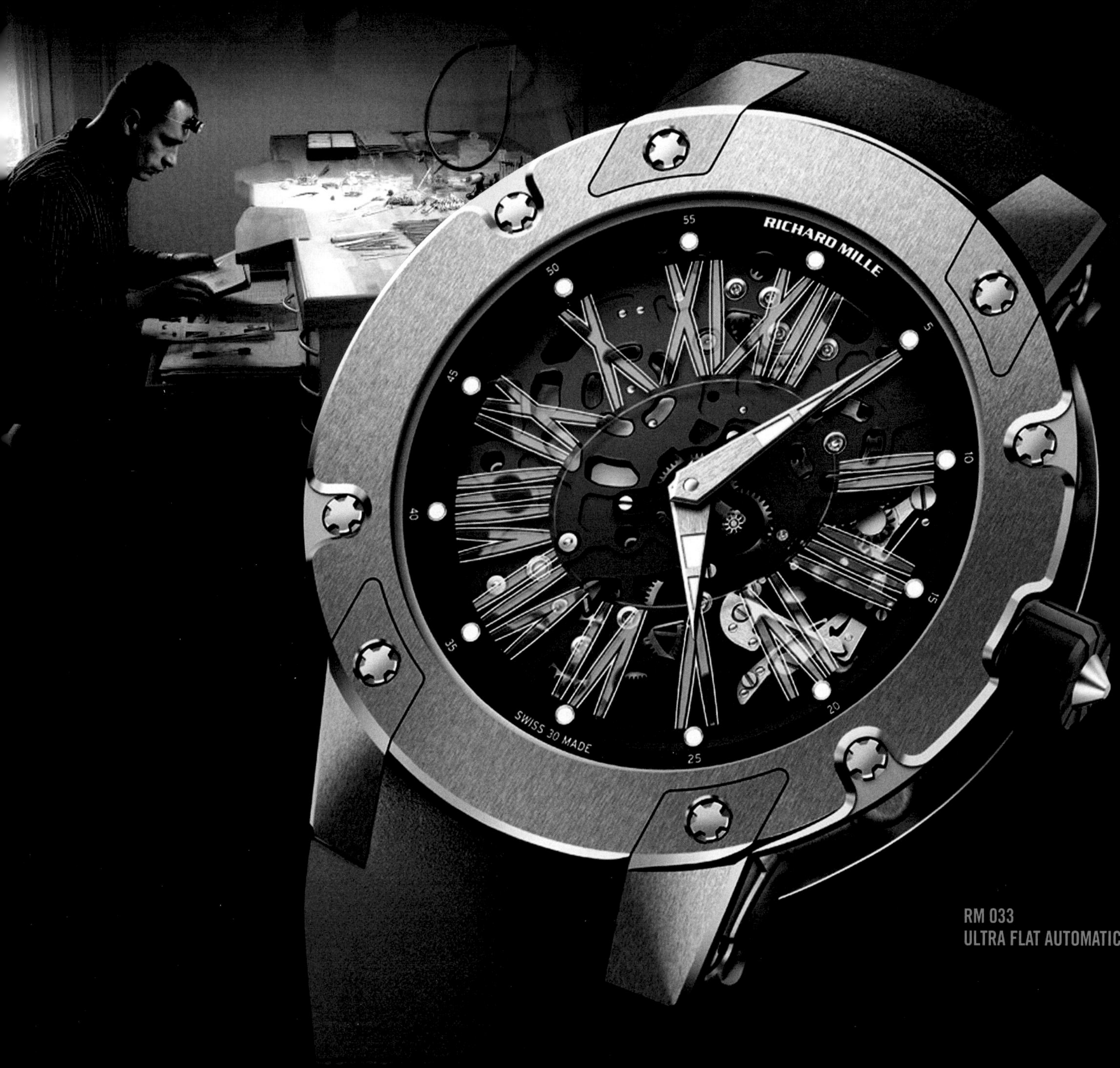

RM 033
ULTRA FLAT AUTOMATIC

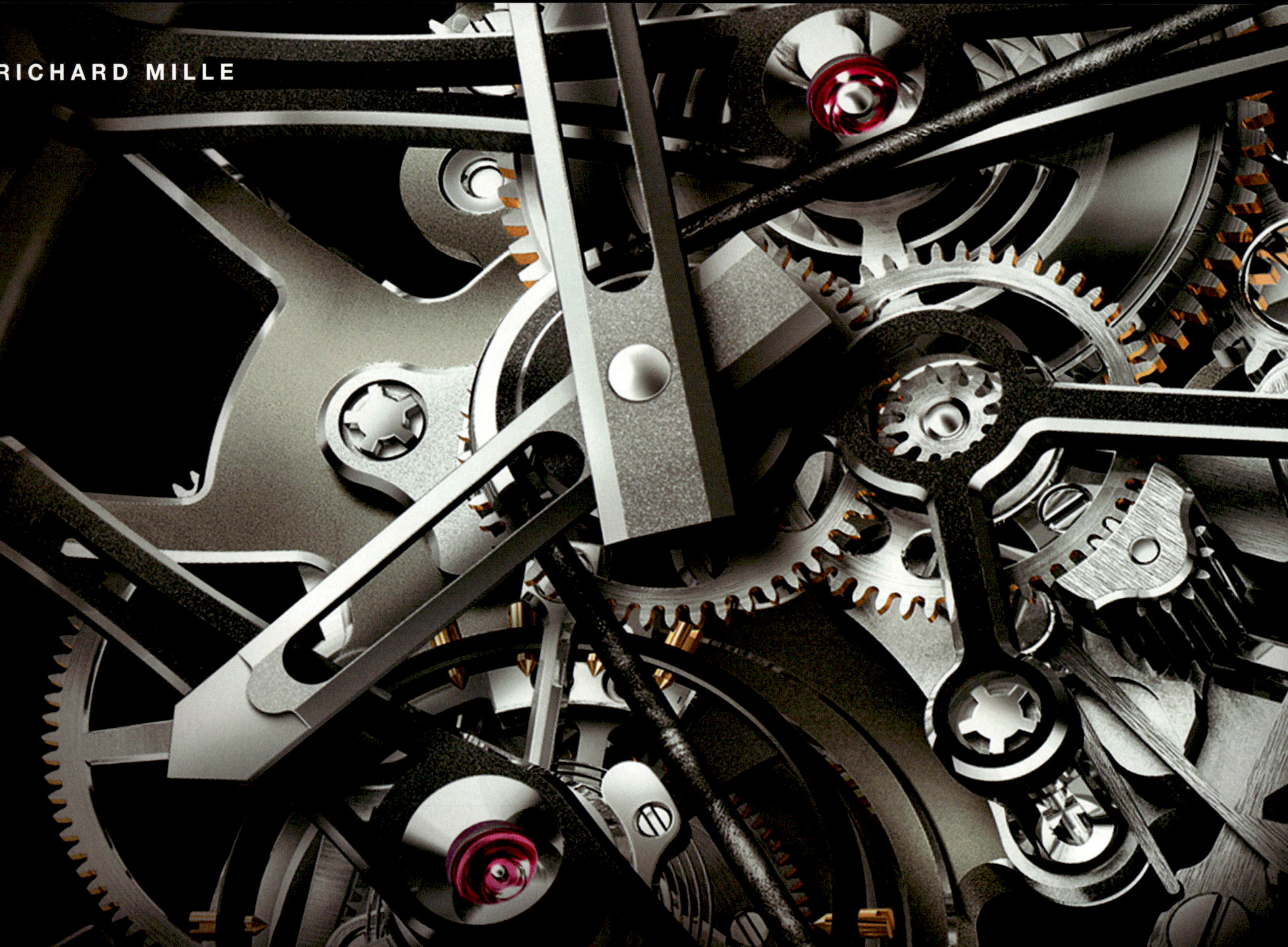

RM 038 TOURBILLON 'BUBBA WATSON'

The manual-winding, skeletonized tourbillon caliber RM 038 'Bubba Watson' beating at the heart of this new creation represents another novel partnership between Richard Mille and the world of sports. The challenge at hand this time was to create a tourbillon able to withstand the specific and exceptional stresses and forces at work within the world of the professional golfer. Not only lightness and extreme shock resistance are at play; the extremes of large, swinging arm movements in opposition to the small delicate manipulations required on the putting green means that the watch must be present, yet never get in the way of any hand, arm or wrist movements whether large or minimal in span, regardless of the level of centrifugal/centripetal forces involved.

The case of 48 mm x 39.70 mm x 12.80 mm encloses the 3Hz tourbillon caliber RM038, with its 19 jewels and grade 5 titanium baseplate and bridges. This allows the whole assembly to be given great rigidity, as well as the precise surface flatness essential for the perfect functioning of the gear train. The extremely skeletonized baseplate was subjected to separate and extensive validation tests to ensure optimal strength requirements under all the conditions to be found on the world's most challenging golf ranges.

The case of the RM 038 is made of an extremely rugged and light magnesium alloy classified as AZ91, composed of aluminum combined with zinc and magnesium plus additional trace metals. The resulting magnesium alloy is more than the sum of the parts, providing a light yet extremely strong material with a dendritic internal crystalline structure making it suitable for extreme applications in the aerospace, telecommunication and automotive industries.

After a long and delicate machining phase, the case is given an electro-plasma treatment named Titalyt II®, covering the surface with a layer of white, crystalline ceramic oxide containing a high ratio of resistant composites. This biocompatible treatment provides an additional layer of high wear and corrosion resistance to the surface of the case's already extreme specifications. The tripartite case is assembled with 12 spline screws in grade 5 titanium and abrasion resistant washers in 316L stainless steel, with the structural water resistance to 50 meters ensured by two Nitril O-ring seals.

The new Richard Mille RM 038 Tourbillon is designed for golfers and sportsmen who appreciate 21st century high-end watchmaking created with refined finishing and details, yet able to cope with extreme conditions. It typifies Richard Mille's revolutionary concepts for the future of watchmaking today.

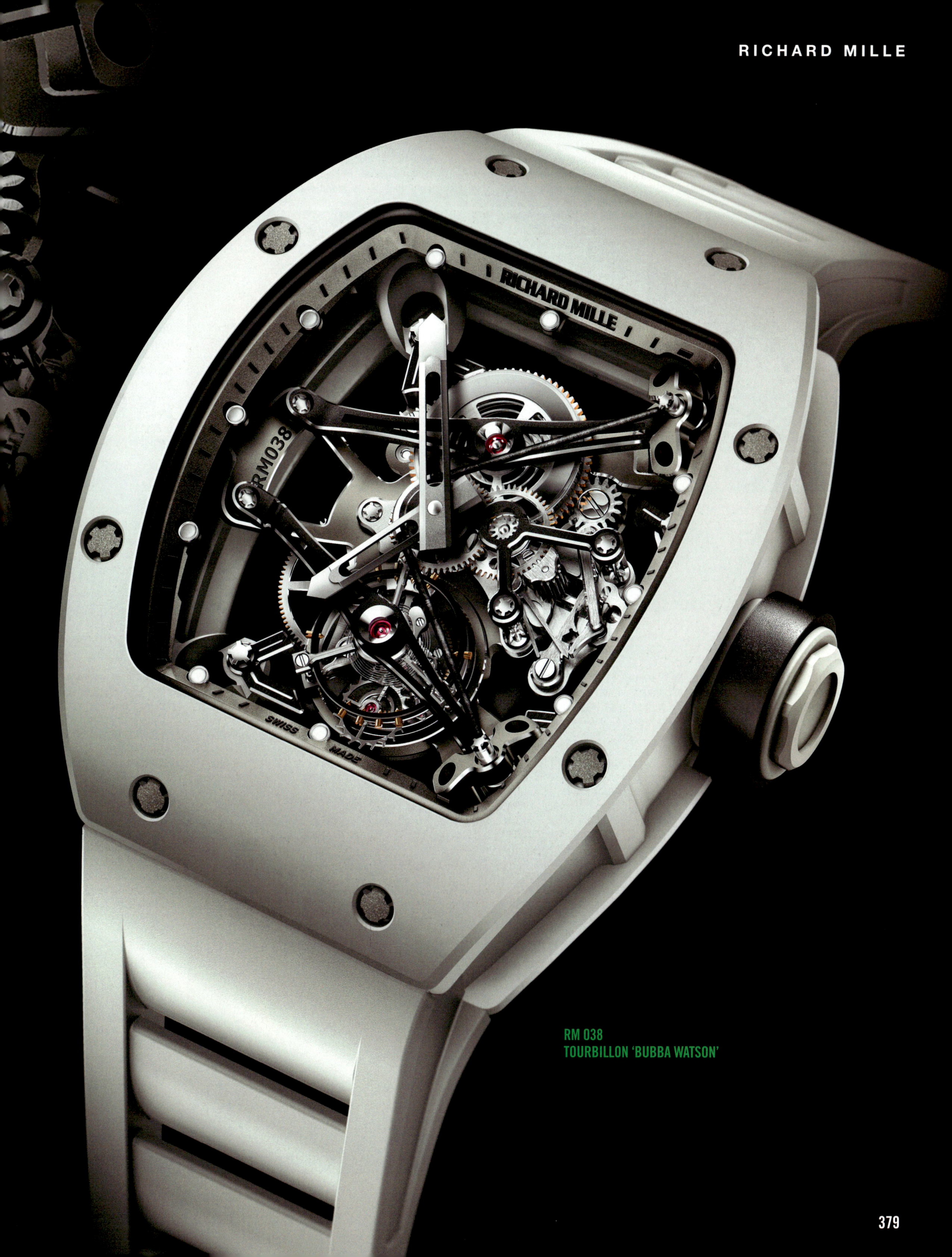

RM 038
TOURBILLON 'BUBBA WATSON'

SPLIT SECONDS CHRONOGRAPH — RM 004-V2

Movement: automatic-winding RM004-V2 caliber; carbon nanofiber baseplate; approx. 60-hour power reserve; titanium column wheels, gear wheels and lever; split-seconds mechanism with improved and patented functions; fast rotating barrel; function indicator; variable inertia balance with overcoil hairspring; newly designed three-tiered titanium bridge with lever escapement; spline screws in grade-5 titanium for the bridges and case; winding barrel and third pinion's teeth with central involute profile.

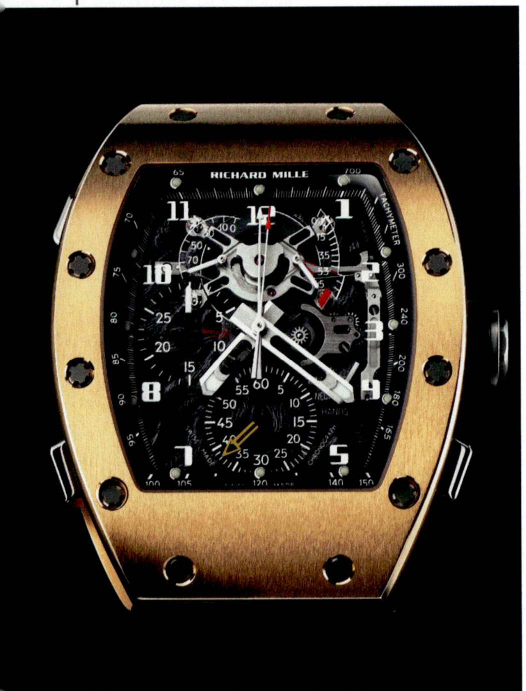

Functions: hours, minutes, seconds; split seconds; chronograph minute counter; power reserve; torque indicator; function indicator.
Case: anatomically curved three-piece case; 48x39.7mm, thickness: 14.95mm; assembled with 20 spline screws in grade-5 titanium; sapphire crystal front and back with double-sided antireflective coating; water resistant to 50 meters.
Dial: sapphire crystal with double-sided antireflective treatment; protected with eight silicon braces in grooved edges.
Strap: leather or crocodile; attached via titanium screws to the case; matching buckle.
Available in: 18K red gold; 18K white gold; titanium; platinum.

AUTOMATIC (TITANIUM VERSION) — RM 007

Movement: automatic-winding RM007 caliber; approx. 38-hour power reserve; rotor fitted with a patented auto-reverse system integrated into the rotor ball bearing; grade-5 titanium screws; date aperture at 6 with sapphire crystal calendar disc treated with double-sided antireflective coating; crown with double-seal O-ring and collar in Alcryn; teeth with central involute profile.
Functions: hours, minutes; date.

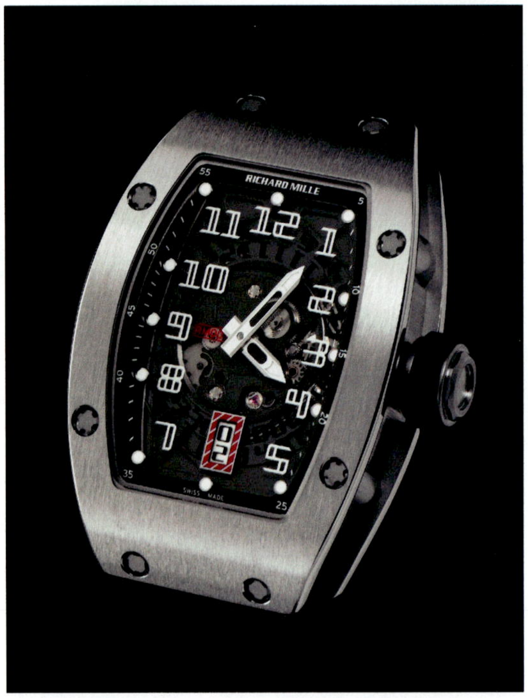

Case: anatomically curved three-piece case; 45x31mm, thickness: 10.95mm; assembled with 12 spline screws in grade-5 titanium; sapphire crystal front and back with double-sided antireflective coating; water resistant to 50 meters.
Dial: sapphire crystal with double-sided antireflective treatment; protected with eight silicon braces in grooved edges.
Strap: leather, crocodile or various fabrics; attached via titanium screws to the case; matching buckle.
Available in: titanium.

AUTOMATIC — RM 007 TITALYT

Movement: automatic-winding RM007 caliber; approx. 38-hour power reserve; rotor fitted with a patented auto-reverse system integrated into the rotor ball bearing; grade-5 titanium screws; date aperture at 6 with sapphire crystal calendar disc treated with double-sided antireflective coating; crown with double-seal O-ring and collar in Alcryn; teeth with central involute profile.
Functions: hours, minutes; date.

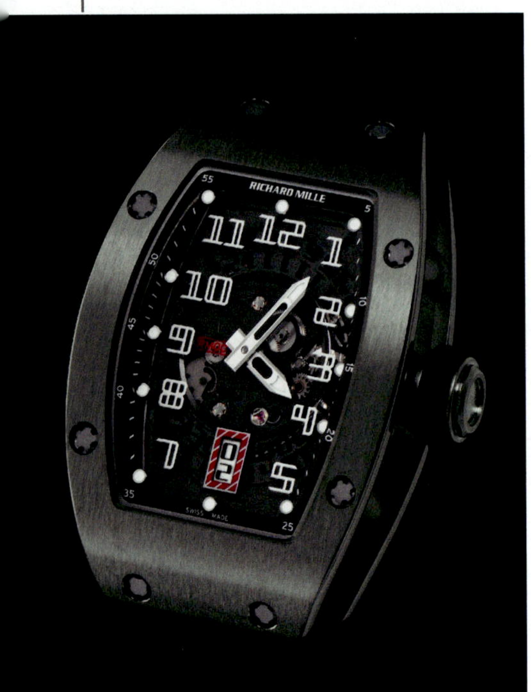

Case: anatomically curved three-piece case with Titalyt surface treatment; 45x31mm, thickness: 10.95mm; assembled with 12 spline screws in grade-5 titanium; sapphire crystal front and back with double-sided antireflective coating; water resistant to 50 meters.
Dial: sapphire crystal with double-sided antireflective treatment; protected with eight silicon braces in grooved edges.
Strap: leather, crocodile or various fabrics; attached via titanium screws to the case; matching buckle.
Available in: titanium.

AUTOMATIC (DIAMOND VERSION) — RM 007

Movement: automatic-winding RM007 caliber; approx. 38-hour power reserve; rotor fitted with a patented auto-reverse system integrated into the rotor ball bearing; rotor segment in sandblasted 18K gold; grade-5 titanium screws; date aperture at 6 with sapphire crystal calendar disc treated with double-sided antireflective coating; crown with double-seal O-ring and collar in Alcryn; teeth with central involute profile.

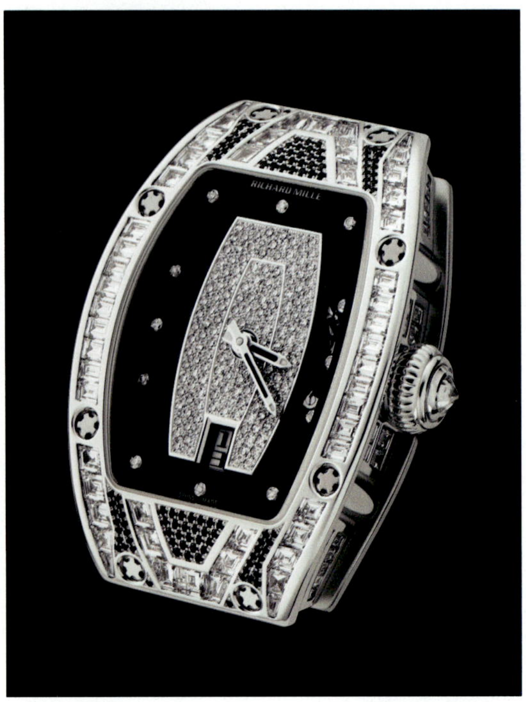

Functions: hours, minutes; date.
Case: anatomically curved three-piece case; 45x31mm, thickness: 10.95mm; bezel and sides set with white diamonds; case columns set with black diamonds; assembled with 12 spline screws in grade-5 titanium; sapphire crystal front and back with double-sided antireflective coating; water resistant to 50 meters.
Dial: central field with full diamond setting.
Strap: crocodile or various fabrics; attached via titanium screws to the case; matching buckle.
Available in: 18K red gold; 18K white gold; titanium; platinum.

TOURBILLON SPLIT SECONDS CHRONOGRAPH — RM 008-V2

Movement: manual-winding tourbillon RM008 caliber; carbon nanofiber baseplate; approx. 60-hour power reserve; titanium column wheels, gear wheels and lever; split-seconds mechanism with improved and patented functions; fast rotating barrel; function indicator; variable inertia balance with overcoil; in-line lever escapement; spline screws in grade-5 titanium for the bridges and case; winding barrel and third pinion teeth with central involute profile.
Functions: hours, minutes, seconds; split seconds; chronograph minute counter; power reserve indicator; torque indicator; function indicator.
Case: anatomically curved three-piececase;48x39.7mm, thickness: 14.95mm; assembled with 20 spline screws in grade-5 titanium; sapphire crystal front and back with double-sided antireflective coating; water resistant to 50 meters.
Dial: sapphire crystal with double sided antireflective treatment; protected with eight silicon braces in grooved edges.
Strap: leather or crocodile; attached via titanium screws to case; with matching buckle.
Available in: 18K red gold; 18K white gold; titanium; platinum.

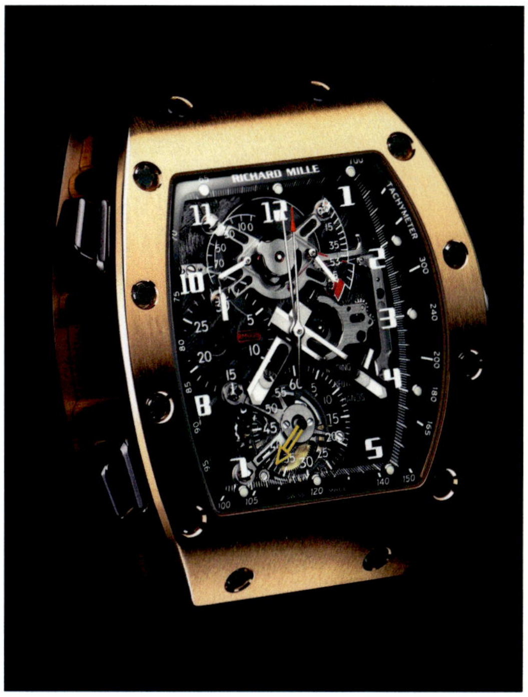

AUTOMATIC — RM 010

Movement: automatic-winding skeletonized RM005-S caliber; approx. 55-hour power reserve; rotor with variable geometry via white-gold wings adjustable to six positions; ceramic rotor ball bearings; PVD-coated titanium baseplate, bridges and balance cock; crown in sandblasted grade-5 titanium with double-seal O-ring and collar in Alcryn; double-winding barrel; grade-5 titanium spline screws for movement and case.
Functions: hours, minutes, seconds; date.
Case: anatomically curved three-piececase;48x39.3mm, thickness: 13.84mm; assembled with 12 spline screws in grade-5 titanium; sapphire crystal front and back with double-sided antireflective coating; water resistant to 100 meters.
Dial: sapphire crystal with double-sided antireflective treatment; protected with eight silicon braces in grooved edges.
Strap: leather or crocodile; attached via titanium screws to the case; matching buckle.
Available in: 18K red gold; 18K white gold; titanium.

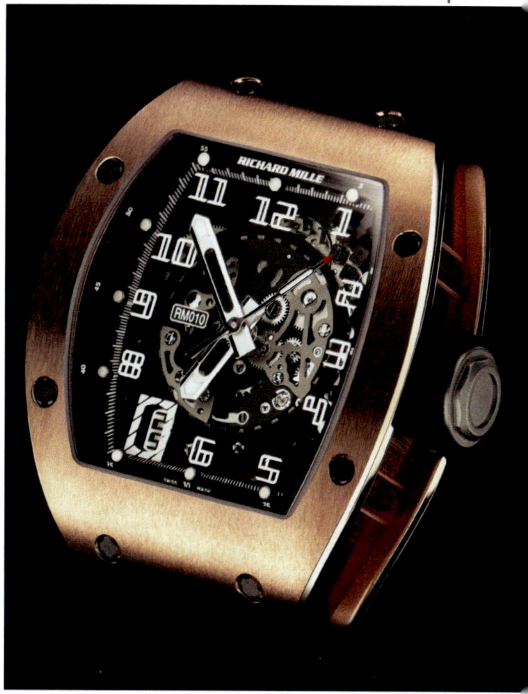

FELIPE MASSA FLYBACK CHRONOGRAPH — RM 011

Movement: automatic-winding skeletonized chronograph RM011 caliber; approx. 55-hour power reserve; rotor with variable geometry via white-gold wings adjustable to six positions; ceramic rotor ball bearings; PVD-coated titanium baseplate, bridges and balance cock; large date; double-winding barrel; titanium column wheel, gear wheels and lever; split-seconds mechanism with improved and patented functions; crown in sandblasted grade-5 titanium with double-seal O-ring and collar in Alcryn; grade-5 titanium spline screws for movement and case.
Functions: hours, minutes, seconds; large date; month; annual calendar; flyback chronograph: 60-minute count-down timer, 12-hour totalizer.
Case: central case ring; anatomically curved three-piece case; 50x40mm, thickness: 16.15mm; assembled with 20 spline screws in grade-5 titanium; sapphire crystal front and back with double-sided antireflective coating; water resistant to 100 meters.
Dial: sapphire crystal with double-sided antireflective treatment; protected with eight silicon braces in grooved edges.
Strap: leather or crocodile; attached via titanium screws to the case; matching buckle.
Available in: 18K red gold; 18K white gold; titanium.

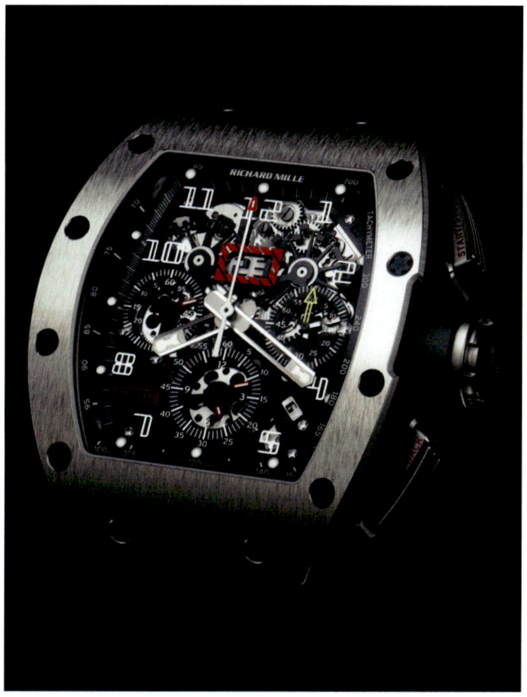

AUTOMATIC FLYBACK CHRONOGRAPH — RM 011 TITALYT

Movement: automatic-winding skeletonized chronograph RM011 caliber; approx. 55-hour power reserve; rotor with variable geometry via white-gold wings adjustable to six positions; ceramic rotor ball bearings; Titalyt-coated titanium baseplate, bridges and balance cock; large date; double-winding barrel; titanium column wheel, gear wheels and lever; split-seconds mechanism with improved and patented functions; crown in sandblasted grade-5 titanium with double-seal O-ring and collar in Alcryn; grade-5 titanium spline screws for movement and case.
Functions: hours, minutes, seconds; large date; month; annual calendar; flyback chronograph: 60-minute countdown timer, 12-hour totalizer.
Case: Titalyt-treated; central case ring; anatomically curved three-piece case; 50x40mm, thickness: 16.15mm; Titalyt-treated crown; assembled with 20 spline screws in grade-5 titanium; sapphire crystal front and back with double-sided antireflective coating; water resistant to 100 meters.
Dial: sapphire crystal with double-sided antireflective treatment; protected with eight silicon braces in grooved edges.
Strap: leather or crocodile; attached via titanium screws to the case; matching buckle.
Available in: titanium.

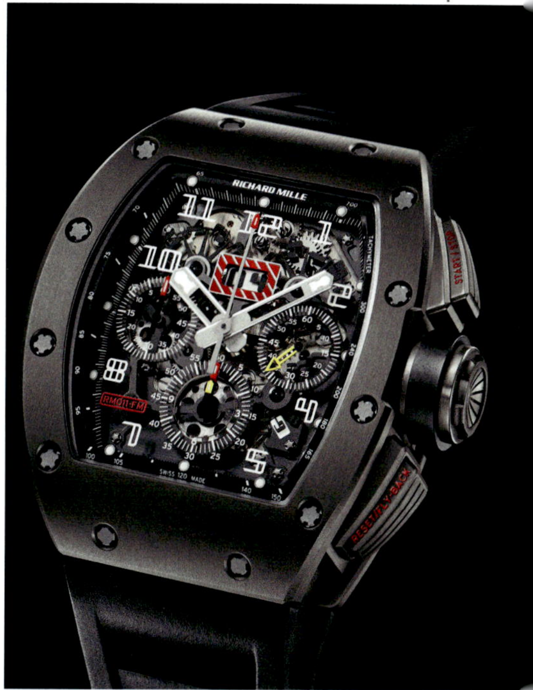

TOURBILLON PERINI NAVI CUP — RM 014

Movement: manual-winding marine tourbillon RM014 caliber; carbon nanofiber baseplate; nautical pattern-finished case, screws and crown; approx. 70-hour power reserve; variable inertia balance with overcoil hairspring; fast rotating barrel; function selector gearbox with indicator; ceramic tourbillon endstone; central bridge in rigidified INOX; spline screws in grade-5 titanium for the bridges and case; winding barrel and third pinion's teeth with central involute profile; jewels set in white-gold chatons.

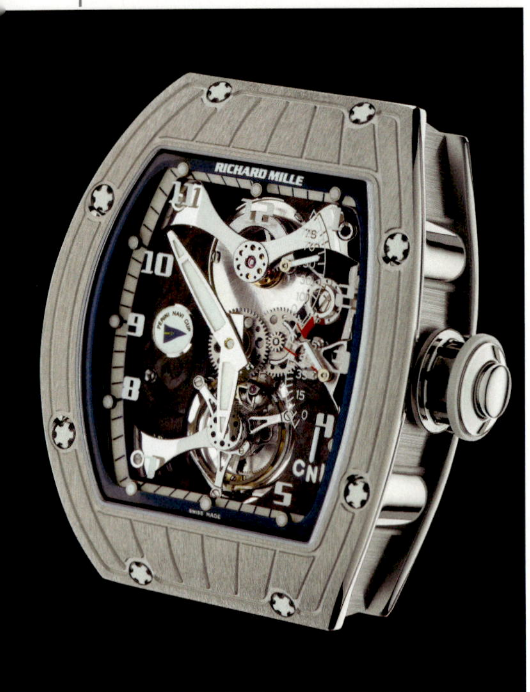

Functions: hours, minutes; power reserve and torque indicator; function selector.
Case: anatomically curved three-piece case; 45x38.9mm, thickness: 11.85mm; assembled with 12 spline screws in grade-5 titanium; sapphire crystal front and back with double-sided antireflective coating; water resistant to 50 meters.
Dial: sapphire crystal with double-sided antireflective treatment; protected with eight silicon braces in grooved edges.
Strap: leather or crocodile; attached via titanium screws to the case; matching buckle.
Available in: 18K red gold; 18K white gold; platinum.

TOURBILLON SECOND TIME ZONE PERINI NAVI CUP — RM 015

Movement: manual-winding marine tourbillon RM015 caliber; carbon nanofiber baseplate; nautical pattern-finished case, screws and crown; approx. 70-hour power reserve; variable inertia balance with overcoil hairspring; fast rotating barrel; function selector gearbox with indicator; ceramic tourbillon endstone; central bridge in rigidified INOX; spline screws in grade-5 titanium for the bridges and case; winding barrel and third pinion's teeth with central involute profile; jewels set in white-gold chatons.

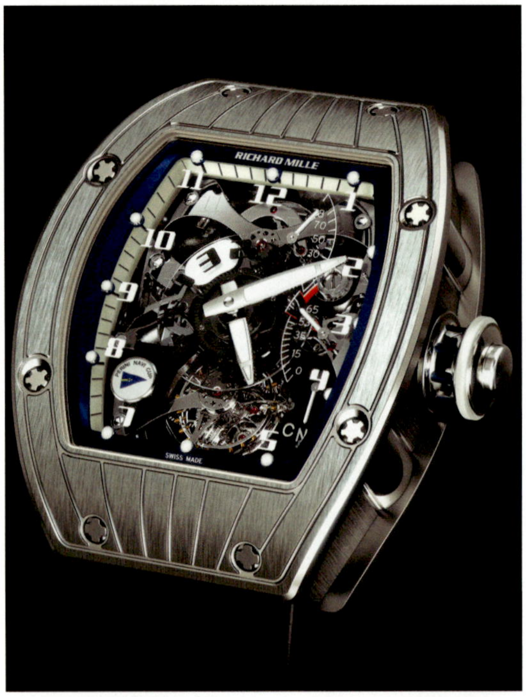

Functions: hours, minutes; second time zone; power reserve and torque indicator; function selector.
Case: anatomically curved three-piece case; 45x38.9mm, thickness: 11.85mm; assembled with 12 spline screws in grade-5 titanium; sapphire crystal front and back with double-sided antireflective coating; water resistant to 50 meters.
Dial: sapphire crystal with double-sided antireflective treatment; protected with eight silicon braces in grooved edges.
Strap: leather or crocodile; attached via titanium screws to the case; matching buckle.
Available in: 18K red gold; 18K white gold; platinum.

AUTOMATIC — RM 016

Movement: automatic-winding skeletonized RM005-S caliber; approx. 55-hour power reserve; rotor with variable geometry via white-gold wings adjustable to six positions; ceramic rotor ball bearings; PVD-coated titanium baseplate, bridges and balance cock; crown in sandblasted grade-5 titanium with double-seal O-ring and collar in Alcryn; double-winding barrel; grade-5 titanium spline screws for movement and case.

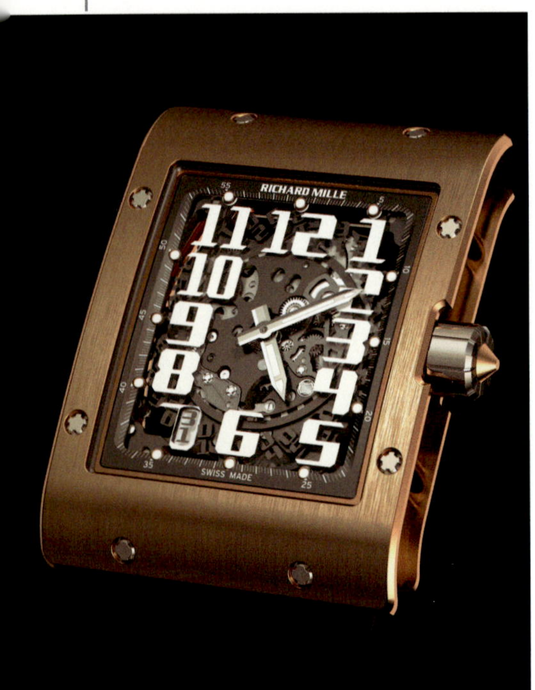

Functions: hours, minutes, seconds; date.
Case: anatomically curved three-piece case; 49.8x38mm, thickness: 8.25mm; assembled with 12 spline screws in grade-5 titanium; sapphire crystal front and back with double-sided antireflective coating; water resistant to 50 meters.
Dial: sapphire crystal with double-sided antireflective treatment; protected with eight silicon braces in grooved edges.
Strap: leather or crocodile; attached via titanium screws to the case; matching buckle.
Available in: 18K red gold; 18K white gold; titanium.

AUTOMATIC — RM 016 TITALYT

Movement: automatic-winding skeletonized RM005-S caliber; approx. 55-hour power reserve; rotor with variable geometry via white-gold wings adjustable to six positions; ceramic rotor ball bearings; Titalyt-coated titanium baseplate, bridges and balance cock; crown in sandblasted grade-5 titanium with double-seal O-ring and collar in Alcryn; double-winding barrel; grade-5 titanium spline screws for movement and case.

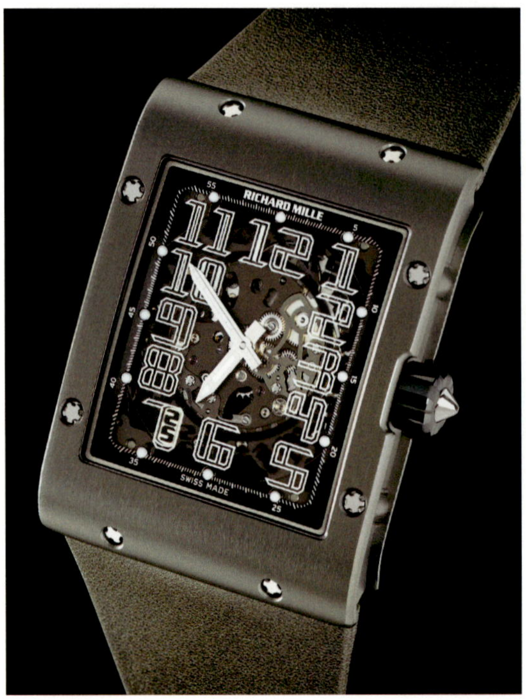

Functions: hours, minutes, seconds; date.
Case: anatomically curved three-piece case with Titalyt surface treatment; 49.8x38mm, thickness: 8.25mm; assembled with 12 spline screws in grade-5 titanium; sapphire crystal front and back with double-sided antireflective coating; water resistant to 50 meters.
Dial: sapphire crystal with double-sided antireflective treatment; protected with eight silicon braces in grooved edges.
Strap: leather or crocodile; attached via titanium screws to the case; matching buckle.
Available in: titanium.

AUTOMATIC — RM 016 DLC

Movement: automatic-winding skeletonized RM005-S caliber; approx. 55-hour power reserve; rotor with variable geometry via white-gold wings adjustable to six positions; ceramic rotor ball bearings; PVD-coated titanium baseplate, bridges and balance cock; crown in sandblasted grade-5 titanium with double-seal O-ring and collar in Alcryn; double-winding barrel; grade-5 titanium spline screws for movement and case.
Functions: hours, minutes, seconds; date.
Case: anatomically curved three-piece case with DLC surface treatment; 49.8x38mm, thickness: 8.25mm; assembled with 12 spline screws in grade-5 titanium; sapphire crystal front and back with double-sided antireflective coating; water resistant to 50 meters.
Dial: sapphire crystal with double-sided antireflective treatment; protected with eight silicon braces in grooved edges.
Strap: leather or crocodile; attached via titanium screws to the case; matching buckle.
Available in: titanium.

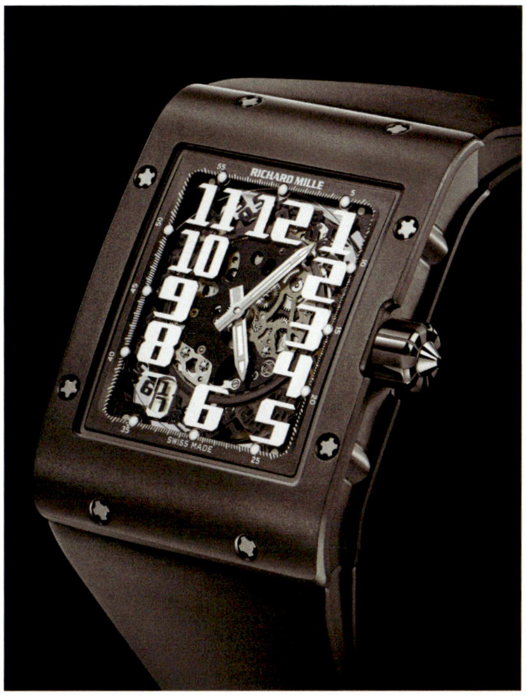

AUTOMATIC WITH FULL DIAMOND SETTING — RM 016

Movement: automatic-winding skeletonized RM005-S caliber; approx. 55-hour power reserve; rotor with variable geometry via white-gold wings adjustable to six positions; ceramic rotor ball bearings; PVD-coated titanium baseplate, bridges and balance cock; crown in sandblasted grade-5 titanium with double-seal O-ring and collar in Alcryn; double-winding barrel; grade-5 titanium spline screws for movement and case.
Functions: hours, minutes, seconds; date.
Case: anatomically curved three-piece case; 49.8x38mm, thickness: 8.25mm; assembled with 12 spline screws in grade-5 titanium; sapphire crystal front and back with double-sided antireflective coating; water resistant to 50 meters.
Dial: sapphire crystal with double-sided antireflective treatment; protected with eight silicon braces in grooved edges.
Strap: leather or crocodile; attached via titanium screws to the case; matching buckle.
Available in: 18K red gold; 18K white gold.

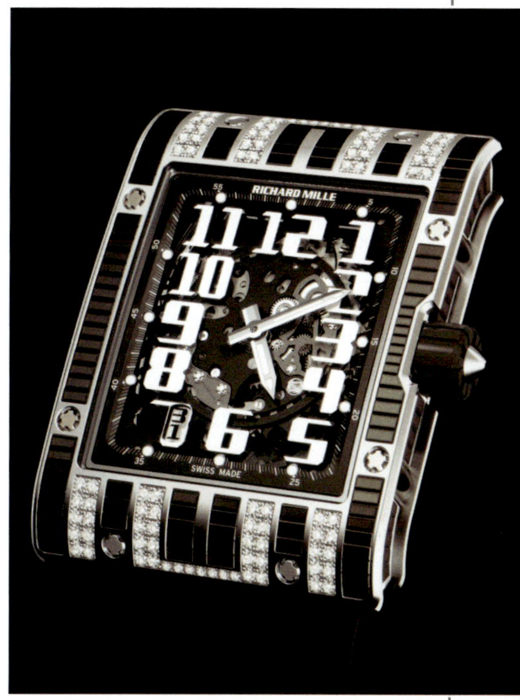

EXTRA FLAT TOURBILLON — RM 017

Movement: manual-winding extra-flat tourbillon RM017 caliber; black PVD-treated titanium baseplate; approx. 70-hour power reserve; variable inertia balance with overcoil; fast rotating barrel; ceramic tourbillon endstone; spline screws in grade-5 titanium for the bridges and case; winding barrel and third pinion's teeth with central involute profile; safety system blocking gear.
Functions: hours, minutes; power reserve indicator; function indicator.
Case: anatomically curved; 49.8x38mm, thickness: 8.7mm; assembled with 12 spline screws in grade-5 titanium; sapphire crystal front and back with double-sided antireflective coating; water resistant to 50 meters.
Dial: sapphire crystal with double-sided antireflective treatment; protected with eight silicon braces in grooved edges.
Strap: crocodile attached via titanium screws to the case; matching buckle.
Available in: 18K red gold; 18K white gold; titanium; gem set.

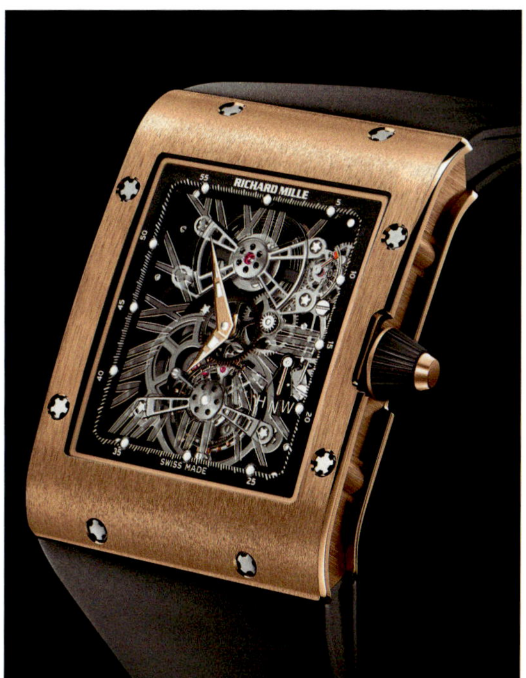

TOURBILLON HOMMAGE A BOUCHERON — RM 018

Movement: manual-winding tourbillon caliber RM018; two-layered synthetic sapphire Al_2O_3 baseplate construction; wheels created from precious and semi-precious stones; approx. 48-hour power reserve; variable inertia balance with overcoil hairspring; fast rotating barrel; ceramic tourbillon endstone; spline screws in grade-5 titanium for the bridges and case; winding barrel and third pinion's teeth with central involute profile; jewels set in white-gold chatons.
Functions: hours, minutes.
Case: 48x39.7mm, thickness: 12.8mm; assembled with 12 spline screws in grade-5 titanium; sapphire crystal front and back with double-sided antireflective coating; water resistant to 50 meters.
Dial: sapphire crystal with double-sided antireflective treatment; protected with eight silicon braces in grooved edges.
Strap: crocodile; attached via titanium screws to the case; matching buckle.
Note: limited to 30 pieces worldwide.
Available in: 18K white gold.

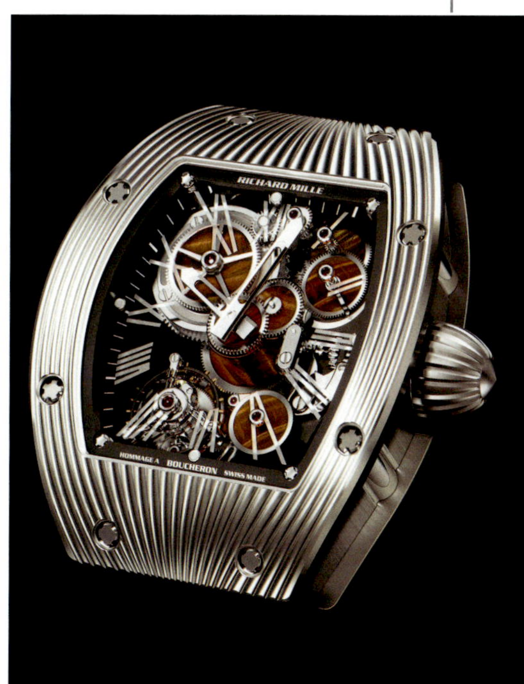

TOURBILLON BLACK ONYX — RM 019

Movement: manual-winding tourbillon RM019 caliber; black onyx baseplate; approx. 48-hour power reserve; variable inertia balance with overcoil hairspring; fast rotating barrel; ceramic tourbillon endstone; spline screws in grade-5 titanium for the bridges and case; winding barrel and third pinion's teeth with central involute profile; jewels set in white-gold chatons.
Functions: hours, minutes; power reserve indicator.

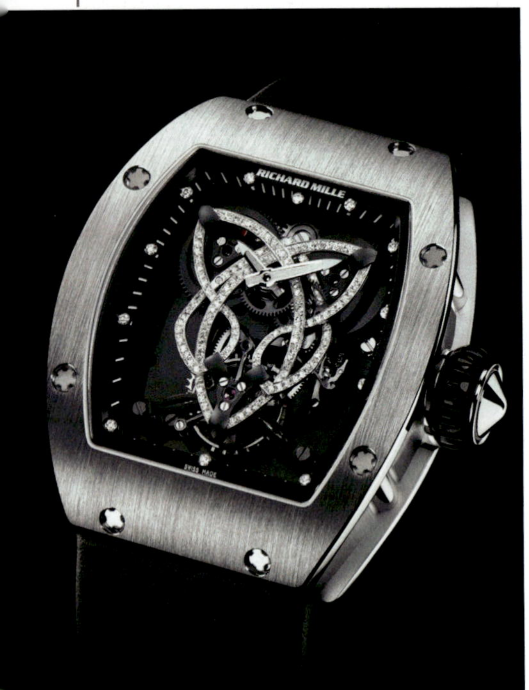

Case: 48x39.3mm, thickness: 12.85mm; assembled with 12 spline screws in grade-5 titanium; sapphire crystal front and back with double-sided antireflective coating; water resistant to 50 meters.
Dial: sapphire crystal with double-sided antireflective treatment; protected with eight silicon braces in grooved edges.
Strap: leather or crocodile; attached via titanium screws to the case; matching buckle.
Note: limited to 30 pieces.
Available in: 18K red gold; 18K white gold.

TOURBILLON POCKET WATCH — RM 020

Movement: manual-winding tourbillon RM020 caliber; carbon nanofiber baseplate; approx. 10-day power reserve via two winding barrels; variable inertia balance with overcoil hairspring; fast rotating barrel; function selector gearbox with indicator; ceramic tourbillon endstone; central bridge in rigidified ARCAP; spline screws in grade-5 titanium for the bridges and case; winding barrel and third pinion teeth with central involute profile; jewels set in gold chatons.

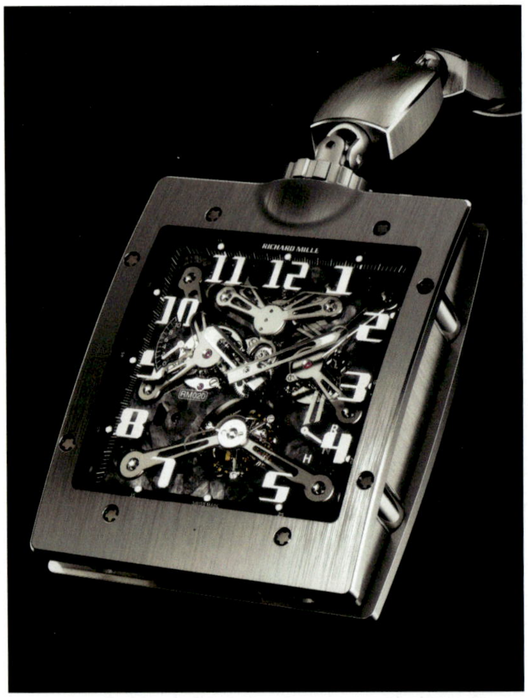

Functions: hours, minutes; power reserve and torque indicator; function indicator.
Case: central case ring with both front and back bezels; 62x52mm, thickness: 15.6mm; assembled with 20 spline screws in grade-5 titanium; sapphire crystal front and back with double-sided antireflective coating; water resistant to 50 meters.
Dial: sapphire crystal with double-sided antireflective treatment; protected with eight silicon braces in grooved edges.
Note: supplied with specially designed titanium chain with quick-release mechanism.
Available in: 18K red gold and titanium; 18K white gold and titanium; titanium and titanium.

TOURBILLON AERODYNE — RM 021

Movement: manual-winding tourbillon RM021 caliber; movement baseplate of titanium and honeycombed orthorhombic titanium aluminide with carbon nanofiber; approx. 70-hour power reserve; variable inertia balance with overcoil hairspring; fast rotating barrel; function selector gearbox with indicator; ceramic tourbillon endstone; central bridge in rigidified ARCAP; spline screws in grade-5 titanium for the bridges and case; winding barrel and third pinion's teeth with central involute profile; jewels set in gold chatons.

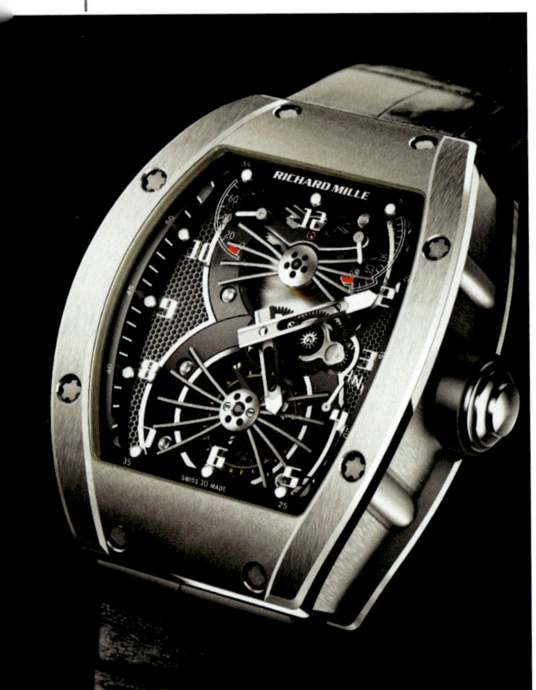

Functions: hours, minutes; power reserve and torque indicator; function selector.
Case: anatomically curved three-piece case; 48.18x39.7mm, thickness: 13.85mm; assembled with 12 spline screws in grade-5 titanium; sapphire crystal front and back with double-sided antireflective coating; water resistant to 50 meters.
Dial: sapphire crystal with double-sided antireflective treatment; protected with eight silicon braces in grooved edges.
Strap: leather or crocodile attached via titanium screws to the case; matching buckle.
Available in: 18K red gold; 18K white gold.

TOURBILLON AERODYNE SECOND TIME ZONE — RM 022

Movement: manual-winding tourbillon RM022 caliber; movement baseplate of titanium and honeycombed orthorhombic titanium aluminide with carbon nanofiber; approx. 70-hour power reserve; variable inertia balance with overcoil hairspring; fast rotating barrel; function selector gearbox with indicator; ceramic tourbillon endstone; central bridge in rigidified ARCAP; spline screws in grade-5 titanium for the bridges and case; winding barrel and third pinion's teeth with central involute profile; jewels set in gold chatons.

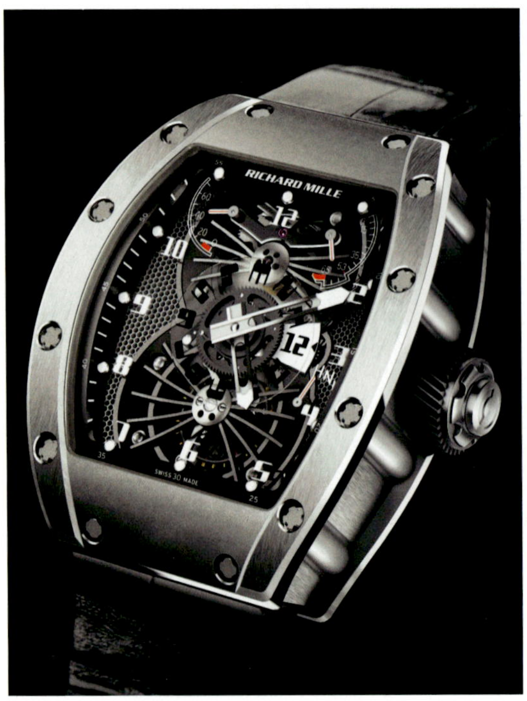

Functions: hours, minutes; second time zone; power reserve indicator; function selector and torque indicator.
Case: anatomically curved three-piece case; 48.18x39.7mm, thickness: 13.85mm; assembled with 20 spline screws in grade-5 titanium; sapphire crystal front and back with double-sided antireflective coating; water resistant to 50 meters.
Dial: sapphire crystal with double-sided antireflective treatment; protected with eight silicon braces in grooved edges.
Strap: leather or crocodile attached via screws to the case; matching buckle.
Available in: 18K red gold; 18K white gold.

AUTOMATIC — RM 023

Movement: automatic-winding partially skeletonized caliber; approx. 55-hour power reserve; rotor with variable geometry via white-gold wings adjustable to six positions; ceramic rotor ball bearings; PVD-coated titanium baseplate, bridges and balance cock; crown in sandblasted grade-5 titanium with double-seal O-ring and collar in Alcryn; double-winding barrel; grade-5 titanium spline screws for movement and case.
Functions: hours, minutes, seconds; date.
Case: anatomically curved three-piece case; 45x37.8mm, thickness: 11.45mm; assembled with 12 spline screws in grade-5 titanium; sapphire crystal front and back with double-sided antireflective coating; water resistant to 50 meters.
Dial: sapphire crystal with double-sided antireflective treatment; protected with eight silicon braces in grooved edges.
Strap: leather or crocodile; attached to the case via titanium screws; matching buckle.
Available in: 18K red gold; 18K white gold; titanium.

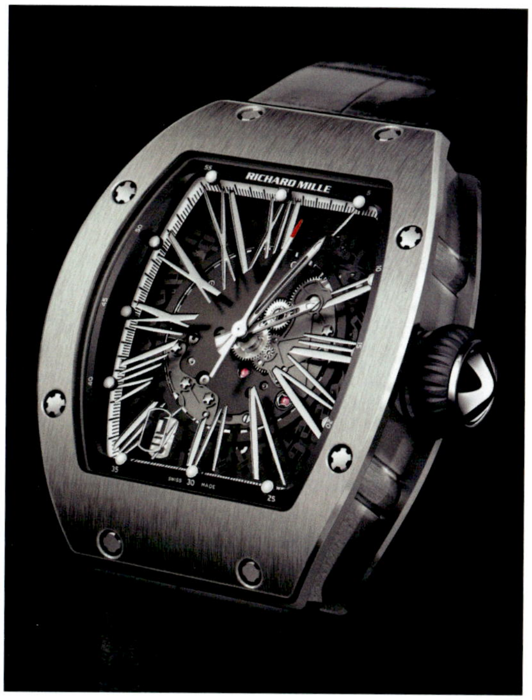

AUTOMATIC — RM 023

Movement: automatic-winding partially skeletonized caliber; approx. 55-hour power reserve; rotor with variable geometry via white-gold wings adjustable to six positions; ceramic rotor ball bearings; PVD-coated titanium baseplate, bridges and balance cock; crown in sandblasted grade-5 titanium with double-seal O-ring and collar in Alcryn; double-winding barrel; grade-5 titanium spline screws for movement and case.
Functions: hours, minutes, seconds; date.
Case: anatomically curved polished three-piece case; 45x37.8mm, thickness: 11.45mm; assembled with 12 spline screws in grade-5 titanium; sapphire crystal front and back with double-sided antireflective coating; water resistant to 50 meters.
Dial: sapphire crystal with double-sided antireflective treatment; protected with eight silicon braces in grooved edges.
Strap: leather or crocodile; attached to the case via screws; matching buckle.
Available in: 18K red gold; 18K white gold; titanium.

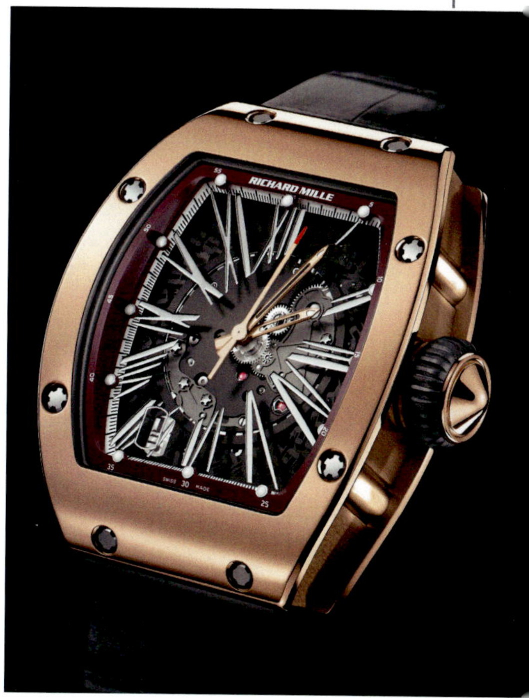

TOURBILLON CHRONOGRAPH DIVER'S WATCH — RM 025

Movement: manual-winding RM025 caliber; carbon nanofiber baseplate; approx. 70-hour power reserve; titanium column wheel; gear wheels and lever; chronograph mechanism with improved and patented functions; fast rotating barrel; variable inertia balance with overcoil hairspring; newly designed in-line lever escapement; spline screws in grade-5 titanium for the bridges and case; screw-in crown; winding barrel and third pinion's teeth central involute profile.
Functions: hours, minutes, seconds; chronograph minute counter; power reserve and torque indicator; function indicator.
Case: anatomically curved three-piece case; Ø 50.7mm, thickness: 19.1mm; assembled with 20 torque screws in grade-5 titanium; unidirectional turning timing bezel; screw-in crown; sapphire crystal front and back with double-sided antireflective coating; water resistant to 300 meters (according to ISO 6425).
Dial: sapphire crystal with double-sided antireflective treatment protected with silicon braces in grooved edges.
Strap: special composite with matching buckle.
Available in: titanium with 18K red-gold lugs.

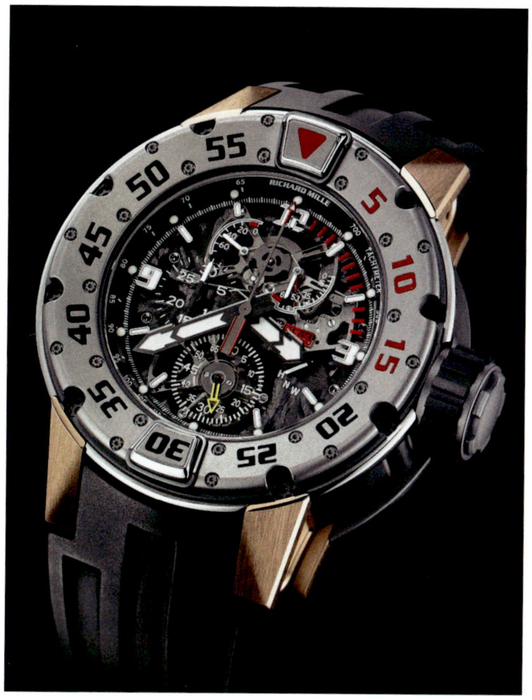

TOURBILLON — RM 026

Movement: manual-winding tourbillon RM026 caliber; black onyx baseplate; approx. 48-hour power reserve; variable inertia balance with overcoil hairspring; ceramic tourbillon endstone; spline screws in grade-5 titanium for the bridges and case; winding barrel and third pinion teeth with central involute profile; jewels set in chatons.
Functions: hours, minutes; power reserve indicator.
Case: 45x39.7mm, thickness: 12.6mm; assembled with 12 spline screws in grade-5 titanium; sapphire crystal front and back with double-sided antireflective coating; water resistant to 50 meters.
Dial: sapphire crystal with double-sided antireflective treatment; protected with eight silicon braces in grooved edges.
Strap: leather or crocodile; attached via titanium screws to the case; matching buckle.
Available in: 18K white gold.
Note: limited edition of 15 numbered unique pieces.

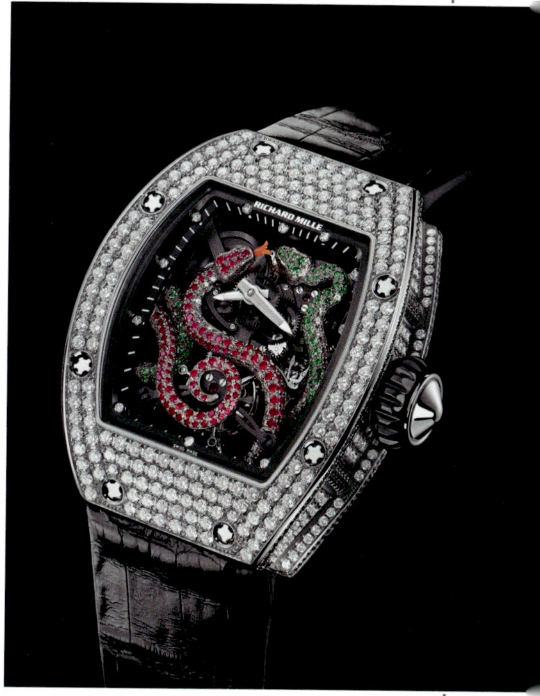

RAFAEL NADAL RM 027

Movement: highly skeletonized titanium and LITAL® alloy, a high lithium content alloy containing aluminium, copper, magnesium and zirconium, possessing a density of 2.55 g/cm³; movement weight 3.83g; 48-hour power reserve; free sprung balance; fast rotating barrel; variable inertia balance with overcoil hairspring; fast rotating barrel; ceramic tourbillon endstone; spline screws in grade-5 titanium for the bridges and case; winding barrel and third pinion teeth with central involute profile; lightest tourbillon wristwatch ever made (circa 13g without strap).
Functions: hours, minutes.
Case: monobloc carbon composite; curved three-piece case; 48x39.7mm, thickness: 11.85mm; assembled with six spline screws; transparent composite crystal.
Dial: sapphire crystal with doubled-sided antireflective treatment; protected with eight silicon braces in grooved edges.
Strap: special composite material with polyurethane fastening.
Available in: carbon composite.
Note: limited edition of 50 numbered pieces.

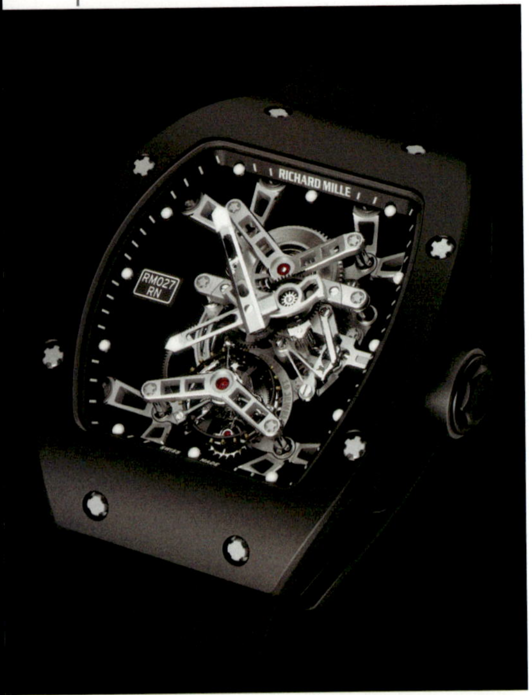

AUTOMATIC DIVER'S WATCH RM 028

Movement: automatic-winding partially skeletonized caliber; approx. 55-hour power reserve; rotor with variable geometry via white-gold wings adjustable to six positions; ceramic rotor ball bearings; PVD-coated titanium baseplate, bridges and balance cock; crown in sandblasted grade-5 titanium with double-seal O-ring and collar in Alcryn; double-winding barrel; unidirectional turning and locking three-piece bezel fastened with 22 special spline screws.
Functions: hours, minutes, seconds; date.
Case: anatomically curved three-piece case; Ø 47, thickness: 14.6mm (thickest area); assembled with 20 spline screws in grade-5 titanium; sapphire crystal front and back with double-sided antireflective coating; water resistant to 300 meters (according to ISO 6425).
Dial: sapphire crystal with double-sided antireflective treatment; protected with eight silicon braces in grooved edges.
Strap: special rubber strap attached with screws to the case; matching buckle.
Available in: 18K red gold; titanium.

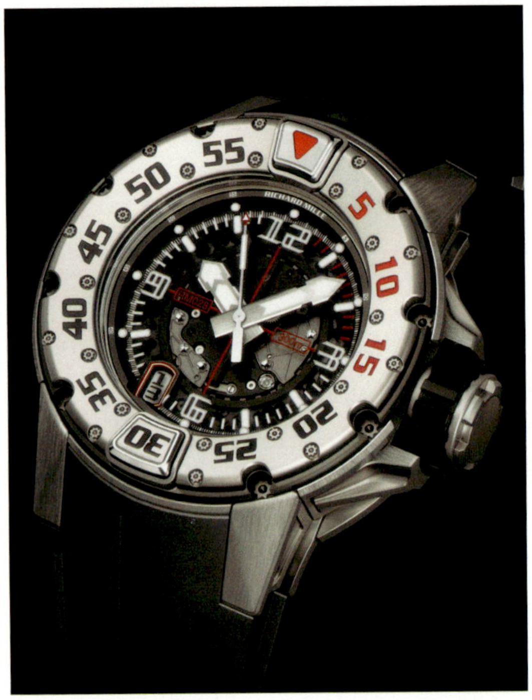

AUTOMATIC OVERSIZE DATE RM 029

Movement: automatic-winding skeletonized RMAS7 caliber; approx. 55-hour power reserve; rotor with variable geometry via wings adjustable to six positions; ceramic rotor ball bearings; titanium PVD-coated baseplate, bridges and balance cock; crown in grade-5 sandblasted titanium with double-seal O-ring and collar case.
Functions: hours, minutes, seconds; oversize date.
Case: anatomically curved three-piece case; 48x39.7mm, thickness: 12.6mm; assembled with 12 spline screws in grade-5 titanium; sapphire crystal front and back with double-sided antireflective coating; water resistant to 50 meters.
Dial: sapphire crystal with double-sided antireflective treatment; protected with eight silicon braces in grooved edges.
Strap: leather or crocodile; attached via titanium screws to the case; matching buckle.
Available in: 18K red gold; 18K white gold; titanium.

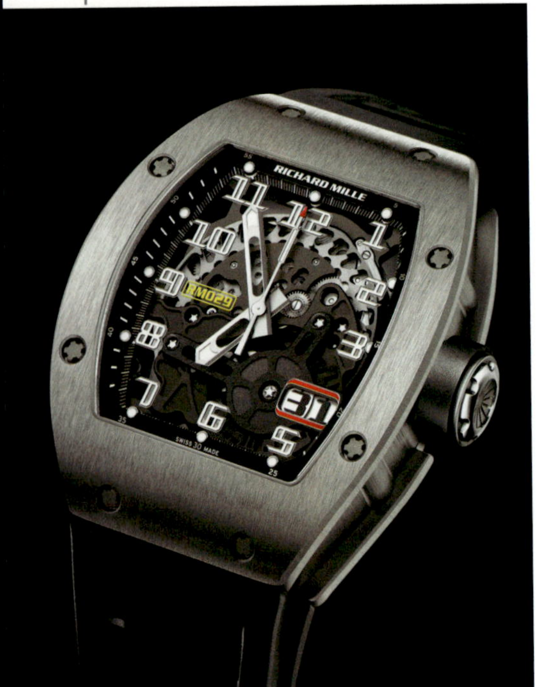

AUTOMATIC WITH DECLUTCHABLE ROTOR RM 030

Movement: automatic-winding skeletonized RMAR1 caliber; special declutching mechanism; approx. 55-hour power reserve; rotor with variable geometry via white-gold wings adjustable to six positions; ceramic rotor ball bearings; titanium PVD-coated baseplate, bridges and balance cock; crown in grade-5 sandblasted titanium with double-seal O-ring and collar in Alcryn; double-winding barrel; grade-5 titanium spline screws for movement and case.
Functions: hours, minutes, seconds; date.
Case: anatomically curved three-piece case; 50x42.7mm, thickness: 13.95mm; assembled with 20 spline screws in grade-5 titanium; sapphire crystal front and back with double-sided antireflective coating; water resistant to 50 meters.
Dial: sapphire crystal with double-sided antireflective treatment; protected with eight silicon braces in grooved edges.
Strap: leather or crocodile; attached via titanium screws to the case; matching buckle.
Available in: 18K red gold; 18K white gold; titanium.

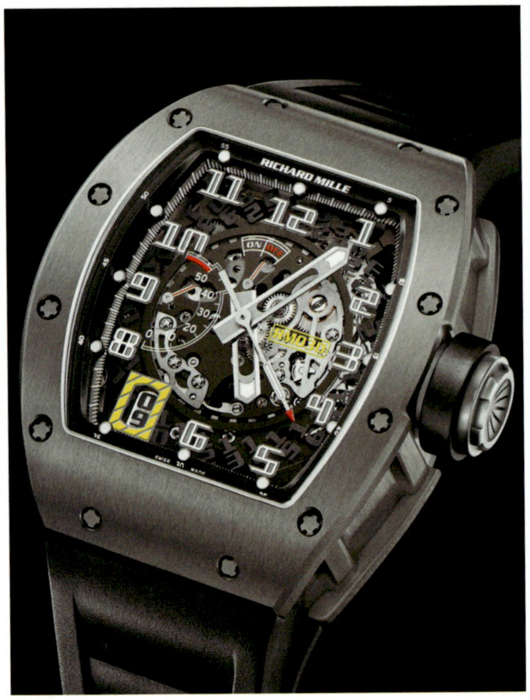

AUTOMATIC CHRONOGRAPH DIVER'S WATCH — RM 032

Movement: automatic-winding skeletonized chronograph RMAC2 caliber; approx. 55-hour power reserve; rotor with variable geometry via white-gold wings adjustable to six positions; ceramic rotor ball bearings; PVD-coated titanium baseplate, bridges and balance cock; large date; double-winding barrel; titanium column wheel, gear wheels and lever; split-seconds mechanism with improved and patented functions; crown in sandblasted grade-5 titanium with double-seal O-ring and collar in Alcryn; grade-5 titanium spline screws for movement and case.
Functions: hours, minutes, central seconds; flyback chronograph: hour, minute and seconds counters; large date; month, annual calendar; running indicator.
Case: anatomically curved three-piece case; Ø 50mm, thickness: 17.8mm; assembled with 20 spline screws in grade-5 titanium; sapphire crystal front and back with double-sided antireflective coating; water resistant to 300 meters (according to ISO 6425).
Dial: sapphire crystal with double-sided antireflective treatment; protected with eight silicon braces in grooved edges.
Strap: special composite with matching buckle.
Available in: 18K red gold; 18K white gold; titanium.

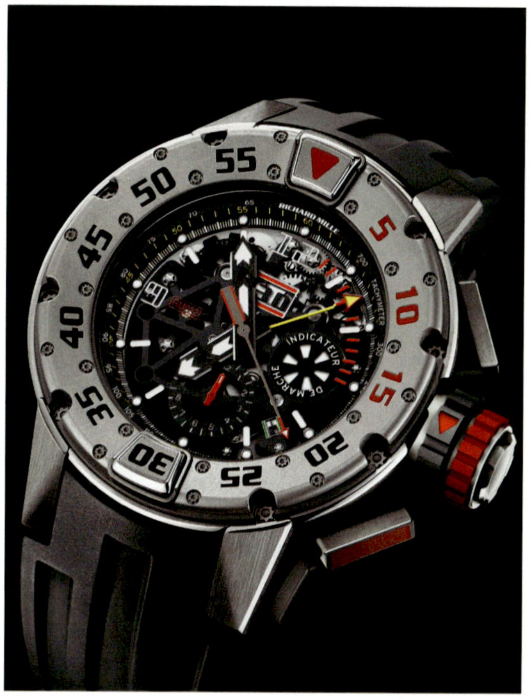

EXTRA FLAT AUTOMATIC — RM 033

Movement: automatic-winding skeletonized RMXP1 caliber with monoblock platinum microrotor; free sprung balance with variable inertia; approx. 42-hour power reserve; Titalyt® coated baseplate; PVD-coated bridges and balance cock; crown in ceramic with double seal O-ring and detailing in titanium.
Functions: hours, minutes.
Case: anatomically curved three-piece case; Ø 45.7mm, thickness: 6.3mm; assembled with 16 spline screws in grade-5 titanium; sapphire crystal front and back with double-sided antireflective coating; water resistant to 30 meters.
Dial: sapphire crystal with double-sided antireflective treatment; protected with eight silicon braces in grooved edges.
Strap: special composite with matching buckle.
Available in: 18K red gold; 18K white gold; titanium.

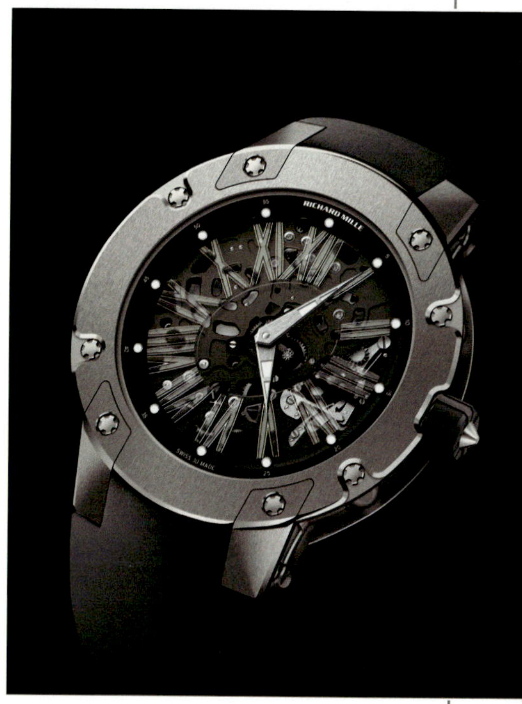

RAFAEL NADAL CHRONOFIABLE® — RM 035

Movement: manual-winding skeletonized chronometer RMUL1 caliber; certified Chronofiable® under extensive and extreme testing conditons; weight of the movement 4.3g; approx. 55-hour power reserve; PVD-coated titanium baseplate, bridges and balance cock; crown in sandblasted grade-5 titanium with double-seal O-ring and collar in Alcryn; double-winding barrel; grade-5 titanium spline screws for movement and case.
Functions: hours, minutes, seconds.
Case: anatomically curved three-piece case made from special Magnesium-Aluminum alloy; 48x39.7mm, thickness: 12.25mm; assembled with 12 spline screws in grade-5 titanium; sapphire crystal front with double-sided antireflective coating; water resistant to 50 meters.
Dial: sapphire crystal with double-sided antireflective treatment; protected with eight silicon braces in grooved edges.
Strap: special composite with matching buckle.
Available in: Magnesium-Aluminum alloy AZ91 with plasma treatment.

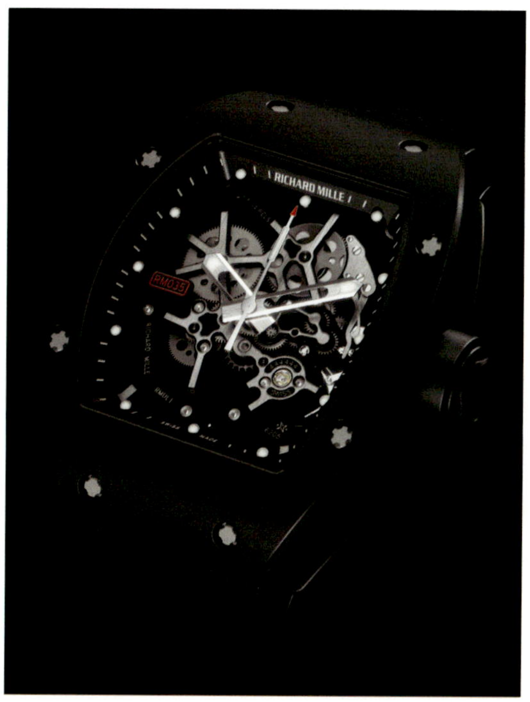

TOURBILLON 'BUBBA WATSON' — RM 038

Movement: manual-winding highly skeletonized tourbillon RM038 caliber; approx. 48-hour power reserve; skeletonized baseplate and bridge framework of grade 5 titanium; fast rotating barrel; crown with double-seal O-ring and collar in Alcryn; grade-5 titanium spline screws for movement and case.
Functions: hours, minutes.
Case: anatomically curved three-piece case made from special Magnesium-Aluminum alloy with white plasma treatment; 48x39.7mm, thickness:12.8mm; assembled with 12 spline screws in grade-5 titanium; sapphire crystal front and back with double-sided antireflective coating; water resistant to 50 meters.
Dial: sapphire crystal with double-sided antireflective treatment; protected with eight silicon braces in grooved edges.
Strap: special composite with matching buckle.
Available in: Magnesium-Aluminum alloy AZ91 with plasma treatment.
Note: limited numbered edition.

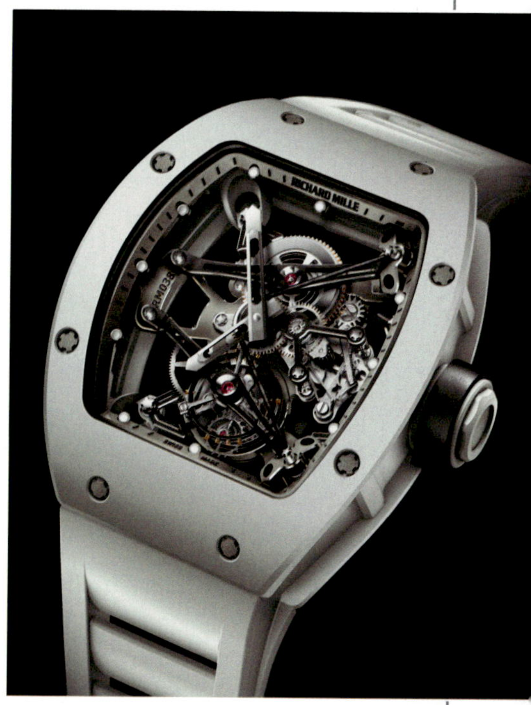

ROGER DUBUIS

MIGHTIER THAN THE SWORD

Evoking the name of the legendary Arthurian sword, Roger Dubuis's Excalibur collection has evolved rapidly since its 2005 debut into a dynamic showcase that illustrates the depth of the Geneva manufacture's creativity and ingenuity through its assertive design and technical refinement.

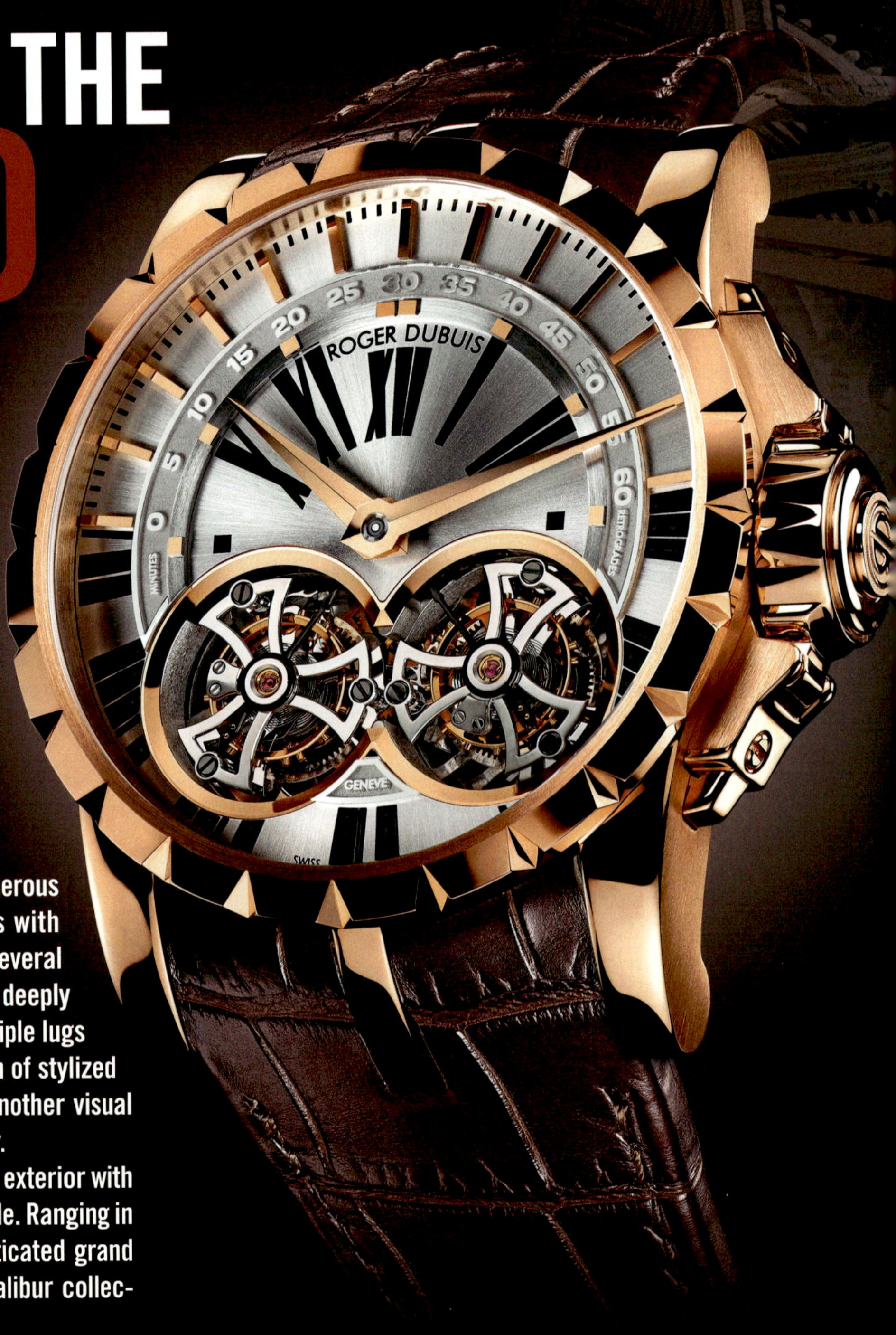

Distinguished by its bold character and generous dimensions, the Excalibur case bristles with masculine energy. It is magnified by several signature visual flourishes like the fluting cleaved deeply into the bezel's outer edge and the distinctive triple lugs that secure the straps to the case. The inclusion of stylized Roman numerals on every Excalibur provides another visual leitmotif that shapes the collection's personality.

Roger Dubuis complements this self-assured exterior with fourteen different manufacture movements inside. Ranging in complexity from a basic automatic to a sophisticated grand complication, each caliber featured in the Excalibur collection bears the Geneva Seal.

Established in 1886 and modified through the years, this voluntary certification process—administered by the Geneva Watchmaking School—provides an independent review of the concept and finishing applied to mechanical movements.

The 45mm pink-gold Excalibur Double Tourbillon indicates the minutes using a retrograde display and the hours with a jumping hand. Also available in platinum, both versions are offered in a limited series of 28 pieces each.

To be considered, a movement must be assembled and adjusted in the canton of Geneva. To earn the prestigious seal, the quality of all components and their finishing must adhere to 12 criteria. For example, all steel parts must have polished angles, longitudinally polished flanks and smooth visible surfaces.

In 2010, the Excalibur family included fourteen different manufacture movements. Of those, half featured a flying tourbillon. The complex mechanism—designed to compensate for errors in chronometric precision caused by the force of gravity on the balance—has become a Roger Dubuis specialty.

The firm delighted horolophiles with a weakness for the complication in 2005 with the debut of the Excalibur Flying Double Tourbillon. The watch returned in 2010, powered by a newly redesigned movement (RD 01).

To better showcase the twin flying tourbillons, Roger Dubuis uses a retrograde indicator for the minutes. This restricts the hand's movement to the upper half of the dial so it will not obscure the flying tourbillons as it travels across the dial's lower half. The company will produce the 45mm Flying Double Tourbillon in a limited series that includes 28 pieces each in pink gold and platinum.

Roger Dubuis also offers a skeletonized version of the Excalibur Flying Double Tourbillon. A classic example of addition by subtraction, the dial's absence provides a stunning view of the anthracite-colored movement (RD01SQ). At the company's workshop, accomplished artisans remove large sections of the mainplate and bridges, leaving behind a star-shaped structure decorated elaborately with perlage. This skeletonization enhances the visibility of all the movement's meticulously hand-finished components that earned the timepiece its Geneva Seal.

To read the time, the flange is set with black diamonds for the hours and red dots for the minutes. Like its sister model, the 45mm pink-gold Excalibur Flying Double Tourbillon Skeleton is offered in a limited edition of 28 pieces.

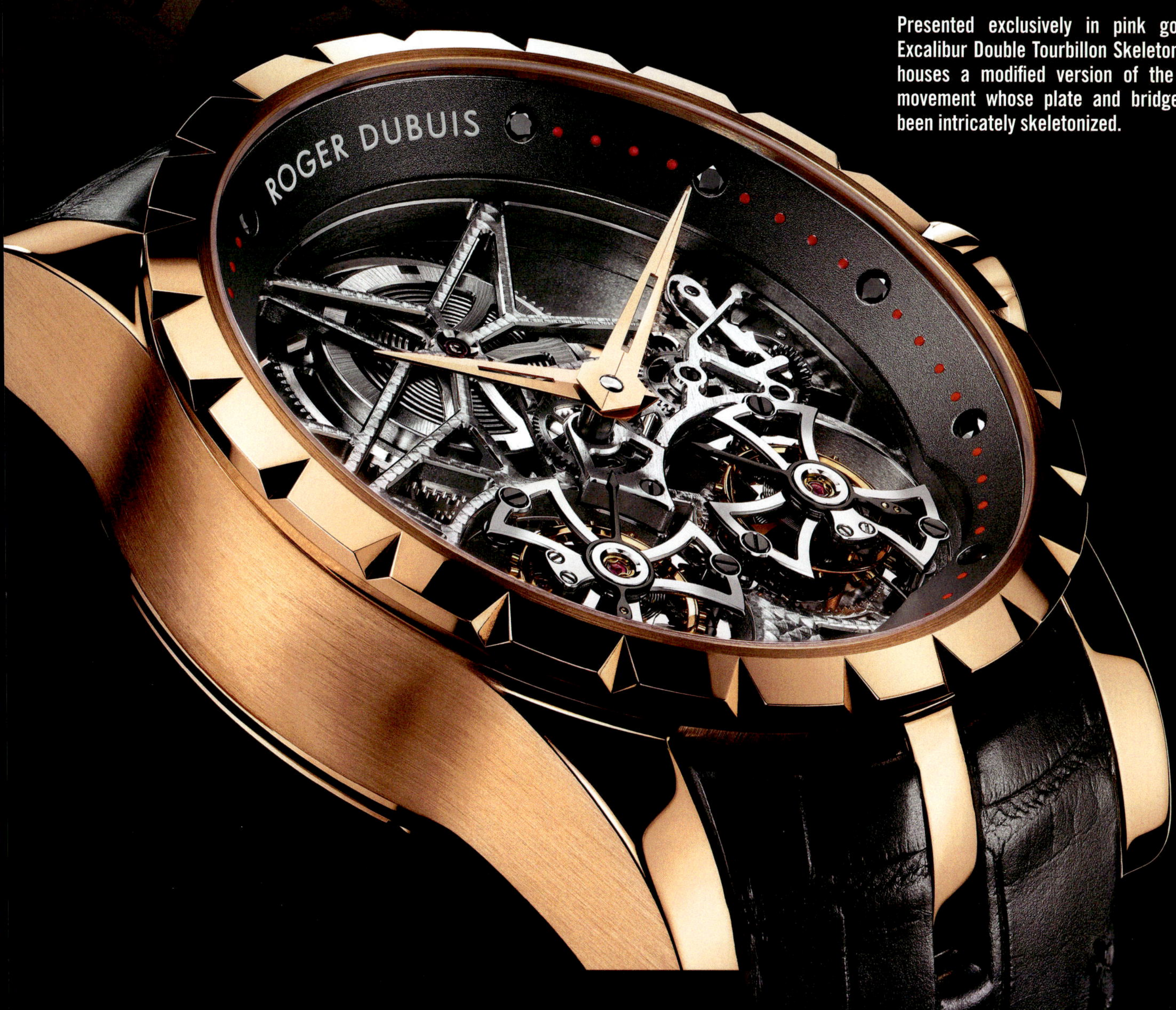

Presented exclusively in pink gold, the Excalibur Double Tourbillon Skeleton's case houses a modified version of the RD 01 movement whose plate and bridges have been intricately skeletonized.

Since its 2005 debut, Roger Dubuis's Excalibur collection has underscored the Geneva manufacture's horological expertise with nearly fourteen complex movements, all of which have earned the prestigious Geneva Seal.

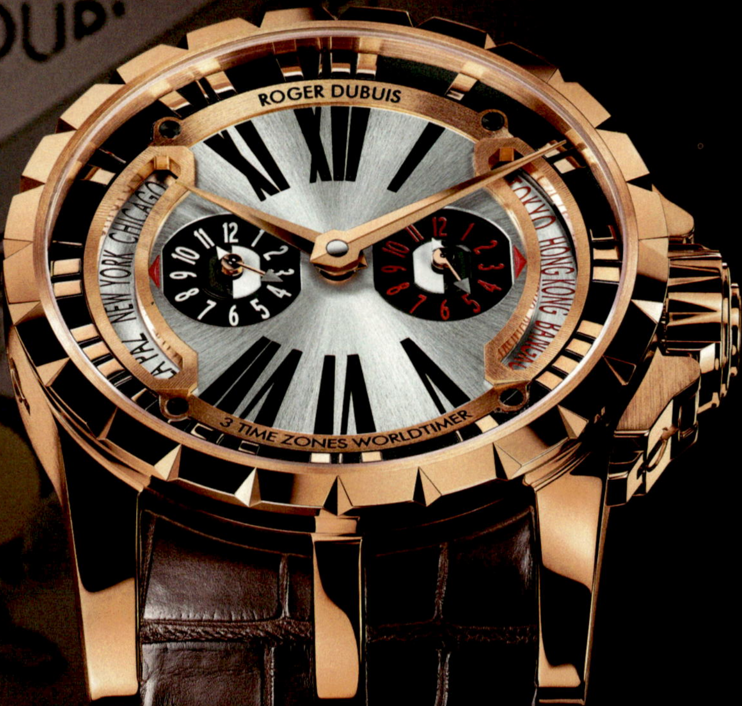

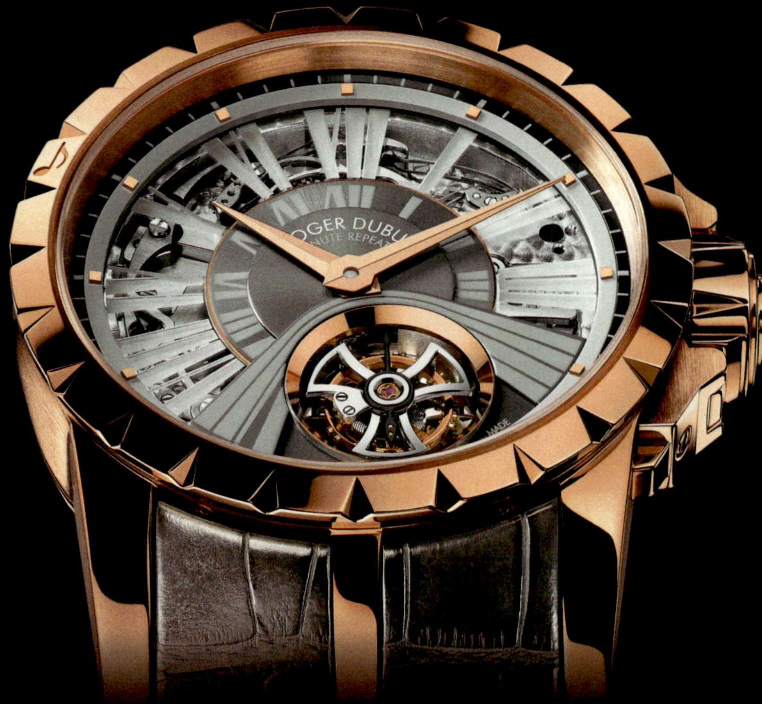

Roger Dubuis offers a global perspective with its Excalibur World Time – Triple Time Zone. The automatic RD 1448 movement displays the local time centrally while simultaneously calculating and showing the current time for two additional time zones.

The caliber incorporates two separate rings, each inscribed with the names of 12 different cities. Curved openings on opposite sides of the rhodium-plated dial display the two locations selected by the owner, who can adjust the cities using correctors inset on the side of the case. These correctors can be set using the corner of a simple credit card. The time for each location is indicated by an adjacent 12-hour display, which features a small hand to specify if the time is ante or post meridiem.

Roger Dubuis confirms its status as an elite manufacture with the Excalibur Minute Repeater—Perpetual Calendar and Tourbillon, a grand complication that combines an on-demand minute repeater, instantaneous perpetual calendar, moonphase, second time zone and a flying tourbillon that is visible through the transparent caseback. The sapphire crystal lens also affords a view of the Côtes de Genève finish that adorns the movement, as well as the two engraved micro-rotors that power the automatic movement's remarkable 60-hour power reserve. The Excalibur Minute Repeater—Perpetual Calendar and Tourbillon is available exclusively in a 45mm platinum case, in a limited edition of eight pieces.

The company continues to articulate the time aurally with its Excalibur Minute Repeater. Along with the gongs and hammers, the movement (RD 08) also features a flying tourbillon topped by a seconds hand. Instead of occupying its traditional spot at 6 o'clock, the flying tourbillon drifts slightly to the right, adding a subtle visual twist to the classic complication. Roger Dubuis presents two versions of the Excalibur Minute Repeater, both produced in limited runs of 28 pieces each. The first comes in platinum with a rhodium-plated dial, while the other is available in pink gold with a dial made partially from sapphire crystal.

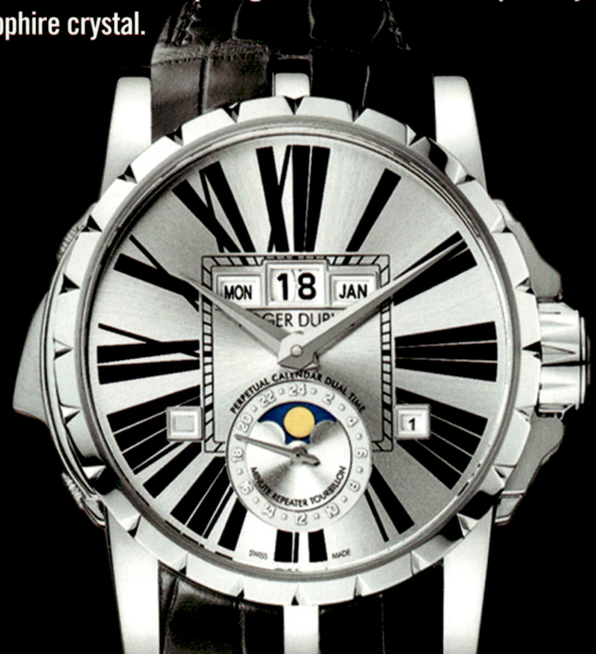

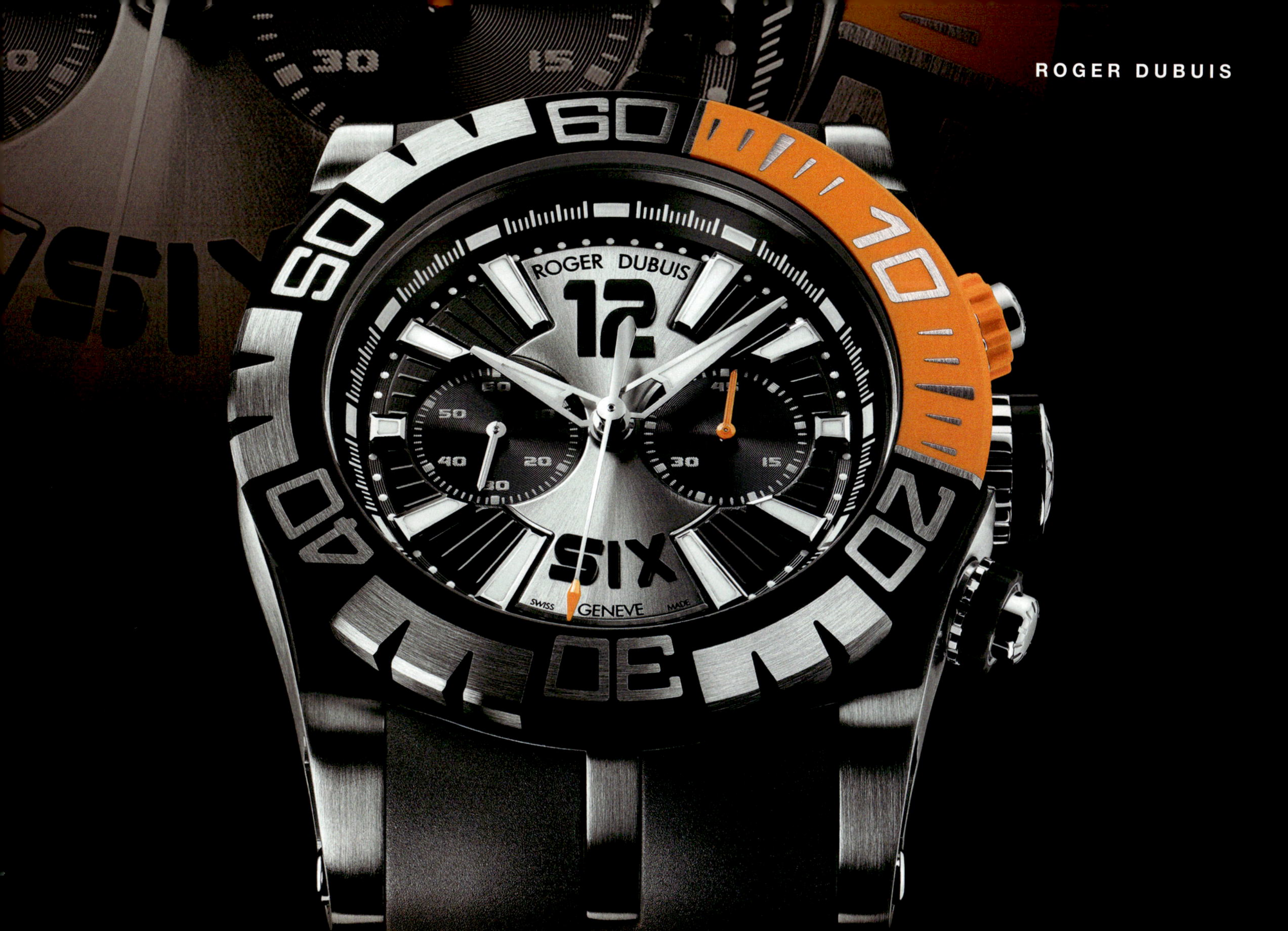

Certainly the Excalibur collection's array of high complications is impressive, but so is the EasyDiver's rare combination of style and strength. Introduced in 2004, the collection specializes in aquatic timepieces that offer water resistance to 300 meters. This ability surpasses the 100-meter minimum mandated by ISO 6425 diver's watch regulations.

United aesthetically by fluted bezels, rubber accents, triple lugs and Geneva Seal movements, the EasyDiver collection encompasses a number of distinct models. The latest incarnations range from a classic three-hand, to a gem-set version and another equipped with a column-wheel chronograph.

Roger Dubuis stakes out different areas of the horological spectrum with the extroverted EasyDiver and cerebral Excalibur. Beneath their exteriors, however, these seeming opposites bear the same Geneva Seal that declares their deep kinship.

FACING PAGE

TOP LEFT In addition to the centrally displayed local time, the pink-gold Excalibur World Time – Triple Time Zone indicates the time in two additional locales using a pair of subsidiary 12-hour counters.

TOP RIGHT The pink-gold version of the Excalibur Minute Repeater features a section of the dial made from sapphire crystal, offering a partial view of the RD 08 movement. A platinum version without the transparent dial is also available.

BOTTOM RIGHT At the push of a button, the platinum Excalibur Minute Repeater – Perpetual Calendar and Tourbillon chimes the hours, quarter-hours and minutes. Roger Dubuis will limit production of the watch to just eight pieces.

THIS PAGE

ABOVE The orange and black elements on the front of the stainless steel case, and the view of the column-wheel chronograph from the back, combine to form the EasyDiver Chronograph's memorable design.

RIGHT This stainless steel EasyDiver for ladies includes a fluted bezel set with 36 diamonds. Mother-of-pearl sections give the purple dial an iridescent glow.

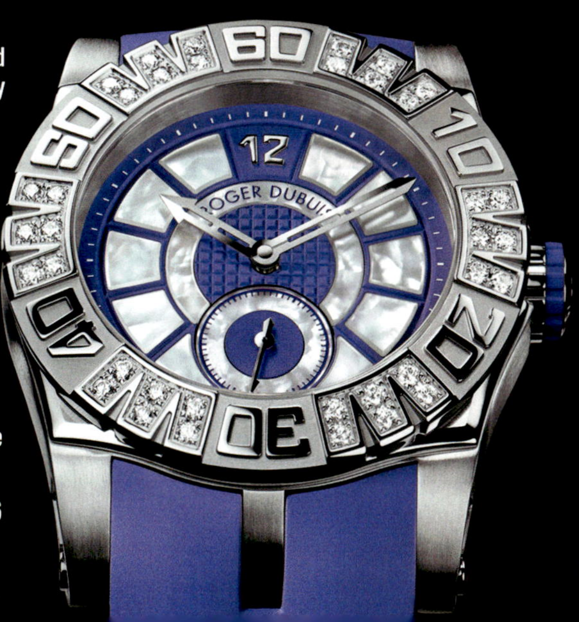

EXCALIBUR CHRONOGRAPH — REF. EX45-78-90-00/09R01/B

Movement: automatic-winding RD78 caliber; chronograph with micro-rotor; 42-hour power reserve; Ø 13.75mm, thickness: 5.8mm; 303 components; 36 jewels; 28,800 vph; finely adjusted in five positions; rhodium-plated, circular-grained plates; Côtes de Genève motif; stamped with the Poinçon de Genève quality hallmark.
Functions: hours, minutes, seconds; chronograph: 45-minute counter at 3, small seconds at 9.

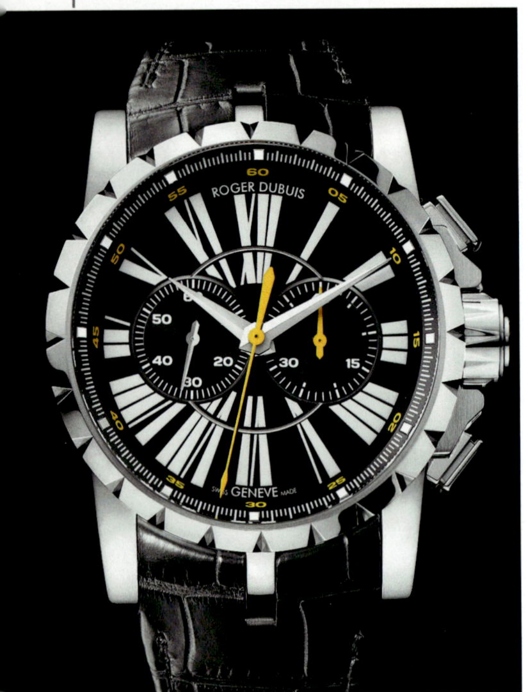

Case: stainless steel; Ø 45mm; water resistant to 5atm.
Dial: black; white Roman numerals; black chronograph counters at 3 and 9; black ring; white index markers; black bottom flange; yellow Arabic numerals; black top flange with white-gold minute-track transfers.
Strap: hand-sewn black genuine alligator; adjustable steel folding buckle.
Note: limited to 280 pieces.
Suggested price: $28,800
Also available: stainless steel with white dial.

EXCALIBUR CHRONOGRAPH — REF. EX45-781-20-00/0ER00/B

Movement: automatic-winding RD781 caliber; double-pusher column-wheel chronograph; 42-hour power reserve; Ø 13.75mm, thickness: 5.8mm; 307 components; 36 jewels; 28,800 vph; finely adjusted in five positions; rhodium-plated, circular-grained plates; Côtes de Genève motif; COSC-certified chronograph; stamped with the Poinçon de Genève quality hallmark.
Functions: hours, minutes, seconds; chronograph: 45-minute counter at 3, small seconds at 9.

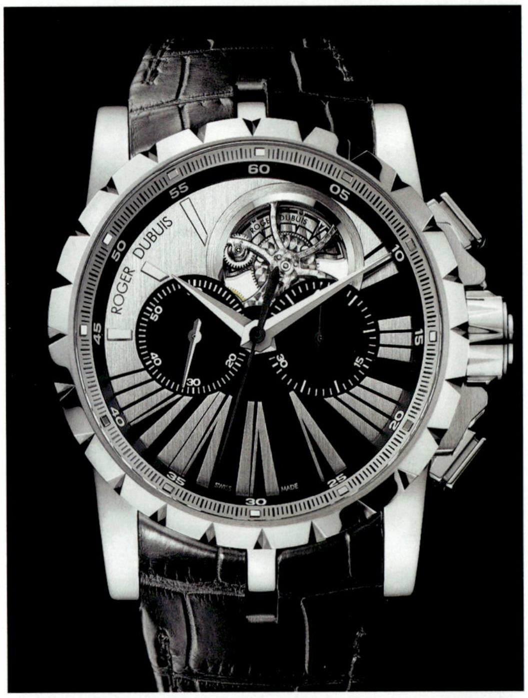

Case: white gold; Ø 45mm; water resistant to 5atm.
Dial: charcoal gray; openworked; rhodium-plated Arabic numerals; rotor aperture at 1; charcoal gray chronograph counters at 3 and 9; black ring; white index markers; applied rhodium-plated white-gold double flange.
Strap: hand-sewn black genuine alligator; adjustable white-gold folding buckle.
Note: limited to 88 pieces.
Suggested price: $51,900

EASYDIVER CHRONOGRAPH — REF. SED46-78-9C-00/03A01/A

Movement: automatic-winding RD78 caliber; double-pusher column-wheel chronograph with micro-rotor; 42-hour power reserve; Ø 13.75mm, thickness: 5.8mm; 303 components; 36 jewels; 28,800 vph; finely adjusted in five positions; rhodium-plated, circular-grained plates; Côtes de Genève motif; stamped with the Poinçon de Genève quality hallmark.
Functions: hours, minutes, seconds; chronograph: 45-minute counter at 3, small seconds at 9.

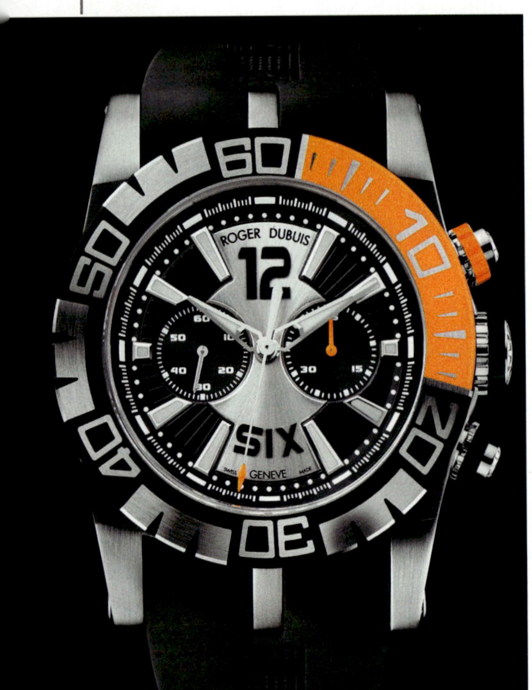

Case: stainless steel; Ø 46mm; two-tone molded rubber bezel, crown and pushers; water resistant to 30atm.
Dial: silver sunburst; applied black numeral at 12 and "SIX" at 6; anthracite transfer; white SuperLumiNova.
Strap: black rubber; adjustable steel folding buckle.
Note: limited to 280 pieces.
Suggested price: $32,500
Also available: solid black version.

EASYDIVER AUTOMATIC — REF. SED46-821-91-00/03A01/A

Movement: automatic-winding RD821 caliber; 48-hour power reserve; Ø 11.5mm, thickness: 3.34mm; 168 components; 33 jewels; 28,800 vph; finely adjusted to five positions; rhodium-plated, circular-grained plates; Côtes de Genève motif; stamped with the Poinçon de Genève quality hallmark.
Functions: hours, minutes; small seconds at 6.
Case: stainless steel; Ø 46mm; water resistant to 30atm.

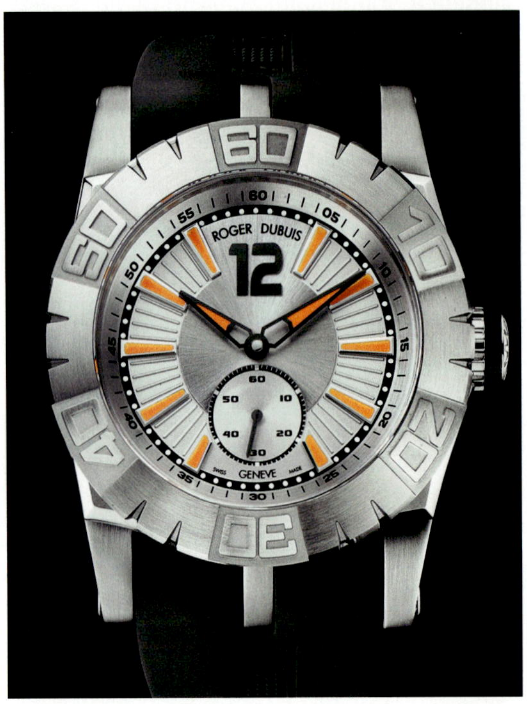

Dial: silver; applied black and rhodium-plated Arabic numeral at 12; orange SuperLumiNova indexes.
Strap: black rubber; adjustable steel folding buckle.
Note: limited to 888 pieces.
Suggested price: $12,900
Also available: black dial with white SuperLumiNova.

EXCALIBUR AUTOMATIC — REF. EX42-77-50-00/0RR00/B

Movement: automatic-winding RD77 caliber; 42-hour power reserve; Ø 13.75mm, thickness: 4mm; 179 components; 29 jewels; 28,800 vph; finely adjusted in five positions; rhodium-plated, circular-grained plates; Côtes de Genève motif; stamped with the Poinçon de Genève quality hallmark.
Functions: hours, minutes; small seconds at 9.
Case: rose gold; Ø 42mm; water resistant to 5atm.
Dial: gray rhodium-plated; black Roman numerals; applied rhodium-plated rose-gold double flange; black ring; white indexes.
Strap: hand-sewn dark brown genuine alligator; adjustable rose-gold folding buckle.
Note: limited to 88 pieces.
Suggested price: $35,500

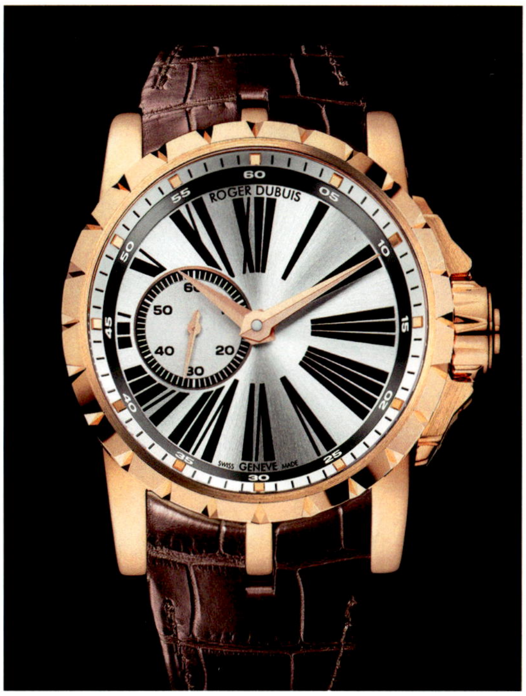

EASYDIVER LADIES — REF. SED40-821-9A-10-0FA10/A

Movement: automatic-winding RD821 caliber; 48-hour power reserve; Ø 11.5mm, thickness: 3.34mm; 168 components; 33 jewels; 28,800 vph; finely adjusted to five positions; rhodium-plated, circular-grained plates; Côtes de Genève motif; stamped with the Poinçon de Genève quality hallmark.
Functions: hours, minutes; small seconds at 6.
Case: stainless steel; set with 36 diamonds (1 carat); Ø 40mm; stamped bezel and caseback; water resistant to 30atm.
Dial: powder beige; Clous de Paris center surrounded by mother-of-pearl; 10 white mother-of-pearl sectors; white Arabic numerals; small seconds counter in mother-of-pearl at 6.
Strap: powder beige rubber; adjustable steel folding buckle.
Note: limited to 888 pieces.
Suggested price: $15,700
Also available: purple version.

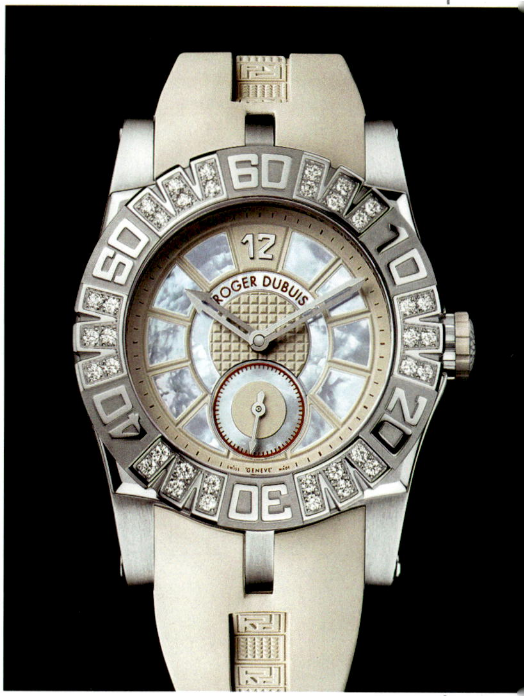

KINGSQUARE LADIES — REF. KS36-14-75-10/S1R00/G

Movement: automatic-winding RD14 caliber; 11 lines; 48-hour power reserve; 171 components; 33 jewels; 28,800 vph; Côtes de Genève motif; stamped with the Poinçon de Genève quality hallmark.
Functions: hours, minutes.
Case: titanium and rose gold; 36x36mm; bezel set with 62 diamonds; water resistant to 5atm.
Dial: white sunburst guilloché; white mother-of-pearl center edged with diamonds; applied Roman numerals; white flange set with white sapphires.
Strap: gray satin.
Note: limited to 88 pieces.
Suggested price: $29,300
Also available: white gold with rose or white dial.

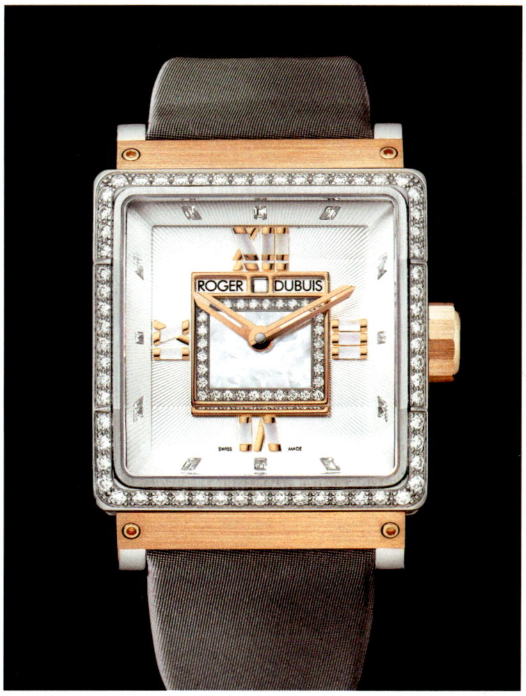

KINGSQUARE AUTOMATIC — REF. KS40-14-51-00/SGR00/B

Movement: manual-winding RD14 caliber; stamped with the Poinçon de Genève quality hallmark.
Functions: hours, minutes; small seconds.
Case: rose gold; 40x40mm.
Dial: organic tortoise shell effect; rose-gold Roman numerals; white ROGER DUBUIS transfer; black small seconds counter at 6; flange pavé with red garnet and white fillet.
Strap: hand-sewn brown genuine alligator; adjustable rose-gold folding clasp.
Note: limited to 88 pieces.
Suggested price: $36,700
Also available: assorted metals and dials.

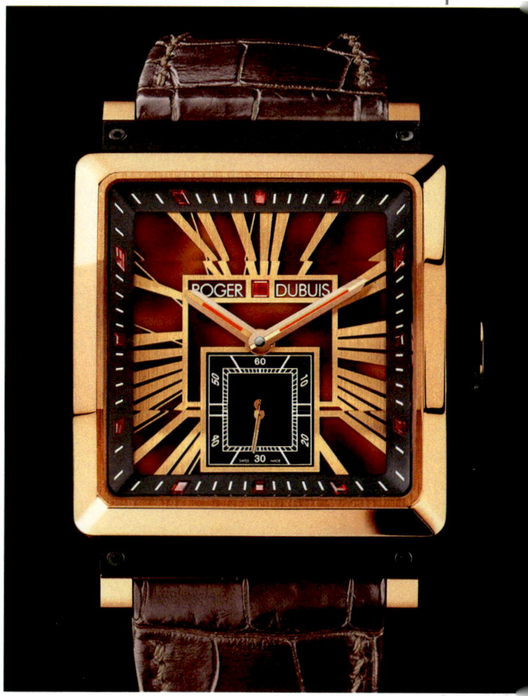

ROLAND ITEN
MECHANICAL LUXURY FOR GENTLEMEN™

DISCREET EXTRAVAGANCE

Swiss designer Roland Iten uses his flair for clever mechanics to transform quotidian items like belt buckles, cufflinks and cardholders into ingenious objects crafted with much of the same precision technology used to make watches.

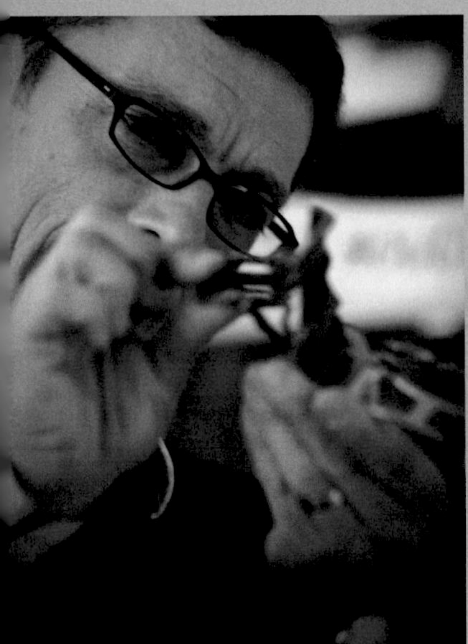

Iten (pronounced ee-TEN) presented his first mechanical belt buckle, the R8, at the Basel Watch and Jewelry Show in 2004. Comprised of more than 100 custom-made components, it was designed to counteract the fluctuation that occurs naturally at the waistline when one sits. "What bothers me about belts is you put them on you when you stand, and most of the time you're sitting." Iten explains. "And they're uncomfortable when you sit for a while."

Iten's solution was a multi-axle mechanism that allows the wearer—with the flip of a finger—to quickly loosen or tighten their belt by 35mm, which is roughly the two-thumb measurement a tailor factors into the waistband of a bespoke pair of trousers.

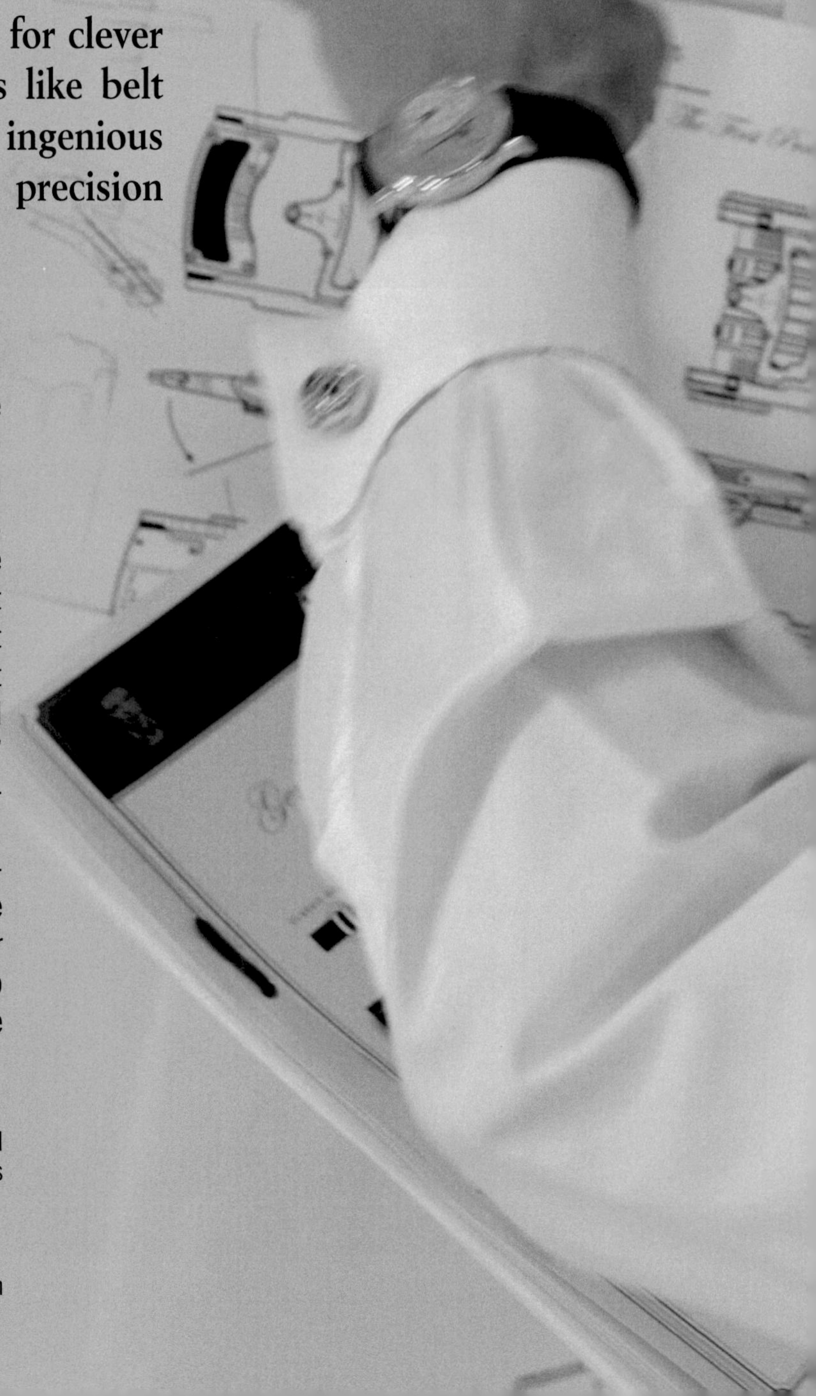

ABOVE
After designing the world's first mechanical belt buckle in 2003, Roland Iten continues to create mechanical toys like cufflinks and card holders that appeal to the little boy in every man.

RIGHT
Swiss designer Roland Iten at work in his studio, which is located in Mont-sur-Lausanne and overlooks Lake Geneva.

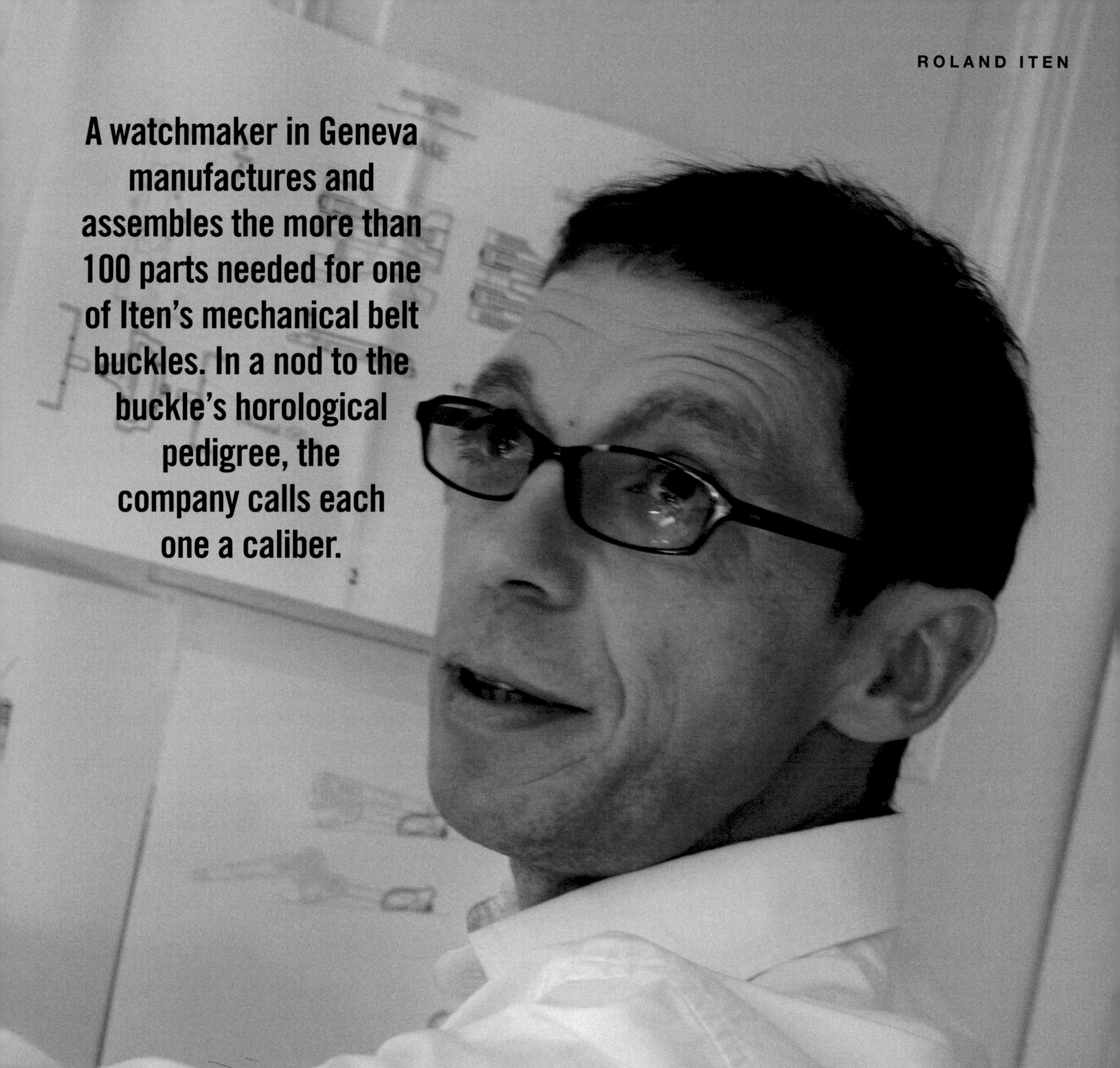

A watchmaker in Geneva manufactures and assembles the more than 100 parts needed for one of Iten's mechanical belt buckles. In a nod to the buckle's horological pedigree, the company calls each one a caliber.

To create parts with the precision necessary to ensure the buckle's smooth operation, Iten turned to legendary watchmaker François-Paul Journe. It is his atelier in Geneva that manufactures and assembles the buckles to Iten's exacting standards. In a nod to the buckle's horological pedigree, the company refers to them as calibers.

"Each of my belt buckle collections is created from individually designed, custom-made, moveable mechanical…pieces." Iten adds: "The kick is that they are touchable mechanics. You can hold it in your hand, inspect it, move it and say to yourself, 'Hey, I get that—I know how it works.'"

The buckle collection currently encompasses several different designs, each crafted in gold, titanium or stainless steel and produced in a limited and numbered series of no more than 100 pieces.

Among them is the R8 Sport Sedan series, which is marked by a lightweight construction that makes it easy to forget the sophisticated mechanism attached to one's belt. The design measures 30mm across and projects a handsome masculinity thanks to its rose-gold accents and a black Tahitian mother-of-pearl inlay.

"The sport version of my original R8 complicated mechanical belt buckle is made with the same engineered performance and is based on the same multi-axle expansion mechanism as the R8 Authentic Precious collection," Iten says. "In this derivation, the solid gold clip and flipper is replaced by a scratch-proof, stainless steel and titanium construction that is lightweight and more performance-oriented for active sports."

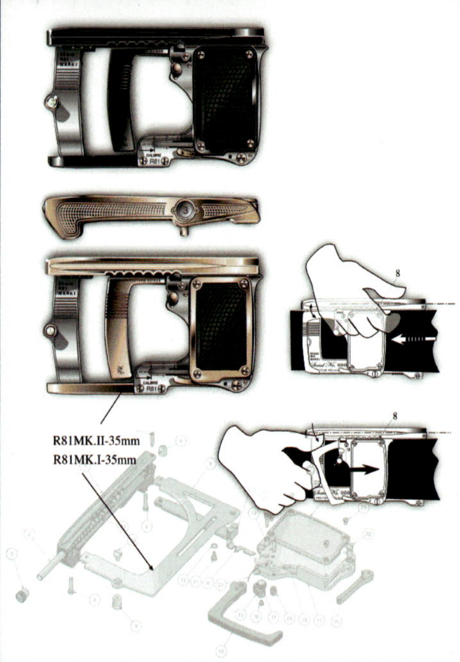

One of the latest creations from Roland Iten is Calibre R81 Spring Loaded, a buckle nicknamed Goldfinger. The idea for it grew out of the designer's recent collaboration with a purveyor of fine custom firearms.

"I toured their factory and saw how their guns open up, felt the power of the springs and this inspired me to create a spring-loaded belt and to develop one with eight positions."

What made this idea possible was the creation of a patent-pending trigger mechanism that allows for adjustments up to 25mm. Unlike the other buckles that expand and contract by flipping over, the Spring Loaded makes adjustments by sliding side to side. "A lot of people wear pullovers or suits, so they don't have open access to flip the buckle," Iten says. "To address that, I created a buckle for the slides so when you're wearing a suit you can maintain discretion while making an adjustment."

In keeping with the gun motif, the trigger curves toward the black Tahitian mother-of-pearl inlay, which is decorated with a lattice pattern that calls to mind the texture of a pistol's grip. "When you have eight positions to choose from, you never have your hand far from the trigger," Iten says.

The Roland Iten collection goes beyond belt buckles with the RC81 mechanical cufflinks.

When threaded through the cuff, these dashing accoutrements lock into place when the lever on top of the cufflink is turned 180 degrees. "The joy of this little mechanical operation also results in an optimal force translation—so that with a slight movement of your finger, the 16 twisting, turning, flipping and pirouetting parts in the internal gearbox turn and lock the link into your cuff."

These cufflinks possess dual personalities thanks to that same lever. When flipped to one side, the look is cool confidence with solid gold. Pushing the lever the other way reveals a circle of diamonds with enough flash to light up the night.

But Iten may have created the ultimate toy for boys who like gadgets with his RCD81, a mechanized credit card holder worthy of James Bond. When its trigger mechanism is activated, up to four credit cards jump to attention from the top of the aluminum or titanium case with a sonorous click. Pulling the trigger again completes the transaction by stowing the cards back inside their protective home.

From the waist to the wrist to the pocket, Iten celebrates functionality, unique craft and timeless beauty with a new generation of mechanical men's accessories.

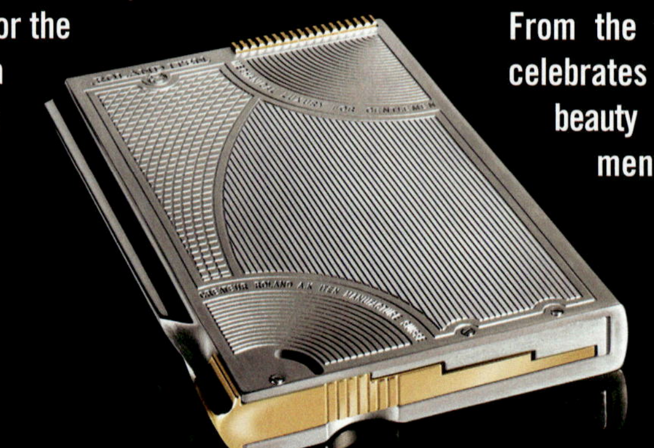

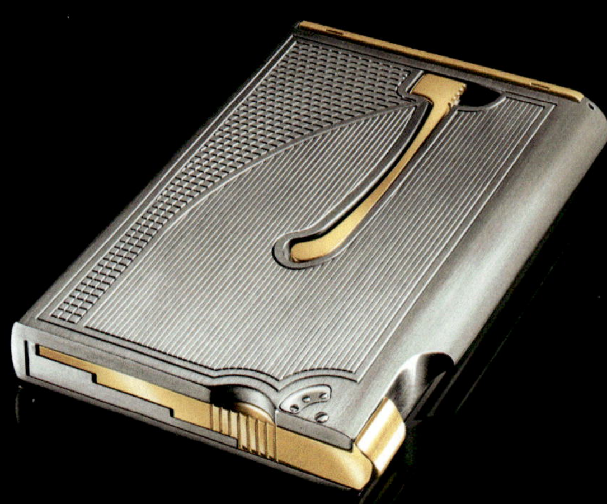

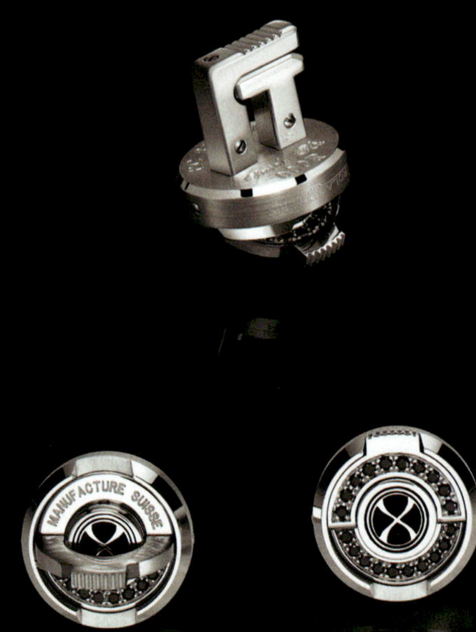

TOP LEFT

The Calibre R81 Spring Loaded uses a patent-pending trigger mechanism that allows the belt to be tightened or loosed by up to 25mm.

RIGHT

Pulling the hidden trigger on the RCD81 opens the top of the aluminum case, allowing up to four credit cards to spring forth. Pulling the trigger a second time stows the cards safely back in the case.

FAR RIGHT

When threaded through the cuff, Iten's RC81 mechanical cufflinks lock into place by turning the lever on top 180 degrees. The lever also flips to give two different looks, solid gold or diamond-pavé.

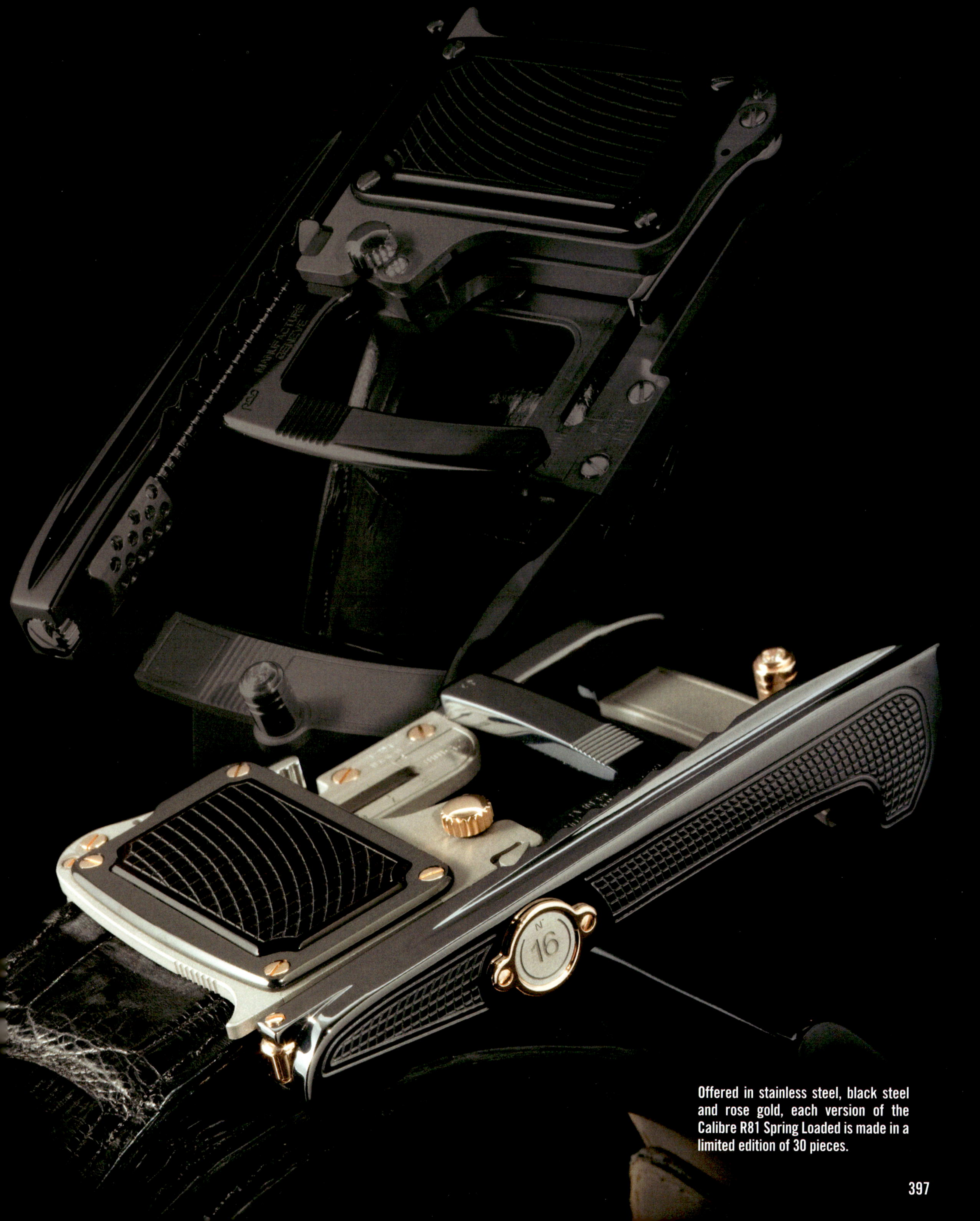

Offered in stainless steel, black steel and rose gold, each version of the Calibre R81 Spring Loaded is made in a limited edition of 30 pieces.

CALLING

Among the few true icons of watchmaking, the Rolex Submariner made an unforgettable splash when it was introduced in 1954 as the first timepiece that could be safely worn underwater to a depth of 330 feet (100 meters).

Professional divers quickly adopted the watch, drawn not only by the case's ability to thwart the infiltration of water, but also by its rotating bezel for timing dives and luminous markers that made it possible to read the dial even in murky waters.

The Submariner entered the cultural vernacular in 1962, when the watch appeared in the first James Bond film, *Dr. No.* After its big screen debut, the watch appeared in nearly a dozen Bond films over a span of 27 years.

While the Submariner's rugged functionality fueled its initial popularity among divers and spies, Rolex broadened the watch's appeal as a fashionable accessory in the late 1960s with the addition of a date function. Indeed, the watch's signature balance of sport and dress has made the Submariner a perennial favorite among collectors for more than half a century.

In 2009, Rolex introduced a new version of the Submariner (reference 116613) that succeeded the last Submariner (reference 16613), one of the company's most popular models.

The refreshed design returned a year later in 2010 as Rolex welcomed two versions of the Submariner (reference 116610) in stainless steel—one with the dial and bezel in black and the other with those elements in green.

These new models feature the same technical and aesthetic innovations introduced in 2009, including an automatic movement (caliber 3135) whose chronometric precision has been certified by the Official Swiss Chronometer Testing Institute. The escapement at the heart of the movement is equipped with a hairspring made from Parachrom, a magnetic and shock-resistant material exclusive to Rolex. This blue-colored coil can be seen when the watch's screw-down caseback is removed.

The new Submariner's bezel offers another upgrade over its predecessor. Gone is the aluminum insert, replaced here by one that glistens with Cerachrom. Developed by Rolex this ceramic-based material will not fade from UV exposure and resists both corrosion and scratches.

Rolex uses another proprietary material that makes it easy to pick out the latest generation of Submariners in the dark. Instead of the pale green glow emitted by SuperLumiNova, the company treats the watch's hour markers and hands with Chromalight, a substance that glows blue.

While the Submariner's performance and design have evolved through the years, the watch has always stayed true to the refined masculinity of its ancestors.

Rolex returns to the roots of its formidable reputation with refreshed versions of the Submariner and Explorer.

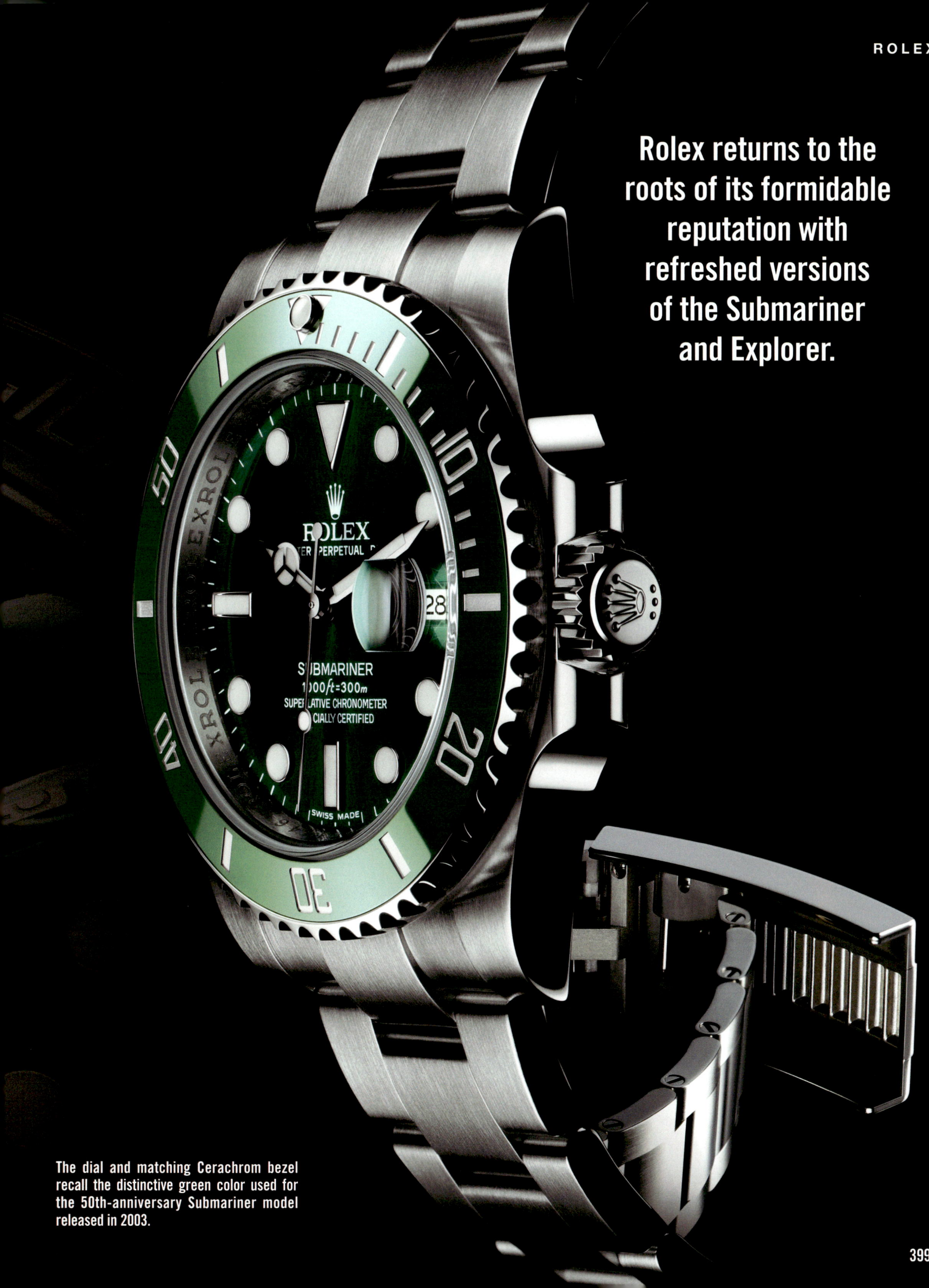

The dial and matching Cerachrom bezel recall the distinctive green color used for the 50th-anniversary Submariner model released in 2003.

Another historic model received a redesign last year as Rolex revamped the Oyster Perpetual Explorer, a wristwatch that accompanied the first Himalayan expedition to successfully scale Mount Everest in 1953.

The 2010 version is presented in a larger case, expanding the diameter from 36mm to a more modern 39mm. While this gives the watch a bit more presence on the wrist, it does nothing to detract from the design's comfortable fit or understated elegance. The other modification made last year can be seen on the black dial, where Rolex has increased the size of the hands, making it easier to read the time.

In keeping with the Explorer's link to the rough and tumble world of adventure, its case is hewn from a solid block of 904L steel, a metal alloy that is highly resistant to corrosion. This production method creates a vault-like enclosure that is not only water resistant to 330 feet, but also optimized to protect the automatic movement, which is made in-house by Rolex. A certified chronometer, caliber 3132 features several of Rolex's proprietary innovations, including Paraflex shock absorbers and a Parachrom hairspring.

Rolex creates visual tension with the Explorer's design, using the smooth surface of the polished bezel to contrast with the brushed texture of the case, lugs and bracelet.

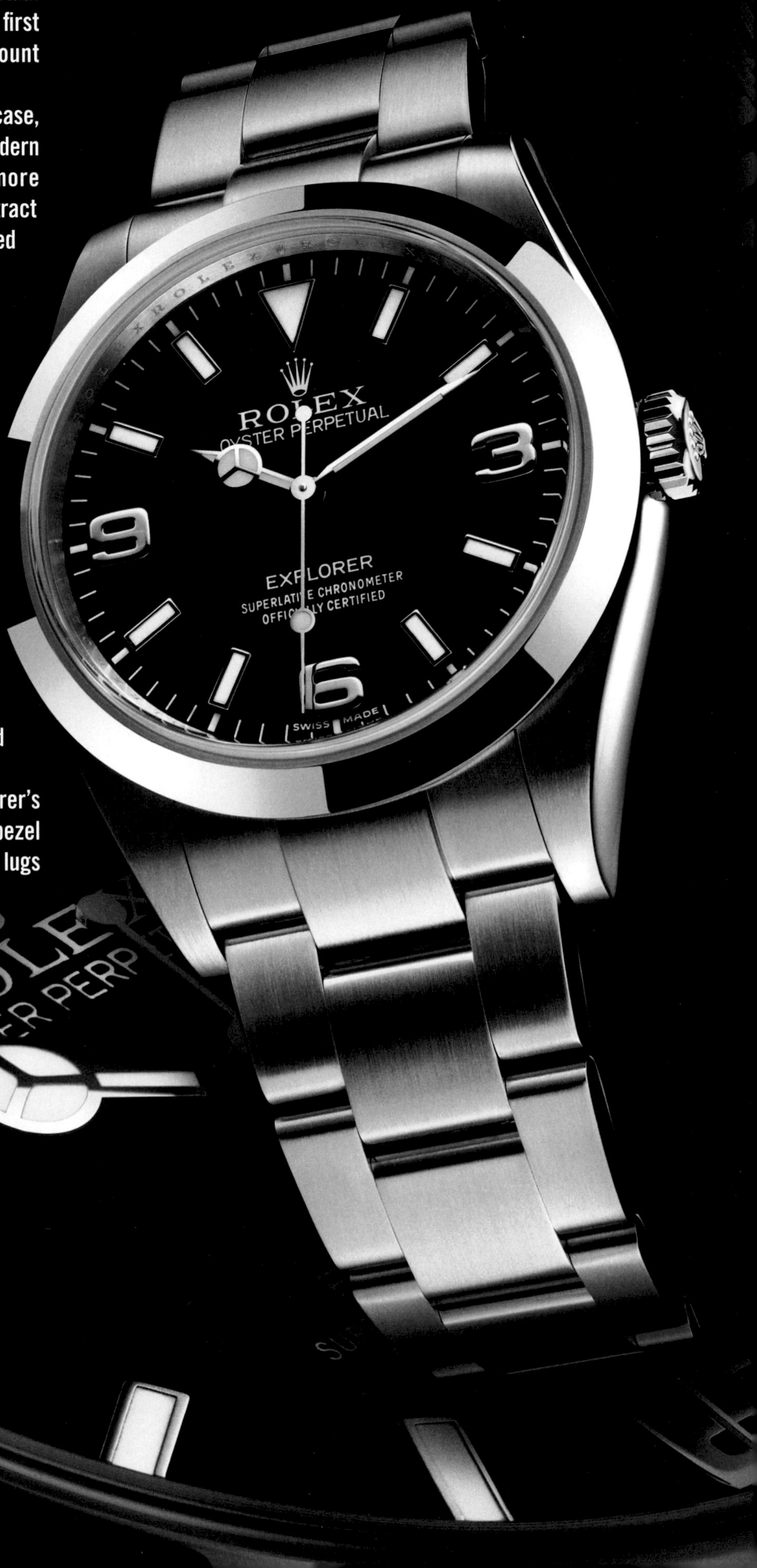

Perpetual Datejust Lady—with three distinctive Rolesor models. These chic siblings project unique personalities thanks to their different metal combinations, but all inherit the same unassailable technical characteristics.

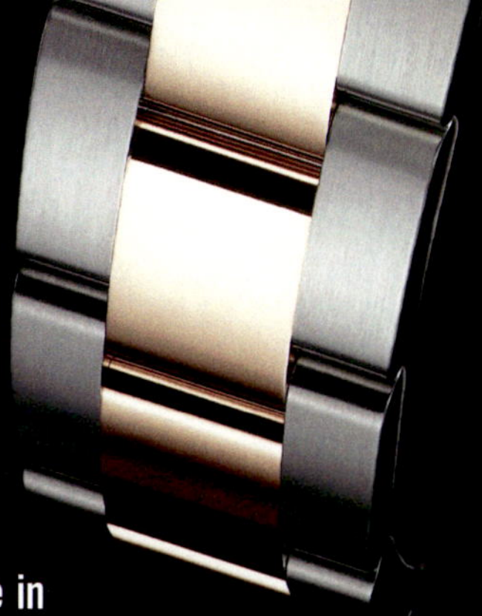

The trio shares identical movements, a chronometer-certified automatic (caliber 2235) with a 48-hour power reserve. The mechanism includes Rolex's trademark Datejust, a date display that advances the date instantly at midnight. Visible through an aperture on the dial, the date is magnified two-and-a-half times by a Cyclops lens in the sapphire crystal.

Rolex presents the Oyster Perpetual Datejust Lady's 31mm case in yellow, white or Everose Rolesor, offering a number of stylistic choices for each version to satisfy just about any whim.

Three configurations in particular highlight the range of options available to women. To showcase its signature Everose alloy, Rolex selects a matching domed bezel set with 24 white diamonds. The watch's chocolate-colored dial features Roman numerals, including a diamond-set "VI."

Rolex evokes a look synonymous with the company by pairing the yellow Rolesor case and matching Oyster bracelet with a silver dial and yellow-gold Roman numerals. To accentuate the 46 sparkling brilliants on the bezel, the firm secures the white diamonds in a yellow-gold setting.

Rolex shifts gears a bit with a white Rolesor model on a Jubilee bracelet that features a dark rhodium dial decorated with flowers. To make these blossoms bloom, the company uses an electroforming process that creates the petals in brilliant relief.

FACING PAGE

Rolex expands the Explorer's 904L steel case to a modern diameter of 39mm while also updating the dial with larger hands.

THIS PAGE

The 31mm Oyster Perpetual DateJust Lady in Everose Rolesor features a domed bezel set with 24 white brilliants.

OYSTER PERPETUAL SUBMARINER DATE — REF. 116610 LN / 97200

Movement: automatic-winding perpetual rotor 3135 caliber; 48-hour power reserve; 28,800 vph; COSC-certified; Parachrom hairspring with Breguet overcoil.
Functions: hours, minutes, seconds; date, instantaneous change and rapid setting.
Case: 904L steel; Ø 40mm; unidirectional rotating bezel with black Cerachrom insert, platinum graduations; Triplock winding crown, shoulders to protect the crown; sapphire crystal, cyclops lens with antireflective coating; water resistant to 30atm.
Dial: luminescent Chromalight hands and hour markers.
Bracelet: 904L steel; Rolex Glidelock clasp.

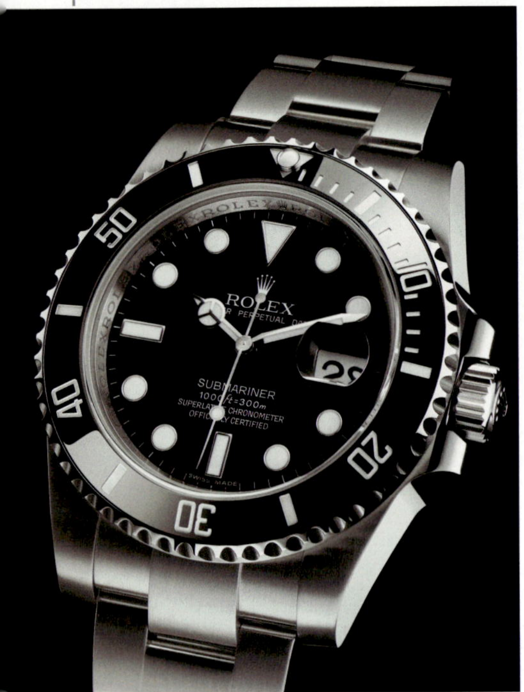

OYSTER PERPETUAL SUBMARINER DATE — REF. 116610 LV / 97200

Movement: automatic-winding perpetual rotor 3135 caliber; 48-hour power reserve; 28,800 vph; COSC-certified; Parachrom hairspring with Breguet overcoil.
Functions: hours, minutes, seconds; date, instantaneous change and rapid setting.
Case: 904L steel; Ø 40mm; unidirectional rotating bezel with green Cerachrom insert, platinum graduations; Triplock winding crown, shoulders to protect the crown; sapphire crystal, cyclops lens with antireflective coating; water resistant to 30atm.
Dial: green gold; luminescent Chromalight hands and hour markers.
Bracelet: 904L steel; Rolex Glidelock clasp.

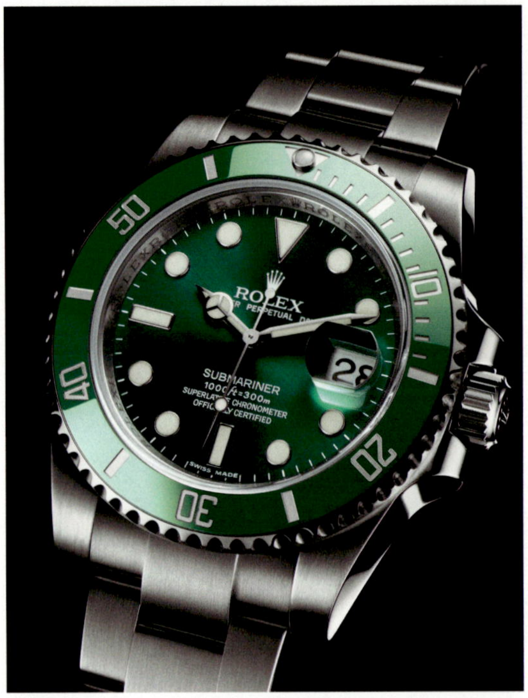

OYSTER PERPETUAL EXPLORER — REF. 214270 / 77200

Movement: automatic-winding perpetual rotor 3132 caliber; 48-hour power reserve; 28,800 vph; COSC-certified; Parachrom hairspring with Breguet overcoil, Paraflex shock absorbers.
Functions: hours, minutes, seconds.
Case: 904L steel; Ø 39mm; fixed, Twinlock winding crown; smooth bezel; sapphire crystal caseback; water resistant to 10atm.
Dial: luminescent Chromalight hands and hour markers.
Bracelet: 904L steel; Oysterlock with Easylink comfort extension link.

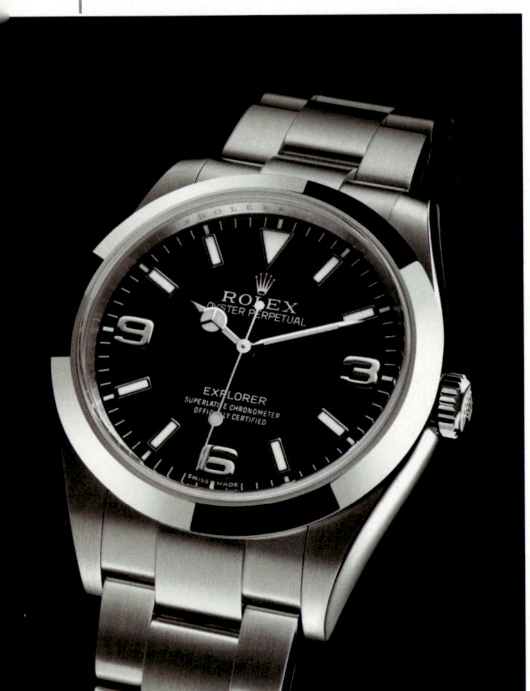

OYSTER PERPETUAL SUBMARINER DATE — REF. 116613 LN

Movement: automatic-winding; 31 jewels; COSC-certified.
Functions: hours, minutes, seconds; date at 3.
Case: stainless steel and yellow gold; Ø 40mm; black ceramic rotating bezel; sapphire crystal; water resistant to 30atm.
Dial: black; luminescent hour markers.
Bracelet: 18K oyster; Oysterlock with Easylink comfort extension link.
Also available: stainless steel with black dial (ref. 16610); stainless steel and yellow gold with blue dial (ref. 116613LB.

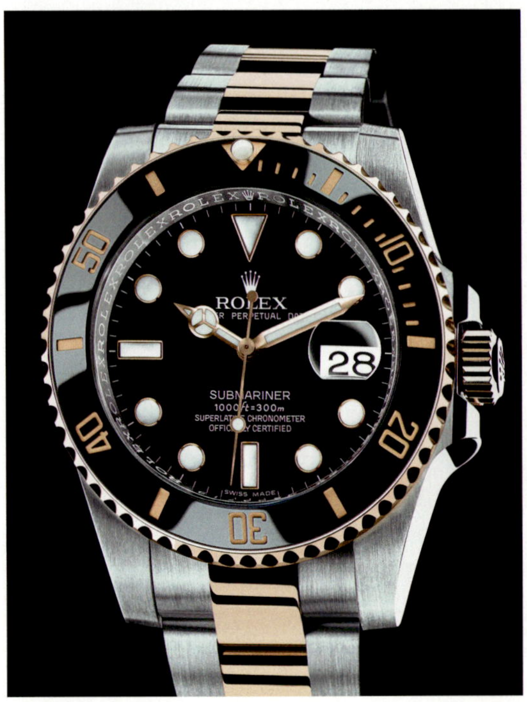

OYSTER PERPETUAL DATEJUST LADY — REF. 178341 / 72161

Movement: automatic-winding perpetual rotor 2235 caliber; 48-hour power reserve; 28,800 vph; COSC-certified; hairspring with Breguet overcoil.
Functions: hours, minutes, seconds; date at 3, instantaneous change and rapid setting.
Case: Everose Rolesor; Ø 31mm; domed bezel set with 24 brilliant diamonds; Twinlock winding crown; sapphire crystal, Cyclops lens with antireflective coating; water resistant to 10atm.
Dial: chocolate brown; Roman numerals, gem-set Roman numeral at 6.
Bracelet: Everose Rolesor; Oyster clasp with Easylink comfort extension link.
Also available: purple dial, Roman numerals, gem-set Roman numeral at 6; white mother-of-pearl dial, Roman numerals, gem-set Roman numeral at 6; white mother-of-pearl dial, maxi Roman numerals; pink dial, electroformed tone-on-tone floral motifs, Arabic numeral at 6.

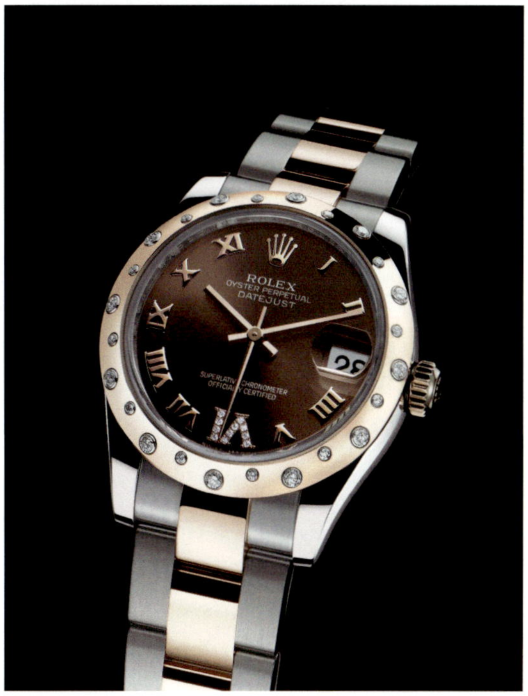

OYSTER PERPETUAL DATEJUST LADY — REF. 178383 / 72163

Movement: automatic-winding perpetual rotor 2235 caliber; 48-hour power reserve; 28,800 vph; COSC-certified; hairspring with Breguet overcoil.
Functions: hours, minutes, seconds; date at 3, instantaneous change and rapid setting.
Case: yellow Rolesor; Ø 31mm; domed bezel set with 46 brilliant diamonds; Twinlock winding crown; sapphire crystal, Cyclops lens with antireflective coating; water resistant to 10atm.
Dial: silver; Roman numerals, gem-set Roman numeral at 6.
Bracelet: yellow Rolesor; Oysterclasp with Easylink comfort extension link.
Also available: olive green dial, Roman numerals, gem-set Roman numeral at 6; white mother-of-pearl dial, maxi Roman numerals; champagne dial, electroformed tone-on-tone floral motifs, Arabic numeral at 6.

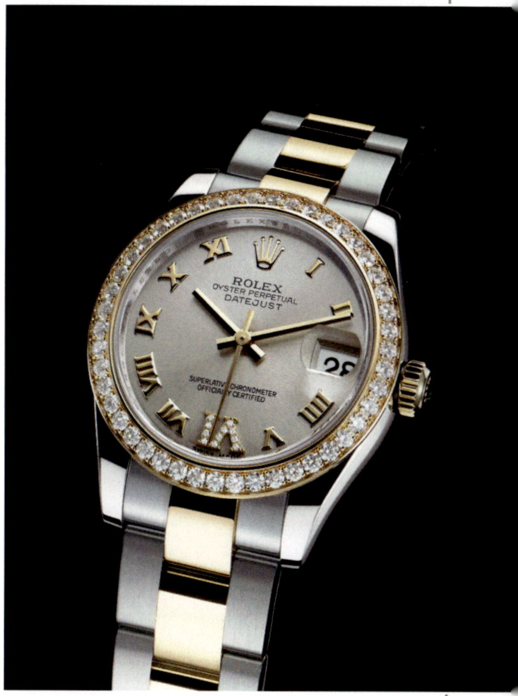

OYSTER PERPETUAL DATEJUST LADY — REF. 178274 / 63160

Movement: automatic-winding perpetual rotor 2235 caliber; 48-hour power reserve; 28,800 vph; COSC-certified; hairspring with Breguet overcoil.
Functions: hours, minutes, seconds; date at 3, instantaneous change and rapid setting.
Case: white Rolesor; Ø 31mm; fluted bezel; Twinlock winding crown; sapphire crystal, Cyclops lens with antireflective coating; water resistant to 10atm.
Dial: dark rhodium; electroformed white rhodium tone-on-tone floral motifs; Arabic numeral at 6.
Bracelet: 904L steel; Oyster clasp.
Also available: bronze dial, Roman numerals, gem-set Roman numeral at 6; purple dial, Roman numerals, gem-set Roman numeral at 6; white mother-of-pearl dial, maxi Roman numerals; white mother-of-pearl dial, Roman numerals, gem-set Roman numeral at 6.

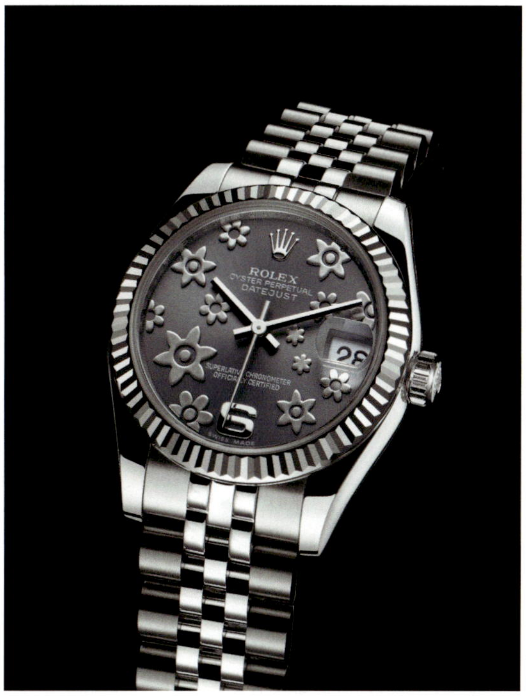

OYSTER PERPETUAL YACHT-MASTER II — REF. 116688

Movement: automatic-winding; COSC-certified.
Functions: hours, minutes, seconds; chronograph.
Case: 18K yellow gold; Ø 44mm; ceramic ring command bezel with scratch-resistant blue Cerachrom disc; sapphire crystal; water resistant to 10atm.
Dial: white; gold luminescent hands and markers; yellow-gold rimmed seconds subdial; red countdown sweep seconds hand; blue rimmed regatta countdown indicator.
Bracelet: 18K yellow gold Oysterlock; Oysterclasp with Easylink.
Also available: 18K white gold with white dial (ref. 116689).

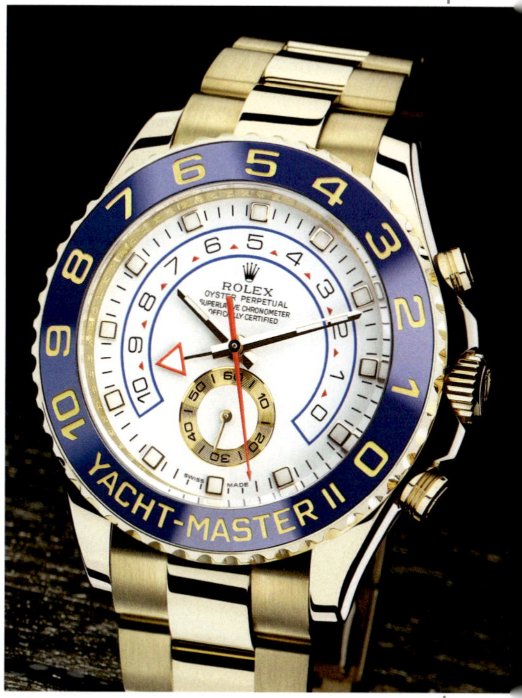

TAG Heuer

SWISS AVANT-GARDE SINCE 1860

PIONEERING SPEED FOR 150 YEARS

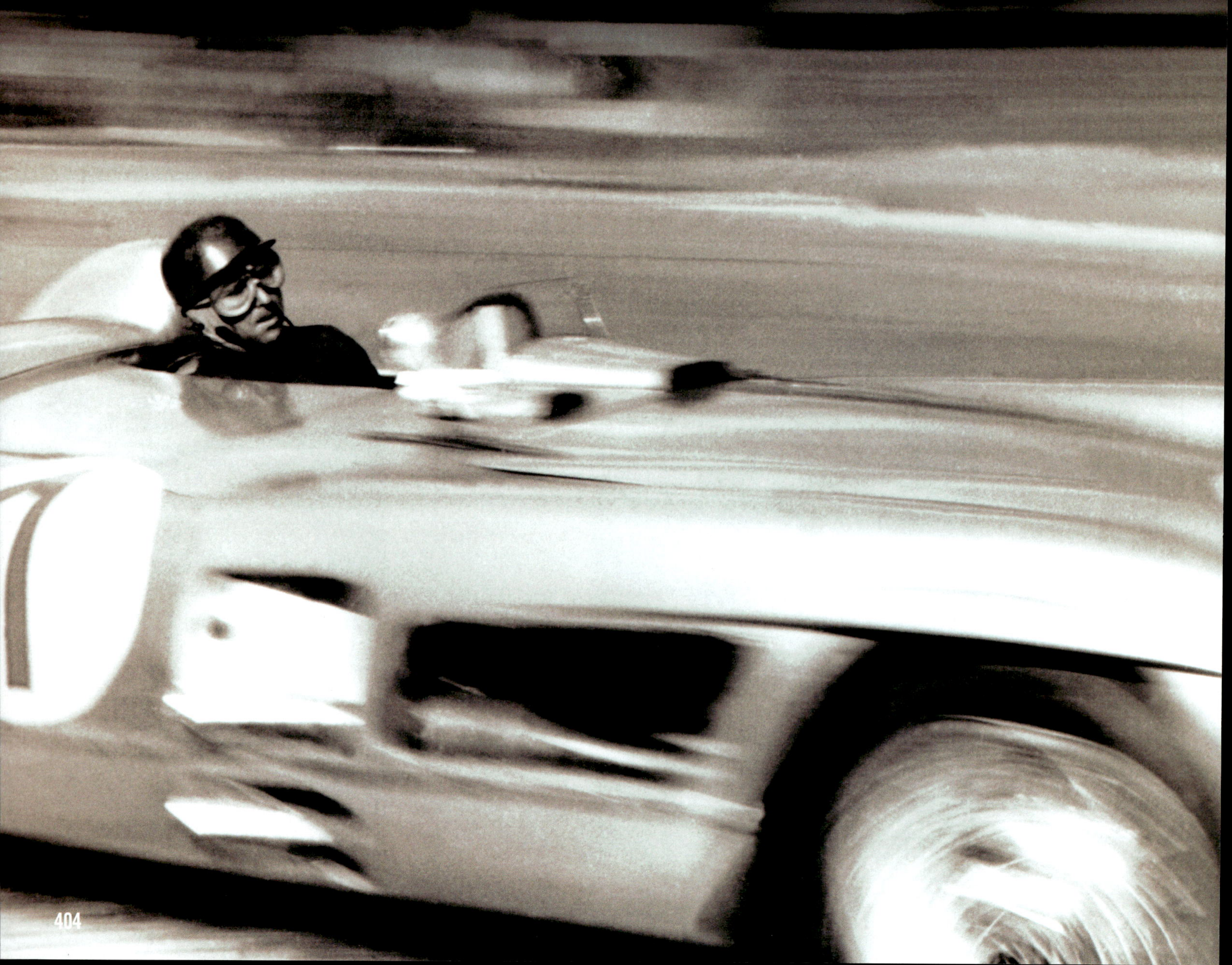

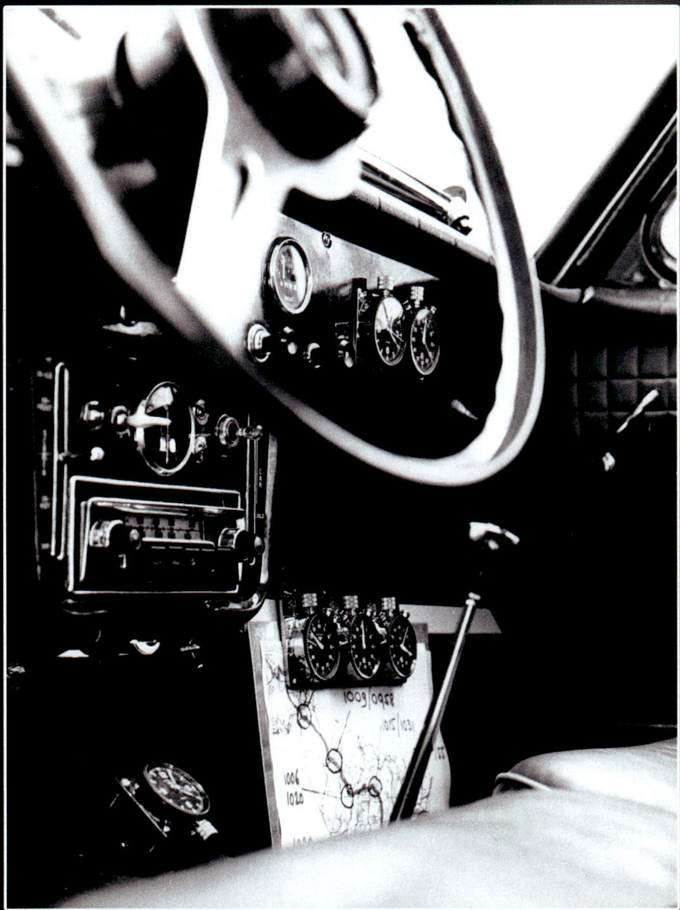

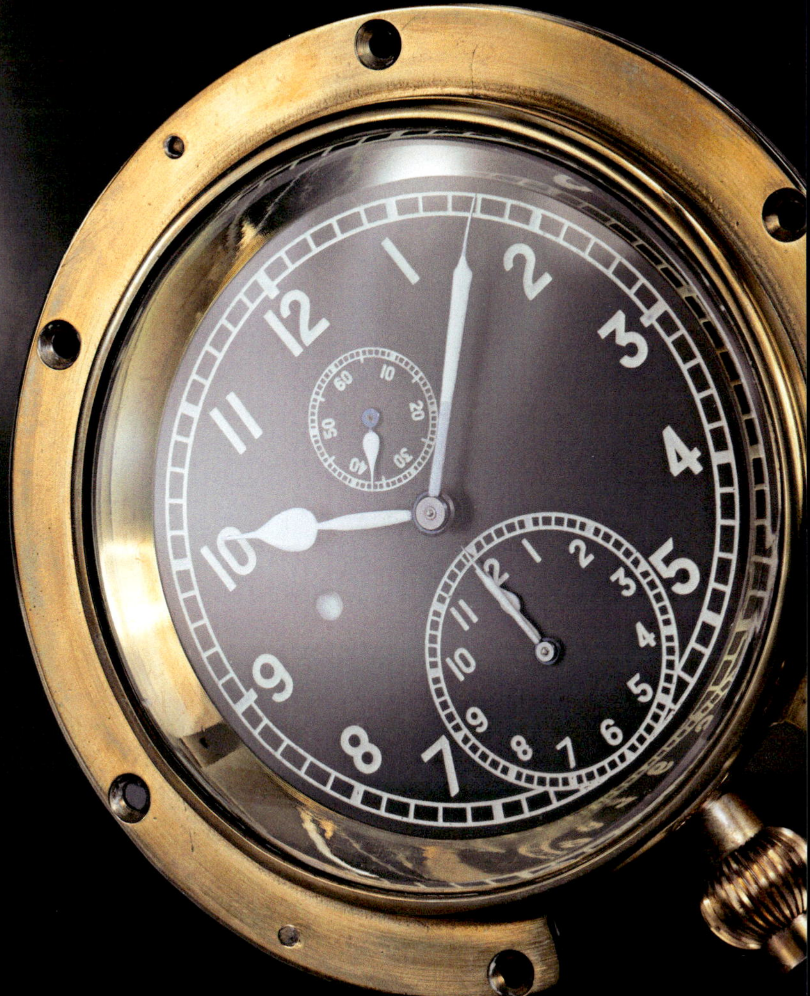

Time has fascinated philosophers for centuries, as the desire to master it through measurement entails mind and machine, perception and precision instruments.

For over 150 years, this has been TAG Heuer territory: designing chronographs to meet the demands of competitive sports in which technology, time and style are paramount. Sporty to its core, TAG Heuer launches a diverse selection of timepieces in early 2011 that reference TAG Heuer's dedicated and superior involvement in the world's most prestigious, historic and glamorous motor races.

For haute horology connoisseurs more classical in style and historical in taste, the Heuer CARRERA MIKROGRAPH 1/100th Second Chronograph, in a rose-gold limited edition of only 150 models, mixes the iconic Carrera with a 1916 Heuer invention, the Mikrograph, which was the first stopwatch to measure 1/100th of a second.

And exclusively for the ladies, the TAG Heuer Formula 1 Lady Steel and Ceramic Chronograph brings the glamorous energy of Formula 1 racing to purely chic timepieces. A chronograph larger in circumference than the first Steel & Ceramic watches launched last year, it debuts in four styles, three of which feature diamonds, with either black or white dials and sleek ceramic bezels.

The first to develop chronographs specifically for sports cars and to break barriers in measuring 1/10,000th of a second digitally and 1/100th of a second mechanically, TAG Heuer is at the top of its game. In the quest for mastering time, TAG Heuer claims over 150 years of innovation-driven history.

FACING PAGE
1954: Juan Manuel Fangio racing in his Mercedes-Benz.

THIS PAGE
TOP LEFT TAG Heuer has always been inspired by automotive design.
TOP RIGHT The Time of Trip, launched in 1911.

TAG HEUER FORMULA 1 LADY STEEL AND CERAMIC CHRONOGRAPH

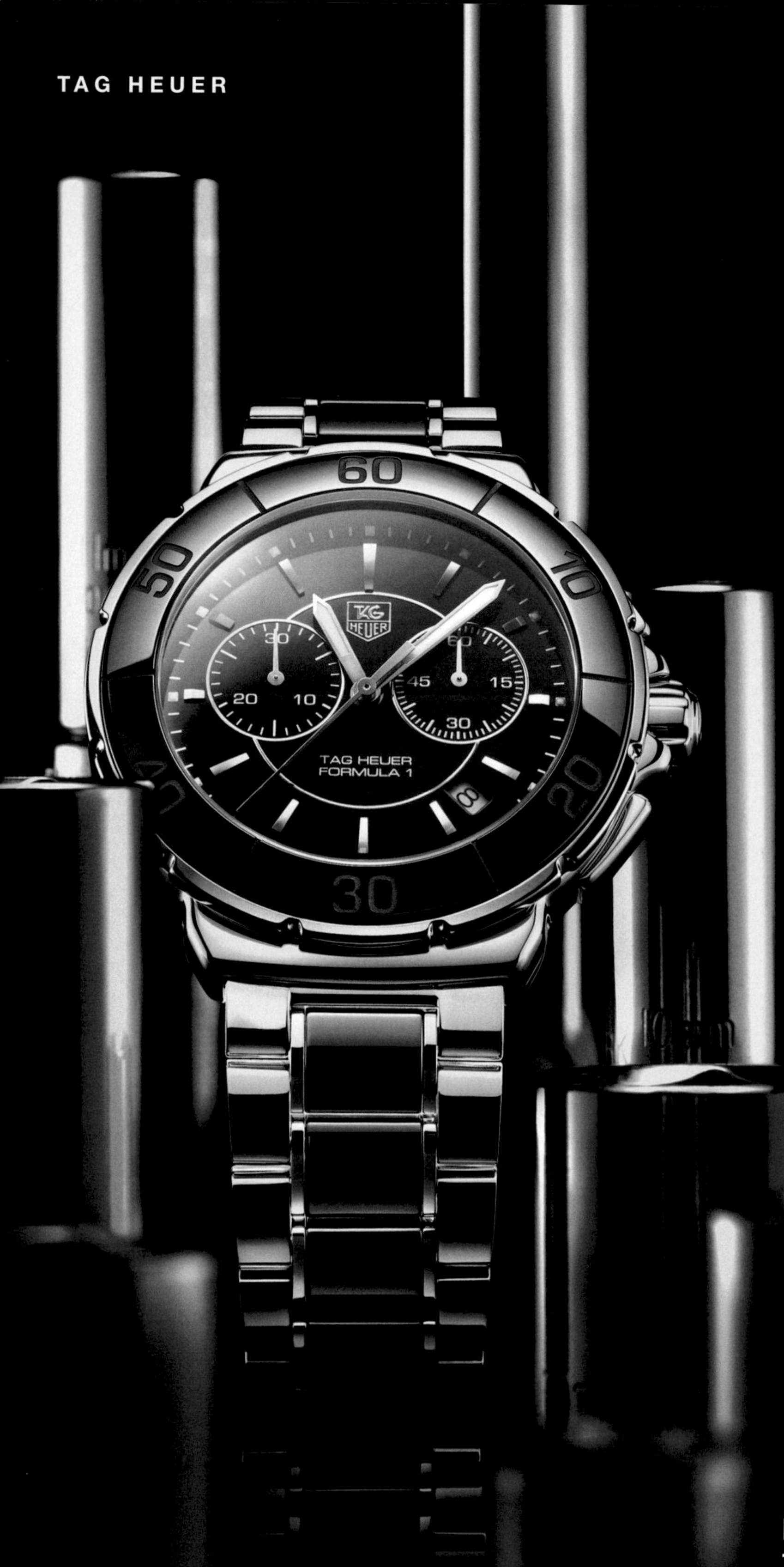

THIS PAGE

TAG Heuer Formula 1 Lady steel and ceramic chronograph.

FACING PAGE

The first mechanical timepiece with 1/100th of a second display by a central hand.

Dazzling, dynamic and audacious, the TAG Heuer Formula 1 Lady Steel & Ceramic Chronograph is the latest in TAG Heuer's evolution of feminine design that is bold yet far from flashy, understated yet full of sex appeal. Four monochromatic models, with a larger 41mm chronograph circumference, extend TAG Heuer's Steel & Ceramic watch collection, which debuted with immediate success in 2010.

With signature style, sophistication and powerful appeal, TAG Heuer's Formula 1 ladies' timepieces are contemporary classics in the making.

HEUER CARRERA MIKROGRAPH 1/100TH SECOND CHRONOGRAPH

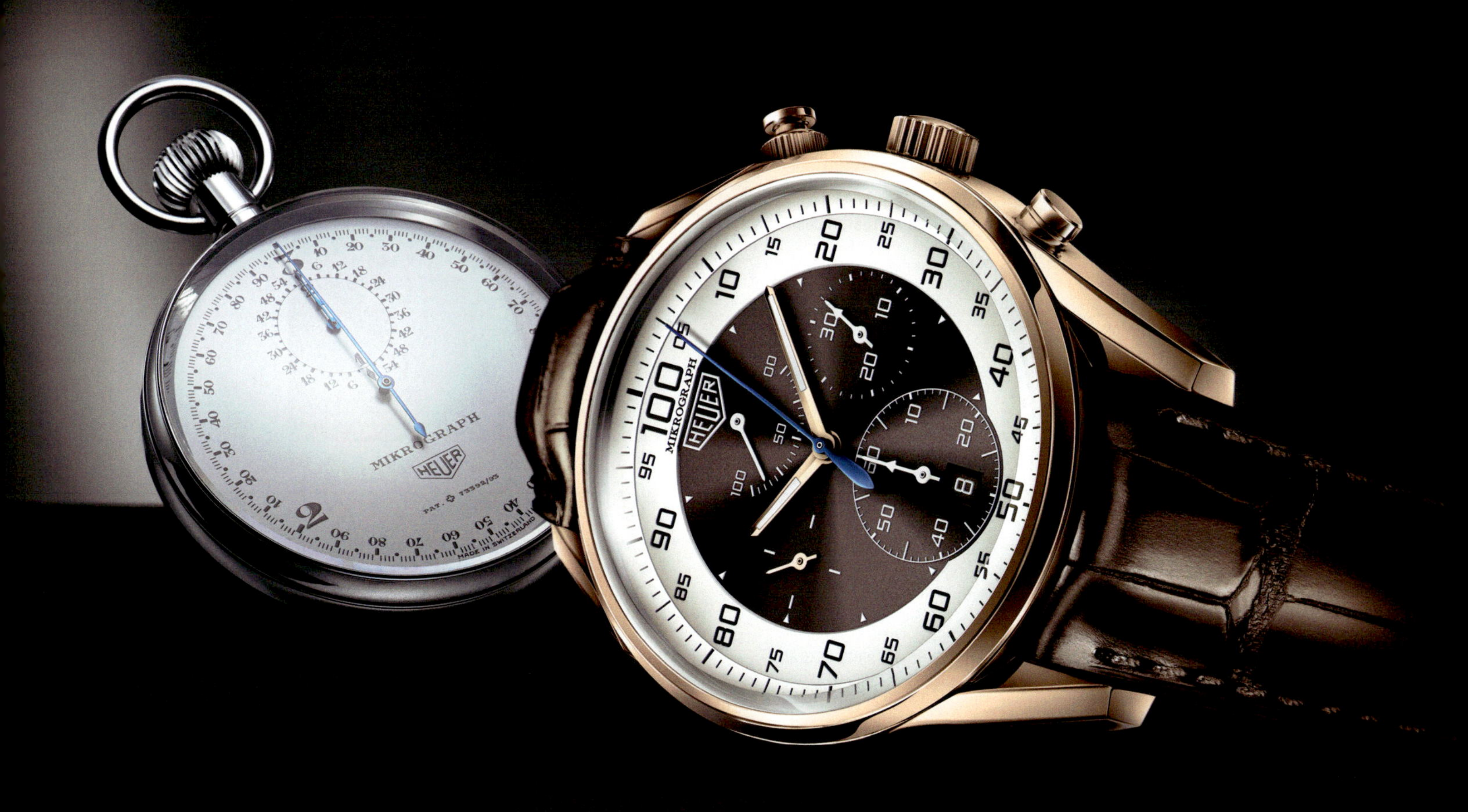

In 1916, Heuer developed the Mikrograph, the first sports stopwatch accurate to 1/50th and 1/100th of a second when other timing instruments could only measure to the nearest 1/5th of a second. This technical innovation changed the future of racing events management, by gaining greater accuracy of a second—a mere moment that can count for everything between striving professionals. This groundbreaking core technology catapulted Heuer ahead as official timekeeper to the world's most prominent competitive sporting events ever since.

Just five years only after the revolutionary Calibre 360 Chronograph, TAG Heuer literally re-invents the high-frequency dual assortment mechanical movement, and pays a tribute to the legendary Heuer Mikrograph stopwatch of 1916, which made history for more than 50 years in timing high speed sports with its 25 and 50 hertz frequencies.

With two assortments, 62 jewels and 396 components, the HEUER CARRERA MIKROGRAPH 1/100th Second Chronograph is a new masterpiece of Swiss haute horology, setting a new milestone in grand complications.

MONACO V4 ROSE GOLD AND SILICON NITRIDE — REF. WAW2040.FC6288

Movement: first-ever automatic belt-driven transmission watch; tungsten ingot linear mass; two pairs of barrels in series, set in parallel and linked by belts.
Functions: hours, minutes, seconds.
Case: bi-material: polished solid rose gold and fine-brushed silicon nitride; Ø 41mm, thickness: 17mm; polished solid rose-gold crown; beveled sapphire crystal with double-sided antireflective treatment; sapphire crystal caseback in three sections; water resistant to 50 meters.

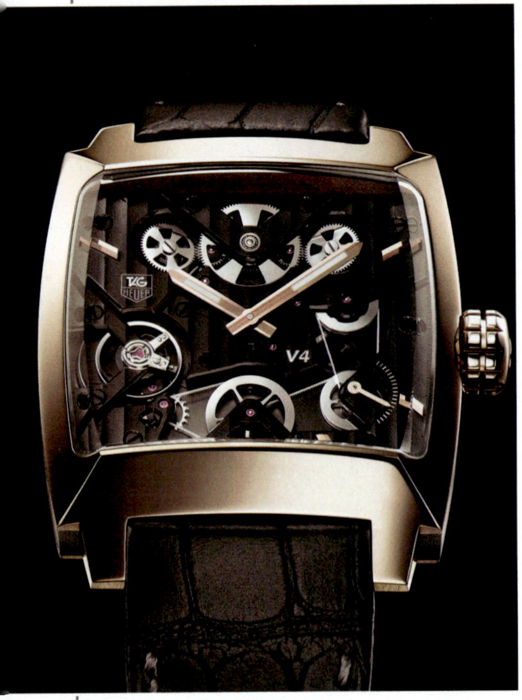

Dial: seven fine-brushed bridges coated with black PVD; Côtes de Genève and haute horology hand-finishings; escapement and belt-driven transmission visible from the front; hand-applied faceted indexes; fine-brushed rose-gold minute and hour hands with white luminescent treatment; solid rose-gold small seconds hand at 4; white "V4" engraving; engraved white TAG Heuer logo.
Strap: hand-sewn anthracite alligator, soft-touch effect; solid rose-gold folding buckle with safety pushbuttons.
Note: limited edition of 60 pieces.

MONACO VINTAGE CALIBRE 11 — REF. CAW211B.FC6241

Movement: automatic-winding TAG Heuer Calibre 11.
Functions: hours, minutes, seconds; date; chronograph with two counters: small seconds at 3; minutes at 9.
Case: fine-brushed and polished stainless steel; Ø 39mm, thickness: 13.8mm; stainless steel polished crown at 9; sapphire crystal; polished and fine-brushed stainless steel pushbuttons; sapphire caseback; water resistant to 100 meters.

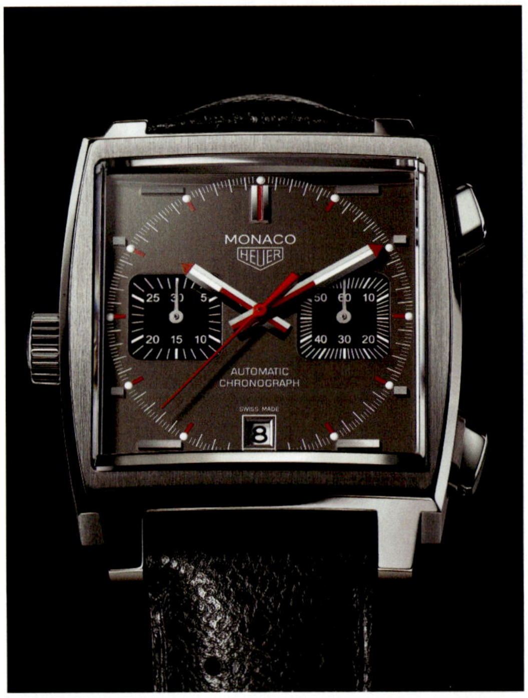

Dial: unique vintage design to celebrate TAG Heuer's 150th anniversary; hand-applied faceted and fine-brushed horizontal indexes; diamond-faceted minute and hour hands with a touch of red and luminescent treatment; red chronograph seconds hand; monochrome printed TAG Heuer logo.
Strap: black punched calfskin; folding buckle with safety pushbuttons.
Note: limited edition of 1,860 pieces.

MONACO TWENTY FOUR CALIBRE 36 CHRONOGRAPH — REF. CAL5110.FC6265

Movement: automatic-winding TAG Heuer Calibre 36; 36,000 vph; advanced dynamic absorber system protecting the movement; annular oscillating mass.
Functions: hours, minutes, seconds; date; chronograph with two counters: minutes at 3 and seconds at 9.
Case: fine-brushed and polished black titanium carbide-coated case; Ø 40.5mm, thickness: 16.8mm; polished stainless steel crown at 3; beveled sapphire crystal; polished stainless steel pushbuttons; sapphire crystal caseback; water resistant to 100 meters.

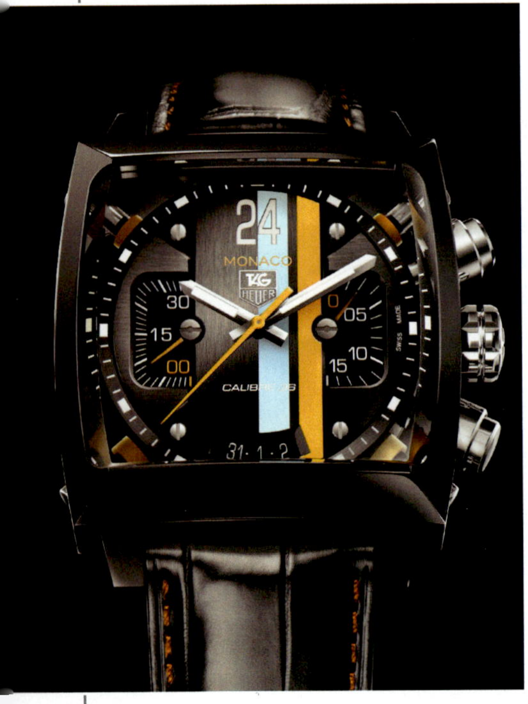

Dial: fine-brushed black dial; oversized "24" at 12, in honor of the 24 of Le Mans; unique two-part transparent dial; faceted polished rhodium-plated minute and hour hands with luminescent treatment; orange chronograph seconds hand; monochrome hand-applied TAG Heuer logo.
Strap: black alligator; orange stitching; titanium folding buckle with safety pushbuttons.

LINK AUTOMATIC WATCH CALIBRE 5 DAY DATE — REF. WAT2011.BA0951

Movement: automatic-winding TAG Heuer Calibre 5.
Functions: hours, minutes, seconds; day and date at 6.
Case: polished and fine-brushed stainless steel; Ø 42mm, thickness: 12.4mm; screw-in polished steel crown; curved scratch-resistant sapphire crystal with double-sided antireflective treatment; sapphire crystal caseback; water resistant to 100 meters.
Dial: silver dial with vertical streak effect; hand-applied curved, faceted and polished indexes; faceted polished rhodium-plated minute and hour hands with luminescent treatment; hand-applied monochrome TAG Heuer logo.

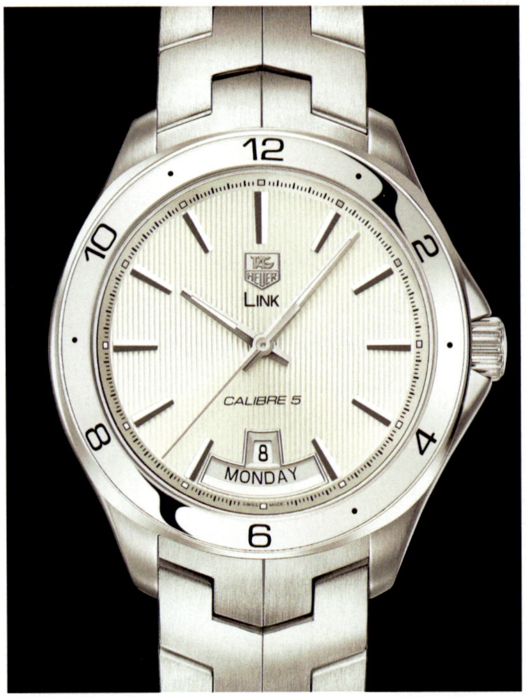

Bracelet: fine-brushed stainless steel bracelet with polished edges; solid steel folding clasp with safety pushbuttons.

LINK AUTOMATIC WATCH CALIBRE 6 — REF. WAT2110.BA0950

Movement: automatic-winding TAG Heuer Calibre 6.
Functions: hours, minutes; seconds and date at 6.
Case: polished and fine-brushed stainless steel; Ø 40mm, thickness: 11.4mm; screw-in polished steel crown; curved scratch-resistant sapphire crystal with double-sided antireflective treatment; sapphire crystal caseback; water resistant to 100 meters.
Dial: black dial with vertical streak effect; hand-applied curved, faceted and polished indexes; faceted polished rhodium-plated minute and hour hands with luminescent treatment; hand-applied monochrome TAG Heuer logo.
Bracelet: fine-brushed stainless steel bracelet with polished edges; solid steel folding clasp with safety pushbuttons.

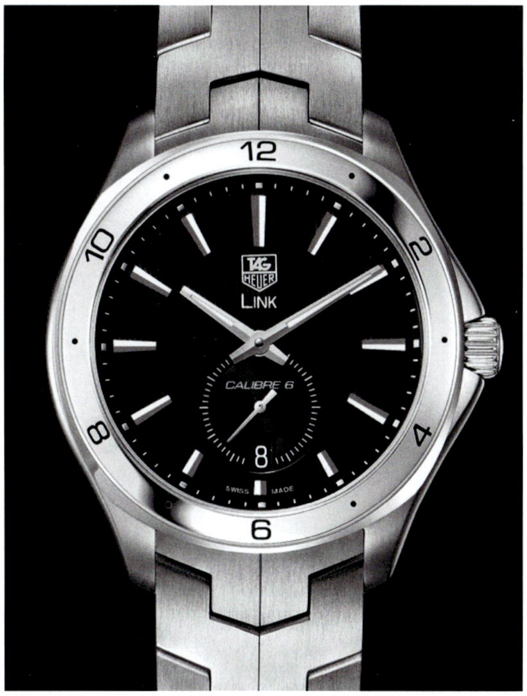

LINK AUTOMATIC WATCH CALIBRE S — REF. CAT7011.BA0952

Movement: TAG Heuer Calibre S – Electro-mechanical Chronograph; invented, patented, developed and manufactured by TAG Heuer.
Functions: hours, minutes, seconds; perpetual retrograde calendar until 2099; time and chronograph display using central hour, minute, seconds hands; flyback chronograph with 1/100th-of-a-second accuracy; 1/100th-of-a-second retrograde counter at 4:30; 1/10th of-a-second retrograde counter at 7:30.
Case: polished and fine-brushed stainless steel case; Ø 43mm, thickness: 13.2mm; polished stainless steel fixed bezel with black tachometric scale; polished pushbutton crown to switch from watch mode to chronograph mode; curved scratch-resistant sapphire crystal with double-sided antireflective treatment; water resistant to 100 meters.
Dial: silver dial with vertical streak effect; hand-applied curved, faceted and polished indexes; faceted polished rhodium-plated minute and hour hands; hand-applied monochrome TAG Heuer logo.
Bracelet: fine-brushed stainless steel bracelet with polished edges; double safety clasp with folding buckle.

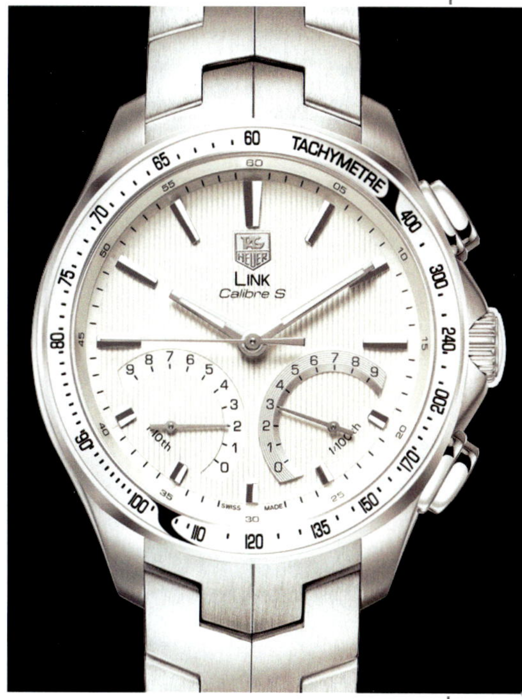

LINK AUTOMATIC CHRONOGRAPH CALIBRE 16 — REF. CAT2010.BA0952

Movement: automatic-winding TAG Heuer Calibre 16.
Functions: hours, minutes, seconds; date at 3; chronograph with three counters: minutes at 12, hours at 6, running seconds at 9.
Case: polished and fine-brushed steel; Ø 43mm, thickness: 15.55mm; polished fixed bezel with black tachometric scale; polished steel pushbuttons and screw-in crown; curved scratch-resistant sapphire crystal with double-sided antireflective treatment; screw-in caseback with engraved decoration and TAG Heuer logo; water resistant to 100 meters.
Dial: black dial with vertical streak effect; hand-applied curved, faceted and polished indexes; faceted polished rhodium-plated minute and hour hands with luminescent treatment; luminescent treatment on the flange; hand-applied monochrome TAG Heuer logo.
Bracelet: fine-brushed stainless steel bracelet with polished edges; solid steel folding clasp with safety pushbuttons.

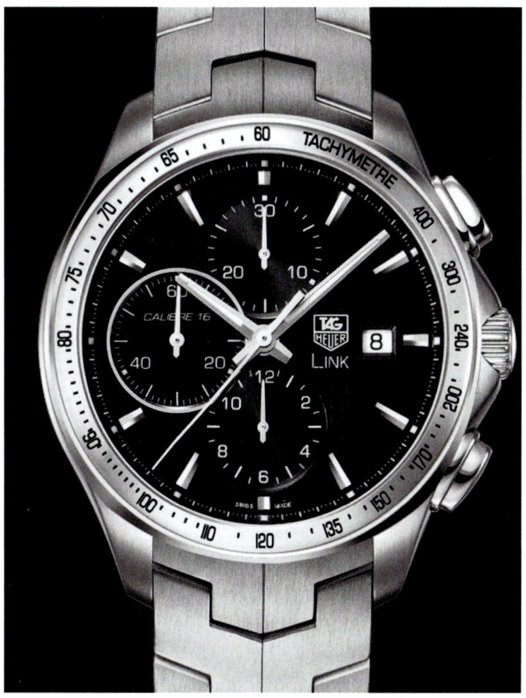

AQUARACER AUTOMATIC WATCH CALIBRE 5 — REF. WAP2011.BA0830

Movement: automatic-winding TAG Heuer Calibre 5.
Functions: hours, minutes, seconds; date at 3.
Case: polished and fine-brushed stainless steel; Ø 41mm, thickness: 11.6mm; unidirectional turning bezel in fine-brushed steel with polished studs; polished screw-in crown; scratch-resistant sapphire crystal; screw-in caseback with a special diver decoration; water resistant to 300 meters.
Dial: silver with horizontal streak effect; hand-applied indexes with polished facets; diamond-shaped hands with polished facets; luminescent treatment on hands and indexes; monochrome TAG Heuer logo.
Bracelet: three-row fine-brushed steel bracelet; polished edges; pushbuttons; solid end piece.

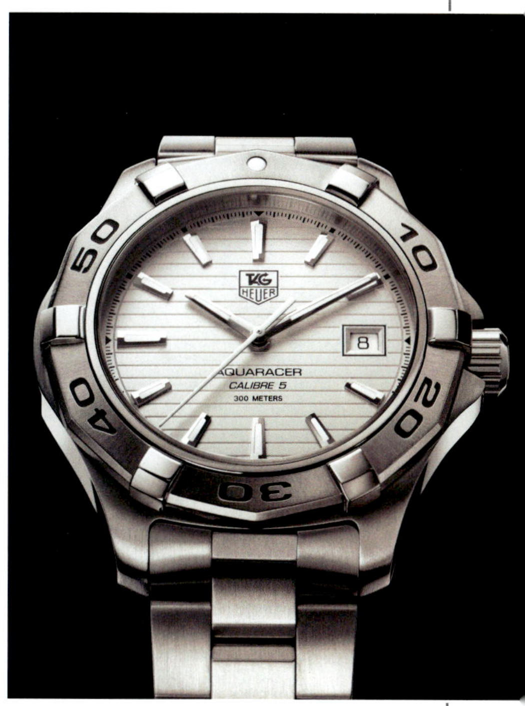

AQUARACER WATCH QUARTZ REF. WAP1112.BA0831

Movement: quartz.
Functions: hours, minutes, seconds; date at 3.
Case: fine-brushed and polished stainless steel case; Ø 39mm, thickness: 9.95mm; unidirectional turning bezel with engraved, black lacquered numerals on the base of the bezel and luminescent dot at 12; polished screw-in crown; scratch-resistant sapphire crystal; screw-in caseback with a special diver decoration; water resistant to 300 meters.
Dial: blue with sunray effect; hand-applied indexes with polished facets; diamond-shaped hands with polished facets; luminescent treatment on hands and indexes; monochrome TAG Heuer logo.
Bracelet: three-row fine-brushed steel bracelet; polished edges; double safety clasp; diving extension system.

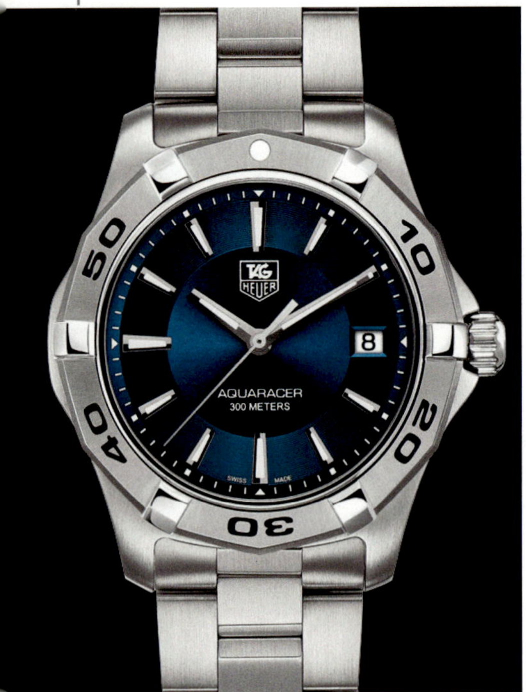

AQUARACER AUTOMATIC CHRONOGRAPH CALIBRE 16 REF. CAP2110.BA0833

Movement: automatic-winding TAG Heuer Calibre 16.
Functions: hours, minutes, seconds; date at 3; chronograph with three counters: minutes at 12, hours at 6, small seconds at 9.
Case: polished and fine-brushed stainless steel case; Ø 42mm, thickness 15.3mm; unidirectional turning bezel with engraved, black lacquered numerals on the base of the bezel and luminescent dot at 12; polished screw-in crown; screw-in caseback with a special diver decoration; water resistant to 300 meters.
Dial: black dial with horizontal streak effect; hand-applied indexes with polished facets; diamond-shaped hands with polished facets; luminescent treatment on hands and indexes; monochrome TAG Heuer logo.
Bracelet: three-row fine-brushed steel bracelet; polished edges; folding buckle; diving extension with safety pushbuttons.

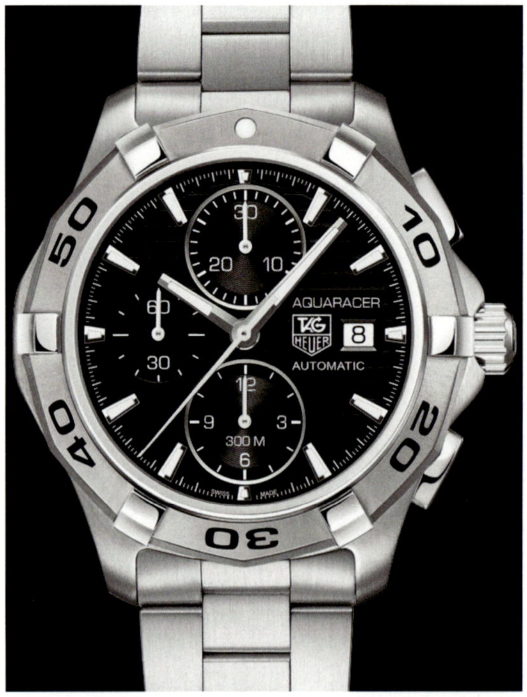

AQUARACER LADY DIAMOND DIAL & DIAMOND BEZEL REF. WAF1313.BA0819

Movement: quartz.
Functions: hours, minutes, seconds; date at 3.
Case: fine-brushed steel with polished edges; Ø 32mm, thickness: 9.55mm; unidirectional turning bezel with polished steel base set with 42 Top Wesselton diamonds: 35 diamonds with Ø 1.5mm, seven diamonds with Ø 1.4mm (total 0.567 carat); polished screw-in crown; scratch-resistant sapphire crystal; screw-in caseback with stamped diver decoration; water resistant to 300 meters.
Dial: white mother-of-pearl; hand-applied curved numeral at 12; 10 Top Wesselton diamonds with Ø 1.3mm (total 0.098 carat); polished finished hands with luminescent treatment; polished and protruded TAG Heuer logo.
Bracelet: five-row alternate fine-brushed and polished steel bracelet; solid steel folding clasp with safety pushbuttons.

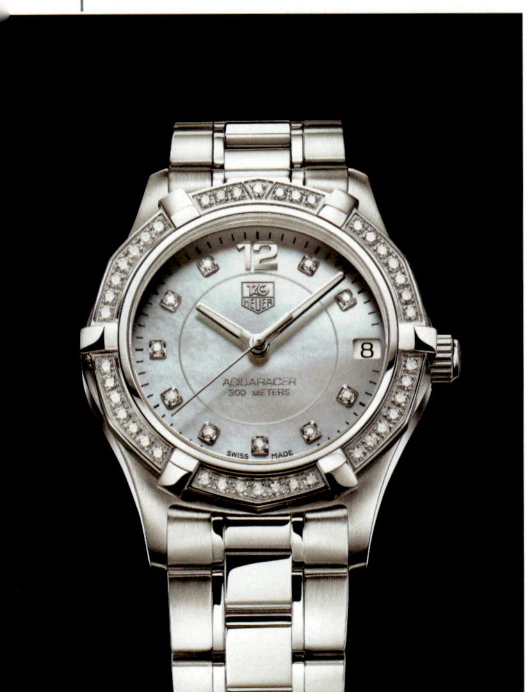

AQUARACER 500M AUTOMATIC CHRONOGRAPH CALIBRE 16 REF. CAJ2110.FT6023

Movement: automatic-winding TAG Heuer Calibre 16.
Functions: hours, minutes, seconds; date at 3 with a magnifying lens; chronograph with three counters: minutes at 12, hours at 6, running seconds at 9.
Case: polished and fine-brushed steel case; Ø 44mm, thickness: 16mm; unidirectional turning bezel in fine-brushed steel with polished studs and soft touch black coating; fine-brushed stainless steel numerals on the bezel and luminescent dot at 12; scratch-resistant sapphire crystal with antireflective treatment; polished screw-in crown; screw-in caseback with a special diver decoration; water resistant to 500 meters.
Dial: black dial with vertical streak effect; hand-applied indexes with polished facets; polished finished hands; seconds hand with a touch of orange at the tip; luminescent treatment on hands and indexes; hand-applied TAG Heuer logo.
Strap: black rubber; solid steel clasp with safety pushbuttons; solid end piece.

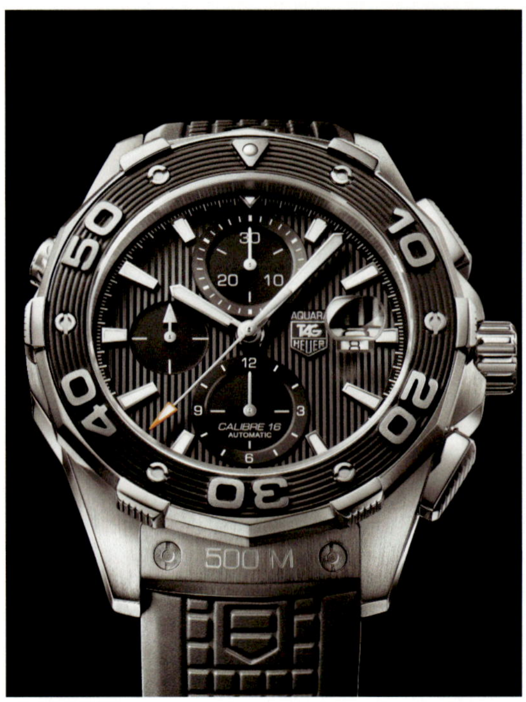

GRAND CARRERA CALIBRE 17 RS2 CHRONOGRAPH TI2 — REF. CAV518B.FC6237

Movement: automatic-winding TAG Heuer Calibre 17 RS; COSC-certified; two Rotating Systems (RS).
Functions: hours, minutes; small seconds at 3; date at 6; chronograph; minute counter at 9.
Case: sandblasted black grade-2 titanium; Ø 43mm, thickness: 14.83mm; curved horns; sandblasted black grade-2 titanium bezel with tachometric scale; oversizedblack grade-2 titanium screw-in solid pushbuttons; oversizedblack grade-2 titanium screw-in crown; curved sapphire crystal with double-sided antireflective treatment; black grade-2 titanium caseback sealed with six screws; smoked double sapphire crystal caseback; water resistant to 100 meters.
Dial: black; opaline central area; external spiral effect area; two rotating systems with black-gold coating, decorated with Côtes de Genève and diamond-polished facets; hand-applied curved faceted indexes with double finishing and black-gold coating; hand-applied TAG Heuer logo with black-gold coating; polished hands with polished facets and black-gold coating; luminescent treatment on hour and minute hands; hand-applied date window with black-gold coating.
Strap: high-tech soft-touch black alligator; red stitching and lining; solid titanium folding clasp with safety pushbuttons; applied TAG Heuer logo.

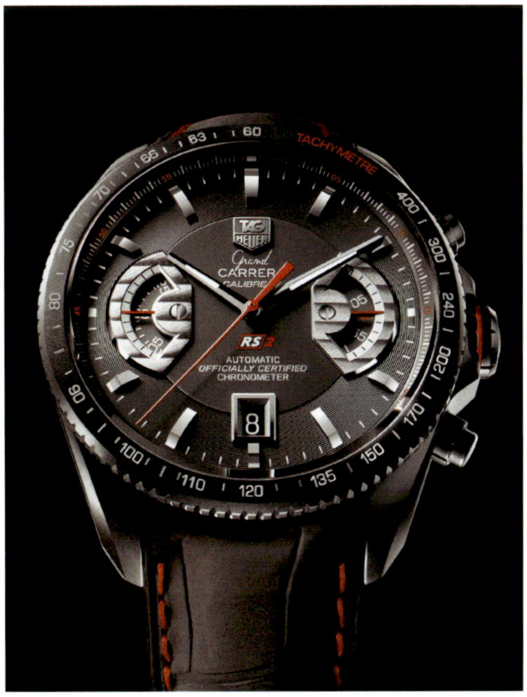

GRAND CARRERA CALIBRE 36 RS CALIPER CHRONOGRAPH — REF. CAV5115.BA0902

Movement: automatic-winding TAG Heuer Calibre 36 RS; COSC-certified; two Rotating Systems (RS).
Functions: hours, minutes, small linear seconds at 9; date at 4:30; chronograph: minutes at 3, hours at 6.
Case: fine-brushed and polished stainless steel; Ø 43mm, thickness: 15.5mm; fine-brushed pushbuttons with polished facets; fine-brushed and polished bezel with tachometric scale; oversized screw-in crown with black line; oversized crown with red line at 10 allowing use of the caliper rotating scale; curved sapphire crystal with double-sided antireflective treatment; double sapphire crystal caseback; caseback sealed by six screws; water resistant to 100 meters.
Dial: black; two rotating systems decorated with Côtes de Genève and diamond-polished facets; hand-applied curved faceted indexes with double finishing; hand-applied TAG Heuer logo; polished hands with polished facets; luminescent treatment on hour and minute hands; caliper rotating scale magnifying the reading of 1/10th of a second driven by the crown at 10.
Strap: fine-brushed and polished steel bracelet; folding buckle with safety pushbuttons.
Also available: black rubber strap with steel end piece.

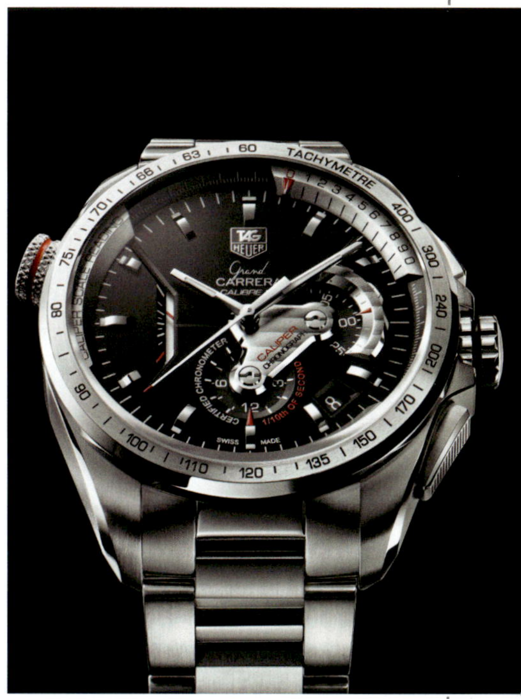

CARRERA CALIBRE 6 HERITAGE — REF. WAS2112.FC6181

Movement: automatic-winding TAG Heuer Calibre 6 – Automatic Watch.
Functions: hours, minutes; small seconds and date at 6.
Case: polished stainless steel; Ø 39mm, thickness: 12.25mm; polished steel fixed bezel; polished crown with TAG Heuer logo on the face; scratch-resistant curved sapphire crystal with double antireflective treatment, scratch-resistant sapphire caseback; water resistant to 100 meters.
Dial: silver with flinqué effect; embossed small seconds counter with azurage at 6; protruded polished rose-gold-colored Arabic numerals; polished solid 18K 5N rose gold hour and minute hands; polished blue running seconds hand; protruded polished rose-gold-colored TAG Heuer logo; "CARRERA Calibre 6" lettering on the dial.
Strap: brown alligator; solid steel folding clasp with safety pushbuttons.

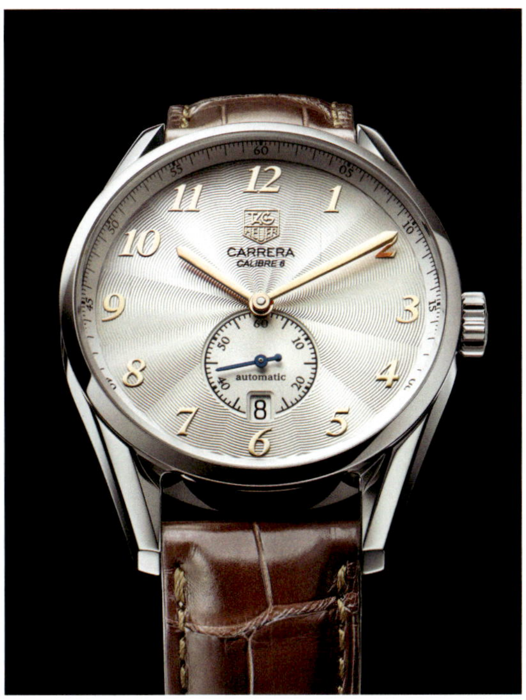

CARRERA CALIBRE 16 HERITAGE CHRONOGRAPH — REF. CAS2110.BA0730

Movement: automatic-winding TAG Heuer Calibre 16 – Automatic Chronograph.
Functions: hours, minutes; small seconds at 9; date at 6; chronograph: minute counter at 12, hour counter at 6.
Case: polished steel; Ø 41mm, thickness: 15.95mm; polished steel fixed bezel; polished steel crown with TAG HEUER logo on the face; polished pushbuttons; scratch-resistant curved sapphire crystal with double-sided antireflective treatment; scratch-resistant sapphire caseback; water resistant to 100 meters.
Dial: silver with flinqué effect; embossed chronograph counters with azurage at 12 and 6; protruded polished blue Arabic numerals; polished silver watch and chronograph hands; protruded polished blue TAG Heuer logo; "CARRERA automatic" lettering on the dial.
Strap: five-row alternate fine-brushed and polished steel bracelet; solid steel folding clasp with safety pushbuttons.
Also available: blue alligator strap with solid steel folding clasp with safety pushbuttons.

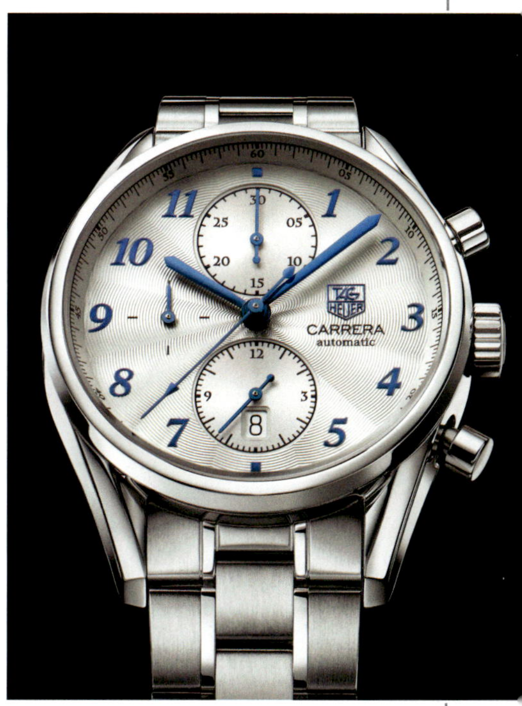

CARRERA CALIBRE 16 RACING CHRONOGRAPH REF. CV2014.FT6014

Movement: automatic-winding TAG Heuer Calibre 16 – Automatic Chronograph.
Functions: hours, minutes, seconds; date at 3; chronograph with three counters: minute counter at 12, hour counter at 6 with red hand, small seconds at 9.
Case: polished steel; Ø 41mm, thickness: 15.85mm; black tachometric scale on a fixed aluminum bezel; scratch-resistant sapphire crystal; scratch-resistant sapphire crystal caseback; water resistant to 100 meters.

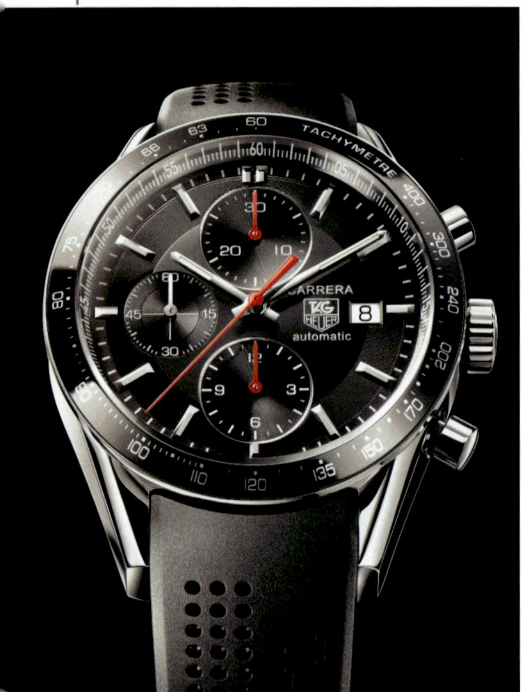

Dial: black; sunray-effect center; spiral-effect outer band; hand-applied faceted indexes; polished finished hour and minute hands with luminescent treatment; red central chronograph hand; monochrome TAG Heuer logo.
Strap: thick black perforated rubber; embossed TAG Heuer and polished steel folding clasp with safety pushbuttons.
Also available: five-row alternate fine-brushed and polished steel bracelet and solid steel folding clasp with safety pushbuttons.

CARRERA CALIBRE 16 DAY-DATE CHRONOGRAPH REF. CV2A10.BA0796

Movement: automatic-winding TAG Heuer Calibre 16 Day-Date.
Functions: hours, minutes, seconds; day-date at 3; chronograph with three counters: minute counter at 12, hour counter at 6, small seconds at 9.
Case: solid steel with polished finishing; Ø 43mm, thickness: 16.3mm; polished steel fixed bezel with tachometric scale; polished oversized crown and pushbuttons; scratch-resistant domed sapphire crystal with double-sided antireflective treatment; scratch-resistant sapphire crystal caseback; water resistant to 100 meters.

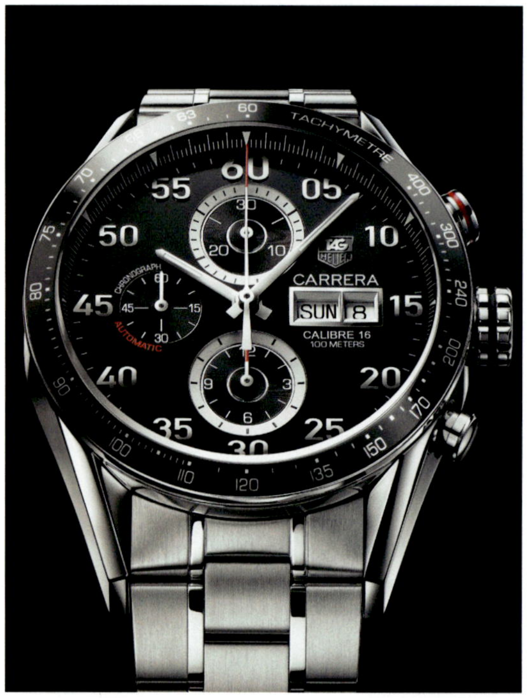

Dial: black; hand-applied numerals; polished finished hour and minute hands with luminescent treatment; polished finished seconds hand and hour and minute counters' hands with red at the tip; silver-ringed hour and minute counters; monochrome TAG Heuer logo.
Strap: five-row alternate fine-brushed and polished steel bracelet; solid steel folding clasp with safety pushbuttons.
Also available: black and brown dial; black or brown alligator strap with polished steel folding clasp with safety pushbuttons.

HEUER CARRERA MIKROGRAPH 1/100TH SECOND CHRONOGRAPH REF. CAR5040.FC8177

Movement: automatic-winding TAG Heuer Mikrograph 1/100th second; manufacture movement; chronograph (360,000 vph), COSC-certified.
Functions: hours, minutes, small seconds at 9; date at 6; chronograph: minutes counter at 3, seconds counter at 6; 1/100th of a second chronograph; chronograph power reserve percentage indicator at 12.
Case: polished solid 18K 5N rose gold; Ø 43mm, thickness: 16.5mm; curved sapphire crystal with double-sided antireflective treatment; solid 18K 5N rose-gold pushbuttons; solid 18K 5N rose-gold crown; solid 18K 5N rose-gold and sapphire caseback to allow direct view of the movement and the specific "limited edition XX/150" engraved oscillating weight; water resistant to 100 meters.

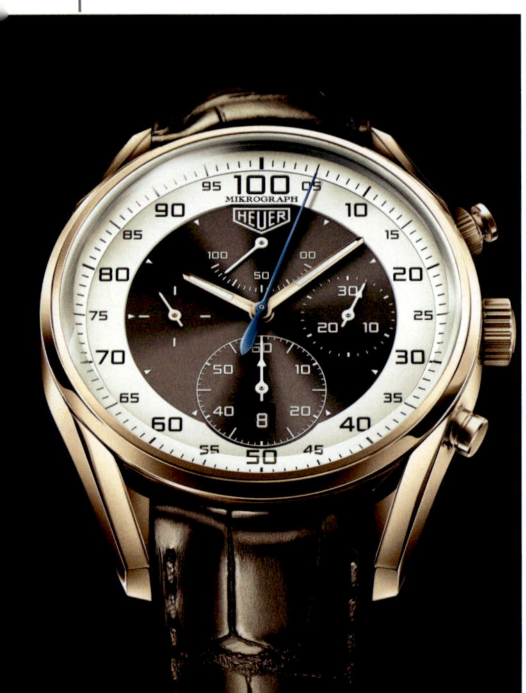

Dial: brown and cream; black Arabic numerals; solid 18K 5N rose-gold hour and minute hands with luminescent treatment; blue central 1/100th of a second chronograph hand; cream chronograph hands and power reserve hand at 12. solid 18K 5N rose-gold small seconds hand, monochrome vintage Heuer logo.
Bracelet: hand-sewn brown alligator; solid 18K 5N rose-gold pin buckle.

CARRERA CALIBRE 1887 CHRONOGRAPH REF. CAR2110.BA0720

Movement: automatic-winding TAG Heuer Calibre 1887; manufacture movement; chronograph.
Functions: hours, minutes; small seconds at 9; date at 6; chronograph: minute counter at 12, hour counter at 6.
Case: polished stainless steel; polished bezel; Ø 41mm, thickness: 15.55mm; polished steel crown and pushbuttons; curved scratch-resistant sapphire crystal with double-sided antireflective treatment; scratch-resistant sapphire caseback; water resistant to 100 meters.

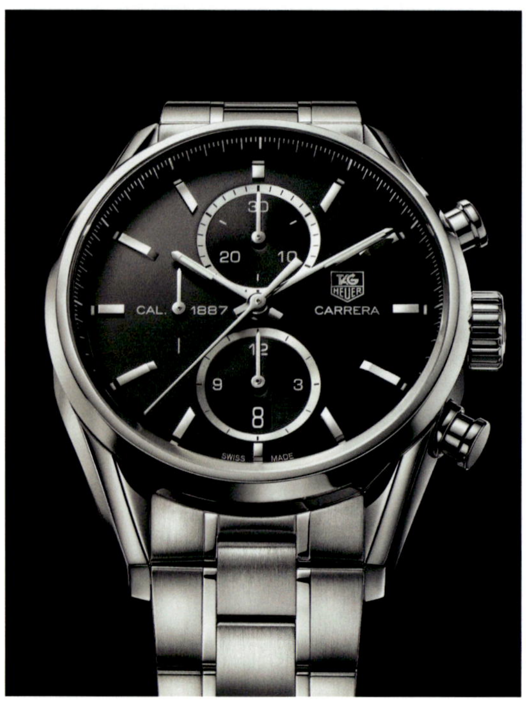

Dial: black; hand-applied faceted indexes; polished silver hands; hour and minute hands with luminescent treatment; monochrome TAG Heuer logo; tachometric scale on the flange; "CARRERA – CAL. 1887 – SWISS MADE" lettering on the dial.
Bracelet: five-row alternate fine-brushed and polished steel bracelet; solid steel folding clasp with safety pushbuttons.
Also available: black or brown alligator strap.

TAG HEUER FORMULA 1 LADY STEEL & CERAMIC AND DIAMONDS REF. WAH1213.BA0861

Movement: quartz.
Functions: hours, minutes, seconds; date at 3.
Case: polished stainless steel; Ø 37mm, thickness: 9.85mm; polished fixed ceramic and steel bezel with 60 Wesselton diamonds with Ø 1.1mm (0.35 carat); polished stainless steel bumpers protecting the crown at 3; polished screw-in crown; sapphire crystal; circular fine-brushed screw-in caseback; water resistant to 200 meters.
Dial: white; hand-applied indexes and Arabic numeral at 12; luminescent treatment on faceted minute and hour hands and above indexes; protruded monochrome TAG Heuer logo.
Bracelet: five-row alternate steel and ceramic (color according to dial); new solid steel butterfly folding clasp with safety pushbuttons.
Also available: black dial and ceramic; color according to dial.

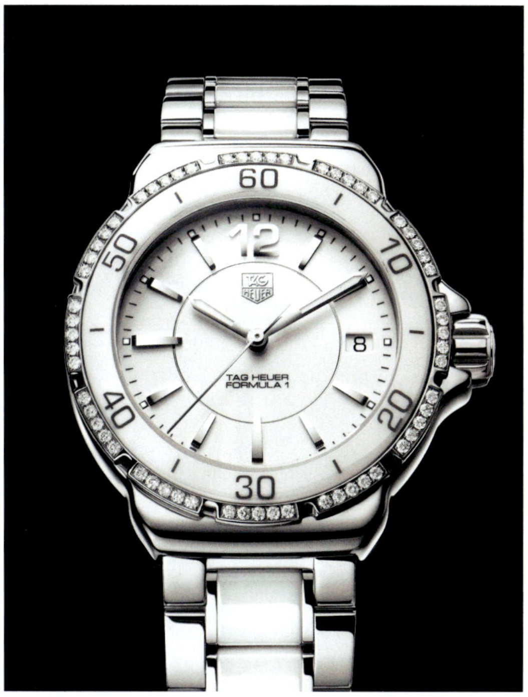

TAG HEUER FORMULA 1 LADY STEEL & CERAMIC REF. WAH1210.BA0859

Movement: quartz.
Functions: hours, minutes, seconds; date at 3.
Case: polished stainless steel; Ø 37mm, thickness: 9.85mm; polished fixed stainless steel and ceramic bezel; polished stainless steel bumpers protecting the crown at 3; polished screw-in crown; sapphire crystal; polished screw-in caseback; water resistant to 200 meters.
Dial: black; hand-applied indexes and Arabic numeral at 12; luminescent treatment on faceted minute and hour hands and above indexes; protruded monochrome TAG Heuer logo.
Bracelet: five-row alternate steel and ceramic (color according to dial); solid steel butterfly folding clasp with safety pushbuttons.
Also available: white dial and ceramic; color according to dial.

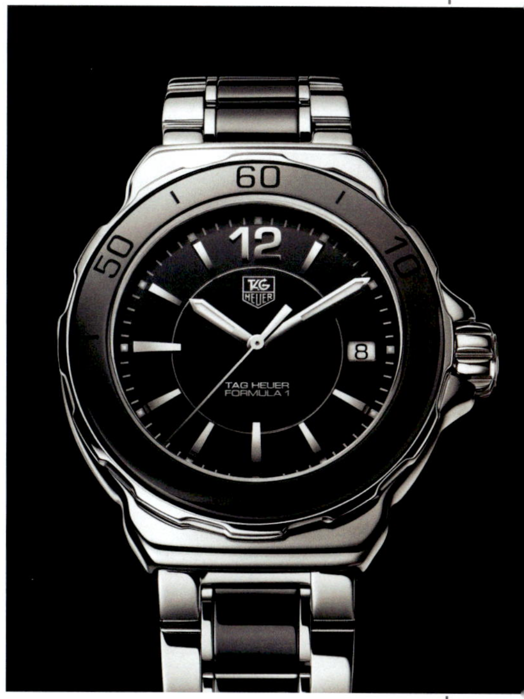

TAG HEUER FORMULA 1 LADY STEEL & CERAMIC CHRONOGRAPH DDDB REF. CAH1213.BA0863

Movement: quartz; chronograph.
Functions: hours, minutes, seconds; date at 4:30; chronograph: central seconds, minute counter at 9.
Case: polished stainless steel; Ø 41mm, thickness: 11.6mm; polished fixed stainless steel and ceramic bezel with 60 diamonds with Ø 1.2mm (0.44 carat) ; polished screw-in crown; sapphire crystal; polished screw-in caseback, water resistant to 200 meters.
Dial: white diamond; 12 Wesselton diamond indexes with Ø 1.2mm (0.9 carat); silver hands; luminescent treatment on minute and hour hands; protruded monochrome TAG Heuer logo; "TAG Heuer Formula 1" lettering on the dial.
Bracelet: five-row alternate steel and ceramic bracelet; solid steel butterfly folding clasp with safety pushbuttons.
Also available: black dial and ceramic, color according to dial.

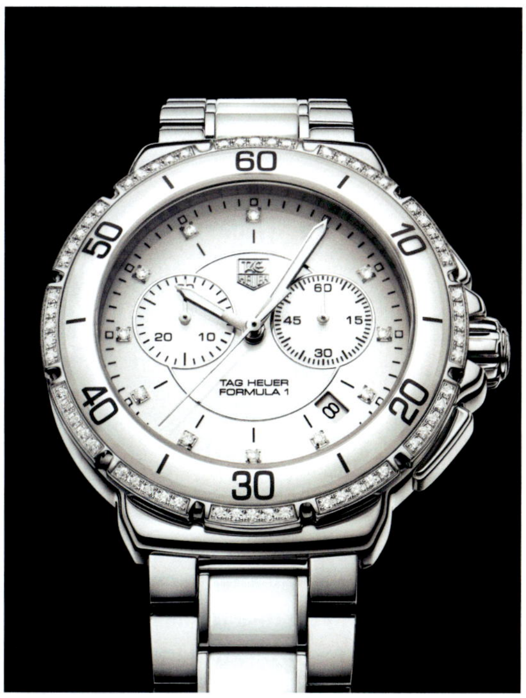

CARRERA LADY DIAMOND DIAL REF. WV1417.BA0793

Movement: quartz.
Functions: hours, minutes, seconds; date at 3.
Case: polished steel; Ø 27mm, thickness: 9.07mm; polished steel fixed bezel; polished crown; scratch-resistant sapphire crystal; polished steel caseback; water resistant to 50 meters.
Dial: pink mother-of-pearl; diamond dial with spiral effect in outer area; 13 Top Wesselton diamonds: 12 diamonds with Ø 1.2mm, one diamond with Ø 1.1mm (total 0.0981 carat); polished finished hands with luminescent treatment; polished and protruded TAG Heuer logo.
Bracelet: five-row alternate fine-brushed and polished steel bracelet; solid steel folding clasp with safety pushbuttons.
Also available: white mother-of-pearl diamond dial; black diamond dial.

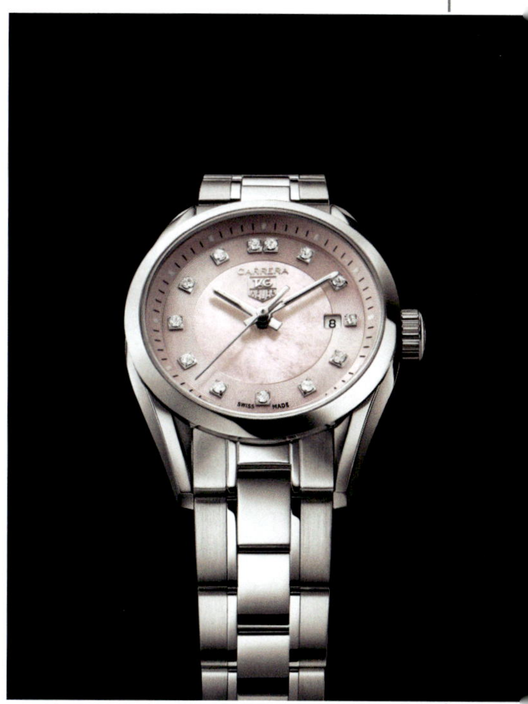

ULYSSE NARDIN

SINCE 1846 LE LOCLE - SUISSE

DEVIL IN THE DETAILS

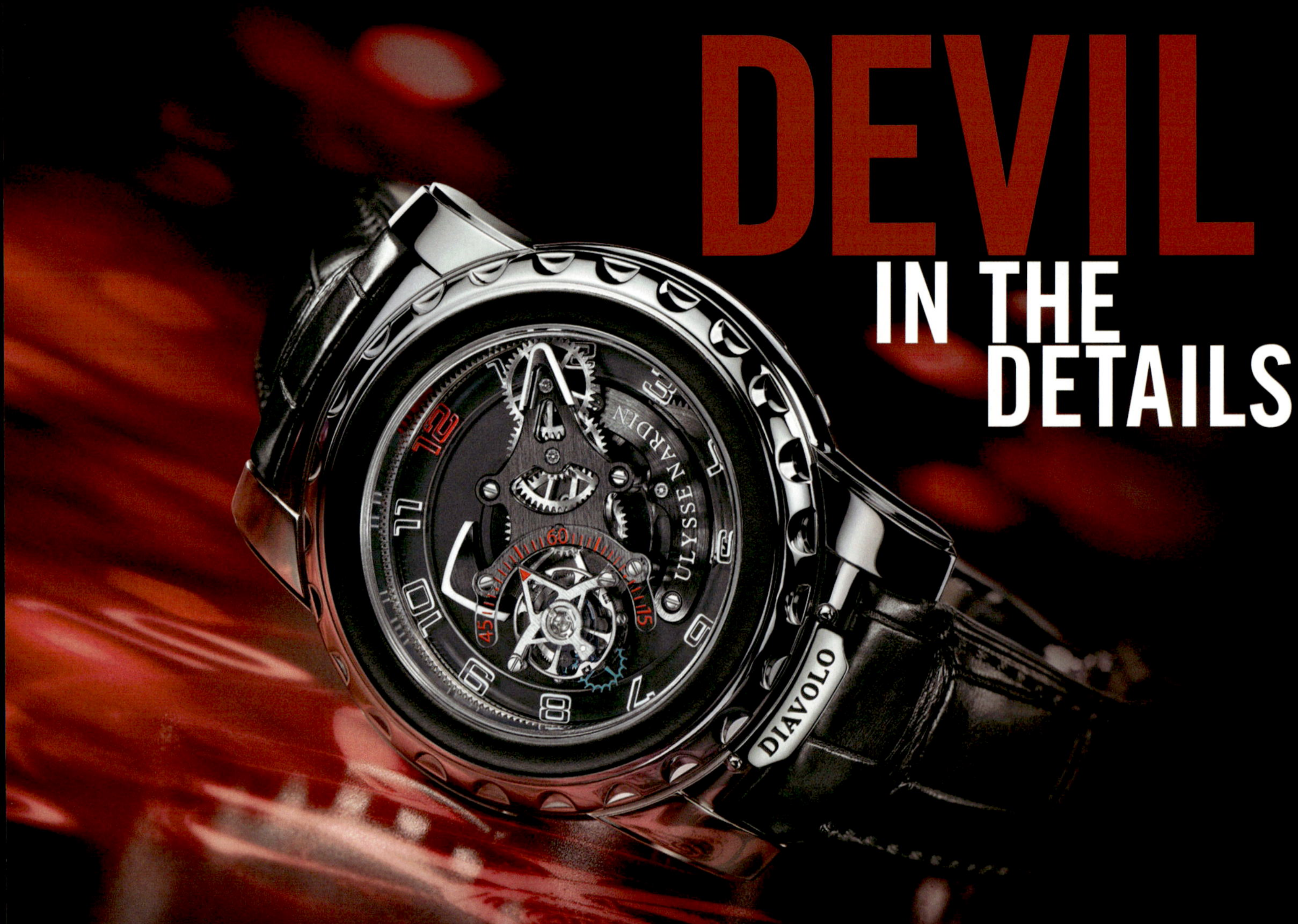

Ulysse Nardin cloaks the Freak Diavolo in darkness, conjuring an air of mystery around its latest incarnation of the revolutionary Freak. Rather than obscure the watch's technical achievements, the dark complexion throws them into bold relief.

The most recognizable advancement since the original Freak's 2001 debut is the addition of a flying tourbillon that doubles as seconds indicator—both firsts for the Freak. Perched atop the tourbillon's cage, a red arrow points to the nearby semicircle scale as it completes a 360-degree rotation once a minute.

This nontraditional rendering of the seconds is entirely in keeping with the unconventional manner in which the Freak conveys time. In lieu of hands or a dial, the watch's carousel tourbillon movement pulls double duty. Not only does it drive the watch's timekeeping function, but it also serves as its display. To read the minutes, an arrow is fixed to the end of the escapement bridge, which rotates around the center of the dial once an hour. Simultaneously, a pointer affixed to the barrel indicates the hours as the mainspring steadily unwinds.

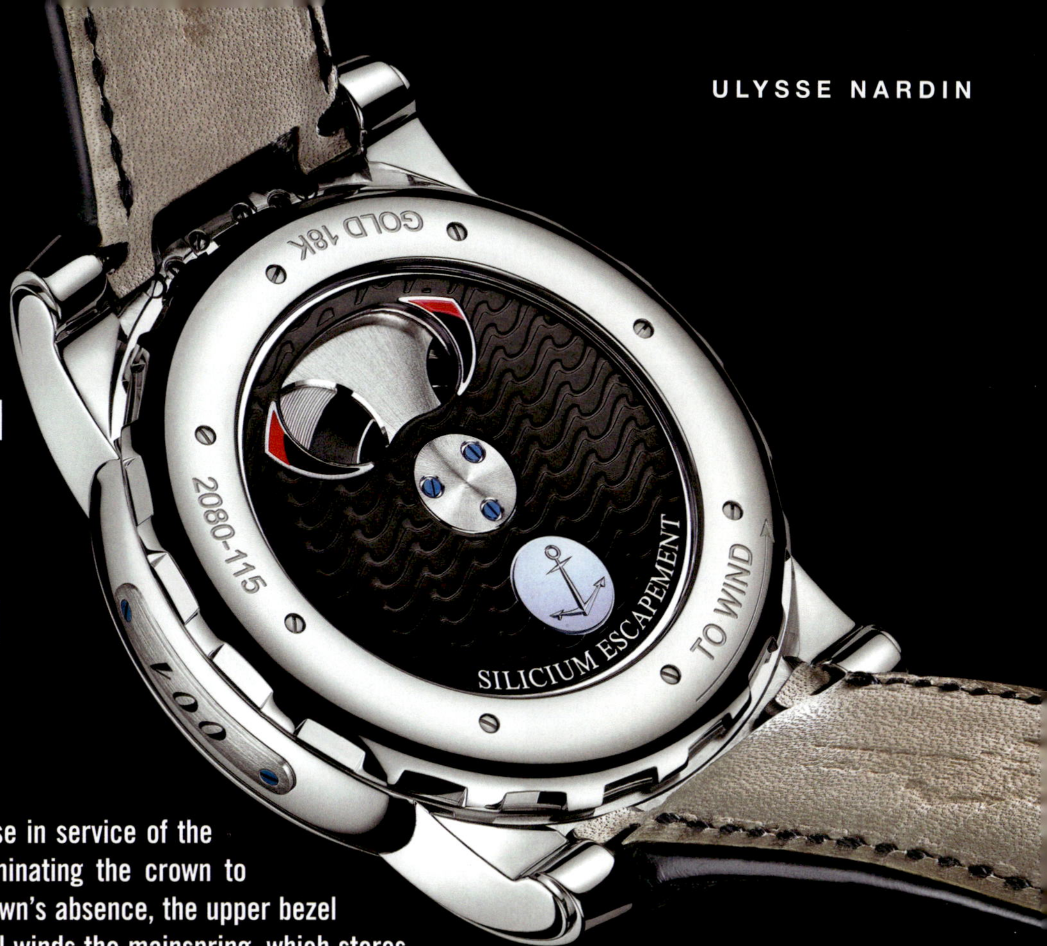

The Freak Diavolo, the newest member of Jlysse Nardin's influential Freak collection, is the first to integrate a silicium hairspring and a flying tourbillon.

Ulysse Nardin uses its technical expertise in service of the Freak's minimalist design once again, eliminating the crown to preserve the case's sleek profile. In the crown's absence, the upper bezel s used to set the time while the lower bezel winds the mainspring, which stores nore than eight days of reserve power. As if to illustrate that the devil is truly in he details, the Diavolo's rotating caseback is decorated with dark waves ɔunctuated by two fiendish-looking red horns that guard the winding aperture.

The Freak Diavolo arrives nearly a decade after Ulysse Nardin unveiled the ɔriginal Freak, which was the first timepiece ever to integrate escape wheels nade from silicium (aka silicon).

Since the Freak's debut, Ulysse Nardin's ongoing commitment to emerging echnologies has fueled a series of advancements that spurred the watch's evolution, including: Freak 28,800 v/h (2004), Freak Diamond Heart (2005), Freak DIAMonSIL (2007), and Freak Blue Phantom (2008).

The Diavolo refines what has come before to create something new, adding a ilicium hairspring whose design is being considered for a patent. Ulysse Nardin echnical Director Pierre Gygax has played an instrumental role in the adoption of silicium for watchmaking purposes.

Because silicium is incredibly strong with a low mass, it provides substan-ial advantages over traditional metal parts. It is ideal, he says, for hairspring production. "It has the necessary elasticity for a hairspring and has the ability to unction well without lubrication. The latter is especially important to the person vearing the watch because it means less regular maintenance."

Through the years, watchmaking has seen its share of innovations come and go. Gygax believes the advanced production techniques pioneered in the Freak line—from silicium and photolithography to LIGA and diamond coating on ilicium parts—will stand the test of time.

"The trend of offering new materials as a kind of gimmick is fading," he says. "An innovation is only important if it provides a lasting value to what you're trying o achieve. The gimmicks quickly fall away and the important things remain."

Indeed, that sentiment of ingenuity with purpose has been one of the brand's guiding principles since Rolf Schnyder acquired Ulysse Nardin in 1983.

FACING PAGE

The Freak Diavolo's carousel tourbillon movement indicates the minutes while the arrow found on the watch's barrel indicates the hours as the mainspring unwinds. It is the first Freak to feature a small seconds display, which rotates above the flying tourbillon. Instead of a crown, the Diavolo's upper bezel is used to set the time. An aperture on the caseback is used to wind the mainspring, which offers more than eight days of reserve power.

ABOVE

"Silicium Escapement" is emblazoned on the Diavolo's caseback, offering a hint at the groundbreaking innovation contained within the white-gold case.

CAPRICE REF. 136-91FC/309

Movement: UN-13.
Functions: hours, minutes; date.
Case: 18K rose gold; 34x35.4mm; diamond-set case and bezel; cabochon-set crown; exhibition caseback.
Dial: gray.
Strap: galuchat.
Also available: on a bracelet.

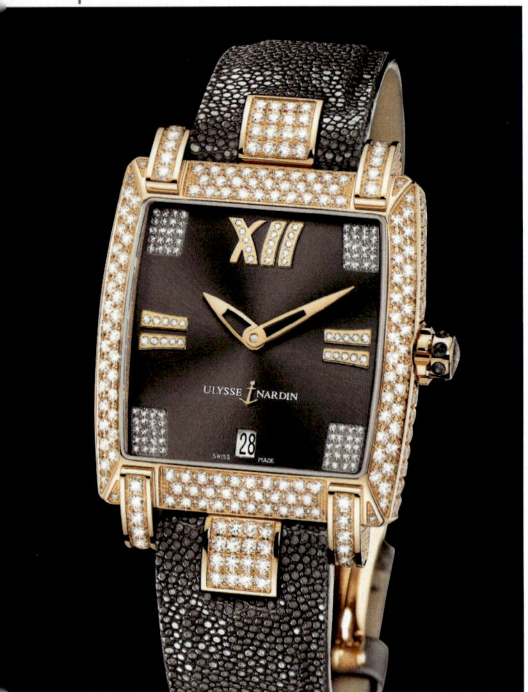

CAPRICE TIGER REF. 130-91FC-8C/TIGER

Movement: UN-13.
Functions: hours, minutes.
Case: 18K white gold; 34x35.4mm; diamond-set case and bezel; cabochon-set crown; exhibition caseback.
Dial: diamond tiger.
Bracelet: 18K white gold.
Also available: satin strap.

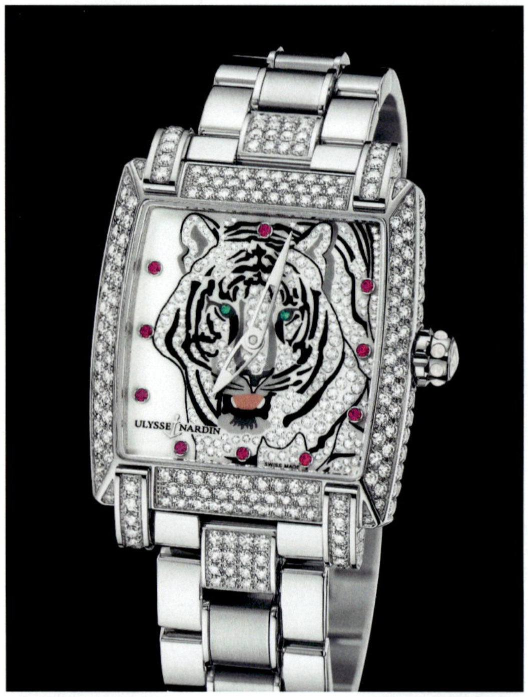

EXECUTIVE DUAL TIME REF. 243-00-3/421

Movement: UN-24; manual-winding; 42-hour power reserve; 34 jewels.
Functions: hours, minutes; small seconds; second time zone on main dial with patented quickset; permanent home time in window at 9; patented large date.
Case: stainless steel; Ø 43mm; ceramic bezel and pushers; screw-down crown; exhibition caseback; water resistant to 10atm.
Strap: black rubber with folding buckle.
Also available: alligator strap.

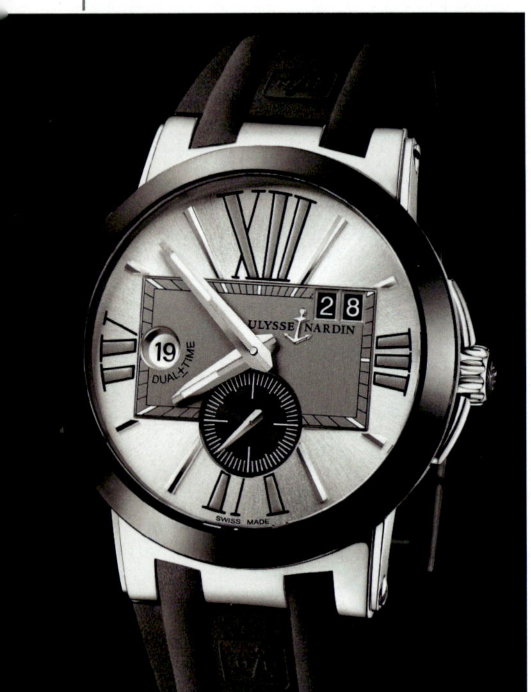

EXECUTIVE DUAL TIME REF. 246-00-421

Movement: UN-24; manual-winding; 42-hour power reserve; 34 jewels; COSC-certified.
Functions: hours, minutes; small seconds; second time zone on main dial with patented quickset; permanent home time in window at 9; patented big date display.
Case: 18K rose gold; Ø 43mm; ceramic bezel and pushers; screw-down crown; exhibition caseback; water resistant to 10atm.
Strap: alligator leather with folding buckle.
Also available: rubber strap.

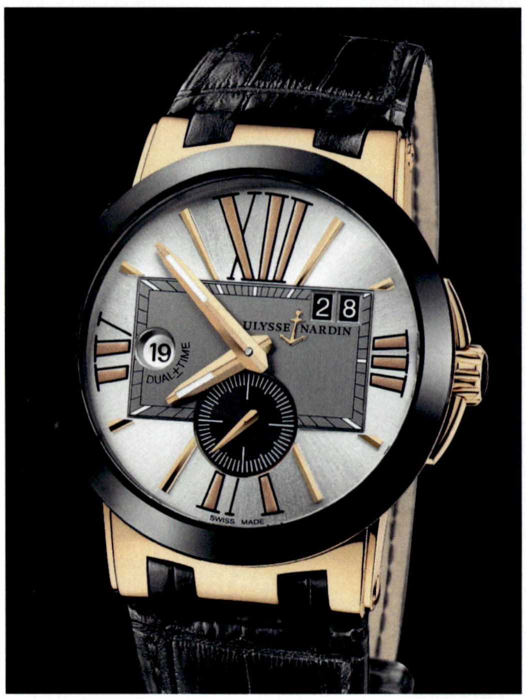

EXECUTIVE LADY REF. 243-10/30-07

Movement: UN-24.
Functions: hours, minutes; small seconds; second time zone on main dial with patented quickset; permanent home time in window at 9.
Case: stainless steel; Ø 40mm; ceramic bezel and pushers; exhibition caseback.
Strap: white rubber.
Also available: white alligator strap.

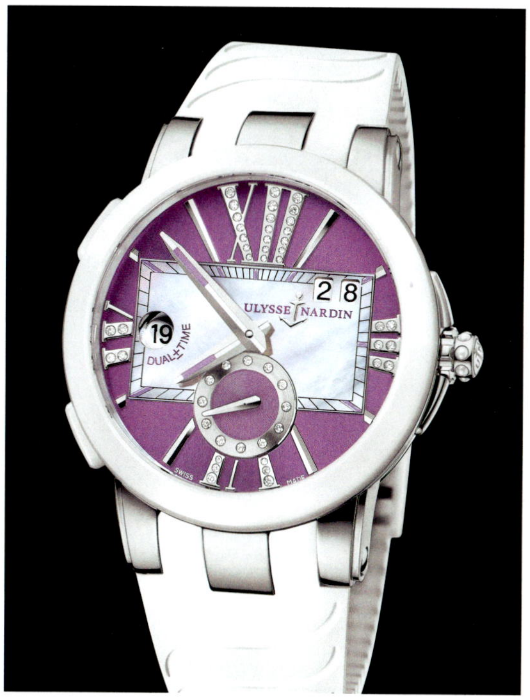

EXECUTIVE LADY REF. 246-10-3/391

Movement: UN-24.
Functions: second time zone on main dial with patented quickset; permanent home time in window at 9.
Case: 18K rose gold; Ø 40mm; ceramic bezel and pushers; exhibition caseback.
Strap: white alligator.
Also available: white rubber strap.

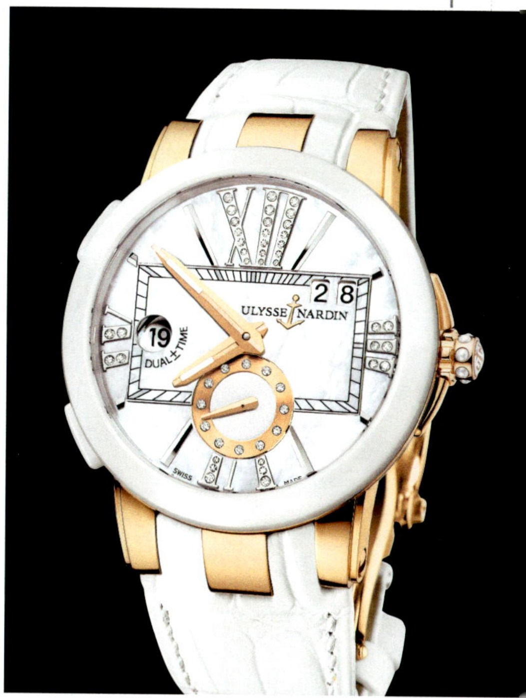

FREAK DIAVOLO REF. 2080-115

Movement: UN-208; eight-day carrousel tourbillon; anchor escapement; flying tourbillon.
Case: 18K white gold; Ø 44.5mm.
Strap: black alligator.

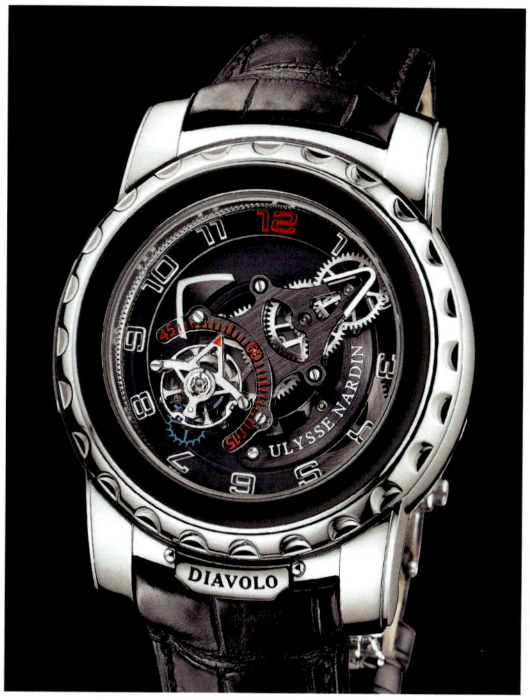

DUAL TIME REF. 243-55/62

Movement: UN-24.
Functions: hours, minutes; second time zone on main dial with patented quickset; permanent home time in window at 9; large date in double window.
Case: stainless steel; Ø 42mm; exhibition caseback.
Strap: black alligator.
Also available: on a bracelet.

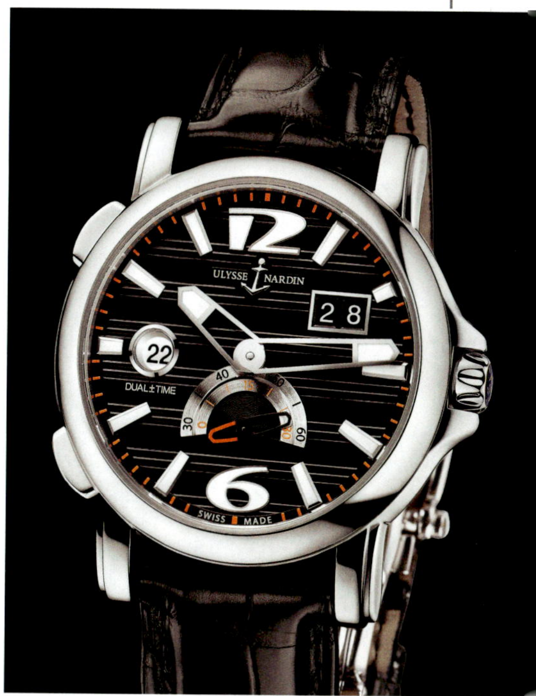

DUAL TIME — REF. 246-55/69

Movement: UN-24.
Functions: hours, minutes; second time zone on main dial with patented quickset; permanent home time in window at 9; large date in double window.
Case: 18K rose gold; Ø 42mm; exhibition caseback.
Strap: black alligator.
Also available: on a bracelet.

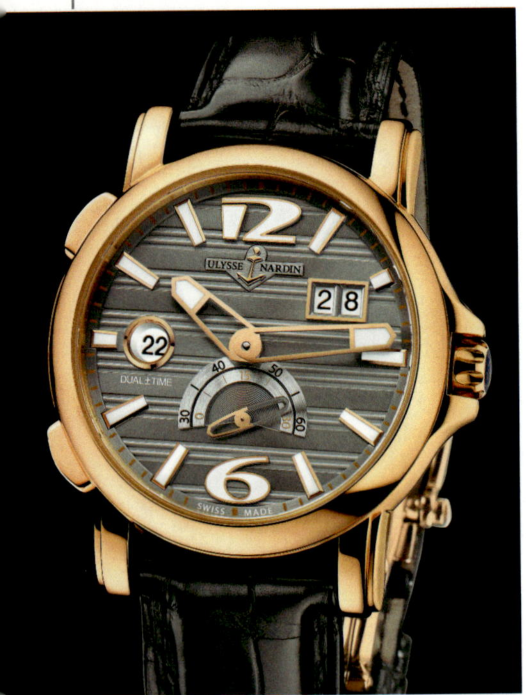

EL TORO — REF. 322-00-3

Movement: UN-32; automatic-winding; 45-hour power reserve; 34 jewels; COSC-certified.
Function: second time zone on main dial with patented quickset; permanent home time indicated by third hand; large date in double window; perpetual calendar.
Case: 18K rose gold; Ø 43mm; ceramic bezel; screw-down crown; antireflective sapphire crystal caseback; water resistant to 10atm.
Dial: perpetual calendar adjustable backwards and forwards from a single crown.
Strap: rubber with ceramic deployant clasp.
Note: limited edition of 500 pieces.
Also available: platinum; leather strap with folding buckle.

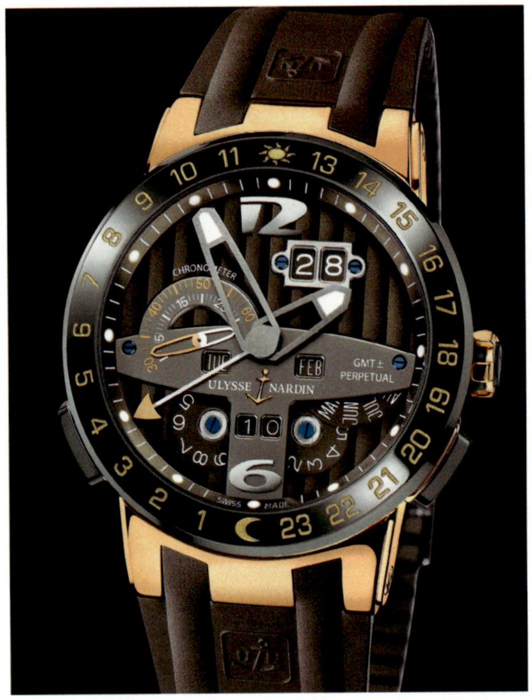

LADY DIVER STARRY NIGHT — REF. 8103-101E-3C/22

Movement: UN-810; automatic-winding; 42-hour power reserve; 21 jewels; 28,800 vph.
Functions: hours, minutes, seconds; date at 6.
Case: stainless steel; Ø 40mm; set with 40 diamonds (0.77 carat); exhibition caseback; water resistant to 10atm.
Dial: black; set with 27 diamonds.
Strap: exclusive rubber.

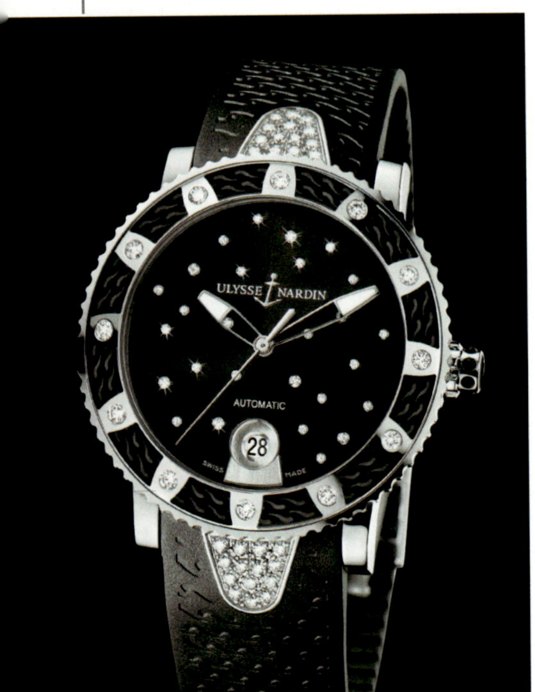

LADY DIVER STARRY NIGHT — REF. 8103-101EC-3C/20

Movement: UN-810; automatic-winding; 42-hour power reserve; 21 jewels; 28,800 vph.
Functions: hours, minutes, seconds; date at 6.
Case: stainless steel; Ø 40mm; set with 40 diamonds (0.77 carat); exhibition caseback; water resistant to 10atm.
Dial: white mother-of-pearl; set with 27 diamonds.
Strap: exclusive rubber.

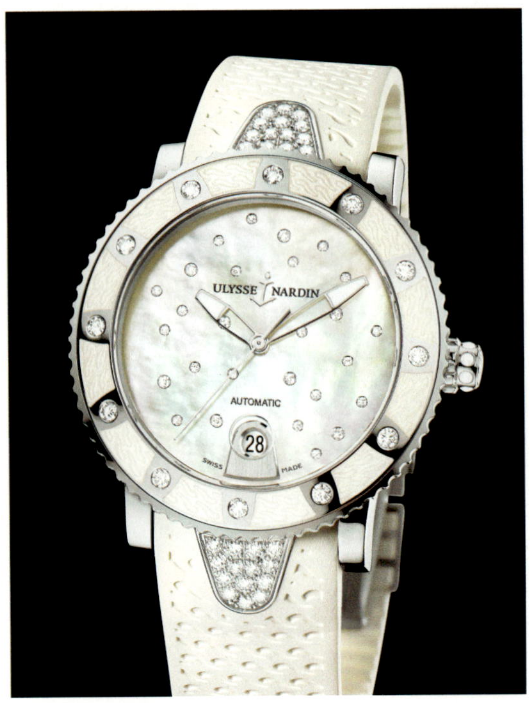

HAMMERHEAD SHARK — REF. 263-91LE-3

Movement: UN-26.
Functions: hours, minutes; date.
Case: titanium; Ø 45mm; stainless steel rotating bezel; titanium caseback.
Note: limited edition of 999 pieces.

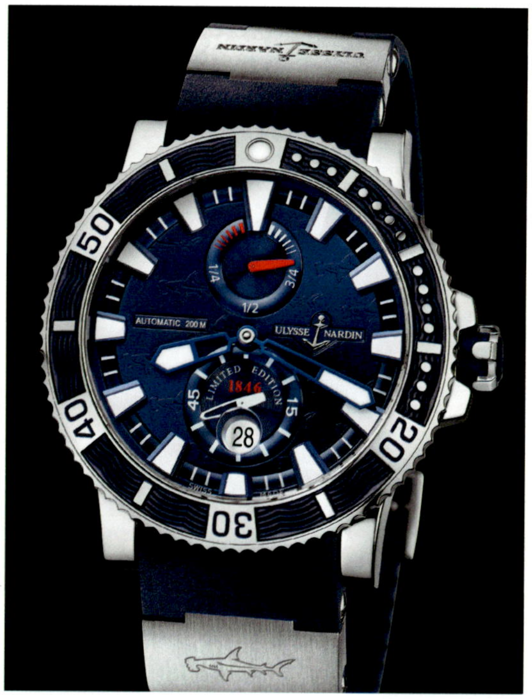

HAMMERHEAD SHARK — REF. 265-91LE-3

Movement: UN-26.
Functions: hours, minutes; date.
Case: titanium; Ø 45mm; 18K rose-gold rotating bezel; titanium caseback.
Note: limited edition of 350 pieces.

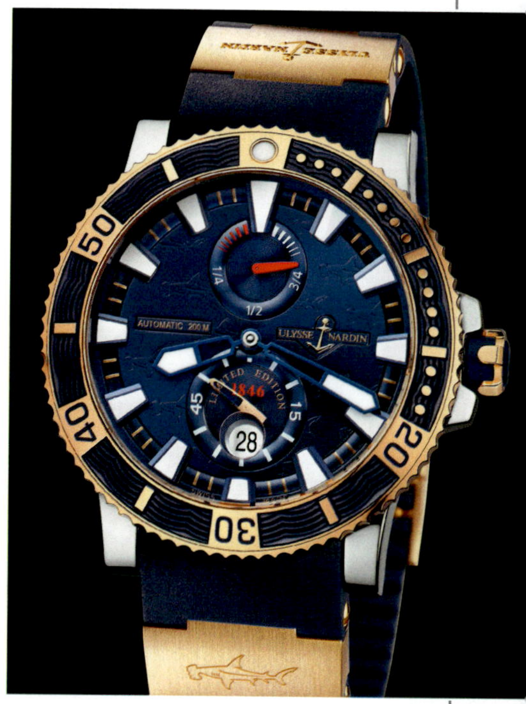

MOONSTRUCK — REF. 1069-113

Movement: UN-106; automatic-winding; 50-hour power reserve.
Functions: hours, minutes; astronomical watch; indication of position of sun and moon in relation to Earth; scientifically accurate moonphase; representation of solar time; indication of tides; instant time zone adjuster with patented quick setting device.
Case: platinum; Ø 46mm; ceramic bezel; screw-down crown; antireflective sapphire crystal caseback; water resistant to 10atm.
Dial: hand-painted mother-of-pearl; hand-painted earth.
Strap: alligator leather with folding buckle.
Note: limited edition of 500 pieces in rose gold and 500 pieces in platinum.

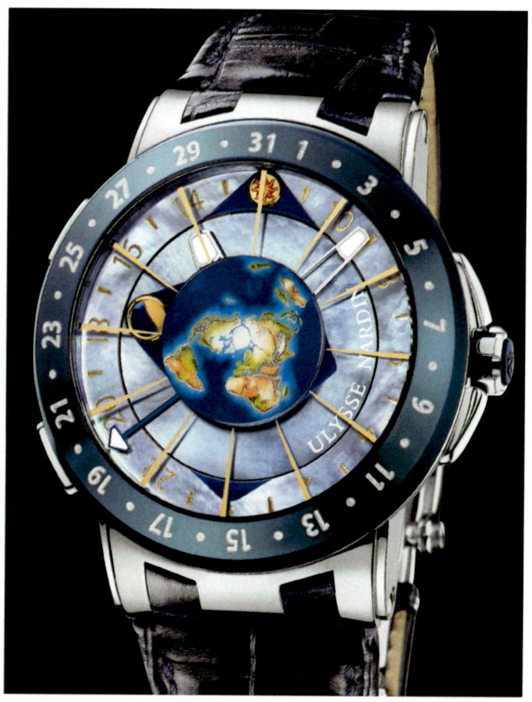

MAXI SKELETON — REF. 3012-200

Movement: UN-301; hand-engraved and chiseled skeleton movement.
Functions: hours, minutes.
Case: 18K rose-gold; Ø 45mm.
Note: limited edition of 50 pieces.
Also available: white gold.

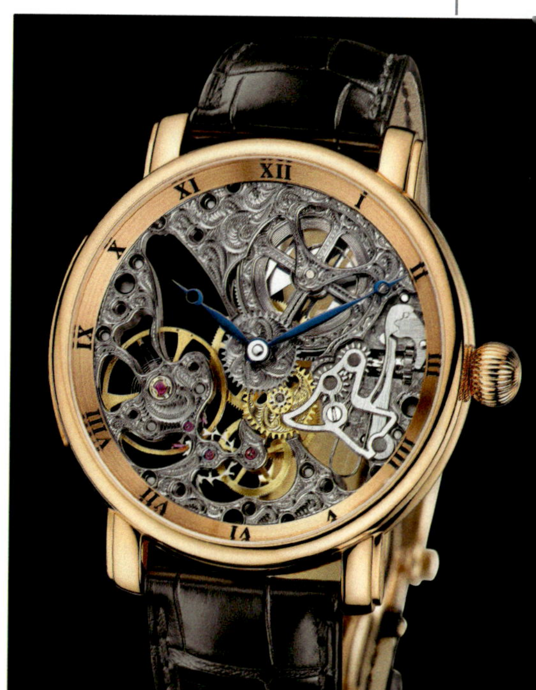

URWERK®

BAUMGARTNER & FREI/GENEVE

ADVANCING THE TIMELINE: LINEAR THINKING

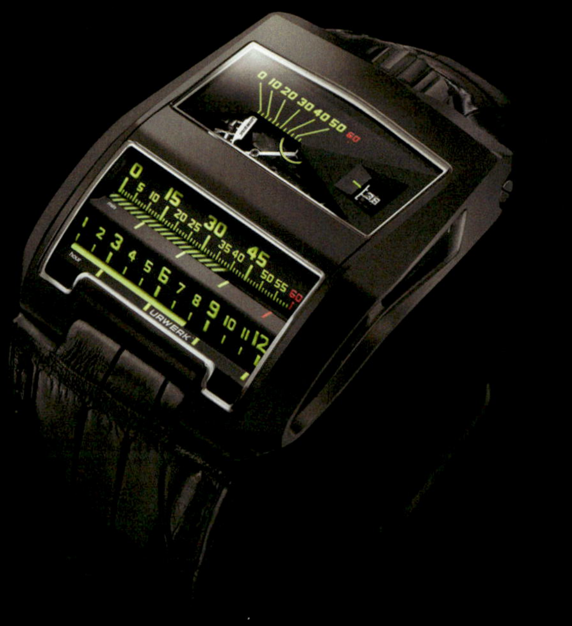

Urwerk's kinetic sculptures express time in an original way that betrays the passion for unconventional engineering and otherworldly design shared by company founders Felix Baumgartner and Martin Frei.

THIS PAGE

Nicknamed The Black Cobra, the UR-CC1 gets its menacing appellation thanks to its white-gold case, which is coated with AlTiN to give it a dark glow.

FACING PAGE

With the UR-CC1, Urwerk overcame a formidable technical challenge to create the first-ever production timepiece to feature linear displays for the hours and minutes.

Among the creative partnership's latest triumphs is the UR-CC1, the first production timepiece to successfully replace the near-ubiquitous 360-degree indication of hours and minutes with linear displays for jumping hours and retrograde minutes.

It is a testament to the true complexity of this mechanism that until Frei and Baumgartner first introduced the UR-CC1 in 2009, no one had unraveled this mechanical riddle and put its solution into production.

True, Gilbert Albert and Louis Cottier did patent a movement with the first linear display in 1959, but the watch—dubbed "The Cobra"—was destined to become part of a museum's collection instead of a collector's. Although the watch served as inspiration for Urwerk's UR-CC1, Baumgartner says it was not the initial spark.

"I'm not a big fan of nostalgia, but I have always loved the linear speedometers found on old cars," he recalls. "My older brother had a 1960s Volvo and it was that which gave us the idea for a horological linear indication."

The genesis of the idea began in 1998, the year after Baumgartner, a third-generation watchmaker and alumni of Schaffhausen's esteemed watchmaking school, formed Urwerk with Frei, who studied painting and sculpture at Lucerne's college of art and design.

The idea remained theoretical until 2006 when Baumgartner and Frei revisited the project's original sketches and began researching what it would take to develop the concept into a watch. Three years later, Urwerk presented its UR-CC1, the "CC" appellation in honor of "Cottier's Cobra." In 2010, the brand unveiled a second model nicknamed the Black Cobra, a reference to the watch's white-gold case, which is treated with AlTiN (aluminum titanium nitride) to produce a dark radiance.

For Frei, the UR-CC1 is a means to explore our perception of time. "Physicists tell us that time can be warped or stretched," he explains. "But I am also intrigued that time can be ordered, even straitjacketed, to flow in a linear direction—a straight line from the past, through the present, to the future. And because this can represent an individual's lifeline, I feel this linear format can be a very human way to look at time."

Three years in the making, UR-CC1's groundbreaking linear displays represent a skillful concentration of mechanical ingenuity and artistic vision aided by the latest production techniques.

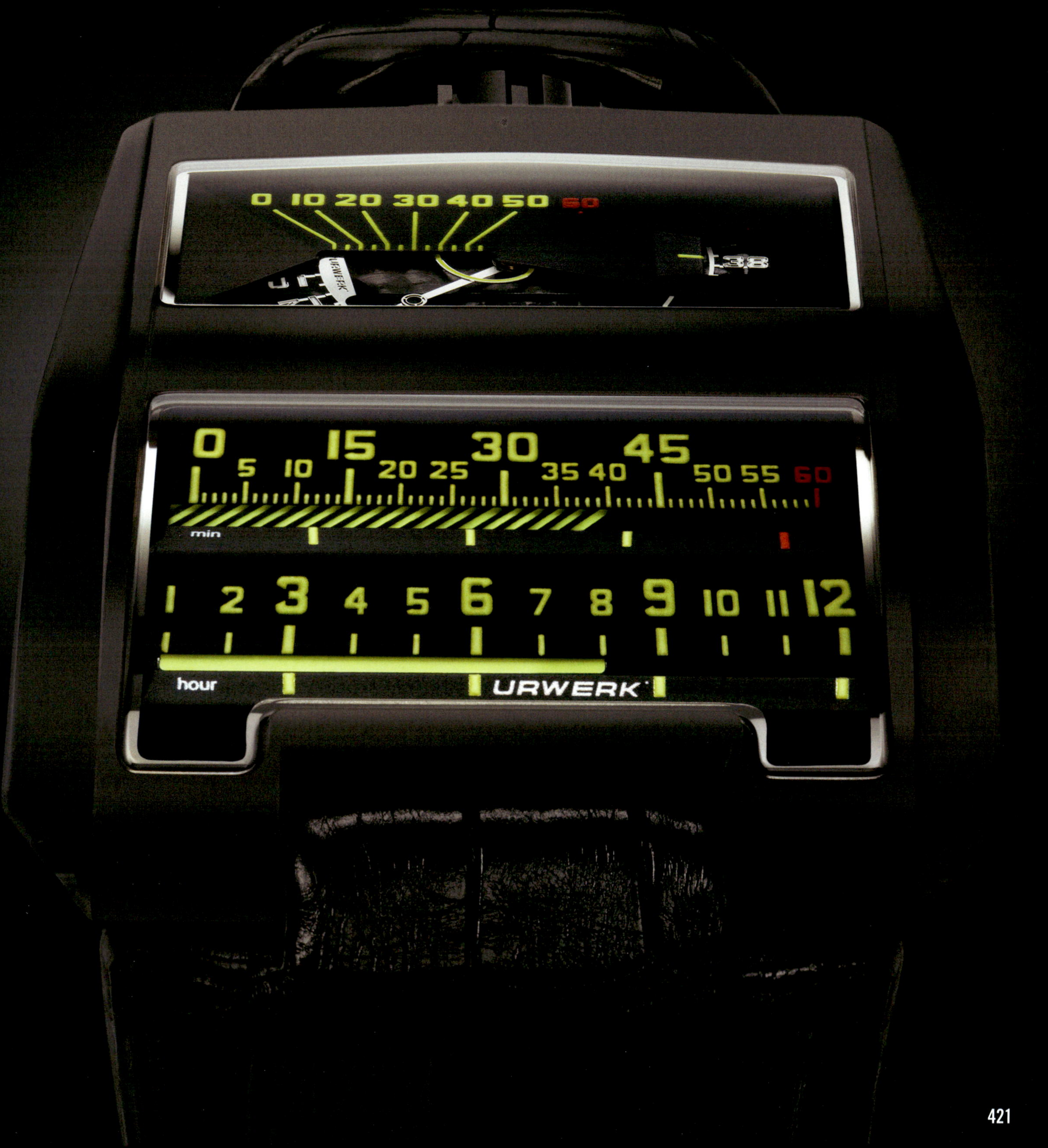

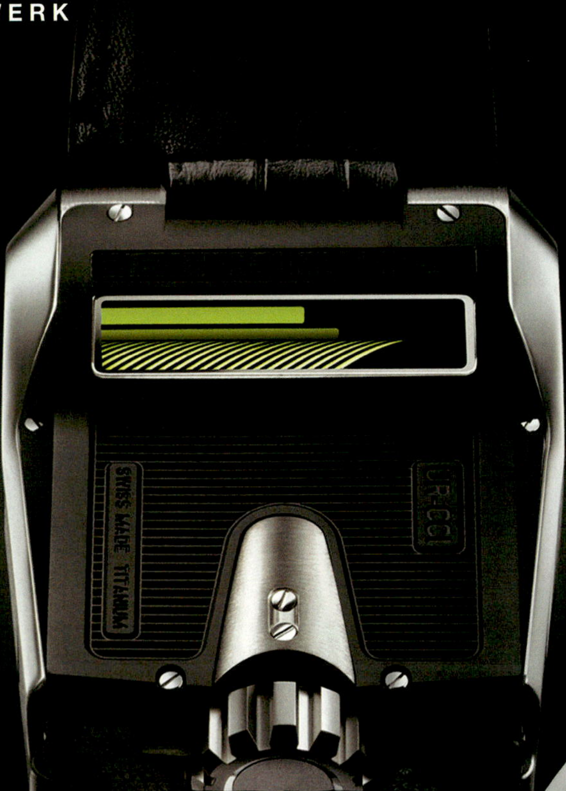

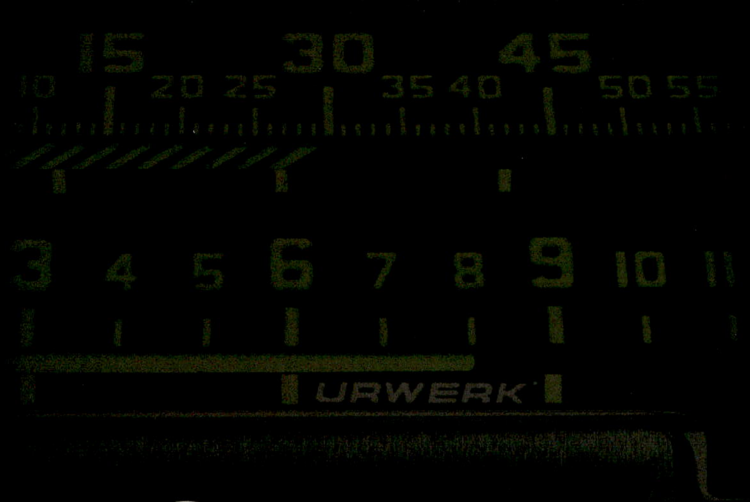

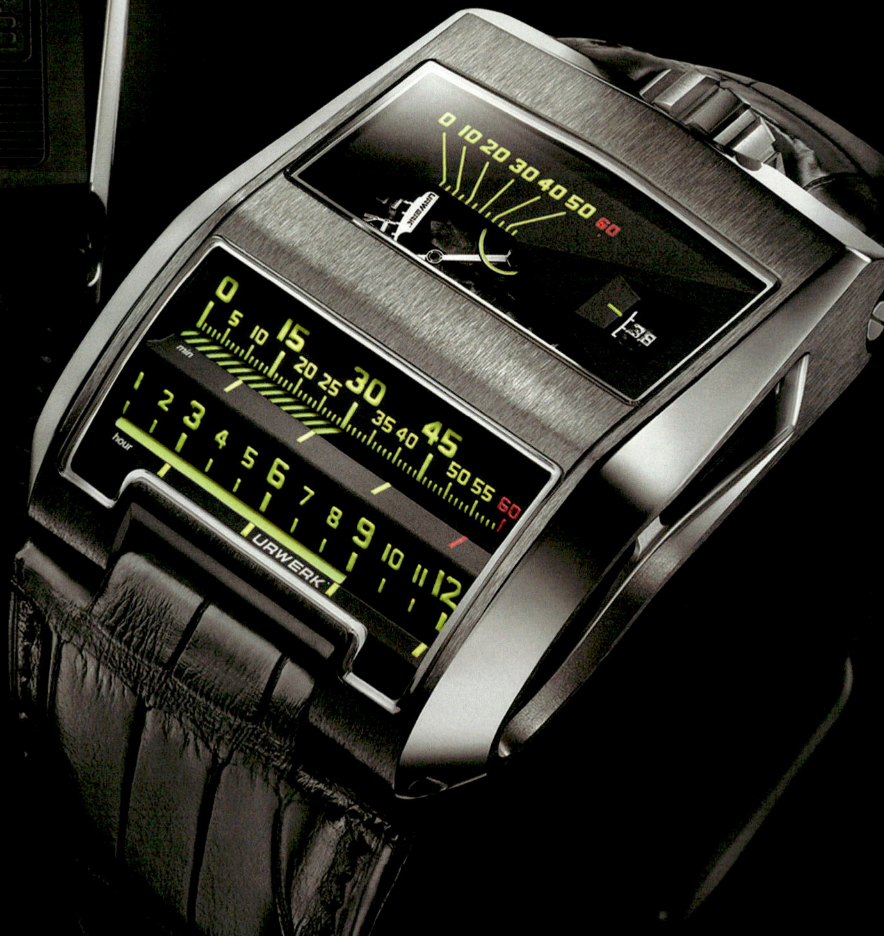

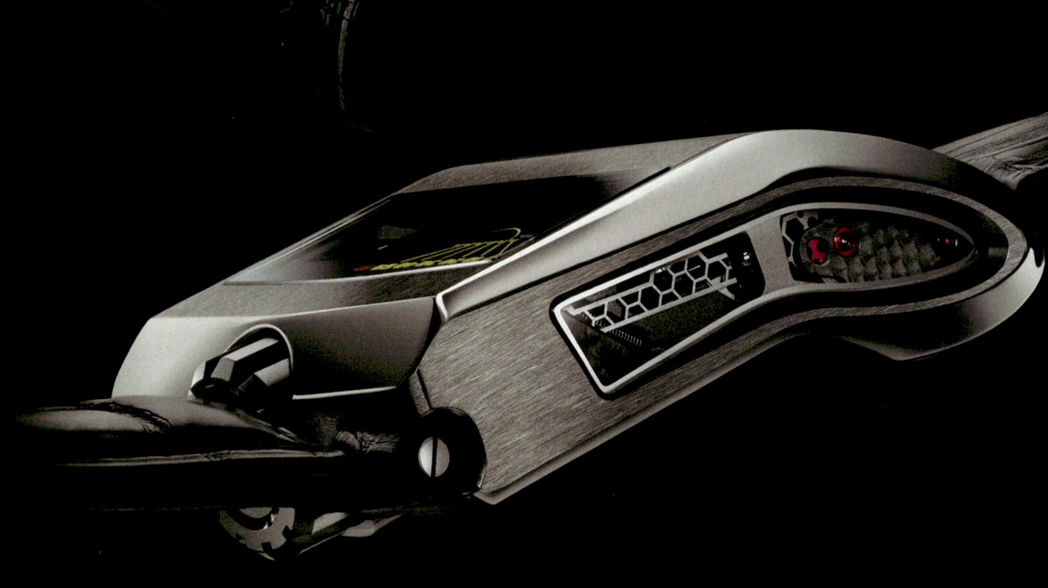

ABOVE

What appears to be an oversized crown is actually a selector switch that regulates Urwerk's pneumatic braking system, which uses air friction to control the rate of the UR-CC1's automatic winding.

CENTER

Shown here in white gold, the UR-CC1's case measures 53.9x42.6mm and is 15.4mm thick.

RIGHT

The sapphire crystal on the side of the UR-CC1's case reveals the honeycomb-shaped lever in motion as it rotates the retrograde minutes cylinder.

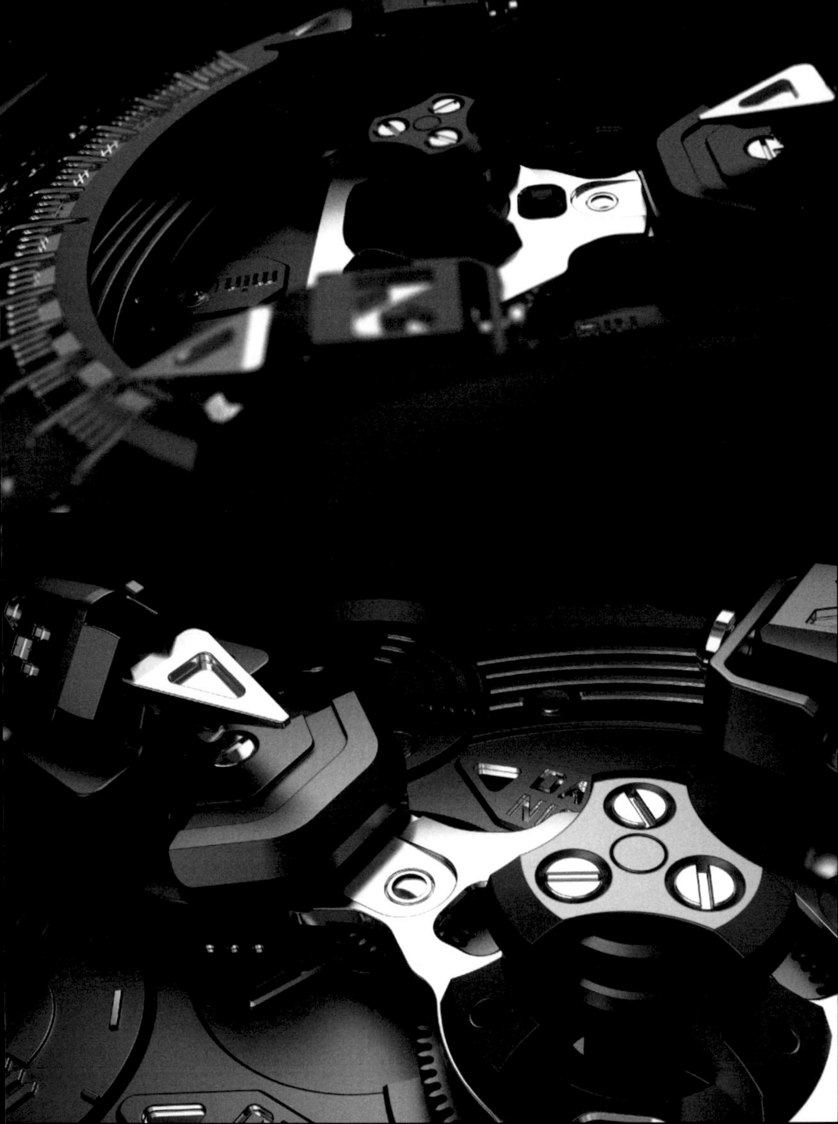

The UR-CC1's groundbreaking displays represent a skillful concentration of mechanical ingenuity and artistic vision aided by the latest production techniques.

At the heart of the watch's movement is a bronze beryllium cam that rotates once every three hours. Its constant rotation powers a toothed lever that rotates the retrograde minutes cylinder. When the minutes reset back to zero, it also advances the jumping hours.

Much of this mechanical procession takes place behind a sapphire crystal embedded in the side of the case. The window offers a prime view of the lever in action, which is easily recognized by its honeycomb pattern. More than a decorative flourish, its construction is specifically engineered to maximize strength and minimize mass.

To achieve this elusive balance, Urwerk enlisted Mimotec, a company that specializes in manufacturing ultra-precise parts with photolithography, an advanced technique capable of producing any kind of pattern for watch components, even patterns too complex to machine.

The process was also required to forge the watch's groundbreaking seconds wheel, which is the first ever to indicate seconds both linearly and digitally. For the digital display on the right, the wheel is edged with even numbers from 2 to 60. Meanwhile, the wheel is also topped with a spiral. As the wheel spins, the line moves to indicate the seconds in the linear display on the left.

Perched above the seconds displays like an oversized crown is a selector switch that regulates Urwerk's "rotor fly brake." This pneumatic braking system uses air friction to control the rate of the movement's automatic winding. Another benefit realized by this system—which was inspired by a technique to regulate chiming clocks in the 18th century—is that the air friction also helps protect the mechanism from unnecessary wear and sudden jolts.

Both versions of the UR-CC1—white gold (King Cobra) and white gold treated with AlTiN (Black Cobra)—are available in a limited series of 25 pieces each.

Urwerk continues to refine its concept for displaying time using three revolving hour satellites with its latest incarnation, the UR-110.

As the hour satellites orbit the dial, one shows the current hour as it passes next to a 60-minute arc spanning the watch's lower edge. To enhance readability, the pointer at the end of the satellite extends as it traces the index's curve.

All three satellites are mounted on epicyclical gearing that allows them to maintain a parallel formation as they rotate around the dial. The watch's open design provides ample space for Urwerk to include a trio of additional functions on the dial's surface, including a day/night disc, a service indicator that rotates once every five years, and a display that uses three arms and three concentric arcs to indicate the seconds.

The watch's technical expression projects a refined industrial chic amplified by the contrasts found throughout the design, including the mix of dark and light tones and smooth and satin textures.

While the UR-110 and the UR-CC1 are fundamentally different in terms of their mechanics and aesthetics, both watches stem from the same creative impulse that drives Urwerk to re-imagine the way we tell time.

TOP LEFT

To indicate the time, one of the UR-110's orbiting satellites shows the hour as its telescopic hand points to the minute on the 60-minute arc that curves along the bottom of the dial.

LEFT CENTER

A detailed view of the UR-110's dial reveals the design's contrasting tones and textures.

VACHERON CONSTANTIN

Manufacture Horlogère. Genève, depuis 1755.

ENRICHING TRADITION WITH INNOVATION

Empowered by a pedigree of progress that extends unrivaled and uninterrupted for more than a quarter-millennium, Vacheron Constantin distills the essence of the watchmaker's art with works of mechanical and artistic originality.

Last year the company unveiled three Patrimony Traditionnelle models encased in platinum, using the metal's rarity and purity to accentuate the noble character of these timepieces.

The Geneva-based manufacture began by pairing the precious metal with one of its most acclaimed movements, the Patrimony Traditionnelle Chronograph Perpetual Calendar Calibre 1141QP. Looking through the crystal caseback at the elegant symphony of gears that harmonize to render this hand-wound mechanism, it's clear why the movement commands such a loyal following.

The pattern of graceful design continues on the opposite side, where a thin bezel encircles a slate gray dial whose rich tone provides a pleasing visual contrast to the pale shimmer of the 43mm platinum case. The watch's namesake complications are arranged across the dial with the chronograph counters lined up horizontally and the calendar displays bisecting the gray field vertically. The snailed pattern that fills the date ring's interior opens at the top to reveal the moonphase, which is indicated by a rotating plate of solid platinum engraved with the moon and stars.

The perpetual calendar returns once again in the Patrimony Traditionnelle Calibre 2755. In this model, Vacheron Constantin teams its venerable calendar with two of the most sophisticated complications in haute horology, a tourbillon and minute repeater.

The movement for which the timepiece is named represents the most complex movement currently offered by the company, requiring 602 components to complete. More than the sum of its parts, however, the watch demonstrates Vacheron Constantin's dedication to constant innovation with a minute repeater that includes a new chiming-rate regulator. Significantly quieter than similar devices, this new mechanism can be seen spinning through the caseback alongside the repeater's hammers and finely tuned gongs.

The caseback also provides a window onto the intensive workmanship that elevates the movement to an elite class, including the base plate's angled edges and Côtes de Genève decoration. The Hallmark of Geneva inscribed on the bridge provides independent confirmation of its quality, attesting to its compliance with exacting requirements for traditional finishing as well as precision.

The dial—available with a silvered or slate finish—is home to a trio of subsidiary dials that indicate the perpetual calendar's date, month and day, as well as a window to highlight the leap year. This mechanized calendar will remain true to the Gregorian calendar for 400 years before requiring an adjustment.

Below the calendar, the Patrimony Traditionnelle Calibre 2755 incorporates a tourbillon to compensate for gravity's constant tug on the balance's hairspring. Vacheron Constantin enhances the complication's already outstanding visual appeal by adding a Maltese Cross, a symbol long associated with the firm.

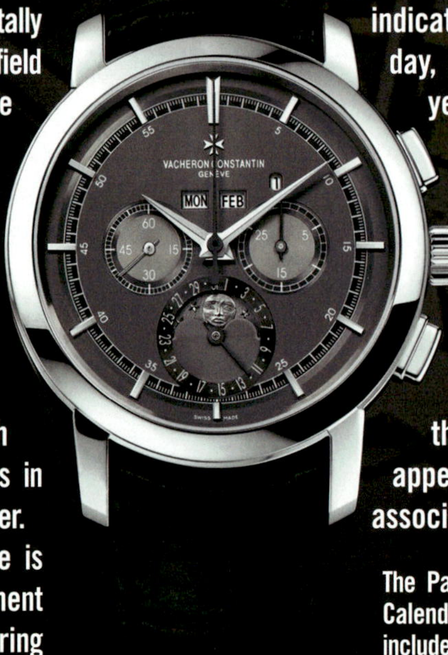

The Patrimony Traditionnelle Chronograph Perpetual Calendar's slate gray dial (also available in silver) includes a moonphase disc made from solid platinum.

Vacheron Constantin illuminates a trio of technically advanced and aesthetically refined movements from its Patrimony Traditionnelle collection with the noble glow of platinum.

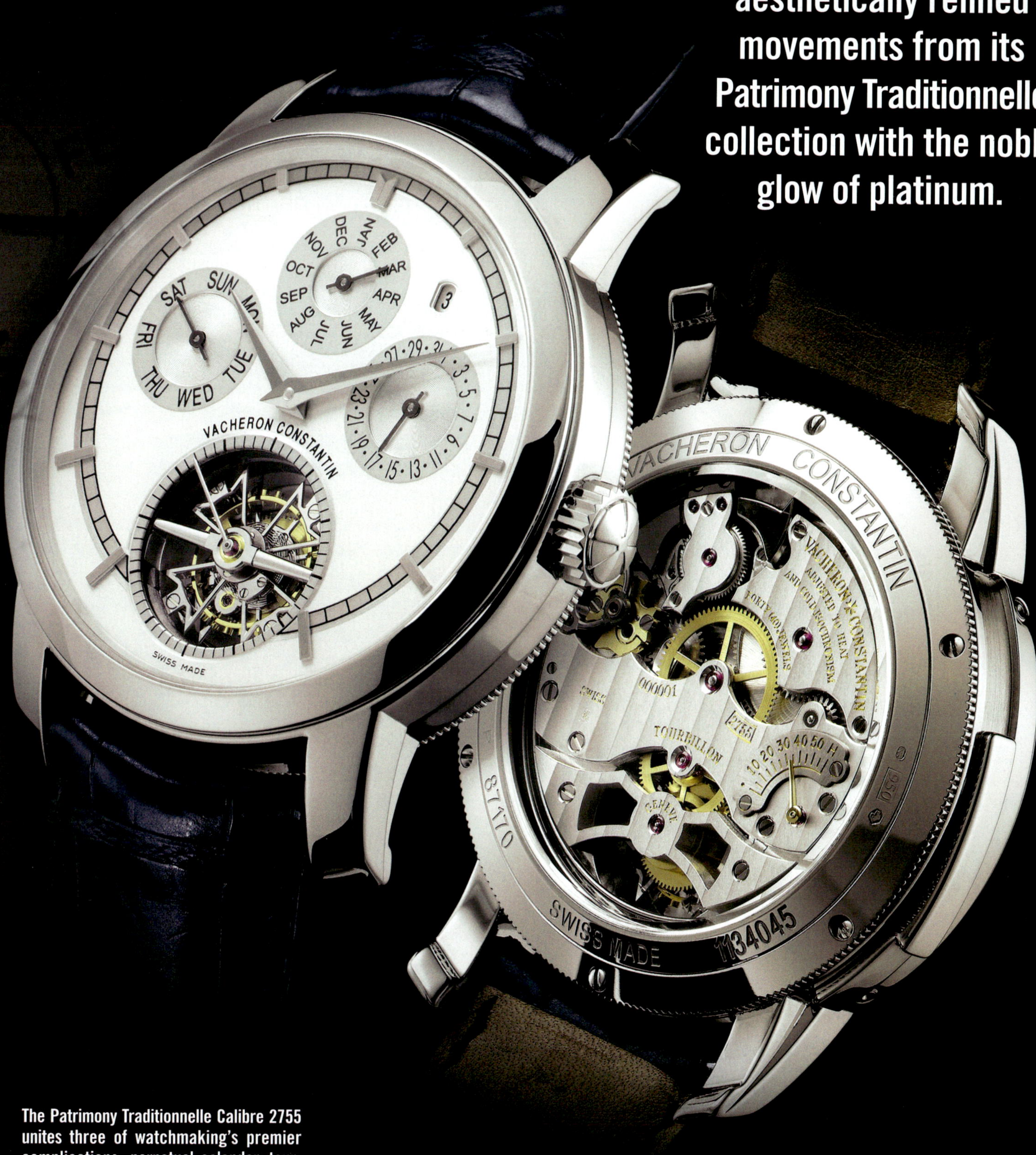

The Patrimony Traditionnelle Calibre 2755 unites three of watchmaking's premier complications: perpetual calendar, tourbillon and minute repeater.

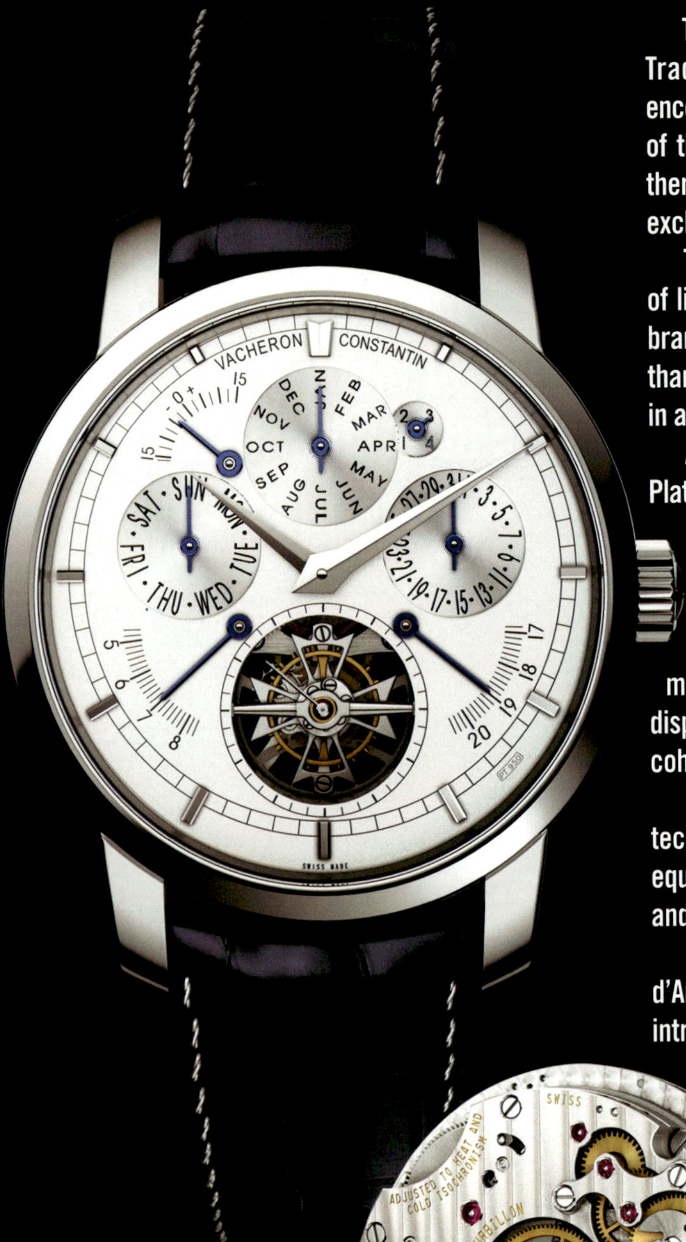

The perpetual calendar receives a third encore in the Patrimony Traditionnelle Calibre 2253. In addition to the calendar, the watch encompasses two more astronomical complications, including an equation of time and displays for sunrise and sunset times. Rather than stopping there, the brand also incorporates a tourbillon, which was developed exclusively by Vacheron Constantin's workshops.

The watch is part of the Collection Excellence Platine, an elite class of limited editions Vacheron Constantin launched in 2006. Now, when the brand introduces a platinum watch, its production is restricted to no more than 150 pieces. Befitting its complexity, the Calibre 2253 will be issued in a series of just ten models.

As a badge of membership, watches in the Collection Excellence Platine feature a rare design element in platinum. The Patrimony Traditionnelle Calibre 2253 boasts a brushed platinum dial and dauphine hour and minute hands made from the precious metal, as well as a blue alligator strap sewn with a combination of silk and platinum threads.

Calibre 2253 proves it is worthy of this distinction with a refinement that skillfully weaves the tourbillon together with seven individual displays—not counting hours and minutes—to create a legible and cohesive design.

Beyond its deeply felt commitment to perpetuating watchmaking's technical traditions through constant innovation, Vacheron Constantin is equally dedicated to preserving decorative arts like enameling, engraving and gem-setting that have enriched horology for centuries.

Nowhere is this devotion more evident than the brand's Métiers d'Art collection, which has beguiled collectors since Vacheron Constantin introduced the Tribute to the Great Explorers and Masques series, in 2004 and 2007 respectively.

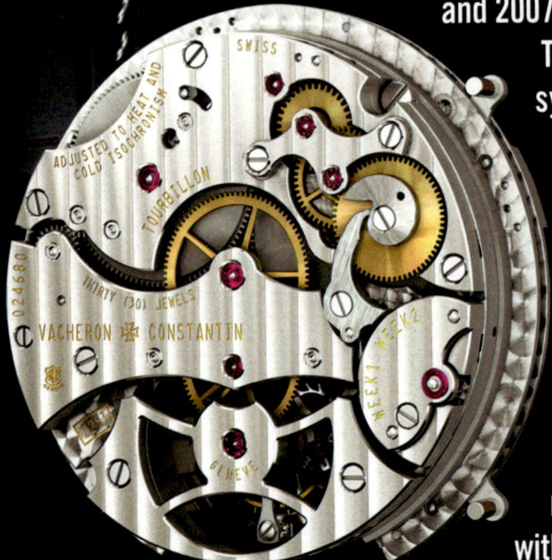

The company launched a new series in 2010 with La symbolique des laques, a collection that unites watchmaking with the traditional Japanese lacquer technique called maki-e. To create a design using maki-e, which means "sprinkled picture," an artisan carefully shakes silver or gold dust over wet lacquer.

To create La symbolique des laques, Vacheron Constantin partnered with Zôhiko, one of Japan's oldest lacquer companies, which will decorate the cases in Japan. Once the maki-e is applied, the cases will be returned to Geneva where the watchmaker will equip each with a skeletonized version of its ultra-thin Caliber 1003.

The first series, dubbed "The Three Friends of Winter," will spotlight a pine tree and a crane; bamboo and a sparrow; as well as a plum tree and a nightingale. Like the previous Métiers d'Art collections, La symbolique des laques will span three years, starting in 2010. Each year, Vacheron will offer a new set of three watches in a limited series of 20.

With its innovative cross-pollination of historic and modern techniques, La symbolique des laques neatly encapsulates more than 250 years of Vacheron Constantin's watchmaking values.

A limited edition of ten pieces, the Patrimony Traditionnelle Calibre 2253 includes a case, dial and central hands all made from platinum. Even the blue alligator strap is sewn with silk and platinum threads.

Newly developed by Vacheron Constantin's Geneva workshops, Calibre 2253 incorporates a tourbillon, perpetual calendar and equation of time, as well as sunset and sunrise times.

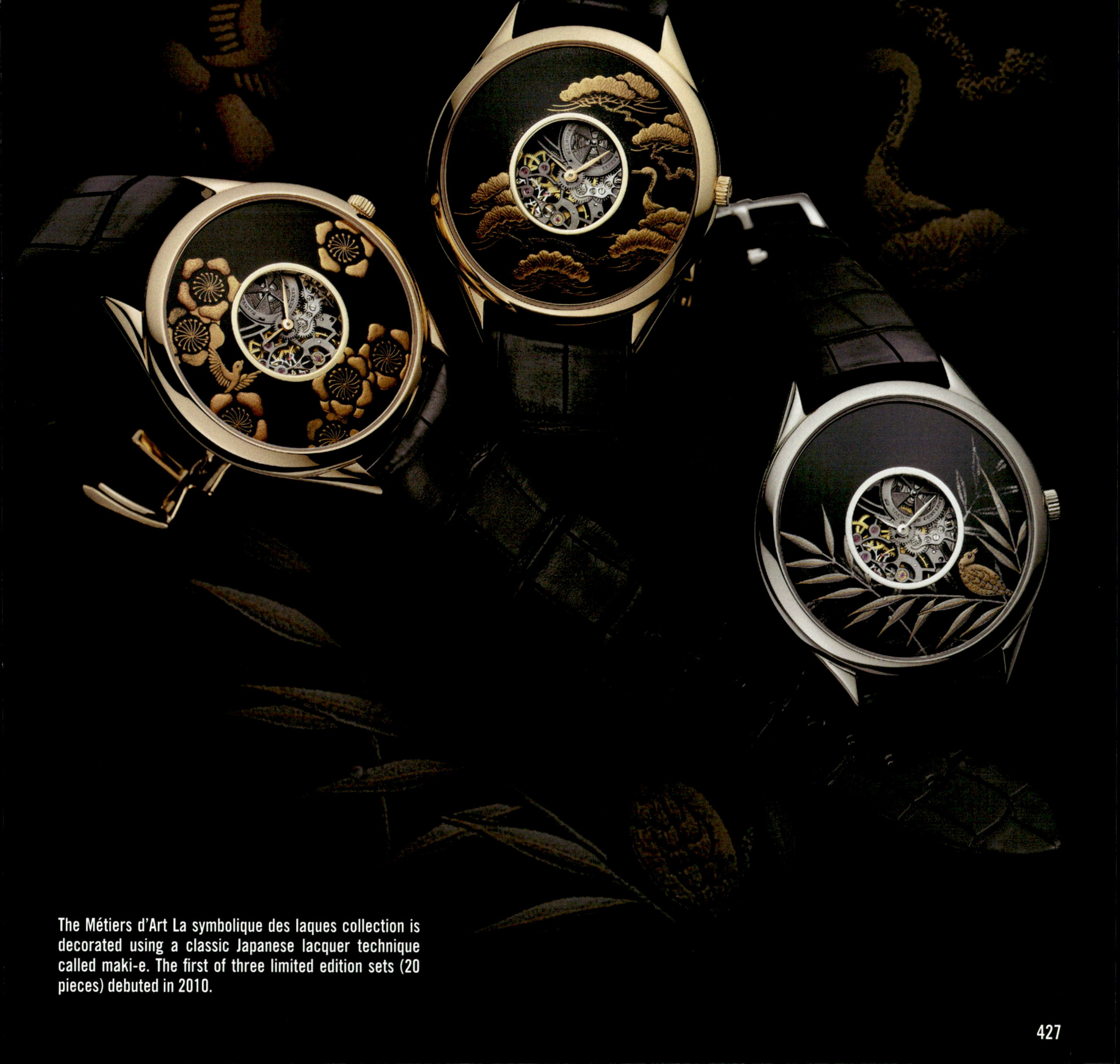

The Métiers d'Art La symbolique des laques collection is decorated using a classic Japanese lacquer technique called maki-e. The first of three limited edition sets (20 pieces) debuted in 2010.

PATRIMONY TRADITIONNELLE CALIBRE 2253 REF. 88172/000P-9495

Movement: manual-winding Vacheron Constantin 2253 caliber; approx. 336-hour power reserve; 30 jewels; 18,000 vph; hallmarked with the Geneva Seal.
Functions: hours, minutes; small seconds at 6; tourbillon; equation of time; sunset/sunrise time; perpetual calendar; power reserve indication.
Case: platinum 950; Ø 44mm; convex sapphire crystal with antireflective coating on the inside; transparent sapphire crystal caseback with screws; water resistant to 3atm.

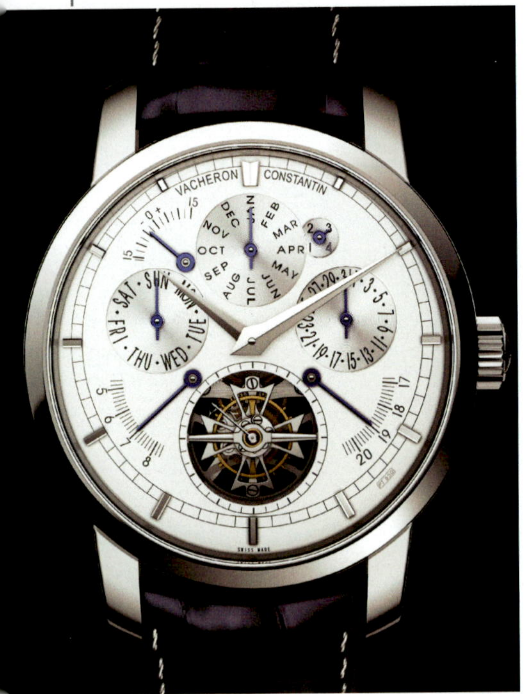

Dial: platinum, sand-blasted; black painted minute track.
Strap: dark blue platinum 950 hand-stitched, saddle-finished, square-scaled Mississippi alligator.
Suggested price: $449,000
Note: limited to 10 pieces.

PATRIMONY TRADITIONNELLE CALIBRE 2755 REF. 80172/000P-9505

Movement: manual-winding Vacheron Constantin 2755 caliber; approx. 58-hour power reserve; 40 jewels; 18,000 vph; hallmarked with the Geneva Seal.
Functions: hours, minutes; small seconds at 6; tourbillon; minute repeater; perpetual calendar; power reserve indication.
Case: platinum 950; Ø 44mm; convex sapphire crystal with antireflective coating on the inside; transparent sapphire crystal caseback with screws.

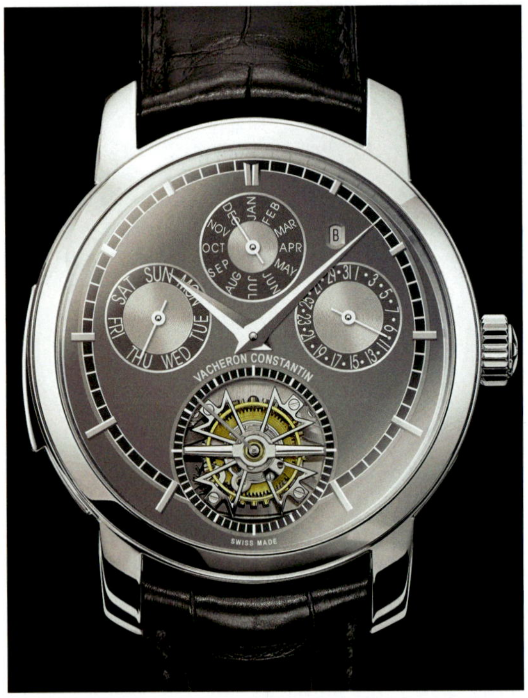

Dial: slate-colored opaline; white painted minute track; snailed counters centers.
Strap: black hand-stitched, saddle-finished, square-scaled Mississippi alligator.
Suggested price: $639,000
Also available: pink gold.

PATRIMONY TRADITIONNELLE CHRONOGRAPH PERPETUAL CALENDAR REF. 47292/000P-9510

Movement: manual-winding Vacheron Constantin 1141 QP caliber; approx. 48-hour power reserve; 21 jewels; 18,000 vph.
Functions: hours, minutes; small seconds at 9; column-wheel chronograph: center chronograph hand, 30-minute counter at 3; day and month at 12; date and precision moonphase at 6.
Case: platinum 950; Ø 43mm; convex sapphire crystal with antireflective coating on the inside; transparent sapphire crystal caseback with screws; water resistant to 3atm.

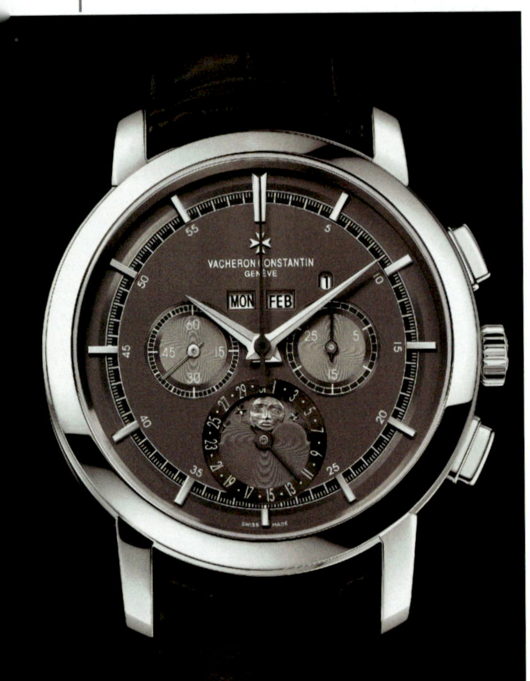

Dial: slate-colored opaline; snailed counters; white painted minute track.
Strap: black hand-stitched, saddle-finished, square-scaled alligator leather.
Suggested price: $127,500
Also available: pink gold.

PATRIMONY TRADITIONNELLE CHRONOGRAPH REF. 47192/000G-9504

Movement: manual-winding Vacheron Constantin 1141 caliber; approx. 48-hour power reserve; 21 jewels; 18,000 vph.
Functions: hours, minutes; small seconds at 9; column-wheel chronograph: 30-minute counter at 3, central chronograph seconds.
Case: 18K white gold; Ø 42mm; convex sapphire crystal with antireflective coating on the inside; transparent sapphire crystal caseback with screws; water resistant to 3atm.

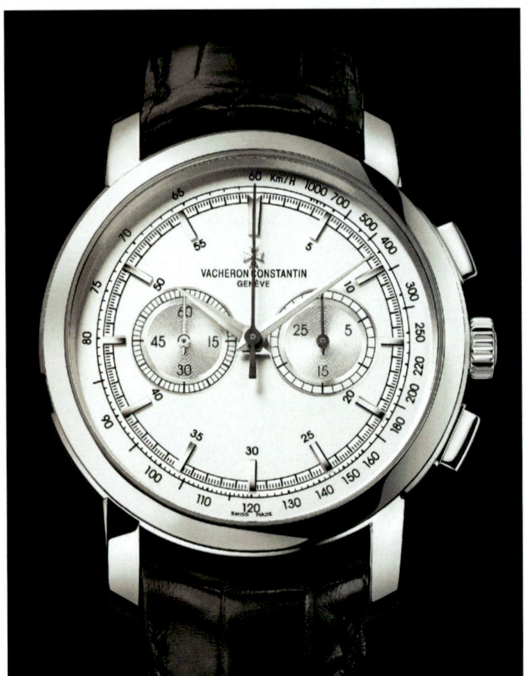

Dial: silvered opaline; snailed counters; black painted minute track.
Strap: black hand-stitched, saddle-finished, square-scaled alligator leather.
Suggested price: $44,900
Also available: pink gold.

PATRIMONY TRADITIONNELLE MANUAL-WINDING REF. 82172/000G-9383

Movement: manual-winding Vacheron Constantin 4400 caliber; approx. 65-hour power reserve; 21 jewels; 28,800 vph; hallmarked with the Geneva Seal.
Functions: hours, minutes; small seconds at 9.
Case: 18K white gold; Ø 38mm; convex sapphire crystal with antireflective coating on the inside; transparent sapphire crystal caseback with screws; water resistant to 3atm.
Dial: silvered opaline; snailed counter; black painted minute and second tracks; internal zones painted in white; 12 applied hour markers in 18K white gold.
Strap: black hand-stitched, saddle-finished, square scaled alligator leather.
Suggested price: $17,200
Also available: pink gold.

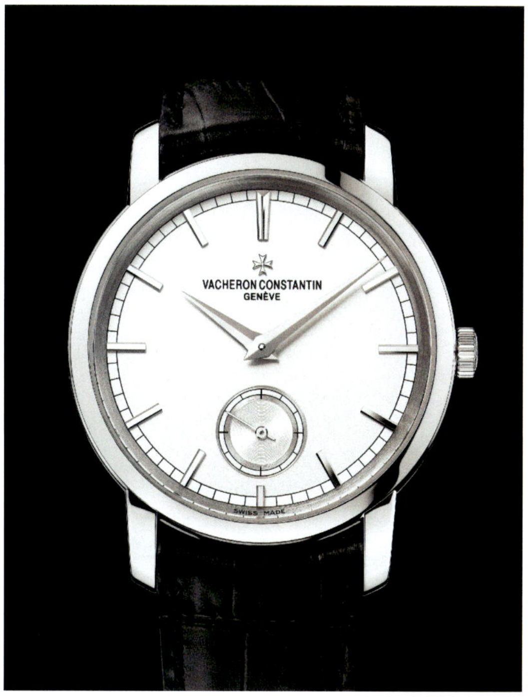

PATRIMONY CONTEMPORAINE RETROGRADE REF. 86020/000G-9508

Movement: automatic-winding Vacheron Constantin 2460 R31R7 caliber; approx. 40-hour power reserve; 27 jewels; 28,800 vph; hallmarked with the Geneva Seal.
Functions: hours, minutes; retrograde date and day.
Case: 18K white gold; Ø 42.5mm, thickness: approx. 10.1mm; polished finish; convex sapphire crystal with antireflective coating on the inside; transparent sapphire crystal caseback; water resistant to 3atm.
Dial: silvered opaline; convex external zone; circular-grained minute track.
Strap: black hand-stitched, saddle-finished, square-scaled Mississippi alligator.
Suggested price: $37,900
Also available: pink gold.

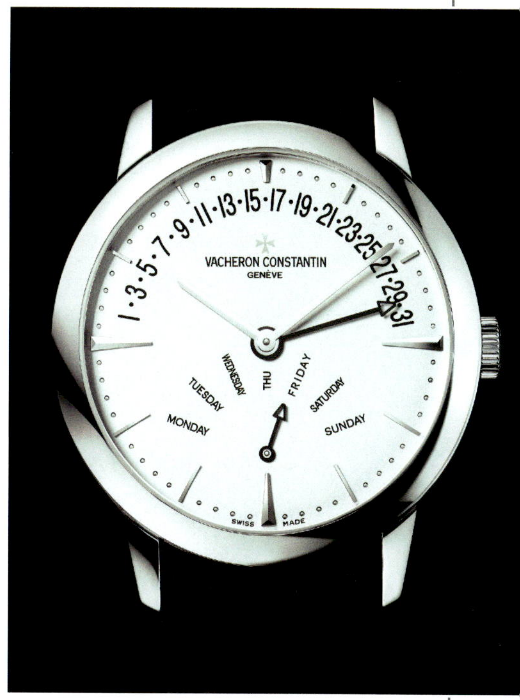

PATRIMONY CONTEMPORAINE REF. 81180/000P-9539

Movement: manual-winding Vacheron Constantin 1400 caliber; approx. 40-hour power reserve; 20 jewels; 28,800 vph; hallmarked with the Geneva Seal.
Functions: hours, minutes.
Case: platinium 950; Ø 40mm; convex sapphire crystal with antireflective coating on the inside; solid caseback; water resistant to 3atm.
Dial: slate-colored opaline; convex external zone; circular-grained minute track.
Strap: black hand-stitched, saddle-finished, square-scaled Mississippi alligator.
Suggested price: $25,500
Also available: white, pink or yellow gold.

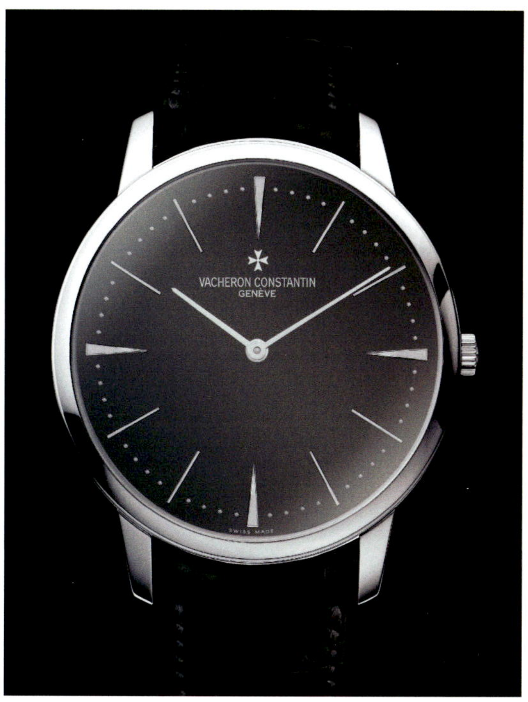

HISTORIQUES AMERICAN 1921 REF. 82035/000R-9359

Movement: manual-winding Vacheron Constantin 4400 caliber; approx. 65-hour power reserve; 21 jewels; 28,800 vph; thickness: 2.8mm; hallmarked with the Geneva Seal.
Functions: hours, minutes; off-center small seconds.
Case: 18K 5N pink gold; Ø 40mm; off-center crown; convex sapphire crystal with antireflective coating; transparent sapphire crystal caseback with screws; water resistant to 3atm.
Dial: sand-blasted finishing; painted Arabic numerals and minute track; black oxidized 18K gold hands.
Strap: black hand-stitched, saddle-finished, square-scaled alligator leather, 18K 5N pink-gold buckle with polished half Maltese cross.
Suggested price: $24,900

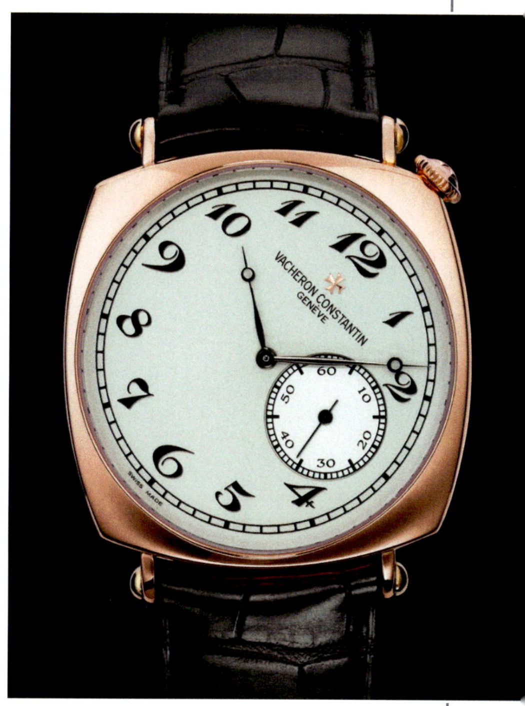

OVERSEAS DUAL TIME — REF. 47450/000W-9511

Movement: automatic-winding Vacheron Constantin 1222 SC caliber; approx. 40-hour power reserve; 34 jewels; 28,800 vph.
Functions: hours, minutes, seconds; date; second time zone with day/night indication; power reserve indication.
Case: stainless steel; Ø 42mm; titanium bezel and pushpiece protector; sapphire crystal with antireflective coating on the inside; flat, solid caseback stamped with Overseas medallion, with screws; water resistant to 3atm.

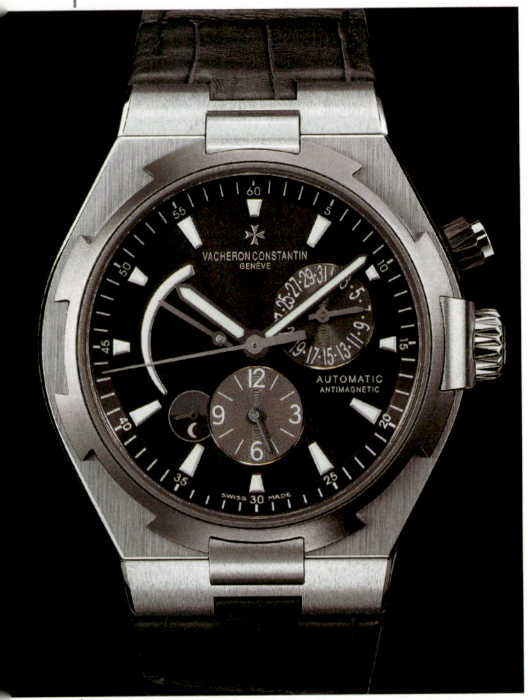

Dial: slate-colored; sunray-brushed; painted exterior minute track; snailed counters with diamond-polished filets.
Strap: dark gray hand-stitched, saddle-finished, square-scaled Mississippi alligator.
Suggested price: $14,400
Also available: white-, pink- or yellow gold.

OVERSEAS CHRONOGRAPH — REF. 49150/000W-9501

Movement: automatic-winding Vacheron Constantin 1137 caliber; approx. 40-hour power reserve; 37 jewels; 21,600 vph; antimagnetic protection.
Functions: hours, minutes, seconds; large date at 12; column-wheel chronograph: 12-hour and 30-minute counters.
Case: stainless steel; Ø 42mm; titanium bezel; solid caseback stamped with Overseas medallion, with screws; water resistant to 15atm.

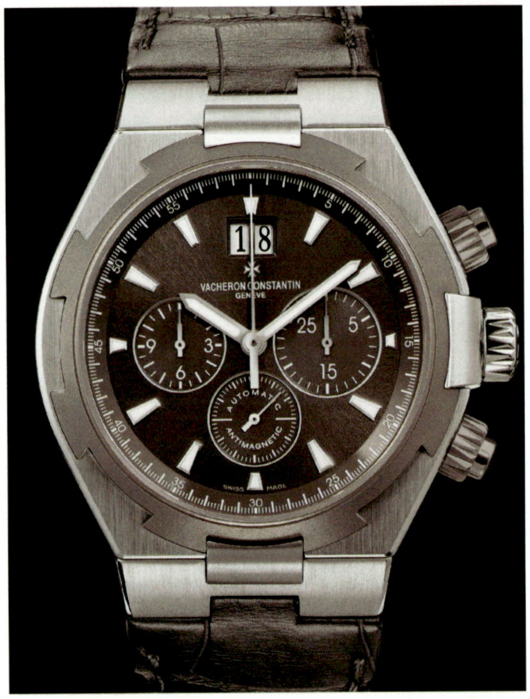

Dial: slate gray; sunraybrushed; circular satin-finishing; painted exterior minute track, snailed counters with diamond-polished filets; 12 applied hour markers in 18K white gold with white luminescent strip.
Strap: dark gray hand-stitched alligator leather.
Suggested price: $16,200
Also available: pink- and yellow-gold.

HISTORIQUES ULTRA-FINE 1955 — REF. 33155/000R-9588

Movement: manual-winding Vacheron Constantin 1003 caliber; approx. 30-hour power reserve; 18 jewels; 18,000 vph; thinnest in the world at just 1.64mm thick; hallmarked with the Geneva Seal.
Functions: hours, minutes.
Case: 18K 4N pink gold; Ø 36mm, thickness: 4.1mm; transparent sapphire crystal caseback with screws; water resistant to 3atm.

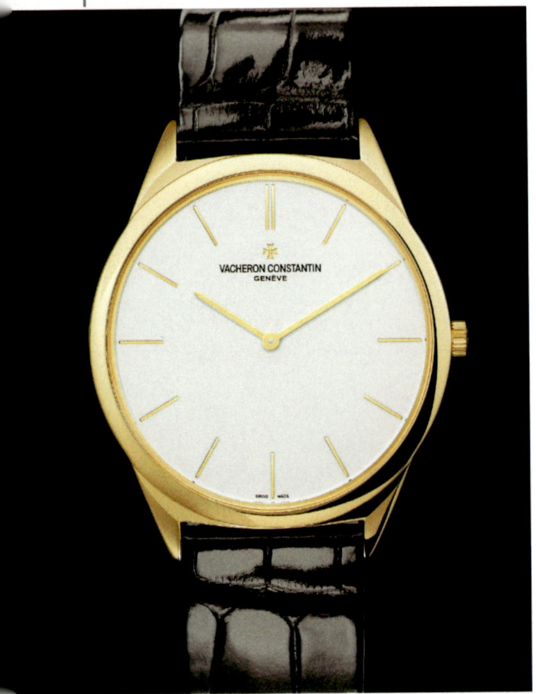

Dial: silvered opaline; mirror-polished 18K gold Maltese Cross and indexes.
Strap: black hand-stitched, saddle-finished, square-scaled alligator leather.
Suggested price: $22,900

HISTORIQUES ULTRA-FINE 1968 — REF. 43043/000R-9592

Movement: manual-winding Vacheron Constantin 1120 caliber; approx. 38-hour power reserve; 36 jewels; 19,800 vph; hallmarked with the Geneva Seal.
Functions: hours, minutes.
Case: 18K 4N pink gold; 39.6x49.5mm, thickness: approx. 5.5mm; convex sapphire crystal with antireflective coating on the inside; solid caseback with screws; water resistant to 3atm.

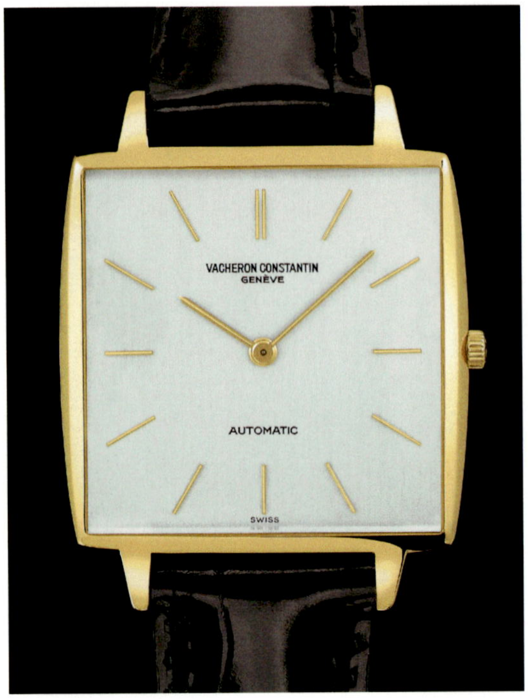

Dial: metal; silvered vertical satin finish.
Strap: black, large square-scaled Mississippi alligator.
Suggested price: $28,200

QUAI DE L'ILE DAY-DATE AND POWER RESERVE SELF-WINDING REF. 85050/000R-9340

Movement: automatic-winding Vacheron Constantin 2475 SC caliber; approx. 43-hour power reserve; 27 jewels; 28,800 vph; hallmarked with the Geneva Seal.
Functions: hours, minutes, seconds; date and day indicated by hands; power reserve indicator.
Case: 18K pink gold; Ø 41mm; screw-down back with sapphire crystal; water resistant to 3atm.
Dial: sapphire crystal; security transparent film (intaglio printing, security inks and micro-printing); numerals 3, 6, 9 and 12 are in galvanic growth of nickel; other numerals are engraved and inked in black or white.
Strap: brown hand-stitched, saddle-finished, square-scaled, high-shine alligator leather; triple-blade palladium folding clasp; polished half Maltese cross.
Suggested price: $41,300
Note: delivered with a second strap in black or brown hand-stitched, saddle-finish, square-scaled, high-shine alligator leather.
Also available: palladium and titanium.

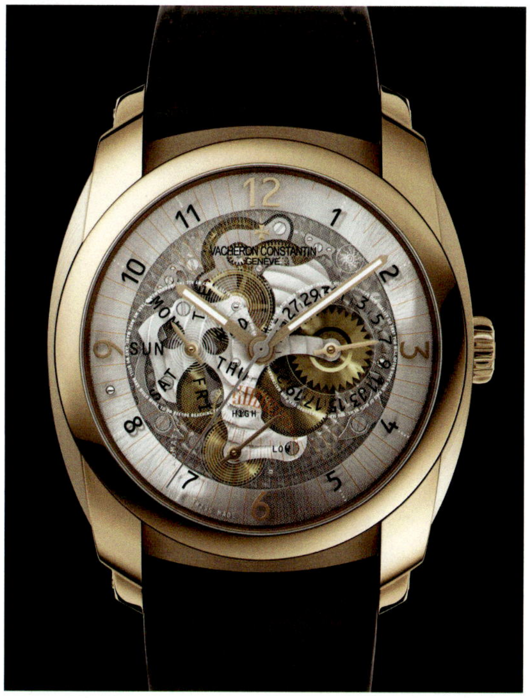

QUAI DE L'ILE DATE SELF-WINDING REF. 86050/000R-9342

Movement: automatic-winding Vacheron Constantin 2460 QH caliber; approx. 43-hour power reserve; 27 jewels; 28,800 vph; hallmarked with the Geneva Seal.
Functions: hours, minutes, seconds; date disc with optimal legibility (numerals engraved and inked on the sapphire dial) and ruthenium-coated with black marking.
Case: 18K pink gold; Ø 41mm; screw-down back with sapphire crystal; water resistant to 3atm.
Dial: sapphire crystal; security transparent film (intaglio printing, security inks and micro-printing); numerals 3, 6, 9 and 12 are in galvanic growth of nickel; other numerals are engraved and inked in black or white.
Strap: brown hand-stitched, saddle-finished, square-scaled, high-shine alligator leather; triple-blade palladium folding clasp, polished half Maltese cross.
Suggested price: $31,500
Note: delivered with a second strap in black or brown hand-stitched, saddle-finish, square-scaled, high-shine alligator leather.
Also available: palladium and titanium.

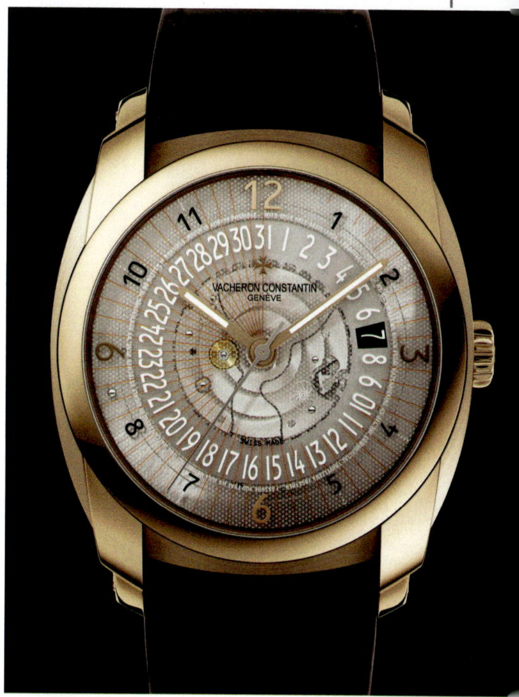

MALTE MOON PHASE AND POWER RESERVE REF. 83080/000G-9408

Movement: manual-winding Vacheron Constantin 1410 caliber; 40-hour power reserve; 22 jewels; 28,800 vph; hallmarked with the Geneva Seal.
Functions: hours, minutes; small seconds at 6; precision moonphase; power reserve indicator.
Case: 18K white gold; 39x49mm; tonneau shaped; water resistant to 3atm.
Dial: silvered Clous de Paris hand-guilloché interior zone; vertical satin-finished exterior zone; applied 18K white-gold Maltese cross.
Strap: black hand-stitched, saddle-finished, square-scaled alligator leather.
Suggested price: $34,500
Also available: 5N pink gold.

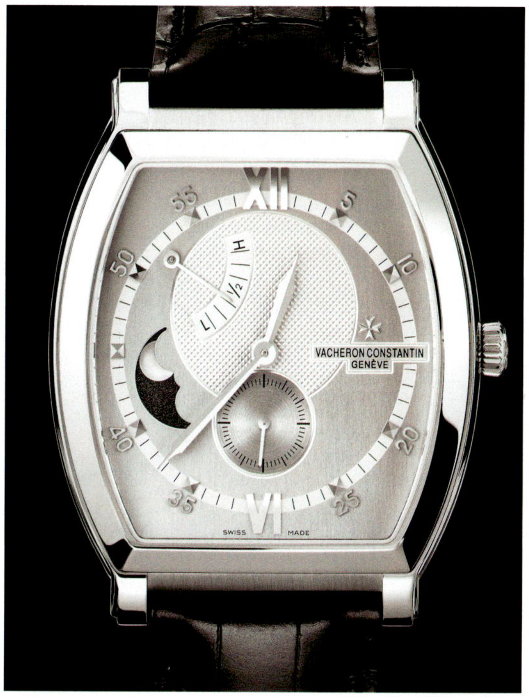

MALTE TONNEAU CHRONOGRAPH REF. 49180/000R-9361

Movement: automatic-winding Vacheron Constantin 1137 caliber; 40-hour power reserve; 37 jewels; 21,600 vph.
Functions: hours, minutes; running seconds at 6; large date at 12; center chronograph seconds; chronograph mechanism to 1/6 of a second; 30-minute and 12-hour totalizers at 3 and 9.
Case: 18K white gold; 40x50mm; water resistant to 3atm.
Dial: guilloché Clous de Paris interior zone; vertical satin-finished exterior zone.
Strap: black hand-stitched, square-scaled alligator leather; white-gold buckle.
Suggested price: $38,300
Also available: 18K pink-gold; brown alligator leather strap.

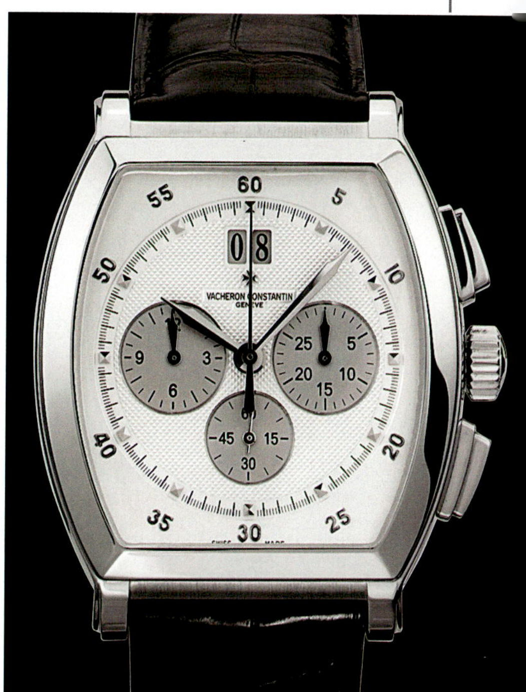

POETRY IN MOTION

Soon after Van Cleef & Arpels began welcoming guests to its fashionable address at Place Vendôme in 1906, the venerable Parisian jeweler offered its first timepieces to the world.

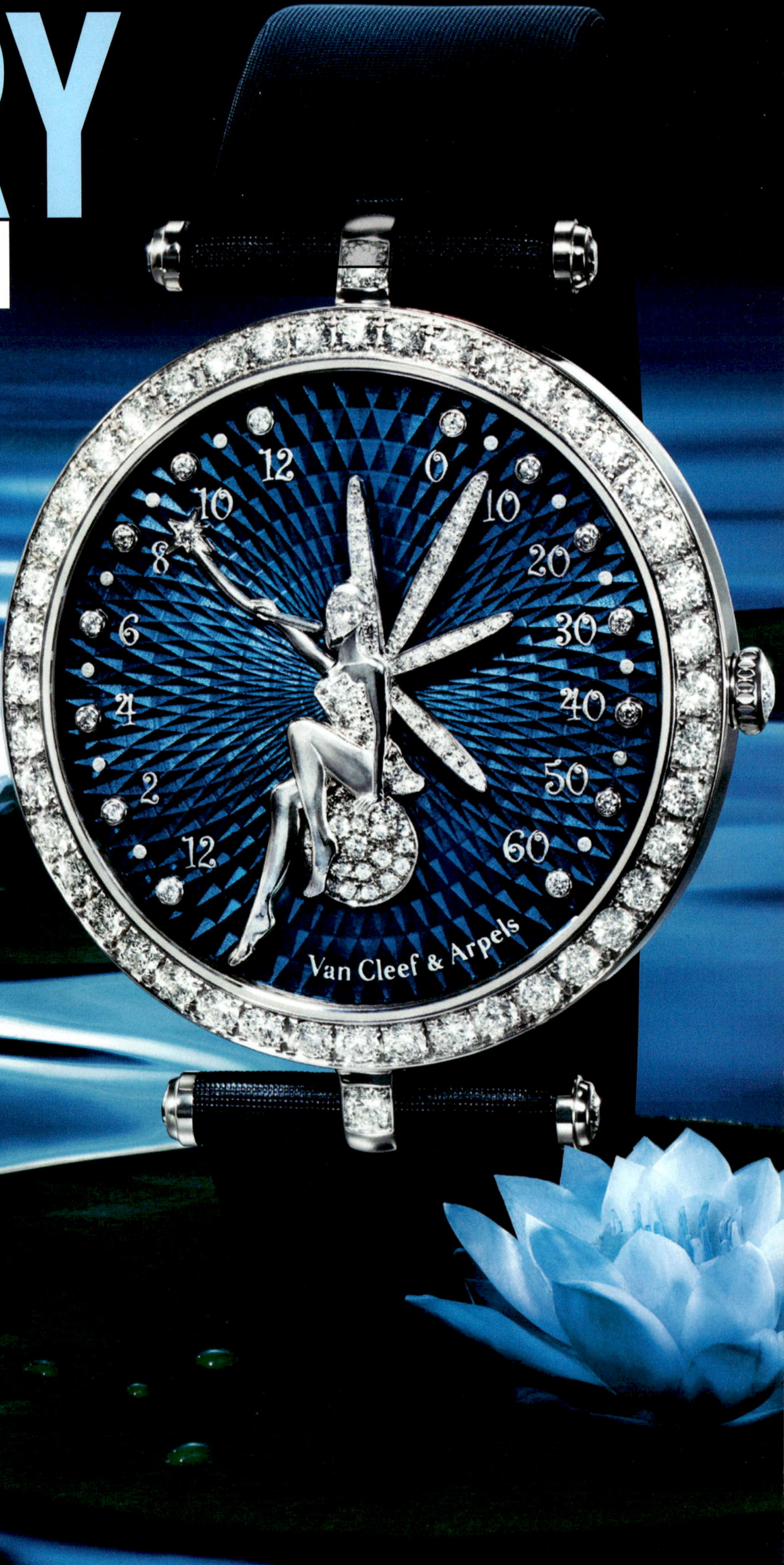

THIS PAGE

Diamonds abound on the Lady Arpels Fairy, adorning her wings and wand, which indicate the minutes and hours respectively.

FACING PAGE

The retrograde movement that powers Le Pont des Amoureux propels two sweethearts as they cross the white-gold bridge and meet in the middle.

Like all the watches in Van Cleef & Arpels' poetic Complications collection, the Lady Arpels Fairy and Le Pont des Amoureux models express time with a distinctive technical and artistic savoir-faire.

Now as then, a chic jeweler's sensibility can be found at work in the details that define the company's watch collection, from the gems that decorate many of its cases and dials, to the aesthetic and intellectual workmanship manifest in its hand-finished movements.

A particularly beguiling example, the Lady Arpels Fairy watch, keeps alive the nearly lost art of enameling with a stunning blue guilloché dial that serves as home to a time-telling fairy. Crafted from white gold and covered in diamonds, this precious pixie doubles as a retrograde display, showing the minutes with her wings and the hours with her wand.

The key, watchmaker Jean-Marc Wiederrecht said during a recent interview, was finding a movement powerful enough to move the unusual wing and wand indicators. "Usually you use light materials for the hands," he explained. "For the Fairy, it is gold. Now imagine the weight of a wing with six or seven diamonds on it." To compensate for the extra heft, a retrograde movement based was created especially for Van Cleef & Arpels. Its powerful design ensures the wand and wings snap back instantaneously after each completes its respective arc.

The Lady Arpels Fairy timepiece is part of Van Cleef & Arpels' poetic Complication collection, an elite family of timepieces whose members are designed to express time in an unexpected way through an outstanding balance of technical and creative savoir-faire.

It is joined by the Le Pont des Amoureux timepiece—the Lovers' Bridge—a second model powered by a retrograde movement. Here, the mechanism moves a man and woman to the center of a white-gold bridge once every 12 hours for a sweet kiss beneath a starry sky. Along their journey, the gentleman indicates the minutes with the flower tucked behind his back while the mademoiselle shows the hours with the tip of her umbrella. While similar to the mechanism powering the Lady Arpels Fairy, Wiederrecht says the movement used in Le Pont des Amoureux is a "real step ahead in the watchmaking world." "The issue is that the movement has to be slow because the lady is walking towards the point in twelve hours," he explains. "It may look simple, but from a watchmaker's point of view, it's very complicated."

These intricate machinations are concealed in a white-gold case whose diamond-set bezel twinkles brightly like the stars pictured on the dial. Here, Van Cleef & Arpels artisans create the dial's moonlit cityscape utilizing the contre-jour technique of enameling, which uses only black and white enamel.

In a telling twist, part of the charm of the Le Pont des Amoureux timepiece is its refusal to share all its secrets. inside—hidden to everyone but the watchmaker who assembled the movement—the caliber is engraved with the silhouettes of the man and woman featured on the dial. "But this is the signature of the Maison," Wiederrecht exclaims, "to care about each single detail, even when no one can see."

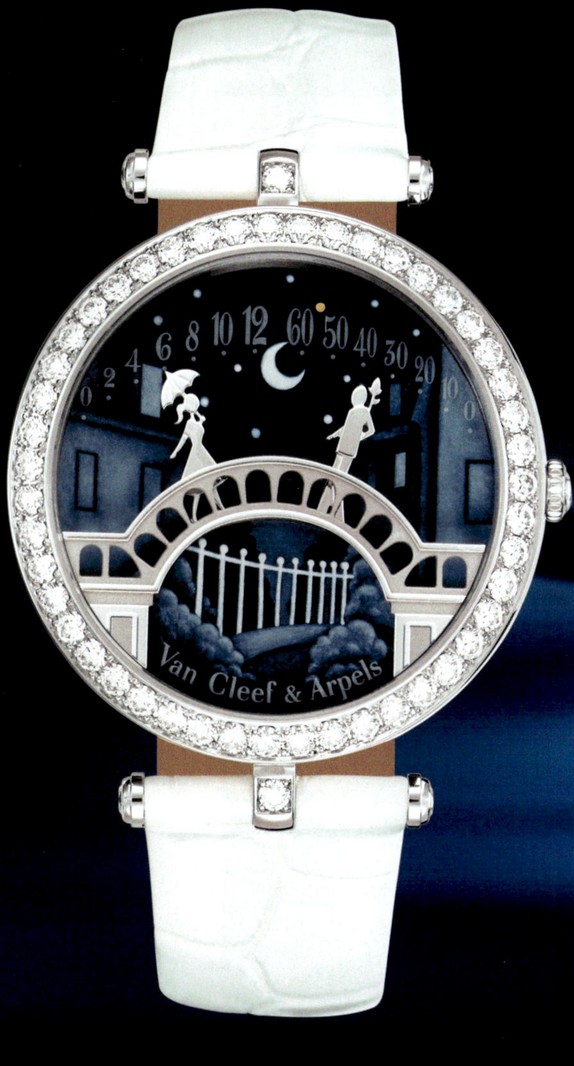

LADY ARPELS FEERIE — REF. VCARF80600

Movement: Swiss mechanical.
Functions: retrograde hours and minutes.
Case: white gold; set with diamonds (2.82 carats); Ø 38mm; scratch-proof sapphire crystal; water resistant to 3atm.
Dial: blue enamel; hand engraved guilloché; diamond-set fairy.
Strap: deep blue satin; white-gold buckle set with diamonds.

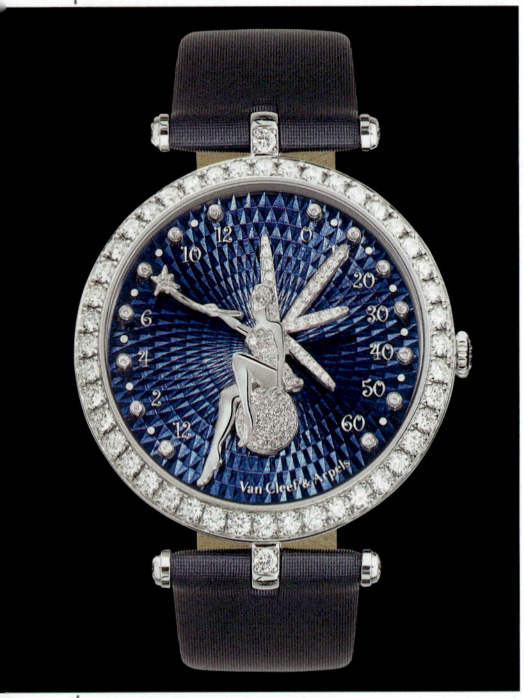

PONT DES AMOUREUX — REF. VCARN9VI00

Movement: Swiss mechanical.
Functions: retrograde hours and minutes.
Case: white gold; set with round diamonds; Ø 38mm.
Dial: backlit enamel; white-gold bridge; engraving on the back.
Strap: alligator; white-gold buckle set with diamonds.
Note: numbered edition.
Also available: checkered links.

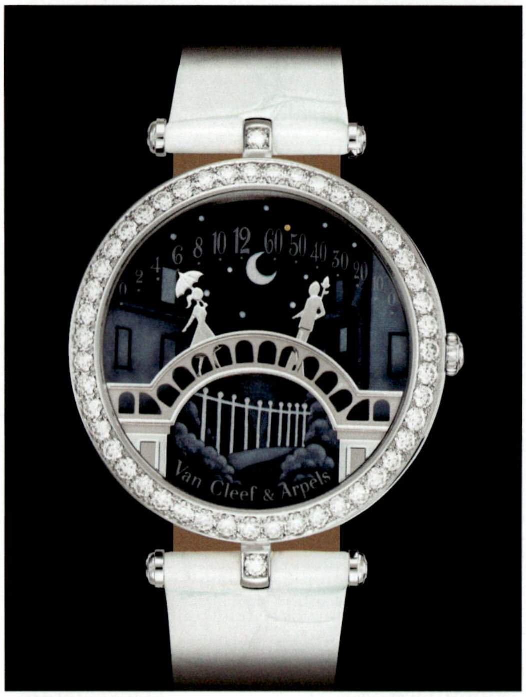

BUTTERFLY SYMPHONY — REF. VCARN9VG00

Movement: Swiss mechanical.
Functions: retrograde hours and minutes.
Case: white gold; set with round diamonds; Ø 38mm.
Dial: mother-of-pearl, onyx and sculpted gold; white-gold bridge; engraving on the back.
Strap: alligator; white-gold buckle set with diamonds.
Note: numbered edition.
Also available: checkered links.

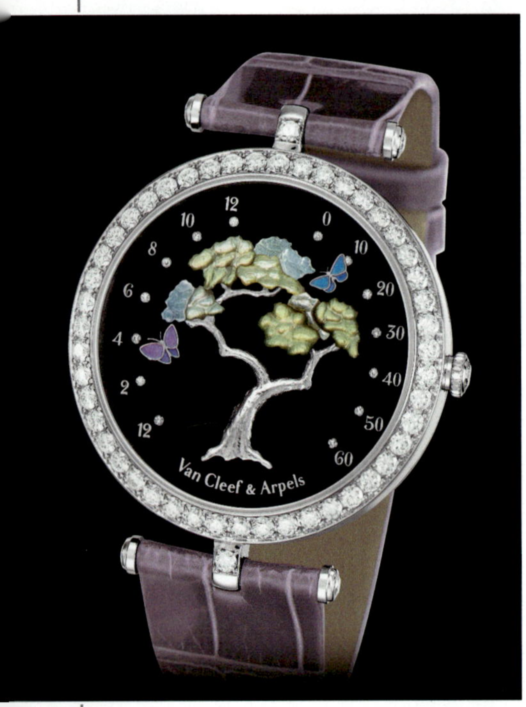

MIDNIGHT CALIFORNIA REVERIE — REF. VCARN9V300

Movement: Swiss automatic-winding.
Case: white gold; Ø 42mm.
Dial: stone inlay; mother-of-pearl and enamel.
Strap: alligator; white-gold buckle.
Note: one of five watches presented in the Extraordinary Cabinet "California Rêverie"; limited edition of eight cabinets.

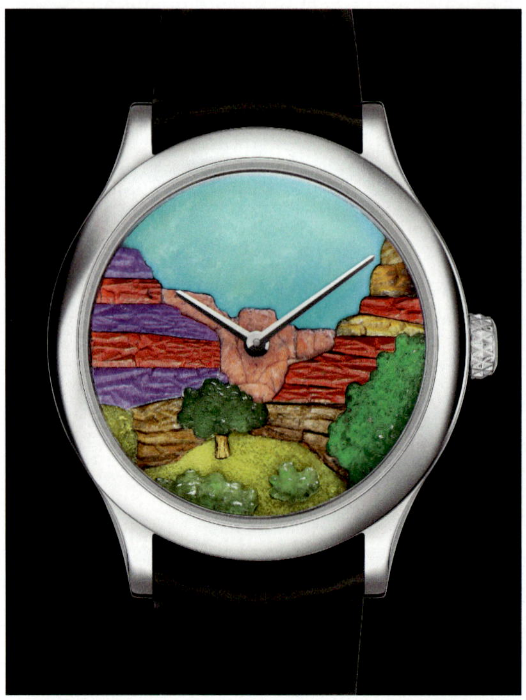

CHARMS PAVE — REF. VCARM95400

Movement: Swiss quartz.
Case: white gold; set with three rows of diamonds (3.16 carats); Ø 38mm.
Dial: white Alhambra guilloché; sunburst effect; white-gold indexes; Roman numerals.
Strap: interchangeable black satin strap set with diamonds.
Also available: pink gold or white gold.

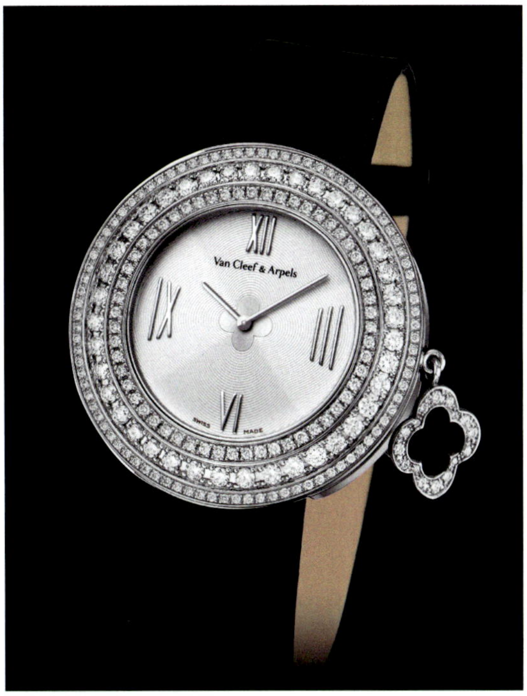

CHARMS MINI — REF. VCARN9UX00

Movement: Swiss quartz.
Case: pink gold; set with two rows of diamonds; Ø 25mm.
Dial: Alhambra guilloché motif; sunburst effect.
Strap: satin; pink-gold buckle set with diamonds.
Also available: white-gold version; fully paved with diamonds; alligator strap; white-gold buckle set with diamonds.

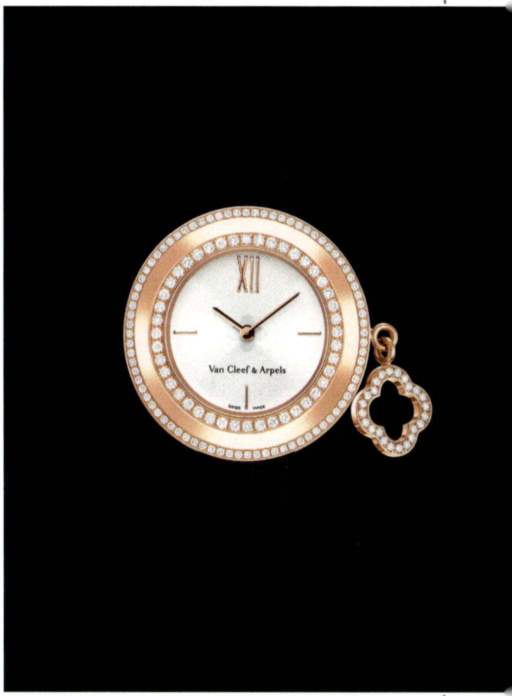

TIMELESS XL — REF. VCARN9VC00

Movement: Swiss quartz.
Case: 18K white gold; set with round diamonds; crown set with a diamond.
Dial: white lacquer guilloché; sunburst effect; white-gold index set with diamonds.
Strap: alligator.
Also available: pink-gold case with white lacquer guilloché dial; white-gold case with midnight blue lacquer guilloché dial.

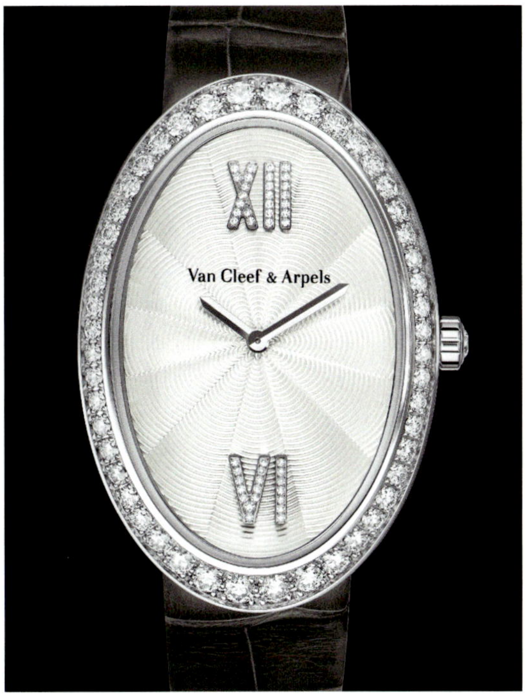

ALHAMBRA VINTAGE BRACELET — REF. VCARF53500

Movement: Swiss quartz.
Case: yellow gold; scratch-proof sapphire crystal; water resistant to 3atm.
Dial: mother-of-pearl.
Bracelet: seven Alhambra motifs.

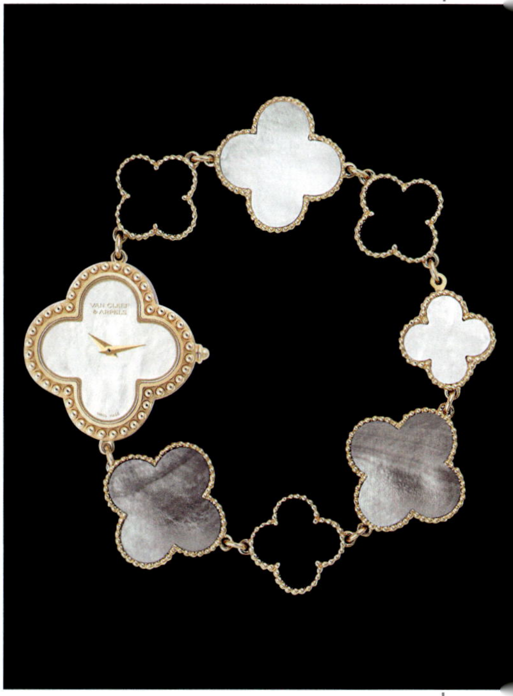

ZANNETTI
HANDMADE WATCHES

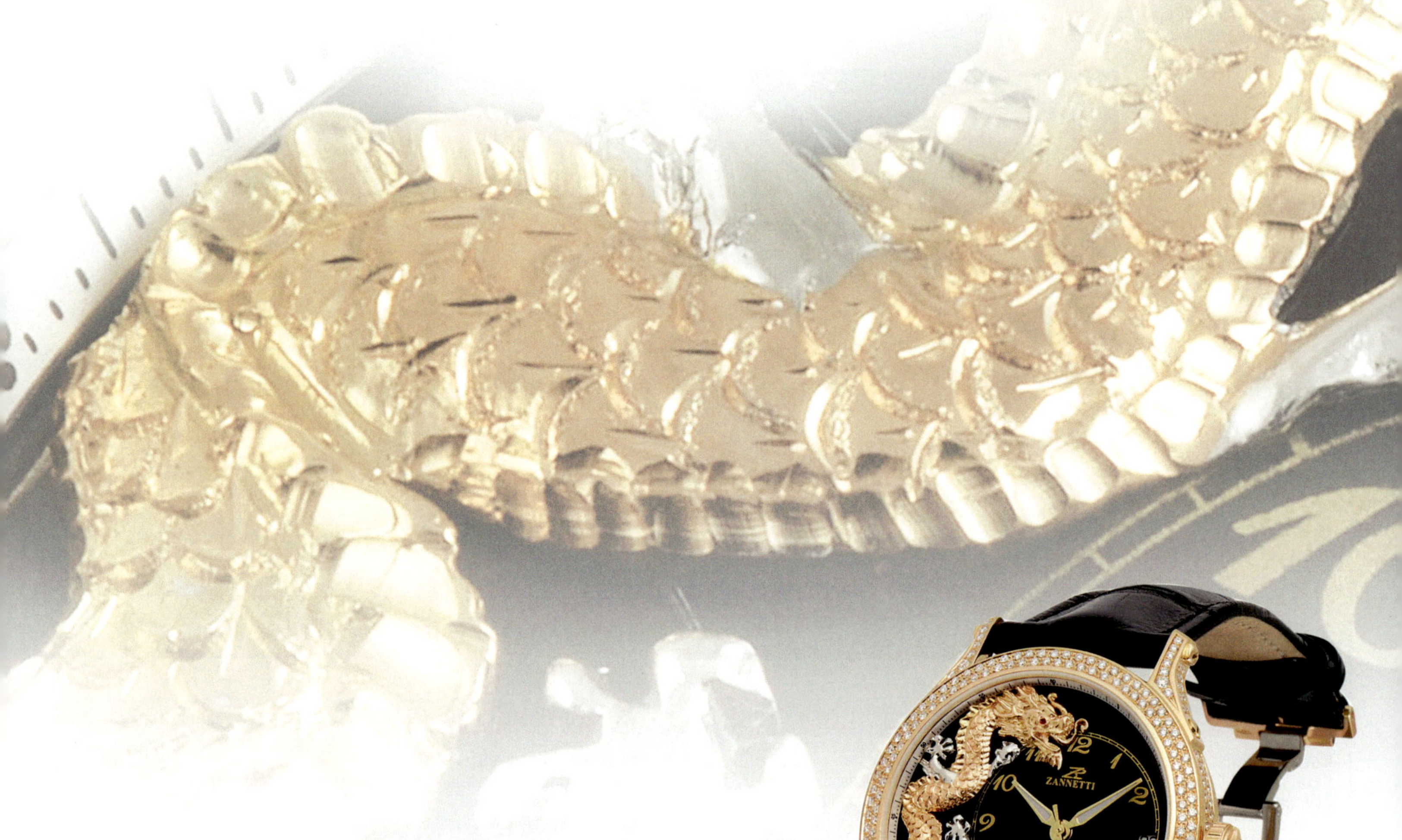

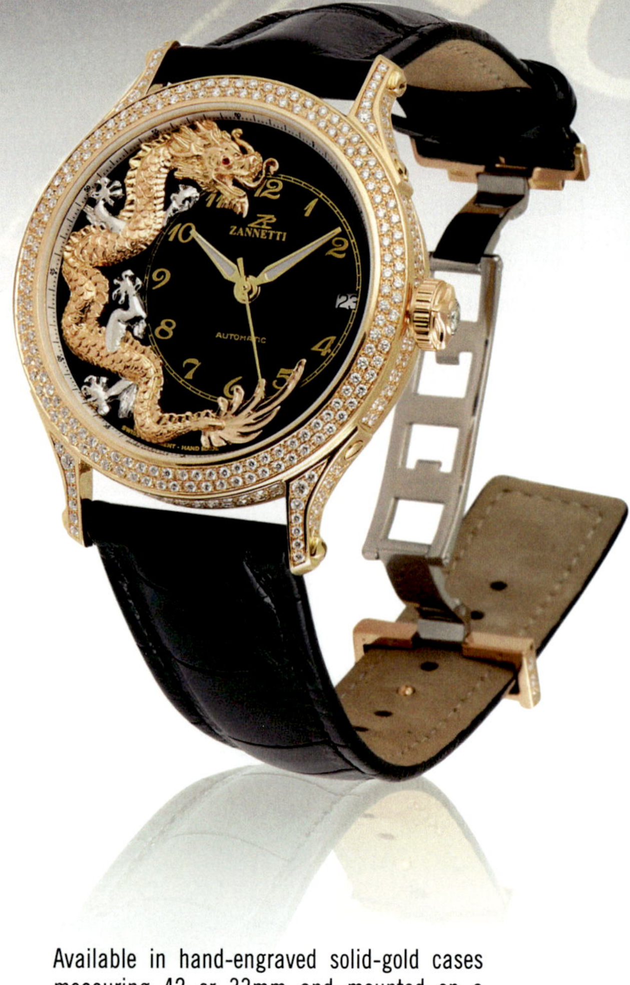

ENTER THE DRAGON

The Italian watchmaker Zannetti has long held a well-earned reputation for inventiveness and humor that punctures the inflated sense of momentousness of more self-serious horological brands. The fun continues with playful designs covering Swiss-made, Zannetti-elaborated mechanical movements.

Available in hand-engraved solid-gold cases measuring 42 or 33mm and mounted on a hand-sewn Louisiana alligator leather strap, the Regent Dragon Joaillerie can also be ordered with a personalized dial color.

Portrayed in the East Asian tradition, Zannetti's dragon curves around the dial mischievously; the three-dimensional effect of the bas-relief gives the creature a sense of tangible reality.

One of Zannetti's most tradition-tweaking designs returns in new flavors of decadence, namely the Brain Orgy, Tree Orgy and Bonsai Orgy. Tiny human figures couple in various acrobatic poses, forming an overall design that becomes more apparent from a distance. The Brain Orgy wittily reminds us of the single largest erogenous zone on the human body, while Tree Orgy and Bonsai Orgy present us with the spectacle of real-life nymphs and satyrs frolicking in the treetops and within the branches of the table-top arborescent plant. Whimsical eroticism carries the day on these hand-engraved dials, which start with a silver base and take on translucent red, blue and black tints that result in a work of art in pink, pale blue and gray. Each subject has been rendered in a limited edition of only 500 examples for each piece. The attention to detail does not end at the dial, however. Each Orgy watch possesses a three-piece stainless steel case that is water resistant to 50 meters. The hands are plated in yellow gold, and the strap is crafted in hand-sewn Lousiana alligator leather.

In a less whimsical but equally playful vein, Zannetti has added a precious dragon to its lineup: the Regent Dragon Joaillerie from the Regent Dragon Collection. The timepiece gleams in 18-karat pink gold and diamonds (a steel version, without diamonds, is also available). The glossy black enameled dial hosts not only an off-center display for the hours, minutes and seconds, but also an impressively fierce dragon, carved in bas-relief from 18-karat gold. Portrayed in the East Asian tradition, in which the mythical beasts are revered as intermediaries between heaven and earth, Zannetti's dragon curves around the dial mischievously, hinting that it refrains from interfering with the watch as a personal favor to the wearer. The three-dimensional effect of the technique gives the creature a sense of tangible reality. One might also see a nod to the European dragon tradition, in which the beasts often guard an enormous hoard of treasure, including precious gems. The Regent Dragon Joaillerie boasts a case that is fully pavé with diamonds, including the lugs and the crown. Inside all of this horological showmanship beats an automatic mechanical movement that was made in Switzerland and completed in Italy, where Zannetti put its unique stamp on the movement's personality. An off-center sapphire crystal opening in the caseback reveals the idiosyncrasies of the Regent Dragon's movement.

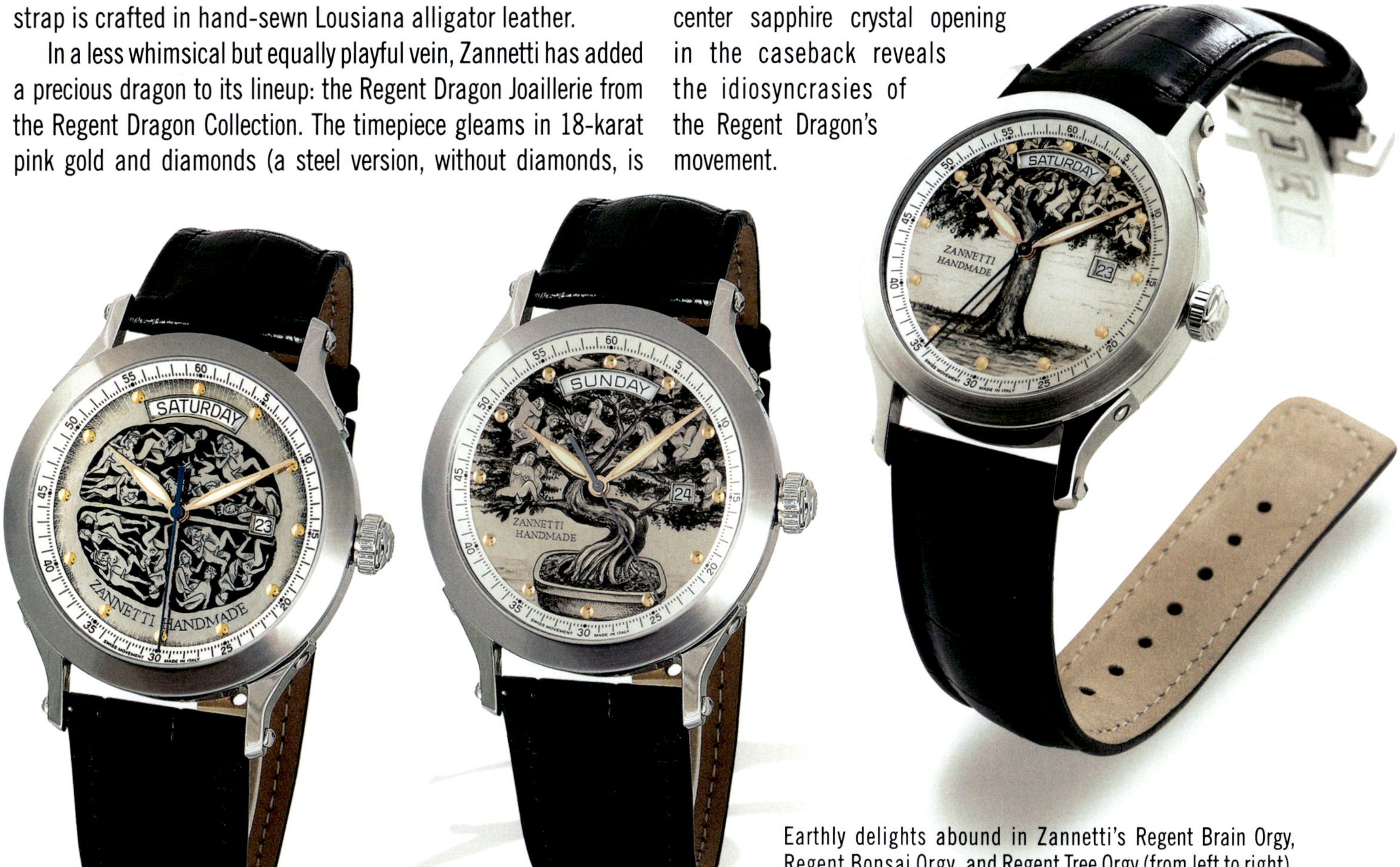

Earthly delights abound in Zannetti's Regent Brain Orgy, Regent Bonsai Orgy and Regent Tree Orgy (from left to right), each one encased in a three-piece stainless steel case.

5-MINUTE REPEATER — REF. RGR.184.431

Movement: automatic-winding 5-minute repeater; Swiss made; Zannetti re-elaborated; totally skeletonized and hand-engraved.
Functions: hours, minutes; 5-minute repetition ringing mechanism activated at any moment via a pushpiece and marking hours and its divisions.
Case: 18K pink gold; three-piece; Ø 44mm, thickness: 15mm; new case with redesigned handles; engraved totally by hand; hand-personalized pressured closed crown; gold octagonal, engraved pusher at 8 for repeater; antireflective sapphire crystal; pink-gold screws with central sapphire crystal opening; water resistant to 2atm.
Dial: skeletonized; completely hand-made; pink-gold dart-style hands.
Strap: black hand-sewn Louisiana alligator leather; Zannetti-personalized 18K pink-gold ardillon buckle.
Note: each model is bespoke and custom-made to the client's request.

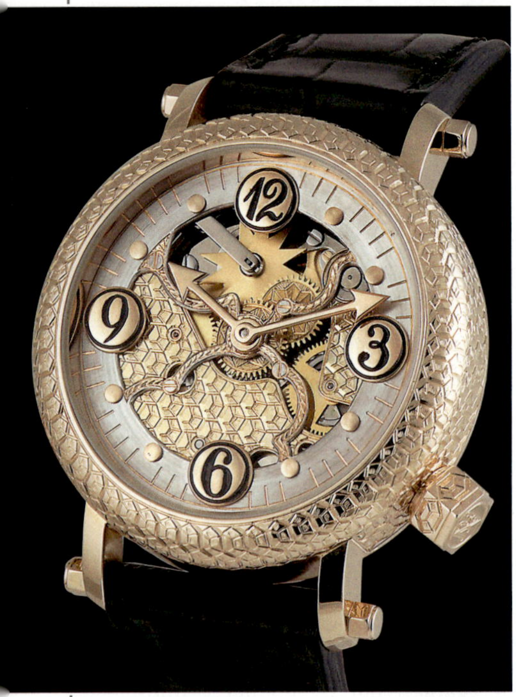

REGENT DRAGON BLACK DIAMONDS — REF. REDRA.51710.334

Movement: automatic-winding.
Functions: off-centered hours and minutes.
Case: 18K pink gold; three-piece; set with round diamonds; Ø 42mm, thickness: 10mm; hand-personalized pressured closed crown; antireflective sapphire crystal with engraved logo; 18K pink-gold caseback with decentralized sapphire crystal opening and fastened with six screws; water resistant to 5atm.
Dial: hand-engraved solid gold; transparent colored enamel; handmade 18K gold dragon figure; yellow-gold-plated indexes.
Strap: black hand-sewn Louisiana alligator leather; Zannetti-personalized 18K gold deployant buckle set with round diamonds.
Also available: steel case, personalized dial color.

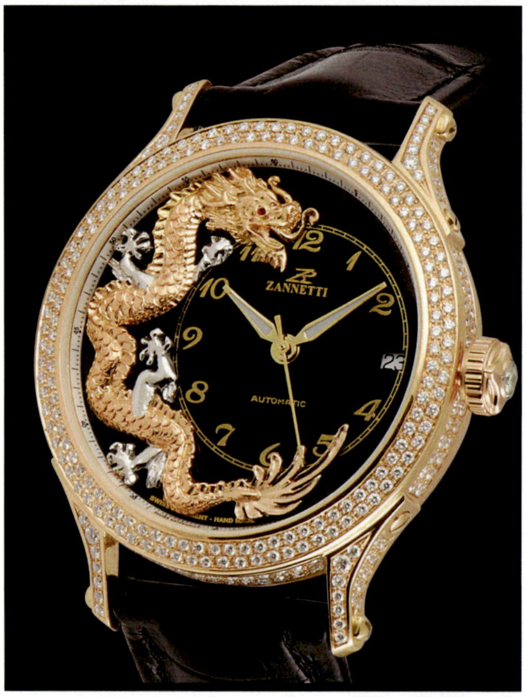

SQUELETTE SILVER — REF. SQFA.160.337

Movement: automatic-winding 2892A2 ETA caliber; Swiss made; movement and rotor totally skeletonized and hand-engraved.
Functions: hours, minutes, seconds.
Case: steel; three-piece; Ø 41mm, thickness: 9.5mm; jointed central attachment bezel with hand-engraved Arabic numerals; hand-personalized screw-down crown; antireflective flat sapphire crystal with engraved logo; back fastened with six screws, numbered, displaying the movement through a sapphire crystal; water resistant to 3atm.
Dial: hand-engraved white-gold flange; four round applied markers; rhodium treatment; leaf-style steel hands with SuperLumiNova.
Strap: black hand-sewn Louisiana alligator leather; Zannetti-personalized steel folding clasp.
Also available: 18K pink-gold case.

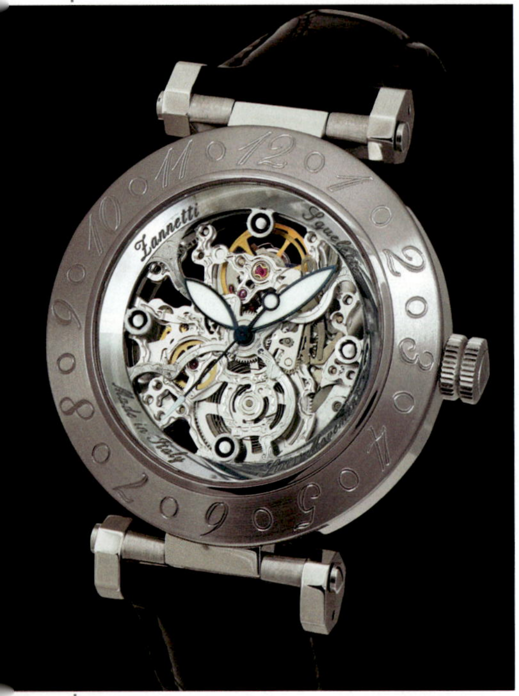

TIME OF DRIVERS RACING ED. BLACK — REF. TODAV.210.337

Movement: automatic-winding 7750 Valjoux caliber chronograph; Swiss made; Zannetti re-elaborated.
Functions: hours, minutes; date at 3; chronograph with two counters: minutes at 12, small seconds at 6.
Case: stainless steel; three-piece; Ø 42.5mm, thickness: 15.3mm; bezel with hand-engraved numbered indexes; black PVD treatment; hand-personalized pressured closed crown; curved antireflective sapphire crystal with engraved logo; stainless steel caseback fastened with five screws, central sapphire crystal opening; water resistant to 3atm.
Dial: black Côtes de Genève; numerals in bombe-applied enamel; leaf-style hands with SuperLumiNova.
Strap: black hand-sewn Louisiana alligator leather, covered with rubber; polished steel folding clasp with safety pushbuttons and engraved Zannetti logo.
Also available: blue or silver dial.

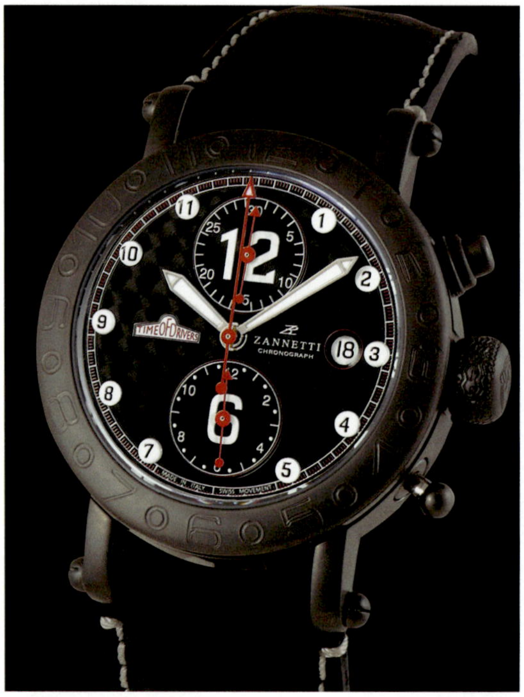

TIME OF DRIVERS LIMITED ED. JAGUAR — REF. TODAV.203.337M

Movement: automatic-winding 7750 Valjoux caliber chronograph; Swiss made; Zannetti re-elaborated.
Functions: hours, minutes; date at 3; chronograph with two counters: minutes at 12, small seconds at 6. **Case:** stainless steel; three-piece; Ø 42.5mm, thickness: 15.3mm; bezel with hand-engraved numbered indexes; hand-personalized pressured closed crown; curved antireflective sapphire crystal with engraved logo; stainless steel caseback fastened with five screws, central sapphire crystal opening; water resistant to 3atm.
Dial: hand-engraved; XL leaf-style hands with Super-LumiNova.
Strap: black hand-sewn Louisiana alligator leather; polished steel folding clasp with safety pushbuttons and engraved Zannetti logo.
Also available: Maserati, Mercedes, Fangio, Ascari, Alfa or traditional double-layer full black, blue or argentè dial.

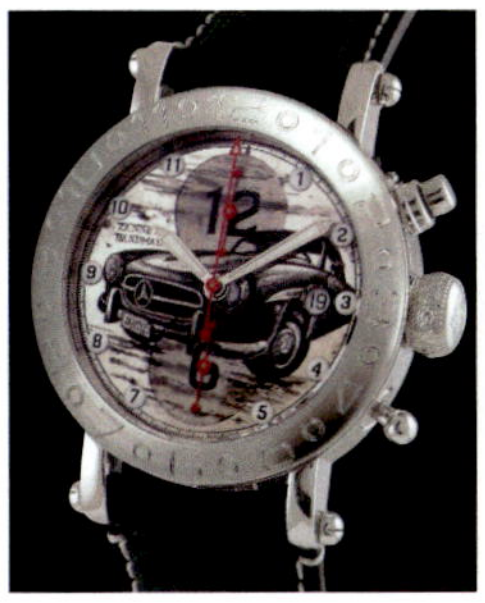

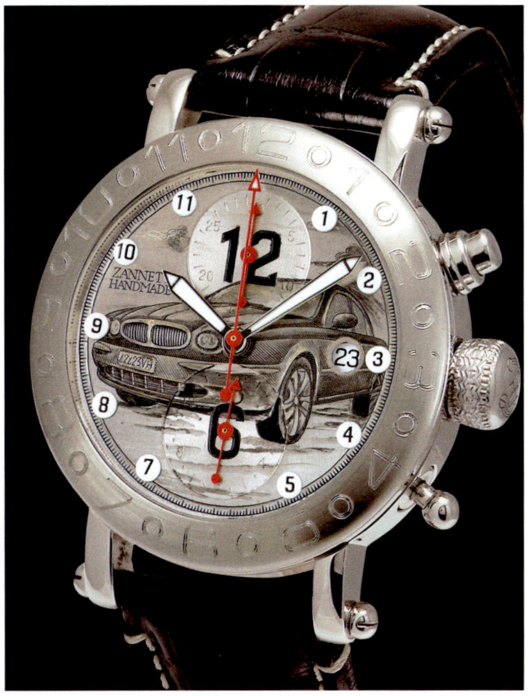

REGENT TREE ORGY — REF. RBOAD.117.14.337

Movement: automatic-winding ETA 2834 caliber; Swiss made; Zannetti re-elaborated; rhodium and perlage plate; Côtes de Genève; blued steel screws.
Functions: hours, minutes, seconds; day at 12; date at 3.
Case: steel; three-piece; Ø 42mm, thickness: 10mm; hand-personalized pressured closed crown; antireflective sapphire crystal; stainless steel caseback with decentralized sapphire crystal opening and fastened with six screws; water resistant to 5atm.
Dial: silver; transparent colored nuances; hand-engraved, yellow-gold-plated alpha hands.
Strap: black hand-sewn Louisiana alligator leather; Zannetti-personalized steel deployant buckle.
Note: limited edition to 100 pieces.
Also available: Bonsai Orgy; Brain Orgy.

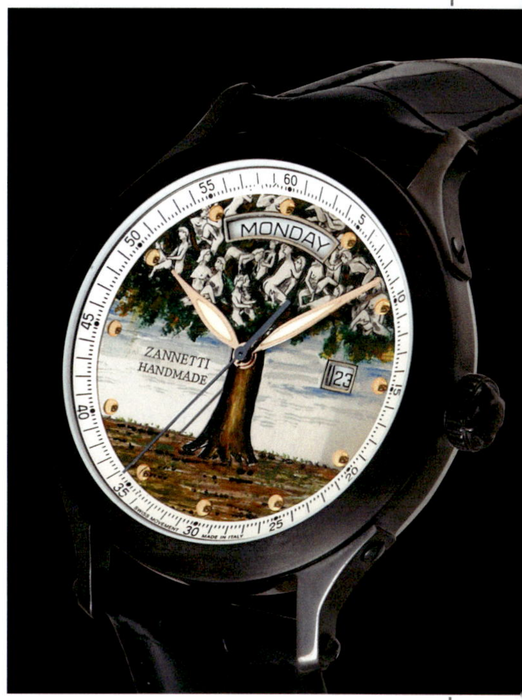

FULL SKY — REF. REFSAA.118.11.137

Movement: automatic-winding 2824 ETA; Swiss made; Zannetti re-elaborated; rhodium and perlage plate; Côtes de Genève; blued steel screws.
Functions: hours, minutes, seconds; date.
Case: steel; three-piece; Ø 42mm, thickness: 10mm; hand-personalized pressured closed crown; antireflective sapphire crystal; stainless steel caseback with decentralized sapphire crystal opening and fastened with six screws; water resistant to 5atm.
Dial: natural mammoth bone; hand-enameled full-sky motif; yellow-gold-plated alpha hands with SuperLumiNova.
Strap: black hand-sewn Louisiana alligator leather; Zannetti-personalized steel deployant buckle.
Also available: Rosa Ventorum.

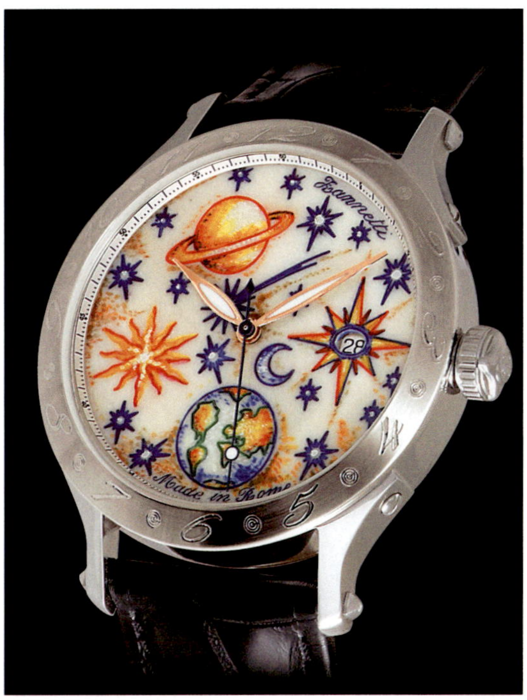

PALATINO HARLEQUIN — REF. PQAA.112.0338

Movement: automatic-winding 2824 ETA; Swiss made; Zannetti re-elaborated; rhodium and perlage plate; Côtes de Genève; blued steel screws.
Functions: hours, minutes, seconds.
Case: steel; three-piece; Ø 44mm, thickness: 12mm; hand-engraved and enameled triangle; hand-personalized closed crown; antireflective crystal fastened with four screws; water resistant to 3atm.
Dial: natural mammoth bone; hand-enameled harlequin triangle motif.
Strap: black hand-sewn Louisiana alligator leather; Zannetti-personalized steel deployant buckle.
Also available: in blue; black and red; green and orange.

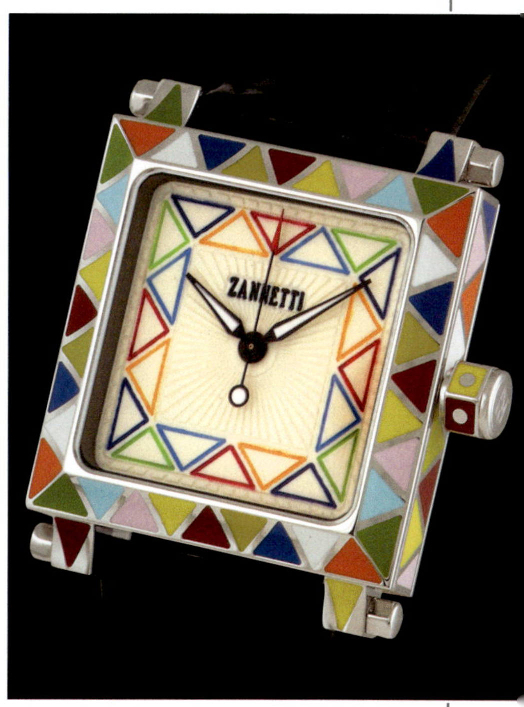

ZENITH

SWISS WATCH MANUFACTURE

SINCE 1865

MAPPING UNCHARTED WATERS

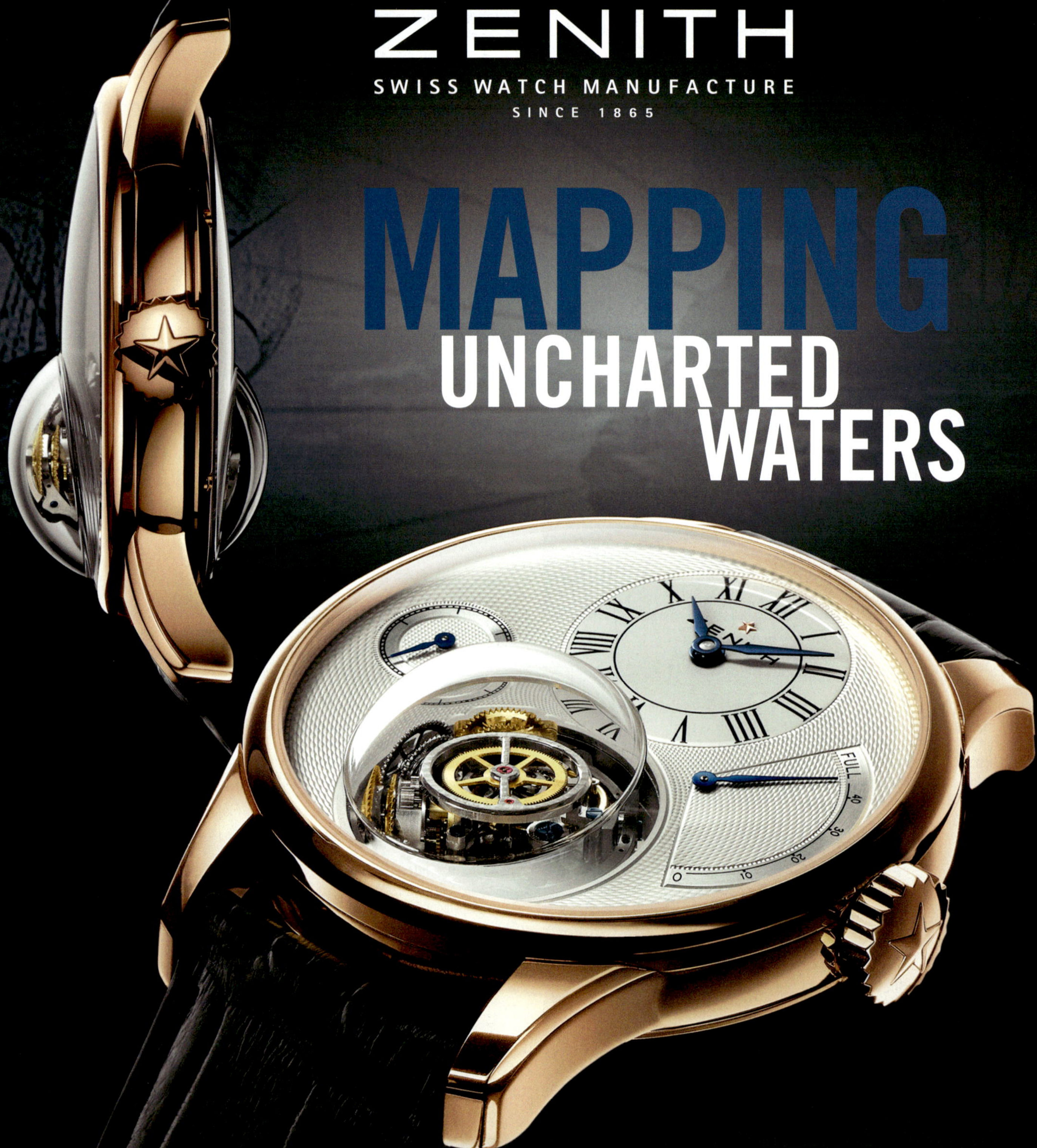

Zenith defies the laws of gravity that have vexed wristwatch designers for years with the Zenith Christophe Colomb, a timepiece equipped with a technically advanced gyroscopic system inspired by marine chronometers.

To achieve the El Primero movement's high level of precision and reliability, Zenith's manufacture workshops in Le Locle spend nine months producing and assembling its components.

The watch shares the same bold spirit as the daring Italian navigator for which it is named, exploring uncharted horological waters with its inventive design. The prominent domed crystal showcases this engineering feat, which was five years in the making at Zenith's manufacture workshops in Le Locle.

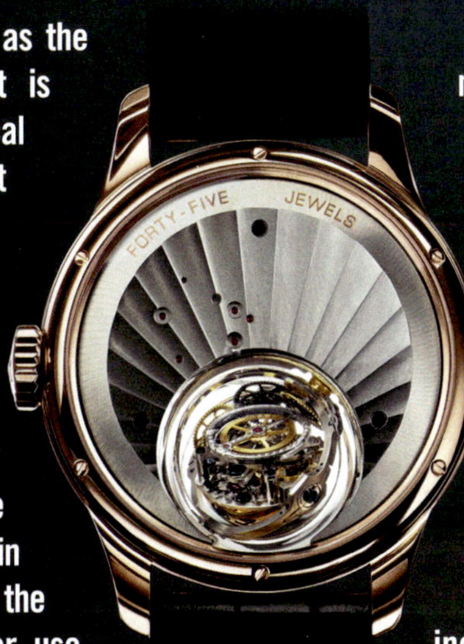

In the 16th century, seafarers began to take advantage of an innovation called the "Cardan suspension" or gimbal, which allows an object to rotate around a single axis. This allowed a ship's compass to remain horizontal even as the ship pitched on the waves. Zenith has adapted this system for use within its Christophe Colomb.

Gravity has always had a negative effect on an escapement's chronometric precision, a problem usually addressed by a tourbillon. However, Zenith's engineers realized that they could circumvent the gravitational problem altogether, simply by maintaining the escapement and regulating organ in a horizontal position. Zenith's groundbreaking gyroscopic system constantly adjusts to keep the regulating organ flat despite the wearer's constant movements. The advantage is made clear when you consider that Zenith's system prevents gravity's harmful effects before they occur, rather than compensating for them after the fact like a tourbillon. Another significant different between the gyroscopic complication and the tourbillon is its level of complexity: Zenith's development comprises 166 components, compared to 66 for a standard tourbillon.

Zenith will produce the Zenith Christophe Colomb as a limited edition that includes 25 pieces each in rose, white and yellow gold.

FACING PAGE

The 42mm rose-gold Christophe Colomb achieves an impressive level of chronometric precision thanks to a self-adjusting system inspired by marine chronometers. Zenith's innovative gyroscopic system is contained within a domed sapphire crystal.

THIS PAGE

TOP Like the sun rising over the horizon, rays of guilloché emanate from the gyroscopic system's domed crystal.

BOTTOM The El Primero Striking 10th measures to one tenth of a second, the smallest increment of time measured by a serially produced mechanical movement.

First introduced in 1969, Zenith's El Primero movement is still celebrated today as a paragon of horological ingenuity. Not only was it the world's first automatic chronograph to beat at a rate of 10 vibrations per second (36,000 vph), the El Primero continues to be the world's most accurate serially produced movement.

Zenith enriches its El Primero collection with a new model that exemplifies this tradition of precision. El Primero Striking 10th features a central chronograph seconds hand that measures time to the tenth of a second, an increment that represents a single beat of the movement's heart.

To display this tiny fraction of time in a legible manner, the blued seconds hand completes a rotation around the dial once every 10 seconds. The measurement is clearly marked by a scale engraved along the outer edge of the silver sunray-brushed dial. A subsidiary dial at 3 o'clock keeps a running total of the chronograph's seconds as it makes its rapid revolutions.

Because the seconds hand starts and stops 10 times a second—or 600 times a minute—it consumes a great deal of energy. To optimize its power reserves, the El Primero Striking 10th uses a number of components made from silicon, a resilient and light material that requires less energy to operate.

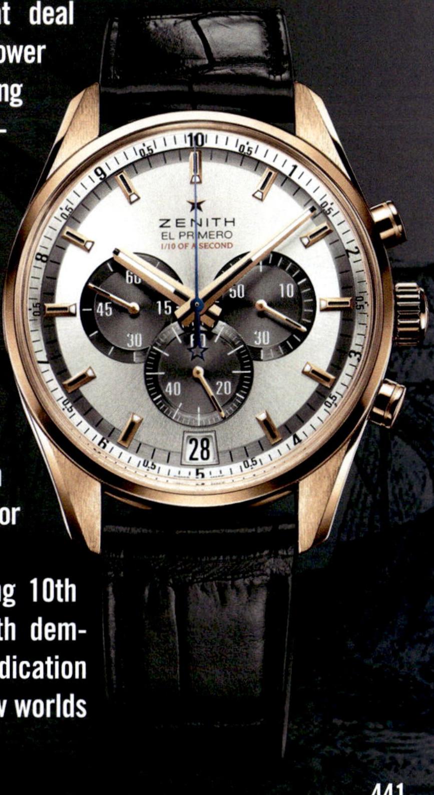

Zenith houses the automatic movement that makes all this possible—El Primero 4052 B—in a 42mm case that is available as a limited edition in either rose gold (500 pieces) or stainless steel (1,969 pieces).

With its El Primero Striking 10th and Christophe Colomb, Zenith demonstrates its unshakable dedication to the exploration of brave new worlds of precision.

EL PRIMERO STRIKING 10TH — REF. 18.2040.4052/21.C496

Movement: El Primero 4052 B automatic; 50-hour power reserve; Ø 30mm, thickness: 6.6mm; 326 components; 31 jewels; 36,000 vph; oscillating weight with Côtes de Genève pattern.
Functions: hours, minutes; small seconds at 9; date at 6; 1/10th of a second chronograph: 60-minute counter at 6, 60-second counter at 3, 1/10th of a second indication by the chronograph hand.

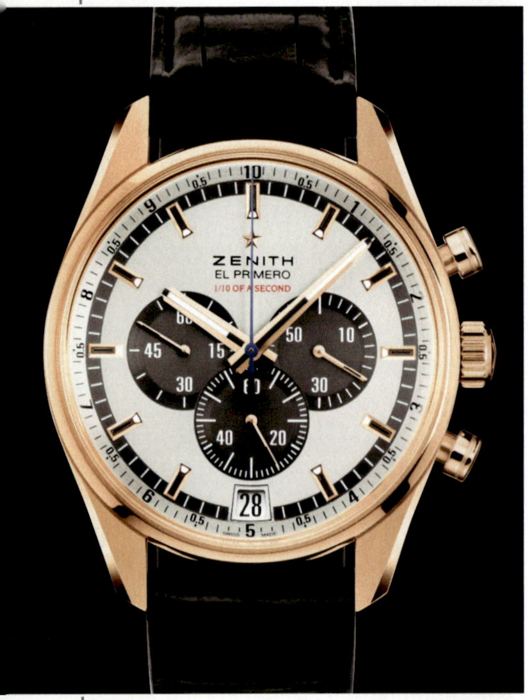

Case: 18K rose gold ; Ø 42mm, thickness: 12.75mm; curved sapphire crystal with antireflective treatment on both sides; sapphire crystal caseback; water resistant to 10atm.
Dial: silver sunray; three-color counters; rhodium-faceted hands and indexes with SuperLumiNova SLN C1 coating.
Strap: black alligator leather lined with rubber; 18K rose-gold buckle.
Note: limited edition of 500 pieces.

EL PRIMERO STRIKING 10TH — REF. 03.2041.4052/69.C496

Movement: El Primero 4052 B automatic; 50-hour power reserve; Ø 30mm, thickness: 6.6mm; 326 components; 31 jewels; 36,000 vph; oscillating weight with Côtes de Genève pattern.
Functions: hours, minutes; small seconds at 9; date at 6; 1/10th of a second chronograph: 60-minute counter at 6, 60-second counter at 3, 1/10th of a second indication by the chronograph hand.

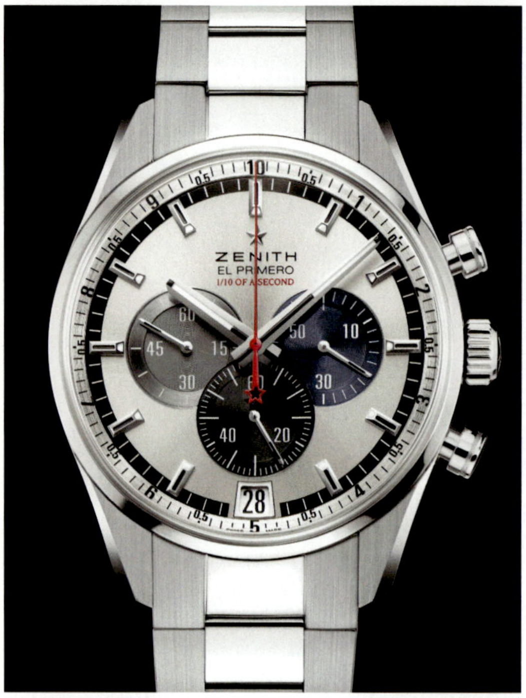

Case: stainless steel; Ø 42mm, thickness: 12.75mm; curved sapphire crystal with antireflective treatment on both sides; sapphire crystal caseback; water resistant to 10atm.
Dial: silver sunray; nickel circular satined zones; rhodium-faceted hands and indexes with SuperLumiNova SLN C1 coating.
Bracelet: metal; stainless steel triple-folding buckle
Note: limited edition of 1,969 pieces.

EL PRIMERO 36,000 VPH "TRIBUTE TO CHARLES VERMOT" — REF. 03.2041.400/51.C496

Movement: El Primero 400 B automatic; 50-hour power reserve; Ø 30mm, thickness: 6.6mm; 326 components; 31 jewels; 36,000 vph; COSC-certified; oscillating weight with Côtes de Genève pattern.
Functions: hours, minutes; small seconds at 9; date at 6; three-counter chronograph: central chronograph hand, 30-minute counter at 3 and 12-hour counter at 6.
Case: stainless steel; Ø 42mm, thickness: 12.75mm; tachometric scale on the flange; curved sapphire crystal with antireflective treatment on both sides; sapphire crystal caseback; water resistant to 10atm.

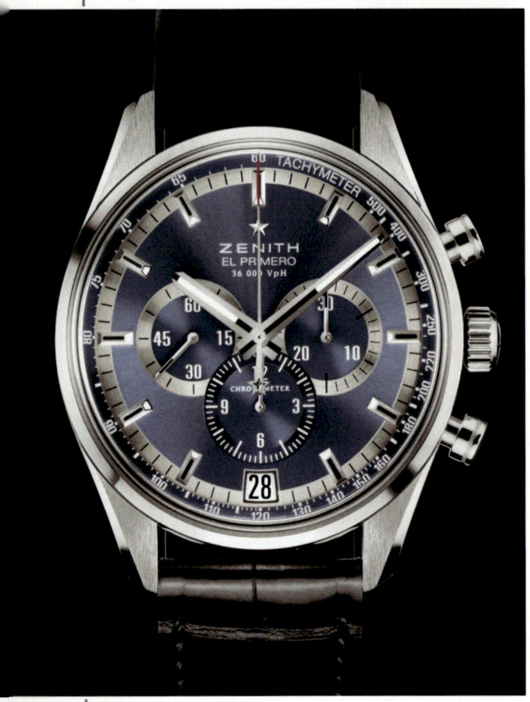

Dial: blue sunray with nickel; circular satined zones; tribute to Charles Vermot; rhodium-faceted hands and indexes with Super-LumiNova SLN C1 coating.
Strap: black alligator leather lined with rubber; stainless steel buckle.
Note: limited edition of 1975 pieces.

EL PRIMERO 36,000 VPH — REF. 03.2040.400/21.M2040

Movement: El Primero 400 B automatic; 50-hour power reserve; Ø 30mm, thickness: 6.6mm; 326 components; 31 jewels; 36,000 vph; COSC-certified; oscillating weight with Côtes de Genève pattern.
Functions: hours, minutes; small seconds at 9; date at 6; three-counter chronograph: central chronograph hand, 30-minute counter at 3 and 12-hour counter at 6.
Case: stainless steel; Ø 42mm, thickness: 12.75mm; tachometric scale on the flange; curved sapphire crystal with antireflective treatment on both sides; sapphire crystal caseback; water resistant to 10atm.

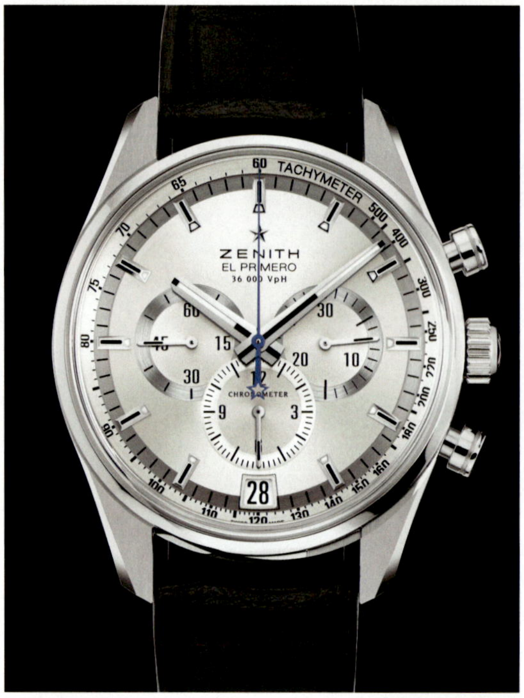

Dial: silver sunray with nickel; circular satined zones; rhodium-faceted hands and indexes with SuperLumiNova SLN C1 coating.
Strap: black alligator leather lined with rubber; stainless steel buckle.

EL PRIMERO 36,000 VPH — REF. 18.2040.400/02.C494

Movement: El Primero 400 B automatic; 50-hour power reserve; Ø 30mm, thickness: 6.6mm; 326 components; 31 jewels; 36,000 vph; COSC-certified; oscillating weight with Côtes de Genève pattern.
Functions: hours, minutes; small seconds at 9; date at 6; three-counter chronograph: central chronograph hand, 30-minute counter at 3 and 12-hour counter at 6.
Case: 18K rose gold; Ø 42mm, thickness: 12.75mm; tachometric scale on the flange; curved sapphire crystal with antireflective treatment on both sides; sapphire crystal caseback; water resistant to 10atm.
Dial: silver sunray with nickel; circular satined zones.
Strap: brown alligator leather lined with rubber; 18K rose-gold pin buckle.

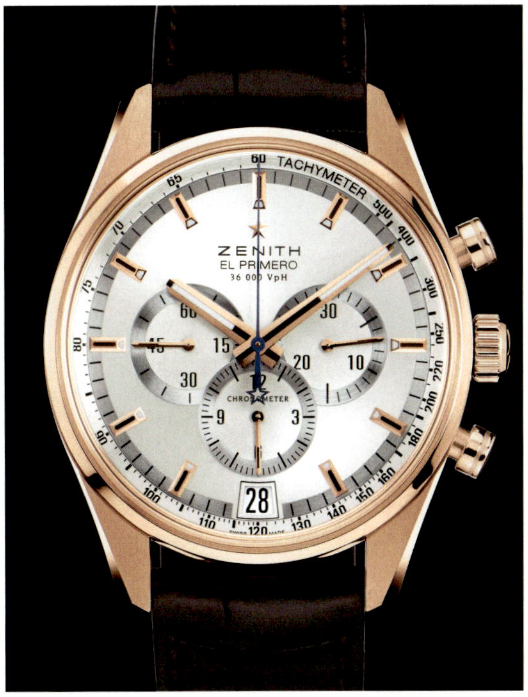

EL PRIMERO RETROTIMER — REF. 75.2030.4055/21.R580

Movement: El Primero 4055 B automatic; 50-hour power reserve; Ø 30mm, thickness: 6.6mm; 281 components; 31 jewels; 36,000 vph; oscillating weight with Côtes de Genève pattern.
Functions: hours, minutes; date at 6; flyback chronograph: central flyback chronograph hand, 30-minute counter at 3.
Case: black PVD; Ø 42mm, thickness: 12.75mm; curved sapphire crystal with antireflective treatment on both sides; sapphire crystal caseback; water resistant to 10atm.
Dial: transferred carbon; rhodium-faceted indexes and hands with Super-LumiNova SLN C1.
Strap: black rubber; black PVD triple-folding buckle.

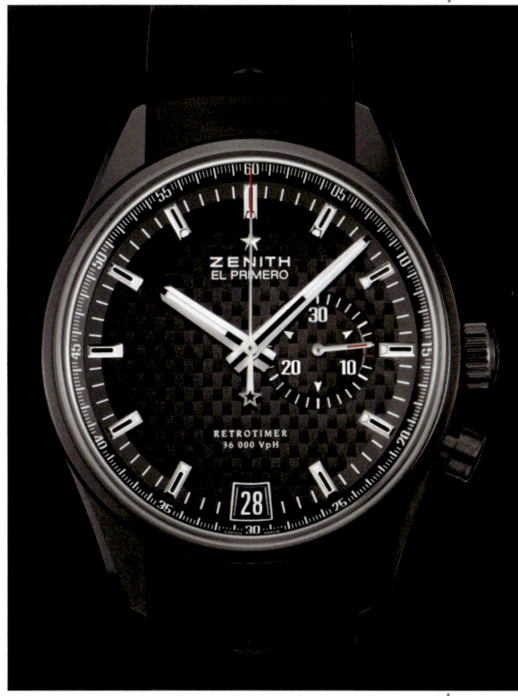

EL PRIMERO RATTRAPANTE — REF. 03.2050.4026/91.C630

Movement: El Primero 4026 automatic; 50-hour power reserve; Ø 30mm, thickness: 9.35mm; 346 components; 32 jewels; 36,000 vph; COSC-certified; oscillating weight with Côtes de Genève pattern.
Functions: hours, minutes; small seconds at 9; large date at 6; split-seconds chronograph: split-seconds and chronograph hand, 30-minute counter at 3.
Case: stainless steel; Ø 44mm, thickness: 16mm; curved sapphire crystal with antireflective treatment on both sides; sapphire crystal caseback; water resistant to 10atm.
Dial: transferred carbon; rhodium-faceted hands and indexes with SuperLumiNova SLN C1.
Strap: black alligator leather lined with rubber; stainless steel triple-folding buckle.

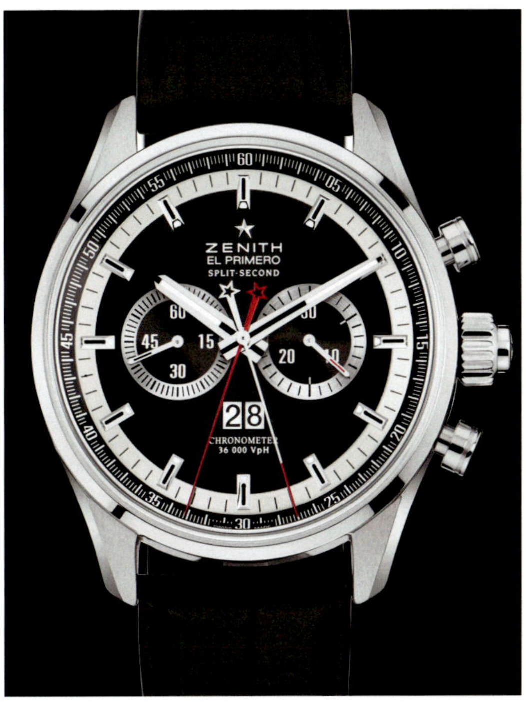

EL PRIMERO RATTRAPANTE — REF. 78.2050.4026/91.R530

Movement: El Primero 4026 automatic; 50-hour power reserve; Ø 30mm, thickness: 9.35mm; 346 components; 32 jewels; 36,000 vph; COSC-certified; oscillating weight with Côtes de Genève pattern.
Functions: hours, minutes; small seconds at 9; large date at 6; split-seconds chronograph: split-seconds and chronograph hand, 30-minute counter at 3.
Case: PVD and rose gold; Ø 44mm, thickness: 16mm; curved sapphire crystal with antireflective treatment on both sides; sapphire crystal caseback; water resistant to 10atm.
Dial: black sunray with nickel; circular satined zones; rose-gold-plated hands and indexes with SuperLumiNova SLN C1.
Strap: integrated black rubber; black PVD triple-folding buckle.

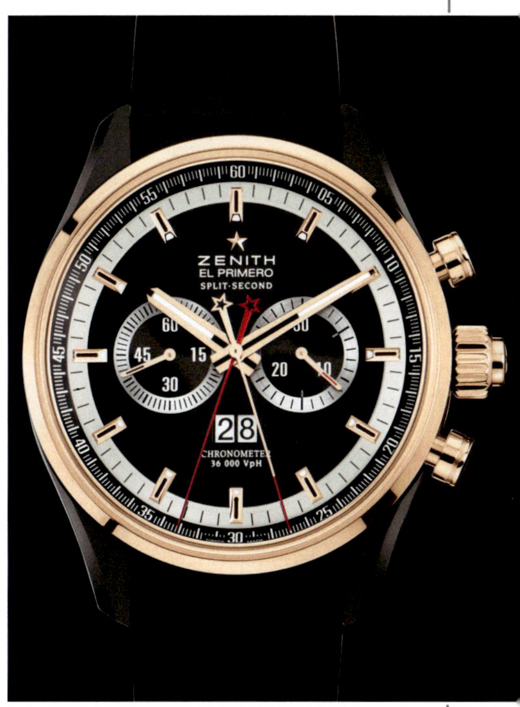

EL PRIMERO CAPTAIN REF. 51.2110.400/01.C498

Movement: El Primero 400 B automatic; 50-hour power reserve; Ø 30mm, thickness: 6.6mm; 326 components; 31 jewels; 36,000 vph; COSC-certified; oscillating weight with Côtes de Genève pattern.
Functions: hours, minutes; small seconds at 9; date at 6; three-counter chronograph: central chronograph hand, 30-minute counter at 3 and 12-hour counter at 6.
Case: bi-color rose gold and steel; Ø 42mm, thickness: 11.8mm; curved sapphire crystal with antireflective treatment on both sides; sapphire crystal caseback; water resistant to 5atm.
Dial: silver sunray; rhodium-faceted indexes and hands with gold plating.
Strap: dark brown alligator leather lined with rubber; steel pin buckle.

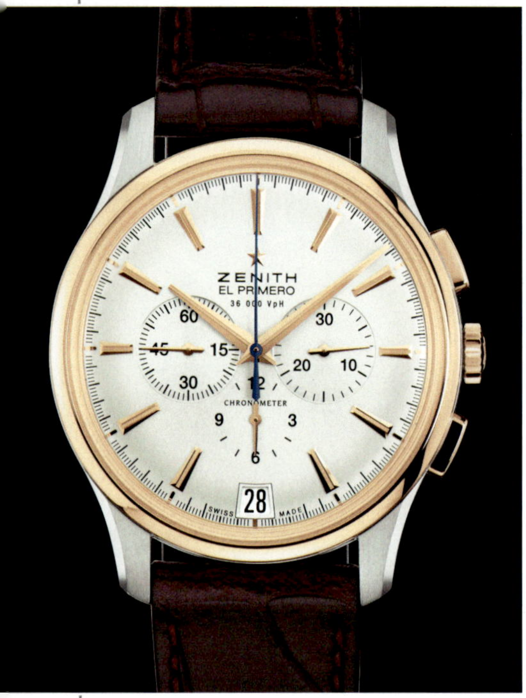

EL PRIMERO CAPTAIN REF. 03.2110.400/21.C493

Movement: El Primero 400 B automatic; 50-hour power reserve; Ø 30mm, thickness: 6.6mm; 326 components; 31 jewels; 36,000 vph; COSC-certified oscillating weight with Côtes de Genève pattern.
Functions: hours, minutes; small seconds at 9; date at 6; three-counter chronograph: central chronograph hand, 30-minute counter at 3 and 12-hour counter at 6.
Case: stainless steel; Ø 42mm, thickness: 11.8mm; curved sapphire crystal with antireflective treatment on both sides; sapphire crystal caseback; water resistant to 5atm.
Dial: black sunray; rhodium-faceted indexes and hands with gold plating.
Strap: black alligator leather lined with rubber; steel pin buckle.

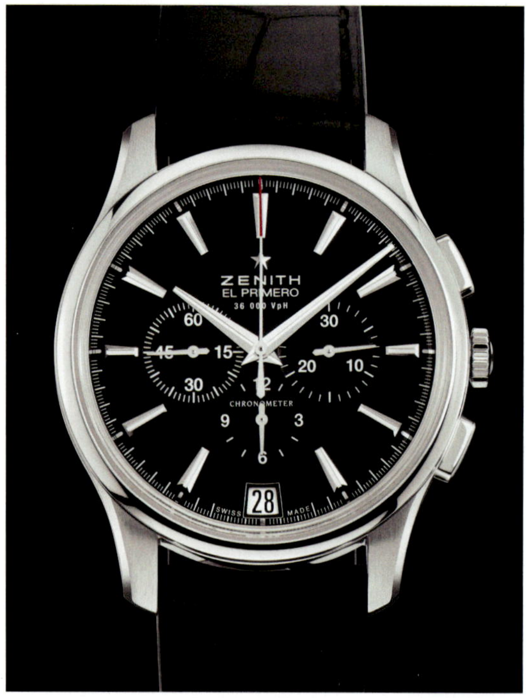

EL PRIMERO TOURBILLON REF. 03.2050.4035/21.C630

Movement: El Primero 4035 D automatic; 50-hour power reserve; Ø 37mm, thickness: 7.55mm; 325 components; 35 jewels; 36,000 vph; oscillating weight with Côtes de Genève pattern.
Functions: hours, minutes; tourbillon; chronograph: central seconds hand, 30-minute counter at 3 and 12-hour counter at 6.
Case: stainless steel; Ø 44mm; curved sapphire crystal with antireflective treatment on both sides; sapphire crystal caseback; water resistant to 10atm.
Dial: black sunray; rhodium-faceted hands and indexes with SuperLumiNova SLN C1; tourbillon carriage at 11, makes one turn per minute, small seconds on the carriage, date is positioned around the carriage.
Strap: black alligator leather; stainless steel triple-folding buckle.
Note: limited edition of 250 pieces.

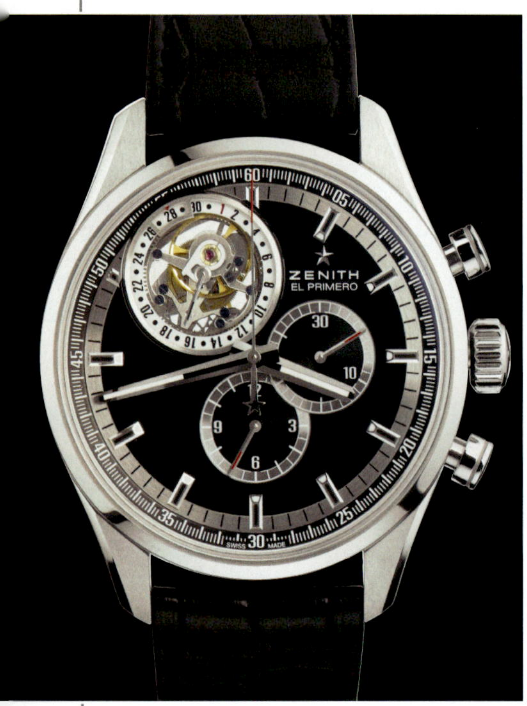

EL PRIMERO TOURBILLON REF. 18.2050.4035/01.C630

Movement: El Primero 4035 D automatic; 50-hour power reserve; Ø 37mm, thickness: 7.55mm; 325 components; 35 jewels; 36,000 vph; oscillating weight with Côtes de Genève pattern.
Functions: hours, minutes; tourbillon; chronograph: central seconds hand, 30-minute counter at 3 and 12-hour counter at 6.
Case: rose gold; Ø 44mm; curved sapphire crystal with antireflective treatment on both sides; sapphire crystal caseback; water resistant to 10atm.
Dial: silver sunray; rose-gold-plated hands and indexes with SuperLumiNova SLN C1; tourbillon carriage at 11, carriage makes one turn per minute, small seconds on the carriage, date is positioned around the carriage.
Strap: dark brown alligator leather lined with rubber; rose-gold triple-folding buckle.
Note: limited edition of 250 pieces.
Also available: black alligator leather.

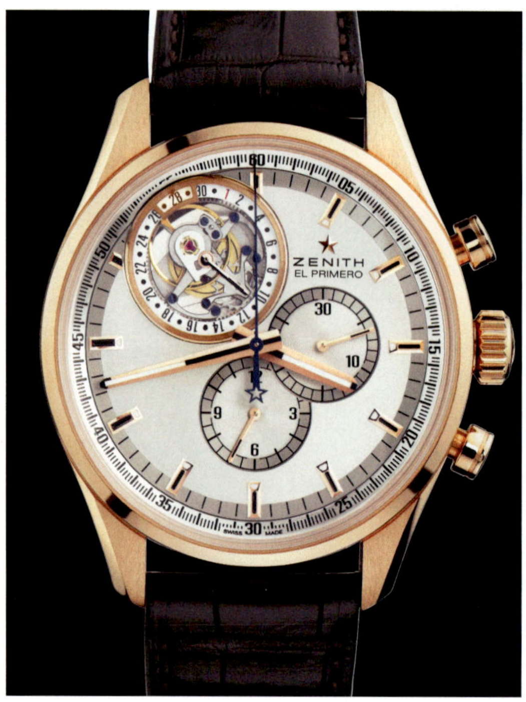

ELITE ULTRA THIN REF. 03.2010.681/01.C493

Movement: Elite 681 automatic; 50-hour power reserve; Ø 25.6mm, thickness: 3.81mm; 128 components; 27 jewels; 28,800 vph; oscillating weight with Côtes de Genève pattern.
Functions: hours, minutes; small seconds at 9.
Case: stainless steel; Ø 40mm, thickness: 7.6mm; curved sapphire crystal with anti-reflective treatment on both sides; sapphire crystal caseback; water resistant to 5atm.
Dial: silver sunray; rhodium-faceted hands and indexes.
Strap: black alligator leather lined with rubber; stainless steel pin buckle.

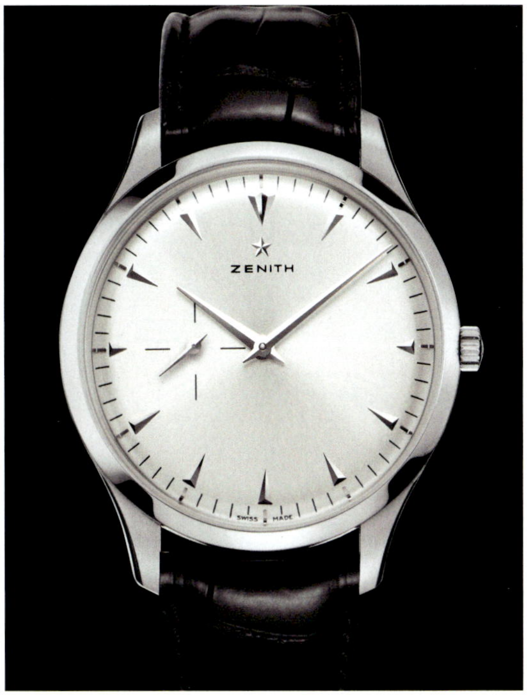

ELITE ULTRA THIN REF. 18.2010.681/01.C498

Movement: Elite 681 automatic; 50-hour power reserve; Ø 25.6mm, thickness: 3.81mm; 128 components; 27 jewels; 28,800 vph; oscillating weight with Côtes de Genève pattern.
Functions: hours, minutes; small seconds at 9.
Case: 18K rose gold; Ø 40mm, thickness: 7.6mm; curved sapphire crystal with anti-reflective treatment on both sides; sapphire crystal caseback; water resistant to 5atm.
Dial: silver sunray; faceted gold-plated hands and indexes.
Strap: dark brown alligator leather lined with rubber; 18K rose-gold pin buckle.

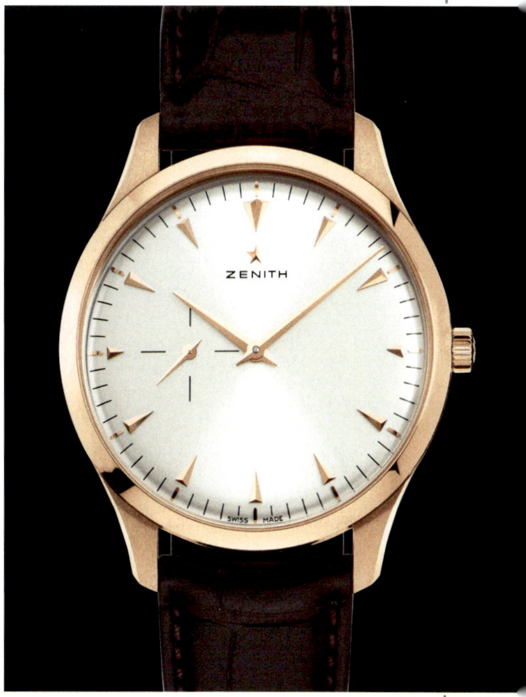

ELITE ULTRA THIN REF. 03.2010.681/02.C493

Movement: Elite 681 automatic; 50-hour power reserve; Ø 25.6mm, thickness: 3.81mm; 128 components; 27 jewels; 28,800 vph; oscillating weight with Côtes de Genève pattern.
Functions: hours, minutes; small seconds at 9.
Case: stainless steel; Ø 40mm, thickness: 7.6mm; curved sapphire crystal with anti-reflective treatment on both sides; sapphire crystal caseback; water resistant to 5atm.
Dial: silver sunray; set with diamonds (0.1 carat); rhodium-faceted hands and indexes.
Strap: black alligator leather lined with rubber; stainless steel pin buckle.
Also available: 18K rose-gold version.

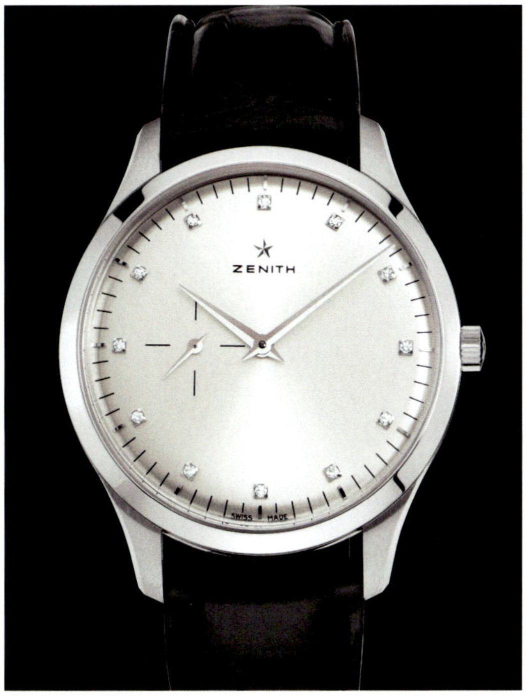

ELITE ULTRA THIN REF. 18.2010.681/91.C493

Movement: Elite 681 automatic; 50-hour power reserve; Ø 25.6mm, thickness: 3.81mm; 128 components; 27 jewels; 28,800 vph; oscillating weight with Côtes de Genève pattern.
Functions: hours, minutes; small seconds at 9.
Case: 18K rose gold; Ø 40mm, thickness: 7.6mm; curved sapphire crystal with anti-reflective treatment on both sides; sapphire crystal caseback; water resistant to 5atm.
Dial: slate-gray sunray; rhodium-faceted hands and indexes with gold plating.
Strap: black alligator leather lined with rubber; 18K rose-gold pin buckle.
Also available: stainless steel version.

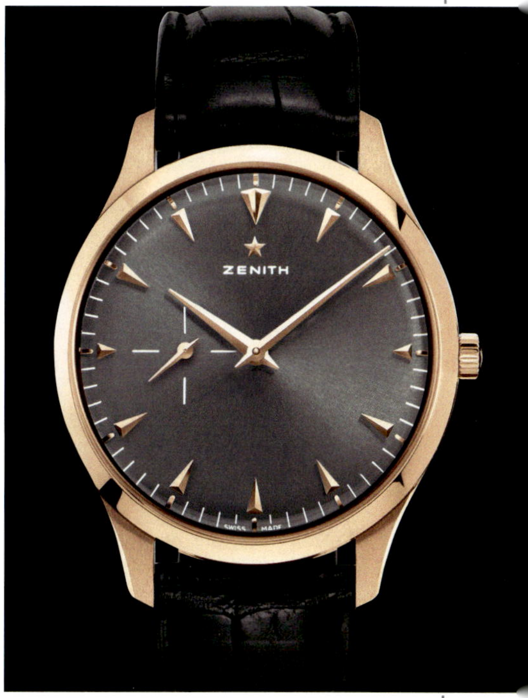

ELITE ULTRA THIN — REF. 18.2010.681/11.C498

Movement: Elite 681 automatic; 50-hour power reserve; Ø 25.6mm, thickness: 3.81mm; 128 components; 27 jewels; 28,800 vph; oscillating weight with Côtes de Genève pattern.
Functions: hours, minutes; small seconds at 9.
Case: 18K rose gold; Ø 40mm, thickness: 7.6mm; curved sapphire crystal with antireflective treatment on both sides; sapphire crystal caseback; water resistant to 5atm.
Dial: white lacquered; black transferred indexes and numerals; rhodium-faceted hands with gold plating.
Strap: dark brown alligator leather lined with rubber; 18K rose-gold pin buckle.
Also available: stainless steel version; black alligator leather strap.

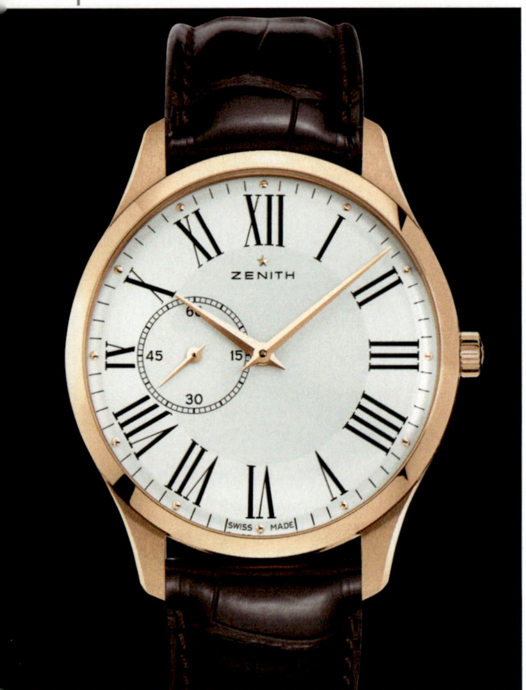

ELITE ULTRA THIN LADY AUTOMATIQUE — REF. 22.1025.680/11.C674

Movement: Elite 680 automatic; 50-hour power reserve; Ø 25.6mm, thickness: 3.28mm; 143 components; 26 jewels; 28,800 vph; oscillating weight with Grain d'Orge pattern.
Functions: hours, minutes; small seconds at 9.
Case: 18K rose gold; Ø 33mm; set with 72 full-cut Top Wesselton VVS-VS diamonds (0.52 carat); curved sapphire crystal with antireflective treatment on both sides; sapphire crystal caseback; water resistant to 3atm.
Dial: white lacquered; rhodium-faceted hands with gold plating; black transferred indexes and numerals.
Strap: dark brown alligator leather lined with silky Alzavel calfskin; 18K rose-gold pin buckle.
Also available: brown silk alligator leather strap.

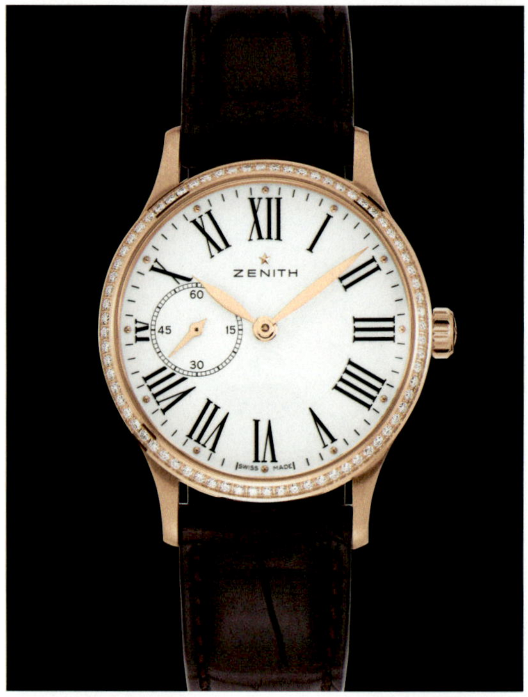

ELITE CAPTAIN CENTRAL SECOND — REF. 03.2020.670/01.C498

Movement: Elite 670 automatic; 50-hour power reserve; Ø 25.6mm, thickness: 3.47mm; 144 components; 27 jewels; 28,800 vph; oscillating weight with Côtes de Genève pattern.
Functions: hours, minutes; seconds; date at 6.
Case: stainless steel; Ø 40mm, thickness: 8.1mm; curved sapphire crystal with antireflective treatment on both sides; sapphire crystal caseback; water resistant to 5atm.
Dial: silver sunray; rhodium-faceted hands and indexes with gold plating.
Strap: dark brown alligator leather lined with rubber; stainless steel pin buckle.
Also available: black alligator leather strap.

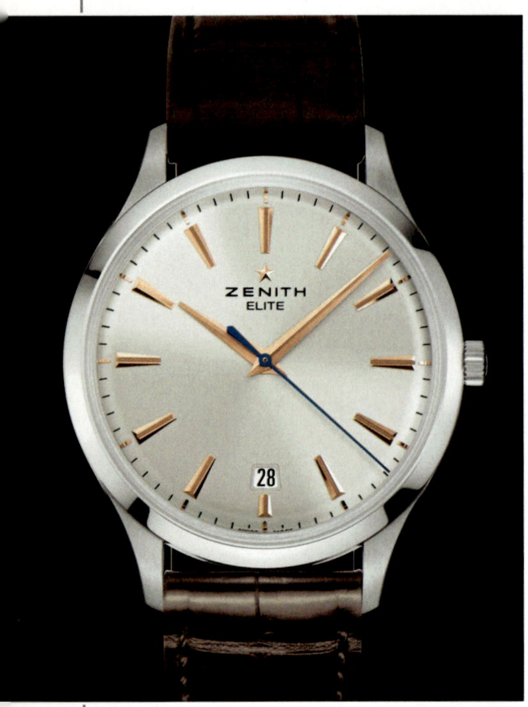

ELITE CAPTAIN CENTRAL SECOND — REF. 03.2020.670/21.M2020

Movement: Elite 670 automatic; 50-hour power reserve; Ø 25.6mm, thickness: 3.47mm; 144 components; 27 jewels; 28,800 vph; oscillating weight with Côtes de Genève pattern.
Functions: hours, minutes; seconds; date at 6.
Case: stainless steel; Ø 40mm, thickness: 8.1mm; curved sapphire crystal with antireflective treatment on both sides; sapphire crystal caseback; water resistant to 5atm.
Dial: black sunray; rhodium-faceted hands and indexes with gold plating.
Bracelet: metal.

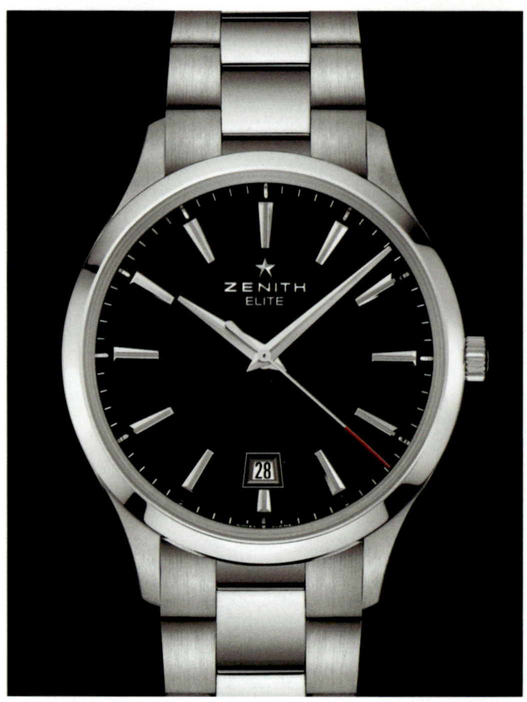

ELITE CAPTAIN CENTRAL SECOND REF. 18.2020.670/01.C498

Movement: Elite 670 automatic; 50-hour power reserve; Ø 25.6mm, thickness: 3.47mm; 144 components; 27 jewels; 28,800 vph; oscillating weight with Côtes de Genève pattern.
Functions: hours, minutes; seconds; date at 6.
Case: 18K rose gold; Ø 40mm, thickness: 8.1mm; curved sapphire crystal with antireflective treatment on both sides; sapphire crystal caseback; water resistant to 5atm.
Dial: silver sunray; rhodium-faceted hands and indexes with gold plating.
Strap: dark brown alligator leather lined with rubber; 18K rose-gold pin buckle.
Also available: black alligator leather strap.

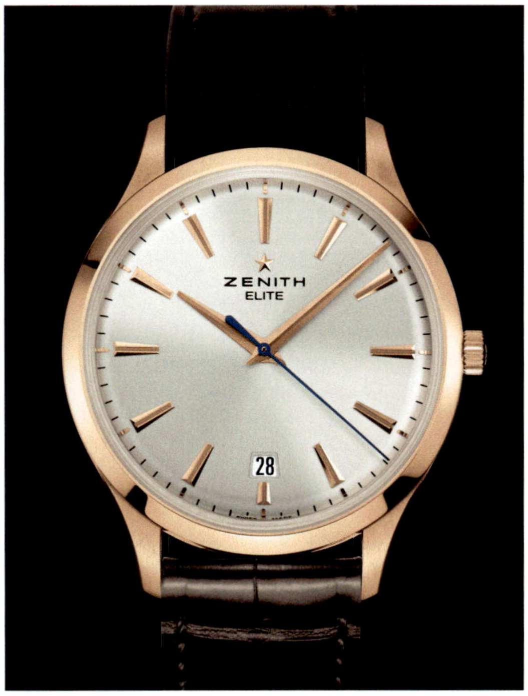

ELITE BABY STAR OPEN REF. 03.1220.68/03.C664

Movement: Elite 68 automatic; 50-hour power reserve; Ø 25.6mm, thickness: 3.81mm; 126 components; 28 jewels; 28,800 vph; oscillating weight decorated with stamped ZENITH numerals and stars.
Functions: hours, minutes; small seconds at 9.
Case: stainless steel; Ø 32mm; curved sapphire crystal with antireflective treatment on both sides; sapphire crystal caseback; water resistant to 3atm.
Dial: silver guilloché; heart open dial at 10, revealing the Elite caliber; sanded ruthenium leaves; small seconds hand symbolized with a red heart.
Strap: white crocodile leather lined with silky Alzavel calfskin; stainless steel pin buckle.

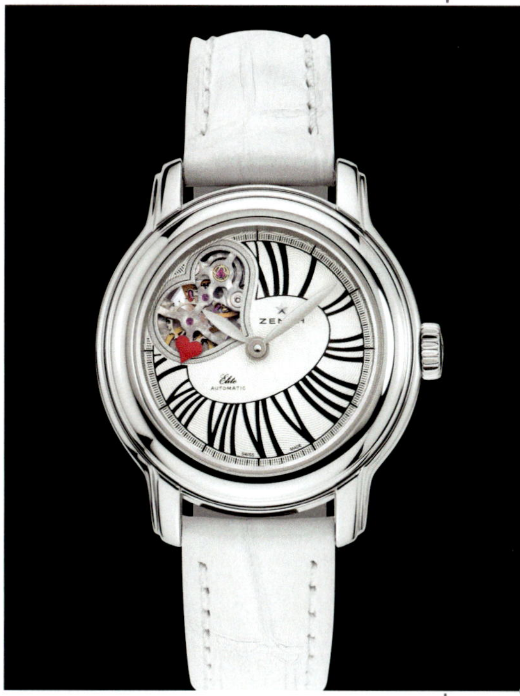

EL PRIMERO CHRONOMASTER STAR OPEN LOVE REF. 22.1230.4021/84.C665

Movement: El Primero 4021 automatic; 50-hour power reserve; Ø 30mm, thickness: 7.75mm; 248 components; 39 jewels; 36,000 vph; oscillating weight with Côtes de Genève pattern.
Functions: hours, minutes; small seconds at 9; chronograph: central second hand, 30-minute counter at 3.
Case: rose gold; Ø 37.5mm; bezel set with diamonds (0.69 carat); curved sapphire crystal with antireflective treatment on both sides; sapphire crystal with engraved Zenith stars; water resistant to 3atm.
Dial: silver guilloché; set with diamonds on the heart (0.1 carat); heart opening at 10 revealing the El Primero caliber; gold-plated hands; small seconds hand symbolized with a red heart.
Strap: dark brown alligator leather lined with silky Alzavel calfskin; rose-gold triple-folding buckle.
Also available: black alligator leather strap.

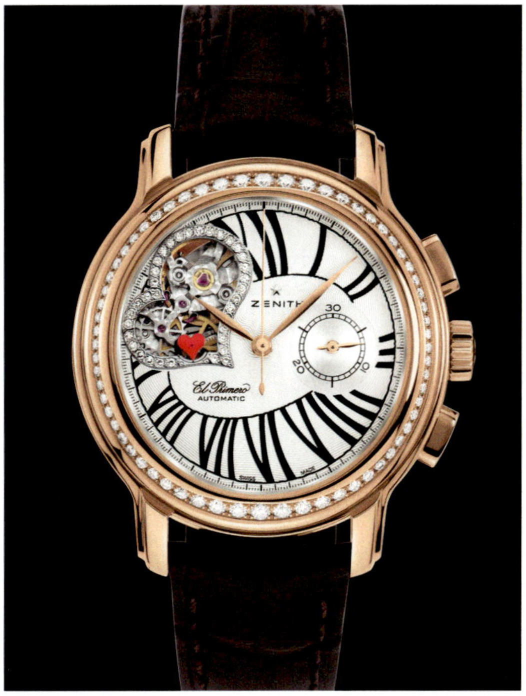

EL PRIMERO NEW VINTAGE 1969 LADY REF. 03.1969.401/02.C510

Movement: El Primero 469 automatic; 50-hour power reserve; Ø 30mm, thickness: 6.5mm; 278 components; 31 jewels; 36,000 vph; oscillating weight with Côtes de Genève pattern.
Functions: hours, minutes; small seconds at 9; date at 4:30; chronograph: central seconds hand, 30-minute counter at 3 and 12-hour counter at 6.
Case: stainless steel; Ø 40mm; tachometric scale; curved sapphire crystal with antireflective treatment on both sides; sapphire crystal caseback; water resistant to 5atm.
Dial: white; applied hand-mounted rhodium indexes with orange SuperLumi-Nova; silver-sanded hands with orange SuperLumi-Nova.
Strap: white alligator leather lined with rubber; stainless steel pin buckle.
Also available: stainless steel bracelet with diamonds.

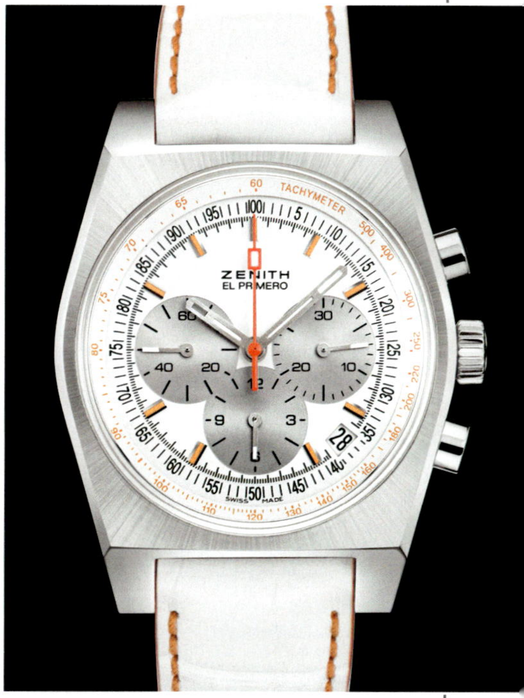

Brand Directory

A. LANGE & SÖHNE
Altenberger Strasse 15
01768 Glashütte
Germany
Tel: 49 35053 440
USA: 800 408 8147

ALPINA
8 Chemin de la Galaise
1228 Plan-les-Ouates
Switzerland
Tel: 41 22 860 87 40
USA: 877 619 2824

AUDEMARS PIGUET
1348 Le Brassus
Switzerland
Tel: 41 21 845 14 00
USA: 212 758 8400

BEDAT & CO.
45 Rue Agasse
1211 Geneva, 17
Switzerland
Tel: 41 22 718 01 83
USA: 305 674 9670

BELL & ROSS
8 Rue Copernic
75016 Paris
France
Tel: 33 1 73 73 93 00
USA: 888 307 7887

BLANCPAIN
Le Rocher 12
1348 Le Brassus
Switzerland
Tel: 41 21 796 36 36
USA: 877 520 1735

BOUCHERON
20 Rue de la Paix
75002 Paris
France
Tel: 33 1 42 44 42 44
USA: 866 983 3747

BREGUET
1344 L'Abbaye
Switzerland
Tel: 41 21 841 90 90
USA: 866 458 7488

BUBEN & ZÖRWEG
Hauptstrasse 515
8962 Gröbming
Austria
Tel: 43 3685 224 80
USA: 310 205 5555

BVLGARI
Rue de Monruz 34,
2000 Neuchâtel
Switzerland
Tel: 41 32 722 78 78
USA: 212 315 9700

CARL F. BUCHERER
1805 South Metro Parkway
Dayton, OH 45459
USA: 800 395 4306

CARTIER SA
Boulevard James-Fazy 8
1201 Geneva
Switzerland
Tel: 41 22 721 24 00
USA: 212 446 3400

CHANEL
25 Place du Marché St. Honoré
75001 Paris
France
Tel: 33 1 55 35 50 00
USA: 212 688 5055

CHOPARD
Rue de Veyrot 8
1217 Meyrin-Geneva 2
Switzerland
Tel: 41 22 719 31 31
USA: 212 821 0300

CHRISTOPHE CLARET
Route du Soleil d'Or 2
2400 Le Locle
Switzerland
Tel: 41 32 933 80 80
USA: 954 610 2234

CLERC
Rue de Lausanne 37A
1201 Geneva
Switzerland
Tel: 41 22 716 25 50
USA: 212 605 0163

CONCORD
MGI Luxury Group SA
Rue de Nidau 35
2501 Bienne
Switzerland
Tel: 41 32 329 34 00
USA: 800 547 4073

DE GRISOGONO
176 bis Route de St. Julien
1228 Plan-les-Ouates
Switzerland
Tel: 41 22 817 81 00
USA: 212 439 4220

DeWITT
Rue du Pré de la Fontaine 2
Satigny 1217 Meyrin 2
Switzerland
Tel: 41 22 750 97 97
USA: 305 572 9812

DIOR HORLOGERIE
44 Rue François 1er
75008 Paris
France
Tel: 33 1 40 73 54 44
USA: 212 931 2700

ETERNA
Schützengasse 46
2540 Grenchen
Switzerland
Tel: 41 32 654 72 11
USA: 212 308 1786

FRANCK MULLER
22 Route de Malagny
1294 Genthod
Switzerland
Tel: 41 22 959 88 88
France: 33 1 53 67 44 39

FRÉDÉRIQUE CONSTANT SA
Chemin du Champ des Filles 32
1228 Plan-les-Ouates
Switzerland
Tel: 41 22 860 04 40
USA: 877 619 2824

GIANTTO
18380 Ventura Blvd.
Tarzana, CA 91356
USA: 818 343 0966

GIRARD-PERREGAUX
Place Girardet 1
2301 La Chaux-de-Fonds
Switzerland
Tel: 41 32 911 33 33
France: 33 1 72 25 65 41

GRAHAM-LONDON
Boulevard des Eplatures 38
CH 2300 La Chaux-de-Fonds
Switzerland
Tel: 41 32 910 98 88
USA: 213 622 1716

GREUBEL FORSEY
Eplatures-Grise 16
2301 La Chaux-de-Fonds
Switzerland
Tel: 41 32 925 45 45
USA: 310 205 5555

GUY ELLIA
21 Rue de la Paix
75002 Paris
France
Tel: 33 1 53 30 25 25
CA: 310 470 1388
NY: 212 888 0505

H. MOSER & CIE.
Rundbuckstrasse 10
8212 Neuhausen am Rheinfall
Switzerland
Tel: 41 52 674 0050
USA: 561 330 0088

HAMILTON WATCHES
Chemin du Long-Champ 119
2504 Biel/Bienne
Switzerland
Tel: 41 32 343 40 04
USA: 866 382 2477

HARRY WINSTON SA
8 Chemin du Tourbillon
1228 Plan-les-Ouates
Switzerland
Tel: 41 22 716 29 00
USA: 212 245 2000

HERMÈS
Erlenstrasse 31A
2555 Brügg
Switzerland
Tel: 41 32 366 70 50
USA: 212 759 7585

HUBLOT
Route de Divonne, 14
1260 Nyon 2
Switzerland
Tel: 41 22 990 90 00
USA: 800 536 0636

IWC SCHAFFHAUSEN
Baumgartenstrasse 15
8201 Schaffhausen
Switzerland
Tel: 41 52 635 62 37
USA: 1 800 492 6755

JACOB & CO
Route de Thonon 146
1222 Vésenaz
Switzerland
Tel: 41 22 752 49 40
USA: 212 888 2330

JAEGER LeCOULTRE
Rue de la Golisse, 8
1347 Le Sentier
Switzerland
Tel: 41 21 845 02 02
USA: 212 308 2525

LONGINES
Saint-Imier 2610
Switzerland
Tel: 41 32 942 54 25
USA: 201 271 1400

LOUIS VUITTON
2 Rue du Pont Neuf
75001 Paris
France
Tel: 33 1 55 80 32 00

MONTBLANC MONTRE
Hellgrundweg 100
22525 Hamburg
Germany
Tel: 49 40 84 00 10
USA: 908 508 2300

PANERAI
Via Ludovico di Breme 44/45
20156 Milan
Italy
Tel: 39 02 363138
USA: 212 888 8788

PARMIGIANI
Rue du Temple 11
2114 Fleurier
Switzerland
Tel: 41 32 862 66 30
USA: 305 260 7770

PATEK PHILIPPE
Chemin du Pont du Centenaire 141
1228 Plan-les-Ouates
Switzerland
Tel: 41 22 884 20 20
USA: 212 218 1263

PIAGET
37 Chemin du Champ-des-Filles
1228 Plan-les-Ouates
Switzerland
Tel: 41 22 884 48 44
USA: 800 628 4344

PORSCHE DESIGN
Schützengasse 46
2540 Grenchen
Switzerland
Tel: 41 32 654 72 11
USA: 212 308 1786

RALPH LAUREN
8 Chemin de Blandonnet
1214 Vernier Geneva
Switzerland
Tel: 41 22 595 59 00
USA: 212 318 7000

RAYMOND WEIL SA
Avenue Eugène-Lance 36-38
1211 Geneva 26
Switzerland
Tel: 41 22 884 00 55
USA: 212 355 3720

REBELLION TIMEPIECES
Chemin du Bief
1027 Lonay
Switzerland
Tel: 41 21 802 33 04

RICHARD MILLE
11 rue du Jura
2345 Les Breuleux Jura
Switzerland
Tel: 41 32 959 43 53
USA: 310 205 5555

ROGER DUBUIS
1217 Meyrin 2 Geneva
Switzerland
Tel: 41 22 783 28 28
USA: 888 738 2847

ROLAND ITEN
Mechanical Luxury SA
Route de Lausane 68
Lausanne 1052
Switzerland
Tel: 41 21 862 1841
USA: 310 205 5555

ROLEX
Rue François Dussaud 3-7
1211 Geneva 24
Switzerland
Tel: 41 22 302 22 00
USA: 212 758 7700

TAG HEUER
Louis-Joseph Chevrolet 6A
2300 La Chaux-de-Fonds
Switzerland
Tel: 41 32 919 80 00
USA: 973 467 1890

ULYSSE NARDIN
3 Rue du Jardin
2400 Le Locle
Switzerland
Tel: 41 32 930 74 00
USA: 561 988 8600

URWERK
34 rue des Noirettes
1227 Carouge-Geneva
Switzerland
Tel: 41 21 900 20 25
USA: 310 205 5555

VACHERON CONSTANTIN
Rue des Moulins 1
1204 Geneva
Switzerland
Tel: 41 22 930 20 05
USA: 212 713 0707

VAN CLEEF & ARPELS
31 Rue Danielle Casanova
75001 Paris
France
Tel: 33 1 53 45 45 40
USA: 212 644 9500

ZANNETTI
Via Monte d'Oro 19
00186 Rome
Italy
Tel: 39 06 68 192 566

ZENITH
2400 Le Locle
Switzerland
Tel: 41 32 930 62 62
USA: 973 467 1890